BARRON'S

SAT *I

HOW TO PREPARE FOR THE SAT I

BARRON'S

SAT*I

HOW TO PREPARE FOR THE SAT I

21ST EDITION

Sharon Weiner Green
Former Instructor in English
Merritt College
Oakland, California

Ira K. Wolf, Ph.D.
President, PowerPrep, Inc.
Former High School Teacher, College Professor,
and University Director of Teacher Preparation

DEDICATION

In memory of Mitchel Weiner and Samuel Brownstein, who first brought college entrance test preparation to the high school students of America.

S.W.G.

To Elaine, my wife and best friend, for all of your support and love.

I.K.W.

Contents

Preface

In writing this book, we have aimed to give you the advantages on the SAT I that the students we tutor privately (or teach in classes) have enjoyed for decades. Therefore, we'd like you to think of this study guide as your personal SAT I tutor, because that's precisely what it is. Like any good tutor, it will work closely with you, prompting you and giving you pointers to improve your testing skills. It will help you pinpoint your trouble spots and show you how to work on them, and it will point out your strengths as well. After working with your tutor, you should see marked improvement in your performance.

Your personal tutor will be available to work with you whenever you like, for as long or short as you like. Working with your tutor, you can go as quickly or as slowly as you like, repeating sections as often as you need, skipping over sections you already know well. Your tutor will give you explanations, not just correct answers, when you make mistakes, and will be infinitely patient and adaptable.

Here are just a few of the things your tutor offers you:

- It takes you step-by-step through thousands of verbal and mathematical questions, showing you how to solve them and how to avoid going wrong.
- It offers you dozens of clear-cut Testing Tactics and shows you how to use them to attack every question type you will find on the SAT I.
- It enables you to simulate actual testing conditions, providing you with a diagnostic test and seven model tests—all with answers fully explained—each of which follows the format of the SAT I exactly.

- It provides comprehensive mathematics review in arithmetic, algebra, and geometry—the three math areas you need to know to do well on the SAT I.
- It pinpoints specific sources of SAT I reading passages, naming authors and books and magazines, and provides a college-level reading list that can guide you to these works and more.
- It gives you the 365-word High Frequency Word List, 365 words from abridge to zealot that have been shown by computer analysis to occur and reoccur on actual published SATs, plus Barron's 3,500-word Basic Word List, your best chance to acquaint yourself with the whole range of college-level vocabulary you will face on the SAT I.
- It even gives you your own set of high-frequency word list flash cards in a convenient tear-out section at the back of the book. More than 200 words that have appeared regularly on previous SAT exams are presented, each with its part of speech, pronunciation, definition, and illustrative sentence. Separate the cards and carry some with you to study in spare moments. Or devise a competitive game, and use them with a partner.

No other book offers you as much. Your personal tutor embodies Barron's ongoing commitment to provide you with the best possible coaching for the SAT I and every other important test you take. It has benefited from the dedicated labors of Linda Turner and other members of the editorial staff of Barron's, all of whom wish you the best as you settle down with your tutor to work on the SAT I.

Countdown to the SAT I

The day before you take the test, don't do practice tests. Do look over all the math and verbal tactics listed below so they will be fresh in your mind.

BEFORE THE TEST

Set out your test kit the night before. You will need your admission ticket, a photo ID (a driver's license or a non-driver picture ID, a passport, or a school ID), your calculator, four or five sharp No. 2 pencils (with erasers), plus a map or directions showing how to get to the test center.

Get a good night's sleep so you are well rested and alert.

Wear comfortable clothes. Dress in layers. Bring a sweater in case the room is cold.

Bring an accurate watch—not one that beeps—in case the room has no clock.

Bring a small snack for quick energy.

Don't be late. Allow plenty of time for getting to the test site. You want to be in your seat, relaxed, before the test begins.

DURING THE TEST

Do not waste any time reading the directions or looking at the sample problems at the beginning of every section. You already know all of the rules for answering each question type that appears on the SAT I. They will not change.

First answer all the easy questions; then tackle the hard ones if you have time.

Pace yourself. Don't work so fast that you start making careless errors. On the other hand, don't get bogged down on any one question.

Play the percentages: guess whenever you can eliminate one or more of the answers.

Make educated guesses, not random ones. As a rule, don't mark down answers when you haven't even looked at the questions.

Watch out for eye-catchers, answer choices that are designed to tempt you into guessing wrong.

Change answers only if you have a reason for doing so; don't change them on a last-minute hunch or whim.

Check your assumptions. Make sure you are answering the question asked and not the one you thought was going to be asked.

Remember that you are allowed to write in the test booklet. Use it to do your math computations and to draw diagrams. Underline key words in sentence completion questions and reading passages. Cross out any answer choices you are sure are wrong. Circle questions you want to return to.

Be careful not to make any stray marks on your answer sheet. The test is graded by a machine, and a machine cannot tell the difference between an accidental mark and a filled-in answer.

Check frequently to make sure you are answering the questions in the right spots.

Remember that you don't have to answer every question to do well.

TIPS FOR THE VERBAL QUESTIONS

Read all the answer choices before you decide which is best.

Think of a context for unfamiliar words; the context may help you come up with the word's meaning.

Break down unfamiliar words into recognizable parts.

Consider secondary meanings of words. If none of the answer choices seem right to you, take another look. A word may have more than one meaning.

Sentence Completion Questions

First, read the sentence carefully to get a feel for its meaning.

Before you look at the choices, think of a word that makes sense.

Watch for words that signal a contrast (like but, although, and however) or indicate the continuation of a thought (like additionally, besides, and furthermore). These signal words are clues that can help you figure out what the sentence actually means.

Look for words that signal the unexpected, such as abnormal, illogical, and ironic. These words indicate that something unexpected, possibly even unwanted, exists or has occurred.

In double-blank sentences, go through the answers, testing the first word in each choice (and eliminating those that don't fit).

Analogy Questions

Before you look at the answer choices, try to state the relationship between the capitalized words in a good, clear sentence.

If more than one answer fits the relationship in your sentence, look for a narrower approach.

Watch out for answer choices that reverse the original grammatical relationship. For example, although PILOT:STEER and SOLDIER:COMMAND may at first look like a good match, they do not relate in the same way. Always ask yourself who is doing what to whom. In this case, the pilot actually does the steering, whereas the soldier does not do the commanding, but is commanded.

Eliminate answer choices that don't express a specific, dictionary-defined relationship.

Critical Reading Questions

When you have a choice, tackle reading passages with familiar subjects before passages with unfamiliar ones.

Make use of the introductions to acquaint yourself with the text.

First read the passage; then read the questions.

Read as rapidly as you can with understanding, but do not force yourself.

As you read the opening sentence, try to anticipate what the passage will be about.

When you tackle the questions, use the line references in the questions to be sure you've gone back to the correct spot, to verify your choice of answer.

Base your answer only on what is written in the passage, not on what you know from other books or courses.

In answering questions on the paired reading passages, first read one passage and answer the questions based on it; then read the second passage and tackle the remaining questions.

Try to answer all the questions on a particular passage.

TIPS FOR THE MATHEMATICS QUESTIONS

Whenever you know how to answer a question directly, just do it. The tactics that are reviewed below should be used only when you need them.

Memorize all the formulas you need to know. Even though some of them are printed on the first page of each math section, during the test you do not want to waste any time referring back to that reference material.

Be sure to bring a calculator, but use it only when you need it. Don't use it for simple arithmetic that you can easily do in your head.

Remember that no problem requires lengthy or difficult computations. If you find yourself doing a lot of arithmetic, stop and reread the question. You are probably not answering the question asked.

Answer every question you attempt. Even if you can't solve it, you can almost always eliminate two or more choices. Often you know that an answer must be negative, but two or three of the choices are positive, or an answer must be even, and some of the choices are odd.

Unless a diagram is labeled "<u>Note</u>: Figure not drawn to scale," it is perfectly accurate, and you can trust it in making an estimate.

When a diagram has not been provided, draw one, especially on any geometry problem.

If a diagram has been provided, feel free to label it, mark it up in any way, including adding line segments, if necessary.

Answer any question for which you can estimate the answer, even if you are not sure you are correct.

Don't panic when you see a strange symbol in a question, It will always be defined. Getting the correct answer just involves following the directions given in the definition.

When a question involves two equations, either add them or subtract them. If there are three or more, just add them.

Never make unwarranted assumptions. Do not assume numbers are positive or integers. If a question refers to two numbers, do not assume that they have to be different. If you know a figure has four sides, do not assume that it is a rectangle.

Be sure to work in consistent units. If the width and length of a rectangle are 8 inches and 2 feet, respectively, either convert the 2 feet to 24 inches or the 8 inches to two-thirds of a foot before calculating the area or perimeter.

Standard Multiple-Choice Questions

Whenever you answer a question by backsolving, start with Choice C.

When you replace variables with numbers, choose easy-to-use numbers, whether or not they are realistic.

Choose appropriate numbers. The best number to use in percent problems is 100. In problems involving fractions, the best number to use is the least common denominator.

When you have no idea how to solve a problem, eliminate all of the absurd choices and guess.

Quantitative Comparison Questions

There are only four possible answers to a quantitative comparison question: A, B, C, or D. E can never be the correct choice.

If the quantity in each column is a number (there are no variables), then the answer cannot be D.

Remember that you do not need to calculate the values in each column; you only have to compare them.

Replace variables with numbers. The best numbers to try are 1, 0, and −1. Occasionally, fractions between 0 and 1 and large numbers, such as 10 or 100, are useful.

Make the problem easier by doing the same thing to each column. You can always add the same number to each column or subtract the same number from each column. You can multiply or divide each column by the same number, if you know that the number is positive.

Ask "Could the columns be equal?" and "Must the columns be equal?"

Student-Produced Response (Grid-in) Questions

Write your answer in the four spaces at the top of the grid, and carefully grid in your answer below. No credit is given for a correct answer if it has been gridded improperly.

Remember that the answer to a grid-in question can never be negative.

You can never grid in a mixed number—you must convert it to an improper fraction or a decimal.

Never round off your answers and never reduce fractions. If a fraction can fit in the four spaces of the grid, enter it. If not, use your calculator to convert it to a decimal (by dividing) and enter a decimal point followed by the first three decimal digits.

When gridding a decimal, do not write a 0 before the decimal point.

If a question has more than one possible answer, only grid in one of them.

There is no penalty for wrong answers on grid-in questions, so you should grid in anything that seems reasonable, rather than leave out a question.

SAT I FORMAT

TOTAL TIME: 3 HOURS*

Section 1: Verbal—30 Questions *Time—30 minutes*	9 Sentence Completion 6 Analogy 15 Reading Comprehension
Section 2: Mathematics—25 Questions *Time—30 minutes*	25 Standard Multiple-Choice
Section 3: Verbal—35 Questions *Time—30 minutes*	10 Sentence Completion 13 Analogy 12 Reading Comprehension
Section 4: Mathematics—25 Questions *Time—30 minutes*	15 Quantitative Comparison 10 Student-Produced Response Questions (Grid-in)
Section 5: Verbal—13 Questions *Time—15 minutes*	13 Reading Comprehension
Section 6: Mathematics—10 Questions *Time—15 minutes*	10 Standard Multiple-Choice

SAT I TEST DATES

Test Dates	Registration Deadlines	
	Regular	**Late**
2001 March 31 May 5 June 2 October 13 November 3 December 1	February 23 March 29 April 27 September 11 September 28 October 26	March 7 April 13 May 9 September 15 October 10 November 7
2002 January 26 March 16 May 4 June 1	December 21 February 8 March 29 April 26	January 2 March 2 April 10 May 8

*<u>Note</u>: The 2½-hour format shown above is followed by all of the Model Tests in this book, including the Diagnostic Test. An actual SAT I takes three hours because there is a fifth 30-minute section. The format of this "experimental" section, which can be math or verbal, is identical to one of the other 30-minute sections. This section, which permits the test-makers to try out new questions, does not count in your score, but because there is no way to know which of the five 30-minute sections is experimental, you must do your best on every section. Also, the sections can come in any order, except that the two 15-minute sections are always last.

ACKNOWLEDGMENTS

The authors gratefully acknowledge the following copyright holders for permission to reprint material used in the reading passages.

Page 5: From *A Handbook to Literature* by C. Hugh Holman, ©1995. Reprinted by permission of Prentice Hall, Inc.

Pages 30–31: From *Black Boy* by Richard Wright. Copyright ©1937, 1942, 1944, 1945 by Richard Wright. Renewed 1973 by Ellen Wright. Reprinted by permission of HarperCollins, Inc.

Pages 31–32: From *King Solomon's Ring* by Konrad Z. Lorenz, ©1952 Harper & Row. Reprinted with permission of HarperCollins Publishers, Inc.

Pages 39–40: From *Bury My Heart at Wounded Knee: An Indian History of the American West* by Dee Brown ©1970 by Dee Brown. Reprinted with permission of Henry Holt & Co., LLC.

Page 47: From "Let's Say You Wrote Badly This Morning" in *The Writing Habit* by David Huddle, ©1989, 1994 University Press of New England.

Pages 47–48: From "My Two One-Eyed Coaches" by George Garrett, ©1987. Reprinted with permission of *The Virginia Quarterly Review*, Spring 1987, Vol. 63, No. 2.

Page 113: From *Summer of '49* by David Halberstam, ©1989. Reprinted with permission of William Morrow & Co.

Page 113–114: From *Take Time For Paradise* ©1989 by the Estate of A. Bartlett Giamatti. Reprinted by permission of Estate of A.B. Giamatti.

Pages 123–124: From *Sculpture/Inuit*, ©1971. Reprinted with permission of the Canadian Eskimo Arts Council and James Houston.

Page 127: From "Renaissance to Modern Tapestries in the Metropolitan Museum of Art" in the *Metropolitan Museum of Art Bulletin*, Spring 1987, by Edith Appleton Standen, copyright ©1987 by the Metropolitan Museum of Art. Reprinted courtesy of the Metropolitan Museum of Art.

Pages 128–129: From "I Love Paul Revere Whether He Rode or Not" by Richard Shenkman. Copyright ©1991 by Richard Shenkman.

Pages 129–130: From *One Writer's Beginnings* by Eudora Welty, Reprinted with permission of Faber and Faber Limited. Copyright ©1983 by Eudora Welty.

Pages 131–132: From "African Sculpture Speaks," by Ladislas Segy, ©1958 by permission of Dover Publications.

Pages 132–133: From "Yonder Peasant, Who Is He?" in *Memories of a Catholic Girlhood*, ©1948 and renewed 1975 by Mary McCarthy, reprinted with permission of Harcourt, Inc.

Page 133: From *Reinventing Womanhood* by Caroline G. Heilbrun. Copyright ©1979 by Carolyn G. Heilbrun. Reprinted with permission of W.W. Norton & Co., Inc.

Page 500: From *Take Time for Paradise* ©1989 by the Estate of A. Bartlett Giamatti. Reprinted by permission of Estate of A.B. Giamatti.

Pages 500–501: From *City* by William H. Whyte. Copyright ©1989 by William Whyte. Used by permission of Doubleday, a division of Random House, Inc.

Pages 526–527: From *The Waning of the Middle Ages* by J. Huizinga. Reprinted with permission of Edward Arnold.

Pages 527–528: From *Hunger of Memory* by Richard Rodriquez. Reprinted with permission of David R. Godine, Publishers, Inc. Copyright ©1982 by Richard Rodriquez.

Pages 535–536: From *Teaching a Stone to Talk* by Annie Dillard. Copyright ©1982 by Annie Dillard. Reprinted by permission of HarperCollins, Inc.

Page 543: From "The Guilty Vicarage" in *The Dyer's Hand and Other Essays* by W.H. Auden. Copyright ©1948 by W.H. Auden. Reprinted with permission of Random House, Inc.

Pages 543–544: From *Modus Operandi: An Excursion into Detective Fiction* by Robin W. Winks, ©1982, pp. 118–119. Reprinted by permission of Robin W. Winks.

Pages 568–569: From *Athabasca* by Alistair MacLean. Copyright ©1980 by Alistair MacLean. Reprinted by permission of Doubleday, a division of Random House, Inc.

Pages 569–570: From *The Uses of Enchantment* by Bruno Bettelheim. Copyright ©1975, 1976 by Bruno Bettelheim. Reprinted with permission of Alfred A. Knopf.

Page 584: From *Native Stranger: A Black American's Journey into the Heart of Africa* by Eddy L. Harris, ©1992. Reprinted by permission of Simon & Schuster.

Pages 584–585: From *Turning Japanese* by David Mura, ©1991 by David Mura. Reprinted by permission of Grove/Atlantic, Inc.

Pages 608–609: From *The Overworked American: The Unexpected Decline of Leisure* by Juliet B. Schor. Copyright ©1991 by BasicBooks, a division of HarperCollins Publishers, Inc. Reprinted by permission of BasicBooks, a member of Perseus Books, L.L.C.

Page 625: From *The Soul of the Night* by Chet Raymo, ©1985. Reprinted by permission of Chet Raymo.

Pages 649–650: From *The Indian in America (New American Nation Series)* by Wilcomb E. Washburn. Copyright ©1975 by Wilcomb E. Washburn. Reprinted with permission of HarperCollins, Inc.

Pages 657–658: From "The Art of Mickey Mouse" edited by Craig Yoe and Janet Morra-Yoe. Introduction by John Updike. Copyright ©1991 by The Walt Disney Company. Introduction ©1991 by John Updike. Reprinted by permission of Disney Editions, an imprint of Disney Publishing Worldwide.

Pages 665–666: From *The Greenpeace Book of Dolphins* by John May, ©1990. Reprinted with permission of Greenpeace © Greenpeace.

Pages 688–689: From *Civilisation* by Kenneth Clark. Copyright ©1969 by Kenneth C. Clark. Reprinted with permission of HarperCollins, Inc.

Pages 689–690: From "Huge Conservation Effort Aims to Save Vanishing Architect of the Savanna" by William K. Stevens, ©1989 by The New York Times Co. Reprinted with permission.

Page 705: From "Tradition and Practice" in *George Santayana's America: Essays on Literature and Culture*, James C. Ballowe, editor. ©1966 Reprinted with permission of the University of Illinois Press, Urbana.

Pages 705–706: From "Postscript: The Almighty Dollar" in *The Dyer's Hand and Other Essays* by W.H. Auden. Copyright ©1948 by W.H. Auden. Reprinted with permission of Random House, Inc.

Pages 728–729: From "Medicine's Home Front" in *The Economist*, ©1987 The Economist Newspaper Group, Inc. Reprinted with permission. Further reproduction prohibited. www.economist.com

Pages 729–730: From "Ruin" in *A Dove of the East and Other Stories* by Mark Helprin, ©1975. Reprinted with permission of Alfred A. Knopf.

Pages 737–738: From *Slavery to Freedom* by John Hope Franklin. Copyright ©1980 by Alfred A. Knopf. Reprinted by permission of the publisher.

Page 745: From "The Feeling of Flying" by Samuel Hynes. First published in *The Sewanee Review*, vol. 95 no. 1, Winter 1987. Copyright 1987 by Samuel Hynes. Reprinted with permission of the editor and the author.

Pages 745–746: From "The Stunt Pilot" in *The Best American Essays* by Annie Dillard, ©1989. Reprinted by permission of Annie Dillard.

PART ONE

Get Acquainted with the SAT I

1 Let's Look at the SAT I

- ■ The Verbal Sections
- ■ The Mathematics Sections
- ■ The Use of Calculators on the SAT I

What Is the SAT I?

Many colleges and universities require their applicants to take a three-hour standardized examination called the SAT I. Consequently, most of you as high school juniors or seniors will take this test as part of the college admissions process. The SAT I, which is written and administered by the Educational Testing Service (ETS), purports to evaluate students' verbal and quantitative reasoning abilities. As a result, you will actually get two scores: a verbal score and a math score, each of which lies between 200 and 800. For both the verbal and the math tests, the median score is 500, meaning that about 50 percent of all students score below 500 and about 50 percent score 500 or above. In discussing their results, students often add the two scores (the sums range from 400 to 1600, with a median of about 1000) and say, "John got a 950," or "Mary got a 1300."

Why Do So Many Colleges Require You to Take the SAT I?

In the United States, we have no national education standards, so a B+ from one teacher doesn't necessarily represent the same level of accomplishment as does a B+ from another teacher, even in the same school. Given how hard it is to compare the academic achievements of students within one school, consider the difficulty of evaluating students who come from public and private schools in urban, suburban, and rural areas throughout the United States. The SAT I provides college admissions officers with a quick way to compare applicants from thousands of different high schools. On one day, hundreds of thousands of students throughout the United States (and in many foreign countries) take the exact same version of the SAT I, and a verbal score of 670 means exactly the same thing at a private school in Massachusetts as it does in a public school in California.

How Do I Sign Up to Take the SAT I?

Your high school guidance office should have copies of the SAT Program Registration Bulletin, which provides informa-

tion on how to register for the test by mail. If your school is out of them, you can get copies from:

College Board SAT I
P. O. Box 6200
Princeton NJ 08541-6200

You can ask to have a bulletin sent to you by phoning the College Board office in Princeton from 8:00 A.M. to 9:45 P.M. Eastern time on weekdays (9:00 A.M. to 4:45 P.M. on Saturdays). The number is (609) 771-7588.

In addition to registering by mail, you can also register for the SAT I on-line. To take advantage of this service, go to: www.collegeboard.org. You will need to have your social security number and/or your date of birth, plus a major credit card. On-line registration is fast and efficient. However, not everyone is eligible to use it. If you plan to pay with a check, money order, or fee waiver, you must register by mail. Similarly, if you are signing up for Sunday testing, or if you have a visual, hearing, or learning disability and plan to take advantage of the Services for Students with Disabilities Program, you must register by mail.

What Does the SAT I Test?

The verbal sections test your critical reading skills and your vocabulary. One goal of the exam is to determine whether when you read a passage you understand what the author is saying and can make valid conclusions based on the text. Another goal is to determine if the level of your vocabulary is sufficiently high for you to be able to read college-level texts. The verbal sections contain three types of questions: sentence completion questions, analogy questions, and critical reading questions. This book will teach you the strategies that will enable you to attack each question intelligently and will help you to develop the high-level vocabulary you need to score well on the verbal sections of the SAT I.

The quantitative sections of the SAT I are less a test of your knowledge of arithmetic, geometry, and algebra than they are of your ability to reason logically. What many students find difficult about these questions is not the level of mathematics—much of the exam is based on grade school arithmetic, and almost every question is based on mathematics that is taught by the ninth grade. Rather, the difficulty lies in the way that the students must use the mathematics they already know as they reason through the solution. In this book, you will learn all the strategies you need to decipher these quantitative questions successfully.

Beyond your vocabulary, reading ability, and reasoning skills, the SAT I tests something else: your ability to take standardized tests. Some students are naturally good test-takers. They instinctively know how to use standardized tests to their advantage. They never freeze, and when they guess they are correct far more often than the laws of averages would suggest. You probably have at least a few classmates who are no brighter than you and who don't study any more than you, but who consistently earn higher test grades—and you hate them! Don't. Just learn their secrets. In classes, in private tutorials, and through previous editions of this and other books, we have helped millions of students to become better test-takers. Now it's your turn.

How Important Is the SAT I?

In addition to your application form, the essays you write, and the letters of recommendation that your teachers and guidance counselor write, colleges receive two important pieces of numerical data. One is your high school transcript, which shows the grades you have earned in all your courses during a three-year period. The other is your SAT I scores, which show how well you did during a three-hour period one Saturday morning. Which is more important? Your transcript, by far. However, your scores on the SAT I definitely do count, and it is precisely because you want your SAT I scores to be as high as possible that you purchased this book. If you use this book wisely, you will not be disappointed.

What Is the Format of the SAT I?

The SAT I is a three-hour exam, divided into seven sections, but because you should arrive a little early and because time is required to pass out materials, read instructions, collect the test, and give you short breaks between the sections, you should assume that you will be in the testing room for about three and a half to four hours.

Although the SAT I consists of seven sections, your scores are based on only six of them. They are four 30-minute sections (two math and two verbal) and two 15-minute sections (one math and one verbal). The seventh section is either a third 30-minute math section or a third 30-minute verbal section. It is what the ETS calls an "equating" section, but is commonly referred to as the "experimental" section. It is used to test out new questions for use on future exams. However, because this extra section is identical in format to one of the other sections, there is no way for you to know which section is the experimental one, and so you must do your best on every section.

The Verbal Sections

There are three types of questions on the verbal portion of the SAT I: (i) sentence completion questions, (ii) analogy questions, and (iii) critical reading questions.

Examples of each type appear in this chapter. Later, in Chapters 4, 5, and 6, you will learn several important strategies for handling each one. There are 78 questions in all, divided into three sections, each of which has its own format. You should expect to see, although not necessarily in this order:

35-Question Verbal Section
Questions 1–10   sentence completion questions
Questions 11–23   analogy questions
Questions 24–35   critical reading questions

30-Question Verbal Section
Questions 1–9   sentence completion questions
Questions 10–15   analogy questions
Questions 16–30   critical reading questions

13-Question Verbal Section
Questions 1–13   critical reading questions on paired
                    passages

As you see, the three verbal sections typically contain a total of 19 sentence completion questions, 19 analogies, and 40 critical reading questions. More than half the verbal questions on the SAT I directly test your reading.

Pay particular attention to how the first two of these sections are organized. These sections contain groups of sentence completion questions followed by groups of analogy questions. The groups of questions are arranged roughly in order of difficulty: they start out with easy warm-up questions and get more and more difficult as they go along. The critical reading questions, however, are not arranged in order of difficulty. Instead, they are arranged to follow the passage's organization: questions about material found early in the passage come before questions about material occurring later. This information will be helpful to you in pacing yourself during the test, as you will see in Chapter 2.

> **NOTE:** If the 30-minute experimental section on your SAT I is a verbal section, it will follow exactly the same format as one of the two 30-minute sections described above. Since, however, there will be no way for you to know which one of the 30-minute verbal sections on your test is experimental, you must do your best on each one.

Here are examples of the specific types of verbal questions you can expect.

Sentence Completions

Sentence completion questions ask you to fill in the blanks. Your job is to find the word or phrase that best completes the sentence's meaning.

> **Directions:** Choose the word or set of words that, when inserted in the sentence, *best* fits the meaning of the sentence as a whole.
>
> Brown, this biography suggests, was an _____ employer, giving generous bonuses one day, ordering pay cuts the next.
>
> (A) indifferent (B) objective (C) unpredictable
>
> (D) ineffectual (E) unobtrusive

Note how the phrases immediately following the word employer give you an idea of Brown's character and help you come up with the missing word. Clearly, someone who switches back and forth in this manner would be a difficult employer, but the test-makers want the precise word that characterizes Brown's arbitrary behavior.

Insert the different answer choices in the sentence to see which make the most sense. Was Brown an indifferent (uncaring or mediocre) employer? Not necessarily: he may or may not have cared about what sort of job he did. Was Brown an objective (fair and impartial) employer? We don't know: we have no information about his fairness and impartiality. Was Brown an unpredictable employer? Definitely. A man who gives bonuses one day and orders pay cuts the next clearly is unpredictable—no one can tell what he's going to do next. The correct answer appears to be Choice C.

To confirm your answer, check the remaining two choices. Was Brown an ineffectual (weak and ineffective) employer. Not necessarily: though his employees probably disliked not knowing from one day to the next how much pay they would receive, he still may have been an effective boss. Was Brown an unobtrusive (hardly noticeable; low-profile) employer? We don't know: we have no information about his visibility in the company. The best answer definitely is Choice C.

Sometimes sentence completion questions contain two blanks rather than one. In answering these double-blank sentences, you must be sure that both words in your answer choice make sense in the original sentence.

For a complete discussion of all the tactics used in handling sentence completion questions, turn to Chapter 4.

Analogies

An analogy is a likeness. Your job is to figure out the relationship between a pair of words and then find the pair of words whose relationship is most like the one linking the original pair.

> **Directions:** Select the lettered pair that *best* expresses a relationship similar to that expressed in the original pair.

WOLF:PACK:: (A) horse:saddle   (B) goose:flock
(C) fox:lair   (D) dog:sled   (E) lion:cub

Find a simple sentence that concisely expresses the relationship between the two capitalized words: "A wolf is a member of a pack," or "A pack by definition is a group of wolves." Now look at the five answer choices. In which one of them is the first word a member of a group and the second word the name of the group? Is a horse a member of a

saddle? No. Eliminate Choice A. Is a goose a member of a flock? Yes. A flock by definition is a group of geese. This is probably the correct answer, but to be sure, check the other choices. Is a fox a member of lair? No. A fox lives in a lair or den, but it is not a member of one. Eliminate Choice C. Similarly, a dog is not a member of a sled, and a lion is not a member of a cub. Both Choices D and E are incorrect. As we thought, the correct answer is Choice B.

You'll get a thorough briefing on analogy questions in Chapter 5, including a valuable list illustrating many of the possible relationships that can exist between the pairs of words.

Critical Reading

Typically, a 30-question verbal section has two reading passages; a 35-question verbal section usually has only one. Each of these passages is followed by from 5 to 13 critical reading questions. They ask about the passage's main idea or specific details, the author's attitude to the subject, the author's logic and techniques, the implications of the discussion, or the meaning of specific words.

> **Directions:** The passage below is followed by questions based on its content. Answer the questions on the basis of what is *stated* or *implied* in that passage.

(The following passage is considerably shorter than those on the SAT I.)

Certain qualities common to the sonnet should be noted. Its definite restrictions make it a challenge to the artistry of the poet and call for all the technical
Line skill at the poet's command. The more or less set
(5) rhyme patterns occurring regularly within the short space of fourteen lines afford a pleasant effect on the ear of the reader, and can create truly musical effects. The rigidity of the form precludes a too great economy or too great prodigality of words. Emphasis is placed
(10) on exactness and perfection of expression. The brevity of the form favors concentrated expression of ideas or passion.

1. The author's primary purpose is to
   (A) contrast different types of sonnets
   (B) criticize the limitations of the sonnet
   (C) identify the characteristics of the sonnet
   (D) explain why the sonnet lost popularity as a literary form
   (E) encourage readers to compose formal sonnets

The first question asks you to find the author's main idea. In the opening sentence, the author says certain qualities of the sonnet should be noted. In other words, he intends to call attention to certain of its characteristics, identifying them. The correct answer is Choice C. You can eliminate the other answers with ease. The author is upbeat about the sonnet: he doesn't say that the sonnet has limitations or that it has become less popular. You can cross out Choices B and D. Similarly the author doesn't mention any different types of sonnets; therefore, he cannot be contrasting them. You can cross out Choice A. And although the author talks about the challenge of composing formal sonnets, he never invites his readers to try to write them. You can cross out Choice E.

> **NOTE:** Even if you felt uneasy about eliminating all four of these incorrect answer choices, you should have been comfortable eliminating two or three of them. Thus, even if you were not absolutely sure of the correct answer, you would have been in an excellent position to guess. You will learn more about guessing tactics on the SAT I in the next chapter.

2. The word "afford" in line 6 means
   (A) initiate
   (B) exaggerate
   (C) are able to pay for
   (D) change into
   (E) provide

The second question asks you to figure out a word's meaning from its context. Substitute each of the answer choices in the original sentence and see which word or phrase makes most sense. Some make no sense at all: the rhyme patterns that the reader hears certainly are not able to pay for any pleasant effect. You can definitely eliminate Choice C. What is it exactly that these rhyme patterns do? The rhyme patterns have a pleasant effect on the ear of the listener; indeed, they provide (furnish or afford) this effect. The correct answer is Choice E.

> **NOTE:** Because you can eliminate at least one of the answer choices, you are in a good position to guess the correct answer to this question. Again, you'll find information on guessing in Chapter 2.

3. The author's attitude toward the sonnet form can best be described as one of
   (A) amused toleration
   (B) grudging admiration
   (C) strong disapprobation
   (D) effusive enthusiasm
   (E) scholarly appreciation

The third question asks you to figure out how the author feels about his subject. All the author's comments about the sonnet form are positive: he approves of this poetic form. You can immediately eliminate Choice C, strong disapprobation or disapproval. You can also eliminate Choice A, amused toleration or forbearance: the author is not simply putting up with the sonnet form in a good-humored, somewhat patronizing way; he thinks wells of it. Choices B and D are somewhat harder to eliminate. The author does seem to admire the sonnet form. However, his admiration is unforced: it is not grudging or reluctant. You can eliminate Choice B. Likewise, the author is enthusiastic about the sonnet. However, he doesn't go so far as to gush: he's not effusive. The only answer that reflects this attitude is Choice E, scholarly appreciation.

Note that the 15-minute verbal section contains a pair of passages on a single topic, and that some of the questions on this section ask you to compare the two of them.

See Chapter 6 for tactics that will help you handle the entire range of critical reading questions.

The Mathematics Sections

There are three types of questions on the mathematics portion of the SAT I: (i) multiple-choice questions, (ii) quantitative comparison questions, and (iii) grid-in questions.

Examples of each type appear in this chapter. Later, in Chapters 9, 10, and 11, you will learn several important strategies for handling each one. There are 60 questions in all, divided into three sections, each of which has its own format. You should expect to see, although not necessarily in this order:

- a 30-minute section with 25 multiple-choice questions,
- a 30-minute section with 15 quantitative comparisons followed by 10 student-produced-response questions (grid-ins),
- a 15-minute section with 10 multiple-choice questions.

> **NOTE:** If the 30-minute experimental section on your SAT I is a mathematics section, it will follow exactly the same format as one of the two 30-minute sections described above. Since, however, there will be no way for you to know which section is experimental, you must do your best on each one.

Within each section the questions are arranged in order of increasing difficulty. The first few multiple-choice questions are quite easy; they are followed by several of medium difficulty; and the last few are considered hard. The quantitative comparisons and grid-ins also proceed from easy to difficult. As a result, the amount of time you spend on any one question will vary greatly. We will discuss time management in detail in Chapter 2, where you will learn the best way to pace yourself.

Multiple-Choice Questions

Of the 60 mathematics questions on the SAT I, 35 are multiple-choice questions. Although you have certainly taken multiple-choice tests before, the SAT I uses a few different types of questions, and you must become familiar with all of them. By far, the most common type of question is one in which you are asked to solve a problem. The straightforward way to answer such a question is to do the necessary work, get the solution, then look at the five choices and choose the one that corresponds to your answer. In Chapter 9 we will discuss other techniques for answering these questions, but now let's look at a couple of examples.

Example 1.

What is the average (arithmetic mean) of all the even integers between −5 and 7?

(A) 0 (B) $\frac{5}{6}$ (C) 1 (D) $\frac{6}{5}$ (E) 3

To solve this problem requires only that you know how to find the average of a set of numbers. Ignore the fact that this is a multiple-choice question. Don't even look at the choices.

- List the even integers whose average you need: –4, –2, 0, 2, 4, 6. (Be careful not to leave out 0, which is an even integer.)

- Calculate the average by adding the six integers and dividing by 6.

$$\frac{\pm 4 + \pm 2 + 0 + 2 + 4 + 6}{6} = \frac{6}{6} = 1.$$

- Having found the average to be 1, look at the five choices, see that 1 is choice C, and blacken **C** on your answer sheet.

Example 2.

A necklace is formed by stringing 133 colored beads on a thin wire in the following order: red, orange, yellow, green, blue, indigo, violet; red, orange, yellow, green, blue, indigo, violet. If this pattern continues, what will be the color of the 101st bead on the string?

(A) orange (B) yellow (C) green (D) blue (E) indigo

Again, you are not helped by the fact that the question, which is less a test of your arithmetic skills than of your ability to reason, is a multiple-choice question. You need to determine the color of the 101st bead, and then select the choice that matches your answer.

The seven colors keep repeating in exactly the same order.

Color: red orange yellow green blue indigo violet

Bead
number: 1   2   3   4   5   6   7

      8   9   10   11   12   13   14   etc.

- The violet beads are in positions 7, 14, 21, . . . , 70, . . . , that is, the multiples of 7.

- If 101 were a multiple of 7, the 101st bead would be violet.

- But when 101 is divided by 7, the quotient is 14 and the remainder is 3.

- Since $14 \times 7 = 98$, the 98th bead completes the 14th cycle, and hence is violet.

- The 99th bead starts the next cycle; it is red. The 100th bead is orange, and the 101st bead is yellow.

- The answer is **B**.

NOTE:

1. You could have just pointed at the colors as you quickly counted up to 101. Had there been 500 or 1000 beads, however, that would not have been practical, whereas the solution given will work with any number.

2. Did you notice that the solution didn't use the fact that the necklace consisted of 133 beads? This is unusual; occasionally, but not often, a problem contains information you don't need.

In contrast to Examples 1 and 2, some questions require you to look at all five choices in order to find the answer.

Consider Example 3.

Example 3.

If a and b are both odd integers, which of the following could be an odd integer?

(A) $a + b$ (B) $a^2 + b^2$ (C) $(a + 1)^2 + (b - 1)^2$

(D) $(a + 1)(b - 1)$ (E) $\dfrac{a + 1}{b \pm 1}$

The words which of the following alert you to the fact that you are going to have to examine each of the five choices to determine which one satisfies the stated condition, in this case that the quantity could be odd. Check each choice.

- The sum of two odd integers is always even. Eliminate A.

- The square of an odd integer is odd; So a^2 and b^2 are each odd, and their sum is even. Eliminate B.

- Since a and b are odd, $(a + 1)$ and $(b - 1)$ are even; so $(a + 1)^2$ and $(b - 1)^2$ are also even, as is their sum. Eliminate C.

- The product of two even integers is even. Eliminate D.

- Having eliminated A, B, C, and D you know that the answer must be E. Check to be sure: $\dfrac{a + 1}{b \pm 1}$ need not even be an integer (e.g., if a = 1 and b = 5), but it could be. For example, if a = 3 and b = 5, then

$$\frac{a + 1}{b \pm 1} = \frac{3 + 1}{5 \pm 1} = \frac{4}{4} = 1,$$

which is an odd integer. The answer is **E**.

Another kind of multiple-choice question that appears on the SAT I is the Roman numeral-type question. These questions actually consist of three statements labeled I, II, and III. The five answer choices give various possibilities for which statement or statements are true. Here is a typical example.

Example 4.

If x is negative, which of the following must be true?

$$\text{I. } x^3 < x^2$$

$$\text{II. } x + \frac{1}{x} < 0$$

$$\text{III. } x = \sqrt{x^2}$$

(A) I only   (B) II only   (C) I and II only
(D) II and III only   (E) I, II, and III

- To solve this problem examine each statement independently.

I. If x is negative, x^3 is negative and must be less than x^2, which is positive. I is true.

II. If x is negative, so is $\dfrac{1}{x}$, and the sum of two negative numbers is negative. II is true.

III. The square root of a number is never negative, and so could not possibly equal x. III is false.

- Only I and II are true. The answer is **C**.

NOTE: You should almost never leave out a Roman numeral-type question. Even if you can't solve the problem completely, there should be at least one of the three Roman numeral statements that you know to be true or false. Based on that information, you should be able to eliminate two or three of the answer choices given. For instance, in Example 4, if all you know for sure is that Statement I is true, you can eliminate Choices B and D. Similarly, if all you know is that Statement II is false, you can eliminate Choices D and E. Then, as you will learn in Chapter 2, you must guess between the remaining choices.

Quantitative Comparison Questions

Of the 60 mathematics questions on the SAT I, 15 are what is known as quantitative comparisons. Unless you have already taken an SAT I or a PSAT, it is very likely that you have never seen such questions before, so read this explanation very carefully.

In these questions there are two quantities in boxes, one in Column A and one in Column B, and it is your job to compare these quantities. There are only four possible answers to quantitative comparison questions: A, B, C, and D. E is never the answer, and blackening E on the answer sheet is equivalent to omitting the question. The correct answer to a quantitative comparison question is:

A   if the quantity in Column A is greater all the time, no matter what;

B   if the quantity in Column B is greater all the time, no matter what;

C   if the two quantities are equal all the time, no matter what;

D   if the answer is not A, B, or C.

In some of the questions, information concerning one or both of the quantities is centered above the two boxes. This information must be taken into consideration when comparing the two quantities. If a symbol appears in both columns, it represents the same thing in each column.

In Chapter 10 you will learn several important strategies for handling quantitative comparisons. Here, let's look at a few examples to make sure that you understand the concepts involved.

Column A	Column B
$(4 + 5)^2$	$4^2 + 5^2$

Example 5.

- Evaluate each column: $(4 + 5)^2 = 9^2 = 81$, whereas $4^2 + 5^2 = 16 + 25 = 41$.
- Compare the quantities. Since $81 > 41$, the quantity in Column A is greater. The answer is **A.**

Column A	Column B
	$a + b = 16$
The average (arithmetic mean) of a and b	8

Example 6.

- The quantity in Column A is the average of a and b: $\frac{a + b}{2}$. Since $a + b = 16$, the quantity in Column A is

$$\frac{a + b}{2} = \frac{16}{2} = 8.$$

- Therefore, the quantities in Columns A and B are equal. The answer is **C.**

NOTE: We cannot determine the value of either a or b; all we know is that their sum is 16. Perhaps $a = 10$ and $b = 6$, or $a = 0$ and $b = 16$, or $a = -4$ and $b = 20$. It doesn't matter. The average of 10 and 6 is 8; the average of 0 and 16 is 8; and the average of -4 and 20 is 8. Since $a + b$ is 16, the average of a and b is 8, all the time, no matter what. The answer, therefore, is C.

Column A	Column B
m^4	m^2

Example 7.

- If $m = 1$, then $m^4 = 1$ and $m^2 = 1$. In this case, the quantities in the two columns are equal.
- This means that the answer to this problem cannot be A or B. Why?
- The answer can be A (or B) only if the quantity in Column A (or B) is greater all the time, no matter what. But it isn't—not when $m = 1$.
- Then is the answer C? Maybe. But for the answer to be C, the quantities would have to be equal all the time, no matter what. Are they?
- No. If $m = 2$, $m^4 = 16$ and $m^2 = 4$. In this case, the two quantities are not equal.
- The answer, therefore, is **D.**

Grid-in Questions

Ten of the 60 mathematics questions on the SAT I are what the College Board calls Student-Produced Response Questions. Since the answers to these questions are entered on a special grid, they are usually referred to as grid-in questions. Except for the method of entering your answer, this type of question is probably the one with which you are most familiar. In your math class, most of your homework problems and test questions require you to determine an answer and write it down, and this is what you will do on the grid-in problems. The only difference is that, once you have figured out an answer, it must be recorded on a special grid, such as the one shown at the right, so that it can be read by a computer. Here is a typical grid-in question.

Example 8.

At the diner, John ordered a sandwich for $3.95 and a soda for 85¢. A sales tax of 5% was added to his bill, and he left the waitress a $1 tip. What was the total cost, in dollars, of John's lunch?

Calculate the cost of the food:

$$\$3.95 + \$0.85 = \$4.80$$

Calculate the tax (5% of $4.80):

$$.05 \times \$4.80 = \$0.24$$

Add the cost of the food, tax, and tip:

$$\$4.80 + \$0.24 + \$1.00 = \$6.04$$

To enter this answer, you write 6.04 (without the dollar sign) in the four spaces at the top of the grid, and blacken the appropriate oval under each space. In the first column, under the 6, you blacken the oval marked 6; in the second column, under the decimal point, you blacken the oval with the decimal point; in the third column, under the 0, you blacken the oval marked 0; and, finally, in the fourth column, under the 4, you blacken the oval marked 4.

Always read each grid-in question very carefully. Example 8 might have asked for the total cost of John's lunch in cents. In that case, the correct answer would have been 604, which would be gridded in, without a decimal point, using only three of the four columns (see below).

Note that the only symbols that appear in the grid are the digits from 0 to 9, a decimal point, and a fraction bar (/). The grid does not have a minus sign, so answers to grid-in problems can never be negative. In Chapter 11, you will learn some important tactics for answering grid-in questions and will be able to practice filling in grids. You will also learn the special rules concerning the proper way to grid in fractions, mixed numbers, and decimals that won't fit in the grid's four columns. When you take the diagnostic test in Chapter 3, just enter your answers exactly as was done in Example 8.

NOTE: Any multiple-choice question whose answer is a positive number less than 10,000 could be a grid-in question. If Example 1 had been a grid-in question, you would have solved it in exactly the same way: you would have determined that the average of the six numbers is 1; but then, instead of looking for 1 among the five choices you would have entered the number 1 on a grid. The mathematics is no harder on grid-in questions than on multiple-choice questions. However, if you don't know how to solve a problem correctly, it is harder to guess at the right answer, since there are no choices to eliminate.

The Use of Calculators on the SAT I

There isn't a single question on any section of the SAT I for which a calculator is required. In fact, on most questions a calculator is completely useless. There are several questions, however, for which a calculator could be used; and since calculators are permitted, you should definitely bring one with you when you take the SAT I. As you go through the hundreds of practice math questions in this book, you should have available the calculator you intend to take to the test, and should use it whenever you think it is appropriate. You will probably use it more at the beginning of your review because, as you go through this book, you will learn more and more strategies to help you solve problems easily without doing tedious calculations.

If you forget to bring a calculator to the actual test, you will not be able to use one, since none will be provided and you will not be allowed to share one with a friend. For the same reason, be sure that you have new batteries in your calculator or that you bring a spare, because if your calculator fails during the test, you will have to finish without one.

What Calculator Should You Use?

Almost any four-function, scientific, or graphic calculator is acceptable. Since you don't "need" a calculator at all, you don't "need" any particular type. There is absolutely no advantage to having a graphic calculator; but we do recommend a scientific calculator, since it is occasionally useful to have parentheses keys, ( ); a reciprocal key, $\frac{1}{x}$; and an exponent key, y^x or $\wedge$. All scientific calculators have these features. If you tend to make mistakes in working with fractions, you may want to get a calculator that can do fractional arithmetic. With such a calculator, for example, you can add $\frac{1}{3}$ and $\frac{1}{5}$ by entering 1 / 3 + 1 / 5; the readout will be 8/15, not the decimal 0.5333333. Such calculators can also reduce fractions. Some, but not most, scientific calculators have this capability.

CAUTION: Do not buy a new calculator right before you take the SAT I. If you don't have one, or you want to get a different one, buy it now and become familiar with it. Do all the practice exams in this book with the same calculator you intend to take to the test.

When Should Calculators Be Used?

If you have strong math skills and are a good test-taker, you will probably use your calculator infrequently, if at all. One reason is that strong math students can do a lot of basic arithmetic just as accurately, and faster, in their heads or on paper than with a calculator. A less obvious, but more important, reason is that students who are good test-takers will realize that many problems can be solved without doing any calculations at all (mental, written, or with a calculator); they will solve these problems in less time than it takes to pick up a calculator. On the other hand, if you are less confident about your mathematical ability or your test-taking skills, you will probably find your calculator a useful tool.

Throughout this book, the icon will be placed next to a problem where the use of a calculator is recommended. As you will see, this judgment is very subjective. Sometimes a question can be answered in a few seconds, with no calculations whatsoever, if you see the best approach. In that case, the use of a calculator is not recommended. If you don't see the easy way, however, and have to do some arithmetic, you may prefer to use a calculator.

Let's look at a few sample questions on which some students would use calculators a lot, others a little, and still others not at all.

Example 1.

If $16 \times 25 \times 36 = (4a)^2$, what is the value of a?

   (A) 6   (B) 15   (C) 30   (D) 36   (E) 60

(i)   **Heavy calculator use:** WITH A CALCULATOR multiply: $16 \times 25 \times 36 = 14{,}400$. Observe that $(4a)^2 = 16a^2$, and so $16a^2 = 14{,}400$. WITH A CALCULATOR divide: $a^2 = 14{,}400 \div 16 = 900$. Finally, WITH A CALCULATOR take the square root: $a = \sqrt{900} = 30$. The answer is **C**.

(ii)   **Light calculator use:** Immediately notice that you can "cancel" the 16 on the left-hand side with the 4^2 on the right-hand side. WITH A CALCULATOR multiply: $25 \times 36 = 900$, and WITH A CALCULATOR take the square root of 900: $\sqrt{900} = 30$.

(iii)   **No calculator use:** "Cancel" the 16 and the 4^2. Notice that $25 = 5^2$ and $36 = 6^2$, so $a^2 = 5^2 \times 6^2 = 30^2$, and $a = 30$.

Example 2.

Of the following, which has the greatest value when $w = 0.0001$?

(A) $1000w$ (B) w^2 (C) w (D) $\sqrt{w}$ (E) $\dfrac{1}{w}$

(i)   **Heavy calculator use:** WITH A CALCULATOR evaluate each of the five choices and compare:

   (A) 0.1 (B) 0.00000001 (C) 0.0001 (D) 0.01 (E) 10,000

The decision is not even close. The answer is **E**.

(ii)   **No calculator use:** Observe that, when w is very small, $\dfrac{1}{w}$ is very large, whereas the other numbers are small.

Example 3 (Grid-in).

If the length of a diagonal of a rectangle is 13, and if one of the sides is 5, what is the perimeter?

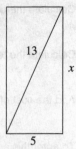

(i)   **Heavy calculator use:** By the Pythagorean theorem, $x^2 + 5^2 = 13^2$. Observe that $5^2 = 25$, and WITH A CALCULATOR evaluate: $13^2 = 169$. Then WITH A CALCULATOR subtract: $169 - 25 = 144$, so $x^2 = 144$. Hit the square-root key on your CALCULATOR to get $x = 12$. Finally, WITH A CALCULATOR add to find the perimeter: $5 + 12 + 5 + 12 = 34$.

(ii)   **Light calculator use:** The steps are the same as in (i) except that some of the calculations are done mentally: taking the square root of 144 and adding at the end.

(iii)   **No calculator use:** All calculations are done mentally. Better yet, no calculations are done at all, because you immediately see that each half of the rectangle is a 5-12-13 right triangle, and you add the sides mentally.

Column A	Column B
$(-15)(-43)$	$(-4)(-9)(-18)$

Example 4.

(i)   **Using a calculator.** Do both multiplications, making sure to enter the negative signs on the CALCULATOR. Compare the answers: 645 versus −648. Column **A** is greater.

(ii)   **No calculator use:** Column A is positive since it is the product of two negative numbers, whereas Column B, which is the product of three negative numbers, is negative.

Column A	Column B
$\dfrac{5}{9} \div \dfrac{9}{7}$	$\dfrac{5}{7}$

Example 5.

(i)   **Heavy calculator use:** WITH A CALCULATOR evaluate $\dfrac{5}{9} = 0.5555\ldots$ and $\dfrac{9}{7} = 1.2857\ldots$. WITH A CALCULATOR divide: $.5555 \div 1.2857 = 0.432$. WITH A CALCULATOR evaluate: $\dfrac{5}{7} = 0.714$. Since $0.714 > 0.432$, the answer is **B**.

(ii)   **Light calculator use:** Rewrite and multiply:

$$\frac{5}{9} \div \frac{9}{7} = \frac{5}{9} \times \frac{7}{9} = \frac{35}{81}.$$

WITH A CALCULATOR evaluate: $\dfrac{35}{81} = 0.432$ and $\dfrac{5}{7} = 0.714$.

(iii)   **Using a calculator with fraction capability:** Enter 5 / 9 ÷ 9 / 7 = . The readout will be 35/81. Now hit the key that converts fractions to decimals, and the readout will be 0.432 . . . Finally, compare that to 5 / 7, which equals 0.714. . . .

(iv) **No calculator use:** Rewrite and multiply:

$$\frac{5}{9} \div \frac{9}{7} = \frac{5}{9} \times \frac{7}{9} = \frac{35}{81}.$$

Observe that $\frac{35}{81}$ is clearly less than $\frac{1}{2}$, whereas $\frac{5}{7}$ is more than $\frac{1}{2}$.

(iv) **Alternative solution with no calculator use:**

Since $\frac{9}{7} > 1$, $\frac{5}{9} \div \frac{9}{7} < \frac{5}{9}$, which is less than $\frac{5}{7}$.

Who should use a calculator to find the average of 3, 4, and 5? No one. This arithmetic you can do in your head: $3 + 4 + 5 = 12$, and $12 \div 3 = 4$. You can do that faster than you can push the buttons on your calculator. Who should use a calculator to find the average of –3, –4, and –5? Anyone who is uncomfortable with negative numbers or tends to make mistakes when using them. By the way, after reading Section E in Chapter 12, you won't use a calculator on either problem—you won't even do any arithmetic. You'll know that the average of any three consecutive integers is the middle one.

Here are three final comments on the use of calculators:

1. The reason that calculators are of limited value on the SAT I is that no calculator can do mathematics. You have to know the mathematics and the way to apply it. No calculator can tell you, for example, that on a particular question you should use the Pythagorean theorem. All the calculator is good for is to calculate 13^2 in 5 seconds instead of the 10 seconds it would take you to do the calculation on paper. If, on the other hand, you had to calculate 6789^2, the calculator would save you a lot of time, but you will never have to do such a calculation on the SAT I.

2. No SAT I problem ever requires a lot of tedious calculation. However, if you don't see how to avoid calculating, just do it—don't spend a _lot_ of time looking for a shortcut that will save you a _little_ time!

3. Most students use calculators more than they should; but, if you can solve a problem with a calculator that you might otherwise miss, use the calculator.

2 Winning Tactics for the SAT I

- **Setting Goals**
- **Pacing Yourself**
- **Guessing**
- **Tactics for the Test**

Everyone wants to be a winner. In this chapter we present our winning tactics for the SAT I.

How can *you* become a winner on the SAT I? First, you have to decide just what winning is for you. For one student, winning means breaking 1000; for another, only a total score of 1400 will do. So the first thing you have to do is set *your* goals.

Second, you must learn to pace yourself during the test. You need to know how many questions to attempt to answer, how many to spend a little extra time on, and how many simply to skip.

Third, you need to understand the rewards of guessing—how educated guesses can boost your scores dramatically. If you doubt this statement, or if the idea of guessing troubles you, work your way through the section on guessing later in this chapter. It will convince you that guessing is an important strategy in helping you to reach your goal.

Finally, you have to master 16 practical, reliable tactics that will help you improve your performance on the SAT I. Memorize these tactics: they will work for you on this test, and on other tests to come.

Setting Goals

Before beginning your course of study for the SAT I, it is very important that you set a realistic goal for yourself. In order to do that, you need to know your math and verbal scores on one actual PSAT or SAT I to use as a reference or starting point.

1. If you have already taken an SAT and will be using this book to help you prepare to retake it, use your actual scores from that test.
2. If you have already taken the PSAT, but have not yet taken the SAT I, use your most recent actual PSAT scores, being sure to add a zero to the end of each score (changing a 55 to a 550, for example).

3. If you have not yet taken an actual PSAT or SAT I, do the following:
   - Reread Chapter 1 of this book to familiarize yourself with each type of question that is used on the SAT I.
   - Get a copy of the College Board's SAT I booklet from your guidance office, and then read the introductory material.
   - Find a quiet place where you can work for three hours without interruptions.
   - Take the SAT I in the booklet under true exam conditions: time yourself on each of the six sections; take no more than a two-minute break between sections; after finishing three sections, take a five-minute break.
   - Carefully follow the instructions in the booklet to grade the test and convert your total raw scores on each part (math and verbal) to a scaled score.
   - Use these scores as your starting point.

If for some reason you feel that your actual PSAT or SAT I scores do not provide an accurate picture of where you are (because you were sick the day you took the test, or for some other reason), instead of using those scores, take another sample test following the instructions in number 3 above.

The College Board reports that about a third of all students earn lower scores on the SAT I than they did on the PSAT; but by virtue of being more familiar with the test, having been in school for six more months, and having done some test preparation, two-thirds of all students earn higher scores on the SAT I than they did on the PSAT. However, the overall average increase is less than 25 points on each section. The College Board reports similar results for students who take the SAT I in the spring of their junior year and then again in the fall of their senior year. In 1994, the average change was an increase of 13 points on the verbal score and 10 points on the math score, a total of 23 points.

The statistics cited in the last paragraph are not very encouraging. Fortunately for you, students who conscientiously go through this book, learning the material, mastering the various tactics, and practicing on the model tests, have *much better results* than the College Board's averages. Using these techniques, we have helped thousands of students increase their scores by hundreds of points each.

It is now time to set a goal that would please you, but at the same time is reasonable. If you earned a 470 on the verbal portion of the PSAT, for example, you might *like* to get a 700 on the SAT I, but unfortunately, that's not a realistic goal. On the other hand, you certainly shouldn't accept as your goal the increase of only 20 points or so that the College Board says is about average. How much you can improve depends on three factors:

1. How high your previous scores are. It is much easier to go up 100 points from 450 to 550 than from 650 to 750.
2. How well prepared you were when you last took the PSAT or SAT I. If you studied extensively and are already familiar with the format of the test and know some of the basic tactics, you probably have less room for improvement than someone who has not yet learned any good test-taking strategies.
3. How much effort you are willing to devote to getting the highest possible scores. If you are committed to learning the material in this book and are willing to work diligently, you should set your goals higher than if you plan to spend just a few hours practicing and are not intending to devote the time necessary to get full benefit from this book.

Subject to the conditions mentioned and the fact that it is slightly easier to raise your math score than your verbal score, the following guidelines are reasonable for your *initial* goals.

Current score	Goal	Current score	Goal
300	400	550	620
350	450	600	660
400	500	650	700
450	540	700	740
500	580	750	780

So if your PSAT grades were 470 verbal and 520 math, we would recommend setting your goals at about 550 verbal and 600 math, an increase of about 80 on each part, for a total increase of 160 points. Clearly, this is far more than the College Board's guidelines, but it is absolutely realistic. If you set your goals higher than this, you risk being continually frustrated by falling far short of your target. Of course, if after using this book for several weeks it appears to you that you will easily reach your goals, do what thousands of our students have done: revise your goals upward. For example, if your initial math score was a 500 and it appears that you will easily reach your goal of 580, then push it to 600 or even 620. Later, you could even revise it again.

Why is it so important to set a goal? Why not just try to get the highest score you can by correctly answering as many questions as possible? The answer is that your goal tells you how many questions you should try to answer. *The single most common tactical error that students make is trying to answer too many questions.* Surprising as it may be, the following statement is true for almost all students:

THE BEST WAY TO INCREASE YOUR SCORE ON THE SAT I IS TO ANSWER FEWER QUESTIONS.

To understand why this is so, let's look at two hypothetical students. The first is John, an average student who expects to graduate in the middle of his class. His grade point average is in the low 80s, higher than about half of the students in his school and lower than the other half. On the SAT I, he would expect to do about the same, but he sets his sights a little higher, hoping to be in about the 60th percentile, scoring higher than 60 percent of the students taking the exam and lower than the other 40 percent.

What would have happened to John if on his final exam in math last year there were 60 questions, and he worked very slowly and carefully, making no mistakes, but answering only 35 of the questions, leaving the other 25 out? It would have been a disaster. He would have failed the final. Now let's look at the result if he does exactly that on the SAT I. He will earn 1 point for each of the 35 questions he answers correctly and nothing for the 25 he omits, so his raw score will be 35. That raw score will then be converted to a scaled score of about 540. For John, that's not a disaster at all; that's great! His score of 540 is not failing; it places him in the top third of all students taking the SAT I. If this occurs, John will exceed his goal, even though he is leaving out more than 40 percent of the questions on the test.

Actually, John is not a hypothetical student; he is real. And here's what really happened to him. In May of his junior year, he earned a 470 on the math portion of the SAT I. Naturally, he had missed a lot of the more difficult questions toward the end of each section. But he had also missed some of the easier questions. One morning, we had him do a sample SAT I for us. On the math section with 25 multiple-choice questions, he finished the first 16 questions in about 15 minutes and used the remaining 15 minutes for the 9 harder questions. On the first 16 questions, he got 11 right and 5 wrong; on the last 9, he got 2 right and 6 wrong, and he omitted 1. We recommended that he slow down and not even attempt the hard problems at the end. Our advice was to spend all 30 minutes on the first 16 questions. We gave him similar guidelines for each section of the test—math and verbal. The very next day, he returned and took another complete SAT I, following our suggestions. The difference was remarkable.

Leaving out the last 9 questions, he earned no points for them at all. That actually represented a *small loss,* because the previous day he earned $\frac{1}{2}$ point of raw score for them—2 points for the 2 right answers minus $\frac{6}{4}$ or $1\frac{1}{2}$ points from those annoying $\frac{1}{4}$ point penalties for each of the 6 questions he missed. (See pages 15–16 to learn how to calculate raw scores.) However, by taking the full 30 minutes on the early questions, he was able to eliminate all of his careless errors and wound up getting 15 out of 16 right. And that really helped his score *a lot.* Changing 4 wrong answers to 4 right answers raised his raw score by 5 points (plus 4 instead of minus 1). The net change on that one section was enough to raise his math score 40 points. He had similar results on the other sections, and *in one day* his math score went up 90 points. His verbal score also increased, by about 50 points.

John's success didn't stop there. He soon found that he could actually get the first 16 questions right (occasionally missing one), in about 24 to 25 minutes, rather than 30. Then, using the tactics from this book, he figured out which one or two of the remaining questions he had the best chance of answering correctly, and spent 5 to 6 minutes working on them. He made comparable improvements on the other math sections as well. In particular, he learned that it was always possible to make an educated guess on quantitative comparison questions, so he picked up a few additional points there. When he finally took the SAT I in the fall of his senior year, he left out 15 of the 60 math questions (a quarter of the test) but only missed two. His score of 620 was 150 points higher than the score he had earned the previous May!

Our second not-so-hypothetical student is Mary. She is a very good student, with an average in the low 90s. She isn't one of the few best in her school, but she is in the top 10 to 15 percent of her class. Her best subjects are math and science, and when she took the SAT I in her junior year, her math score was 710. However, she was disappointed in her verbal score, which was only 620. She desperately wanted to "break" 1400, and so decided to retake the SAT I in the fall. It turned out that although she understood virtually everything she read, she was a slow reader, and in order to finish the test, wound up skimming some passages rather than reading them. This resulted in her missing too many critical reading questions. She also missed some analogies and sentence completions she shouldn't have because she was racing to get to the reading, which she knew would require extra time.

We recommended that she slow down, just as we had for John. In particular, on the verbal section with two passages, we recommended that instead of reading both passages quickly, she skip the 5-question passage entirely, and read the 10-question passage more slowly and carefully. For several weeks, she resisted. Students used to getting 90s and 95s never intentionally leave out questions on a test, and, of course, leaving out questions on a test in school would be a terrible strategy. So she concentrated on practicing the tactics discussed in this book on both verbal analogies and sentence completions. Her score did improve, but not as much as she wanted it to. Finally, she agreed to try it our way. The results were stunning and immediate. Her verbal score shot up 50 points.

When Mary finally took the SAT I for the second time, she left out 10 verbal questions, and earned exactly 700 points. Note that although she was only in the top 10 to 15 percent of her class, her verbal SAT I score was in the top 2 to 3 percent of all the students in the country.

The advice in this section is so important that it is worth repeating:

THE BEST WAY TO INCREASE YOUR SCORE ON THE SAT I IS TO ANSWER FEWER QUESTIONS.

CAUTION: This advice does *not* imply that you should leave out questions without ever trying to guess. Later in this chapter, you will learn that if you have worked on a problem and have eliminated some choices, you *must* guess. Answering fewer questions *never* means omitting questions that you have worked on and on which you can make an educated guess. Answering fewer questions means not even reading certain questions because you are pacing yourself properly and taking more time on other questions. If, as you go through this book, you discover that certain patterns of questions *consistently* stump you, consider skipping them entirely to give yourself more time to answer the rest. However, once you've started work on any problem and have ruled out some answer choices, go for that educated guess.

How Many Questions Should You Answer?

Suppose that your current verbal score is 400 and that your initial goal is 500. To get a 500, you need a raw score of about 34 or 35, less than half of the 78 points available. Look at the following chart, which shows several ways to get a raw score of 35. Which way do you think is best?

Number answered	Number omitted	Number correct	Number wrong	Raw score
35	43	35	0	35
40	38	36	4	35
45	33	37	8	35
50	28	38	12	35
55	23	39	16	35
60	18	40	20	35
65	13	41	24	35

Going very slowly and answering only 35 questions is not the best strategy. Even working very carefully, you still might misinterpret a critical reading question, or miss a sentence completion question because you get confused about a vocabulary word you think you know. So you might wind up missing 2 or 3 questions. If you miss 3, your raw score would drop to 31 and you would fall short of your goal by 20 or 30 points.

Your best strategy would be to answer 40 to 45 questions (still omitting more than 40 percent of the test). This allows you to miss 4 to 8 questions and still reach your goal.

To see how to apply this strategy, carefully read the next section on pacing yourself.

Pacing Yourself

Once you have determined your goal and know how many questions in a particular section you have to answer to get the score you want, then you can work out how to pace yourself during the test.

Consider an actual section. The 15-minute math section contains 10 multiple-choice questions. To answer all 10, you would have to average 1.5 minutes per question. Going that fast, you might miss several. If, on the other hand, you attempted only 5 of them, you could average 3 minutes per question. At that rate, you might not miss any. If your math goal is a 550, for example, you need to get 6 correct answers in those 15 minutes. Our advice to you for that section would be to spend your time as follows:

Questions 1 and 2	1.5 minutes each
Questions 3, 4, 5, and 6	3 minutes each
Questions 7, 8, 9, and 10	don't even read them

Pacing yourself in this way would give you your best chance of getting the first 6 questions right. However, if you finish all 6 in 12 or 13 minutes, and still have 2 or 3 minutes left, use 30 seconds to read Questions 7 and 8. Quickly decide which one you think you have a better chance of getting right or making an educated guess on, and use your remaining time on that one question. Unless you are consistently getting all of the first 6 questions right, do not go any faster than this.

As you see, the general rule is first do the easy questions at the beginning of a section or set; then do the harder questions that follow. In the 25-multiple-choice-question math section, for example, you would generally be best off answering the questions in the exact order in which they appear. In the 30-question verbal section, however, you might be better off answering the first 5 of the 9 sentence completion questions in order and then skipping to Question 10 to start work on the easy analogy questions that begin the next set.

There are some exceptions to this general rule. In the 25-multiple-choice-question math section, suppose you have completed the first 18 questions and have only 6 minutes to go. Because you only have enough time to answer 2 (or at most 3) more questions, don't automatically try numbers 19 and 20. Take a few seconds to glance at the questions remaining and pick the 2 or 3 that *you* like best. Perhaps you may want to do the geometry questions and avoid the algebra ones (or vice versa). Similarly, in the other 30-minute math section, even though the last few quantitative comparison questions will be hard and the first few grid-ins easy, do not skip to the grid-ins. Instead, finish the quantitative comparisons first, because, as you will learn in Chapter 10, even on hard quantitative comparison questions you can almost always make an educated guess. Likewise, on the verbal section with two reading comprehension passages, glance at both passages and choose which one you want to read *first*. Pick the one you think will be easier or more congenial. Perhaps you prefer reading scientific passages to reading excerpts from novels (or vice versa).

The biggest issue in pacing yourself properly is deciding how many questions you are going to attempt in each section, and how many you are going to skip. As you have just seen in the previous section, this depends on the goal you have set for yourself.

To start the process, get the most recent copy of the College Board's booklet *Taking the SAT I Reasoning Test,* available in your school's guidance office, or the College Board's book *10 Real SATs,* available in bookstores and possibly in your school or public library. Look at an actual score conversion table. Find the raw scores corresponding to your scaled score goals, and on each part (math and verbal) the number of questions you should plan to answer is that raw score plus 5 or 6. For example, if the initial verbal goal that you set for yourself was 550, you would need a raw score of about 44. The simplest way to get a raw score of 44 is to answer exactly 44 questions and get all of them right. A more realistic way would be to answer 50 questions, so that even if you miss 5, your raw score would still be 44. Because there are 78 verbal questions, answering 50 means omitting 28. Therefore, plan to omit about 12 on each 30-minute section and 4 on the 15-minute section. A reasonable strategy on a 30-minute verbal section might be to just ignore the 4 or 5 hardest analogies and sentence completions and to omit a few critical reading questions.

Now do a couple of model tests in this book, pacing yourself to answer only the required number of questions in each section. You will quickly determine how fast or slow you have to go in order to answer the correct number of questions in the allotted time. If you don't finish, try to go a little faster the next time. If you finish early, don't answer more questions; go back and look over any questions you guessed at or about which you were unsure. Only when you can *consistently* reach your goal should you raise it and try to answer more questions.

Guessing

If you don't know the answer to a question on the SAT I, should you guess?

There is probably more controversy surrounding the issue of guessing than any other. If you ask several people for advice, you will surely get conflicting answers. However, the answer to the above question is very simple: in general, *it pays to guess*. To understand why this is so and why so many people are confused about it, you must understand how the SAT I is scored.

On the SAT I, every question is worth exactly the same amount: one point. A correct answer to a critical reading question for which you might have to reread a whole paragraph is worth no more than a correct answer to a verbal analogy that you can answer in a few seconds. You get no more credit for a correct answer to the hardest math question than you do for the easiest. For each question that you answer correctly, you receive one raw score point. Your total raw score on the math and verbal sections are then converted to scaled scores between 200 and 800. Because the three verbal sections of the SAT I have a total of 78 questions, the maximum raw score you could get would be a 78, which you would obtain by answering every question correctly (a feat achieved by fewer than one student in a thousand), and that raw score would be converted to a scaled score of 800.

Consider the following scenario. Suppose you work very slowly and carefully and answer only half (39) of the verbal questions, and get each of them correct. Your raw score would be 39, and that would be converted to a scaled score of about 520. If that were the whole story, then you should take the last minute of the test and quickly fill in an answer to each of the other 39 questions. Because each question has 5 choices, you should get about one-fifth of them right. Surely, you would get *some* of them right—most likely between 5 and 11. Say you get 8 of them right. Then your raw score would go from 39 to 47, and your scaled score would now be about 570. Your verbal score would increase 50 points due to one minute of wild guessing! Clearly, this is not what the College Board wants to happen. To counter this, there is a so-called *guessing penalty,* which adjusts your scores for wrong answers, and makes it unlikely that you will profit from wild guessing.

The penalty for each incorrect answer on the three verbal sections is a reduction of $\frac{1}{4}$ of a point. What effect would this penalty have in the example just discussed? Recall that by wildly guessing at 39 questions, you got 8 right and 31 wrong. Those 8 extra right answers caused your raw score to go up by 8 points. But now you lose $\frac{1}{4}$ of a point for each of the 31 problems you missed—a total reduction of $\frac{31}{4}$ or $7\frac{3}{4}$ points, which is rounded up to 8 points. So you broke even: you gained 8 points and lost 8 points. Your raw score, and hence your scaled score, didn't change at all.

Notice that the guessing *penalty* didn't actually penalize you. It prevented you from making a big gain that you didn't deserve, but it didn't punish you by lowering your score. It's not a very harsh penalty after all. In fairness, we should point out that wild guessing *could* have lowered your score. It is possible that instead of getting 8 correct answers, you only got 6, and as a result, your scaled score dropped from 520 to 510. On the other hand, it is actually slightly more likely that you would have gotten 10 rather than 6 right, and that your scaled score would have increased from 520 to 530 or 540. But, on average, *wild guessing does not affect your score on the SAT I.*

Educated guessing on the other hand can have an enormous effect on your score: it can increase it dramatically! Let's look at what we mean by educated guessing and see how it can improve your score on the SAT I.

Consider the following verbal analogy question.

TOLERANCE:BIGOTRY::
(A) prodigality:ribaldry
(B) magnanimity:parsimony
(C) exigency:urgency
(D) emulation:rivalry
(E) patience:conformity

Let's assume you know that *tolerance* is the opposite of *bigotry.* Suppose that looking at the choices, you realize that (C) is wrong because *exigency* and *urgency* mean the same thing, and that there doesn't seem to be much connection between the words in (D) and (E)—they're certainly not opposites. You now know that the correct answer

must be (A) or (B), but unfortunately you have no idea what *prodigality* or *parsimony* means. You *could* guess, but you don't want to be wrong; after all, there's that penalty for incorrect answers. So, should you leave it out? Absolutely not. *You must guess!* We'll explain why and how in a moment, but first let's look at one more example, this time a math one.

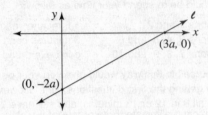

What is the slope of line ℓ in the figure above?

(A) $-\frac{2}{3}$ (B) $-\frac{3}{2}$ (C) 0   (D) $\frac{2}{3}$ (E) $\frac{3}{2}$

Suppose that you have completely forgotten how to calculate the slope of a line, but you do remember that lines that go up (↗) have positive slopes and that lines that go down (↘) have negative slopes. So you know the answer must be (D) or (E). What do you do? Do you guess and risk incurring the guessing penalty, or do you leave it out, because you're not sure which answer is correct? *You must guess!*

Suppose that you are still working slowly and carefully on the verbal sections, and that of the 78 questions, you are sure of the answers to 39 of them; in 15 of them you are able to eliminate 3 of the choices, but you have no idea which of the remaining 2 choices is correct; and the remaining 24 questions you don't even look at. You already know what would happen if you guessed wildly on the last 24 questions—you would probably break even. But what about the 15 questions you narrowed down to 2 choices? If you guess on those, you should get about half right and half wrong. Is that good or bad? *It's very good!* Assume you got 7 right and 8 wrong. For the 7 correct answers, you would receive 7 points, and for the 8 incorrect answers, you would lose $\frac{8}{4} = 2$ points. This is a net gain of 5 raw score points, for which your verbal SAT I score would go from 520 to 550. It would be a shame to throw away those 30 points just because you were afraid of the guessing penalty.

At this point, many students protest that they are unlucky and that they never guess right. They are wrong. *There is no such thing as a poor guesser.* We'll prove that to you in a minute. For the sake of argument, however, suppose you were a poor guesser, and that when you guessed on those 15 questions, you got twice as many wrong (10) as you got right (5). In that case you would have received 5 points for the correct ones and lost $\frac{10}{4} = 2\frac{1}{2}$ points for the incorrect ones. Your raw score would have increased from 39 to $41\frac{1}{2}$, which would be rounded up to 42, and your scaled score would still have increased: from 520 to 540. So even if you think you're a poor guesser, you should guess.

Actually, the real guessing penalty is not the one that the College Board uses to prevent you from profiting from wild guesses. *The real guessing penalty is the one you impose on yourself by not guessing when you should.*

Occasionally, you can even eliminate 4 of the 5 choices! Suppose that in the analogy given above, you realize that you do know what *prodigality* means, and that it can't be the answer. You still have no idea about *parsimony,* and you may be hesitant to answer a question with a word you never heard of; but you must. If in the previous math question, only one of the choices were positive, it would have to be correct. Don't leave it out because you can't verify the answer by calculating the slope yourself. You must choose the only answer you haven't eliminated.

What if you can't eliminate three or four of the choices? You should guess if you can eliminate even one choice. Assume that there are 20 questions whose answers you are unsure of. The following table indicates the most likely outcome if you guess at each of them.

| Number of choices eliminated | Most Likely Effect | | | | |
| | Number correct | Number wrong | Raw score | Scaled Score | |
				Verbal	Math
0	4	16	+0	+0	+0
1	5	15	+1.25	+10	+15
2	7	13	+3.75	+30	+40
3	10	10	+7.50	+50	+70
4	20	0	+20	+120	+150

On an actual test, there would be some questions on which you could eliminate 1 or 2 choices and others where you could eliminate 3 or 4. No matter what the mix, guessing pays.

The scoring of the math sections is somewhat different from the scoring of the verbal. The 35 multiple-choice questions have the same $1/4$-point penalty for incorrect answers as do all the verbal questions. Because the quantitative comparison questions have only 4 choices, however, the penalty is a little greater—$1/3$ of a point for each wrong answer. However, as you will see in Chapter 10, you can almost always eliminate 2 of the 4 choices, so you should *definitely guess on quantitative comparisons.* There is *no penalty* on grid-in questions, so you can surely guess on those. Of course, because you can grid in any number from .001 to 9999, it is very unlikely that a wild guess will be correct. But as you will see in Chapter 11, sometimes a grid-in

question will ask for the smallest integer that satisfies a certain property (the length of the side of a particular triangle, for example), and you know that the answer must be greater than 1 and less than 10. So guess.

It's time to prove to you that you are not a poor guesser; in fact, no one is. Take out a sheet of paper and number from 1 to 20. This is your answer sheet. Assume that for each of 20 questions you have eliminated 3 of the 5 choices (B, C, and E), so you know that the correct answer is either A or D. Now guess. Next to each number write either A or D. When you are done, turn to page 18. Tests 1, 2, and 3 list the order in which the first 20 A's and D's appeared on three actual SAT I's. Check to see how many right answers you would have had on each test. On each test, if you got 10 out of 20 correct, your SAT I score would have gone up by about 60 points as a result of your guessing. If you got more than 10 right, add 10 points for each extra one you got correct; if you got fewer than 10 right, subtract 10 points for each extra one you missed. So if you had 13 right, your SAT I score increased by 90 points, and if you only got 7 right, it still increased by 30 points. Probably, for the three tests, your average number of correct answers was very close to 10. You couldn't have missed all of them if you wanted to. You simply cannot afford not to guess.

You can repeat this experiment as often as you like. Ask a friend to write down a list of 20 A's and D's, and then compare your list and his. Or just go to the answer keys to the Model Tests in the back of the book, and read down any column, ignoring the B's, C's, and E's.

Would you like to see how well you do if you can eliminate only 2 choices? Do the same thing, except this time eliminate B and D and choose A, C, or E. Check your answers against the correct answers in Tests 4, 5, and 6 on page 18. Give yourself 1 raw score point for each correct answer and deduct $1/4$ of a point for each wrong answer. Multiply your raw score by 8 to get approximately how many points you gained by guessing.

A few final comments about guessing. If it is really a guess, don't agonize over it. Don't spend 30 seconds thinking, "Should I pick A? The last time I guessed, I chose A; maybe this time I should pick D. I'm really not sure. But I haven't had too many A answers lately; so, maybe it's time." STOP! A guess is just that—a guess. You can decide right now how you are going to guess on the actual SAT I you take. For example, you could just always guess the letter closest to A: if A is in the running, choose it; if not, pick B, and so on. If you'd rather start with E, that's OK, too. If you are down to 2 choices and you have a hunch, play it. But if you have no idea and it is truly a guess, do not take more than two seconds to choose, and move on to the next question.

TEST 1

1. A	11. D
2. D	12. D
3. D	13. A
4. A	14. D
5. A	15. A
6. D	16. D
7. D	17. A
8. A	18. D
9. A	19. A
10. A	20. D

TEST 2

1. D	11. D
2. A	12. A
3. D	13. D
4. A	14. D
5. D	15. A
6. A	16. A
7. A	17. D
8. D	18. D
9. A	19. D
10. A	20. A

TEST 3

1. A	11. D
2. D	12. D
3. D	13. D
4. A	14. A
5. D	15. A
6. D	16. D
7. D	17. A
8. A	18. A
9. A	19. D
10. D	20. D

TEST 4

1. A	11. E
2. C	12. A
3. A	13. E
4. C	14. E
5. E	15. C
6. E	16. C
7. C	17. C
8. A	18. E
9. E	19. E
10. C	20. A

TEST 5

1. C	11. C
2. A	12. E
3. A	13. E
4. A	14. E
5. C	15. A
6. E	16. E
7. A	17. C
8. C	18. C
9. C	19. C
10. C	20. E

TEST 6

1. C	11. C
2. C	12. E
3. E	13. A
4. E	14. C
5. A	15. A
6. A	16. A
7. C	17. A
8. E	18. C
9. E	19. E
10. A	20. E

Tactics for the Test

Here are 16 tactics to help you maximize your SAT I scores. Practice using them on every model test you do. That way, by the time you take your SAT I, they will be second nature to you.

1   Keep careful track of your time.

Bring a watch. Even if there is a clock in the room, it is better for you to have a watch on your desk. Before you start each section, set your watch to 12:00. It is easier to know that a section will be over when your watch reads 12:30 than to have a section start at 9:37 and have to remember

that it will be over at 10:07. Your job will be even easier if you have a digital stopwatch that you start at the beginning of each section; either let it count down from 30 (or 15) to zero or start it at 0 and know that your time will be up after 15 or 30 minutes.

2   Don't read the directions or look at the sample questions.

For each section of the SAT I, the directions given in this book are identical to the directions you will see on your

actual exam. Learn them now. Do not waste even a few seconds of your valuable test time reading them.

3   Answer the easy questions first; then tackle the hard ones.

Because the questions in each section (except the critical reading questions) proceed from easy to hard, this usually

means you should answer the questions in the order in which they appear.

4   Be aware of the difficulty level of each question.

Easy questions (the first few in each section) can usually be answered very quickly. Don't read too much into them. On these questions, your first hunch is probably right. Difficult questions (the last few in a section or group) usually require

a bit of thought. Be wary of an answer that strikes you immediately. You may have made an incorrect assumption or fallen into a trap. Reread the question and check the other choices before answering too quickly.

In the verbal sections, read each choice before choosing your answer.

Unlike math questions, which always have exactly one correct answer, verbal questions are more subjective. You are looking for the *best* choice. If A or B looks good, still check out the others; D or E might be better.

If you aren't sure of an answer, guess if you can eliminate even one of the choices (which should almost always be the case).

Remember that educated guessing can significantly increase your scores. In particular, don't leave out any critical reading questions if you have read the passage; you can always eliminate some of the choices. Most math questions contain at least one or two choices that are absurd (for example, negative choices when you know the answer must be positive); eliminate them and guess.

Fill in the answers on your answer sheet in blocks.

This is an important time-saving technique. For example, suppose that the first page of a math section has four questions. As you answer each question, circle the correct answer in your question book. Then before going on to the next page, enter your four answers on your answer sheet. This is more efficient than moving back and forth between your question booklet and answer sheet after each question. This technique is particularly valuable on the critical reading sections, where entering your answers after each question may interrupt your train of thought about the passage.

> **CAUTION:** When you get to the last two or three minutes of each section, enter your answers as you go. You don't want to be left with a block of questions that you have answered but not yet entered when the proctor announces that time is up.

Make sure that you answer the question asked.

Sometimes a math question requires you to solve an equation, but instead of asking for the value of x, the question asks for the value of x^2 or $x - 5$. Similarly, sometimes a critical reading question requires you to determine the LEAST likely outcome of an action; still another may ask you to find the exception to something, as in "The author uses all of the following EXCEPT." To avoid answering the wrong question, circle or underline what you have been asked for.

Answer questions based only on the information provided—never on what you think you already know.

On critical reading questions, base your answer only on the material in the passage, not on what you think you know about the subject matter. On data interpretation questions, base your answer only on the information given in the chart or table.

Remember that you are allowed to write anything you want in your test booklet.

Circle questions you skip, and put big question marks next to questions you answer but are unsure about. If you have time left at the end, you want to be able to locate those questions quickly to go over them. In sentence completion questions, circle or underline key words such as *although, therefore, not,* and so on. In reading passages, underline or put a mark in the margin next to any important point. On math questions, mark up diagrams, adding lines when necessary. And, of course, use all the space provided to solve the problem. In every section, math and verbal, cross out every choice that you *know* is wrong. In short, write anything that will help you, using whatever symbols you like. But remember, the only thing that counts is what you enter on your answer sheet. No one will ever see anything that you write in your booklet.

Be careful not to make any stray pencil marks on your answer sheet.

The SAT I is scored by a computer that cannot distinguish between an accidental mark and a filled-in answer. If the computer registers two answers where there should be only one, it will mark that question wrong.

Don't change answers capriciously.

If you have time to return to a question and realize that you made a mistake, by all means correct it, making sure you *completely* erase the first mark you made. However, don't change answers on a last-minute hunch or whim, or for fear there have been too many A's and not enough B's. In such cases, more often than not, students change right answers to wrong ones.

Use your calculator only when you need to.

As explained in Chapter 1, many students actually waste time using their calculators on questions that do not require them. Use your calculator whenever you feel it will help, but don't overuse it. And remember, no problem on the SAT I requires lengthy, tedious calculations.

When you use your calculator, don't go too quickly.

Your calculator leaves no trail. If you accidentally hit the wrong button, and get a wrong answer, there is no way to look at your work and find your mistake. You just have to do it all over.

Remember your pacing strategies: never get bogged down on any one question, and don't rush.

Using the techniques in this chapter, you should set realistic goals for how many questions you can answer in the

allotted time. Stick to your plan. Don't panic and try to race through more questions.

Remember that you don't have to answer every question to do well.

Reread the sections on setting goals and pacing. You know you don't have to answer all the questions to do well. It is possible to omit more than half of the questions and still be

in the top half of all students taking the test; similarly, you can omit more than 30 questions and earn a 1300. After you set your final goal, pace yourself to reach it.

Now you have the general tactics you'll need to deal with SAT I. In the next chapter, apply them: take our Diagnostic Test and see how you do. Then move on to Part Three,

where you will learn tactics for handling each specific question type.

PART TWO

Pinpoint Your Trouble Spots

3 A Diagnostic SAT I

- ■ **Diagnostic Test**
- ■ **Answer Key**
- ■ **Self-Evaluation**
- ■ **Answer Explanations**

The diagnostic test in this chapter is a multipurpose tool. First, it is a tool to help you identify your problem areas and skills. Take the test, evaluate your results following our charts, and you will discover your strengths and weaknesses. You will know what to study.

Second, this test is a tool to help you design a study plan that's right for you. Use the information you get from this test to tailor a study plan to fit your particular needs. If you find you need extra time on a certain topic, build time in. You are in charge of your study program—make it work for you.

Third, this test is your introduction to the format and content of the actual SAT I. There is nothing like working your way through actual SAT I-type questions for two-and-a-half hours to teach you how much stamina you need and how much speed.

Finally, this test is your chance to learn how to profit from your mistakes. It will expose you to the sorts of traps the test-makers set for you and the sorts of shortcuts we recommend you take. Read the answer explanations for every question you miss or omit. You'll be amazed to see how much you'll learn.

You are about to take a Diagnostic Test that can change the way you do on the SAT I. You have two-and-a-half hours to get through the six sections. Make every minute pay.

Answer Sheet—Diagnostic Test

If a section has fewer than 35 questions, leave the extra spaces blank.

Remove answer sheet by cutting on dotted line

Section 1

1 Ⓐ Ⓑ Ⓒ Ⓓ Ⓔ	8 Ⓐ Ⓑ Ⓒ Ⓓ Ⓔ	15 Ⓐ Ⓑ Ⓒ Ⓓ Ⓔ	22 Ⓐ Ⓑ Ⓒ Ⓓ Ⓔ	29 Ⓐ Ⓑ Ⓒ Ⓓ Ⓔ
2 Ⓐ Ⓑ Ⓒ Ⓓ Ⓔ	9 Ⓐ Ⓑ Ⓒ Ⓓ Ⓔ	16 Ⓐ Ⓑ Ⓒ Ⓓ Ⓔ	23 Ⓐ Ⓑ Ⓒ Ⓓ Ⓔ	30 Ⓐ Ⓑ Ⓒ Ⓓ Ⓔ
3 Ⓐ Ⓑ Ⓒ Ⓓ Ⓔ	10 Ⓐ Ⓑ Ⓒ Ⓓ Ⓔ	17 Ⓐ Ⓑ Ⓒ Ⓓ Ⓔ	24 Ⓐ Ⓑ Ⓒ Ⓓ Ⓔ	31 Ⓐ Ⓑ Ⓒ Ⓓ Ⓔ
4 Ⓐ Ⓑ Ⓒ Ⓓ Ⓔ	11 Ⓐ Ⓑ Ⓒ Ⓓ Ⓔ	18 Ⓐ Ⓑ Ⓒ Ⓓ Ⓔ	25 Ⓐ Ⓑ Ⓒ Ⓓ Ⓔ	32 Ⓐ Ⓑ Ⓒ Ⓓ Ⓔ
5 Ⓐ Ⓑ Ⓒ Ⓓ Ⓔ	12 Ⓐ Ⓑ Ⓒ Ⓓ Ⓔ	19 Ⓐ Ⓑ Ⓒ Ⓓ Ⓔ	26 Ⓐ Ⓑ Ⓒ Ⓓ Ⓔ	33 Ⓐ Ⓑ Ⓒ Ⓓ Ⓔ
6 Ⓐ Ⓑ Ⓒ Ⓓ Ⓔ	13 Ⓐ Ⓑ Ⓒ Ⓓ Ⓔ	20 Ⓐ Ⓑ Ⓒ Ⓓ Ⓔ	27 Ⓐ Ⓑ Ⓒ Ⓓ Ⓔ	34 Ⓐ Ⓑ Ⓒ Ⓓ Ⓔ
7 Ⓐ Ⓑ Ⓒ Ⓓ Ⓔ	14 Ⓐ Ⓑ Ⓒ Ⓓ Ⓔ	21 Ⓐ Ⓑ Ⓒ Ⓓ Ⓔ	28 Ⓐ Ⓑ Ⓒ Ⓓ Ⓔ	35 Ⓐ Ⓑ Ⓒ Ⓓ Ⓔ

Section 2

1 Ⓐ Ⓑ Ⓒ Ⓓ Ⓔ	8 Ⓐ Ⓑ Ⓒ Ⓓ Ⓔ	15 Ⓐ Ⓑ Ⓒ Ⓓ Ⓔ	22 Ⓐ Ⓑ Ⓒ Ⓓ Ⓔ	29 Ⓐ Ⓑ Ⓒ Ⓓ Ⓔ
2 Ⓐ Ⓑ Ⓒ Ⓓ Ⓔ	9 Ⓐ Ⓑ Ⓒ Ⓓ Ⓔ	16 Ⓐ Ⓑ Ⓒ Ⓓ Ⓔ	23 Ⓐ Ⓑ Ⓒ Ⓓ Ⓔ	30 Ⓐ Ⓑ Ⓒ Ⓓ Ⓔ
3 Ⓐ Ⓑ Ⓒ Ⓓ Ⓔ	10 Ⓐ Ⓑ Ⓒ Ⓓ Ⓔ	17 Ⓐ Ⓑ Ⓒ Ⓓ Ⓔ	24 Ⓐ Ⓑ Ⓒ Ⓓ Ⓔ	31 Ⓐ Ⓑ Ⓒ Ⓓ Ⓔ
4 Ⓐ Ⓑ Ⓒ Ⓓ Ⓔ	11 Ⓐ Ⓑ Ⓒ Ⓓ Ⓔ	18 Ⓐ Ⓑ Ⓒ Ⓓ Ⓔ	25 Ⓐ Ⓑ Ⓒ Ⓓ Ⓔ	32 Ⓐ Ⓑ Ⓒ Ⓓ Ⓔ
5 Ⓐ Ⓑ Ⓒ Ⓓ Ⓔ	12 Ⓐ Ⓑ Ⓒ Ⓓ Ⓔ	19 Ⓐ Ⓑ Ⓒ Ⓓ Ⓔ	26 Ⓐ Ⓑ Ⓒ Ⓓ Ⓔ	33 Ⓐ Ⓑ Ⓒ Ⓓ Ⓔ
6 Ⓐ Ⓑ Ⓒ Ⓓ Ⓔ	13 Ⓐ Ⓑ Ⓒ Ⓓ Ⓔ	20 Ⓐ Ⓑ Ⓒ Ⓓ Ⓔ	27 Ⓐ Ⓑ Ⓒ Ⓓ Ⓔ	34 Ⓐ Ⓑ Ⓒ Ⓓ Ⓔ
7 Ⓐ Ⓑ Ⓒ Ⓓ Ⓔ	14 Ⓐ Ⓑ Ⓒ Ⓓ Ⓔ	21 Ⓐ Ⓑ Ⓒ Ⓓ Ⓔ	28 Ⓐ Ⓑ Ⓒ Ⓓ Ⓔ	35 Ⓐ Ⓑ Ⓒ Ⓓ Ⓔ

Section 3

1 Ⓐ Ⓑ Ⓒ Ⓓ Ⓔ	8 Ⓐ Ⓑ Ⓒ Ⓓ Ⓔ	15 Ⓐ Ⓑ Ⓒ Ⓓ Ⓔ	22 Ⓐ Ⓑ Ⓒ Ⓓ Ⓔ	29 Ⓐ Ⓑ Ⓒ Ⓓ Ⓔ
2 Ⓐ Ⓑ Ⓒ Ⓓ Ⓔ	9 Ⓐ Ⓑ Ⓒ Ⓓ Ⓔ	16 Ⓐ Ⓑ Ⓒ Ⓓ Ⓔ	23 Ⓐ Ⓑ Ⓒ Ⓓ Ⓔ	30 Ⓐ Ⓑ Ⓒ Ⓓ Ⓔ
3 Ⓐ Ⓑ Ⓒ Ⓓ Ⓔ	10 Ⓐ Ⓑ Ⓒ Ⓓ Ⓔ	17 Ⓐ Ⓑ Ⓒ Ⓓ Ⓔ	24 Ⓐ Ⓑ Ⓒ Ⓓ Ⓔ	31 Ⓐ Ⓑ Ⓒ Ⓓ Ⓔ
4 Ⓐ Ⓑ Ⓒ Ⓓ Ⓔ	11 Ⓐ Ⓑ Ⓒ Ⓓ Ⓔ	18 Ⓐ Ⓑ Ⓒ Ⓓ Ⓔ	25 Ⓐ Ⓑ Ⓒ Ⓓ Ⓔ	32 Ⓐ Ⓑ Ⓒ Ⓓ Ⓔ
5 Ⓐ Ⓑ Ⓒ Ⓓ Ⓔ	12 Ⓐ Ⓑ Ⓒ Ⓓ Ⓔ	19 Ⓐ Ⓑ Ⓒ Ⓓ Ⓔ	26 Ⓐ Ⓑ Ⓒ Ⓓ Ⓔ	33 Ⓐ Ⓑ Ⓒ Ⓓ Ⓔ
6 Ⓐ Ⓑ Ⓒ Ⓓ Ⓔ	13 Ⓐ Ⓑ Ⓒ Ⓓ Ⓔ	20 Ⓐ Ⓑ Ⓒ Ⓓ Ⓔ	27 Ⓐ Ⓑ Ⓒ Ⓓ Ⓔ	34 Ⓐ Ⓑ Ⓒ Ⓓ Ⓔ
7 Ⓐ Ⓑ Ⓒ Ⓓ Ⓔ	14 Ⓐ Ⓑ Ⓒ Ⓓ Ⓔ	21 Ⓐ Ⓑ Ⓒ Ⓓ Ⓔ	28 Ⓐ Ⓑ Ⓒ Ⓓ Ⓔ	35 Ⓐ Ⓑ Ⓒ Ⓓ Ⓔ

Section 4

1 Ⓐ Ⓑ Ⓒ Ⓓ Ⓔ	4 Ⓐ Ⓑ Ⓒ Ⓓ Ⓔ	7 Ⓐ Ⓑ Ⓒ Ⓓ Ⓔ	10 Ⓐ Ⓑ Ⓒ Ⓓ Ⓔ	13 Ⓐ Ⓑ Ⓒ Ⓓ Ⓔ
2 Ⓐ Ⓑ Ⓒ Ⓓ Ⓔ	5 Ⓐ Ⓑ Ⓒ Ⓓ Ⓔ	8 Ⓐ Ⓑ Ⓒ Ⓓ Ⓔ	11 Ⓐ Ⓑ Ⓒ Ⓓ Ⓔ	14 Ⓐ Ⓑ Ⓒ Ⓓ Ⓔ
3 Ⓐ Ⓑ Ⓒ Ⓓ Ⓔ	6 Ⓐ Ⓑ Ⓒ Ⓓ Ⓔ	9 Ⓐ Ⓑ Ⓒ Ⓓ Ⓔ	12 Ⓐ Ⓑ Ⓒ Ⓓ Ⓔ	15 Ⓐ Ⓑ Ⓒ Ⓓ Ⓔ

Section 4 (continued)

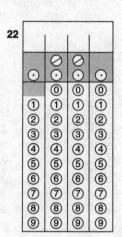

Section 5

1 Ⓐ Ⓑ Ⓒ Ⓓ Ⓔ	8 Ⓐ Ⓑ Ⓒ Ⓓ Ⓔ	15 Ⓐ Ⓑ Ⓒ Ⓓ Ⓔ	22 Ⓐ Ⓑ Ⓒ Ⓓ Ⓔ	29 Ⓐ Ⓑ Ⓒ Ⓓ Ⓔ
2 Ⓐ Ⓑ Ⓒ Ⓓ Ⓔ	9 Ⓐ Ⓑ Ⓒ Ⓓ Ⓔ	16 Ⓐ Ⓑ Ⓒ Ⓓ Ⓔ	23 Ⓐ Ⓑ Ⓒ Ⓓ Ⓔ	30 Ⓐ Ⓑ Ⓒ Ⓓ Ⓔ
3 Ⓐ Ⓑ Ⓒ Ⓓ Ⓔ	10 Ⓐ Ⓑ Ⓒ Ⓓ Ⓔ	17 Ⓐ Ⓑ Ⓒ Ⓓ Ⓔ	24 Ⓐ Ⓑ Ⓒ Ⓓ Ⓔ	31 Ⓐ Ⓑ Ⓒ Ⓓ Ⓔ
4 Ⓐ Ⓑ Ⓒ Ⓓ Ⓔ	11 Ⓐ Ⓑ Ⓒ Ⓓ Ⓔ	18 Ⓐ Ⓑ Ⓒ Ⓓ Ⓔ	25 Ⓐ Ⓑ Ⓒ Ⓓ Ⓔ	32 Ⓐ Ⓑ Ⓒ Ⓓ Ⓔ
5 Ⓐ Ⓑ Ⓒ Ⓓ Ⓔ	12 Ⓐ Ⓑ Ⓒ Ⓓ Ⓔ	19 Ⓐ Ⓑ Ⓒ Ⓓ Ⓔ	26 Ⓐ Ⓑ Ⓒ Ⓓ Ⓔ	33 Ⓐ Ⓑ Ⓒ Ⓓ Ⓔ
6 Ⓐ Ⓑ Ⓒ Ⓓ Ⓔ	13 Ⓐ Ⓑ Ⓒ Ⓓ Ⓔ	20 Ⓐ Ⓑ Ⓒ Ⓓ Ⓔ	27 Ⓐ Ⓑ Ⓒ Ⓓ Ⓔ	34 Ⓐ Ⓑ Ⓒ Ⓓ Ⓔ
7 Ⓐ Ⓑ Ⓒ Ⓓ Ⓔ	14 Ⓐ Ⓑ Ⓒ Ⓓ Ⓔ	21 Ⓐ Ⓑ Ⓒ Ⓓ Ⓔ	28 Ⓐ Ⓑ Ⓒ Ⓓ Ⓔ	35 Ⓐ Ⓑ Ⓒ Ⓓ Ⓔ

Section 6

1 Ⓐ Ⓑ Ⓒ Ⓓ Ⓔ	8 Ⓐ Ⓑ Ⓒ Ⓓ Ⓔ	15 Ⓐ Ⓑ Ⓒ Ⓓ Ⓔ	22 Ⓐ Ⓑ Ⓒ Ⓓ Ⓔ	29 Ⓐ Ⓑ Ⓒ Ⓓ Ⓔ
2 Ⓐ Ⓑ Ⓒ Ⓓ Ⓔ	9 Ⓐ Ⓑ Ⓒ Ⓓ Ⓔ	16 Ⓐ Ⓑ Ⓒ Ⓓ Ⓔ	23 Ⓐ Ⓑ Ⓒ Ⓓ Ⓔ	30 Ⓐ Ⓑ Ⓒ Ⓓ Ⓔ
3 Ⓐ Ⓑ Ⓒ Ⓓ Ⓔ	10 Ⓐ Ⓑ Ⓒ Ⓓ Ⓔ	17 Ⓐ Ⓑ Ⓒ Ⓓ Ⓔ	24 Ⓐ Ⓑ Ⓒ Ⓓ Ⓔ	31 Ⓐ Ⓑ Ⓒ Ⓓ Ⓔ
4 Ⓐ Ⓑ Ⓒ Ⓓ Ⓔ	11 Ⓐ Ⓑ Ⓒ Ⓓ Ⓔ	18 Ⓐ Ⓑ Ⓒ Ⓓ Ⓔ	25 Ⓐ Ⓑ Ⓒ Ⓓ Ⓔ	32 Ⓐ Ⓑ Ⓒ Ⓓ Ⓔ
5 Ⓐ Ⓑ Ⓒ Ⓓ Ⓔ	12 Ⓐ Ⓑ Ⓒ Ⓓ Ⓔ	19 Ⓐ Ⓑ Ⓒ Ⓓ Ⓔ	26 Ⓐ Ⓑ Ⓒ Ⓓ Ⓔ	33 Ⓐ Ⓑ Ⓒ Ⓓ Ⓔ
6 Ⓐ Ⓑ Ⓒ Ⓓ Ⓔ	13 Ⓐ Ⓑ Ⓒ Ⓓ Ⓔ	20 Ⓐ Ⓑ Ⓒ Ⓓ Ⓔ	27 Ⓐ Ⓑ Ⓒ Ⓓ Ⓔ	34 Ⓐ Ⓑ Ⓒ Ⓓ Ⓔ
7 Ⓐ Ⓑ Ⓒ Ⓓ Ⓔ	14 Ⓐ Ⓑ Ⓒ Ⓓ Ⓔ	21 Ⓐ Ⓑ Ⓒ Ⓓ Ⓔ	28 Ⓐ Ⓑ Ⓒ Ⓓ Ⓔ	35 Ⓐ Ⓑ Ⓒ Ⓓ Ⓔ

DIAGNOSTIC TEST   1 1 1 1 1 1   1

**Time—30 Minutes
30 Questions** **Select the best answer to the following questions, then fill in
the appropriate space on your Answer Sheet.**

Each of the following sentences contains one or two blanks; these blanks indicate that a word or set of words has been left out. Below the sentence are five words or phrases, lettered A through E. Select the word or set of words that best completes the sentence.

Example:

Fame is ----; today's rising star is all too soon tomorrow's washed-up has-been.

(A) rewarding   (B) gradual
 (C) essential   (D) spontaneous
  (E) transitory

 Ⓐ Ⓑ Ⓒ Ⓓ ●

---

1. Because of their frequent disarray, confusion, and loss of memory, those hit by lightning while alone are sometimes ---- victims of assault.

   (A) mistaken for
   (B) attracted to
   (C) unaware of
   (D) avoided by
   (E) useful to

2. Having published more than three hundred books in less than fifty years, science fiction writer Isaac Asimov may well be the most ---- author of our day.

   (A) fastidious
   (B) insecure
   (C) outmoded
   (D) prolific
   (E) indigenous

3. Because his time was limited, Weng decided to read the ---- novel *War and Peace* in ---- edition.

   (A) wordy...an unedited
   (B) lengthy...an abridged
   (C) famous...a modern
   (D) romantic...an autographed
   (E) popular...a complete

4. In giving a speech, the speaker's goal is to communicate ideas clearly and ----, so that the audience will be in no ---- about the meaning of the speech.

   (A) effectively...haste
   (B) indirectly...distress
   (C) vigorously...discomfort
   (D) unambiguously...confusion
   (E) tactfully...suspense

5. Although gregarious by nature, Lisa became quiet and ---- after she was unexpectedly laid off from work.

   (A) autonomous   (B) susceptible   (C) assertive
   (D) withdrawn   (E) composed

6. The increasingly popular leader of America's second largest tribe, Cherokee Chief Wilma Mankiller, has ---- the myth that only males could be leaders in American Indian government.

   (A) shattered   (B) perpetuated   (C) exaggerated
   (D) confirmed   (E) venerated

7. The commission of inquiry censured the senator for his ---- expenditure of public funds, which they found to be ----.

   (A) flagrant...cursory
   (B) improper...vindicated
   (C) lavish...unjustifiable
   (D) judicious...blameworthy
   (E) arbitrary...critical

8. During the Battle of Trafalgar, Admiral Nelson remained ---- and in full command of the situation in spite of the hysteria and panic all around him.

   (A) impassable   (B) imperturbable
   (C) overbearing   (D) frenetic
    (E) lackadaisical

9. Although he had spent many hours at the computer trying to solve the problem, he was the first to admit that the final solution was ---- and not the ---- of his labor.

   (A) trivial...cause
   (B) incomplete...intent
   (C) adequate...concern
   (D) schematic...fault
   (E) fortuitous...result

GO ON TO THE NEXT PAGE ➤

1   1   1   1   1   1   1   1   1   1   1

The analogies questions present two words or phrases that are related in some way. Determine which A-through-E answer choice below has a relationship *most* similar to that of the original words or phrases.

Example:

YAWN:BOREDOM::   (A) dream:sleep
(B) anger:madness   (C) smile:amusement
(D) face:expression   (E) impatience:rebellion

Ⓐ Ⓑ ● Ⓓ Ⓔ

10. CONSTITUTION:PREAMBLE::
    (A) prelude:overture
    (B) legislation:introduction
    (C) opera:intermezzo
    (D) book:preface
    (E) play:epilogue

11. QUARRY:MARBLE::
    (A) metal:silver
    (B) ore:gold
    (C) mine:coal
    (D) prey:rabbit
    (E) necklace:diamonds

12. JOY:ECSTASY::
    (A) rain:drought
    (B) breeze:hurricane
    (C) river:creek
    (D) deluge:flood
    (E) jazz:opera

13. DEPTH:FISSURE::
    (A) breadth:scope
    (B) height:peak
    (C) velocity:road
    (D) weight:diet
    (E) length:duration

14. BLATANT:OBTRUSIVENESS::
    (A) cynical:anger
    (B) weary:hopelessness
    (C) erudite:ignorance
    (D) lavish:extravagance
    (E) arrogant:humility

15. STRIDENT:VOICE::
    (A) muted:music
    (B) smooth:texture
    (C) acrid:taste
    (D) fragrant:odor
    (E) tuned:instrument

Read each of the passages below, and then answer the questions that follow each passage. The correct response may be stated outright or merely suggested in the passage.

Questions 16–21 are based on the following passage.

In this excerpt from Richard Wright's 1937 novel Black Boy, *the young African-American narrator confronts a new world in the books he illegally borrows from the "whites-only" public library.*

That night in my rented room, while letting the hot water run over my can of pork and beans in the sink, I opened Mencken's *A Book of*
Line *Prejudices* and began to read. I was jarred and
(5) shocked by the style, the clear, clean, sweeping sentences. Why did he write like that? And how did one write like that? I pictured the man as a raging demon, slashing with his pen, consumed with hate, denouncing everything American,
(10) extolling everything European, laughing at the weaknesses of people, mocking God, authority. What was this? I stood up, trying to realize what reality lay behind the meaning of the words. Yes, this man was fighting, fighting with words. He
(15) was using words as a weapon, using them as one would use a club. Could words be weapons? Well, yes, for here they were. Then, maybe, per-

haps, a Negro could use them as a weapon? No. It frightened me. I read on, and what amazed me
(20) was not what he said, but how on earth anybody had the courage to say it.

What strange world was this? I concluded the book with the conviction that I had somehow overlooked something terribly important in life. I
(25) had once tried to write, had once reveled in feeling, had let my crude imagination roam, but the impulse to dream had been slowly beaten out of me by experience. Now it surged up again and I hungered for books, new ways of looking and
(30) seeing. It was not a matter of believing or disbelieving what I read, but of feeling something new, of being affected by something that made the look of the world different.

GO ON TO THE NEXT PAGE

1   1   1   1   1   1   1   1   1   1   1

As dawn broke I ate my pork and beans, feel-
(35) ing dopey, sleepy. I went to work, but the mood
of the book would not die; it lingered, coloring
everything I saw, heard, did. I now felt that I
knew what the white men were feeling. Merely
because I had read a book that had spoken of how
(40) they lived and thought, I identified myself with
that book. I felt vaguely guilty. Would I, filled
with bookish notions, act in a manner that would
make the whites dislike me?

I forged more notes and my trips to the library
(45) became frequent. Reading grew into a passion.
My first serious novel was Sinclair Lewis's *Main
Street*. It made me see my boss, Mr. Gerald, and
identify him as an American type. I would smile
when I saw him lugging his golf bags into the
(50) office. I had always felt a vast distance separating
me from the boss, and now I felt closer to him,
though still distant. I felt now that I knew him,
that I could feel the very limits of his narrow life.
This had happened because I had read a novel
(55) about a mythical man called George F. Babbitt.
But I could not conquer my sense of guilt, my
feeling that the white men around me knew that I
was changing, that I had begun to regard them
differently.

16. The narrator's initial reaction to Mencken's prose
can best be described as one of

(A) wrath
(B) disbelief
(C) remorse
(D) laughter
(E) disdain

17. To the narrator, Mencken appeared to be all of the
following EXCEPT

(A) intrepid
(B) articulate
(C) satiric
(D) reverent
(E) opinionated

18. As used in line 36, "coloring" most nearly means

(A) reddening
(B) sketching
(C) blushing
(D) affecting
(E) lying

19. The narrator's attitude in lines 28–30 is best
described as one of

(A) dreamy indifference
(B) sullen resentment
(C) impatient ardor
(D) wistful anxiety
(E) quiet resolve

20. The passage suggests that, when he saw Mr. Gerald
carrying the golf clubs, the narrator smiled out of a
sense of

(A) relief
(B) duty
(C) recognition
(D) disbelief
(E) levity

21. The passage as a whole is best characterized as

(A) an impassioned argument in favor of increased
literacy for blacks
(B) a description of a youth's gradual introduction
to racial prejudice
(C) a comparison of the respective merits of
Mencken's and Lewis's literary styles
(D) an analysis of the impact of ordinary life on art
(E) a portrait of a youth's response to expanding
intellectual horizons

Questions 22–30 are based on the following passage.

*The following passage about pond-dwellers is excerpted
from an essay on natural history written in 1952 by the
zoologist Konrad Lorenz.*

There are some terrible robbers in the pond
world, and, in our aquarium, we may witness all
the cruelties of an embittered struggle for exis-
Line   tence enacted before our very eyes. If you have
(5) introduced to your aquarium a mixed catch, you
will soon see an example of such conflicts, for,
amongst the new arrivals, there will probably be a
larva of the water-beetle Dytiscus. Considering
their relative size, the voracity and cunning with
(10) which these animals destroy their prey eclipse the
methods of even such notorious robbers as tigers,
lions, wolves, or killer whales. These are all as
lambs compared with the Dytiscus larva.

It is a slim, streamlined insect, rather more
(15) than two inches long. Its six legs are equipped
with stout fringes of bristles, which form broad
oar-like blades that propel the animal quickly and
surely through the water. The wide, flat head
bears an enormous, pincer-shaped pair of jaws
(20) that are hollow and serve not only as syringes for
injecting poison, but also as orifices of ingestion.
The animal lies in ambush on some waterplant;
suddenly it shoots at lightning speed towards its
prey, darts underneath it, then quickly jerks up its
(25) head and grabs the victim in its jaws. "Prey," for

GO ON TO THE NEXT PAGE

1 1 1 1 1 1 1 1 1 1 1

these creatures, is all that moves or that smells of "animal" in any way. It has often happened to me that, while standing quietly in the water of a pond, I have been "eaten" by a Dytiscus larva.
(30) Even for man, an injection of the poisonous digestive juice of this insect is extremely painful.
  These beetle larvae are among the few animals that digest "out of doors." The glandular secretion that they inject, through their hollow forceps, into
(35) their prey, dissolves the entire inside of the latter into a liquid soup, which is then sucked in through the same channel by the attacker. Even large victims, such as fat tadpoles or dragon-fly larvae, which have been bitten by a Dytiscus
(40) larva, stiffen after a few defensive moments, and their inside, which, as in most water animals, is more or less transparent, becomes opaque as though fixed by formalin. The animal swells up first, then gradually shrinks to a limp bundle of
(45) skin that hangs from the deadly jaws, and is finally allowed to drop. In the confines of an aquarium, a few large Dytiscus larvae will, within days, eat all living things over a quarter of an inch long. What happens then? They will eat each other, if
(50) they have not already done so; this depends less on who is bigger and stronger than upon who succeeds in seizing the other first. I have often seen two nearly equal sized Dytiscus larvae each seize the other simultaneously and both die a quick
(55) death by inner dissolution. Very few animals, even when threatened with starvation, will attack an equal sized animal of their own species with the intention of devouring it. I only know this to be definitely true of rats and a few related
(60) rodents; that wolves do the same thing, I am much inclined to doubt, on the strength of some observations of which I shall speak later. But Dytiscus larvae devour animals of their own breed and size, even when other nourishment is at hand, and that
(65) is done, as far as I know, by no other animal.

22. By robbers (line 1), the author refers to
   (A) thieves
   (B) plagiarists
   (C) people who steal fish
   (D) creatures that devour their prey
   (E) unethical scientific observers

23. As used in line 5, a "mixed catch" most likely is
   (A) a device used to shut the aquarium lid temporarily
   (B) a disturbed group of water beetle larvae
   (C) a partially desirable prospective denizen of the aquarium
   (D) a random batch of creatures taken from a pond
   (E) a theoretical drawback that may have positive results

24. The presence of Dytiscus larvae in an aquarium most likely would be of particular interest to naturalists studying
   (A) means of exterminating water-beetle larvae
   (B) predatory patterns within a closed environment
   (C) genetic characteristics of a mixed catch
   (D) the effect of captivity on aquatic life
   (E) the social behavior of dragon-fly larvae

25. The author's primary purpose in lines 14–21 is to
   (A) depict the typical victim of a Dytiscus larva
   (B) point out the threat to humans represented by Dytiscus larvae
   (C) describe the physical appearance of an aquatic predator
   (D) refute the notion of the aquarium as a peaceful habitat
   (E) clarify the method the Dytiscus larva uses to dispatch its prey

26. The passage mentions all of the following facts about Dytiscus larvae EXCEPT that they
   (A) secrete digestive juices
   (B) attack their fellow larvae
   (C) are attracted to motion
   (D) provide food for amphibians
   (E) have ravenous appetites

27. By digesting "out of doors" (line 33), the author is referring to the Dytiscus larva's
   (A) preference for open-water ponds over confined spaces
   (B) metabolic elimination of waste matter
   (C) amphibious method of locomotion
   (D) extreme voraciousness of appetite
   (E) external conversion of food into absorbable form

28. According to the author, which of the following is (are) true of the victim of a Dytiscus larva?
   I. Its interior increases in opacity.
   II. It shrivels as it is drained of nourishment.
   III. It is beheaded by the larva's jaws.
   (A) I only
   (B) II only
   (C) III only
   (D) I and II only
   (E) II and III only

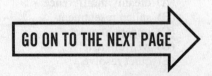

GO ON TO THE NEXT PAGE

29. In the final paragraph, the author mentions rats and related rodents in order to emphasize which point about Dytiscus larvae?

(A) Unless starvation drives them, they will not resort to eating members of their own species.

(B) They are reluctant to attack equal-sized members of their own breed.

(C) They are capable of resisting attacks from much larger animals.

(D) They are one of extremely few species given to devouring members of their own breed.

(E) Although they are noted predators, Dytiscus larvae are less savage than rats.

30. The author indicates that in subsequent passages he will discuss

(A) the likelihood of cannibalism among wolves

(B) the metamorphosis of dragon-fly larvae into dragon-flies

(C) antidotes to cases of Dytiscus poisoning

(D) the digestive processes of killer whales

(E) the elimination of Dytiscus larvae from aquariums

YOU MAY GO BACK AND REVIEW THIS SECTION IN THE REMAINING TIME, BUT DO NOT WORK IN ANY OTHER SECTION UNTIL TOLD TO DO SO.

STOP

2   2 2 2 2 2 2 2 2 2   2

SECTION 2

Time—30 Minutes
25 Questions

For each problem in this section determine which of the five choices is correct and blacken in that choice on your answer sheet. You may use any blank space on the page for your work.

Notes:

- You may use a calculator whenever you feel it will be helpful.
- Use the diagrams provided to help you solve the problems. Unless you see the words "Note: Figure not drawn to scale" under a diagram, it has been drawn as accurately as possible. Unless it is stated that a figure is three-dimensional, you may assume it lies in a plane.

Reference Information

| Area Facts | Volume Facts | Triangle Facts | Angle Facts |

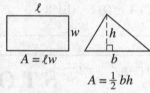

$A = \ell w$

$A = \frac{1}{2} bh$

$A = \pi r^2$
$C = 2\pi r$

$V = \ell w h$

$V = \pi r^2 h$

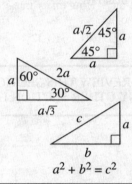

$a^2 + b^2 = c^2$

$x + y + z = 180$

1. Every Sunday Greg jogs 3 miles. For the rest of the week, each day he jogs 1 mile more than the previous day. How many miles does Greg jog in 2 weeks?

   (A) 42   (B) 63   (C) 84   (D) 98   (E) 117

2.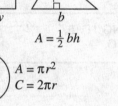

   In the figure above, what is the value of x?

   (A) 50   (B) 60   (C) 70   (D) 110
   (E) It cannot be determined from the information given.

3. The following table lists the prices of eight types of sandwiches:

Sandwich	Price	Sandwich	Price
Roast beef	$5.25	Tuna fish	$4.25
Corned beef	$5.00	Salami	$4.50
BLT	$4.00	Grilled cheese	$3.95
Egg salad	$3.50	Club	$5.75

   If the price of a tuna fish sandwich is increased 75¢ and the price of every other sandwich is increased 50¢, how many sandwiches will be more expensive than the tuna fish?

   (A) 0   (B) 1   (C) 2   (D) 3   (E) 4

4. When a gymnast competes at the Olympics, each of six judges awards a score between 0 and 10. The highest and lowest scores are discarded, and the gymnast's final mark is the average (arithmetic mean) of the remaining scores. What would be a gymnast's mark if the judges' scores were 9.6, 9.4, 9.5, 9.7, 9.2, and 9.6?

   (A) 9.5   (B) 9.525   (C) 9.55   (D) 9.575
   (E) 9.6

5.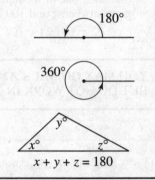

   In parallelogram $ABCD$, above, what is the value of x?

   (A) 2   (B) 4   (C) 6   (D) 20   (E) 60

6. If a speed of 1 meter per second is equal to a speed of k kilometers per hour, what is the value of k? (1 kilometer = 1000 meters)

   (A) 0.036   (B) 0.06   (C) 0.36   (D) 0.6   (E) 3.6

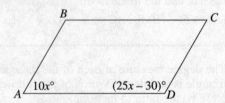
GO ON TO THE NEXT PAGE

2 2 2 2 2 2 2 2 2 2 2

7. Three lines are drawn in a plane. Which of the following could NOT be the total number of points of intersection?

(A) 0   (B) 1   (C) 2   (D) 3
(E) They all could.

8. If $a - b = 10$, and $a^2 - b^2 = 20$, what is the value of b?

(A) –6   (B) –4   (C) 4   (D) 6
(E) It cannot be determined from the information given.

9. An integer is called "octal" if it is divisible by 8 or if at least one of its digits is an 8. How many integers between 1 and 100 are octal?

(A) 22   (B) 24   (C) 27   (D) 30   (E) 32

10. If $x = 9$ is a solution of the equation $x^2 - a = 0$, which of the following is a solution of $x^4 - a = 0$?

(A) –81   (B) –3   (C) 0   (D) 9   (E) 81

11. The following table shows the hourly wages earned by the employees of a small company and the number of employees who earn each wage.

Wages per Hour	Number of Employees
$6	3
8	5
10	4
13	4

What is the average (arithmetic mean) of the median and the mode of this set of data?

(A) 4.5   (B) 8   (C) 8.5   (D) 9   (E) 9.5

12. The degree measure of each of the three angles of a triangle is an integer. Which of the following could NOT be the ratio of their measures?

(A) 2:3:4   (B) 3:4:5   (C) 4:5:6   (D) 5:6:7
(E) 6:7:8

13. In 1985, twice as many boys as girls at Adams High School earned varsity letters. From 1985 to 1995, the number of girls earning varsity letters increased by 25% while the number of boys earning varsity letters decreased by 25%. What was the ratio in 1995 of the number of girls to the number of boys who earned varsity letters?

(A) $\frac{5}{3}$ (B) $\frac{6}{5}$ (C) $\frac{1}{1}$ (D) $\frac{5}{6}$ (E) $\frac{3}{5}$

14. If $3x + 2y = 11$ and $2x + 3y = 17$, what is the average (arithmetic mean) of x and y?

(A) 2.5   (B) 2.8   (C) 5.6   (D) 5.8   (E) 14

Questions 15–16 refer to the following definition.

W	X
Y	Z

is a *number square* if $W + Z = X + Y$ and $2W = 3X$.

15. If

3	X
Y	7

is a *number square*, what is the value of Y?

(A) 0   (B) 2   (C) 4   (D) 6   (E) 8

16. If

W	X
Y	W

is a *number square*, $Y =$

(A) $\frac{3}{4}W$ (B) W (C) $\frac{4}{3}W$ (D) $3W$ (E) $4W$

17. When the price of gold went up, a jeweler raised the prices on certain rings by 60%. On one ring, however, the price was accidentally reduced by 60%. By what percent must the incorrect price be increased to reflect the proper new price?

(A) 60%   (B) 120%   (C) 300%   (D) 400%
(E) It depends on the original price of the ring

18.
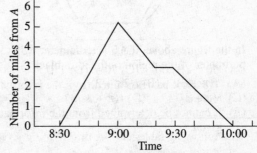

John rode his bicycle 5 miles along a straight road from A to B and back. The graph above shows how far he was from A at any given time. Not counting the time he stopped, what was John's average speed, in miles per hour, for the round trip?

(A) $6\frac{2}{3}$ (B) $7\frac{1}{2}$ (C) $8\frac{4}{7}$ (D) 10

(E) It cannot be determined from the graph.

GO ON TO THE NEXT PAGE

2　　2　2　2　2　2　2　2　2　2　　2

19. Let A, B, and C be three points in a plane such that $AB:BC = 3:5$. Which of the following could be the ratio $AB:AC$?

    I. 1:2
    II. 1:3
    III. 3:8

    (A) I only　　(B) II only　　(C) III only
    (D) I and III only　　(E) I, II, and III

20. If the average (arithmetic mean) of a, b, c, and d is equal to the average of a, b, and c, what is d in terms of a, b, and c?

    (A) $a + b + c$　　(B) $\dfrac{a+b+c}{3}$　　(C) $\dfrac{4(a+b+c)}{3}$

    (D) $\dfrac{3(a+b+c)}{4}$　　(E) $\dfrac{(a+b+c)}{4}$

21. To what percent of $60\sqrt{5}$ is $\sqrt{3}\%$ of $5\sqrt{60}$ equal?

    (A) 0.5%　　(B) $\sqrt{3}\%$　　(C) 1%　　(D) 3%
    (E) 100%

22.

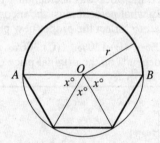

    In the figure above, if AB is a diameter, what is the perimeter of the region outlined in black?

    (A) $r(\pi + 3)$　　(B) $r(2\pi + 3)$
    (C) $r(\pi + 3\sqrt{2})$　　(D) $r(\pi + 3\sqrt{3})$
    (E) It cannot be determined from the information given.

23. If a and b are the lengths of the legs of a right triangle whose hypotenuse is 10 and whose area is 20, what is the value of $(a + b)^2$?

    (A) 100　　(B) 120　　(C) 140　　(D) 180　　(E) 200

24. Because her test turned out to be more difficult than she intended it to be, a teacher decided to adjust the grades by deducting only half the number of points a student missed. For example, if a student missed 10 points, she received a 95 instead of a 90. Before the grades were adjusted, the class average was A. What was the average after the adjustment?

    (A) $50 + \dfrac{A}{2}$　　(B) $\dfrac{50+A}{2}$　　(C) $100 - \dfrac{A}{2}$

    (D) $\dfrac{100-A}{2}$　　(E) $A + 25$

25. On the verbal portion of the SAT I, the raw score is calculated as follows: 1 point is awarded for each correct answer, and $\dfrac{1}{4}$ point is deducted for each wrong answer. If Ellen answered all q questions on the test and earned a raw score of 10, how many questions did she answer correctly?

    (A) $q - 10$　　(B) $\dfrac{q}{5}$　　(C) $\dfrac{q}{5} - 10$　　(D) $\dfrac{q-10}{5}$

    (E) $8 + \dfrac{q}{5}$

YOU MAY GO BACK AND REVIEW THIS SECTION IN THE REMAINING TIME, BUT DO NOT WORK IN ANY OTHER SECTION UNTIL TOLD TO DO SO.　　**STOP**

3   3 3 3 3 3 3 3 3 3 3   3

SECTION 3   **Time—30 Minutes**
35 Questions   **Select the best answer to the following questions, then fill in the appropriate space on your Answer Sheet.**

Each of the following sentences contains one or two blanks; these blanks indicate that a word or set of words has been left out. Below the sentence are five words or phrases, lettered A through E. Select the word or set of words that best completes the sentence.

Example:

Fame is ----; today's rising star is all too soon tomorrow's washed-up has-been.

(A) rewarding   (B) gradual
 (C) essential   (D) spontaneous
  (E) transitory

Ⓐ Ⓑ Ⓒ Ⓓ ●

1. Despite the ---- of the materials with which he worked, many of Tiffany's glass masterpieces have survived for more than seventy years.

   (A) beauty   (B) translucence   (C) abundance
    (D) majesty   (E) fragility

2. Although similar to mice in many physical characteristics, voles may be ---- mice by the shortness of their tails.

   (A) distinguished from
   (B) classified with
   (C) related to
   (D) categorized as
   (E) enumerated with

3. No summary of the behavior of animals toward reflected images is given, but not much else that is ---- seems missing from this comprehensive yet compact study of mirrors and mankind.

   (A) redundant   (B) contemplative
    (C) relevant   (D) peripheral
     (E) disputable

4. Dr. Charles Drew's technique for preserving and storing blood plasma for emergency use proved so ---- that it became the ---- for the present blood bank system used by the American Red Cross.

   (A) irrelevant...inspiration
   (B) urgent...pattern
   (C) effective...model
   (D) innocuous...excuse
   (E) complex...blueprint

5. The likenesses of language around the Mediterranean were sufficiently marked to ---- ease of movement both of men and ideas: it took relatively few alterations to make a Spanish song intelligible in Italy, and an Italian trader could, without much difficulty, make himself at home in France.

   (A) eliminate   (B) facilitate   (C) hinder
    (D) clarify   (E) aggravate

6. Because he saw no ---- to the task assigned him, he worked at it in a very ---- way.

   (A) function...systematic
   (B) method...dutiful
   (C) purpose...diligent
   (D) end...rigid
   (E) point...perfunctory

7. Pain is the body's early warning system: loss of ---- in the extremities leaves a person ---- injuring himself unwittingly.

   (A) agony...incapable of
   (B) sensation...vulnerable to
   (C) consciousness...desirous of
   (D) feeling...habituated to
   (E) movement...prone to

8. Much of the clown's success may be attributed to the contrast between the ---- manner he adopts and the general ---- that characterizes the circus.

   (A) giddy...sobriety
   (B) lugubrious...hilarity
   (C) gaudy...clamor
   (D) joyful...hysteria
   (E) frenetic...excitement

9. Fortunately, she was ---- her accomplishments, properly unwilling to ---- them before her friends.

   (A) excited by...parade
   (B) immodest about...discuss
   (C) deprecatory about...flaunt
   (D) uncertain of...concede
   (E) unaware of...conceal

GO ON TO THE NEXT PAGE ⟩

3   3   3   3   3   3   3   3   3   3   3   3

10. Despite their ---- of Twain's *Huckleberry Finn* for its stereotyped portrait of the slave Jim, even the novel's ---- agreed it was a masterpiece of American prose.

   (A) admiration...critics
   (B) denunciation...supporters
   (C) criticism...detractors
   (D) defense...censors
   (E) praise...advocates

The analogies questions present two words or phrases that are related in some way. Determine which A-through-E answer choice below has a relationship *most* similar to that of the original words or phrases.

Example:

   YAWN:BOREDOM::   (A) dream:sleep
   (B) anger:madness   (C) smile:amusement
   (D) face:expression   (E) impatience:rebellion

---

11. PLAY:ACTS::

   (A) opera:arias
   (B) novel:chapters
   (C) poem:rhymes
   (D) essay:topics
   (E) game:athletes

12. GEOLOGY:SCIENCE::

   (A) biology:laboratory
   (B) astronomy:galaxy
   (C) fashion:style
   (D) fir:tree
   (E) theory:practice

13. SIGNATURE:PORTRAIT::

   (A) title:novel
   (B) negative:photograph
   (C) autograph:celebrity
   (D) postscript:letter
   (E) byline:article

14. PLANE:SMOOTH::

   (A) boat:sink
   (B) arc:circle
   (C) cheese:grate
   (D) axe:sharpen
   (E) wrench:twist

15. FUNDS:EMBEZZLED::

   (A) loot:buried
   (B) writings:plagiarized
   (C) ransom:demanded
   (D) money:deposited
   (E) truth:exaggerated

16. UNCOUTH:GRACELESSNESS::

   (A) petulant:agreement
   (B) avaricious:greed
   (C) impassive:feeling
   (D) malicious:dishonesty
   (E) reticent:shamelessness

17. ELEVATOR:SHAFT::

   (A) electricity:outlet
   (B) water:conduit
   (C) escalator:step
   (D) railroad:train
   (E) skyscraper:foundation

18. PARSIMONY:FRUGALITY::

   (A) agony:pain
   (B) steam:water
   (C) anger:wrath
   (D) warmth:flame
   (E) pleasure:gloom

19. DILETTANTE:DABBLE::

   (A) coquette:flirt
   (B) gymnast:exercise
   (C) soldier:drill
   (D) embezzler:steal
   (E) benefactor:donate

20. INDIFFERENT:CONCERN::

   (A) intrepid:bravery
   (B) arrogant:modesty
   (C) unbigoted:tolerance
   (D) unnatural:emotion
   (E) incomparable:relevance

21. TACITURNITY:LACONIC::

   (A) improvisation:unrehearsed
   (B) verbosity:pithy
   (C) silence:golden
   (D) ballet:ungainly
   (E) vacation:leisurely

GO ON TO THE NEXT PAGE

3 3 3 3 3 3 3 3 3 3 3 3

22. SLANDER:DEFAMATORY::
  (A) fraud:notorious
  (B) tenet:devotional
  (C) elegy:sorrowful
  (D) edict:temporary
  (E) exhortation:cautionary

23. SLOUGH:SKIN::
  (A) shed:hair
  (B) polish:teeth
  (C) shade:eyes
  (D) tear:ligaments
  (E) remove:tonsils

Read the passage below, and then answer the questions that follow the passage. The correct response may be stated outright or merely suggested in the passage.

Questions 24–35 are based on the following passage.

The passage below is excerpted from the introduction to "Bury My Heart at Wounded Knee," *written in 1970 by the Native American historian Dee Brown.*

Since the exploratory journey of Lewis and Clark to the Pacific Coast early in the nineteenth century, the number of published accounts
Line describing the "opening" of the American West
(5) has risen into the thousands. The greatest concentration of recorded experience and observation came out of the thirty-year span between 1860 and 1890—the period covered by this book. It was an incredible era of violence, greed, audacity,
(10) sentimentality, undirected exuberance, and an almost reverential attitude toward the ideal of personal freedom for those who already had it.

During that time the culture and civilization of the American Indian was destroyed, and out of
(15) that time came virtually all the great myths of the American West—tales of fur traders, mountain men, steamboat pilots, goldseekers, gamblers, gunmen, cavalrymen, cowboys, harlots, missionaries, schoolmarms, and homesteaders. Only
(20) occasionally was the voice of the Indian heard, and then more often than not it was recorded by the pen of a white man. The Indian was the dark menace of the myths, and even if he had known how to write in English, where would he have
(25) found a printer or a publisher?

Yet they are not all lost, those Indian voices of the past. A few authentic accounts of American western history were recorded by Indians either in pictographs or in translated English, and some
(30) managed to get published in obscure journals, pamphlets, or books of small circulation. In the late nineteenth century, when the white man's curiosity about Indian survivors of the wars reached a high point, enterprising newspaper
(35) reporters frequently interviewed warriors and chiefs and gave them an opportunity to express their opinions on what was happening in the West. The quality of these interviews varied greatly, depending upon the abilities of the inter-
(40) preters, or upon the inclination of the Indians to speak freely. Some feared reprisals for telling the truth, while others delighted in hoaxing reporters with tall tales and shaggy-dog stories. Contemporary newspaper statements by Indians
(45) must therefore be read with skepticism, although some of them are masterpieces of irony and others burn with outbursts of poetic fury.

Among the richest sources of first-person statements by Indians are the records of treaty
(50) councils and other formal meetings with civilian and military representatives of the United States government. Isaac Pitman's new stenographic system was coming into vogue in the second half of the nineteenth century, and when Indians spoke
(55) in council a recording clerk sat beside the official interpreter.

Even when the meetings were in remote parts of the West, someone usually was available to write down the speeches, and because of the
(60) slowness of the translation process, much of what was said could be recorded in longhand. Interpreters quite often were half-bloods who knew spoken languages but seldom could read or write. Like most oral peoples they and the Indians
(65) depended upon imagery to express their thoughts, so that the English translations were filled with graphic similes and metaphors of the natural world. If an eloquent Indian had a poor interpreter, his words might be transformed to flat
(70) prose, but a good interpreter could make a poor speaker sound poetic.

Most Indian leaders spoke freely and candidly in councils with white officials, and as they became more sophisticated in such matters during
(75) the 1870s and 1880s, they demanded the right to choose their own interpreters and recorders. In this latter period, all members of the tribes were free to speak, and some of the older men chose such opportunities to recount events they had wit-
(80) nessed in the past, or sum up the histories of their peoples. Although the Indians who lived through

GO ON TO THE NEXT PAGE

this doom period of their civilization have vanished from the earth, millions of their words are
preserved in official records. Many of the more
(85) important council proceedings were published in
government documents and reports.

    Out of all these sources of almost forgotten
oral history, I have tried to fashion a narrative of
the conquest of the American West as the victims
(90) experienced it, using their own words whenever
possible. Americans who have always looked
westward when reading about this period should
read this book facing eastward.

    This is not a cheerful book, but history has a
(95) way of intruding upon the present, and perhaps
those who read it will have a clearer understanding of what the American Indian is, by knowing
what he was. They may learn something about
their own relationship to the earth from a people
(100) who were true conservationists. The Indians knew
that life was equated with the earth and its
resources, that America was a paradise, and they
could not comprehend why the intruders from the
East were determined to destroy all that was
(105) Indian as well as America itself.

24. The author finds the period of 1860–1890 noteworthy because

  (A) the journals of the Lewis and Clark expedition
were made public during this time
  (B) in that period the bulk of original accounts of
the "winning of the West" were produced
  (C) during these years American Indians made
great strides in regaining their lands
  (D) only a very few documents dating from this
period are still extant
  (E) people still believed in personal freedom as an
ideal

25. The author most likely uses quotation marks
around the word "opening" (line 4) because

  (A) the West was closed rather than opened during
this period of time
  (B) the American West actually was opened for
settlement much earlier in the century
  (C) from a Native American perspective it is an
inaccurate term
  (D) he is citing an authoritative source
  (E) he has employed it in its figurative sense

26. A main concern of the author in this passage is to

  (A) denounce the white man for his untrustworthi-
ness and savagery
  (B) evaluate the effectiveness of the military treaty
councils
  (C) argue for the improved treatment of Indians
today

  (D) suggest that Indian narratives of the conquest
of the West are similar to white accounts
  (E) introduce the background of the original
source materials for his text

27. The word "concentration" in lines 5–6 means

  (A) memory
  (B) attention
  (C) diligence
  (D) imprisonment
  (E) cluster

28. In describing the ideal of freedom revered by the
pioneers as "personal freedom for those who
already had it" (line 12), the author is being

  (A) enthusiastic
  (B) ironic
  (C) prosaic
  (D) redundant
  (E) lyrical

29. According to the passage, nineteenth-century newspaper accounts of interviews with Indians may contain inaccuracies for which of the following reasons?

  I. Lack of skill on the part of the translators
  II. The tendency of the reporters to overstate what
they were told by the Indians
  III. The Indians' misgivings about possible
retaliations

  (A) I only
  (B) III only
  (C) I and II only
  (D) I and III only
  (E) I, II, and III

30. The author's tone in describing the Indian survivors
can best be described as

  (A) skeptical
  (B) detached
  (C) elegiac
  (D) obsequious
  (E) impatient

31. The author is most impressed by which aspect of
the English translations of Indian speeches?

  (A) Their vividness of imagery
  (B) Their lack of frankness
  (C) The inefficiency of the process
  (D) Their absence of sophistication
  (E) Their brevity of expression

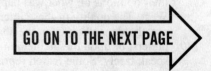

GO ON TO THE NEXT PAGE

32. The word "flat" in line 69 means

    (A) smooth
    (B) level
    (C) pedestrian
    (D) horizontal
    (E) unequivocal

33. In treaty councils before 1870, most Indians did not ask for their own interpreters and recorders because

    (A) they could not afford to hire people to take down their words
    (B) the white officials provided these services as a matter of course
    (C) they were unaware that they had the option to demand such services
    (D) they preferred speaking for themselves without the help of translators
    (E) they were reluctant to have their words recorded for posterity

34. The author most likely suggests that Americans should read this book facing eastward

    (A) in an inappropriate attempt at levity
    (B) out of respect for Western superstitions
    (C) in order to read by natural light
    (D) because the Indians came from the East
    (E) to identify with the Indians' viewpoint

35. The phrase "equated with" in line 101 means

    (A) reduced to an average with
    (B) necessarily tied to
    (C) numerically equal to
    (D) fulfilled by
    (E) differentiated by

YOU MAY GO BACK AND REVIEW THIS SECTION IN THE REMAINING TIME, BUT DO NOT WORK IN ANY OTHER SECTION UNTIL TOLD TO DO SO.

S T O P

4   4   4   4   4   4   4   4   4   4   4   4

SECTION 4

Time—30 Minutes
25 Questions

You have 30 minutes to answer the 15 Quantitative Comparison questions and 10 Student-Produced Response questions in this section. You may use any blank space on the page for your work.

Notes:

- You may use a calculator whenever you feel it will be helpful.
- Use the diagrams provided to help you solve the problems. Unless you see the words "Note: Figure not drawn to scale" under a diagram, it has been drawn as accurately as possible. Unless it is stated that a figure is three-dimensional, you may assume it lies in a plane.

Reference Information

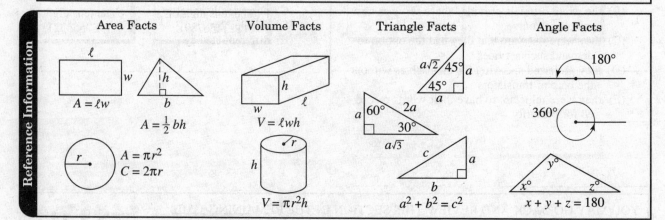

Area Facts

$A = \ell w$

$A = \frac{1}{2} bh$

$A = \pi r^2$
$C = 2\pi r$

Volume Facts

$V = \ell wh$

$V = \pi r^2 h$

Triangle Facts

$a^2 + b^2 = c^2$

Angle Facts

$x + y + z = 180$

Directions for Quantitative Comparison Questions

In each of questions 1–15, two quantities appear in boxes: one in Column A and one in Column B. You must compare them. The correct answer to a question is

- A if the quantity in Column A is greater;
- B if the quantity in Column B is greater;
- C if the two quantities are equal;
- D if it is impossible to determine which quantity is greater.

Notes:

- *The correct answer is never E.*
- Sometimes information about one or both of the quantities is centered above the two boxes.
- If the same symbol appears in both columns, it represents the same thing each time.
- All variables represent real numbers.

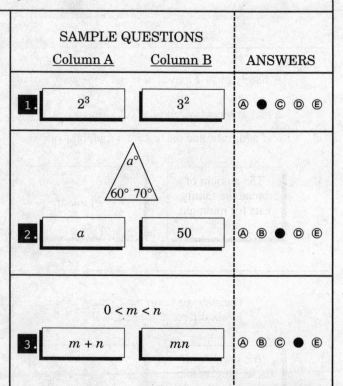

SAMPLE QUESTIONS

Column A	Column B	ANSWERS
1. 2^3	3^2	Ⓐ ● Ⓒ Ⓓ Ⓔ

2. a | 50 | Ⓐ Ⓑ ● Ⓓ Ⓔ

$0 < m < n$

3. $m + n$ | mn | Ⓐ Ⓑ Ⓒ ● Ⓔ

GO ON TO THE NEXT PAGE

4   4 4 4 4 4 4 4 4 4 4   4

SUMMARY DIRECTIONS FOR QUANTITATIVE COMPARISON QUESTIONS

<u>Answer</u>: A if the quantity in Column A is greater;
         B if the quantity in Column B is greater;
         C if the two quantities are equal;
         D if it is impossible to determine which quantity is greater.

<u>Column A</u>   <u>Column B</u>   <u>Column A</u>   <u>Column B</u>

1. $\dfrac{3}{11}$ of 7 $\dfrac{7}{11}$ of 3

6.   The tens digit of $(123456789)^2$ The tens digit of $(987654321)^2$

$y = x + 10$

2. $x + 5$ $y - 5$

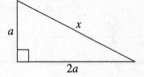

7. x $a\sqrt{3}$

$a > 0$

3. $a^4 a^5$ $(a^3)^2$

8.   The volume of a cylinder whose height is 10   The volume of a cone whose height is 10

A family buys 2 loaves of bread and eats $\dfrac{5}{12}$ of a loaf at breakfast, $\dfrac{5}{8}$ of a loaf at lunch, $\dfrac{5}{6}$ of a loaf at dinner, and the rest for a midnight snack.

$3 < a < 4$
$0 < b < 1$

4.   The amount of bread the family eats for midnight snack $\dfrac{1}{5}$ of a loaf

9. ab $\dfrac{a}{b}$

The average (arithmetic mean) of six different integers is 10.

Line ℓ passes through Quadrants I, II, and IV.
$\ell \perp k$

5.   The number of these integers that are greater than 10   3

10.   The slope of ℓ The slope of k

GO ON TO THE NEXT PAGE

4   4 4 4 4 4 4 4 4 4 4   4

SUMMARY DIRECTIONS FOR QUANTITATIVE COMPARISON QUESTIONS

<u>Answer</u>: A if the quantity in Column A is greater;
B if the quantity in Column B is greater;
C if the two quantities are equal;
D if it is impossible to determine which quantity is greater.

Column A   Column B

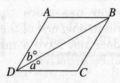

In parallelogram *ABCD*, all four sides
have the same length.

11.   *a*   *b*

$$ABA$$
$$\times\ \ A$$
$$DCD$$

In the multiplication problem above,
each letter represents a different digit.

12.   *B*   5

Column A   Column B

$$p = \frac{3}{5}s, \quad q = \frac{4}{3}s, \quad r = \frac{3}{8}q$$

13.   5*p*   6*r*

14. | The area of a | The area of a |
45-45-90 right triangle whose hypotenuse is 2 vs 30-60-90 right triangle whose hypotenuse is 2

$$a + 2b = 6d$$
$$c - b = 5d$$

15.   The average
(arithmetic mean)
of *a*, *b*, *c*, and *d*   3*d*

GO ON TO THE NEXT PAGE

4   4 4 4 4 4 4 4 4 4 4   4

Directions for Student-Produced Response Questions (Grid-ins)

In questions 16–25, first solve the problem, and then enter your answer on the grid provided on the answer sheet. The instructions for entering your answers are as follows:

- First, write your answer in the boxes at the top of the grid.
- Second, grid your answer in the columns below the boxes.
- Use the fraction bar in the first row or the decimal point in the second row to enter fractions and decimal answers.

- Grid only one space in each column.
- Entering the answer in the boxes is recommended as an aid in gridding, but is not required.
- The machine scoring your exam can read only what you grid, so you **must grid in your answers correctly to get credit.**
- If a question has more than one correct answer, grid in only one of them.
- The grid does not have a minus sign, so no answer can be negative.
- A mixed number *must* be converted to an improper fraction or a decimal before it is gridded. Enter $1\frac{1}{4}$ as 5/4 or 1.25; the machine will interpret 1 1/4 as $\frac{11}{4}$ and mark it wrong.
- **All decimals must be entered as accurately as possible.** Here are the three acceptable ways of gridding

$$\frac{3}{11} = 0.272727...$$

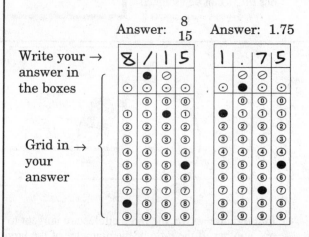

Answer: $\frac{8}{15}$ Answer: 1.75

Write your → answer in the boxes

Grid in → your answer

Answer: 100

Either position is acceptable

3/11   .272   .273

- Note that rounding to .273 is acceptable, because you are using the full grid, but you would receive **no credit** for .3 or .27, because they are less accurate.

---

16. Pencils that were selling at three for 25 cents are now on sale at five for 29 cents. How much money, in cents, would you save by buying 60 pencils at the sale price?

17. If $1 < 3x - 5 < 2$, what is one possible value for x?

GO ON TO THE NEXT PAGE →

18. What is the largest integer, x, such that $x < 10,000$ and $\dfrac{\sqrt{x}}{5}$ is an even integer?

19. Ellie is dropping marbles into a box one at a time in the following order: red, white, white, blue, blue, blue; red, white, white, blue, blue, blue; .... How many marbles will be in the box right after the 100th blue one is put in?

20. Four 3-4-5 right triangles and a square whose sides are 5 are arranged to form a second square. What is the perimeter of that square?

Questions 21–22 refer to the following definition.

For any positive integer a: $\langle\langle a \rangle\rangle = \dfrac{1}{2^{a+1}}$.

21. What is the value of $\langle\langle 3 \rangle\rangle - \langle\langle 4 \rangle\rangle$?

22. What is the ratio of $\langle\langle a + 3 \rangle\rangle$ to $\langle\langle a \rangle\rangle$?

23. Each of 100 cards has none, one, or two of the letters A and C written on it. If 75 cards have the letter A, 30 have the letter C, and fewer than 15 are blank, what is the largest possible number of cards that have both A and C written on them?

24. To use a certain cash machine, you need a Personal Identification Code (PIC). If each PIC consists of two letters followed by one of the digits from 1 to 9 (such as AQ7 or BB3) or one letter followed by two digits (such as Q37 or J88), how many different PIC's can be assigned?

25.

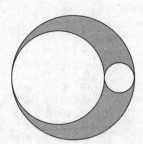

In the figure above, the three circles are tangent to one another. If the ratio of the diameter of the large white circle to the diameter of the small white circle is 3:1, what fraction of the largest circle has been shaded?

YOU MAY GO BACK AND REVIEW THIS SECTION IN THE REMAINING TIME, BUT DO NOT WORK IN ANY OTHER SECTION UNTIL TOLD TO DO SO.   **S T O P**

5

The questions that follow the two passages in this section relate to the content of both, and to their relationship. The correct response may be stated outright in the passages or merely suggested.

Questions 1–13 are based on the following passages.

The following passages are excerpted from two recent essays that make an analogy between writing and sports. The author of Passage 1 discusses the sorts of failures experienced by writers and ballplayers. The author of Passage 2 explores how his involvement in sports affected his writing career.

Passage 1

In consigning this manuscript to a desk drawer, I am comforted by the behavior of baseball players. There are *no* pitchers who do not give up home
Line runs, there are *no* batters who do not strike out.
(5) There are *no* major league pitchers or batters who have not somehow learned to survive giving up home runs and striking out. That much is obvious.

What seems to me less obvious is how these "failures" must be digested, or put to use, in the
(10) overall experience of the player. A jogger once explained to me that the nerves of the ankle are so sensitive and complex that each time a runner sets his foot down, hundreds of messages are conveyed to the runner's brain about the nature of the
(15) terrain and the requirements for weight distribution, balance, and muscle-strength. I'm certain that the ninth-inning home run that Dave Henderson hit off Donny Moore registered complexly and permanently in Moore's mind and
(20) body and that the next time Moore faced Henderson, his pitching was informed by his awful experience of October 1986. Moore's continuing baseball career depended to some extent on his converting that encounter with Henderson
(25) into something useful for his pitching. I can also imagine such an experience destroying an athlete, registering in his mind and body in such a negative way as to produce a debilitating fear.

Of the many ways in which athletes and artists
(30) are similar, one is that, unlike accountants or plumbers or insurance salesmen, to succeed at all they must perform at an extraordinary level of excellence. Another is that they must be willing to extend themselves irrationally in order to achieve
(35) that level of performance. A writer doesn't have to write all-out all the time, but he or she must be ready to write all-out any time the story requires it. Hold back and you produce what just about any literate citizen can produce, a "pretty good" piece

(40) of work. Like the cautious pitcher, the timid writer can spend a lifetime in the minor leagues.

And what more than failure—the strike out, the crucial home run given up, the manuscript criticized and rejected—is more likely to produce
(45) caution or timidity? An instinctive response to painful experience is to avoid the behavior that produced the pain. To function at the level of excellence required for survival, writers, like athletes, must go against instinct, must absorb their
(50) failures and become stronger, must endlessly repeat the behavior that produced the pain.

Passage 2

The athletic advantages of this concentration, particularly for an athlete who was making up for the absence of great natural skill, were consider-
(55) able. Concentration gave you an edge over many of your opponents, even your betters, who could not isolate themselves to that degree. For example, in football if they were ahead (or behind) by several touchdowns, if the game itself seemed to have
(60) been settled, they tended to slack off, to ease off a little, certainly to relax their own concentration. It was then that your own unwavering concentration and your own indifference to the larger point of view paid off. At the very least you could deal out
(65) surprise and discomfort to your opponents.

But it was more than that. Do you see? The ritual of physical concentration, of acute engagement in a small space while disregarding all the clamor and demands of the larger world, was the
(70) best possible lesson in precisely the kind of selfish intensity needed to create and to finish a poem, a story, or a novel. This alone mattered while all the world going on, with and without you, did not.

I was learning first in muscle, blood, and bone,
(75) not from literature and not from teachers of literature or the arts or the natural sciences, but from coaches, in particular this one coach who paid me enough attention to influence me to teach some things to myself. I was learning about art and life

GO ON TO THE NEXT PAGE

5

(80) through the abstraction of athletics in much the same way that a soldier is, to an extent, prepared for war by endless parade ground drill. His body must learn to be a soldier before heart, mind, and spirit can.

(85)   Ironically, I tend to dismiss most comparisons of athletics to art and to "the creative process." But only because, I think, so much that is claimed for both is untrue. But I have come to believe— indeed I have to believe it insofar as I believe in

(90) the validity and efficacy of art—that what comes to us first and foremost through the body, as a sensuous affective experience, is taken and transformed by mind and self into a thing of the spirit. Which is only to say that what the body learns

(95) and is taught is of enormous significance—at least until the last light of the body fails.

1. Why does the author of Passage 1 consign his manuscript to a desk drawer?

   (A) To protect it from the inquisitive eyes of his family
   (B) To prevent its getting lost or disordered
   (C) Because his publisher wishes to take another look at it
   (D) Because he chooses to watch a televised baseball game
   (E) To set it aside as unmarketable in its current state

2. Why is the author of Passage 1 "comforted by the behavior of baseball players" (line 2)?

   (A) He treasures the timeless rituals of America's national pastime.
   (B) He sees he is not alone in having to confront failure and move on.
   (C) He enjoys watching the frustration of the batters who strike out.
   (D) He looks at baseball from the viewpoint of a behavioral psychologist.
   (E) He welcomes any distraction from the task of revising his novel.

3. What function in the passage is served by the discussion of the nerves in the ankle in lines 11–16?

   (A) It provides a momentary digression from the overall narrative flow.
   (B) It emphasizes how strong a mental impact Henderson's home run must have had on Moore.
   (C) It provides scientific confirmation of the neuromuscular abilities of athletes.
   (D) It illustrates that the author's interest in sports is not limited to baseball alone.
   (E) It conveys a sense of how confusing it is for the mind to deal with so many simultaneous messages.

4. The word "registered" in line 18 means

   (A) enrolled formally
   (B) expressed without words
   (C) corresponded exactly
   (D) made an impression
   (E) qualified officially

5. The attitude of the author of Passage 1 to accountants, plumbers, and insurance salesmen (lines 30–33) can best be described as

   (A) respectful   (B) cautious   (C) superior
    (D) cynical   (E) hypocritical

6. In the final two paragraphs of Passage 1, the author appears to

   (A) romanticize the writer as someone heroic in his or her accomplishments
   (B) deprecate athletes for their inability to react to experience instinctively
   (C) minimize the travail that artists and athletes endure to do their work
   (D) advocate the importance of literacy to the common citizen
   (E) suggest that a cautious approach would reduce the likelihood of future failure

7. The author of Passage 2 prizes

   (A) his innate athletic talent
   (B) the respect of his peers
   (C) his ability to focus
   (D) the gift of relaxation
   (E) winning at any cost

8. The word "settled" in line 60 means

   (A) judged   (B) decided   (C) reconciled
    (D) pacified   (E) inhabited

9. What does the author mean by "indifference to the larger point of view" (line 63)?

   (A) Inability to see the greater implications of the activity in which you were involved
   (B) Hostility to opponents coming from larger, better trained teams
   (C) Reluctance to look beyond your own immediate concerns
   (D) Refusing to care how greatly you might be hurt by your opponents
   (E) Being more concerned with the task at hand than with whether you win or lose

GO ON TO THE NEXT PAGE

5

10. What is the function of the phrase "to an extent" in line 81?

(A) It denies a situation
(B) It conveys a paradox
(C) It qualifies a statement
(D) It represents a metaphor
(E) It minimizes a liability

11. The author finds it ironic that he tends to "dismiss most comparisons of athletics to art" (lines 85–86) because

(A) athletics is the basis for great art
(B) he finds comparisons generally unhelpful
(C) he is making such a comparison
(D) he typically is less cynical
(E) he rejects the so-called "creative process"

12. The authors of both passages would agree that

(A) the lot of the professional writer is more trying than that of the professional athlete
(B) athletics has little to do with the actual workings of the creative process
(C) both artists and athletes learn hard lessons in the course of mastering their art

(D) it is important to concentrate on the things that hurt us in life
(E) participating in sports provides a distraction from the isolation of a writer's life

13. How would the author of Passage 2 respond to the author of Passage 1's viewpoint that a failure such as giving up a key home run can destroy an athlete?

(A) An athlete learns through his body that failure is enormously significant and affects him both physically and spiritually.
(B) Athletes of great natural skill suffer less from the agonies of failure than less accomplished athletes do.
(C) If an athlete plays without holding back, he will surpass athletes who are more inherently adept.
(D) If the athlete focuses on the job at hand and not on past errors, he will continue to function successfully.
(E) Athletes are highly sensitive performers who need to be sheltered from the clamor and demands of the larger world.

YOU MAY GO BACK AND REVIEW THIS SECTION IN THE REMAINING TIME, BUT DO NOT WORK IN ANY OTHER SECTION UNTIL TOLD TO DO SO.   **S T O P**

6   6   6   6   6   6   6   6   6   6   6

SECTION **6**

Time—15 Minutes
10 Questions

For each problem in this section determine which of the five choices is correct and blacken in that choice on your answer sheet. You may use any blank space on the page for your work.

Notes:

- You may use a calculator whenever you feel it will be helpful.
- Use the diagrams provided to help you solve the problems. Unless you see the words "Note: Figure not drawn to scale" under a diagram, it has been drawn as accurately as possible. Unless it is stated that a figure is three-dimensional, you may assume it lies in a plane.

Reference Information

Area Facts

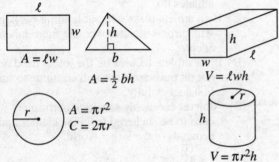

$A = \ell w$

$A = \frac{1}{2} bh$

$A = \pi r^2$
$C = 2\pi r$

Volume Facts

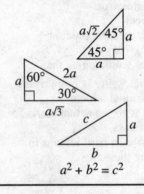

$V = \ell wh$

$V = \pi r^2 h$

Triangle Facts

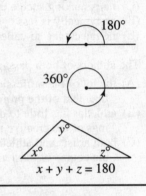

$a^2 + b^2 = c^2$

Angle Facts

$180°$

$360°$

$x + y + z = 180$

1.

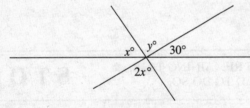

In the figure above, what is the value of y?

(A) 50   (B) 70   (C) 100   (D) 140
(E) It cannot be determined from the information given.

---

2. In a laboratory a solution was being heated. In 90 minutes, the temperature rose from –8° to 7°. What was the average hourly increase in temperature?

(A) 5°   (B) 7.5°   (C) 10°   (D) 15°   (E) 22.5°

---

3. For how many integers, n, is it true that $n^2 - 30$ is negative?

(A) 5   (B) 6   (C) 10   (D) 11
(E) Infinitely many

---

4. Which of the following is NOT a solution of $2a^2 + 3b = 5$?

(A) $a = 0$ and $b = \dfrac{5}{3}$ (B) $a = 1$ and $b = 1$

(C) $a = 2$ and $b = -1$ (D) $a = 3$ and $b = -4$
(E) $a = 4$ and $b = -9$

---

5. If the measures of the angles of a triangle are in the ratio of 1:2:3, what is the ratio of the lengths of the sides?

(A) 1:2:3   (B) 1:1: $\sqrt{2}$ (C) 1: $\sqrt{3}$:2   (D) 3:4:5
(E) It cannot be determined from the information given.

---

6. A googol is the number that is written as 1 followed by 100 zeros. If g represents a googol, how many digits are there in g^2?

(A) 102   (B) 103   (C) 199   (D) 201   (E) 202

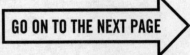

GO ON TO THE NEXT PAGE

6   6   6   6   6   6   6   6   6   6   6

7. Which of the following expresses the area of a circle in terms of C, its circumference?

(A) $\dfrac{C^2}{4\pi}$ (B) $\dfrac{C^2}{2\pi}$ (C) $\dfrac{\sqrt{C}}{2\pi}$ (D) $\dfrac{C\pi}{4}$ (E) $\dfrac{C}{4\pi}$

8. To get to a business meeting, Joanna drove m miles in h hours, and arrived $\dfrac{1}{2}$ hour early. At what rate should she have driven to arrive exactly on time?

(A) $\dfrac{m}{2h}$ (B) $\dfrac{2m+h}{2h}$ (C) $\dfrac{2m-h}{2h}$ (D) $\dfrac{2m}{2h-1}$

(E) $\dfrac{2m}{2h+1}$

9.

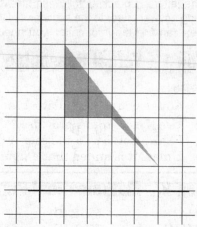

In the figure above, what is the area of the shaded region?

(A) 4   (B) 5   (C) 5.5   (D) 6   (E) 7

10. What is the average (arithmetic mean) of 3^{30}, 3^{60}, and 3^{90}?

(A) 3^{60} (B) 3^{177} (C) $3^{10} + 3^{20} + 3^{30}$
(D) $3^{27} + 3^{57} + 3^{87}$ (E) $3^{29} + 3^{59} + 3^{89}$

YOU MAY GO BACK AND REVIEW THIS SECTION IN THE REMAINING TIME, BUT DO NOT WORK IN ANY OTHER SECTION UNTIL TOLD TO DO SO.   **S T O P**

Answer Key

Note: The letters in brackets following the Mathematical Reasoning answers refer to the sections of Chapter 12 in which you can find the information you need to answer the questions. For example, **1. C [E]**, means that the answer to question 1 is C, and that the solution requires information found in Section 12-E: Averages.

Section 1   Verbal Reasoning

1. A	7. C	13. B	19. C	25. C
2. D	8. B	14. D	20. C	26. D
3. B	9. E	15. C	21. E	27. E
4. D	10. D	16. B	22. D	28. D
5. D	11. C	17. D	23. D	29. D
6. A	12. B	18. D	24. B	30. A

Section 2   Mathematical Reasoning

1. C [A]	6. E [D]	11. C [E]	16. C [G]	21. A [A, C]
2. C [I, J]	7. E [I]	12. E [D, J]	17. C [C]	22. A [J, L]
3. D [A, Q]	8. B [F]	13. D [C, D]	18. B [H, Q]	23. D [J, F]
4. B [E]	9. C [P, Q]	14. B [E, G]	19. D [D, I]	24. A [E]
5. C [G, K]	10. B [G]	15. E [G]	20. B [E, G]	25. E [G, H]

Section 3   Verbal Reasoning

1. E	8. B	15. B	22. C	29. D
2. A	9. C	16. B	23. A	30. C
3. C	10. C	17. B	24. B	31. A
4. C	11. B	18. A	25. C	32. C
5. B	12. D	19. A	26. E	33. C
6. E	13. E	20. B	27. E	34. E
7. B	14. E	21. A	28. B	35. B

Section 4   Mathematical Reasoning

Quantitative Comparison Questions

1. C [B]	4. B [B]	7. A [J]	10. B [N]	13. C [B, G]
2. C [G]	5. D [E]	8. D [M]	11. C [I, K]	14. A [J]
3. D [A]	6. B [A]	9. B [A]	12. B [P]	15. C [E, G]

Grid-in Questions

16. [A]   **1 5 2**

17. [G]   **2 . 1**

18. [A]   **8 1 0 0**

19. [O, P]   **2 0 2**

20. [J, K]   **2 8**

$2.01 \le x \le 2.33$

21.
[A, B] **1 / 3 2**

22.
[B, D] **1 / 8**

23.
[P] **1 9**

24.
[O] **8 1 9 0**

25.
[D, L] **3 / 8**   or   **. 3 7 5**

Section 5   Verbal Reasoning

1. E
2. B
3. B
4. D
5. C
6. A
7. C
8. B
9. E
10. C
11. C
12. C
13. D

Section 6   Mathematical Reasoning

1. C [I]
2. C [E]
3. D [A, O]
4. D [G]
5. C [D, J]
6. D [A, P]
7. A [L]
8. E [B, H]
9. A [J, K, N]
10. E [A, E]

Self-Evaluation

Now that you have completed the Diagnostic Test, evaluate your performance. Identify your strengths and weaknesses, and then plan a practical study program based on what you have discovered. Follow these steps to evaluate your work on the Diagnostic Test. (Note: You'll find the charts referred to in steps 1–5 on the next three pages.)

■ **STEP 1**   Use the Answer Key to check your answers for each section.

■ **STEP 2**   For each section, count the number of correct and incorrect answers (remember that you don't count omitted answers), and enter the numbers on the appropriate lines of the chart "Calculate Your Raw Score." Then do the indicated calculations to get your Raw Verbal Reasoning Score and your Raw Mathematical Reasoning Score.

■ **STEP 3**   Consult the chart "Evaluate Your Performance" to see how well you did.

■ **STEP 4**   To pinpoint the specific areas in which you need to improve, circle the numbers of the questions that you either left blank or got wrong on the "Identify Your Weaknesses" charts. This will tell you where to concentrate your efforts to get the most out of your study time. The chart for the math sections gives you page references for review and practice by skill areas. The charts for the verbal sections refer you to the appropriate chapters to study for each question type.

■ **STEP 5**   Do the review and practice indicated on the charts wherever you had a concentration of circles.

Important: Remember that, in addition to evaluating your scores, you should read all of the answer explanations for questions you answered incorrectly, questions you omitted, and questions you answered correctly but found difficult. Reviewing the answer explanations will help you understand concepts and strategies, and may point out shortcuts.

Calculate Your Raw Score

Verbal Reasoning

Section 1 $\dfrac{}{\text{number correct}} - \dfrac{1}{4}\left(\dfrac{}{\text{number incorrect}}\right) = \underline{}$ (A)

Section 3 $\dfrac{}{\text{number correct}} - \dfrac{1}{4}\left(\dfrac{}{\text{number incorrect}}\right) = \underline{}$ (B)

Section 5 $\dfrac{}{\text{number correct}} - \dfrac{1}{4}\left(\dfrac{}{\text{number incorrect}}\right) = \underline{}$ (C)

Raw Verbal Reasoning Score = (A) + (B) + (C) = $\underline{}$

Mathematical Reasoning

Section 2 $\dfrac{}{\text{number correct}} - \dfrac{1}{4}\left(\dfrac{}{\text{number incorrect}}\right) = \underline{}$ (D)

Section 4
Part I
(1–15) $\dfrac{}{\text{number correct}} - \dfrac{1}{3}\left(\dfrac{}{\text{number incorrect}}\right) = \underline{}$ (E)

Part II
(16–25) $\dfrac{}{\text{number correct}} = \underline{}$ (F)

Section 6 $\dfrac{}{\text{number correct}} - \dfrac{1}{4}\left(\dfrac{}{\text{number incorrect}}\right) = \underline{}$ (G)

Raw Mathematical Reasoning Score = (D) + (E) + (F) + (G) = $\underline{}$

Evaluate Your Performance

	Verbal Reasoning	Mathematical Reasoning
Superior	67–78	51–60
Very Good	60–66	45–50
Good	52–59	40–44
Satisfactory	44–51	35–39
Average	36–43	30–34
Needs Further Study	29–35	25–29
Needs Intensive Study	21–28	20–24
Inadequate	0–20	0–19

Identify Your Weaknesses

Verbal Reasoning

Question Type	Question Numbers			Chapter to Study
	Section 1	Section 3	Section 5	
Sentence Completion	1, 2, 3, 4, 5, 6, 7, 8, 9	1, 2, 3, 4, 5, 6, 7, 8, 9, 10		Chapter 4
Analogy	10, 11, 12, 13, 14, 15	11, 12, 13, 14, 15, 16, 17, 18, 19, 20, 21, 22, 23		Chapter 5
Reading Comprehension	16, 17, 18, 19, 20, 21, 22, 23, 24	24, 25, 26, 27, 28, 29, 30	1, 2, 3, 4, 5, 6, 7, 8, 9, 10, 11, 12, 13	Chapter 6

Identify Your Weaknesses

Mathematical Reasoning

Skill Area	Question Numbers			Pages to Study
	Section 2	Section 4	Section 6	
Basics of Arithmetic	1, 21	3, 6, 9, 16, 18, 21	3, 6, 10	331–338
Fractions and Decimals		1, 4, 13, 22	8	344–352
Percents	13, 17, 21			358–361
Ratios	6, 12, 13, 19	22, 25	5	366–370
Averages	4, 11, 14, 24	5, 15	2, 10	376–378
Polynomials	8, 23			383–386
Equations and Inequalities	5, 10, 14, 15, 16, 20, 24, 25	2, 13, 15, 17	4	389–394
Word Problems	2, 15, 16, 18		8	399–402
Lines and Angles	2, 7, 19	11	1	407–410
Triangles	12, 22, 23	7, 14, 20	5, 9	414–418
Quadrilaterals	5	11, 20	9	425–428
Circles	22	25	7	432–435
Solid Geometry		8		440–442
Coordinate Geometry		10	9	446–448
Counting and Probability	9	19, 24	3	452–456
Logical Reasoning	9	12, 19, 23	6	462–464
Data Interpretation	3, 9, 18			468–471

Answer Explanations

Section 1   Verbal Reasoning

1. A. Because lightning victims are so battered and confused, they seem like assault victims. Thus, they are often *mistaken for* victims of assault.   (Cause and Effect Signal)

2. D. Anyone who has produced more than three hundred books in a single lifetime is an enormously productive or *prolific* writer. Writers are often described as prolific, but few, if any, have been as prolific as the late Dr. Asimov. Beware Eye-Catchers: Choice A is incorrect. *Fastidious* means painstakingly careful; it has nothing to do with writing fast.   (Examples)

3. B. Time limitations would cause problems for you if you were reading a *lengthy* book. To save time, you might want to read it in an *abridged* or shortened form.
   Remember to watch for signal words that link one part of the sentence to another. The use of "because" in the opening clause is a cause signal.   (Cause and Effect Signal)

4. D. Speakers wish to communicate *unambiguously* in order that there may be no *confusion* about their meaning.
   Remember to watch for signal words that link one part of the sentence to another. The presence of *and* linking two items in a series indicates that the missing word may be a synonym or near-synonym for the other linked word. In this case, *unambiguously* is a synonym for *clearly*. Similarly, the use of "so that" in the second clause signals cause and effect.   (Argument Pattern)

5. D. Lisa was normally *gregarious* or sociable. When she unexpectedly lost her job, she became quiet and *withdrawn* (distant; unsociable). Note how the signal word *Although* indicates a contrast between her normally sociable and presently unsociable states.   (Contrast Pattern)

6. A. Wilma Mankiller, a female, heads a major American Indian tribe. She performs her role successfully: she is "increasingly popular." By her success, she has *shattered* or exploded a myth of male supremacy.   (Argument Pattern)

7. C. The commission censured or condemned the senator for doing something wrong. They condemned him *because* his expenditures of public funds were *lavish* or extravagant; he spent the public's money in an *unjustifiable*, unwarranted way.   (Cause and Effect Pattern)

8. B. Nelson remained calm and in control in spite of the panic of battle. In other words, he was *imperturbable*, not capable of being agitated or perturbed.
   Note how the phrase *in spite of* signals the contrast between the subject's calm and the surrounding panic. Similarly, note how other signal words link one part of the sentence to another. The presence of *and* linking two items in a series indicates that the missing word should be similar in meaning to the phrase "in full command."   (Contrast Pattern)

9. E. Despite his hard work trying to solve the problem, the solution was not the *result* or outcome of his labor. Instead, it was *fortuitous* or accidental.
   Remember to watch for signal words that link one part of the sentence to another. The use of the "was...and not..." structure sets up a contrast. The missing words must be antonyms or near-antonyms.   (Contrast Pattern)

10. D. A *constitution* is introduced by a *preamble*. A *book* is introduced by a *preface*.   (Sequence)

11. C. A *quarry* is a place from which one extracts or digs *marble*. A *mine* is a place from which one extracts or digs *coal*.
                (Defining Characteristic)

12. B. *Ecstasy* is an extreme form of *joy*; a *hurricane* is an extreme form of a wind or *breeze*.
                (Degree of Intensity)

13. B. A *fissure* (cleft) is a geographical feature measured in terms of its *depth*; a *peak* is a geographical feature measured in terms of its *height*.   (Defining Characteristic)

14. D. Something *blatant* (obtrusive; brazenly obvious) is characterized by *obtrusiveness* (conspicuousness). Something *lavish* (prodigal; excessive) is characterized by *extravagance*.
                (Synonym Variant)

15. C. Neither a *strident* (unpleasantly grating; shrill) *voice* nor an *acrid* (bitterly sharp) *taste* appeals to the senses.
                (Defining Characteristic)

16. B. The author describes himself as "jarred and shocked" (lines 4 and 5). He asks himself, "What strange world was this?" His initial reaction to Mencken's prose is one of *disbelief*. Choice A is incorrect. Mencken rages; the narrator does not. Choice C is incorrect. It is unsupported by the passage. Choices D and E are incorrect. Again, these terms apply to Mencken, not to the narrator.

17. D.   The narrator does *not* portray Mencken as reverent or respectful of religious belief. Instead, he says that Mencken mocks God. Choice A is incorrect. The narrator portrays Mencken as intrepid (brave); he wonders where Mencken gets his courage. Choice B is incorrect. The narrator portrays Mencken as articulate (verbally expressive); he says Mencken writes clear, clean sentences. Choice C is incorrect. The narrator portrays Mencken as satiric (mocking); he says Mencken makes fun of people's weaknesses. Choice E is incorrect. The narrator portrays Mencken as opinionated (stubborn about his opinions; prejudiced). Mencken's book, after all, is *A Book of Prejudices*.
Remember, when asked about specific information in the passage, spot key words in the question and scan the passage to find them (or their synonyms).

18. D.   The mood of the book colored or *affected* the narrator's perceptions.
Remember, when answering a vocabulary-in-context question, test each answer choice, substituting it in the sentence for the word in quotes.

19. C.   The narrator feels a hunger for books that surges up in him. In other words, he is filled with *impatient ardor* or eagerness. Choice A is incorrect. The narrator has his dreams, but he is involved rather than indifferent. Choices B and D are incorrect. There is nothing in the lines to suggest them. Choice E is incorrect. The narrator is determined, but his resolve is active and eager rather than quiet.
Remember, when asked to determine the author's attitude or tone, look for words that convey emotion or paint pictures.

20. C.   The narrator is able to identify Mr. Gerald as an American type. He feels closer to Mr. Gerald, familiar with the limits of his life. This suggests that he smiles out of a sense of *recognition*. Choices A, B, D, and E are incorrect. There is nothing in the passage to suggest them.
Remember, when asked to make inferences, base your answers on what the passage implies, not what it states directly.

21. E.   Phrases like "feeling something new, being affected by something that made the look of the world different" and "filled with bookish notions" reflect the narrator's response to the new books he reads. You have here a portrait of a youth's response to his expanding intellectual horizons. Choice A is incorrect. The narrator is not arguing in favor of a cause; he is recounting an episode from his life. Choice B is incorrect. The narrator was aware of racial prejudice long before he read Mencken.

Choice C is incorrect. The passage is not about Mencken's and Lewis's styles; it is about their effect in opening up the world to the narrator. Choice D is incorrect. The passage is more about the impact of art on life than about the impact of life on art. Remember, when asked to find the main idea, be sure to check the opening and summary sentences of each paragraph.

22. D.   The terrible robbers in the pond world are the cruel creatures who, in the course of the struggle to exist, devour their fellows.

23. D.   Here, "catch" is used as in fishing: "a good catch of fish." Suppose you want to collect a sample of pond-dwellers. You lower a jar into the nearest pond and capture a random batch of creatures swimming by—fish, tadpoles, full-grown insects, larvae—in other words, a mixed catch.

24. B.   The opening paragraph states that the introduction of the Dytiscus larvae to the aquarium will result in a struggle for existence in which the larvae will destroy their prey. The larvae, thus, are predators (hunters of prey). This suggests that their presence would be of particular interest to naturalists studying predatory patterns at work within a closed environment such as an aquarium.

25. C.   The author is describing how the Dytiscus larva looks: slim body, six legs, flat head, huge jaws. Choice A is incorrect. All the details indicate the author is describing the killer, not the victim.

26. D.   Though the passage mentions amphibians—tadpoles—and food, it states that the tadpoles provide food for the larvae, not vice versa. The passage nowhere states that the larvae are a source of food for amphibians. Choice A is incorrect. The passage states that the larvae secrete digestive juices; it mentions secretion in line 33. Choice B is incorrect. The passage states that the larvae attack one another; they seize and devour their own breed (lines 53–63). Choice C is incorrect. The passage states that the larvae are attracted to motion; prey for them "is all that moves." Choice E is incorrect. The passage states that the larvae have ravenous appetites: their "voracity" is unique. Remember, when asked about specific information in the passage, spot key words in the question and scan the passage to find them (or their synonyms).

27. E.   Digesting "out of doors" refers to the larva's external conversion of food into absorbable form. Look at the sentence immediately

following line 33. Break down the process step by step. The larva injects a secretion into the victim. The secretion dissolves the victim's insides. That is the start of the digestive process. It takes place inside the victim's body; in other words, *outside* the larva's body—"out of doors." Only then does the larva begin to suck up the dissolved juices of his prey.

28. **D.** Choice D is correct. You can arrive at it by the process of elimination. Statement I is true. The inside of the victim "becomes opaque" (line 42); it increases in opacity. Therefore, you can eliminate Choices B, C, and E. Statement II is also true. As it is drained, the victim's body shrivels or "shrinks to a limp bundle of skin." Therefore, you can eliminate Choice A. Statement III has to be untrue. The victim's head must stay on; otherwise, the dissolving interior would leak out. Only Choice D is left. It is the correct answer.

29. **D.** The author mentions rats because a rat will attack and devour other rats. He is sure rodents do this; he's not sure any other animals do so. Thus, he mentions rats and related rodents to point up an uncommon characteristic also found in Dytiscus larvae.

30. **A.** In line 62 the author mentions some "observations of which I shall speak later." These observations deal with whether wolves try to devour other wolves. Thus, the author clearly intends to discuss the likelihood of cannibalism among wolves.
In answering questions about what may be discussed in subsequent sections of the text, pay particular attention to words that are similar in meaning to subsequent: *following, succeeding, successive, later.*

Section 2 Mathematical Reasoning

1. **C.** Just quickly add up the number of miles Greg jogs each week:

$$3 + 4 + 5 + 6 + 7 + 8 + 9 = 42.$$

In 2 weeks he jogs **84** miles.

2. **C.** In the figure at the right, $x + y + z = 180$. Since $y = 60$ and $z = 50$, then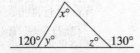

$$x = 180 - (50 + 60) = 180 - 110 = \textbf{70}.$$

3. **D.** After an increase of 75¢, a tuna fish sandwich will cost $5.00. The only sandwiches that, after a 50¢ increase, will be more expensive than the tuna fish are the **3** that now cost *more than* $4.50.

4. **B.** Discard the scores of 9.2 and 9.7, and take the average of the other four scores:

$$\frac{9.4 + 9.5 + 9.6 + 9.6}{4} = \frac{38.1}{4} = \textbf{9.525}.$$

5. **C.** The sum of the measures of two adjacent angles of a parallelogram is 180°. Therefore, $180 = 10x + 25x - 30 = 35x - 30$, which implies that $35x = 210$ and $x = \textbf{6}$.

6. **E.** Set up a proportion:

$$\frac{1 \text{ meter}}{1 \text{ second}} = \frac{k \text{ kilometers}}{1 \text{ hour}} = \frac{1000k \text{ meters}}{60 \text{ minutes}} =$$

$$\frac{1000k \text{ meters}}{3600 \text{ seconds}} = \frac{10k \text{ meters}}{36 \text{ seconds}}$$

Cross-multiplying the first and last ratios, we get $10k = 36$, and so $k = \textbf{3.6}$.

7. **E.** The figures below show that **all** of the choices **are possible**.

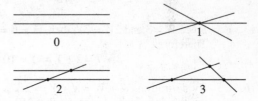

8. **B.** Since $a^2 - b^2 = (a - b)(a + b)$, then:

$$20 = a^2 - b^2 = (a - b)(a + b) = 10(a + b).$$

Therefore, $a + b = 2$. Adding the equations $a + b = 2$ and $a - b = 10$, we get

$$2a = 12 \Rightarrow a = 6 \Rightarrow b = \textbf{-4}.$$

9. **C.** Between 1 and 100 there are 12 multiples of 8 (8, 16, 24, ..., 96), each of which is octal. Each of the 10 integers whose units digit is an 8 (8, 18, ..., 98) is also octal; but 3 of them (8, 48, and 88) are already included as multiples, so there are 7 more. Finally, there are the 10 integers whose tens digit is an 8 (80, 81, 82, ..., 89); but 2 of them (80 and 88) have already been counted, so there are 8 more. In total there are $12 + 7 + 8 = 27$ octal numbers between 1 and 100.

10. **B.** Since 9 is a solution of $x^2 - a = 0$, then $81 - a = 0 \Rightarrow a = 81$. Now solve the equation:

$$x^4 - 81 = 0 \Rightarrow x^4 = 81 \Rightarrow x^2 = 9 \Rightarrow x = 3 \text{ or } \textbf{-3}.$$

11. **C.** The mode is 8, since more people earn $8 an hour than any other salary. Also, since there are 16 employees, the median is the average of the 8th and 9th items of data: $8 and $10, so the median is 9. Finally, the average of 8 and 9 is **8.5**.

12. E. If the ratio were $a:b:c$, then

$$180 = ax + bx + cx = (a + b + c)x.$$

Since each of the choices is written in lowest terms, $a + b + c$ must be a factor of 180. This is the case in choices A–D. Only choice E, **6:7:8**, fails: $6 + 7 + 8 = 21$, which is not a divisor of 180.

13. D. Pick easy-to-use numbers. Assume that in 1985 200 boys and 100 girls earned varsity letters. Then in 1995, there were 150 boys and 125 girls. The ratio of girls to boys was $125:150 = 5:6$ or $\dfrac{\mathbf{5}}{\mathbf{6}}$.

14. B. Adding the two equations, we get $5x + 5y = 28$. Then $x + y = \dfrac{28}{5}$, and the average of x and y is

$$\frac{x+y}{2} = \frac{\dfrac{28}{5}}{2} = \frac{28}{10} = \mathbf{2.8}.$$

15. E. Since $W = 3$ and $2W = 3X$, then $3X = 6 \Rightarrow X = 2$. Therefore

$$3 + 7 = 2 + Y \Rightarrow Y = 10 - 2 = \mathbf{8}.$$

16. C. By definition, $W + W = X + Y \Rightarrow 2W = X + Y$; but the definition also states that $2W = 3X$, so $X = \dfrac{2}{3}W$. Therefore

$$2W = \frac{2}{3}W + Y \Rightarrow Y = \frac{\mathbf{4}}{\mathbf{3}}\mathbf{W}.$$

17. C. If the ring was originally priced at $100, it was accidentally marked $40 instead of $160. The incorrect price of $40 must be increased by $120, which is 3 times, or **300%** of, the incorrect price.

18. B. John's average speed is calculated by dividing his total distance of 10 miles by the total time he spent riding his bicycle. Each tick mark on the horizontal axis of the graph represents 10 minutes. He left at 8:30 and arrived back home $1\dfrac{1}{2}$ hours later, at 10:00. However, he stopped for 10 minutes, from 9:20 to 9:30, so he was riding for only 1 hour and 20 minutes, or $\dfrac{4}{3}$ hours. Finally, $10 \div \dfrac{4}{3} = 10 \times \dfrac{3}{4} = 7\dfrac{\mathbf{1}}{\mathbf{2}}$.

19. D. Assume $AB = 3$ and $BC = 5$. The least that AC can be is 2, if A is on line BC, between B and C; and the most AC can be is 8, if A is on line BC, so that B is between A and C. In fact, AC can be any length between 2 and 8.

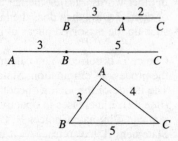

Therefore the ratio $AB:AC$ can be any number between $3:2$ $(= 1.5)$ and $3:8$ $(= 0.375)$. In particular, it can be $1:2$ $(= 0.5)$ and $3:8$. (I and III are true.) It cannot be $1:3$ $(= 0.333)$. (II is false.) Statements **I and III only** are true.

20. B. The easiest observation is that, if adding a fourth number, d, to a set doesn't change the average, then d is equal to the existing average. If you don't realize that, solve for d:

$$\frac{a+b+c+d}{4} = \frac{a+b+c}{3} \Rightarrow$$
$$3a + 3b + 3c + 3d = 4a + 4b + 4c \Rightarrow$$
$$3d = a + b + c \Rightarrow d = \frac{\mathbf{a+b+c}}{\mathbf{3}}.$$

21. A. Set up the equation:

$$\frac{\sqrt{3}}{100}(5\sqrt{60}) = \frac{x}{100}(60\sqrt{5}).$$

Multiply both sides by 100 to get rid of the fractions: $\sqrt{3}(5\sqrt{60}) = 60\sqrt{5}x$. Divide both sides by $60\sqrt{5}$ and simplify:

$$x = \frac{5\sqrt{3}\sqrt{60}}{60\sqrt{5}} = \frac{\sqrt{3}\sqrt{12}}{12} = \frac{\sqrt{36}}{12} = \frac{6}{12} = \frac{1}{2}$$

or **0.5%**.

22. A. Since $3x = 180$, then $x = 60$, and each triangle is equilateral with sides of r. The curved portion of the region is a semicircle of radius r, and its length is one-half the circumference: $\dfrac{1}{2}(2\pi r) = \pi r$. The total perimeter is $\pi r + 3r = \mathbf{r(\pi + 3)}$.

23. D. Expand:

$$(a + b)^2 = a^2 + 2ab + b^2 = (a^2 + b^2) + 2ab.$$

By the Pythagorean theorem, $a^2 + b^2 = 10^2 = 100$; and since the area is 20, $\frac{1}{2}ab = 20$ $\Rightarrow ab = 40$, and $2ab = 80$. Then

$$(a^2 + b^2) + 2ab = 100 + 80 = \mathbf{180}.$$

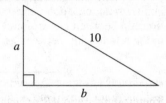

24. A. If a student earned a grade of G, she missed $(100 - G)$ points. In adjusting the grades, the teacher decided to deduct only half that number: $\frac{100 - G}{2}$, so the student's new grade was

$$100 - \left(\frac{100 - G}{2}\right) = 100 - 50 + \frac{G}{2} = 50 + \frac{G}{2}.$$

Since this was done to each student's grade, the effect on the average was exactly the same. The new average was $\mathbf{50 + \dfrac{A}{2}}$.

25. E. To earn 10 points, Ellen needed to get 10 correct answers and then earn no more points on the remaining $q - 10$ questions. To earn no points on a set of questions, she had to miss 4 questions (thereby losing $4 \times \frac{1}{4} = 1$ point) for every 1 question she got right in that set. She answered $\frac{1}{5}$ of the $q - 10$ questions correctly (and $\frac{4}{5}$ of them incorrectly). The total number of correct answers was

$$10 + \frac{q - 10}{5} = 10 + \frac{q}{5} - \frac{10}{5} = \mathbf{8 + \dfrac{q}{5}}.$$

Alternative Solution: Let c be the number of questions Ellen answered correctly, and $q - c$ the number she missed. Then her raw score is $c - \frac{1}{4}(q - c)$, which equals 10, so

$$4c - q + c = 40 \Rightarrow 5c - q = 40 \Rightarrow 5c = 40 + q$$
$$\Rightarrow c = \frac{40 + q}{5} = 8 + \frac{q}{5}.$$

Section 3   Verbal Reasoning

1. E. Tiffany's works of art have survived in spite of their *fragility* (tendency to break). Remember to watch for signal words that link one part of the sentence to another. The use of "despite" in the opening phrase sets up a contrast. *Despite* signals you that Tiffany's glass works were unlikely candidates to survive for several decades.   (Contrast Signal)

2. A. Voles are similar to mice; however, they are also different from them, and may be *distinguished from* them.
Note how the use of "although" in the opening phrase sets up the basic contrast here.
                (Contrast Signal)

3. C. A comprehensive or thorough study would not be missing *relevant* or important material. Remember to watch for signal words that link one part of the sentence to another. The use of "but" in the second clause sets up a contrast.
                (Contrast Signal)

4. C. Because Dr. Drew's method proved *effective*, it became a *model* for other systems. Remember to watch for signal words that link one part of the sentence to another. The "so...that" structure signals cause and effect.
                (Cause and Effect Signal)

5. B. The fact that the languages of the Mediterranean area were markedly (strikingly) alike eased or *facilitated* the movement of people and ideas from country to country. Note how the specific examples in the second part of the sentence clarify the idea stated in the first part.   (Examples)

6. E. Feeling that a job was *pointless* might well lead you to perform it in a *perfunctory* (indifferent or mechanical) manner. Remember, watch for signal words that link one part of the sentence to another. The use of "because" in the opening clause is a cause signal.   (Cause and Effect Signal)

7. B. Pain is a sensation. Losing the ability to feel pain would leave the body vulnerable, defenseless, lacking its usual warnings against impending bodily harm. Note how the second clause serves to clarify or explain what is meant by pain's being an "early warning system."   (Definition)

8. B. A *lugubrious* (exaggeratedly gloomy) appearance may create laughter because it is so inappropriate in the *hilarity* (noisy gaiety) of the circus. The clown's success stems from a contrast. The missing words must be antonyms or

near-antonyms. You can immediately eliminate Choices C, D, and E as nonantonym
pairs. In addition, you can eliminate Choice A;
sobriety or seriousness is an inappropriate
term for describing circus life.
                                    (Contrast Pattern)

9. C.   If she *deprecated* her accomplishments
        (diminished them or saw nothing praiseworthy
        in them), she would show her unwillingness
        to boast about them or *flaunt* them. Note the
        use of "properly" to describe her unwilling-
        ness to do something. This suggests that the
        second missing word would have negative
        associations.   (Definition)

10. C. A stereotyped or oversimplified portrait of a
        slave would lead sensitive readers to *criticize*
        it for dismissing the issue of slavery so casual-
        ly. Thus, they normally would be *detractors* of
        the novel. However, *Huckleberry Finn* is such
        a fine work that even its critics acknowledge
        its greatness. Signal words are helpful here.
        Despite in the first clause implies a contrast,
        and *even* in the second clause implies that the
        subjects somewhat reluctantly agree that the
        novel is a masterpiece.   (Contrast Signal)

11. B. A *play* is made up of *acts*. A *novel* is made up
        of *chapters*.   (Part to Whole)

12. D. *Geology* is an example of a *science*. A *fir* tree
        is an example of a *tree*.   (Class and Member)

13. E. A *signature* on a *portrait* establishes who
        painted it. A *byline* on an *article* establishes
        who wrote it.   (Function)

14. E. A *plane* is a tool used to *smooth* objects; a
        wrench is a tool used to grip and *twist* objects.
        Note that *plane* here is used in a somewhat
        uncommon sense. Be on the alert for unfamil-
        iar secondary meanings of words.
        Remember to watch out for errors stemming
        from grammatical or logical reversals. Choice
        D is incorrect. An axe is sharpened. It does
        not sharpen; it hews or chops.
                                        (Tool and Action)

15. B. *Funds* that are *embezzled* are appropriated or
        taken fraudulently. Similarly, *writings* that are
        plagiarized are appropriated fraudulently.
        Note that Choices A, C, and D are eye-catch-
        ers. Because *money*, *ransom*, and *loot* all have
        some relationship to *funds*, these answers may
        tempt you into making an incorrect choice.
                                    (Defining Characteristic)

16. B. *Uncouth* is a synonym for *graceless*.
        Therefore, gracelessness is the quality of
        being uncouth. Similarly, *avaricious* is a

synonym for *greedy*. Therefore, greed is the
quality of being avaricious.
                                    (Synonym Variant)

17. B. An *elevator* moves through a *shaft*. *Water*
        moves through a *conduit* (a pipe or channel
        for fluids).
        Beware Eye-Catchers: Choice C is incorrect.
        Just because elevators and escalators have
        similar functions, don't expect that the rela-
        tionship between *elevator* and *shaft* is similar
        to the relationship between *escalator* and *step*.
                                        (Location)

18. A. *Parsimony* (stinginess) is extreme thrift or *fru-
        gality*. *Agony* is extreme suffering or *pain*.
                                    (Degree of Intensity)

19. A. A *dilettante* is not serious about art; he or she
        merely *dabbles*. A *coquette* is not serious
        about her affairs of the heart; she merely *flirts*.
                                        (Definition)

20. B. Someone *indifferent* is uncaring or uncon-
        cerned; he or she is lacking in *concern*.
        Someone *arrogant* is proud and immodest; he
        or she is lacking in *modesty*.
                                    (Antonym Variant)

21. A. *Laconic* (brief, curt in speech) is similar in
        meaning to *taciturn* (disinclined to talk). Thus,
        taciturnity has the quality of being laconic.
        Similarly, *unrehearsed* is similar in meaning
        to *improvised* (composed and performed with-
        out preparation). Thus, improvisation has the
        quality of being unrehearsed.
                                    (Synonym Variant)

22. C. *Slander* is by its nature *defamatory* (injurious
        to one's reputation); an *elegy* (poem or song
        of mourning) is by nature *sorrowful*.
                                    (Defining Characteristic)

23. A. A snake *sloughs* or casts off its dead *skin*;
        people and animals *shed* their unneeded *hair*.
                                        (Function)

24. B. The author is writing a book about the effect
        of the opening of the West on the Indians liv-
        ing there. As a historian, he needs primary
        source materials—firsthand accounts of the
        period written by men and women living at
        that time. Thus, he finds the period of
        1860–1890 worth mentioning because in that
        period the "greatest concentration of recorded
        experience and observation" was created.

25. C. Only the white settlers looked on their intru-
        sion into Indian territory as the opening of the
        West. To the Native Americans, it was an
        invasion. Thus, "opening" *from a Native
        American perspective is an inaccurate term.*

26. E.   Throughout the passage the author presents and comments on the nature of the original documents that form the basis for his historical narrative. Thus, it is clear that a major concern of his is to *introduce* these "sources of almost forgotten oral history" to his readers. Choice A is incorrect. The author clearly regrets the fate of the Indians. However, he does not take this occasion to denounce or condemn the white man. Choice B is incorrect. While the author discusses the various treaty councils, he does not evaluate or judge how effective they were. Choice C is incorrect. The author never touches on the current treatment of Indians. Choice D is incorrect. The author indicates no such thing.

27. E.   Of all the thousands of published descriptions of the opening of the West, the greatest concentration or *cluster* of accounts date from the period of 1860 to 1890.

28. B.   The author is describing a period in which Native Americans lost their land and much of their personal freedom to the same pioneers who supposedly revered the ideal of freedom. Thus, in describing the ideal of freedom revered by the pioneers as "personal freedom for those who already had it" (in other words, personal freedom for the pioneers, not the Indians), the author is being *ironic*.

29. D.   You can arrive at the correct choice by the process of elimination.
Statement I is true. The passage states that the quality of the interviews depended on the interpreters' abilities. Inaccuracies could creep in because of the translators' lack of skill. Therefore, you can eliminate Choice B. Statement II is untrue. The passage indicates that the Indians sometimes exaggerated, telling the reporters tall tales. It does not indicate that the reporters in turn overstated what they had been told. Therefore, you can eliminate Choices C and E. Statement III is true. The passage indicates that the Indians sometimes were disinclined to speak the whole truth because they feared reprisals (retaliation) if they did. Therefore, you can eliminate Choice A. Only Choice D is left. It is the correct answer.

30. C.   Brown speaks of the Indians who lived through the "doom period of their civilization," the victims of the conquest of the American West. In doing so, his tone can best be described as *elegiac*, expressing sadness about their fate and lamenting their vanished civilization.

31. A.   In the fifth paragraph Brown comments upon the "graphic similes and metaphors of the natural world" found in the English translations of Indian speeches. Thus, he is impressed by their *vividness of imagery*.

32. C.   Commenting about inadequate interpreters who turned eloquent Indian speeches into "flat" prose, Brown is criticizing the translations for their *pedestrian*, unimaginative quality.

33. C.   Lines 73–76 state that, as the Indian leaders became more sophisticated or knowledgeable about addressing treaty councils, "they demanded the right to choose their own interpreters and recorders." Until they had become familiar with the process, *they were unaware that they had the option to demand such services*.

34. E.   Brown has tried to create a narrative of the winning of the West from the victims' perspective. This suggests that, in asking his readers to read the book facing eastward (the way the Indians would have been looking when they first saw the whites headed west), he is asking them metaphorically to look at things from the Indians' point of view.

35. B.   In the sentence immediately preceding the one in which this phrase appears, Brown calls the Indians "true conservationists." Such conservationists know that life is *necessarily tied to* the earth and to its resources, and that by destroying these resources, by imbalancing the equation, so to speak, you destroy life itself.

Section 4   Mathematical Reasoning
Quantitative Comparison Questions

1. C.   Multiply: each column is $\frac{21}{11}$. The columns are equal (C).

2. C.   Subtract 5 from each side of the equation $y = x + 10$: $y - 5 = x + 5$.
Alternatively, add 5 to each column. Then Column A becomes $x + 10$ and Column B becomes y, and it is given that $y = x + 10$. The columns are equal (C).

3. D.   By the laws of exponents, Column A is $a^4 a^5 = a^9$, and Column B is $(a^3)^2 = a^6$. If a had to be greater than 1, then Column A would be greater. When $a = 1$, however, the columns are equal, and if a is less than 1, Column B is greater. Neither column is *always* greater, and the columns are not *always* equal (D).

4. B.   Add to get the amount of bread, in fractions of a loaf, eaten at the three meals:

$$\frac{5}{12} + \frac{5}{8} + \frac{5}{6} = \frac{10}{24} + \frac{15}{24} + \frac{20}{24} = \frac{45}{24}.$$

Then $2 - \dfrac{45}{24} = \dfrac{48}{24} - \dfrac{45}{24} = \dfrac{3}{24} = \dfrac{1}{8}$ loaf was left for midnight snack, and $\dfrac{1}{8} < \dfrac{1}{5}$. Column B is greater.

5. **D.** If the average of six numbers is 10, the sum of the numbers is 60. If the six numbers were 3, 4, 5, 15, 16, 17, Column A would be 3; but if the six numbers were 1, 2, 3, 4, 5, 45, Column A would be only 1. Neither column is *always* greater, and the columns are not *always* equal (D).

6. **B.** In each column, the tens digit will be the same as the tens digit obtained by squaring just the last two digits of the number given. Since $89^2 = 7921$ and $21^2 = 441$, Column B is greater.

7. **A.** By the Pythagorean theorem, $a^2 + (2a)^2 = x^2$, so
$$x^2 = a^2 + (2a)^2 = a^2 + 4a^2 = 5a^2.$$
Therefore, $x = a\sqrt{5}$, which is greater than $a\sqrt{3}$. Column A is greater.

8. **D.** Since we have no information as to the area of the base of the cylinder or of the cone, we cannot tell which has the larger volume. The radius 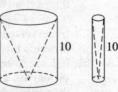 of the cylinder could be 0.001 or 10,000,000. Neither column is *always* greater, and the columns are not *always* equal (D).

9. **B.** Since $0 < b < 1$, then $b < \dfrac{1}{b}$. Multiplying each side by a gives
$$ab < a\left(\dfrac{1}{b}\right) = \dfrac{a}{b}$$
Column B is greater.

10. **B.** As shown in the figure, the slope of ℓ is negative and the slope of k is positive. Column B is greater.

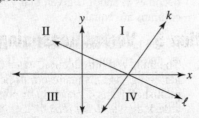

11. **C.** Since $AB = AD$, $\triangle ABD$ is isosceles, and $b = c$. But BD is a transversal cutting parallel sides

AB and CD, so $a = c$. Therefore, $a = b$. The columns are equal (**C**).

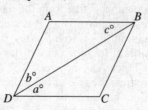

12. **B.** Since A times ABA is a three-digit number, A has to be less than 4; but 1 times ABA is ABA, so $A \ne 1$. Therefore, $A = 2$ or $A = 3$.

$$\begin{array}{c} 2B2 \\ \times\ 2 \\ \hline 4C4 \end{array} \quad \text{or} \quad \begin{array}{c} 3B3 \\ \times\ 3 \\ \hline 9C9 \end{array}$$

Since there is no carrying, either $2 \times B = C$, a one-digit number, and $B < 5$, or $3 \times B = C$, and $B < 3$. In either case, column B is greater.

13. **C.** Since $q = \dfrac{4}{3}s$, we can replace q by $\dfrac{4}{3}s$ in the equation $r = \dfrac{3}{8}q$:
$$r = \dfrac{\overset{1}{\cancel{3}}}{\underset{2}{\cancel{8}}} \times \dfrac{\overset{1}{\cancel{4}}}{\underset{1}{\cancel{3}}}s \Rightarrow r = \dfrac{1}{2}s \Rightarrow 2r = s \Rightarrow 6r = 3s.$$
From the first given equation, however, $5p = 3s$, so $5p = 6r$. The columns are equal (**C**).

14. **A.** Column A: Since the hypotenuse is 2, the length of each leg is $\dfrac{2}{\sqrt{2}} = \sqrt{2}$, and the area is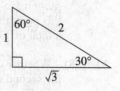
$$\dfrac{1}{2}\left(\sqrt{2}\right)\left(\sqrt{2}\right) = \dfrac{1}{2}(2) = 1.$$
Column B: Since the hypotenuse is 2, the shorter leg is 1, the longer leg is $\sqrt{3}$, and the area is
$$\dfrac{1}{2}(1)\left(\sqrt{3}\right) = \dfrac{\sqrt{3}}{2} \approx 0.866.$$
Column A is greater.

15. **C.** Adding the two given equations, we get $a + b + c = 11d$. Then
$$a + b + c + d = 11d + d = 12d \Rightarrow$$
$$\dfrac{a + b + c + d}{4} = \dfrac{12d}{4} = 3d.$$
The columns are equal (**C**).

Grid-in Questions

16. (152) Normally, to get 60 pencils you would need to buy 20 sets of three at 25 cents per set, a total expenditure of $20 \times 25 = 500$ cents. On sale, you could get 60 pencils by buying 12 sets of five at 29 cents per set, for a total cost of $12 \times 29 = 348$ cents. This is a savings of $500 - 348 = \mathbf{152}$ cents.

17. (any decimal between 2.01 and 2.33 or $\dfrac{13}{6}$)

It is given that: $1 < 3x - 5 < 2$
Add 5 to each expression: $6 < 3x < 7$
Divide each expression by 3: $2 < x < \dfrac{7}{3}$

Grid in any decimal number between 2 and 2.33: **2.1**, for example. You could also grid in the fraction $\dfrac{13}{6}$, which is the average of

$2 = \dfrac{12}{6}$ and $\dfrac{7}{3} = \dfrac{14}{6}$.

18. (8100) $x < 10{,}000 \Rightarrow \sqrt{x} < \sqrt{10{,}000} = 100 \Rightarrow$

$$\frac{\sqrt{x}}{5} < \frac{100}{5} = 20$$

Since $\dfrac{\sqrt{x}}{5}$ must be an even integer, the

greatest possible value of $\dfrac{\sqrt{x}}{5}$ is 18:

$$\frac{\sqrt{x}}{5} = 18 \Rightarrow \sqrt{x} = 90 \Rightarrow x = 8100$$

19. (202) After 33 repetitions of the pattern—red, white, white, blue, blue, blue—there will be $6 \times 33 = 198$ marbles in the box, of which 99 will be blue. When these are followed by 4 more marbles (1 red, 2 whites, and 1 blue), at this point there will be 100 blue marbles, and a total of $198 + 4 = \mathbf{202}$ marbles in all.

20. (28) Whether or not you can visualize (or draw) the second (large) square, you can calculate its area. The area of each of the four triangles is $\dfrac{1}{2}(3)(4) = 6$, for a total of 24, and the area of the 5×5 square is 25. Then, the area of the large square is $24 + 25 = 49$. Each side of the square is 7, and the perimeter is **28**.

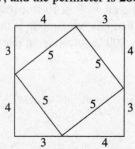

21. $\left(\dfrac{1}{32}\right)$ $\langle\langle 3 \rangle\rangle - \langle\langle 4 \rangle\rangle = \dfrac{1}{2^{3+1}} - \dfrac{1}{2^{4+1}} = \dfrac{1}{2^4} - \dfrac{1}{2^5} =$

$\dfrac{1}{16} - \dfrac{1}{32} = \dfrac{1}{\mathbf{32}}$

22. $\left(\dfrac{1}{8}\right)$ $\langle\langle a + 3 \rangle\rangle : \langle\langle a \rangle\rangle = \dfrac{1}{2^{(a+3)+1}} : \dfrac{1}{2^{a+1}} = \dfrac{1}{2^{a+4}} : \dfrac{1}{2^{a+1}} =$

$\dfrac{1}{2^{a+4}} \div \dfrac{1}{2^{a+1}} = \dfrac{1}{2^{a+4}} \times \dfrac{2^{a+1}}{1} = \dfrac{1}{2^3} = \dfrac{1}{\mathbf{8}}$.

23. (19) There are at most 14 blank cards, so at least 86 of the 100 cards have one or more letters on them. If x is the number of cards with both letters on them, then

$$75 + 30 - x \le 86 \Rightarrow x \ge 105 - 86 = 19.$$

This is illustrated in the Venn diagram below.

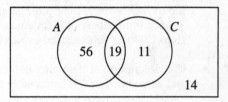

24. (8190) There are $26 \times 26 \times 9 = 6084$ PIC's with two letters and one digit, and there are $26 \times 9 \times 9 = 2106$ PIC's with one letter and two digits, for a total of $6084 + 2106 = \mathbf{8190}$.

25. $\left(\dfrac{3}{8} \text{ or } .375\right)$ If the diameter of the small white

circle is d, then the diameter of the large white circle is $3d$, and the diameter of the largest circle is $d + 3d = 4d$. Then the ratio of the diameters, and hence of the radii, of the three circles is 4:3:1. Assume the radii are 4, 3, and 1. Then the areas of the circles are 16π, 9π, and π. The sum of the areas of the white circles is 10π, the shaded region is

$16\pi - 10\pi = 6\pi$, and $\dfrac{6\pi}{16\pi} = \dfrac{3}{8}$.

Section 5 Verbal Reasoning

1. E. The italicized introduction states that the author has had his manuscript rejected by his publisher. He is consigning or committing it to a desk drawer *to set it aside as unmarketable.*

2. B. The rejected author identifies with these baseball players, who constantly must face "failure." *He sees he is not alone in having to confront failure and move on.*

3. B.   The author uses the jogger's comment to make a point about the *mental impact Henderson's home run must have had on Moore*. He reasons that, if each step a runner takes sends so many complex messages to the brain, then Henderson's ninth-inning home run must have flooded Moore's brain with messages, impressing its image indelibly in Moore's mind.

4. D.   The author is talking of the impact of Henderson's home run on Moore's mind. Registering in Moore's mind, the home run *made an impression* on him.

5. C.   The author looks on himself as someone who "to succeed at all..must perform at an extraordinary level of excellence." This level of excellence, he maintains, is not demanded of accountants, plumbers, and insurance salesmen, and he seems to pride himself on belonging to such a demanding profession. Thus, his attitude to members of less demanding professions can best be described as *superior*.

6. A.   The description of the writer defying his pain and extending himself irrationally to create a "masterpiece" despite the rejections of critics and publishers is a highly romantic one that elevates *the writer as someone heroic in his or her accomplishments*.

7. C.   The author of Passage 2 discusses the advantages of his ability to concentrate. Clearly, he prizes *his ability to focus* on the task at hand.

8. B.   When one football team is ahead of another by several touchdowns and there seems to be no way for the second team to catch up, the outcome of the game appears *decided* or settled.

9. E.   The "larger point of view" focuses on what to most people is the big question: the outcome of the game. The author is indifferent to this larger point of view. Concentrating on his own performance, he is *more concerned with the task at hand than with* winning or losing the game.

10. C.   Parade ground drill clearly does not entirely prepare a soldier for the reality of war. It only does so "to an extent." By using this phrase, the author is *qualifying his statement*, making it less absolute.

11. C.   One would expect someone who dismisses or rejects most comparisons of athletics to art to avoid making such comparisons. The author,

however, *is making such a comparison*. This reversal of what would have been expected is an instance of irony.

12. C.   To learn to overcome failure, to learn to give one's all in performance, to learn to focus on the work of the moment, to learn to have "the selfish intensity" that can block out the rest of the world—these are hard lessons that *both athletes and artists learn*.

13. D.   Throughout Passage 2, the author stresses the advantages and the power of concentration. He believes that, if you concentrate intensely on the job at hand, you will reduce the chances of your dwelling on past failures and psyching yourself out. Thus, he is not particularly swayed by the Passage 1 author's contention that a failure such as giving up a key home run can destroy an athlete.

Section 6   Mathematical Reasoning

1. C.   Replacing y by $2x$ in the equation $x + y + 30 = 180$, we get
$$x + 2x + 30 = 180 \Rightarrow 3x = 150 \Rightarrow$$
$$x = 50 \Rightarrow y = 2x = \mathbf{100}.$$

2. C.   The temperature rose $8 - (-7) = 8 + 7 = 15°$ in 1.5 hours. The average hourly increase was $15° \div 1.5 = \mathbf{10°}$.

3. D.   The expression $n^2 - 30$ is negative whenever $n^2 < 30$. This is true for all integers between -5 and 5 inclusive, **11** in all.

4. D.   The only thing to do is to test each set of values to see which ones work and which one doesn't. In this case, choice D, $a = 3$ and $b = -4$, does not work:
$2(3)^2 + 3(-4) = 18 - 12 = 6$, not 5.
The other choices all work.

5. C.   For some number x, the measures of the angles are x, $2x$, and $3x$; so
$$180 = x + 2x + 3x = 6x \Rightarrow x = 30.$$
Therefore, the triangle is a 30-60-90 triangle, and the ratio of the sides is $\mathbf{1:\sqrt{3}:2}$.

6. D.   By definition, a googol is equal to 10^{100}. Therefore, $g^2 = 10^{100} \times 10^{100} = 10^{200}$, which, when it is written out, is the digit 1 followed by 200 0s, creating an integer with 201 digits.

7. A.   Since $C = 2\pi r$, then $r = \dfrac{C}{2\pi}$, and

area of circle $= \pi r^2 = \pi \left(\dfrac{C}{2\pi} \right)^2 =$

$\pi \left(\dfrac{C^2}{4\pi^2} \right) = \dfrac{C^2}{4\pi}$.

8. E.   Joanna needed to drive the m miles in $h + \dfrac{1}{2}$ hours. Since $r = \dfrac{d}{t}$, to find her rate, we divide the distance, m, by the time, $\left(h + \dfrac{1}{2} \right)$:

$\dfrac{m}{h + \dfrac{1}{2}} = \dfrac{2m}{2h + 1}$.

9. A.   The area of $\triangle ABC$ is $\dfrac{1}{2}(4)(5) = 10$. Then the area of the shaded region is 10 minus the areas of the small white square and triangle: $10 - 4 - 2 = \mathbf{4}$.

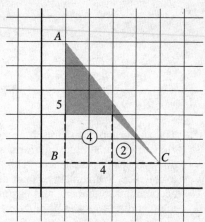

10. E.   To find the average of three numbers, divide their sum by 3: $\dfrac{3^{30} + 3^{60} + 3^{90}}{3}$. To simplify this fraction, divide each term in the numerator by 3:

$\dfrac{3^{30}}{3} + \dfrac{3^{60}}{3} + \dfrac{3^{90}}{3} = \mathbf{3^{29} + 3^{59} + 3^{89}}$.

PART THREE

Tactics, Strategies, Practice: Verbal

4 The Sentence Completion Question

- ■ **Testing Tactics**
- ■ **Long-Range Strategies**
- ■ **Practice Exercises**
- ■ **Answer Key**

Two of the three verbal sections start with "fill-in-the-blank" sentence completion questions. Consider them warm-up exercises: to answer them correctly, you'll have to use both your reading comprehension and vocabulary skills. You will then be prepared for the critical reading portions of the test.

The sentence completion questions ask you to choose the best way to complete a sentence from which one or two words have been omitted. The sentences deal with the sorts of topics you've probably encountered in your general reading: ballet, banking, tarantulas, thunderstorms, paintings, plagues. However, this is *not* a test of your general knowledge, although you may feel more comfortable if you are familiar with the topic the sentence is discussing. If you're unfamiliar with the topic, don't worry about it. You should be able to answer any of the questions using what you know about how the English language works.

Here is a set of directions for the sentence completion questions that has appeared on actual SAT I exams for several years. From time to time the SAT-makers come up with different sentences as examples. However, the basic directions vary hardly at all. Master them now. Don't waste your test time re-reading familiar directions. Spend that time answering additional questions. That's the way to boost your score!

Each sentence below has one or two blanks, each blank indicating that something has been omitted. Beneath the sentence are five lettered words or sets of words. Choose the word or set of words that <u>best</u> fits the meaning of the sentence as a whole.

Example:

Medieval kingdoms did not become constitutional republics overnight; on the contrary, the change was ----.

(A) unpopular   (B) unexpected   (C) advantageous
(D) sufficient   (E) gradual

Ⓐ Ⓑ Ⓒ Ⓓ ●

The phrase *on the contrary* is your key to the correct answer. It is what we call a **signal word**: it signals a contrast. *On the contrary* sets up a contrast between a hypothetical change—the change you might have assumed took place—and the actual change. Did medieval kingdoms turn into republics *overnight*? No, they did not. Instead of happening overnight, the actual change took time: it was *gradual*. The correct answer is Choice E, *gradual*.

Now that you know what to expect on sentence completion questions, work through the following tactics and learn to spot the signals that will help you fill in the blanks. Then do the practice exercises at the end of the chapter.

Testing Tactics

First, Read the Sentence Carefully to Get a Feel for Its Meaning.

Have you ever put together a jigsaw puzzle and wound up missing one final piece? There you are, staring at the almost complete picture. You know the shape of the missing piece. You can see where it fits. You know what its coloration must be. You know, *because you've looked hard at the incomplete picture, and you've got a sense of what's needed to make it whole.*

That's the position you're in when you're working with sentence completion questions. You have to look hard at that incomplete sentence, to read it carefully to get a sense of its drift. Once you've got a feel for the big picture, you'll be ready to come up with an answer choice that fits.

Before You Look at the Choices, Think of a Word That Makes Sense.

Your problem here is to find a word that best completes the sentence's thought. Before you look at the answer choices, try to come up with a word that makes logical sense in this context. Then look at all five choices supplied by the SAT-makers. If the word you thought of is one of your five choices, select it as your answer. If the word you thought of is *not* one of your five choices, look for a synonym of that word.

See how the process works in dealing with the following sentence.

> The psychologist set up the experiment to test the rat's -----; he wished to see how well the rat adjusted to the changing conditions it had to face.

Note how the part of the sentence following the semi-colon (the second clause, in technical terms) is being used to define or clarify what the psychologist is trying to test. He is trying to see how well the rat *adjusts*. What words does this suggest to you? *Flexibility*, possibly, or *adaptability*. Either of these words could complete the sentence's thought.

Here are the five answer choices given.

> (A) reflexes   (B) communicability   (C) stamina
> (D) sociability   (E) adaptability

The answer clearly is *adaptability*, Choice E.

Look at All the Possible Answers Before You Make Your Final Choice.

You are looking for the word that *best* fits the meaning of the sentence as a whole. Don't be hasty in picking an answer. Test each answer choice, substituting it for the missing word. That way you can satisfy yourself that you have come up with the answer that best fits.

Follow this tactic as you work through a question from an actual, published SAT.

> Physical laws do not, of course, in themselves force bodies to behave in a certain way, but merely ---- how, as a matter of fact, they do behave.
> (A) determine   (B) preclude   (C) counteract
> (D) describe   (E) commend

When you looked at the answer choices, did you find that one seemed to leap right off the page? Specifically, did Choice A, *determine*, catch your eye?

A hasty reader might easily focus on Choice A, but in this sentence *determine* doesn't really work. However, there are reasons for its appeal.

Determine often appears in a scientific context. It's a word you may have come across in class discussions of experiments: "By flying a kite during a lightning storm, Ben Franklin tried to *determine* (find out; discover) just how lightning worked."

Here, determine is an eye-catcher, an answer choice set up to tempt the unwary into guessing wrong. Eye-catchers are words that somehow come to mind after reading the statement. They're related in a way; they feel as if they belong in the statement, as if they're dealing with the same field.

Because you have seen *determine* previously in a scientific context, you may want to select it as your answer without thinking the sentence through. However, you *must* take time to think it through, to figure out what it is about. Here it's about physical laws (the law of gravity, for example). It says physical laws *don't* force bodies to act in a specific way. (The *law* of gravity didn't make the apple fall on Isaac Newton's head; the *force* of gravity did.)

The sentence goes on to clarify what physical laws actually do. What *do* they do? Do physical laws make discoveries about how bodies behave? No. *People* make discoveries about how bodies behave. Then people write down physical laws to describe what they have discovered. The correct answer to this question is Choice D, *describe*. Be suspicious of answer choices that come too easily.

Watch Out for Negative Words and Prefixes.

No, not, none; non-, un-, in-. These negative words and word parts are killers, especially in combination.

> The damage to the car was insignificant.
> ("Don't worry about it—it's just a scratch.")
> The damage to the car was not insignificant.
> ("Oh, no, Bart! We totaled Mom's car!")

Watch out for *not*: it's easy to overlook, but it's a key word, as the following sentence clearly illustrates.

> Madison was not ---- person and thus made few public addresses; but those he made were memorable, filled with noble phrases.
>
> (A) a reticent   (B) a stately   (C) an inspiring
>   (D) an introspective   (E) a communicative

What would happen if you overlooked *not* in this question? Probably you'd wind up choosing Choice A: Madison was a *reticent* (quiet; reserved) man. *For this reason* he made few public addresses.

Unfortunately, you'd have gotten things backward. The sentence isn't telling you what Madison was like. It's telling you what he was *not* like. And he was not a *communicative* person; he didn't express himself freely. However, when he did get around to expressing himself, he had valuable things to say. Choice E is the correct answer.

Use Your Knowledge of Context Clues to Get at the Meanings of Unfamiliar Words.

If a word used in a sentence is unfamiliar, or if an answer choice is unknown to you, look at its context in the sentence to see whether the context provides a clue to the meaning of the word. Often authors will use an unfamiliar word and then immediately define it within the same sentence.

> The ---- of Queen Elizabeth I impressed her contemporaries: she seemed to know what dignitaries and foreign leaders were thinking.
>
> (A) symbiosis (B) malevolence (C) punctiliousness
>   (D) consternation   (E) perspicacity

Looking at the five answer choices, you may feel unequipped to try to tackle the sentence at all. However, the clause that immediately follows the colon ("she seemed to know what...leaders were thinking") is there to explain and clarify that missing word. The two groups of words are juxtaposed—set beside one another—to make their

relationship clear. The missing word has something to do with the queen's ability to see through those foreign leaders and practically read their thoughts.

Now that you know the missing word's general meaning, go through the answer choices to see which one makes sense. *Symbiosis* means living together cooperatively or intimately (as in "a symbiotic relationship"). It has nothing to do with being insightful or astute; you can eliminate Choice A. *Malevolence* means ill-will. The queen's ability shows her perceptiveness, not her ill-will; you can eliminate Choice B. *Punctiliousness* means carefulness about observing all the proper formalities; you can eliminate Choice C. *Consternation* means amazement or alarm. Elizabeth was clear-sighted, not confused or amazed; you can eliminate Choice D. Only Choice E is left, *perspicacity*. Elizabeth's ability to know the thoughts of foreign leaders demonstrates her acute mental vision or discernment, in other words, her perspicacity. The correct answer is Choice E.

Break Down Unfamiliar Words Into Recognizable Parts.

If you're having vocabulary trouble, look for familiar parts—prefixes, suffixes, and roots—in unfamiliar words.

Note that your knowledge of word parts could have helped you answer the previous question. Suppose you had been able to eliminate two of the answer choices and were trying to decide among three unfamiliar words, *symbiosis*, *punctiliousness*, and *perspicacity*. By using what you know about word parts, you still could have come up with the correct answer. Take a good look at *perspicacity*. Do you know any

other words that begin with the letters *per-*? What about *pervade*, to spread through? The prefix *per-* means thoroughly or through. Next look at the letters *spic*. What other words contain those letters? Take *despicable*, for example, or *conspicuous*. A despicable person deserves to be looked down on. A conspicuous object is noticeable; it must be looked at. the root *spic* means to look at or see. Queen Elizabeth I had the ability to *see through* surfaces and perceive people's inner thoughts. In a word, she had *perspicacity*.

Watch for Signal Words That Link One Part of the Sentence to Another.

Writers use transitions to link their ideas logically. These transitions or signal words are clues that can help you figure out what the sentence actually means.

Contrast Signals

Look for words or phrases that indicate a contrast between one idea and another. In such cases an antonym or near-antonym for another word in the sentence should be the correct answer.

Signal Words

although	in contrast	on the other hand
but	in spite of	rather than
despite	instead of	still
even though	nevertheless	yet
however	on the contrary	

See how a contrast signal works in an easy question from a recent SAT I.

> In sharp contrast to the previous night's revelry, the wedding was ---- affair.
>
> (A) a fervent   (B) a dignified   (C) a chaotic
> (D) an ingenious   (E) a jubilant

In sharp contrast signals you explicitly to look for an antonym or near-antonym of another word or idea in the sentence. The wedding, it suggests, is *different in character* from the party the night before. What was that party like? It was *revelry*: wild, noisy, even drunken partying. The wedding, therefore, was *not* wild and noisy. Instead, it was calm and formal; it was *dignified* (stately, decorous). The correct answer is Choice B, *dignified*.

Support Signals

Look for words or phrases that indicate that the omitted portion of the sentence supports or continues a thought developed elsewhere in the sentence. In such cases, a synonym

or near-synonym for another word in the sentence should be the correct answer.

Signal Words

additionally	furthermore
also	in addition
and	likewise
besides	moreover

See how *and* works as a support signal in the following SAT question.

> During the Middle Ages, plague and other ---- decimated the populations of entire towns.
>
> (A) pestilences   (B) immunizations   (C) proclivities
> (D) indispositions   (E) demises

The presence of *and* linking two items in a series indicates that the missing word may be a synonym or near-synonym for the other linked word. In this case, *pestilences* are, like the *plague*, deadly epidemic diseases: the medieval Black Plague was one type of pestilence. The correct answer is Choice A.

Note, by the way, that the missing word, like *plague*, must be a word with *extremely* negative associations. Therefore, you can eliminate any word with positive or neutral ones. You can even eliminate words with *mildly* negative connotations. *Immunizations* (processes giving the ability to resist a disease) have positive effects: you may dislike your flu shot, but you prefer it to coming down with the flu. You can eliminate Choice B. *Proclivities* (natural tendencies), in themselves, are neutral (you can have a proclivity for championing the rights of underdogs, or a proclivity for neatness, or a proclivity for violence); they are not *by definition* inevitably negative. Therefore, you can eliminate Choice C. Similarly, while *indispositions* (slight illnesses; minor unwillingness) are negative, they are only mildly so. You can eliminate Choice D. Choice E, *demises* (deaths) also fails to work in this context. Thus, you are left with the correct answer, Choice A.

Cause and Effect Signals

Look for words or phrases that indicate that one thing causes another.

Signal Words

accordingly	in order to
because	so...that
consequently	therefore
for	thus
hence	when...then

See how a cause and effect signal works in a question from a recent SAT I.

> Tarantulas apparently have little sense of ----, for a hungry one will ignore a loudly chirping cricket placed in its cage unless the cricket happens to get in its way.
>
> (A) touch   (B) time   (C) hearing
> (D) self-preservation   (E) temperature

For sets up a relationship of cause and effect. Why does the tarantula ignore the loudly chirping cricket? *Because*, it seems, the tarantula does not hear the cricket's chirps. Apparently, it has little sense of *hearing*. The correct answer is Choice C.

Look for Words That Signal the Unexpected.

Some words indicate that something unexpected, possibly even unwanted, exists or has occurred. These words signal a built-in contrast.

Words That Signal the Unexpected

abnormal	ironic
anomalous	odd
curious (odd)	paradoxical
illogical	surprising
incongruous	unexpected

See how such a word works in the following SAT I question.

> The historian noted irony in the fact that developments considered ---- by people of that era are now viewed as having been ----.
>
> (A) inspirational...impetuous
> (B) bizarre...irrational
> (C) intuitive...uncertain
> (D) actual...grandiose
> (E) improbable...inevitable

Before you consider the answer choices, think through the sentence. Remember, something unexpected has taken place. People of some earlier period had one idea of certain developments during that time. With hindsight, however, people today view them in an unexpected, different light. The two views actually contradict each other.

Only one answer choice presents such a mutually contradictory pair of words, Choice E. People in days gone by looked on certain developments as *improbable*, unlikely. Today we view these very developments as *inevitable*, inescapable. To a historian, such a mismatch in opinions is ironic.

In Double-Blank Sentences, Go Through the Answers, Testing the *First* Word in Each Choice (and Eliminating Those That Don't Fit).

In a sentence completion question with two blanks, read through the entire sentence. Then insert the first word of each answer pair in the sentence's first blank. Ask yourself whether this particular word makes sense in this blank. If the initial word of an answer pair makes no sense in the sentence, you can eliminate that answer pair.

> The author portrays research psychologists not as disruptive ---- in the field of psychotherapy, but as effective ---- working ultimately toward the same ends as the psychotherapists.
>
> (A) proponents...opponents
> (B) antagonists...pundits
> (C) interlocutors...surrogates
> (D) meddlers...usurpers
> (E) intruders...collaborators

If you test the first word in each choice, you can eliminate some choices. The adjective "disruptive" suggests that the first missing word is negative in tone. *Proponents* (supporters, advocates) and *interlocutors* (people engaged in a dialogue; questioners) are largely neutral terms. You can most likely eliminate Choices A and C.

Turn to the second part of the sentence. Both the contrast signal *but* and the adjective "effective" indicate the second missing word must be positive. *Usurpers* is a negative term: a usurper is someone who seizes someone else's power or rank or position. You can eliminate Choice D. *Pundits* (authorities on a subject; experts) and *collaborators* (people who work cooperatively with others) are both positive terms. However, research psychologists are described as "working…toward the same ends as the psychotherapists." Thus, they are in effect *collaborating* with the psychotherapists to achieve a common goal. The correct answer is Choice E.

Here is a second, more difficult SAT I question that you can solve using this same tactic.

The author inadvertently undermined his thesis by allowing his biases to ---- his otherwise ---- scholarship.

(A) bolster...superior
(B) cloud...unfocused
(C) compromise...judicious
(D) confirm...exhaustive
(E) falsify...questionable

The author has undermined or weakened his thesis (the point he's trying to make). How has he done this? He has let his prejudices affect his work as a scholar *in a negative way*. Your first missing word must have a negative meaning; you can eliminate any answer choice whose first word has only a positive sense.

Bolster or support is wholly positive; so is *confirm*. You can eliminate Choices A and D. The three other choices need closer examination. To *cloud* someone's scholarship, obscuring or tarnishing it, would be damaging; to *falsify* scholarly work would be damaging as well. To *compromise* someone's scholarship also is damaging: if you compromise your standards, you fail to live up to the high scholarly standards expected of you. You thus endanger your scholarly reputation. (Note that this is a secondary, relatively unfamiliar meaning of *compromise*; the SAT-makers love words with multiple meanings like this.)

Now examine the context of the second missing word. Rephrase the sentence, breaking it down. The author has let his prejudices damage his scholarship, which was otherwise *good*. The second missing word must be positive in meaning.

Check out the second word of Choices B, C, and E. *Unfocused*, vague scholarly work isn't good. Neither is *questionable*, doubtful scholarship. *Judicious*, thoughtful work, however, *is* good. The correct answer is Choice C.

Remember, in double-blank sentences, the right answer must correctly fill *both* blanks. A wrong answer choice often includes one correct and one incorrect answer. Always test the second word.

Long-Range Strategies

Although you certainly will wish to consult "Build Your Vocabulary," Chapter 8, and work on the vocabulary-development methods there, answering sentence completion questions involves more than recognizing individual words. You need to know idiomatic expressions—groups of words always used together—particularly those involving prepositions, and those used so frequently in formal prose that they seem clichés. Similarly, you need to know the typical patterns that writers follow in developing their thoughts.

Familiarize Yourself With Idiomatic Expressions and Clichés

In their general tips for answering sentence completion questions, the SAT-makers say, "Don't select an answer simply because it is a popular cliché or 'sounds good.'" The key word here is *simply*. If an answer is a popular cliché, it may well be right. *Don't* disregard an answer just because it's a cliché.

If you look at the answers to the sentence completion questions in *10 SATs* and *5 SATs*, the College Board's own publications, you will swiftly discover a high proportion of the correct answers are, in fact, clichés—set phrases an experienced reader will find extremely familiar. Consider, for example, phrases like *avert disaster*, *cavalier treatment*, *render unnecessary*, *overt acts*. The more formal prose you read, the more you will encounter set phrases such as these.

Learn to Spot Typical Sentence Patterns

Definitions

In a definition, the author restates a word or phrase to clarify its meaning. The author commonly will set the definition beside the word being defined, juxtaposing them. Commas, hyphens, and parentheses are used to signal definitions.

1. The rebec, a medieval stringed instrument played with a bow, has only three strings.

2. Paleontologists—students of fossil remains—explore the earth's history.

3. Most mammals are quadrupeds (four-footed animals).

Definitions also follow forms of the verb "to be" and other connecting verbs.

1. A *stoic* **is** a person who is indifferent to pleasure or pain.

2. A three-pronged spear **is called** a *trident*.

Often an unfamiliar word in one clause of a sentence will be defined in the sentence's other clause.

1. That Barbie doll is a *lethal* weapon; your daughter nearly killed me with it!

2. The early morning dew had frozen, and everything was covered with a thin coat of *rime*.

Examples

By presenting specific, concrete examples, an author makes a general, abstract word come to life.

1. Crates of coins, paintings by Rubens and Renoir, diamond tiaras and rings of rubies and gold—I never realized the extent of President Marcos' *affluence* until I read the accounts of what he brought with him from the Philippines.

2. Cowards, we use *euphemisms* when we cannot bear the truth, calling our dead "the dear departed," as if they have just left the room.

3. I'm impressed by Trudy's business *acumen*: she buys sound but aging houses, renovates them relatively inexpensively, and then rents them out for fabulous sums.

Comparisons

Just as concrete examples make abstract words come to life, in the same way the use of a familiar object in a comparison can bring home the meaning of an unfamiliar word or phrase.

1. Some *circumstantial evidence* is very strong, as when you find a trout in the milk. — Thoreau.

2. Our impact on this world is as *evanescent* as a skywriter's impact on the sky.

Contrasts

You can learn a great deal about what something *is* if you come to terms with what it *is not*. Notice the signal words at work in the sentences that follow.

1. **Although** America's total Vietnamese population is *minuscule*, the number of Vietnamese students attending major American universities is surprisingly high.

2. Marriage has many pains, **but** *celibacy* has no pleasures. — Johnson.

3. **In place of** *complacency*, I give you unrest; in place of sameness I give you variety.

Often a writer contrasts two ideas without using a signal word. The contrast is implicit in the juxtaposition of the two clauses.

1. The *optimist* proclaims that we live in the best of all possible worlds; the *pessimist* fears this is true.
   — Cabell.

2. Lord, make me an instrument of Your peace.
   Where there is hatred, let me sow love;
   Where there is injury, pardon;
   Where there is doubt, faith;
   Where there is despair, hope;
   Where there is darkness, light; and
   Where there is sadness, joy. —St. Francis

Arguments

Sentences that present arguments often follow the pattern of cause and effect. You must try to follow the author's reasoning as you work towards his or her conclusion.

1. When *tillage* begins, other arts follow. The farmers, **therefore**, are the founders of human civilization.
   — Webster.

2. A man ought to read just as *inclination* leads him; **for** what he reads as a task will do him little good.
   — Johnson.

Practice Exercises

Use the following practice exercises as a warm-up before you go on to the model tests. Check your answers against the answer key. For every answer you get incorrect, follow this procedure:

1. Review the unfamiliar words. Check them out in the Basic Word List in Chapter 7, or look them up in your dictionary. Again, remember that these are SAT-level words. Make use of this chance to go over what they mean.

2. Once you know the meaning of the words, see if you can spot signal words or context clues that might have helped you get the answer right. Note any word parts that you can find in the unfamiliar words.

3. Go over your guessing tactics. If you eliminated any answer choices, see whether you were correct in eliminating them. Remember, if you *can* eliminate one or two answer choices, you *should* guess. Even if you get a particular question wrong, in the long run, if you use the process of elimination correctly, you'll come out ahead of the game.

Sentence Completion Exercise A

Each sentence below has one or two blanks, each blank indicating that something has been omitted. Beneath the sentence are five lettered words or sets of words. Choose the word or set of words that best fits the meaning of the sentence as a whole.

Example:

Although its publicity has been ----, the film itself is intelligent, well-acted, handsomely produced, and altogether ---- .

(A) tasteless..respectable (B) extensive..moderate
  (C) sophisticated..amateur (D) risqué..crude
    (E) perfect..spectacular

1. The selection committee for the exhibit was amazed to see such fine work done by a mere ----.

    (A) connoisseur   (B) artist   (C) amateur
    (D) entrepreneur   (E) exhibitionist

2. The teacher suspected cheating as soon as he noticed the pupil's ---- glances at his classmate's paper.

    (A) futile   (B) sporadic   (C) furtive   (D) cold
      (E) inconsequential

3. Known for his commitment to numerous worthy causes, the philanthropist deserved ---- for his ----.

    (A) recognition..folly
    (B) blame..hypocrisy
    (C) reward..modesty
    (D) admonishment..wastefulness
    (E) credit..altruism

4. Miss Watson termed Huck's behavior --- because in her opinion nothing could excuse his deliberate disregard of her commands.

    (A) devious   (B) intolerant   (C) irrevocable
      (D) indefensible   (E) boisterous

5. Either the surfing at Maui is ----, or I went there on an off day.

    (A) consistent   (B) thrilling   (C) invigorating
      (D) overrated   (E) scenic

6. Your ---- remarks spoil the effect of your speech; try not to stray from your subject.

    (A) innocuous   (B) digressive   (C) derogatory
      (D) persistent   (E) enigmatic

7. We need both ornament and implement in our society; we need the artist and the ----.

    (A) beautician   (B) writer   (C) politician
      (D) artisan   (E) model

8. When such ---- remarks are circulated, we can only blame and despise those who produce them.

    (A) adulatory   (B) chance   (C) rhetorical
      (D) redundant   (E) reprehensible

9. The stereotypical image of masculinity assumes that weeping is ---- "unmanly" behavior, and not simply a human reaction which may be ---- by either sex.

    (A) inexplicably..repented
    (B) excessively..discerned
    (C) essentially..defined
    (D) inherently..adopted
    (E) intentionally..exaggerated

10. We need more men and women of culture and enlightenment in our society; we have too many ---- among us.

    (A) pedants (B) philistines (C) ascetics (D) paragons (E) apologists

11. There was a hint of carelessness about her appearance, as though the cut of her blouse or the fit of her slacks was a matter of ---- to her.

    (A) satisfaction (B) aesthetics (C) indifference (D) significance (E) controversy

12. Many educators argue that a ---- grouping of students would improve instruction because it would limit the range of student abilities in the classroom.

    (A) heterogeneous (B) systematic (C) homogeneous (D) sporadic (E) fragmentary

13. As news of his indictment spread through the town, the citizens began to ---- him and to avoid meeting him.

    (A) ostracize (B) congratulate (C) desecrate (D) minimize (E) harass

14. After years of talking down to his students as if they couldn't understand a word, the teacher finally acknowledged that his attitude was ---- .

    (A) colloquial (B) condescending (C) professorial (D) justifiable (E) logical

15. There are too many ---- and not enough serious workers.

    (A) sycophants (B) kleptomaniacs (C) novices (D) dilettantes (E) zealots

16. Unlike W. E. B. Dubois, who was ---- of the vocational emphasis in black education, Booker T. Washington favored ---- the limited funds available for educating blacks to programs that prepared people for practical jobs.

    (A) critical..restricting
    (B) aware..confining
    (C) suspicious..denying
    (D) protective..allotting
    (E) appreciative..allocating

17. Many elderly people are capable of working, but they are kept from gainful employment by the ----

of those employers who mistakenly believe that young people alone can give them adequate service.

    (A) philosophy (B) parsimony (C) conservatism (D) rationalizations (E) short-sightedness

18. The college president made the ---- statement that no student athlete on academic probation, not even the top-scorer of the varsity team, would be allowed to participate in intercollegiate sports.

    (A) impertinent (B) uncontroversial (C) opinionated (D) categorical (E) equivocal

19. The fire marshalls spend many hours seeking the cause of the ---- in which so many people were killed and so many others hospitalized with major burns.

    (A) maelstrom (B) labyrinth (C) conflagration (D) torpor (E) carnage

20. If you come to the conference table with such an ---- attitude, we cannot expect to reach any harmonious agreement.

    (A) exemplary (B) iridescent (C) indolent (D) obdurate (E) unwonted

21. I can vouch for his honesty; I have always found him ---- and carefully observant of the truth.

    (A) arbitrary (B) plausible (C) volatile (D) veracious (E) innocuous

22. This well-documented history is of importance because it carefully ---- the ---- accomplishments of Indian artists who are all too little known to the public at large.

    (A) recognizes..negligible
    (B) overlooks..purported
    (C) scrutinizes..illusory
    (D) distorts..noteworthy
    (E) substantiates..considerable

23. Perhaps because he feels ---- by an excess of parental restrictions and rules, at adolescence the repressed child may break out dramatically.

    (A) nurtured (B) appeased (C) confined (D) fascinated (E) liberated

24. Sue felt that Jack's ---- in the face of the compelling evidence which she had presented was an example of his ---- mind.

    (A) truculence..unbiased
    (B) skepticism..open
    (C) incredulity..closed
    (D) acquiescence..keen
    (E) reluctance..impartial

25. As a girl, Emily Dickinson was ---- but also ---- : extraordinarily intense about her poetry yet exceptionally inhibited socially.

    (A) zealous..gregarious
    (B) ardent..repressed
    (C) prudent..reserved
    (D) rash..intrusive
    (E) impulsive..dedicated

26. The good night's sleep had ---- effect on the weary climber, who woke refreshed and eager to resume the ascent.

    (A) an innocuous   (B) a tonic
    (C) a minor   (D) an enervating
    (E) a detrimental

27. She is an interesting ----, an infinitely shy person who, in apparent contradiction, possesses an enormously intuitive ---- for understanding people.

    (A) aberration..disdain
    (B) caricature..talent
    (C) specimen..loathing
    (D) phenomenon..disinclination
    (E) paradox..gift

28. The coach's harsh rebuke deeply wounded the star quarterback, who had never been ---- like that before.

    (A) summoned   (B) reprimanded
    (C) stimulated   (D) placated
    (E) ignored

29. At the present time, we are suffering from ---- of stories about the war; try writing about another subject.

    (A) a calumny   (B) a dearth   (C) an insurgence
    (D) a plethora   (E) an inhibition

30. Because he was ----, he shunned human society.

    (A) a misanthrope   (B) an oligarch   (C) an anomaly
    (D) a stereotype   (E) a nonentity

31. The police feel that the ---- shown by the judges to first offenders unfortunately ---- many youngsters to embark on a life of crime.

    (A) understanding..condemns
    (B) clemency.. encourages
    (C) harshness..predisposes
    (D) indifference..directs
    (E) intolerance..induces

32. Ernest Hemingway's prose is generally esteemed for its ---- ; as one critic puts it, Hemingway "cuts out unneeded words."

    (A) sensitivity   (B) economy   (C) gusto
    (D) breadth   (E) intricacy

33. After Bob had broken the punch bowl, we sensed the extent of his ---- from the way he shamefacedly avoided meeting his hostess's eye.

    (A) composure   (B) perspicacity
    (C) discomfiture   (D) forbearance
    (E) benevolence

34. Crowther maintained that the current revival was the most fatuous and ---- production of the entire theatrical season.

    (A) gripping   (B) inane   (C) prophetic
    (D) memorable   (E) salubrious

35. His olfactory sense was so highly developed that he was often called in to judge ----.

    (A) productivity   (B) colors   (C) litigation
    (D) perfume   (E) acoustics

36. Jean Georges was famous for his ---- cuisine, which brought together ingredients from many cooking traditions—Thai, Chinese, French—and combined them in innovative ways.

    (A) aesthetic   (B) clandestine
    (C) homogeneous   (D) eclectic
    (E) conventional

37. Believing that all children possess a certain natural intelligence, the headmaster exhorted the teachers to discover and ---- each student's ---- talents.

    (A) suppress..unrecognized
    (B) develop..intrinsic
    (C) redirect..specious
    (D) belittle..dormant
    (E) cultivate..gratuitous

38. Micawber's habit of spending more than he earned left him in a state of perpetual ----, but he ---- hoping to see a more affluent day.

    (A) indigence..persevered in
    (B) confusion..compromised by
    (C) enervation..retaliated by
    (D) motion..responded by
    (E) opulence..insisted on

39. The ---- of such utopian notions is reflected by the quick disintegration of the idealistic community at Brooke Farm.

    (A) timeliness   (B) creativity
    (C) impracticability   (D) effervescence
    (E) vindication

40. We were amazed that a man who had been heretofore the most ---- of public speakers could, in a single speech, electrify an audience and bring them cheering to their feet.

    (A) enthralling   (B) accomplished   (C) pedestrian
    (D) auspicious   (E) masterful

41. Despite the mixture's ---- nature, we found that by lowering its temperature in the laboratory we could dramatically reduce its tendency to vaporize.

    (A) resilient   (B) volatile   (C) homogeneous
    (D) insipid   (E) acerbic

42. Surrounded by a host of besiegers and unable to ---- their supplies, the defenders of the castle feared their food would soon be ----.

    (A) replenish..exhausted
    (B) consume..hoarded
    (C) replace..obtainable
    (D) estimate..superfluous
    (E) deplete..rationed

43. Fitness experts claim that jogging is ----; once you begin to jog regularly, you may be unable to stop, because you are sure to love it more and more all the time.

    (A) exhausting   (B) illusive   (C) addictive
    (D) exotic   (E) overrated

44. Although newscasters often use the terms Chicano and Latino ----, students of Hispanic-American culture are profoundly aware of the ---- the two.

    (A) interchangeably..dissimilarities between
    (B) indifferently..equivalence of
    (C) deprecatingly..controversies about
    (D) unerringly..significance of
    (E) confidently..origins of

45. She maintained that the proposed legislation was ---- because it simply established an affirmative action task force without making any appropriate provision to fund such a force.

    (A) inevitable   (B) inadequate   (C) prudent
    (D) necessary   (E) beneficial

46. The faculty senate warned that, if its recommendations were to go unheeded, the differences between the administration and the teaching staff would be ---- and eventually rendered irreconcilable.

    (A) rectified   (B) exacerbated   (C) imponderable
    (D) eradicated   (E) alienated

47. Hroswitha the nun, though hidden among the cloisters and ---- time, is now considered an important literary figure of the medieval period.

    (A) oppressed by   (B) fighting against
    (C) celebrated throughout   (D) elapsed from
    (E) obscured by

48. Famed athlete Bobby Orr was given his first pair of skates by a ---- Canadian woman who somehow "knew" he would use them to attain sporting greatness.

    (A) prosperous   (B) prescient   (C) notorious
    (D) skeptical   (E) fallible

49. The supervisor's evaluation was ---- , for she noted the employee's strong points and limitations without overly emphasizing either.

    (A) equitable   (B) laudatory   (C) practicable
    (D) slanted   (E) dogmatic

50. She has sufficient tact to ---- the ordinary crises of diplomatic life; however, even her diplomacy is insufficient to enable her to ---- the current emergency.

    (A) negotiate..comprehend
    (B) survive..exaggerate
    (C) handle..weather
    (D) ignore..transform
    (E) aggravate..resolve

Sentence Completion Exercise B

Each sentence below has one or two blanks, each blank indicating that something has been omitted. Beneath the sentence are five lettered words or sets of words. Choose the word or set of words that best fits the meaning of the sentence as a whole.

Example:

Although its publicity has been ----, the film itself is intelligent, well-acted, handsomely produced, and altogether ---- .

(A) tasteless. .respectable (B) extensive. .moderate
(C) sophisticated..amateur (D) risqué..crude
(E) perfect..spectacular

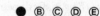

1. Because he is so ----, we can never predict what course he will take at any moment.

    (A) incoherent   (B) superficial   (C) capricious
    (D) deleterious   (E) conventional

2. The bank teller's ---- of the funds went undiscovered until the auditors examined the accounts and found that huge sums were missing.

    (A) extradition   (B) embezzlement
    (C) subordination   (D) scrutiny
    (E) verification

3. He was so convinced that people were driven by ---- motives that he believed there was no such thing as a purely unselfish act.

    (A) sentimental   (B) personal   (C) altruistic
    (D) ulterior   (E) intrinsic

4. Because he was ---- by nature, he preferred reading a book in the privacy of his own study to visiting a nightclub with friends.

   (A) an exhibitionist   (B) a hedonist
   (C) an adversary   (D) an egoist   (E) an introvert

5. Surprisingly enough, it is more difficult to write about the ---- than about the ---- and strange.

   (A) specific..foreign
   (B) abstract..prosaic
   (C) commonplace..exotic
   (D) simple..routine
   (E) ludicrous..dejected

6. The plot of this story is so ---- that I can predict the outcome.

   (A) intricate   (B) theoretical   (C) pivotal
   (D) trite   (E) fictitious

7. The fundraising ball turned out to be a ---- : it started late, attracted too few dancers, and lost almost a million dollars.

   (A) debacle   (B) blockbuster   (C) deluge
   (D) gala   (E) milestone

8. She was pleased by the accolades she received; like everyone else, she enjoyed being ----.

   (A) entertained   (B) praised   (C) playful
   (D) vindicated   (E) charitable

9. Safire as a political commentator is patently never ----; he writes ---- editorials about every action the government takes.

   (A) content..deferential
   (B) querulous..biased
   (C) amazed..bemused
   (D) overawed..flattering
   (E) satisfied..peevish

10. Although frugal by nature, on this special occasion he refused to ---- , but instead feasted his guests ---- .

    (A) splurge..munificently
    (B) conserve..intangibly
    (C) stint..lavishly
    (D) temporize..austerely
    (E) cooperate..exorbitantly

11. The tapeworm is an example of ---- organism, one that lives within or on another creature, deriving some or all of its nutriment from its host.

    (A) a hospitable   (B) an exemplary
    (C) a parasitic   (D) an autonomous
    (E) a protozoan

12. He found himself in the ---- position of appearing to support a point of view that he abhorred.

    (A) obvious   (B) innocuous   (C) anomalous
    (D) enviable   (E) auspicious

13. The younger members of the company resented the domineering and ---- manner of the office manager.

    (A) urbane   (B) prudent   (C) convivial
    (D) imperious   (E) objective

14. Bluebeard was noted for his ---- jealousy, a jealousy so extreme that it passed all reasonable bounds.

    (A) transitory   (B) rhetorical   (C) stringent
    (D) callous   (E) inordinate

15. I regret that my remarks seemed ----; I never intended to belittle you.

    (A) inadequate   (B) justified   (C) unassailable
    (D) disparaging   (E) shortsighted

16. A ---- glance pays ---- attention to details.

    (A) furtive..meticulous   (B) cursory..little
    (C) cryptic..close   (D) keen..scanty
    (E) fleeting..vigilant

17. With its elaborately carved, convoluted lines, furniture of the Baroque period was highly ---- .

    (A) functional   (B) primitive   (C) linear
    (D) spare   (E) ornate

18. His overweening pride in his accomplishments was ---- : he had accomplished little if anything at all.

    (A) unjustified   (B) innocuous   (C) systematic
    (D) rational   (E) critical

19. A ---- relationship links the rhinoceros and the oxpecker (or rhinoceros bird), for the two are mutually dependent.

    (A) monolithic   (B) superficial   (C) symbiotic
    (D) debilitating   (E) stereotypical

20. When we saw black smoke billowing from the wing of the plane, we were certain that disaster was ----.

    (A) unlikely   (B) opportune   (C) imminent
    (D) undeserved   (E) averted

21. Upon realizing that his position was ----, the general ---- his men to retreat to a neighboring hill.

    (A) valuable..admonished
    (B) untenable..ordered
    (C) overrated..forbade
    (D) exposed..urged
    (E) salubrious..commanded

22. The seriousness of the drought could only be understood by those who had seen the ---- crops in the fields.

    (A) copious (B) deluged (C) wilted
    (D) bumper (E) diversified

23. As ecologists recently ---- in studying the effects of naturally induced forest fires, some phenomena that appear on the surface to be destructive often have a hidden ---- effect on balance.

    (A) disproved..beneficial
    (B) discovered..positive
    (C) hypothesized..catastrophic
    (D) disclosed..unecological
    (E) determined..disastrous

24. The dispute became so ---- that we were afraid the adversaries would come to blows.

    (A) ironic (B) generalized (C) didactic
    (D) articulate (E) acrimonious

25. With the rift between the two sides apparently widening, analysts said they considered the likelihood of a merger between the two corporations to be ----.

    (A) deteriorating (B) substantial
    (C) coincidental (D) legitimate (E) plausible

26. Fossils may be set in stone, but their interpretation is not; a new find may necessitate the ---- of a traditional theory.

    (A) ambiguity (B) revision (C) formulation
    (D) validation (E) assertion

27. In attempting to reconcile estranged spouses, counselors try to foster a spirit of ---- rather than one of stubborn implacability.

    (A) disillusionment (B) ambivalence
    (C) compromise (D) antagonism
    (E) independence

28. Shakespeare's reference to clocks in "Julius Caesar" is an example of ----; that is, it is chronologically out of place.

    (A) timeliness (B) antiquarianism
    (C) anachronism (D) synchronization
    (E) ignorance

29. A diligent scholar, she devoted herself ---- to the completion of the book.

    (A) assiduously (B) ingenuously
    (C) theoretically (D) voluminously
    (E) sporadically

30. He was ---- success, painting not for the sake of fame or monetary reward, but for the sheer love of art.

    (A) indifferent to (B) destined for (C) avid for
    (D) jaded by (E) enamored of

31. The thought of being trapped in a stalled elevator terrifies me; it brings out all my ---- fears of small, enclosed places.

    (A) agoraphobic (B) kleptomaniac
    (C) hypochondriac (D) therapeutic
    (E) claustrophobic

32. Crows are extremely ---- : their cries easily drown out the songs of neighboring birds.

    (A) fickle (B) swarthy (C) raucous
    (D) cordial (E) versatile

33. The gardener had planted such a wide variety of flowering trees and shrubs in the courtyard that it seemed a virtual ---- .

    (A) wasteland (B) cloister (C) panorama
    (D) arboretum (E) granary

34. You should ---- this paragraph in order to make your essay more ----.

    (A) delete..succinct (B) enlarge..redundant
    (C) remove..discursive (D) revise..abstruse
    (E) excise..legible

35. Sharon's childhood can best be termed ---- : she had never been farther west than Philadelphia until she turned sixteen.

    (A) provincial (B) transitory (C) nomadic
    (D) utilitarian (E) eclectic

36. His submissiveness of manner and general air of self-effacement made it ---- he would be ---- to take command of the firm.

    (A) unlikely..selected (B) implausible..hesitant
    (C) clear..designated (D) puzzling..disinclined
    (E) probable..demoted

37. She was accused of plagiarism in a dispute over a short story, and, though ----, she never recovered from the accusation and the scandal.

    (A) indicted (B) verified (C) exonerated
    (D) retaliated (E) convinced

38. The patient is subject to emotional ---- : she is utterly ecstatic one minute and thoroughly ---- the next.

    (A) impoverishment..enervated
    (B) upheavals..euphoric
    (C) extremes..downcast
    (D) deviations..wayward
    (E) stability..unresponsive

39. The king's champion was a ---- foe, one whose mighty presence on the field of battle struck fear in the hearts of his prospective adversaries.

    (A) methodical (B) rancorous
    (C) timorous (D) redoubtable
    (E) questionable

40. Watching the hang gliders soar above the fields, I marveled at how they seemed to ---- gravity, hovering in the sky like rainbow-colored birds.

    (A) release   (B) adorn   (C) defy   (D) emulate
        (E) abet

41. Her novel published to universal acclaim, her literary gifts acknowledged by the chief figures of the Harlem Renaissance, her reputation as yet ---- by envious slights, Hurston clearly was at the ---- of her career.

    (A) undamaged..ebb   (B) untarnished..zenith
     (C) untainted..extremity   (D) blackened..mercy
        (E) unmarred..brink

42. In *Anne of Green Gables,* the heroine turns down a prestigious scholarship so that the young hero may receive it; once more, the woman ---- her own ---- to those of the man.

    (A) prefers..ambitions   (B) sacrifices..losses
     (C) surrenders..talents   (D) accommodates..beliefs
        (E) subordinates..interests

43. Having envisioned atomic weapons a decade before, Leo Szilard felt horror and guilt at the bombings of Hiroshima and Nagasaki, calling them "a flagrant ---- of our own moral standards."

    (A) violation   (B) exposition   (C) punishment
        (D) vindication   (E) agitation

44. From the lunch counter sit-ins and bus boycotts to the historic freedom march from Selma to Montgomery, this fine volume shows how ---- Americans from every walk of life fought ---- battle for "liberty and justice for all."

    (A) revolutionary..an unnecessary
    (B) typical..an ignoble
    (C) progressive..a vainglorious
    (D) ordinary..an inspiring
    (E) pugnacious..a dubious

45. Despite an affected ---- which convinced casual observers that he was indifferent about his painting and enjoyed only frivolity, Warhol cared deeply about his art and labored at it ----.

    (A) nonchalance..diligently
    (B) empathy..methodically
    (C) fervor..secretly
    (D) gloom..intermittently
    (E) hysteria..sporadically

46. Cancer cells are normal cells run riot, growing and multiplying out of ----.

    (A) spite   (B) danger   (C) control   (D) apathy
        (E) range

47. Science progresses by building on what has come before; important findings thus form the basis of ---- experiments.

    (A) gradual   (B) subsequent   (C) ingenious
        (D) repetitive   (E) perfunctory

48. The Internal Revenue Service agent was a ---- for accuracy, insisting that taxpayers provide exact figures for every deduction they claimed.

    (A) martyr   (B) scoundrel
        (C) stickler   (D) procrastinator
        (E) candidate

49. Even if you do not ---- what I have to say, I would appreciate your listening to me with an open mind.

    (A) concur with   (B) reject   (C) clarify
        (D) deviate from   (E) anticipate

50. Paradoxically, Helen, who had been a strict mother to her children, proved ---- mistress to her cats.

    (A) a harsh   (B) an indolent   (C) an ambivalent
        (D) a cautious   (E) a lenient

Answer Key

Sentence Completion Exercise A

1.	C	9.	D	17.	E	25.	B	33.	C	41.	B	49.	A
2.	C	10.	B	18.	D	26.	B	34.	B	42.	A	50.	C
3.	E	11.	C	19.	C	27.	E	35.	D	43.	C		
4.	D	12.	C	20.	D	28.	B	36.	D	44.	A		
5.	D	13.	A	21.	D	29.	D	37.	B	45.	B		
6.	B	14.	B	22.	E	30.	A	38.	A	46.	B		
7.	D	15.	D	23.	C	31.	B	39.	C	47.	E		
8.	E	16.	A	24.	C	32.	B	40.	C	48.	B		

Sentence Completion Exercise B

1.	C	9.	E	17.	E	25.	A	33.	D	41.	B	49.	A
2.	B	10.	C	18.	A	26.	B	34.	A	42.	E	50.	E
3.	D	11.	C	19.	C	27.	C	35.	A	43.	A		
4.	E	12.	C	20.	C	28.	C	36.	A	44.	D		
5.	C	13.	D	21.	B	29.	A	37.	C	45.	A		
6.	D	14.	E	22.	C	30.	A	38.	C	46.	C		
7.	A	15.	D	23.	B	31.	E	39.	D	47.	B		
8.	B	16.	B	24.	E	32.	C	40.	C	48.	C		

Sentence Completion Wrap-up

1. First, read the sentence carefully to get a feel for its meaning.

2. Before you look at the choices, think of a word that makes sense.

3. Look at all the possible answers before you make your final choice.

4. Watch out for negative words and prefixes.

5. Use your knowledge of context clues to get at the meanings of unfamiliar words.

6. Break down unfamiliar words into recognizable parts.

7. Watch for signal words that link one part of the sentence to another.

8. Look for words that signal the unexpected.

9. In double-blank sentences, go through the answers, testing the *first* word in each choice (and eliminating those that don't fit).

5 The Analogy Question

- ■ **Testing Tactics**
- ■ **Long-Range Strategies**
- ■ **Practice Exercises**
- ■ **Answer Key**

Analogy questions ask you to determine the relationship in a pair of words and then recognize a similar or parallel relationship in a different pair of words. You are given one pair of words. You must choose from the five pairs given as answer choices another pair that is related in the same way. The relationship between the words in the original pair will always be specific and precise; the same is true for the relationship between the words in the correct answer pair.

Here are the standard directions for the analogy questions. Learn them now. The test time you would spend reading the directions can be better spent answering questions.

Each question below consists of a related pair of words or phrases, followed by five lettered pairs of words or phrases labeled A through E. Select the pair that <u>best</u> expresses a relationship similar to that expressed in the original pair.

Example:

CRUMB:BREAD::   (A) ounce:unit
(B) splinter:wood   (C) water:bucket
  (D) twine:rope   (E) cream:butter

Ⓐ ● Ⓒ Ⓓ Ⓔ

Just as a crumb is a fragment of bread, a splinter is a fragment of wood. The one is broken off from the other. Choice B is correct. Choice E is not. Though cream and butter, like bread, are things people eat, cream is the substance out of which one makes butter. One makes bread out of flour or meal mixed with liquid, not out of crumbs.

Note how an SAT I analogy question is set up. First you have the two capitalized words linked by a symbol. Take a look at a few examples.

ACTOR:STAGE

An actor is related to a stage. How? An actor works or performs on a stage.

SCRIBBLE:WRITE

Scribble is related to write. How? To scribble is to write hastily, even carelessly.

DOG:POODLE

Dog is related to poodle. How? A poodle is a kind of dog. Notice the wording of the last sentence. You could equally have said "One kind of dog is a poodle" and maintained the word order of the analogy. However, as in the discussion of CRUMB:BREAD, it sometimes is easier to express a relationship if you reverse the order of the words.

Some of the analogy questions on SAT I are as clearcut as the ones above. Others are far more complex. In some questions, for example, you are asked to carry an analogy from a concrete example to a more abstract or less tangible one.

SURGEON:SCALPEL::satirist:words

A surgeon *literally* uses a scalpel to make an incision, to cut. A satirist (a writer of literary satire) uses words to cut and ridicule the pride and folly of his subjects. As you can see, answering such questions correctly involves more than knowing single meanings of words. You'll find practice exercises containing both straightforward and tricky analogies at the end of this chapter.

Analogy questions are a bit like riddles; they're a kind of word game. At first analogies may seem a stumbling block to you, but once you master our tactics for solving them, you may even find them fun.

Testing Tactics

Before You Look at the Choices, Try to State the Relationship Between the Capitalized Words in a Good Sentence.

In answering an analogy question, your first problem is to determine the exact nature of the relationship that exists between the two capitalized words. *Before you look at the answer pairs,* make up a sentence that shows how these capitalized words are related. Then test the possible answers by seeing how well they fit in your sentence.

Take, for example, this analogy question.

> CONSTELLATION:STARS::   (A) prison:bars
> (B) assembly:speaker   (C) troupe:actors
> (D) mountain:peak   (E) flock:shepherds

A *constellation* is made up of *stars*. A *troupe* (not *troop* but *troupe*) is made up of *actors*. Choice C is correct.

Don't let Choice E fool you: a flock is made up of sheep, not of shepherds.

Note, by the way, the characteristics of the analogy you have just analyzed. CONSTELLATION:STARS. It is a good analogy. The relationship between the words is built-in; if you look up *constellation* in a dictionary, you will see that a constellation is a group of stars. The words are related *by definition*.

Your correct answer choice has got to have the same characteristics as the original pair. The words must have a clear relationship. They must be related *by definition*. If you substitute them in your test sentence, they must fit it exactly.

If You Are Stumped by an Unfamiliar Word, Try Thinking of It in a Context.

Don't let unfamiliar-looking words puzzle you. If you come across a word you don't recognize, try to think of a phrase or sentence in which you have heard it used. The context may help you come up with the word's meaning.

See how this tactic works in the following example.

> COMPOSER:SYMPHONY::   (A) porter:terminal
> (B) writer:plagiarism   (C) coach:team
> (D) painter:mural   (E) doctor:stethoscope

First, come up with a test sentence: "A composer creates a symphony." You are looking for a relationship between a worker and something he or she has created. You can easi-

ly eliminate choices A and E: a porter works *at* a terminal; a doctor works *with* a stethoscope. You can also eliminate choice C: no coach literally *creates* a team in the same way that a composer creates a symphony.

Writers and painters, however, both create works of art. Which answer is better, B or D? If you know the meanings of *plagiarism* and *mural*, the question is easy. Suppose you don't.

Try thinking of contexts for *plagiarism* and *mural*. Someone is "guilty of plagiarism." From this you can infer that *plagiarism* is a crime (passing off someone else's work as your own), not a created work. "Colorful murals." A mural is a picture painted on a wall. The correct answer is Choice D.

If More Than One Answer Fits the Relationship in Your Sentence, Look for a Narrower Approach.

When you try to express the relationship between the two capitalized words in sentence form, make sure you include enough details to particularize your analogy. Otherwise, more than one answer may fit the relationship, and you will have to go back to the original pair of words and study them more.

Consider this actual analogy from a recent SAT I.

> TENTACLES:OCTOPUS::   (A) petals:flower
> (B) tadpoles:frog   (C) claws:crab
> (D) algae:seaweed   (E) quills:porcupine

Suppose your original sentence is "An octopus has tentacles." That sentence is far too broad. It could equally well fit Choices A, C, and E.

Go back to the original pair of words for more details. How does an octopus use its tentacles? What function do they serve? "An octopus uses its tentacles for grasping." Try the answer choices in this new test sentence. "A flower uses its petals for grasping." False. "A porcupine uses its quills for grasping." False. "A crab uses its claws for grasping." Choice C clearly is best.

Note, by the way, that in making your test sentence it was easier to express the relationship of TENTACLES: OCTO-PUS by switching the order of the words. Whenever you do so, you must be sure to switch the order of the words in the answer choices when you try them out in your test sentence.

Whether or not you reverse the order of the words in your test sentence, your sentence should reflect the relationship between the two capitalized words *exactly*. If it doesn't, try again.

Here is another recent SAT I question to examine.

> TYRANT:GOVERN::   (A) inspector:examine
> (B) inquisitor:question   (C) cynic:believe
> (D) fugitive:escape   (E) volunteer:work

Suppose your original sentence was "A tyrant by definition rules or governs." Again, that framework is too broad: it could work equally well for Choice A ("An inspector by definition investigates or examines"), Choice B ("An inquisitor by definition inquires or questions") or Choice D ("A fugitive by definition escapes or flees"). According to the dictionary definition, however, a tyrant is a very *specific* sort of ruler, one who governs in a particular manner. A tyrant governs people harshly, even brutally. Likewise, an inquisitor questions people harshly, even brutally. The correct answer is Choice B.

Remember, in answering analogy questions on SAT I, pay special attention to how a dictionary would define the words involved.

Watch Out for Errors Caused by Eye-Catchers.

Sometimes the test-makers set out to tempt you into making a mistake. They come up with incorrect answer choices *designed* to catch your eye. These eye-catchers can distract your attention from the *real* answer—but not if you're aware of the test-makers' game.

Try this next SAT I analogy question to see just how an eye-catcher works.

> EBB:TIDE::   (A) receive: radio
> (B) splash:wave   (C) blossom:flower
> (D) wane:moon   (E) hibernate:bear

When you look at these answer choices, does Choice B seem to leap right off the page? If it does, watch out—

you've run into an eye-catcher. Eye-catchers grab your attention because they somehow remind you of one (or both) of the capitalized words. In this case, *splash* and *wave* are both related to *water;* they immediately remind you of *tide*. The words feel as if they belong together, and your immediate impulse may be to mark down Choice B.

Choice B, however, is wrong. When the tide ebbs, the waters recede or diminish. When a wave splashes, the water spatters, scattering and falling in droplets. You are looking for a relationship in which something appears to diminish. In this case, the correct answer is Choice D. When the moon wanes, it appears to diminish, decreasing in phase or intensity.

Watch Out for Answer Choices That Reverse the Original Relationship.

In an analogy you have two capitalized words that relate in a set way. In setting up the answer choices, the SAT-makers will often tempt you with pairs of words that relate in a grammatically or logically opposite way. See how it works in an example from a recently published SAT I.

> PERCEPTIVE:DISCERN::   (A) determined:hesitate
> (B) authoritarian:heed   (C) persistent: persevere
> (D) abandoned:neglect   (E) restrained:rebel

At first glance, several of these answers may seem to work. "A perceptive person is someone who discerns or sees

clearly." "An abandoned person is someone who is neglected or forsaken." Ask yourself *who is doing what to whom?* In the original pair, the perceptive person is doing something; he or she is actively discerning or seeing something. In Choice D, the abandoned person is *not* a person actively doing something; he or she is the person to whom something is being done. The abandoned person is being neglected; he or she doesn't get to neglect others. In other words, the abandoned person is the object of the verb *neglect,* not the verb's subject. The original grammatical relationship is reversed. A similar flaw eliminates Choice B: an authoritarian person is someone who seeks to be heeded or obeyed; he or she does not necessarily seek to heed someone else. Again, the original relationship is turned inside out.

The correct answer to this question is Choice C. *By definition,* a perceptive person is someone who discerns. In the same way, *by definition,* a persistent person is someone who perseveres.

Use this same tactic to rule out an eye-catching incorrect answer to a second, more difficult SAT I question.

> CENSURE:REPREHENSIBLE::
>   (A) prize:valuable   (B) provide:supportive
>   (C) applaud:enthusiastic   (D) inquire:informed
>   (E) continue:initial

Again, ask yourself who is doing what to whom. You censure or condemn something because *it* is reprehensible (blameworthy; objectionable). You applaud something, however, because *you* are enthusiastic or strongly excited about it, not because *it* is enthusiastic. Choice C has switched relationships on you. In addition, it is an eye-catcher: the words *applaud* and *censure* feel related because they typically occur in the context of judging something and expressing approval or disapproval of it.

Choice C is incorrect. The correct answer is Choice A. Just as you censure something because it is reprehensible, you prize or treasure something because it is valuable.

Be Guided by the Parts of Speech.

Grammatical information can help you recognize analogy types and spot the use of unfamiliar or secondary meanings of words. In SAT analogy questions, the relationship between the parts of speech of the capitalized words and the parts of speech of the answer choices is consistent. If your capitalized words are a noun and a verb, each one of your answer pairs will be a noun and a verb. If they are an adjective and a noun, each one of your answer pairs will be an adjective and a noun. If you can recognize the parts of speech in a single answer pair, you know the parts of speech of every other answer pair, and of the original pair as well. Consider the analogy you faced in the previous tactic, CENSURE:REPREHENSIBLE. If you hadn't been alert, you might have thought you were dealing with a noun and an adjective; for your test sentence, you might have settled on "Something reprehensible deserves censure." With that test sentence, you never would have chosen Choice A as the correct answer: it makes no sense to say that something valuable deserves a prize. Instead, looking at the first word of the other answer choices, you could see that they were all verbs. Thus, *prize* and *censure* had to be verbs as well.

See how this tactic works in a somewhat difficult question the test-makers once released.

> HUSBAND:RESOURCES::   (A) conserve:energy
>   (B) spend:salary   (C) predict:hurricane
>   (D) analyze:statement   (E) revise:story

At first glance, *husband* and *resources* seem only vaguely related. After all, a husband is a married man; he may have resources, or he may not. However, take a look at the answer pairs. *Conserve, spend,* they're verbs, not nouns. *Husband* must be a verb as well.

You now know you're dealing with an unfamiliar meaning of *husband.* However, you also know that husbanding is an action that has something to do with *resources* or assets. Typically, you do one of two things with resources or assets: save them or expend them. You've just narrowed things down to a decision between Choice A, *conserve:energy,* and Choice B, *spend:salary.* Choice B, however, is an eye-catcher: it's set up to remind you that "husbands" earn a *salary.* The correct answer is Choice A. To husband resources is to use them economically, conserving them as much as you can. This is comparable to conserving energy.

Consider Secondary Meanings of Words as Well as Their Primary Meanings.

How can you tell that you are dealing with an unfamiliar secondary meaning of an apparently familiar word? Simple. When you come across the word in an analogy, it makes no sense.

At that point, what do you do? First, try to think of other contexts for the problem word. Make up new sentences using it. Reverse the grammatical order of the pair. If the problem word is part of the capitalized pair, look over the answer pairs to see whether you can come up with any clues to the relationship linking the capitalized pair.

See how this tactic works in handling a recent SAT I question involving apparently familiar words.

> MYSTIFY:UNDERSTANDING::
>   (A) nip:maturation   (B) insure:disaster
>   (C) rearrange:order   (D) intensify:endurance
>   (E) reciprocate:interchange

At first glance, this analogy is simple. To mystify is to bewilder someone intentionally, to block that person's understanding. The relationship between the capitalized words is clear. However, this is the last question of a set, typically the hardest analogy question in that section. Its simplicity is deceptive: this is a very easy question *to get wrong.* The problem lies not in the original analogy but in the answer pairs.

Consider the answer choices closely. Choices C, D, and E seem clear enough. To rearrange something is to alter the order in which you find it. To intensify endurance is to increase stamina. To reciprocate is to make a mutual exchange or interchange. None of these possibilities fit the test sentence. Choice B is a bit more complex. Two possibilities for the relationship between *insure* and *disaster* exist. One, to insure disaster is to make disaster certain or inevitable: if you leave your picnic basket and all your food at home, you insure disaster for your picnic. Two, to insure oneself is to protect oneself financially from loss caused by death or some other disaster This second possible sentence

may seem appealing, but Choice B is incorrect. Insuring yourself against disaster does not prevent the disaster from taking place; it merely reduces the financial risk involved.

Having eliminated all the other choices, take another look at Choice A. Compared to Choices B, C, D, and E, it seems far out. How does *nipping* or biting relate to *maturation,* the process of reaching full growth and development? A puppy nips at his owner's ankle, but that has nothing to do with the dog's growing up!

Coming across such a weird pairing, most people just shrug their shoulders and skip to the next answer choice. In this case, they'd be making a big mistake. Choice A is the correct answer: to *nip* something, as used here, is to destroy its progress or fulfillment (as in the phrase "nipped in the bud": when the FBI nips a conspiracy in the bud, they prevent the plot from achieving completion). Just as to mystify someone is to block his or her understanding, to nip something is to block its full growth or maturation.

Eliminate Answer Choices That Don't Express a Specific Relationship.

One of your basic SAT strategies is to eliminate as many wrong answer choices as you can. One way to spot a wrong answer in an analogy question is to look for answer pairs whose terms are only vaguely linked.

In the capitalized pairs, the words are always clearly linked:

An OCTOPUS uses its TENTACLES for grasping.
A PERCEPTIVE person is someone who DISCERNS.
To MYSTIFY someone is to block that person's UNDERSTANDING.

In the answer pairs, the relationship between the words may sometimes seem casual at best, as in the following relatively simple analogy from an SAT.

> ACT:STAGE::   (A) play:concert
> (B) lecture:program   (C) swim:pool
> (D) watch:solitude   (E) sketch:subject

Most of these answer choices are easy to express in clear sentences that reflect the words' dictionary definitions. By definition, a *concert* is a musical performance in which musicians

play. A *pool* is a place in which people *swim.* A *subject* is a scene, person, or object that an artist chooses to represent or *sketch.* But what about Choices B and D? A *program* or schedule of events may include *lecturing,* but not necessarily so. Similarly, *solitude* may be a time for *watching,* but it's not defined as such. There is no necessary, specific connection to link the words in either of these choices. Therefore, eliminate Choices B and D. Which of the other answer choices is correct? The answer is of course Choice C. Just as a *stage* is a place where people *act,* a *pool* is a place where people *swim.*

One word of caution. There is a difference between words that *seem* to be related but are actually only casually linked and words that, at first glance, seem to have no relationship at all. When you first looked at the answer choice *nip:maturation* (in Tactic 7), it looked completely absurd. You couldn't even begin to come up with a sentence linking *nip* (in the sense of bite or pinch) and *maturation. Don't* automatically eliminate such off-the-wall answer choices, especially if you find them in the harder analogies toward the end of the set. Study them to see if a secondary meaning is involved.

Familiarize Yourself with Common Analogy Types.

Analogies tend to fall into certain common basic types. Do not go overboard and try to memorize these types. Just try to get a feel for them, so that you'll be able to recognize how each pair of words is linked.

Common Analogy Types
Definition
REFUGE:SHELTER
A *refuge* (place of asylum) by definition *shelters.*

NOMAD:WANDER
A *nomad* by definition *wanders*.

HAGGLER:BARGAIN
A *haggler*, a person who argues over prices, by definition *bargains*.

Defining Characteristic

TIGER:CARNIVOROUS
A *tiger* is defined as a *carnivorous* or meat-eating animal.

ENTOMOLOGIST:INSECTS
An *entomologist* is defined as a person who studies *insects*.

HIVE:BEE
A *hive* is defined as a home for *bees*.

Class and Member

RODENT:SQUIRREL
A *squirrel* is a kind of *rodent*.

SOFA:FURNITURE
A *sofa* belongs to the category known as *furniture*.

SONNET:POEM
A *sonnet* is a kind of *poem*.

Group and Member

DANCER:ENSEMBLE
A *dancer* is a member of an *ensemble* or troupe.

LION:PRIDE
A *lion* is a member of a *pride* or company.

GAGGLE:GEESE
A *gaggle* is a group or flock of *geese*.

Antonyms

Antonyms are words that are opposite in meaning. Both words belong to the same part of speech.

CONCERNED:INDIFFERENT
Indifferent means *unconcerned*.

WAX:WANE
Wax, to grow larger, and *wane*, to dwindle, are opposites.

ANARCHY:ORDER
Anarchy is the opposite of *order*.

Antonym Variants

In an Antonym Variant, the words are not strictly antonyms; however, their meanings are opposed. Take the adjective *nervous*. A strict antonym for the adjective *nervous* would be the adjective *poised*. However, where an Antonym would put the adjective *poised*, an Antonym Variant puts the noun *poise*. It looks like this:

NERVOUS:POISE
Nervous means lacking in *poise*.

WICKED:VIRTUE
Something *wicked* lacks *virtue*. It is the opposite of virtuous.

WILLFUL:OBEDIENCE
Willful means lacking in *obedience*. It is the opposite of obedient.

Synonyms

Synonyms are words that have the same meaning. Both words belong to the same part of speech.

MAGNIFICENT:GRANDIOSE
Grandiose means *magnificent*.

NARRATE:TELL
To *narrate* is to *tell*.

EDIFICE:BUILDING
An *edifice* is a *building*.

Synonym Variants

In a Synonym Variant, the words are not strictly synonyms; however, their meanings are similar. For example, take the adjective *willful*. A strict synonym for the adjective *willful* would be the adjective *unruly*. However, where a Synonym would put the adjective *unruly*, a Synonym Variant would put the noun *unruliness*. It looks like this:

WILLFUL:UNRULINESS
Willful means exhibiting *unruliness*.

VERBOSE:WORDINESS
Someone *verbose* is wordy; he or she exhibits *wordiness*.

FRIENDLY:AMICABILITY
Someone *friendly* is amicable; he or she shows *amicability*.

Degree of Intensity

LUKEWARM:BOILING
Lukewarm is less extreme than *boiling*.

FLURRY:BLIZZARD
A *flurry* or shower of snow is less extreme than a *blizzard*.

ANNOYED:FURIOUS
To be *annoyed* is less intense an emotion than to be *furious*.

Part to Whole

ISLAND:ARCHIPELAGO
Many *islands* make up an *archipelago*.

LETTER:ALPHABET
The English *alphabet* is made up of 26 *letters*.

FINGER:HAND
The *finger* is part of the *hand*.

Function

ASYLUM:REFUGE
An *asylum* provides *refuge* or protection.

FEET:MARCH
A function of *feet* is to *march*.

LULL:STORM
A *lull* temporarily interrupts a *storm*.

Manner

MUMBLE:SPEAK
To *mumble* is to *speak* indistinctly, that is, to speak in an indistinct manner.

STRUT:WALK
To *strut* is to *walk* proudly, that is, to walk in a proud manner.

STRAINED:WIT
Wit that is *strained* is forced in manner.

Worker and Article Created

POET:SONNET
A *poet* creates a *sonnet*.

ARCHITECT:BLUEPRINT
An *architect* designs a *blueprint*.

MASON:WALL
A *mason* builds a *wall*.

Worker and Tool

PAINTER:BRUSH
A *painter* uses a *brush.*

GOLFER:CLUB
A *golfer* uses a *club* to strike the ball.

CARPENTER:VISE
A *carpenter* uses a *vise* to hold the object being worked on.

Worker and Action

ACROBAT:CARTWHEEL
An *acrobat* performs a *cartwheel.*

FINANCIER:INVEST
A *financier* invests.

TENOR:ARIA
A *tenor* sings an *aria.*

Worker and Workplace

TEACHER:CLASSROOM
A *teacher* works in a *classroom.*

SCULPTOR:STUDIO
A *sculptor* works in a *studio.*

DRUGGIST:PHARMACY
A *druggist* works in a *pharmacy.*

Tool and Object It Acts Upon

KNIFE:BREAD
A *knife* cuts *bread.*

PEN:PAPER
A *pen* writes on *paper.*

RAKE:LEAVES
A *rake* gathers *leaves.*

Tool and Its Action

SAW:CUT
A *saw* is a tool used to *cut* wood.

CROWBAR:PRY
A *crowbar* is a tool used to *pry* things apart.

SIEVE:SIFT
A *sieve* is a tool used to strain or *sift.*

Action and Its Significance

HUG:AFFECTION
A *hug* is a sign of *affection.*

NOD:ASSENT
A *nod* signifies *assent* or agreement.

WINCE:PAIN
A *wince* is a sign that one feels *pain.*

Less Common Analogy Types

Cause and Effect

VIRUS:INFLUENZA
A *virus* causes *influenza.*

Time Sequence

FIRST:LAST
First and *last* mark the beginning and end of a sequence.

Spatial Sequence

ATTIC:BASEMENT
The *attic* is the highest point in the house; the *basement,* the lowest point.

Gender

DOE:STAG
A *doe* is a female deer; a *stag,* a male deer.

Age

COLT:STALLION
A *colt* is a young *stallion.*

Symbol and Abstraction It Represents

DOVE:PEACE
A *dove* is the symbol of *peace.*

Long-Range Strategies

Not many words of the vocabulary in the analogy section come from Latin. Generally speaking, the words are more concrete than abstract.

You need to know the names of everyday objects and parts of objects, names that the testmakers assume are in your everyday vocabulary but that nonetheless may be unfamiliar to you. You need to know that hawks have talons and trout have gills, that a group of islands is called an archipelago and a group of lions is called a pride. You need to know that calipers measure and that augers bore, that painters paint murals, and that poets write odes.

How can you build up the sort of wide-ranging, concrete vocabulary you need to see the variety of relationships possible between words? The words are there; they're yours for the taking.

Words for the Taking

To meet new words, branch out in your reading. Try magazines in fields you haven't pursued before. Geology, geography, natural history, astronomy, art—terms from these disciplines appear again and again. Branch out in your viewing as well. You can watch *National Geographic* specials and other documentaries on television and build your vocabulary by attaching the names of objects to the things themselves: people need pictures as well as words.

Unabridged dictionaries often provide pictures of everyday objects: color plates of insects and flowers, birds and fish; line drawings of tools and machines. Picture dictionaries also exist. There is even a splendid visual glossary entitled *What's What,* consisting of hundreds of illustrations of everyday objects—from paper clips to passenger ships—carefully labeled to identify every part.

Learn by Doing

As you expand your vocabulary, try constructing some analogies using your new words. Look up one of the words on our High-Frequency or Hot Prospects Word Lists in an unabridged dictionary. See if you can spot a key word in the definitions given. Use it to construct an analogy of your own. For example, if you look up *amorphous*, you will find it defined as "without form or shape." Based on this definition, a good analogy would be AMORPHOUS:SHAPE.

Something *amorphous* lacks *shape*.

Go through the list of analogy types, modeling your analogies on the samples given. You should have no difficulty constructing innumerable variants on synonyms and antonyms. Challenge yourself. Try to construct analogies where the relationship is one of cause and effect or one of a part to the whole. The better able you are to create good analogies of your own, the better able you will be to analyze the analogies of others.

Practice Exercises

Use the exercises that follow to practice handling analogy questions. When you've completed an exercise, check your answers against the answer key on page 99. Then, read the answer explanations for any questions you either answered incorrectly or omitted.

The answer explanations will show you how to state the relationship in each analogy in a good sentence; they'll provide definitions for words you might not have known; and they'll point out the analogy type for each question. So, if you missed a question because you didn't know the meaning of a word, you'll learn the meaning of that word. If you

missed a question because you didn't understand the relationship between the two words, you'll see what that relationship was.

Spot the Analogy

For each of the following pairs of words, name the common analogy type to which it belongs. Use your dictionary if you need to check a definition before you decide on an analogy type. Then check your answers against the answers on page 93. Any given analogy type may be used once, twice, or not at all.

1. SURGEON:SCALPEL   Worker and tool
2. BARK:TREE   Part to whole
3. FLOWER:PEONY   Class and member
4. DRILL:BORE
5. MINUTE:HOUR
6. COW:HERBIVOROUS
7. TENT:SHELTER
8. EWE:RAM
9. SHOAT:PIG
10. LAUREL:VICTORY
11. FAWN:DEER
12. MEAL:LUNCH
13. SCULPTOR:STATUE
14. TELLER:BANK
15. DISPERSE:ASSEMBLE
16. DRENCHED:MOIST
17. ADORE:LOATHE
18. SCULPTOR:MALLET
19. VERACIOUS:TRUTHFUL
20. ANGLER:FISH
21. BUTCHER:CLEAVER
22. RIDDLE:CRYPTIC
23. KAYAK:BOAT
24. BROOM:SWEEP
25. SOPORIFIC:SLEEP

Answers to Spot the Analogy Practice

4. Tool and its action. A drill is a tool used to bore holes.

5. Part to whole. A minute is part of an hour.

6. Defining characteristic. A cow is defined as herbivorous.

7. Class and member. A tent is a kind of shelter.

8. Defining Characteristic. A ewe is a female sheep; a ram, a male sheep.

9. Defining Characteristic. A shoat is a young pig.

10. Symbol and what it represents. The laurel is the symbol of victory.

11. Defining Characteristic. A fawn is a young deer.

12. Class and member. One example of a meal is lunch.

13. Worker and article created. A sculptor creates a statue.

14. Worker and workplace. A teller works in a bank.

15. Antonyms. Disperse (scatter) and assemble are opposites.

16. Degree of intensity. Drenched means extremely wet; moist, only moderately so.

17. Antonyms. Adore and loathe (hate) are opposites.

18. Worker and tool. A sculptor uses a mallet.

19. Synonyms. Veracious and truthful have the same meaning.

20. Function. An angler tries to catch fish.

21. Worker and tool. A butcher uses a cleaver.

22. Defining characteristic. A riddle is by definition cryptic (mysterious).

23. Class and member. A kayak is a kind of boat.

24. Tool and object. A broom is a tool used to sweep.

25. Cause and effect. Something soporific induces sleep.

Analogy Exercise A

Each question below consists of a related pair of words or phrases, followed by five lettered pairs of words or phrases. Select the lettered pair that <u>best</u> expresses a relationship similar to that expressed in the original pair.

Example:

YAWN:BOREDOM::   (A) dream:sleep
(B) anger:madness   (C) smile:amusement
(D) face:expression   (E) impatience:rebellion

1. FISH:TROUT::   (A) ocean:wave
    (B) mammal:whale   (C) bird:aviary
    (D) antenna:insect   (E) stag:doe

2. FISH:SCALES::   (A) plane:wings
    (B) bird:feathers   (C) cat:claws
    (D) snake:fangs   (E) song:notes

3. FISH:SCHOOL::   (A) book:education
    (B) team:practice   (C) dog:sled
    (D) bear:lair   (E) lion:pride

4. CLOCK:TIME::   (A) watch:wrist
    (B) odometer:speed   (C) hourglass:sand
    (D) yardstick:distance   (E) radio:sound

5. DOCTOR:DISEASE::
    (A) moron:imbecility
    (B) pediatrician:senility
    (C) psychiatrist:maladjustment
    (D) broker:stocks
    (E) charlatan:truth

6. SCISSORS:SEVER::   (A) scales:average
    (B) barrel:roll   (C) eraser:smudge
    (D) millstone:grind   (E) match:strike

7. HONE:SHARP::   (A) polish:shiny
    (B) whet:blunt   (C) memorize:minor
    (D) erode:moist   (E) varnish:sticky

8. PATRON:SUPPORT::
    (A) spouse:divorce
    (B) restaurant:management
    (C) counselor:advice
    (D) host:hostility
    (E) artist:imitation

9. DIMMED:LIGHT::   (A) bleached:texture
    (B) muffled:sound   (C) measured:weight
    (D) fragrant:smell   (E) garish:color

10. STETHOSCOPE:PHYSICIAN::
    (A) kaleidoscope:mortician
    (B) microscope:astronomer
    (C) plot:author
    (D) studio:sculptor
    (E) transit:surveyor

11. DAUNTLESS:COURAGE::
    (A) ruthless:compassion
    (B) affable:suspicion
    (C) unruffled:composure
    (D) energetic:indifference
    (E) dutiful:sympathy

12. CUMULONIMBUS:CLOUD::
    (A) grasshopper:insect
    (B) rainbow:shower
    (C) twilight:dusk
    (D) omnibus:road
    (E) bough:tree

13. OCEAN:BAY::   (A) archipelago:atoll
    (B) island:inlet   (C) headland:promontory
     (D) continent:peninsula   (E) comet:galaxy

14. INTREPID:VALOR::   (A) clever:ingenuity
    (B) boisterous:grief   (C) timorous:haste
     (D) frivolous:fervor   (E) derelict:duty

15. LEOPARD:CARNIVOROUS::
    (A) tiger:ominous
    (B) cat:feline
    (C) cow:herbivorous
    (D) quadruped:four-legged
    (E) crab:crustacean

16. VACCINE:PREVENT::   (A) wound:heal
    (B) victim:attend   (C) antidote:counteract
     (D) diagnosis:cure   (E) antiseptic:infect

17. ANARCHY:GOVERNMENT::
    (A) penury:wealth
    (B) chaos:disorder
    (C) monarchy:republic
    (D) verbosity:words
    (E) ethics:philosophy

18. CIRCUITOUS:DIRECTNESS::
    (A) cautious:duplicity
    (B) religious:faith
    (C) faulty:impropriety
    (D) inexact:accuracy
    (E) sentimental:hypocrisy

19. IMPECUNIOUS:MONEY::
    (A) generous:charity
    (B) impeccable:flaws
    (C) honest:integrity
    (D) bankrupt:industry
    (E) mendacious:dreams

20. DELUGE:SHOWER::   (A) ecstasy:joy
    (B) sophistication:naivete   (C) opinion:notion
     (D) breeze:air   (E) inception:termination

21. ROBIN:NEST::   (A) animal:cave
    (B) horse:stall   (C) alligator:swamp
     (D) clam:shell   (E) rabbit:burrow

22. SILO:STORAGE::   (A) sanctuary:refuge
    (B) oasis:mirage   (C) restaurant:corkage
     (D) fine:damage   (E) butcher:carnage

23. TIRADE:ABUSIVE::   (A) diatribe:familial
    (B) satire:pungent   (C) panegyric:laudatory
     (D) eulogy:regretful   (E) elegy:religious

24. PRICK:STAB::   (A) point:thrust
    (B) lend:borrow   (C) sip:gulp
     (D) thread:sew   (E) push:shove

25. INTEREST:FASCINATE::   (A) vex:enrage
    (B) vindicate:condemn   (C) regret:rue
     (D) appall:bother   (E) weary:fatigue

26. INDUSTRIOUS:ASSIDUOUS::
    (A) affluent:impoverished
    (B) mendacious:beggarly
    (C) fortuitous:fortunate
    (D) impecunious:poor
    (E) impartial:biased

27. INDUSTRY:BEAVER::
    (A) ferocity:lion
    (B) cowardice:tiger
    (C) indolence:wolf
    (D) forgetfulness:elephant
    (E) pride:peacock

28. KANGAROO:MARSUPIAL::   (A) rose:hybrid
    (B) antelope:gazelle   (C) bee:drone
     (D) quail:bevy   (E) mushroom:fungus

29. HELMET:HEAD::   (A) insignia:office
    (B) amulet:shoulder   (C) scepter:crown
     (D) gauntlet:hand   (E) planet:sun

30. VENISON:DEER::   (A) bison:cattle
    (B) mutton:sheep   (C) mallard:duck
     (D) antler:stag   (E) fawn:doe

31. SOLDIER:REGIMENT::   (A) colonel:martinet
    (B) dancer:balletomane   (C) singer:chorus
     (D) trooper:rifle   (E) student:professor

32. LIGHT YEAR:DISTANCE::
    (A) decibel:sound
    (B) black hole:proximity
    (C) meteor:intensity
    (D) microphone:volume
    (E) heat wave:brightness

33. DEBATER:LARYNGITIS::
    (A) actor:stage fright
    (B) pedestrian:sprained ankle
    (C) doctor:tonsillitis
    (D) writer:thesis
    (E) swimmer:aquacade

34. TEAM:ATHLETES::
    (A) game:series
    (B) alliance:nations
    (C) delegates:alternates
    (D) congregation:preachers
    (E) term:holidays

35. ENTREPRENEUR:PROFITS::
    (A) laborer:wages
    (B) manager:employees
    (C) moonlighter:debts
    (D) arbitrator:complaints
    (E) financier:mortgages

36. ANATHEMA:CURSE::
    (A) benediction:song
    (B) admonition:reproach
    (C) supposition:proof
    (D) exhortation:flattery
    (E) homage:disrespect

37. GUSTATORY:TASTE::   (A) kinesthetic:sight
    (B) olfactory:smell   (C) hortatory:hearing
    (D) myopic:vision   (E) palpable:touch

38. STUBBORN:MULISH::   (A) coy:kittenish
    (B) fierce:doglike   (C) contrite:lionhearted
    (D) devoted:sheepish   (E) glib:fishy

39. RUSE:DECEIVE::   (A) policy:change
    (B) argument:persuade   (C) subterfuge:revenge
    (D) strategy:gamble   (E) denial:confuse

40. DRAB:COLOR::   (A) resonant:sound
    (B) insipid:flavor   (C) pungent:smell
    (D) pert:liveliness   (E) dismal:size

41. RATTLE:COMPOSE::   (A) spatter:spill
    (B) brush:touch   (C) disperse:collect
    (D) crash:collide   (E) clatter:knock

42. LARIAT:COWBOY::   (A) rink:skater
    (B) apron:chef   (C) oasis:nomad
    (D) chariot:charioteer   (E) snare:trapper

43. PREAMBLE:CONSTITUTION::
    (A) amendment:bill
    (B) prologue:play
    (C) episode:serial
    (D) by-line:article
    (E) premonition:omen

44. DISBAND:ARMY::   (A) convene:assembly
    (B) muster:platoon   (C) dissolve:corporation
    (D) abandon:navy   (E) countermand:order

45. DETRITUS:GLACIERS::   (A) thaw:snowfall
    (B) snow:ice cap   (C) silt:rivers
    (D) range:mountain   (E) foliage:trees

46. DECREPIT:RENOVATION::
    (A) enervated:invigoration
    (B) languid:confrontation
    (C) pallid:purification
    (D) gullible:vehemence
    (E) tearful:reconciliation

47. SILO:CORN::   (A) mill:grain
    (B) reservoir:water   (C) acre:wheat
    (D) paddy:rice   (E) furrow:seed

48. STATIC:MOVEMENT::
    (A) humdrum:excitement
    (B) chronic:timeliness
    (C) ecstatic:decay
    (D) diligent:industry
    (E) prestigious:wealth

49. SIDEREAL:STARS::
    (A) ethereal:planets
    (B) central:earth
    (C) chimerical:matter
    (D) horticultural:plants
    (E) supernatural:heavens

50. DESCRY:DISTANT::   (A) mourn:lost
    (B) whisper:muted   (C) discern:subtle
    (D) destroy:flagrant   (E) entrap:hostile

Analogy Exercise B

Each question below consists of a related pair of words or phrases, followed by five lettered pairs of words or phrases. Select the lettered pair that best expresses a relationship similar to that expressed in the original pair.

Example:

  YAWN:BOREDOM::   (A) dream:sleep
  (B) anger:madness   (C) smile:amusement
  (D) face:expression   (E) impatience:rebellion

  Ⓐ Ⓑ ● Ⓓ Ⓔ

1. TELLER:BANK::   (A) artist:museum
   (B) cashier:check   (C) waiter:restaurant
   (D) borrower:loan   (E) mourner:funeral

2. INNING:BASEBALL::   (A) round:boxing
   (B) puck:hockey   (C) touchdown:football
   (D) serve:tennis   (E) outing:hiking

3. DEGREE:TEMPERATURE::   (A) ounce:weight
   (B) fathom:volume   (C) mass:energy
   (D) time:length   (E) light:heat

4. PICK:GUITAR::   (A) peg:ukelele
(B) string:banjo   (C) pipe:organ
 (D) bow:violin   (E) head:tambourine

5. FRAGILE:BREAK::   (A) vital:destroy
(B) hostile:invite   (C) vivid:grow
 (D) flexible:bend   (E) fertile:smell

6. SPOKE:WHEEL::   (A) square:circle
(B) balance:lever   (C) door:latch
 (D) book:shelf   (E) rung:ladder

7. VESSEL:FLEET::   (A) wolf:pack
(B) forest:clearing   (C) vehicle:truck
 (D) carriage:horse   (E) squadron:rank

8. PICADOR:BULL::   (A) heckler:speaker
(B) executioner:victim   (C) shepherd:sheep
 (D) singer:song   (E) matador:cow

9. CORPULENCE:STOUT::
(A) baldness:hirsute
(B) erudition:learned
(C) gauntness:beautiful
(D) steadfastness:mercurial
(E) competence:strict

10. ASYLUM:SHELTER::
(A) harbor:concealment
(B) palisade:display
(C) stronghold:defense
(D) hospice:exile
(E) cloister:storage

11. MOTION PICTURE:SCENARIO::
(A) drama:setting
(B) play:plot
(C) theater:program
(D) ballet:pirouette
(E) recital:review

12. MILDEW:DANKNESS::
(A) gangrene:infection
(B) dew:sunshine
(C) dawn:darkness
(D) canker:blossom
(E) rust:hardness

13. CALLOW:MATURITY::
(A) fallow:productivity
(B) crusty:incivility
(C) eager:anxiety
(D) spoiled:common sense
(E) callous:growth

14. ENIGMA:PUZZLING::
(A) dilemma:compelling
(B) labyrinth:disorienting
(C) sphinx:massive
(D) riddle:humorous
(E) maze:extensive

15. KERNEL:CORN::   (A) neck:bottle
(B) eye:storm   (C) grain:wheat
 (D) stem:carrot   (E) nose:bouquet

16. FLABBY:FIRMNESS::
(A) definite:accuracy
(B) tired:fatigue
(C) solvent:wealth
(D) defiant:strength
(E) humble:arrogance

17. ARCHIPELAGO:ISLAND::
(A) peninsula:strait
(B) cluster:star
(C) border:nation
(D) nucleus:atom
(E) skyscraper:building

18. HOBBLE:WALK::   (A) gallop:run
(B) stammer:speak   (C) stumble:fall
 (D) sniff:smell   (E) amble:stroll

19. EXUBERANT:DOWNCAST::
(A) exiled:overthrown
(B) extravagant:lavish
(C) effusive:undemonstrative
(D) parsimonious:eager
(E) formidable:dismal

20. MINISTER:SERMON::
(A) politician:promises
(B) heckler:interruptions
(C) doctor:diagnosis
(D) lecturer:speech
(E) curator:museum

21. HOBNOB:COMPANIONS::
(A) conspire:plotters
(B) kowtow:servants
(C) blackmail:police
(D) kidnap:victims
(E) quarrel:friends

22. GOURMET:DELICACY::
(A) clairvoyant:seance
(B) connoisseur:masterpiece
(C) socialite:seclusion
(D) commoner:aristocracy
(E) chef:scullery

23. INADVERTENT:THOUGHT::
(A) gauche:grace
(B) clandestine:secrecy
(C) lugubrious:gloom
(D) wealthy:money
(E) curious:opinion

24. GAGGLE:GEESE::   (A) coop:chickens
(B) muzzle:dogs   (C) gill:fish
 (D) swarm:bees   (E) waddle:ducks

25. TIFF:QUARREL::
    (A) conflagration:fire
    (B) truce:battle
    (C) peccadillo:offense
    (D) reconciliation:divorce
    (E) fib:argument

26. UNEMPLOYED:WORKER::
    (A) unknown:artist
    (B) fallow:field
    (C) renovated:house
    (D) observant:spectator
    (E) unconscious:sleeper

27. DISCONSOLATE:GRIEF::
    (A) fatuous:weight
    (B) incurable:disease
    (C) explicit:statement
    (D) perfunctory:sympathy
    (E) solitary:confinement

28. CATCALL:DERISION::
    (A) wolf whistle:admiration
    (B) horselaugh:dismay
    (C) snort:approval
    (D) mutter:indifference
    (E) sputter:sympathy

29. CRACK:CIPHER::   (A) break:platter
    (B) divide:number   (C) strike:hammer
    (D) unriddle:mystery   (E) detonate:revolver

30. PAN:CAMERA::   (A) ban:book
    (B) tune:radio   (C) charge:battery
    (D) filter:lens   (E) rotate:periscope

31. HAIR:SCALP::   (A) dimple:cheek
    (B) elbow:knee   (C) tooth:gum
    (D) beard:moustache   (E) waist:torso

32. BUSTLE:MOVE::   (A) hum:sing
    (B) shuffle:walk   (C) lope:run
    (D) glide:dance   (E) chatter:talk

33. TOLERANCE:BIGOTRY::
    (A) prodigality:ribaldry
    (B) magnanimity:parsimony
    (C) exigency:urgency
    (D) emulation:rivalry
    (E) patience:conformity

34. BUNGLER:COMPETENCE::
    (A) beggar:influence
    (B) jester:wit
    (C) meddler:patience
    (D) grumbler:satisfaction
    (E) cobbler:leather

35. ABHOR:DISLIKE::   (A) calcify:petrify
    (B) torture:discomfort   (C) rebuke:ridicule
    (D) admire:disdain   (E) magnify:enlarge

36. BULLY:BLUSTER::
    (A) coward:rant
    (B) charlatan:snivel
    (C) cutthroat:mutter
    (D) stool pigeon:squeal
    (E) blackguard:cringe

37. CARESS:AFFECTION::
    (A) curtsy:respect
    (B) salute:admiration
    (C) handshake:indifference
    (D) wink:suspicion
    (E) wave:agitation

38. FOOLHARDY:CAUTION::
    (A) hardhearted:fear
    (B) careworn:anxiety
    (C) high-strung:tension
    (D) thick-skinned:sensitivity
    (E) spendthrift:resource

39. VERTEX:CONE::   (A) perimeter:rectangle
    (B) whirlpool:pond   (C) pod:seed
    (D) peak:mountain   (E) step:staircase

40. GEOLOGIST:FELDSPAR::
    (A) meteorologist:orbit
    (B) botanist:zinnia
    (C) architect:monolith
    (D) cosmetologist:space
    (E) philanthropist:stamp

41. FELON:PENITENTIARY::
    (A) perjurer:perjury
    (B) conniver:constabulary
    (C) malefactor:sanctuary
    (D) juvenile delinquent:reformatory
    (E) hedonist:confessional

42. TRAVELER:ITINERARY::
    (A) tourist:vacation
    (B) lecturer:outline
    (C) pedestrian:routine
    (D) explorer:safari
    (E) soldier:furlough

43. AERIE:EAGLE::
    (A) hawk:falcon
    (B) viper:reptile
    (C) venom:rattlesnake
    (D) lair:wolf
    (E) fang:adder

44. IMPROMPTU:REHEARSAL::
    (A) practiced:technique
    (B) makeshift:whim
    (C) offhand:premeditation
    (D) glib:fluency
    (E) numerical:calculation

45. EVANESCENT:VANISH AWAY::
    (A) volatile:vaporize
    (B) incandescent:flee
    (C) ethereal:drift
    (D) celestial:disappear
    (E) transient:gravitate

46. RILE:ANGER::
    (A) intimidate:fear
    (B) suppress:rebellion
    (C) disappoint:expectation
    (D) avenge:insult
    (E) soothe:annoyance

47. STICKLER:INSIST::
    (A) mumbler:enunciate
    (B) trickster:risk
    (C) haggler:concede
    (D) laggard:outlast
    (E) braggart:boast

48. PLUMAGE:BIRD::
    (A) foliage:horse
    (B) fleece:sheep
    (C) forage:cattle
    (D) hive:bee
    (E) carnage:beast

49. RAREFY:DENSE::
    (A) amplify:loud
    (B) inoculate:infectious
    (C) mystify:obscure
    (D) condense:compact
    (E) soften:hard

50. ABOLITIONIST:SLAVERY::
    (A) capitalist:commerce
    (B) militarist:war
    (C) pugilist:victory
    (D) conservationist:wildlife
    (E) prohibitionist:liquor

Answer Key

Analogy Exercise A

1.	B	11.	C	21.	E	31.	C	41.	C
2.	B	12.	A	22.	A	32.	A	42.	E
3.	E	13.	D	23.	C	33.	B	43.	B
4.	D	14.	A	24.	C	34.	B	44.	C
5.	C	15.	C	25.	A	35.	A	45.	C
6.	D	16.	C	26.	D	36.	B	46.	A
7.	A	17.	A	27.	E	37.	B	47.	B
8.	C	18.	D	28.	E	38.	A	48.	A
9.	B	19.	B	29.	D	39.	B	49.	D
10.	E	20.	A	30.	B	40.	B	50.	C

Analogy Exercise B

1.	C	11.	B	21.	A	31.	C	41.	D
2.	A	12.	A	22.	B	32.	E	42.	B
3.	A	13.	A	23.	A	33.	B	43.	D
4.	D	14.	B	24.	D	34.	D	44.	C
5.	D	15.	C	25.	C	35.	B	45.	A
6.	E	16.	E	26.	B	36.	D	46.	A
7.	A	17.	B	27.	B	37.	A	47.	E
8.	A	18.	B	28.	A	38.	D	48.	B
9.	B	19.	C	29.	D	39.	D	49.	E
10.	C	20.	D	30.	E	40.	B	50.	E

Answer Explanations

Analogy Exercise A

1. B. A *trout* is a kind of *fish*. A *whale* is a kind of *mammal*. (Class and Member)

2. B. The body of a *fish* is covered with *scales*. The body of a *bird* is covered with *feathers*. (Defining Characteristic)

3. E. A *school* is a group of *fish*. A *pride* is a group of *lions*. (Part to Whole)

4. D. A *clock* measures *time*. A *yardstick* measures *distance*. (Function)

5. C. A *doctor* attempts to treat a *disease*. A *psychiatrist* attempts to treat a *maladjustment*. (Function)

6. D. *Scissors* by definition cut or *sever*. A *millstone* by definition *grinds*. (Tool and Action)

7. A. One *hones* or sharpens something to make it *sharp*. One *polishes* something to make it *shiny*. (Cause and Effect)

8. C. A *patron* by definition provides patronage or *support*. A *counselor* by definition provides *advice*. (Defining Characteristic)

9. B. *Light* that is *dimmed* is lessened in brightness. *Sound* that is *muffled* is lessened in volume. (Manner)

10. E. A *stethoscope* is the tool of a *physician*. A *transit* (measuring instrument) is the tool of a *surveyor*. (Worker and Tool)

11. C. Someone *dauntless* (unable to be frightened) possesses *courage*. Someone *unruffled* (not flustered) possesses *composure* (poise). (Synonym Variant)

12. A. A *cumulonimbus* is a kind of *cloud*. A *grasshopper* is a kind of *insect*. (Class and Member)

13. D. A *bay* is an inlet, part of an *ocean* or sea that projects out into the land. A *peninsula* is a point of land, part of a *continent* that projects out into the water. (Part to Whole)

14. A. Someone *intrepid* (brave) shows *valor* (bravery). Someone *clever* shows *ingenuity* (cleverness). (Synonym Variant)

15. C. A *leopard* is a *carnivorous* (meat-eating) animal. A *cow* is a *herbivorous* (grass-eating) animal. (Defining Characteristic)

16. C. A *vaccine's* purpose is to *prevent* the harmful development of disease-causing microorganisms. An *antidote's* purpose is to *counteract* the harmful effects of poison. (Function)

17. A. *Anarchy* is the absence of *government*. *Penury* (poverty) is the absence of *wealth*. (Antonyms)

18. D. Something *circuitous* (roundabout) is lacking in *directness*. Something *inexact* (inaccurate) is lacking in *accuracy*. (Antonym Variant)

19. B. *Impecunious* (impoverished) means without money. *Impeccable* (flawless) means without flaws. (Antonym Variant)

20. A. A *deluge* (flood; drenching rainburst) is more intense than a *shower*. *Ecstasy* (rapture) is more intense than *joy*. (Degree of Intensity)

21. E. A *robin* constructs a *nest* to live in. A *rabbit* digs out a *burrow* to live in. (Defining Characteristic)

22. A. The function of a *silo* is to provide *storage* space. The function of a *sanctuary* is to provide *refuge* or shelter. (Function)

23. C. A *tirade* (bitter, condemnatory speech) is by definition *abusive*. A *panegyric* (speech of praise) is by definition *laudatory*. (Defining Characteristic)

24. C. To *prick* someone is not as extreme as to *stab* him. To *sip* something is not as extreme as to *gulp* it. (Degree of Intensity)

25. A. To *fascinate* (interest strongly) is to involve more intensely than merely to *interest*. To *enrage* (anger deeply) is more intense than merely to *vex* (annoy). (Degree of Intensity)

26. D. *Industrious* (hard-working) and *assiduous* are synonyms. *Impoverished* and *poor* are synonyms also. (Synonyms)

27. E. The *beaver* is a symbol of *industry* ("busy as a beaver"). The *peacock* is a symbol of *pride* ("proud as a peacock"). (Symbol and Abstraction It Represents)

28. E. A *kangaroo* is a kind of *marsupial*. A *mushroom* is a kind of *fungus*. (Class and Member)

29. D. A *helmet* protects the *head*. A *gauntlet* (armored glove) protects the *hand*. (Function)

30. B. *Venison* is the meat of a *deer*. *Mutton* is the meat of a *sheep*. (Defining Characteristic)

31. C. A *soldier* is part of a *regiment* (military unit). A *singer* is part of a *chorus*. (Part to Whole)

32. A. A *light year* is a measure of *distance*. A *decibel* is a measure of *sound*. (Function)

33. B. *Laryngitis* is a physical ailment that could prevent a *debater* (public speaker) from functioning. A *sprained ankle* is a physical ailment that could prevent a *pedestrian* (walker) from functioning. (Function)

34. B. A *team* is made up of *athletes*. An *alliance* is made up of *nations*. (Group and Member)

35. A. An *entrepreneur* (organizer of a business) works for *profits*. A *laborer* works for *wages*. (Person and Objective)

36. B. An *anathema* is a *curse*. An *admonition* is a *reproach* or scolding. (Synonyms)

37. B. *Gustatory* by definition means related to the sense of *taste*. *Olfactory* by definition means related to the sense of *smell*. (Defining Characteristic)

38. A. *Stubborn* and *mulish* are synonyms. *Coy* (flirtatious; artfully shy) and *kittenish* are synonyms. (Synonyms)

39. B. The purpose of a *ruse* (trick or stratagem) is to *deceive*. The purpose of an *argument* is to *persuade*. (Function)

40. B. *Drab* (dull, colorless) means lacking in *color*. *Insipid* (bland) means lacking in *flavor*. (Antonym Variant)

41. C. To *rattle* or fluster is the opposite of to *compose* or calm. To *disperse* or scatter is the opposite of to gather or *collect*. (Antonyms)

42. E. A *lariat* or lasso is a tool a *cowboy* uses to catch animals. Similarly, a *snare* is a tool a *trapper* uses to catch animals. (Worker and Tool)

43. B. A *preamble* or preface introduces a *constitution*. A *prologue* or introduction introduces a *play*. (Part to Whole)

44. C. To break up an *army* is to *disband* it. To break up a *corporation* is to *dissolve* it. (Function)

45. C. *Detritus* is disintegrated debris found deposited in the path of a *glacier*. *Silt* is disintegrated rock particles found deposited in the path of a *river*. (Defining Characteristic)

46. A. Something *decrepit* (worn out; broken down) needs *renovation*. Someone *enervated* (exhausted; tired out) needs *invigoration*. (Antonym Variant)

47. B. A *silo* is built to store or hold *corn* or grain. A *reservoir* is built to store or hold *water*. (Function)

48. A. Something *static* (unmoving) lacks *movement*. Something *humdrum* (dull) lacks *excitement*. (Antonym Variant)

49. D. *Sidereal* means pertaining to the *stars*. *Horticultural* means pertaining to the cultivation of *plants*. (Defining Characteristic)

50. C. To *descry* something is to make out or see something that is *distant*. To *discern* something is to make out or see something that is *subtle*. (Defining Characteristic)

Analogy Exercise B

1. C. A *teller* works in a *bank*. A *waiter* works in a *restaurant*. (Worker and Workplace)

2. A. An *inning* is a division of a *baseball* game. A *round* is a division of a *boxing* match. (Part to Whole)

3. A. A *degree* is a measure of *temperature*. An *ounce* is a measure of *weight*. (Function)

4. D. A *pick* is a device used to pluck or sound the strings of a *guitar*. A *bow* is an instrument used to play or sound the strings of a *violin*. (Function)

5. D. Something *fragile* or delicate is able to *break*. Something *flexible* is able to *bend*. (Definition)

6. E. A *spoke* is part of a *wheel*. A *rung* is part of a *ladder*. (Part to Whole)

7. A. A *fleet* is made up of *vessels*. A *pack* is made up of *wolves*. (Part to Whole)

8. A. A *picador* physically jabs at a *bull* to annoy it. A *heckler* verbally jabs at a *speaker* to annoy him. (Function)

9. B. *Corpulence* (fatness) is the state of being *stout*. *Erudition* (scholarliness) is the state of being *knowledgeable* or learned. (Synonym Variant)

10. C. An *asylum* provides refuge or *shelter*. A *stronghold* or fortress provides *defense*. (Function)

11. B.   A *scenario* is the story line of a *motion picture*. A *plot* is the story line of a *play*.
(Defining Characteristic)

12. A.   *Dankness* or dampness leads to *mildew* (spreading discoloration, as of fabric). *Infection* leads to *gangrene* (spreading tissue rot).   (Cause and Effect)

13. A.   A *callow* (immature) person is lacking in *maturity*. A *fallow* (uncultivated) field is lacking in *productivity*.   (Antonym Variant)

14. B.   An *enigma* or puzzle is by definition *puzzling*. A *labyrinth* or maze is by definition *disorienting*.   (Defining Characteristic)

15. C.   A *kernel* is a seed of *corn*. A *grain* is a seed of *wheat*.   (Defining Characteristic)

16. E.   *Flabby* means lacking *firmness*. *Humble* means lacking *arrogance*; modest.
(Antonym Variant)

17. B.   An *archipelago* is a group of *islands*. A *cluster* is a group of *stars*.   (Part to Whole)

18. B.   To *hobble* is to *walk* laboriously and with difficulty. To *stammer* is to *speak* laboriously and with difficulty.   (Manner)

19. C.   *Exuberant* or extremely high-spirited is the opposite of *downcast*. *Effusive* or emotionally unrestrained is the opposite of *undemonstrative*.   (Antonyms)

20. D.   A *sermon* is a religious discourse delivered by a *minister*. A *speech* is a formal discourse delivered by a *lecturer*.
(Defining Characteristic)

21. A.   *Companions* by definition socialize or *hobnob* with one another. *Plotters* by definition *conspire* or scheme with one another.
(Definition)

22. B.   A *gourmet* is an appreciator and judge of food delicacies. A *connoisseur* is an appreciator and judge of *masterpieces* of art.
(Defining Characteristic)

23. A.   Something *inadvertent* or unintentional is lacking in *thought*. Something *gauche* or clumsy is lacking in *grace*. (Antonym Variant)

24. D.   A *gaggle* is a group of *geese*. A *swarm* is a group of *bees*.   (Group and Member)

25. C.   A *tiff* is a slight or petty *quarrel*. A *peccadillo* is a slight or petty sin or *offense*.
(Degree of Intensity)

26. B.   A *worker* that is *unemployed* by definition is not being productive. A *field* that is *fallow* (uncultivated) by definition is not being productive.   (Function)

27. B.   A *grief* that is *disconsolate* is not able to be eased or consoled. A *disease* that is *incurable* is not able to be cured.   (Manner)

28. A.   A *catcall* expresses *derision* or disapproval. A *wolf whistle* expresses *admiration*.
(Action and Significance)

29. D.   To *crack* a *cipher* (code) is to solve or decode it. To *unriddle* a *mystery* is to puzzle it out or solve it.   (Function)

30. E.   To *pan* a *camera* is to rotate it to get a comprehensive view. To *rotate* a *periscope* is to turn it to get a comprehensive view. (Function)

31. C.   *Hair* grows from the *scalp*. A *tooth* grows from the *gum*.   (Location)

32. E.   To *bustle* is to *move* in a hurried manner, with more fuss than productivity. To *chatter* is to *talk* in a hurried manner, with more sound than sense.   (Function)

33. B.   *Tolerance* is the opposite of prejudice or *bigotry*. *Magnanimity* (greatness of spirit; generosity) is the opposite of *parsimony* or stinginess.   (Antonyms)

34. D.   A *bungler* (fumbler; person who botches things) lacks *competence* or skill. A *grumbler* (complainer) lacks contentment or *satisfaction*.   (Antonym Variant)

35. B.   To *abhor* (greatly hate) someone is more intense than to *dislike* him. To *torture* someone is more intense than merely to *discomfort* or disturb him.   (Degree of Intensity)

36. D.   A *bully* by definition is someone who *blusters* or storms around uttering threats. A *stool pigeon* (informer or tattletale) by definition is someone who *squeals*.   (Definition)

37. A.   A *caress* or embrace is a sign of *affection*. A *curtsy* is a sign of politeness or *respect*.
(Action and Significance)

38. D.   Someone *foolhardy* (rash, unthinking) lacks *caution*. Someone *thick-skinned* lacks *sensitivity*.   (Antonym Variant)

39. D.   The *vertex* is defined as the top part of a *cone*. A *peak* is defined as the top part of a *mountain*.   (Part to Whole)

40. B. A *geologist* studies rocks; *feldspar* is a kind of rock. A *botanist* studies plants; a *zinnia* is a kind of plant.   (Defining Characteristic)

41. D. A *felon* (major offender) is confined in a *penitentiary*. A *juvenile delinquent* (youthful offender) is confined in a *reformatory*.
          (Function)

42. B. A *traveler* follows an *itinerary* (plan of a journey). A *lecturer* follows an *outline* (lecture plan).   (Defining Characteristic)

43. D. An *aerie* is the resting place of an *eagle*. A *lair* is the resting place of a *wolf*.   (Function)

44. C. Something *impromptu* or improvised is performed without *rehearsal*. Something *offhand* is said or done without *premeditation* or advance thought.   (Antonym Variant)

45. A. Something *evanescent* tends to *vanish away* or disappear. Something *volatile* tends to *vaporize* or evaporate.
          (Definition)

46. A. To *rile* someone is by definition to arouse *anger*. To *intimidate* someone is by definition to arouse *fear*.
          (Defining Characteristic)

47. E. A *stickler* (person who insists on something) by definition *insists*. A *braggart* (boaster) by definition *boasts*.   (Definition)

48. B. A *bird's plumage* is its feathery outer covering. A *sheep's fleece* is its wooly outer covering.   (Defining Characteristic)

49. E. To *rarefy* something is by definition to make it less *dense* (like a gas). To *soften* something is by definition to make it less *hard*.
          (Antonym Variant)

50. E. An *abolitionist* is a person who seeks to put an end to the practice of *slavery*. A *prohibitionist* is a person who seeks to put an end to the use of hard *liquor*.   (Defining Characteristic)

Analogies Wrap-up

1. Before you look at the answer choices, try to state the relationship between the capitalized words in a good sentence.

2. If you are stumped by an unfamiliar word, try thinking of it in a context.

3. If more than one answer fits the relationship in the sentence, look for a narrower approach.

4. Watch out for errors caused by eye-catchers.

5. Watch out for answer choices that reverse the original relationship.

6. Be guided by the parts of speech in the answer choices in deciding the grammatical relationship of the original pair of words.

7. Consider secondary meanings of words as well as their primary meanings.

8. Eliminate answer choices that don't express a specific relationship.

9. Familiarize yourself with common analogy types.

6 The Critical Reading Question

- ■ **Testing Tactics**
- ■ **Long-Range Strategies**
- ■ **Practice Exercises**
- ■ **Answer Key**
- ■ **Answer Explanations**

SAT I critical reading questions test your ability to understand what you read—both content and technique. Each verbal section on the SAT I will include one or two reading passages of different length, followed by six to thirteen questions of assorted types. One passage on the test will be **narrative**: a passage from a novel, a short story, an autobiography, or a personal essay. One will deal with the **sciences** (including medicine, botany, zoology, chemistry, physics, geology, astronomy); another with the **humanities** (including art, literature, music, philosophy, folklore); a third, with the **social sciences** (including history, economics, sociology, government.) Some passages may be what the College Board calls **argumentative**; these passages present a definite point of view on a subject. One passage will most likely be **ethnic** in content: whether it is a history passage, a personal narrative, or a passage on music, art, or literature, it will deal with concerns of a particular minority group.

Your SAT I test will contain three verbal sections (not counting any experimental verbal part). They will generally follow these three basic patterns.

30-question section
1 400- to 500-word reading passage
1 500- to 600-word reading passage
15 reading comprehension questions

35-question section
1 800- to 900-word reading passage
12 critical reading questions

or

2 reading passages totalling 800–900 words
4 critical reading questions on Passage 1
4 critical reading questions on Passage 2
4 critical reading questions comparing the two passages

13-question section
2 reading passages totalling 800–900 words

5 critical reading questions on Passage 1
5 critical reading questions on Passage 2
3 critical reading questions comparing the two passages

or

1 800- to 900-word reading passage
13 critical reading questions

Do not worry if the test you take doesn't exactly match the above model. The SAT-makers occasionally seem to be playing games, but they are just fine-tuning their new format. Once they put together a test made up of a 31-question section (16 critical reading questions), a 36-question section (13 critical reading questions on a long passage), and an 11-question section comparing two passages. However, the total number of reading questions students had to answer on the test—40—remained the same.

Unlike the sentence completion and analogy questions, the questions that come after each reading passage are *not* arranged in order of difficulty. They are arranged to suit the way the passage's content is organized. (A question based on information found at the beginning of the passage will come before a question based on information at the passage's end.) If you are stumped by a tough reading question, do not skip the other questions on that passage. A tough question may be just one question away from an easy one.

This chapter contains three published SAT reading passages that are somewhat shorter than the ones you will face on the SAT I. However, the questions that follow the passages are just like the questions on the SAT I. Some of the questions ask you about specific details in the passages. Others ask you to interpret the passages, to make judgments about them. Many of these questions are actual questions from the old SAT. Others are brand new, created for this book and modeled on questions on SAT I.

The chapter begins with basic advice about the SAT I critical reading sections. Tactics 1–6 tell you how to deal with SAT I reading questions in general. Tactics 7–13 give you the answers to the questions on the three SAT passages, plus solid hints about how to answer each type of question and short lists of key words you are sure to meet in certain question types. Finally, Tactic 14 shows you how to deal with the new, unfamiliar paired passages you'll face in SAT I's third verbal reasoning section.

The directions for the critical reading section on the SAT I are minimal. They are:

> Each passage below is followed by questions based on its content. Answer all questions following a passage on the basis of what is <u>stated</u> or <u>implied</u> in that passage.

Testing Tactics

Make Use of the New Introductions to Acquaint Yourself with the Text.

Almost every reading passage is preceded by an italicized introduction. Don't skip it. As you read the italicized introductory material and tackle the passage's opening sentences, try to anticipate what the passage will be about. You'll be in a better position to understand what you read.

Use the Line References in the Questions to Be Sure You've Gone Back to the Correct Spot in the Passage.

The reading passages on the current SAT I tend to be longer than those on the old SAT. Fortunately, the lines are numbered, and the questions often refer you to specific lines in the passage by number. It takes less time to locate a line number than to spot a word or phrase. Use the line numbers to orient yourself in the text.

When You Have a Choice, Tackle Passages with Familiar Subjects Before Passages with Unfamiliar Ones.

Build on what you already know and like. It's only common sense: if you know very little about botany or are uninterested in it, you are all too likely to run into trouble reading a passage about plant life.

It is hard to concentrate when you read about something that is wholly unfamiliar to you. Give yourself a break. When you have more than one reading passage in a section, start with one that interests you or that deals with a topic you know well. There is nothing wrong in skipping questions. Just remember to check the numbering of your answer sheet. You should, of course, go back to the questions you skipped if you have time.

First Read the Passage; Then Read the Questions.

Students often ask whether it is better to read the passage first or the questions first. Those who want to read the questions before they read the passage think it will save time. Ninety-nine times out of a hundred they are wrong.

Reading all the questions before you read the passage generally will not save you time. It will cost you time. If you read the questions first, when you turn to the passage you will have a number of question words and phrases dancing around in your head. These phrases won't focus you; they'll distract you. You will be so involved in trying to spot the places that they occur in the passage that you'll be unable to concentrate on comprehending the passage as a whole. Why increase your anxiety and decrease your capacity to think? First read the passage using the following technique:

1. Read as rapidly as you can with understanding, but do not force yourself. Do not worry about the time element. If you worry about not finishing the test, you will begin to take short cuts and miss the correct answer in your haste.

2. As you read the opening sentences, try to anticipate what the passage will be about. Who or what is the author talking about?

3. As you continue reading, notice in what part of the passage the author makes major points. In that way, even when a question does not point you to a particular line or paragraph, you should be able to head for the right section of the text *without* having to reread the entire passage. Underline key words and phrases—sparingly!

Try to Answer *All* the Questions on a Particular Passage.

Don't let yourself get bogged down on any one question; you can't afford to get stuck on one question when you have eleven more on the same passage to answer. Skip the one that's got you stumped, but make a point of coming back to it later, after you've answered one or two more questions on the passage. Often, working through other questions on the same passage will provide you with information you can use to answer any questions that stumped you the first time around. If the question still stumps you, move on. It's just fine to skip an individual reading question, especially if it resembles other reading questions that you've had trouble with before.

Learn to Spot the Major Reading Question Types.

Just as it will help you to know the directions for the analogy and sentence completion questions on SAT I, it will also help you to familiarize yourself with the major types of reading questions on the test.

If you can recognize just what a given question is asking you to do, you'll be better able to tell which particular reading tactic to apply.

Here are six categories of reading questions you are sure to face.

1. **Main Idea** Questions that test your ability to find the central thought of a passage or to judge its significance often take the following form:

The main point of the passage is to

The passage is primarily concerned with

The author's primary purpose in this passage is to

The chief theme of the passage can be best described as

Which of the following titles best describes the content of the passage?

Which of the following statements best expresses the main idea of the passage?

2. **Specific Details** Questions that test your ability to understand what the author states *explicitly* are often worded:

According to the author

The author states all of the following EXCEPT

According to the passage, which of the following is true of the

According to the passage, the chief characteristic of the subject is

Which of the following statements is (are) best supported by the passage?

Which of the following is NOT cited in the passage as evidence of

3. **Inferences** Questions that test your ability to go beyond the author's explicit statements and see what these statements imply may be worded:

It can be inferred from the passage that

The passage suggests that the author would support which of the following views?

The author implies that

The author apparently feels that

According to the passage, it is likely that

The passage is most likely directed toward an audience of

Which of the following statements about...can be inferred from the passage?

4. **Tone/Attitude** Questions that test your ability to sense an author's or character's emotional state often take the form:

The author's attitude to the problem can best be described as

Which of the following best describes the author's tone in the passage?

The author's tone in the passage is that of a person attempting to

The author's presentation is marked by a tone of

The passage indicates that the author experiences a feeling of

5. **Vocabulary in Context** Questions that test your ability to work out the meaning of words from their context often are worded:

As it is used in the passage, the term...can best be described as

The phrase...is used in the passage to mean that

In the passage, the word...means

The author uses the phrase...to describe

6. **Technique** Questions that test your ability to recognize a passage's method of organization or technique often are worded:

Which of the following best describes the development of this passage?

In presenting the argument, the author does all of the following EXCEPT...

The relationship between the second paragraph and the first paragraph can best be described as...

As you become familiar with these major reading question types, you may find that some question types cause you more trouble than others. Make particular note of these types: if you always get technique questions wrong, for example, these may be good questions for you to skip.

Tactic 7

When Asked to Find the Main Idea, Be Sure to Check the Opening and Summary Sentences of Each Paragraph.

The opening and closing sentences of each paragraph are key sentences for you to read. They can serve as guideposts for you, pointing out the author's main idea.

Whenever you are asked to determine a passage's main idea, *always* check each paragraph's opening and summary sentences. Typically, in each paragraph, authors provide readers with a sentence that expresses the paragraph's main idea succinctly. Although such *topic sentences* may appear anywhere in the paragraph, experienced readers customarily look for them in the opening or closing sentences.

Notice the impact of words like *furthermore, moreover, notably,* and *significantly* in the passage. These signal words may call your attention to the main idea.

Note that in SAT I reading passages, topic sentences are sometimes implied rather than stated directly. If you cannot find a topic sentence, ask yourself these questions:

1. Whom or what is this passage about?

2. What aspect of this subject is the author talking about?

3. What is the author trying to get across about this aspect of the subject?

Read the following ethnic reading passage from a published SAT and apply this tactic.

   Lois Mailou Jones is one example of an answer to the charge that there are no Black or female American artists to include in art history textbooks and classes. Beginning her formal art education at the School of the Museum of Fine Arts in Boston, Lois Jones found herself strongly attracted to design rather than fine arts. After teaching for a while, she went to Paris to study, on the advice of the sculptor Meta Warrick Fuller.

   It was in Paris that she first felt free to paint. Following her return to this country in 1938, Jones had an exhibit at the Vose Gallery in Boston, a major breakthrough for a Black artist at that time. Her work during this period consisted of excellent impressionist scenes of Paris. It was not until the early 1940s, after she met the Black aesthetician Alain Locke, that she began to paint works like *Mob Victim*, which explicitly dealt with her own background as a Black American. Later, in the fifties, she went often to Haiti, which had yet another influence on her style. Then a sabbatical leave in Africa again changed her imagery. Indeed, the scope of this distinguished artist's career so well spans the development of twentieth-century art that her work could be a textbook in itself.

Now look at a question on this passage. It's a good example of a main idea question.

> The passage primarily focuses on the
>
> (A) influence of Lois Jones on other artists
> (B) recognition given to Lois Jones for her work
> (C) experiences that influenced the work of Lois Jones
> (D) obstacles that Lois Jones surmounted in her career
> (E) techniques that characterize the work of Lois Jones

Look at the opening and summary sentences of the two paragraphs that make up the passage: "Lois Mailou Jones is one example of...Black or female American artists to include in art history textbooks and classes," "It was in Paris that she first felt free to paint," "Indeed, the scope of [her] career spans the development of twentieth-century art. . ." Note particularly the use of the signal word "indeed" to call your attention to the author's point. Lois Jones has had a vast range of experiences that have contributed to her work as an artist. The correct answer is Choice C.

Choice A is incorrect. The passage talks of influences on Lois Jones, not of Lois Jones's influence on others. Choice B is incorrect. The passage mentions recognition given to Jones only in passing. Choice D is incorrect. There is nothing in the passage to support it. Choice E is incorrect. The passage never deals with specific questions of craft or technique.

Certain words come up again and again in questions on a passage's purpose or main idea. You probably know most of these words, but if you're shaky about any of their meanings, look them up in a good dictionary and familiarize yourself with how they are used. It would be silly to miss an answer not because you misunderstood the passage's meaning but because you failed to recognize a common question word.

Important Words in Questions on Main Idea or Purpose

bolster (verb)	endorse
delineate	exemplify
depict	illustrate
discredit	refute
document (verb)	speculate
elaborate (verb)	verify

Familiarize Yourself with the Technical Terms Used to Describe a Passage's Organization.

Another part of understanding the author's point is understanding how the author organizes what he or she has to say. To do so, often you have to figure out how the opening sentence or paragraph is connected to the passage as a whole.

Try this question on the author's technique, based on the previous passage about Lois Mailou Jones.

> Which of the following best summarizes the relationship of the first sentence to the rest of the passage?
>
> (A) Assertion followed by supporting evidence
> (B) Challenge followed by debate pro and con
> (C) Prediction followed by analysis
> (D) Specific instance followed by generalizations
> (E) Objective reporting followed by personal reminiscences

The correct answer is Choice A. The author makes an assertion (a positive statement) about Jones's importance and then proceeds to back it up with specific details from her career.

Choice B is incorrect. There is no debate for and against the author's thesis or point about Jones; the only details given support that point. Choice C is incorrect. The author does not predict or foretell something that is going to happen; the author asserts or states positively something that is an accomplished fact. Choice D is incorrect. The author's opening general assertion is followed by specific details to support it, not the reverse. Choice E is incorrect. The author shares no personal memories or reminiscences of Jones; the writing is objective throughout.

Important Words in Questions on Technique or Style

abstract	explanatory
analogy	expository
antithesis	generalization
argumentative	narrative
assertion	persuasive
cite	rhetorical
concrete	thesis
evidence	

When Asked to Choose a Title, Watch Out for Choices That Are Too Specific or Too Broad.

Someone once defined a paragraph as a group of sentences revolving around a central theme. A proper title for a paragraph, therefore, should include this central theme that each of the sentences in the paragraph is developing. It has to fit: it should be neither too broad in scope, nor too narrow; it should be specific and yet comprehensive enough to include all the essentials.

A good title for a longer passage of two or more paragraphs follows the same rules. It expresses the theme of the whole passage. It is specific, yet comprehensive. It includes the thoughts of ALL the paragraphs.

This third question on the Jones passage is a title question. Note how it resembles questions on the passage's purpose or main idea.

> Which of the following is the best title for the passage?
>
> (A) Unsung Black Artists of America
> (B) A Hard Row to Hoe: The Struggles of Lois Jones
> (C) Locke and Jones: Two Black Artistic Pioneers
> (D) African and Haitian Influences on Lois Mailou Jones
> (E) The Making of an Artist: Lois Mailou Jones

When you are trying to select the best title for a passage, watch out for words that come straight out of the passage. They may not always be your best choice. Consider Choice C. Though the author mentions Alain Locke and suggests the importance of his influence in prompting Jones to use her experiences as a black American in her art, the passage as a whole is about Jones, not about Locke and Jones. Likewise, although the passage refers to African and Haitian influences on her imagery and style, the passage is about how Jones's experiences formed her as an artist, not about the specific influences on her style. Choice D is too narrow in scope to be a good title for this text.

Choice A has the opposite problem. As a title for this passage, *Unsung Black Artists of America* is far too broad. This passage concerns itself with a particular black artist whose fame deserves to be sung.

While Choice B limits itself to Jones, it too has a flaw. The passage clearly does not dwell on Jones's struggles; instead, it focuses on influences on her artistic growth.

Of the titles suggested, Choice E is best. The passage refers to the many and varied experiences that have made Jones an important figure in the world of art. Following her progress step by step, it portrays "the making of an artist."

When Asked About Specific Details in the Passage, Spot Key Words in the Question and Scan the Passage to Find Them (or Their Synonyms).

In developing the main idea of a passage, a writer will make statements to support his or her point. To answer questions about such supporting details, you *must* find a word or group of words in the passage that supports your choice of answer. The words "according to the passage" or "according to the author" should focus your attention on what the passage explicitly states. Do not be misled into choosing an answer (even one that makes good sense) if you cannot find it supported in the text.

Often detail questions ask about a particular phrase or line. The new SAT I generally provides numbered line references to help you locate the relevant section of the passage. Occasionally it fails to do so. In such instances, use the following technique:

1. Look for key words (nouns or verbs) in the answer choices.

2. Run your eye down the passage, looking for those key words or their synonyms. (This is called *scanning*. It is what you do when you look up someone's number in the phone book.)

3. When you find a key word or its synonym, reread the sentence to make sure the test-writer hasn't used the original wording to mislead you.

Read the following scientific passage from a recently published SAT and apply this tactic.

Prostaglandins are short-lived hormonelike substances made by most cells in the body after injury or shock. They are responsible for a number of physiological reactions. Prostaglandins have been shown to influence blood pressure, muscle contraction, and blood coagulation and are involved in producing pain, fever, and inflammation. When released from platelets—minute discs in the blood—a prostaglandin derivative called thromboxane makes the platelets clump together and thus initiates clotting.

In 1971, John Vane, a British researcher, discovered that aspirin interferes with the synthesis of prostaglandins. Scientists now know that aspirin relieves pain by inactivating cyclooxygenase, an enzyme that aids in initiating the synthesis of prostaglandins. When scientists realized that aspirin can also interfere with clotting, they began to wonder whether it could help prevent heart attacks and strokes, which are often caused by blood clots that block arteries in the chest and neck. Studies now indicate that low daily doses of aspirin can cut the risk of a second heart attack by about twenty percent and the risk of a second stroke by nearly half. It seems logical to assume that if the drug can prevent second heart attacks, it can also ward off an attack the first time around. Therefore, many doctors recommend an aspirin tablet every other day to people

who have high blood pressure or other symptoms that increase the risk of heart attacks.

Now look at a question on a significant detail in the passage.

> According to the passage, prostaglandins play a role in all of the following EXCEPT the
> (A) clotting of blood
> (B) sensation of pain
> (C) contraction of muscles
> (D) manufacture of platelets
> (E) inflammation of tissue

Watch out for questions containing the word EXCEPT. To answer them, you must go through each answer choice in turn, checking to see if you can find it supported in the passage. If you can find support for it, then you must rule it out. When you find an answer choice *without* support in the passage, that's the answer you want.

The last two sentences in the first paragraph are the key to this question. These two sentences cite the physiological reactions caused by prostaglandins. Check each of the answer choices against these lines.

Choice A is incorrect. Prostaglandins influence "blood coagulation" or *clotting*. Note the use of *clotting*, a synonym for *coagulation*, rather than the passage's original wording.

Choice B is incorrect. Prostaglandins are involved in producing pain.

Choice C is incorrect. Prostaglandins influence muscle contraction.

Choice E is incorrect. Prostaglandins are involved in producing inflammation.

The correct answer is Choice D. While prostaglandins do have an influence on platelets, they play a role in causing platelets to clump or gather together, *not* in manufacturing them.

Important Words in Questions on Specific Detail

aesthetic	indicative
allusion	inherent
assumption	innate
attribute	innovative
divergent	misconception
fluctuate	phenomenon
hypothetical	preclude
incompatible	

Tactic 11

When Asked to Make Inferences, Base Your Answers on What the Passage Implies, Not What It States Directly.

In *Language in Thought and Action*, S.I. Hayakawa defines an inference as "a statement about the unknown made on the basis of the known."

Inference questions require you to use your own judgment. You must not take anything directly stated by the author as an inference. Instead, you must look for clues in the passage that you can use in coming up with your own conclusion. You should choose as your answer a statement which is a logical development of the information the author has provided.

Try this fairly easy inference question, based on the previous passage about prostaglandins.

> The passage suggests that which of the following would be most likely to initiate the production of prostaglandins?
>
> (A) Taking an aspirin
> (B) Spraining an ankle
> (C) Climbing stairs
> (D) Flexing a muscle
> (E) Running a fever

The justification for Choice B as an answer comes in the opening sentence, which states that prostaglandins are produced in response to injury or shock. Choice B, *spraining an ankle*, is an example of an injury. As such, it is likely to initiate or set into motion the production of prostaglandins. None of the other choices is an example of an injury or shock. Thus, you can logically infer they are unlikely to start prostaglandin production going. Taking an aspirin, in fact, would interfere with or block prostaglandin production. Only Choice B is logical to suggest.

Now read this SAT fiction passage, taken from the novel *The Heart of the Matter* by Graham Greene.

"Imagine. Forty days in the boats!" cried Mrs. Perrot. Everything over the river was still and blank.

"The French behaved well this time at least," Dawson remarked.

"They've only brought in the dying," the doctor retorted. "They could hardly have done less."

Dawson exclaimed and struck at his hand. "Come inside," Mrs. Perrot said, "The windows are netted." The stale air was heavy with the coming rains.

"There are some cases of fever," said the doctor, "but most are just exhaustion—the worst disease. It's what most of us die of in the end."

Mrs. Perrot turned a knob; music from the London Orpheum filtered in. Dawson shifted uncomfortably; the Wurlitzer organ moaned and boomed. It seemed to him outrageously immodest.

Wilson came in to a welcome from Mrs. Perrot. "A surprise to see *you*, Major Dawson."

"Hardly, Wilson." Mr. Perrot injected. "I told you he'd be here." Dawson looked across at Wilson and saw him blush at Perrot's betrayal, saw too that his eyes gave the lie to his youth.

"Well," sneered Perrot, "any scandals from the big city?" Like a Huguenot imagining Rome, he built up a picture of frivolity, viciousness, and corruption. "We bush-folk live quietly."

Mrs. Perrot's mouth stiffened in the effort to ignore her husband in his familiar part. She pretended to listen to the old Viennese melodies.

"None," Dawson answered, watching Mrs. Perrot with pity. "People are too busy with the war."

"So many files to turn over," said Perrot. "Growing rice down here would teach them what work is."

The first question based on this passage is an inference question. Note the use of the terms "suggests" and "most likely." The passage never tells you directly where the story takes place. You must put two and two together and see what you get.

> The evidence in the passage suggests that the story most likely takes place
>
> (A) on a boat during a tropical storm
> (B) at a hospital during a wartime blackout
> (C) in a small town in France
> (D) near a rice plantation in the tropics
> (E) among a group of people en route to a large Asian city

Go through the answer choices one by one. Remember that in answering inference questions you must go beyond the obvious, go beyond what the author explicitly states, to look for logical implications of what the author says.

The correct answer is Choice D, *near a rice plantation in the tropics*. Several lines in the passage suggest it: Perrot's reference to "bush-folk," people living in a tropical jungle or similar uncleared wilderness; Perrot's comment about the work involved in growing rice; the references to fever and the coming rains.

Choice A is incorrect. The people rescued have been in the boats for forty days. The story itself is not set on a boat.

Choice B is incorrect. Although the presence of a doctor and the talk of dying patients suggests a hospital and Dawson's comment implies that people elsewhere are concerned with a war, nothing in the passage suggests that it is set in a wartime blackout. The windows are not covered or blacked out to prevent light from getting out; instead, they are netted to prevent mosquitos from getting in. (Note how Dawson exclaims and swats his hand; he has just been bitten by a mosquito).

Choice C is incorrect. Although the French are mentioned, nothing suggests that the story takes place in France, a European country not noted for uncleared wilderness or tropical rains.

Choice E is incorrect. Nothing in the passage suggests these people are en route elsewhere. In addition, Wilson could not logically pretend to be surprised by Dawson's presence if they were companions on a tour.

Important Words in Inference Questions

criterion	likelihood
derive	overrated
excerpt	plausible
implication	suggestive
imply	tentative

Tactic 12

When Asked About an Attitude, Mood, or Tone, Look for Words That Convey Emotion, Express Values, or Paint

In figuring out the attitude, mood, or tone of an author or character, take a close look at the specific language used. Is the author using adjectives to describe the subject? If so, are they words like *fragrant, tranquil, magnanimous*—words with positive connotations? Or are they words like *fetid, ruffled, stingy*—words with negative connotations?

When we speak, our tone of voice conveys our mood—frustrated, cheerful, critical, gloomy, angry. When we write, our images and descriptive phrases get our feelings across.

The second question on the Greene passage is a tone question. Note the question refers you to specific lines in which a particular character speaks. Those lines are repeated here so that you can easily refer to them.

"They've only brought in the dying," the doctor retorted. "They could hardly have done less."

"There are some cases of fever," said the doctor, "but most are just exhaustion—the worst disease. It's what most of us die of in the end."

> The tone of the doctor's remarks (lines 5–6, 10–12) indicates that he is basically
>
> (A) unselfish
> (B) magnanimous
> (C) indifferent
> (D) rich in patience
> (E) without illusions

Note the doctor's use of "only" and "hardly," words with a negative sense. The doctor is deprecating or belittling what the French have done for the sufferers from the boats, the people who are dying from the exhaustion of their forty-day journey. The doctor is *retorting*: he is replying sharply to Dawson's positive remark about the French having behaved well. The doctor has judged the French. In his eyes, they have not behaved well.

Go through the answer choices one by one to see which choice comes closest to matching your sense of the doctor's tone.

Choice A is incorrect. Nothing in the passage specifically suggests selfishness or unselfishness on his part, merely irritability.

Choice B is incorrect. The doctor sounds irritable, critical, sharp-tempered. He feels resentment for the lack of care received by the victims. He does not sound like a magnanimous, forgiving man.

Choice C is incorrect. The doctor is not indifferent or uncaring. If he did not care, he would not be so sharp in challenging Dawson's innocent remark.

Choice D is also incorrect. The doctor is quick to counter Dawson, quick to criticize the French. Impatience, not patience, distinguishes him.

The correct answer is Choice E. The doctor is without illusions. Unlike Dawson, he cannot comfort himself with the illusion that things are going well. He has no illusions about life or death: most of us, he points out unsentimentally, die of exhaustion in the end.

When you are considering questions of attitude and tone, bear in mind the nature of SAT I. It is a standardized test aimed at a wide variety of test-takers—heavy metal fans, political activists, 4-H members, computer hacks, readers of *GQ*. It is taken by Native Americans and Chinese refugees, evangelical Christians and Orthodox Jews, Buddhists and Hindus, Hispanics and blacks, New Yorkers and Nebraskans—a typically American mix.

The SAT-makers are very aware of this diversity. As members of their staff have told us, they are particularly concerned to avoid using material on the tests that might upset students (and possibly adversely affect their scores). For this reason, the goal is to be noncontroversial: to present material that won't offend *anyone*. Thus, in selecting potential reading passages, the SAT-makers tend to avoid subjects that are sensitive in favor of ones that are bland. In fact, if a passage doesn't start out bland, they revise it and cut out the spice. One SAT test, for example, includes Kenneth Clark's comment about the "sharp wits" of Romans, but cuts out his comment about their "hard heads." Another uses a passage from Mary McCarthy's prickly *Memories of a Catholic Girlhood*, but cuts out every reference to Catholic and Protestant interaction—and much of the humor, too.

How does this affect the sort of tone and attitude questions the SAT-makers ask? As you can see, the SAT-makers attempt to respect the feelings of minority group members. Thus, you can expect minority group members to be portrayed in SAT I reading passages in a favorable light. If, for example, there had been an attitude question based on the Lois Mailou Jones passage, it might have been worded like this:

> The author's attitude toward the artistic achievements mentioned in the passage can best be described as one of
>
> (A) incredulity
> (B) suspicion
> (C) condescension
> (D) indifference
> (E) admiration

Admiration is the only possible choice.

When Asked to Give the Meaning of an Unfamiliar Word, Look for Nearby Context Clues.

Every student who has ever looked into a dictionary is aware that many words have more than one meaning. A common question that appears on the new SAT I tests your ability to determine the correct meaning of a word from its context. Sometimes the word is a common one, and you must determine its exact meaning as used by the author. At other times, the word is uncommon. You can determine its meaning by a careful examination of the text.

As always, use your knowledge of context clues and word parts (Chapter 5) to help you discover the meanings of unfamiliar words.

One question based on the Lois Mailou Jones passage asks you to determine which exact meaning of a common word is used in a particular sentence. Here is the sentence in which the word appears.

> Lois Mailou Jones is one example of an answer to the charge that there are no black or female American artists to include in art history textbooks and classes.

> The word "charge" in line 2 means
>
> (A) fee
> (B) duty
> (C) onslaught
> (D) allegation
> (E) care

To answer this question, simply substitute each of the answer choices for the quoted word in its original context. Clearly, both black and female American artists exist. Thus, the statement that there are no black or female American artists to include in art history texts or classes is an *allega-*

Important Words in Questions on Attitude and Tone

aloof	indifference
ambivalent	ironic
brusque	judicious
cautionary	naive
compassionate	nostalgia
condescension	objective
cynical	optimism
defensive	pedantic
detachment	pessimism
didactic	pomposity
disdain	prosaic
disparaging	resigned (adjective)
dispassionate	sarcasm
esteem	satirical
flippant	skeptical
grudging	trite
hypocritical	whimsical

tion (unproven accusation) that our black and female artists are not good enough to be included in the texts. Jones, however, *is* good enough. Therefore, she is an example of an answer to this false accusation or charge.

A second vocabulary question, this one based on the Greene passage, concerns an uncommon, unfamiliar word. Here is the paragraph in which the word appeared.

> "Well," sneered Perrot, "any scandals from the big city?" Like a Huguenot imagining Rome, he built up a picture of frivolity, viciousness, and corruption. "We bush-folk live quietly."

> A Huguenot, as used in the passage, is most likely
>
> (A) a person dying of exhaustion
> (B) a doctor angered by needless suffering
> (C) an admirer of the Roman aristocracy
> (D) a city-dweller scornful of country ways
> (E) a puritan who suspects others of immorality

What is a Huguenot? It's certainly not an everyday word. You may never have encountered the term before you read this passage. But you can figure it out. A Huguenot is someone who, when he thinks of Rome, thinks of it in terms of vice and lack of seriousness. He disapproves of it for its wickedness and frivolity. Thus, he is a puritan of sorts, a person who condemns practices which he regards as impure or corrupt. The correct answer is Choice E. Look at the words in the immediate vicinity of the word you are defining. They will give you a sense of the meaning of the unfamiliar word.

When Dealing with the New Double Passages, Tackle Them One at a Time.

If the double passage section has you worried, relax. It's not that formidable, especially if you deal with it our way. Read the lines in italics introducing both passages. Then look at the two passages. Their lines will be numbered as if they were one *enormous* passage: if Passage 1 ends on line 42, Passage 2 will begin on line 43. However, they are two separate passages. Tackle them one at a time.

The questions are organized sequentially: questions about Passage 1 come before questions about Passage 2. So, do things in order. *First* read Passage 1; then jump straight to the questions and answer all those based on Passage 1. *Next* read Passage 2; then answer all the questions based on Passage 2. (The line numbers in the questions will help you spot where the questions on Passage 1 end and those on Passage 2 begin.) *Finally*, tackle the two or three questions that refer to *both* passages. Go back to both passages as needed.

Occasionally a couple of questions referring to *both* passages will precede the questions focusing on Passage 1. Do not let this minor hitch throw you. Use your common sense. You've just read the first passage. Skip the one or two questions on both passages, and head for those questions about Passage 1. Answer them. Then read Passage 2. Answer the questions on Passage 2. Finally, go back to those questions you skipped and answer them and any other questions at the end of the set that refer to both passages. Remember, however: whenever you skip from question to question, or from passage to passage, *be sure you're filling in the right ovals on your answer sheet.*

Here is an example of a double passage. Go through the questions that follow, applying the tactics you've just learned.

The following passages are excerpted from books on America's national pastime, baseball. Passage 1 is taken from an account of a particularly memorable season. Passage 2 is from a meditation on the game written in 1989 by the late literary scholar A. Bartlett Giamatti, then commissioner of baseball.

Passage 1

DiMaggio had size, power, and speed. McCarthy, his longtime manager, liked to say that DiMaggio might have stolen 60 bases a season if he had given
Line him the green light. Stengel, his new manager, was
(5) equally impressed, and when DiMaggio was on base he would point to him as an example of the perfect base runner. "Look at him," Stengel would say as DiMaggio ran out a base hit, "he's always watching the ball. He isn't watching second base.
(10) He isn't watching third base. He knows they haven't been moved. He isn't watching the ground, because he knows they haven't built a canal or a swimming pool since he was last there. He's watching the

ball and the outfielder, which is the one thing that
(15) is different on every play."

DiMaggio complemented his natural athletic ability with astonishing physical grace. He played the outfield, he ran the bases, and he batted not just effectively but with rare style. He would glide
(20) rather than run, it seemed, always smooth, always ending up where he wanted to be just when he wanted to be there. If he appeared to play effortlessly, his teammates knew otherwise. In his first season as a Yankee, Gene Woodling, who played
(25) left field, was struck by the sound of DiMaggio chasing a fly ball. He sounded like a giant truck horse on the loose, Woodling thought, his feet thudding down hard on the grass. The great, clear noises in the open space enabled Woodling to measure
(30) the distances between them without looking.

He was the perfect Hemingway hero, for Hemingway in his novels romanticized the man who exhibited grace under pressure, who withheld any emotion lest it soil the purer statement of his
(35) deeds. DiMaggio was that kind of hero; his grace and skill were always on display, his emotions always concealed. This stoic grace was not achieved without a terrible price: DiMaggio was a man wound tight. He suffered from insomnia and ulcers.
(40) When he sat and watched the game he chain-smoked and drank endless cups of coffee. He was ever conscious of his obligation to play well. Late in his career, when his legs were bothering him and the Yankees had a comfortable lead in a pennant
(45) race, columnist Jimmy Cannon asked him why he played so hard—the games, after all, no longer meant so much. "Because there might be somebody out there who's never seen me play before," he answered.

Passage 2

(50) Athletes and actors—let actors stand for the set of performing artists—share much. They share the need to make gesture as fluid and economical as possible, to make out of a welter of choices the single, precisely right one. They share the need for
(55) thousands of hours of practice in order to train the body to become the perfect, instinctive instrument to express. Both athlete and actor, out of that abundance of emotion, choice, strategy, knowledge of the terrain, mood of spectators, condition of others
(60) in the ensemble, secret awareness of injury or weakness, and as nearly an absolute *concentration* as possible so that all externalities are integrated, all distraction absorbed to the self, must be able to change the self so successfully that it changes us.
(65) When either athlete or actor can bring all these skills to bear and focus them, then he or she will

achieve that state of complete intensity and complete relaxation—complete coherence or integrity
between what the performer wants to do and what
(70) the performer has to do. Then, the performer is free;
for then, all that has been learned, by thousands of
hours of practice and discipline and by repetition of
pattern, becomes natural. Then intellect is upgraded
to the level of an instinct. The body follows com-
(75) mands that precede thinking.

When athlete and artist achieve such self-
knowledge that they transform the self so that we
are re-created, it is finally an exercise in power.
The individual's power to dominate, on stage or
(80) field invests the whole arena around the locus of
performance with his or her power. We draw from
the performer's energy, just as we scrutinize the
performer's vulnerabilities, and we criticize as if
we were equals (we are not) what is displayed. This
(85) is why all performers dislike or resent the audience
as much as they need and enjoy it. Power flows in
a mysterious circuit from performer to spectator (I
assume a "live" performance) and back, and while
cheers or applause are the hoped-for outcome of
(90) performing, silence or gasps are the most desired,
for then the moment has occurred—then domination is complete, and as the performer triumphs, a
unity rare and inspiring results.

1. In Passage 1, Stengel is most impressed by DiMaggio's

   (A) indifference to potential dangers
   (B) tendency to overlook the bases in his haste
   (C) ability to focus on the variables
   (D) proficiency at fielding fly balls
   (E) overall swiftness and stamina

2. Stengel's comments in lines 7–15 serve chiefly to

   (A) point up the stupidity of the sort of error he
       condemns
   (B) suggest the inevitability of mistakes in running
       bases
   (C) show it is easier to spot problems than to come
       up with answers
   (D) answer the criticisms of DiMaggio's base running
   (E) modify his earlier position on DiMaggio's ability

3. By quoting Woodling's comment on DiMaggio's
   running (lines 26–28), the author most likely intends
   to emphasize

   (A) his teammates' envy of DiMaggio's natural gifts
   (B) how much exertion went into DiMaggio's moves
   (C) how important speed is to a baseball player
   (D) Woodling's awareness of his own slowness
   (E) how easily DiMaggio was able to cover territory

4. The phrase "a man wound tight" (line 39) means a man

   (A) wrapped in confining bandages
   (B) living in constricted quarters
   (C) under intense emotional pressure
   (D) who drank alcohol to excess
   (E) who could throw with great force

5. In the last paragraph of Passage 1, the author acknowl-
   edges which negative aspect of DiMaggio's heroic stature?

   (A) His overemphasis on physical grace
   (B) His emotional romanticism
   (C) The uniformity of his performance
   (D) The obligation to answer the questions of reporters
   (E) The burden of living up to his reputation

6. Which best describes what the author is doing in the
   parenthetical comment "let actors stand for the set
   of performing artists" (lines 50–51)?

   (A) Indicating that actors should rise out of respect
       for the arts
   (B) Defining the way in which he is using a particular
       term
   (C) Encouraging actors to show tolerance for their
       fellow artists
   (D) Emphasizing that actors are superior to other
       performing artists
   (E) Correcting a misinterpretation of the role of actors

7. The phrase "bring all these skills to bear" in lines
   65–66 is best taken to mean that the athlete

   (A) comes to endure these skills
   (B) carries the burden of his talent
   (C) applies these skills purposefully
   (D) causes himself to behave skillfully
   (E) influences himself to give birth to his skills

8. To the author of Passage 2, freedom for performers
   depends on

   (A) their subjection of the audience
   (B) their willingness to depart from tradition
   (C) the internalization of all they have learned
   (D) their ability to interpret material independently
   (E) the absence of injuries or other weaknesses

9. The author's attitude toward the concept of the equality
   of spectators and performers (lines 83–84) is one of

   (A) relative indifference
   (B) mild skepticism
   (C) explicit rejection
   (D) strong embarrassment
   (E) marked perplexity

10. Why, in lines 86–87, does the author of Passage 2
    assume a "live" performance?

    (A) His argument assumes a mutual involvement
        between performer and spectator that can only
        occur when both are present.
    (B) He believes that televised and filmed images give
        a false impression of the performer's ability to
        the spectators.
    (C) He fears the use of "instant replay" and other
        broadcasting techniques will cause performers
        to resent spectators even more strongly.
    (D) His argument dismisses the possibility of com-
        bining live performances with filmed segments.
    (E) He prefers audiences not to have time to reflect
        about the performance they have just seen.

11. The author of Passage 2 would most likely react to the characterization of DiMaggio presented in lines 41–49 by pointing out that DiMaggio probably

    (A) felt some resentment of the spectator whose good opinion he supposedly sought
    (B) never achieved the degree of self-knowledge that would have transformed him
    (C) was unaware that his audience was surveying his weak points
    (D) was a purely instinctive natural athlete
    (E) was seldom criticized by his peers

12. Which of the following attributes of the ideal athlete mentioned in Passage 2 is NOT illustrated by the anecdotes about DiMaggio in Passage 1?

    (A) knowledge of the terrain
    (B) secret awareness of injury or weakness
    (C) consciousness of the condition of other teammates
    (D) ability to make gestures fluid and economical
    (E) absolute powers of concentration

13. Which of the following statements is best supported by a comparison of the two excerpts?

    (A) Both excerpts focus on the development of a specific professional athlete.
    (B) The purpose of both excerpts is to compare athletes with performing artists.
    (C) The development of ideas in both excerpts is similar.
    (D) Both excerpts examine the nature of superior athletic performance.
    (E) Both excerpts discuss athletic performance primarily in abstract terms.

DOUBLE PASSAGE ANSWER KEY

1. **C**	5. **E**	9. **C**	13. **D**
2. **A**	6. **B**	10. **A**	
3. **B**	7. **C**	11. **A**	
4. **C**	8. **C**	12. **C**	

1. **C.** Stengel's concluding sentence indicates that DiMaggio watches "the one thing that is different on every play." In other words, DiMaggio *focuses on the variables*, the factors that change from play to play.

2. **A.** Stengel's sarcastic comments about the mistakes DiMaggio *doesn't* make indicate just how dumb he thinks it is to look down at the ground when you should have your attention on the outfielder and the ball. Clearly, if one of his players made such an error, Stengel's response would be to say, "What's the matter, stupid? Are you afraid you're going to fall in a canal down there?"

3. **B.** Note the context of the reference to Woodling. In the sentence immediately preceding, the author says that, if DiMaggio "appeared to play effortlessly, his teammates knew otherwise." The author then introduces a comment by Woodling, one of DiMaggio's teammates. Woodling knew a great deal of effort went into DiMaggio's playing: he describes how DiMaggio's feet pounded as he ran. Clearly, the force of DiMaggio's running is mentioned to illustrate *how much exertion went into DiMaggio's moves*.

4. **C.** Look at the sentences following this phrase. They indicate that DiMaggio was a man *under intense emotional pressure*, one who felt so much stress that he developed ulcers and had problems getting to sleep.

5. **E.** In the final paragraph, the author describes DiMaggio pushing himself to play hard despite his injuries. DiMaggio does so because he is trying to live up to the image his public has of him. He feels *the burden of living up to his reputation*.

6. **B.** At this point, the questions on Passage 2 begin. In this brief aside, the author is taking a moment away from his argument to make sure the reader knows exactly who the subjects of his comparison are. He wishes to use the word *actors* to stand for or *represent* all other performers. This way every time he makes his comparison between athletes and performers he won't have to list all the various sorts of performing artists (actors, dancers, singers, acrobats, clowns) who resemble athletes in their need for physical grace, extensive rehearsal, and total concentration. Thus, in his side comment, he is *defining* how he intends to use the word *actors* throughout the discussion.

7. **C.** The author has been describing the wide range of skills a performer utilizes in crafting an artistic or athletic performance. It is by taking these skills and *applying them purposefully* and with concentration to the task at hand that the performer achieves his or her goal.

8. **C.** Performers are free when all they have learned becomes so natural, so internalized, that it seems instinctive. In other words, freedom depends on *the internalization* of what they have learned.

9. **C.** The author bluntly states that we spectators are not the performers' equals. Thus, his attitude toward the concept is one of *explicit rejection*.

10. **A.** While a spectator may feel powerfully involved with a filmed or televised image of a performer, the filmed image is unaffected by the spectator's feelings. Thus, for power to "flow in a mysterious circuit" from performer to spectator *and back*, the assumption is that both performer and spectator *must be present* in the flesh.

11. A. Passage 1 indicates DiMaggio always played hard to live up to his reputation and to perform well for anyone in the stands who had never seen him play before. Clearly, he wanted the spectators to have a good opinion of him. Passage 2, however, presents a more complex picture of the relationship between the performer and his audience. On the one hand, the performer needs the audience, needs its good opinion and its applause. On the other hand, the performer also resents the audience, resents the way spectators freely point out his weaknesses and criticize his art. Thus, the author of Passage 2 might well point out that DiMaggio *felt some resentment* of the audience whom he hoped to impress with his skill.

12. C. Though DiMaggio's teammates clearly were aware of *his* condition (as the Woodling anecdote illustrates), none of the anecdotes in Passage 1 indicate or even imply that DiMaggio was specifically *conscious of his teammates' condition.* You can answer this question by using the process of elimination. In running bases, DiMaggio never lets himself be distracted by looking at the bases or down at the ground; as Stengel says, he knows where they are. Clearly, he *knows the terrain*. You can eliminate Choice A. When DiMaggio's legs are failing him late in his career, he still pushes himself to perform well for the fan in the stands who hasn't seen him play before. In doing so, he takes into account his *secret awareness* of his legs' weakness. You can eliminate Choice B. Gliding rather than running, always smooth, never wasting a glance on inessentials, DiMaggio clearly exhibits *fluidity and economy* in his movements. You can eliminate Choice D. Running bases, DiMaggio always keeps his eye on the ball and the outfielder; he *concentrates absolutely* on them. You can eliminate Choice E. Only Choice C is left. It is the correct answer.

13. D. Though one passage presents an abstract discussion of the nature of the ideal athlete and the other describes the achievements and character of a specific superior athlete, both passages *examine the nature of superior athletic performance.*

Long-Range Strategies

Are you a good reader? Do you read twenty-five or more books a year in addition to those books assigned in school? When you read light fiction, do you cover a page per minute? Do you read only light fiction, or have you begun to read "heavy" books—books on science, political theory, literary criticism, art? Do you browse regularly through magazines and newspapers?

Faced with the above questions, students frequently panic. Accustomed to gathering information from television and radio rather than from books, they don't know how to get back on the track. But getting back on the track is easier than they think.

Read, Read, Read!

Just do it.

There is no substitute for extensive reading as a preparation for SAT I and for college work. The only way to obtain proficiency in reading is by reading books of all kinds. As you read, you will develop speed, stamina, and the ability to comprehend the printed page. But if you want to turn yourself into the kind of reader the colleges are looking for, you must develop the habit of reading—every day.

25 Books a Year

Suppose you're an average reader; you read an ordinary book at about 300 words a minute. In 20 minutes, how many words can you read? Six thousand, right?

In a week of reading 20 minutes per day, how many words can you read? Seven days, 42,000 words.

Now get out your calculator. In 52 weeks of reading 20 minutes per day, how many words can you read? That's 52 times 42,000, a grand total of 2,184,000 words!

Now here comes the hard part. Full-length books usually contain 60,000 to 100,000 words. Say the average book runs about 75,000 words. If reading 20 minutes a day you can read 2,184,000 words in a year, how many average, 75,000-word books can you read in a year?

The answer is a little over 29. Twenty-nine books in a year. So don't panic at the thought of reading 25 books a year. Anybody can find twenty minutes a day, and if you can do that, you can read *more than* 25 books a year. The trick is always to have your book on hand, so that you don't have to waste time hunting around for it if you suddenly find yourself with some free time.

Schedule a set time for nonschool reading. Make the 20-minute-a-day plan part of your life.

Speed Up Your Reading

If you have trouble getting through a typical verbal section in 30 minutes, you may want to work on ways to build up your reading speed.

One thing you should be aware of is that to build speed you have to practice with easy materials. Most slow readers are used to reading everything—technical material, sports columns, comics—at one slow, careful speed. To build up speed, you have to get your eyes and brain accustomed to moving rapidly, and that means working with passages that are easy for you. Given sufficiently easy material, there are all sorts of techniques that you can try: you can draw a line down the middle of a newspaper column, for example, and then, focusing your eye on the line, try to get the meanings of the words on each side as you read straight down the column. It's a great exercise for your peripheral vision.

One major cause of slow reading is that sometimes you don't focus. Your eyes keep moving down the page, but your mind is out to lunch. Then bang! You wake up from your daydream and say, "Hey! What was I reading?" And your eyes jump back to an earlier spot on the page and you wind up rereading the whole thing.

Obviously, regressing, going back and rereading words or whole passages you've already supposedly read, slows you down. Regressing is a habit, but like any other habit, you can break it.

One way to reduce regressions is to preview a passage before you read it. A quick look at the introductory sentences of paragraphs, at titles and section headings, at words in italics and other key words, will give you an idea of what you're about to read. At that point, you have a sense of the material and you come to read the passage with some questions in mind—you read actively, not passively.

A second way to reduce regressions is to make it impossible to look back. Take a 3 × 5 card and use it like a shutter to cover what you've already read. That way you force yourself to keep going. You have to concentrate: you have no choice.

One last speed-reading technique you should be aware of is called clustering or phrase-reading. Have you ever watched somebody's eyes when he or she is busy reading? Do it sometime. You'll see the eyes move, then come to a stop, then dart back for a second, stop, then sweep forward again, stop, and so on. The stops last only for a fraction of a second, but they're important: it's only when the eyes stop that you actually read. In that fraction-of-a-second stop, or fixation, your eyes *fix* on a word. If you're skilled at clustering, however, in that one stop your eyes fix on not one, but a group of words. Clustering, phrase-reading, prevents word-by-word reading. It speeds you up where word-by-word reading slows you down.

Here's how to practice clustering. First, find something easy to read. Don't start out with SAT I tests. Divide up the passage into three or four word phrases. Next read it trying to see those three or four words in a single fixation. Then reread it at your normal speed to catch anything you've missed.

One final, crucial point: These pointers on how to build up your reading speed are long-range strategies. They are not specific tactics for how to go about dealing with the SAT I test you're going to face in the near future. SAT I is no time for you to try out new techniques that you've heard of but have yet to master.

Upgrade What You Read

Challenge yourself. Don't limit your reading to light fiction and biography as so many high school students do. Branch out a bit. Go beyond *People* magazine. Try to develop an interest in as many fields as you can. Sample some of the quality magazines: *The New Yorker, Smithsonian, Scientific American, National Geographic, Harper's, Newsweek, Time*. In these magazines, you'll find articles on literature, music, science, philosophy, history, the arts—the whole range of fields touched on by the SAT. If you take time to acquaint yourself with the contents of these magazines, you won't find the subject matter of the reading passages on the examination so strange.

Be sure to take a look at *Scientific American*. The SAT-makers used to use excerpts from *Scientific American* articles regularly on their tests. Now, however, the new SAT I has cut down on excessively technical, dry reading passages. Most science passages on SAT I will be easier to read than the average *Scientific American* article you face. Don't feel you have to read entire articles: if you can make sense out of the first page or two of an article, you're doing fine; you're reading to get acquainted with the subject matter, not to master every experimental detail.

Read good newspapers, too. *The Washington Post, The Christian Science Monitor, The New York Times*—these and other major papers offer excellent coverage of the arts and sciences as well as current events.

Reader's Guide to SAT I

The reading passages you will face on SAT I are excerpts from the sorts of books your college instructors will assign you in your freshman and sophomore years. You can get a head start on college (and on SAT I) by beginning to read college-level material now—today.

The following reading list is divided into seven sections:

1. Fiction
2. Personal Narrative
3. Ethnic (autobiography, biography, art, music, history)
4. Literary Criticism
5. Humanities (art, music, drama, dance)
6. Science (biology, chemistry, physics, mathematics, geology, astronomy)
7. Social Sciences (history, political science, archaeology, sociology)

A number of the subjects on this list have been the source of passages on published SATs.

Follow these steps in working through the list. Choose material from areas with which you feel unfamiliar. Do not worry if the first book you tackle seems difficult to you. Try working your way through a short section—the first chapter should be enough to give you a sense of what the author has to say. *Remember that this is college-level material*: it is bound to be challenging to you; be glad you're getting a chance at it so soon.

If you get stuck, work your way up to the level of the book, taking it step by step. If Edith Wharton's novel *The Age of Innocence* seems hard, try reading it after you've seen the award-winning movie of the same name. If an article in the Scientific American book *The Brain* seems hard, try reading it after you've read Isaac Asimov's popular *The Human Brain*. Get introductory books on your subject from the high school library or from the Young Adults section of the local public library. There isn't one of these books that's beyond you; you just need to fill in some background first.

(Note that books marked with an asterisk [*] have been the sources for reading passages used in published SAT tests; books marked M or TV have been made into excellent motion pictures or television shows.)

Fiction

James Agee, *A Death in the Family*
Kingsley Amis, *Lucky Jim* (M)
Jane Austen, *Emma* (M)
   Lady Susan
   Pride and Prejudice (M) *
James Baldwin, *Go Tell It on the Mountain* (TV)
Charlotte Bronte, *Jane Eyre* (M)
   Villette
Joseph Conrad, *The Heart of Darkness*
Stephen Crane, "The Open Boat" *
Charles Dickens, *Barnaby Rudge* *
   Great Expectations (M)
   Little Dorritt (TV) *
   Nicholas Nickelby (TV)
   Our Mutual Friend *
Margaret Drabble, *A Summer Bird-Cage*
George Eliot, *Middlemarch* *
Ralph Ellison, *The Invisible Man* (M)
William Faulkner, *Collected Stories of William Faulkner*
   Intruder in the Dust (M)
   Sartoris
F. Scott Fitzgerald, *Babylon Revisited*
   The Great Gatsby (M)
E.M. Forster, *A Room with a View* (M)
Elizabeth Gaskell, *Cranford*
   Sylvia's Lovers *
William Golding, *Lord of the Flies* (M)
Graham Greene, *The Heart of the Matter* * (M)
   Our Man in Havana (M)
   The Power and the Glory
   The Third Man (M)
Thomas Hardy, *Far from the Madding Crowd* (M)
   Jude the Obscure
Ernest Hemingway, *A Farewell to Arms* (M)
   For Whom the Bell Tolls (M)
   The Nick Adams Stories, "The Last Good Country" *
   The Sun Also Rises (M)
Wm. Dean Howells, *A Modern Instance* *
Henry James, *The American* *
   Daisy Miller
   The Portrait of a Lady *
   The Turn of the Screw
   Washington Square *
James Joyce, *Dubliners*, "Araby" *
Arthur Koestler, *Darkness at Noon*
D.H. Lawrence, *Sons and Lovers* (M)
   Women in Love (M)

C.S. Lewis, *The Screwtape Letters*
Herman Melville, *Billy Budd* (M)
   Moby Dick (M)
George Orwell, *Animal Farm* (M)
   1984 (M)
William Makepeace Thackeray, *Vanity Fair* (TV)
Anthony Trollope, *Barchester Towers* (TV)
   The Warden (TV)
Mark Twain, *The Adventures of Huckleberry Finn* (M, TV)
   "The Man That Corrupted Hadleyburg" *
Robert Penn Warren, *All the King's Men* (M)
Evelyn Waugh, *Brideshead Revisited* (TV)
   Men at Arms
Mary Webb, *The House in Dormer Forest* *
Edith Wharton, *The Age of Innocence* (M) *
   The House of Mirth *
Virginia Woolf, *Orlando* (M)
   To the Lighthouse

Personal Narrative

Elizabeth Bishop, *Efforts of Affection: A Memoir of*
   Marianne Moore *
Pablo Casals, *Joys and Sorrows*
M.F.K. Fisher, *As They Were*
Janet Flanner, *Paris Journal/1944–1965*
Gail Godwin, "My Face" *
Robert Graves, *Goodbye to All That*
Lillian Hellman, *An Unfinished Life*
C.S. Lewis, *A Grief Observed* (TV)
Mary McCarthy, *Memories of a Catholic Girlhood* *
   How I Grew
George Orwell, *Such, Such Were the Joys*
Arthur Rubinstein, *My Young Years*
Gertrude Stein, *The Autobiography of Alice B. Toklas*
Gloria Steinem, *Outrageous Acts and Everyday Rebellions*

Ethnic

Maya Angelou, *I Know Why the Caged Bird Sings* (TV)
   The Heart of a Woman
   "Shades and Slashes of Light" in *Black Women Writers* *
James Baldwin, *The Fire Next Time*
   Nobody Knows My Name
   No Name in the Street
Vine Deloria, *Custer Died for Your Sins*
Frederick Douglass, *Narrative of the Life of an*
   American Slave
W.E.B. DuBois, *The Souls of Black Folk*
Ralph Ellison, *Going to the Territory*
John Hope Franklin, *From Slavery to Freedom*
Jamake Highwater, *Songs from the Earth: American*
   Indian Painting
   Words in the Blood: Contemporary Indian Writers
Nathan I. Huggins, *Black Odyssey*
   Harlem Renaissance
   Slave and Citizen: The Life of Frederick Douglass
Leroi Jones, *Blues People* (music)
Maxine Hong Kingston, *China Men*
   The Woman Warrior
Samella Lewis, *Art: African American*
H. Brett Melendy, *Asians in America*
William Peterson, *Japanese Americans*

Alan Riding, *Our Distant Neighbors*
Richard Rodriguez, *The Hunger of Memory* *
Lesley Byrd Simpson, *Many Mexicans*
Eileen Southern, *Music of Black Americans*
Stan Steiner, *La Raza: The Mexican Americans*
Wilcomb E. Washburn, *The Indian in America*
Richard Wright, *American Hunger* *
    Black Boy

Literary Criticism

Marchette Chute, *Geoffrey Chaucer of England*
John Ciardi, *How Does a Poem Mean*
E.M. Forster, *Aspects of the Novel*
Arnold Kettle, *An Introduction to the English Novel**
D.H. Lawrence, *Studies in Classic American Literature*
J.R.R. Tolkien, "*Beowulf, the Monsters, & the Critics*"*
Dorothy Van Ghent, *The English Novel*
Virginia Woolf, *The Second Common Reader*

Humanities

Sally Barnes, *Terpsichore in Sneakers* (dance)
Bruno Bettelheim, *The Uses of Enchantment*
Kenneth Clark, *Civilization* (TV)*
Marcia Davenport, *Mozart*
John Gassner, *Masters of the Drama*
Harley Granville-Barker, *Prefaces to Shakespeare*
S. I. Hayakawa, *Language in Thought and Action* *
Joseph Kerman, *Contemplating Music*
Beaumont Newhall, *The History of Photography*
Marcia B. Siegal, *The Shapes of Change* (dance)
C.P. Snow, *The Two Cultures*
Walter Sorell, *Dance in its Time*

Science

Isaac Asimov, *The Human Body*
    The Human Brain
Eric T. Bell, *The Development of Mathematics*
Jeremy Bernstein, *Experiencing Science*
    Science Observed
Jacob Bronowski, *The Ascent of Man*
N.P. Davis, *Lawrence and Oppenheimer*
Adrian Desmond, *The Hot-Blooded Dinosaurs*
Gerald Durrell, *My Family and Other Animals*
    Fauna and Family

Richard Feynman, *Surely You're Joking, Mr. Feynman*
Karl von Frisch, *Animal Architecture*
George Gamow, *Mr. Tompkins* (series)
    One, Two, Three...Infinity
Jane Goodall, *In the Shadow of Man*
Stephen Jay Gould, *Ever Since Darwin*
Arthur Koestler, *The Case of the Midwife Toad*
Aldo Leopold, *Sand County Almanac*
Konrad Lorenz, *King Solomon's Ring*
    On Aggression
Jonathan Miller, *The Body in Question*
Scientific American Books,   *The Biosphere*
    The Brain
    Energy and Power
    Evolution
    *The Ocean**
    The Solar System
    *Volcanoes and the Earth's Interior**
James Watson, *The Double Helix*
Gary Zukav, *The Dancing Wu Li Masters*

Social Sciences

Frederick Lewis Allen, *Only Yesterday*
Corelli Barnet, *The Desert Generals*
    The Sword Bearers
Peter Berger, *Invitation to Sociology*
Fritjof Capra, *The Turning Point*
Vincent Cronin, *Napoleon*
Will and Ariel Durant, *The Story of Civilization*
Einhard and Notken the Stammerer, *Two Lives of*
    Charlemagne
J. Huizinga, *The Waning of the Middle Ages*
Joseph P. Lash, *Eleanor and Franklin* (TV)
Joe McGinniss, *The Selling of the President, 1968*
Paul MacKendrick, *The Mute Stones Speak*
Nancy Mitford, *Frederick the Great*
Johannes Nohl, *The Black Death*
Eileen Power, *Medieval People*
Diane Ravitch, *The Democracy Reader* *
Josephine Tey, *The Daughter of Time*
Barbara Tuchman, *A Distant Mirror*
    The Guns of August (M)
T.H. White, *The Making of the President* (series)
Edmund Wilson, *To the Finland Station*
Michael Wood, *In Search of the Trojan War* (TV)

Practice Exercises

On the following pages you will find four reading exercises. Allow about 30 minutes for each group. The correct answers, as well as answer explanations, are given at the end of the chapter. Practice the testing tactics you have learned as you work. Your reading score will improve.

Exercise A

Each of the following passages comes from a novel or short story collection that has provided reading passages on prior SATs. Use this exercise to acquaint yourself with the sort of fiction you will confront on the test and to practice answering critical reading questions based on literature.

The following passage is taken from Great Expectations *by Charles Dickens. In it, the hero, Pip, recollects a dismal period in his youth during which he for a time lost hope of ever bettering his fortunes.*

It is a most miserable thing to feel ashamed of home. There may be black ingratitude in the thing, and the punishment may be retributive and well
Line deserved; but, that it is a miserable thing, I can
(5) testify. Home had never been a very pleasant place to me, because of my sister's temper. But Joe had sanctified it and I believed in it. I had believed in the best parlor as a most elegant salon; I had believed in the front door as a mysterious portal of the Temple
(10) of State whose solemn opening was attended with a sacrifice of roast fowls; I had believed in the kitchen as a chaste though not magnificent apartment; I had believed in the forge as the glowing road to manhood. Now, it was all coarse and com-
(15) mon, and I would not have had Miss Havisham and Estella see it on any account.

Once, it had seemed to me that when I should at last roll up my shirt sleeves and go into the forge, Joe's 'prentice, I should be distinguished and happy.
(20) Now the reality was in my hold, I only felt that I was dusty with the dust of small coal, and that I had a weight upon my daily remembrance to which the anvil was a feather. There have been occasions in my later life (I suppose as in most lives) when I have
(25) felt for a time as if a thick curtain had fallen on all its interest and romance, to shut me out from any thing save dull endurance any more. Never has that curtain dropped so heavy and blank, as when my way in life lay stretched out straight before me through
(30) the newly-entered road of apprenticeship to Joe.

I remember that at a later period of my "time," I used to stand about the churchyard on Sunday evenings, when night was falling, comparing my own perspective with the windy marsh view, and
(35) making out some likeness between them by thinking how flat and low both were, and how on both there came an unknown way and a dark mist and then the sea. I was quite as dejected on the first working-day of my apprenticeship as in that after
(40) time; but I am glad to know that I never breathed a murmur to Joe while my indentures lasted. It is about the only thing I *am* glad to know of myself in that connection.

For, though it includes what I proceed to add,
(45) all the merit of what I proceed to add was Joe's. It was not because I was faithful, but because Joe was faithful, that I never ran away and went for a soldier or a sailor. It was not because I had a strong sense of the virtue of industry, but because
(50) Joe had a strong sense of the virtue of industry, that I worked with tolerable zeal against the grain. It is not possible to know how far the influence of any amiable honest-hearted duty-going man flies out into the world; but it is very possible to know
(55) how it has touched one's self in going by, and I know right well that any good that intermixed itself

with my apprenticeship came of plain contented Joe, and not of restless aspiring discontented me.

1. The passage as a whole is best described as
   (A) an analysis of the reasons behind a change in attitude
   (B) an account of a young man's reflections on his emotional state
   (C) a description of a young man's awakening to the harsh conditions of working class life
   (D) a defense of a young man's longings for romance and glamour
   (E) a criticism of young people's ingratitude to their elders

2. It may be inferred from the passage that the young man has been apprenticed to a
   (A) cook
   (B) forger
   (C) coal miner
   (D) blacksmith
   (E) grave digger

3. In the passage, Joe is portrayed most specifically as
   (A) distinguished
   (B) virtuous
   (C) independent
   (D) homely
   (E) coarse

4. The passage suggests that the narrator's increasing discontent with his home during his apprenticeship was caused by
   (A) a new awareness on his part of how his home would appear to others
   (B) the increasing heaviness of the labor involved
   (C) the unwillingness of Joe to curb his sister's temper
   (D) the narrator's lack of an industrious character
   (E) a combination of simple ingratitude and sinfulness

5. According to the passage, the narrator gives himself a measure of credit for
   (A) working diligently despite his unhappiness
   (B) abandoning his hope of a military career
   (C) keeping his menial position secret from Miss Havisham
   (D) concealing his despondency from Joe
   (E) surrendering his childish beliefs

The following passage is excerpted from the short story "Clay" in Dubliners *by James Joyce. In this passage, tiny, unmarried Maria oversees tea for the washerwomen, all the while thinking of the treat in store for her: a night off.*

The matron had given her leave to go out as soon as the women's tea was over and Maria looked forward to her evening out. The kitchen was spick
Line and span: the cook said you could see yourself in
(5) the big copper boilers. The fire was nice and bright

and on one of the side-tables were four very big barmbracks. These barmbracks seemed uncut; but if you went closer you would see that they had been cut into long thick even slices and were ready
(10) to be handed round at tea. Maria had cut them herself.

Maria was a very, very small person indeed but she had a very long nose and a very long chin. She talked a little through her nose, always soothingly: "*Yes, my dear,*" and "*No, my dear.*" She was always
(15) sent for when the women quarrelled over their tubs and always succeeded in making peace. One day the matron had said to her:

"Maria, you are a veritable peace-maker!"

And the sub-matron and two of the Board ladies
(20) had heard the compliment. And Ginger Mooney was always saying what she wouldn't do to the dummy who had charge of the irons if it wasn't for Maria. Everyone was so fond of Maria.

When the cook told her everything was ready,
(25) she went into the women's room and began to pull the big bell. In a few minutes the women began to come in by twos and threes, wiping their steaming hands in their petticoats and pulling down the sleeves of their blouses over their red steaming
(30) arms. They settled down before their huge mugs which the cook and the dummy filled up with hot tea, already mixed with milk and sugar in huge tin cans. Maria superintended the distribution of the barmbrack and saw that every woman got her four
(35) slices. There was a great deal of laughing and joking during the meal. Lizzie Fleming said Maria was sure to get the ring and, though Fleming had said that for so many Hallow Eves, Maria had to laugh and say she didn't want any ring or man either; and
(40) when she laughed her grey-green eyes sparkled with disappointed shyness and the tip of her nose nearly met the tip of her chin. Then Ginger Mooney lifted her mug of tea and proposed Maria's health while all the other women clattered with their mugs on
(45) the table, and said she was sorry she hadn't a sup of porter to drink it in. And Maria laughed again till the tip of her nose nearly met the tip of her chin and till her minute body nearly shook itself asunder because she knew that Mooney meant well though,
(50) of course, she had the notions of a common woman.

6. The author's primary purpose in the second paragraph is to

(A) introduce the character of a spinster
(B) describe working conditions in a public institution
(C) compare two women of different social classes
(D) illustrate the value of peace-makers in society
(E) create suspense about Maria's fate

7. The language of the passage most resembles the language of

(A) a mystery novel
(B) an epic
(C) a fairy tale
(D) institutional board reports
(E) a sermon

8. It can be inferred from the passage that Maria would most likely view the matron as which of the following?

(A) A political figurehead
(B) An inept administrator
(C) A demanding taskmaster
(D) An intimate friend
(E) A benevolent superior

9. We may infer from the care with which Maria has cut the barmbracks (lines 7–10) that

(A) she fears the matron
(B) she is in a hurry to leave
(C) she expects the Board members for tea
(D) it is a dangerous task
(E) she takes pride in her work

10. It can be inferred from the passage that all the following are characteristic of Maria EXCEPT

(A) a deferential nature
(B) eagerness for compliments
(C) respect for authority
(D) dreams of matrimony
(E) reluctance to compromise

The following passage is taken from Jane Austen's novel Mansfield Park. *This excerpt presents Sir Thomas Bertram, owner of Mansfield Park, who has just joined the members of his family.*

Sir Thomas was indeed the life of the party, who at his suggestion now seated themselves round the fire. He had the best right to be the talker; and the
Line delight of his sensations in being again in his own
(5) house, in the center of his family, after such a separation, made him communicative and chatty in a very unusual degree; and he was ready to answer every question of his two sons almost before it was put. All the little particulars of his proceedings and
(10) events, his arrivals and departures, were most promptly delivered, as he sat by Lady Bertram and looked with heartfelt satisfaction at the faces around him—interrupting himself more than once, however, to remark on his good fortune in finding
(15) them all at home—coming unexpectedly as he did —all collected together exactly as he could have wished, but dared not depend on.

By not one of the circle was he listened to with such unbroken unalloyed enjoyment as by his wife,
(20) whose feelings were so warmed by his sudden arrival, as to place her nearer agitation than she had been for the last twenty years. She had been *almost* fluttered for a few minutes, and still remained so sensibly animated as to put away her work, move
(25) Pug from her side, and give all her attention and all the rest of her sofa to her husband. She had no anxieties for anybody to cloud *her* pleasure; her own time had been irreproachably spent during his absence; she had done a great deal of carpet work
(30) and made many yards of fringe; and she would have

answered as freely for the good conduct and useful
pursuits of all the young people as for her own. It
was so agreeable to her to see him again, and hear
him talk, to have her ear amused and her whole
(35)   comprehension filled by his narratives, that she
began particularly to feel how dreadfully she must
have missed him, and how impossible it would have
been for her to bear a lengthened absence.

Mrs. Norris was by no means to be compared in
(40)   happiness to her sister. Not that *she* was incommod-
ed by many fears of Sir Thomas's disapprobation
when the present state of his house should be known,
for her judgment had been so blinded, that she could
hardly be said to show any sign of alarm; but she
(45)   was vexed by the *manner* of his return. It had left
her nothing to do. Instead of being sent for out of
the room, and seeing him first, and having to spread
the happy news through the house, Sir Thomas,
with a very reasonable dependence perhaps on the
(50)   nerves of his wife and children, had sought no confidant but the butler, and had been following him
almost instantaneously into the drawing-room. Mrs.
Norris felt herself defrauded of an office on which
she had always depended, whether his arrival or
(55)   his death were to be the thing unfolded; and was
now trying to be in a bustle without having any
thing to bustle about. Would Sir Thomas have con-
sented to eat, she might have gone to the housekeeper with troublesome directions; but Sir Thomas
(60)   resolutely declined all dinner; he would take nothing,
nothing till tea came—he would rather wait for tea.
Still Mrs. Norris was at intervals urging something
different; and in the most interesting moment of
his passage to England, when the alarm of a French
(65)   privateer was at the height, she burst through his
recital with the proposal of soup. "Sure, my dear
Sir Thomas, a basin of soup would be a much better
thing for you than tea. Do have a basin of soup."

Sir Thomas could not be provoked. "Still the
(70)   same anxiety for everybody's comfort, my dear
Mrs. Norris," was his answer. "But indeed I would
rather have nothing but tea."

11. We can infer from the opening paragraph that Sir
Thomas is customarily

(A) unwelcome at home
(B) tardy in business affairs
(C) dissatisfied with life
(D) more restrained in speech
(E) lacking in family feeling

12. The passage suggests that Sir Thomas's sudden
arrival

(A) was motivated by concern for his wife
(B) came as no surprise to Lady Bertram
(C) was timed by him to coincide with a family
reunion
(D) was expected by the servants
(E) was received with mixed emotions

13. Which of the following titles best describes the passage?

(A) An Unexpected Return
(B) The Conversation of the Upper Class
(C) Mrs. Norris's Grievance
(D) A Romantic Reunion
(E) An Account of a Voyage Abroad

14. The author's tone in her description of Lady
Bertram's sensations (lines 20–26) is

(A) markedly scornful
(B) mildly bitter
(C) gently ironic
(D) manifestly indifferent
(E) warmly sympathetic

15. By stressing that Lady Bertram "had no anxieties
for anybody to cloud *her* pleasure" (lines 26–27),
the author primarily intends to imply that

(A) Lady Bertram was hardhearted in ignoring the
sufferings of others
(B) it was unusual for Lady Bertram to be so
unconcerned
(C) others in the company had reason to be anxious
(D) Sir Thomas expected his wife to be pleased to
see him
(E) Lady Bertram lived only for pleasure

16. Sir Thomas's attitude toward Mrs. Norris can best
be described as one of

(A) sharp irritation
(B) patient forbearance
(C) solemn disapproval
(D) unreasoned alarm
(E) unmixed delight

17. The office of which Mrs. Norris feels herself
defrauded is most likely that of

(A) butler
(B) housekeeper
(C) wife
(D) world traveler
(E) message-bearer

---

*The following passage is taken from Edith Wharton's
novel,* The Age of Innocence. *In this excerpt, the
American hero has an unexpected encounter during the
course of a visit to the Louvre Museum in Paris.*

Newman promised himself to pay Mademoiselle
Noemie another visit at the Louvre. He was curious
about the progress of his copies, but it must be added
Line   that he was still more curious about the progress
(5)   of the young lady herself. He went one afternoon
to the great museum, and wandered through several
of the rooms in fruitless quest of her. He was bending his steps to the long hall of the Italian masters,
when suddenly he found himself face to face with
(10)   Valentin de Bellegarde. The young Frenchman

greeted him with ardor, and assured him that he was
a godsend. He himself was in the worst of humors
and he wanted someone to contradict.

"In a bad humor among all these beautiful things?"
(15) said Newman "I thought you were so fond of pictures, especially the old black ones. There are two
or three here that ought to keep you in spirits."

"Oh, today," answered Valentin, "I am not in a
mood for pictures, and the more beautiful they are
(20) the less I like them. Their great staring eyes and
fixed positions irritate me. I feel as if I were at some
big, dull party, in a room full of people I shouldn't
wish to speak to. What should I care for their beauty?
It's a bore, and, worse still, it's a reproach. I have
(25) a great many *ennuis*; I feel vicious."

"If the Louvre has so little comfort for you, why
in the world did you come here?" Newman asked.

"That is one of my *ennuis*. I came to meet my
cousin—a dreadful English cousin, a member of my
(30) mother's family—who is in Paris for a week with
her husband, and who wishes me to point out the
'principal beauties.' Imagine a woman who wears
a green crepe bonnet in December and has straps
sticking out of the ankles of her interminable boots!
(35) My mother begged I would do something to oblige
them. I have undertaken to play *valet de place* this
afternoon. They were to have met me here at two
o'clock, and I have been waiting for them twenty
minutes. Why doesn't she arrive? She has at least
(40) a pair of feet to carry her. I don't know whether to
be furious at their playing me false, or delighted to
have escaped them."

"I think in your place I would be furious," said
Newman, "because they may arrive yet, and then
(45) your fury will still be of use to you. Whereas if you
were delighted and they were afterwards to turn up,
you might not know what to do with your delight."

"You give me excellent advice, and I already
feel better. I will be furious; I will let them go to

(50) the deuce and I myself will go with you—unless
by chance you too have a rendezvous."

18. The passage indicates that Newman has gone to the
Louvre in order to
(A) meet Valentin
(B) look at the paintings
(C) explore Paris
(D) keep an appointment
(E) see Mademoiselle Noemie

19. According to the passage, Valentin is unhappy
about being at the Louvre because he
(A) hates the paintings of the Italian masters
(B) has accidentally met Newman in the long hall
(C) wishes to be at a party
(D) feels that beauty should be that of nature
(E) is supposed to guide his cousin through it

20. It can be inferred from the passage that in lines
32–39 Valentin is expressing his annoyance by
(A) walking out of the Louvre in a fit of temper
(B) making insulting remarks about a woman
(C) not accepting Newman's advice
(D) criticizing the paintings
(E) refusing to do as his mother wishes

21. With which of the following statements would
Valentin most likely agree?
   I. Clothes make the man.
  II. Blood is thicker than water.
 III. Better late than never.
(A) I only   (B) II only   (C) III only
   (D) I and II only   (E) I, II, and III

22. Newman's role in the conversation is that of
(A) a heckler   (B) a gossiper   (C) a confidant
   (D) an enemy   (E) a doubter

Exercise B

This exercise provides you with a mixture of reading passages similar in variety to what you will encounter on
the SAT I. Answer all questions on the basis of what is <u>stated</u> or <u>implied</u> in the passages.

The best Eskimo carvings of all ages seem to
possess a powerful ability to reach across the great
barriers of language and time and communicate
Line directly with us. The more we look at these carvings,
(5) the more life we perceive hidden within them. We
discover subtle living forms of the animal, human,
and mystical world. These arctic carvings are not
the cold sculptures of a frozen world. Instead, they
reveal to us the passionate feelings of a vital people
(10) well aware of all the joys, terrors, tranquility, and
wildness of life around them.

Eskimo carvers are people moved by dreams. In
spite of all their new contacts with the outsiders, they
are still concerned with their own kind of mystical
(15) imagery. The most skillful carvers possess a bold

confidence, a direct approach to their art that has a
freedom unsullied by any kind of formalized training.
Eskimo carvers have strong, skilled hands, used to
forcing hard materials with their simple tools. Their
(20) hunting life and the northern environment invigorates
them. Bad weather often imposes a special kind of
leisure, giving them time in which to perfect their
carvings.

They are among the last of the hunting societies
(25) that have retained some part of the keen sense of
observation that we have so long forgotten. The
carvers are also butchers of meat, and therefore
masters in the understanding of animal anatomy.
Flesh and bones and sheaths of muscle seem to move
(30) in their works. They show us how to drive the

caribou, how to hold a child, how to walk cautiously
on thin ice. Through their eyes we understand the
dangerous power of a polar bear. In the very best
of Eskimo art we see vibrant animal and human

(35) forms that stand quietly or tensely, strongly radiating
a sense of life. We can see, and even feel with our
hands, the cold sleekness of seals, the hulking weight
of walrus, the icy swiftness of trout, the flowing
rhythm in a flight of geese. In their art we catch

(40) brief glimpses of a people who have long possessed
a very different approach to the whole question of
life and death.

In Eskimo art there is much evidence of humor
which the carvers have in abundance. Some of the

(45) carvings are caricatures of themselves, of ourselves,
and of situations, or records of ancient legends. Their
laughter may be subtle, or broad and Chaucerian.

Perhaps no one can accurately define the right
way or wrong way to create a carving. Each carver

(50) must follow his own way, in his own time. Technique in itself is meaningless unless it serves to
express content. According to the Eskimo, the best
carvings possess a sense of movement that seems
to come from within the material itself, a feeling

(55) of tension, a living excitement.

1. The author is primarily concerned with
   (A) showing how Eskimo carvings achieve their
       effects
   (B) describing how Eskimo artists resist the
       influence of outsiders
   (C) discussing the significant characteristics of
       Eskimo art
   (D) explaining how Eskimo carvers use their
       strength to manipulate hard materials
   (E) interpreting the symbolism of Eskimo art

2. The author's attitude toward Eskimo art is one of
   (A) condescension (B) awe (C) admiration
   (D) regret (E) bewilderment

3. With which of the following statements would the
   author most likely agree?
   (A) Formal training may often destroy an artist's
       originality.
   (B) Artists should learn their craft by studying the
       work of experts.
   (C) The content of a work of art is insignificant.
   (D) Caricatures have no place in serious art.
   (E) Eskimo art is interesting more as an expression
       of a life view than as a serious art form.

4. The author gives examples of the subjects of
   Eskimo carvings primarily to
   (A) show that they have no relevance to modern life
   (B) indicate the artist's lack of imagination
   (C) imply that other artists have imitated them
   (D) prove that the artists' limited experience of life
       has been a handicap
   (E) suggest the quality and variety of the work

5. According to the passage, Eskimo carvings have all
   the following EXCEPT
   (A) wit (B) subtlety (C) emotional depth
   (D) stylistic uniformity (E) anatomical accuracy

Charlotte Stanhope was at this time about thirty-
five years old; and, whatever may have been her
faults, she had none of those which belong to old

Line young ladies. She neither dressed young, nor talked
(5) young, nor indeed looked young. She appeared to
be perfectly content with her time of life, and in no
way affected the graces of youth. She was a fine
young woman; and had she been a man, would have
been a fine young man. All that was done in the

(10) house, and was not done by servants, was done by
her. She gave the orders, paid the bills, hired and
dismissed the domestics, made the tea, carved the
meat, and managed everything in the Stanhope
household. She, and she alone, could ever induce her

(15) father to look into the state of his worldly concerns.
She, and she alone, could in any degree control the
absurdities of her sister. She, and she alone, prevented
the whole family from falling into utter disrepute and
beggary. It was by her advice that they now found

(20) themselves very unpleasantly situated in Barchester.
So far, the character of Charlotte Stanhope is not
unprepossessing. But it remains to be said, that the
influence which she had in her family, though it had
been used to a certain extent for their worldly well-

(25) being, had not been used to their real benefit, as it
might have been. She had aided her father in his
indifference to his professional duties, counselling
him that his livings were as much his individual
property as the estates of his elder brother were the

(30) property of that worthy peer. She had for years past
stifled every little rising wish for a return to England
which the reverend doctor had from time to time
expressed. She had encouraged her mother in her
idleness in order that she herself might be mistress

(35) and manager of the Stanhope household. She had
encouraged and fostered the follies of her sister,
though she was always willing, and often able, to
protect her from their probable result. She had done
her best, and had thoroughly succeeded in spoiling

(40) her brother, and turning him loose upon the world
an idle man without a profession, and without a
shilling that he could call his own.
Miss Stanhope was a clever woman, able to talk
on most subjects, and quite indifferent as to what

(45) the subject was. She prided herself on her freedom
from English prejudice, and she might have added,
from feminine delicacy. On religion she was a pure
freethinker, and with much want of true affection,
delighted to throw out her own views before the

(50) troubled mind of her father. To have shaken what
remained of his Church of England faith would have
gratified her much; but the idea of his abandoning
his preferment in the church had never once presented itself to her mind. How could he indeed, when

(55) he had no income from any other source?

6. The passage as a whole is best characterized as

   (A) a description of the members of a family
   (B) a portrait of a young woman's moral and intellectual temperament
   (C) an illustration of the evils of egotism
   (D) an analysis of family dynamics in aristocratic society
   (E) a contrast between a virtuous daughter and her disreputable family

7. The tone of the passage is best described as

   (A) self-righteous and moralistic
   (B) satirical and candid
   (C) sympathetic and sentimental
   (D) bitter and disillusioned
   (E) indifferent and unfeeling

8. On the basis of the passage, which of the following statements about Dr. Stanhope can most logically be made?

   (A) He is even more indolent than his wife.
   (B) He resents having surrendered his authority to his daughter.
   (C) He feels remorse for his professional misconduct.
   (D) He has little left of his initial religious beliefs.
   (E) He has disinherited his son without a shilling.

9. It can be inferred from the passage that Charlotte's mother (lines 33–35) is which of the following?

   I. An affectionate wife and mother
   II. A model of the domestic arts
   III. A woman of unassertive character

   (A) I only
   (B) II only
   (C) III only
   (D) I and III only
   (E) II and III only

10. The passage suggests that Charlotte possesses all of the following characteristics EXCEPT

   (A) an inappropriate flirtatiousness
   (B) a lack of reverence
   (C) a materialistic nature
   (D) a managing disposition
   (E) a touch of coarseness

The following passage on the nature of the surface of the earth is taken from a basic geology text.

Of the 197 million square miles making up the surface of the globe, 71 percent is covered by inter-connecting bodies of marine water; the Pacific Ocean
Line alone covers half the earth and averages near 14,000
(5) feet in depth. The *continents*—Eurasia, Africa, North America, South America, Australia, and Antarctica —are the portions of the *continental masses* rising above sea level. The submerged borders of the continental masses are the *continental shelves,* beyond
(10) which lie the deep-sea basins.

The oceans attain their greatest depths not in their central parts, but in certain elongated furrows, or long narrow troughs, called *deeps*. These profound troughs have a peripheral arrangement,
(15) notably around the borders of the Pacific and Indian oceans. The position of the deeps near the continental masses suggests that the deeps, like the highest mountains, are of recent origin, since otherwise they would have been filled with waste from the
(20) lands. This suggestion is strengthened by the fact that the deeps are frequently the sites of world-shaking earthquakes. For example, the "tidal wave" that in April, 1946, caused widespread destruction along Pacific coasts resulted from a strong earth-
(25) quake on the floor of the Aleutian Deep.

The topography of the ocean floors is none too well known, since in great areas the available soundings are hundreds or even thousands of miles apart. However, the floor of the Atlantic is becoming fairly
(30) well known as a result of special surveys since 1920. A broad, well-defined ridge—the mid-Atlantic ridge—runs north and south between Africa and the two Americas, and numerous other major irregularities diversify the Atlantic floor. Closely spaced
(35) soundings show that many parts of the oceanic floors are as rugged as mountainous regions of the continents. Use of the recently perfected method of echo sounding is rapidly enlarging our knowledge of submarine topography. During World War II great
(40) strides were made in mapping submarine surfaces, particularly in many parts of the vast Pacific basin.

The continents stand on the average 2870 feet—slightly more than half a mile—above sea level. North America averages 2300 feet; Europe averages
(45) only 1150 feet; and Asia, the highest of the larger continental subdivisions, averages 3200 feet. The highest point on the globe, Mount Everest in the Himalayas, is 29,000 feet above the sea; and as the greatest known depth in the sea is over 35,000 feet,
(50) the maximum *relief* (that is, the difference in altitude between the lowest and highest points) exceeds 64,000 feet, or exceeds 12 miles. The continental masses and the deep-sea basins are relief features of the first order; the deeps, ridges, and volcanic
(55) cones that diversify the sea floor, as well as the plains, plateaus, and mountains of the continents, are relief features of the second order. The lands are unendingly subject to a complex of activities summarized in the term *erosion*, which first sculp-
(60) tures them in great detail and then tends to reduce them ultimately to sealevel. The modeling of the landscape by weather, running water, and other agents is apparent to the keenly observant eye and causes thinking people to speculate on what must
(65) be the final result of the ceaseless wearing down of the lands. Long before there was a science of geology, Shakespeare wrote "the revolution of the times makes mountains level."

11. It can be inferred from lines 1–4 that the largest ocean is the

    (A) Atlantic
    (B) Pacific
    (C) Indian
    (D) Aleutian Deep
    (E) Arctic

12. According to lines 15–17, the peripheral furrows or *deeps* are found

    (A) only in the Pacific and Indian oceans
    (B) near earthquakes
    (C) near the shore
    (D) in the center of the ocean
    (E) to be 14,000 feet in depth in the Pacific

13. The passage indicates that the continental masses

    (A) comprise 29 percent of the earth's surface
    (B) consist of six continents
    (C) rise above sea level
    (D) are partially underwater
    (E) are relief features of the second order

14. The "revolution of the times" as used in the final sentence means

    (A) the passage of years
    (B) the current rebellion
    (C) the science of geology
    (D) the action of the ocean floor
    (E) the overthrow of natural forces

15. From this passage, it can be inferred that earthquakes

    (A) occur only in the peripheral furrows
    (B) occur more frequently in newly formed land or sea formations
    (C) are a prime cause of soil erosion
    (D) will ultimately "make mountains level"
    (E) are caused by the weight of water pressing on the earth's surface

---

Ever since America's founding fathers established the legislative branch of our government, the Senate and House of Representatives have been the target of periodic criticisms. In this speech dating from the 1950s, we learn of one accusation made against the House.

Mr. Speaker, ours is an open society. It is a pluralistic society. Its strength lies in its institutions. Those institutions remain viable only as long as the
Line majority of our citizens retain a meaningful belief
(5) in them. As long as Americans feel that their institutions are responsive to the wishes of the people, we shall endure and prevail.

Everyone will admit freely that today there is a crisis in our institutions and the faith people have in
(10) them. No institution is more basic than the Congress —in this case the House of Representatives, in which we have the privilege to serve.

Over the past year or so, the Nation has been awakened to the fact that the House—this House—
(15) our institution—has been less than responsive to the requirements of modern times. The Nation has read one article after the other that finds this institution wanting. One of the most pertinent and irrefutable accusations has to do with the fact that the House
(20) operates with too great an emphasis on secrecy, with too great an imbalance of power and too little attention paid to the wishes of the majority of its Members. In effect, this House of the people has been operating all too often in an undemocratic
(25) manner.

We cannot pretend to stand for pluralistic democracy for the Nation if we daily deny the democratic process in our procedures and deliberations. This is what is going on each day, nonetheless. It is folly
(30) to deny the need for reform. We only add fuel to the fires already being set by reactionaries of every stripe who have a vested interest in the failure of democracy. They anticipate reaction, claiming our lack of response as reason enough for seeking the
(35) overthrow of the society we are all a part of. Reform on our part in response to a proven need will cut short the fuse of rebellion, cut short those who seek the defeat of democracy.

Such reform can only be accomplished through
(40) existing institutions; it can only be accomplished through reform of them, beginning with the rules and procedures of the House of Representatives. We must let the people and their news media see what is transpiring here in their name, rather than shut
(45) them out in the name of fear and breach of security. This is their House, and they have a right to know what is happening here.

Mr. Speaker, we should have little to hide from the people. The national security argument has been
(50) worked to death. Recently, an article in the *Wall Street Journal* by Dr. Edward Teller, no raving liberal, attacks secrecy for its own sake. We defeat our own purposes by being overly secretive.

By closing the House of the people to those very
(55) same people, we only alienate growing segments of society, stifle the democratic process and undermine the foundations of the institution and the Nation we all love so deeply. If we do not take the initiative in instituting reform, we merely reaffirm
(60) the worst that has been stated about the lack of progressivism in the Congress. We add strength to the arguments of the radical revolutionaries among us. We contribute to the erosion of this House and its role.

16. Which of the following does the author appear to value LEAST?

    (A) Legislative reforms
    (B) Press coverage of Congressional sessions
    (C) His responsiveness to his constituents
    (D) The rhetoric of left wing extremists
    (E) The opinion of Dr. Edward Teller

17. The author's primary purpose in this passage is to

   (A) encourage Congress to limit the powers of the media
   (B) call for an end to undemocratic practices in Congress
   (C) answer the radicals who want to overthrow the government
   (D) define the powers of Congressional committees
   (E) analyze the needs for security of governmental agencies

18. The phrase "stand for" in line 26 means

   (A) tolerate
   (B) withstand
   (C) surpass
   (D) advocate
   (E) arise

19. The author's attitude toward closed Congressional hearings is one of

   (A) cautious skepticism
   (B) grudging tolerance
   (C) outright rejection
   (D) wholehearted acceptance
   (E) fundamental indifference

20. The tone of the passage as a whole is best described as

   (A) satirical
   (B) cautionary
   (C) alienated
   (D) objective
   (E) elegiac

Exercise C

This exercise provides you with a mixture of reading passages similar in variety to what you will encounter on the SAT I. Answer all questions on the basis of what is <u>stated</u> or <u>implied</u> in the passages.

The following passage is taken from the introduction to the catalog of a major exhibition of Flemish tapestries.

Tapestries are made on looms. Their distinctive weave is basically simple: the colored weft threads interface regularly with the monochrome warps, as
Line in darning or plain cloth, but as they do so, they form
(5) a design by reversing their direction when a change of color is needed. The wefts are beaten down to cover the warps completely. The result is a design or picture that is the fabric itself, not one laid upon a ground like an embroidery, a print, or brocading.
(10) The back and front of a tapestry show the same design. The weaver always follows a preexisting model, generally a drawing or painting, known as the cartoon, which in most cases he reproduces as exactly as he can. Long training is needed to become a pro-
(15) fessional tapestry weaver. It can take as much as a year to produce a yard of very finely woven tapestry.

Tapestry-woven fabrics have been made from China to Peru and from very early times to the present day, but large wall hangings in this technique,
(20) mainly of wool, are typically Northern European. Few examples predating the late fourteenth century have survived, but from about 1400 tapestries were an essential part of aristocratic life. The prince or great nobleman sent his plate and his tapestries
(25) ahead of him to furnish his castles before his arrival as he traveled through his domains; both had the same function, to display his wealth and social position. It has frequently been suggested that tapestries helped to heat stone-walled rooms, but
(30) this is a modern idea; comfort was of minor importance in the Middle Ages. Tapestries were portable grandeur, instant splendor, taking the place, north of the Alps, of painted frescoes further south. They were hung without gaps between them, covering

(35) entire walls and often doors as well. Only very occasionally were they made as individual works of art such as altar frontals. They were usually commissioned or bought as sets, or "chambers," and constituted the most important furnishings of any grand room,
(40) except for the display of plate, throughout the Middle Ages and the sixteenth century. Later, woven silks, ornamental wood carving, stucco decoration, and painted leather gradually replaced tapestry as expensive wall coverings, until at last wallpaper was
(45) introduced in the late eighteenth century and eventually swept away almost everything else.

By the end of the eighteenth century, the "tapestry-room" [a room with every available wall surface covered with wall hangings] was no longer fashion-
(50) able: paper had replaced wall coverings of wool and silk. Tapestries, of course, were still made, but in the nineteenth century they often seem to have been produced mainly as individual works of art that astonish by their resemblance to oil paintings, tours
(55) de force woven with a remarkably large number of wefts per inch. In England during the second half of the century, William Morris attempted to reverse this trend and to bring tapestry weaving back to its true principles, those he considered to
(60) have governed it in the Middle Ages. He imitated medieval tapestries in both style and technique, using few warps to the inch, but he did not make sets; the original function for which tapestry is so admirably suited—completely covering the walls
(65) of a room and providing sumptuous surroundings for a life of pomp and splendor—could not be revived. Morris's example has been followed, though with less imitation of medieval style, by many weavers of the present century, whose coarsely
(70) woven cloths hang like single pictures and can be admired as examples of contemporary art.

1. Tapestry weaving may be characterized as which of the following?
   I.   Time-consuming
   II. Spontaneous in concept
   III. Faithful to an original

   (A) I only
   (B) III only
   (C) I and II only
   (D) I and III only
   (E) II and III only

2. The word "distinctive" in line 1 means
   (A) characteristic
   (B) stylish
   (C) discriminatory
   (D) eminent
   (E) articulate

3. Renaissance nobles carried tapestries with them to demonstrate their
   (A) piety
   (B) consequence
   (C) aesthetic judgment
   (D) need for privacy
   (E) dislike for cold

4. The word "ground" in line 9 means
   (A) terrain
   (B) dust
   (C) thread
   (D) base
   (E) pigment

5. In contrast to nineteenth century tapestries, contemporary tapestries
   (A) are displayed in sets of panels
   (B) echo medieval themes
   (C) faithfully copy oil paintings
   (D) have a less fine weave
   (E) indicate the owner's social position

6. The primary purpose of the passage is to
   (A) explain the process of tapestry making
   (B) contrast Eastern and Western schools of tapestry
   (C) analyze the reasons for the decline in popularity of tapestries
   (D) provide a historical perspective on tapestry making
   (E) advocate a return to a more colorful way of life

The following passage is taken from a book of popular history written in 1991.

The advantage of associating the birth of democracy with the Mayflower Compact is that it is easy to do so. The public loves a simple explanation, and
Line none is simpler than the belief that on November 11,
(5) 1620—the day the compact was approved—a cornerstone of American democracy was laid. Certainly it makes it easier on schoolchildren. Marking the start of democracy in 1620 relieves students of the responsibility of knowing what happened in the
(10) hundred some years before, from the arrival of the *Santa Maria* to the landing of the *Mayflower*.

The compact, to be sure, demonstrated the Englishman's striking capacity for self-government. And in affirming the principle of majority rule, the
(15) Pilgrims showed how far they had come from the days when the king's whim was law and nobody dared say otherwise.

But the emphasis on the compact is misplaced. Scholarly research in the last half century indicates
(20) that the compact had nothing to do with the development of self-government in America. In truth, the Mayflower Compact was no more a cornerstone of American democracy than the Pilgrim hut was the foundation of American architecture. As Samuel Eliot
(25) Morison so emphatically put it, American democracy "was not born in the cabin of the *Mayflower*."

The Pilgrims indeed are miscast as the heroes of American democracy. They spurned democracy and would have been shocked to see themselves
(30) held up as its defenders. George Willison, regarded as one of the most careful students of the Pilgrims, states that "the merest glance at the history of Plymouth" shows that they were not democrats.

The mythmakers would have us believe that
(35) even if the Pilgrims themselves weren't democratic, the Mayflower Compact itself was. But in fact the compact was expressly designed to curb freedom, not promote it. The Pilgrim governor and historian, William Bradford, from whom we have gotten
(40) nearly all of the information there is about the Pilgrims, frankly conceded as much. Bradford wrote that the purpose of the compact was to control renegades aboard the *Mayflower* who were threatening to go their own way when the ship reached
(45) land. Because the Pilgrims had decided to settle in an area outside the jurisdiction of their royal patent, some aboard the *Mayflower* had hinted that upon landing they would "use their owne libertie, for none had power to command them." Under the
(50) terms of the compact, they couldn't; the compact required all who lived in the colony to "promise all due submission and obedience" to it.

Furthermore, despite the compact's mention of majority rule, the Pilgrim fathers had no intention
(55) of turning over the colony's government to the people. Plymouth was to be ruled by the elite. And the elite wasn't bashful in the least about advancing its claims to superiority. When the Mayflower Compact was signed, the elite signed first. The
(60) second rank consisted of the "goodmen." At the bottom of the list came four servants' names. No women or children signed.

Whether the compact was or was not actually hostile to the democratic spirit, it was deemed suf-
(65) ficiently hostile that during the Revolution the Tories put it to use as "propaganda for the crown." The monarchists made much of the fact that the Pilgrims

had chosen to establish an English-style government that placed power in the hands of a governor, not a
(70) cleric, and a governor who owed his allegiance not to the people or to a church but to "our dread Sovereign Lord King James." No one thought it significant that the Tories had adopted the principle of majority rule. Tory historian George Chalmers, in a work
(75) published in 1780, claimed the central meaning of the compact was the Pilgrims' recognition of the necessity of royal authority. This may have been not only a convenient argument but a true one. It is at least as plausible as the belief that the compact
(80) stood for democracy.

7. The author's attitude toward the general public (lines 3–11) can best be described as

(A) egalitarian
(B) grateful
(C) sympathetic
(D) envious
(E) superior

8. The phrase "held up" in line 30 means

(A) delayed
(B) cited
(C) accommodated
(D) carried
(E) waylaid

9. According to the passage (lines 45–53), the compact's primary purpose was to

(A) establish legal authority within the colony
(B) outlaw non-Pilgrims among the settlers
(C) preach against heretical thinking
(D) protect each individual's civil rights
(E) countermand the original royal patent

10. The author of the passage can best be described as

(A) an iconoclast
(B) an atheist
(C) a mythmaker
(D) an elitist
(E) an authoritarian

11. In lines 58–63, the details about the signers of the Mayflower Compact are used to emphasize

(A) the Pilgrims' respect for the social hierarchy
(B) the inclusion of servants among those signing
(C) their importance to American history
(D) the variety of social classes aboard
(E) the lack of any provision for minority rule

In this excerpt from her autobiography, One Writer's Beginnings, *the short-story writer Eudora Welty introduces her parents.*

My father loved all instruments that would instruct and fascinate. His place to keep things was the drawer in the "library table" where lying on top

Line of his folded maps was a telescope with brass exten-
(5) sions, to find the moon and the Big Dipper after supper in our front yard, and to keep appointments with eclipses. In the back of the drawer you could find a magnifying glass, a kaleidoscope, and a gyroscope kept in a black buckram box, which he
(10) would set dancing for us on a string pulled tight. He had also supplied himself with an assortment of puzzles composed of metal rings and intersecting links and keys chained together, impossible for the rest of us, however patiently shown, to take apart;
(15) he had an almost childlike love of the ingenious.

In time, a barometer was added to our dining room wall, but we didn't really need it. My father had the country boy's accurate knowledge of the weather and its skies. He went out and stood on
(20) our front steps first thing in the morning and took a good look at it and a sniff. He was a pretty good weather prophet.

"Well, I'm *not*," my mother would say, with enormous self-satisfaction.
(25) He told us children what to do if we were lost in a strange country. "Look for where the sky is brightest along the horizon," he said. "That reflects the nearest river. Strike out for a river and you will find habitation." Eventualities were much on his
(30) mind. In his care for us children he cautioned us to take measures against such things as being struck by lightning. He drew us all away from the windows during the severe electrical storms that are common where we live. My mother stood apart, scoffing at
(35) caution as a character failing. "Why, I always loved a storm! High winds never bothered me in West Virginia! Just listen at that! I wasn't a bit afraid of a little lightning and thunder! I'd go out on the mountain and spread my arms wide and *run* in a
(40) good big storm!"

So I developed a strong meteorological sensibility. In years ahead when I wrote stories, atmosphere took its influential role from the start. Commotion in the weather and the inner feelings aroused by
(45) such a hovering disturbance emerged connected in dramatic form. (I tried a tornado first, in a story called "The Winds.")

From our earliest Christmas times, Santa Claus brought us toys that instruct boys and girls (sepa-
(50) rately) how to build things—stone blocks cut to the castle-building style, Tinker Toys, and Erector sets. Daddy made for us himself elaborate kites that needed to be taken miles out of town to a pasture long enough (and my father was not afraid of horses
(55) and cows watching) for him to run with and get up on a long cord to which my mother held the spindle, and then we children were given it to hold, tugging like something alive at our hands. They were beautiful, sound, shapely box kites, smelling delicately
(60) of office glue for their entire short lives. And of course, as soon as the boys attained anywhere near the right age, there was an electric train, the engine with its pea-sized working headlight, its line of cars, tracks equipped with switches, semaphores, its

(65) station, its bridges, and its tunnel, which blocked off all other traffic in the upstairs hall. Even from downstairs, and through the cries of excited children, the elegant rush and click of the train could be heard through the ceiling, running around and
(70) around its figure eight.

All of this, but especially the train, represents my father's fondest beliefs—in progress, in the future. With these gifts, he was preparing his children.

And so was my mother with her different gifts.
(75) I learned from the age of two or three that any room in our house, at any time of day, was there to read in, or be read to. My mother read to me. She'd read to me in the big bedroom in the mornings, when we were in her rocker together, which ticked in
(80) rhythm as we rocked, as though we had a cricket accompanying the story. She'd read to me in the dining room on winter afternoons in front of the coal fire, with our cuckoo clock ending the story with "Cuckoo," and at night when I'd got in my own
(85) bed. I must have given her no peace. Sometimes she read to me in the kitchen while she sat churning, and the churning sobbed along with *any* story. It was my ambition to have her read to me while *I* churned; once she granted my wish, but she read
(90) off my story before I brought her butter. She was an expressive reader. When she was reading "Puss in Boots," for instance, it was impossible not to know that she distrusted *all* cats.

12. In saying that her father used the telescope to "keep appointments with eclipses" (lines 6–7), Welty means that

(A) the regularity of eclipses helped him avoid missing engagements

(B) his attempts at astronomical observation met with failure

(C) he made a point of observing major astronomical phenomena

(D) he tried to instruct his children in the importance of keeping appointments

(E) he invented ingenious new ways to use the telescope

13. We can infer from lines 19–23 that Welty's father stood on the front steps and sniffed first thing in the morning

(A) because he disapproved of the day's weather

(B) because he suffered from nasal congestion

(C) to enjoy the fragrance of the flowers

(D) to detect signs of changes in the weather

(E) in an instinctive response to fresh air

14. The word "measures" in line 31 means

(A) legislative actions

(B) preventative steps

(C) yardsticks

(D) food rations

(E) warnings

15. When Welty's mother exclaims "Just listen at that!" (line 37), she wants everyone to pay attention to

(A) her husband's advice

(B) her memories of West Virginia

(C) the sounds of the storm

(D) her reasons for being unafraid

(E) the noise the children are making

16. Compared to Welty's father, her mother can best be described as

(A) more literate and more progressive

(B) proud of her knowledge of the weather, but imprudent about storms

(C) unafraid of ordinary storms, but deeply disturbed by tornadoes

(D) more protective of her children, but less patient with them

(E) less apt to foresee problems, but more apt to enjoy the moment

17. The word "fondest" in line 72 means

(A) most affectionate

(B) most foolish

(C) most radical

(D) most cherished

(E) most credulous

18. By the phrase "brought her butter" (line 90), Welty means that she

(A) manufactured butter

(B) fetched butter

(C) spread butter

(D) purchased butter

(E) melted butter

19. Why does Welty recount these anecdotes about her parents?

(A) She wishes to prove that theirs was an unhappy marriage of opposites

(B) The anecdotes are vivid illustrations of truths that she holds dear

(C) She seeks to provide advice for travelers lost in the wilderness

(D) She envisions her parents chiefly as humorous subjects for ironic characterization

(E) She wishes to provide background on early influences on her as a writer

Exercise D

This exercise provides you with a mixture of reading passages similar in variety to what you will encounter on the SAT I. Answer all questions on the basis of what is <u>stated</u> or <u>implied</u> in the passages.

The following passage analyzes the contributions of the Mexican cowboy to American culture and to the English language.

The near-legendary history of the American West might have been quite different had the Mexican not brought cattle-raising to New Mexico and Texas.
Line The Spanish style of herding cattle on open ranges
(5) was different from the style of other Europeans, particularly the English. The American *rancho* was possible because of the lack of enough water for normal agricultural practices, and because of the easy availability of large amounts of land. This land-
(10) extensive form of cattle-raising required different techniques and brought forth the *vaquero*, the cowboy (from the Spanish *vaca*, cow) who tended the widely-scattered herds of Spanish longhorn cattle. Because of the American penchant to be consider-
(15) ed the inventors of nearly everything, the wide-open style of cattle-ranching was appropriated from the Mexican originators. As popular a folk-hero as the American cowboy is, he owes his development to the Spanish and the Mexicans, not the English.
(20) It is quite probable, as McWilliams asserts, that "with the exception of the capital required to expand the industry, there seems to have been nothing the American rancher or cowboy contributed to the development of cattle-raising in the
(25) Southwest."
Other contributions of the Mexican cowboy were: the western-style saddle with a large, ornate horn; *chaparejos*, or chaps; *lazo*, lasso; *la reata*, lariat; the cinch; the halter; the *mecate*, or horse-
(30) hair rope; chin strap for the hat; feed bag for the horse; ten-gallon hat (which comes from a mistranslation of a Spanish phrase "su sombrero galoneado" that really meant a "festooned" or "galooned" hat). Cowboy slang came from such
(35) words as: *juzgado*, hoosegow; *ranchero*, rancher; *estampida*, stampede; *calabozo*, calaboose; and *pinto* for a painted horse.
Just as the Mexican association for the protection of the rights of sheepherders gave rise to the
(40) American Sheepman's Association, the Spanish system of branding range animals and registering these brands became standard practice among Anglo stockmen. The idea of brands originated in North Africa and was brought to Spain by the Moors,
(45) along with their stocky ponies. The Mexican brands are of great antiquity, having been copied from earlier Indian signs which include symbols of the sky—sun, moon, and stars. Hernando Cortez is said to have been the first to use a brand on the
(50) continent.

1. Which of the following would be the best title for this passage?
   (A) How to Herd Cattle
   (B) The American Cowboy: A Romantic Figure
   (C) Farming Practices in Europe and America
   (D) Hispanic Contributions to Western Ranching
   (E) Spanish Influence on American Culture

2. It can be inferred from lines 8–9 that American ranches developed in the West rather than the East because
   (A) more Spanish-speaking people lived in the West
   (B) there was more money available in the West
   (C) people in the East were more bound by tradition
   (D) many jobless men in the East wanted to become cowboys
   (E) there was more unsettled land available in the West

3. The author gives examples of cowboy slang (lines 34–37) in order to
   (A) arouse the reader's interest
   (B) show that he is familiar with the subject
   (C) prove that many cowboys lacked education
   (D) point out the differences between America's East and West
   (E) demonstrate how these terms originated

4. According to the author, which of the following did Mexicans contribute to ranching?
   I. Money to buy ranches
   II. Methods of handling animals
   III. Items of riding equipment
   (A) I only   (B) II only   (C) III only
   (D) I and II only   (E) II and III only

5. Which of the following best describes the development of this passage?
   (A) Major points, minor points
   (B) Statement of problem, examples, proposed solution
   (C) Introduction, positive factors, negative factors
   (D) Cause, effects
   (E) Comparison, contrast

In this introduction to a pictorial survey of African art, the author describes the impact of African sculpture.

When you first saw a piece of African art, it impressed you as a unit; you did not see it as a collection of shapes or forms. This, of course, means
Line that the shapes and volumes within the sculpture
(5) itself were coordinated so successfully that the viewer was affected emotionally.
It is entirely valid to ask how, from a purely

artistic point of view, this unity was achieved. And we must also inquire whether there is a recurrent
(10) pattern or rules or a plastic language and vocabulary which is responsible for the powerful communication of emotion which the best African sculpture achieves. If there is such a pattern or rules, are these rules applied consciously or instinctively to obtain
(15) so many works of such high artistic quality?

It is obvious from the study of art history that an intense and unified emotional experience, such as the Christian credo of the Byzantine or 12th or 13th century Europe, when expressed in art forms, gave
(20) great unity, coherence, and power to art. But such an integrated feeling was only the inspirational element for the artist, only the starting point of the creative act. The expression of this emotion and its realization in the work could be done only with
(25) discipline and thorough knowledge of the craft. And the African sculptor was a highly trained workman. He started his apprenticeship with a master when a child, and he learned the tribal styles and the use of the tools and the nature of woods so thoroughly
(30) that his carving became what Boas calls "motor action." He carved automatically and instinctively.

The African carver followed his rules without thinking of them; indeed, they never seem to have been formulated in words. But such rules existed,
(35) for accident and coincidence cannot explain the common plastic language of African sculpture. There is too great a consistency from one work to another. Yet, although the African, with amazing insight into art, used these rules, I am certain that he
(40) was not conscious of them. This is the great mystery of such a traditional art: talent, or the ability certain people have, without conscious effort, to follow the rules which later the analyst can discover only from the work of art which has already been created.

6. The author is primarily concerned with

(A) discussing how African sculptors achieved their effects
(B) listing the rules followed in African art
(C) relating African art to the art of 12th- or 13th-century Europe
(D) integrating emotion and realization
(E) expressing the beauty of African art

7. According to the passage, one of the outstanding features of African sculpture is

(A) its subject matter
(B) the feelings it arouses
(C) the training of the artists
(D) its strangeness
(E) its emphasis on movement

8. The word "plastic" in line 10 means

(A) synthetic
(B) linguistic
(C) consistent
(D) sculptural
(E) repetitive

9. According to the information in the passage, an African carver can be best compared to a

(A) chef following a recipe
(B) fluent speaker of English who is just beginning to study French
(C) batter who hits a homerun in his or her first baseball game
(D) concert pianist performing a well-rehearsed concerto
(E) writer who is grammatically expert but stylistically uncreative

10. Which of the following titles best summarizes the content of the passage?

(A) The Apprenticeship of the African Sculptor
(B) The History of African Sculpture
(C) How African Art Achieves Unity
(D) Analyzing African Art
(E) The Unconscious Rules of African Art

The following passages present two portraits of grandmothers. In Passage 1 Mary McCarthy shares her memories of her Catholic grandmother, who raised McCarthy and her brother after their parents' death. In Passage 2 Caroline Heilbrun tells of her Jewish grandmother, who died when Heilbrun was 10.

Passage 1

Luckily, I am writing a memoir and not a work of fiction, and therefore I do not have to account for my grandmother's unpleasing character and look
Line for the Oedipal fixation or the traumatic experience
(5) which would give her that clinical authenticity that is nowadays so desirable in portraiture. I do not know how my grandmother got the way she was; I assume, from family photographs and from the inflexibility of her habits, that she was always the
(10) same, and it seems as idle to inquire into her childhood as to ask what was ailing Iago or look for the error in toilet-training that was responsible for Lady Macbeth. My grandmother's sexual history, bristling with infant mortality in the usual style of her period,
(15) was robust and decisive: three tall, handsome sons grew up, and one attentive daughter. Her husband treated her kindly. She had money, many grandchildren, and religion to sustain her. White hair, glasses, soft skin, wrinkles, needlework—all the
(20) paraphernalia of motherliness were hers; yet it was a cold, grudging, disputatious old woman who sat all day in her sunroom making tapestries from a pattern, scanning religious periodicals, and setting her iron jaw against any infraction of her ways.
(25) Combativeness was, I suppose, the dominant trait in my grandmother's nature. An aggressive churchgoer, she was quite without Christian feeling; the mercy of the Lord Jesus had never entered her heart. Her piety was an act of war against the
(30) Protestant ascendancy. The religious magazines on her table furnished her not with food for meditation

but with fresh pretexts for anger; articles attacking birth control, divorce, mixed marriages, Darwin, and secular education were her favorite reading.
(35) The teachings of the Church did not interest her, except as they were a rebuke to others; "Honor thy father and thy mother", a commandment she was no longer called upon to practice, was the one most frequently on her lips. The extermination of
(40) Protestantism, rather than spiritual perfection, was the boon she prayed for. Her mind was preoccupied with conversion; the capture of a soul for God much diverted her fancy—it made one less Protestant in the world. Foreign missions, with
(45) their overtones of good will and social service, appealed to her less strongly; it was not a *harvest* of souls that my grandmother had in mind.

   This pugnacity of my grandmother's did not confine itself to sectarian enthusiasm. There was
(50) the defence of her furniture and her house against the imagined encroachments of visitors. With her, this was not the gentle and tremulous protectiveness endemic in old ladies, who fear for the safety of their possessions with a truly touching anxiety,
(55) inferring the fragility of all things from the brittleness of their old bones and hearing the crash of mortality in the perilous tinkling of a tea-cup. My grandmother's sentiment was more autocratic: she hated having her chairs sat in or her lawns stepped
(60) on or the water turned on in her basins, for no reason at all except pure officiousness; she even grudged the mailman his daily promenade up her sidewalk. Her home was a center of power, and she would not allow it to be derogated by easy or democratic usage.
(65) Under her jealous eye, its social properties had atrophied, and it functioned in the family structure simply as a political headquarters. The family had no friends, and entertaining was held to be a foolish and unnecessary courtesy as between blood relations.
(70) Holiday dinners fell, as a duty, on the lesser members of the organization: the daughters and daughters-in-law (converts from the false religion) offered up Baked Alaska on a platter like the head of John the Baptist, while the old people sat enthroned at
(75) the table, and only their digestive processes acknowledged, with rumbling, enigmatic salvos, the festal day.

Passage 2

   My grandmother, one of Howe's sustaining women, not only ruled the household with an arm
(80) of iron, but kept a store to support them all, her blond, blue-eyed husband enjoying life rather than struggling through it. My grandmother was one of those powerful women who know that they stand between their families and an outside world filled
(85) with temptations to failure and shame. I remember her as thoroughly loving. But there can be no question that she impaired her six daughters for

autonomy as thoroughly as if she had crippled them —more so. The way to security was marriage; the
(90) dread that stood in the way of this was sexual dalliance, above all pregnancy. The horror of pregnancy in an unmarried girl is difficult, perhaps, to recapture now. For a Jewish girl not to be a virgin on marriage was failure. The male's rights were
(95) embodied in her lack of sexual experience, in the knowledge that he was the first, the owner.

   All attempts at autonomy had to be frustrated. And of course, my grandmother's greatest weapon was her own vulnerability. She had worked hard,
(100) only her daughters knew how hard. She could not be comforted or repaid—as *my* mother would feel repaid—by a daughter's accomplishments, only by her marriage.

11. McCarthy's attitude toward her grandmother is best described as

   (A) tolerant
   (B) appreciative
   (C) indifferent
   (D) nostalgic
   (E) sardonic

12. The word "idle" in line 10 means

   (A) slothful
   (B) passive
   (C) fallow
   (D) useless
   (E) unoccupied

13. According to McCarthy, a portrait of a character in a work of modern fiction must have

   (A) photographic realism
   (B) psychological validity
   (C) sympathetic attitudes
   (D) religious qualities
   (E) historical accuracy

14. McCarthy's primary point in describing her grandmother's physical appearance (lines 18–19) is best summarized by which of the following axioms?

   (A) Familiarity breeds contempt.
   (B) You can't judge a book by its cover.
   (C) One picture is worth more than ten thousand words.
   (D) There's no smoke without fire.
   (E) Blood is thicker than water.

15. By describing (in lines 52–58) the typical old woman's fear for the safety of her possessions, McCarthy emphasizes that

   (A) her grandmother feared the approach of death
   (B) old women have dangerously brittle bones
   (C) her grandmother possessed considerable wealth
   (D) her grandmother had different reasons for her actions
   (E) visitors were unwelcome in her grandmother's home

16. The word "properties" in line 65 means
    - (A) belongings
    - (B) aspects
    - (C) holdings
    - (D) titles
    - (E) acreage

17. Heilbrun is critical of her grandmother primarily because
    - (A) she would not allow her husband to enjoy himself
    - (B) she could not accept her own vulnerability
    - (C) she fostered a sense of sexual inadequacy
    - (D) she discouraged her daughters' independence
    - (E) she physically injured her children

18. By describing the extent of the feeling against pregnancy in unmarried girls (lines 91–96), Heilbrun helps the reader understand
    - (A) her fear of being scorned as an unwed mother
    - (B) why her grandmother strove to limit her daughters' autonomy
    - (C) her disapproval of contemporary sexual practices
    - (D) her awareness of her mother's desire for happiness
    - (E) how unforgiving her grandmother was

19. In stating that her grandmother's greatest weapon was her own vulnerability (lines 98–99), Heilbrun implies that her grandmother got her way by exploiting her children's
    - (A) sense of guilt
    - (B) innocence of evil
    - (C) feeling of indifference
    - (D) abdication of responsibility
    - (E) lack of experience

20. Each passage mentions which of the following as being important to the writer's grandmother?
    - (A) governing the actions of others
    - (B) contributing to religious organizations
    - (C) protecting her children's virtue
    - (D) marrying off her daughters
    - (E) being surrounded by a circle of friends

21. McCarthy would most likely react to the characterization of her grandmother, like Heilbrun's grandmother, as one of the "sustaining women" (lines 78–79) by pointing out that
    - (A) this characterization is not in good taste
    - (B) the characterization fails to account for her grandmother's piety
    - (C) the details of the family's social life support this characterization
    - (D) her grandmother's actual conduct is not in keeping with this characterization
    - (E) this characterization slightly exaggerates her grandmother's chief virtue

Answer Key

Exercise A

1.	B	6.	A	11.	D	16.	B	21.	D
2.	D	7.	C	12.	E	17.	E	22.	C
3.	B	8.	E	13.	A	18.	E		
4.	A	9.	E	14.	C	19.	E		
5.	D	10.	E	15.	C	20.	B		

Exercise B

1.	C	5.	D	9.	C	13.	D	17.	B
2.	C	6.	B	10.	A	14.	A	18.	D
3.	A	7.	B	11.	B	15.	B	19.	C
4.	E	8.	D	12.	C	16.	D	20.	B

Exercise C

1.	D	5.	D	9.	A	13.	D	17.	D
2.	A	6.	D	10.	A	14.	B	18.	A
3.	B	7.	E	11.	A	15.	C	19.	E
4.	D	8.	B	12.	C	16.	E		

Exercise D

1.	D	6.	A	11.	E	16.	B	21.	D
2.	E	7.	B	12.	D	17.	D		
3.	E	8.	D	13.	B	18.	B		
4.	E	9.	D	14.	B	19.	A		
5.	A	10.	E	15.	D	20.	A		

Answer Explanations

Exercise A

1. **B.** The opening lines indicate that the narrator is *reflecting on his feelings*. Throughout the passage he uses words like "miserable," "ashamed," and "discontented" to describe his emotional state.
   Choice A is incorrect. The narrator does not analyze or dissect a change in attitude; he describes an ongoing attitude.
   Choice C is incorrect. The passage gives an example of emotional self-awareness, not of political consciousness.
   Choice D is incorrect. The narrator condemns rather than defends the longings that brought him discontentment.
   Choice E is incorrect. The narrator criticizes himself, not young people in general.

2. **D.** The references to the forge (line 13) and the anvil (line 23) support Choice D. None of the other choices are suggested by the passage.

3. **B.** Note the adjectives used to describe Joe: "faithful," "industrious," "kind." These are virtues, and Joe is fundamentally *virtuous*.
   Choice A is incorrect. Joe is plain and hard-working, not eminent and distinguished.
   Choice C is incorrect. The passage portrays not Joe but the narrator as desiring to be independent.
   Choice D is incorrect. It is unsupported by the passage.
   Choice E is incorrect. The narrator thinks his life is coarse; he thinks Joe is virtuous.

4. **A.** Choice A is supported by lines 15–16 in which the narrator states he "would not have had Miss Havisham and Estella see (his home) on any account."
   Choices B and C are incorrect. Nothing in the passage suggests either might be the case.
   Choice D is incorrect. Though the narrator may not show himself as hard-working, nothing in the passage suggests laziness led to his discontent.
   Choice E is incorrect. Nothing in the passage suggests sinfulness has prompted his discontent. In addition, although ingratitude may play a part in his discontent, shame at his background plays a far greater part.

5. **D.** In lines 40–41, the narrator manages to say something good about his youthful self: "I am glad to know I never breathed a murmur to Joe." He gives himself credit for *concealing his despondency*.
   Choices A and B are incorrect. The narrator gives Joe all the credit for his having worked industriously and for his not having run away to become a soldier.
   Choices C and E are incorrect. They are unsupported by the passage.

6. **A.** Throughout the second paragraph, the author pays particular attention to Maria's appearance, her behavior, her effect on others. If she had been *introduced* previously in the text, there would be no need to present these details about her at this point in the passage.

7. **C.** The descriptions of the bright and shiny kitchen where you "could see yourself in the big copper boilers" and of tiny, witch-like Maria with her long nose and long chin belong to the realm of *fairy tales*.

8. **E.** The passage mentions the matron twice: once, in the opening line, where she gives Maria permission to leave work early; once, in lines 17–18, where she pays Maria a compliment. Given this context, we can logically infer that Maria views the matron positively, finding her a *benevolent or kindly supervisor*.
   Choices A, B, and C are incorrect. Nothing in the passage suggests Maria has a negative view of the matron.
   Choice D is incorrect. Given Maria's relatively menial position, it is unlikely she and the matron would be close or intimate friends.

9. **E.** To slice loaves so neatly and invisibly takes a great deal of care. The author specifically states that Maria has cut the loaves. Not only that, he emphasizes the importance of her having done so by placing this statement at the end of the paragraph (a key position). As the subsequent paragraphs point up, Maria is hungry for compliments. Just as she takes pride in her peacemaking, she takes pride in her ability to slice barmbracks evenly.

10. **E.** Maria helps others to compromise or become reconciled; she herself is not necessarily unwilling to compromise.
    The passage suggests that Choice A is characteristic of Maria. She speaks soothingly and respectfully. Therefore, Choice A is incorrect.
    The passage suggests that Choice B is characteristic of Maria. Maria's response to Ginger Mooney's toast shows her enjoyment of being noticed in this way. Therefore, Choice B is incorrect.
    The passage suggests that Choice C is characteristic of Maria. Maria's obedience to the cook and to the matron shows her respect for authority. Therefore, Choice C is incorrect.
    The passage suggests that Choice D is characteristic of Maria. Maria's disappointed shyness and her forced laughter about a wedding ring and husband show that she has wistful dreams of marriage. Therefore, Choice D is incorrect.

11. **D.** By stating that his joy at his return "made him communicative and chatty in a very unusual degree" (lines 6–7), the opening paragraph

implies that Sir Thomas is usually *more restrained in speech*. Choice D is correct.

Choice A is incorrect. Nothing in the passage suggests he is usually unwelcome in his own home.

Choices B and C are incorrect. Neither is supported by the opening paragraph.

Choice E is incorrect. Sir Thomas's delight at finding his family together "exactly as he could have wished" indicates he does not lack family feeling.

Remember, when asked to make inferences, base your answers on what the passage implies, not what it states directly.

12. E.   The opening sentence of the second paragraph states that none of the members of his family listened to him with such "unbroken unalloyed enjoyment" as his wife did. Her enjoyment was complete and unmixed with other emotions. This suggests that others in the group face Sir Thomas's arrival not with complete pleasure but *with mixed emotions*.

Choice A is incorrect. It is unsupported by the passage.

Choice B is incorrect. Lady Bertram's fluttered or discomposed state on his arrival indicates her surprise.

Choice C is incorrect. Lines 14–15 indicate that Sir Thomas did not expect to find his whole family at home. Therefore, he had not timed his arrival to coincide with a reunion.

Choice D is incorrect. Sir Thomas has had to seek out the butler and confide the news of his arrival to him (lines 50–51). Therefore, the servants had not expected his arrival.

13. A.   The phrases "coming unexpectedly as he did" (line 15) and "his sudden arrival" (lines 20–21) support the idea that Sir Thomas has returned unexpectedly. Note that these key phrases are found in the closing sentence of the first paragraph and in the opening sentence of the second paragraph. Sir Thomas's unexpected return is central to the passage.

Choice B is incorrect. Although the persons talking belong to the upper classes, as a title "The Conversation of the Upper Class" is too vague.

Choice C is incorrect. Mrs. Norris's complaint or grievance (the subject of the third paragraph) is too narrow in scope to be an appropriate title for the passage as a whole.

Choice D is incorrect. Although Lady Bertram is quite pleased to have her husband home again, their reunion is placid rather than emotional or romantic.

Choice E is incorrect. Although Sir Thomas gives an account of his voyage in the first paragraph, the passage places its emphasis on the reactions of his family to his surprising return.

Remember, when asked to choose a title, watch out for choices that are too specific or too broad.

14. C.   Examine Lady Bertram's behavior carefully. She is not agitated (though she is "nearer agitation than she had been for the last twenty years"). She is so moved by her husband's return that she actually moves her lap dog from the sofa and makes room for her husband. Clearly, the author is making fun of Lady Bertram's idiosyncratic behavior, describing her quirky reactions in a lightly mocking, *gently ironic* way.

15. C.   The author italicizes the word *her* for emphasis. Lady Bertram had no worries to take away from her pleasure at Sir Thomas's return. However, she is unusual in this. The author's emphasis on her happiness *serves to suggest that others in the group have reason to be less happy about Sir Thomas's arrival*.

16. B.   Refusing to be provoked by Mrs. Norris's interruptions, Sir Thomas demonstrates *patient forbearance* or restraint.

Choice A is incorrect. Line 69 states that Sir Thomas "could not be provoked." Therefore, he showed no irritation.

Choice C is incorrect. Sir Thomas remarks courteously on Mrs. Norris's anxiety for everybody's comfort (lines 69–71). This implies that he in general approves rather than disapproves of her concern.

Choice D is incorrect. It is unsupported by the passage.

Choice E is incorrect. Given Mrs. Norris's interruptions of his story, it is unlikely Sir Thomas would view her with *unmixed delight*.

17. E.   Mrs. Norris has looked forward to spreading the news of Sir Thomas's return (or of his death!). The office she has lost is that of herald or *message-bearer*.

Choice A is incorrect. Mrs. Norris wishes to give orders to the butler, not to be the butler.

Choice B is incorrect for much the same reason.

Choice C is incorrect. Mrs. Norris is the sister of Sir Thomas's wife; the passage does not indicate that she has any desire to be his wife.

Choice D is incorrect. Mrs. Norris wishes to give news of the traveler, not to be the traveler.

18. E.   The first sentence of the passage states that Newman's purpose is to see Mademoiselle Noemie, to pay her another visit. Indeed, in lines 6–7, he is described as roaming "through several of the rooms in fruitless quest of her."

19. E.   In lines 35–36, Valentin explains that, giving in to his mother's entreaties, he has reluctantly agreed to guide his cousin through the Louvre. The prospect bores him—playing tour guide is one of his *ennuis*. He is even more bored than usual, for his cousin is late.

20. B. Valentin shows what a bad mood he is in by *making insulting comments* about his cousin's poor taste in clothes, huge feet, and lack of punctuality.
    Choice A is incorrect. Though Valentin's cousin is late, he has not yet stalked off in a fit of temper.
    Choice C is incorrect. Valentin is quite ready to accept Newman's advice.
    Choice D is incorrect. He is criticizing his English cousin's choice of clothes, not his mother's.
    Choice E is incorrect. Though he is about to offer to go off with Newman, Valentin has not yet refused to do as his mother wished. Up to now, he has been a very obedient, though disgruntled, son.

21. D. Use the process of elimination to answer this question.
    Valentin would most likely agree with Statement I. His concern for fashionable clothing is evident from the disparaging remarks he makes about his cousin's clothes. Therefore, you can eliminate Choices B and C.
    Valentin would most likely also agree with Statement II. He respects family relationships, for he has agreed to his mother's request to show the cousin around. Therefore, you can eliminate Choice A.
    Valentin would probably *not* agree with Statement III. He is furious that his cousin is late. Therefore, you can eliminate Choice E.
    Only Choice D is left. It is the correct answer.

22. C. Valentin confides in Newman, telling the American why he is so irritated. He speaks extremely frankly, making disparaging comments about his English cousin, for he is sure that his trusted friend or *confidant* will not betray these confidences.

Exercise B

1. C. Each paragraph discusses some important feature or *significant characteristic* of Eskimo art (its mystical quality, realistic understanding of anatomy, humor, etc.).

2. C. The author's use of such terms as "powerful ability" (line 2), "masters in the understanding of animal anatomy" (line 28), and "living excitement" (line 55) indicates an *admiration* for the art.

3. A. The author's comment in line 17 that Eskimo art "has a special freedom unsullied (unstained or undefiled) by any kind of formalized training" suggests that he would agree that formal training might defile or *destroy an artist's originality* and freedom of expression.

4. E. Each example the author provides describes a type of Eskimo sculpture (man driving a caribou, woman holding a child, geese flying, polar bear charging) and gives the reader a sense of its *quality and variety*.

5. D. Use the process of elimination to answer this question.
    Choice A is incorrect. Line 43 states "there is much evidence of humor" in Eskimo art.
    Choice B is incorrect. Humor in Eskimo carvings "may be subtle" (lines 46–47).
    Choice C is incorrect. Eskimo carvings reveal "the passionate feelings of a vital people" (line 9); they possess *emotional depth*.
    Choice E is incorrect. Eskimo sculptors are "masters in the understanding of animal anatomy" (line 28). Their works are characterized by *anatomical accuracy*.
    Only Choice D is left. It is the correct answer. If "no one can accurately define the right way or wrong way to create a carving" (lines 48–49), clearly Eskimo carving lacks *stylistic uniformity*.

6. B. The passage as a whole is a portrait of Charlotte Stanhope's moral and intellectual temperament or character. The opening sentence of each paragraph describes some aspect of her behavior or character which the paragraph then goes on to develop.
    Remember, when asked to find the main idea, be sure to check the opening and summary sentences of each paragraph.
    Choice A is incorrect. While the various members of the family are described, they are described only in relationship to Charlotte.
    Choice C is incorrect. Although Charlotte may well be selfish or egotistical, she does do some good for others. The passage does not illustrate the evils of egotism.
    Choice D is incorrect. The passage analyzes Charlotte; it discusses the members of her family only in relationship to her.
    Choice E is incorrect. While Charlotte has her virtues, the passage stresses her faults. While her family may not be described as admirable, nothing suggests that they are disreputable (not well-esteemed or well-regarded).

7. B. The author presents Charlotte *candidly* and openly: her faults are not concealed. The author also presents her *satirically*: her weaknesses and those of her family are mocked or made fun of. If you find the characters in a passage foolish or pompous, the author may well be writing satirically.
    Choice A is incorrect. While the author is concerned with Charlotte's moral character, he is not *moralistic* or *self-righteous*; he is describing her character, not preaching a sermon against her.
    Choice C is incorrect. The author is unsympathetic to Charlotte's faults and he is not *sentimental* or

emotionally excessive about her.

Choice D is incorrect. *Bitterness* is too strong a term to describe the author's tone. He has no reason to be bitter.

Choice E is incorrect. While the author's tone is not highly emotional, it is better to describe it as satiric than as *unfeeling*.

8. D. Lines 50–51 mention the troubled mind of Dr. Stanhope, and state that Charlotte would have enjoyed shaking "*what remained* of his Church of England faith." The phrase "what remained" implies that little is left of Dr. Stanhope's original religious faith.

Choice A is incorrect. There is no comparison made between the two elder Stanhopes. Both are *indolent* (lazy).

Choice B is incorrect. Since only Charlotte could persuade her father to look after his affairs (lines 14–15), he apparently was willing to let her manage matters for him and willingly surrendered his authority.

Choice C is incorrect. There is no evidence in the passage that Dr. Stanhope feels regret or remorse.

Choice E is incorrect. While Charlotte's brother is described as moneyless (lines 41–42), there is no evidence in the passage that Dr. Stanhope has disinherited him.

9. C. There is no evidence in the passage that Charlotte's mother is an affectionate wife and mother; similarly, there is no evidence that she is excellent in the "domestic arts" (making tea; managing the household—the very tasks assumed by Charlotte).

Statements I and II are incorrect. Only Statement III is correct. The sole mention of Charlotte's mother (lines 33–35) states that she was encouraged in her idleness by Charlotte. She lacks the willpower to resist Charlotte's encouragements. Thus, she shows herself to be a woman of unassertive, pliable character.

10. A. The first paragraph emphasizes that Charlotte "in no way affected the graces of youth." Her manner is that of an assured mistress of a household, not a flirt.

Choice B is incorrect. Charlotte is a free-thinker (one who denies established beliefs) and thus lacks reverence or respect for religion.

Choice C is incorrect. Charlotte is concerned with her family's worldly well-being and makes her father attend to his material concerns. Thus, she has a materialistic nature.

Choice D is incorrect. Charlotte manages everything and everybody.

Choice E is incorrect. Charlotte's coarseness (vulgarity; crudeness) is implied in the reference to her "freedom...from feminine delicacy" (lines 45–47).

11. B. We are told that 71 percent of the earth is covered by water and that the Pacific Ocean covers half the earth. The Pacific is obviously the largest ocean.

12. C. The peripheral furrows or *deeps* are discussed in lines 13–25. We are told that these deeps are near the continental masses, and, therefore, near the shore.

13. D. The last sentence of the first paragraph discusses the submerged or *underwater* portions of the continental masses.

Key Words: masses, percent, sea level, submerged, relief.

14. A. Terms such as "unendingly," "ultimately," and "ceaseless" indicate that the mountains are made level over an enormous *passage of years*.

15. B. The passage states that the *deeps*, the site of frequent earthquakes, are of recent origin: they were formed comparatively recently. This suggests that newly formed land and sea formations may have a greater frequency of earthquake occurrence than older, more stable formations. Remember, when asked to make inferences, base your answers on what the passage implies, not what it states directly.

16. D. The author does *not* value the rhetoric of left wing extremists. He does not want to "add strength to the arguments of the radical revolutionaries among us" (lines 61–63).

Choice A is incorrect. The author values *legislative reform*; he argues in its favor throughout the passage.

Choice B is incorrect. The author values *press coverage of Congressional sessions*: he advocates letting "the people and their news media see what is transpiring here" in lines 43–44.

Choice C is incorrect. The author values his *responsiveness to his constituents*, his ability to respond to the wishes of the people. He maintains in lines 5–7 that it is this responsiveness on the part of our institutions that makes our way of life prevail.

Choice E is incorrect. The author apparently values *the opinion of Dr. Edward Teller*: he quotes Teller in order to back up his argument against Congressional secretiveness.

17. B. Throughout the passage the author repeatedly calls for reform. He points out the failings of the House. In particular, he asserts that "this House of the people has been operating...in an undemocratic manner" (lines 23–25). Such *undemocratic practices* must come to an end.

Choice A is incorrect. The author wishes to grant the media access to Congress (lines 42–47); he does not seek to limit their powers.

Choice C is incorrect. While he mentions the radical revolutionaries in our midst, he does so only in passing (lines 61–63): his primary purpose is not to answer their arguments, but to make an argument of his own.

Choice D is incorrect. The author never mentions stregthening the powers of Congressional committees.

Choice E is incorrect. Although the author mentions in passing the needs for security of governmental agencies, he dismisses these needs as less important than the public's need (and right) to know what's going on.

18. D. The author has just accused the House of operating in an undemocratic manner. He now asserts that he and his fellow Representatives cannot pretend to *advocate* or support democracy to the American people if they act undemocratically.

19. C. In lines 26–30 the author directly rejects closed Congressional hearings. Closed hearings undermine the very foundations of Congress and of democracy itself. He demands reform. His attitude is one of outright, complete rejection.

Choice A is incorrect. The author is not merely being skeptical (suspicious, unwilling to believe) when he discusses closed hearings.

Choice B is incorrect. The author attacks closed hearings. He does not accept or tolerate them grudgingly (reluctantly).

Choice D is incorrect. The author certainly does not accept closed hearings enthusiastically or wholeheartedly.

Choice E is incorrect. The author is not basically indifferent to closed hearings; he would not have spent so much time arguing against them if he were.

20. B. Choice B is correct. The passage is *cautionary* in tone. The author is warning his audience, giving them lots of advice.

Choice A is incorrect. *Satirical* means ironic, mocking, critical in a witty or humorous manner. The author is far too involved in the issue to make witty, mocking remarks.

Choice C is incorrect. The author is concerned. He has not been made indifferent or *alienated*.

Choice D is incorrect. *Objective* means fair, unprejudiced, undistorted by emotion. The author's prejudices against "radical revolutionaries" and his use of emotionally loaded phrases like "stifle the democratic process" and "Nation we all love so deeply" make his lack of objectivity clear.

Choice E is incorrect. The author is not *elegiac*, sorrowfully lamenting a death. He is issuing a warning.

Exercise C

1. D. Tapestry weaving is time-consuming, taking "as much as a year to produce a yard." In addition, it is faithful to the original ("The weaver always follows a preexisting model.") It is not, however, spontaneous in concept.

2. A. The author mentions tapestry's distinctive or *characteristic* weave as something that distinguishes tapestry-woven materials from other fabrics (prints, brocades, etc.).

3. B. By using tapestries "to display his wealth and social position," the nobleman is using them to demonstrate his *consequence* or importance.

4. D. The "ground" upon which embroidery is laid is the cloth *base* upon which the embroiderer stitches a design.

5. D. In comparison to the tightly-woven tapestries of the nineteenth century, present day wall-hangings are described as "coarsely woven cloths." Thus, they *have a less fine weave* than their predecessors.

6. D. The passage explains the process of tapestry making and mentions that large wall-hangings are Western rather than Eastern in origin. Choices A and B do not reflect the passage's primary purpose. This purpose is to *provide an historical perspective on tapestry making*.

7. E. By stating that the public loves a simple explanation and by commenting on how much easier it is for schoolchildren to ignore what happened on the American continent from 1492 to 1620, the historian-author reveals a *superior* attitude toward the public at large, who are content with easy answers.

8. B. The democracy-rejecting Pilgrims would have been amazed to find themselves held up or *cited* as defenders of democracy.

9. A. The Pilgrims had been given a royal patent legally empowering them to settle in a certain area. Because they had decided to colonize a different area, some of the group felt that once they were ashore no laws would bind them. The compact bound the signers to obey the laws of the colony. It thus served to *establish legal authority within the colony*.

10. A. In debunking the image of the Mayflower Compact as the cornerstone of American democracy, the author reveals himself to be an *iconoclast*, an attacker of established beliefs.

11. A. According to the passage, the Pilgrims signed the Mayflower Compact in order of rank: first, the gentlemen; next, the "goodmen" or yeoman-farmers; finally, the servants. In doing so they showed their *respect for the social hierarchy*.

12. C. Welty's father used his telescope to observe the moon and the Big Dipper. An eager amateur astronomer, he clearly *made a point of observing* eclipses and other major astronomical phenomena.

13. D. Welty calls her father a "pretty good weather prophet," saying he had "the country boy's accurate knowledge of the weather and its skies." In support of this, she describes his going out on the porch first thing in the morning for a look at the weather and a sniff. This suggests he sniffed the air *to detect signs of changes in the weather*.

14. B. Caring for his children, the father warned them to take *preventative steps* (such as moving away from the windows during electrical storms) to avoid being hit by lightning.

15. C. Exhilarated by the thunderstorm (she "always loved a storm!"), the mother stands apart from the rest of the family, urging them to share her excitement over *the sounds of the storm*.

16. E. Running through thunderstorms unworried by lightning bolts, Welty's mother was clearly *less apt to foresee problems* than Welty's father was; she also was *more apt to enjoy the moment*.

17. D. Welty's father held dear his beliefs in progress and in the future; these were his fondest, *most cherished* beliefs.

18. A. Welty's ambition was to beat the milk in the churn and make butter while her mother read to her; her mother finished reading the story before Welty finished *manufacturing butter* for her.

19. E. Welty calls her autobiography *One Writer's Beginnings*. In this passage she shows how her father and mother, with their different gifts, were preparing her for life, especially for the life of a writer. Her father gave her his love of ingenious devices, his country-boy's knowledge of terrain. Her mother gave her books, a love of reading, a sense of the sound of words. Both parents helped form her "strong meteorological sensibility" that affected her later tales.

Exercise D

1. D. The topic discussed throughout this passage is Hispanic (Spanish and Mexican) contributions to Western ranching.

2. E. The first paragraph notes that ranches can develop where large amounts of land are available. It can be inferred that more unsettled land was available in the West than in the East.

3. E. The use of only Mexican terms suggests that the author is using these examples of cowboy slang to demonstrate the origins of the words and prove how much Mexicans contributed.

4. E. The first paragraph tells of the adoption of Mexican methods of handling animals, and the second speaks of Mexican contributions to riding equipment. The quotation at the end of the first paragraph implies that the money for the ranching industry was provided by Americans.

5. A. The passage starts with the major Mexican contribution of the whole concept of ranching, goes on, in the second paragraph, to discuss lesser contributions of equipment and slang, and ends, in the third paragraph, with the relatively minor contribution of branding.

6. A. Each paragraph of the passage discusses how African sculptors achieved their effects.

7. B. Both the first and second paragraphs mention the emotions aroused by African sculpture.

8. D. The passage discusses sculpture, so it can be inferred that "the common plastic language" means the common *sculptural* language.

9. D. We are told that the African sculptor was highly trained and followed the rules without thinking about them. Similarly, a well-rehearsed pianist can perform a concerto without worrying too much about the notes. Both artists have become free to concentrate on mood or creativity.

10. E. Throughout the passage, the author discusses the rules of African art. He concludes that they were unconscious.

11. E. In candidly exposing her grandmother's flaws, the author exhibits a *sardonic* or scornful and sarcastic attitude.

12. D. McCarthy sees as little point in speculating about her grandmother's childhood as she does in wondering about the toilet-training of a fictional character like Lady Macbeth. Such speculations are, to McCarthy's mind, idle or *useless*.

13. B. The author states (somewhat ironically) that modern fictional characters must have "clinical authenticity." In other words, they must appear to be genuine or *valid* in *psychological* terms.

14. B. Although the grandmother's outward appearance was soft and motherly, her essential nature was hard as nails. Clearly, you cannot judge a book (person) by its cover (outward appearance).

15. D. McCarthy is building up a portrait of her grandmother as a pugnacious, autocratic person. She describes the fear old ladies have for their belongings as a very human (and understandable) reaction: aware of their own increasing fragility (and eventual death), the old ladies identify with their fragile possessions and are protective of them. McCarthy's grandmother was also protective of her belongings, but she was not the typical "gentle and tremulous" elderly woman. She was a petty tyrant and had decidedly *different reasons for her actions*.

16. B. Because her grandmother was more interested in maintaining her power than in being hospitable, the social properties or *aspects* of the family home had withered and decayed till no real sociability existed.

17. D. Heilbrun's central criticism is that her grandmother "impaired her six daughters for autonomy" or independence. In other words, *she discouraged her daughters' independence*.

18. B. Heilbrun realizes that people nowadays may have difficulty understanding what motivated her grandmother to control her daughters' lives and restrict their autonomy so thoroughly. By describing how great the horror of pregnancy in an unmarried girl was, she helps the reader understand *why her grandmother* acted as she did.

19. A. By dwelling on how hard she had worked to support her daughters and how much she would be hurt if they failed to pay her back by making good marriages, Heilbrun's grandmother exploited their *sense of guilt*.

20. A. The common factor in both grandmothers' lives is their need to *govern the actions of others*. McCarthy's grandmother tyrannized everyone from the mailman to her daughters and daughters-in-law; Heilbrun's grandmother "ruled the household with an arm of iron," governing her daughters' lives.

21. D. While Heilbrun's grandmother was a "sustaining woman" who provided for her family, allowing her husband to live a life of relative leisure, McCarthy's grandmother was a grudging woman, not a sustaining one. Thus, McCarthy would most likely point out that *her grandmother's actual conduct is not in keeping with this characterization*.

7 Build Your Vocabulary

- ■ **The SAT I High-Frequency Word List**
- ■ **The SAT I Hot Prospects Word List**
- ■ **The 3,500 Basic Word List**
- ■ **Basic Word Parts**

The more you study actual SAT I verbal questions, the more you realize one thing: *the key to doing well on the verbal part of SAT I is a strong working vocabulary of college-level words*. And the key to building that strong working vocabulary can be summed up in one word: READ.

Read widely, read deeply, read daily. If you do, your vocabulary will grow. If you don't it won't.

Reading widely, however, may not always help you remember the words you read. You may have the words in your passive vocabulary and be able to recognize them when you see them in a context and yet be unable to define them clearly or think of synonyms for them. In addition, unless you have already begun to upgrade your reading to the college level, reading widely also may not acquaint you most efficiently with college-level words.

What are college-level words? In going through the preceding three chapters, you have examined dozens of questions taken from recently published SATs. Some of the words in these questions—*govern* and *tyrant*—have been familiar to you; others—*pundit* and *interlocutor*—have not. Still others—*husband* and *nip*—have looked familiar, but have turned out to be defined in unexpected ways. All these words belong in your college-level vocabulary; any of them may turn up when you take SAT I.

Use the vocabulary and word parts lists in this chapter to upgrade your vocabulary to a college level. They are all excellent vocabulary building tools.

No matter how little time you have before you take SAT I, you can familiarize yourself with the sort of vocabulary you will be facing on the test. First, look over the words on our SAT I High-Frequency Word List, which you'll find on the following pages. Each of these words has appeared (as answer choices or as question words) from eight to forty times on SATs published in the past two decades.

Next, look over the words on our new Hot Prospects List, which appears immediately after the High-Frequency List. Though these words don't appear as often as the high-frequency words do, when they do appear, the odds are that they're *key* words in questions. As such, they deserve your special attention.

Now you're ready to master the words on the High-Frequency and Hot Prospects Word Lists. First, check off those words you think you know. Then, look up all the words and their definitions in our 3,500 Basic Word List. Pay particular attention to the words you thought you knew. See whether any of them are defined in an unexpected way. If they are, make a special note of them. As you know from the preceding chapters, SAT I often stumps students with questions based on unfamiliar meanings of familiar-looking words.

Use the flash cards in the back of this book and create others for the words you want to master. Work up memory tricks to help yourself remember them. Try using them on your parents and friends. Not only will going over these high-frequency words reassure you that you *do* know some SAT-type words, but also it may well help you on the actual day of the test. These words have turned up on recent tests; some of them may well turn up on the test you take.

The SAT I High-Frequency Word List*

abridge	compile	disseminate	guile	materialism
abstemious	complacency	dissent	gullible	methodical
abstract	compliance	divergent	hamper (V)	meticulous
abstruse	composure	doctrine	hardy	miserly
accessible	comprehensive	document (V)	haughtiness	mitigate
acclaim	concede	dogmatic	hedonist	morose
acknowledge	conciliatory	dubious	heresy	mundane
adulation	concise	duplicity	hierarchy	negate
adversary	concur	eclectic	homogeneous	nonchalance
adversity	condone	egotism	hypocritical	notoriety
advocate	conflagration	elated	hypothetical	novelty
aesthetic	confound	eloquence	idiosyncrasy	nurture
affable	consensus	elusive	illusory	obliterate
affirmation	constraint	embellish	immutable	oblivion
alleviate	contend	emulate	impair	obscure (V)
aloof	contentious	endorse	impeccable	obstinate
altruistic	contract (V)	enhance	impede	ominous
ambiguous	conviction	enigma	implausible	opaque
ambivalence	cordial	enmity	implement (V)	opportunist
analogous	corroborate	ephemeral	impudence	optimist
anarchist	credulity	equivocal	inadvertent	opulence
anecdote	criterion	erroneous	inane	orator
animosity	cryptic	erudite	incisive	ostentatious
antagonism	cursory	esoteric	incite	pacifist
antidote	curtail	eulogy	inclusive	partisan
antiquated	decorum	euphemism	incongruous	peripheral
apathy	deference	exacerbate	inconsequential	perpetuate
appease	degradation	exalt	incorrigible	pervasive
apprehension	delineate	execute	indict	pessimism
arbitrary	denounce	exemplary	indifferent	phenomena
archaic	deplore	exemplify	indiscriminate	philanthropist
arrogance	depravity	exhaustive	induce	piety
articulate	deprecate	exhilarating	inert	placate
artifact	deride	exonerate	ingenious	ponderous
artisan	derivative	expedient	inherent	pragmatic
ascendancy	despondent	expedite	innate	preclude
ascetic	detached	explicit	innocuous	precocious
aspire	deterrent	exploit (V)	innovation	predator
astute	detrimental	extol	insipid	predecessor
attribute (V)	devious	extraneous	instigate	presumptuous
augment	devise	extricate	insularity	pretentious
austere	diffuse	exuberance	integrity	prevalent
authoritarian	digression	facilitate	intervene	prodigal
autonomous	diligence	fallacious	intimidate	profane
aversion	diminution	fanaticism	intrepid	profound
belie	discerning	fastidious	inundate	profusion
benevolent	disclose	feasible	invert	proliferation
bolster	discordant	fervor	ironic	prolific
braggart	discount (V)	flagrant	lament	provincial
brevity	discrepancy	frivolous	laud	proximity
cajole	discriminating	frugality	lavish (ADJ)	prudent
calculated	disdain	furtive	lethargic	qualified
candor	disinclination	garrulous	levity	quandary
capricious	dismiss	glutton	linger	ramble
censorious	disparage	gratify	listless	rancor
censure	disparity	gratuitous	lofty	ratify
coercion	disperse	gravity	malicious	rebuttal
commemorate	disputatious	gregarious	marred	recluse

recount	resolve (N)	seclusion	superfluous	turmoil
rectify	restraint	servile	surpass	undermine
redundant	reticence	skeptic	surreptitious	uniformity
refute	retract	sluggish	susceptible	unwarranted
relegate	reverent	somber	sustain	usurp
remorse	rhetorical	sporadic	sycophant	vacillate
renounce	rigor	squander	taciturn	venerate
repel	robust	stagnant	temper (V)	verbose
reprehensible	sage	static (ADJ)	tentative	vigor
reprimand	sanction (V)	submissive	terse	vilify
reprove	satirical	subordinate (ADJ)	thrive	vindicate
repudiate	saturate	subside	tranquillity	virtuoso
reserve (N)	scanty	substantiate	transient	volatile
resigned	scrupulous	succinct	trite	whimsical
resolution	scrutinize	superficial	turbulence	zealot

*This word list has been updated to include all released SAT I exams through January 2000.

The SAT I Hot Prospects Word List

abate	colloquial	fallow	mercenary (ADJ)	recant
accolade	combustible	falter	mercurial	remission
acquiesce	complementary	fathom (V)	mirth	replete
acrid	confluence	fell (V)	misanthrope	repugnant
acrimony	conjecture	fitful	misnomer	rescind
aggregate (V)	converge	florid	mollify	respite
amorphous	corrode	foolhardy	mosaic	resplendent
anachronistic	corrugated	glacial	munificent	savory
anomaly	culpable	hackneyed	nefarious	sedentary
antediluvian	debilitate	hyperbole	nuance	soporific
antipathy	debunk	iconoclastic	obdurate	spurious
apocryphal	dehydrate	ignominy	odious	spurn
arable	deleterious	illicit	ornate	steadfast
ardent	depose	impecunious	pariah	stolid
assiduous	desiccate	impregnable	parody	strident
assuage	diffidence	incidental	parsimony	stupefy
atrophy	dilatory	incontrovertible	paucity	supplant
audacious	discourse	indefatigable	penury	surfeit
avarice	discrepancy	indolent	perfunctory	swagger
avert	disquiet	ineffable	pernicious	tantamount
aviary	distend	inexorable	pitfall	tenacity
beguile	dupe	insolvent	pithy	terrestrial
bequeath	ebullient	insuperable	polemical	threadbare
bleak	edify	intractable	prattle	tirade
blighted	efface	irreproachable	precarious	torpor
bombastic	effervesce	jocular	profligate (ADJ)	trepidation
buttress	elegy	labyrinth	quagmire	trifling
cacophonous	elicit	laconic	quell	truncate
cardiologist	elucidate	laggard	querulous	unkempt
carping	emaciated	lampoon	quiescent	unprecedented
certitude	emend	lassitude	rant	vaporize
charlatan	equanimity	lithe	rarefy	viable
circumlocution	equitable	lurid	raucous	virulent
cliché	evanescent	luxuriant	ravenous	voluble
coalesce	excerpt	meander	raze	witticism

The 3,500 Basic Word List

The 3,500 Basic Word List begins on the following page. *Do not let this list overwhelm you.* You do not need to memorize every word.

The more than 3,500 words in this list have been compiled from various sources. They have been taken from the standard literature read by high school students throughout the country and from the many tests taken by high school and college students. Ever since this book first appeared in 1954, countless students have reported that working with this list has been of immense value in the taking of all kinds of college entrance and scholarship tests. It has been used with profit by people preparing for civil service examinations, placement tests, and promotional examinations in many industrial fields. Above all, it has been used with profit by people studying for SAT.

Even before the College Board began publishing its own SAT sample examinations, the Basic Word List was unique in its ability to reflect, and often predict, the actual vocabulary appearing on the SAT. Today, thanks to our ongoing research and computer analysis of published SAT materials, we believe our 3,500 Basic Word List is the best in the field.

For those of you who wish to work your way through the *entire* word list and feel the need for a plan, we recommend that you follow the procedure described below in order to use the lists and the exercises most profitably:

1. Allot a definite time each day for the study of a list.
2. Devote at least one hour to each list.
3. First go through the list looking at the flagged High-Frequency and Hot Prospects words and the short, simple-looking words (7 letters at most). Mark those you don't know. In studying, pay particular attention to them.
4. Go through the list again looking at the longer words. Pay particular attention to words with more than one meaning and familiar-looking words that have unusual definitions that come as a surprise to you. Study these secondary definitions.
5. List unusual words on index cards that you can shuffle and review from time to time, along with the flash cards in this book.
6. Use the illustrative sentences in the list as models and make up new sentences of your own.

For each word, the following is provided:
1. The word (printed in heavy type).
2. Its part of speech (abbreviated).
3. A brief definition.
4. A sentence illustrating the word's use.
5. Whenever appropriate, related words are provided, together with their parts of speech.

The word lists are arranged in strict alphabetical order. In each word list, High-Frequency words are marked with a square bullet (■), Hot Prospects with a round one (●).

Basic Word List

Word List 1   abase-adroit

abase   V. lower; humiliate. Defeated, Queen Zenobia was forced to *abase* herself before the conquering Romans, who made her march in chains before the emperor in the procession celebrating his triumph. abasement, N.

abash   V. embarrass. He was not at all *abashed* by her open admiration.

● **abate**   V. subside; decrease, lessen. Rather than leaving immediately, they waited for the storm to *abate*. abatement, N.

abbreviate   V. shorten. Because we were running out of time, the lecturer had to *abbreviate* her speech.

abdicate   V. renounce; give up. When Edward VIII *abdicated* the British throne to marry the woman he loved, he surprised the entire world.

abduction   N. kidnapping. The movie *Ransom* describes the attempts to rescue a multimillionaire's son after the child's *abduction* by kidnappers. abduct, V.

aberrant   N. abnormal or deviant. Given the *aberrant* nature of the data, we doubted the validity of the entire experiment. also N.

abet   V. aid, usually in doing something wrong; encourage. She was unwilling to *abet* him in the swindle he had planned.

abeyance   N. suspended action. The deal was held in *abeyance* until her arrival.

abhor   V. detest; hate. She *abhorred* all forms of bigotry. abhorrence, N.

abject   ADJ. wretched; lacking pride. On the streets of New York the homeless live in *abject* poverty, huddling in doorways to find shelter from the wind.

abjure   V. renounce upon oath. He *abjured* his allegiance to the king. abjuration, N.

ablution   N. washing. His daily *ablutions* were accompanied by loud noises that he humorously labeled "Opera in the Bath."

abnegation   N. repudiation; self-sacrifice. No act of *abnegation* was more pronounced than his refusal of any rewards for his discovery.

abolish   V. cancel; put an end to. The president of the college refused to *abolish* the physical education requirement. abolition, N.

abominable   ADJ. detestable; extremely unpleasant; very bad. Mary liked John until she learned he was dating Susan; then she called him an *abominable* young man, with *abominable* taste in women.

aboriginal   ADJ., N. being the first of its kind in a region; primitive; native. Her studies of the primitive art forms of the *aboriginal* Indians were widely reported in the scientific journals. aborigines, N.

abortive   ADJ. unsuccessful; fruitless. Attacked by armed troops, the Chinese students had to abandon their *abortive* attempt to democratize Beijing peacefully. abort, V.

abrade   V. wear away by friction; scrape; erode. The sharp rocks *abraded* the skin on her legs, so she put iodine on her *abrasions*.

abrasive   ADJ. rubbing away; tending to grind down. Just as *abrasive* cleaning powders can wear away a shiny finish, *abrasive* remarks can wear away a listener's patience. abrade, V.

■ **abridge**   V. condense or shorten. Because the publishers felt the public wanted a shorter version of *War and Peace*, they proceeded to *abridge* the novel.

abrogate   ADJ. abolish. He intended to *abrogate* the decree issued by his predecessor.

abscond   V. depart secretly and hide. The teller who *absconded* with the bonds went uncaptured until someone recognized him from his photograph on "America's Most Wanted."

absolute   ADJ. complete; totally unlimited; certain. Although the King of Siam was an *absolute* monarch, he did not want to behead his unfaithful wife without *absolute* evidence of her infidelity.

absolve   V. pardon (an offense). The father confessor *absolved* him of his sins. absolution, N.

absorb   V. assimilate or incorporate; suck or drink up; wholly engage. During the nineteenth century, America *absorbed* hordes of immigrants, turning them into productive citizens. Can Huggies diapers *absorb* more liquid than Pampers can? This question does not *absorb* me; instead, it bores me. absorption, N.

abstain   V. refrain; hold oneself back voluntarily from an action or practice. After considering the effect of alcohol on his athletic performance, he decided to *abstain* from drinking while he trained for the race. abstinence, N.

■ **abstemious**   ADJ. sparing in eating and drinking; temperate. Concerned whether her vegetarian son's *abstemious* diet provided him with sufficient protein, the worried mother pressed food on him.

abstinence   N. restraint from eating or drinking. The doctor recommended total *abstinence* from salted foods. abstain, V.

■ **abstract**   ADJ. theoretical; not concrete; nonrepresentational. To him, hunger was an *abstract* concept; he had never missed a meal.

■ **abstruse**   ADJ. obscure; profound; difficult to understand. She carries around *abstruse* works of philosophy, not because she understands them but because she wants her friends to think she does.

abundant ADJ. plentiful; possessing riches or resources. At his immigration interview, Ivan listed his *abundant* reasons for coming to America: the hope of religious freedom, the prospect of employment, the promise of a more *abundant* life.

abusive ADJ. coarsely insulting; physically harmful. An *abusive* parent damages a child both mentally and physically.

abut V. border upon; adjoin. Where our estates *abut,* we must build a fence.

abysmal ADJ. bottomless. His arrogance is exceeded only by his *abysmal* ignorance.

abyss N. enormous chasm; vast bottomless pit. Darth Vader seized the evil emperor and hurled him down into the *abyss.*

academic ADJ. related to a school; not practical or directly useful. The dean's talk about reforming the college admissions system was only an *academic* discussion: we knew little, if anything, would change.

accede V. agree. If I *accede* to this demand for blackmail, I am afraid that I will be the victim of future demands.

accelerate V. move faster. In our science class, we learn how falling bodies *accelerate.*

accentuate V. emphasize; stress. If you *accentuate* the positive and eliminate the negative, you may wind up with an overoptimistic view of the world.

■ **accessible** ADJ. easy to approach; obtainable. We asked our guide whether the ruins were *accessible* on foot.

accessory N. additional object; useful but not essential thing. She bought an attractive handbag as an *accessory* for her dress. also ADJ.

■ **acclaim** V. applaud; announce with great approval. The NBC sportscasters *acclaimed* every American victory in the Olympics and decried every American defeat. also N.

acclimate V. adjust to climate. One of the difficulties of our present air age is the need of travelers to *acclimate* themselves to their new and often strange environments.

acclivity N. sharp upslope of a hill. The car would not go up the *acclivity* in high gear.

● **accolade** N. award of merit. In Hollywood, an "Oscar" is the highest *accolade.*

accommodate V. oblige or help someone; adjust or bring into harmony; adapt. Mitch always did everything possible to *accommodate* his elderly relatives, from driving them to medical appointments to helping them with paperwork. (secondary meaning)

accomplice N. partner in crime. Because he had provided the criminal with the lethal weapon, he was arrested as an *accomplice* in the murder.

accord N. agreement. She was in complete *accord* with the verdict.

accost V. approach and speak first to a person. When the two young men *accosted* me, I was frightened because I thought they were going to attack me.

accoutre V. equip. The fisherman was *accoutred* with the best that the sporting goods store could supply. accoutrements, N.

accretion N. growth; increase. The *accretion* of wealth marked the family's rise in power.

accrue V. come about by addition. You must pay the interest that has *accrued* on your debt as well as the principal sum. accrual, N.

acerbity N. bitterness of speech and temper. The meeting of the United Nations General Assembly was marked with such *acerbity* that informed sources held out little hope of reaching any useful settlement of the problem. acerbic, ADJ.

acetic ADJ. vinegary. The salad had an exceedingly *acetic* flavor.

acidulous ADJ. slightly sour; sharp, caustic. James was unpopular because of his sarcastic and *acidulous* remarks.

■ **acknowledge** V. recognize; admit. Although I *acknowledge* that the Beatles' tunes sound pretty dated today, I still prefer them to the "gangsta rap" songs my brothers play.

acme N. top; pinnacle. His success in this role marked the *acme* of his career as an actor.

acoustics N. science of sound; quality that makes a room easy or hard to hear in. Carnegie Hall is liked by music lovers because of its fine *acoustics.*

● **acquiesce** V. assent; agree without protesting. Although she appeared to *acquiesce* to her employer's suggestions, I could tell she had reservations about the changes he wanted made. acquiescence, N.; acquiescent, ADJ.

acquire V. obtain; get. Frederick Douglass was determined to *acquire* an education despite his master's efforts to prevent his doing so.

acquittal N. deliverance from a charge. His *acquittal* by the jury surprised those who had thought him guilty. acquit, V.

● **acrid** ADJ. sharp; bitterly pungent. The *acrid* odor of burnt gunpowder filled the room after the pistol had been fired.

● **acrimonious** ADJ. bitter in words or manner. The candidate attacked his opponent in highly *acrimonious* terms. acrimony, N.

acrophobia N. fear of heights. A born salesman, he could convince someone with a bad case of *acrophobia* to sign up for a life membership in a sky-diving club.

actuarial ADJ. calculating; pertaining to insurance statistics. According to recent *actuarial* tables, life expectancy is greater today than it was a century ago.

actuate V. motivate. I fail to understand what *actuated* you to reply to this letter so nastily.

acuity N. sharpness. In time his youthful *acuity* of vision failed him, and he needed glasses.

acumen N. mental keenness. His business *acumen* helped him to succeed where others had failed.

acute ADJ. quickly perceptive; keen; brief and severe. The *acute* young doctor realized immediately that the gradual deterioration of her patient's once *acute* hearing was due to a chronic illness, not an *acute* one.

adage   N. wise saying; proverb. There is much truth in the old *adage* about fools and their money.

adamant   ADJ. hard; inflexible. Bronson played the part of a revenge-driven man, *adamant* in his determination to punish the criminals who destroyed his family. adamancy, N.

adapt   V. alter; modify. Some species of animals have become extinct because they could not *adapt* to a changing environment.

addendum   N. an addition or supplement. As an *addendum* to the minutes, let me point out that Susan moved to appoint Kathy and Arthur to the finance committee.

addiction   N. compulsive, habitual need. His *addiction* to drugs caused his friends much grief.

addle   V. muddle; drive crazy; become rotten. This idiotic plan is confusing enough to *addle* anyone. addled, ADJ.

address   V. direct a speech to; deal with or discuss. Due to *address* the convention in July, Brown planned to *address* the issue of low-income housing in his speech.

adept   ADJ. expert at. She was *adept* at the fine art of irritating people. also N.

adhere   V. stick fast. I will *adhere* to this opinion until proof that I am wrong is presented. adhesion, N.

adherent   N. supporter; follower. In the wake of the scandal, the senator's one-time *adherents* quickly deserted him.

adjacent   ADJ. adjoining; neighboring; close by. Philip's best friend Jason lived only four houses down the block, close but not immediately *adjacent*.

adjunct   N. something added on or attached (generally nonessential or inferior). Although I don't absolutely need a second computer, I plan to buy a laptop to serve as an *adjunct* to my desktop model.

admonish   V. warn; reprove. He *admonished* his listeners to change their wicked ways. admonition, N.

admonition   N. warning. After the student protesters repeatedly rejected Chairman Deng's *admonitions*, the government issued an ultimatum: either the students would end the demonstration at once or the soldiers would fire on the crowd.

adorn   V. decorate. Wall paintings and carved statues *adorned* the temple. adornment, N.

adroit   ADJ. skillful. His *adroit* handling of the delicate situation pleased his employers.

Word List 2   adulation–amend

■ **adulation**   N. flattery; admiration. The rock star thrived on the *adulation* of his groupies and yes men. adulate, V.

adulterate   V. make impure by adding inferior or tainted substances. It is a crime to *adulterate* foods without informing the buyer; when consumers learned that Beech-Nut had *adulterated* their apple juice by mixing it with water, they protested vigorously.

advent   N. arrival. Most Americans were unaware of the *advent* of the Nuclear Age until the news of Hiroshima reached them.

adventitious   ADJ. accidental; casual. He found this *adventitious* meeting with his friend extremely fortunate.

■ **adversary**   N. opponent. The young wrestler struggled to defeat his *adversary*.

adverse   ADJ. unfavorable; hostile. The recession had a highly *adverse* effect on Father's investment portfolio: he lost so much money that he could no longer afford the butler and the upstairs maid. adversity, N.

■ **adversity**   N. poverty; misfortune. We must learn to meet *adversity* gracefully.

advocacy   N. support; active pleading on something's behalf. No threats could dissuade Bishop Desmond Tutu from his *advocacy* of the human rights of black South Africans.

■ **advocate**   V. urge; plead for. The abolitionists *advocated* freedom for the slaves. also N.

aerie   N. nest of a large bird of prey (eagle, hawk). The mother eagle swooped down on the unwitting rabbit and bore it off to her *aerie* high in the Rocky Mountains.

■ **aesthetic**   ADJ. artistic; dealing with or capable of appreciation of the beautiful. The beauty of Tiffany's stained glass appealed to Esther's *aesthetic* sense. aesthete, N.

■ **affable**   ADJ. easily approachable; warmly friendly. Accustomed to cold, aloof supervisors, Nicholas was amazed at how *affable* his new employer was.

affected   ADJ. artificial; pretended; assumed in order to impress. His *affected* mannerisms—his "Harvard" accent, his air of boredom, his use of obscure foreign words—bugged us: he acted as if he thought he was too good for his old high school friends. affectation, N.

affidavit   N. written statement made under oath. The court refused to accept his statement unless he presented it in the form of an *affidavit*.

affiliation   N. joining; associating with. His *affiliation* with the political party was of short duration for he soon disagreed with his colleagues.

affinity   N. kinship. She felt an *affinity* with all who suffered; their pains were her pains.

■ **affirmation**   N. positive assertion; confirmation; solemn pledge by one who refuses to take an oath. Despite Tom's *affirmations* of innocence, Aunt Polly still suspected he had eaten the pie.

affix v. fasten; attach; add on. First the registrar had to *affix* her signature to the license; then she had to *affix* her official seal.

affliction N. state of distress; cause of suffering. Even in the midst of her *affliction*, Elizabeth tried to keep up the spirits of those around her.

affluence N. abundance; wealth. Foreigners are amazed by the *affluence* and luxury of the American way of life.

affront N. insult; offense; intentional act of disrespect. When Mrs. Proudie was not seated beside the Archdeacon at the head table, she took it as a personal *affront* and refused to speak to her hosts for a week. also v.

aftermath N. consequences; outcome; upshot. People around the world wondered what the *aftermath* of China's violent suppression of the student protests would be.

agenda N. items of business at a meeting. We had so much difficulty agreeing upon an *agenda* that there was very little time for the meeting.

agent N. means or instrument; personal representative; person acting in an official capacity. "I will be the *agent* of America's destruction," proclaimed the beady-eyed villain, whose *agent* had gotten him the role. With his face, he could never have played the part of the hero, a heroic F.B.I. *agent*.

agglomeration N. collection; heap. It took weeks to assort the *agglomeration* of miscellaneous items she had collected on her trip.

aggrandize v. increase or intensify. The history of the past quarter century illustrates how a President may *aggrandize* his power to act aggressively in international affairs without considering the wishes of Congress.

● **aggregate** v. gather; accumulate. Before the Wall Street scandals, dealers in so-called junk bonds managed to *aggregate* great wealth in short periods of time. aggregation, N.

aggressor N. attacker. Before you punish both boys for fighting, see whether you can determine which one was the *aggressor*.

aghast ADJ. horrified. He was *aghast* at the nerve of the speaker who had insulted his host.

agility N. nimbleness. The *agility* of the acrobat amazed and thrilled the audience.

agitate v. stir up; disturb. Her fiery remarks *agitated* the already angry mob.

agnostic N. one who is skeptical of the existence or knowability of a god or any ultimate reality. *Agnostics* say we can neither prove nor disprove the existence of god; we simply just can't know. also ADJ.

agrarian ADJ. pertaining to land or its cultivation. The country is gradually losing its *agrarian* occupation and turning more and more to an industrial point of view.

alacrity N. cheerful promptness. Phil and Dave were raring to get off to the mountains; they packed up their ski gear and climbed into the van with *alacrity*.

alchemy N. medieval chemistry. The changing of baser metals into gold was the goal of the students of *alchemy*. alchemist, N.

alcove N. nook; small, recessed section of a room. Though their apartment lacked a full-scale dining room, an *alcove* adjacent to the living room made an adequate breakfast nook for the young couple.

alias N. an assumed name. John Smith's *alias* was Bob Jones. also ADV.

alienate v. make hostile; separate. Her attempts to *alienate* the two friends failed because they had complete faith in each other.

alimentary ADJ. supplying nourishment. The *alimentary* canal in our bodies is so named because digestion of foods occurs there. When asked for the name of the digestive tract, Sherlock Holmes replied, "*Alimentary*, my dear Watson."

alimony N. payment by a husband to his divorced wife (or vice versa). Mrs. Jones was awarded $200 monthly *alimony* by the court when she was divorced from her husband.

allay v. calm; pacify. The crew tried to *allay* the fears of the passengers by announcing that the fire had been controlled.

allege v. state without proof. Although it is *alleged* that she has worked for the enemy, she denies the *allegation* and, legally, we can take no action against her without proof. allegation, N.

allegiance N. loyalty. Not even a term in prison could shake Lech Walesa's *allegiance* to Solidarity, the Polish trade union he had helped to found.

allegory N. story in which characters are used as symbols; fable. *Pilgrim's Progress* is an *allegory* of the temptations and victories of man's soul. allegorical, ADJ.

■ **alleviate** v. relieve. This should *alleviate* the pain; if it does not, we shall have to use stronger drugs.

alliteration N. repetition of beginning sound in poetry. "The furrow followed free" is an example of *alliteration*.

allocate v. assign. Even though the Red Cross had *allocated* a large sum for the relief of the sufferers of the disaster, many people perished.

alloy N. a mixture as of metals. *Alloys* of gold are used more frequently than the pure metal.

alloy v. mix; make less pure; lessen or moderate. Our delight at the Yankees' victory was *alloyed* by our concern for Dwight Gooden, who injured his pitching arm in the game.

allude v. refer indirectly. Try not to mention divorce in Jack's presence because he will think you are *alluding* to his marital problems with Jill.

allure v. entice; attract. *Allured* by the song of the sirens, the helmsman steered the ship toward the reef. also N.

allusion N. indirect reference. When Amanda said to the ticket scalper, "One hundred bucks? What do you want, a pound of flesh?," she was making an *allusion* to Shakespeare's *Merchant of Venice*.

aloft ADV. upward. The sailor climbed *aloft* into the rigging. To get into a loft bed, you have to climb *aloft*.

■ **aloof** ADJ. apart; reserved. Shy by nature, she remained *aloof* while all the rest conversed.

altercation N. noisy quarrel; heated dispute. In that hot-tempered household, no meal ever came to a peaceful conclusion; the inevitable *altercation* might even end in blows.

■ **altruistic** ADJ. unselfishly generous; concerned for others. In providing tutorial assistance and college scholarships for hundreds of economically disadvantaged youths, Eugene Lang performed a truly *altruistic* deed. altruism, N.

amalgamate V. combine; unite in one body. The unions will attempt to *amalgamate* their groups into one national body.

amass V. collect. The miser's aim is to *amass* and hoard as much gold as possible.

ambidextrous ADJ. capable of using either hand with equal ease. A switch-hitter in baseball should be naturally *ambidextrous*.

ambience N. environment; atmosphere. She went to the restaurant not for the food but for the *ambience*.

■ **ambiguous** ADJ. unclear or doubtful in meaning. His *ambiguous* instructions misled us; we did not know which road to take. ambiguity, N.

■ **ambivalence** N. the state of having contradictory or conflicting emotional attitudes. Torn between loving her parents one minute and hating them the next, she was confused by the *ambivalence* of her feelings. ambivalent, ADJ.

amble N. moving at an easy pace. When she first mounted the horse, she was afraid to urge the animal to go faster than a gentle *amble*. also V.

ambulatory ADJ. able to walk; not bedridden. Juan was a highly *ambulatory* patient; not only did he refuse to be confined to bed, but he insisted on riding his skateboard up and down the halls.

ameliorate V. improve. Many social workers have attempted to *ameliorate* the conditions of people living in the slums.

amenable ADJ. readily managed; willing to be led. He was *amenable* to any suggestions that came from those he looked up to; he resented advice from his inferiors.

amend V. correct; change, generally for the better. Hoping to *amend* his condition, he left Vietnam for the United States.

Word List 3   amenities-apostate

amenities N. convenient features; courtesies. In addition to the customary *amenities* for the business traveler—fax machines, modems, a health club—the hotel offers the services of a butler versed in the social *amenities*.

amiable ADJ. agreeable; lovable; warmly friendly. In *Little Women*, Beth is the *amiable* daughter whose loving disposition endears her to all who know her.

amicable ADJ. politely friendly; not quarrelsome. Beth's sister Jo is the hot-tempered tomboy who has a hard time maintaining *amicable* relations with those around her. Jo's quarrel with her friend Laurie finally reaches an *amicable* settlement, but not because Jo turns amiable overnight.

amiss ADJ. wrong; faulty. Seeing her frown, he wondered if anything were *amiss*. also ADV.

amity N. friendship. Student exchange programs such as the Experiment in International Living were established to promote international *amity*.

amnesia N. loss of memory. Because she was suffering from *amnesia*, the police could not get the young girl to identify herself.

amnesty N. pardon. When his first child was born, the king granted *amnesty* to all in prison.

amoral ADJ. nonmoral. The *amoral* individual lacks a code of ethics; he cannot tell right from wrong. The immoral person can tell right from wrong; he chooses to do something he knows is wrong.

amorous ADJ. moved by sexual love; loving. "Love them and leave them" was the motto of the *amorous* Don Juan.

● **amorphous** ADJ. formless; lacking shape or definition. As soon as we have decided on our itinerary, we shall send you a copy; right now, our plans are still *amorphous*.

amphibian ADJ. able to live both on land and in water. Frogs are classified as *amphibian*. also N.

amphitheater N. oval building with tiers of seats. The spectators in the *amphitheater* cheered the gladiators.

ample ADJ. abundant. Bond had *ample* opportunity to escape. Why did he let us catch him?

amplify V. broaden or clarify by expanding; intensify; make stronger. Charlie Brown tried to *amplify* his remarks, but he was drowned out by jeers from the audience. Lucy was smarter: she used a loudspeaker to *amplify* her voice.

amputate V. cut off part of body; prune. When the doctors had to *amputate* the young man's leg to prevent the spread of cancer, he did not let the loss of a limb keep him from participating in sports.

amulet N. charm; talisman. Around her neck she wore the *amulet* that the witch doctor had given her.

● **anachronistic** ADJ. having an error involving time in a story. The reference to clocks in *Julius Caesar* is *anachronistic*: clocks did not exist in Caesar's time. anachronism, N.

analgesic ADJ. causing insensitivity to pain. The *analgesic* qualities of this lotion will provide temporary relief.

■ **analogous** ADJ. comparable. She called our attention to the things that had been done in an *analogous* situation and recommended that we do the same.

analogy   N. similarity; parallelism. A well-known *analogy* compares the body's immune system with an army whose defending troops are the lymphocytes or white blood cells.

■ **anarchist**   N. person who seeks to overturn the established government; advocate of abolishing authority. Denying she was an *anarchist*, Katya maintained she wished only to make changes in our government, not to destroy it entirely. anarchy, N.

anarchy   N. absence of governing body; state of disorder. The assassination of the leaders led to a period of *anarchy*.

anathema   N. solemn curse; someone or something regarded as a curse. The Ayatolla Khomeini heaped *anathema* upon "the Great Satan," that is, the United States. To the Ayatolla, America and the West were *anathema*; he loathed the democratic nations, cursing them in his dying words. anathematize, V.

ancestry   N. family descent. David can trace his *ancestry* as far back as the seventeenth century, when one of his *ancestors* was a court trumpeter somewhere in Germany. ancestral, ADJ.

anchor   V. secure or fasten firmly; be fixed in place. We set the post in concrete to *anchor* it in place. anchorage, N.

ancillary   ADJ. serving as an aid or accessory; auxiliary. In an *ancillary* capacity, Doctor Watson was helpful; however, Holmes could not trust the good doctor to solve a perplexing case on his own. also N.

■ **anecdote**   N. short account of an amusing or interesting event. Rather than make concrete proposals for welfare reform, President Reagan told *anecdotes* about poor people who became wealthy despite their impoverished backgrounds.

anemia   N. condition in which blood lacks red corpuscles. The doctor ascribes her tiredness to *anemia*. anemic, ADJ.

anesthetic   N. substance that removes sensation with or without loss of consciousness. His monotonous voice acted like an *anesthetic*; his audience was soon asleep. anesthesia, N.

anguish   N. acute pain; extreme suffering. Visiting the site of the explosion, the governor wept to see the *anguish* of the victims and their families.

angular   ADJ. sharp-cornered; stiff in manner. Mr. Spock's features, though *angular*, were curiously attractive, in a Vulcan way.

animated   ADJ. lively; spirited. Jim Carrey's facial expressions are highly *animated*: when he played Ace Ventura, he looked practically rubber-faced.

■ **animosity**   N. active enmity. He incurred the *animosity* of the ruling class because he advocated limitations of their power.

animus   N. hostile feeling or intent. The *animus* of the speaker became obvious to all when he began to indulge in sarcastic and insulting remarks.

annals   N. records; history. In the *annals* of this period, we find no mention of democratic movements.

annex   V. attach; take possession of. Mexico objected to the United States' attempts to *annex* the territory that later became the state of Texas.

annihilate   V. destroy. The enemy in its revenge tried to *annihilate* the entire population.

annotate   V. comment; make explanatory notes. In the appendix to the novel, the editor sought to *annotate* many of the author's more esoteric references.

annuity   N. yearly allowance. The *annuity* he set up with the insurance company supplements his social security benefits so that he can live very comfortably without working.

annul   V. make void. The parents of the eloped couple tried to *annul* the marriage.

anoint   V. consecrate. The prophet Samuel *anointed* David with oil, crowning him king of Israel.

anomalous   ADJ. abnormal; irregular. He was placed in the *anomalous* position of seeming to approve procedures which he despised.

● **anomaly**   N. irregularity. A bird that cannot fly is an *anomaly*.

anonymity   N. state of being nameless; anonymousness. The donor of the gift asked the college not to mention him by name; the dean readily agreed to respect his *anonymity*.

anonymous   ADJ. having no name. She tried to ascertain the identity of the writer of the *anonymous* letter.

■ **antagonism**   N. hostility; active resistance. Barry showed his *antagonism* toward his new stepmother by ignoring her whenever she tried talking to him. antagonistic, ADJ.

antecede   V. precede. The invention of the radiotelegraph *anteceded* the development of television by a quarter of a century.

antecedents   N. preceding events or circumstances that influence what comes later; ancestors or early background. Susi Bechhofer's ignorance of her Jewish background had its *antecedents* in the chaos of World War II. Smuggled out of Germany and adopted by a Christian family, she knew nothing of her birth and *antecedents* until she was reunited with her family in 1989.

● **antediluvian**   ADJ. antiquated; extremely ancient. Looking at his great-aunt's antique furniture, which must have been cluttering up her attic since the time of Noah's flood, the young heir exclaimed, "Heavens! How positively *antediluvian*!"

anthem   N. song of praise or patriotism. Let us now all join in singing the national *anthem*.

anthology   N. book of literary selections by various authors. This *anthology* of science fiction was compiled by the late Isaac Asimov. anthologize, V.

anthropocentric   ADJ. regarding human beings as the center of the universe. Without considering any evidence that might challenge his *anthropocentric* viewpoint, Hector categorically maintained that dolphins could not be as intelligent as men. anthropocentrism, N.

anthropoid   ADJ. manlike. The gorilla is the strongest of the *anthropoid* animals. also N.

anthropologist   N. a student of the history and science of mankind. *Anthropologists* have discovered several relics of prehistoric man in this area.

anthropomorphic   ADJ. having human form or characteristics. Primitive religions often have deities with *anthropomorphic* characteristics. anthropomorphism, N.

anticlimax   N. letdown in thought or emotion. After the fine performance in the first act, the rest of the play was an *anticlimax*. anticlimactic, ADJ.

■ **antidote**   N. medicine to counteract a poison or disease. When Marge's child accidentally swallowed some cleaning fluid, the local poison control hotline instructed Marge how to administer the *antidote*.

● **antipathy**   N. aversion; dislike. Tom's extreme *antipathy* for disputes keeps him from getting into arguments with his temperamental wife. Noise in any form is *antipathetic* to him. Among his other *antipathies* are honking cars, boom boxes, and heavy metal rock.

■ **antiquated**   ADJ. old-fashioned; obsolete. Philip had grown so accustomed to editing his papers on word processors that he thought typewriters were too *antiquated* for him to use.

antiseptic   N. substance that prevents infection. It is advisable to apply an *antiseptic* to any wound, no matter how slight or insignificant. also ADJ.

antithesis   N. contrast; direct opposite of or to. This tyranny was the *antithesis* of all that he had hoped for, and he fought it with all his strength.

■ **apathy**   N. lack of caring; indifference. A firm believer in democratic government, she could not understand the *apathy* of people who never bothered to vote. apathetic, ADJ.

ape   V. imitate or mimic. He was suspended for a week because he had *aped* the principal in front of the whole school.

aperture   N. opening; hole. She discovered a small *aperture* in the wall, through which the insects had entered the room.

apex   N. tip; summit; climax. He was at the *apex* of his career: he had climbed to the top of the heap.

aphasia   N. loss of speech due to injury or illness. After the automobile accident, the victim had periods of *aphasia* when he could not speak at all or could only mumble incoherently.

aphorism   N. pithy maxim. An *aphorism* differs from an adage in that it is more philosophical or scientific. "The proper study of mankind is man" is an *aphorism*. "There's no smoke without a fire" is an adage. aphoristic, ADJ.

apiary   N. a place where bees are kept. Although he spent many hours daily in the *apiary*, he was very seldom stung by a bee.

aplomb   N. poise; assurance. Gwen's *aplomb* in handling potentially embarrassing moments was legendary around the office; when one of her clients broke a piece of her best crystal, she coolly picked up her own goblet and hurled it into the fireplace.

apocalyptic   ADJ. prophetic; pertaining to revelations. The crowd jeered at the street preacher's *apocalyptic* predictions of doom. The *Apocalypse* or *Book of Revelations* of Saint John prophesies the end of the world as we know it and foretells marvels and prodigies that signal the coming doom.

● **apocryphal**   ADJ. untrue; made up. To impress his friends, Tom invented *apocryphal* tales of his adventures in the big city.

apogee   N. highest point. When the moon in its orbit is farthest away from the earth, it is at its *apogee*.

apolitical   ADJ. having an aversion or lack of concern for political affairs. It was hard to remain *apolitical* during the Vietnam War; even people who generally ignored public issues felt they had to take political stands.

apologist   N. one who writes in defense of a cause or institution. Rather than act as an *apologist* for the current regime in Beijing and defend its brutal actions, the young diplomat decided to defect to the West.

apostate   N. one who abandons his religious faith or political beliefs. Because he switched from one party to another, his former friends shunned him as an *apostate*. apostasy, N.

Word List 4   apotheosis–astigmatism

apotheosis   N. elevation to godhood; an ideal example of something. The *apotheosis* of a Roman emperor was designed to insure his eternal greatness: people would worship at his altar forever. The hero of the musical *How to Succeed in Business*…was the *apotheosis* of yuppieness: he was the perfect upwardly-bound young man on the make.

appall   V. dismay; shock. We were *appalled* by the horrifying conditions in the city's jails.

apparatus   N. equipment. Firefighters use specialized *apparatus* to fight fires.

apparition   N. ghost; phantom. On the castle battlements, an *apparition* materialized and spoke to Hamlet, warning him of his uncle's treachery. In *Ghostbusters*, hordes of *apparitions* materialized, only to be dematerialized by the specialized apparatus wielded by Bill Murray.

■ **appease**   V. pacify or soothe; relieve. Tom and Jody tried to *appease* the crying baby by offering him one toy after another, but he would not calm down until they *appeased* his hunger by giving him a bottle.

appellation   N. name; title. Macbeth was startled when the witches greeted him with an incorrect *appellation*. Why did they call him Thane of Cawdor, he wondered, when the holder of that title still lived?

append   V. attach. When you *append* a bibliography to a text, you have just created an *appendix*.

application N. diligent attention. Pleased with how well Tom had whitewashed the fence, Aunt Polly praised him for his *application* to the task. apply, V. (secondary meaning)

apposite ADJ. appropriate; fitting. He was always able to find the *apposite* phrase, the correct expression for every occasion.

appraise V. estimate value of. It is difficult to *appraise* the value of old paintings; it is easier to call them priceless. appraisal, N.

appreciate V. be thankful for; increase in worth; be thoroughly conscious of. Little Orphan Annie truly *appreciated* the stocks Daddy Warbucks gave her, which *appreciated* in value considerably over the years.

apprehend V. arrest (a criminal); dread; perceive. The police will *apprehend* the culprit and convict him before long.

■ **apprehension** N. fear. His nervous glances at the passersby on the deserted street revealed his *apprehension*.

apprenticeship N. time spent as a novice learning a trade from a skilled worker. As a child, Pip had thought it would be wonderful to work as Joe's *apprentice*; now he hated his *apprenticeship* and scorned the blacksmith's trade.

apprise V. inform. When he was *apprised* of the dangerous weather conditions, he decided to postpone his trip.

approbation N. approval. She looked for some sign of *approbation* from her parents, hoping her good grades would please them.

appropriate V. acquire; take possession of for one's own use. The ranch owners *appropriated* the lands that had originally been set aside for the Indians' use.

apropos PREP. with reference to; regarding. I find your remarks *apropos* of the present situation timely and pertinent. also ADJ. and ADV.

aptitude N. fitness; talent. The counselor gave him an *aptitude* test before advising him about the career he should follow.

aquatic ADJ. pertaining to water. Paul enjoyed *aquatic* sports such as scuba diving and snorkeling.

aquiline ADJ. curved, hooked. He can be recognized by his *aquiline* nose, curved like the beak of the eagle.

● **arable** ADJ. fit for growing crops. The first settlers wrote home glowing reports of the New World, praising its vast acres of *arable* land ready for the plow.

arbiter N. a person with power to decide a dispute; judge. As an *arbiter* in labor disputes, she has won the confidence of the workers and the employers.

■ **arbitrary** ADJ. capricious; randomly chosen; tyrannical. Tom's *arbitrary* dismissal angered him; his boss had no reason to fire him. He threw an *arbitrary* assortment of clothes into his suitcase and headed off, not caring where he went.

arbitrator N. judge. Because the negotiating teams had been unable to reach a contract settlement, an outside *arbitrator* was called upon to mediate the dispute between union and management. arbitration, N.

arboretum N. place where different tree varieties are exhibited. Walking along the tree-lined paths of the *arbore-tum*, Rita noted poplars, firs, and some particularly fine sycamores.

arcade N. a covered passageway, usually lined with shops. The *arcade* was popular with shoppers because it gave them protection from the summer sun and the winter rain.

arcane ADJ. secret; mysterious; known only to the initiated. Secret brotherhoods surround themselves with *arcane* rituals and trappings to mystify outsiders. So do doctors. Consider the *arcane* terminology they use and the impression they try to give that what is *arcane* to us is obvious to them.

archaeology N. study of artifacts and relics of early mankind. The professor of *archaeology* headed an expedition to the Gobi Desert in search of ancient ruins.

■ **archaic** ADJ. antiquated. "Methinks," "thee," and "thou" are *archaic* words that are no longer part of our normal vocabulary.

archetype N. prototype; primitive pattern. The Brooklyn Bridge was the *archetype* of the many spans that now connect Manhattan with Long Island and New Jersey.

archipelago N. group of closely located islands. When Gauguin looked at the map and saw the *archipelagoes* in the South Seas, he longed to visit them.

archives N. public records; place where public records are kept. These documents should be part of the *archives* so that historians may be able to evaluate them in the future.

● **ardent** ADJ. intense; passionate; zealous. Katya's *ardor* was contagious; soon all her fellow demonstrators were busily making posters and handing out flyers, inspired by her *ardent* enthusiasm for the cause. ardor, N.

arduous ADJ. hard; strenuous. Her *arduous* efforts had sapped her energy.

aria N. operatic solo. At her Metropolitan Opera audition, Marian Anderson sang an *aria* from *Norma*.

arid ADJ. dry; barren. The cactus has adapted to survive in an *arid* environment.

aristocracy N. hereditary nobility; privileged class. Americans have mixed feelings about hereditary *aristocracy*: we say all men are created equal, but we describe particularly outstanding people as natural *aristocrats*.

armada N. fleet of warships. Queen Elizabeth's navy defeated the mighty *armada* that threatened the English coast.

aromatic ADJ. fragrant. Medieval sailing vessels brought *aromatic* herbs from China to Europe.

arousal N. awakening; provocation (of a response). On *arousal*, Papa was always grumpy as a bear. The children tiptoed around the house, fearing they would *arouse* his anger by waking him up.

arraign V. charge in court; indict. After his indictment by the Grand Jury, the accused man was *arraigned* in the County Criminal Court.

array V. marshal; draw up in order. His actions were bound to *array* public sentiment against him. also N.

array V. clothe; adorn. She liked to watch her mother *array* herself in her finest clothes before going out for the evening. also N.

arrears N. being in debt. He was in *arrears* with his payments on the car.

arrest V. stop or slow down; catch someone's attention. Slipping, the trapeze artist plunged from the heights until a safety net luckily *arrested* his fall. This near-disaster *arrested* the crowd's attention.

■ **arrogance** N. pride; haughtiness. Convinced that Emma thought she was better than anyone else in the class, Ed rebuked her for her *arrogance*.

arroyo N. gully. Until the heavy rains of the past spring, this *arroyo* had been a dry bed.

arsenal N. storage place for military equipment. People are forbidden to smoke in the *arsenal* for fear that a stray spark might set off the munitions stored there.

■ **articulate** ADJ. effective; distinct. Her *articulate* presentation of the advertising campaign impressed her employers. also V.

■ **artifact** N. object made by human beings, either handmade or mass-produced. Archaeologists debated the significance of the *artifacts* discovered in the ruins of Asia Minor but came to no conclusion about the culture they represented.

artifice N. deception; trickery. The Trojan War proved to the Greeks that cunning and *artifice* were often more effective than military might.

■ **artisan** N. manually skilled worker; craftsman, as opposed to artist. A noted *artisan*, Arturo was known for the fine craftsmanship of his inlaid cabinets.

artless ADJ. without guile; open and honest. Sophisticated and cynical, Jack could not believe Jill was as *artless* and naive as she appeared to be.

■ **ascendancy** N. controlling influence; domination. Leaders of religious cults maintain *ascendancy* over their followers by methods that can verge on brainwashing.

ascertain V. find out for certain. Please *ascertain* her present address.

■ **ascetic** ADJ. practicing self-denial; austere. The wealthy, self-indulgent young man felt oddly drawn to the strict, *ascetic* life led by members of some monastic orders. also N.

ascribe V. refer; attribute; assign. I can *ascribe* no motive for her acts.

aseptic ADJ. preventing infection; having a cleansing effect. Hospitals succeeded in lowering the mortality rate as soon as they introduced *aseptic* conditions.

ashen ADJ. ash-colored. Her face was *ashen* with fear.

asinine ADJ. stupid. Your *asinine* remarks prove that you have not given this problem any serious consideration.

askance ADJ. with a sideways or indirect look. Looking *askance* at her questioner, she displayed her scorn.

askew ADJ. crookedly; slanted; at an angle. When he placed his hat *askew* upon his head, his observers laughed.

asperity N. sharpness (of temper). These remarks, spoken with *asperity*, stung the boys to whom they had been directed.

aspirant N. seeker after position or status. Although I am an *aspirant* for public office, I am not willing to accept the dictates of the party bosses. also ADJ.

■ **aspire** V. seek to attain; long for. Because he *aspired* to a career in professional sports, Philip enrolled in a graduate program in sports management. aspiration, N.

assail V. assault. He was *assailed* with questions after his lecture.

assay V. analyze; evaluate. When they *assayed* the ore, they found that they had discovered a very rich vein. also N.

assent V. agree; accept. It gives me great pleasure to *assent* to your request.

assert V. declare or state with confidence; put oneself forward boldly. Malcolm *asserted* that if Reese quit acting like a wimp and *asserted* himself a bit more, he'd improve his chances of getting a date. assertion, N.

assessment N. evaluation; judgment. Your SAT I score plays a part in the admission committee's *assessment* of you as an applicant.

● **assiduous** ADJ. diligent. He was *assiduous*, working at this task for weeks before he felt satisfied with his results. assiduity, N.

assimilate V. absorb; cause to become homogeneous. The manner in which the United States was able to *assimilate* the hordes of immigrants during the nineteenth and early twentieth centuries will always be a source of pride to Americans. The immigrants eagerly *assimilated* new ideas and customs; they soaked them up, the way plants soak up water.

● **assuage** V. ease or lessen (pain); satisfy (hunger); soothe (anger). Jilted by Jane, Dick tried to *assuage* his heartache by indulging in ice cream. One gallon later, he had *assuaged* his appetite but not his grief.

assumption N. something taken for granted; taking over or taking possession of. The young princess made the foolish *assumption* that the regent would not object to her *assumption* of power. assume, V.

assurance N. promise or pledge; certainty; self-confidence. When Guthrie gave Guinness his *assurance* that rehearsals were going well, he spoke with such *assurance* that Guinness felt relieved. assure, V.

asteroid N. small planet. *Asteroids* have become commonplace to the readers of interstellar travel stories in science fiction magazines.

astigmatism N. eye defect that prevents proper focus. As soon as his parents discovered that the boy suffered from *astigmatism*, they took him to the optometrist for corrective glasses.

Word List 5   astral-barb

astral   ADJ. relating to the stars. She was amazed at the number of *astral* bodies the new telescope revealed.

astringent   ADJ. binding; causing contraction. The *astringent* quality of the unsweetened lemon juice made swallowing difficult. also N.

astronomical   ADJ. enormously large or extensive. The government seems willing to spend *astronomical* sums on weapons development.

■ **astute**   ADJ. wise; shrewd; keen. The painter was an *astute* observer, noticing every tiny detail of her model's appearance and knowing exactly how important each one was.

asunder   ADV. into parts; apart. A fierce quarrel split the partnership *asunder*: the two partners finally sundered their connections because their points of view were poles *asunder*.

asylum   N. place of refuge or shelter; protection. The refugees sought *asylum* from religious persecution in a new land.

asymmetric   ADJ. not identical on both sides of a dividing central line. Because one eyebrow was set markedly higher than the other, William's face had a particularly *asymmetric* appearance.

atavism   N. resemblance to remote ancestors rather than to parents; deformity returning after passage of two or more generations. The doctors ascribed the child's deformity to an *atavism*.

atheistic   ADJ. denying the existence of God. His *atheistic* remarks shocked the religious worshippers.

atlas   N. a bound volume of maps, charts, or tables. Embarrassed at being unable to distinguish Slovenia from Slovakia, George W. finally consulted an *atlas*.

atone   V. make amends for; pay for. He knew no way in which he could *atone* for his brutal crime.

atrocity   N. brutal deed. In time of war, many *atrocities* are committed by invading armies.

● **atrophy**   N. wasting away. Polio victims need physiotherapy to prevent the *atrophy* of affected limbs. also V.

attain   V. achieve or accomplish; gain. The scarecrow sought to *attain* one goal: he wished to obtain a brain.

attentive   ADJ. alert and watchful; considerate; thoughtful. Spellbound, the *attentive* audience watched the final game of the tennis match, never taking their eyes from the ball. A cold wind sprang up; Stan's *attentive* daughter slipped a sweater over his shoulders without distracting his attention from the game.

attenuate   V. make thin; weaken. By withdrawing their forces, the generals hoped to *attenuate* the enemy lines.

attest   V. testify, bear witness. Having served as a member of the Grand Jury, I can *attest* that our system of indicting individuals is in need of improvement.

attribute   N. essential quality. His outstanding *attribute* was his kindness.

■ **attribute**   V. ascribe; explain. I *attribute* her success in science to the encouragement she received from her parents.

attrition   N. gradual decrease in numbers; reduction in the work force without firing employees; wearing away of opposition by means of harassment. In the 1960s urban churches suffered from *attrition* as members moved from the cities to the suburbs. Rather than fire staff members, church leaders followed a policy of *attrition*, allowing elderly workers to retire without replacing them.

atypical   ADJ. not normal. The child psychiatrist reassured Mrs. Keaton that playing doctor was not *atypical* behavior for a child of young Alex's age. "Yes," she replied, "but not charging for house calls!"

● **audacious**   ADJ. daring; bold. Audiences cheered as Luke Skywalker and Princess Leia made their *audacious*, death-defying leap to freedom, escaping Darth Vader's troops. audacity, N.

audit   N. examination of accounts. When the bank examiners arrived to hold their annual *audit*, they discovered the embezzlements of the chief cashier. also V.

auditory   ADJ. pertaining to the sense of hearing. Audrey suffered from *auditory* hallucinations: she thought Elvis was speaking to her from the Great Beyond.

■ **augment**   V. increase; add to. Armies *augment* their forces by calling up reinforcements; teachers *augment* their salaries by taking odd jobs.

augury   N. omen; prophecy. He interpreted the departure of the birds as an *augury* of evil. augur, V.

august   ADJ. impressive; majestic. Visiting the palace at Versailles, she was impressed by the *august* surroundings in which she found herself.

aureole   N. sun's corona; halo. Many medieval paintings depict saintly characters with *aureoles* around their heads.

auroral   ADJ. pertaining to the aurora borealis. The *auroral* display was particularly spectacular that evening.

auspicious   ADJ. favoring success. With favorable weather conditions, it was an *auspicious* moment to set sail. Thomas, however, had doubts about sailing: a paranoid, he became suspicious whenever conditions seemed *auspicious*.

■ **austere**   ADJ. forbiddingly stern; severely simple and unornamented. The headmaster's *austere* demeanor tended to scare off the more timid students, who never visited his study willingly. The room reflected the man, *austere* and bare, like a monk's cell, with no touches of luxury to moderate its *austerity*.

authenticate   V. prove genuine. An expert was needed to *authenticate* the original Van Gogh painting, distinguishing it from its imitation.

■ **authoritarian**   ADJ. subordinating the individual to the state; completely dominating another's will. The leaders of the *authoritarian* regime ordered the suppression of the democratic protest movement. After years of submitting to the will of her *authoritarian* father, Elizabeth Barrett ran away from home with the poet Robert Browning.

authoritative   ADJ. having the weight of authority; peremptory and dictatorial. Impressed by the young researcher's well-documented presentation, we accepted her analysis of the experiment as *authoritative*.

autocratic   ADJ. having absolute, unchecked power; dictatorial. Someone accustomed to exercising authority may become *autocratic* if his or her power is unchecked. Dictators by definition are *autocrats*. Bosses who dictate behavior as well as letters can be *autocrats* too.

automaton   N. mechanism that imitates actions of humans. Long before science fiction readers became aware of robots, writers were presenting stories of *automatons* who could outperform men.

■ **autonomous**   ADJ. self-governing. Although the University of California at Berkeley is just one part of the state university system, in many ways Cal Berkeley is *autonomous*, for it runs several programs that are not subject to outside control. autonomy, N.

autopsy   N. examination of a dead body; post-mortem. The medical examiner ordered an *autopsy* to determine the cause of death. also V.

auxiliary   ADJ. helper, additional or subsidiary. To prepare for the emergency, they built an *auxiliary* power station. also N.

avalanche   N. great mass of falling snow and ice. The park ranger warned the skiers to stay on the main trails, where they would be in no danger of being buried beneath a sudden *avalanche*.

● **avarice**   N. greediness for wealth. King Midas is a perfect example of *avarice*, for he was so greedy that he wished everything he touched would turn to gold.

avenge   V. take vengeance for something (or on behalf of someone). Hamlet vowed he would *avenge* his father's murder and punish Claudius for his horrible crime.

averse   ADJ. reluctant; disinclined. The reporter was *averse* to revealing the sources of his information.

■ **aversion**   N. firm dislike. Bert had an *aversion* to yuppies; Alex had an *aversion* to punks. Their mutual *aversion* was so great that they refused to speak to one another.

● **avert**   V. prevent; turn away. She *averted* her eyes from the dead cat on the highway.

● **aviary**   N. enclosure for birds. The *aviary* at the zoo held nearly 300 birds.

avid   ADJ. greedy; eager for. He was *avid* for learning and read everything he could get. avidity, N.

avocation   N. secondary or minor occupation. His hobby proved to be so fascinating and profitable that gradually he abandoned his regular occupation and concentrated on his *avocation*.

avow   V. declare openly. Lana *avowed* that she never meant to steal Debbie's boyfriend, but no one believed her *avowal* of innocence.

avuncular   ADJ. like an uncle. *Avuncular* pride did not prevent him from noticing his nephew's shortcomings.

awe   N. solemn wonder. The tourists gazed with *awe* at the tremendous expanse of the Grand Canyon.

awry   ADV. distorted; crooked. He held his head *awry*, giving the impression that he had caught cold in his neck during the night. also ADJ.

axiom   N. self-evident truth requiring no proof. Before a student can begin to think along the lines of Euclidean geometry, he must accept certain principles or *axioms*.

azure   ADJ. sky blue. *Azure* skies are indicative of good weather.

babble   V. chatter idly. The little girl *babbled* about her doll. also N.

bacchanalian   ADJ. drunken. Emperor Nero attended the *bacchanalian* orgy.

badger   V. pester; annoy. She was forced to change her telephone number because she was *badgered* by obscene phone calls.

badinage   N. teasing conversation. Her friends at work greeted the news of her engagement with cheerful *badinage*.

baffle   V. frustrate; perplex. The new code *baffled* the enemy agents.

bait   V. harass; tease. The school bully *baited* the smaller children, terrorizing them.

baleful   ADJ. deadly; having a malign influence; ominous. The fortune teller made *baleful* predictions of terrible things to come.

balk   V. foil or thwart; stop short; refuse to go on. When the warden learned that several inmates were planning to escape, he took steps to *balk* their attempt. However, he *balked* at punishing them by shackling them to the walls of their cells.

ballast   N. heavy substance used to add stability or weight. The ship was listing badly to one side; it was necessary to shift the *ballast* in the hold to get her back on an even keel. also V.

balm   N. something that relieves pain. Friendship is the finest *balm* for the pangs of disappointed love.

balmy   ADJ. mild; fragrant. A *balmy* breeze refreshed us after the sultry blast.

banal   ADJ. hackneyed; commonplace; trite; lacking originality. The hack writer's worn-out clichés made his comic sketch seem *banal*. He even resorted to the *banality* of having someone slip on a banana peel!

bandy   V. discuss lightly or glibly; exchange (words) heatedly. While the president was happy to *bandy* patriotic generalizations with anyone who would listen to him, he refused to *bandy* words with unfriendly reporters at the press conference.

bane   N. cause of ruin; curse. Lucy's little brother was the *bane* of her existence: his attempts to make her life miserable worked so well that she could have poisoned him with ratsbane for having such a *baneful* effect.

bantering   ADJ. good-natured ridiculing. They resented his *bantering* remarks because they thought he was being sarcastic.

barb   N. sharp projection from fishhook, etc.; openly cutting remark. If you were a politician, which would you prefer, being caught on the *barb* of a fishhook or being subjected to malicious verbal *barbs*? Who can blame the president if he's happier fishing than back in the capitol listening to his critics' *barbed* remarks?

Word List 6   bard-bluff

bard   N. poet. The ancient *bard* Homer sang of the fall of Troy.

baroque   ADJ. highly ornate. Accustomed to the severe lines of contemporary buildings, the architecture students found the flamboyance of *baroque* architecture amusing. They simply didn't go for *baroque*.

barrage   N. barrier laid down by artillery fire. The company was forced to retreat through the *barrage* of heavy cannons.

barren   ADJ. desolate; fruitless and unproductive; lacking. Looking out at the trackless, *barren* desert, Indiana Jones feared that his search for the missing expedition would prove *barren*.

barricade   N. hastily put together defensive barrier; obstacle. Marius and his fellow students hurriedly improvised a rough *barricade* to block police access to the students' quarter. Malcolm and his brothers *barricaded* themselves in their bedroom to keep their mother from seeing the hole in the bedroom floor. also v.

barterer   N. trader. The *barterer* exchanged trinkets for the natives' furs. It seemed smarter to *barter* than to pay cash.

bask   V. luxuriate; take pleasure in warmth. *Basking* on the beach, she relaxed so completely that she fell asleep.

bastion   N. fortress; defense. The villagers fortified the town hall, hoping this improvised *bastion* could protect them from the guerillas' raids.

bate   V. let down; restrain. Until it was time to open the presents, the children had to *bate* their curiosity. bated, ADJ.

bauble   N. trinket; trifle. The child was delighted with the *bauble* she had won in the grab bag.

bawdy   ADJ. indecent; obscene. Jack took offense at Jill's *bawdy* remarks. What kind of young man did she think he was?

beam   N. ray of light; long piece of metal or wood; course of a radio signal. V. smile radiantly. If a *beam* of light falls on you, it illuminates you; if a *beam* of iron falls on you, it eliminates you. (No one feels like *beaming* when crushed by an iron *beam*.)

beatific   ADJ. giving bliss; blissful. The *beatific* smile on the child's face made us very happy.

beatitude   N. blessedness; state of bliss. Growing closer to God each day, the mystic achieved a state of indescribable *beatitude*.

bedizen   V. dress with vulgar finery. The witch doctors were *bedizened* in all their gaudiest costumes.

bedraggle   V. wet thoroughly; stain with mud. We were so *bedraggled* by the severe storm that we had to change into dry clothing. bedraggled, ADJ.

beeline   N. direct, quick route. As soon as the movie was over, Jim made a *beeline* for the exit.

befuddle   V. confuse thoroughly. His attempts to clarify the situation succeeded only in *befuddling* her further.

beget   V. father; produce; give rise to. One good turn may deserve another; it does not necessarily *beget* another.

begrudge   V. resent. I *begrudge* every minute I have to spend attending meetings; they're a complete waste of time.

● **beguile**   V. mislead or delude; pass time. With flattery and big talk of easy money, the con men *beguiled* Kyle into betting his allowance on the shell game. Broke, he *beguiled* himself during the long hours by playing solitaire.

behemoth   N. huge creature; monstrous animal. Sportscasters nicknamed the linebacker "The *Behemoth*."

belabor   V. explain or go over excessively or to a ridiculous degree; attack verbally. The debate coach warned her student not to bore the audience by *belaboring* her point.

belated   ADJ. delayed. He apologized for his *belated* note of condolence to the widow of his friend and explained that he had just learned of her husband's untimely death.

beleaguer   V. besiege or attack; harassed. The babysitter was surrounded by a crowd of unmanageable brats who relentlessly *beleaguered* her.

■ **belie**   V. contradict; give a false impression. His coarse, hard-bitten exterior *belied* his inner sensitivity.

belittle   V. disparage or depreciate; put down. Parents should not *belittle* their children's early attempts at drawing, but should encourage their efforts. Barry was a put-down artist: he was a genius at *belittling* people and making them feel small.

bellicose   ADJ. warlike. His *bellicose* disposition alienated his friends.

belligerent   ADJ. quarrelsome. Whenever he had too much to drink, he became *belligerent* and tried to pick fights with strangers. belligerence, N.

bemoan   V. lament; express disapproval of. The widow *bemoaned* the death of her beloved husband. Although critics *bemoaned* the serious flaws in the author's novels, each year his latest book topped the best-seller list.

bemused   ADJ. confused; lost in thought; preoccupied. Jill studied the garbled instructions with a *bemused* look on her face.

benediction   N. blessing. The appearance of the sun after the many rainy days was like a *benediction*.

benefactor   N. gift giver; patron. Scrooge later became Tiny Tim's *benefactor* and gave him gifts.

beneficial   ADJ. helpful; useful. Tiny Tim's cheerful good nature had a *beneficial* influence on Scrooge's once-uncharitable disposition.

beneficiary   N. person entitled to benefits or proceeds of an insurance policy or will. In Scrooge's will, he made Tiny Tim his *beneficiary*: everything he left would go to young Tim.

■ **benevolent**   ADJ. generous; charitable. Mr. Fezziwig was a *benevolent* employer, who wished to make Christmas merrier for young Scrooge and his other employees.

benign   ADJ. kindly; favorable; not malignant. Though her *benign* smile and gentle bearing made Miss Marple seem a sweet little old lady, in reality she was a tough-minded, shrewd observer of human nature. benignity, N.

bent   ADJ; N. determined; natural talent or inclination. *Bent* on advancing in the business world, the secretary-heroine of *Working Girl* has a true *bent* for high finance.

● **bequeath**   V. leave to someone by a will; hand down. Though Maud had intended to *bequeath* the family home to her nephew, she died before changing her will. bequest, N.

berate   V. scold strongly. He feared she would *berate* him for his forgetfulness.

bereavement   N. state of being deprived of something valuable or beloved. His friends gathered to console him upon his sudden *bereavement*.

bereft   ADJ. deprived of; lacking; desolate because of a loss. The foolish gambler soon found himself *bereft* of funds.

berserk   ADV. frenzied. Angered, he went *berserk* and began to wreck the room.

beseech   V. beg; plead with. The workaholic executive's wife *beseeched* him to spend more time with their son.

beset   V. harass or trouble; hem in. Many vexing problems *beset* the American public school system. Sleeping Beauty's castle was *beset* on all sides by dense thickets that hid it from view.

besiege   V. surround with armed forces; harass (with requests). When the bandits *besieged* the village, the villagers holed up in the town hall and prepared to withstand a long siege. Members of the new administration were *besieged* with job applications from people who had worked on the campaign.

besmirch   V. soil, defile. The scandalous remarks in the newspaper *besmirch* the reputations of every member of the society.

bestial   ADJ. beastlike; brutal. According to legend, the werewolf was able to abandon its human shape and take on a *bestial* form.

bestow   V. give. He wished to *bestow* great honors upon the hero.

betoken   V. signify; indicate. The well-equipped docks, tall piles of cargo containers, and numerous vessels being loaded all *betoken* Oakland's importance as a port.

betray   V. be unfaithful; reveal (unconsciously or unwillingly). The spy *betrayed* his country by selling military secrets to the enemy. When he was taken in for questioning, the tightness of his lips *betrayed* his fear of being caught.

betroth   V. become engaged to marry. The announcement that they had become *betrothed* surprised their friends who had not suspected any romance. betrothal, N.

bevy   N. large group. The movie actor was surrounded by a *bevy* of starlets.

biased   ADJ. slanted; prejudiced. Because the judge played golf regularly with the district attorney's father, we feared he might be *biased* in the prosecution's favor. bias, N.

bicameral   ADJ. two-chambered, as a legislative body. The United States Congress is a *bicameral* body.

bicker   V. quarrel. The children *bickered* morning, noon, and night, exasperating their parents.

biennial   ADJ. every two years. Seeing no need to meet more frequently, the group held *biennial* meetings instead of annual ones. Plants that bear flowers *biennially* are known as *biennials*.

bigotry   N. stubborn intolerance. Brought up in a democratic atmosphere, the student was shocked by the *bigotry* and narrowness expressed by several of his classmates.

bilious   ADJ. suffering from indigestion; irritable. His *bilious* temperament was apparent to all who heard him rant about his difficulties.

bilk   V. swindle; cheat. The con man specialized in *bilking* insurance companies.

billowing   ADJ. swelling out in waves; surging. Standing over the air vent, Marilyn Monroe tried vainly to control her *billowing* skirts.

bivouac   N. temporary encampment. While in *bivouac*, we spent the night in our sleeping bags under the stars. also V.

bizarre   ADJ. fantastic; violently contrasting. The plot of the novel was too *bizarre* to be believed.

blanch   V. bleach; whiten. Although age had *blanched* his hair, he was still vigorous and energetic.

bland   ADJ. soothing or mild; agreeable. Jill tried a *bland* ointment for her sunburn. However, when Jack absent-mindedly patted her on the sunburned shoulder, she couldn't maintain a *bland* disposition.

blandishment   N. flattery. Despite the salesperson's *blandishments,* the customer did not buy the outfit.

blare   N. loud, harsh roar or screech; dazzling blaze of light. I don't know which is worse: the steady *blare* of a boom box deafening your ears or a sudden *blare* of flashbulbs dazzling your eyes.

blasé   ADJ. bored with pleasure or dissipation. Although Beth was as thrilled with the idea of a trip to Paris as her classmates were, she tried to act super cool and *blasé*, as if she'd been abroad hundreds of times.

blasphemy   N. irreverence; sacrilege; cursing. In my father's house, the Dodgers were the holiest of holies; to cheer for another team was to utter words of *blasphemy*. blasphemous, ADJ.

blatant   ADJ. flagrant; conspicuously obvious; loudly offensive. To the unemployed youth from Dublin, the "No Irish Need Apply" placard in the shop window was a *blatant* mark of prejudice.

● **bleak** ADJ. cold or cheerless; unlikely to be favorable. The frigid, inhospitable Aleutian Islands are *bleak* military outposts. It's no wonder that soldiers assigned there have a *bleak* attitude toward their posting.

● **blighted** ADJ. suffering from a disease; destroyed. The extent of the *blighted* areas could be seen only when viewed from the air.

blithe ADJ. gay; joyous; heedless. Shelley called the skylark a *"blithe* spirit" because of its happy song.

bloated ADJ. swollen or puffed as with water or air. Her *bloated* stomach came from drinking so much water.

bludgeon N. club; heavy-headed weapon. Attacked by Dr. Moriarty, Holmes used his walking stick as a *bludgeon* to defend himself. "Watson," he said, "I fear I may have *bludgeoned* Moriarty to death."

bluff ADJ. rough but good-natured. Jack had a *bluff* and-hearty manner that belied his actual sensitivity; he never let people know how thin-skinned he really was.

bluff N. pretense (of strength); deception; high cliff. Claire thought Lord Byron's boast that he would swim the Hellespont was just a *bluff;* she was astounded when he dove from the high *bluff* into the waters below.

Word List 7   blunder-canter

blunder N. error. The criminal's fatal *blunder* led to his capture. also v.

blurt v. utter impulsively. Before she could stop him, he *blurted* out the news.

bluster v. blow in heavy gusts; threaten emptily; bully. "Let the stormy winds *bluster*," cried Jack, "we'll set sail tonight." Jill let Jack *bluster:* she wasn't going anywhere, no matter what he said.

bode v. foreshadow; portend. The gloomy skies and the sulphurous odors from the mineral springs seemed to *bode* evil to those who settled in the area.

bogus ADJ. counterfeit; not authentic. The police quickly found the distributors of the *bogus* twenty-dollar bills.

bohemian ADJ. unconventional (in an artistic way). Gertrude Stein ran off to Paris to live an eccentric, *bohemian* life with her writer friends. Oakland was not *bohemian:* it was too bourgeois, too middle-class.

boisterous ADJ. violent; rough; noisy. The unruly crowd became even more *boisterous* when he tried to quiet them.

■ **bolster** v. support; reinforce. The debaters amassed file boxes full of evidence to *bolster* their arguments.

bolt N. door bar; fastening pin or screw; length of fabric. The carpenter shut the workshop door, sliding the heavy metal *bolt* into place. He sorted through his toolbox for the nuts and *bolts* and nails he would need. Before he cut into the *bolt* of canvas, he measured how much fabric he would need.

bolt v. dash or dart off; fasten (a door); gobble down. Jack was set to *bolt* out the front door, but Jill *bolted* the door. "Eat your breakfast," she said, "don't *bolt* your food."

bombardment N. attack with missiles. The enemy *bombardment* demolished the town. Members of the opposition party *bombarded* the prime minister with questions about the enemy attack.

bombastic ADJ. pompous; using inflated language. Puffed up with conceit, the orator spoke in such a *bombastic* manner that we longed to deflate him. bombast, N.

booming ADJ. deep and resonant; flourishing, thriving. "Who needs a microphone?" cried the mayor in his *boom-*

ing voice. Cheerfully he *boomed* out that, thanks to him, the city's economy was *booming*. boom, v.

boon N. blessing; benefit. The recent rains that filled our empty reservoirs were a *boon* to the whole community.

boorish ADJ. rude; clumsy; ungentlemanly. Natasha was embarrassed by her fellow spy's *boorish* behavior. "If you cannot act like a gentleman, Boris, go back to Russia: espionage is no job for clumsy *boors*." boor, N.

boundless ADJ. unlimited; vast. Mike's energy was *boundless:* the greater the challenge, the more vigorously he tackled the job.

bountiful ADJ. abundant; graciously generous. Thanks to the good harvest, we had a *bountiful* supply of food and we could be as *bountiful* as we liked in distributing food to the needy.

bourgeois ADJ. middle class; selfishly materialistic; dully conventional. Technically, anyone who belongs to the middle class is *bourgeois*, but, given the word's connotations, most people resent it if you call them that.

bovine ADJ. cowlike; placid and dull. Nothing excites Esther; even when she won the state lottery, she still preserved her air of *bovine* calm.

bowdlerize v. expurgate. After the film editors had *bowdlerized* the language in the script, the motion picture's rating was changed from "R" to "PG."

boycott v. refrain from buying or using. To put pressure on grape growers to stop using pesticides that harmed the farm workers' health, Cesar Chavez called for consumers to *boycott* grapes.

■ **braggart** N. boaster. Modest by nature, she was no *braggart*, preferring to let her accomplishments speak for themselves.

brandish v. wave around; flourish. Alarmed, Doctor Watson wildly *brandished* his gun until Holmes told him to put the thing away before he shot himself.

bravado N. swagger; assumed air of defiance. The *bravado* of the young criminal disappeared when he was confronted by the victims of his brutal attack.

brawn N. muscular strength; sturdiness. It takes *brawn* to become a champion weightlifter. brawny, ADJ.

brazen ADJ. insolent. Her *brazen* contempt for authority angered the officials.

breach N. breaking of contract or duty; fissure or gap. Jill sued Jack for *breach* of promise, claiming he had broken his promise to marry her. They found a *breach* in the enemy's fortifications and penetrated their lines. also V.

breadth N. width; extent. We were impressed by the *breadth* of her knowledge.

■ **brevity** N. conciseness. *Brevity* is essential when you send a telegram or cablegram; you are charged for every word.

brindled ADJ. tawny or grayish with streaks or spots. He was disappointed in the litter because the puppies were *brindled;* he had hoped for animals of a uniform color.

bristling ADJ. rising like bristles; showing irritation. The dog stood there, *bristling* with anger.

brittle ADJ. easily broken; difficult. My employer's self-control was as *brittle* as an egg-shell. Her *brittle* personality made it difficult for me to get along with her.

broach V. introduce; open up. Jack did not even try to *broach* the subject of religion with his in-laws. If you *broach* a touchy subject, it may cause a breach.

brochure N. pamphlet. This *brochure* on farming was issued by the Department of Agriculture.

brooch N. ornamental clasp. She treasured the *brooch* because it was an heirloom.

browbeat V. bully; intimidate. Billy resisted Ted's attempts *browbeat* him into handing over his lunch money.

browse V. graze; skim or glance at casually. "How now, brown cow, *browsing* in the green, green grass." I remember lines of verse that I came across while *browsing* through the poetry section of the local bookstore.

brunt N. main impact or shock. Tom Sawyer claimed credit for painting the fence, but the *brunt* of the work fell on others. However, he bore the *brunt* of Aunt Polly's complaints when the paint began to peel.

brusque ADJ. blunt; abrupt. Was Bruce too *brusque* when he brushed off Bob's request with a curt "Not now!"?

buccaneer N. pirate. At Disneyland the Pirates of the Caribbean sing a song about their lives as bloody *buccaneers*.

bucolic ADJ. rustic; pastoral. Filled with browsing cows and bleating sheep, the meadow was a charmingly *bucolic* sight.

buffet N. table with food set out for people to serve themselves; meal at which people help themselves to food that's been set out. Please convey the soufflé on the tray to the *buffet*. (*Buffet* rhymes with tray.)

buffet V. slap; batter; knock about. To *buffet* something is to rough it up. (*Buffet* rhymes with Muffett.) Was Miss Muffett *buffeted* by the crowd on the way to the buffet tray?

buffoonery N. clowning. In the Ace Ventura movies, Jim Carrey's *buffoonery* was hilarious: like Bozo the Clown, he's a natural *buffoon*.

bullion N. gold and silver in the form of bars. Much *bullion* is stored in the vaults at Fort Knox.

bulwark N. earthwork or other strong defense; person who defends. The navy is our principal *bulwark* against invasion.

bumptious ADJ. self-assertive. His classmates called him a show-off because of his *bumptious* airs.

bungalow N. small cottage. Every summer we rent a *bungalow* on Cape Cod for our vacation home. The rent is high, the roof is low—it's a basic *bungalow*.

bungle V. mismanage; blunder. Don't botch this assignment, Bumstead; if you *bungle* the job, you're fired!

buoyant ADJ. able to float; cheerful and optimistic. When the boat capsized, her *buoyant* life jacket kept Jody afloat. Scrambling back on board, she was still in a *buoyant* mood, certain that despite the delay she'd win the race.

bureaucracy N. over-regulated administrative system marked by red tape. The Internal Revenue Service is the ultimate *bureaucracy*: taxpayers wasted so much paper filling out IRS forms that the IRS *bureaucrats* printed up a new set of rules requiring taxpayers to comply with the Paperwork Reduction Act.

burgeon V. grow forth; send out buds. In the spring, the plants that *burgeon* are a promise of the beauty that is to come.

burlesque V. give an imitation that ridicules. In *Spaceballs*, Rick Moranis *burlesques* Darth Vader of *Star Wars*, outrageously parodying Vader's stiff walk and hollow voice.

burly ADJ. husky; muscular. The *burly* mover lifted the packing crate with ease.

burnish V. make shiny by rubbing; polish. The maid *burnished* the brass fixtures until they reflected the lamplight.

bustle V. move about energetically; teem. David and the children *bustled* about the house getting in each other's way as they tried to pack for the camping trip. The whole house *bustled* with activity.

● **buttress** V. support; prop up. The attorney came up with several far-fetched arguments in a vain attempt to *buttress* his weak case. also N.

buxom ADJ. plump; vigorous; jolly. The soldiers remembered the *buxom* nurse who had always been so pleasant to them.

cabal N. small group of persons secretly united to promote their own interests. The *cabal* was defeated when their scheme was discovered.

cache N. hiding place. The detectives followed the suspect until he led them to the *cache* where he had stored his loot. He had *cached* the cash in a bag for trash: it was a hefty sum.

● **cacophonous** ADJ. discordant; inharmonious. Do the students in the orchestra enjoy the *cacophonous* sounds they make when they're tuning up? I don't know how they can stand the racket. cacophony, N.

cadaver N. corpse. In some states, it is illegal to dissect *cadavers*.

cadaverous ADJ. like a corpse; pale. By his *cadaverous* appearance, we could see how the disease had ravaged him.

cadence N. rhythmic rise and fall (of words or sounds); beat. Marching down the road, the troops sang out, following the *cadence* set by the sergeant.

■ **cajole** V. coax; wheedle. Diane tried to *cajole* her father into letting her drive the family car. cajolery, N.

calamity N. disaster; misery. As news of the *calamity* spread, offers of relief poured in to the stricken community.

■ **calculated** ADJ. deliberately planned; likely. Lexy's choice of clothes to wear to the debate tournament was carefully *calculated*. Her conventional suit was one *calculated* to appeal to the conservative judges.

caldron N. large kettle. "Why, Mr. Crusoe," said the savage heating the giant *caldron*, "we'd love to have you for dinner!"

caliber N. ability; quality. Einstein's cleaning the blackboards again? Albert, quit it! A man of your *caliber* shouldn't have to do such menial tasks.

calligraphy N. beautiful writing; excellent penmanship. As we examine ancient manuscripts, we become impressed with the *calligraphy* of the scribes.

callous ADJ. hardened; unfeeling. He had worked in the hospital for so many years that he was *callous* to the suffering in the wards. callus, N.

callow ADJ. youthful; immature; inexperienced. As a freshman, Jack was sure he was a man of the world; as a sophomore, he made fun of freshmen as *callow* youths. In both cases, his judgment showed just how *callow* he was.

calorific ADJ. heat-producing. Coal is much more *calorific* than green wood.

calumny N. malicious misrepresentation; slander. He could endure his financial failure, but he could not bear the *calumny* that his foes heaped upon him.

camaraderie N. good-fellowship. What he loved best about his job was the sense of *camaraderie* he and his co-workers shared.

cameo N. shell or jewel carved in relief; star's special appearance in a minor role in a film. Don't bother buying *cameos* from the street peddlers in Rome: the carvings they sell are clumsy jobs. Did you enjoy Bill Murray's *cameo* in *Little Shop of Horrors*? He was onscreen for only a minute, but he cracked me up.

camouflage V. disguise; conceal. In order to rescue Han Solo, Princess Leia *camouflaged* herself in the helmet and cloak of a space bandit.

■ **candor** N. frankness; open honesty. Jack can carry *candor* too far: when he told Jill his honest opinion of her, she nearly slapped his face. candid, ADJ.

canine ADJ. related to dogs; dog-like. Some days the *canine* population of Berkeley seems almost to outnumber the human population.

canny ADJ. shrewd; thrifty. The *canny* Scotsman was more than a match for the swindlers.

cant N. insincere expressions of piety; jargon of thieves. Shocked by news of the minister's extramarital love affairs, the worshippers dismissed his talk about the sacredness of marriage as mere *cant*. *Cant* is a form of hypocrisy: those who can, pray; those who *cant*, pretend.

cantankerous ADJ. ill humored; irritable. Constantly complaining about his treatment and refusing to cooperate with the hospital staff, he was a *cantankerous* patient.

cantata N. story set to music, to be sung by a chorus. The choral society sang the new *cantata* composed by its leader.

canter N. slow gallop. Because the racehorse had outdistanced its competition so easily, the reporter wrote that the race was won in a *canter*. also V.

Word List 8   canto-chameleon

canto N. division of a long poem. Dante's poetic masterpiece *The Divine Comedy* is divided into *cantos*.

canvass V. determine votes, etc. After *canvassing* the sentiments of his constituents, the congressman was confident that he represented the majority opinion of his district. also N.

capacious ADJ. spacious. In the *capacious* rotunda of the railroad terminal, thousands of travelers lingered while waiting for their train.

capacity N. mental or physical ability; role; ability to accommodate. Mike had the *capacity* to handle several jobs at once. In his *capacity* as president of SelecTronics he marketed an electronic dictionary with a *capacity* of 200,000 words.

capitulate V. surrender. The enemy was warned to *capitulate* or face annihilation.

caprice N. sudden, unexpected fancy; whim. On a *caprice*, Jack tried drag-racing, but paid the price—his father took his Chevy Caprice away from him.

■ **capricious** ADJ. unpredictable; fickle. The storm was *capricious*: it changed course constantly. Jill was *capricious*, too: she changed boyfriends almost as often as she changed clothes.

caption N. title; chapter heading; text under illustration. The *captions* that accompany *The Far Side* cartoons are almost as funny as the pictures. also V.

captivate V. charm or enthrall. Bart and Lisa were *captivated* by their new nanny's winning manner.

carat N. unit of weight for precious stones; measure of fineness of gold. He gave her a three-*carat* diamond mounted in an eighteen-*carat* gold band.

cardinal ADJ. chief. If you want to increase your word power, the *cardinal* rule of vocabulary-building is to read.

● **cardiologist** N. doctor specializing in the heart. When the pediatrician noticed Philip had a slight heart murmur, she referred him to a *cardiologist* for further tests.

careen   V. lurch; sway from side to side. The taxicab *careened* wildly as it rounded the corner.

caricature   N. distortion; burlesque. The *caricatures* he drew always emphasized a personal weakness of the people he burlesqued. also V.

carnage   N. destruction of life. The film *The Killing Fields* vividly depicts the *carnage* wreaked by Pol Pot's followers in Cambodia.

carnal   ADJ. fleshly. Is the public more interested in *carnal* pleasures than in spiritual matters? Compare the number of people who read *Playboy* daily to the number of those who read the Bible or Koran every day.

carnivorous   ADJ. meat-eating. The lion's a *carnivorous* beast. A hunk of meat makes up his feast. A cow is not a *carnivore*. She likes the taste of grain, not gore.

● **carping**   ADJ. finding fault. A *carping* critic is a nit-picker: he loves to point out flaws. If you don't like this definition, feel free to *carp*.

cartographer   N. map-maker. Though not a professional *cartographer*, Tolkien was able to construct a map of his fictional world.

cascade   N. small waterfall. We were too tired to appreciate the beauty of the many *cascades* because we had to detour around them to avoid being drenched by the water *cascading* down.

castigate   V. criticize severely; punish. When the teacher threatened that she would *castigate* the mischievous boys if they didn't behave, they shaped up in a hurry.

casualty   N. serious or fatal accident. The number of automotive *casualties* on this holiday weekend was high.

cataclysm   N. upheaval; deluge. A *cataclysm* such as the French Revolution affects all countries. cataclysmic, ADJ.

catalyst   N. agent which brings about a chemical change while it remains unaffected and unchanged. Many chemical reactions cannot take place without the presence of a *catalyst*.

catapult   N. slingshot; a hurling machine. Airplanes are sometimes launched from battleships by *catapults*. also V.

cataract   N. great waterfall; eye abnormality. She gazed with awe at the mighty *cataract* known as Niagara Falls.

catastrophe   N. calamity; disaster. The 1906 San Francisco earthquake was a *catastrophe* that destroyed most of the city. A similar earthquake striking today could have even more *catastrophic* results.

catcall   N. shout of disapproval; boo. Every major league pitcher has off days during which he must learn to ignore the *catcalls* and angry hisses from the crowd.

catechism   N. book for religious instruction; instruction by question and answer. He taught by engaging his pupils in a *catechism* until they gave him the correct answer.

categorical   ADJ. without exceptions; unqualified; absolute. Though the captain claimed he was never, never sick at sea, he finally had to qualify his *categorical* denial: he was "hardly ever" sick at sea.

cater to   V. supply something desired (whether good or bad). The chef was happy to *cater to* the tastes of his highly sophisticated clientele. Critics condemned the movie industry for *catering to* the public's ever-increasing appetite for violence.

catharsis   N. purging or cleansing of any passage of the body. Aristotle maintained that tragedy created a *catharsis* by purging the soul of base concepts.

catholic   ADJ. broadly sympathetic; liberal. He was extremely *catholic* in his taste and read everything he could find in the library.

caucus   N. private meeting of members of a party to select officers or determine policy. At the opening of Congress, the members of the Democratic Party held a *caucus* to elect the Majority Leader of the House and the Party Whip.

caulk   V. make watertight by filling in cracks. Jack had to *caulk* the tiles in the shower stall to stop the leak into the basement below.

causal   ADJ. implying a cause-and-effect relationship. The psychologist maintained there was a *causal* relationship between the nature of one's early childhood experiences and one's adult personality. causality, N.

caustic   ADJ. burning; sarcastically biting. The critic's *caustic* remarks angered the hapless actors who were the subjects of his sarcasm.

cavalcade   N. procession; parade. As described by Chaucer, the *cavalcade* of Canterbury pilgrims was a motley group.

cavalier   ADJ. offhand or casual; haughty. The disguised prince resented the *cavalier* way in which the palace guards treated him. How dared they handle a member of the royal family so unceremoniously!

cavil   V. make frivolous objections. It's fine when you make sensible criticisms, but it really bugs me when you *cavil* about unimportant details. also N.

cede   V. yield (title, territory) to; surrender formally. Eventually the descendants of England's Henry II were forced to *cede* their French territories to the King of France.

celebrated   ADJ. famous; well-known. Thanks to their race to break Roger Maris's home-run record, Sammy Sosa and Mark McGwire are two of America's most *celebrated* baseball players. celebrity, N.

celerity   N. speed; rapidity. Hamlet resented his mother's *celerity* in remarrying within a month after his father's death.

celestial   ADJ. heavenly. She spoke of the *celestial* joys that awaited virtuous souls in the hereafter.

celibate   ADJ. unmarried; abstaining from sexual intercourse. The perennial bachelor vowed to remain *celibate*. celibacy, N.

censor   N. overseer of morals; person who reads to eliminate inappropriate remarks. Soldiers dislike having their mail read by a *censor* but understand the need for this precaution. also V.

■ **censorious**   ADJ. critical. *Censorious* people delight in casting blame.

■ **censure** V. blame; criticize. The senator was *censured* for behavior inappropriate to a member of Congress. also N.

centigrade ADJ. measure of temperature used widely in Europe. On the *centigrade* thermometer, the freezing point of water is zero degrees.

centrifugal ADJ. radiating; departing from the center. Many automatic drying machines remove excess moisture from clothing by *centrifugal* force.

centripetal ADJ. tending toward the center. Does *centripetal* force or the force of gravity bring orbiting bodies to the earth's surface?

centurion N. Roman army officer. Because he was in command of a company of one hundred soldiers, he was called a *centurion.*

cerebral ADJ. pertaining to the brain or intellect. The content of philosophical works is *cerebral* in nature and requires much thought.

cerebration N. thought. Mathematics problems sometimes require much *cerebration.*

ceremonious ADJ. marked by formality. Ordinary dress would be inappropriate at so *ceremonious* an affair.

● **certitude** N. certainty. Though there was no *certitude* of his getting the job, Lou thought he had a good chance of doing so.

cessation N. stoppage. The airline's employees threatened a *cessation* of all work if management failed to meet their demands. cease, V.

cession N. yielding to another; ceding. The *cession* of Alaska to the United States is discussed in this chapter.

chafe V. warm by rubbing; make sore (by rubbing). Chilled, he *chafed* his hands before the fire. The collar of his school uniform *chafed* Tom's neck, but not as much the school's strict rules *chafed* his spirit. also N.

chaff N. worthless products of an endeavor. When you separate the wheat from the *chaff,* be sure you throw out the *chaff.*

chaffing ADJ. bantering; joking. Sometimes Chad's flippant, *chaffing* remarks annoy us. Still, Chad's *chaffing* keeps us laughing. also N.

chagrin N. vexation (caused by humiliation or injured pride); disappointment. Embarrassed by his parents' shabby, working-class appearance, Doug felt their visit to his school would bring him nothing but *chagrin.* Someone filled with *chagrin* doesn't grin: he's too mortified.

chalice N. goblet; consecrated cup. In a small room adjoining the cathedral, many ornately decorated *chalices* made by the most famous European goldsmiths were on display.

chameleon N. lizard that changes color in different situations. Like the *chameleon,* he assumed the political thinking of every group he met.

Word List 9   champion-colander

champion V. support militantly. Martin Luther King, Jr., won the Nobel Peace Prize because he *championed* the oppressed in their struggle for equality.

chaotic ADJ. in utter disorder. He tried to bring order into the *chaotic* state of affairs. chaos, N.

charisma N. divine gift; great popular charm or appeal of a political leader Political commentators have deplored the importance of a candidate's *charisma* in these days of television campaigning.

● **charlatan** N. quack; pretender to knowledge. When they realized that the Wizard didn't know how to get them back to Kansas, Dorothy and her companions were indignant that they'd been duped by a *charlatan.*

chary ADJ. cautious; sparing or restrained about giving. A prudent, thrifty, New Englander, DeWitt was as *chary* of investing money in junk bonds as he was *chary* of paying people unnecessary compliments.

chasm N. abyss. They could not see the bottom of the *chasm.*

chassis N. framework and working parts of an automobile. Examining the car after the accident, the owner discovered that the body had been ruined but that the *chassis* was unharmed.

chaste ADJ. pure. Her *chaste* and decorous garb was appropriately selected for the solemnity of the occasion. chastity, N.

chasten V. discipline; punish in order to correct. Whom God loves, God *chastens.*

chastise V. punish. I must *chastise* you for this offense.

chauvinist N. blindly devoted patriot. A *chauvinist* cannot recognize any faults in his country, no matter how flagrant they may be. Likewise, a male *chauvinist* cannot recognize his bias in favor of his own sex, no matter how flagrant that may be. chauvinistic, ADJ.

check V. stop motion; curb or restrain. Thrusting out her arm, Grandma *checked* Bobby's lunge at his sister. "Young man," she said, "you'd better *check* your temper." (secondary meaning)

checkered ADJ. marked by changes in fortune. During his *checkered* career he had lived in palatial mansions and in dreary boardinghouses.

cherubic ADJ. angelic; innocent-looking. With her cheerful smile and rosy cheeks, she was a particularly *cherubic* child.

chicanery N. trickery; deception. Those sneaky lawyers misrepresented what occurred, made up all sorts of implausible alternative scenarios to confuse the jurors, and in general depended on *chicanery* to win the case.

chide V. scold. Grandma began to *chide* Steven for his lying.

chimerical   ADJ. fantastically improbable; highly unrealistic; imaginative. As everyone expected, Ted's *chimerical* scheme to make a fortune by raising ermines in his back yard proved a dismal failure.

chisel   N. wedgelike tool for cutting. With his hammer and *chisel*, the sculptor chipped away at the block of marble.

chisel   V. swindle or cheat; cut with a chisel. That crook *chiseled* me out of a hundred dollars when he sold me that "marble" statue he'd *chiseled* out of some cheap hunk of rock.

chivalrous   ADJ. courteous; faithful; brave. *Chivalrous* behavior involves noble words and good deeds.

choleric   ADJ. hot-tempered. His flushed, angry face indicated a *choleric* nature.

choreography   N. art of representing dances in written symbols; arrangement of dances. Merce Cunningham has begun to use a computer in designing *choreography*: a software program allows him to compose arrangements of possible moves and immediately view them onscreen.

chortle   V. chuckle with delight. When she heard that her rival had just been jailed for embezzlement, she *chortled* with joy. She was *not* a nice lady.

chronic   ADJ. long established as a disease. The doctors were finally able to attribute his *chronic* headaches and nausea to traces of formaldehyde gas in his apartment.

chronicle   V. report; record (in chronological order). The gossip columnist was paid to *chronicle* the latest escapades of the socially prominent celebrities. also N.

churlish   ADJ. boorish; rude. Dismayed by his *churlish* manners at the party, the girls vowed never to invite him again.

cipher   N. secret code. Lacking his code book, the spy was unable to decode the message sent to him in *cipher*.

cipher   N. nonentity; worthless person or thing. She claimed her ex-husband was a total *cipher* and wondered why she had ever married him.

circuitous   ADJ. roundabout. To avoid the traffic congestion on the main highways, she took a *circuitous* route. circuit, N.

● **circumlocution**   N. indirect or roundabout expression. He was afraid to call a spade a spade and resorted to *circumlocutions* to avoid direct reference to his subject.

circumscribe   V. limit; confine. Although I do not wish to *circumscribe* your activities, I must insist that you complete this assignment before you start anything else.

circumspect   ADJ. prudent; cautious. Investigating before acting, she tried always to be *circumspect*.

circumvent   V. outwit; baffle. In order to *circumvent* the enemy, we will make two preliminary attacks in other sections before starting our major campaign.

cistern   N. reservoir or water tank. The farmers were able to withstand the dry season by using rainwater they had stored in an underground *cistern*.

citadel   N. fortress. The *citadel* overlooked the city like a protecting angel.

cite   V. quote; command. She could *cite* passages in the Bible from memory. citation, N.

civil   ADJ. having to do with citizens or the state; courteous and polite. Although Internal Revenue Service agents are *civil* servants, they are not always *civil* to suspected tax cheats.

clairvoyant   ADJ., N. having foresight; fortuneteller. Cassandra's *clairvoyant* warning was not heeded by the Trojans. clairvoyance, N.

clamber   V. climb by crawling. She *clambered* over the wall.

clamor   N. noise. The *clamor* of the children at play outside made it impossible for her to take a nap. also V.

clandestine   ADJ. secret. After avoiding their chaperon, the lovers had a *clandestine* meeting.

clangor   N. loud, resounding noise. The blacksmith was accustomed to the *clangor* of hammers on steel.

clapper   N. striker (tongue) of a bell. Wishing to be undisturbed by the bell, Dale wound his scarf around the *clapper* to muffle the noise of its striking.

clasp   N. fastening device; firm grip. When the *clasp* on Judy's bracelet broke, Fred repaired it, bending the hook back into shape. He then helped her slip on the bracelet, holding it firm in the sure *clasp* of his hand.

claustrophobia   N. fear of being locked in. His fellow classmates laughed at his *claustrophobia* and often threatened to lock him in his room.

cleave   V. split or sever; cling to; remain faithful to. With her heavy cleaver, Julia Child can *cleave* a whole roast duck in two. Soaked through, the soldier tugged at the uniform that *cleaved* annoyingly to his body. He would *cleave* to his post, come rain or shine.

cleft   N. split. Trying for a fresh handhold, the mountainclimber grasped the edge of a *cleft* in the sheer rockface. also ADJ.

clemency   N. disposition to be lenient; mildness, as of the weather. The lawyer was pleased when the case was sent to Judge Smith's chambers because Smith was noted for her *clemency* toward first offenders.

clench   V. close tightly; grasp. "Open wide," said the dentist, but Clint *clenched* his teeth even more tightly than before.

● **cliché**   N. phrase dulled in meaning by repetition. High school compositions are often marred by such *clichés* as "strong as an ox."

clientele   N. body of customers. The rock club attracted a young, stylish *clientele*.

climactic   ADJ. relating to the highest point. When he reached the *climactic* portions of the book, he could not stop reading. climax, N.

clime   N. region; climate. His doctor advised him to move to a milder *clime*.

clip   N. section of filmed material. Phil's job at Fox Sports involved selecting *clips* of the day's sporting highlights for later broadcast. also V.

clique   N. small exclusive group. Fitzgerald wished that he belonged to the *clique* of popular athletes and big men on campus who seemed to run Princeton's social life.

cloister N. monastery or convent. The nuns lived a secluded life in the *cloister*.

clout N. great influence (especially political or social). Gatsby wondered whether he had enough *clout* to be admitted to the exclusive club.

cloying ADJ. distasteful (because excessive); excessively sweet or sentimental. Disliking the *cloying* sweetness of standard wedding cakes, Jody and Tom chose to have homemade carrot cake at the reception. cloy, V.

clump N. cluster or close group (of bushes, trees); mass; sound of heavy treading. Hiding behind the *clump* of bushes, the fugitives waited for the heavy *clump* of the soldiers' feet to fade away.

coagulate V. thicken; congeal; clot. Even after you remove the pudding from the burner, it will continue to *coagulate* as it stands; therefore, do not overcook the pudding, lest it become too thick.

● **coalesce** V. combine; fuse. The brooks *coalesce* into one large river. When minor political parties *coalesce*, their *coalescence* may create a major coalition.

coalition N. partnership; league; union. The Rainbow *Coalition* united people of all races in a common cause.

coddle V. to treat gently. Don't *coddle* the children so much; they need a taste of discipline.

codicil N. supplement to the body of a will. Miss Havisham kept her lawyers busy drawing up *codicils* to add to her already complicated will.

codify V. arrange (laws, rules) as a code; classify. We need to take the varying rules and regulations of the different health agencies and *codify* them into a national health code.

■ **coercion** N. use of force to get someone to obey. The inquisitors used both physical and psychological *coercion* to force Joan of Arc to deny that her visions were sent by God. coerce, V.

cogent ADJ. convincing. It was inevitable that David chose to go to Harvard: he had several *cogent* reasons for doing so, including a full-tuition scholarship. Katya argued her case with such *cogency* that the jury had to decide in favor of her client.

cogitate V. think over. *Cogitate* on this problem; the solution will come.

cognate ADJ. related linguistically: allied by blood: similar or akin in nature. The English word "mother" is *cognate* to the Latin word "mater," whose influence is visible in the words "maternal" and "maternity." also N.

cognitive ADJ. having to do with knowing or perceiving; related to the mental processes. Though Jack was emotionally immature, his *cognitive* development was admirable; he was very advanced intellectually.

cognizance N. knowledge. During the election campaign, the two candidates were kept in full *cognizance* of the international situation.

cohere V. stick together. Solids have a greater tendency to *cohere* than liquids.

cohesion N. tendency to keep together. A firm believer in the maxim "Divide and conquer," the evil emperor, by means of lies and trickery, sought to disrupt the *cohesion* of the federation of free nations.

coiffure N. hairstyle. You can make a statement with your choice of *coiffure*: in the sixties many African-Americans affirmed their racial heritage by wearing their hair in Afros.

coin V. make coins; invent or fabricate. Mints *coin* good money; counterfeiters *coin* fakes. Slanderers *coin* nasty rumors; writers *coin* words. A neologism is an expression that's been newly-*coined*.

coincidence N. two or more things occurring at the same time by chance. Was it just a *coincidence* that John and she had chanced to meet at the market for three days running, or was he deliberately trying to seek her out? coincidental, ADJ.

colander N. utensil with perforated bottom used for straining. Before serving the spaghetti, place it in a *colander* to drain it.

Word List 10 collaborate-congenital

collaborate V. work together. Two writers *collaborated* in preparing this book.

collage N. work of art put together from fragments. Scraps of cloth, paper doilies, and old photographs all went into her *collage*.

collate V. examine in order to verify authenticity; arrange in order. They *collated* the newly found manuscripts to determine their age.

collateral N. security given for loan. The sum you wish to borrow is so large that it must be secured by *collateral*.

● **colloquial** ADJ. pertaining to conversational or common speech. Some of the new, less formal reading passages on SAT I have a *colloquial* tone that is intended to make them more appealing to students.

collusion N. conspiring in a fraudulent scheme. The swindlers were found guilty of *collusion*.

colossal ADJ. huge. Radio City Music Hall has a *colossal* stage.

comatose ADJ. in a coma; extremely sleepy. The long-winded orator soon had his audience in a *comatose* state.

● **combustible** ADJ. easily burned. After the recent outbreak of fires in private homes, the fire commissioner ordered that all *combustible* materials be kept in safe containers. also N.

comely ADJ. attractive; agreeable. I would rather have a poor and *comely* wife than a rich and homely one.

comeuppance N. rebuke; deserts. After his earlier rudeness, we were delighted to see him get his *comeuppance*.

commandeer   V. to draft for military purposes; to take for public use. The policeman *commandeered* the first car that approached and ordered the driver to go to the nearest hospital.

■ **commemorate**   V. honor the memory of. The statue of the Minute Man *commemorates* the valiant soldiers who fought in the Revolutionary War.

commensurate   ADJ. equal in extent. Your reward will be *commensurate* with your effort.

commiserate   V. feel or express pity or sympathy for. Her friends *commiserated* with the widow.

commodious   ADJ. spacious and comfortable. After sleeping in small roadside cabins, they found their hotel suite *commodious*.

communal   ADJ. held in common; of a group of people. When they were divorced, they had trouble dividing their *communal* property.

compact   N. agreement; contract. The signers of the Mayflower *Compact* were establishing a form of government.

compact   ADJ. tightly packed; firm; brief. His short, *compact* body was better suited to wrestling than to basketball.

comparable   ADJ. similar. People whose jobs are *comparable* in difficulty should receive *comparable* pay.

compatible   ADJ. harmonious; in harmony with. They were *compatible* neighbors, never quarreling over unimportant matters. compatibility, N.

compelling   ADJ. overpowering; irresistible in effect. The prosecutor presented a well-reasoned case, but the defense attorney's *compelling* arguments for leniency won over the jury.

compensatory   ADJ. making up for; repaying. Can a *compensatory* education program make up for the inadequate schooling he received in earlier years?

■ **compile**   V. assemble; gather; accumulate. We planned to *compile* a list of the words most frequently used on SAT I examinations.

■ **complacency**   N. self-satisfaction; smugness. Full of *complacency* about his latest victories, he looked smugly at the row of trophies on his mantelpiece. complacent, ADJ.

complaisant   ADJ. trying to please; obliging. The courtier obeyed the king's orders in a *complaisant* manner.

complement   V. complete; consummate; make perfect. The waiter recommended a glass of port to *complement* the cheese. also N.

● **complementary**   ADJ. serving to complete something. John and Lisa's skills are *complementary*: he's good at following a daily routine, while she's great at improvising and handling emergencies. Together they make a great team.

■ **compliance**   N. readiness to yield; conformity in fulfilling requirements. Bullheaded Bill was not noted for easy *compliance* with the demands of others. As an architect, however, Bill recognized that his design for the new school had to be in *compliance* with the local building code.

compliant   ADJ. yielding. Because Joel usually gave in and went along with whatever his friends desired, his mother worried that he might be too *compliant*.

complicity   N. participation; involvement. You cannot keep your *complicity* in this affair secret very long; you would be wise to admit your involvement immediately.

component   N. element; ingredient. I wish all the *components* of my stereo system were working at the same time.

■ **composure**   N. mental calmness. Even the latest work crisis failed to shake her *composure*.

compound   V. combine; constitute; pay interest; increase. The makers of the popular cold remedy *compounded* a nasal decongestant with an antihistamine. also N.

■ **comprehensive**   ADJ. thorough; inclusive. This book provides a *comprehensive* review of verbal and math skills for the SAT.

compress   V. close; squeeze; contract. She *compressed* the package under her arm.

comprise   V. include; consist of. If the District of Columbia were to be granted statehood, the United States of America would *comprise* fifty-one states, not just fifty.

compromise   V. adjust or settle by making mutual concessions; endanger the interests or reputation of. Sometimes the presence of a neutral third party can help adversaries *compromise* their differences. Unfortunately, you're not neutral; therefore, your presence here *compromises* our chances of reaching an agreement. also N.

compunction   N. remorse. The judge was especially severe in his sentencing because he felt that the criminal had shown no *compunction* for his heinous crime.

compute   V. reckon; calculate. He failed to *compute* the interest, so his bank balance was not accurate. computation, N.

concave   ADJ. hollow. The back-packers found partial shelter from the storm by huddling against the *concave* wall of the cliff.

■ **concede**   V. admit; yield. Despite all the evidence Monica had assembled, Mark refused to *concede* that she was right.

conceit   N. vanity or self-love; whimsical idea; extravagant metaphor. Although Jack was smug and puffed up with *conceit*, he was an entertaining companion, always expressing himself in amusing *conceits* and witty turns of phrase.

concentric   ADJ. having a common center. The target was made of *concentric* circles.

conception   N. beginning; forming of an idea. At the first *conception* of the work, he was consulted. conceive, V.

concerted   ADJ. mutually agreed on; done together. All the Girl Scouts made a *concerted* effort to raise funds for their annual outing. When the movie star appeared, his fans let out a *concerted* sigh.

concession   N. an act of yielding. Before they could reach an agreement, both sides had to make certain *concessions*.

■ **conciliatory**   ADJ. reconciling; soothing. She was still angry despite his *conciliatory* words. conciliate, V.

■ **concise**   ADJ. brief and compact. When you define a new word, be *concise*: the shorter the definition, the easier it is to remember.

conclusive ADJ. decisive; ending all debate. When the stolen books turned up in John's locker, we finally had *conclusive* evidence of the identity of the mysterious thief.

concoct V. prepare by combining; make up in concert. How did the inventive chef ever *concoct* such a strange dish? concoction, N.

concomitant N. that which accompanies. Culture is not always a *concomitant* of wealth. also ADJ.

concord N. harmony; agreement between people or things. Watching Tweedledum and Tweedledee battle, Alice wondered at their lack of *concord.*

■ **concur** V. agree. Did you *concur* with the decision of the court or did you find it unfair?

concurrent ADJ. happening at the same time. In America, the colonists were resisting the demands of the mother country; at the *concurrent* moment in France, the middle class was sowing the seeds of rebellion.

condemn V. censure; sentence; force or limit to a particular state. In *My Cousin Vinnie*, Vinnie's fiancée *condemned* Vinnie for mishandling his cousin Tony's defense. If Vinnie didn't do a better job defending Tony, the judge would *condemn* Tony to death, and Vinnie would be *condemned* to cleaning toilets for a living.

condense V. make more compact or dense; shorten or abridge; reduce into a denser form. If you squeeze a slice of Wonder Bread, taking out the extra air, you can *condense* it into a pellet the size of a sugar cube. If you cut out the unnecessary words from your essay, you can *condense* it to a paragraph. As the bathroom cooled down, the steam from the shower *condensed* into droplets of water.

condescend V. bestow courtesies with a superior air. The king *condescended* to grant an audience to the friends of the condemned man. condescension, N.

condiments N. seasonings; spices. Spanish food is full of *condiments.*

condole V. express sympathetic sorrow. His friends gathered to *condole* with him over his loss. condolence, N.

■ **condone** V. overlook; forgive; give tacit approval; excuse. Unlike Widow Douglass, who *condoned* Huck's minor offenses, Miss Watson did nothing but scold.

conducive ADJ. contributive; tending to. Rest and proper diet are *conducive* to good health.

conduit N. aqueduct; passageway for fluids. Water was brought to the army in the desert by an improvised *conduit* from the adjoining mountain.

confidant N. trusted friend. He had no *confidants* with whom he could discuss his problems at home.

confine V. shut in; restrict. The terrorists had *confined* their prisoner in a small room. However, they had not chained him to the wall or done anything else to *confine* his movements further. confinement, N.

confirm V. corroborate; verify; support. I have several witnesses who will *confirm* my account of what happened.

confiscate V. seize; commandeer. The army *confiscated* all available supplies of uranium.

■ **conflagration** N. great fire. In the *conflagration* that followed the 1906 earthquake, much of San Francisco was destroyed.

● **confluence** N. flowing together; crowd. They built the city at the *confluence* of two rivers.

conformity N. harmony; agreement. In *conformity* with our rules and regulations, I am calling a meeting of our organization.

■ **confound** V. confuse; puzzle. No mystery could *confound* Sherlock Holmes for long.

confrontation N. act of facing someone or something; encounter, often hostile. Morris hoped to avoid any *confrontations* with his ex-wife, but he kept on running into her at the health club. How would you like to *confront* someone who can bench press 200 pounds? confront, V., confrontational, ADJ.

congeal V. freeze; coagulate. His blood *congealed* in his veins as he saw the dread monster rush toward him.

congenial ADJ. pleasant; friendly. My father loved to go out for a meal with *congenial* companions.

congenital ADJ. existing at birth. Were you born stupid, or did you just turn out this way? In other words, is your idiocy acquired or *congenital*? Doctors are able to cure some *congenital* deformities such as cleft palates by performing operations on infants.

Word List 11   conglomeration-countermand

conglomeration N. mass of material sticking together. In such a *conglomeration* of miscellaneous statistics, it was impossible to find a single area of analysis.

congruent ADJ. in agreement; corresponding. In formulating a hypothesis, we must keep it *congruent* with what we know of the real world; it cannot disagree with our experience.

conifer N. pine tree; cone-bearing tree. According to geologists, the *conifers* were the first plants to bear flowers.

● **conjecture** N. surmise; guess. I will end all your *conjectures;* I admit I am guilty as charged. also V.

conjugal ADJ. pertaining to marriage. Their dreams of *conjugal* bliss were shattered as soon as their temperaments clashed.

conjure V. summon a devil; practice magic; imagine or invent. Sorcerers *conjure* devils to appear. Magicians *conjure* white rabbits out of hats. Political candidates *conjure* up images of reformed cities and a world at peace.

connivance N. assistance; pretense of ignorance of something wrong; permission to offend. With the *connivance* of his friends, he plotted to embarrass the teacher. connive, V.

connoisseur N. person competent to act as a judge of art, etc.; a lover of an art. She had developed into a *connoisseur* of fine china.

connotation N. suggested or implied meaning of an expression. Foreigners frequently are unaware of the *connotations* of the words they use.

connubial ADJ. pertaining to marriage or the matrimonial state. In his telegram, he wished the newlyweds a lifetime of *connubial* bliss.

conscientious ADJ. scrupulous; careful. A *conscientious* editor, she checked every definition for its accuracy.

consecrate V. dedicate; sanctify. We shall *consecrate* our lives to this noble purpose.

■ **consensus** N. general agreement. The *consensus* indicates that we are opposed to entering into this pact.

consequential ADJ. pompous; important; self-important. Convinced of his own importance, the actor strutted about the dressing room with a *consequential* air.

conservatory N. school of the fine arts (especially music or drama). A gifted violinist, Marya was selected to study at the *conservatory*.

consign V. deliver officially; entrust; set apart. The court *consigned* the child to her paternal grandmother's care. consignment, N.

consistency N. absence of contradictions; dependability; uniformity; degree of thickness. Holmes judged puddings and explanations on their *consistency:* he liked his puddings without lumps and his explanations without improbabilities.

console V. lessen sadness or disappointment; give comfort. When her father died, Marius did his best to *console* Cosette.

consolidation N. unification; process of becoming firmer or stronger. The recent *consolidation* of several small airlines into one major company has left observers of the industry wondering whether room still exists for the "little guy" in aviation. consolidate, V.

consonance N. harmony; agreement. Her agitation seemed out of *consonance* with her usual calm.

consort V. associate with. We frequently judge people by the company with whom they *consort*.

consort N. husband or wife. The search for a *consort* for the young Queen Victoria ended happily.

conspicuous ADJ. easily seen; noticeable; striking. Janet was *conspicuous* both for her red hair and for her height.

conspiracy N. treacherous plot. Brutus and Cassius joined in the *conspiracy* to kill Julius Caesar. conspire, V.

constituent N. supporter. The congressman received hundreds of letters from angry *constituents* after the Equal Rights Amendment failed to pass.

■ **constraint** N. compulsion; repression of feelings. There was a feeling of *constraint* in the room because no one dared to criticize the speaker. constrain, V.

construe V. explain; interpret. If I *construe* your remarks correctly, you disagree with the theory already advanced.

consummate ADJ. complete. I have never seen anyone who makes as many stupid errors as you do; you must be a *consummate* idiot. also V.

contagion N. infection. Fearing *contagion,* they took great steps to prevent the spread of the disease.

contaminate V. pollute. The sewage system of the city so *contaminated* the water that swimming was forbidden.

contemporary N. person belonging to the same period. Though Charlotte Brontë and George Eliot were *contemporaries,* the two novelists depicted their Victorian world in markedly different ways. also ADJ.

contempt N. scorn; disdain. The heavyweight boxer looked on ordinary people with *contempt*, scorning them as weaklings who couldn't hurt a fly. We thought it was *contemptible* of him to be *contemptuous* of people for being weak.

■ **contend** V. struggle; compete; assert earnestly. Sociologist Harry Edwards *contends* that young black athletes are exploited by some college recruiters.

contention N. claim; thesis. It is our *contention* that, if you follow our tactics, you will boost your score on the SAT. contend, V.

■ **contentious** ADJ. quarrelsome. Disagreeing violently with the referees' ruling, the coach became so *contentious* that they threw him out of the game.

contest V. dispute. The defeated candidate attempted to *contest* the election results.

context N. writings preceding and following the passage quoted. Because these lines are taken out of *context*, they do not convey the message the author intended.

contiguous ADJ. adjacent to; touching upon. The two countries are *contiguous* for a few miles; then they are separated by the gulf.

continence N. self-restraint; sexual chastity. At the convent, Connie vowed to lead a life of *continence*. The question was, could Connie be content with always being *continent*?

contingent ADJ. dependent on; conditional. Caroline's father informed her that any raise in her allowance was *contingent* on the quality of her final grades. contingency, N.

contingent N. group that makes up part of a gathering. The New York *contingent* of delegates at the Democratic National Convention was a boisterous, sometimes rowdy lot.

contortions N. twistings; distortions. As the effects of the opiate wore away, the *contortions* of the patient became more violent and demonstrated how much pain she was enduring.

contraband N. ADJ. illegal trade; smuggling. The Coast Guard tries to prevent traffic in *contraband* goods.

■ **contract** V. compress or shrink; make a pledge; catch a disease. Warm metal expands; cold metal *contracts*.

contravene V. contradict; oppose; infringe on or transgress. Mr. Barrett did not expect his frail daughter Elizabeth to *contravene* his will by eloping with Robert Browning.

contrite ADJ. penitent. Her *contrite* tears did not influence the judge when he imposed sentence. contrition, N.

contrived ADJ. forced; artificial; not spontaneous. Feeling ill at ease with his new in-laws, James made a few *contrived* attempts at conversation and then retreated into silence.

controvert V. oppose with arguments; attempt to refute; contradict. The witness's testimony was so clear and her reputation for honesty so well-established that the defense attorney decided it was wiser to make no attempt to *controvert* what she said.

contusion N. bruise. Black and blue after her fall, Sue was treated for *contusions* and abrasions.

conundrum N. riddle. During the long car ride, she invented *conundrums* to entertain the children.

convene V. assemble. Because much needed legislation had to be enacted, the governor ordered the legislature to *convene* in special session by January 15.

convention N. social or moral custom; established practice. Flying in the face of *convention*, George Sand shocked society by taking lovers and wearing men's clothes.

conventional ADJ. ordinary; typical. His *conventional* upbringing left him wholly unprepared for his wife's eccentric family.

● **converge** V. approach; tend to meet; come together. African-American men from all over the United States *converged* on Washington to take part in the historic Million Men march.

conversant ADJ. familiar with. The lawyer is *conversant* with all the evidence.

converse N. opposite. The inevitable *converse* of peace is not war but annihilation.

converse V. chat; talk informally. Eva was all ears while Lulu and Lola *conversed*. Wasn't it rude of her to eavesdrop on their *conversation*? conversation, N.

convert N. one who has adopted a different religion or opinion. On his trip to Japan, though the President spoke at length about the virtues of American automobiles, he made few *converts* to his beliefs. also V.

convex ADJ. curving outward. He polished the *convex* lens of his telescope.

conveyance N. vehicle; transfer. During the transit strike, commuters used various kinds of *conveyances*.

■ **conviction** N. judgment that someone is guilty of a crime; strongly held belief. Even her *conviction* for murder did not shake Peter's *conviction* that Harriet was innocent of the crime.

convivial ADJ. festive; gay; characterized by joviality. The *convivial* celebrators of the victory sang their college songs.

convoke V. call together. Congress was *convoked* at the outbreak of the emergency. convocation, N.

convoluted ADJ. coiled around; involved; intricate. His argument was so *convoluted* that few of us could follow it intelligently.

copious ADJ. plentiful. She had *copious* reasons for rejecting the proposal.

coquette N. flirt. Because she refused to give him an answer to his proposal of marriage, he called her a *coquette*. also V.

■ **cordial** ADJ. gracious; heartfelt. Our hosts greeted us at the airport with a *cordial* welcome and a hearty hug.

cordon N. extended line of men or fortifications to prevent access or egress. The police *cordon* was so tight that the criminals could not leave the area. also V.

cornucopia N. horn overflowing with fruit and grain; symbol of abundance. The encyclopedia salesman claimed the new edition was a veritable *cornucopia* of information, an inexhaustible source of knowledge for the entire family.

corollary N. consequence; accompaniment. Brotherly love is a complex emotion, with sibling rivalry its natural *corollary*.

coronation N. ceremony of crowning a queen or king. When the witches told Macbeth he would be king, they failed to warn him he would lose his crown soon after his *coronation*.

corporeal ADJ. bodily; material. The doctor had no patience with spiritual matters: his job was to attend to his patients' *corporeal* problems, not to minister to their souls.

corpulent ADJ. very fat. The *corpulent* man resolved to reduce. corpulence, N.

correlation N. mutual relationship. He sought to determine the *correlation* that existed between ability in algebra and ability to interpret reading exercises. correlate, V., N.

■ **corroborate** V. confirm; support. Though Huck was quite willing to *corroborate* Tom's story, Aunt Polly knew better than to believe either of them.

● **corrode** V. destroy by chemical action. The girders supporting the bridge *corroded* so gradually that no one suspected any danger until the bridge suddenly collapsed. corrosion, N.

corrosive ADJ. eating away by chemicals or disease. Stainless steel is able to withstand the effects of *corrosive* chemicals. corrode, V.

● **corrugated** ADJ. wrinkled; ridged. She wished she could smooth away the wrinkles from his *corrugated* brow.

cosmic ADJ. pertaining to the universe; vast. *Cosmic* rays derive their name from the fact that they bombard the earth's atmosphere from outer space. cosmos, N.

cosmopolitan ADJ. sophisticated. Her years in the capitol had transformed her into a *cosmopolitan* young woman highly aware of international affairs.

coterie N. group that meets socially; select circle. After his book had been published, he was invited to join the literary *coterie* that lunched daily at the hotel.

countenance V. approve; tolerate. He refused to *countenance* such rude behavior on their part.

countenance N. face. When Jose saw his newborn daughter, a proud smile spread across his *countenance*.

countermand V. cancel; revoke. The general *countermanded* the orders issued in his absence.

Word List 12   counterpart-decelerate

counterpart N. a thing that completes another; things very much alike. Night and day are *counterparts*, complementing one another.

coup N. highly successful action or sudden attack. As the news of his *coup* spread throughout Wall Street, his fellow brokers dropped by to congratulate him.

couple V. join; unite. The Flying Karamazovs *couple* expert juggling and amateur joking in their nightclub act.

courier N. messenger. The publisher sent a special *courier* to pick up the manuscript.

covenant N. agreement. We must comply with the terms of the *covenant*.

covert ADJ. secret; hidden; implied. Investigations of the Central Intelligence Agency and other secret service networks reveal that such *covert* operations can get out of control.

covetous ADJ. avaricious; eagerly desirous of. The child was *covetous* by nature and wanted to take the toys belonging to his classmates. covet, V.

cow V. terrorize; intimidate. The little boy was so *cowed* by the hulking bully that he gave up his lunch money without a word of protest.

cower V. shrink quivering, as from fear. The frightened child *cowered* in the corner of the room.

coy ADJ. shy; modest; coquettish. Reluctant to commit herself so early in the game, Kay was *coy* in her answers to Ken's offer.

cozen V. cheat; hoodwink; swindle. He was the kind of individual who would *cozen* his friends in a cheap card game but remain eminently ethical in all business dealings.

crabbed ADJ. sour; peevish. The *crabbed* old man was avoided by the children because he scolded them when they made noise.

craftiness N. slyness; trickiness. In many Native American legends, the coyote is the clever trickster, the embodiment of *craftiness*. crafty, N.

crass ADJ. very unrefined; grossly insensible. The film critic deplored the *crass* commercialism of movie-makers who abandon artistic standards in order to make a quick buck.

craven ADJ. cowardly. Lillian's *craven* refusal to join the protest was criticized by her comrades, who had expected her to be brave enough to stand up for her beliefs.

credence N. belief. Do not place any *credence* in his promises.

credibility N. believability. Because the candidate had made some pretty unbelievable promises, we began to question the *credibility* of everything she said.

credo N. creed. I believe we may best describe his *credo* by saying that it approximates the Golden Rule.

■ **credulity** N. belief on slight evidence; gullibility; naivete. Con artists take advantage of the *credulity* of inexperienced investors to swindle them out of their savings. credulous, ADJ.

creed N. system of religious or ethical belief. Any loyal American's *creed* must emphasize love of democracy.

crescendo N. increase in the volume or intensity, as in a musical passage; climax. I love it when a piece of music suddenly shifts its mood, dramatically switching from a muted, contemplative passage to a *crescendo* with blaring trumpets and clashing cymbals.

crest N. highest point of a hill; foamy top of a wave. Fleeing the tidal wave, the islanders scrambled to reach the *crest* of Mount Lucinda. With relief, they watched the *crest* of the wave break well below their vantage point.

crestfallen ADJ. dejected; dispirited. We were surprised at his reaction to the failure of his project; instead of being *crestfallen*, he was busily engaged in planning new activities.

crevice N. crack; fissure. The mountain climbers found footholds in the tiny *crevices* in the mountainside.

cringe V. shrink back, as if in fear. The dog *cringed*, expecting a blow.

■ **criterion** N. standard used in judging. What *criterion* did you use when you selected this essay as the prizewinner? criteria, PL.

crop V. cut off unwanted parts of a photograph; graze. With care, David *cropped* the picture until its edges neatly framed the flock of sheep *cropping* the grass.

crotchety ADJ. eccentric; whimsical. Although he was reputed to be a *crotchety* old gentleman, I found his ideas substantially sound and sensible.

crux N. crucial point. This is the *crux* of the entire problem: everything centers on its being resolved.

crypt N. secret recess or vault, usually used for burial. Until recently, only bodies of rulers and leading statesmen were interred in this *crypt*.

■ **cryptic** ADJ. mysterious; hidden; secret. Thoroughly baffled by Holmes's *cryptic* remarks, Watson wondered whether Holmes was intentionally concealing his thoughts about the crime.

cubicle N. small chamber used for sleeping. After his many hours of intensive study in the library, he retired to his *cubicle*.

cuisine N. style of cooking. French *cuisine* is noted for its use of sauces and wines.

culinary ADJ. relating to cooking. Many chefs attribute their *culinary* skill to the wise use of spices.

cull V. pick out; reject. Every month the farmer *culls* the nonlaying hens from his flock and sells them to the local butcher. also N.

culminate V. attain the highest point; climax. George Bush's years of service to the Republican Party *culminated* in his being chosen as the Republican candidate for the presidency. His subsequent inauguration as President of the United States marked the *culmination* of his political career.

● **culpable** ADJ. deserving blame. Corrupt politicians who condone the activities of the gamblers are equally *culpable*.

culvert   N. artificial channel for water. If we build a *culvert* under the road at this point, we will reduce the possibility of the road's being flooded during the rainy season.

cumbersome   ADJ. heavy; hard to manage. He was burdened down with *cumbersome* parcels.

cumulative   ADJ. growing by addition. Vocabulary building is a *cumulative* process: as you go through your flash cards, you will add new words to your vocabulary, one by one.

cupidity   N. greed. The defeated people could not satisfy the *cupidity* of the conquerors, who demanded excessive tribute.

curator   N. superintendent; manager. The members of the board of trustees of the museum expected the new *curator* to plan events and exhibitions that would make the museum more popular.

curmudgeon   N. churlish, miserly individual. Although he was regarded by many as a *curmudgeon*, a few of us were aware of the many kindnesses and acts of charity that he secretly performed.

cursive   ADJ. flowing, running. In normal writing we run our letters together in *cursive* form; in printing, we separate the letters.

■ **cursory**   ADJ. casual; hastily done. Because a *cursory* examination of the ruins indicates the possibility of arson, we believe the insurance agency should undertake a more extensive investigation of the fire's cause.

■ **curtail**   V. shorten; reduce. When Herb asked Diane for a date, she said she was really sorry she couldn't go out with him, but her dad had ordered her to *curtail* her social life.

cynical   ADJ. skeptical or distrustful of human motives. *Cynical* from birth, Sidney was suspicious whenever anyone gave him a gift "with no strings attached." cynic, N.

cynosure   N. the object of general attention. As soon as the movie star entered the room, she became the *cynosure* of all eyes.

dabble   V. work at in a non-serious fashion; splash around. The amateur painter *dabbled* at art, but seldom produced a finished piece. The children *dabbled* their hands in the bird bath, splashing one another gleefully.

dais   N. raised platform for guests of honor. When he approached the *dais*, he was greeted by cheers from the people who had come to honor him.

dank   ADJ. damp. The walls of the dungeon were *dank* and slimy.

dapper   ADJ. neat and trim. In "The Odd Couple" TV show, Tony Randall played Felix Unger, an excessively *dapper* soul who could not stand to have a hair out of place.

dappled   ADJ. spotted. The sunlight filtering through the screens created a *dappled* effect on the wall.

daub   V. smear (as with paint). From the way he *daubed* his paint on the canvas, I could tell he knew nothing of oils. also N.

daunt   V. intimidate; frighten. "Boast all you like of your prowess. Mere words cannot *daunt* me," the hero answered the villain.

dauntless   ADJ. bold. Despite the dangerous nature of the undertaking, the *dauntless* soldier volunteered for the assignment.

dawdle   V. loiter; waste time. We have to meet a deadline so don't *dawdle*; just get down to work.

deadlock   N. standstill; stalemate. Because negotiations had reached a *deadlock*, some of the delegates had begun to mutter about breaking off the talks. also V.

deadpan   ADJ. wooden; impersonal. We wanted to see how long he could maintain his *deadpan* expression.

dearth   N. scarcity. The *dearth* of skilled labor compelled the employers to open trade schools.

debacle   N. sudden downfall; complete disaster. In the *Airplane* movies, every flight turns into a *debacle*, with passengers and crew members collapsing, engines falling apart, and carry-on baggage popping out of the overhead bins.

debase   V. reduce in quality or value; lower in esteem; degrade. In *The King and I*, Anna refuses to kneel down and prostrate herself before the king, for she feels that to do so would *debase* her position, and she will not submit to such *debasement*.

debauch   V. corrupt; seduce from virtue. Did Socrates' teachings lead the young men of Athens to be virtuous citizens, or did they *debauch* the young men, causing them to question the customs of their fathers? Clearly, Socrates' philosophical talks were nothing like the wild *debauchery* of the toga parties in *Animal House*.

● **debilitate**   V. weaken; enfeeble. Michael's severe bout of the flu *debilitated* him so much that he was too tired to go to work for a week.

debonair   ADJ. friendly; aiming to please. The *debonair* youth was liked by all who met him, because of his cheerful and obliging manner.

debris   N. rubble. A full year after the earthquake in Mexico City, they were still carting away the *debris*.

● **debunk**   V. expose as false, exaggerated, worthless, etc; ridicule. Pointing out that he consistently had voted against strengthening anti-pollution legislation, reporters *debunked* the candidate's claim that he was a fervent environmentalist.

debutante   N. young woman making formal entrance into society. As a *debutante*, she was often mentioned in the society columns of the newspapers.

decadence   N. decay. The moral *decadence* of the people was reflected in the lewd literature of the period.

decapitate   V. behead. They did not hang Lady Jane Grey; they *decapitated* her. "Off with her head!" cried the Duchess, eager to *decapitate* poor Alice.

decelerate   V. slow down. Seeing the emergency blinkers in the road ahead, he *decelerated* quickly.

Word List 13   deciduous-dermatologist

deciduous   ADJ. falling off as of leaves. The oak is a *deciduous* tree; in winter it looks quite bare.

decimate   V. kill, usually one out of ten. We do more to *decimate* our population in automobile accidents than we do in war.

decipher   V. interpret secret code. Lacking his code book, the spy was unable to *decipher* the scrambled message sent to him from the KGB.

declivity   N. downward slope. The children loved to ski down the *declivity.*

decolleté   ADJ. having a low-necked dress. Current fashion decrees that evening gowns be *decolleté* this season; bare shoulders are again the vogue.

decomposition   N. decay. Despite the body's advanced state of *decomposition,* the police were able to identify the murdered man.

■ **decorum**   N. propriety; orderliness and good taste in manners. Even the best-mannered students have trouble behaving with *decorum* on the last day of school. decorous, ADJ.

decoy   N. lure or bait. The wild ducks were not fooled by the *decoy.* also V.

decrepit   ADJ. worn out by age. The *decrepit* car blocked traffic on the highway.

decrepitude   N. state of collapse caused by illness or old age. I was unprepared for the state of *decrepitude* in which I had found my old friend; he seemed to have aged twenty years in six months.

decry   V. express strong disapproval of; disparage. The founder of the Children's Defense Fund, Marian Wright Edelman, strongly *decries* the lack of financial and moral support for children in America today.

deducible   ADJ. derived by reasoning. If we accept your premise, your conclusions are easily *deducible.*

deface   V. mar; disfigure. If you *deface* a library book, you will have to pay a hefty fine.

defame   V. harm someone's reputation; malign; slander. If you try to *defame* my good name, my lawyers will see you in court. If rival candidates persist in *defaming* one another, the voters may conclude that all politicians are crooks. defamation, N.

default   N. failure to act. When the visiting team failed to show up for the big game, they lost the game by *default.* When Jack failed to make the payments on his Jaguar, the dealership took back the car because he had *defaulted* on his debt.

defeatist   ADJ. attitude of one who is ready to accept defeat as a natural outcome. If you maintain your *defeatist* attitude, you will never succeed. also N.

defection   N. desertion. The children, who had made him an idol, were hurt most by his *defection* from our cause.

defer   V. delay till later; exempt temporarily. In wartime, some young men immediately volunteer to serve; others *defer* making plans until they hear from their draft boards. During the Vietnam War, many young men, hoping to be *deferred,* requested student *deferments.*

defer   V. give in respectfully; submit. When it comes to making decisions about purchasing software, we must *defer* to Michael, our computer guru; he gets the final word. Michael, however, can *defer* these questions to no one; only he can decide.

■ **deference**   N. courteous regard for another's wish. In *deference* to the minister's request, please do not take photographs during the wedding service.

defiance   N. refusal to yield; resistance. When John reached the "terrible two's," he responded to every parental request with howls of *defiance.* defy, V.

defile   V. pollute; profane. The hoodlums *defiled* the church with their scurrilous writing.

definitive   ADJ. final; complete. Carl Sandburg's *Abraham Lincoln* may be regarded as the *definitive* work on the life of the Great Emancipator.

deflect   V. turn aside. His life was saved when his cigarette case *deflected* the bullet.

defoliate   V. destroy leaves. In Vietnam the army made extensive use of chemical agents to *defoliate* the woodlands.

defray   V. pay the costs of. Her employer offered to *defray* the costs of her postgraduate education.

deft   ADJ. neat; skillful. The *deft* waiter uncorked the champagne without spilling a drop.

defunct   ADJ. dead; no longer in use or existence. The lawyers sought to examine the books of the *defunct* corporation.

defuse   V. remove the fuse of a bomb; reduce or eliminate a threat. Police negotiators are trained to *defuse* dangerous situations by avoiding confrontational language and behavior.

degenerate   V. become worse; deteriorate. As the fight dragged on, the champion's style *degenerated* until he could barely keep on his feet.

■ **degradation**   N. humiliation; debasement; degeneration. Some secretaries object to fetching the boss a cup of coffee because they resent the *degradation* of being made to do such lowly tasks. degrade, V.

● **dehydrate**   V. remove water from; dry out. Running under a hot sun quickly *dehydrates* the body; joggers soon learn to carry water bottles and to drink from them frequently.

deify   V. turn into a god; idolize. Admire Elvis Presley all you want; just don't *deify* him.

deign   V. condescend; stoop. The celebrated fashion designer would not *deign* to speak to a mere seamstress; his overburdened assistant had to convey the master's wishes to the lowly workers assembling his great designs.

delectable   ADJ. delightful; delicious. We thanked our host for a most *delectable* meal.

delete v. erase; strike out. Less is more: if you *delete* this paragraph, your whole essay will have greater appeal.

● **deleterious** ADJ. harmful. If you believe that smoking is *deleterious* to your health (and the Surgeon General certainly does), then quit!

deliberate v. consider; ponder. Offered the new job, she asked for time to *deliberate* before she told them her decision.

■ **delineate** v. portray; depict; sketch. Using only a few descriptive phrases, Austen *delineates* the character of Mr. Collins so well that we can predict his every move. delineation, N.

delirium N. mental disorder marked by confusion. In his *delirium*, the drunkard saw pink panthers and talking pigs. Perhaps he wasn't *delirious*: he might just have wandered into a movie.

delude v. deceive. His mistress may have *deluded* herself into believing that he would leave his wife and marry her.

deluge N. flood; rush. When we advertised the position, we received a *deluge* of applications.

delusion N. false belief; hallucination. Don suffers from *delusions* of grandeur: he thinks he's a world-famous author when he's published just one paperback book.

delve v. dig; investigate. *Delving* into old books and manuscripts is part of a researcher's job.

demagogue N. person who appeals to people's prejudice; false leader of people. He was accused of being a *demagogue* because he made promises that aroused futile hopes in his listeners.

demean v. degrade; humiliate. Standing on his dignity, he refused to *demean* himself by replying to the offensive letter. If you truly believed in the dignity of labor, you would not think it would *demean* you to work as a janitor.

demeanor N. behavior; bearing. His sober *demeanor* quieted the noisy revelers.

demented ADJ. insane. Doctor Demento was a lunatic radio personality who liked to act as if he were truly *demented*. If you're *demented*, your mental state is out of whack; in other words, you're wacky.

demise N. death. Upon the *demise* of the dictator, a bitter dispute about succession to power developed.

demolition N. destruction. One of the major aims of the air force was the complete *demolition* of all means of transportation by bombing of rail lines and terminals. demolish, v.

demoniac ADJ. fiendish. The Spanish Inquisition devised many *demoniac* means of torture. demon, N.

demur v. object (because of doubts, scruples); hesitate. When offered a post on the board of directors, David *demurred*: he had scruples about taking on the job because he was unsure he could handle it in addition to his other responsibilities.

demure ADJ. grave; serious; coy. She was *demure* and reserved, a nice modest girl whom any young man would be proud to take home to his mother.

demystify v. clarify; free from mystery or obscurity. Helpful doctors *demystify* medical procedures by describing them in everyday language, explaining that a myringotomy, for example, is an operation involving making a small hole in one's eardrum.

denigrate v. blacken. All attempts to *denigrate* the character of our late president have failed; the people still love him and cherish his memory.

denizen N. inhabitant or resident; regular visitor. In *The Untouchables*, Eliot Ness fights Al Capone and the other *denizens* of Chicago's underworld. Ness's fight against corruption was the talk of all the *denizens* of the local bars.

denotation N. meaning; distinguishing by name. A dictionary will always give us the *denotation* of a word; frequently, it will also give us the connotations. denote, v.

denouement N. outcome; final development of the plot of a play. The play was childishly written; the *denouement* was obvious to sophisticated theatergoers as early as the middle of the first act.

■ **denounce** v. condemn; criticize. The reform candidate *denounced* the corrupt city officers for having betrayed the public's trust. denunciation, N.

depict v. portray. In this sensational exposé, the author *depicts* Beatle John Lennon as a drug-crazed neurotic. Do you question the accuracy of this *depiction* of Lennon?

deplete v. reduce; exhaust. We must wait until we *deplete* our present inventory before we order replacements.

■ **deplore** v. regret; disapprove of. Although I *deplore* the vulgarity of your language, I defend your right to express yourself freely.

deploy v. spread out [troops] in an extended though shallow battle line. The general ordered the battalion to *deploy* in order to meet the enemy offensive.

● **depose** v. dethrone; remove from office. The army attempted to *depose* the king and set up a military government.

deposition N. testimony under oath. He made his *deposition* in the judge's chamber.

■ **depravity** N. extreme corruption; wickedness. The *depravity* of Caligula's behavior came to sicken even those who had willingly participated in his earlier, comparatively innocent orgies.

■ **deprecate** v. express disapproval of; protest against; belittle. A firm believer in old-fashioned courtesy, Miss Post *deprecated* the modern tendency to address new acquaintances by their first names. deprecatory, ADJ.

depreciate v. lessen in value. If you neglect this property, it will *depreciate*.

depredation N. plundering. After the *depredations* of the invaders, the people were penniless.

deranged ADJ. insane. He had to be institutionalized because he was mentally *deranged*.

derelict ADJ. abandoned; negligent. The *derelict* craft was a menace to navigation. Whoever abandoned it in the middle of the harbor was *derelict* in living up to his responsibilities as a boat owner. also N.

■ **deride** V. ridicule; make fun of. The critics *derided* his pretentious dialogue and refused to consider his play seriously. derision, N.

■ **derivative** ADJ. unoriginal; derived from another source. Although her early poetry was clearly *derivative* in nature,

the critics thought she had promise and eventually would find her own voice.

dermatologist N. one who studies the skin and its diseases. I advise you to consult a *dermatologist* about your acne.

Word List 14   derogatory-disgruntle

derogatory ADJ. expressing a low opinion. I resent your *derogatory* remarks.

descant V. discuss fully. He was willing to *descant* upon any topic of conversation, even when he knew very little about the subject under discussion. also N.

descry V. catch sight of. In the distance, we could barely *descry* the enemy vessels.

desecrate V. profane; violate the sanctity of. Shattering the altar and trampling the holy objects underfoot, the invaders *desecrated* the sanctuary.

● **desiccate** V. dry up. A tour of this smokehouse will give you an idea of how the pioneers used to *desiccate* food in order to preserve it.

desolate ADJ. unpopulated. After six months in the crowded, bustling metropolis, David was so sick of people that he was ready to head for the most *desolate* patch of wilderness he could find.

desolate V. rob of joy; lay waste to; forsake. The bandits *desolated* the countryside, burning farms and carrying off the harvest.

despise V. look on with scorn; regard as worthless or distasteful. Mr. Bond, I *despise* spies; I look down on them as mean, *despicable*, honorless men, whom I would wipe from the face of the earth with as little concern as I would scrape dog droppings from the bottom of my shoe.

despoil V. plunder. If you do not yield, I am afraid the enemy will *despoil* the countryside.

■ **despondent** ADJ. depressed; gloomy. To the dismay of his parents, William became seriously *despondent* after he broke up with Jan; they despaired of finding a cure for his gloom. despondency, N.

despot N. tyrant; harsh, authoritarian ruler. How could a benevolent king turn overnight into a *despot*?

destitute ADJ. extremely poor. Because they had no health insurance, the father's costly illness left the family *destitute*.

desultory ADJ. aimless; haphazard; digressing at random. In prison Malcolm X set himself the task of reading straight through the dictionary; to him, reading was purposeful, not *desultory*.

■ **detached** ADJ. emotionally removed; calm and objective; physically unconnected. A psychoanalyst must maintain a *detached* point of view and stay uninvolved with his or her patients' personal lives. To a child growing up in an apartment or a row house, to live in a *detached* house was an unattainable dream.

detergent N. cleansing agent. Many new *detergents* have replaced soap.

determination N. resolve; measurement or calculation; decision. Nothing could shake his *determination* that his children would get the best education that money could buy. Thanks to my pocket calculator, my *determination* of the answer to the problem took only seconds of my time.

■ **deterrent** N. something that discourages; hindrance. Does the threat of capital punishment serve as a *deterrent* to potential killers? deter, V.

detonation N. explosion. The *detonation* of the bomb could be heard miles away.

detraction N. slandering; aspersion. He is offended by your frequent *detractions* of his ability as a leader.

■ **detrimental** ADJ. harmful; damaging. The candidate's acceptance of major financial contributions from a well-known racist ultimately proved *detrimental* to his campaign, for he lost the backing of many of his early grassroots supporters. detriment, N.

deviate V. turn away from (a principle, norm); depart; diverge. Richard never *deviated* from his daily routine: every day he set off for work at eight o'clock, had his sack lunch (peanut butter on whole wheat) at 12:15, and headed home at the stroke of five.

■ **devious** ADJ. roundabout; erratic; not straightforward. The Joker's plan was so *devious* that it was only with great difficulty we could follow its shifts and dodges.

■ **devise** V. think up; invent; plan. How clever he must be to have *devised* such a devious plan! What ingenious inventions might he have *devised* if he had turned his mind to science and not to crime.

devoid ADJ. lacking. You may think her mind is a total void, but she's actually not *devoid* of intelligence. She just sounds like an airhead.

devotee N. enthusiastic follower. A *devotee* of the opera, he bought season tickets every year.

devout ADJ. pious. The *devout* man prayed daily.

dexterous ADJ. skillful. The magician was so *dexterous* that we could not follow him as he performed his tricks.

diabolical ADJ. devilish. "What a fiend I am, to devise such a *diabolical* scheme to destroy Gotham City," chortled the Joker gleefully.

diagnosis N. art of identifying a disease; analysis of a condition. In medical school Margaret developed her skill at *diagnosis*, learning how to read volumes from a rapid pulse or a hacking cough. diagnose, V.; diagnostic, ADJ.

dialectical ADJ. relating to the art of debate; mutual or reciprocal. The debate coach's students grew to develop great forensic and *dialectical* skill. Teaching, however, is inherently a *dialectical* situation: the coach learned at least as much from her students as they learned from her. dialectics, N.

diaphanous ADJ. sheer; transparent. They saw the burglar clearly through the *diaphanous* curtain.

diatribe N. bitter scolding; invective. During the lengthy *diatribe* delivered by his opponent he remained calm and self-controlled.

dichotomy N. split; branching into two parts (especially contradictory ones). Willie didn't know how to resolve the *dichotomy* between his ambition to go to college and his childhood longing to run away and join the circus. Then he heard about Ringling Brothers Circus College, and he knew he'd found the perfect school.

dictum N. authoritative and weighty statement; saying; maxim. University administrations still follow the old *dictum* of "Publish or perish." They don't care how good a teacher you are; if you don't publish enough papers, you're out of a job.

didactic ADJ. teaching; instructional. Pope's lengthy poem *An Essay on Man* is too *didactic* for my taste: I dislike it when poets turn preachy and moralize.

differentiate V. distinguish; perceive a difference between. Tweedledum and Tweedledee were like two peas in a pod; not even Mother Tweedle could *differentiate* the one from the other.

● **diffidence** N. shyness. You must overcome your *diffidence* if you intend to become a salesperson.

■ **diffuse** ADJ. wordy; rambling; spread out (like a gas). If you pay authors by the word, you tempt them to produce *diffuse* manuscripts rather than brief ones. diffusion, N.

■ **digression** N. wandering away from the subject. Nobody minded when Professor Renoir's lectures wandered away from their official theme; his *digressions* were always more fascinating than the topic of the day. digress, V.

dilapidated ADJ. ruined because of neglect. The *dilapidated* old building needed far more work than just a new coat of paint. dilapidation, N.

dilate V. expand. In the dark, the pupils of your eyes *dilate*.

● **dilatory** ADJ. delaying. Your *dilatory* tactics may compel me to cancel the contract.

dilemma N. problem; choice of two unsatisfactory alternatives. In this *dilemma*, he knew no one to whom he could turn for advice.

dilettante N. aimless follower of the arts; amateur; dabbler. He was not serious in his painting; he was rather a *dilettante*.

■ **diligence** N. steadiness of effort; persistent hard work. Her employers were greatly impressed by her *diligence* and offered her a partnership in the firm. diligent, ADJ.

dilute V. make less concentrated; reduce in strength. She preferred to *dilute* her coffee with milk.

■ **diminution** N. lessening; reduction in size. Old Jack was as sharp at eighty as he had been at fifty; increasing age led to no *diminution* of his mental acuity.

din N. continued loud noise. The *din* of the jackhammers outside the classroom window drowned out the lecturer's voice. also V.

dinghy N. small ship's boat. In the film *Lifeboat*, an ill-assorted group of passengers from a sunken ocean liner are marooned at sea in a *dinghy*.

dingy ADJ. dull; not fresh; cheerless. Refusing to be depressed by her *dingy* studio apartment, Bea spent the weekend polishing the floors and windows and hanging bright posters on the walls.

dint N. means; effort. By *dint* of much hard work, the volunteers were able to place the raging forest fire under control.

diorama N. life-size three-dimensional scene from nature or history. Because they dramatically pose actual stuffed animals against realistic painted landscapes, the *dioramas* at the Museum of Natural History particularly impress high school biology students.

dire ADJ. disastrous. People ignored her *dire* predictions of an approaching depression.

dirge N. lament with music. The funeral *dirge* stirred us to tears.

disabuse V. correct a false impression; undeceive. I will attempt to *disabuse* you of your impression of my client's guilt; I know he is innocent.

disaffected ADJ. disloyal. Once the most loyal of Gorbachev's supporters, Sheverdnaze found himself becoming increasingly *disaffected*.

disapprobation N. disapproval; condemnation. The conservative father viewed his daughter's radical boyfriend with *disapprobation*.

disarray N. a disorderly or untidy state. After the New Year's party, the once orderly house was in total *disarray*.

disavowal N. denial; disclaiming. His *disavowal* of his part in the conspiracy was not believed by the jury. disavow, V.

disband V. dissolve; disperse. The chess club *disbanded* after its disastrous initial season.

disburse V. pay out. When you *disburse* money on the company's behalf, be sure to get a receipt.

discernible ADJ. distinguishable; perceivable. The ships in the harbor were not *discernible* in the fog. discern, V.

■ **discerning** ADJ. mentally quick and observant; having insight. Though no genius, the star was sufficiently *discerning* to tell her true friends from the countless phonies who flattered her.

disclaim V. disown; renounce claim to. If I grant you this privilege, will you *disclaim* all other rights?

■ **disclose** V. reveal. Although competitors offered him bribes, he refused to *disclose* any information about his company's forthcoming product. disclosure, N.

discombobulated ADJ. confused; discomposed. The novice square dancer became so *discombobulated* that he wandered into the wrong set.

discomfit V. put to rout; defeat; disconcert. This ruse will *discomfit* the enemy. discomfiture, N. discomfited, ADJ.

discomposure N. agitation; loss of poise. Perpetually poised, Agent 007 never exhibited a moment's *discomposure*.

disconcert V. confuse; upset; embarrass. The lawyer was *disconcerted* by the evidence produced by her adversary.

disconsolate ADJ. sad. The death of his wife left him *disconsolate*.

discord N. conflict; lack of harmony. Watching Tweedledum battle Tweedledee, Alice wondered what had caused this pointless *discord*.

■ **discordant** ADJ. not harmonious; conflicting. Nothing is quite so *discordant* as the sound of a junior high school orchestra tuning up.

■ **discount** V. disregard; dismiss. Be prepared to *discount* what he has to say about his ex-wife.

● **discourse** N. formal discussion; conversation. The young Plato was drawn to the Agora to hear the philosophical *discourse* of Socrates and his followers. also V.

discredit V. defame; destroy confidence in; disbelieve. The campaign was highly negative in tone; each candidate tried to *discredit* the other.

● **discrepancy** N. lack of consistency; difference. The police noticed some *discrepancies* in his description of the crime and did not believe him.

discrete ADJ. separate; unconnected. The universe is composed of *discrete* bodies.

discretion N. prudence; ability to adjust actions to circumstances. Use your *discretion* in this matter and do not discuss it with anyone. discreet, ADJ.

■ **discriminating** ADJ. able to see differences; prejudiced. A superb interpreter of Picasso, she was sufficiently *discriminating* to judge the most complex works of modern art. (secondary meaning) discrimination, N.

discursive ADJ. digressing; rambling. As the lecturer wandered from topic to topic, we wondered what if any point there was to his *discursive* remarks.

■ **disdain** V. view with scorn or contempt. In the film *Funny Face*, the bookish heroine *disdained* fashion models for their lack of intellectual interests. also N.

disembark V. go ashore; unload cargo from a ship. Before the passengers could *disembark*, they had to pick up their passports from the ship's purser.

disenfranchise V. deprive of a civil right. The imposition of the poll tax effectively *disenfranchised* poor Southern blacks, who lost their right to vote.

disengage V. uncouple; separate; disconnect. A standard movie routine involves the hero's desperate attempt to *disengage* a railroad car from a moving train.

disfigure V. mar in beauty; spoil. An ugly frown *disfigured* his normally pleasant face.

disgorge V. surrender something; eject; vomit. Unwilling to *disgorge* the cash he had stolen from the pension fund, the embezzler tried to run away.

disgruntle V. make discontented. The passengers were *disgruntled* by the numerous delays.

Word List 15   dishearten–duplicity

dishearten V. discourage; cause to lose courage or hope. His failure to pass the bar exam *disheartened* him.

disheveled ADJ. untidy. Your *disheveled* appearance will hurt your chances in this interview.

■ **disinclination** N. unwillingness. Some mornings I feel a great *disinclination* to get out of bed.

disingenuous ADJ. lacking genuine candor; insincere. Now that we know the mayor and his wife are engaged in a bitter divorce fight, we find their earlier remarks regretting their lack of time together remarkably *disingenuous*.

disinter V. dig up; unearth. They *disinterred* the body and held an autopsy.

disinterested ADJ. unprejudiced. Given the judge's political ambitions and the lawyers' financial interest in the case, the only *disinterested* person in the courtroom may have been the court reporter.

disjointed ADJ. disconnected. His remarks were so *disjointed* that we could not follow his reasoning.

dislodge V. remove (forcibly). Thrusting her fist up under the choking man's lower ribs, Margaret used the Heimlich maneuver to *dislodge* the food caught in his throat.

dismantle V. take apart. When the show closed, they *dismantled* the scenery before storing it.

dismay V. discourage; frighten. The huge amount of work she had left to do *dismayed* her. also N.

dismember V. cut into small parts. When the Austrian Empire was *dismembered*, several new countries were established.

■ **dismiss** V. put away from consideration; reject. Believing in John's love for her, she *dismissed* the notion that he might be unfaithful. (secondary meaning)

■ **disparage** V. belittle. A doting mother, Emma was more likely to praise her son's crude attempts at art than to *disparage* them.

disparate ADJ. basically different; unrelated. Unfortunately, Tony and Tina have *disparate* notions of marriage: Tony sees it as a carefree extended love affair, while Tina sees it as a solemn commitment to build a family and a home.

■ **disparity** N. difference; condition of inequality. Their *disparity* in rank made no difference at all to the prince and Cinderella.

dispassionate ADJ. calm; impartial. Known in the company for his cool judgment, Bill could impartially examine the causes of a problem, giving a *dispassionate* analysis of what had gone wrong, and go on to suggest how to correct the mess.

dispatch N. speediness; prompt execution; message sent with all due speed. Young Napoleon defeated the enemy with all possible *dispatch;* he then sent a *dispatch* to headquarters informing his commander of the great victory. also V.

dispel V. scatter; drive away; cause to vanish. The bright sunlight eventually *dispelled* the morning mist.

■ **disperse** V. scatter. The police fired tear gas into the crowd to *disperse* the protesters. dispersion, N.

dispirited ADJ. lacking in spirit. The coach used all the tricks at his command to buoy up the enthusiasm of his team, which had become *dispirited* at the loss of the star player.

■ **disputatious** ADJ. argumentative; fond of arguing. Convinced he knew more than his lawyers, Alan was a *disputatious* client, ready to argue about the best way to conduct the case. disputant, N.

disquiet V. make uneasy or anxious. Holmes's absence for a day, slightly *disquieted* Watson; after a week with no word, however, Watson's uneasiness about his missing friend had grown into a deep fear for his safety. disquietude, N.

dissection N. analysis; cutting apart in order to examine. The *dissection* of frogs in the laboratory is particularly unpleasant to some students.

dissemble V. disguise; pretend. Even though John tried to *dissemble* his motive for taking modern dance, we all knew he was there not to dance but to meet girls.

■ **disseminate** V. distribute; spread; scatter (like seeds). By their use of the Internet, propagandists have been able to *disseminate* their pet doctrines to new audiences around the globe.

■ **dissent** V. disagree. In the recent Supreme Court decision, Justice O'Connor *dissented* from the majority opinion. also N.

dissertation N. formal essay. In order to earn a graduate degree from many of our universities, a candidate is frequently required to prepare a *dissertation* on some scholarly subject.

dissident ADJ. dissenting; rebellious. In the purge that followed the student demonstrations at Tiananmen Square, the government hunted down the *dissident* students and their supporters. also N.

dissimulate V. pretend; conceal by feigning. She tried to *dissimulate* her grief by her exuberant attitude.

dissipate V. squander; waste; scatter. He is a fine artist, but I fear he may *dissipate* his gifts if he keeps wasting his time playing games.

dissolute ADJ. loose in morals. The *dissolute* life led by the ancient Romans is indeed shocking.

dissolution N. breaking of a union; decay; termination. Which caused King Lear more suffering: the *dissolution* of his kingdom into warring factions, or the *dissolution* of his aged, failing body?

dissonance N. discord. Composer Charles Ives often used *dissonance*—clashing or unresolved chords—for special effects in his musical works.

dissuade V. persuade not to do; discourage. Since Tom could not *dissuade* Huck from running away from home, he decided to run away with him. dissuasion, N.

distant ADJ. reserved or aloof; cold in manner. His *distant* greeting made me feel unwelcome from the start. (secondary meaning)

● **distend** V. expand; swell out. I can tell when he is under stress by the way the veins *distend* on his forehead.

distill V. extract the essence; purify; refine. A moonshiner *distills* mash into whiskey; an epigrammatist *distills* thoughts into quips.

distinction N. honor; contrast; discrimination. A holder of the Medal of Honor, George served with great *distinction* in World War II. He made a *distinction*, however, between World War II and Vietnam, which he considered an immoral conflict.

distort V. twist out of shape. It is difficult to believe the newspaper accounts of the riots because of the way some reporters *distort* and exaggerate the actual events. distortion, N.

distraught ADJ. upset; distracted by anxiety. The *distraught* parents frantically searched the ravine for their lost child.

diurnal ADJ. daily. A farmer cannot neglect his *diurnal* tasks at any time; cows, for example, must be milked regularly.

diva N. operatic singer; prima donna. Although world famous as a *diva,* she did not indulge in fits of temperament.

diverge V. vary; go in different directions from the same point. The spokes of the wheel *diverge* from the hub.

■ **divergent** ADJ. differing; deviating. Since graduating from medical school, the two doctors have taken *divergent* paths, one going on to become a nationally prominent surgeon, the other dedicating himself to a small family practice in his home town. divergence, N.

diverse ADJ. differing in some characteristics; various. The professor suggested *diverse* ways of approaching the assignment and recommended that we choose one of them. diversity, N.

diversion N. act of turning aside; pastime. After studying for several hours, he needed a *diversion* from work. divert, V.

diversity N. variety; dissimilitude. The *diversity* of colleges in this country indicates that many levels of ability are being cared for.

divest V. strip; deprive. He was *divested* of his power to act and could no longer govern. divestiture, N.

divine V. perceive intuitively; foresee the future. Nothing infuriated Tom more than Aunt Polly's ability to *divine* when he was telling the truth.

divulge V. reveal. No lover of gossip, Charlotte would never *divulge* anything that a friend told her in confidence.

docile ADJ. obedient; easily managed. As *docile* as he seems today, that old lion was once a ferocious, snarling beast. docility, N.

doctrinaire   ADJ. unable to compromise about points of doctrine; dogmatic; unyielding. Weng had hoped that the student-led democracy movement might bring about change in China, but the repressive response of the *doctrinaire* hard-liners crushed his dreams of democracy.

■ **doctrine**   N. teachings, in general; particular principle (religious, legal, etc.) taught. He was so committed to the *doctrines* of his faith that he was unable to evaluate them impartially.

■ **document**   V. provide written evidence. She kept all the receipts from her business trip in order to *document* her expenses for the firm. also N.

doff   V. take off. A gentleman used to *doff* his hat to a lady.

dogged   ADJ. determined; stubborn. *Les Miserables* tells of Inspector Javert's long, *dogged* pursuit of the criminal Jean Valjean.

doggerel   N. poor verse. Although we find occasional snatches of genuine poetry in her work, most of her writing is mere *doggerel*.

■ **dogmatic**   ADJ. opinionated; arbitrary; doctrinal. We tried to discourage Doug from being so *dogmatic*, but never could convince him that his opinions might be wrong.

doldrums   N. blues; listlessness; slack period. Once the excitement of meeting her deadline was over, she found herself in the *doldrums*.

doleful   ADJ. sorrowful. He found the *doleful* lamentations of the bereaved family emotionally disturbing and he left as quickly as he could.

dolt   N. stupid person. I thought I was talking to a mature audience; instead, I find myself addressing a pack of *dolts* and idiots.

domicile   N. home. Although his legal *domicile* was in New York City, his work kept him away from his residence for many years. also V.

domineer   V. rule over tyrannically. Students prefer teachers who guide, not ones who *domineer*.

don   V. put on. When Clark Kent has to *don* his Superman outfit, he changes clothes in a convenient phone booth.

doodle   V. scribble or draw aimlessly; waste time. Art's teachers scolded him when he *doodled* all over the margins of his papers.

dormant   ADJ. sleeping; lethargic; latent. At fifty her long-*dormant* ambition to write flared up once more; within a year she had completed the first of her great historical novels.

dormer   N. window projecting from roof. In remodeling the attic into a bedroom, we decided that we needed to put in *dormers* to provide sufficient ventilation for the new room.

dossier   N. file of documents on a subject. Ordered by J. Edgar Hoover to investigate the senator, the FBI compiled a complete *dossier* on him.

dote   V. be excessively fond of; show signs of mental decline. Not only grandmothers bore you with stories about their brilliant grandchildren; grandfathers *dote* on the little

rascals, too. Poor old Alf clearly *doted*: the senile old *dotard* was past it; in fact, he was in his *dotage*.

douse   V. plunge into water; drench; extinguish. They *doused* each other with hoses and water balloons.

dowdy   ADJ. slovenly; untidy. She tried to change her *dowdy* image by buying a new fashionable wardrobe.

downcast   ADJ. disheartened; sad. Cheerful and optimistic by nature, Beth was never *downcast* despite the difficulties she faced.

drab   ADJ. dull; lacking color; cheerless. The Dutch woman's *drab* winter coat contrasted with the distinctive, colorful native costume she wore beneath it.

draconian   ADJ. extremely severe. When the principal canceled the senior prom because some seniors had been late to school that week, we thought the *draconian* punishment was far too harsh for such a minor violation of the rules.

dregs   N. sediment; worthless residue. David poured the wine carefully to avoid stirring up the *dregs*.

drivel   N. nonsense; foolishness. Why do I have to spend my days listening to such idiotic *drivel*? *Drivel* is related to *dribble*: think of a dribbling, *driveling* idiot.

droll   ADJ. queer and amusing. He was a popular guest because his *droll* anecdotes were always entertaining.

drone   N. idle person; male bee. Content to let his wife support him, the would-be writer was in reality nothing but a *drone*.

drone   V. talk dully; buzz or murmur like a bee. On a gorgeous day, who wants to be stuck in a classroom listening to the teacher *drone*?

dross   N. waste matter; worthless impurities. Many methods have been devised to separate the valuable metal from the *dross*.

drudgery   N. menial work. Cinderella's fairy godmother rescued her from a life of *drudgery*.

■ **dubious**   ADJ. questionable; filled with doubt. Many critics of SAT I contend the test is of *dubious* worth. Jay claimed he could get a perfect 1600 on SAT I, but Ellen was *dubious*: she knew he hadn't cracked a book in three years.

ductile   ADJ. malleable; flexible; pliable. Copper is an extremely *ductile* material: you can stretch it into the thinnest of wires, bend it, even wind it into loops.

dulcet   ADJ. sweet sounding. The *dulcet* sounds of the birds at dawn were soon drowned out by the roar of traffic passing our motel.

dumbfound   V. astonish. Egbert's perfect 1600 on his SAT I exam *dumbfounded* his classmates, who had always found him to be perfectly dumb.

● **dupe**   N. someone easily fooled. While the gullible Watson often was made a *dupe* by unscrupulous parties, Sherlock Holmes was far more difficult to fool. also V.

■ **duplicity**   N. double-dealing; hypocrisy. When Tanya learned that Mark had been two-timing her, she was furious at his *duplicity*.

Word List 16 duration-encroachment

duration N. length of time something lasts. Because she wanted the children to make a good impression on the dinner guests, Mother promised them a treat if they'd behave for the *duration* of the meal.

duress N. forcible restraint, especially unlawfully. The hostages were held under *duress* until the prisoners' demands were met.

dutiful ADJ. respectful; obedient. When Mother told Billy to kiss Great-Aunt Hattie, the boy obediently gave the old woman a *dutiful* peck on her cheek.

dwarf V. cause to seem small. The giant redwoods and high cliffs *dwarfed* the elegant Ahwahnee Hotel, making it appear a modest lodge rather than an imposing hostelry.

dwindle V. shrink; reduce. The food in the life boat gradually *dwindled* away to nothing; in the end, they ate the ship's cook.

dynamic ADJ. energetic; vigorously active. The *dynamic* aerobics instructor kept her students on the run; she was a little *dynamo*.

earthy ADJ. unrefined; coarse. His *earthy* remarks often embarrassed the women in his audience.

ebb V. recede; lessen. Sitting on the beach, Mrs. Dalloway watched the tide *ebb*: the waters receded, drawing away from her as she sat there all alone. also N.

● **ebullient** ADJ. showing excitement; overflowing with enthusiasm. Amy's *ebullient* nature could not be repressed; she was always bubbling over with excitement. ebullience, N.

eccentric ADJ. irregular; odd; whimsical; bizarre. The comet veered dangerously close to the earth in its *eccentric* orbit. People came up with some *eccentric* ideas for dealing with the emergency: someone even suggested tieing a knot in the comet's tail!

eccentricity N. oddity; idiosyncrasy. Some of his friends tried to account for his rudeness to strangers as the *eccentricity* of genius.

ecclesiastic ADJ. pertaining to the church. The minister donned his *ecclesiastic* garb and walked to the pulpit. also N.

■ **eclectic** ADJ. composed of elements drawn from disparate sources. His style of interior decoration was *eclectic*: bits and pieces of furnishings from widely divergent periods, strikingly juxtaposed to create a unique decor. eclecticism, N.

eclipse V. darken; extinguish; surpass. The new stock market high *eclipsed* the previous record set in 1995.

ecologist N. a person concerned with the interrelationship between living organisms and their environment. The *ecologist* was concerned that the new dam would upset the natural balance of the creatures living in Glen Canyon.

economy N. efficiency or conciseness in using something. Reading the epigrams of Pope, I admire the *economy* of his verse: in few words he conveys worlds of meaning. (secondary meaning)

ecstasy N. rapture; joy; any overpowering emotion. When Allison received her long-hoped-for letter of acceptance from Harvard, she was in *ecstasy*. ecstatic, ADJ.

eddy N. swirling current of water, air, etc. The water in the tide pool was still, except for an occasional *eddy*.

edict N. decree (especially issued by a sovereign); official command. The emperor issued an *edict* decreeing that everyone should come see him model his magnificent new clothes.

● **edify** V. instruct; correct morally. Although his purpose was to *edify* and not to entertain his audience, many of his listeners were amused rather than enlightened.

eerie ADJ. weird. In that *eerie* setting, it was easy to believe in ghosts and other supernatural beings.

● **efface** V. rub out. The coin had been handled so many times that its date had been *effaced*.

effectual ADJ. able to produce a desired effect; valid. Medical researchers are concerned because of the development of drug-resistant strains of bacteria; many once useful antibiotics are no longer *effectual* in curing bacterial infections.

● **effervescence** N. inner excitement or exuberance; bubbling from fermentation or carbonation. Nothing depressed Sue for long; her natural *effervescence* soon reasserted itself. Soda that loses its *effervescence* goes flat. effervescent, ADJ. effervesce, V.

efficacy N. power to produce desired effect. The *efficacy* of this drug depends on the regularity of the dosage. efficacious, ADJ.

effigy N. dummy. The mob showed its irritation by hanging the judge in *effigy*.

effrontery N. shameless boldness. She had the *effrontery* to insult the guest.

effusive ADJ. pouring forth; gushing. Her *effusive* manner of greeting her friends finally began to irritate them. effusion, N.

egoism N. excessive interest in one's self; belief that one should be interested in one's self rather than in others. His *egoism* prevented him from seeing the needs of his colleagues.

■ **egotistical** ADJ. excessively self-centered; self-important; conceited. Typical *egotistical* remark: "But enough of this chit-chat about you and your little problems. Let's talk about what's really important: *Me!*"

egregious ADJ. notorious; conspicuously bad or shocking. She was an *egregious* liar; we all knew better than to believe a word she said. Ed's housekeeping was *egregious*: he let his dirty dishes pile up so long that they were stuck together with last week's food.

egress N. exit. Barnum's sign "To the *Egress*" fooled many people who thought they were going to see an animal and instead found themselves in the street.

ejaculation N. exclamation. He could not repress an *ejaculation* of surprise when he heard the news.

elaboration N. addition of details; intricacy. Tell what happened simply, without any *elaboration*. elaborate, v.

■ **elated** ADJ. overjoyed; in high spirits. Grinning from ear to ear, Bonnie Blair was clearly *elated* by her fifth Olympic gold medal. elation, N.

● **elegy** N. poem or song expressing lamentation. On the death of Edward King, Milton composed the *elegy* "Lycidas." elegiacal, ADJ.

● **elicit** V. draw out by discussion. The detectives tried to *elicit* where he had hidden his loot.

elixir N. cure-all; something invigorating. The news of her chance to go abroad acted on her like an *elixir*.

ellipsis N. omission of words from a text. Sometimes an *ellipsis* can lead to a dangling modifier, as in the sentence "Once dressed, you should refrigerate the potato salad."

elliptical ADJ. oval; ambiguous, either purposely or because key words have been left out. An *elliptical* billiard ball wobbles because it is not perfectly round; an *elliptical* remark baffles because it is not perfectly clear.

■ **eloquence** N. expressiveness; persuasive speech. The crowds were stirred by Martin Luther King's *eloquence*. eloquent, ADJ.

● **elucidate** V. explain; enlighten. He was called upon to *elucidate* the disputed points in his article.

■ **elusive** ADJ. evasive; baffling; hard to grasp. Trying to pin down exactly when the contractors would be finished remodeling the house, Nancy was frustrated by their *elusive* replies. elude, v.

● **emaciated** ADJ. thin and wasted. His long period of starvation had left him *emaciated*.

emanate V. issue forth. A strong odor of sulphur *emanated* from the spring.

emancipate V. set free. At first, the attempts of the Abolitionists to *emancipate* the slaves were unpopular in New England as well as in the South.

embargo N. ban on commerce or other activity. As a result of the *embargo*, trade with the colonies was at a standstill.

embark V. commence; go on board a boat or airplane; begin a journey. In devoting herself to the study of gorillas, Dian Fossey *embarked* on a course of action that was to cost her her life.

embed V. enclose; place in something. Tales of actual historical figures like King Alfred have become *embedded* in legends.

■ **embellish** V. adorn; ornament. The costume designer *embellished* the leading lady's ball gown with yards and yards of ribbon and lace.

embezzlement N. stealing. The bank teller confessed his *embezzlement* of the funds.

embody V. personify; make concrete; incorporate. Cheering on his rival Mark McGwire's efforts to break Roger Maris's home run record, Sammy Sosa *embodied* the spirit of true sportsmanship.

embrace V. hug; adopt or espouse; accept readily; encircle; include. Clasping Maid Marian in his arms, Robin Hood *embraced* her lovingly. In joining the outlaws in Sherwood Forest, she had openly *embraced* their cause.

embroider V. decorate with needlework; ornament with fancy or fictitious details. For her mother's birthday, Beth *embroidered* a lovely design on a handkerchief. When asked what made her late getting home, Jo *embroidered* her account with tales of runaway horses and rescuing people from a ditch. embroidery, N.

embroil V. throw into confusion; involve in strife; entangle. He became *embroiled* in the heated discussion when he tried to arbitrate the dispute.

embryonic ADJ. undeveloped; rudimentary. The evil of class and race hatred must be eliminated while it is still in an *embryonic* state; otherwise, it may grow to dangerous proportions.

● **emend** V. correct; correct by a critic. The critic *emended* the book by selecting the passages which he thought most appropriate to the text.

emendation N. correction of errors; improvement. Please initial all the *emendations* you have made in this contract.

eminent ADJ. high; lofty. After his appointment to this *eminent* position, he seldom had time for his former friends.

emissary N. agent; messenger. The secretary of state was sent as the president's special *emissary* to the conference on disarmament.

emollient N. soothing or softening remedy. The nurse applied an *emollient* to the inflamed area. also ADJ.

empathy N. ability to identify with another's feelings, ideas, etc. What made Ann such a fine counselor was her *empathy*, her ability to put herself in her client's place and feel his emotions as if they were her own. empathize, v.

empirical ADJ. based on experience. He distrusted hunches and intuitive flashes; he placed his reliance entirely on *empirical* data.

■ **emulate** V. imitate; rival. In a brief essay, describe a person you admire, someone whose virtues you would like to *emulate*.

enamored ADJ. in love. Narcissus became *enamored* of his own beauty.

encipher V. encode; convert a message into code. One of Bond's first lessons was how to *encipher* the messages he sent to Miss Moneypenny so that none of his other lady friends could decipher them.

enclave N. territory enclosed within an alien land. The Vatican is an independent *enclave* in Italy.

encomium N. high praise; eulogy. Uneasy with the *encomiums* expressed by his supporters, Tolkien felt unworthy of such high praise.

encompass V. surround. Although we were *encompassed* by enemy forces, we were cheerful for we were well stocked and could withstand a siege until our allies joined us.

encroachment N. gradual intrusion. The *encroachment* of the factories upon the neighborhood lowered the value of the real estate.

Word List 17 encumber-etymology

encumber V. burden. Some people *encumber* themselves with too much luggage when they take short trips.

endearment N. fond statement. Your gifts and *endearments* cannot make me forget your earlier insolence.

endemic ADJ. prevailing among a specific group of people or in a specific area or country. This disease is *endemic* in this part of the world; more than 80 percent of the population are at one time or another affected by it.

■ **endorse** V. approve; support. Everyone waited to see which one of the rival candidates for the city council the mayor would *endorse*. (secondary meaning) endorsement, N.

enduring ADJ. lasting; surviving. Keats believed in the *enduring* power of great art, which would outlast its creators' brief lives.

energize V. invigorate; make forceful and active. Rather than exhausting Maggie, dancing *energized* her.

enervate V. weaken. She was slow to recover from her illness; even a short walk to the window would *enervate* her.

enfranchise V. to admit to the rights of citizenship (especially the right to vote). Although Blacks were *enfranchised* shortly after the Civil War, women did not receive the right to vote until 1920.

engage V. attract; hire; pledge oneself; confront. "Your case has *engaged* my interest, my lord," said Holmes. "You may *engage* my services."

engaging ADJ. charming; attractive. Everyone liked Nancy's pleasant manners and *engaging* personality.

engender V. cause; produce. To receive praise for real accomplishments *engenders* self-confidence in a child.

engross V. occupy fully. John was so *engrossed* in his studies that he did not hear his mother call.

■ **enhance** V. increase; improve. You can *enhance* your chances of being admitted to the college of your choice by learning to write well; an excellent essay can *enhance* any application.

■ **enigma** N. puzzle; mystery. "What *do* women want?" asked Dr. Sigmund Freud. Their behavior was an *enigma* to him.

enigmatic ADJ. obscure; puzzling. Many have sought to fathom the *enigmatic* smile of the *Mona Lisa*.

■ **enmity** N. ill will; hatred. At Camp David, President Carter labored to bring an end to the *enmity* that prevented the peaceful coexistence of Egypt and Israel.

ennui N. boredom. The monotonous routine of hospital life induced a feeling of *ennui* that made him moody and irritable.

enormity N. hugeness (in a bad sense). He did not realize the *enormity* of his crime until he saw what suffering he had caused.

enrapture V. please intensely. The audience was *enraptured* by the freshness of the voices and the excellent orchestration.

ensconce V. settle comfortably. Now that their children were *ensconced* safely in the private school, the jet-setting parents decided to leave for Europe.

ensemble N. group of (supporting) players; organic unity; costume. As a dancer with the Oakland Ballet, Benjamin enjoyed being part of the *ensemble*. Having acted with one another for well over a decade, the cast members have developed a true sense of *ensemble*: They work together seamlessly. Mitzi wore a charming two-piece *ensemble* designed by Donna Karan.

entail V. require; necessitate; involve. Building a college-level vocabulary will *entail* some work on your part.

enterprising ADJ. full of initiative. By coming up with fresh ways to market the company's products, Mike proved himself to be an *enterprising* businessman.

enthrall V. capture; enslave. From the moment he saw her picture, he was *enthralled* by her beauty.

entice V. lure; attract; tempt. She always tried to *entice* her baby brother into mischief.

entitlement N. right to claim something; right to benefits. While Bill was *entitled* to use a company car while he worked for the firm, the company's lawyers questioned his *entitlement* to the vehicle once he'd quit his job.

entity N. real being. As soon as the Charter was adopted, the United Nations became an *entity* and had to be considered as a factor in world diplomacy.

entomology N. study of insects. Kent found *entomology* the most annoying part of his biology course; studying insects bugged him.

entourage N. group of attendants; retinue. Surrounded by the members of his *entourage*, the mayor hurried into city hall, shouting a brusque "No comment!" to the reporters lining the steps.

entrance V. put under a spell; carry away with emotion. Shafts of sunlight on a wall could *entrance* her and leave her spellbound.

entreat V. plead; ask earnestly. She *entreated* her father to let her stay out till midnight.

entrepreneur N. businessman; contractor. Opponents of our present tax program argue that it discourages *entrepreneurs* from trying new fields of business activity.

enumerate V. list; mention one by one. Huck hung his head in shame as Miss Watson *enumerated* his many flaws.

enunciate V. speak distinctly. Stop mumbling! How will people understand you if you do not *enunciate*?

eon N. long period of time; an age. It has taken *eons* for our civilization to develop.

■ **ephemeral** ADJ. short-lived; fleeting. The mayfly is an *ephemeral* creature: its adult life lasts little more than a day.

epic N. long heroic poem, or similar work of art. Kurosawa's film *Seven Samurai* is an *epic* portraying the struggle of seven warriors to destroy a band of robbers. also ADJ.

epicure   N. connoisseur of food and drink. *Epicures* fre-. quent this restaurant because it features exotic wines and dishes. epicurean, ADJ.

epigram   N. witty thought or saying, usually short. Poor Richard's *epigrams* made Benjamin Franklin famous.

epilogue   N. short speech at conclusion of dramatic work. The audience was so disappointed in the play that many did not remain to hear the *epilogue.*

episodic   ADJ. loosely connected; divided into incidents. Though he tried to follow the plot of *Gravity's Rainbow,* John found the novel too *episodic;* he enjoyed individual pas-sages, but had trouble following the work as a whole.

epistolary   ADJ. consisting of letters. Mark Harris's *Wake Up, Stupid!* is a modern *epistolary* novel that uses letters, telegrams, and newspaper clippings to tell the hero's story. The movie *You've Got Mail* tells a story using e-mail; does that make it an *e-pistolary* movie? epistle, N.

epitaph   N. inscription in memory of a dead person. In his will, he dictated the *epitaph* he wanted placed on his tomb-stone.

epithet   N. word or phrase characteristically used to describe a person or thing. So many kings of France were named Charles that you could tell them apart only by their *epithets*: Charles the Wise was someone far different from Charles the Fat.

epitome   N. perfect example or embodiment. Singing "I am the very model of a modern Major-General," in *The Pirates of Penzance,* Major-General Stanley proclaimed himself the *epitome* of an officer and a gentleman.

epoch   N. period of time. The glacial *epoch* lasted for thou-sands of years.

equable   ADJ. tranquil; steady; uniform. After the hot sum-mers and cold winters of New England, he found the cli-mate of the West Indies *equable* and pleasant.

● **equanimity**   N. calmness of temperament; composure. Even the inevitable strains of caring for an ailing mother did not disturb Bea's *equanimity.*

equestrian   N. rider on horseback. These paths in the park are reserved for *equestrians* and their steeds. also ADJ.

equilibrium   N. balance. After the divorce, he needed some time to regain his *equilibrium.*

equine   ADJ. resembling a horse. His long, bony face had an *equine* look to it.

equinox   N. period of equal days and nights; the beginning of Spring and Autumn. The vernal *equinox* is usually marked by heavy rainstorms.

● **equitable**   ADJ. fair; impartial. I am seeking an *equitable* solution to this dispute, one that will be fair and acceptable to both sides.

equity   N. fairness; justice. Our courts guarantee *equity* to all.

■ **equivocal**   ADJ. ambiguous; intentionally misleading. Rejecting the candidate's *equivocal* comments on tax reform, the reporters pressed him to state clearly where he stood on the issue. equivocate, V.

equivocate   V. lie; mislead; attempt to conceal the truth. The audience saw through his attempts to *equivocate* on the subject under discussion and ridiculed his remarks.

erode   V. eat away. The limestone was *eroded* by the drip-ping water until only a thin shell remained. erosion, N.

erotic   ADJ. pertaining to passionate love. The *erotic* pas-sages in this novel should be removed as they are merely pornographic.

erratic   ADJ. odd; unpredictable. Investors become anxious when the stock market appears *erratic.*

■ **erroneous**   ADJ. mistaken; wrong. I thought my answer was correct, but it was *erroneous.*

■ **erudite**   ADJ. learned; scholarly. Though his fellow students thought him *erudite,* Paul knew he would have to spend many years in serious study before he could consider him-self a scholar.

escapade   N. prank; flighty conduct. The headmaster could not regard this latest *escapade* as a boyish joke and expelled the young man.

escapism   N. avoiding reality by diverting oneself with amusements. Before you criticize her constant reading as mere *escapism,* note how greatly her vocabulary has improved since she began spending her days buried in books.

eschew   V. avoid. Hoping to present himself to his girlfriend as a totally reformed character, he tried to *eschew* all the vices, especially chewing tobacco and drinking bathtub gin.

■ **esoteric**   ADJ. hard to understand; known only to the cho-sen few. *The New Yorker* short stories often include *esoteric* allusions to obscure people and events: the implication is, if you are in the in-crowd, you'll get the reference; if you come from Cleveland, you won't.

espionage   N. spying. In order to maintain its power, the government developed a system of *espionage* that pene-trated every household.

espouse   V. adopt; support. She was always ready to *espouse* a worthy cause.

esteem   V. respect; value. Jill *esteemed* Jack's taste in music, but she deplored his taste in clothes.

estranged   ADJ. separated; alienated. The *estranged* wife sought a divorce. estrangement, N.

ethereal   ADJ. light; heavenly; unusually refined. In Shake-speare's *The Tempest,* the spirit Ariel is an *ethereal* crea-ture, too airy and unearthly for our mortal world.

ethnic   ADJ. relating to races. Intolerance between *ethnic* groups is deplorable and usually is based on lack of infor-mation.

ethos   N. underlying character of a culture, group, etc. Seeing how tenderly ordinary Spaniards treated her small daughter made author Barbara Kingsolver aware of how greatly children were valued in the Spanish *ethos.*

etymology   N. study of word parts. A knowledge of *etymol-ogy* can help you on many English tests: if you know what the roots and prefixes mean, you can determine the mean-ings of unfamiliar words.

Word List 18 eulogy-faculty

■ **eulogy** N. expression of praise, often on the occasion of someone's death. Instead of delivering a spoken *eulogy* at Genny's memorial service, Jeff sang a song he had written in her honor.

■ **euphemism** N. mild expression in place of an unpleasant one. The expression "he passed away" is a *euphemism* for "he died."

euphonious ADJ. pleasing in sound. *Euphonious* even when spoken, the Italian language is particularly pleasing to the ear when sung. euphony. N.

euphoria N. feeling of great happiness and well-being (sometimes exaggerated). Delighted with her SAT scores, sure that the university would accept her, Allison was filled with *euphoria*. euphoric, ADJ.

● **evanescent** ADJ. fleeting; vanishing. Brandon's satisfaction in his new job was *evanescent*, for he immediately began to notice its many drawbacks. evanescence, N.

evasive ADJ. not frank; eluding. Your *evasive* answers convinced the judge that you were withholding important evidence. evade, V.

evenhanded ADJ. impartial; fair. Do men and women receive *evenhanded* treatment from their teachers, or, as recent studies suggest, do teachers pay more attention to male students than to females?

evince V. show clearly. When he tried to answer the questions, he *evinced* his ignorance of the subject matter.

evocative ADJ. tending to call up (emotions, memories). Scent can be remarkably *evocative*: the aroma of pipe tobacco *evokes* the memory of my father; a whiff of talcum powder calls up images of my daughter as a child.

ewe N. female sheep. The flock of sheep was made up of dozens of *ewes*, together with only a handful of rams.

■ **exacerbate** V. worsen; embitter. The latest bombing *exacerbated* England's already existing bitterness against the IRA, causing the prime minister to break off the peace talks abruptly.

exacting ADJ. extremely demanding. Cleaning the ceiling of the Sistine Chapel was an *exacting* task, one that demanded extremely meticulous care on the part of the restorers. exaction, N.

■ **exalt** V. raise in rank or dignity; praise. The actor Alec Guinness was *exalted* to the rank of knighthood by the queen.

exasperate V. vex. Johnny often *exasperates* his mother with his pranks.

exceptionable ADJ. objectionable. Do you find the punk rock band Green Day a highly *exceptionable*, thoroughly distasteful group, or do you think they are exceptionally talented performers?

● **excerpt** N. selected passage (written or musical). The cinematic equivalent of an *excerpt* from a novel is a clip from a film. also V.

excise V. cut away; cut out. When you *excise* the dead and dying limbs of a tree, you not only improve its appear-

ance but also enhance its chances of bearing fruit. excision. N.

exclaim V. cry out suddenly. "Watson! Behind you!" Holmes *exclaimed*, seeing the assassin hurl himself on his friend.

excoriate V. scold with biting harshness; strip the skin off. Seeing the holes in Bill's new pants, his mother furiously *excoriated* him for ruining his good clothes. The tight, starched collar chafed and *excoriated* his neck, rubbing it raw.

exculpate V. clear from blame. He was *exculpated* of the crime when the real criminal confessed.

execrable ADJ. very bad. The anecdote was in such *execrable* taste that it revolted the audience.

■ **execute** V. put into effect; carry out. The choreographer wanted to see how well she could *execute* a pirouette. (secondary meaning) execution, N.

exegesis N. explanation; interpretation, especially of a biblical text. The minister based her sermon on her *exegesis* of a difficult passage from the book of Job. exegetical, ADJ.

■ **exemplary** ADJ. serving as a model; outstanding. At commencement the dean praised Ellen for her *exemplary* behavior as class president.

■ **exemplify** V. serve as an example of; embody. For a generation of balletgoers, Rudolf Nureyev *exemplified* the ideal of masculine grace.

exempt ADJ. not subject to a duty, obligation. Because of his flat feet, Foster was *exempt* from serving in the armed forces. also V.

exertion N. effort; expenditure of much physical work. The *exertion* spent in unscrewing the rusty bolt left her exhausted.

■ **exhaustive** ADJ. thorough; comprehensive. We have made an *exhaustive* study of all published SAT tests and are happy to share our research with you.

■ **exhilarating** ADJ. invigorating and refreshing; cheering. Though some of the hikers found tramping through the snow tiring, Jeffrey found the walk on the cold, crisp day *exhilarating*.

exhort V. urge. The evangelist *exhorted* all the sinners in his audience to reform. exhortation, N.

exhume V. dig out of the ground; remove from the grave. Could evidence that might identify the serial killer have been buried with his victim? To answer this question, the police asked the authorities for permission to *exhume* the victim's body.

exigency N. urgent situation. In this *exigency*, we must look for aid from our allies.

exodus N. departure. The *exodus* from the hot and stuffy city was particularly noticeable on Friday evenings.

■ **exonerate** V. acquit; exculpate. The defense team feverishly sought fresh evidence that might *exonerate* their client.

exorbitant ADJ. excessive. The people grumbled at his *exorbitant* prices but paid them because he had a monopoly.

exorcise V. drive out evil spirits. By incantation and prayer, the medicine man sought to *exorcise* the evil spirits which had taken possession of the young warrior.

exotic ADJ. not native; strange. Because of his *exotic* headdress, he was followed in the streets by small children who laughed at his strange appearance.

expansive ADJ. outgoing and sociable; broad and extensive; able to increase in size. Mr. Fezziwig was in an *expansive* humor, cheerfully urging his guests to join in the Christmas feast. Looking down on his *expansive* paunch, he sighed: if his belly *expanded* any further, he'd need an *expansive* waistline for his pants.

expatriate N. exile; someone who has withdrawn from his native land. Henry James was an American *expatriate* who settled in England.

■ **expedient** ADJ. suitable; practical; politic. A pragmatic politician, he was guided by what was *expedient* rather than by what was ethical. expediency, N.

■ **expedite** V. hasten. Because we are on a tight schedule, we hope you will be able to *expedite* the delivery of our order. The more *expeditious* your response is, the happier we'll be.

expenditure N. payment or expense; output. When you are operating on an expense account, you must keep receipts for all your *expenditures*. If you don't save your receipts, you won't get repaid without the *expenditure* of a lot of energy arguing with the firm's accountants.

expertise N. specialized knowledge; expert skill. Although she was knowledgeable in a number of fields, she was hired for her particular *expertise* in computer programming.

expiate V. make amends for (a sin). He tried to *expiate* his crimes by a full confession to the authorities.

expletive N. interjection; profane oath. The sergeant's remarks were filled with *expletives* that offended the new recruits.

explicate V. explain; interpret; clarify. Harry Levin *explicated* James Joyce's often bewildering novels with such clarity that even *Finnegan's Wake* seemed comprehensible to his students.

■ **explicit** ADJ. totally clear; definite; outspoken. Don't just hint around that you're dissatisfied: be *explicit* about what's bugging you.

exploit N. deed or action, particularly a brave deed. Raoul Wallenberg was noted for his *exploits* in rescuing Jews from Hitler's forces.

■ **exploit** V. make use of, sometimes unjustly. Cesar Chavez fought attempts to *exploit* migrant farmworkers in California. exploitation, N. exploitative, ADJ.

expository ADJ. explanatory; serving to explain. The manual that came with my VCR was no masterpiece of *expository* prose: its explanations were so garbled that I couldn't even figure out how to rewind a tape. exposition, N.

exposure N. risk, particularly of being exposed to disease or to the elements; unmasking; act of laying something open. *Exposure* to sun and wind had dried out her hair and weathered her face. She looked so changed that she no longer feared *exposure* as the notorious Irene Adler, one-time antagonist of Sherlock Holmes.

expropriate V. take possession of. He questioned the government's right to *expropriate* his land to create a wildlife preserve.

expunge V. cancel; remove. If you behave, I will *expunge* this notation from your record.

expurgate V. clean; remove offensive parts of a book. The editors felt that certain passages in the book had to be *expurgated* before it could be used in the classroom.

extant ADJ. still in existence. Although the book is out of print, some copies are still *extant*. Unfortunately, all of them are in libraries or private collections; none are for sale.

extent N. degree; magnitude; scope. What is the *extent* of the patient's injuries? If they are not too *extensive*, we can treat him on an outpatient basis.

extenuate V. weaken; mitigate. It is easier for us to *extenuate* our own shortcomings than those of others.

■ **extol** V. praise; glorify. The president *extolled* the astronauts, calling them the pioneers of the Space Age.

extort V. wring from; get money by threats, etc. The blackmailer *extorted* money from his victim.

extradition N. surrender of prisoner by one state to another. The lawyers opposed the *extradition* of their client on the grounds that for more than five years he had been a model citizen.

■ **extraneous** ADJ. not essential; superfluous. No wonder Ted can't think straight! His mind is so cluttered up with *extraneous* trivia, he can't concentrate on the essentials.

extrapolation N. projection; conjecture. Based on their *extrapolation* from the results of the primaries on Super Tuesday, the networks predicted that Bob Dole would be the Republican candidate for the presidency. extrapolate, V.

■ **extricate** V. free; disentangle. Icebreakers were needed to *extricate* the trapped whales from the icy floes that closed them in.

extrinsic ADJ. external; not essential; extraneous. A critically acclaimed *extrinsic* feature of the Chrysler Building is its ornate spire. The judge would not admit the testimony, ruling that it was *extrinsic* to the matter at hand.

extrovert N. person interested mostly in external objects and actions. A good salesman is usually an *extrovert*, who likes to mingle with people.

extrude V. force or push out. Much pressure is required to *extrude* these plastics.

■ **exuberance** N. overflowing abundance; joyful enthusiasm; flamboyance; lavishness. I was bowled over by the *exuberance* of Amy's welcome. What an enthusiastic greeting!

exude V. discharge; give forth. We get maple syrup from the sap that *exudes* from the trees in early spring. exudation, N.

exult V. rejoice. We *exulted* when our team won the victory.

fabricate V. build; lie. If we *fabricate* the buildings in this project out of standardized sections, we can reduce construction costs considerably. Because of Jack's tendency to *fabricate*, Jill had trouble believing a word he said.

facade N. front (of building); superficial or false appearance. The ornate *facade* of the church was often photographed by tourists, who never bothered to walk around the building to view its other sides. Susan seemed super-confident, but that was just a *facade* she put on to hide her insecurity.

facet N. small plane surface (of a gem); a side. The stone-cutter decided to improve the rough diamond by providing it with several *facets*.

facetious ADJ. joking (often inappropriately); humorous. I'm serious about this project; I don't need any *facetious*, smart-alecky cracks about do-gooder little rich girls.

facile ADJ. easily accomplished; ready or fluent; superficial. Words came easily to Jonathan: he was a *facile*

speaker and prided himself on being ready to make a speech at a moment's notice.

■ **facilitate** V. help bring about; make less difficult. Rest and proper nourishment should *facilitate* the patient's recovery.

facsimile N. copy. Many museums sell *facsimiles* of the works of art on display.

faction N. party; clique; dissension. The quarrels and bickering of the two small *factions* within the club disturbed the majority of the members.

faculty N. mental or bodily powers; teaching staff. As he grew old, Professor Twiggly feared he might lose his *faculties* and become unfit to teach. However, he had tenure: whether or not he was in full possession of his *faculties*, the school couldn't kick him off the *faculty*.

Word List 19 fallacious-flinch

■ **fallacious** ADJ. false; misleading. Paradoxically, *fallacious* reasoning does not always yield erroneous results: even though your logic may be faulty, the answer you get may nevertheless be correct. fallacy, N.

fallible ADJ. liable to err. I know I am *fallible*, but I feel confident that I am right this time.

● **fallow** ADJ. plowed but not sowed; uncultivated. Farmers have learned that it is advisable to permit land to lie *fallow* every few years.

● **falter** V. hesitate. When told to dive off the high board, she did not *falter*, but proceeded at once.

■ **fanaticism** N. excessive zeal; extreme devotion to a belief or cause. When Islamic fundamentalists demanded the death of Salman Rushdie because his novel questioned their faith, world opinion condemned them for their *fanaticism*.

fancy N. notion; whim; inclination. Martin took a *fancy* to paint his toenails purple. Assuming he would outgrow such *fanciful* behavior, his parents ignored his *fancy* feet. also ADJ.

fanfare N. call by bugles or trumpets. The exposition was opened with a *fanfare* of trumpets and the firing of cannon.

farce N. broad comedy; mockery. Nothing went right; the entire interview degenerated into a *farce*. farcical, ADJ.

■ **fastidious** ADJ. difficult to please; squeamish. Bobby was such a *fastidious* eater that he would eat a sandwich only if his mother first cut off every scrap of crust.

fatalism N. belief that events are determined by forces beyond one's control. With *fatalism*, he accepted the hardships that beset him. fatalistic, ADJ.

● **fathom** V. comprehend; investigate. I find his motives impossible to *fathom*; in fact, I'm totally clueless about what goes on in his mind.

fatuous ADJ. foolish; inane. He is far too intelligent to utter such *fatuous* remarks.

fauna N. animals of a period or region. The scientist could visualize the *fauna* of the period by examining the skeletal remains and the fossils.

fawning ADJ. courting favor by cringing and flattering. She was constantly surrounded by a group of *fawning* admirers who hoped to win some favor. fawn, V.

faze V. disconcert; dismay. No crisis could *faze* the resourceful hotel manager.

■ **feasible** ADJ. practical. Is it *feasible* to build a new stadium for the Yankees on New York's West Side? Without additional funding, the project is clearly unrealistic.

fecundity N. fertility; fruitfulness. The *fecundity* of his mind is illustrated by the many vivid images in his poems.

feign V. pretend. Lady Macbeth *feigned* illness although she was actually healthy.

feint N. trick; shift; sham blow. The boxer was fooled by his opponent's *feint* and dropped his guard. also V.

felicitous ADJ. apt; suitably expressed; well chosen. He was famous for his *felicitous* remarks and was called upon to serve as master-of-ceremonies at many a banquet. felicity, N.

felicity N. happiness; appropriateness (of a remark, choice, etc.). She wrote a note to the newlyweds wishing them great *felicity* in their wedded life.

fell ADJ. cruel; deadly. The newspapers told of the tragic spread of the *fell* disease.

● **fell** V. cut or knock down; bring down (with a missile). Crying "Timber!" Paul Bunyan *felled* the mighty redwood tree. Robin Hood loosed his arrow and *felled* the king's deer.

felon N. person convicted of a grave crime. A convicted *felon* loses the right to vote.

feral ADJ. not domestic; wild. Abandoned by their owners, dogs may revert to their *feral* state, roaming the woods in packs.

ferment N. agitation; commotion. With the breakup of the Soviet Union, much of Eastern Europe was in a state of *ferment*.

ferret V. drive or hunt out of hiding. She *ferreted* out their secret.

fervent ADJ. ardent; hot. She felt that the *fervent* praise was excessive and somewhat undeserved.

fervid ADJ. ardent. Her *fervid* enthusiasm inspired all of us to undertake the dangerous mission.

■ **fervor** N. glowing ardor; intensity of feeling. At the protest rally, the students cheered the strikers and booed the dean with equal *fervor*.

fester V. rankle; produce irritation or resentment. Joe's insult *festered* in Anne's mind for days, and made her too angry to speak to him.

festive ADJ. joyous; celebratory. Their wedding in the park was a *festive* occasion.

fetid ADJ. malodorous. The neglected wound became *fetid*.

fetter V. shackle. The prisoner was *fettered* to the wall.

fiasco N. total failure. Our ambitious venture ended in a *fiasco* and we were forced to flee.

fickle ADJ. changeable; faithless. As soon as Romeo saw Juliet, he forgot all about his old girlfriend Rosaline. Was Romeo *fickle*?

fictitious ADJ. imaginary. Although this book purports to be a biography of George Washington, many of the incidents are *fictitious*.

fidelity N. loyalty. A dog's *fidelity* to its owner is one of the reasons why that animal is a favorite household pet.

figment N. invention; imaginary thing. That incident never took place; it is a *figment* of your imagination.

figurative ADJ. not literal, but metaphorical; using a figure of speech. "To lose one's marbles" is a *figurative* expression; if you're told that Jack has lost his marbles, no one expects you to rush out to buy him a replacement set.

figurine N. small ornamental statuette. In *The Maltese Falcon*, Sam Spade was hired to trace the missing *figurine* of a black bird.

filament N. fine thread or fiber; threadlike structure within a light bulb. A ray of sunlight illuminated the *filaments* of the spider web, turning the web into a net of gold.

filch V. steal. The boys *filched* apples from the fruit stand.

filial ADJ. pertaining to a son or daughter. Many children forget their *filial* obligations and disregard the wishes of their parents.

filibuster V. to block legislation by making long speeches. Even though we disapproved of Senator Foghorn's political goals, we were impressed by his ability to *filibuster* endlessly to keep an issue from coming to a vote.

finale N. conclusion. It is not until we reach the *finale* of this play that we can understand the author's message.

finesse N. delicate skill. The *finesse* and adroitness with which the surgeon wielded her scalpel impressed all the observers in the operating room.

finicky ADJ. too particular; fussy. The little girl was *finicky* about her food, leaving over anything that wasn't to her taste.

firebrand N. hothead: troublemaker. The police tried to keep track of all the local *firebrands* when the President came to town.

fissure N. crevice. The mountain climbers secured footholds in tiny *fissures* in the rock.

● **fitful** ADJ. spasmodic; intermittent. After several *fitful* attempts, he decided to postpone the start of the project until he felt more energetic.

flabbergasted ADJ. astounded; astonished; overcome with surprise. In the film *Flubber,* the hero invents a remarkable substance whose amazing properties leave his coworkers *flabbergasted.* flabbergast, V.

flaccid ADJ. flabby. His sedentary life had left him with *flaccid* muscles.

flag V. droop; grow feeble. When the opposing hockey team scored its third goal only minutes into the first quarter, the home team's spirits *flagged*. flagging, ADJ.

■ **flagrant** ADJ. conspicuously wicked; blatant; outrageous. The governor's appointment of his brother-in-law to the State Supreme Court was a *flagrant* violation of the state laws against nepotism (favoritism based on kinship).

flair N. talent. She has an uncanny *flair* for discovering new artists before the public has become aware of their existence.

flamboyant ADJ. ornate. Modern architecture has discarded the *flamboyant* trimming on buildings and emphasizes simplicity of line.

flaunt V. display ostentatiously. Mae West saw nothing wrong with showing off her considerable physical charms, saying, "Honey, if you've got it, *flaunt* it!"

fleck V. spot. Her cheeks, *flecked* with tears, were testimony to the hours of weeping.

fledgling ADJ. inexperienced. While it is necessary to provide these *fledgling* poets with an opportunity to present their work, it is not essential that we admire everything they write. also N.

fleece N. wool coat of a sheep. They shear sheep of their *fleece,* which they then comb into separate strands of wool.

fleece V. rob; plunder. The tricksters *fleeced* him of his inheritance.

flick N. light stroke as with a whip. The horse needed no encouragement; one *flick* of the whip was all the jockey had to apply to get the animal to run at top speed.

flinch V. hesitate, shrink. He did not *flinch* in the face of danger but fought back bravely.

Word List 20 flippant-gaffe

flippant ADJ. lacking proper seriousness. When Mark told Mona he loved her, she dismissed his earnest declaration with a *flippant* "Oh, you say that to all the girls!" flippancy, N.

flit V. fly; dart lightly; pass swiftly by. Like a bee *flitting* from flower to flower, Rose *flitted* from one boyfriend to the next.

floe N. mass of floating ice. The ship made slow progress as it battered its way through the ice *floes*.

flora N. plants of a region or era. Because she was a botanist, she spent most of her time studying the *flora* of the desert.

● **florid** ADJ. ruddy; reddish; flowery. If you go to Florida and get a sunburn, your complexion will look *florid*.

flounder V. struggle and thrash about; proceed clumsily or falter. Up to his knees in the bog, Floyd *floundered* about, trying to regain his footing. Bewildered by the new software, Flo *floundered* until Jan showed her how to get started.

flourish V. grow well; prosper; decorate with ornaments. The orange trees *flourished* in the sun.

flout V. reject; mock. The headstrong youth *flouted* all authority; he refused to be curbed.

fluctuate V. waver; shift. The water pressure in our shower *fluctuates* wildly; you start rinsing yourself off with a trickle, and, two minutes later, a blast of water nearly knocks you down.

fluency N. smoothness of speech. He spoke French with *fluency* and ease.

fluke N. unlikely occurrence; stroke of fortune. When Douglas defeated Tyson for the heavyweight championship, some sportscasters dismissed his victory as a *fluke*.

fluster V. confuse. The teacher's sudden question *flustered* him and he stammered his reply.

flux N. flowing; series of changes. While conditions are in such a state of *flux*, I do not wish to commit myself too deeply in this affair.

fodder N. coarse food for cattle, horses, etc. One of Nancy's chores at the ranch was to put fresh supplies of *fodder* in the horses' stalls.

foible N. weakness; slight fault. We can overlook the *foibles* of our friends; no one is perfect.

foil N. contrast. In *Star Wars*, dark, evil Darth Vader is a perfect *foil* for fair-haired, naive Luke Skywalker.

foil V. defeat; frustrate. In the end, Skywalker is able to *foil* Vader's diabolical schemes.

foliage N. masses of leaves. Every autumn before the leaves fell he promised himself he would drive through New England to admire the colorful fall *foliage*.

foment V. stir up; instigate. Cheryl's archenemy Heather spread some nasty rumors that *fomented* trouble in the club. Do you think Cheryl's foe meant to *foment* such discord?

● **foolhardy** ADJ. rash. Don't be *foolhardy*. Get the advice of experienced people before undertaking this venture.

fop N. dandy; man excessively concerned with his clothes. People who dismissed young Mizrahi as a *fop* felt chagrined when he turned into one of the top fashion designers of his day. foppish, ADJ.

forbearance N. patience. We must use *forbearance* in dealing with him because he is still weak from his illness.

ford N. place where a river can be crossed on foot. Rather than risk using the shaky rope bridge, David walked a half-mile downstream until he came to the nearest *ford*. also V.

forebears N. ancestors. Reverence for one's *forebears* (sometimes referred to as ancestor worship) plays an important part in many Oriental cultures.

foreboding N. premonition of evil. Suspecting no conspiracies against him, Caesar gently ridiculed his wife's *forebodings* about the Ides of March.

forensic ADJ. suitable to debate or courts of law. In her best *forensic* manner, the lawyer addressed the jury. forensics, N.

foreshadow V. give an indication beforehand; portend; prefigure. In retrospect, political analysts realized that Yeltsin's defiance of the attempted coup *foreshadowed* his emergence as the dominant figure of the new Russian republic.

foresight N. ability to foresee future happenings; prudence. A wise investor, she had the *foresight* to buy land just before the current real estate boom.

forestall V. prevent by taking action in advance. By setting up a prenuptial agreement, the prospective bride and groom hoped to *forestall* any potential arguments about money in the event of a divorce.

forgo V. give up; do without. Determined to lose weight for the summer, Ida decided to *forgo* dessert until she could fit into a size eight again.

forlorn ADJ. sad and lonely; wretched. Deserted by her big sisters and her friends, the *forlorn* child sat sadly on the steps awaiting their return.

formality N. ceremonious quality; something done just for form's sake. The president received the visiting heads of state with due *formality*: flags waving, honor guards standing at attention, anthems sounding at full blast. Signing this petition is a mere *formality*; it does not obligate you in any way.

formidable ADJ. menacing; threatening. We must not treat the battle lightly for we are facing a *formidable* foe.

forsake V. desert; abandon; renounce. No one expected Foster to *forsake* his wife and children and run off with another woman.

forswear V. renounce; abandon. The captured knight could escape death only if he agreed to *forswear* Christianity and embrace Islam as the one true faith.

forte N. strong point or special talent. I am not eager to play this rather serious role, for my *forte* is comedy.

forthright ADJ. outspoken; straightforward; frank. Never afraid to call a spade a spade, she was perhaps too *forthright* to be a successful party politician.

fortitude   N. bravery; courage. He was awarded the medal for his *fortitude* in the battle.

fortuitous   ADJ. accidental; by chance. Though he pretended their encounter was *fortuitous*, he'd actually been hanging around her usual haunts for the past two weeks, hoping she'd turn up.

forum   N. place of assembly to discuss public concerns; meeting for discussion. The film opens with a shot of the ancient *Forum* in Rome, where several senators are discussing the strange new sect known as Christians. At the end of the movie, its director presided over a *forum* examining new fashions in filmmaking.

foster   V. rear; encourage. According to the legend, Romulus and Remus were *fostered* by a she-wolf who raised the abandoned infants with her own cubs. also ADJ.

founder   V. fail completely; sink. After hitting the submerged iceberg, the *Titanic* started taking in water rapidly and soon *foundered*.

founder   N. person who establishes (an organization, business). Among those drowned when the *Titanic* sank was the *founder* of the Abraham & Straus department store.

fracas   N. brawl, melee. The military police stopped the *fracas* in the bar and arrested the belligerents.

fractious   ADJ. unruly; disobedient; irritable. Bucking and kicking, the *fractious* horse unseated its rider.

frail   ADJ. weak. The delicate child seemed too *frail* to lift the heavy carton. frailty, N.

franchise   N. right granted by authority; right to vote; business licensed to sell a product in a particular territory. The city issued a *franchise* to the company to operate surface transit lines on the streets for ninety-nine years. For most of American history women lacked the right to vote: not until the early twentieth century was the *franchise* granted to women. Stan owns a Carvel's ice cream *franchise* in Chinatown.

frantic   ADJ. wild. At the time of the collision, many people became *frantic* with fear.

fraternize   V. associate in a friendly way. After the game, the members of the two teams *fraternized* as cheerfully as if they had never been rivals.

fraudulent   ADJ. cheating; deceitful. The government seeks to prevent *fraudulent* and misleading advertising.

fraught   ADJ. filled. Since this enterprise is *fraught* with danger, I will ask for volunteers who are willing to assume the risks.

fray   N. brawl. The three musketeers were in the thick of the *fray*.

frenetic   ADJ. frenzied; frantic. His *frenetic* activities convinced us that he had no organized plan of operation.

frenzied   ADJ. madly excited. As soon as they smelled smoke, the *frenzied* animals milled about in their cages.

fresco   N. painting on plaster (usually fresh). The cathedral is visited by many tourists who wish to admire the *frescoes* by Giotto.

fret   V. to be annoyed or vexed. To *fret* over your poor grades is foolish; instead, decide to work harder in the future.

friction   N. clash in opinion; rubbing against. At this time when harmony is essential, we cannot afford to have any *friction* in our group.

frigid   ADJ. intensely cold. Alaska is in the *frigid* zone.

■ **frivolous**   ADJ. lacking in seriousness; self-indulgently carefree; relatively unimportant. Though Nancy enjoyed Bill's *frivolous*, lighthearted companionship, she sometimes wondered whether he could ever be serious. frivolity, N.

frolicsome   ADJ. prankish; gay. The *frolicsome* puppy tried to lick the face of its master.

frond   N. fern leaf; palm or banana leaf. After the storm the beach was littered with the *fronds* of palm trees.

■ **frugality**   N. thrift; economy. In economically hard times, anyone who doesn't learn to practice *frugality* risks bankruptcy. frugal, ADJ.

fruition   N. bearing of fruit; fulfillment; realization. This building marks the *fruition* of all our aspirations and years of hard work.

frustrate   V. thwart; defeat. We must *frustrate* this dictator's plan to seize control of the government.

fugitive   ADJ. fleeting or transitory; roving. The film brought a few *fugitive* images to her mind, but on the whole it made no lasting impression upon her.

fulcrum   N. support on which a lever rests. If we use this stone as a *fulcrum* and the crowbar as a lever, we may be able to move this boulder.

fulsome   ADJ. disgustingly excessive. His *fulsome* praise of the dictator revolted his listeners.

fundamental   V. basic; primary; essential. The committee discussed all sorts of side issues without ever getting down to addressing the *fundamental* problem.

furlough   N. leave of absence; vacation granted a soldier or civil servant. Dreaming of her loved ones back in the States, the young soldier could hardly wait for her upcoming *furlough*.

furor   N. frenzy; great excitement. The story of her embezzlement of the funds created a *furor* on the Stock Exchange.

■ **furtive**   ADJ. stealthy; sneaky. Noticing the *furtive* glance the customer gave the diamond bracelet on the counter, the jeweler wondered whether he had a potential shoplifter on his hands.

fusion   N. union; coalition. The opponents of the political party in power organized a *fusion* of disgruntled groups and became an important element in the election.

futile   ADJ. useless; hopeless; ineffectual. It is *futile* for me to try to get any work done around here while the telephone is ringing every thirty seconds. futility, N.

gadfly   N. animal-biting fly; an irritating person. Like a *gadfly*, he irritated all the guests at the hotel; within forty-eight hours, everyone regarded him as an annoying busybody.

gaffe   N. social blunder. According to Miss Manners, to call your husband by your lover's name is worse than a mere *gaffe*; it is a tactical mistake.

Word List 21   gainsay-gory

gainsay   v. deny. She was too honest to *gainsay* the truth of the report.

gait   N. manner of walking or running; speed. The lame man walked with an uneven *gait*.

galaxy   N. large, isolated system of stars, such as the Milky Way; any collection of brilliant personalities. Science fiction stories speculate about the possible existence of life in other *galaxies*. The deaths of such famous actors as John Candy and George Burns tells us that the *galaxy* of Hollywood superstars is rapidly disappearing.

gale   N. windstorm; gust of wind; emotional outburst (laughter, tears). The Weather Channel warned viewers about a rising *gale*, with winds of up to sixty miles per hour.

gall   N. bitterness; nerve. The knowledge of his failure filled him with *gall*.

gall   v. annoy; chafe. Their taunts *galled* him.

galleon   N. large sailing ship. The Spaniards pinned their hopes on the *galleon*, the large warship; the British, on the smaller and faster pinnace.

galvanize   v. stimulate by shock; stir up; revitalize. News that the prince was almost at their door *galvanized* the ugly stepsisters into a frenzy of combing and primping.

gambit   N. opening in chess in which a piece is sacrificed. The player was afraid to accept his opponent's *gambit* because he feared a trap which as yet he could not see.

gambol   v. skip; leap playfully. Watching children *gamboling* in the park is a pleasant experience. also N.

gamely   ADV. bravely; with spirit. Because he had fought *gamely* against a much superior boxer, the crowd gave him a standing ovation when he left the arena.

gamut   N. entire range. In this performance, the leading lady was able to demonstrate the complete *gamut* of her acting ability.

gape   v. open widely; stare open-mouthed. The huge pit *gaped* before him; if he stumbled, he would fall in. Slack-jawed in wonder, Huck *gaped* at the huge stalactites hanging down from the ceiling of the limestone cavern.

garbled   ADJ. mixed up; jumbled; distorted. A favorite party game involves passing a whispered message from one person to another until, by the time it reaches the last player, the message is totally *garbled*.

gargantuan   ADJ. huge; enormous. The *gargantuan* wrestler was terrified of mice.

garish   ADJ. over-bright in color; gaudy. She wore a gaudy rhinestone necklace with an excessively *garish* gold lamé dress.

garner   v. gather; store up. She hoped to *garner* the world's literature in one library.

garnish   v. decorate. Parsley was used to *garnish* the boiled potato. also N.

■ **garrulous**   ADJ. loquacious; wordy; talkative. My Uncle Henry can out-talk any three people I know. He is the most *garrulous* person in Cayuga County. garrulity, N.

gauche   ADJ. clumsy; coarse and uncouth. Compared to the sophisticated young ladies in their elegant gowns, tomboyish Jo felt *gauche* and out of place.

gaudy   ADJ. flashy; showy. The newest Trump skyscraper is typically *gaudy*, covered in gilded panels that gleam in the sun.

gaunt   ADJ. lean and angular; barren. His once round face looked surprisingly *gaunt* after he had lost weight.

gavel   N. hammerlike tool; mallet. "Sold!" cried the auctioneer, banging her *gavel* on the table to indicate she'd accepted the final bid.

gawk   v. stare foolishly; look in open-mouthed awe. The country boy *gawked* at the skyscrapers and neon lights of the big city.

genealogy   N. record of descent; lineage. He was proud of his *genealogy* and constantly referred to the achievements of his ancestors.

generality   N. vague statement. This report is filled with *generalities*; be more specific in your statements.

generate   v. cause; produce; create. In his first days in office, President Clinton managed to *generate* a new mood of optimism; we just hoped he could generate some new jobs.

generic   ADJ. characteristic of an entire class or species. Sue knew so many computer programmers who spent their spare time playing fantasy games that she began to think that playing Dungeons & Dragons was a *generic* trait.

genesis   N. beginning; origin. Tracing the *genesis* of a family is the theme of *Roots*.

geniality   N. cheerfulness; kindliness; sympathy. This restaurant is famous and popular because of the *geniality* of the proprietor who tries to make everyone happy.

genre   N. particular variety of art or literature. Both a short story writer and a poet, Langston Hughes proved himself equally skilled in either *genre*.

genteel   ADJ. well-bred; elegant. We are looking for a man with a *genteel* appearance who can inspire confidence by his cultivated manner.

gentility   N. those of gentle birth; refinement. Her family was proud of its *gentility* and elegance.

gentry   N. people of standing; class of people just below nobility. The local *gentry* did not welcome the visits of the summer tourists and tried to ignore their presence in the community.

germane   ADJ. pertinent; bearing upon the case at hand. The judge refused to allow the testimony to be heard by the jury because it was not *germane* to the case.

germinal   ADJ. pertaining to a germ; creative. Such an idea is *germinal*; I am certain that it will influence thinkers and philosophers for many generations.

germinate   v. cause to sprout; sprout. After the seeds *germinate* and develop their permanent leaves, the plants may be removed from the cold frames and transplanted to the garden.

gesticulation   N. motion; gesture. Operatic performers are trained to make exaggerated *gesticulations* because of the large auditoriums in which they appear.

ghastly   ADJ. horrible. The murdered man was a *ghastly* sight.

gibberish   N. nonsense; babbling. Did you hear that fool boy spouting *gibberish* about monsters from outer space? gibber, V.

gibe   V. mock. As you *gibe* at their superstitious beliefs, do you realize that you, too, are guilty of similarly foolish thoughts?

giddy   ADJ. light-hearted; dizzy. He felt his *giddy* youth was past.

gingerly   ADV. very carefully. To separate egg whites, first crack the egg *gingerly*.

girth   N. distance around something; circumference. It took an extra-large cummerbund to fit around Andrew Carnegie's considerable *girth*.

gist   N. essence. She was asked to give the *gist* of the essay in two sentences.

● **glacial**   ADJ. like a glacier; extremely cold. Never a warm person, when offended John could seem positively *glacial*.

glaring   ADJ. highly conspicuous; harshly bright. *Glaring* spelling or grammatical errors in your resumé will unfavorably impress potential employers.

glaze   V. cover with a thin and shiny surface. The freezing rain *glazed* the streets and made driving hazardous. also N.

glib   ADJ. fluent; facile; slick. Keeping up a steady patter to entertain his customers, the kitchen gadget salesman was a *glib* speaker, never at a loss for a word.

glimmer   V. shine erratically; twinkle. In the darkness of the cavern, the glowworms hanging from the cavern roof *glimmered* like distant stars.

gloat   V. express evil satisfaction; view malevolently. As you *gloat* over your ill-gotten wealth, do you think of the many victims you have defrauded?

glossary   N. brief explanation of words used in the text. I have found the *glossary* in this book very useful; it has eliminated many trips to the dictionary.

gloss over   V. explain away. No matter how hard he tried to talk around the issue, President Bush could not *gloss over* the fact that he had raised taxes after all.

glossy   ADJ. smooth and shining. I want this photograph printed on *glossy* paper, not matte.

glower   V. scowl. The angry boy *glowered* at his father.

glut   V. overstock; fill to excess. The many manufacturers *glutted* the market and could not find purchasers for the excess articles they had produced. also N.

■ **glutton**   N. someone who eats too much. When Mother saw that Bobby had eaten all the cookies, she called him a little *glutton*. gluttonous, ADJ.

gnarled   ADJ. twisted. The *gnarled* oak tree had been a landmark for years and was mentioned in several deeds.

gnome   N. dwarf; underground spirit. In medieval mythology, *gnomes* were the special guardians and inhabitants of subterranean mines.

goad   V. urge on. He was *goaded* by his friends until he yielded to their wishes. also N.

gorge   N. small, steep-walled canyon. The white-water rafting guide warned us about the rapids farther downstream, where the river cut through a narrow *gorge*.

gorge   V. stuff oneself. The gluttonous guest *gorged* himself with food as though he had not eaten for days.

gory   ADJ. bloody. The audience shuddered as they listened to the details of the *gory* massacre.

Word List 22   gouge-hiatus

gouge   V. tear out. In that fight, all the rules were forgotten; the adversaries bit, kicked, and tried to *gouge* each other's eyes out.

gourmand   N. epicure; person who takes excessive pleasure in food and drink. *Gourmands* lack self-restraint; if they enjoy a particular cuisine, they eat far too much of it.

gourmet   N. connoisseur of food and drink. The *gourmet* stated that this was the best onion soup she had ever tasted.

graduated   ADJ. arranged by degrees (of height, difficulty, etc.). Margaret loved her *graduated* set of Russian hollow wooden dolls; she spent hours happily putting the smaller dolls into their larger counterparts.

graft   N. piece of transplanted tissue; portion of plant inserted in another plant. After the fire, Greg required skin *grafts* to replace the badly damaged areas on his forearms. also V.

grandeur   N. impressiveness; stateliness; majesty. No matter how often he hiked through the mountains, David never failed to be struck by the *grandeur* of the Sierra Nevada range.

grandiloquent   ADJ. pompous; bombastic; using high-sounding language. The politician could never speak simply; she was always *grandiloquent*.

grandiose   ADJ. pretentious; high-flown; ridiculously exaggerated; impressive. The aged matinee idol still had *grandiose* notions of his supposed importance in the theatrical world.

granulate   V. form into grains. Sugar that has been *granulated* dissolves more readily than lump sugar. granule, N.

graphic   ADJ. pertaining to the art of delineating; vividly described. I was particularly impressed by the *graphic* presentation of the storm.

grapple   V. wrestle; come to grips with. He *grappled* with the burglar and overpowered him.

grate V. make a harsh noise; have an unpleasant effect; shred. The screams of the quarreling children *grated* on her nerves.

■ **gratify** V. please. Lori's parents were *gratified* by her successful performance on the SAT.

gratis ADJ. free. The company offered to give one package *gratis* to every purchaser of one of their products. also ADJ.

■ **gratuitous** ADJ. given freely; unwarranted; uncalled for. Quit making *gratuitous* comments about my driving; no one asked you for your opinion.

■ **gravity** N. seriousness. We could tell we were in serious trouble from the *gravity* of the principal's expression. (secondary meaning) grave, ADJ.

■ **gregarious** ADJ. sociable. Typically, partygoers are *gregarious*; hermits are not.

grievance N. cause of complaint. When her supervisor ignored her complaint, she took her *grievance* to the union.

grill V. question severely. In violation of the Miranda law, the police *grilled* the suspect for several hours before reading him his rights. (secondary meaning)

grimace N. a facial distortion to show feeling such as pain, disgust, etc. Even though he remained silent, his *grimace* indicated his displeasure. also V.

grisly ADJ. ghastly. She shuddered at the *grisly* sight.

grouse V. complain; fuss. Students traditionally *grouse* about the abysmal quality of "mystery meat" and similar dormitory food.

grotesque ADJ. fantastic; comically hideous. On Halloween people enjoy wearing *grotesque* costumes.

grove N. group of trees (smaller than a forest); orchard. To the child, the small *grove* of oaks was as vast as Sherwood Forest, in which he played that legendary hero, Robin Hood.

grovel V. crawl or creep on ground; remain prostrate. Even though we have been defeated, we do not have to *grovel* before our conquerors.

grudging ADJ. unwilling; reluctant; stingy. We received only *grudging* support from the mayor despite his earlier promises of aid.

gruel N. liquid food made by boiling oatmeal, etc., in milk or water. Our daily allotment of *gruel* made the meal not only monotonous but also unpalatable.

grueling ADJ. exhausting. The marathon is a *grueling* race.

gruesome ADJ. grisly; horrible. His face was the stuff of nightmares: all the children in the audience screamed when Freddy Kruger's *gruesome* countenance was flashed on the screen.

gruff ADJ. rough-mannered. Although he was blunt and *gruff* with most people, he was always gentle with children.

guffaw N. boisterous laughter. The loud *guffaws* that came from the closed room indicated that the members of the committee had not yet settled down to serious business. also V.

■ **guile** N. deceit; duplicity; wiliness; cunning. Iago uses considerable *guile* to trick Othello into believing that Desdemona has been unfaithful.

guileless ADJ. without deceit. He is naive, simple, and *guileless*; he cannot be guilty of fraud.

guise N. appearance; costume. In the *guise* of a plumber, the detective investigated the murder case.

■ **gullible** ADJ. easily deceived. Overly *gullible* people have only themselves to blame if they fall for con artists repeatedly. As the saying goes, "Fool me once, shame on you. Fool me twice, shame on *me*."

gustatory ADJ. affecting the sense of taste. The Thai restaurant offered an unusual *gustatory* experience for those used to a bland cuisine.

gusto N. enjoyment; enthusiasm. He accepted the assignment with such *gusto* that I feel he would have been satisfied with a smaller salary.

gusty ADJ. windy. The *gusty* weather made sailing precarious.

● **hackneyed** ADJ. commonplace; trite. When the reviewer criticized the movie for its *hackneyed* plot, we agreed; we had seen similar stories hundreds of times before.

haggard ADJ. wasted away; gaunt. After his long illness, he was pale and *haggard*.

haggle V. argue about prices. I prefer to shop in a store that has a one-price policy because, whenever I *haggle* with a shopkeeper, I am never certain that I paid a fair price for the articles I purchased.

hallowed ADJ. blessed; consecrated. Although the dead girl's parents had never been active churchgoers, they insisted that their daughter be buried in *hallowed* ground.

hallucination N. delusion. I think you were frightened by a *hallucination* you created in your own mind.

halting ADJ. hesitant; faltering. Novice extemporaneous speakers often talk in a *halting* fashion as they grope for the right words.

■ **hamper** V. obstruct. The new mother didn't realize how much the effort of caring for an infant would *hamper* her ability to keep an immaculate house.

haphazard ADJ. random; by chance. His *haphazard* reading left him unacquainted with the authors of the books.

harangue N. noisy speech. In her lengthy *harangue*, the principal berated the offenders. also V.

harass V. to annoy by repeated attacks. When he could not pay his bills as quickly as he had promised, he was *harassed* by his creditors.

harbinger N. forerunner. The crocus is an early *harbinger* of spring.

harbor V. provide a refuge for; hide. The church *harbored* illegal aliens who were political refugees.

■ **hardy** ADJ. sturdy; robust; able to stand inclement weather. We asked the gardening expert to recommend particularly *hardy* plants that could withstand our harsh New England winters.

harrowing ADJ. agonizing; distressing; traumatic. At first the former prisoner did not wish to discuss his *harrowing* months of captivity as a political hostage.

■ **haughtiness** N. pride; arrogance. When she realized that Darcy believed himself too good to dance with his inferiors, Elizabeth took great offense at his *haughtiness*.

hazardous ADJ. dangerous. Your occupation is too *hazardous* for insurance companies to consider your application.

hazy ADJ. slightly obscure. In *hazy* weather, you cannot see the top of this mountain.

headlong ADJ. hasty; rash. The slave seized the unexpected chance to make a *headlong* dash across the border to freedom.

headstrong ADJ. stubborn; willful; unyielding. Because she refused to marry the man her parents had chosen for her, everyone scolded Minna and called her a foolish *headstrong* girl.

heckler N. person who harasses others. The *heckler* kept interrupting the speaker with rude remarks. heckle, V.

■ **hedonist** N. one who believes that pleasure is the sole aim in life. A thoroughgoing *hedonist*, he considered only his own pleasure and ignored any claims others had on his money or time.

heed V. pay attention to; consider. We hope you *heed* our advice and get a good night's sleep before the test. also N.

heedless ADJ. not noticing; disregarding. He drove on, *heedless* of the danger warnings placed at the side of the road.

heinous ADJ. atrocious; hatefully bad. Hitler's *heinous* crimes will never be forgotten.

herbivorous ADJ. grain-eating. Some *herbivorous* animals have two stomachs for digesting their food.

■ **heresy** N. opinion contrary to popular belief; opinion contrary to accepted religion. Galileo's assertion that the earth moved around the sun directly contradicted the religious teachings of his day; as a result, he was tried for *heresy*. heretic, N.

hermetic ADJ. sealed by fusion so as to be airtight. After you sterilize the bandages, place them in a container and seal it with a *hermetic* seal to protect them from contamination by airborne bacteria.

hermitage N. home of a hermit. Even in his remote *hermitage* he could not escape completely from the world.

heterodox ADJ. unorthodox; unconventional. To those who upheld the belief that the earth did not move, Galileo's theory that the earth circled the sun was disturbingly *heterodox*.

heterogeneous ADJ. dissimilar; mixed. This year's entering class is a remarkably *heterogeneous* body: it includes students from forty different states and twenty-six foreign countries, some the children of billionaires, others the offspring of welfare families. heterogenity, N.

heyday N. time of greatest success; prime. In their *heyday*, the San Francisco Forty-Niners won the Super Bowl two years running.

hiatus N. gap; interruption in duration or continuity; pause. During the summer *hiatus*, many students try to earn enough money to pay their tuition for the next school year.

Word List 23   hibernal-imbibe

hibernal ADJ. wintry. Bears prepare for their long *hibernal* sleep by overeating.

hibernate V. sleep throughout the winter. Bears are one of the many species of animals that *hibernate*. hibernation, N.

■ **hierarchy** N. arrangement by rank or standing; authoritarian body divided into ranks. To be low man on the totem pole is to have an inferior place in the *hierarchy*.

hilarity N. boisterous mirth. This *hilarity* is improper on this solemn day of mourning.

hindrance N. block; obstacle. Stalled cars along the highway are a *hindrance* to traffic that tow trucks should remove without delay. hinder, V.

histrionic ADJ. theatrical. He was proud of his *histrionic* ability and wanted to play the role of Hamlet. histrionics, N.

hoard V. stockpile; accumulate for future use. Whenever there are rumors of a food shortage, many people are tempted to *hoard* food. also N.

hoary ADJ. white with age. The man was *hoary* and wrinkled when he was 70.

hoax N. trick; practical joke. Embarrassed by the *hoax*, he reddened and left the room. also V.

hodgepodge N. jumble; mixture of ill-suited elements. The reviewer roundly condemned the play as a *hodgepodge* of random and purposeless encounters carried out by a cast lacking any uniformity of accent or style.

holster N. pistol case. Even when he was not in uniform, he carried a *holster* and pistol under his arm.

homage N. honor; tribute. In her speech she tried to pay *homage* to a great man.

■ **homogeneous** ADJ. of the same kind. Because the student body at Elite Prep was so *homogeneous*, Sara and James decided to send their daughter to a school that offered greater cultural diversity. homogenize, V.

hone V. sharpen. To make shaving easier, he *honed* his razor with great care.

hoodwink V. deceive; delude. Having been *hoodwinked* once by the fast-talking salesman, he was extremely cautious when he went to purchase a used car.

horde N. crowd. Just before Christmas the stores are filled with *hordes* of shoppers.

horticultural ADJ. pertaining to cultivation of gardens. When he bought his house, he began to look for flowers and decorative shrubs, and began to read books dealing with *horticultural* matters.

host N. great number; person entertaining guests; animal or plant from which a parasite gets its nourishment. You must attend to a *host* of details if you wish to succeed as *host* of a formal dinner party. Leeches are parasites that cling to their *hosts* and drink their *hosts'* blood.

hostility N. unfriendliness; hatred. A child who has been the sole object of his parents' affection often feels *hostility* toward a new baby in the family, resenting the newcomer who has taken his place.

hovel N. shack; small, wretched house. He wondered how poor people could stand living in such a *hovel*.

hover V. hang about; wait nearby. The police helicopter *hovered* above the accident.

hue N. color; aspect. The aviary contained birds of every possible *hue*.

hulking ADJ. massive; bulky; great in size. Despite his *hulking* build, the heavyweight boxing champion was surprisingly light on his feet. hulk, N.

humane ADJ. marked by kindness or consideration. It is ironic that the *Humane* Society sometimes must show its compassion toward mistreated animals by killing them to put them out of their misery.

humdrum ADJ. dull; monotonous. After his years of adventure, he could not settle down to a *humdrum* existence.

humid ADJ. damp. She could not stand the *humid* climate and moved to a drier area.

humility N. humbleness of spirit. He spoke with a *humility* and lack of pride that impressed his listeners.

hurtle V. crash; rush. The runaway train *hurtled* toward disaster.

husband V. use sparingly; conserve; save. Marathon runners must *husband* their energy so that they can keep going for the entire distance.

hybrid N. mongrel; mixed breed. Mendel's formula explains the appearance of *hybrids* and pure species in breeding. also ADJ.

hydrophobia N. rabies; fear of water. A dog that bites a human being must be observed for symptoms of *hydrophobia*.

hyperbole N. exaggeration; overstatement. As far as I'm concerned, Apple's claims about the new computer are pure *hyperbole*: no machine is that good!

hypercritical ADJ. excessively exacting. You are *hypercritical* in your demands for perfection; we all make mistakes.

hypochondriac N. person unduly worried about his health; worrier without cause about illness. The doctor prescribed chocolate pills for his patient who was a *hypochondriac*.

■ **hypocritical** ADJ. pretending to be virtuous; deceiving. Believing Eddie to be interested only in his own advancement, Greg resented his *hypocritical* posing as a friend. hypocrisy, N.

■ **hypothetical** ADJ. based on assumptions or hypotheses; supposed. Suppose you are accepted by Harvard, Stanford, and Brown. Which one would you choose to attend?

Remember, this is only a *hypothetical* situation. hypothesis, N.

ichthyology N. study of fish. Jacques Cousteau's programs about sea life have advanced the cause of *ichthyology*.

icon N. religious image; idol. The *icons* on the walls of the church were painted in the 13th century.

● **iconoclastic** ADJ. attacking cherished traditions. Deeply *iconoclastic*, Jean Genet deliberately set out to shock conventional theatergoers with his radical plays.

ideology N. system of ideas of a group. For people who had grown up believing in the communist *ideology*, it was hard to adjust to capitalism.

idiom N. expression whose meaning as a whole differs from the meanings of its individual words; distinctive style. The phrase "to lose one's marbles" is an *idiom*: if I say that Joe's lost his marbles, I'm not asking you to find some for him. I'm telling you *idiomatically* that he's crazy.

■ **idiosyncrasy** N. individual trait, usually odd in nature; eccentricity. One of Richard Nixon's little *idiosyncrasies* was his liking for ketchup on cottage cheese. One of Hannibal Lecter's little *idiosyncrasies* was his liking for human flesh. idiosyncratic, ADJ.

idolatry N. worship of idols; excessive admiration. Such *idolatry* of singers of country music is typical of the excessive enthusiasm of youth.

ignite V. kindle; light. When Desi crooned, "Baby, light my fire," literal-minded Lucy looked around for some paper to *ignite*.

ignoble ADJ. of lowly origin; unworthy. This plan is inspired by *ignoble* motives and I must, therefore, oppose it.

● **ignominy** N. deep disgrace; shame or dishonor. To lose the Ping-Pong match to a trained chimpanzee! How could Rollo stand the *ignominy* of his defeat? ignominious, ADJ.

● **illicit** ADJ. illegal. The defense attorney maintained that his client had never performed any *illicit* action.

illimitable ADJ. infinite. Man, having explored the far corners of the earth, is now reaching out into *illimitable* space.

illuminate V. brighten; clear up or make understandable; enlighten. Just as a lamp can *illuminate* a dark room, a perceptive comment can *illuminate* a knotty problem.

illusion N. misleading vision. It is easy to create an optical *illusion* in which lines of equal length appear different.

■ **illusory** ADJ. deceptive; not real. Unfortunately, the costs of running the lemonade stand were so high that Tom's profits proved *illusory*.

imbalance N. lack of balance or symmetry; disproportion. To correct racial *imbalance* in the schools, school boards have bussed black children into white neighborhoods and white children into black ones.

imbibe V. drink in. The dry soil *imbibed* the rain quickly.

Word List 24   immaculate-incessant

immaculate   ADJ. spotless; flawless; absolutely clean. Ken and Jessica were wonderful tenants and left the apartment in *immaculate* condition when they moved out.

imminent   ADJ. near at hand; impending. Rosa was such a last-minute worker that she could never start writing a paper till the deadline was *imminent*.

immobility   N. state of being immovable. Modern armies cannot afford the luxury of *immobility*, as they are vulnerable to attack while standing still.

immune   ADJ. resistant to; free or exempt from. Fortunately, Florence had contracted chicken pox as a child and was *immune* to it when her baby broke out in spots.

■ **immutable**   ADJ. unchangeable. All things change over time; nothing is *immutable*.

■ **impair**   V. injure; hurt. Drinking alcohol can *impair* your ability to drive safely; if you're going to drink, don't drive.

impale   V. pierce. He was *impaled* by the spear hurled by his adversary.

impalpable   ADJ. imperceptible; intangible. The ash is so fine that it is *impalpable* to the touch but it can be seen as a fine layer covering the window ledge.

impart   V. reveal or tell; grant. Polly begged Grandma to *impart* her recipe for rugeleh, but her grandmother wouldn't say a word.

impartial   ADJ. not biased; fair. Knowing she could not be *impartial* about her own child, Jo refused to judge any match in which Billy was competing.

impassable   ADJ. not able to be traveled or crossed. A giant redwood had fallen across the highway, blocking all four lanes: the road was *impassable*.

impasse   N. predicament from which there is no escape; deadlock. In this *impasse*, all turned to prayer as their last hope.

impassive   ADJ. without feeling; imperturbable; stoical. Refusing to let the enemy see how deeply shaken he was by his capture, the prisoner kept his face *impassive*.

impeach   V. charge with crime in office; indict. The angry congressman wanted to *impeach* the president for his misdeeds.

■ **impeccable**   ADJ. faultless. The uncrowned queen of the fashion industry, Diana was acclaimed for her *impeccable* taste.

● **impecunious**   ADJ. without money. Though Scrooge claimed he was too *impecunious* to give alms, he easily could have afforded to be charitable.

■ **impede**   V. hinder; block; delay. A series of accidents *impeded* the launching of the space shuttle.

impediment   N. hindrance; stumbling-block. She had a speech *impediment* that prevented her speaking clearly.

impel   V. drive or force onward. A strong feeling of urgency *impelled* her; if she failed to finish the project right then, she knew that she would never get it done.

impenetrable   ADJ. not able to be pierced or entered; beyond understanding. How could the murderer have gotten into the locked room? To Watson, the mystery, like the room, was *impenetrable*.

impending   ADJ. nearing; approaching. The entire country was saddened by the news of his *impending* death.

impenitent   ADJ. not repentant. We could see from his tough guy attitude that he was *impenitent*.

imperative   ADJ. absolutely necessary; critically important. It is *imperative* that you be extremely agreeable to Great-Aunt Maud when she comes to tea: otherwise she might not leave you that million dollars in her will. also N.

imperceptible   ADJ. unnoticeable; undetectable. Fortunately, the stain on the blouse was *imperceptible* after the blouse had gone through the wash.

imperial   ADJ. like an emperor; related to an empire. When hotel owner Leona Helmsley appeared in ads as Queen Leona standing guard over the Palace Hotel, her critics mocked her *imperial* fancies.

imperious   ADJ. domineering; haughty. Jane rather liked a man to be masterful, but Mr. Rochester seemed so bent on getting his own way that he was actually *imperious*!

impermeable   ADJ. impervious; not permitting passage through its substance. This new material is *impermeable* to liquids.

impertinent   ADJ. insolent; rude. His neighbors' *impertinent* curiosity about his lack of dates angered Ted. It was downright rude of them to ask him such personal questions.

imperturbable   ADJ. calm; placid; composed. In the midst of the battle, the Duke of Wellington remained *imperturbable* and in full command of the situation despite the hysteria and panic all around him. imperturbability, N.

impervious   ADJ. impenetrable; incapable of being damaged or distressed. The carpet salesman told Simone that his most expensive brand of floor covering was warranted to be *impervious* to ordinary wear and tear. Having read so many negative reviews of his acting, the movie star had learned to ignore them, and was now *impervious* to criticism.

impetuous   ADJ. violent; hasty; rash. "Leap before you look" was the motto suggested by one particularly *impetuous* young man.

impetus   N. incentive; stimulus; moving force. A new federal highway program would create jobs and give added *impetus* to our economic recovery.

impiety   N. irreverence; lack of respect for God. When members of the youth group draped the church in toilet paper one Halloween, the minister reprimanded them for their *impiety*.

impinge   V. infringe; touch; collide with. How could they be married without *impinging* on one another's freedom?

impious   ADJ. irreverent. The congregation was offended by her *impious* remarks.

implacable   ADJ. incapable of being pacified. Madame Defarge was the *implacable* enemy of the Evremonde family.

■ **implausible**   ADJ. unlikely; unbelievable. Though her alibi seemed *implausible*, it in fact turned out to be true.

■ **implement**   V. put into effect; supply with tools. The mayor was unwilling to *implement* the plan until she was sure it had the governor's backing. also N.

implicate   V. incriminate; show to be involved. Here's the deal: if you agree to take the witness stand and *implicate* your partners in crime, the prosecution will recommend that the judge go easy in sentencing you.

implication   N. something hinted at or suggested. When Miss Watson said she hadn't seen her purse since the last time Jim was in the house, the *implication* was that she suspected Jim had taken it. imply, v.

implicit   ADJ. understood but not stated. Jack never told Jill he adored her; he believed his love was *implicit* in his actions.

implore   V. beg. He *implored* her to give him a second chance.

imply   V. suggest a meaning not expressed; signify. When Aunt Millie said, "My! That's a big piece of pie, young man!" was she *implying* that Bobby was being a glutton in helping himself to such a huge piece?

importunate   ADJ. urging; demanding. He tried to hide from his *importunate* creditors until his allowance arrived.

importune   V. beg persistently. Democratic and Republican phone solicitors *importuned* her for contributions so frequently that she decided to give nothing to either party.

impostor   N. someone who assumes a false identity. Holmes exposed the doctor as an *impostor*.

impotent   ADJ. weak; ineffective. Although he wished to break the nicotine habit, he found himself *impotent* in resisting the craving for a cigarette.

impoverished   ADJ. poor. The loss of their farm left the family *impoverished* and without hope.

● **impregnable**   ADJ. invulnerable. Until the development of the airplane as a military weapon, the fort was considered *impregnable*.

impromptu   ADJ. without previous preparation; off the cuff; on the spur of the moment. The judges were amazed that she could make such a thorough, well-supported presentation in an *impromptu* speech.

impropriety   N. improperness; unsuitableness. Because of the *impropriety* of the punk rocker's slashed T-shirt and jeans, the management refused to admit him to the hotel's very formal dining room.

improvident   ADJ. thriftless. He was constantly being warned to mend his *improvident* ways and begin to "save for a rainy day." improvidence, N.

improvise   V. compose on the spur of the moment. She would sit at the piano and *improvise* for hours on themes from Bach and Handel.

imprudent   ADJ. lacking caution; injudicious. It is *imprudent* to exercise vigorously and become overheated when you are unwell.

■ **impudence**   N. impertinence; insolence. Kissed on the cheek by a perfect stranger, Lady Catherine exclaimed, "Of all the nerve! Young man, I should have you horse-whipped for your *impudence*."

impugn   V. dispute or contradict (often in an insulting way); challenge; gainsay. Our treasurer was furious when the finance committee's report *impugned* the accuracy of his financial records and recommended that he should take bonehead math.

impunity   N. freedom from punishment or harm. A 98-pound weakling can't attack a beachfront bully with *impunity*: the poor, puny guy is sure to get mashed.

■ **inadvertently**   ADV. unintentionally; by oversight; carelessly. Judy's great fear was that she might *inadvertently* omit a question on the exam and mismark her whole answer sheet.

inalienable   ADJ. not to be taken away; nontransferable. The Declaration of Independence mentions the *inalienable* rights that all of us possess.

■ **inane**   ADJ. silly; senseless. There's no point to what you're saying. Why are you bothering to make such *inane* remarks?

inanimate   ADJ. lifeless. She was asked to identify the still and *inanimate* body.

inarticulate   ADJ. speechless; producing indistinct speech. He became *inarticulate* with rage and uttered sounds without meaning.

inaugurate   V. start; initiate; install in office. The airline decided to *inaugurate* its new route to the Far East with a special reduced fare offer. inaugural, ADJ.

incandescent   ADJ. strikingly bright; shining with intense heat. If you leave on an *incandescent* light bulb, it quickly grows too hot to touch.

incantation   N. singing or chanting of magic spells; magical formula. Uttering *incantations* to make the brew more potent, the witch doctor stirred the liquid in the caldron.

incapacitate   V. disable. During the winter, many people were *incapacitated* by respiratory ailments.

incarcerate   V. imprison. The civil rights workers were willing to be arrested and even *incarcerated* if by their imprisonment they could serve the cause.

incarnation   N. act of assuming a human body and human nature. The *incarnation* of Jesus Christ is a basic tenet of Christian theology.

incendiary   N. arsonist. The fire spread in such an unusual manner that the fire department chiefs were certain that it had been set by an *incendiary*. also ADJ.

incense   V. enrage; infuriate. Cruelty to defenseless animals *incensed* Kit: the very idea brought tears of anger to her eyes.

incentive   N. spur; motive. Mike's strong desire to outshine his big sister was all the *incentive* he needed to do well in school.

inception   N. start; beginning. She was involved with the project from its *inception*.

incessant   ADJ. uninterrupted; unceasing. In a famous TV commercial, the frogs' *incessant* croaking goes on and on until eventually it turns into a single word: "Bud-weis-er."

Word List 25 inchoate-ingenious

inchoate ADJ. recently begun; rudimentary; elementary. Before the Creation, the world was an *inchoate* mass.

incidence N. rate of occurrence; particular occurrence. Health professionals expressed great concern over the high *incidence* of infant mortality in major urban areas.

● **incidental** ADJ. not essential; minor. The scholarship covered his major expenses at college and some of his *incidental* expenses as well.

incipient ADJ. beginning; in an early stage. I will go to sleep early for I want to break an *incipient* cold.

■ **incisive** ADJ. cutting; sharp. His *incisive* remarks made us see the fallacy in our plans.

■ **incite** V. arouse to action; goad; motivate; induce to exist. In a fiery speech, Mario *incited* his fellow students to go out on strike to protest the university's anti-affirmative action stand.

inclement ADJ. stormy; unkind. In *inclement* weather, I like to curl up on the sofa with a good book and listen to the storm blowing outside.

incline N. slope; slant. The architect recommended that the nursing home's ramp be rebuilt because its *incline* was too steep for wheelchairs.

inclined ADJ. tending or leaning toward; bent. Though I am *inclined* to be skeptical, the witness's manner *inclines* me to believe his story. also V.

■ **inclusive** ADJ. tending to include all. The comedian turned down the invitation to join the Players' Club, saying any club that would let him in was too *inclusive* for him.

incoherent ADJ. unintelligible; muddled; illogical. The excited fan blushed and stammered, her words becoming almost *incoherent* in the thrill of meeting her favorite rock star face to face. incoherence, N.

incompatible ADJ. inharmonious. The married couple argued incessantly and finally decided to separate because they were *incompatible*. incompatibility, N.

■ **incongruous** ADJ. not fitting; absurd. Dave saw nothing *incongruous* about wearing sneakers with his tuxedo; he couldn't understand why his date took one look at him and started to laugh. incongruity, N.

■ **inconsequential** ADJ. insignificant; unimportant. Brushing off Ali's apologies for having broken the wineglass, Tamara said, "Don't worry about it; it's *inconsequential*."

inconsistency N. state of being self-contradictory; lack of uniformity or steadiness. How are lawyers different from agricultural inspectors? While lawyers check *inconsistencies* in witnesses' statements, agricultural inspectors check *inconsistencies* in Grade A eggs. inconsistent, ADJ.

incontinent ADJ. lacking self-restraint; licentious. His *incontinent* behavior off stage so shocked many people that they refused to attend the plays and movies in which he appeared.

● **incontrovertible** ADJ. indisputable; not open to question. Unless you find the evidence against my client absolutely *incontrovertible*, you must declare her not guilty of this charge.

incorporate V. introduce something into a larger whole; combine; unite. Breaking with precedent, President Truman ordered the military to *incorporate* blacks into every branch of the armed services. also ADJ.

incorporeal ADJ. lacking a material body; insubstantial. While Casper the friendly ghost is an *incorporeal* being, nevertheless he and his fellow ghosts make quite an impact on the physical world.

■ **incorrigible** ADJ. not correctable. Though Widow Douglass hoped to reform Huck, Miss Watson called him *incorrigible* and said he would come to no good end.

incredulous ADJ. withholding belief; skeptical. When Jack claimed he hadn't eaten the jelly doughnut, Jill took an *incredulous* look at his smeared face and laughed. incredulity, N.

increment N. increase. The new contract calls for a 10 percent *increment* in salary for each employee for the next two years.

incriminate V. accuse. The evidence gathered against the racketeers *incriminates* some high public officials as well.

incrustation N. hard coating or crust. In dry dock, we scraped off the *incrustation* of dirt and barnacles that covered the hull of the ship.

incubate V. hatch; scheme. Inasmuch as our supply of electricity is cut off, we shall have to rely on the hens to *incubate* these eggs.

inculcate V. teach; instill. In an effort to *inculcate* religious devotion, the officials ordered that the school day begin with the singing of a hymn.

incumbent ADJ. obligatory; currently holding an office. It is *incumbent* upon all *incumbent* elected officials to keep accurate records of expenses incurred in office. also N.

incur V. bring upon oneself. His parents refused to pay any future debts he might *incur*.

incursion N. temporary invasion. The nightly *incursions* and hit-and-run raids of our neighbors across the border tried the patience of the country to the point where we decided to retaliate in force.

● **indefatigable** ADJ. tireless. Although the effort of taking out the garbage tired Wayne out for the entire morning, when it came to partying, he was *indefatigable*.

indelible ADJ. not able to be erased. The *indelible* ink left a permanent mark on my shirt. Young Bill Clinton's meeting with President Kennedy made an *indelible* impression on the youth.

indentation N. notch; deep recess. You can tell one tree from another by examining their leaves and noting the differences in the *indentations* along the edges of the leaves. indent, V.

indenture V. bind as servant or apprentice to master. Many immigrants could come to America only after they had *indentured* themselves for several years. also N.

indeterminate ADJ. uncertain; not clearly fixed; indefinite. That interest rates shall rise appears certain; when they will do so, however, remains *indeterminate.*

indicative ADJ. suggestive; implying. A lack of appetite may be *indicative* of a major mental or physical disorder.

indices N. PL. signs; indications. Many college admissions officers believe that SAT scores and high school grades are the best *indices* of a student's potential to succeed in college. N. SG. index.

■ **indict** V. charge. The district attorney didn't want to *indict* the suspect until she was sure she had a strong enough case to convince a jury. indictment, N.

■ **indifferent** ADJ. unmoved or unconcerned by; mediocre. Because Ann felt no desire to marry, she was *indifferent* to Carl's constant proposals. Not only was she *indifferent* to him personally, but she felt that, given his general silliness, he would make an *indifferent* husband.

indigenous ADJ. native. Cigarettes are made of tobacco, a plant *indigenous* to the New World.

indigent ADJ. poor; destitute. Someone who is truly *indigent* can't even afford to buy a pack of cigarettes. [Don't mix up *indigent* and *indigenous*. See previous sentence.]

indignation N. anger at an injustice. He felt *indignation* at the ill-treatment of helpless animals.

indignity N. offensive or insulting treatment. Although he seemed to accept cheerfully the *indignities* heaped upon him, he was inwardly very angry.

indiscretion N. lack of tactfulness or sound judgment. Terrified that the least *indiscretion* could jeopardize his political career, the novice politician never uttered an unguarded word. indiscreet, ADJ.

■ **indiscriminate** ADJ. choosing at random; confused. She disapproved of her son's *indiscriminate* television viewing and decided to restrict him to educational programs.

indisputable ADJ. too certain to be disputed. In the face of these *indisputable* statements, I withdraw my complaint.

indissoluble ADJ. permanent. The *indissoluble* bonds of marriage are all too often being dissolved.

indoctrinate V. instruct in a doctrine or ideology. Cuban-Americans resisted sending Elian Gonzalez back to Cuba because he would be *indoctrinated* there with Communist principles.

● **indolent** ADJ. lazy. Couch potatoes lead an *indolent* life lying back on their Lazyboy recliners watching TV. indolence, N.

indomitable ADJ. unconquerable; unyielding. Focusing on her game despite all her personal problems, tennis champion Steffi Graf proved she had an *indomitable* will to win.

indubitable ADJ. unable to be doubted; unquestionable. Auditioning for the chorus line, Molly was an *indubitable* hit: the director fired the leading lady and hired Molly in her place!

■ **induce** V. persuade; bring about. After the quarrel, Tina said nothing could *induce* her to talk to Tony again. inducement, N.

indulgent ADJ. humoring; yielding; lenient. Jay's mom was excessively *indulgent*: she bought him every Nintendo cartridge and video game on the market. She *indulged* Jay so much, she spoiled him rotten.

industrious ADJ. diligent; hard-working. Look busy when the boss walks by your desk; it never hurts to appear *industrious*. industry, N.

inebriated ADJ. habitually intoxicated; drunk. Abe was *inebriated* more often than he was sober. Because of his *inebriety*, he was discharged from his job as a bus driver.

● **ineffable** ADJ. unutterable; cannot be expressed in speech. Such *ineffable* joy must be experienced; it cannot be described.

ineffectual ADJ. not effective; weak. Because the candidate failed to get across his message to the public, his campaign was *ineffectual.*

inefficacious ADJ. not effective; unable to produce a desired result. All Lois's coaxing and urging was *inefficacious*: Clark still refused to join her and Superman for dinner. inefficacy, N.

inept ADJ. lacking skill; unsuited; incompetent. The *inept* glovemaker was all thumbs.

inequity N. unfairness. In demanding equal pay for equal work, women protest the basic *inequity* of a system that gives greater financial rewards to men.

■ **inert** ADJ. inactive; lacking power to move. "Get up, you lazybones," she cried to her husband, who lay in bed *inert*. inertia, N.

inevitable ADJ. unavoidable. Though death and taxes are both supposedly *inevitable*, some people avoid paying taxes for years.

● **inexorable** ADJ. relentless; unyielding; implacable. After listening to the pleas for clemency, the judge was *inexorable* and gave the convicted man the maximum punishment allowed by law.

infallible ADJ. unerring. We must remember that none of us is *infallible;* we all make mistakes.

infamous ADJ. notoriously bad. Charles Manson and Jeffrey Dahmer are both *infamous* killers.

infantile ADJ. childish. When will he outgrow such *infantile* behavior?

infer V. deduce; conclude. From the students' glazed looks, it was easy for me to *infer* that they were bored out of their minds. inference, N.

infernal ADJ. pertaining to hell; devilish. Batman was baffled: he could think of no way to hinder the Joker's *infernal* scheme to destroy the city.

infidel N. unbeliever. The Saracens made war against the *infidels.*

infiltrate V. pass into or through; penetrate (an organization) sneakily. In order to be able to *infiltrate* enemy lines at night without being seen, the scouts darkened their faces and wore black coveralls. infiltrator, N.

infinitesimal ADJ. very small. In the twentieth century, physicists have made their greatest discoveries about the characteristics of *infinitesimal* objects like the atom and its parts.

infirmity N. weakness. Her greatest *infirmity* was lack of willpower.

inflated ADJ. exaggerated; pompous; enlarged (with air or gas). His claims about the new product were *inflated*; it did not work as well as he had promised.

influx N. flowing into. The *influx* of refugees into the country has taxed the relief agencies severely.

informal ADJ. absence of ceremony; casual. The English teacher preferred *informal* discussions to prepared lectures.

infraction N. violation (of a rule or regulation); breach. When Dennis Rodman butted heads with that referee, he committed a clear *infraction* of NBA rules.

infuriate V. enrage; anger. Her big brother's teasing always *infuriated* Margaret; no matter how hard she tried to keep her temper, he always got her goat.

infusion N. act of introducing or instilling a quality; liquid solution. The rookie quarterback brought an *infusion* of new life and vigor to the tired team. infuse, V.

■ **ingenious** ADJ. clever; resourceful. Kit admired the *ingenious* way that her computer keyboard opened up to reveal the built-in CD-ROM below. ingenuity, N.

Word List 26 ingenue-invigorate

ingenue N. an artless girl; an actress who plays such parts. Although she was forty, she still insisted that she be cast as an *ingenue* and refused to play more mature roles.

ingenuous ADJ. naive and trusting; young; unsophisticated. The woodsman had not realized how *ingenuous* Little Red Riding Hood was until he heard that she had gone off for a walk in the woods with the Big Bad Wolf.

ingrained ADJ. deeply established; firmly rooted. Try as they would, the missionaries were unable to uproot the *ingrained* superstitions of the natives.

ingrate N. ungrateful person. That *ingrate* Bob sneered at the tie I gave him.

ingratiate V. become popular with. He tried to *ingratiate* himself into her parents' good graces.

■ **inherent** ADJ. firmly established by nature or habit. Katya's *inherent* love of justice caused her to champion anyone she considered treated unfairly by society.

inhibit V. restrain; retard or prevent. Only two things *inhibited* him from taking a punch at Mike Tyson: Tyson's left hook, and Tyson's right jab. The protective undercoating on my car *inhibits* the formation of rust.

inimical ADJ. unfriendly; hostile; harmful; detrimental. I've always been friendly to Martha. Why is she so *inimical* to me?

inimitable ADJ. matchless; not able to be imitated. We admire Auden for his *inimitable* use of language; he is one of a kind.

iniquitous ADJ. wicked; immoral; unrighteous. Whether or not King Richard III was responsible for the murder of the two young princes in the Tower, it was an *iniquitous* deed. iniquity, N.

initiate V. begin; originate; receive into a group. The college is about to *initiate* a program in reducing math anxiety among students.

injurious ADJ. harmful. Smoking cigarettes can be *injurious* to your health.

inkling N. hint. This came as a complete surprise to me as I did not have the slightest *inkling* of your plans.

■ **innate** ADJ. inborn. Mozart's parents soon recognized young Wolfgang's *innate* talent for music.

■ **innocuous** ADJ. harmless. An occasional glass of wine with dinner is relatively *innocuous* and should have no ill effect on you.

■ **innovation** N. change; introduction of something new. Although Richard liked to keep up with all the latest technological *innovations*, he didn't always abandon tried and true techniques in favor of something new. innovate, V.

innovative ADJ. novel; introducing a change. The establishment of our SAT I computer data base has enabled us to come up with some *innovative* tactics for doing well on the SAT.

innuendo N. hint; insinuation. I can defend myself against direct accusations; *innuendos* and oblique attacks on my character are what trouble me.

inopportune ADJ. untimely; poorly chosen. A rock concert is an *inopportune* setting for a quiet conversation.

inordinate ADJ. unrestrained; excessive. She had an *inordinate* fondness for candy, eating two or three boxes in a single day.

inquisitor N. questioner (especially harsh); investigator. Fearing being grilled ruthlessly by the secret police, Masha faced her *inquisitors* with trepidation.

insalubrious ADJ. unwholesome; not healthful. The mosquito-ridden swamp was an *insalubrious* place, a breeding ground for malarial contagion.

insatiable ADJ. not easily satisfied; unquenchable; greedy. David's appetite for oysters was *insatiable*: he could easily eat four dozen at a single sitting.

inscrutable ADJ. impenetrable; not readily understood; mysterious. Experienced poker players try to keep their expressions *inscrutable*, hiding their reactions to the cards behind a so-called "poker face."

insensible ADJ. unconscious; unresponsive. Sherry and I are very different; at times when I would be covered with embarrassment, she seems *insensible* to shame.

insidious ADJ. treacherous; stealthy; sly. The fifth column is *insidious* because it works secretly within our territory for our defeat.

insightful ADJ. discerning; perceptive. Sol thought he was very *insightful* about human behavior, but he was actually clueless as to why people acted the way they did.

insinuate V. hint; imply; creep in. When you said I looked robust, did you mean to *insinuate* that I'm getting fat?

■ **insipid** ADJ. lacking in flavor; dull. Flat prose and flat ginger ale are equally *insipid*: both lack sparkle.

insolence N. impudent disrespect; haughtiness. How dare you treat me so rudely! The manager will hear of your *insolence*. insolent, ADJ.

● **insolvent** ADJ. bankrupt; unable to repay one's debts. Although young Lord Widgeon was *insolvent*, he had no fear of being thrown into debtors' prison, for he was sure that if his creditors pressed him for payment his wealthy parents would repay what he owed. insolvency, N.

insomnia N. wakefulness; inability to sleep. He refused to join us in a midnight cup of coffee because he claimed it gave him *insomnia*.

■ **instigate** V. urge; start; provoke. Rumors of police corruption led the mayor to *instigate* an investigation into the department's activities.

insubordination N. disobedience; rebelliousness. At the slightest hint of *insubordination* from the sailors of the *Bounty*, Captain Bligh had them flogged; finally, they mutinied.

insubstantial ADJ. lacking substance; insignificant; frail. His hopes for a career in acting proved *insubstantial*; no one would cast him, even in an *insubstantial* role.

■ **insularity** N. narrow-mindedness; isolation. The *insularity* of the islanders manifested itself in their suspicion of anything foreign. insular, ADJ.

insulated ADJ. set apart; isolated. A well-to-do bachelor, James spent his money freely, *insulated* from the cares of his friends, who had families to support.

● **insuperable** ADJ. insurmountable; unbeatable. Though the odds against their survival seemed *insuperable*, the Apollo 13 astronauts reached earth safely.

insurgent ADJ. rebellious. Because the *insurgent* forces had occupied the capital and had gained control of the railway lines, several of the war correspondents covering the uprising predicted a rebel victory.

insurmountable ADJ. overwhelming; unbeatable; insuperable. Faced by almost *insurmountable* obstacles, the members of the underground maintained their courage and will to resist.

insurrection N. rebellion; uprising. In retrospect, given how badly the British treated the American colonists, the eventual *insurrection* seems inevitable.

intangible ADJ. not able to be perceived by touch; vague. Though the financial benefits of his Oxford post were meager, Lewis was drawn to it by its *intangible* rewards: prestige, intellectual freedom, the fellowship of his peers.

integral ADJ. complete; necessary for completeness. Physical education is an *integral* part of our curriculum; a sound mind and a sound body are complementary.

integrate V. make whole; combine; make into one unit. She tried to *integrate* all their activities into one program.

■ **integrity** N. uprightness; wholeness. Lincoln, whose personal *integrity* has inspired millions, fought a civil war to maintain the *integrity* of the Republic, that these United States might remain undivided for all time.

intellect N. higher mental powers. He thought college would develop his *intellect*.

intelligentsia N. the intelligent and educated classes [often used derogatorily]. She preferred discussions about sports and politics to the literary conversations of the *intelligentsia*.

intemperate ADJ. immoderate; excessive; extreme. In a temper, Tony refused to tone down his *intemperate* remarks.

inter V. bury. They are going to *inter* the body tomorrow at Broadlawn Cemetery.

interim N. meantime. The company will not consider our proposal until next week; in the *interim*, let us proceed as we have in the past.

interloper N. intruder; unwanted meddler. The merchant thought of his competitors as *interlopers* who were stealing away his trade.

interment N. burial. *Interment* will take place in the church cemetery at 2 P.M. Wednesday.

interminable ADJ. endless. Although his speech lasted for only twenty minutes, it seemed *interminable* to his bored audience.

intermittent ADJ. periodic; on and off. The outdoor wedding reception had to be moved indoors to avoid the *intermittent* showers that fell on and off all afternoon.

interrogate V. question closely; cross-examine. Knowing that the Nazis would *interrogate* him about his background, the secret agent invented a cover story that would help him meet their questions.

■ **intervene** V. come between. When two close friends get into a fight, be careful if you try to *intervene*; they may join forces to gang up on you.

intimacy N. closeness, often affectionate; privacy; familiarity. In a moment of rare *intimacy*, the mayor allowed the reporters a glimpse of his personal feelings about his family. intimate, ADJ.

intimate V. hint; suggest. Was Dick *intimating* that Jane had bad breath when he asked if she'd like a breath mint?

■ **intimidate** V. frighten. I'll learn karate and then those big bullies won't be able to *intimidate* me any more.

● **intractable** ADJ. unruly; stubborn; unyielding. Charlie Brown's friend Pigpen was *intractable*: he absolutely refused to take a bath.

intransigence N. refusal of any compromise; stubbornness. The negotiating team had not expected such *intransigence* from the striking workers, who rejected any hint of a compromise. intransigent, ADJ.

■ **intrepid** ADJ. fearless. For her *intrepid* conduct nursing the wounded during the war, Florence Nightingale was honored by Queen Victoria.

intricate ADJ. complex; knotty; tangled. Philip spent many hours designing mazes so *intricate* that none of his classmates could solve them. intricacy, N.

intrinsic ADJ. essential; inherent; built-in. Although my grandmother's china has little *intrinsic* value, I shall always cherish it for the memories it evokes.

introspective ADJ. looking within oneself. Though young Francis of Assisi led a wild and worldly life, even then he had *introspective* moments during which he examined his soul.

introvert N. one who is introspective; inclined to think more about oneself. In his poetry, he reveals that he is an *introvert* by his intense interest in his own problems. also V.

intrude V. trespass; enter as an uninvited person. She hesitated to *intrude* on their conversation.

intuition N. immediate insight; power of knowing without reasoning. Even though Tony denied that anything was wrong, Tina trusted her *intuition* that something was bothering him. intuitive, ADJ.

■ **inundate** V. overwhelm; flood; submerge. This semester I am *inundated* with work: You should see the piles of paperwork flooding my desk. Until the great dam was built, the waters of the Nile used to *inundate* the river valley like clockwork every year.

inured ADJ. accustomed; hardened. She became *inured* to the Alaskan cold.

invalidate V. weaken; destroy. The relatives who received little or nothing sought to *invalidate* the will by claiming that the deceased had not been in his right mind when he had signed the document.

invasive ADJ. tending to spread aggressively; intrusive. Giving up our war with the *invasive* blackberry vines that had taken over the back yard, we covered the lawn with concrete. invade, V.

invective N. abuse. He had expected criticism but not the *invective* that greeted his proposal. inveigh, V.

inverse ADJ. opposite. There is an *inverse* ratio between the strength of light and its distance.

■ **invert** V. turn upside down or inside out. When he *inverted* his body in a handstand, he felt the blood rush to his head.

inveterate ADJ. deep-rooted; habitual. An *inveterate* smoker, Bob cannot seem to break the habit, no matter how hard he tries.

invidious ADJ. designed to create ill will or envy. We disregarded her *invidious* remarks because we realized how jealous she was.

invigorate V. energize; stimulate. A quick dip in the pool *invigorated* Meg, and with renewed energy she got back to work.

Word List 27   invincible-laggard

invincible ADJ. unconquerable. Superman is *invincible*.

inviolable ADJ. secure from corruption, attack, or violation; unassailable. Batman considered his oath to keep the people of Gotham City *inviolable*: nothing on earth could make him break this promise.

invocation N. prayer for help; calling upon as a reference or support. The service of Morning Prayer opens with an *invocation* during which we ask God to hear our prayers.

invoke V. call upon; ask for. She *invoked* her advisor's aid in filling out her financial aid forms.

invulnerable ADJ. incapable of injury. Achilles was *invulnerable* except in his heel.

iota N. very small quantity. She hadn't an *iota* of common sense.

irascible ADJ. irritable; easily angered. Miss Minchin's *irascible* temper intimidated the younger schoolgirls, who feared she'd burst into a rage at any moment.

irate ADJ. angry. When John's mother found out he had overdrawn his checking account for the third month in a row, she was so *irate* she could scarcely speak to him.

ire N. anger. The waiter tried unsuccessfully to placate the *ire* of the diner who had found a cockroach in her soup.

iridescent ADJ. exhibiting rainbowlike colors. She admired the *iridescent* hues of the oil that floated on the surface of the water.

irksome ADJ. annoying; tedious. He found working on the assembly line *irksome* because of the monotony of the operation he had to perform. irk, V.

■ **ironic** ADJ. resulting in an unexpected and contrary outcome. It is *ironic* that his success came when he least wanted it.

irony N. hidden sarcasm or satire; use of words that seem to mean the opposite of what they actually mean. Gradually his listeners began to realize that the excessive praise he was lavishing on his opponent was actually *irony*; he was in fact ridiculing the poor fool.

irrational ADJ. illogical; lacking reason; insane. Many people have such an *irrational* fear of snakes that they panic at the sight of a harmless garter snake.

irreconcilable ADJ. incompatible; not able to be resolved. Because the separated couple were *irreconcilable*, the marriage counselor recommended a divorce.

irrefutable ADJ. indisputable; incontrovertible; undeniable. No matter how hard I tried to find a good comeback for her argument, I couldn't think of one: her logic was *irrefutable*.

irrelevant ADJ. not applicable; unrelated. No matter how *irrelevant* the patient's mumblings may seem, they give us some indications of what he has on his mind.

irremediable ADJ. incurable; uncorrectable. The error she made was *irremediable*; she could see no way to repair it.

irreparable ADJ. not able to be corrected or repaired. Your apology cannot atone for the *irreparable* damage you have done to her reputation.

irrepressible ADJ. unable to be restrained or held back. My friend Kitty's curiosity was *irrepressible*: she poked her nose into everybody's business and just laughed when I warned her that curiosity killed the cat.

● **irreproachable** ADJ. blameless; impeccable. Homer's conduct at the office party was *irreproachable*; even Marge didn't have anything bad to say about how he behaved.

irresolute ADJ. uncertain how to act; weak. Once you have made your decision, don't waver; a leader should never appear *irresolute*.

irretrievable ADJ. impossible to recover or regain; irreparable. The left fielder tried to retrieve the ball, but it flew over the fence, bounced off a wall, and fell into the sewer: it was *irretrievable*.

irreverence N. lack of proper respect. Some audience members were amused by the *irreverence* of the comedian's jokes about the Pope; others felt offended by his lack of respect for their faith. irreverent, ADJ.

irrevocable ADJ. unalterable; irreversible. As Sue dropped the "Dear John" letter into the mailbox, she suddenly had second thoughts and wanted to take it back, but she could not: her action was *irrevocable*.

itinerant ADJ. wandering; traveling. He was an *itinerant* peddler and traveled through Pennsylvania and Virginia selling his wares. also N.

itinerary N. plan of a trip. Disliking sudden changes in plans when she traveled abroad, Ethel refused to make any alterations in her *itinerary*.

jabber V. chatter rapidly or unintelligibly. Why does the fellow insist on *jabbering* away in French when I can't understand a word he says?

jaded ADJ. fatigued; surfeited. He looked for exotic foods to stimulate his *jaded* appetite.

jargon N. language used by a special group; technical terminology; gibberish. The computer salesmen at the store used a *jargon* of their own that we simply couldn't follow; we had no idea what they were jabbering about.

jaundiced ADJ. prejudiced (envious, hostile or resentful); yellowed. Because Sue disliked Carolyn, she looked at Carolyn's paintings with a *jaundiced* eye, calling them formless smears. Newborn infants afflicted with *jaundice* look slightly yellow: they have *jaundiced* skin.

jaunt N. trip; short journey. He took a quick *jaunt* to Atlantic City.

jaunty ADJ. lighthearted; animated; easy and carefree. In *An American in Paris*, Gene Kelly sang and danced his way through "Singing in the Rain" in a properly *jaunty* style.

jeopardize V. endanger; imperil; put at risk. You can't give me a D in chemistry: you'll *jeopardize* my chances of getting into M.I.T. jeopardy, N.

jettison V. throw overboard. In order to enable the ship to ride safely through the storm, the captain had to *jettison* much of his cargo.

jingoist N. extremely aggressive and militant patriot; warlike chauvinist. Always bellowing "America first!," the congressman was such a *jingoist* you could almost hear the sabers rattling as he marched down the halls. jingoism, N.

jocose ADJ. given to joking. The salesman was so *jocose* that many of his customers suggested that he become a "stand-up" comic.

● **jocular** ADJ. said or done in jest. Although Bill knew the boss hated jokes, he couldn't resist making one *jocular* remark.

jollity N. gaiety; cheerfulness. The festive Christmas dinner was a merry one, and old and young alike joined in the general *jollity*.

jostle V. shove; bump. In the subway he was *jostled* by the crowds.

jovial ADJ. good-natured; merry. A frown seemed out of place on his invariably *jovial* face.

jubilation N. rejoicing. There was great *jubilation* when the armistice was announced. jubilant, ADJ.

judicious ADJ. sound in judgment; wise. At a key moment in his life, he made a *judicious* investment that was the foundation of his later wealth.

juncture N. crisis; joining point. At this critical *juncture*, let us think carefully before determining the course we shall follow.

junta N. group of men joined in political intrigue; cabal. As soon as he learned of its existence, the dictator ordered the execution of all of the members of the *junta*.

jurisprudence N. science of law. He was more a student of *jurisprudence* than a practitioner of the law.

justification N. good or just reason; defense; excuse. The jury found him guilty of the more serious charge because they could see no possible *justification* for his actions.

kaleidoscope N. tube in which patterns made by the reflection in mirrors of colored pieces of glass, etc., produce interesting symmetrical effects. People found a new source of entertainment while peering through the *kaleidoscope*; they found the ever-changing patterns fascinating.

kernel N. central or vital part; whole seed (as of corn). "Watson, buried within this tissue of lies there is a *kernel* of truth; when I find it, the mystery will be solved."

killjoy N. grouch; spoilsport. At breakfast we had all been enjoying our bacon and eggs until that *killjoy* John started talking about how bad animal fats were for our health.

kindle V. start a fire; inspire. One of the first things Ben learned in the Boy Scouts was how to *kindle* a fire by rubbing two dry sticks together. Her teacher's praise for her poetry *kindled* a spark of hope inside Maya.

kindred ADJ. related; belonging to the same family. Tom Sawyer and Huck Finn were two *kindred* spirits. also N.

kinetic ADJ. producing motion. Designers of the electric automobile find that their greatest obstacle lies in the development of light and efficient storage batteries, the source of the *kinetic* energy needed to propel the vehicle.

kleptomaniac N. person who has a compulsive desire to steal. They discovered that the wealthy customer was a *kleptomaniac* when they caught her stealing some cheap trinkets.

knave N. untrustworthy person; rogue; scoundrel. Any politician nicknamed Tricky Dick clearly has the reputation of a *knave*. knavery, N.

knit V. contract into wrinkles; grow together. Whenever David worries, his brow *knits* in a frown. When he broke his leg, he sat around the house all day waiting for the bones to *knit*.

knoll N. little round hill. Robert Louis Stevenson's grave is on a *knoll* in Samoa; to reach the grave site, you must climb uphill and walk a short distance along a marked path.

knotty ADJ. intricate; difficult; tangled. What to Watson had been a *knotty* problem, to Sherlock Holmes was simplicity itself.

kudos N. honor; glory; praise. The singer complacently received *kudos* from his entourage on his performance.

laborious ADJ. demanding much work or care; tedious. In putting together his dictionary of the English language, Doctor Johnson undertook a *laborious* task.

● **labyrinth** N. maze. Hiding from Indian Joe, Tom and Becky soon lost themselves in the *labyrinth* of secret underground caves. labyrinthine, ADJ.

laceration N. torn, ragged wound. The stock car driver needed stitches to close up the *lacerations* he received in the car crash.

lachrymose ADJ. producing tears. His voice has a *lachrymose* quality more appropriate to a funeral than a class reunion.

lackadaisical ADJ. lacking purpose or zest; halfhearted; languid. Because Gatsby had his mind more on his love life than on his finances, he did a very *lackadaisical* job of managing his money.

lackluster ADJ. dull. We were disappointed by the *lackluster* performance.

● **laconic** ADJ. brief and to the point. Many of the characters portrayed by Clint Eastwood are *laconic* types: strong men of few words.

● **laggard** ADJ. slow; sluggish. The sailor had been taught not to be *laggard* in carrying out orders. lag, N., V.

Word List 28   lament-low

■ **lament** V. grieve; express sorrow. Even advocates of the war *lamented* the loss of so many lives in combat. lamentation, N.

● **lampoon** V. ridicule. This article *lampoons* the pretensions of some movie moguls. also N.

languid ADJ. weary; sluggish; listless. Her siege of illness left her *languid* and pallid.

languish V. lose animation; lose strength. Left at Miss Minchin's school for girls while her father went off to war, Sarah Crewe refused to *languish*; instead, she hid her grief and actively befriended her less fortunate classmates.

languor N. lassitude; depression. His friends tried to overcome the *languor* into which he had fallen by taking him to parties and to the theater.

lap V. take in food or drink with one's tongue; splash gently. The kitten neatly *lapped* up her milk. The waves softly *lapped* against the pier.

larceny N. theft. Because of the prisoner's record, the district attorney refused to reduce the charge from grand *larceny* to petty *larceny*.

larder N. pantry; place where food is kept. The first thing Bill did on returning home from school was to check what snacks his mother had in the *larder*.

largess N. generous gift. Lady Bountiful distributed *largess* to the poor.

● **lassitude** N. languor; weariness. After a massage and a long soak in the hot tub, I gave in to my growing *lassitude* and lay down for a nap.

latent ADJ. potential but undeveloped; dormant; hidden. Polaroid pictures are popular at parties, because you can see the *latent* photographic image gradually appear before your eyes.

lateral ADJ. coming from the side. In order to get good plant growth, the gardener must pinch off all *lateral* shoots.

latitude N. freedom from narrow limitations. I think you have permitted your son too much *latitude* in this matter.

■ **laud** V. praise. The NFL *lauded* Boomer Esiason's efforts to raise money to combat cystic fibrosis. laudable, laudatory, ADJ.

■ **lavish** ADJ. liberal; wasteful. The actor's *lavish* gifts pleased her. also V.

lax ADJ. careless. We dislike restaurants where the service is *lax* and inattentive.

leaven V. cause to rise or grow lighter; enliven. As bread dough is *leavened*, it puffs up, expanding in volume.

lechery N. lustfulness; impurity in thought and deed. In his youth he led a life of *lechery* and debauchery; he did not mend his ways until middle age. lecherous, ADJ.

leery ADJ. suspicious; cautious. Don't eat the sushi at this restaurant; I'm a bit *leery* about how fresh the raw fish is.

legacy N. a gift made by a will. Part of my *legacy* from my parents is an album of family photographs.

legend N. explanatory list of symbols on a map. The *legend* at the bottom of the map made it clear which symbols stood for rest areas along the highway and which stood for public camp sites. (secondary meaning)

legerdemain N. sleight of hand. The magician demonstrated his renowned *legerdemain*.

leniency N. mildness; permissiveness. Considering the gravity of the offense, we were surprised by the *leniency* of the sentence.

lethal ADJ. deadly. It is unwise to leave *lethal* weapons where children may find them.

■ **lethargic** ADJ. drowsy; dull. The stuffy room made her *lethargic*: she felt as if she was about to nod off.

levitate V. float in the air (especially by magical means). As the magician passed his hands over the recumbent body of his assistant, she appeared to rise and *levitate* about three feet above the table.

■ **levity** N. lack of seriousness; lightness. Stop giggling and wriggling around in the pew: such *levity* is improper in church.

levy V. impose (a fine); collect (a payment). Crying "No taxation without representation," the colonists demonstrated against England's power to *levy* taxes.

lewd ADJ. lustful. They found his *lewd* stories objectionable.

lexicographer N. compiler of a dictionary. The new dictionary is the work of many *lexicographers* who spent years compiling and editing the work.

lexicon N. dictionary. I cannot find this word in any *lexicon* in the library.

liability N. drawback; debts. Her lack of an extensive vocabulary was a *liability* that she was eventually able to overcome.

liaison N. contact keeping parts of an organization in communication; go-between; secret love affair. As the *liaison* between the American and British forces during World War II, the colonel had to ease tensions between the leaders of the two armies. Romeo's romantic *liaison* with Juliet ended in tragedy.

libel N. defamatory statement; act of writing something that smears a person's character. If Batman wrote that the Joker was a dirty, rotten, mass-murdering criminal, could the Joker sue Batman for *libel*?

liberator N. one who sets free. Simon Bolivar, who led the South American colonies in their rebellion against Spanish rule, is known as the great *liberator*. liberate, V.

libretto N. text of an opera. The composer of an opera's music is remembered more frequently than the author of its *libretto*.

licentious ADJ. amoral; lewd and lascivious; unrestrained. Unscrupulously seducing the daughter of his host, Don Juan felt no qualms about the immorality of his *licentious* behavior.

lilliputian ADJ. extremely small. Tiny and delicate, the model was built on a *lilliputian* scale. also N.

limber ADJ. flexible. Hours of ballet classes kept him *limber*.

limerick N. humorous short verse. The *limerick* form is the best; its meter is pure anapest. A *limerick's* fun for most everyone, and the word may occur on your test.

limpid ADJ. clear. A *limpid* stream ran through his property.

linchpin N. something that holds or links various parts together. The *linchpin* in the district attorney's case was a photograph showing the defendant shaking hands with the hired killer.

lineage N. descent; ancestry. He traced his *lineage* back to Mayflower days.

■ **linger** V. loiter or dawdle; continue or persist. Hoping to see Juliet pass by, Romeo *lingered* outside the Capulet house for hours. Though Mother made stuffed cabbage on Monday, the smell *lingered* around the house for days.

linguistic ADJ. pertaining to language. The modern tourist will encounter very little *linguistic* difficulty as English has become an almost universal language.

liniment N. ointment; lotion; salve. The trainer carefully applied the *liniment* to the quarterback's bruise, gently rubbing it into the skin.

lionize V. treat as a celebrity. She enjoyed being *lionized* and adored by the public.

liquidate V. settle accounts; clearup. He was able to *liquidate* all his debts in a short period of time.

list V. tilt; lean over. That flagpole should be absolutely vertical; instead, it *lists* to one side. (secondary meaning)

■ **listless** ADJ. lacking in spirit or energy. We had expected him to be full of enthusiasm and were surprised by his *listless* attitude.

litany N. supplicatory prayer. On this solemn day, the congregation responded to the prayers of the priest during the *litany* with fervor and intensity.

● **lithe** ADJ. flexible; supple. Her figure was *lithe* and willowy.

litigation N. lawsuit. Try to settle this amicably; I do not want to become involved in *litigation.* litigant, N.

livid ADJ. lead-colored; black and blue; enraged. His face was so *livid* with rage that we were afraid that he might have an attack of apoplexy.

loath ADJ. reluctant; disinclined. Romeo and Juliet were both *loath* for him to go.

loathe V. detest. Booing and hissing, the audience showed how much they *loathed* the wicked villain.

■ **lofty** ADJ. very high. Though Barbara Jordan's fellow students used to tease her about her *lofty* ambitions, she rose to hold one of the highest positions in the land.

log N. record of a voyage or flight; record of day to day activities. "Flogged two seamen today for insubordination" wrote Captain Bligh in the *Bounty's log*. To see how much work I've accomplished recently, just take a look at the number of new files listed on my computer *log*.

loiter V. hang around; linger. The policeman told him not to *loiter* in the alley.

loll V. lounge about. They *lolled* around in their chairs watching television.

longevity N. long life. When he reached ninety, the old man was proud of his *longevity*.

loom V. appear or take shape (usually in an enlarged or distorted form). The shadow of the gallows *loomed* threateningly above the small boy.

lope v. gallop slowly. As the horses *loped* along, we had an opportunity to admire the ever-changing scenery.

loquacious ADJ. talkative. Though our daughter barely says a word to us these days, put a phone in her hand and see how *loquacious* she can be: our phone bills are out of sight! loquacity, N.

lout N. clumsy person. That awkward *lout* dropped my priceless vase!

low v. moo. From the hilltop, they could see the herd like ants in the distance; they could barely hear the cattle *low*.

Word List 29   lucid-maul

lucid ADJ. easily understood; clear; intelligible. Ellen makes an excellent teacher: her explanations of technical points are *lucid* enough for a child to grasp.

lucrative ADJ. profitable. He turned his hobby into a *lucrative* profession.

ludicrous ADJ. laughable; trifling. Let us be serious; this is not a *ludicrous* issue.

lugubrious ADJ. mournful. The *lugubrious* howling of the dogs added to our sadness.

lull N. moment of calm. Not wanting to get wet, they waited under the awning for a *lull* in the rain.

lull v. soothe; cause one to relax one's guard; subside. The mother's gentle song *lulled* the child to sleep. Malcolm tried to come up with a plausible story to *lull* his mother's suspicions, but she didn't believe a word he said.

lumber v. move heavily or clumsily. Still somewhat torpid after its long hibernation, the bear *lumbered* through the woods.

luminary N. celebrity; dignitary. A leading light of the American stage, Ethel Barrymore was a theatrical *luminary* whose name lives on.

luminous ADJ. shining; issuing light. The sun is a *luminous* body.

lummox N. big, clumsy, often stupid person. Because he was highly overweight and looked ungainly, John Candy often was cast as a slow-witted *lummox*.

lunar ADJ. pertaining to the moon. *Lunar* craters can be plainly seen with the aid of a small telescope.

lunge v. quick forward dive or reach; thrust. The wide receiver *lunged* forward to grab the football. With his sword, Dartagnan *lunged* at his adversary.

● **lurid** ADJ. wild; sensational; graphic; gruesome. Do the *lurid* cover stories in the *Enquirer* actually attract people to buy that trashy tabloid?

lurk v. stealthily lie in waiting; slink; exist unperceived. "Who knows what evil *lurks* in the hearts of men? The Shadow knows."

luscious ADJ. pleasing to taste or smell. The ripe peach was *luscious*.

luster N. shine; gloss. The soft *luster* of the silk in the dim light was pleasing.

lustrous ADJ. shining. Her large and *lustrous* eyes lent a touch of beauty to an otherwise plain face.

● **luxuriant** ADJ. abundant; rich and splendid; fertile. Lady Godiva was completely covered by her *luxuriant* hair.

machinations N. evil schemes or plots. Fortunately, Batman saw through the wily *machinations* of the Riddler and saved Gotham City from destruction by the forces of evil.

madrigal N. pastoral song. His program of folk songs included several *madrigals* which he sang to the accompaniment of a lute.

maelstrom N. whirlpool. The canoe was tossed about in the *maelstrom*.

magnanimous ADJ. generous; great-hearted. Philanthropists by definition are *magnanimous*; misers, by definition, are not. Cordelia was too *magnanimous* to resent her father's unkindness to her; instead, she generously forgave him. magnanimity, N.

magnate N. person of prominence or influence. Growing up in Pittsburgh, Annie Dillard was surrounded by the mansions of the great steel and coal *magnates* who set their mark on that city.

magnitude N. greatness; extent. It is difficult to comprehend the *magnitude* of his crime.

maim v. mutilate; injure. The hospital could not take care of all who had been wounded or *maimed* in the railroad accident.

maladroit ADJ. clumsy; bungling. How *maladroit* it was of me to mention seeing you out partying last night! From the look on his face, I take it that your boyfriend thought you were otherwise occupied.

malady N. illness. A mysterious *malady* swept the country, filling doctors' offices with feverish, purple-spotted patients.

malaise N. uneasiness; vague feeling of ill health. Feeling slightly queasy before going onstage, Carol realized that this touch of *malaise* was merely stage fright.

malapropism N. comic misuse of a word. When Mrs. Malaprop accuses Lydia of being "as headstrong as an allegory on the banks of the Nile," she confuses "allegory" and "alligator" in a typical *malapropism*.

malcontent N. person dissatisfied with existing state of affairs. One of the few *malcontents* in Congress, he constantly voiced his objections to the presidential program. also ADJ.

malediction N. curse. When the magic mirror revealed that Snow White was still alive, the wicked queen cried out in rage and uttered dreadful *maledictions*.

malefactor N. evildoer; criminal. Mighty Mouse will save the day, hunting down *malefactors* and rescuing innocent mice from peril.

malevolent ADJ. wishing evil. Iago is a *malevolent* villain who takes pleasure in ruining Othello.

malfeasance N. wrongdoing. The authorities did not discover the campaign manager's *malfeasance* until after he had spent most of the money he had embezzled.

■ **malicious** ADJ. hateful; spiteful. Jealous of Cinderella's beauty, her *malicious* stepsisters expressed their spite by forcing her to do menial tasks. malice, N.

malign V. speak evil of; bad-mouth; defame. Putting her hands over her ears, Rose refused to listen to Betty *malign* her friend Susan.

malignant ADJ. injurious; tending to cause death; aggressively malevolent. Though many tumors are benign, some are *malignant*, growing out of control and endangering the life of the patient.

malingerer N. one who feigns illness to escape duty. The captain ordered the sergeant to punish all *malingerers* and force them to work. malinger, V.

malleable ADJ. capable of being shaped by pounding; impressionable. Gold is a *malleable* metal, easily shaped into bracelets and rings. Fagin hoped Oliver was a *malleable* lad, easily shaped into a thief.

malodorous ADJ. foul-smelling. The compost heap was most *malodorous* in summer.

mammal N. a vertebrate animal whose female suckles its young. Many people regard the whale as a fish and do not realize that it is a *mammal.*

mammoth ADJ. gigantic; enormous. To try to memorize every word on this vocabulary list would be a *mammoth* undertaking; take on projects that are more manageable in size.

mandate N. order; charge. In his inaugural address, the president stated that he had a *mandate* from the people to seek an end to social evils such as poverty. also V.

mandatory ADJ. obligatory. These instructions are *mandatory*; any violation will be severely punished.

maniacal ADJ. raging mad; insane. Though Mr. Rochester had locked his mad wife in the attic, he could still hear her *maniacal* laughter echoing throughout the house.

manifest ADJ. evident; visible; obvious. Digby's embarrassment when he met Madonna was *manifest*: his ears turned bright pink, he kept scuffing one shoe in the dirt, and he couldn't look her in the eye.

manifesto N. declaration; statement of policy. The *Communist Manifesto* by Marx and Engels proclaimed the principles of modern communism.

manipulate V. operate with one's hands; control or play upon (people, forces, etc.) artfully. Jim Henson understood how to *manipulate* the Muppets. Madonna understands how to *manipulate* men (and publicity).

mannered ADJ. affected; not natural. Attempting to copy the style of his wealthy neighbors, Gatsby adopted a *mannered*, artificial way of speech.

marital ADJ. pertaining to marriage. After the publication of his book on *marital* affairs, he was often consulted by married people on the verge of divorce.

maritime ADJ. bordering on the sea; nautical. The *Maritime* Provinces depend on the sea for their wealth.

marked ADJ. noticeable or pronounced; targeted for vengeance. He walked with a *marked* limp, a souvenir of an old I.R.A. attack. As British ambassador, he knew he was a *marked* man, for he knew the Irish Republican Army wanted him dead.

marquee N. canopy above an entrance, under which one can take shelter; rooflike shelter above a theater entrance. On stormy days, the hotel doorman keeps dry by standing directly beneath the *marquee.* The title of Arthur Kopit's play *Oh Dad, Poor Dad, Momma's Hung You in the Closet and I'm Feeling So Sad* was too long to fit on the *marquee.*

■ **marred** ADJ. damaged; disfigured. She had to refinish the *marred* surface of the table. mar, V.

marshal V. put in order. At a debate tournament, extemporaneous speakers have only a minute or two to *marshal* their thoughts before they address their audience.

marsupial N. one of a family of mammals that nurse their offspring in a pouch. The most common *marsupial* in North America is the opossum.

martial ADJ. warlike. The sound of *martial* music inspired the young cadet with dreams of military glory.

martinet N. strict disciplinarian. No talking at meals! No mingling with the servants! Miss Minchin was a *martinet* who insisted that the schoolgirls in her charge observe each regulation to the letter.

martyr N. one who voluntarily suffers death for his or her religion or cause; great sufferer. By burning her at the stake, the English made Joan of Arc a *martyr* for her faith. Mother played the *martyr* by staying home cleaning the house while the rest of the family went off to the beach.

masochist N. person who enjoys his own pain. The *masochist* begs, "Hit me." The sadist smiles and says, "I won't."

material ADJ. made of physical matter; unspiritual; important. Probing the mysteries of this *material* world has always fascinated physicist George Whitesides. Reporters nicknamed Madonna the *Material* Girl because, despite her name, she seemed wholly uninterested in spiritual values. Lexy's active participation made a *material* difference to the success of the fund-raiser.

■ **materialism** N. preoccupation with physical comforts and things. By its nature, *materialism* is opposed to idealism, for where the materialist emphasizes the needs of the body, the idealist emphasizes the needs of the soul.

maternal ADJ. motherly. Many animals display *maternal* instincts only while their offspring are young and helpless.

matriarch N. woman who rules a family or larger social group. The *matriarch* ruled her gypsy tribe with a firm hand.

matriculate V. enroll (in college or graduate school). Incoming students formally *matriculate* at our college in a special ceremony during which they sign the official register of students.

maudlin ADJ. effusively sentimental. Whenever a particularly *maudlin* tearjerker was playing at the movies, Marvin would embarrass himself by weeping copiously.

maul V. handle roughly. The rock star was *mauled* by his over-excited fans.

Word List 30   maverick-misrepresent

maverick   N. rebel; nonconformist. To the masculine literary establishment, George Sand with her insistence on wearing trousers and smoking cigars was clearly a *maverick* who fought her proper womanly role.

mawkish   ADJ. mushy and gushy; icky-sticky sentimental; maudlin. Whenever Gigi and her boyfriend would sigh and get all lovey-dovey, her little brother would shout, "Yuck!" protesting their *mawkish* behavior.

maxim   N. proverb; a truth pithily stated. Aesop's fables illustrate moral *maxims*.

meager   ADJ. scanty; inadequate. Still hungry after his *meager* serving of porridge, Oliver Twist asked for a second helping.

● **meander**   V. wind or turn in its course. Needing to stay close to a source of water, he followed every twist and turn of the stream as it *meandered* through the countryside.

meddlesome   ADJ. interfering. He felt his marriage was suffering because of his *meddlesome* mother-in-law.

mediate   V. settle a dispute through the services of an outsider. King Solomon was asked to *mediate* a dispute between two women, each of whom claimed to be the mother of the same child.

mediocre   ADJ. ordinary; commonplace. We were disappointed because he gave a rather *mediocre* performance in this role.

meditation   N. reflection; thought. She reached her decision only after much *meditation*.

medley   N. mixture. To avoid boring dancers by playing any one tune for too long, bands may combine three or four tunes into a *medley*.

meek   ADJ. quiet and obedient; spiritless. Can Lois Lane see through Superman's disguise and spot the superhero hiding behind the guise of *meek*, timorous Clark Kent? Mr. Barrett never expected his *meek* daughter would dare to defy him by eloping with her suitor.

melancholy   ADJ. gloomy; morose; blue. To Eugene, stuck in his small town, a train whistle was a *melancholy* sound, for it made him think of all the places he would never get to see.

mellifluous   ADJ. sweetly or smoothly flowing; melodious. Italian is a *mellifluous* language, especially suited to being sung.

membrane   N. thin soft sheet of animal or vegetable tissue. Each individual section of an orange is covered with a thin, transparent *membrane*. membranous, ADJ.

memento   N. token; reminder. Take this book as a *memento* of your visit.

menagerie   N. collection of wild animals. Whenever the children run wild around the house, Mom shouts, "Calm down! I'm not running a *menagerie*!"

mendacious   ADJ. lying; habitually dishonest. Distrusting Huck from the start, Miss Watson assumed he was *mendacious* and refused to believe a word he said.

mendicant   N. beggar. "O noble sir, give alms to the poor," cried Aladdin, playing the *mendicant*.

menial   ADJ. suitable for servants; lowly; mean. Her wicked stepmother forced Cinderella to do *menial* tasks around the house while her ugly stepsisters lolled around painting their toenails.

mentor   N. teacher. During this very trying period, she could not have had a better *mentor*, for the teacher was sympathetic and understanding.

● **mercenary**   ADJ. interested in money or gain. Andy's every act was prompted by *mercenary* motives: his first question was always "What's in it for me?"

● **mercurial**   ADJ. capricious; changing; fickle. Quick as quicksilver to change, he was *mercurial* in nature and therefore unreliable.

merger   N. combination (of two business corporations). When the firm's president married the director of financial planning, the office joke was that it wasn't a marriage, it was a *merger*.

mesmerize   V. hypnotize. The incessant drone seemed to *mesmerize* him and place him in a trance.

metallurgical   ADJ. pertaining to the art of removing metals from ores. During the course of his *metallurgical* research, the scientist developed a steel alloy of tremendous strength.

metamorphosis   N. change of form; major transformation. The *metamorphosis* of caterpillar to butterfly is typical of many such changes in animal life. metamorphose, V.

metaphor   N. implied comparison. "He soared like an eagle" is an example of a simile; "He is an eagle in flight," a *metaphor*.

metaphysical   ADJ. pertaining to speculative philosophy. The modern poets have gone back to the fanciful poems of the *metaphysical* poets of the seventeenth century for many of their images. metaphysics, N.

■ **methodical**   ADJ. systematic. An accountant must be *methodical* and maintain order among his financial records.

■ **meticulous**   ADJ. excessively careful; painstaking; scrupulous. Martha Stewart was a *meticulous* housekeeper, fussing about each and every detail that went into making up her perfect home.

metropolis   N. large city. Every evening the terminal is filled with thousands of commuters going from this *metropolis* to their homes in the suburbs.

mettle   N. courage; spirit. When challenged by the other horses in the race, the thoroughbred proved its *mettle* by its determination to hold the lead.

miasma   N. swamp gas; heavy, vaporous atmosphere, often emanating from decaying matter; pervasive corrupting influence. The smog hung over Victorian London like a dark cloud; noisome, reeking of decay, it was a visible *miasma*.

microcosm   N. small world; the world in miniature. The small village community that Jane Austen depicts serves as a *microcosm* of English society in her time, for in this small world we see all the social classes meeting and mingling.

migrant ADJ. changing its habitat; wandering. These *migrant* birds return every spring. also N.

migratory ADJ. wandering. The return of the *migratory* birds to the northern sections of this country is a harbinger of spring. migrate, V.

milieu N. environment; means of expression. Surrounded by smooth preppies and arty bohemians, the country boy from Smalltown, USA, felt out of his *milieu*. Although he has produced excellent oil paintings and lithographs, his proper *milieu* is watercolor.

militant ADJ. combative; bellicose. Although at this time he was advocating a policy of neutrality, one could usually find him adopting a more *militant* attitude. also N.

mimicry N. imitation. Her gift for *mimicry* was so great that her friends said that she should be in the theater.

mincing ADJ. affectedly dainty. Yum-Yum walked across the stage with *mincing* steps.

minuscule ADJ. extremely small. Why should I involve myself with a project with so *minuscule* a chance for success?

minute ADJ. extremely small. The twins resembled one another closely; only *minute* differences set them apart.

minutiae N. petty details. She would have liked to ignore the *minutiae* of daily living.

mirage N. unreal reflection; optical illusion. The lost prospector was fooled by a *mirage* in the desert.

mire V. entangle; stick in swampy ground. Their rear wheels became *mired* in mud. also N.

● **mirth** N. merriment; laughter. Sober Malvolio found Sir Toby's *mirth* improper.

● **misanthrope** N. one who hates mankind. In *Gulliver's Travels*, Swift portrays an image of humanity as vile, degraded beasts; for this reason, various critics consider him a *misanthrope*.

misapprehension N. error; misunderstanding. To avoid *misapprehension,* I am going to ask all of you to repeat the instructions I have given.

miscellany N. mixture of writings on various subjects. This is an interesting *miscellany* of nineteenth-century prose and poetry.

mischance N. ill luck. By *mischance,* he lost his week's salary.

misconception N. mistaken idea. "Sir, you are suffering from a *misconception*. I do not wish to marry you in the least!"

misconstrue V. interpret incorrectly; misjudge. She took the passage seriously rather than humorously because she *misconstrued* the author's ironic tone.

misdemeanor N. minor crime. The culprit pleaded guilty to a *misdemeanor* rather than face trial for a felony.

■ **miserly** ADJ. stingy; mean. Transformed by his vision on Christmas Eve, mean old Scrooge ceased being *miserly* and became a generous, kind old man.

misgivings N. doubts. Hamlet described his *misgivings* to Horatio but decided to fence with Laertes despite his foreboding of evil.

mishap N. accident. With a little care you could have avoided this *mishap*.

● **misnomer** N. wrong name; incorrect designation. His tyrannical conduct proved to all that his nickname, King Eric the Just, was a *misnomer*.

misrepresent V. give a false or incorrect impression, often deliberately; serve unsatisfactorily as a representative. In his job application, Milton *misrepresented* his academic background; he was fired when his employers discovered the truth. The reformers accused Senator Gunbucks of *misrepresenting* his constituents and claimed he took bribes from the NRA.

Word List 31 missile-natty

missile N. object to be thrown or projected. After carefully folding his book report into a paper airplane, Beavis threw the *missile* across the classroom at Butthead. Rocket scientists are building guided *missiles*; Beavis and Butthead can barely make unguided ones.

missive N. letter. The ambassador received a *missive* from the secretary of state.

mite N. very small object or creature; small coin. Gnats are annoying *mites* that sting.

■ **mitigate** V. appease; moderate. Nothing Jason did could *mitigate* Medea's anger; she refused to forgive him for betraying her.

mnemonic ADJ. pertaining to memory. He used *mnemonic* tricks to master new words.

mobile ADJ. movable; not fixed. The *mobile* blood bank operated by the Red Cross visited our neighborhood today. mobility, N.

mock V. ridicule; imitate, often in derision. It is unkind to *mock* anyone; it is stupid to *mock* anyone significantly bigger than you. mockery, N.

mode N. prevailing style; manner; way of doing something. The rock star had to have her hair done in the latest *mode*: frizzed, with occasional moussed spikes for variety. Henry plans to adopt a simpler *mode* of life: he is going to become a mushroom hunter and live off the land.

modicum N. limited quantity. Although his story is based on a *modicum* of truth, most of the events he describes are fictitious.

modulate V. tone down in intensity; regulate; change from one key to another. Always singing at the top of her lungs, the budding Brunhilde never learned to *modulate* her voice.

molecule N. the smallest particle (one or more atoms) of a substance, having all the properties of that substance. In chemistry, we study how atoms and *molecules* react to form new substances.

● **mollify**   v. soothe. The airline customer service representative tried to *mollify* the angry passenger by offering her a seat in first class.

molt   v. shed or cast off hair or feathers. When Molly's canary *molted*, he shed feathers all over the house.

molten   ADJ. melted. The city of Pompeii was destroyed by volcanic ash rather than by *molten* lava flowing from Mount Vesuvius.

momentous   ADJ. very important. When Marie and Pierre Curie discovered radium, they had no idea of the *momentous* impact their discovery would have upon society.

momentum   N. quantity of motion of a moving body; impetus. The car lost *momentum* as it tried to ascend the steep hill.

monarchy   N. government under a single ruler. Though England today is a *monarchy*, there is some question whether it will be one in twenty years, given the present discontent at the prospect of Prince Charles as king.

monastic   ADJ. related to monks or monasteries; removed from worldly concerns. Withdrawing from the world, Thomas Merton joined a contemplative religious order and adopted the *monastic* life.

monetary   ADJ. pertaining to money. Jane held the family purse strings: she made all *monetary* decisions affecting the household.

monochromatic   ADJ. having only one color. Most people who are color blind actually can distinguish several colors; some, however, have a truly *monochromatic* view of a world all in shades of gray.

monolithic   ADJ. solidly uniform; unyielding. Knowing the importance of appearing resolute, the patriots sought to present a *monolithic* front.

monosyllabic   ADJ. having only one syllable. No matter what he was asked, the taciturn New Englander answered with a *monosyllabic* "Yep" or "Nope." monosyllable, N.

monotony   N. sameness leading to boredom. What could be more deadly dull than the *monotony* of punching numbers into a computer hour after hour?

montage   N. photographic composition combining elements from different sources. In one early *montage*, Beauchamp brought together pictures of broken mannequins and newspaper clippings about the Vietnam War.

monumental   ADJ. massive. Writing a dictionary is a *monumental* task.

moodiness   N. fits of depression or gloom. Her recurrent *moodiness* left her feeling as if she had fallen into a black hole.

moratorium   N. legal delay of payment. If we declare a *moratorium* and delay collection of debts for six months, I am sure the farmers will be able to meet their bills.

morbid   ADJ. given to unwholesome thought; moody; characteristic of disease. People who come to disaster sites just to peer at the grisly wreckage are indulging their *morbid* curiosity.

mores   N. conventions; moral standards; customs. In America, Benazir Bhutto dressed as Western women did; in Pakistan, however, she followed the *mores* of her people, dressing in traditional veil and robes.

moribund   ADJ. dying. Hearst took a *moribund*, failing weekly newspaper and transformed it into one of the liveliest, most profitable daily papers around.

■ **morose**   ADJ. ill-humored; sullen; melancholy. Forced to take early retirement, Bill acted *morose* for months; then, all of a sudden, he shook off his sullen mood and was his usual cheerful self.

mortician   N. undertaker. The *mortician* prepared the corpse for burial.

mortify   v. humiliate; punish the flesh. She was so *mortified* by her blunder that she ran to her room in tears.

● **mosaic**   N. picture made of colorful small inlaid tiles. The mayor compared the city to a beautiful *mosaic* made up of people of every race and religion on earth.

mote   N. small speck. The tiniest *mote* in the eye is very painful.

motif   N. theme. This simple *motif* runs throughout the entire score.

motley   ADJ. multi-colored; mixed. The jester wore a *motley* tunic, red and green and blue and gold all patched together haphazardly. Captain Ahab had gathered a *motley* crew to sail the vessel: old sea dogs and runaway boys, pillars of the church and drunkards, even a tattooed islander who terrified the rest of the crew.

mottled   ADJ. blotched in coloring; spotted. When old Falstaff blushed, his face was *mottled* with embarrassment, all pink and purple and red.

muddle   v. confuse; mix up. His thoughts were *muddled* and chaotic. also N.

muggy   ADJ. warm and damp. August in New York City is often *muggy*.

multifaceted   ADJ. having many aspects. A *multifaceted* composer, Roger Davidson has recorded original pieces that range from ragtime tangos to choral masses.

multifarious   ADJ. varied; greatly diversified. A career woman and mother, she was constantly busy with the *multifarious* activities of her daily life.

multiform   ADJ. having many forms. Snowflakes are *multiform* but always hexagonal.

multilingual   ADJ. having many languages. Because they are bordered by so many countries, the Swiss people are *multilingual*.

multiplicity   N. state of being numerous. He was appalled by the *multiplicity* of details he had to complete before setting out on his mission.

■ **mundane**   ADJ. worldly as opposed to spiritual; everyday. Uninterested in philosophical or spiritual discussions, Tom talked only of *mundane* matters such as the daily weather forecast or the latest basketball results.

● **munificent**   ADJ. very generous. Shamelessly fawning over a particularly generous donor, the dean kept on referring to her as "our *munificent* benefactor." munificence, N.

mural N. wall painting. The walls of the Chicano Community Center are covered with *murals* painted in the style of Diego Rivera, the great Mexican artist.

murky ADJ. dark and gloomy; thick with fog; vague. The *murky* depths of the swamp were so dark that one couldn't tell the vines and branches from the snakes.

muse V. ponder. For a moment he *mused* about the beauty of the scene, but his thoughts soon changed as he recalled his own personal problems. also N.

mushroom V. expand or grow rapidly. Between 1990 and 1999, the population of Silicon Valley *mushroomed*; with the rapidly increasing demand for housing, home prices skyrocketed as well.

musky ADJ. having the odor of musk. She left a trace of *musky* perfume behind her.

muster V. gather; assemble. Washington *mustered* his forces at Trenton. also N.

musty ADJ. stale; spoiled by age. The attic was dark and *musty*.

mutability N. ability to change in form; fickleness. Going from rags to riches, and then back to rags again, the bankrupt financier was a victim of the *mutability* of fortune.

muted ADJ. silent; muffled; toned down. Thanks to the thick, sound-absorbing walls of the cathedral, only *muted* traffic noise reached the worshippers within.

mutinous ADJ. unruly; rebellious. The captain had to use force to quiet his *mutinous* crew. mutiny, N.

myopic ADJ. nearsighted; lacking foresight. Stumbling into doors despite the coke bottle lenses on his glasses, the nearsighted Mr. Magoo is markedly *myopic*. In playing all summer long and ignoring to store up food for winter, the grasshopper in Aesop's fable was *myopic* as well.

myriad N. very large number. *Myriads* of mosquitoes from the swamps invaded our village every twilight. also ADJ.

mystify V. bewilder purposely. When doctors speak in medical jargon, they often *mystify* their patients, who have little knowledge of medical terminology.

nadir N. lowest point. Although few people realized it, the Dow-Jones averages had reached their *nadir* and would soon begin an upward surge.

naiveté N. quality of being unsophisticated; simplicity; artlessness; gullibility. Touched by the *naiveté* of sweet, convent-trained Cosette, Marius pledges himself to protect her innocence. naive, ADJ.

narcissist N. conceited person; someone in love with his own image. A *narcissist* is her own best friend.

narrative ADJ. related to telling a story. A born teller of tales, Tillie Olsen used her impressive *narrative* skills to advantage in her story "I Stand Here Ironing." narrate, V.

nascent ADJ. incipient; coming into being. If we could identify these revolutionary movements in their *nascent* state, we would be able to eliminate serious trouble in later years.

natty ADJ. neatly or smartly dressed. Priding himself on being a *natty* dresser, the gangster Bugsy Siegel collected a wardrobe of imported suits and ties.

Word List 32   nauseate-obsessive

nauseate V. cause to become sick; fill with disgust. The foul smells began to *nauseate* him.

nautical ADJ. pertaining to ships or navigation. The Maritime Museum contains many models of clipper ships, logbooks, anchors and many other items of a *nautical* nature.

navigable ADJ. wide and deep enough to allow ships to pass through; able to be steered. So much sand had built up at the bottom of the canal that the waterway was barely *navigable*.

nebulous ADJ. vague; hazy; cloudy. After twenty years, she had only a *nebulous* memory of her grandmother's face.

necromancy N. black magic; dealings with the dead. The evil sorceror performed feats of *necromancy*, calling on the spirits of the dead to tell the future.

● **nefarious** ADJ. very wicked. The villain's crimes, though various, were one and all *nefarious*.

■ **negate** V. cancel out; nullify; deny. A sudden surge of adrenalin can *negate* the effects of fatigue: there's nothing like a good shock to wake you up.

negligence N. neglect; failure to take reasonable care. Tommy failed to put back the cover on the well after he fetched his pail of water; because of his *negligence*, Kitty fell in.

negligible ADJ. so small, trifling, or unimportant that it may be easily disregarded. Because the damage to his car had been *negligible*, Michael decided he wouldn't bother to report the matter to his insurance company.

nemesis N. someone seeking revenge. Abandoned at sea in a small boat, the vengeful Captain Bligh vowed to be the *nemesis* of Fletcher Christian and his fellow mutineers.

neologism N. new or newly coined word or phrase. As we invent new techniques and professions, we must also invent *neologisms* such as "microcomputer" and "astronaut" to describe them.

neophyte N. recent convert; beginner. This mountain slope contains slides that will challenge experts as well as *neophytes*.

nepotism N. favoritism (to a relative). John left his position with the company because he felt that advancement was based on *nepotism* rather than ability.

nettle V. annoy; vex. Do not let him *nettle* you with his sarcastic remarks.

neutral   ADJ. impartial; not supporting one side over another. Reluctant to get mixed up in someone else's quarrel, Bobby tried to remain *neutral,* but eventually he had to take sides.

nicety   N. precision; minute distinction. I cannot distinguish between such *niceties* of reasoning.

nihilist   N. one who believes traditional beliefs to be groundless and existence meaningless; absolute skeptic; revolutionary terrorist. In his final days, Hitler revealed himself a power-mad *nihilist,* ready to annihilate all of Western Europe, even to destroy Germany itself, in order that his will might prevail. The root of the word *nihilist* is *nihil,* Latin for *nothing.* nihilism, N.

nip   V. stop something's growth or development; snip off; bite; make numb with cold. The twins were plotting mischief, but Mother intervened and *nipped* that plan in the bud. The gardener *nipped* off a lovely rose and gave it to me. Last week a guard dog *nipped* the postman in the leg; this week the extreme chill *nipped* his fingers till he could barely hold the mail.

nirvana   N. in Buddhist teachings, the ideal state in which the individual loses himself in the attainment of an impersonal beatitude. Despite his desire to achieve *nirvana,* the young Buddhist found that even the buzzing of a fly could distract him from his meditation.

nocturnal   ADJ. done at night. Mr. Jones obtained a watchdog to prevent the *nocturnal* raids on his chicken coops.

noisome   ADJ. foul-smelling; unwholesome. The *noisome* atmosphere downwind of the oil refinery not only stank, it damaged the lungs of everyone living in the area.

nomadic   ADJ. wandering. Several *nomadic* tribes of Indians would hunt in this area each year.

nomenclature   N. terminology; system of names. Sharon found Latin word parts useful in translating medical *nomenclature*: when her son had to have a bilateral myringotomy, she figured out that he just needed a hole in each of his eardrums to end the earaches he had.

nominal   ADJ. in name only; trifling. He offered to drive her to the airport for only a *nominal* fee.

■ **nonchalance**   N. indifference; lack of concern; composure. Cool, calm, and collected under fire, James Bond shows remarkable *nonchalance* in the face of danger.

noncommittal   ADJ. neutral; unpledged; undecided. We were annoyed by his *noncommittal* reply for we had been led to expect definite assurances of his approval.

nondescript   ADJ. undistinctive; ordinary. The private detective was a short, *nondescript* fellow with no outstanding features, the sort of person one would never notice in a crowd.

nonentity   N. person of no importance; nonexistence. Because the two older princes dismissed their youngest brother as a *nonentity,* they did not realize that he was quietly plotting to seize the throne.

nonplus   V. bring to halt by confusion; perplex. Jack's uncharacteristic rudeness *nonplussed* Jill, leaving her uncertain how to react.

nostalgia   N. homesickness; longing for the past. My grandfather seldom spoke of life in the old country; he had little patience with *nostalgia.* nostalgic, ADJ.

notable   ADJ. conspicuous; important; distinguished. Normally *notable* for his calm in the kitchen, today the head cook was shaking, for the *notable* chef Julia Child was coming to dinner.

■ **notoriety**   N. disrepute; ill fame. To the starlet, any publicity was good publicity: if she couldn't have a good reputation, she'd settle for *notoriety.* notorious, ADJ.

■ **novelty**   N. something new; newness. The computer is no longer a *novelty* at work; every desk in our office has one. novel, ADJ.

novice   N. beginner. Even a *novice* at working with computers can install *Barron's Computer Study Program for the SAT* by following the easy steps outlined in the user's manual.

noxious   ADJ. harmful. We must trace the source of these *noxious* gases before they asphyxiate us.

● **nuance**   N. shade of difference in meaning or color; subtle distinction. Jody gazed at the Monet landscape for an hour, appreciating every subtle *nuance* of color in the painting.

nullify   V. to make invalid. Once the contract was *nullified,* it no longer had any legal force.

numismatist   N. person who collects coins. The *numismatist* had a splendid collection of antique coins.

nuptial   ADJ. related to marriage. Reluctant to be married in a traditional setting, they decided to hold their *nuptial* ceremony at the carousel in Golden Gate Park.

■ **nurture**   V. nourish; educate; foster. The Head Start program attempts to *nurture* pre-kindergarten children so that they will do well when they enter public school. also N.

nutrient   N. nourishing substance. As a budding nutritionist, Kim has learned to design diets that contain foods rich in important basic *nutrients.*

oaf   N. stupid, awkward person. "Watch what you're doing, you clumsy *oaf*!" Bill shouted at the waiter who had drenched him with iced coffee.

● **obdurate**   ADJ. stubborn. He was *obdurate* in his refusal to listen to our complaints.

obese   ADJ. fat. It is advisable that *obese* people try to lose weight.

obfuscate   V. confuse; muddle; cause confusion; make needlessly complex. Was the president's spokesman trying to clarify the Whitewater mystery, or was he trying to *obfuscate* the issue so the voters would never figure out what went on?

obituary   ADJ. death notice. I first learned of her death when I read the *obituary* column in the newspaper. also N.

objective   ADJ. not influenced by emotions; fair. Even though he was her son, she tried to be *objective* about his behavior.

objective   N. goal; aim. A degree in medicine was her ultimate *objective.*

obligatory ADJ. binding; required. It is *obligatory* that books borrowed from the library be returned within two weeks.

oblique ADJ. indirect; slanting (deviating from the perpendicular or from a straight line). Casting a quick, *oblique* glance at the reviewing stand, the sergeant ordered the company to march "*Oblique* Right."

■ **obliterate** V. destroy completely. The tidal wave *obliterated* several island villages.

■ **oblivion** N. obscurity; forgetfulness. After a decade of popularity, Hurston's works had fallen into *oblivion*; no one bothered to read them any more.

oblivious ADJ. inattentive or unmindful; wholly absorbed. Deep in her book, Nancy was *oblivious* to the noisy squabbles of her brother and his friends.

obnoxious ADJ. offensive. I find your behavior *obnoxious*; please mend your ways.

obscure ADJ. dark; vague; unclear. Even after I read the poem a fourth time, its meaning was still *obscure*. obscurity, N.

■ **obscure** V. darken; make unclear. At times he seemed purposely to *obscure* his meaning, preferring mystery to clarity.

obsequious ADJ. slavishly attentive; servile; sycophantic. Helen liked to be served by people who behaved as if they respected themselves; nothing irritated her more than an excessively *obsequious* waiter or a fawning salesclerk.

obsessive ADJ. related to thinking about something constantly; preoccupying. Ballet, which had been a hobby, began to dominate his life: his love of dancing became *obsessive*. obsession, N.

Word List 33 obsolete-pacifist

obsolete ADJ. no longer useful; outmoded; antiquated. The invention of the pocket calculator made the slide rule used by generations of engineers *obsolete*.

obstetrician N. physician specializing in delivery of babies. In modern times, the delivery of children has passed from the midwife to the more scientifically trained *obstetrician*.

■ **obstinate** ADJ. stubborn; hard to control or treat. We tried to persuade him to give up smoking, but he was *obstinate* and refused to change. Blackberry stickers are the most *obstinate* weeds I know: once established in a yard, they're extremely hard to root out. obstinacy, N.

obstreperous ADJ. boisterous; noisy. What do you do when an *obstreperous* horde of drunken policemen goes carousing through your hotel, crashing into potted plants and singing vulgar songs?

obtrude V. push (oneself or one's ideas) forward or intrude; butt in; stick out or extrude. Because Fanny was reluctant to *obtrude* her opinions about child-raising upon her daughter-in-law, she kept a close watch on her tongue. obtrusive, ADJ.

obtuse ADJ. blunt; stupid. What can you do with somebody who's so *obtuse* that he can't even tell that you're insulting him?

obviate V. make unnecessary; get rid of. I hope this contribution will *obviate* any need for further collections of funds.

● **odious** ADJ. hateful; vile. Cinderella's ugly stepsisters had the *odious* habit of popping their zits in public.

odium N. detestation; hatefulness; disrepute. Prince Charming could not express the *odium* he felt toward Cinderella's stepsisters because of their mistreatment of poor Cinderella.

odorous ADJ. having an odor. This variety of hybrid tea rose is more *odorous* than the one you have in your garden.

odyssey N. long, eventful journey. The refugee's journey from Cambodia was a terrifying *odyssey*.

offensive ADJ. attacking; insulting; distasteful. Getting into street brawls is no minor matter for professional boxers, who are required by law to restrict their *offensive* impulses to the ring.

offhand ADJ. casual; done without prior thought. Expecting to be treated with due propriety by her hosts, Great-Aunt Maud was offended by their *offhand* manner.

officious ADJ. meddlesome; excessively pushy in offering one's services. Judy wanted to look over the new computer models on her own, but the *officious* salesman kept on butting in with "helpful" advice until she was ready to walk out of the store.

ogle V. look at amorously; make eyes at. At the coffee house, Walter was too shy to *ogle* the pretty girls openly; instead, he peeked out at them from behind a rubber plant.

olfactory ADJ. concerning the sense of smell. A wine taster must have a discriminating palate and a keen *olfactory* sense, for a good wine appeals both to the taste buds and to the nose.

oligarchy N. government by a privileged few. One small clique ran the student council: what had been intended as a democratic governing body had turned into an *oligarchy*.

■ **ominous** ADJ. threatening. Those clouds are *ominous*; they suggest a severe storm is on the way.

omnipotent ADJ. all-powerful. The monarch regarded himself as *omnipotent* and responsible to no one for his acts.

omnipresent ADJ. universally present; ubiquitous. On Christmas Eve, Santa Claus is *omnipresent*.

omniscient ADJ. all-knowing. I do not pretend to be *omniscient*, but I am positive about this fact.

omnivorous ADJ. eating both plant and animal food; devouring everything. Some animals, including man, are *omnivorous* and eat both meat and vegetables; others are either carnivorous or herbivorous.

onerous ADJ. burdensome. He asked for an assistant because his work load was too *onerous*.

onset N. beginning; attack. Caught unprepared by the sudden *onset* of the storm, we rushed around the house closing windows and bringing the garden furniture into shelter. Caught unprepared by the enemy *onset*, the troops scrambled to take shelter.

onus N. burden; responsibility. The emperor was spared the *onus* of signing the surrender papers; instead, he relegated the assignment to his generals.

opalescent ADJ. iridescent; lustrous. The oil slick on the water had an *opalescent*, rainbow-like sheen.

■ **opaque** ADJ. dark; not transparent. The *opaque* window shade kept the sunlight out of the room. opacity, N.

opiate N. medicine to induce sleep or deaden pain; something that relieves emotions or causes inaction. To say that religion is the *opiate* of the people is to condemn religion as a drug that keeps the people quiet and submissive to those in power.

opportune ADJ. timely; well-chosen. Sally looked at her father struggling to balance his checkbook; clearly this would not be an *opportune* moment to ask him for a raise in her allowance.

■ **opportunist** N. individual who sacrifices principles for expediency by taking advantage of circumstances. Joe is such an *opportunist* that he tripled the price of bottled water at his store as soon as the earthquake struck. Because it can break water pipes, an earthquake is, to most people, a disaster; to Joe, it was an *opportunity*.

optician N. maker and seller of eyeglasses. The patient took the prescription given him by his oculist to the *optician*.

■ **optimist** N. person who looks on the good side. The pessimist says the glass is half-empty; the *optimist* says it is half-full.

optimum ADJ. most favorable. If you wait for the *optimum* moment to act, you may never begin your project. also N.

optional ADJ. not obligatory; left to one's choice. Most colleges require applicants to submit SAT I scores; at some colleges, however, submitting SAT I scores is *optional*.

■ **opulence** N. extreme wealth; luxuriousness; abundance. The glitter and *opulence* of the ballroom took Cinderella's breath away. opulent, ADJ.

opus N. work. Although many critics hailed his Fifth Symphony as his major work, he did not regard it as his major *opus*.

oracular ADJ. prophetic; uttered as if with divine authority; mysterious or ambiguous. Like many others who sought divine guidance from the *oracle* at Delphi, Oedipus could not understand the enigmatic *oracular* warning he received.

■ **orator** N. public speaker. The abolitionist Frederick Douglass was a brilliant *orator* whose speeches brought home to his audience the evils of slavery.

ordain V. decree or command; grant holy orders; predestine. The king *ordained* that no foreigner should be allowed to enter the city. The Bishop of Michigan *ordained* David a deacon in the Episcopal Church. The young lovers felt that fate had *ordained* their meeting.

ordeal N. severe trial or affliction. June was so painfully shy that it was an *ordeal* for her to speak up when the teacher called on her in class.

ordinance N. decree. Passing a red light is a violation of a city *ordinance*.

ordination N. ceremony making someone a minister. At the young priest's *ordination*, the members of the congregation presented him with a set of vestments. ordain, V.

orgy N. wild, drunken revelry; unrestrained indulgence in a tendency. The Roman emperor's *orgies* were far wilder than the toga party in the movie *Animal House*. When her income tax refund check finally arrived, Sally indulged in an *orgy* of shopping.

orient V. get one's bearings; adjust. Philip spent his first day in Denver *orienting* himself to the city.

orientation N. act of finding oneself in society. Freshman *orientation* provides the incoming students with an opportunity to learn about their new environment and their place in it.

● **ornate** ADJ. excessively or elaborately decorated. With its elaborately carved, convoluted lines, furniture of the Baroque period was highly *ornate*.

ornithologist N. scientific student of birds. Audubon's drawings of American bird life have been of interest not only to the *ornithologists* but also to the general public.

ornithology N. study of birds. Audubon's studies of American birds greatly influenced the course of *ornithology*.

orthodox ADJ. traditional; conservative in belief. Faced with a problem, he preferred to take an *orthodox* approach rather than shock anyone. orthodoxy, N.

oscillate V. vibrate pendulumlike; waver. It is interesting to note how public opinion *oscillates* between the extremes of optimism and pessimism.

ossify V. change or harden into bone. When he called his opponent a "bonehead," he implied that his adversary's brain had *ossified* to the point that he was incapable of clear thinking.

ostensible ADJ. apparent; professed; pretended. Although the *ostensible* purpose of this expedition is to discover new lands, we are really interested in finding new markets for our products.

■ **ostentatious** ADJ. showy; pretentious; trying to attract attention. Donald Trump's latest casino in Atlantic City is the most *ostentatious* gambling palace in the East: it easily outglitters its competitors. ostentation, N.

ostracize V. exclude from public favor; ban. As soon as the newspapers carried the story of his connection with the criminals, his friends began to *ostracize* him. ostracism, N.

oust V. expel; drive out. The world wondered if Aquino would be able to *oust* Marcos from office. ouster, N.

outlandish ADJ. bizarre; peculiar; unconventional. The eccentric professor who engages in markedly *outlandish* behavior is a stock figure in novels with an academic setting.

outmoded ADJ. no longer stylish; old-fashioned. Unconcerned about keeping in style, Lenore was perfectly happy to wear *outmoded* clothes as long as they were clean and unfrayed.

outskirts N. fringes; outer borders. We lived, not in central London, but in one of those peripheral suburbs that spring up on the *outskirts* of a great city.

outspoken ADJ. candid; blunt. The candidate was too *outspoken* to be a successful politician; he had not yet learned to weigh his words carefully.

outstrip V. surpass; outdo. Jesse Owens easily *outstripped* his white competitors to win the gold medal at the Olympic Games.

outwit V. outsmart; trick. By disguising himself as an old woman, Holmes was able to *outwit* his pursuers and escape capture.

ovation N. enthusiastic applause. When the popular tenor Placido Domingo came on stage in the first act of *La Boheme*, he was greeted by a tremendous *ovation*.

overbearing ADJ. bossy and arrogant; decisively important. Certain of her own importance, and of the unimportance of everyone else, Lady Bracknell was intolerably *overbearing* in her manner. "In choosing a husband," she said, "good birth is of *overbearing* importance; compared to that, neither wealth nor talent signifies."

overt ADJ. open to view. According to the United States Constitution, a person must commit an *overt* act before he may be tried for treason.

overwrought ADJ. extremely agitated; hysterical. When Kate heard the news of the sudden tragedy, she became too *overwrought* to work and had to leave the office early.

pachyderm N. thick-skinned animal. The elephant is probably the best-known *pachyderm*.

■ **pacifist** N. one opposed to force; antimilitarist. Shooting his way through the jungle, Rambo was clearly not a *pacifist*.

Word List 34   pacify-peccadillo

pacify V. soothe; make calm or quiet; subdue. Dentists criticize the practice of giving fussy children sweets to *pacify* them.

pact N. agreement; treaty. Tweedledum and Tweedledee made a *pact* not to quarrel anymore.

paean N. song of praise or joy. *Paeans* celebrating the victory filled the air.

painstaking ADJ. showing hard work; taking great care. The new high-frequency word list is the result of *painstaking* efforts on the part of our research staff.

palatable ADJ. agreeable; pleasing to the taste. Neither Jack's underbaked opinions nor his overcooked casseroles were *palatable* to Jill.

paleontology N. study of prehistoric life. The *paleontology* instructor had a superb collection of fossils.

palette N. board on which painter mixes pigments. At the present time, art supply stores are selling a paper *palette* that may be discarded after use.

pall V. grow tiresome. The study of word lists can eventually *pall* and put one to sleep.

palliate V. lessen the violence of (a disease); alleviate; moderate intensity; gloss over with excuses. Not content merely to *palliate* the patient's sores and cankers, the researcher sought a means of wiping out the disease. palliative, ADJ.

pallid ADJ. pale; wan. Because his job required that he work at night and sleep during the day, he had an exceptionally *pallid* complexion.

palpable ADJ. tangible; easily perceptible; unmistakable. The patient's enlarged spleen was *palpable:* even the first year medical student could feel it.

palpitate V. throb; flutter. As he became excited, his heart began to *palpitate* more and more erratically.

paltry ADJ. insignificant; petty; trifling. One hundred dollars for a genuine imitation Rolex watch! Lady, this is a *paltry* sum to pay for such a high-class piece of jewelry.

pan V. criticize harshly. Hoping for a rave review of his new show, the playwright was miserable when the critics *panned* it unanimously.

panacea N. cure-all; remedy for all diseases. The rich youth cynically declared that the *panacea* for all speeding tickets was a big enough bribe.

panache N. flair; flamboyance. Many performers imitate Noel Coward, but few have his *panache* and sense of style.

pandemic ADJ. widespread; affecting the majority of people. They feared the AIDS epidemic would soon reach *pandemic* proportions.

pandemonium N. wild tumult. When the ships collided in the harbor, *pandemonium* broke out among the passengers.

pander V. cater to the low desires of others. The reviewer accused the makers of *Lethal Weapon* of *pandering* to the masses' taste for violence.

panegyric N. formal praise. Blushing at all the praise heaped upon him by the speakers, the modest hero said, "I don't deserve such *panegyrics*."

panoramic ADJ. related to an unobstructed and comprehensive view. On a clear day, from the top of the World Trade Center you can get a *panoramic* view of New York City and parts of New Jersey and Long Island. panorama, N.

pantomime N. acting without dialogue. Because he worked in *pantomime*, the clown could be understood wherever he appeared. also V.

papyrus N. ancient paper made from stem of papyrus plant. The ancient Egyptians were among the first to write on *papyrus*.

parable N. short, simple story teaching a moral. Let us apply to our own conduct the lesson that this *parable* teaches.

paradigm   N. model; example; pattern. Pavlov's experiment in which he trains a dog to salivate on hearing a bell is a *paradigm* of the conditioned-response experiment in behavioral psychology. Barron's *How to Prepare for College Entrance Examinations* was a *paradigm* for all the SAT-prep books that followed.

paradox   N. something apparently contradictory in nature; statement that looks false but is actually correct. Richard presents a bit of a *paradox*, for he is a card-carrying member of both the National Rifle Association and the relatively pacifist American Civil Liberties Union.

paragon   N. model of perfection. Her fellow students disliked Lavinia because Miss Minchin always pointed her out as a *paragon* of virtue.

parallelism   N. state of being parallel; similarity. Although the twins were separated at birth and grew up in different adoptive families, a striking *parallelism* exists between their lives.

paramount   ADJ. foremost in importance; supreme. Proper nutrition and hygiene are of *paramount* importance in adolescent development and growth.

paranoia   N. psychosis marked by delusions of grandeur or persecution. Suffering from *paranoia*, Don claimed everyone was out to get him; ironically, his claim was accurate: even *paranoids* have enemies.

paraphernalia   N. equipment; odds and ends. His desk was cluttered with paper, pen, ink, dictionary and other *paraphernalia* of the writing craft.

paraphrase   V. restate a passage in one's own words while retaining thought of author. In 250 words or less, *paraphrase* this article. also N.

parasite   N. animal or plant living on another; toady; sycophant. The tapeworm is an example of the kind of *parasite* that may infest the human body.

parched   ADJ. extremely dry; very thirsty. The *parched* desert landscape seemed hostile to life.

● **pariah**   N. social outcast. If everyone ostracized singer Mariah Carey, would she then be Mariah the *pariah*?

parity   N. equality in status or amount; close resemblance. Unfortunately, some doubt exists whether women's salaries will ever achieve *parity* with men's.

parochial   ADJ. narrow in outlook; provincial; related to parishes. Although Jane Austen sets her novels in small rural communities, her concerns are universal, not *parochial*.

● **parody**   N. humorous imitation; spoof; takeoff; travesty. The show *Forbidden Broadway* presents *parodies* spoofing the year's new productions playing on Broadway.

paroxysm   N. fit or attack of pain, laughter, rage. When he heard of his son's misdeeds, he was seized by a *paroxysm* of rage.

parry   V. ward off a blow; deflect. Unwilling to injure his opponent in such a pointless clash, Dartagnan simply tried to *parry* his rival's thrusts. What fun it was to watch Katherine Hepburn and Spencer Tracy *parry* each other's verbal thrusts in their classic screwball comedies!

● **parsimony**   N. stinginess; excessive frugality. Furious because her father wouldn't let her buy out the clothing store, Annie accused him of *parsimony*.

partial   ADJ. incomplete; having a liking for something. In this issue we have published only a *partial* list of contributors because we lack space to acknowledge everyone. I am extremely *partial* to chocolate eclairs.

partiality   N. inclination; bias. As a judge, not only must I be unbiased, but I must also avoid any evidence of *partiality* when I award the prize.

■ **partisan**   ADJ. one-sided; prejudiced; committed to a party. On certain issues of principle, she refused to take a *partisan* stand, but let her conscience be her guide. Rather than joining forces to solve our nation's problems, the Democrats and Republicans spend their time on *partisan* struggles. also N.

partition   V. divide into parts. Before their second daughter was born, Jason and Lizzie decided each child needed a room of her own, and so they *partitioned* a large bedroom into two small but separate rooms. also N.

passive   ADJ. not active; acted upon. Mahatma Gandhi urged his followers to pursue a program of *passive* resistance as he felt that it was more effective than violence and acts of terrorism.

passport   N. legal document identifying the bearer as a citizen of a country and allowing him or her to travel abroad. In arranging your first trip abroad, be sure to allow yourself enough time to apply for and receive your *passport*: you won't be allowed to travel without one.

pastiche   N. imitation of another's style in musical composition or in writing. We cannot even say that her music is a: *pastiche* of this composer or that; it is, rather, reminiscent of many musicians.

pastoral   ADJ. rural. In these stories of *pastoral* life, we find an understanding of the daily tasks of country folk.

patent   ADJ. open for the public to read; obvious. It was *patent* to everyone that the witness spoke the truth. also N.

pathetic   ADJ. causing sadness, compassion, pity; touching. Everyone in the auditorium was weeping by the time he finished his *pathetic* tale about the orphaned boy.

pathological   ADJ. related to the study of disease; diseased or markedly abnormal. Jerome's *pathological* fear of germs led him to wash his hands a hundred times a day. pathology, N.

pathos   N. tender sorrow; pity; quality in art or literature that produces these feelings. The quiet tone of *pathos* that ran through the novel never degenerated into the maudlin or the overly sentimental.

patina   N. green crust on old bronze works; tone slowly taken by varnished painting. Judging by the *patina* on this bronze statue, we can conclude that this is the work of a medieval artist.

patriarch   N. father and ruler of a family or tribe. In many primitive tribes, the leader and lawmaker was the *patriarch*.

patrician   ADJ. noble; aristocratic. We greatly admired her well-bred, *patrician* elegance. also N.

patronize V. support; act superior toward; be a customer of. Penniless artists hope to find some wealthy art-lover who will *patronize* them. If some condescending wine steward *patronized* me because he saw I knew nothing about fine wine, I'd refuse to *patronize* his restaurant.

● **paucity** N. scarcity. They closed the restaurant because the *paucity* of customers made it uneconomical to operate.

pauper N. very poor person. Though Widow Brown was living on a reduced income, she was by no means a *pauper*.

peccadillo N. slight offense. When Peter Piper picked a peck of Polly Potter's pickles, did Pete commit a major crime or just a *peccadillo*?

Word List 35 pecuniary-philanderer

pecuniary ADJ. pertaining to money. Seldom earning enough to cover their expenses, folk dance teachers work because they love dancing, not because they expect any *pecuniary* reward.

pedagogy N. teaching; art of education. Though Maria Montessori gained fame for her innovations in *pedagogy*, it took years before her teaching techniques were common practice in American schools.

pedant N. scholar who overemphasizes book learning or technicalities. Her insistence that the book be memorized marked the teacher as a *pedant* rather than a scholar.

pedantic ADJ. showing off learning; bookish. Leavening his decisions with humorous, down-to-earth anecdotes, Judge Walker was not at all the *pedantic* legal scholar. pedant, pedantry, N.

pedestrian ADJ. ordinary; unimaginative. Unintentionally boring, he wrote page after page of *pedestrian* prose.

pediatrician N. expert in children's diseases. The family doctor advised the parents to consult a *pediatrician* about their child's ailment.

peerless ADJ. having no equal; incomparable. The reigning operatic tenor of his generation, to his admirers Luciano Pavarotti was *peerless*: no one could compare with him.

pejorative ADJ. negative in connotation; having a belittling effect. Instead of criticizing Clinton's policies, the Republicans made *pejorative* remarks about his character.

pellucid ADJ. transparent; limpid; easy to understand. After reading these stodgy philosophers, I find Bertrand Russell's *pellucid* style very enjoyable.

penchant N. strong inclination; liking. Dave has a *penchant* for taking risks: one semester he went steady with three girls, two of whom were stars on the school karate team.

pendant N. ornament (hanging from a necklace, etc.) The grateful team presented the coach with a silver chain and *pendant* engraved with the school's motto.

penitent ADJ. repentant. When he realized the enormity of his crime, he became remorseful and *penitent*. also N.

pensive ADJ. dreamily thoughtful; thoughtful with a hint of sadness; contemplative. The *pensive* lover gazed at the portrait of his beloved and deeply sighed.

● **penury** N. severe poverty; stinginess. When his pension fund failed, George feared he would end his days in *penury*. He became such a penny pincher that he turned into a closefisted, *penurious* miser.

perceptive ADJ. insightful; aware; wise. Although Maud was a generally *perceptive* critic, she had her blind spots: she could never see flaws in the work of her friends.

percussion ADJ. striking one object against another sharply. The drum is a *percussion* instrument. also N.

perdition N. damnation; complete ruin. Praying for salvation, young Steven Daedalus feared he was damned to eternal *perdition*.

peregrination N. journey. Auntie Mame was a world traveler whose *peregrinations* took her from Tiajuana to Timbuctoo.

peremptory ADJ. demanding and leaving no choice. From Jack's *peremptory* knock on the door, Jill could tell he would not give up until she let him in.

perennial N. something that is continuing or recurrent. These plants are hardy *perennials* and will bloom for many years. also ADJ.

perfidious ADJ. treacherous; disloyal. When Caesar realized that Brutus had betrayed him, he reproached his *perfidious* friend. perfidy, N.

perforate V. pierce; put a hole through. Before you can open the aspirin bottle, you must first *perforate* the plastic safety seal that covers the cap.

● **perfunctory** ADJ. superficial; not thorough; lacking interest, care, or enthusiasm. The auditor's *perfunctory* inspection of the books overlooked many errors. Giving the tabletop only a *perfunctory* swipe with her dust cloth, Betty promised herself she'd clean it more thoroughly tomorrow.

perimeter N. outer boundary. To find the *perimeter* of any quadrilateral, we add the lengths of the four sides.

■ **peripheral** ADJ. marginal; outer. We lived, not in central London, but in one of those *peripheral* suburbs that spring up on the outskirts of a great city.

periphery N. edge, especially of a round surface. He sensed that there was something just beyond the *periphery* of his vision.

perjury N. false testimony while under oath. Rather than lie under oath and perhaps be indicted for *perjury*, the witness chose to take the Fifth Amendment, refusing to answer any questions on the grounds that he might incriminate himself.

permeable ADJ. penetrable; porous; allowing liquids or gas to pass through. If your jogging clothes weren't made out of *permeable* fabric, you'd drown in your own perspiration (figuratively speaking).

permeate V. pass through; spread. The odor of frying onions *permeated* the air.

● **pernicious** ADJ. very destructive. Crack cocaine has had a *pernicious* effect on urban society: it has destroyed families, turned children into drug dealers, and increased the spread of violent crimes.

perpetrate V. commit an offense. Only an insane person could *perpetrate* such a horrible crime.

perpetual ADJ. everlasting. Ponce de Leon hoped to find the legendary fountain of *perpetual* youth.

■ **perpetuate** V. make something last; preserve from extinction. Some critics attack *The Adventures of Huckleberry Finn* because they believe Twain's book *perpetuates* a false image of Blacks in this country.

perquisite N. any gain above stipulated salary. The *perquisites* attached to this job make it even more attractive than the salary indicates.

persona N. public personality or facade. Offstage the comedian was a sullen, irritable grumbler, a far cry from his ever-cheerful adopted stage *persona*.

personable ADJ. attractive. The man I am seeking to fill this position must be *personable* since he will be representing us before the public.

perspicacious ADJ. having insight; penetrating; astute. The brilliant lawyer was known for his *perspicacious* deductions. perspicacity, N.

pert ADJ. impertinent; forward. I think your *pert* and impudent remarks call for an apology.

pertinacious ADJ. stubborn; persistent. He is bound to succeed because his *pertinacious* nature will not permit him to quit.

pertinent ADJ. to the point; relevant. Virginia Woolf's words on women's rights are as *pertinent* today as they were when she wrote them nearly a century ago.

perturb V. disturb greatly. The thought that electricity might be leaking out of the empty light bulb sockets *perturbed* my aunt so much that at night she crept about the house screwing fresh bulbs in the vacant spots. perturbation, N.

peruse V. read with care. After the conflagration that burned down her house, Joan closely *perused* her home insurance policy to discover exactly what benefits her coverage provided her. perusal, N.

■ **pervasive** ADJ. pervading; spread throughout every part. Despite airing them for several hours, Martha could not rid her clothes of the *pervasive* odor of mothballs that clung to them. pervade, V.

perverse ADJ. stubbornly wrongheaded; wicked and perverted. When Jack was in a *perverse* mood, he would do the opposite of whatever Jill asked him. When Hannibal Lecter was in a *perverse* mood, he ate the flesh of his victims. Jack acted out of *perversity*. Hannibal's act proved his *perversion*.

■ **pessimism** N. belief that life is basically bad or evil; gloominess. Considering how well you have done in the course so far, you have no real reason for such *pessimism* about your final grade.

petrify V. turn to stone. His sudden and unexpected appearance seemed to *petrify* her.

petty ADJ. trivial; unimportant; very small. She had no major complaints to make about his work, only a few *petty* quibbles that were almost too minor to state.

petulant ADJ. touchy; peevish. If you'd had hardly any sleep for three nights and people kept phoning and waking you up, you'd sound pretty *petulant*, too.

■ **phenomena** N. observable facts; subjects of scientific investigation. We kept careful records of the *phenomena* we noted in the course of these experiments.

philanderer N. faithless lover; flirt. Swearing he had never so much as looked at another woman, Ralph assured Alice he was no *philanderer*.

Word List 36   philanthropist-precedent

■ **philanthropist** N. lover of mankind; doer of good. In his role as *philanthropist* and public benefactor, John D. Rockefeller, Sr., donated millions to charity; as an individual, however, he was a tight-fisted old man.

philistine N. narrow-minded person, uncultured and exclusively interested in material gain. We need more men of culture and enlightenment; we have too many *philistines* among us.

philology N. study of language. The professor of *philology* advocated the use of Esperanto as an international language.

phlegmatic ADJ. calm; not easily disturbed. The nurse was a cheerful but *phlegmatic* person, unexcited in the face of sudden emergencies.

phobia N. morbid fear. Her fear of flying was more than mere nervousness; it was a real *phobia*.

phoenix N. symbol of immortality or rebirth. Like the legendary *phoenix* rising from its ashes, the city of San Francisco rose again after its destruction during the 1906 earthquake.

phylum N. major class of plants; primary branch of animal kingdom; division. In sorting out her hundreds of packets of seeds, Katya decided to file them by *phylum*.

physiological ADJ. pertaining to the science of the function of living organisms. To understand this disease fully, we must examine not only its *physiological* aspects but also its psychological elements.

picaresque ADJ. pertaining to rogues in literature. *Tom Jones* has been hailed as one of the best *picaresque* novels in the English language.

piebald ADJ. mottled; spotted. You should be able to identify Polka Dot in this race; it is the only *piebald* horse running.

piecemeal ADV. one piece at a time; gradually. Tolstoy's *War and Peace* is too huge to finish in one sitting; I'll have to read it *piecemeal*.

pied ADJ. variegated; multicolored. The *Pied* Piper of Hamelin got his name from the multicolored clothing he wore.

■ **piety** N. religious devotion; godliness. The nuns in the convent were noted for their *piety;* they spent their days in worship and prayer. pious, ADJ.

pigment N. coloring matter. Van Gogh mixed various *pigments* with linseed oil to create his paints.

pillage V. plunder. The enemy *pillaged* the quiet village and left it in ruins.

pine V. languish, decline; long for, yearn. Though she tried to be happy living with Clara in the city, Heidi *pined* for the mountains and for her gruff but loving grandfather.

pinnacle N. peak. We could see the morning sunlight illuminate the *pinnacle* while the rest of the mountain lay in shadow.

pious ADJ. devout; religious. The challenge for church people today is how to be *pious* in the best sense, that is, to be devout without becoming hypocritical or sanctimonious. piety, N.

piquant ADJ. pleasantly tart-tasting; stimulating. The *piquant* sauce added to our enjoyment of the meal. piquancy, N.

pique N. irritation; resentment. She showed her *pique* at her loss by refusing to appear with the other contestants at the end of the competition. also V.

pique V. provoke or arouse; annoy. "I know something *you* don't know," said Lucy, trying to *pique* Ethel's interest.

● **pitfall** N. hidden danger; concealed trap. Her parents warned young Sophie against the many *pitfalls* that lay in wait for her in the dangerous big city.

● **pithy** ADJ. concise; meaningful; substantial; meaty. While other girls might have gone on and on about how uncool Elton was, Liz summed it up in one *pithy* remark: "He's bogus!"

pittance N. a small allowance or wage. He could not live on the *pittance* he received as a pension and had to look for an additional source of revenue.

pivotal ADJ. crucial; key; vital. The new "smart weapons" technology played a *pivotal* role in the quick resolution of the war with Iraq.

■ **placate** V. pacify; conciliate. The store manager tried to *placate* the angry customer, offering to replace the damaged merchandise or to give back her money right away.

placebo N. harmless substance prescribed as a dummy pill. In a controlled experiment, fifty volunteers were given aspirin tablets; the control group received only *placebos.*

placid ADJ. peaceful; calm. After his vacation in this *placid* section, he felt soothed and rested.

plagiarism N. theft of another's ideas or writings passed off as original. The editor recognized the *plagiarism* and rebuked the culprit who had presented the manuscript as original.

plagiarize V. steal another's ideas and pass them off as one's own. The teacher could tell that the student had *pla-*giarized parts of his essay; she could recognize whole paragraphs straight from *Barron's Book Notes.*

plaintive ADJ. mournful. The dove has a *plaintive* and melancholy call.

plasticity N. ability to be molded. When clay dries out, it loses its *plasticity* and becomes less malleable.

platitude N. trite remark; commonplace statement. In giving advice to his son, old Polonius expressed himself only in *platitudes;* every word out of his mouth was a commonplace.

plaudit N. enthusiastically worded approval; round of applause. The theatrical company reprinted the *plaudits* of the critics in its advertisements. plauditory, ADJ.

plausible ADJ. having a show of truth but open to doubt; specious. Your mother made you stay home from school because she needed you to program the VCR? I'm sorry, you'll have to come up with a more *plausible* excuse than that.

plenitude N. abundance; completeness. Looking in the pantry, we admired the *plenitude* of fruits and pickles we had preserved during the summer.

plethora N. excess; overabundance. She offered a *plethora* of excuses for her shortcomings.

pliable ADJ. flexible; yielding; adaptable. In remodeling the bathroom, we have replaced all the old, rigid lead pipes with new, *pliable* copper tubing.

pliant ADJ. flexible; easily influenced. Pinocchio's disposition was *pliant;* he was like putty in his tempters' hands.

plight N. condition, state (especially a bad state or condition); predicament. Many people feel that the federal government should do more to alleviate the *plight* of the homeless. Loggers, unmoved by the *plight* of the spotted owl, plan to continue logging whether or not they ruin the owl's habitat.

plumb ADJ. checking perpendicularity; vertical. Before hanging wallpaper it is advisable to drop a *plumb* line from the ceiling as a guide. also N. and V.

plumage N. feathers of a bird. Bird watchers identify different species of bird by their characteristic songs and distinctive *plumage.*

plummet V. fall sharply. Stock prices *plummeted* as Wall Street reacted to the crisis in the economy.

plutocracy N. society ruled by the wealthy. From the way the government caters to the rich, you might think our society is a *plutocracy* rather than a democracy.

podiatrist N. doctor who treats ailments of the feet. He consulted a *podiatrist* about his fallen arches.

podium N. pedestal; raised platform. The audience applauded as the conductor made his way to the *podium.*

poignancy N. quality of being deeply moving; keenness of emotion. Watching the tearful reunion of the long-separated mother and child, the social worker was touched by the *poignancy* of the scene. poignant, ADJ.

polarize V. split into opposite extremes or camps. The abortion issue has *polarized* the country into pro-choice and anti-abortion camps. polarization, N.

● **polemical** ADJ. aggressive in verbal attack; disputatious. Lexy was a master of *polemical* rhetoric; she should have worn a T-shirt with the slogan "Born to Debate."

politic ADJ. expedient; prudent; well advised. Even though he was disappointed by the size of the bonus he was offered, he did not think it *politic* to refuse it.

polygamist N. one who has more than one spouse at a time. He was arrested as a *polygamist* when his two wives filed complaints about him.

polyglot ADJ. speaking several languages. New York City is a *polyglot* community because of the thousands of immigrants who settle there.

pomposity N. self-important behavior; acting like a stuffed shirt. Although the commencement speaker had some good things to say, we had to laugh at his *pomposity* and general air of parading his own dignity. pompous, ADJ.

■ **ponderous** ADJ. weighty; unwieldy. His humor lacked the light touch; his jokes were always *ponderous*.

pontifical ADJ. pertaining to a bishop or pope; pompous or pretentious. From his earliest days at the seminary, John seemed destined for a high *pontifical* office. However, he sounded so pompous when he *pontificated* that he never was chosen *pontiff* after all.

pore V. study industriously; ponder; scrutinize. Determined to become a physician, Beth spent hours *poring* over her anatomy text.

porous ADJ. full of pores; like a sieve. Dancers like to wear *porous* clothing because it allows the ready passage of water and air.

portend V. foretell; presage. The king did not know what these omens might *portend* and asked his soothsayers to interpret them.

portent N. sign; omen; forewarning. He regarded the black cloud as a *portent* of evil.

portly ADJ. stately; stout. The overweight gentleman was referred to as *portly* by the polite salesclerk.

poseur N. person who pretends to be sophisticated, elegant, etc., to impress others. Some thought Salvador Dali was a brilliant painter; others dismissed him as a *poseur*.

posterity N. descendants; future generations. We hope to leave a better world to *posterity*.

posthumous ADJ. after death (as of child born after father's death or book published after author's death). The critics ignored his works during his lifetime; it was only after the *posthumous* publication of his last novel that they recognized his great talent.

postulate N. essential premise; underlying assumption. The basic *postulate* of democracy, set forth in the Declaration of Independence, is that all men are created equal.

potable ADJ. suitable for drinking. The recent drought in the Middle Atlantic states has emphasized the need for extensive research in ways of making sea water *potable*. also N.

potent ADJ. powerful; persuasive; greatly influential. Looking at the expiration date on the cough syrup bottle, we wondered whether the medication would still be *potent*. potency, N.

potentate N. monarch; sovereign. The *potentate* spent more time at Monte Carlo than he did at home on his throne.

potential ADJ. expressing possibility; latent. This juvenile delinquent is a *potential* murderer. also N.

potion N. dose (of liquid). Tristan and Isolde drink a love *potion* in the first act of the opera.

practicable ADJ. feasible. The board of directors decided that the plan was *practicable* and agreed to undertake the project.

practical ADJ. based on experience; useful. He was a *practical* man, opposed to theory.

practitioner N. someone engaged in a profession (law, medicine). In need of a hip replacement, Carl sought a *practitioner* with considerable experience performing this particular surgery.

■ **pragmatic** ADJ. practical (as opposed to idealistic); concerned with the practical worth or impact of something. This coming trip to France should provide me with a *pragmatic* test of the value of my conversational French class.

pragmatist N. practical person. No *pragmatist* enjoys becoming involved in a game he can never win.

prank N. mischievous trick. Is tipping over garbage cans on Halloween merely a childish *prank*, or is it vandalism?

prate V. speak foolishly; boast idly. Let us not *prate* about our good qualities; rather, let our virtues speak for themselves.

● **prattle** V. babble. Baby John *prattled* on and on about the cats and his ball and the Cookie Monster.

preamble N. introductory statement. In the *Preamble* to the Constitution, the purpose of the document is set forth.

● **precarious** ADJ. uncertain; risky. Saying the stock would be a *precarious* investment, the broker advised her client against purchasing it.

precedent N. something preceding in time that may be used as an authority or guide for future action. If I buy you a car for your sixteenth birthday, your brothers will want me to buy them cars when they turn sixteen, too; I can't afford to set such an expensive *precedent*. The law professor asked Jill to state which famous case served as a *precedent* for the court's decision in *Brown II*.

Word List 37   precept-propitiate

precept   N. practical rule guiding conduct. "Love thy neighbor as thyself" is a worthwhile *precept*.

precinct   N. district or division of a city. Ed McBain's detective novels set in the 87th *precinct* provide an exciting picture of police work.

precipice   N. cliff; dangerous position. Suddenly Indiana Jones found himself dangling from the edge of a *precipice*.

precipitate   ADJ. rash; premature; hasty; sudden. Though I was angry enough to resign on the spot, I had enough sense to keep myself from quitting a job in such a *precipitate* fashion.

precipitate   V. throw headlong; hasten. The removal of American political support appears to have *precipitated* the downfall of the Marcos regime.

precipitous   ADJ. steep; overhasty. This hill is difficult to climb because it is so *precipitous*; one slip, and our descent will be *precipitous* as well.

précis   N. concise summing up of main points. Before making her presentation at the conference, Ellen wrote up a neat *précis* of the major elements she would cover.

precise   ADJ. exact. If you don't give me *precise* directions and a map, I'll never find your place.

■ **preclude**   V. make impossible; eliminate. The fact that the band was already booked to play in Hollywood on New Year's Eve *precluded* their accepting the New Year's Eve gig in London they were offered.

■ **precocious**   ADJ. advanced in development. Listening to the grown-up way the child discussed serious topics, we couldn't help remarking how *precocious* she was. precocity, N.

precursor   N. forerunner. Though Gray and Burns share many traits with the Romantic poets who followed them, most critics consider them *precursors* of the Romantic Movement, not true Romantics.

■ **predator**   N. creature that seizes and devours another animal; person who robs or exploits others. Not just cats, but a wide variety of *predators*—owls, hawks, weasels, foxes—catch mice for dinner. A carnivore is by definition *predatory*, for he *preys* on weaker creatures.

■ **predecessor**   N. former occupant of a post. I hope I can live up to the fine example set by my late *predecessor* in this office.

predetermine   V. predestine; settle or decide beforehand; influence markedly. Romeo and Juliet believed that Fate had *predetermined* their meeting. Bea gathered estimates from caterers, florists, and stationers so that she could *predetermine* the costs of holding a catered buffet. Philip's love of athletics *predetermined* his choice of a career in sports marketing.

predicament   N. tricky or dangerous situation; dilemma. Tied to the railroad tracks by the villain, Pauline strained against her bonds. How would she escape from this terrible *predicament*?

predilection   N. partiality; preference. Although I have written all sorts of poetry over the years, I have a definite *predilection* for occasional verse.

predispose   V. give an inclination toward; make susceptible to. Oleg's love of dressing up his big sister's Barbie doll may have *predisposed* him to become a fashion designer. Genetic influences apparently *predispose* people to certain forms of cancer.

preeminent   ADJ. outstanding; superior. The king traveled to Boston because he wanted the *preeminent* surgeon in the field to perform the operation.

preempt   V. head off; forestall by acting first; appropriate for oneself; supplant. Hoping to *preempt* any attempts by the opposition to make educational reform a hot political issue, the candidate set out her own plan to revitalize the public schools. preemptive, ADJ.

preen   V. make oneself tidy in appearance; feel self-satisfaction. As Kitty *preened* before the mirror, carefully smoothing her shining hair, she couldn't help *preening* over how pretty she looked.

prehensile   ADJ. capable of grasping or holding. Monkeys use not only their arms and legs but also their *prehensile* tails in traveling through the trees.

prelate   N. church dignitary. The archbishop of Moscow and other high-ranking *prelates* visited the Russian Orthodox seminary.

prelude   N. introduction; forerunner. I am afraid that this border raid is the *prelude* to more serious attacks.

premeditate   V. plan in advance. She had *premeditated* the murder for months, reading about common poisons and buying weed killer that contained arsenic.

premise   N. assumption; postulate. Based on the *premise* that there's no fool like an old fool, P. T. Barnum hired a ninety-year-old clown for his circus.

premonition   N. forewarning. We ignored these *premonitions* of disaster because they appeared to be based on childish fears.

preposterous   ADJ. absurd; ridiculous. When he tried to downplay his youthful experiments with marijuana by saying he hadn't inhaled, we all thought, "What a *preposterous* excuse!"

prerogative   N. privilege; unquestionable right. The president cannot levy taxes; that is the *prerogative* of the legislative branch of government.

presage   V. foretell. The vultures flying overhead *presaged* the discovery of the corpse in the desert.

prescience   N. ability to foretell the future. Given the current wave of Japan-bashing, it does not take *prescience* for me to foresee problems in our future trade relations with Japan.

presentiment   N. feeling something will happen; anticipatory fear; premonition. Saying goodbye at the airport, Jack had a sudden *presentiment* that this was the last time he would see Jill.

prestige N. impression produced by achievements or reputation. Many students want to go to Harvard College not for the education offered but for the *prestige* of Harvard's name.

■ **presumptuous** ADJ. overconfident; impertinently bold; taking liberties. Matilda thought it was somewhat *presumptuous* of the young man to have addressed her without first having been introduced. Perhaps manners were freer here in the New World.

■ **pretentious** ADJ. ostentatious; pompous; making unjustified claims; overly ambitious. None of the other prize winners are wearing their medals; isn't it a bit *pretentious* of you to wear yours?

preternatural ADJ. beyond what is normal in nature. Malcolm's mother's total ability to tell when he was lying struck him as almost *preternatural.*

pretext N. excuse. He looked for a good *pretext* to get out of paying a visit to his aunt.

prevail V. induce; triumph over. He tried to *prevail* on her to type his essay for him.

■ **prevalent** ADJ. widespread; generally accepted. A radical committed to social change, Reed had no patience with the conservative views *prevalent* in the America of his day.

prevaricate V. lie. Some people believe that to *prevaricate* in a good cause is justifiable and regard such a statement as a "white lie."

prey N. target of a hunt; victim. In *Stalking the Wild Asparagus*, Euell Gibbons has as his *prey* not wild beasts but wild plants. also v.

prim ADJ. very precise and formal; exceedingly proper. Many people commented on the contrast between the *prim* attire of the young lady and the inappropriate clothing worn by her escort.

primordial ADJ. existing at the beginning (of time); rudimentary. The Neanderthal Man is one of our *primordial* ancestors.

primp V. groom oneself with care; adorn oneself. The groom stood by idly while his nervous bride-to-be *primped* one last time before the mirror.

pristine ADJ. characteristic of earlier times; primitive; unspoiled. This area has been preserved in all its *pristine* wildness.

privation N. hardship; want. In his youth, he knew hunger and *privation.*

probe V. explore with tools. The surgeon *probed* the wound for foreign matter before suturing it. also N.

problematic ADJ. doubtful; unsettled; questionable; perplexing. Given the way building costs have exceeded estimates for the job, whether the arena will ever be completed is *problematic.*

proclivity N. inclination; natural tendency. Watching the two-year-old voluntarily put away his toys, I was amazed by his *proclivity* for neatness.

procrastinate V. postpone; delay or put off. Looking at four years of receipts and checks he still had to sort through, Bob was truly sorry he had *procrastinated* for so long and not finished filing his taxes long ago.

prod V. poke; stir up; urge. If you *prod* him hard enough, he'll eventually clean his room.

■ **prodigal** ADJ. wasteful; reckless with money. Don't be so *prodigal* spending my money; when you've earned some money yourself, you can waste it as much as you want! also N.

prodigious ADJ. marvelous; enormous. Watching the champion weight lifter heave the weighty barbell to shoulder height and then boost it overhead, we marveled at his *prodigious* strength.

prodigy N. marvel; highly gifted child. Menuhin *was a prodigy*, performing wonders on his violin when he was barely eight years old.

■ **profane** V. violate; desecrate; treat unworthily. The members of the mysterious Far Eastern cult sought to kill the British explorer because he had *profaned* the sanctity of their holy goblet by using it as an ashtray. also ADJ.

● **profligate** ADJ. dissipated; wasteful; wildly immoral. Although surrounded by wild and *profligate* companions, she nevertheless managed to retain some sense of decency.

■ **profound** ADJ. deep; not superficial; complete. Freud's remarkable insights into human behavior caused his fellow scientists to honor him as a *profound* thinker. profundity, N.

■ **profusion** N. overabundance; lavish expenditure; excess. Freddy was so overwhelmed by the *profusion* of choices on the menu that he knocked over his wine glass and soaked his host. He made *profuse* apologies to his host, the waiter, the bus boy, the people at the next table, and the attendant handing out paper towels.

progenitor N. ancestor. The Roth family, whose *progenitors* emigrated from Germany early in the nineteenth century, settled in Peru, Illinois.

progeny N. children; offspring. He was proud of his *progeny* in general, but regarded George as the most promising of all his children.

prognosis N. forecasted course of a disease; prediction. If the doctor's *prognosis* is correct, the patient will be in a coma for at least twenty-four hours.

projectile N. missile. Man has always hurled *projectiles* at his enemy whether in the form of stones or of highly explosive shells.

proletarian N. member of the working class; blue collar person. "Workers of the world, unite! You have nothing to lose but your chains" is addressed to *proletarians*, not preppies. So is *Blue Collar Holler.* proletariat, N.

■ **proliferation** N. rapid growth; spread; multiplication. Times of economic hardship inevitably encourage the *proliferation* of countless get-rich-quick schemes. proliferate, V.

■ **prolific** ADJ. abundantly fruitful. My editors must assume I'm a *prolific* writer: they expect me to revise six books this year!

prolixity N. tedious wordiness; verbosity. A writer who suffers from *prolixity* tells his readers everything they *never* wanted to know about his subject (or were too bored to ask). prolix, ADJ.

prologue N. introduction (to a poem or play). In the *prologue* to *Romeo and Juliet*, Shakespeare introduces the audience to the feud between the Montagues and the Capulets.

prolong V. make longer; draw out; lengthen. In their determination to discover ways to *prolong* human life, doctors fail to take into account that longer lives are not always happier ones.

prominent ADJ. conspicuous; notable; sticking out. Have you ever noticed that Prince Charles's *prominent* ears make him look like the big-eared character in *Mad* comics?

promiscuous ADJ. mixed indiscriminately; haphazard; irregular, particularly sexually. In the opera *La Bohème*, we get a picture of the *promiscuous* life led by the young artists of Paris.

promontory N. headland. They erected a lighthouse on the *promontory* to warn approaching ships of their nearness to the shore.

promote V. help to flourish; advance in rank; publicize. Founder of the Children's Defense Fund, Marian Wright Edelman ceaselessly *promotes* the welfare of young people everywhere.

prompt V. cause; provoke; provide a cue for an actor. Whatever *prompted* you to ask for such a big piece of cake when you're on a diet?

promulgate V. proclaim a doctrine or law; make known by official publication. When Moses came down from the mountain top all set to *promulgate* God's commandments, he freaked out on discovering his followers worshipping a golden calf.

prone ADJ. inclined to; prostrate. She was *prone* to sudden fits of anger during which she would lie *prone* on the floor, screaming and kicking her heels.

propagate V. multiply; spread. Since bacteria *propagate* more quickly in unsanitary environments, it is important to keep hospital rooms clean.

propellants N. substances that propel or drive forward. The development of our missile program has forced our scientists to seek more powerful *propellants*.

propensity N. natural inclination. Convinced of his own talent, Sol has an unfortunate *propensity* to belittle the talents of others.

prophetic ADJ. foretelling the future. I have no magical *prophetic* powers; when I predict what will happen, I base my predictions on common sense. prophesy, V.

propinquity N. nearness; kinship. Their relationship could not be explained as being based on mere *propinquity;* they were more than relatives, they were true friends.

propitiate V. appease. The natives offered sacrifices to *propitiate* the gods.

Word List 38 propitious-quarry

propitious ADJ. favorable; fortunate; advantageous. Chloe consulted her horoscope to see whether Tuesday would be a *propitious* day to dump her boyfriend.

proponent N. supporter; backer; opposite of opponent. In the Senate, *proponents* of the universal health care measure lobbied to gain additional support for the controversial legislation.

propound V. put forth for analysis. In your discussion, you have *propounded* several questions; let us consider each one separately.

propriety N. fitness; correct conduct. Miss Manners counsels her readers so that they may behave with due *propriety* in any social situation and not embarrass themselves.

propulsive ADJ. driving forward. The jet plane has a greater *propulsive* power than the engine-driven plane.

prosaic ADJ. dull and unimaginative; matter-of-fact; factual. Though the ad writers came up with an original way to publicize the product, the head office rejected it for a more *prosaic*, ordinary slogan.

proscribe V. ostracize; banish; outlaw. Antony, Octavius, and Lepidus *proscribed* all those who had conspired against Julius Caesar.

proselytize V. convert to a religion or belief. In these interfaith meetings, there must be no attempt to *proselytize; we* must respect all points of view.

prosperity N. good fortune; financial success; physical well-being. Promising to stay together "for richer, for poorer," the newlyweds vowed to be true to one another in *prosperity* and hardship alike.

prostrate V. stretch out full on ground. He *prostrated* himself before the idol. also ADJ.

protean ADJ. versatile; able to take on many shapes. A remarkably *protean* actor, Alec Guinness could take on any role.

protégé N. person receiving protection and support from a patron. Born with an independent spirit, Cyrano de Bergerac refused to be a *protégé* of Cardinal Richelieu.

protocol N. diplomatic etiquette. We must run this state dinner according to *protocol* if we are to avoid offending any of our guests.

prototype N. original work used as a model by others. The crude typewriter on display in this museum is the *prototype* of the elaborate machines in use today.

protract V. prolong. Seeking to delay the union members' vote, the management team tried to *protract* the negotiations endlessly.

protrude V. stick out. His fingers *protruded* from the holes in his gloves. protrusion, N.

protuberance N. protrusion; bulge. A ganglionic cyst is a fluid-filled tumor that develops near a joint membrane or tendon sheath, and that bulges beneath the skin, forming a *protuberance*.

provident ADJ. displaying foresight; thrifty; preparing for emergencies. In his usual *provident* manner, he had insured himself against this type of loss.

■ **provincial** ADJ. pertaining to a province; limited in outlook; unsophisticated. As *provincial* governor, Sir Henry administered the Queen's law in his remote corner of Canada. Caught up in local problems, out of touch with London news, he became sadly *provincial*.

provisional ADJ. tentative. Kim's acceptance as an American Express card holder was *provisional*: before issuing her a card, American Express wanted to check her employment record and credit history.

provocative ADJ. arousing anger or interest; annoying. In a typically *provocative* act, the bully kicked sand into the weaker man's face.

provoke V. stir to anger; cause retaliation. In order to prevent a sudden outbreak of hostilities, we must not *provoke* our foe. provocation, N; provocative, ADJ.

prowess N. extraordinary ability; military bravery. Performing triple axels and double lutzes at the age of six, the young figure skater was world famous for her *prowess* on the ice.

■ **proximity** N. nearness. Blind people sometimes develop a compensatory ability to sense the *proximity* of objects around them.

proxy N. authorized agent. Please act as my *proxy* and vote for this slate of candidates in my absence.

prude N. excessively modest person. The X-rated film was definitely not for *prudes*. prudish, ADJ.

■ **prudent** ADJ. cautious; careful. A miser hoards money not because he is *prudent* but because he is greedy. prudence, N.

prune V. cut away; trim. With the help of her editor, she was able to *prune* her overlong manuscript into publishable form.

prurient ADJ. having or causing lustful thoughts and desires. Aroused by his *prurient* impulses, the dirty old man leered at the sweet young thing and offered to give her a sample of his "prowess."

pseudonym N. pen name. Samuel Clemens' *pseudonym* was Mark Twain.

psyche N. soul; mind. It is difficult to delve into the *psyche* of a human being.

pterodactyl N. extinct flying reptile. The remains of *pterodactyls* indicate that these flying reptiles had a wingspan of as much as twenty feet.

puerile ADJ. childish. His *puerile* pranks sometimes offended his more mature friends.

pugilist N. boxer. The famous *pugilist* Cassius Clay changed his name to Muhammed Ali.

pugnacity N. combativeness; disposition to fight. "Put up your dukes!" he cried, making a fist to show his *pugnacity*. pugnacious, ADJ.

pulchritude N. beauty; comeliness. I do not envy the judges who have to select this year's Miss America from this collection of female *pulchritude*.

pulverize V. crush or grind into dust. Before sprinkling the dried herbs into the stew, Michael first *pulverized* them into a fine powder.

pummel V. beat or pound with fists. Swinging wildly, Pam *pummeled* her brother around the head and shoulders.

punctilious ADJ. laying stress on niceties of conduct or form; minutely attentive to fine points (perhaps too much so). Percy is *punctilious* about observing the rules of etiquette whenever Miss Manners invites him to stay. punctiliousness, N.

pundit N. authority on a subject; learned person; expert. Some authors who write about SAT I as if they are *pundits* actually know very little about the test.

pungent ADJ. stinging; sharp in taste or smell; caustic. The *pungent* odor of ripe Limburger cheese appealed to Simone but made Stanley gag.

punitive ADJ. punishing. He asked for *punitive* measures against the offender.

puny ADJ. insignificant; tiny; weak. Our *puny* efforts to stop the flood were futile.

purchase N. firm grasp or footing. The mountaineer struggled to get a proper *purchase* on the slippery rock. (secondary meaning)

purge V. remove or get rid of something unwanted; free from blame or guilt; cleanse or purify. When the Communist government *purged* the party to get rid of members suspected of capitalist sympathies, they sent the disloyal members to labor camps in Siberia.

purported ADJ. alleged; claimed; reputed or rumored. The *purported* Satanists sacrificing live roosters in the park turned out to be a party of Shriners holding a chicken barbecue.

purse V. pucker; contract into wrinkles. Miss Watson *pursed* her lips to show her disapproval of Huck's bedraggled appearance.

purveyor N. furnisher of foodstuffs; caterer. As *purveyor* of rare wines and viands, he traveled through France and Italy every year in search of new products to sell.

pusillanimous ADJ. cowardly; fainthearted. You should be ashamed of your *pusillanimous* conduct during this dispute.

putrid ADJ. foul; rotten; decayed. The gangrenous condition of the wound was indicated by the *putrid* smell when the bandages were removed. putrescence, N.

pyromaniac N. person with an insane desire to set things on fire. The detectives searched the area for the *pyromaniac* who had set these costly fires.

quack N. charlatan; impostor. Do not be misled by the exorbitant claims of this *quack*; he cannot cure you.

quadruped N. four-footed animal. Most mammals are *quadrupeds*.

quaff V. drink with relish. As we *quaffed* our ale, we listened to the lively songs of the students in the tavern.

● **quagmire** N. soft wet boggy land; complex or dangerous situation from which it is difficult to free oneself. Up to her knees in mud, Myra wondered how on earth she was going to extricate herself from this *quagmire*.

quail   V. cower; lose heart. The Cowardly Lion was afraid that he would *quail* in the face of danger.

quaint   ADJ. odd; old-fashioned; picturesque. Her *quaint* clothes and old-fashioned language marked her as an eccentric.

■ **qualified**   ADJ. limited; restricted. Unable to give the candidate full support, the mayor gave him only a *qualified* endorsement. (secondary meaning)

qualms   N. misgivings; uneasy fears, especially about matters of conscience. I have no *qualms* about giving this assignment to Helen; I know she will handle it admirably.

■ **quandary**   N. dilemma. When both Harvard and Stanford accepted Laura, she was in a *quandary* as to which school she should attend.

quarantine   N. isolation of person or ship to prevent spread of infection. We will have to place this house under *quarantine* until we determine the exact nature of the disease. also V.

quarry   N. victim; object of a hunt. The police closed in on their *quarry*.

quarry   V. dig into. They *quarried* blocks of marble out of the hillside. also N.

Word List 39   quay-recurrent

quay   N. dock; landing place. Because of the captain's carelessness, the ship crashed into the *quay*.

queasy   ADJ. easily nauseated; squeamish. Remember that great chase movie, the one with the carsick passenger? That's right: *Queasy Rider*!

● **quell**   V. extinguish; put down; quiet. Miss Minchin's demeanor was so stern and forbidding that she could *quell* any unrest among her students with one intimidating glance.

quench   V. douse or extinguish; assuage or satisfy. No matter how much water the hiker drank, she could not *quench* her thirst.

● **querulous**   ADJ. fretful; whining. Even the most agreeable toddlers can begin to act *querulous* if they miss their nap.

query   N. inquiry; question. In her column "Ask Beth," the columnist invites young readers to send her their *queries* about life and love.

quibble   N. minor objection or complaint. Aside from a few hundred teensy-weensy *quibbles* about the set, the script, the actors, the director, the costumes, the lighting, and the props, the hypercritical critic loved the play. also V.

● **quiescent**   ADJ. at rest; dormant; temporarily inactive. After the great eruption, fear of Mount Etna was great; people did not return to cultivate its rich hillside lands until the volcano had been *quiescent* for a full two years. quiescence, N.

quietude   N. tranquility. He was impressed by the air of *quietude* and peace that pervaded the valley.

quintessence   N. purest and highest embodiment. Noel Coward displayed the *quintessence* of wit.

quip   N. taunt. You are unpopular because you are too free with your *quips* and sarcastic comments. also V.

quirk   N. startling twist; caprice. By a *quirk* of fate, he found himself working for the man whom he had discharged years before.

quiver   V. tremble; shake. The bird dog's nose twitched and his whiskers *quivered* as he strained eagerly against the leash. also N.

quiver   N. case for arrows. Robin Hood reached back and plucked one last arrow from his *quiver*. (secondary meaning)

quixotic   ADJ. idealistic but impractical. Constantly coming up with *quixotic*, unworkable schemes to save the world, Simon has his heart in the right place, but his head somewhere in the clouds.

quizzical   ADJ. teasing; bantering; mocking; curious. When the skinny teenager tripped over his own feet stepping into the bullpen, Coach raised one *quizzical* eyebrow, shook his head, and said, "Okay, kid. You're here, let's see what you've got."

quorum   N. number of members necessary to conduct a meeting. The senator asked for a roll call to determine whether a *quorum* was present.

rabid   ADJ. like a fanatic; furious. He was a *rabid* follower of the Dodgers and watched them play whenever he could go to the ball park.

raconteur   N. storyteller. My father was a gifted *raconteur* with an unlimited supply of anecdotes.

rail   V. scold; rant. You may *rail* at him all you want; you will never change him.

raiment   N. clothing. "How can I go to the ball?" asked Cinderella. "I have no *raiment* fit to wear."

rally   V. call up or summon (forces, vital powers, etc.); revive or recuperate. Washington quickly *rallied* his troops to fight off the British attack. The patient had been sinking throughout the night, but at dawn she *rallied* and made a complete recovery.

■ **ramble**   V. wander aimlessly (physically or mentally). Listening to the teacher *ramble*, Judy wondered whether he'd ever get to his point.

ramification   N. branching out; subdivision. We must examine all the *ramifications* of this problem.

ramify   V. divide into branches or subdivisions. When the plant begins to *ramify*, it is advisable to nip off most of the new branches.

ramp   N. slope; inclined plane. The house was built with *ramps* instead of stairs in order to enable the man in the wheelchair to move easily from room to room and floor to floor.

rampant   ADJ. growing in profusion; unrestrained. The *rampant* weeds in the garden choked the flowers until they died.

ramshackle ADJ. rickety; falling apart. The boys propped up the *ramshackle* clubhouse with a couple of boards.

rancid ADJ. having the odor of stale fat. A *rancid* odor filled the ship's galley and nauseated the crew.

■ **rancor** N. bitterness; hatred. Thirty years after the war, she could not let go of the past but was still consumed with *rancor* against the foe.

random ADJ. without definite purpose, plan, or aim; haphazard. Although the sponsor of the raffle claimed all winners were chosen at *random*, people had their suspicions when the grand prize went to the sponsor's brother-in-law.

rankle V. irritate; fester. The memory of having been jilted *rankled* him for years.

● **rant** V. rave; talk excitedly; scold; make a grandiloquent speech. When he heard that I'd totaled the family car, Dad began to *rant* at me like a complete madman.

rapacious ADJ. excessively greedy; predatory. The *rapacious* brigands stripped the villagers of all their possessions. rapacity, N.

rapport N. emotional closeness; harmony. In team teaching, it is important that all teachers in the group have good *rapport* with one another.

rapt ADJ. absorbed; enchanted. Caught up in the wonder of the storyteller's tale, the *rapt* listeners sat motionless, hanging on his every word.

rarefied ADJ. made less dense [of a gas]. The mountain climbers had difficulty breathing in the *rarefied* atmosphere. rarefy, V.

raspy ADJ. grating; harsh. The sergeant's *raspy* voice grated on the recruits' ears.

■ **ratify** V. approve formally; confirm; verify. Party leaders doubted that they had enough votes in both houses of Congress to *ratify* the constitutional amendment.

ratiocination N. reasoning; act of drawing conclusions from premises. While Watson was a man of average intelligence, Holmes was a genius, whose gift for *ratiocination* made him a superb detective.

rationale N. fundamental reason or justification; grounds for an action. Her need to have someplace to hang her earring collection was Dora's *rationale* for piercing fifteen holes in each ear.

rationalize V. give a plausible reason for an action in place of a true, less admirable one; offer an excuse. When David told gabby Gabrielle he couldn't give her a ride to the dance because he had no room in the car, he was *rationalizing*; actually, he couldn't stand being cooped up in a car with anyone who talked as much as she did.

● **raucous** ADJ. harsh and shrill; disorderly and boisterous. The *raucous* crowd of New Year's Eve revelers got progressively noisier as midnight drew near.

rave N. overwhelmingly favorable review. Though critic John Simon seldom has a good word to say about most contemporary plays, his review of *All in the Timing* was a total *rave*.

ravel V. fall apart into tangles; unravel or untwist; entangle. A single thread pulled loose, and the entire scarf started to *ravel*.

● **ravenous** ADJ. extremely hungry. The *ravenous* dog upset several garbage pails in its search for food.

● **raze** V. destroy completely. Spelling is important: to raise a building is to put it up; to *raze* a building is to tear it down.

reactionary ADJ. recoiling from progress; politically ultra-conservative. Opposing the use of English in worship services, *reactionary* forces in the church fought to reinstate the mass in Latin.

realm N. kingdom; field or sphere. In the animal *realm*, the lion is the king of beasts.

reaper N. one who harvests grain. Death, the Grim *Reaper*, cuts down mortal men and women, just as a farmer cuts down the ripened grain. reap, V.

rebuff V. snub; beat back. She *rebuffed* his invitation so smoothly that he did not realize he had been snubbed. also N.

rebuke V. scold harshly; criticize severely. No matter how sharply Miss Watson *rebuked* Huck for his misconduct, he never talked back but just stood there like a stump. also N.

■ **rebuttal** N. refutation; response with contrary evidence. The defense lawyer confidently listened to the prosecutor sum up his case, sure that she could answer his arguments in her *rebuttal*.

recalcitrant ADJ. obstinately stubborn; determined to resist authority; unruly. Which animal do you think is more *recalcitrant*, a pig or a mule?

● **recant** V. disclaim or disavow; retract a previous statement; openly confess error. Those who can, keep true to their faith; those who can't, *recant*. Hoping to make Joan of Arc *recant* her sworn testimony, her English captors tried to convince her that her visions had been sent to her by the Devil.

recapitulate V. summarize. Let us *recapitulate* what has been said thus far before going ahead.

recast V. reconstruct (a sentence, story, etc.); fashion again. Let me *recast* this sentence in terms your feeble brain can grasp: in words of one syllable, you are a fool.

receptive ADJ. quick or willing to receive ideas, suggestions, etc. Adventure-loving Huck Finn proved a *receptive* audience for Tom's tales of buried treasure and piracy.

recession N. withdrawal; retreat; time of low economic activity. The slow *recession* of the flood waters created problems for the crews working to restore power to the area. recede, V.

recidivism N. habitual return to crime. Prison reformers in the United States are disturbed by the high rate of *recidivism*; the number of men serving second and third terms in prison indicates the failure of prisons to rehabilitate the inmates.

recipient N. receiver. Although he had been the *recipient* of many favors, he was not grateful to his benefactor.

reciprocal ADJ. mutual; exchangeable; interacting. The two nations signed a *reciprocal* trade agreement.

reciprocate V. repay in kind. If they attack us, we shall be compelled to *reciprocate* and bomb their territory. reciprocity, N.

■ **recluse**   N. hermit; loner. Disappointed in love, Miss Emily became a *recluse*; she shut herself away in her empty mansion and refused to see another living soul. reclusive, ADJ.

reconcile   V. correct inconsistencies; become friendly after a quarrel. Each month when we try to reconcile our checkbook with the bank statement, we quarrel. However, despite these monthly lovers' quarrels, we always manage to *reconcile*.

reconnaissance   N. survey of enemy by soldiers; reconnoitering. If you encounter any enemy soldiers during your *reconnaissance,* capture them for questioning.

■ **recount**   V. narrate or tell; count over again. A born storyteller, my father loved to *recount* anecdotes about his early years in New York.

recourse   N. resorting to help when in trouble. The boy's only *recourse* was to appeal to his father for aid.

recrimination   N. countercharges. Loud and angry *recriminations* were her answer to his accusations.

■ **rectify**   V. set right; correct. You had better send a check to *rectify* your account before American Express cancels your credit card.

rectitude   N. uprightness; moral virtue; correctness of judgment. The Eagle Scout was a model of *rectitude*.

recumbent   ADJ. reclining; lying down completely or in part. The command "AT EASE" does not permit you to take a *recumbent* position.

recuperate   V. recover. The doctors were worried because the patient did not *recuperate* as rapidly as they had expected.

recurrent   ADJ. occurring again and again. Richard's *recurrent* asthma attacks disturbed us and we consulted a physician.

Word List 40   redolent-rescind

redolent   ADJ. fragrant; odorous; suggestive of an odor. Even though it is February, the air is *redolent* of spring.

redoubtable   ADJ. formidable; causing fear. During the Cold War period, neighboring countries tried not to offend the Russians because they could be *redoubtable* foes.

redress   N. remedy; compensation. Do you mean to tell me that I can get no *redress* for my injuries? also V.

■ **redundant**   ADJ. superfluous; repetitious; excessively wordy. The bottle of wine I brought to Bob's was certainly *redundant*: how was I to know Bob owned a winery? In your essay, you repeat several points unnecessarily; try to be less *redundant* in the future. redundancy, N.

reek   V. emit (odor). The room *reeked* with stale tobacco smoke. also N.

refraction   N. bending of a ray of light. When you look at a stick inserted in water, it looks bent because of the *refraction* of the light by the water.

refractory   ADJ. stubborn; unmanageable. The *refractory* horse was eliminated from the race when he refused to obey the jockey.

refrain   V. abstain from; resist. N. chorus. Whenever he heard a song with a lively chorus, Sol could never *refrain* from joining in on the *refrain*.

refurbish   V. renovate; make bright by polishing. The flood left a deposit of mud on everything; we had to *refurbish* our belongings.

■ **refute**   V. disprove. The defense called several respectable witnesses who were able to *refute* the false testimony of the prosecution's sole witness. refutation, N.

regal   ADJ. royal. Prince Albert had a *regal* manner.

regale   V. entertain. John *regaled* us with tales of his adventures in Africa.

regime   N. method or system of government. When the French mention the Old *Regime,* they refer to the government existing before the revolution.

regimen   N. prescribed diet and habits. I doubt whether the results warrant our living under such a strict *regimen*.

rehabilitate   V. restore to proper condition. We must *rehabilitate* those whom we send to prison.

reimburse   V. repay. Let me know what you have spent and I will *reimburse* you.

reiterate   V. repeat. He *reiterated* the warning to make sure everyone understood it.

rejoinder   N. retort; comeback; reply. When someone has been rude to me, I find it particularly satisfying to come up with a quick *rejoinder*.

rejuvenate   V. make young again. The charlatan claimed that his elixir would *rejuvenate* the aged and weary.

■ **relegate**   V. banish to an inferior position; delegate; assign. After Ralph dropped his second tray of drinks that week, the manager swiftly *relegated* him to a minor post cleaning up behind the bar.

relent   V. give in. When her stern father would not *relent* and allow her to marry Robert Browning, Elizabeth Barrett eloped with her suitor. relentless, ADJ.

relevant   ADJ. pertinent; referring to the case in hand. How *relevant* Virginia Woolf's essays are to women writers today! It's as if Woolf in the 1930s foresaw our current literary struggles. relevancy, N.

relic   N. surviving remnant; memento. Egypt's Department of Antiquities prohibits tourists from taking mummies and other ancient *relics* out of the country. Mike keeps his photos of his trip to Egypt in a box with other *relics* of his travels.

relinquish   V. give up something with reluctance; yield. Denise never realized how hard it would be for her to *relinquish* her newborn son to the care of his adoptive parents. Once you get used to fringe benefits like expense account meals and a company car, it's very hard to *relinquish* them.

relish V. savor; enjoy. Watching Peter enthusiastically chow down, I thought, "Now there's a man who *relishes* a good dinner!" also N.

remediable ADJ. reparable. Let us be grateful that the damage is *remediable*.

remedial ADJ. curative; corrective. Because he was a slow reader, he decided to take a course in *remedial* reading.

reminiscence N. recollection. Her *reminiscences* of her experiences are so fascinating that she ought to write a book.

remiss ADJ. negligent. The guard was accused of being *remiss* in his duty when the prisoner escaped.

● **remission** N. temporary moderation of disease symptoms; cancellation of a debt; forgiveness or pardon. Though the senator had been treated for cancer, his symptoms were in *remission*, and he was considered fit enough to handle the strains of a presidential race.

remnant N. remainder. I suggest that you wait until the store places the *remnants* of these goods on sale.

remonstrance N. protest; objection. The authorities were deaf to the pastor's *remonstrances* about the lack of police protection in the area. remonstrate, V.

■ **remorse** N. guilt; self-reproach. The murderer felt no *remorse* for his crime.

remunerative ADJ. compensating; rewarding. I find my new work so *remunerative* that I may not return to my previous employment. remuneration, N.

rend V. split; tear apart. In his grief, he tried to *rend* his garments. rent, N.

render V. deliver; provide; represent. He *rendered* aid to the needy and indigent.

rendition N. translation; artistic interpretation of a song, etc. The audience cheered enthusiastically as she completed her *rendition* of the aria.

renegade N. deserter; traitor. Because he had abandoned his post and joined forces with the Indians, his fellow officers considered the hero of *Dances with Wolves* a *renegade*. also ADJ.

renege V. deny; go back on. He *reneged* on paying off his debt.

■ **renounce** V. abandon; disown; repudiate. Even though she knew she would be burned at the stake as a witch, Joan of Arc refused to *renounce* her belief that her voices came from God. renunciation, N.

renovate V. restore to good condition; renew. They claim that they can *renovate* worn shoes so that they look like new ones.

renown N. fame. For many years an unheralded researcher, Barbara McClintock gained international *renown* when she won the Nobel Prize in Physiology and Medicine. renowned, ADJ.

rent N. rip; split. Kit did an excellent job of mending the *rent* in the lining of her coat.

reparable ADJ. capable of being repaired. Fortunately, the damages we suffered in the accident were *reparable* and our car looks brand new.

reparation N. amends; compensation. At the peace conference, the defeated country promised to pay *reparations* to the victors.

repast N. meal; feast; banquet. The caterers prepared a delicious *repast* for Fred and Judy's wedding day.

repeal V. revoke; annul. What would the effect on our society be if we decriminalized drug use by *repealing* the laws against the possession and sale of narcotics?

■ **repel** V. drive away; disgust. At first, the Beast's ferocious appearance *repelled* Beauty, but she came to love the tender heart hidden behind that beastly exterior.

repellent ADJ. driving away; unattractive. Mosquitoes find the odor so *repellent* that they leave any spot where this liquid has been sprayed. also N.

repercussion N. rebound; reverberation; reaction. I am afraid that this unfortunate incident will have serious *repercussions*.

repertoire N. list of works of music, drama, etc., a performer is prepared to present. The opera company decided to include *Madame Butterfly* in its *repertoire* for the following season.

replenish V. fill up again. Before she could take another backpacking trip, Carla had to *replenish* her stock of freeze-dried foods.

● **replete** ADJ. filled to the brim or to the point of being stuffed; abundantly supplied. The movie star's memoir was *replete* with juicy details about the love life of half of Hollywood.

replica N. copy. Are you going to hang this *replica* of the Declaration of Independence in the classroom or in the auditorium?

replicate V. reproduce; duplicate. Because he had always wanted a palace, Donald decided to *replicate* the Taj Mahal in miniature on his estate.

repository N. storehouse. Libraries are *repositories* of the world's best thoughts.

■ **reprehensible** ADJ. deserving blame. Shocked by the viciousness of the bombing, politicians of every party uniformly condemned the terrorists' *reprehensible* deed.

repress V. restrain; crush; oppress. Anne's parents tried to curb her impetuosity without *repressing* her boundless high spirits.

reprieve N. temporary stay. During the twenty-four-hour *reprieve*, the lawyers sought to make the stay of execution permanent. also V.

■ **reprimand** V. reprove severely; rebuke. Every time Ermengarde made a mistake in class, she was afraid that Miss Minchin would *reprimand* her and tell her father how badly she was doing in school. also N.

reprisal N. retaliation. I am confident that we are ready for any *reprisals* the enemy may undertake.

reprise N. musical repetition; repeat performance; recurrent action. We enjoyed the soprano's solo in Act I so much that we were delighted by its *reprise* in the finale.

reproach V. express disapproval or disappointment. He never could do anything wrong without imagining how the look on his mother's face would *reproach* him afterwards. reproachful, ADJ.

reprobate N. person hardened in sin; devoid of a sense of decency. I cannot understand why he has so many admirers if he is the *reprobate* you say he is.

■ **reprove** V. censure; rebuke. The principal severely *reproved* the students whenever they talked in the halls.

■ **repudiate** V. disown; disavow. On separating from Tony, Tina announced that she would *repudiate* all debts incurred by her soon-to-be ex-husband.

● **repugnant** ADJ. loathsome; hateful. She found the snake *repugnant* and looked on it with loathing and fear.

repulsion N. distaste; act of driving back. Hating bloodshed, she viewed war with *repulsion*. Even defensive battles distressed her, for the *repulsion* of enemy forces is never accomplished bloodlessly.

reputable ADJ. respectable. If you want to buy antiques, look for a *reputable* dealer; far too many dealers today pass off fakes as genuine antiques.

reputed ADJ. supposed. Though he is the *reputed* father of the child, no one can be sure. repute, N.

requiem N. mass for the dead; dirge. They played Mozart's *Requiem* at the funeral.

requisite N. necessary requirement. Many colleges state that a student must offer three years of a language as a *requisite* for admission.

requite V. repay; revenge. The wretch *requited* his benefactors by betraying them.

● **rescind** V. cancel. Because of the public outcry against the new taxes, the senator proposed a bill to *rescind* the unpopular financial measure.

Word List 41   resentment-sacrosanct

resentment N. indignation; bitterness; displeasure. Not wanting to appear a sore loser, Bill tried to hide his *resentment* of Barry's success.

■ **reserve** N. self-control; formal but distant manner. Although some girls were attracted by Mark's air of *reserve*, Judy was put off by it, for she felt his aloofness indicated a lack of openness. reserved, ADJ.

residue N. remainder; balance. In his will, he requested that after payment of debts, taxes, and funeral expenses, the *residue* be given to his wife. residual, ADJ.

■ **resigned** ADJ. accepting one's fate; unresisting; patiently submissive. *Resigned* to his downtrodden existence, Bob Cratchit was too meek to protest Scrooge's bullying. resignation, N.

resilient ADJ. elastic; having the power of springing back. Highly *resilient*, steel makes excellent bedsprings. resilience, N.

■ **resolution** N. determination; resolve. Nothing could shake his *resolution* that his children would get the best education that money could buy. resolute, ADJ.

■ **resolve** N. determination; firmness of purpose. How dare you question my *resolve* to take up sky-diving! Of course I haven't changed my mind!

resolve V. decide; settle; solve. Holmes *resolved* to travel to Bohemia to *resolve* the dispute between Irene Adler and the king.

resonant ADJ. echoing; resounding; deep and full in sound. The deep, *resonant* voice of the actor James Earl Jones makes him particularly effective when he appears on stage.

respiration N. breathing; exhalation. The doctor found that the patient's years of smoking had adversely affected both his lung capacity and his rate of *respiration*.

● **respite** N. interval of relief; time for rest; delay in punishment. After working nonstop on this project for three straight months, I need a *respite*! For David, the two weeks vaca-

tioning in New Zealand were a delightful *respite* from the pressures of his job.

● **resplendent** ADJ. dazzling; glorious; brilliant. While all the adults were commenting how glorious the emperor looked in his *resplendent* new clothes, one little boy was heard to say, "But he's naked!"

responsiveness N. state of reacting readily to appeals, orders, etc. The audience cheered and applauded, delighting the performers by its *responsiveness*.

restitution N. reparation; indemnification. He offered to make *restitution* for the window broken by his son.

restive ADJ. restlessly impatient; obstinately resisting control. Waiting impatiently in line to see Santa Claus, even the best-behaved children grow *restive* and start to fidget.

■ **restraint** N. moderation or self-control; controlling force; restriction. Control yourself, young lady! Show some *restraint*!

resumption N. taking up again; recommencement. During summer break, Don had not realized how much he missed university life: at the *resumption* of classes, however, he felt marked excitement and pleasure. resume, V.

resurge V. rise again; flow to and fro. It was startling to see the spirit of nationalism *resurge* as the Soviet Union disintegrated into a loose federation of ethnic and national groups. resurgence, N.

retain V. keep; employ. Fighting to *retain* his seat in Congress, Senator Foghorn *retained* a new manager to head his reelection campaign.

retaliation N. repayment in kind (usually for bad treatment). Because everyone knew the Princeton Band had stolen Brown's mascot, the whole Princeton student body expected some sort of *retaliation* from Brown. retaliate, V.

retentive ADJ. holding; having a good memory. The pupil did not need to spend much time studying, for he had a *retentive* mind and remembered all he read.

■ **reticence** N. reserve; uncommunicativeness; inclination to silence. Fearing his competitors might get advance word about his plans from talkative staff members, Hughes preferred *reticence* from his employees to loquacity. reticent, ADJ.

retinue N. following; attendants. The queen's *retinue* followed her down the aisle.

retiring ADJ. modest; shy. Given Susan's *retiring* personality, no one expected her to take up public speaking; surprisingly enough, she became a star of the school debate team.

retort N. quick sharp reply. Even when it was advisable for her to keep her mouth shut, she was always ready with a quick *retort*. also V.

■ **retract** V. withdraw; take back. When I saw how Fred and his fraternity brothers had trashed the frat house, I decided to *retract* my offer to let them use our summer cottage for the weekend. retraction, N.

retrench V. cut down; economize. In order to be able to afford to send their children to college, they would have to *retrench*. retrenchment, N.

retribution N. vengeance; compensation; punishment for offenses. The evangelist maintained that an angry deity would exact *retribution* from the sinners.

retrieve V. recover; find and bring in. The dog was intelligent and quickly learned to *retrieve* the game killed by the hunter.

retroactive ADJ. of a law that dates back to a period before its enactment. Because the law was *retroactive* to the first of the year, we found she was eligible for the pension.

retrograde V. go backwards; degenerate. instead of advancing, our civilization seems to have *retrograded* in ethics and culture. also ADJ.

retrospective ADJ. looking back on the past. The Museum of Graphic Arts is holding a *retrospective* showing of the paintings of Michael Whelan over the past two decades.

revelry N. boisterous merrymaking. New Year's Eve is a night of *revelry*

■ **reverent** ADJ. respectful; worshipful. Though I bow my head in church and recite the prayers, sometimes I don't feel properly *reverent*. revere, V.

reverie N. daydream; musing. He was awakened from his *reverie* by the teacher's question.

revert V. relapse; backslide; turn back to. Most of the time Andy seemed sensitive and mature, but occasionally he would *revert* to his smart-alecky, macho, adolescent self.

revile V. attack with abusive language; vilify. Though most of his contemporaries *reviled* Captain Kidd as a notorious, bloody-handed pirate, some of his fellow merchant-captains believed him innocent of his alleged crimes.

revoke V. cancel; retract. Repeat offenders who continue to drive under the influence of alcohol face having their driver's licenses permanently *revoked*.

revulsion N. sudden violent change of feeling; reaction. Many people in this country who admired dictatorships underwent a *revulsion* when they realized what Hitler and Mussolini were trying to do.

rhapsodize V. to speak or write in an exaggeratedly enthusiastic manner. She greatly enjoyed her Hawaiian vacation and *rhapsodized* about it for weeks.

rhetoric N. art of effective communication; insincere language. All writers, by necessity, must be skilled in *rhetoric*.

■ **rhetorical** ADJ. pertaining to effective communication; insincere in language. To win his audience, the speaker used every *rhetorical* trick in the book.

ribald ADJ. wanton; profane. He sang a *ribald* song that offended many of the more prudish listeners.

riddle V. pierce with holes; permeate or spread throughout. With his machine gun, Tracy *riddled* the car with bullets till it looked like a slice of Swiss cheese. During the proofreaders' strike, the newspaper was *riddled* with typos.

rider N. amendment or clause added to a legislative bill. Senator Foghorn said he would support Senator Filibuster's tax reform bill only if Filibuster agreed to add an antipollution *rider* to the bill.

rife ADJ. abundant; current. In the face of the many rumors of scandal, which are *rife* at the moment, it is best to remain silent.

rift N. opening; break. The plane was lost in the stormy sky until the pilot saw the city through a *rift* in the clouds.

rig V. fix or manipulate. The ward boss was able to *rig* the election by bribing people to stuff the ballot boxes with ballots marked in his candidate's favor.

rigid ADJ. stiff and unyielding; strict; hard and unbending. By living with a man to whom she was not married, George Eliot broke Victorian society's most *rigid* rule of respectable behavior.

■ **rigor** N. severity. Many settlers could not stand the *rigors* of the New England winters.

rigorous ADJ. severe; harsh; demanding; exact. Disliked by his superiors, the officer candidate in *An Officer and a Gentleman* endured an extremely *rigorous* training program.

rile V. vex; irritate; muddy. Red had a hair-trigger temper: he was an easy man to *rile*.

riveting ADJ. absorbing; engrossing. The reviewer described Byatt's novel *Possession* as a *riveting* tale, one so absorbing that he had finished it in a single night.

rivulet N. small stream. As the rains continued, the small trickle of water running down the hillside grew into a *rivulet* that threatened to wash away a portion of the slope.

■ **robust** ADJ. vigorous; strong. After pumping iron and taking karate for six months, the little old lady was so *robust* that she could break a plank with her fist.

roil V. to make liquids murky by stirring up sediment. Be careful when you pour not to *roil* the wine; if you stir up the sediment you'll destroy the flavor.

roster N. list. They print the *roster* of players in the season's program.

rostrum N. platform for speech-making; pulpit. The crowd murmured angrily and indicated that they did not care to listen to the speaker who was approaching the *rostrum*.

rote N. repetition. He recited the passage by *rote* and gave no indication he understood what he was saying.

rotundity N. roundness; sonorousness of speech. Washington Irving emphasized the *rotundity* of the governor by describing his height and circumference.

rousing ADJ. lively; stirring. "And now, let's have a *rousing* welcome for TV's own Roseanne Barr, who'll lead us in a *rousing* rendition of 'The Star-Spangled Banner.'"

rout V. stampede; drive out. The reinforcements were able to *rout* the enemy. also N.

rubble N. broken fragments. Ten years after World War II, some of the *rubble* left by enemy bombings could still be seen.

ruddy ADJ. reddish; healthy-looking. Santa Claus's *ruddy* cheeks nicely complement Rudolph the Reindeer's bright red nose.

rudimentary ADJ. not developed; elementary; crude. Although my grandmother's English vocabulary was limited to a few *rudimentary* phrases, she always could make herself understood.

rue V. regret; lament; mourn. Tina *rued* the night she met Tony and wondered how she ever fell for such a jerk. rueful, ADJ.

ruffian N. bully; scoundrel. The *ruffians* threw stones at the police.

ruminate V. chew over and over (mentally, or, like cows, physically); mull over; ponder. Unable to digest quickly the baffling events of the day, Reuben *ruminated* about them till four in the morning.

rummage V. ransack; thoroughly search. When we *rummaged* through the trunks in the attic, we found many souvenirs of our childhood days. also N.

ruse N. trick; stratagem. You will not be able to fool your friends with such an obvious *ruse*.

rustic ADJ. pertaining to country people; uncouth. The backwoodsman looked out of place in his *rustic* attire.

ruthless ADJ. pitiless; cruel. Captain Hook was a dangerous, *ruthless* villain who would stop at nothing to destroy Peter Pan.

saboteur N. one who commits sabotage; destroyer of property. Members of the Resistance acted as *saboteurs*, blowing up train lines to prevent supplies from reaching the Nazi army.

saccharine ADJ. cloyingly sweet. She tried to ingratiate herself, speaking sweetly and smiling a *saccharine* smile.

sacrilegious ADJ. desecrating; profane. His stealing of the altar cloth was a very *sacrilegious* act.

sacrosanct ADJ. most sacred; inviolable. The brash insurance salesman invaded the *sacrosanct* privacy of the office of the president of the company.

Word List 42   sadistic-sentinel

sadistic ADJ. inclined to cruelty. If we are to improve conditions in this prison, we must first get rid of the *sadistic* warden.

saga N. Scandinavian myth; any legend. This is a *saga* of the sea and the men who risk their lives on it.

sagacious ADJ. perceptive; shrewd; having insight. My father was a *sagacious* judge of character: he could spot a phony a mile away. sagacity, N.

■ **sage** N. person celebrated for wisdom. Hearing tales of a mysterious Master of All Knowledge who lived in the hills of Tibet, Sandy was possessed with a burning desire to consult the legendary *sage*. also ADJ.

salacious ADJ. lascivious; lustful. Chaucer's monk is not pious but *salacious*, a teller of lewd tales and ribald jests.

salient ADJ. prominent. One of the *salient* features of that newspaper is its excellent editorial page.

salubrious ADJ. healthful. Many people with hay fever move to more *salubrious* sections of the country during the months of August and September.

salutary ADJ. tending to improve; beneficial; wholesome. The punishment had a *salutary* effect on the boy, as he became a model student.

salvage V. rescue from loss. All attempts to *salvage* the wrecked ship failed. also N.

salvo N. discharge of firearms; military salute. The boom of the enemy's opening *salvo* made the petrified private jump.

sanctimonious ADJ. displaying ostentatious or hypocritical devoutness. You do not have to be so *sanctimonious* to prove that you are devout.

■ **sanction** V. approve; ratify. Nothing will convince me to *sanction* the engagement of my daughter to such a worthless young man.

sanctuary N. refuge; shelter; shrine; holy place. The tiny attic was Helen's *sanctuary* to which she fled when she had to get away from the rest of her family.

sanguine ADJ. cheerful; hopeful. Let us not be too *sanguine* about the outcome; something could go wrong.

sap V. diminish; undermine. The element kryptonite has an unhealthy effect on Superman: it *saps* his strength.

sarcasm N. scornful remarks; stinging rebuke. Though Ralph pretended to ignore the mocking comments of his supposed friends, their *sarcasm* wounded him deeply.

sardonic ADJ. disdainful; sarcastic; cynical. The *sardonic* humor of nightclub comedians who satirize or ridicule patrons in the audience strikes some people as amusing and others as rude.

sartorial ADJ. pertaining to tailors. He was as famous for the *sartorial* splendor of his attire as he was for his acting.

sate V. satisfy to the full; cloy. Its hunger *sated*, the lion dozed.

satellite N. small body revolving around a larger one. During the first few years of the Space Age, hundreds of *satellites* were launched by Russia and the United States.

satiate   v. satisfy fully. Having stuffed themselves until they were *satiated*, the guests were so full they were ready for a nap.

satire   N. form of literature in which irony, sarcasm, and ridicule are employed to attack vice and folly. *Gulliver's Travels*, which is regarded by many as a tale for children, is actually a bitter *satire* attacking man's folly.

■ **satirical**   ADJ. mocking. The humor of cartoonist Gary Trudeau often is *satirical;* through the comments of the Doonesbury characters, Trudeau ridicules political corruption and folly.

■ **saturate**   v. soak thoroughly. *Saturate* your sponge with water until it can't hold any more.

saturnine   ADJ. gloomy. Do not be misled by his *saturnine* countenance; he is not as gloomy as he looks.

saunter   v. stroll slowly. As we *sauntered* through the park, we stopped frequently to admire the spring flowers.

savant   N. scholar. Our faculty includes many world-famous *savants*.

savor   v. enjoy; have a distinctive flavor, smell, or quality. Relishing his triumph, the actor especially *savored* the chagrin of the critics who had predicted his failure.

● **savory**   ADJ. tasty; pleasing, attractive, or agreeable. Julia Child's recipes enable amateur chefs to create *savory* delicacies for their guests.

scabbard   N. case for a sword blade; sheath. The drill master told the recruit to wipe the blood from his sword before slipping it back into the *scabbard*.

scad   N. a great quantity. Refusing Dave's offer to lend him a shirt, Phil replied, "No, thanks, I've got *scads* of clothes."

scaffold   N. temporary platform for workers; bracing framework; platform for execution. Before painting the house, the workers put up a *scaffold* to allow them to work on the second story.

scale   v. climb up; ascend. In order to locate a book on the top shelf of the stacks, Lee had to *scale* an exceptionally rickety ladder.

scamp   N. rascal. Despite his mischievous behavior, Malcolm was such an engaging *scamp* that his mother almost lacked the heart to punish him.

■ **scanty**   ADJ. meager; insufficient. Thinking his helping of food was *scanty*, Oliver Twist asked for more.

scapegoat   N. someone who bears the blame for others. After the *Challenger* disaster, NASA searched for *scapegoats* on whom they could cast the blame.

scavenge   v. hunt through discarded materials for usable items; search, especially for food. If you need car parts that the dealers no longer stock, try *scavenging* for odd bits and pieces at the auto wreckers' yards. scavenger, N.

scenario   N. plot outline; screenplay; opera libretto. Scaramouche startled the other actors in the commedia troupe when he suddenly departed from their customary *scenario* and began to improvise.

schematic   ADJ. relating to an outline or diagram; using a system of symbols. In working out the solution to this logic puzzle, you may find it helpful to construct a simple *schematic* diagram outlining the order of events.

schism   N. division; split. Let us not widen the *schism* by further bickering.

scintillate   v. sparkle; flash. I enjoy her dinner parties because the food is excellent and the conversation *scintillates*.

scoff   v. mock; ridicule. He *scoffed* at dentists until he had his first toothache.

scourge   N. lash; whip; severe punishment. They feared the plague and regarded it as a deadly *scourge*. also v.

scruple   v. fret about; hesitate, for ethical reasons. Fearing that her husband had become involved in an affair, she did not *scruple* to read his diary. also N.

■ **scrupulous**   ADJ. conscientious; extremely thorough. Though Alfred is *scrupulous* in fulfilling his duties at work, he is less conscientious about his obligations to his family and friends.

■ **scrutinize**   v. examine closely and critically. Searching for flaws, the sergeant *scrutinized* every detail of the private's uniform.

scuffle   v. struggle confusedly; move off in a confused hurry. The twins briefly *scuffled*, wrestling to see which of them would get the toy. When their big brother yelled, "Let go of my Gameboy!" they *scuffled* off down the hall.

scurrilous   ADJ. obscene; indecent. Your *scurrilous* remarks are especially offensive because they are untrue.

scurry   v. move briskly. The White Rabbit had to *scurry* to get to his appointment on time.

scurvy   ADJ. despicable; contemptible. Peter Pan sneered at Captain Hook and his *scurvy* crew.

scuttle   v. scurry; run with short, rapid steps. The bug *scuttled* rapidly across the floor.

scuttle   v. sink. The sailors decided to *scuttle* their vessel rather than surrender it to the enemy.

seamy   ADJ. sordid; unwholesome. In *The Godfather*, Michael Corleone is unwilling to expose his wife and children to the *seamy* side of his life as the son of a Mafia don.

sear   v. char or burn; brand. Accidentally brushing against the hot grill, she *seared* her hand badly.

seasoned   ADJ. experienced. Though pleased with her new batch of rookies, the basketball coach wished she had a few more *seasoned* players on the team.

secession   N. withdrawal. The *secession* of the Southern states provided Lincoln with his first major problem after his inauguration. secede, v.

■ **seclusion**   N. isolation; solitude. One moment she loved crowds; the next, she sought *seclusion*. seclude, v.

secrete   v. hide away; produce and release a substance into an organism. The pack rat *secretes* odds and ends in its nest; the pancreas *secretes* insulin in the islets of Langerhans.

sect   N. separate religious body; faction. As university chaplain, she sought to address universal religious issues and not limit herself to concerns of any one *sect*.

sectarian   ADJ. relating to a religious faction or subgroup; narrow-minded; limited. Far from being broad-minded, the religious leader was intolerant of new ideas, paying attention only to purely *sectarian* interests. sect. N.

secular ADJ. worldly; not pertaining to church matters; temporal. The church leaders decided not to interfere in *secular* matters.

sedate ADJ. composed; grave. The parents were worried because they felt their son was too quiet and *sedate*.

● **sedentary** ADJ. requiring sitting. Disliking the effect of her *sedentary* occupation on her figure, Stacy decided to work out at the gym every other day.

sedition N. resistance to authority; insubordination. His words, though not treasonous in themselves, were calculated to arouse thoughts of *sedition*.

sedulous ADJ. diligent; hardworking. After weeks of patient and *sedulous* labor, we completed our detailed analysis of every published SAT examination.

seedy ADJ. run-down; decrepit; disreputable. I would rather stay in dormitory lodgings in a decent youth hostel than have a room of my own in a *seedy* downtown hotel.

seemly ADJ. proper; appropriate. Lady Bracknell did not think it was *seemly* for Ernest to lack a proper family: no

baby abandoned on a doorstep could grow up to be a fit match for *her* daughter.

seep V. ooze; trickle. During the rainstorm, water *seeped* through the crack in the basement wall and damaged the floor boards. seepage, N.

seethe V. be disturbed; boil. The nation was *seething* with discontent as the noblemen continued their arrogant ways.

seismic ADJ. pertaining to earthquakes. The Richter scale is a measurement of *seismic* disturbances.

seminary N. school for training future ministers; academy for young women. Sure of his priestly vocation, Terrence planned to pursue his theological training at the local Roman Catholic *seminary*.

sensual ADJ. devoted to the pleasures of the senses; carnal; voluptuous. I cannot understand what caused him to abandon his *sensual* way of life and become so ascetic.

sententious ADJ. terse; concise; aphoristic. After reading so many redundant speeches, I find his *sententious* style particularly pleasing.

sentinel N. sentry; lookout. Though camped in enemy territory, Bledsoe ignored the elementary precaution of posting *sentinels* around the encampment.

Word List 43   sequester-solvent

sequester V. isolate; retire from public life; segregate; seclude. Banished from his kingdom, the wizard Prospero *sequestered* himself on a desert island. To prevent the jurors from hearing news broadcasts about the case, the judge decided to *sequester* the jury.

serendipity N. gift for finding valuable or desirable things by accident; accidental good fortune or luck. Many scientific discoveries are a matter of *serendipity*: Newton was not sitting under a tree thinking about gravity when the apple dropped on his head.

serenity N. calmness; placidity. The sound of air raid sirens pierced the *serenity* of the quiet village of Pearl Harbor.

serpentine ADJ. winding; twisting. The car swerved at every curve in the *serpentine* road.

serrated ADJ. having a sawtoothed edge. The beech tree is one of many plants that have *serrated* leaves.

■ **servile** ADJ. slavish; cringing. Constantly fawning on his employer, humble Uriah Heap was a *servile* creature.

servitude N. slavery; compulsory labor. Born a slave, Frederick Douglass resented his life of *servitude* and plotted to escape to the North.

sever V. cut; separate. The released prisoner wanted to begin a new life and *sever* all connections with his criminal past. Dr. Guillotin invented a machine that could neatly *sever* an aristocratic head from its equally aristocratic body. Unfortunately, he couldn't collect any *severance* pay. severance, N.

severity N. harshness; intensity; sternness; austerity. The *severity* of Jane's migraine attack was so great that she took to her bed for a week.

shackle V. chain; fetter. The criminal's ankles were *shackled* to prevent his escape. also N.

sham V. pretend. He *shammed* sickness to get out of going to school. also N.

shambles N. wreck; mess. After the hurricane, the Carolina coast was a *shambles*. After the New Year's Eve party, the apartment was a *shambles*.

shard N. fragment, generally of pottery. The archaeologist assigned several students the task of reassembling earthenware vessels from the *shards* he had brought back from the expedition.

sheaf N. bundle of stalks of grain; any bundle of things tied together. The lawyer picked up a *sheaf* of papers as he rose to question the witness.

shear V. cut or clip (hair; fleece); strip of something. You may not care to cut a sheep's hair, but Sarah *shears* sheep for Little Bo Peep.

sheathe V. place into a case. As soon as he recognized the approaching men, he *sheathed* his dagger and hailed them as friends.

sheer ADJ. very thin or transparent; very steep; absolute. Wearing nothing but an almost *sheer* robe, Delilah draped herself against the *sheer* temple wall. Beholding her, Samson was overcome by her *sheer* beauty. Then she sheared his hair.

shimmer V. glimmer intermittently. The moonlight *shimmered* on the water as the moon broke through the clouds for a moment. also N.

shirk V. avoid (responsibility, work, etc.); malinger. Brian has a strong sense of duty; he would never *shirk* any responsibility.

shoddy ADJ. sham; not genuine; inferior. You will never get the public to buy such *shoddy* material.

shrewd ADJ. clever; astute. A *shrewd* investor, he took clever advantage of the fluctuations of the stock market.

shroud V. hide from view; wrap for burial. Fog *shrouded* Dracula's castle, hiding the ruined tower beneath sheets of mist.

shun V. keep away from. Cherishing his solitude, the recluse *shunned* the company of other human beings.

shyster N. lawyer using questionable methods. On *L.A. Law*, Brackman is horrified to learn that his newly-discovered half brother is nothing but a cheap *shyster*.

sibling N. brother or sister. We may not enjoy being *siblings,* but we cannot forget that we still belong to the same family.

simian ADJ. monkeylike. Lemurs are nocturnal mammals and have many *simian* characteristics, although they are less intelligent than monkeys.

simile N. comparison of one thing with another, using the word *like* or *as*. "My love is like a red, red rose" is a *simile*.

simper V. smirk; smile affectedly. Complimented on her appearance, Stella self-consciously *simpered*.

simplistic ADJ. oversimplified. Though Jack's solution dealt adequately with one aspect of the problem, it was *simplistic* in failing to consider various complications that might arise.

simulate V. feign. He *simulated* insanity in order to avoid punishment for his crime.

sinecure N. well-paid position with little responsibility. My job is no *sinecure*; I work long hours and have much responsibility.

sinewy ADJ. tough; strong and firm. The steak was too *sinewy* to chew.

singular ADJ. unique; extraordinary; odd. Though the young man tried to understand Father William's *singular* behavior, he still found it odd that the old man incessantly stood on his head. singularity, N.

sinister ADJ. evil. We must defeat the *sinister* forces that seek our downfall.

sinuous ADJ. winding; bending in and out; not morally honest. The snake moved in a *sinuous* manner.

■ **skeptic** N. doubter; person who suspends judgment until the evidence supporting a point of view has been examined. I am a *skeptic* about the new health plan; I want some proof that it can work. skepticism, N.

skiff N. small, light sailboat or rowboat. Tom dreamed of owning an ocean-going yacht but had to settle for a *skiff* he could sail in the bay.

skimp V. provide scantily; live very economically. They were forced to *skimp* on necessities in order to make their limited supplies last the winter.

skinflint N. stingy person; miser. Scrooge was an ungenerous old *skinflint* until he reformed his ways and became a notable philanthropist.

skirmish N. minor fight. Custer's troops expected they might run into a *skirmish* or two on maneuvers; they did not expect to face a major battle. also V.

skulk V. move furtively and secretly. He *skulked* through the less fashionable sections of the city in order to avoid meeting any of his former friends.

slacken V. slow up; loosen. As they passed the finish line, the runners *slackened* their pace.

slag N. residue from smelting metal; dross; waste matter. The blast furnace had a special opening at the bottom to allow the workers to remove the worthless *slag*.

slake V. quench; sate. When we reached the oasis, we were able to *slake* our thirst.

slander N. defamation; utterance of false and malicious statements. Considering the negative comments politicians make about each other, it's a wonder that more of them aren't sued for *slander*. also V.

slapdash ADJ. haphazard; careless; sloppy. From the number of typos and misspellings I've found in it, it's clear that Mario proofread the report in a remarkably *slapdash* fashion.

sleeper N. something originally of little value or importance that in time becomes very valuable. Unnoticed by the critics at its publication, the eventual Pulitzer Prize winner was a classic *sleeper*.

sleight N. dexterity. The magician amazed the audience with his *sleight* of hand.

slight N. insult to one's dignity; snub. Hypersensitive and ready to take offense at any discourtesy, Bertha was always on the lookout for real or imaginary *slights*. also V.

slipshod ADJ. untidy or slovenly; shabby. As a master craftsman, the carpenter prided himself on not doing *slipshod* work.

slither V. slip or slide. During the recent ice storm, many people *slithered* down this hill as they walked to the station.

slothful ADJ. lazy. Lying idly on the sofa while others worked, Reggie denied he was *slothful*: "I just supervise better lying down."

slough V. cast off. Each spring, the snake *sloughs* off its skin.

slovenly ADJ. untidy; careless in work habits. Unshaven, sitting around in his bathrobe all afternoon, Gus didn't seem to care about the *slovenly* appearance he presented. The dark ring around the bathtub and the spider webs hanging from the beams proved what a *slovenly* housekeeper she was.

sluggard N. lazy person. "You are a *sluggard,* a drone, a parasite," the angry father shouted at his lazy son.

■ **sluggish** ADJ. slow; lazy; lethargic. After two nights without sleep, she felt *sluggish* and incapable of exertion.

slur v. speak indistinctly; mumble. When Sol has too much to drink, he starts to *slur* his words: "Washamatter? Cansh you undershtand what I shay?"

slur N. insult to one's character or reputation; slander. Polls revealed that the front-runner's standing had been badly damaged by the *slurs* and innuendoes circulated by his opponent's staff. also v. (secondary meaning)

smelt v. melt or blend ores, changing their chemical composition. The furnaceman *smelts* tin with copper to create a special alloy used in making bells.

smirk N. conceited smile. Wipe that *smirk* off your face! also v.

smolder v. burn without flame; be liable to break out at any moment. The rags *smoldered* for hours before they burst into flame.

snicker N. half-stifled laugh. The boy could not suppress a *snicker* when the teacher sat on the tack. also v.

snivel v. run at the nose; snuffle; whine. Don't you come *sniveling* to me complaining about your big brother.

sobriety N. moderation (especially regarding indulgence in alcohol); seriousness. Neither falling-down drunks nor stand-up comics are noted for *sobriety*. sober, ADJ.

sodden ADJ. soaked; dull, as if from drink. He set his *sodden* overcoat near the radiator to dry.

sojourn N. temporary stay. After his *sojourn* in Florida, he began to long for the colder climate of his native New England home.

solace N. comfort in trouble. I hope you will find *solace* in the thought that all of us share your loss.

solder v. repair or make whole by using a metal alloy. The plumber fixed the leak in the pipes by *soldering* a couple of joints from which water had been oozing.

solecism N. construction that is flagrantly incorrect grammatically. I must give this paper a failing mark because it contains many *solecisms.*

solemnity N. seriousness; gravity. The minister was concerned that nothing should disturb the *solemnity* of the marriage service. solemn, ADJ.

solicit v. request earnestly; seek. Knowing she needed to have a solid majority for the budget to pass, the mayor telephoned all the members of the city council to *solicit* their votes.

solicitous ADJ. worried; concerned. The employer was very *solicitous* about the health of her employees as replacements were difficult to get.

soliloquy N. talking to oneself. The *soliloquy* is a device used by the dramatist to reveal a character's innermost thoughts and emotions.

solitude N. state of being alone; seclusion. Much depends on how much you like your own company. What to one person seems fearful isolation to another is blessed *solitude.*

soluble ADJ. able to be dissolved; able to be explained. Sugar is *soluble* in water; put a sugar cube in water and it will quickly dissolve.

solvent ADJ. able to pay all debts. By dint of very frugal living, he was finally able to become *solvent* and avoid bankruptcy proceedings.

Word List 44 somber–sublime

■ **somber** ADJ. gloomy; depressing; dark; drab. From the doctor's grim expression, I could tell he had *somber* news. Dull brown and charcoal gray are pretty *somber* colors; can't you wear something bright?

somnambulist N. sleepwalker. The most famous *somnambulist* in literature is Lady Macbeth; her monologue in the sleepwalking scene is one of the highlights of Shakespeare's play.

somnolent ADJ. half asleep. The heavy meal and the overheated room made us all *somnolent* and indifferent to the speaker.

sonorous ADJ. resonant. His *sonorous* voice resounded through the hall.

sophisticated ADJ. worldly-wise and urbane; complex. When Sophie makes wisecracks, she thinks she sounds *sophisticated*, but instead she sounds sophomoric. The new IBM laptop with the butterfly keyboard and the built-in quadspeed FAX modem is a pretty *sophisticated* machine.

sophistry N. seemingly plausible but fallacious reasoning. Instead of advancing valid arguments, he tried to overwhelm his audience with a flood of *sophistries.*

sophomoric ADJ. immature; half-baked, like a sophomore. Even if you're only a freshman, it's no compliment to be told your humor is *sophomoric*. The humor in *Dumb and Dumber* is *sophomoric* at best.

● **soporific** ADJ. sleep-causing; marked by sleepiness. Professor Pringle's lectures were so *soporific* that even he fell asleep in class. also N.

sordid ADJ. filthy; base; vile. The social worker was angered by the *sordid* housing provided for the homeless.

sovereign ADJ. efficacious; supreme or paramount; self-governing. Professor Pennywhistle claimed his panacea was a *sovereign* cure for all chronic complaints. In medicine the *sovereign* task of the doctor is to do no harm. Rebelling against the mother country, the onetime colony now proclaimed itself a *sovereign* state. also N.

spangle N. small metallic piece sewn to clothing for ornamentation. The thousands of *spangles* on her dress sparkled in the glare of the stage lights.

sparse ADJ. not thick; thinly scattered; scanty. No matter how carefully Albert combed his hair to make it look as full as possible, it still looked *sparse.*

spartan ADJ. avoiding luxury and comfort; sternly disciplined. Looking over the bare, unheated room, with its hard cot, he wondered what he was doing in such *spartan* quarters. Only his *spartan* sense of duty kept him at his post.

spasmodic ADJ. fitful; periodic. The *spasmodic* coughing in the auditorium annoyed the performers.

spat N. squabble; minor dispute. What had started out as a mere *spat* escalated into a full-blown argument.

spate N. sudden flood or strong outburst; a large number or amount. After the *spate* of angry words that came pouring out of him, Mary was sure they would never be reconciled.

spatial ADJ. relating to space. NASA is engaged in an ongoing program of *spatial* exploration. When Jay says he's studying *spatial* relations, that doesn't mean he has relatives in outer space.

spatula N. broad-bladed instrument used for spreading or mixing. The manufacturers of this frying pan recommend the use of a rubber *spatula* to avoid scratching the specially treated surface.

spawn V. lay eggs. Fish ladders had to be built in the dams to assist the salmon returning to *spawn* in their native streams. also N.

specious ADJ. seemingly reasonable but incorrect; misleading (often intentionally). To claim that, because houses and birds both have wings, both can fly, is extremely *specious* reasoning.

spectrum N. colored band produced when beam of light passes through a prism. The visible portion of the *spectrum* includes red at one end and violet at the other.

spendthrift N. someone who wastes money. Easy access to credit encourages people to turn into *spendthrifts* who shop till they drop.

sphinx-like ADJ. enigmatic; mysterious. The Mona Lisa's *sphinx-like* expression has intrigued and mystified art lovers for centuries.

splice V. fasten together; unite. Before you *splice* two strips of tape together, be sure to line them up evenly. also N.

spontaneity N. lack of premeditation; naturalness; freedom from constraint. When Anne and Amy met, Amy impulsively hugged her new colleague, but Anne drew back, unprepared for such *spontaneity*. The cast over-rehearsed the play so much that the eventual performance lacked any *spontaneity*. spontaneous, ADJ.

■ **sporadic** ADJ. occurring irregularly. Although you can still hear *sporadic* outbursts of laughter and singing outside, the big Halloween parade has passed; the party's over till next year.

sportive ADJ. playful. Such a *sportive* attitude is surprising in a person as serious as you usually are.

spry ADJ. vigorously active; nimble. She was eighty years old, yet still *spry* and alert.

● **spurious** ADJ. false; counterfeit; forged; illogical. The antique dealer hero of Jonathan Gash's mystery novels gives the reader tips on how to tell *spurious* antiques from the real thing. Natasha's claim to be the lost heir of the Romanoffs was *spurious*: the only thing Russian about her was the vodka she drank!

● **spurn** V. reject; scorn. The heroine *spurned* the villain's advances.

squabble N. minor quarrel; bickering. Children invariably get involved in petty *squabbles*; wise parents know when to interfere and when to let the children work things out on their own.

squalor N. filth; degradation; dirty, neglected state. Rusted, broken-down cars in its yard, trash piled up on the porch, tar paper peeling from the roof, the shack was the picture of *squalor*. squalid, ADJ.

■ **squander** V. waste. If you *squander* your allowance on candy and comic books, you won't have any money left to buy the new box of crayons you want.

squat ADJ. stocky; short and thick. Tolkien's hobbits are somewhat *squat*, sturdy little creatures, fond of good ale, good music, and good mushrooms.

staccato ADJ. played in an abrupt manner; marked by abrupt sharp sound. His *staccato* speech reminded one of the sound of a machine gun.

■ **stagnant** ADJ. motionless; stale; dull. Mosquitoes commonly breed in ponds of *stagnant* water. Mike's career was *stagnant*; it wasn't going anywhere, and neither was he! stagnate, V.

staid ADJ. sober; sedate. Her conduct during the funeral ceremony was *staid* and solemn.

stalemate N. deadlock. Negotiations between the union and the employers have reached a *stalemate*; neither side is willing to budge from previously stated positions.

stalwart ADJ. strong, brawny; steadfast. His consistent support of the party has proved that he is a *stalwart* and loyal member. also N.

stamina N. strength; staying power. I doubt that she has the *stamina* to run the full distance of the marathon race.

stanch V. check flow of blood. It is imperative that we *stanch* the gushing wound before we attend to the other injuries.

stanza N. division of a poem. Do you know the last *stanza* of "The Star-Spangled Banner"?

■ **static** ADJ. unchanging; lacking development. Why watch chess on TV? I like watching a game with action, not something *static* where nothing seems to be going on.

statute N. law enacted by the legislature. The *statute* of limitations sets the limits on how long you have to take legal action in specific cases.

● **steadfast** ADJ. loyal; unswerving. Penelope was *steadfast* in her affections, faithfully waiting for Ulysses to return from his wanderings.

stealth N. slyness; sneakiness; secretiveness. Fearing detection by the sentries on duty, the scout inched his way toward the enemy camp with great *stealth*.

steep V. soak; saturate. Be sure to *steep* the fabric in the dyebath for the full time prescribed.

stellar ADJ. pertaining to the stars. He was the *stellar* attraction of the entire performance.

stem V. check the flow. The paramedic used a tourniquet to *stem* the bleeding from the slashed artery.

stem from V. arise from. Milton's problems in school *stemmed from* his poor study habits.

stereotype N. fixed and unvarying representation; standardized mental picture, often reflecting prejudice. Critics object to the character of Jim in *The Adventures of Huckleberry Finn* because he seems to reflect the *stereotype* of the happy, ignorant slave.

stifle V. suppress; extinguish; inhibit. Halfway through the boring lecture, Laura gave up trying to *stifle* her yawns.

stigma N. token of disgrace; brand. I do not attach any *stigma* to the fact that you were accused of this crime; the fact that you were acquitted clears you completely.

stigmatize V. brand; mark as wicked. I do not want to *stigmatize* this young offender for life by sending her to prison.

stilted ADJ. bombastic; inflated. His *stilted* rhetoric did not impress the college audience; they were immune to bombastic utterances.

stint N. supply; allotted amount; assigned portion of work. He performed his daily *stint* cheerfully and willingly. also V.

stint V. be thrifty; set limits. "Spare no expense," the bride's father said, refusing to *stint* on the wedding arrangements.

stipend N. pay for services. There is a nominal *stipend* for this position.

stipulate V. make express conditions; specify. Before agreeing to reduce American military forces in Europe, the president *stipulated* that NATO inspection teams be allowed to inspect Soviet bases.

stodgy ADJ. stuffy; boringly conservative. For a young person, Winston seems remarkably *stodgy*: you'd expect someone his age to show a little more life.

stoic ADJ. impassive; unmoved by joy or grief. I wasn't particularly *stoic* when I had my flu shot; I squealed like a stuck pig. also N.

stoke V. stir up a fire; feed plentifully. As a Scout Marisa learned how to light a fire, how to *stoke* it if it started to die down, and how to extinguish it completely.

● **stolid** ADJ. dull; impassive. The earthquake shattered Stuart's usual *stolid* demeanor; trembling, he crouched on the no longer stable ground.

stratagem N. deceptive scheme. We saw through his clever *stratagem*.

stratify V. divide into classes; be arranged into strata. As the economic gap between the rich and the poor increased, Roman society grew increasingly *stratified*.

stratum N. layer of earth's surface; layer of society. Unless we alleviate conditions in the lowest *stratum* of our society, we may expect grumbling and revolt.

strew V. spread randomly; sprinkle; scatter. Preceding the bride to the altar, the flower girl will *strew* rose petals along the aisle.

striated ADJ. marked with parallel bands; grooved. The glacier left many *striated* rocks. striate, V.

stricture N. restriction; adverse criticism. Huck regularly disobeyed Miss Watson's rules and *strictures* upon his behavior: he wouldn't wear shoes, no matter what she said.

● **strident** ADJ. loud and harsh; insistent. Whenever Sue became angry, she tried not to raise her voice; she had no desire to appear *strident*.

stringent ADJ. binding; rigid. I think these regulations are too *stringent*.

strut N. pompous walk; swagger. Looking at his self-important *strut* as he swaggered about the parade ground, I could tell Colonel Blimp thought highly of himself. also V.

strut N. supporting bar. The engineer calculated that the *strut* supporting the rafter needed to be reinforced. (secondary meaning)

studied ADJ. not spontaneous; deliberate; thoughtful. Given Jill's previous slights, Jack felt that the omission of his name from the guest list was a *studied* insult.

stultify V. cause to appear or become stupid or inconsistent; frustrate or hinder. His long hours in the blacking factory left young Dickens numb and incurious, as if the menial labor had *stultified* his brain.

● **stupefy** V. make numb; stun; amaze. Disapproving of drugs in general, Laura refused to take sleeping pills or any other medicine that might *stupefy* her. stupefaction, N.

stupor N. state of apathy; daze; lack of awareness. In his *stupor*, the addict was unaware of the events taking place around him.

stymie V. present an obstacle; stump. The detective was *stymied* by the contradictory evidence in the robbery investigation. also N.

suavity N. urbanity; polish. The elegant actor is particularly good in roles that require *suavity* and sophistication.

subdued ADJ. less intense; quieter. Bob liked the *subdued* lighting at the restaurant because he thought it was romantic. I just thought it was dimly lit.

subjective ADJ. occurring or taking place within the subject; unreal. Your analysis is highly *subjective;* you have permitted your emotions and your opinions to color your thinking.

subjugate V. conquer; bring under control. It is not our aim to *subjugate* our foe; we are interested only in establishing peaceful relations.

sublime ADJ. exalted or noble and uplifting; utter. Lucy was in awe of Desi's *sublime* musicianship, while he was in awe of her *sublime* naiveté.

Word List 45   subliminal-tantamount

subliminal   ADJ. below the threshold. We may not be aware of the *subliminal* influences that affect our thinking.

■ **submissive**   ADJ. yielding; timid. When he refused to permit Elizabeth to marry her poet, Mr. Barrett expected her to be properly *submissive*; instead, she eloped!

■ **subordinate**   ADJ. occupying a lower rank; inferior; submissive. Bishop Proudie's wife expected all the *subordinate* clergy to behave with great deference to the wife of their superior.

suborn   V. persuade to act unlawfully (especially to commit perjury). In *The Godfather*, the mobsters used bribery and threats to *suborn* the witnesses against Don Michael Corleone.

subpoena   N. writ summoning a witness to appear. The prosecutor's office was ready to serve a *subpoena* on the reluctant witness. also V.

subsequent   ADJ. following; later. In *subsequent* lessons, we shall take up more difficult problems.

subservient   ADJ. behaving like a slave; servile; obsequious. He was proud and dignified; he refused to be *subservient* to anyone.

■ **subside**   V. settle down; descend; grow quiet. The doctor assured us that the fever would eventually *subside*.

subsidiary   ADJ. subordinate; secondary. This information may be used as *subsidiary* evidence but is not sufficient by itself to prove your argument. also N.

subsidy   N. direct financial aid by government, etc. Without this *subsidy*, American ship operators would not be able to compete in world markets.

subsistence   N. existence; means of support; livelihood. In these days of inflated prices, my salary provides a mere *subsistence*.

substantial   ADJ. ample; solid; in essentials. The generous scholarship represented a *substantial* sum of money.

■ **substantiate**   V. establish by evidence; verify; support. These endorsements from satisfied customers *substantiate* our claim that Barron's *How to Prepare for the SAT I* is the best SAT-prep book on the market.

substantive   ADJ. essential; pertaining to the substance. Although the delegates were aware of the importance of the problem, they could not agree on the *substantive* issues.

subterfuge   N. pretense; evasion. As soon as we realized that you had won our support by a *subterfuge*, we withdrew our endorsement of your candidacy.

subtlety   N. perceptiveness; ingenuity; delicacy. Never obvious, she expressed herself with such *subtlety* that her remarks went right over the heads of most of her audience. subtle, ADJ.

subversive   ADJ. tending to overthrow; destructive. At first glance, the notion that styrofoam cups may actually be more ecologically sound than paper cups strikes most environmentalists as *subversive*.

■ **succinct**   ADJ. brief; terse; compact. Don't bore your audience with excess verbiage: be *succinct*.

succor   V. aid; assist; comfort. If you believe that con man has come here to *succor* you in your hour of need, you're an even bigger sucker than I thought. also N.

succulent   ADJ. juicy; full of richness. To some people, Florida citrus fruits are more *succulent* than those from California. also N.

succumb   V. yield; give in; die. I *succumb* to temptation whenever I see chocolate.

suffragist   N. advocate of voting rights (for women). In recognition of her efforts to win the vote for women, Congress authorized coining a silver dollar honoring the *suffragist* Susan B. Anthony

sully   V. tarnish; soil. He felt that it was beneath his dignity to *sully* his hands in such menial labor.

sultry   ADJ. sweltering. He could not adjust himself to the *sultry* climate of the tropics.

summation   N. act of finding the total; summary. In his *summation*, the lawyer emphasized the testimony given by the two witnesses.

summit   N. utmost height or pinnacle; highest point (of a mountain, etc.) The *summit* of the amateur mountain climber's aspirations was someday to reach the *summit* of Mount Everest.

sumptuous   ADJ. lavish; rich. I cannot recall when I have had such a *sumptuous* Thanksgiving feast.

sunder   V. separate; part. Northern and southern Ireland are politically and religiously *sundered*.

supercilious   ADJ. arrogant; condescending; patronizing. The *supercilious* headwaiter sneered at customers whom he thought did not fit in at a restaurant catering to an ultra-fashionable crowd.

■ **superficial**   ADJ. trivial; shallow. Since your report gave only a *superficial* analysis of the problem, I cannot give you more than a passing grade.

■ **superfluous**   ADJ. unnecessary; excessive; overabundant. Betsy lacked the heart to tell June that the wedding present she brought was *superfluous*; she and Bob had already received five toasters. Please try not to include so many *superfluous* details in your report; just give me the facts. superfluity, N.

superimpose   V. place over something else. Your attempt to *superimpose* another agency in this field will merely increase the bureaucratic nature of our government.

supersede   V. cause to be set aside; replace; make obsolete. The new bulk mailing postal regulation *supersedes* the old one. If you continue to follow the old regulation, your bulk mailing will be returned to you.

● **supplant**   V. replace; usurp. Bolingbroke, later to be known as King Henry IV, fought to *supplant* his cousin, Richard III, as King of England.

supple ADJ. flexible; pliant. Years of yoga exercises made Grace's body *supple*.

supplicate V. petition humbly; pray to grant a favor. We *supplicate* Your Majesty to grant him amnesty.

supposition N. hypothesis; the act of supposing. I based my decision to confide in him on the *supposition* that he would be discreet. suppose, V.

suppress V. stifle; overwhelm; subdue; inhibit. Too polite to laugh in anyone's face, Roy did his best to *suppress* his amusement at Ed's inane remark.

● **surfeit** V. satiate; stuff; indulge to excess in anything. Every Thanksgiving we are *surfeited* with an overabundance of holiday treats. also N.

surly ADJ. rude; cross. Because of his *surly* attitude, many people avoided his company.

surmise V. guess. I *surmise* that he will be late for this meeting. also N.

surmount V. overcome. Could Helen Keller, blind and deaf since childhood, *surmount* her physical disabilities and lead a productive life?

■ **surpass** V. exceed. Her SAT I scores *surpassed* our expectations.

■ **surreptitious** ADJ. secret; furtive; sneaky; hidden. Hoping to discover where his mom had hidden the Christmas presents, Timmy took a *surreptitious* peek into the master bedroom closet.

surrogate N. substitute. For a fatherless child, a male teacher may become a father *surrogate*.

surveillance N. watching; guarding. The FBI kept the house under constant *surveillance* in the hope of capturing all the criminals at one time.

■ **susceptible** ADJ. impressionable; easily influenced; having little resistance, as to a disease; receptive to. Said the patent medicine man to his very *susceptible* customer: "Buy this new miracle drug, and you will no longer be *susceptible* to the common cold."

■ **sustain** V. experience; support; nourish. He *sustained* such a severe injury that the doctors feared he would be unable to work to *sustain* his growing family.

sustenance N. means of support, food, nourishment. In the tropics, the natives find *sustenance* easy to obtain, due to all the fruit trees.

suture N. stitches sewn to hold the cut edges of a wound or incision; material used in sewing. We will remove the *sutures* as soon as the wound heals. also V.

swagger V. behave arrogantly or pompously; strut or walk proudly. The conquering hero didn't simply stride down the street; he *swaggered*. also N.

swarm N. dense moving crowd; large group of honeybees. At the height of the city hall scandals, a constant *swarm* of reporters followed the mayor everywhere. also V.

swarthy ADJ. dark; dusky. Despite the stereotypes, not all Italians are *swarthy*; many are fair and blond.

swathe V. wrap around; bandage. When I visited him in the hospital, I found him *swathed* in bandages.

swelter V. be oppressed by heat. I am going to buy an air conditioning unit for my apartment as I do not intend to *swelter* through another hot and humid summer.

swerve V. deviate; turn aside sharply. The car *swerved* wildly as the driver struggled to regain control of the wheel.

swill V. drink greedily. Singing "Yo, ho, ho, and a bottle of rum," Long John Silver and his fellow pirates *swilled* their grog.

swindler N. cheat. She was gullible and trusting, an easy victim for the first *swindler* who came along.

sybarite N. lover of luxury. Rich people are not always *sybarites;* some of them have little taste for a life of luxury.

● **sycophant** N. servile flatterer; bootlicker; yes man. Fed up with the toadies and flunkies who made up his entourage, the star cried, "Get out, all of you! I'm sick of *sycophants*!" sycophancy, N.

symbiosis N. interdependent relationship (between groups, species), often mutually beneficial. Both the crocodile bird and the crocodile derive benefit from their *symbiosis*: pecking away at food particles embedded in the crocodile's teeth, the bird receives nourishment; the crocodile, meanwhile, receives proper dental hygiene. symbiotic, ADJ.

symmetry N. arrangement of parts so that balance is obtained; congruity. Something lopsided by definition lacks *symmetry*.

synoptic ADJ. providing a general overview; summary. The professor turned to the latest issue of *Dissertation Abstracts* for a *synoptic* account of what was new in the field. synopsis, N.

synthesis N. combining parts into a whole. Now that we have succeeded in isolating this drug, our next problem is to plan its *synthesis* in the laboratory. synthesize, V.

table V. set aside a resolution or proposal for future consideration. Because we seem unable to agree on this issue at the moment, let us *table* the motion for now and come back to it at a later date.

tacit ADJ. understood; not put into words. We have a *tacit* agreement based on only a handshake.

■ **taciturn** ADJ. habitually silent; talking little. The stereotypical cowboy is a *taciturn* soul, answering lengthy questions with a "Yep" or "Nope."

tactile ADJ. pertaining to the organs or sense of touch. His callused hands had lost their *tactile* sensitivity.

taint V. contaminate; cause to lose purity; modify with a trace of something bad. One speck of dirt on your utensils may contain enough germs to *taint* an entire batch of preserves.

talisman N. charm to bring good luck and avert misfortune. Joe believed the carved pendant he found in Vietnam served him as a *talisman* and brought him safely through the war.

talon N. claw of bird. The falconer wore a leather gauntlet to avoid being clawed by the hawk's *talons*.

tangential ADJ. peripheral; only slightly connected; digressing. Despite Clark's attempts to distract her with *tangential* remarks, Lois kept on coming back to her main question: why couldn't he come out to dinner with Super-man and her?

tangible   ADJ. able to be touched; real; palpable. Although Tom did not own a house, he had several *tangible* assets—a car, a television, a PC—that he could sell if he needed cash.

tanner   N. person who turns animal hides into leather. Using a solution of tanbark, the *tanner* treated the cowhide, transforming it into supple leather.

tantalize   V. tease; torture with disappointment. Tom loved to *tantalize* his younger brother with candy; he knew the boy was forbidden to have it.

● **tantamount**   ADJ. equivalent in effect or value. Though Rudy claimed his wife was off visiting friends, his shriek of horror when she walked into the room was *tantamount* to a confession that he believed she was dead.

Word List 46   tantrum-tonic

tantrum   N. fit of petulance; caprice. The child learned that he could have almost anything if he had a *tantrum*.

tarantula   N. venomous spider. We need an antitoxin to counteract the bite of the *tarantula*.

tarry   V. delay; dawdle. We can't *tarry* if we want to get to the airport on time.

taut   ADJ. tight; ready. The captain maintained that he ran a *taut* ship.

tautological   ADJ. needlessly repetitious. In the sentence "It was visible to the eye, " the phrase "to the eye" is *tautological.*

tautology   N. unnecessary repetition. "Joyful happiness" is an illustration of *tautology.*

tawdry   ADJ. cheap and gaudy. He won a few *tawdry* trinkets in Coney Island.

tedious   ADJ. boring; tiring. The repetitious nature of work on the assembly line made Martin's job very *tedious.* tedium, N.

temerity   N. boldness; rashness. Do you have the *temerity* to argue with me?

■ **temper**   V. moderate; tone down or restrain; toughen (steel). Not even her supervisor's grumpiness could *temper* Nancy's enthusiasm for her new job.

temperament   N. characteristic frame of mind; disposition; emotional excess. Although the twins look alike, they differ markedly in *temperament*: Todd is calm, but Rod is excitable.

temperate   ADJ. restrained; self-controlled; moderate in respect to temperature. Try to be *temperate* in your eating this holiday season; if you control your appetite, you won't gain too much weight.

tempestuous   ADJ. stormy; impassioned; violent. Racket-throwing tennis star John McEnroe was famed for his displays of *tempestuous* temperament.

tempo   N. speed of music. I find the band's *tempo* too slow for such a lively dance.

temporal   ADJ. not lasting forever; limited by time; secular. At one time in our history, *temporal* rulers assumed that they had been given their thrones by divine right.

temporize   V. avoid commiting oneself; gain time. I cannot permit you to *temporize* any longer; I must have a definite answer today.

tenacious   ADJ. holding fast. I had to struggle to break his *tenacious* hold on my arm.

● **tenacity**   N. firmness; persistence. Jean Valjean could not believe the *tenacity* of Inspector Javert. Here all Valjean had done was to steal a loaf of bread, and the inspector had pursued him doggedly for twenty years!

tendentious   ADJ. having an aim; biased; designed to further a cause. The editorials in this periodical are *tendentious* rather than truth-seeking.

tender   V. offer; extend. Although no formal charges had been made against him, in the wake of the recent scandal the mayor felt he should *tender* his resignation.

tenet   N. doctrine; dogma. The agnostic did not accept the *tenets* of their faith.

tensile   ADJ. capable of being stretched. Mountain climbers must know the *tensile* strength of their ropes.

■ **tentative**   ADJ. hesitant; not fully worked out or developed; experimental; not definite or positive. Unsure of his welcome at the Christmas party, Scrooge took a *tentative* step into his nephew's drawing room.

tenuous   ADJ. thin; rare; slim. The allegiance of our allies is held by rather *tenuous* ties.

tenure   N. holding of an office; time during which such an office is held. He has permanent *tenure* in this position and cannot be fired.

tepid   ADJ. lukewarm. During the summer, I like to take a *tepid* bath, not a hot one.

termination   N. end. Though the time for *termination* of the project was near, we still had a lot of work to finish before we shut up shop. terminate, V.

terminology   N. terms used in a science or art. The special *terminology* developed by some authorities in the field has done more to confuse the layman than to enlighten him.

terminus   N. last stop of railroad. After we reached the rail-road *terminus*, we continued our journey into the wilderness on saddle horses.

● **terrestrial**   ADJ. earthly (as opposed to celestial); pertaining to the land. In many science fiction films, alien invaders from outer space plan to destroy all *terrestrial* life.

■ **terse**   ADJ. concise; abrupt; pithy. There is a fine line between speech that is *terse* and to the point and speech that is too abrupt.

testy   ADJ. irritable; short-tempered. My advice is to avoid discussing this problem with him today as he is rather *testy* and may shout at you.

tether   v. tie with a rope. Before we went to sleep, we *tethered* the horses to prevent their wandering off during the night.

thematic   ADJ. relating to a unifying motif or idea. Those who think of *Moby Dick* as a simple adventure story about whaling miss its underlying *thematic* import.

theocracy   N. government run by religious leaders. Though some Pilgrims aboard the *Mayflower* favored the establishment of a *theocracy* in New England, many of their fellow voyagers preferred a nonreligious form of government.

theoretical   ADJ. not practical or applied; hypothetical. Bob was better at applied engineering and computer programming than he was at *theoretical* physics and math. While I can still think of some *theoretical* objections to your plan, you've convinced me of its basic soundness.

therapeutic   ADJ. curative. Now better known for its racetrack, Saratoga Springs first gained attention for the *therapeutic* qualities of its famous "healing waters." therapy, N.

thermal   ADJ. pertaining to heat. The natives discovered that the hot springs made excellent *thermal* baths and began to develop their community as a health resort. also N.

thespian   ADJ. pertaining to drama. Her success in the school play convinced her she was destined for a *thespian* career. also N.

● **threadbare**   ADJ. worn through till the threads show; shabby and poor. The poor adjunct professor hid the *threadbare* spots on his jacket by sewing leather patches on his sleeves.

thrifty   ADJ. careful about money; economical. A *thrifty* shopper compares prices before making major purchases.

■ **thrive**   v. prosper; flourish. Despite the impact of the recession on the restaurant trade, Philip's cafe *thrived.*

throes   N. violent anguish. The *throes* of despair can be as devastating as the spasms accompanying physical pain.

throng   N. crowd. *Throngs* of shoppers jammed the aisles. also V.

thwart   v. baffle; frustrate. He felt that everyone was trying to *thwart* his plans and prevent his success.

tightwad   N. excessively frugal person; miser. Jill called Jack a *tightwad* because he never picked up the check.

tiller   N. handle used to move boat's rudder (to steer). Fearing the wind might shift suddenly and capsize the skiff, Tom kept one hand on the *tiller* at all times.

timidity   N. lack of self-confidence or courage. If you are to succeed as a salesman, you must first lose your *timidity* and fear of failure.

timorous   ADJ. fearful; demonstrating fear. His *timorous* manner betrayed the fear he felt at the moment.

● **tirade**   N. extended scolding; denunciation; harangue. Every time the boss holds a meeting, he goes into a lengthy *tirade*, scolding us for everything from tardiness to padding our expenses.

titanic   ADJ. gigantic. *Titanic* waves beat against the majestic S.S. *Titanic*, driving it against the concealed iceberg.

title   N. right or claim to possession; mark of rank; name (of a book, film, etc.). Though the penniless Duke of Ragwort no longer held *title* to the family estate, he still retained his *title* as head of one of England's oldest families.

titter   N. nervous laugh. Her aunt's constant *titter* nearly drove her mad. also V.

titular   ADJ. nominal holding of title without obligations. Although he was the *titular* head of the company, the real decisions were made by his general manager.

toady   N. servile flatterer; yes man. Never tell the boss anything he doesn't wish to hear: he doesn't want an independent adviser, he just wants a *toady*. also V.

tome   N. large volume. He spent much time in the libraries poring over ancient *tomes.*

tonic   ADJ. invigorating; refreshing. The tart homemade ginger ale had a *tonic* effect on Kit: she perked right up. also N.

Word List 47   topography–ubiquitous

topography   N. physical features of a region. Before the generals gave the order to attack, they ordered a complete study of the *topography* of the region.

● **torpor**   N. lethargy; sluggishness; dormancy. Throughout the winter, nothing aroused the bear from his *torpor*: he would not emerge from hibernation until spring. torpid, ADJ.

torrent   N. rushing stream; flood. Day after day of heavy rain saturated the hillside until the water ran downhill in *torrents*. torrential, ADJ.

torrid   ADJ. passionate; hot or scorching. Harlequin Romances publish *torrid* tales of love affairs, some set in *torrid* climates.

torso   N. trunk of statue with head and limbs missing; human trunk. This *torso*, found in the ruins of Pompeii, is now on exhibition in the museum in Naples.

tortuous   ADJ. winding; full of curves. Because this road is so *tortuous*, it is unwise to go faster than twenty miles an hour on it.

totter   v. move unsteadily; sway, as if about to fall. On unsteady feet, the drunk *tottered* down the hill to the nearest bar.

touchstone   N. stone used to test the fineness of gold alloys; criterion. What *touchstone* can be used to measure the character of a person?

touchy   ADJ. sensitive; irascible. Do not mention his bald spot; he's very *touchy* about it.

tout   v. publicize; praise excessively. I lost confidence in my broker after he *touted* some junk bonds to me that turned out to be a bad investment.

toxic   ADJ. poisonous. We must seek an antidote for whatever *toxic* substance he has eaten. toxicity, N.

tract N. region of land (often imprecisely described); pamphlet. The king granted William Penn a *tract* of land in the New World. Penn then printed a *tract* in which he encouraged settlers to join his colony.

tractable ADJ. docile; easily managed. Although Susan seemed a *tractable* young woman, she had a stubborn streak of independence that occasionally led her to defy the powers-that-be when she felt they were in the wrong.

traduce V. expose to slander. His opponents tried to *traduce* the candidate's reputation by spreading rumors about his past.

trajectory N. path taken by a projectile. The police tried to locate the spot from which the assassin had fired the fatal shot by tracing the *trajectory* of the bullet.

■ **tranquillity** N. calmness; peace. After the commotion and excitement of the city, I appreciate the *tranquillity* of these fields and forests.

transcendent ADJ. surpassing; exceeding ordinary limits; superior. For the amateur chef, dining at the four-star restaurant was a *transcendent* experience: the meal surpassed his wildest dreams.

transcribe V. copy. When you *transcribe* your notes, please send a copy to Mr. Smith and keep the original for our files. transcription, N.

transgression N. violation of a law; sin. Forgive us our *transgressions;* we know not what we do.

■ **transient** ADJ. momentary; temporary; staying for a short time. Lexy's joy at finding the perfect Christmas gift for Phil was *transient;* she still had to find presents for the cousins and Uncle Bob. Located near the airport, this hotel caters to a largely *transient* trade. transience, N.

transition N. going from one state of action to another. During the period of *transition* from oil heat to gas heat, the furnace will have to be shut off.

transitory ADJ. impermanent; fleeting. Fame is *transitory*: today's rising star is all too soon tomorrow's washed-up has-been. transitoriness, N.

translucent ADJ. partly transparent. We could not recognize the people in the next room because of the *translucent* curtains that separated us.

transmute V. change; convert to something different. He was unable to *transmute* his dreams into actualities.

transparent ADJ. easily detected; permitting light to pass through freely. John's pride in his son is *transparent*; no one who sees the two of them together can miss it.

transport N. strong emotion. Margo was a creature of extremes, at one moment in *transports* of joy over a vivid sunset, at another moment in *transports* of grief over a dying bird. also V. (secondary meaning)

trappings N. outward decorations; ornaments. He loved the *trappings* of success: the limousines, the stock options, the company jet.

traumatic ADJ. pertaining to an injury caused by violence. In his nightmares, he kept on recalling the *traumatic* experience of being wounded in battle.

travail N. painful labor. How long do you think a man can endure such *travail* and degradation without rebelling?

traverse V. go through or across. When you *traverse* this field, be careful of the bull.

travesty N. comical parody; treatment aimed at making something appear ridiculous. The ridiculous decision the jury has reached is a *travesty* of justice.

treacly ADJ. sticky sweet; cloyingly sentimental. Irritatingly cheerful, always looking on the bright side, Pollyanna speaks nothing but *treacly* sentimentalities. treacle, N.

treatise N. article treating a subject systematically and thoroughly. He is preparing a *treatise* on the Elizabethan playwrights for his graduate degree.

trek N. travel; journey. The tribe made their *trek* farther north that summer in search of game. also V.

tremor N. trembling; slight quiver. She had a nervous *tremor* in her right hand.

tremulous ADJ. trembling; wavering. She was *tremulous* more from excitement than from fear.

trenchant ADJ. cutting; keen. I am afraid of his *trenchant* wit for it is so often sarcastic.

● **trepidation** N. fear; nervous apprehension. As she entered the office of the dean of admissions, Sharon felt some *trepidation* about how she would do in her interview.

trespass V. unlawfully enter the boundaries of some else's property. The wicked baron flogged any poacher who *trespassed* on his private hunting grounds. also N.

tribute N. tax levied by a ruler; mark of respect. The colonists refused to pay *tribute* to a foreign despot.

● **trifling** ADJ. trivial; unimportant. Why bother going to see a doctor for such a *trifling*, everyday cold?

trigger V. set off. John is touchy today; say one word wrong and you'll *trigger* an explosion.

trinket N. knickknack; bauble. Whenever she traveled abroad, Ethel would pick up costume jewelry and other *trinkets* as souvenirs.

■ **trite** ADJ. hackneyed; commonplace. The *trite* and predictable situations in many television programs turn off many viewers, who, in turn, turn off their sets.

trivial ADJ. unimportant; trifling. Too many magazines ignore newsworthy subjects and feature *trivial* affairs. trivia, N.

trough N. container for feeding farm animals; lowest point (of a wave, business cycle, etc.) The hungry pigs struggled to get at the fresh swill in the *trough*. The surfer rode her board, coasting along in the *trough* between two waves.

truculence N. aggressiveness; ferocity. Tynan's reviews were noted for their caustic attacks and general tone of *truculence*. truculent, ADJ.

truism N. self-evident truth. Many a *truism* is summed up in a proverb; for example, "Marry in haste, repent at leisure."

● **truncate** V. cut the top off. The top of a cone that has been *truncated* in a plane parallel to its base is a circle.

tryst N. meeting. The lovers kept their *tryst* even though they realized their danger.

tumult   N. commotion; riot; noise. She could not make herself heard over the *tumult* of the mob.

tundra   N. rolling, treeless plain in Siberia and arctic North America. Despite the cold, many geologists are trying to discover valuable mineral deposits in the *tundra*.

turbid   ADJ. muddy; having the sediment disturbed. The water was *turbid* after the children had waded through it.

■ **turbulence**   N. state of violent agitation. Warned of approaching *turbulence* in the atmosphere, the pilot told the passengers to fasten their seat belts.

turgid   ADJ. swollen; distended. The *turgid* river threatened to overflow the levees and flood the countryside.

■ **turmoil**   N. great commotion and confusion. Lydia running off with a soldier! Mother fainting at the news! The Bennet household was in *turmoil*.

turncoat   N. traitor. The British considered Benedict Arnold a loyalist; the Americans considered him a *turncoat*.

turpitude   N. depravity. A visitor may be denied admittance to this country if she has been guilty of moral *turpitude*.

tutelage   N. guardianship; training. Under the *tutelage* of such masters of the instrument, she made rapid progress as a virtuoso.

tycoon   N. wealthy leader. John D. Rockefeller was a prominent *tycoon*.

typhoon   N. tropical hurricane or cyclone. If you liked *Twister*, you'll love *Typhoon*!

tyranny   N. oppression; cruel government. Frederick Douglass fought against the *tyranny* of slavery throughout his life.

tyro   N. beginner; novice. For a mere *tyro*, you have produced some wonderfully expert results.

ubiquitous   ADJ. being everywhere; omnipresent. That Christmas "The Little Drummer Boy" seemed *ubiquitous*; David heard the tune everywhere.

Word List 48   ulterior-vehement

ulterior   ADJ. situated beyond; unstated. You must have an *ulterior* motive for your behavior, since there is no obvious reason for it.

ultimate   ADJ. final; not susceptible to further analysis. Scientists are searching for *ultimate* truths.

unaccountable   ADJ. inexplicable; unreasonable or mysterious. I have taken an *unaccountable* dislike to my doctor: "I do not love thee, Doctor Fell. The reason why, I cannot tell."

unanimity   N. complete agreement. We were surprised by the *unanimity* with which members of both parties accepted our proposals. unanimous, ADJ.

unassailable   ADJ. not subject to question; not open to attack. Penelope's virtue was *unassailable*; while she waited for her husband to come back from the war, no other man had a chance.

unassuming   ADJ. modest. He is so *unassuming* that some people fail to realize how great a man he really is.

unbridled   ADJ. violent. She had a sudden fit of *unbridled* rage.

uncanny   ADJ. strange; mysterious. You have the *uncanny* knack of reading my innermost thoughts.

unconscionable   ADJ. unscrupulous; excessive. She found the loan shark's demands *unconscionable* and impossible to meet.

uncouth   ADJ. outlandish; clumsy; boorish. Most biographers portray Lincoln as an *uncouth* and ungainly young man.

unctuous   ADJ. oily; bland; insincerely suave. Uriah Heep disguised his nefarious actions by *unctuous* protestations of his "humility."

underlying   ADJ. fundamental; lying below. The *underlying* cause of the student riot was not the strict curfew rule but the moldy cafeteria food. Miss Marple seems a sweet little old lady at first, but there's an iron will *underlying* that soft and fluffy facade.

■ **undermine**   V. weaken; sap. The recent corruption scandals have *undermined* many people's faith in the city government. The recent torrential rains have washed away much of the cliffside; the deluge threatens to *undermine* the pillars supporting several houses at the edge of the cliff.

underscore   V. emphasize. Addressing the jogging class, Kim *underscored* the importance to runners of good nutrition.

undulating   ADJ. moving with a wavelike motion. The Hilo Hula Festival was an *undulating* sea of grass skirts.

unearth   V. dig up. When they *unearthed* the city, the archeologists found many relics of an ancient civilization.

unequivocal   ADJ. plain; obvious; unmistakable. My answer to your proposal is an *unequivocal* and absolute "No."

unerringly   ADJ. infallibly. My teacher *unerringly* pounced on the one typographical error in my essay.

unfathomable   ADJ. incomprehensible; impenetrable. Unable to get to the bottom of the mystery, Watson declared it was *unfathomable*.

unfetter   V. liberate; free from chains. Chained to the wall for months on end, the hostage despaired that he would ever be *unfettered*.

unfrock   V. to strip a priest or minister of church authority. To disbar a lawyer, to *unfrock* a priest, to suspend a doctor's license to practice—these are extreme steps that the authorities should take only after careful consideration.

ungainly   ADJ. awkward; clumsy; unwieldy. "If you want to know whether Nick's an *ungainly* dancer, check out my bruised feet," said Nora. Anyone who has ever tried to carry a bass fiddle knows it's an *ungainly* instrument.

■ **uniformity** N. sameness; monotony. At *Persons* magazine, we strive for *uniformity* of style; as a result, all our writers wind up sounding exactly alike.

unimpeachable ADJ. blameless and exemplary. Her conduct in office was *unimpeachable* and her record is spotless.

uninhibited ADJ. unrepressed. The congregation was shocked by her *uninhibited* laughter during the sermon.

unintimidating ADJ. unfrightening. Though Phil had expected to feel overawed when he met Steve Young, he found the famous quarterback friendly and *unintimidating*.

unique ADJ. without an equal; single in kind. You have the *unique* distinction of being the only student whom I have had to fail in this course.

universal ADJ. characterizing or affecting all; present everywhere. At first, no one shared Christopher's opinions; his theory that the world was round was met with *universal* disdain.

● **unkempt** ADJ. disheveled; uncared for in appearance. Jeremy hated his neighbor's *unkempt* lawn: he thought its neglected appearance had a detrimental effect on neighborhood property values.

unmitigated ADJ. unrelieved or immoderate; absolute. After four days of *unmitigated* heat, I was ready to collapse from heat prostration. The congresswoman's husband was an *unmitigated* jerk: not only did he abandon her, he took her campaign funds, too!

unobtrusive ADJ. inconspicuous; not blatant. Reluctant to attract notice, the governess took a chair in a far corner of the room and tried to be as *unobtrusive* as possible.

unpalatable ADJ. distasteful; disagreeable. "I refuse to swallow your conclusion," said she, finding his logic *unpalatable*.

● **unprecedented** ADJ. novel; unparalleled. For a first novel, Margaret Mitchell's novel *Gone with the Wind* was an *unprecedented* success.

unprepossessing ADJ. unattractive. During adolescence many attractive young people somehow acquire the false notion that their appearance is *unprepossessing*.

unravel V. disentangle; solve. With equal ease Miss Marple *unraveled* tangled balls of yarn and baffling murder mysteries.

unrequited ADJ. not reciprocated. Suffering the pangs of *unrequited* love, Olivia rebukes Cesario for his hardheartedness.

unruly ADJ. disobedient; lawless. The only way to curb this *unruly* mob is to use tear gas.

unscathed ADJ. unharmed. They prayed he would come back from the war *unscathed*.

unseemly ADJ. unbecoming; indecent; in poor taste. When he put whoopie cushions on all the seats in the funeral parlor, his conduct was most *unseemly*.

unsightly ADJ. ugly. Although James was an experienced emergency room nurse, he occasionally became queasy when faced with a particularly *unsightly* injury.

unstinting ADJ. giving generously; not holding back. The dean praised the donor of the new science building for her *unstinting* generosity.

untenable ADJ. indefensible; not able to be maintained. Wayne is so contrary that the more *untenable* a position is, the harder he'll try to defend it.

■ **unwarranted** ADJ. unjustified; groundless; undeserved. Your assumption that I would accept your proposal is *unwarranted*, sir; I do not want to marry you at all. We could not understand Martin's *unwarranted* rudeness to his mother's guests.

unwieldy ADJ. awkward; cumbersome; unmanageable. The large carton was so *unwieldy* that the movers had trouble getting it up the stairs.

unwitting ADJ. unintentional; not knowing. She was the *unwitting* tool of the swindlers.

upbraid V. severely scold; reprimand. Not only did Miss Minchin *upbraid* Ermengarde for her disobedience, but she hung her up by her braids from a coat rack in the classroom.

uproarious ADJ. marked by commotion; extremely funny; very noisy. The *uproarious* comedy hit *Ace Ventura: Pet Detective* starred Jim Carrey, whose comic mugging provoked gales of *uproarious* laughter from audiences coast to coast.

upshot N. outcome. The *upshot* of the rematch was that the former champion proved that he still possessed all the skills of his youth.

urbane ADJ. suave; refined; elegant. The courtier was *urbane* and sophisticated. urbanity, N.

■ **usurp** V. seize another's power or rank. The revolution ended when the victorious rebel general succeeded in his attempt to *usurp* the throne.

utopia N. ideal place, state, or society. Fed up with this imperfect universe, Don would have liked to run off to Shangri-la or some other imaginary *utopia*. utopian, ADJ.

■ **vacillate** V. waver; fluctuate. Uncertain which suitor she ought to marry, the princess *vacillated*, saying now one, now the other. The big boss likes his people to be decisive: when he asks you for your opinion, whatever you do, don't *vacillate*. vacillation, N.

vacuous ADJ. empty; inane. The *vacuous* remarks of the politician annoyed the audience, who had hoped to hear more than empty platitudes.

vagabond N. wanderer; tramp. In summer, college students wander the roads of Europe like carefree *vagabonds*. also ADJ.

vagrant N. a homeless wanderer. Because he was a stranger in town with no visible means of support, Martin feared he would be jailed as a *vagrant*. vagrancy, N.

valedictory ADJ. pertaining to farewell. I found the *valedictory* address too long; leave-taking should be brief.

valid ADJ. logically convincing; sound; legally acceptable. You're going to have to come up with a better argument if you want to convince me that your reasoning is *valid*.

validate V. confirm; ratify. I will not publish my findings until I *validate* my results.

valor N. bravery. He received the Medal of Honor for his *valor* in battle.

vampire N. ghostly being that sucks the blood of the living. Children were afraid to go to sleep because of the many legends of *vampires* roaming at night.

vanguard N. forerunners; advance forces. We are the *vanguard* of a tremendous army that is following us.

vantage N. position giving an advantage. They fired upon the enemy from behind trees, walls and any other point of *vantage* they could find.

vapid ADJ. dull and unimaginative; insipid and flavorless. "*Bor*-ing!" said Jessica, as she suffered through yet another *vapid* lecture about Dead White Male Poets.

● **vaporize** V. turn into vapor (steam, gas, fog, etc.). "Zap!" went Super Mario's atomic ray gun as he *vaporized* another deadly foe.

variegated ADJ. many-colored. Without her glasses, Gretchen saw the fields of tulips as a *variegated* blur.

veer V. change in direction. After what seemed an eternity, the wind *veered* to the east and the storm abated.

vehement ADJ. forceful; intensely emotional; with marked vigor. Alfred became so *vehement* in describing what was wrong with the Internal Revenue Service that he began jumping up and down and frothing at the mouth. vehemence, N.

Word List 49   velocity-vogue

velocity N. speed. The train went by at considerable *velocity*.

venal ADJ. capable of being bribed. The *venal* policeman cheerfully accepted the bribe offered him by the speeding motorist whom he had stopped.

vendetta N. blood feud. The rival mobs engaged in a bitter *vendetta*.

vendor N. seller. The fruit *vendor* sold her wares from a stall on the sidewalk.

veneer N. thin layer; cover. Casual acquaintances were deceived by his *veneer* of sophistication and failed to recognize his fundamental shallowness.

venerable ADJ. deserving high respect. We do not mean to be disrespectful when we refuse to follow the advice of our *venerable* leader.

■ **venerate** V. revere. In Tibet today, the common people still *venerate* their traditional spiritual leader, the Dalai Lama.

venial ADJ. forgivable; trivial. When Jean Valjean stole a loaf of bread to feed his starving sister, he committed a *venial* offense.

venom N. poison; hatred. Bitten by a rattlesnake on his ankle, the cowboy contortionist curled up like a pretzel and sucked the *venom* out of the wound.

vent N. a small opening; outlet. The wine did not flow because the air *vent* in the barrel was clogged.

vent V. express; utter. The angry teacher *vented* his wrath on his class.

ventriloquist N. someone who can make his or her voice seem to come from another person or thing. This *ventriloquist* does an act in which she has a conversation with a wooden dummy.

venturesome ADJ. bold. A group of *venturesome* women were the first to scale Mt. Annapurna.

veracity N. truthfulness. Asserting his *veracity*, young George Washington proclaimed, "Father, I cannot tell a lie!"

verbalize V. put into words. I know you don't like to talk about these things, but please try to *verbalize* your feelings.

verbatim ADV. word for word. He repeated the message *verbatim*. also ADJ.

verbiage N. pompous array of words. After we had waded through all the *verbiage,* we discovered that the writer had said very little.

■ **verbose** ADJ. wordy. Someone mute can't talk; someone *verbose* can hardly stop talking.

verdant ADJ. green; lush in vegetation. Monet's paintings of the *verdant* meadows were symphonies in green.

verge N. border; edge. Madame Curie knew she was on the *verge* of discovering the secrets of radioactive elements. also V.

verisimilitude N. appearance of truth; likelihood. Critics praised her for the *verisimilitude* of her performance as Lady Macbeth. She was completely believable.

verity N. quality of being true; lasting truth or principle. Did you question the *verity* of Kato Kaelin's testimony about what he heard the night Nicole Brown Simpson was slain? To the skeptic, everything was relative: there were no eternal *verities* in which one could believe.

vernacular N. living language; natural style. Cut out those old-fashioned thee's and thou's and write in the *vernacular*. also ADJ.

versatile ADJ. having many talents; capable of working in many fields. She was a *versatile* athlete, earning varsity letters in basketball, hockey, and track.

vertex N. summit. Let us drop a perpendicular line from the *vertex* of the triangle to the base.

vertigo N. severe dizziness. When you test potential airplane pilots for susceptibility to spells of *vertigo*, be sure to hand out air-sickness bags.

verve N. enthusiasm; liveliness. She approached her studies with such *verve* that it was impossible for her to do poorly.

vestige N. trace; remains. We discovered *vestiges* of early Indian life in the cave. vestigial, ADJ.

vex N. annoy; distress. Please try not to *vex* your mother; she is doing the best she can.

● **viable** ADJ. practical or workable; capable of maintaining life. That idea won't work. Let me see whether I can come up with a *viable* alternative.

vicarious ADJ. acting as a substitute; done by a deputy. Many people get a *vicarious* thrill at the movies by imagining they are the characters on the screen.

vicissitude N. change of fortune. Humbled by life's *vicissitudes*, the last emperor of China worked as a lowly gardener in the palace over which he had once ruled.

vie V. contend; compete. Politicians *vie* with one another, competing for donations and votes.

vigilance N. watchfulness. Eternal *vigilance* is the price of liberty.

vignette N. picture; short literary sketch. The *New Yorker* published her latest *vignette*.

■ **vigor** N. active strength. Although he was over seventy years old, Jack had the *vigor* of a man in his prime. vigorous, ADJ.

■ **vilify** V. slander. Waging a highly negative campaign, the candidate attempted to *vilify* his opponent's reputation. vilification, N.

■ **vindicate** V. clear from blame; exonerate; justify or support. The lawyer's goal was to *vindicate* her client and prove him innocent on all charges. The critics' extremely favorable reviews *vindicate* my opinion that *The Madness of King George* is a brilliant movie.

vindictive ADJ. out for revenge; malicious. I think it's unworthy of Martha to be so *vindictive*; she shouldn't stoop to such petty acts of revenge.

viper N. poisonous snake. The habitat of the horned *viper*, a particularly venomous snake, is in sandy regions like the Sahara or the Sinai peninsula.

virile ADJ. manly. I do not accept the premise that a man proves he's *virile* by being belligerent.

virtual ADJ. in essence; for practical purposes. She is a *virtual* financial wizard when it comes to money matters.

virtue N. goodness, moral excellence; good quality. *Virtue* carried to extremes can turn into vice: humility, for example, can degenerate into servility and spinelessness.

■ **virtuoso** N. highly skilled artist. The child prodigy Yehudi Menuhin grew into a *virtuoso* whose violin performances thrilled millions. virtuosity, N.

● **virulent** ADJ. extremely poisonous; hostile; bitter. Laid up with a *virulent* case of measles, Vera blamed her doctors because her recovery took so long. In fact, she became quite *virulent* on the subject of the quality of modern medical care.

virus N. disease communicator. The doctors are looking for a specific medicine to control this *virus*.

visceral ADJ. felt in one's inner organs. She disliked the *visceral* sensations she had whenever she rode the roller coaster.

viscid ADJ. adhesive; gluey. The trunk of the maple tree was *viscid* with sap.

viscous ADJ. sticky; gluey. Melted tar is a *viscous* substance. viscosity, N.

vise N. tool for holding work in place. Before filing its edges, the locksmith took the blank key and fixed it firmly between the jaws of a *vise*.

visionary ADJ. produced by imagination; fanciful; mystical. She was given to *visionary* schemes that never materialized. also N.

vital ADJ. vibrant and lively; critical; living, breathing. The *vital*, highly energetic first aid instructor stressed that it was *vital* in examining accident victims to note their *vital* signs.

vitriolic ADJ. corrosive; sarcastic. Such *vitriolic* criticism is uncalled for.

vituperative ADJ. abusive; scolding. He became more *vituperative* as he realized that we were not going to grant him his wish.

vivacious ADJ. animated; lively. She had always been *vivacious* and sparkling.

vociferous ADJ. clamorous; noisy. The crowd grew *vociferous* in its anger and threatened to take the law into its own hands.

vogue N. popular fashion. Jeans became the *vogue* on many college campuses.

Word List 50   volatile–zephyr

■ **volatile** ADJ. changeable; explosive; evaporating rapidly. The political climate today is extremely *volatile*: No one can predict what the electorate will do next. Maria Callas's temper was extremely *volatile*: The only thing you could predict was that she was sure to blow up. Acetone is an extremely *volatile* liquid: It evaporates instantly.

volition N. act of making a conscious choice. She selected this dress of her own *volition*.

● **voluble** ADJ. fluent; glib; talkative. The excessively *voluble* speaker suffers from logorrhea: he runs off at the mouth a lot!

voluminous ADJ. bulky; large. A caftan is a *voluminous* garment; most people wearing one look as if they're draped in a small tent.

voluptuous ADJ. gratifying the senses. The nobility during the Renaissance led *voluptuous* lives.

voracious ADJ. ravenous. The wolf is a *voracious* animal, its hunger never satisfied.

vortex N. whirlwind; whirlpool; center of turbulence; predicament into which one is inexorably plunged. Sucked into the *vortex* of the tornado, Dorothy and Toto were carried from Kansas to Oz.

vouchsafe V. grant; choose to give in reply; permit. Occasionally the rock star would drift out onto the balcony and *vouchsafe* the crowd below a glimpse of her celebrated features. The professor *vouchsafed* not a word to the students' questions about what would be covered on the test.

voyeur N. Peeping Tom. Nancy called her brother a *voyeur* when she caught him aiming his binoculars at an upstairs window of the house of the newlyweds next door.

vulnerable ADJ. susceptible to wounds. His opponents could not harm Achilles, who was *vulnerable* only in his heel.

waffle V. speak equivocally about an issue. When asked directly about the governor's involvement in the savings and loan scandal, the press secretary *waffled*, talking all around the issue.

waft V. moved gently by wind or waves. Daydreaming, he gazed at the leaves that *wafted* past his window.

waggish ADJ. mischievous; humorous; tricky. He was a prankster who, unfortunately, often overlooked the damage he could cause with his *waggish* tricks. wag, N.

waif N. homeless child or animal. Although he already had eight cats, he could not resist adopting yet another feline *waif*.

waive V. give up temporarily; yield. I will *waive* my rights in this matter in order to expedite our reaching a proper decision.

wake N. trail of ship or other object through water; path of something that has gone before. The *wake* of the swan gliding through the water glistened in the moonlight. Reporters and photographers converged on South Carolina in the *wake* of the hurricane that devastated much of the eastern seaboard.

wallow V. roll in; indulge in; become helpless. The hippopotamus loves to *wallow* in the mud.

wan ADJ. having a pale or sickly color; pallid. Suckling asked, "Why so pale and *wan*, fond lover?"

wane V. decrease in size or strength; draw gradually to an end. When lit, does a wax candle *wane*?

wanton ADJ. unrestrained; willfully malicious; unchaste. Pointing to the stack of bills, Sheldon criticized Sarah for her *wanton* expenditures. In response, Sarah accused Sheldon of making an unfounded, *wanton* attack.

warble V. sing; babble. Every morning the birds *warbled* outside her window. also N.

warrant V. justify; authorize. Before the judge issues the injunction, you must convince her this action is *warranted*.

warranty N. guarantee; assurance by seller. The purchaser of this automobile is protected by the manufacturer's *warranty* that the company will replace any defective part for five years or 50,000 miles.

wary ADJ. very cautious. The spies grew *wary* as they approached the sentry.

wastrel N. profligate. His neighbors denounced him as a *wastrel* who had dissipated his inheritance.

watershed N. crucial dividing point. The invention of the personal computer proved a historic *watershed*, for it opened the way to today's Information Age.

wax V. increase; grow. With proper handling, his fortunes *waxed* and he became rich.

waylay V. ambush; lie in wait. They agreed to *waylay* their victim as he passed through the dark alley going home.

wean V. accustom a baby to not nurse; give up a cherished activity. He decided he would *wean* himself away from eating junk food and stick to fruits and vegetables.

weather V. endure the effects of weather or other forces. He *weathered* the changes in his personal life with difficulty, as he had no one in whom to confide.

welter N. turmoil; bewildering jumble. The existing *welter* of overlapping federal and state programs cries out for immediate reform.

wheedle V. cajole; coax; deceive by flattery. She knows she can *wheedle* almost anything she wants from her father.

whelp N. young wolf, dog, tiger, etc. This collie *whelp* won't do for breeding, but he'd make a fine pet.

whet V. sharpen; stimulate. The odors from the kitchen are *whetting* my appetite; I will be ravenous by the time the meal is served.

whiff N. puff or gust (of air, scent, etc.); hint. The slightest *whiff* of Old Spice cologne brought memories of George to her mind.

■ **whimsical** ADJ. capricious; fanciful. In *Mrs. Doubtfire*, the hero is a playful, *whimsical* man who takes a notion to dress up as a woman so that he can look after his children, who are in the custody of his ex-wife. whimsy, N.

whinny V. neigh like a horse. When he laughed through his nose, it sounded as if he *whinnied*.

whittle V. pare; cut off bits. As a present for Aunt Polly, Tom *whittled* some clothespins out of a chunk of wood.

willful ADJ. intentional; headstrong. Donald had planned to kill his wife for months; clearly, her death was a case of deliberate, *willful* murder, not a crime of passion committed by a hasty, *willful* youth unable to foresee the consequences of his deeds.

wily ADJ. cunning; artful. She is as *wily* as a fox in avoiding trouble.

wince V. shrink back; flinch. The screech of the chalk on the blackboard made her *wince*.

windfall N. unexpected lucky event. This huge tax refund is quite a *windfall*.

winnow V. sift; separate good parts from bad. This test will *winnow* out the students who study from those who don't bother.

winsome ADJ. agreeable; gracious; engaging. By her *winsome* manner, she made herself liked by everyone who met her.

wispy ADJ. thin; slight; barely discernible. Worried about preserving his few *wispy* tufts of hair, Walter carefully massaged his scalp and applied hair restorer every night.

wistful ADJ. vaguely longing; sadly thoughtful. With a last *wistful* glance at the happy couples dancing in the hall, Sue headed back to her room to study for her exam.

withdrawn ADJ. introverted; remote. Rebuffed by his colleagues, the initially outgoing young researcher became increasingly *withdrawn*.

wither V. shrivel; decay. Cut flowers are beautiful for a day, but all too soon they *wither*.

withhold   v. refuse to give; hold back. The tenants decided to *withhold* a portion of the rent until the landlord kept his promise to renovate the building.

withstand   v. stand up against; successfully resist. If you can *withstand* all the peer pressure in high school to cut classes and goof off, you should survive college just fine.

witless   ADJ. foolish; idiotic. If Beavis is a half-wit, then Butthead is totally *witless*.

● **witticism**   N. witty saying; wisecrack. I don't mean any criticism, but that last *witticism* totally hurt my feelings.

wizardry   N. sorcery; magic. Merlin the Magician amazed the knights with his *wizardry*.

woe   N. deep, inconsolable grief; affliction; suffering. Pale and wan with grief, Wanda was bowed down beneath the burden of her *woes*.

worldly   ADJ. engrossed in matters of this earth; not spiritual. You must leave your *worldly* goods behind you when you go to meet your Maker.

wrath   N. anger; fury. She turned to him, full of *wrath,* and said, "What makes you think I'll accept lower pay for this job than you get?"

wrench   v. pull; strain; twist. She *wrenched* free of her attacker and landed a powerful kick to his kneecap.

writhe   v. twist in coils; contort in pain. In *Dances with Snakes*, the snake dancer wriggled sinuously as her boa constrictor *writhed* around her torso.

wry   ADJ. twisted; with a humorous twist. We enjoy Dorothy Parker's verse for its *wry* wit.

xenophobia   N. fear or hatred of foreigners. When the refugee arrived in America, he was unprepared for the *xenophobia* he found there.

yen   N. longing; urge. She had a *yen* to get away and live on her own for a while.

yield   v. give in; surrender. The wounded knight refused to *yield* to his foe.

yield   N. amount produced; crop; income on investment. An experienced farmer can estimate the annual *yield* of his acres with surprising accuracy. also v.

yoke   v. join together, unite. I don't wish to be *yoked* to him in marriage, as if we were cattle pulling a plow. also N.

yore   N. time past. He dreamed of the elegant homes of *yore,* but gave no thought to their inelegant plumbing.

zany   ADJ. crazy; comic. I can watch the Marx brothers' *zany* antics for hours.

zeal   N. eager enthusiasm. Katya's *zeal* was contagious; soon all her fellow students were busily making posters, inspired by her ardent enthusiasm for the cause. zealous, ADJ.

■ **zealot**   N. fanatic; person who shows excessive zeal. Though Glenn was devout, he was no *zealot*; he never tried to force his beliefs on his friends.

zenith   N. point directly overhead in the sky; summit. When the sun was at its *zenith,* the glare was not as strong as at sunrise and sunset.

zephyr   N. gentle breeze; west wind. When these *zephyrs* blow, it is good to be in an open boat under a full sail.

Basic Word Parts

In addition to reviewing the SAT I High-Frequency Word List, what other quick vocabulary-building tactics can you follow when you face an SAT I deadline?

One good approach is to learn how to build up (and tear apart) words. You know that words are made up of other words: the *room* in which you *store* things is the *storeroom;* the person whose job is to *keep* the *books* is the *bookkeeper.*

Just as words are made up of other words, words are also made up of word parts: prefixes, suffixes, and roots. A knowledge of these word parts and their meanings can help you determine the meanings of unfamiliar words.

Most modern English words are derived from Anglo-Saxon (Old English), Latin, and Greek. Because few students nowadays study Latin and Greek (and even fewer study Anglo-Saxon!), the majority of high school juniors and seniors lack a vital tool for unlocking the meaning of unfamiliar words.

Build your vocabulary by mastering basic word parts. Learning thirty key word parts can help you unlock the meaning of over 10,000 words. Learning fifty key word parts can help you unlock the meaning of over 100,000!

Common Prefixes

Prefixes are syllables that precede the root or stem and change or refine its meaning.

Prefix	Meaning	Illustration
ab, abs	from, away from	*abduct* lead away, kidnap *abjure* renounce *abject* degraded, cast down
ad, ac, af, ag, an, ap, ar, as, at	to, forward	*adit* entrance *adjure* request earnestly *admit* allow entrance *accord* agreement, harmony *affliction* distress *aggregation* collection *annexation* add to *apparition* ghost *arraignment* indictment *assumption* arrogance, the taking for granted *attendance* presence, the persons present
ambi	both	*ambidextrous* skilled with both hands *ambiguous* of double meaning *ambivalent* having two conflicting emotions
an, a	without	*anarchy* lack of government *anemia* lack of blood *amoral* without moral sense
ante	before	*antecedent* preceding event or word *antediluvian* ancient (before the flood) *ante-nuptial* before the wedding
anti	against, opposite	*antipathy* hatred *antiseptic* against infection *antithetical* exactly opposite

Prefix	Meaning	Illustration
arch	chief, first	*archetype* original *archbishop* chief bishop *archeology* study of first or ancient times
be	over, thoroughly	*bedaub* smear over *befuddle* confuse thoroughly *beguile* deceive, charm thoroughly
bi	two	*bicameral* composed of two houses (Congress) *biennial* every two years *bicycle* two-wheeled vehicle
cata	down	*catastrophe* disaster *cataract* waterfall *catapult* hurl (throw down)
circum	around	*circumnavigate* sail around (the globe) *circumspect* cautious (looking around) *circumscribe* limit (place a circle around)
com, co, col, con, cor	with, together	*combine* merge with *commerce* trade with *communicate* correspond with *coeditor* joint editor *collateral* subordinate, connected *conference* meeting *corroborate* confirm
contra, contro	against	*contravene* conflict with *controversy* dispute
de	down, away	*debase* lower in value *decadence* deterioration *decant* pour off
demi	partly, half	*demigod* partly divine being
di	two	*dichotomy* division into two parts *dilemma* choice between two bad alternatives
dia	across	*diagonal* across a figure *diameter* distance across a circle *diagram* outline drawing
dis, dif	not, apart	*discord* lack of harmony *differ* disagree (carry apart) *disparity* condition of inequality; difference
dys	faulty, bad	*dyslexia* faulty ability to read *dyspepsia* indigestion
ex, e	out	*expel* drive out *extirpate* root out *eject* throw out

Prefix	Meaning	Illustration
extra, extro	beyond, outside	*extracurricular* beyond the curriculum *extraterritorial* beyond a nation's bounds *extrovert* person interested chiefly in external *objects* and actions
hyper	above; excessively	*hyperbole* exaggeration *hyperventilate* breathe at an excessive rate
hypo	beneath; lower	*hypoglycemia* low blood sugar
in, il, im, ir	not	*inefficient* not efficient *inarticulate* not clear or distinct *illegible* not readable *impeccable* not capable of sinning; flawless *irrevocable* not able to be called back
in, il, im, ir	in, on, upon	*invite* call in *illustration* something that makes clear *impression* effect upon mind or feelings *irradiate* shine upon
inter	between, among	*intervene* come between *international* between nations *interjection* a statement thrown in
intra, intro	within	*intramural* within a school *introvert* person who turns within himself
macro	large, long	*macrobiotic* tending to prolong life *macrocosm* the great world (the entire universe)
mega	great, million	*megalomania* delusions of grandeur *megaton* explosive force of a million tons of TNT
meta	involving change	*metamorphosis* change of form
micro	small	*microcosm* miniature universe *microbe* minute organism *microscopic* extremely small
mis	bad, improper	*misdemeanor* minor crime; bad conduct *mischance* unfortunate accident *misnomer* wrong name
mis	hatred	*misanthrope* person who hates mankind *misogynist* woman-hater
mono	one	*monarchy* government by one ruler *monotheism* belief in one god
multi	many	*multifarious* having many parts *multitudinous* numerous
neo	new	*neologism* newly coined word *neophyte* beginner; novice

Prefix	Meaning	Illustration
non	not	*noncommittal* undecided *nonentity* person of no importance
ob, oc, of, op	against	*obloquy* infamy; disgrace *obtrude* push into prominence *occlude* close; block out *offend* insult *opponent* someone who struggles against; foe
olig	few	*oligarchy* government by a few
pan	all, every	*panacea* cure-all *panorama* unobstructed view in all directions
para	beyond, related	*parallel* similar *paraphrase* restate; translate
per	through, completely	*permeable* allowing passage through *pervade* spread throughout
peri	around, near	*perimeter* outer boundary *periphery* edge *periphrastic* stated in a roundabout way
poly	many	*polygamist* person with several spouses *polyglot* speaking several languages
post	after	*postpone* delay *posterity* generations that follow *posthumous* after death
pre	before	*preamble* introductory statement *prefix* word part placed before a root/stem *premonition* forewarning
prim	first	*primordial* existing at the dawn of time *primogeniture* state of being the first born
pro	forward, in favor of	*propulsive* driving forward *proponent* supporter
proto	first	*prototype* first of its kind
pseudo	false	*pseudonym* pen name
re	again, back	*reiterate* repeat *reimburse* pay back
retro	backward	*retrospect* looking back *retroactive* effective as of a past date
se	away, aside	*secede* withdraw *seclude* shut away *seduce* lead astray

Prefix	Meaning	Illustration
semi	half, partly	*semiannual* every six months *semiconscious* partly conscious
sub, suc, suf, sug, sup, sus	under, less	*subway* underground road *subjugate* bring under control *succumb* yield; cease to resist *suffuse* spread through *suggest* hint *suppress* put down by force *suspend* delay
super, sur	over, above	*supernatural* above natural things *supervise* oversee *surtax* additional tax
syn, sym, syl, sys	with, together	*synchronize* time together *synthesize* combine together *sympathize* pity; identify with *syllogism* explanation of how ideas relate *system* network
tele	far	*telemetry* measurement from a distance *telegraphic* communicated over a distance
trans	across	*transport* carry across *transpose* reverse, move across
ultra	beyond, excessive	*ultramodern* excessively modern *ultracritical* exceedingly critical
un	not	*unfeigned* not pretended; real *unkempt* not combed; disheveled *unwitting* not knowing; unintentional
under	below	*undergird* strengthen underneath *underling* someone inferior
uni	one	*unison* oneness of pitch; complete accord *unicycle* one-wheeled vehicle
vice	in place of	*vicarious* acting as a substitute *viceroy* governor acting in place of a king
with	away, against	*withhold* hold back; keep *withstand* stand up against; resist

Common Roots and Stems

Roots are basic words which have been carried over into English. *Stems* are varia-tions of roots brought about by changes in declension or conjugation.

Root or Stem	Meaning	Illustration
ac, acr	sharp	*acrimonious* bitter; caustic *acerbity* bitterness of temper *acidulate* to make somewhat acid or sour
aev, ev	age, era	*primeval* of the first age *coeval* of the same age or era *medieval* or *mediaeval* of the middle ages
ag, act	do	*act* deed *agent* doer
agog	leader	*demagogue* false leader of people *pedagogue* teacher (leader of children)
agri, agrari	field	*agrarian* one who works in the field *agriculture* cultivation of fields *peregrination* wandering (through fields)
ali	another	*alias* assumed (another) name *alienate* estrange (turn away from another)
alt	high	*altitude* height *altimeter* instrument for measuring height
alter	other	*altruistic* unselfish, considering others *alter ego* a second self
am	love	*amorous* loving, especially sexually *amity* friendship *amicable* friendly
anim	mind, soul	*animadvert* cast criticism upon *unanimous* of one mind *magnanimity* greatness of mind or spirit
ann, enn	year	*annuity* yearly remittance *biennial* every two years *perennial* present all year; persisting for several years
anthrop	man	*anthropology* study of man *misanthrope* hater of mankind *philanthropy* love of mankind; charity
apt	fit	*aptitude* skill *adapt* make suitable or fit

Root or Stem	Meaning	Illustration
aqua	water	*aqueduct* passageway for conducting water *aquatic* living in water *aqua fortis* nitric acid (strong water)
arch	ruler, first	*archaeology* study of antiquities (study of first things) *monarch* sole ruler *anarchy* lack of government
aster	star	*astronomy* study of the stars *asterisk* star-like type character (*) *disaster* catastrophe (contrary star)
aud, audit	hear	*audible* able to be heard *auditorium* place where people may be heard *audience* hearers
auto	self	*autocracy* rule by one person (self) *automobile* vehicle that moves by itself *autobiography* story of one's own life
belli	war	*bellicose* inclined to fight *belligerent* inclined to wage war *rebellious* resisting authority
ben, bon	good	*benefactor* one who does good deeds *benevolence* charity (wishing good) *bonus* something extra above regular pay
biblio	book	*bibliography* list of books *bibliophile* lover of books *Bible* The Book
bio	life	*biography* writing about a person's life *biology* study of living things *biochemist* student of the chemistry of living things
breve	short	*brevity* briefness *abbreviate* shorten *breviloquent* marked by brevity of speech
cad, cas	to fall	*decadent* deteriorating *cadence* intonation, musical movement *cascade* waterfall
cap, capt, cept, cip	to take	*capture* seize *participate* take part *precept* wise saying (originally a command)
capit, capt	head	*decapitate* remove (cut off) someone's head *captain* chief
carn	flesh	*carnivorous* flesh-eating *carnage* destruction of life *carnal* fleshly

Root or Stem	Meaning	Illustration
ced, cess	to yield, to go	*recede* go back, withdraw *antecedent* that which goes before *process* go forward
celer	swift	*celerity* swiftness *decelerate* reduce swiftness *accelerate* increase swiftness
cent	one hundred	*century* one hundred years *centennial* hundredth anniversary *centipede* many-footed, wingless animal
chron	time	*chronology* timetable of events *anachronism* a thing out of time sequence *chronicle* register events in order of time
cid, cis	to cut, to kill	*incision* a cut (surgical) *homicide* killing of a man *fratricide* killing of a brother
cit, citat	to call, to start	*incite* stir up, start up *excite* stir up *recitation* a recalling (or repeating) aloud
civi	citizen	*civilization* society of citizens, culture *civilian* member of community *civil* courteous
clam, clamat	to cry out	*clamorous* loud *declamation* speech *acclamation* shouted approval
claud, claus, 　clos, clud	to close	*claustrophobia* fear of close places *enclose* close in *conclude* finish
cognosc, cognit	to learn	*agnostic* lacking knowledge, skeptical *incognito* traveling under assumed name *cognition* knowledge
compl	to fill	*complete* filled out *complement* that which completes something *comply* fulfill
cord	heart	*accord* agreement (from the heart) *cordial* friendly *discord* lack of harmony
corpor	body	*incorporate* organize into a body *corporeal* pertaining to the body, fleshly *corpse* dead body
cred, credit	to believe	*incredulous* not believing, skeptical *credulity* gullibility *credence* belief

Root or Stem	Meaning	Illustration
cur	to care	*curator* person who has the care of something *sinecure* position without responsibility *secure* safe
curr, curs	to run	*excursion* journey *cursory* brief *precursor* forerunner
da, dat	to give	*data* facts, statistics *mandate* command *date* given time
deb, debit	to owe	*debt* something owed *indebtedness* debt *debenture* bond
dem	people	*democracy* rule of the people *demagogue* (false) leader of the people *epidemic* widespread (among the people)
derm	skin	*epidermis* skin *pachyderm* thick-skinned quadruped *dermatology* study of skin and its disorders
di, diurn	day	*diary* a daily record of activities, feelings, etc. *diurnal* pertaining to daytime
dic, dict	to say	*abdicate* renounce *diction* speech *verdict* statement of jury
doc, doct	to teach	*docile* obedient; easily taught *document* something that provides evidence *doctor* learned person (originally, teacher)
domin	to rule	*dominate* have power over *domain* land under rule *dominant* prevailing
duc, duct	to lead	*viaduct* arched roadway *aqueduct* artificial waterway
dynam	power, strength	*dynamic* powerful *dynamite* powerful explosive *dynamo* engine making electrical power
ego	I	*egoist* person who is self-interested *egotist* selfish person *egocentric* revolving about self
erg, urg	work	*energy* power *ergatocracy* rule of the workers *metallurgy* science and technology of metals

Root or Stem	Meaning	Illustration
err	to wander	*error* mistake *erratic* not reliable, wandering *knight-errant* wandering knight
eu	good, well, beautiful	*eupeptic* having good digestion *eulogize* praise *euphemism* substitution of pleasant way of saying something blunt
fac, fic, fec, fect	to make, to do	*factory* place where things are made *fiction* manufactured story *affect* cause to change
fall, fals	to deceive	*fallacious* misleading *infallible* not prone to error, perfect *falsify* lie
fer, lat	to bring, to bear	*transfer* bring from one place to another *translate* bring from one language to another *conifer* bearing cones, as pine trees
fid	belief, faith	*infidel* nonbeliever, heathen *confidence* assurance, belief
fin	end, limit	*confine* keep within limits *finite* having definite limits
flect, flex	bend	*flexible* able to bend *deflect* bend away, turn aside
fort	luck, chance	*fortuitous* accidental, occurring by chance *fortunate* lucky
fort	strong	*fortitude* strength, firmness of mind *fortification* strengthening *fortress* stronghold
frag, fract	break	*fragile* easily broken *infraction* breaking of a rule *fractious* unruly, tending to break rules
fug	flee	*fugitive* someone who flees *refuge* shelter, home for someone fleeing
fus	pour	*effusive* gushing, pouring out *diffuse* widespread (poured in many directions)
gam	marriage	*monogamy* marriage to one person *bigamy* marriage to two people at the same time *polygamy* having many wives or husbands at the same time
gen, gener	class, race	*genus* group of animals with similar traits *generic* characteristic of a class *gender* class organized by sex

Root or Stem	Meaning	Illustration
grad, gress	go, step	*digress* go astray (from the main point) *regress* go backwards *gradual* step by step, by degrees
graph, gram	writing	*epigram* pithy statement *telegram* instantaneous message over great distance *stenography* shorthand (writing narrowly)
greg	flock, herd	*gregarious* tending to group together as in a herd *aggregate* group, total *egregious* conspicuously bad; shocking
helio	sun	*heliotrope* flower that faces the sun *heliograph* instrument that uses the sun's rays to send signals
it, itiner	journey, road	*exit* way out *itinerary* plan of journey
jac, jact, jec	to throw	*projectile* missile; something thrown forward *trajectory* path taken by thrown object *ejaculatory* casting or throwing out
jur, jurat	to swear	*perjure* testify falsely *jury* group of men and women sworn to seek the truth *adjuration* solemn urging
labor, laborat	to work	*laboratory* place where work is done *collaborate* work together with others *laborious* difficult
leg, lect, lig	to choose, to read	*election* choice *legible* able to be read *eligible* able to be selected
leg	law	*legislature* law-making body *legitimate* lawful *legal* lawful
liber, libr	book	*library* collection of books *libretto* the "book" of a musical play *libel* slander (originally found in a little book)
liber	free	*liberation* the fact of setting free *liberal* generous (giving freely); tolerant
log	word, study	*entomology* study of insects *etymology* study of word parts and derivations *monologue* speech by one person
loqu, locut	to talk	*soliloquy* speech by one individual *loquacious* talkative *elocution* speech

Root or Stem	Meaning	Illustration
luc	light	*elucidate* enlighten *lucid* clear *translucent* allowing some light to pass through
magn	great	*magnify* enlarge *magnanimity* generosity, greatness of soul *magnitude* greatness, extent
mal	bad	*malevolent* wishing evil *malediction* curse *malefactor* evil-doer
man	hand	*manufacture* create (make by hand) *manuscript* written by hand *emancipate* free (let go from the hand)
mar	sea	*maritime* connected with seafaring *submarine* undersea craft *mariner* seaman
mater, matr	mother	*maternal* pertaining to motherhood *matriarch* female ruler of a family, group, or state *matrilineal* descended on the mother's side
mit, miss	to send	*missile* projectile *dismiss* send away *transmit* send across
mob, mot, mov	move	*mobilize* cause to move *motility* ability to move *immovable* not able to be moved
mon, monit	to warn	*admonish* warn *premonition* foreboding *monitor* watcher (warner)
mori, mort	to die	*mortuary* funeral parlor *moribund* dying *immortal* not dying
morph	shape, form	*amorphous* formless, lacking shape *metamorphosis* change of shape *anthropomorphic* in the shape of man
mut	change	*immutable* not able to be changed *mutate* undergo a great change *mutability* changeableness, inconstancy
nat	born	*innate* from birth *prenatal* before birth *nativity* birth
nav	ship	*navigate* sail a ship *circumnavigate* sail around the world *naval* pertaining to ships

Root or Stem	Meaning	Illustration
neg	deny	*negation* denial *renege* deny, go back on one's word *renegade* turncoat, traitor
nomen	name	*nomenclature* act of naming, terminology *nominal* in name only (as opposed to actual) *cognomen* surname, distinguishing nickname
nov	new	*novice* beginner *renovate* make new again *novelty* newness
omni	all	*omniscient* all knowing *omnipotent* all powerful *omnivorous* eating everything
oper	to work	*operate* work *cooperation* working together
pac	peace	*pacify* make peaceful *pacific* peaceful *pacifist* person opposed to war
pass	feel	*dispassionate* free of emotion *impassioned* emotion-filled *impassive* showing no feeling
pater, patr	father	*patriotism* love of one's country (fatherland) *patriarch* male ruler of a family, group, or state *paternity* fatherhood
path	disease, feeling	*pathology* study of diseased tissue *apathetic* lacking feeling; indifferent *antipathy* hostile feeling
ped, pod	foot	*impediment* stumbling-block; hindrance *tripod* three-footed stand *quadruped* four-footed animal
ped	child	*pedagogue* teacher of children *pediatrician* children's doctor
pel, puls	to drive	*compulsion* a forcing to do *repel* drive back *expel* drive out, banish
pet, petit	to seek	*petition* request *appetite* craving, desire *compete* vie with others
phil	love	*philanthropist* benefactor, lover of humanity *Anglophile* lover of everything English *philanderer* one involved in brief love affairs

Root or Stem	Meaning	Illustration
pon, posit	to place	*postpone* place after *positive* definite, unquestioned (definitely placed)
port, portat	to carry	*portable* able to be carried *transport* carry across *export* carry out (of country)
poten	able, powerful	*omnipotent* all-powerful *potentate* powerful person *impotent* powerless
psych	mind	*psychology* study of the mind *psychosis* mental disorder *psychopath* mentally ill person
put, putat	to trim, to calculate	*putative* supposed (calculated) *computation* calculation *amputate* cut off
quer, ques, quir, quis	to ask	*inquiry* investigation *inquisitive* questioning *query* question
reg, rect	rule	*regicide* murder of a ruler *regent* ruler *insurrection* rebellion; overthrow of a ruler
rid, ris	to laugh	*derision* scorn *risibility* inclination to laughter *ridiculous* deserving to be laughed at
rog, rogat	to ask	*interrogate* question *prerogative* privilege
rupt	to break	*interrupt* break into *bankrupt* insolvent *rupture* a break
sacr	holy	*sacred* holy *sacrilegious* impious, violating something holy *sacrament* religious act
sci	to know	*science* knowledge *omniscient* knowing all *conscious* aware
scop	watch, see	*periscope* device for seeing around corners *microscope* device for seeing small objects
scrib, script	to write	*transcribe* make a written copy *script* written text *circumscribe* write around, limit
sect	cut	*dissect* cut apart *bisect* cut into two pieces

Root or Stem	Meaning	Illustration
sed, sess	to sit	*sedentary* inactive (sitting) *session* meeting
sent, sens	to think, to feel	*consent* agree *resent* show indignation *sensitive* showing feeling
sequi, secut, seque	to follow	*consecutive* following in order *sequence* arrangement *sequel* that which follows *non sequitur* something that does not follow logically
solv, solut	to loosen	*absolve* free from blame *dissolute* morally lax *absolute* complete (not loosened)
somn	sleep	*insomnia* inability to sleep *somnolent* sleepy *somnambulist* sleepwalker
soph	wisdom	*philosopher* lover of wisdom *sophisticated* worldly wise
spec, spect	to look at	*spectator* observer *aspect* appearance *circumspect* cautious (looking around)
spir	breathe	*respiratory* pertaining to breathing *spirited* full of life (breath)
string, strict	bind	*stringent* strict *constrict* become tight *stricture* limit, something that restrains
stru, struct	build	*constructive* helping to build *construe* analyze (how something is built)
tang, tact, ting	to touch	*tangent* touching *contact* touching with, meeting *contingent* depending upon
tempor	time	*contemporary* at same time *extemporaneous* impromptu *temporize* delay
ten, tent	to hold	*tenable* able to be held *tenure* holding of office *retentive* holding; having a good memory
term	end	*interminable* endless *terminate* end
terr	land	*terrestrial* pertaining to earth *subterranean* underground

Root or Stem	Meaning	Illustration
therm	heat	*thermostat* instrument that regulates heat *diathermy* sending heat through body tissues
tors, tort	twist	*distort* twist out of true shape or meaning *torsion* act of twisting *tortuous* twisting
tract	drag, pull	*distract* pull (one's attention) away *intractable* stubborn, unable to be dragged *attraction* pull, drawing quality
trud, trus	push, shove	*intrude* push one's way in *protrusion* something sticking out
urb	city	*urban* pertaining to a city *urbane* polished, sophisticated (pertaining to a city dweller) *suburban* outside of a city
vac	empty	*vacuous* lacking content, empty-headed *evacuate* compel to empty an area
vad, vas	go	*invade* enter in a hostile fashion *evasive* not frank; eluding
veni, vent, ven	to come	*intervene* come between *prevent* stop *convention* meeting
ver	true	*veracious* truthful *verify* check the truth *verisimilitude* appearance of truth
verb	word	*verbose* wordy *verbiage* excessive use of words *verbatim* word for word
vers, vert	turn	*vertigo* turning dizzy *revert* turn back (to an earlier state) *diversion* something causing one to turn aside
via	way	*deviation* departure from the way *viaduct* roadway (arched) *trivial* trifling (small talk at crossroads)
vid, vis	to see	*vision* sight *evidence* things seen *vista* view
vinc, vict, vanq	to conquer	*invincible* unconquerable *victory* winning *vanquish* defeat

Root or Stem	Meaning	Illustration
viv, vit	alive	*vivisection* operating on living animals *vivacious* full of life *vitality* liveliness
voc, vocat	to call	*avocation* calling, minor occupation *provocation* calling or rousing the anger of *invocation* calling in prayer
vol	wish	*malevolent* wishing someone ill *voluntary* of one's own will
volv, volut	to roll	*revolve* roll around *evolve* roll out, develop *convolution* coiled state

Common Suffixes

Suffixes are syllables that are added to a word. Occasionally, they change the meaning of the word; more frequently, they serve to change the grammatical form of the word (noun to adjective, adjective to noun, noun to verb).

Suffix	Meaning	Illustration
able, ible	capable of (adjective suffix)	*portable* able to be carried *interminable* not able to be limited *legible* able to be read
ac, ic	like, pertaining to (adjective suffix)	*cardiac* pertaining to the heart *aquatic* pertaining to the water *dramatic* pertaining to the drama
acious, icious	full of (adjective suffix)	*audacious* full of daring *perspicacious* full of mental perception *avaricious* full of greed
al	pertaining to (adjective or noun suffix)	*maniacal* insane *final* pertaining to the end *logical* pertaining to logic
ant, ent	full of (adjective or noun suffix)	*eloquent* pertaining to fluid, effective speech *suppliant* pleader (person full of requests) *verdant* green
ary	like, connected with (adjective or noun suffix)	*dictionary* book connected with words *honorary* with honor *luminary* celestial body
ate	to make (verb suffix)	*consecrate* to make holy *enervate* to make weary *mitigate* to make less severe

Suffix	Meaning	Illustration
ation	that which is (noun suffix)	*exasperation* irritation *irritation* annoyance
cy	state of being (noun suffix)	*democracy* government ruled by the people *obstinacy* stubbornness *accuracy* correctness
eer, er, or	person who (noun suffix)	*mutineer* person who rebels *lecher* person who lusts *censor* person who deletes improper remarks
escent	becoming (adjective suffix)	*evanescent* tending to vanish *pubescent* arriving at puberty
fic	making, doing (adjective suffix)	*terrific* arousing great fear *soporific* causing sleep
fy	to make (verb suffix)	*magnify* enlarge *petrify* turn to stone *beautify* make beautiful
iferous	producing, bearing (adjective suffix)	*pestiferous* carrying disease *vociferous* bearing a loud voice
il, ile	pertaining to, capable of (adjective suffix)	*puerile* pertaining to a boy or child *ductile* capable of being hammered or drawn *civil* polite
ism	doctrine, belief (noun suffix)	*monotheism* belief in one god *fanaticism* excessive zeal; extreme belief
ist	dealer, doer (noun suffix)	*fascist* one who believes in a fascist state *realist* one who is realistic *artist* one who deals with art
ity	state of being (noun suffix)	*annuity* yearly grant *credulity* state of being unduly willing to believe *sagacity* wisdom
ive	like (adjective suffix)	*expensive* costly *quantitative* concerned with quantity *effusive* gushing
ize, ise	make (verb suffix)	*victimize* make a victim of *rationalize* make rational *harmonize* make harmonious *enfranchise* make free or set free
oid	resembling, like (adjective suffix)	*ovoid* like an egg *anthropoid* resembling man *spheroid* resembling a sphere
ose	full of (adjective suffix)	*verbose* full of words *lachrymose* full of tears

Suffix	Meaning	Illustration
osis	condition (noun suffix)	*psychosis* diseased mental condition *neurosis* nervous condition *hypnosis* condition of induced sleep
ous	full of (adjective suffix)	*nauseous* full of nausea *ludicrous* foolish
tude	state of (noun suffix)	*fortitude* state of strength *beatitude* state of blessedness *certitude* state of sureness

PART THREE

Tactics, Strategies, Practice: Mathematics

Introduction to Part Three

PART THREE consists of five chapters. Chapter 8 presents several important strategies that can be used on any mathematics questions that appear on the SAT I. In each of Chapters 9, 10, and 11 you will find tactics that are specific to one of the three different types of questions. Chapter 12 contains a complete review of all the mathematics you need to know in order to do well on the SAT I, as well as hundreds of sample problems patterned on actual test questions.

Four Types of Tactics

Four different types of tactics are discussed in this book.

1. In Chapter 2 you learned many basic tactics used by all good test-takers; for example, read each question carefully, pace yourself, don't get bogged down on any one question, and never waste time reading the directions. These tactics apply to all of the sections of the SAT I, both verbal and mathematics.

2. In Chapters 4, 5, and 6 you learned the important tactics needed for handling each of the three types of verbal questions.

3. In Chapters 8–11 you will find all of the tactics that apply to the mathematics sections of the SAT I. Chapter 8 deals with techniques that can be applied to all types of mathematics questions, whereas Chapters 9, 10, and 11 present specific strategies to deal with each of the three kinds of mathematics questions found on the SAT I: multiple-choice, quantitative comparison, and grid-in.

4. In Chapter 12 you will learn or review all of the mathematics that is needed for the SAT I, and you will master the tactics and key facts that apply to each of the different mathematical topics.

Using these tactics will enable you to answer more quickly many problems that you already know how to do. The greatest value of these tactics, however, is that they will allow you to answer correctly, or make educated guesses on, problems that you *do not know how to do*.

When to Study Chapter 12

How much time you initially devote to Chapter 12 should depend on how good your math skills are. If you are an excellent student who consistently earns A's in math, you can initially skip the instructional parts of Chapter 12. If, however, while doing the model tests in PART FOUR, you find that you keep making mistakes on certain types of problems (averages, percentages,

geometry, etc.) or if they take you too long, you should then study the appropriate sections of Chapter 12. Even if your math skills are excellent, and you don't need the review, you should do the sample questions in those sections; they are an excellent source of additional SAT I questions. If you know that your math skills are not very good, it is advisable to review the material in Chapter 12, including working out the problems, *before* tackling the model tests in PART FOUR.

No matter how good you are in math, *you should carefully read and do the hundreds of sample problems in Chapters 8, 9, 10, and 11.* For many of these problems, two solutions are given: the most direct mathematical solution and a solution using one or more of the special tactics taught in these chapters.

An Important Symbol

Throughout the book, the symbol "$\Rightarrow$" is used to indicate that one step in the solution of a problem follows *immediately* from the preceding one, and that no explanation is necessary. You should read:

$$2x = 12 \Rightarrow x = 6$$

as $2x = 12$ *implies* (or *which implies*) *that* $x = 6$, or, *since* $2x = 12$, then $x = 6$.

Here is a sample solution, using $\Rightarrow$, to the following problem:

What is the value of $3x^2 - 7$ when $x = -5$?

$$x = -5 \Rightarrow x^2 = (-5)^2 = 25 \Rightarrow 3x^2 = 3(25) = 75 \Rightarrow$$
$$3x^2 - 7 = 75 - 7 = \textbf{68}.$$

When the reason for a step is not obvious, $\Rightarrow$ is not used: rather, an explanation is given, often including a reference to a KEY FACT from Chapter 12. In many solutions, some steps are explained, while others are linked by the $\Rightarrow$ symbol, as in the following example:

In the diagram at the right, if $w = 10$, what is z?

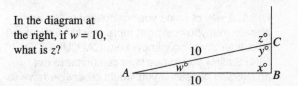

- By KEY FACT J1, $w + x + y = 180$.
- Since $\triangle ABC$ is isosceles, $x = y$ [KEY FACT J5].
- Therefore, $w + 2y = 180 \Rightarrow 10 + 2y = 180 \Rightarrow$ $2y = 170 \Rightarrow y = 85$.
- Finally, since $y + z = 180$ [KEY FACT I3], $85 + z = 180 \Rightarrow z = \textbf{95}$.

Six Important Headings

Throughout all of the chapters in PART THREE, you will see six headings, which will indicate valuable information and help to guide you as you study this book. Here is a brief explanation of each heading.

A useful strategy for attacking a certain type of problem. Some TACTICS give you advice on how to handle multiple-choice or quantitative comparison questions, regardless of the subject matter. Others point out ways to handle specific subject matter, such as finding averages or solving equations, regardless of the type of problem.

Key Fact

An important mathematical fact that you should commit to memory, because it comes up often on the SAT I.

Helpful Hint

A useful idea that will help you solve a problem more easily or avoid a pitfall.

CAUTION: A warning of a potential danger. Often a CAUTION points out a common error or a source of careless mistakes.

Calculator Shortcut

A method of using your calculator, even when it is unnecessary, to help you get an answer faster than you otherwise might. Often this will be an unusual or non-standard way of using your calculator that you might not think of.

 CALCULATOR HINT

Often, a way of using your calculator to get an answer that you could get more quickly without the calculator if you only knew how. CALCULATOR HINTS allow you to use your calculator to get answers to questions you would otherwise have to omit or guess at.

Use of the Calculator

Before doing all the work in PART THREE and the model tests in PART FOUR, you should reread the short discussion in Chapter 1 on the use of calculators on the SAT I. As you do the sample problems in this book, always have available the calculator you intend to

take to the SAT I, and use it whenever you feel it is appropriate. Throughout the rest of the book, whenever the use of a calculator is recommended, the icon has been placed next to the example or question. We stress that no problem *requires* the use of a calculator, but there are several for which it is helpful.

Because students' mathematical knowledge and arithmetic skills vary considerably, the decision as to when to use a calculator is highly subjective. Consider the following rather easy problem. Would you use a calculator?

What is the average (arithmetic mean) of 301, 303, and 305?

Let's analyze the four possibilities:

1. Some students would use their calculators twice: first to add, $301 + 303 + 305 = 909$, and then to divide, $909 \div 3 = 303$.

2. Others would use their calculators just once: to add the numbers; they would then divide mentally.

3. Others would not use their calculators at all, because they could add the three numbers mentally faster than they could on a calculator. (Just say to yourself: 300, 300, and 300 is 900; and $1 + 3 + 5$ is 9 more.)

4. Finally, others would do no calculations whatsoever. Having read Section 12-E, they would know that the average of three consecutive odd integers is always the middle one: 301, **303**, 305.

Note that the more the calculator was used, the *longer* it took to solve the problem. Use your calculator only when it will really save you time or if you think you will make a mistake without it.

Helpful Hint

In general, you should do very little arithmetic longhand. If you can't do a calculation mentally, use your calculator. In particular, avoid long division and multiplication in which the factors have two or more digits. If you know that $13^2 = 169$, terrific; if not, it's better to use your calculator than to multiply with paper and pencil.

Memorize Important Facts and Directions

On the first page of every mathematics section of the SAT I, there is a box labeled "Reference Information" that contains several basic math facts and formulas. In each math section of every Model Test in this book, you will find the exact same information.

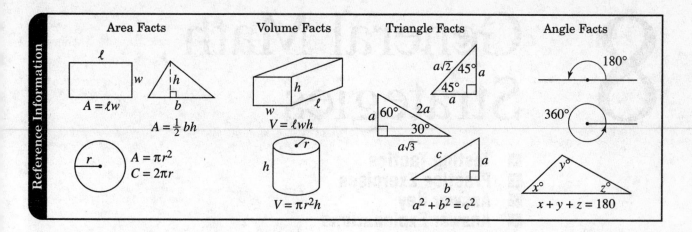

The College Board's official guide, *Taking the SAT I Reasoning Test*, offers the following tip:

> The test doesn't require you to memorize formulas. Commonly used formulas are provided in the test booklet at the beginning of each mathematical section.

If you interpret this to mean "Don't bother memorizing the formulas provided," this is terrible advice. It may be reassuring to know that, if you should forget a basic geometry fact, you can look it up in the box headed "Reference Information," but you should decide right now that you will never have to do that. During the test, you don't want to spend any precious time looking up facts that you can learn now. All of these "commonly used formulas" and other important facts are presented in Chapter 12. As you learn and review these facts, you should commit them to memory.

On the opening pages of Chapters 9, 10, and 11 you will learn the instructions for the three types of mathematics questions on the SAT I. *They will not change.* They will be exactly the same on the test you take.

Helpful Hint

As you prepare for this test, memorize the directions for each section. *When you take the SAT I, do not waste even one second reading directions.*

The purpose of the preceding hint is to save you time. This issue of good time management is critically important. Periodically reread the hints in Chapter 2 on pacing yourself and not spending too much time on any one question.

8 General Math Strategies

- ■ **Testing Tactics**
- ■ **Practice Exercises**
- ■ **Answer Key**
- ■ **Answer Explanations**

In Chapters 9, 10, and 11, you will learn tactics that will help you with the three specific types of math questions on the SAT I. In this chapter you will learn several important strategies that can be used on any of these questions. Mastering these tactics will improve your performance on all mathematics tests.

The first six tactics deal with the best ways of handling diagrams.

TACTIC 8-1.	Draw a diagram.
TACTIC 8-2.	If a diagram has been drawn to scale, trust it.
TACTIC 8-3.	If a diagram has not been drawn to scale, redraw it.
TACTIC 8-4.	Exaggerate or otherwise change a diagram.
TACTIC 8-5.	Add a line to a diagram.
TACTIC 8-6.	Subtract to find shaded regions.

To implement these tactics, you need to be able to draw line segments and angles accurately, and also to be able to look at segments and angles and accurately estimate their measures. Let's look at three variations of the same problem.

a. If the diagonal of a rectangle is twice as long as the shorter side, what is the degree measure of the angle the diagonal makes with the longer side?

b. In the rectangle at the right, what is the value of *x*?

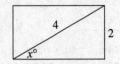

c. In the rectangle at the right, what is the value of *x*?

Note: Figure not drawn to scale

For the moment, let's ignore the correct mathematical way to solve this problem. You should be able to look at the diagram in (b) and "see" that *x* is about 30, *certainly*

between 25 and 35. In (a), however, you aren't given a diagram, and in (c) the diagram is useless because it hasn't been drawn to scale. In each of these cases, you should be able to draw a diagram that looks just like the one in (b); then you can look at *your* diagram and "see" that the measure of the angle in question is about 30°.

If this were a multiple-choice question, and the choices were as follows:

   (A) 15   (B) 30   (C) 45   (D) 60   (E) 75

you would, of course, choose **30**, (**B**). If the choices were

   (A) 20   (B) 25   (C) 30   (D) 35   (E) 40

you would still choose **30**, here (**C**).

If this was a grid-in problem, you should answer **30**, and if it were a quantitative comparison:

<u>Column A</u>	<u>Column B</u>
x	45

you should "know" that, since *x* is approximately 30, Column **B** is greater.

By the way, *x* is *exactly* 30. A right triangle in which one leg is half the hypotenuse must be a 30-60-90 triangle, and that leg is opposite the 30° angle [see KEY FACT J11].

But how can you know the value of *x* just by looking at the diagram in (b)? In this section, you will learn not only how to look at *any* angle and know its measure within 5 or 10°, but also how to draw any angle with the same accuracy. You will also learn how to draw line segments the correct length, so that your diagrams won't be as bad as the one in (c). Do you see what is wrong with that diagram? The diagonal is *labeled* 4 and one of the sides is *labeled* 2, but the diagonal, *as drawn*, isn't nearly twice as long as the side.

Consider the following example:

Example 1.

In the figure at the right, what is the value of *d*?

(A) 2   (B) 2.5   (C) 3
(D) 3.5   (E) 4

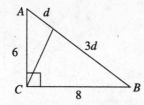

Solution. Since there is no note indicating that the diagram has not been drawn to scale, you can trust it [TACTIC 8-2].

• Clearly, *d* is less than *AC*, which is 6; but all five choices are less than 6, so that doesn't help.
• Actually, it looks as though *d* is less than *half* of *AC*, or 3.
• You assume it is, and eliminate choices C, D, and E.

You could now guess between choices A and B; but if you measure, you'll *know* which is right. However, there's a problem—on the SAT I, you are *not* allowed to use a ruler, a compass, or a protractor. So how can you measure anything? *Use the back of your answer sheet!* Here are two ways to do this, with the procedures illustrated below.

1. Turn your answer sheet over, place one corner of it on point *A* and with your pencil make a small mark to indicate length *d*. Now use this "ruler" to measure *AC*. Put a dot on *AC d* units from *A*; slide the answer sheet, mark off a second segment of length *d*, and do this once more. The third mark is well past *C*, so 3*d* is more than 6; that is, *d* > 2. Eliminate A.

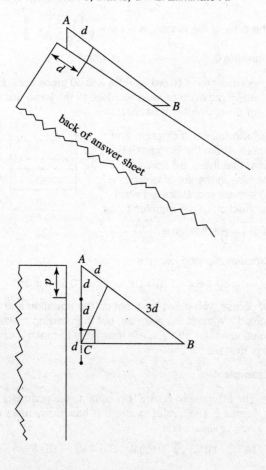

2. On the back of your answer sheet, measure *AC* and *BC* from the same point. The distance between them is 2. Compare 2 to *d*; *d* is longer. Eliminate A.

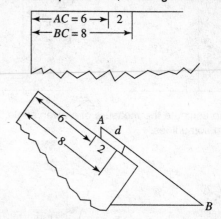

• The answer is **2.5 (B)**.

Finally, erase the dot or mark you made on the back of your answer sheet, so it won't confuse you if you need to make a new "ruler" for another question. Also, there should be no stray pencil marks anywhere on the answer sheet when you hand it in.

To answer this question without TACTIC 8-2, use the Pythagorean theorem to obtain *AB* = 10 (or recognize that this is a 6-8-10 right triangle) and then solve the equation: $d + 3d = 10 \Rightarrow d = 2.5$.

To take full advantage of TACTICS 8-1, 8-2, and 8-3, you need to be able to measure angles as well as line segments. Fortunately, this is very easy. In fact, you should be able to *look* at any angle and know its measure within 5–10°, and be able to *draw* any angle accurately within 10°. Let's see how.

First, you should easily recognize a 90° angle and can probably draw one freehand, or you can always just trace the corner of your answer sheet. Second, to draw a 45° angle, just bisect a 90° angle. Again, you can probably do this freehand. If not, or to be more accurate, draw a right angle, mark off the same distance on each side, draw a square, and then draw in the diagonal.

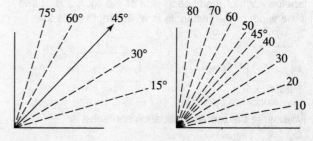

Third, to draw other acute angles, just divide the two 45° angles in the above diagram with as many lines as are necessary.

Finally, to draw an obtuse angle, add an acute angle to a right angle.

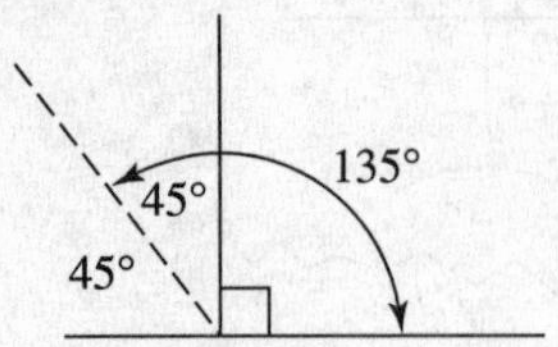

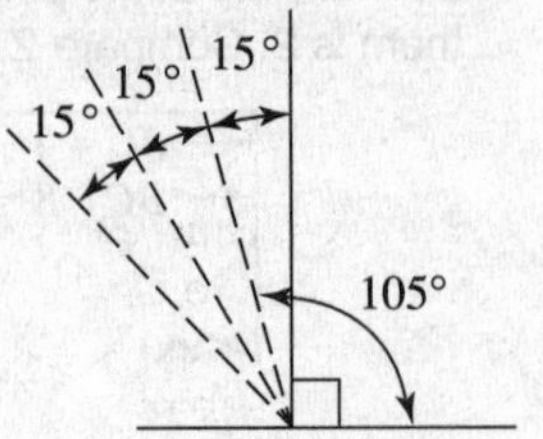

Now, to estimate the measure of a given angle, just draw in some lines.

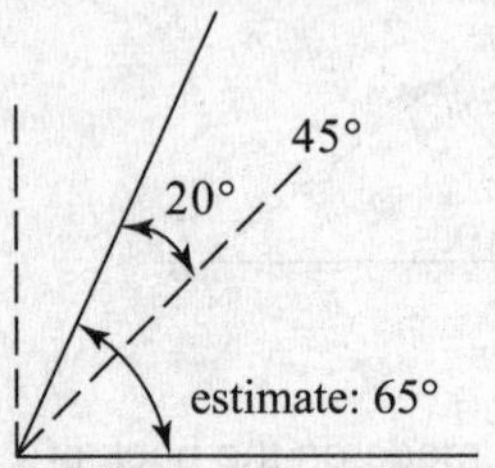

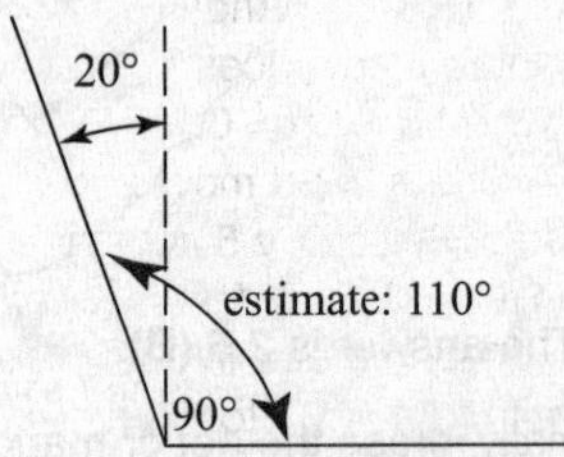

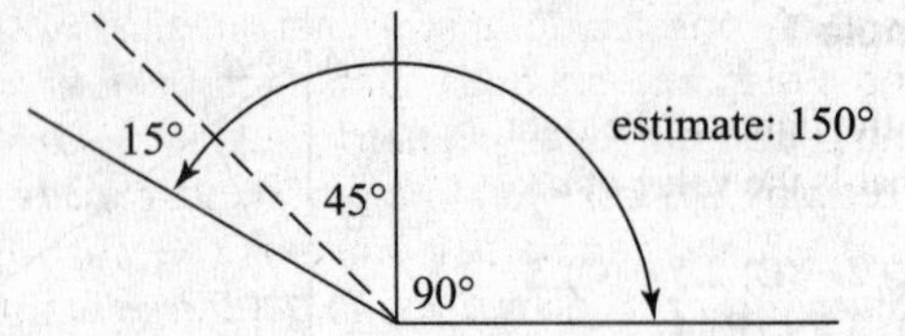

To test yourself, find the measure of each angle shown below. The answers are found below.

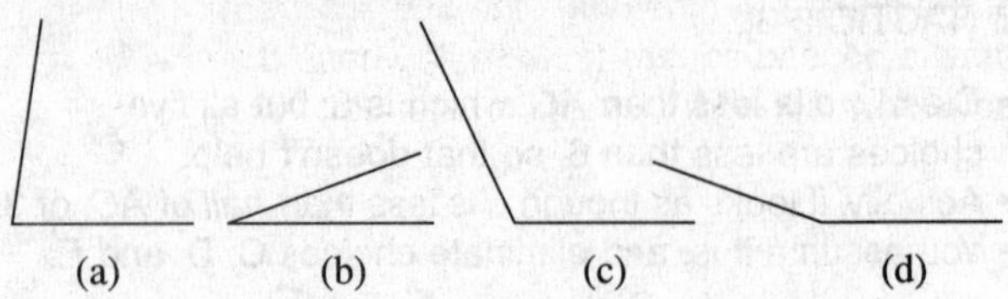

Answers: (a) 80° (b) 20° (c) 115° (d) 160°. Did you come within 10° on each one?

Testing Tactics

Tactic 8-1 Draw a Diagram.

On any geometry question for which a figure is not provided, draw one (as accurately as possible) in your test booklet. Drawings should not be limited, however, to geometry questions; there are many other questions on which drawings will help. Whether you intend to solve a problem directly or to use one of the tactics described in Chapters 9–11, drawing a diagram is the first step.

A good drawing requires no artistic ability. Usually, a few line segments are sufficient.

Let's consider some examples.

Example 2.

What is the area of a rectangle whose length is twice its width and whose perimeter is equal to that of a square whose area is 1?

Solution. Don't even think of answering this question until you have drawn a square and a rectangle and labeled each of them: each side of the square is 1; and if the width of the rectangle is w, its length (ℓ) is $2w$.

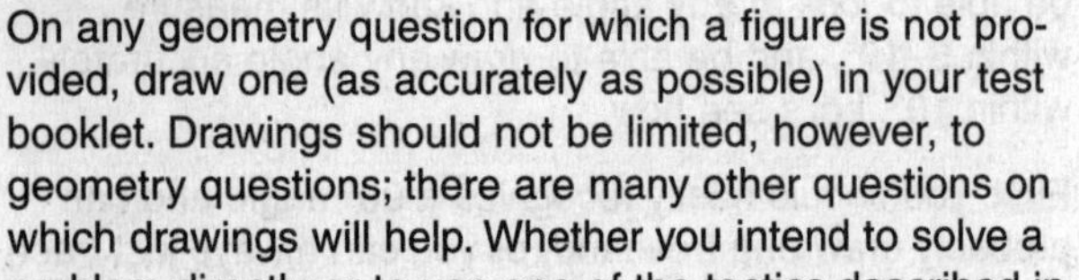

Now, write the required equation and solve it:

$$6w = 4 \Rightarrow w = \frac{4}{6} = \frac{2}{3} \Rightarrow 2w = \frac{4}{3}$$

The area of the rectangle $= \ell w = \left(\frac{4}{3}\right)\left(\frac{2}{3}\right) = \mathbf{\frac{8}{9}}$.

Example 3.

A jar contains 10 red marbles and 30 green ones. How many red marbles must be added to the jar so that 60% of the marbles will be red?

Solution. Draw a diagram and label it. From the diagram it is clear that there are now $40 + x$ marbles in the jar, of which $10 + x$ are red. Since we want the fraction of red marbles to be $60\% \left(= \frac{3}{5}\right)$, we have $\frac{10+x}{40+x} = \frac{3}{5}$.

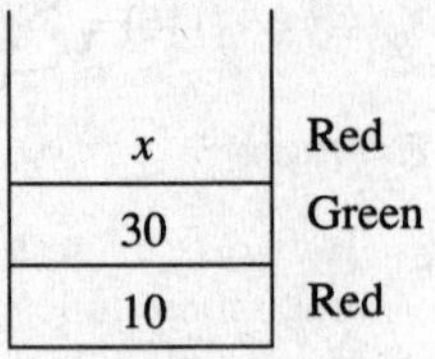

Cross-multiplying, we get:

$$50 + 5x = 120 + 3x \Rightarrow 2x = 70 \Rightarrow x = \mathbf{35}.$$

Of course, you could have set up the equation and solved it without the diagram, but the drawing makes the solution easier and you are less likely to make a careless mistake.

Example 4.

The diagonal of square II is equal to the perimeter of square I. The area of square II is how many times the area of square I?

(A) 2 (B) $2\sqrt{2}$ (C) 4 (D) $4\sqrt{2}$ (E) 8

It is certainly possible to answer this question without drawing a diagram, but don't. Get in the habit of *always* drawing a diagram for a geometry problem. Often a good drawing will lead you to the correct solution; other times, as you will see here, it prevents you from making a careless error or it allows you to get the right answer *even if you don't know how to solve the problem.*

Solution. Draw a small square (square I), and next to it mark off a line segment equal in length to the perimeter of the square (4 times the side of the square). Then draw a second square (square II) whose diagonal is equal to the length of the line segment.

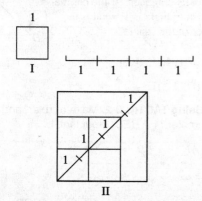

You can see how much larger square II is. In fact, if you draw four squares the size of square I inside square II, you can see that the answer to this question is certainly much more than 4, so eliminate choices A, B, and C. Then, if you don't know how to proceed, just guess between D and E. In fact, $4\sqrt{2} \approx 5.6$, and even that is too small, so you should choose **8 (E)**, the correct answer. [If the side of square I is 1, its perimeter is 4. Then the diagonal of square II is 4. Now use the formula $A = \frac{1}{2}d^2$ to find that the area of square II is $\frac{1}{2}(4)^2 = \frac{1}{2}(16) = 8$, whereas the area of square I is 1.]

Example 5.

Tony drove 8 miles west, 6 miles north, 3 miles east, and 6 more miles north. How far was Tony from his starting place?

(A) 13　(B) 17　(C) 19　(D) 21　(E) 23

Solution. Draw a diagram. Now, extend line segment, *ED* until it intersects *AB* at *F* [see TACTIC 8-5]. Then, *AFE* is a right triangle whose legs are 5 and 12 and, therefore, whose hypotenuse is **13 (A)**.

[If you drew the diagram accurately, you could get the right answer by measuring!]

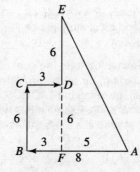

Example 6.

By how many degrees does the angle formed by the hour hand and the minute hand of a clock increase from 1:27 to 1:28?

Solution. Draw a simple picture of a clock. The hour hand makes a complete revolution, 360°, once every 12 hours. Therefore, in 1 hour it goes through $360° \div 12 = 30°$, and in 1 minute it advances through $30° \div 60 = 0.5°$. The minute hand moves through 30° every 5 minutes and 6° each 1 minute. Therefore, in the minute from 1:27 to 1:28 (or any other minute), the *difference* between the hands increases by $6 - 0.5 = $ **5.5** degrees. [Note that it was not necessary, and would have been more time-consuming to determine the angles between the hands at 1:27 and 1:28 (See TACTIC 8-7: Don't do more than you have to).]

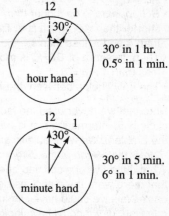

30° in 1 hr.
0.5° in 1 min.

30° in 5 min.
6° in 1 min.

Tactic 8-2 If a Diagram Is Drawn to Scale, Trust It, and Use Your Eyes.

Remember that every diagram that appears on the SAT I has been drawn as accurately as possible *unless* you see "Note: Figure not drawn to scale" written below it.

For figures that are drawn to scale, the following are true: line segments that appear to be the same length *are* the same length; if an angle clearly looks obtuse, it *is* obtuse; and if one angle appears larger than another, you may assume that it *is* larger.

Try Examples 7 and 8, which have diagrams that have been drawn to scale. Both of these examples would be classified as hard questions. On an actual SAT I, questions of comparable difficulty would be answered correctly by at most 20–35% of the students taking the exam. After you master TACTIC 8-2, you should have no trouble with problems like these.

Example 7.

In the figure at the right, *EF*, not shown, is a diagonal of rectangle *AFJE* and a diameter of the circle. *D* is the midpoint of *AE*, *C* is the midpoint of *AD*, and *B* is the midpoint of *AC*.

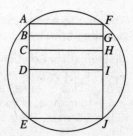

If *AE* is 8 and the radius of the circle is 5, what is the area of rectangle *BGHC*?

(A) 4　(B) 6　(C) 8　(D) 12　(E) 24

Solution. Since there is no note indicating that the diagram has not been drawn to scale, we can trust it.

- The area of rectangle *BGHC* is the product of its width, *BC*, and its length, *BG*.
- *AE* = 8 ⇒ *AD* = 4 ⇒ *AC* = 2 ⇒ *BC* = 1.
- *BG appears* to be longer than *AD*, which is 4, and shorter than *AE*, which is 8. Therefore, *BG is* more than 4 and *is* less than 8.
- Then, the area of *BGHC* is more than 1 × 4 = 4 and less than 1 × 8 = 8.
- The only choice between 4 and 8 is 6. The answer is **B**.

Note that we never used the fact that the radius of the circle is 5, information that is necessary to actually *solve* the problem. We were able to answer this question *merely by looking at the diagram.* Were we just lucky? What if the five choices had been 4, 5, 6, 7, and 8, so that there were three choices between 4 and 8, not just one? Well, we could have eliminated 4 and 8 and guessed, or we could have looked at the diagram even more closely. *BG appears* to be about the same length as *CE*, which is 6. If *BG is* 6, then the area of *BGHC is* exactly 6. How can we be sure? We'll measure the lengths!

On the answer sheet we make two small pencil marks to indicate length *BG*:

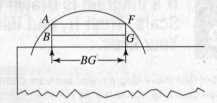

Now, we use that length to measure *CE*:

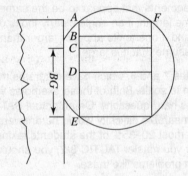

The lengths *are* the same. *BG is* 6; the area *is* 6. It's not a guess after all.

Mathematical Solution. Diameter *EF*, which is 10, is also the hypotenuse of right triangle *EAF*. Since leg *AE* is 8, *AF*, the other leg, is 6 (either you recognize this as a 6-8-10 triangle, or you use the Pythagorean theorem). Since *BG* = *AF*, *BG is* 6, and the area *is* **6**.

If Example 7 had been a grid-in problem instead of a multiple-choice question, we could have used TACTIC 8-2 in exactly the same way, but we would have been

less sure of our answer. If, based on a diagram, we know that the area of a rectangle is about 6 or the measure of an angle is about 30°, we can almost always pick the correct choice, but on a grid-in we can't be certain that the area isn't 6.2 or the angle 31°. Nevertheless, if you can't solve a problem directly, you should always grid in a "simple" number that is consistent with the diagram.

Example 8.

In the figure at the right, square *ABCD* has been divided into four triangles by its diagonals. If the perimeter of each triangle is 1, what is the perimeter of the square?

(A) $\frac{4}{3}$ (B) $4(\sqrt{2} - 1)$

(C) 2   (D) 3   (E) 4

Solution Using TACTIC 8-2. Make a "ruler" and mark off the perimeter of △*BEC*; label that 1.

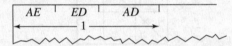

Now, mark off the perimeter of square *ABCD*.

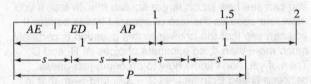

It should be clear that *P* is much less than 2 (eliminate C, D, and E), but more than 1.5 (eliminate A). The answer must be **B**.

Direct Mathematical Solution. Let *s* be a side of the square. Then, since △*BEC* is a 45-45-90 right triangle, *BE* and *EC* are each $\frac{s}{\sqrt{2}}$, which equals $\frac{s\sqrt{2}}{2}$ (see KEY FACT J8). Therefore, the perimeter of △*BEC* is $\frac{s\sqrt{2}}{2} + \frac{s\sqrt{2}}{2} + s$, which equals 1. Solving for *s*, we get

$$s = \frac{1}{\sqrt{2}+1} = \sqrt{2} - 1.$$

Finally, *P* = 4*s* = **4($\sqrt{2}$ – 1)**. Even if you could do this (and most students can't), it is far easier to use TACTIC 8-2.

Remember that the goal of this book is to help you get credit (i) for *all* the problems you know how to do, and (ii), by using the TACTICS, for *many* that you don't know how to do. Example 8 is typical. Most students omit it because it is too hard. *You*, however, can now answer it correctly, even though you may not be able to solve it directly.

TACTIC 8-2 is equally effective on quantitative comparison questions that have diagrams.

Column A   Column B

Example 9.

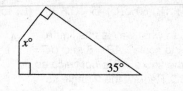

| x | 170 |

Example 10.

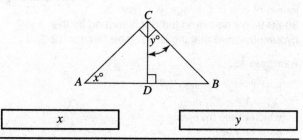

| x | y |

 Solutions 9 and 10.

Direct Calculation	**Solution Using TACTIC 8-2**
9. The sum of the measures of the four angles in *any* quadrilateral is 360° (KEY FACT K1). So 360 = 90 + 90 + 35 + x = 215 + x. Column A: x = 360 − 215 = 145 Column B: 170. The answer is **B**.	9. Since the diagram is drawn to scale, trust it. Look at x: it appears to be *about* 90 + 50 = 140; it is *definitely* less than 170. 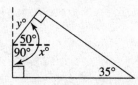 Also, y, drawn above is clearly more than 10, so x is less than 170. Choose **B**.
10. The sums of the measure of the three angles in triangles *ABC* and *CBD* are equal (they are both 180). So 90 + m∠B + x = 90 + m∠B + y ⇒ x = y. The answer is **C**.	10. In the diagram x and y look about the same. In the absence of any reason to think they aren't, just guess **C**.

Now try Examples 11–13, in which the diagrams are drawn to scale, and you need to find the measures of angles. Even if you know that you can solve these problems directly, practice TACTIC 8-2 and estimate the answers. The correct mathematical solutions without using this tactic are also given.

Example 11.

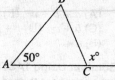

If, in the figure at the right, $AB = AC$, what is the value of x?

(A) 135   (B) 125   (C) 115
(D) 65   (E) 50

Solution Using TACTIC 8-2. *Ignore all the information in the question.* Just "measure" x. Draw *DC* perpendicular to *AB*, and let *EC* divide right angle *DCA* into two 45° angles, ∠*DCE* and ∠*ACE*. Now, ∠*DCB* is about half of ∠*DCE*, say 20–25°. Therefore, your estimate for x should be about 110 (90 + 20) or 115 (90 + 25). Choose **C**.

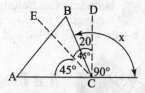

Mathematical Solution. Since △*ABC* is isosceles, with $AB = AC$, the other two angles in the triangle, ∠*B* and ∠*C*, each measure 65°.

Therefore, $x + 65 = 180 \Rightarrow x = \mathbf{115}$.

Example 12.

In the figure at the right, what is the sum of the measures of all of the marked angles?

(A) 360°   (B) 540°
(C) 720°   (D) 900°
(E) 1080°

Solution Using TACTIC 8-2. Make your best estimate of each angle, and add up the values. The five choices are so far apart that, even if you're off by 15° or more on some of the angles, you'll get the right answer. The sum of the estimates shown is 690°, so the correct answer *must* be 720° **(C)**.

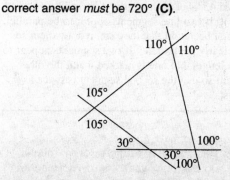

Mathematical Solution. Each of the eight marked angles is an exterior angle of the quadrilateral. If we take one angle from each pair, their sum is 360°; so, taking both angles at each vertex, we find that the sum of the measures is 360° + 360° = **720°**. (KEY FACT K3:

In any polygon the sum of all the exterior angles, taking one at each vertex, is 360°.)

Example 13.

In the diagram at the right, which of the following is equal to $180 - a - b - c$?

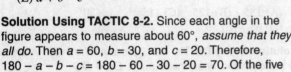

(A) $a + b + c$ (B) $a + c$
(C) $b + c$ (D) $b + 2c$
(E) $a + b - c$

Solution Using TACTIC 8-2. Since each angle in the figure appears to measure about 60°, *assume that they all do.* Then $a = 60$, $b = 30$, and $c = 20$. Therefore, $180 - a - b - c = 180 - 60 - 30 - 20 = 70$. Of the five choices, only **D** is 70 when $a = 60$, $b = 30$, and $c = 20$.

Mathematical Solution. Since $a + 2b + 3c = 180$, subtracting $a + b + c$ from each side yields $b + 2c = 180 - (a + b + c) = 180 - a - b - c$.

Tactic 8-3

If a Diagram Is *Not* Drawn to Scale, Redraw It to Scale, and Then Use Your Eyes.

For figures that have not been drawn to scale, you can make *no* assumptions. Lines that look parallel may not be; an angle that appears to be obtuse may, in fact, be acute; two line segments may have the same length even though one looks twice as long as the other.

In the examples illustrating TACTIC 8-2, all of the diagrams were drawn to scale, and we were able to use the diagrams to our advantage. When diagrams have not been drawn to scale, you must be much more careful. TACTIC 8-3 tells you to redraw the diagram *as accurately as possible*, based on the information you are given, and then to apply the technique of TACTIC 8-2.

Helpful Hint

In order to redraw a diagram to scale, you first have to ask yourself, "What is wrong with the original diagram?" If an angle is marked 45°, but in the figure it looks like a 75° angle, redraw it. If two line segments appear to be parallel, but you have not been told that they are, redraw them so that they are clearly *not* parallel. If two segments appear to have the same length, but one is marked 5 and the other 10, redraw them so that the second segment is twice as long as the first.

CAUTION: Redrawing a diagram, even roughly, takes time. Do this only when you do not see an easy direct solution to the problem.

Example 14.

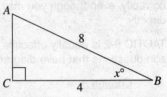

In $\triangle ACB$, what is the value of x?

Note: Figure not drawn to scale

(A) 75   (B) 60   (C) 45   (D) 30   (E) 15

Solution. In what way is this figure not drawn to scale? $AB = 8$ and $BC = 4$, but in the figure AB is *not* twice as long as BC. Redraw the triangle so that AB *is* twice as long as BC. Now, just look: x is about **60 (B)**.

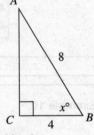

In fact, x is exactly 60. If the hypotenuse of a right triangle is twice the length of one of the legs, you have a 30-60-90 triangle, and the angle formed by the hypotenuse and that leg is 60° (see Section 12-J).

Example 15.

In $\triangle XYZ$ at the right, if $XY < YZ < ZX$, then which of the following must be true?

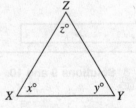

(A) $x < 60$ (B) $z < 60$
(C) $y < z$ (D) $x < z$
(E) $y < x$

Note: Figure not drawn to scale

Solution. As drawn, the diagram is useless. The triangle looks like an equilateral triangle, even though the question states that $XY < YZ < ZX$. Redraw the figure so that the condition is satisfied (that is, ZX is clearly the longest side and XY the shortest).

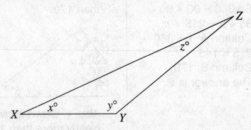

From the redrawn figure, it is clear that y is the largest angle, so eliminate choices C and E. Also, since $z < x$, eliminate D as well. Both x and z appear to be less than 60; but only one answer can be correct. Since $z < x$, if only one of these angles is less than 60, it must be z. Therefore, $z < 60$ **(B)** must be true.

In quantitative comparison questions, too, diagrams are sometimes not drawn to scale, and TACTIC 8-3 works on them, as well.

<u>Column A</u>   <u>Column B</u>

Example 16.

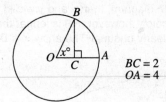

$BC = 2$
$OA = 4$

O is the center of the circle.
<u>Note</u>: Figure not drawn to scale

x	45

Example 17.

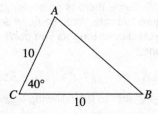

<u>Note</u>: Figure not drawn to scale

AB	10

Solutions 16 and 17.

Direct Calculation	**Solution Using TACTIC 8-3**
16. Since *OB* is a radius, it has the same length as radius *OA*, which is 4. So △*BCO* is a right triangle in which the hypotenuse is twice as long as one leg. This can occur *only* in a 30-60-90 triangle, and the angle opposite that leg measures 30°. Therefore, *x* = 30, which is less than 45. The answer is **B**.	16. 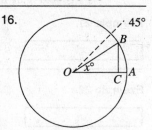 Do you see why the figure isn't drawn to scale? *BC*, which is 2, looks almost as long as *OA*, which is 4. Use TACTIC 8-3. Redraw the diagram, making sure that *BC* is only one-half as long as *OA*. With the diagram drawn to scale, you can *see* that *x* is less than 45. Choose **B**.

Direct Calculation	**Solution Using TACTIC 8-3**
17. Since *AC* = *BC*, the angles opposite these sides (*A* and *B*) have the same measure (KEY FACT Q4), which is clearly more than 40°. (In fact, each angle measures 70°.) Therefore, ∠*C* is the smallest angle, which means that side *AB* is the smallest side (KEY FACT J3). *AB* < 10. The answer is **B**.	17. 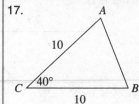 In the given diagram, *AB* is longer than *AC*, which is 10, but *we cannot trust the diagram*. Actually, there are two things wrong: ∠*C* is labeled 40°, but looks much more like 60° or 70°, and *AC* and *BC* are each labeled 10, but *BC* is drawn much longer. Use TACTIC 8-3. Redraw the triangle with a 40° angle and two sides of the same length. Now, it's clear that *AB* < 10. Choose **B**.

Tactic 8-4

Exaggerate or Otherwise Change a Diagram.

Sometimes it is appropriate to do exactly the opposite of TACTIC 8-3. We take a diagram that may (or may not) be drawn to scale and intentionally exaggerate it so that it is not to scale. Why would we do this? Consider the following examples.

<u>Column A</u>   <u>Column B</u>

Example 18.

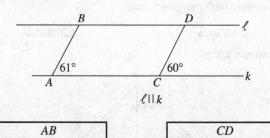

$\ell \| k$

AB	*CD*

Solution. The diagram has been drawn to scale, and it looks as though *AB* and *CD* are the same length. However, angles *A* and *C* also look the same, but they're labeled with different values. If *AB* ≠ *CD*, it must be due to the fact that one angle is smaller than the other.

Exaggerate the diagram: redraw it, making ∠C *much smaller* than ∠A. Now, it's clear: *CD* is longer. The answer is **B**.

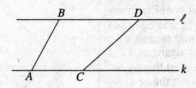

Column A	Column B

Example 19.

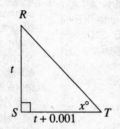

Note: Figure not drawn to scale

x	45

Solution. Since ∠T is opposite the shorter leg of right triangle *RST*, it measures less than 45°, and ∠R measures more than 45° (KEY FACTS J3 and J4). Column **B** is greater.

If you don't know those KEY FACTS, you have to rely on the diagram. It looks as though $x = 45$; but it also looks as though *RS* = *ST*, even though they're not. Exaggerating the diagram to make *ST* clearly longer than *RS* shows that $x < 45$.

When a figure has not been drawn to scale, you can change anything you like as long as your diagram is consistent with the given data.

Column A	Column B

Example 20.

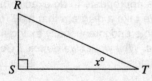

Note: Figure not drawn to scale

x	y

Solution. You may redraw this diagram in any way you like, as long as the two angles that are marked 45° remain 45°. If *PQ* and *PR* were equal, as they appear to be in the given diagram, then *x* and *y* would be equal. In the diagram below, however, *PR* is longer than *PQ*, and *x* and *y* are clearly unequal. The answer is **D**.

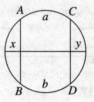

Sometimes you see the notation "Note: Figure not drawn to scale" for a diagram on which there are *no* numbers: there is no 30° angle that has deviously been drawn to look like a 60° angle, nor are there two segments that have been drawn the same length even though they are marked 3 and 5. Since there is no scale, you can't redraw the figure to scale. What you *can* do is to redraw it in any way you like, as long as you don't violate any given conditions.

Column A	Column B

Examples 21–22 refer to the following figure.

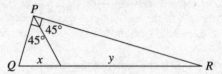

AB ∥ *CD*

Note: Figure not drawn to scale

Example 21.

x	y

Example 22.

a	b

Solutions 21 and 22. Redraw the diagrams, changing them in any way you like, as long as you draw *AB* ∥ *CD*. Clearly, either *x* or *y* could be greater, so the answer to Example 21 is **D**.

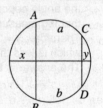

No matter how you draw the diagram, however, *a* and *b* appear to be equal, so choose **C** for Example 22. (In fact, parallel chords *always* cut off equal arcs.)

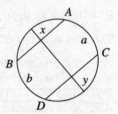

Tactic 8-5 Add a Line to a Diagram.

Occasionally, after staring at a diagram, you still have no idea how to solve the problem to which it applies. It looks as though there isn't enough given information. When this happens, it often helps to draw another line in the diagram.

Example 23.

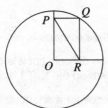

In the figure at the right, Q is a point on the circle whose center is O and whose radius is r, and $OPQR$ is a rectangle. What is the length of diagonal PR?

(A) r (B) r^2 (C) $\dfrac{r^2}{\pi}$ (D) $\dfrac{r\sqrt{2}}{\pi}$

(E) It cannot be determined from the information given.

Solution. If, after staring at the diagram and thinking about rectangles, circles, and the Pythagorean theorem, you're still lost, don't give up. Ask yourself, "Can I add another line to this diagram?" As soon as you think to draw in OQ, the other diagonal, the problem becomes easy: the two diagonals are equal, and, since OQ is a radius, it is equal to **r (A)**.

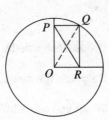

Note that you could also have made a "ruler" and seen that PR is equal to r.

Example 24.

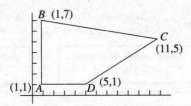

What is the area of quadrilateral $ABCD$?

Solution. Since the quadrilateral is irregular, you don't know any formula to get the answer. However, if you draw in AC, you will divide $ABCD$ into two triangles, each of whose areas can be determined. If you then draw in CE and CF, the height of each triangle, you see that the area of $\triangle ACD$ is $\dfrac{1}{2}(4)(4) = 8$, and the area of $\triangle BAC$ is $\dfrac{1}{2}(6)(10) = 30$. Then the area of $ABCD$ is $30 + 8 = $ **38**.

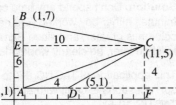

Note that this problem could also have been solved by drawing in lines to create rectangle $ABEF$, and subtracting the areas of $\triangle BEC$ and $\triangle CFD$ from the area of the rectangle.

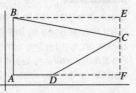

Tactic 8-6 Subtract to Find Shaded Regions.

Whenever part of a figure is white and part is shaded, the straightforward way to find the area of the shaded portion is to find the area of the entire figure and then subtract from it the area of the white region. Of course, if you are asked for the area of the white region, you can, instead, subtract the shaded area from the total area. Occasionally, you may see an easy way to calculate the shaded area directly, but usually you should subtract.

Example 25.

In the figure below, $ABCD$ is a rectangle, and BE and CF are arcs of circles centered at A and D. What is the area of the shaded region?

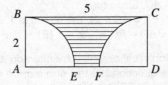

(A) $10 - \pi$ (B) $2(5 - \pi)$ (C) $2(5 - 2\pi)$
(D) $6 + 2\pi$ (E) $5(2 - \pi)$

Solution. The entire region is a 2×5 rectangle whose area is 10. Since each white region is a quarter-circle of radius 2, the combined area of these regions is that of a semicircle of radius 2: $\dfrac{1}{2}\pi(2)^2 = 2\pi$.
Therefore, the area of the shaded region is $10 - 2\pi = $ **$2(5 - \pi)$ (B)**.

Example 26.

In the figure at the right, each side of square $ABCD$ is divided into three equal parts. What is the ratio of the shaded area to the white area?

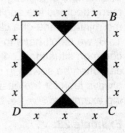

(A) $\dfrac{1}{9}$ (B) $\dfrac{1}{8}$ (C) $\dfrac{1}{6}$

(D) $\dfrac{1}{4}$ (E) $\dfrac{1}{3}$

Solution. Since the answer doesn't depend on the value of x (the *ratio* will be the same no matter what x is), let $x = 1$. Then the area of the whole square is $3^2 = 9$. The area of each shaded triangle or of all the white sections can be calculated, but there's an easier way: notice that, if you slide the four shaded triangles together, they form a square of side 1. Therefore, the total shaded area is 1, and the white area is $9 - 1 = 8$.

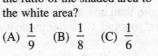

The desired ratio is $\dfrac{1}{8}$ **(B)**.

The idea of subtracting a part from the whole works with line segments as well as areas.

Example 27.

In the figure at the right, the circle with center O is inscribed in square $ABCD$. Line segment AO intersects the circle at P. What is the length of AP?

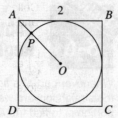

(A) 1   (B) $2 - \sqrt{2}$

(C) $1 - \dfrac{\sqrt{2}}{2}$ (D) $2\sqrt{2} - 2$ (E) $\sqrt{2} - 1$

Solution. First use TACTIC 8-5 and draw some lines. Extend AO to form diagonal AC. Then, since $\triangle ADC$ is an isosceles right triangle, $AC = 2\sqrt{2}$ (Key Fact J8) and AO is half of that, or $\sqrt{2}$. Then draw in diameter EF parallel to AD. Since the diameter is 2 ($EF = AD = 2$), the radius is 1. Finally, subtract: $AP = AO - PO = \sqrt{2} - 1$ **(E)**.

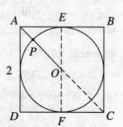

Note: If you don't realize which lines to add and/or you can't reason a question like this one out, *do not* omit it. You can still use TACTIC 8-2: trust the diagram. Since $AB = 2$, then $AE = 1$, and AP is clearly less than 0.5. With your calculator evaluate each choice. A, B, and D are all greater than 0.5. Eliminate them, and guess either C or E.

Tactic 8-7 Don't Do More Than You Have To.

In Example 6, although we needed to know by how many degrees the angle formed by the hour hand and the minute hand of a clock increases between 1:27 and 1:28, we didn't have to calculate either angle. This is a common situation. Look for shortcuts. Since a problem can often be solved in more than one way, you should always look for the easiest method. Consider the following examples.

Example 28.

If $5(3x - 7) = 20$, what is $3x - 8$?

It's not difficult to solve for x:

$$5(3x - 7) = 20 \Rightarrow 15x - 35 = 20 \Rightarrow 15x = 55 \Rightarrow$$
$$x = \frac{55}{15} = \frac{11}{3}.$$

But it's too much work. Besides, once you find that $x = \frac{11}{3}$, you still have to multiply to get $3x$: $3\left(\dfrac{11}{3}\right) = 11$, and then subtract to get $3x - 8$: $11 - 8 = 3$.

Solution. The key is to recognize that you don't need x. Finding $3x - 7$ is easy (just divide the original equation by 5), and $3x - 8$ is just 1 less:

$$5(3x - 7) = 20 \Rightarrow 3x - 7 = 4 \Rightarrow 3x - 8 = 3.$$

Example 29.

If $7x + 3y = 17$ and $3x + 7y = 19$, what is the average (arithmetic mean) of x and y?

The obvious way to do this is to first find x and y by solving the two equations simultaneously and then to take their average. If you are familiar with this method, try it now, before reading further. If you worked carefully, you should have found that $x = \dfrac{31}{20}$ and $y = \dfrac{41}{20}$, and

their average is $\dfrac{\dfrac{31}{20} + \dfrac{41}{20}}{2} = \dfrac{9}{5}$ or **1.8**. This method is not

too difficult; but it is quite time-consuming, and no problem on the SAT I requires you to do that much work.

Look for a shortcut. Is there a way to find the average without first finding x and y? Absolutely! Here's the best way to do this.

 Solution. Add the two equations:

$$
\begin{array}{r}
7x + 3y = 17 \\
+ \ 3x + 7y = 19 \\
\hline
10x + 10y = 36
\end{array}
$$

Divide each side by 10: $x + y = 3.6$

Calculate the average: $\dfrac{x + y}{2} = \dfrac{3.6}{2} = \mathbf{1.8}$

When you learn TACTIC 8-14, you will see that adding two equations, as we did here, is the standard way to attack problems such as this on the SAT I.

Column A	Column B

Example 30.

Zach worked from 9:47 A.M. until 12:11 P.M.
Sam worked from 9:11 A.M. until 12:47 P.M.

The number of minutes Zach worked	The number of minutes Sam worked

Solution. Don't spend any time calculating how many minutes either boy worked. You need to know only which column is greater; and since Sam started earlier and finished later, he clearly worked longer. The answer is **B**.

This application of TACTIC 8-7 to quantitative comparison questions is dealt with at length in Chapter 10 (see TACTIC 10-5).

Tactic 8-8 Pay Attention to Units.

Often the answer to a question must be in units different from those used in the given data. As you read the question, <u>underline</u> exactly what you are being asked. Do the examiners want hours or minutes or seconds, dollars or cents, feet or inches, meters or centimeters?

On multiple-choice questions an answer with the wrong units is almost always one of the choices.

Example 31.

At a speed of 48 miles per hour, how many minutes will be required to drive 32 miles?

(A) $\dfrac{2}{3}$ (B) $\dfrac{3}{2}$ (C) 40   (D) 45   (E) 2400

 Solution. This is a relatively easy question. Just be attentive. Since $\dfrac{32}{48} = \dfrac{2}{3}$, it will take $\dfrac{2}{3}$ of an *hour* to drive 32 miles. Choice A is $\dfrac{2}{3}$; but that is *not* the correct answer because you are asked how many *minutes* will be required. (Did you underline the word "minutes" in the question?) The correct answer is $\dfrac{2}{3}(60) = \mathbf{40\ (C)}$.

Note that you could have been asked how many *seconds* would be needed, in which case the answer would be 40(60) = 2400 (E).

Example 32.

The wholesale price of potatoes is usually 3 pounds for $1.79. How much money, in cents, did a restaurant save when it was able to purchase 600 pounds of potatoes at 2 pounds for $1.15?

Solution. For 600 pounds the restaurant would normally have to buy 200 3-pound bags for $200 \times \$1.79 = \$358$. On sale, it bought 300 2-pound bags for $300 \times \$1.15 = \$345$. Therefore, the restaurant saved 13 dollars. *Do not* grid in 13. If you underline the word "cents" you won't forget to convert the units: 13 dollars is **1300** cents.

Use Your Calculator.

You already know that you can use a calculator on the SAT I. (See Chapter 1 for a complete discussion of calculator usage.) The main reason to use a calculator is that it enables you to do arithmetic more quickly and more accurately than you can by hand on *problems that you know how to solve*. (For instance, in Example 32, you should use your calculator to multiply 200×1.79.) The purpose of TACTIC 8-9 is to show you how to use your calculator to get the right answer to *questions that you do not know how to solve or you cannot solve*.

Example 33.

If $x^2 = 2$, what is the value of $\left(x + \dfrac{1}{x}\right)\left(x - \dfrac{1}{x}\right)$?

(A) 1   (B) 1.5   (C) $1 + \sqrt{2}$ (D) $2 + \sqrt{2}$
(E) $1.5 + 2\sqrt{2}$

Solution. The College Board would consider this a hard question, and most students would either omit it or, worse, miss it. The best approach is to recognize $\left(x + \dfrac{1}{x}\right)\left(x - \dfrac{1}{x}\right)$ as a product of the form $(a + b)(a - b) = a^2 - b^2$. Therefore:

$$\left(x + \frac{1}{x}\right)\left(x - \frac{1}{x}\right) = x^2 - \frac{1}{x^2} = 2 - \frac{1}{2} = \mathbf{1.5\ (B)}.$$

If you don't see this solution, you could still solve the problem by writing $x = \sqrt{2}$ and then trying to multiply and simplify $\left(\sqrt{2} + \dfrac{1}{\sqrt{2}}\right)\left(\sqrt{2} - \dfrac{1}{\sqrt{2}}\right)$. It is likely, however, that you would make a mistake somewhere along the way.

 The better method is to *use your calculator*:
$\sqrt{2} \approx 1.414$ and $\dfrac{1}{\sqrt{2}} \approx 0.707$, so

$$\left(\sqrt{2} + \frac{1}{\sqrt{2}}\right)\left(\sqrt{2} - \frac{1}{\sqrt{2}}\right) \approx (1.414 + 0.707)(1.414 - 0.707) =$$

$(2.121)(0.707) = 1.499547$.

Clearly, choose **1.5**, the small difference being due to the rounding off of $\sqrt{2}$ as 1.414.

If this were a grid-in question, however, you should *not* grid in 1.49, since you know that that's only an approximation. Rather, you should guess a simple number near 1.499, such as 1.5. In fact, if you don't round off, and just use the value your calculator gives for $\sqrt{2}$ (1.414213562, say), you will probably get 1.5 exactly (although you may get 1.49999999 or 1.50000001).

Example 34.

If a and b are positive numbers, with $a^3 = 3$ and $a^5 = 12b^2$, what is the ratio of a to b?

Solution. This is another difficult question that most students would omit or miss. If you think to divide the second equation by the first, however, it's not too bad:

$$\frac{a^5}{a^3} = \frac{12b^2}{3} = 4b^2 \quad \text{and} \quad \frac{a^5}{a^3} = a^2$$

Then

$$a^2 = 4b^2 \Rightarrow \frac{a^2}{b^2} = 4 \Rightarrow \frac{a}{b} = \mathbf{2}.$$

If you don't see this, you can still solve the problem if you are using a *scientific* calculator:

$$a = \sqrt[3]{3} \approx 1.44225 \Rightarrow a^5 \approx 6.24026 \Rightarrow b^2 = \frac{6.24026}{12}$$

$$\approx 0.52 \Rightarrow b \approx \sqrt{0.52} \approx 0.7211 \Rightarrow \frac{a}{b} \approx 2.00007.$$

Grid in 2.

Example 35.

What is the value of $\dfrac{1+\dfrac{7}{5}}{1-\dfrac{5}{7}}$?

Solution. There are two straightforward ways to do this: (i) multiply the numerator and denominator by 35, the LCM of 5 and 7, and (ii) simplify and divide:

(i) $\dfrac{35\left(1+\dfrac{7}{5}\right)}{35\left(1-\dfrac{5}{7}\right)} = \dfrac{35+49}{35-25} = \dfrac{84}{10} = \mathbf{8.4}$.

(ii) $\dfrac{1+\dfrac{7}{5}}{1-\dfrac{5}{7}} = \dfrac{\dfrac{12}{5}}{\dfrac{2}{7}} = \dfrac{\cancel{12}^{\,6}}{5} \times \dfrac{7}{\cancel{2}_{\,1}} = \dfrac{42}{5} = \mathbf{8.4}$.

 However, if you hate working with fractions, you can easily do this on *any* calculator. If your calculator has parentheses, you don't even need memory.

> **CAUTION:** Be sure you know how *your* calculator works. Be sure you can evaluate the given complex fraction and get 8.4.

If this had been a multiple-choice question, the five choices would probably have been fractions, in which case the correct answer would be $\dfrac{42}{5}$. If you had solved this with your calculator, you would then have had to use the calculator to determine which of the fractions offered as choices was equal to 8.4.

Tactic 8-10 Know When *Not* to Use Your Calculator.

Don't get into the habit of using your calculator on every problem involving arithmetic. Since many problems can be solved more easily and faster without a calculator, learn to use your calculator only when you need it (see Chapter 1).

Example 36.

John had $150. He used 85% of it to pay his electric bill and 5% of it on a gift for his mother. How much did he have left?

Solution. Many students would use their calculators on each step of this problem.

Electric bill:	$150 × .85 = $127.50
Gift for mother:	$150 × .05 = $7.50
Total spent:	$127.50 + $7.50 = $135
Amount left:	$150 − $135 = **$15**

Good test-takers would have proceeded as follows, finishing the problem in less time than it takes to calculate

the first percent: John used 90% of his money, so he had 10% left; and 10% of $150 is **$15**.

Column A	Column B

Example 37.

$\left(\dfrac{5}{11}\right)^3$	$\sqrt[3]{\dfrac{5}{11}}$

Solution. With a scientific calculator, it is very easy to evaluate each column. Even with a four-function calculator it is easy to evaluate Column A (.094) and then compare the cubes of the column. It is much easier, however, *not* to use a calculator; you simply have to know that for any number x between 0 and 1, $x^3 < \sqrt[3]{x}$. (See Section 12-A.)

Tactic 8-11 Systematically Make Lists.

When a question asks "how many," often the best strategy is to make a list of all the possibilities. It is important that you make the list in a *systematic* fashion so that you don't inadvertently leave something out. Often, shortly after starting the list, you can see a pattern developing and can figure out how many more entries there will be without writing them all down.

Even if the question does not specifically ask "how many," you may need to count some items to answer it; in this case, as well, the best plan may be to make a list.

Example 38.

For how many positive integers less than 100 is the remainder the same when the integer is divided by 5 and 7?

Solution. First, write down the integers whose remainder is 0 when divided by 5 and 7, the multiples of 35:   0, 35, 70

Next, list the integers whose remainder is 1; they are 1 more than the multiples of 35:   1, 36, 71

The integers whose remainder is 2:   2, 37, 72

The integers whose remainder is 3:   3, 38, 73

The integers whose remainder is 4:   4, 39, 74

No integer has a remainder bigger than 4 when divided by 5, so that's it. We listed 15 integers, but 0 is not positive, so the answer is **14**. (See Section 12-A.)

Example 39.

The product of three positive integers is 300. If one of them is 5, what is the least possible value of the sum of the other two?

Solution. Since one of the integers is 5, the product of the other two is 60 (5 × 60 = 300). Systematically, list all possible pairs, (*a, b*), of positive integers whose product is 60, and check their sums. First, let *a* =1, then 2, and so on.

a	*b*	*a + b*
1	60	61
2	30	32
3	20	23
4	15	19
5	12	17
6	10	16

The answer is **16**.

Example 40.

A palindrome is a number, such as 93539, that reads the same forward and backward. How many palindromes are there between 100 and 1000?

Solution. First, write down the numbers in the 100's that end in 1:   101, 111, 121, 131, 141, 151, 161, 171, 181, 191

Now write the numbers beginning and ending in 2:   202, 212, 222, 232, 242, 252, 262, 272, 282, 292

By now you should see the pattern: there are 10 numbers beginning with 1, and 10 beginning with 2, and there will be 10 beginning with 3, 4, ..., 9 for a total of 9 × 10 = **90** palindromes.

Tactic 8-12 Trust All Grids, Graphs, and Charts.

Figures that show the grid lines of a graph are *always* accurate, whether or not the coordinates of the points are given. For example, in the figure below, you can determine each of the following:

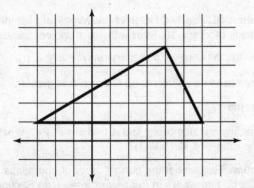

• the lengths of all three sides of the triangle;
• the perimeter of the triangle;
• the area of the triangle;
• the slope of each line segment.

Example 41.

In the grid below, what is the area of quadrilateral *ABCD*?

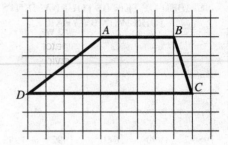

(A) 19.5   (B) 21   (C) 25.5   (D) 27   (E) 34

Solution. *AB* and *CD* are parallel (they're both horizontal), so *ABCD* is a trapezoid. If you know how to find the area of a trapezoid, just do it (area = height × average of the two bases). Count boxes: *AB* = 4 and *DC* = 9, so their average is 6.5; *AE* = 3. Therefore, the area is 3 × 6.5 = **19.5 (B)**.

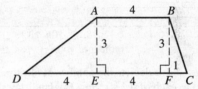

If you don't know the formula, use *AE* and *BF* to divide *ABCD* into a rectangle *(ABFE)* and two right triangles *(AED* and *BFC)*. Their areas are 12, 6, and 1.5, respectively, for a total area of **19.5**.

For sample problems using grids, see Section 12-N on coordinate geometry.

SAT I problems that use any kind of charts or graphs are *always* drawn accurately and can be trusted. For example, suppose that you are told that each of the 1000 students at Central High School studies exactly one foreign language. Then, from the circle graph below, you may conclude that fewer than half of the students study Spanish, but more students study Spanish than any other language; that approximately 250 students study French; that fewer students study German than any other language; and that approximately the same number of students are studying Latin and Italian.

FOREIGN LANGUAGES STUDIED BY 1000 STUDENTS AT CENTRAL HIGH SCHOOL

From the bar graph that follows, you know that in 1990 John won exactly three tournaments, and you can calculate that from 1989 to 1990 the number of tournaments he won decreased by 50%, whereas from 1990 to 1991 the number increased by 200%.

NUMBER OF TENNIS TOURNAMENTS JOHN WON BY YEAR

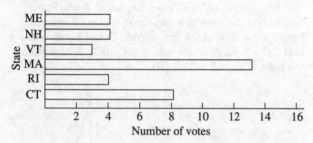

Example 42.

The chart above depicts the number of electoral votes assigned to each of the six New England states. What is the average (arithmetic mean) number of electoral votes, to the <u>nearest tenth</u>, assigned to these states?

(A) 4.0   (B) 5.7   (C) 6.0   (D) 6.5   (E) 6.7

Solution. Since we can trust the chart to be accurate, the total number of electoral votes for the six states is

$$4 + 4 + 3 + 13 + 4 + 8 = 36$$

and the average is $36 \div 6 = $ **6 (C)**.

Several different types of questions concerning bar graphs, circle graphs, line graphs, and various charts and tables can be found in Section 12-Q.

Tactic 8-13   Handle Strange Symbols Properly.

On almost all SAT I's a few questions use symbols, such as: $\oplus$, $\square$, $\odot$, $\maltese$, and $\clubsuit$, that you have never before seen in a mathematics problem. How can you answer such a question? Don't panic! It's easy; you are always told exactly what the symbol means! All you have to do is follow the directions carefully.

Example 43.

If $a \odot b = \dfrac{a+b}{a-b}$, what is the value of $25 \odot 15$?

Solution. The definition of "$\odot$" tells us that, whenever two numbers surround a "happy face," we are to form a

fraction in which the numerator is the sum of the numbers and the denominator is their difference. Here, $25 \odot 15$ is the fraction whose numerator is $25 + 15 = 40$ and whose denominator is $25 - 15 = 10$: $\dfrac{40}{10} = $ **4.**

Sometimes the same symbol is used in two (or even three) questions. In these cases, the first question is easy and involves only numbers; the second is a bit harder and usually contains variables.

Column A	Column B

Examples 44–46 refer to the following definition.

For any real numbers x and y: $x \updownarrow y = x + y^2$

Example 44.

Column A	Column B
$1 \updownarrow 3$	$6 \updownarrow 2$

Example 45.

Column A	Column B
$a \updownarrow 1$	$1 \updownarrow a$

Example 46.

Column A	Column B
The number of pairs, (x, y), of positive integers that are solutions of $x \updownarrow y = 10$	2

Solution 44. Column A: $1 + 3^2 = 1 + 9 = 10$
Column B: $6 + 2^2 = 6 + 4 = 10$
The answer is **C**.

Solution 45.

	Column A	Column B
	$a + 1$	$1 + a^2$
Subtract 1 from each column:	a	a^2

The columns are equal if $a = 1$, but not if $a = 2$. The answer is **D**.

Solution 46. Use TACTIC 8-11: *systematically* list the solutions of $x \updownarrow y = 10$. Start with $y = 1$ and continue:

$$9 + 1^2 = 10; \quad 6 + 2^2 = 10; \quad \text{and} \quad 1 + 3^2 = 10.$$

There are three solutions, so Column **A** is greater.

Example 47.

For any real numbers c and d, $c \maltese d = c^d + d^c$. What is the value of $1 \maltese (2 \maltese 3)$?

Solution. Remember the correct order of operations: always do first what's in the parentheses (see Section 12-A).

$$2 \maltese 3 = 2^3 + 3^2 = 8 + 9 = 17$$
$$\text{and}$$
$$1 \maltese 17 = 1^{17} + 17^1 = 1 + 17 = 18.$$

Grid-in **18.**

Column A   Column B

Examples 48–49 refer to the following definition.

For any even integer n: $\langle n \rangle = n^2 - n$
For any odd integer n: $\langle n \rangle = n^2 + n$

Example 48.

| $\langle 5 \rangle$ | $\langle 6 \rangle$ |

Example 49.

n is even.

| $\dfrac{\langle n \rangle}{\langle n+1 \rangle}$ | $\dfrac{n}{n+1}$ |

Solution 48. Since 5 is odd,

$$\langle 5 \rangle = 5^2 + 5 = 25 + 5 = 30.$$

Since 6 is even,

$$\langle 6 \rangle = 6^2 - 6 = 36 - 6 = 30.$$

The answer is **C**.

Solution 49. Since n is even and $n + 1$ is odd:

$$\frac{\langle n \rangle}{\langle n+1 \rangle} = \frac{n^2 - n}{(n+1)^2 + (n+1)} = \frac{n(n-1)}{(n+1)[(n+1)+1]} = \frac{n(n-1)}{(n+1)(n+2)},$$

which is less than $\dfrac{n}{n+1}$ since $\dfrac{n-1}{n+2}$ is less than 1.
The answer is **B**.

In Chapter 10, you will learn tactics for quantitative comparisons questions that will make Example 49 easier.

8-14   Add Equations.

When a question involves two equations, either add them or subtract them. If there are three or more equations, add them.

Helpful Hint

Very often, answering a question that involves two or more equations does *not* require you to solve the equations. Remember TACTIC 8-7: *Do not do any more than is necessary.*

Example 50.

If $3x + 5y = 14$ and $x - y = 6$, what is the average of x and y?

(A) 0   (B) 2.5   (C) 3   (D) 3.5   (E) 5

Solution. Add the equations:

$$\begin{array}{r} 3x + 5y = 14 \\ + \quad x - y = 6 \\ \hline 4x + 4y = 20 \end{array}$$

Divide each side by 4: $x + y = 5$

The average of x and y is their sum divided by 2:

$$\frac{x + y}{2} = \frac{5}{2} = 2.5$$

The answer is **B**.

Note that you *could have* actually solved for x and y [$x = 5.5$, $y = -0.5$], and then taken their average. However, that would have been time-consuming and unnecessary.

Here are two more problems involving two or more equations.

Example 51.

If $a - b + c = 7$ and $a + b - c = 11$, which of the following statements MUST be true?

I. a is positive   II. $b > c$ III. $bc < 0$

(A) None   (B) I only   (C) II only   (D) III only
(E) I and II only

Example 52.

If $a - b = 1$, $b - c = 2$, and $c - a = d$, what is the value of d?

(A) –3   (B) –1   (C) 1   (D) 3
(E) It cannot be determined from the information given.

Solution 51. Start by adding the two equations:

$$\begin{array}{r} a - b + c = 7 \\ + \quad a + b - c = 11 \\ \hline 2a = 18 \end{array}$$

Therefore, $a = 9$. (I is true.)

Replace a by 9 in each equation to obtain two new equations:

$9 - b + c = 7 \Rightarrow -b + c = -2$
and
$9 + b - c = 11 \Rightarrow b - c = 2$

Since $b - c = 2$, then $b > c$. (II is true.)

As long as $b = c + 2$, however, there are no restrictions on b and c: if $b = 2$ and $c = 0$, $bc = 0$. (III is false.)

The answer is **E**.

Solution 52. Add the three equations:

$$\begin{array}{r} a - b = 1 \\ b - c = 2 \\ + \quad c - a = d \\ \hline 0 = 3 + d \Rightarrow d = -3 \end{array}$$

The answer is **A**.

Practice Exercises

Multiple-Choice Questions

1. In 1995, Diana read 10 English books and 7 French books. In 1996, she read twice as many French books as English books. If 60% of the books that she read during the 2 years were French, how many English and French books did she read in 1996?

    (A) 16   (B) 26   (C) 32   (D) 39   (E) 48

2. In the figure below, if the radius of circle O is 10, what is the length of diagonal AC of rectangle $OABC$?

    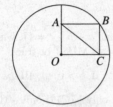

    (A) $\sqrt{2}$ (B) $\sqrt{10}$ (C) $5\sqrt{2}$ (D) 10   (E) $10\sqrt{2}$

3. In the figure below, vertex Q of square $OPQR$ is on a circle with center O. If the area of the square is 8, what is the area of the circle?

    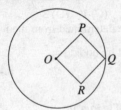

    (A) 8π (B) $8\pi\sqrt{2}$ (C) 16π (D) 32π (E) 64π

4. In the figure below, AB and AC are two chords in a circle of radius 5. What is the sum of the lengths of the two chords?

    Note: Figure not drawn to scale

    (A) 10   (B) 15   (C) 5π (D) 10π
    (E) It cannot be determined from the information given.

5. In the figure below, $ABCD$ is a square and AED is an equilateral triangle. If $AB = 2$, what is the area of the shaded region?

    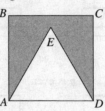

    (A) $\sqrt{3}$ (B) 2   (C) 3   (D) $4 - 2\sqrt{3}$ (E) $4 - \sqrt{3}$

6. In the figure below, equilateral triangle ABC is inscribed in circle O, whose radius is 4. Altitude BD is extended until it intersects the circle at E. What is the length of DE?

    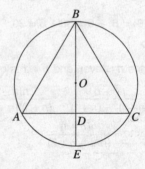

    (A) 1   (B) $\sqrt{3}$ (C) 2   (D) $2\sqrt{3}$ (E) $4\sqrt{3}$

7. If $5x + 13 = 31$, what is the value of $\sqrt{5x + 31}$?

    (A) $\sqrt{13}$ (B) $\sqrt{\dfrac{173}{5}}$ (C) 7   (D) 13   (E) 169

8. At Nat's Nuts a $2\frac{1}{4}$-pound bag of pistachio nuts costs \$6.00. At this rate, what is the cost, in cents, of a bag weighing 9 ounces?

    (A) 1.5   (B) 24   (C) 150   (D) 1350   (E) 2400

9. The map below shows all the roads connecting five towns. How many different ways are there to go from A to E if you may not return to a town after you leave it and you may not go through both C and D?

    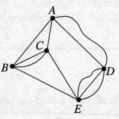

    (A) 8   (B) 12   (C) 16   (D) 24   (E) 32

10. If $12a + 3b = 1$ and $7b - 2a = 9$, what is the average (arithmetic mean) of a and b?

(A) 0.1   (B) 0.5   (C) 1   (D) 2.5   (E) 5

Quantitative Comparison Questions

Column A	Column B

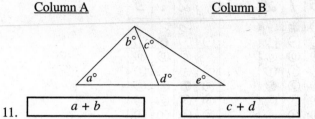

11. | $a + b$ | $c + d$ |

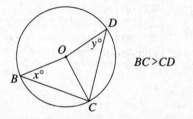

$BC > CD$

Note: Figure not drawn to scale

12. | x | y |

13. | The number of odd positive factors of 30 | The number of even positive factors of 30 |

Questions 14–15 refer to the following definition.

$\{a, b\}$ represents the remainder when a is divided by b.

14. | $\{10^3, 3\}$ | $\{10^5, 5\}$ |

c and d are positive integers with $c < d$.

15. | $\{c, d\}$ | $\{d, c\}$ |

Grid-in Questions

16. What is the degree measure of the smaller angle formed by the hour hand and the minute hand of a clock at 1:15?

17. In writing all of the integers from 1 to 300, how many times is the digit 1 used?

18. If $a + 2b = 14$ and $5a + 4b = 16$, what is the average (arithmetic mean) of a and b?

19. A bag contains 4 marbles, 1 of each color: red, blue, yellow, and green. The marbles are removed at random, 1 at a time. If the first marble is red, what is the probability that the yellow marble is removed before the blue marble?

20. The area of circle O in the above figure is 12. What is the area of the shaded sector?

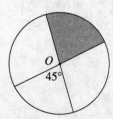

Note: Figure not drawn to scale

Answer Key

1.	E	4.	E	7.	C	10.	B	13. C
2.	D	5.	E	8.	C	11.	B	14. A
3.	C	6.	C	9.	B	12.	B	15. A

16. **5 2 . 5**

17. **1 6 0**

18. **5 / 2** or **2 . 5**

19. **3 / 6** or **1 / 2** or **. 5**

20. **1 2 / 8** or **3 / 2** or **1 . 5**

Answer Explanations

Note: For many problems, an alternative solution, indicated by two asterisks (**), follows the first solution. When this occurs, one of the solutions is the direct mathematical one and the other is based on one of the tactics discussed in this chapter.

1. **E.** Use TACTIC 8-1: draw a diagram representing a pile of books or a bookshelf.

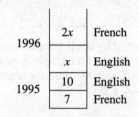

Eng.	Fr.	Eng.	Fr.
10	7	x	2x

1995   1996

In the 2 years the number of French books Diana read was $7 + 2x$, and the total number of books was $17 + 3x$. Then 60% or

$$\frac{3}{5} = \frac{7+2x}{17+3x}.$$ To solve, cross-multiply:

$$35 + 10x = 51 + 9x \Rightarrow x = 16.$$

In 1996, Diana read 16 English books and 32 French books, a total of **48** books.

2. **D.** Even if you can't solve this problem, don't omit it. Use TACTIC 8-2: trust the diagram. AC is clearly longer than OC, and very close to radius OE (measure them).

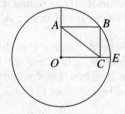

Therefore, AC must be about 10. Either by inspection or with your calculator, check the choices. They are approximately as follows: (A) $\sqrt{2} = 1.4$; (B) $\sqrt{10} = 3.1$; (C) $5\sqrt{2} = 7$; (D) 10; (E) $10\sqrt{2} = 14$. The answer must be **10**.
The answer *is* **10. The two diagonals are equal, and diagonal OB is a radius.

3. **C.** As in question 3, if you get stuck trying to answer this, use TACTIC 8-2: look at the diagram.

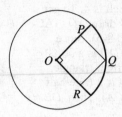

Square $OPQR$, whose area is 8, takes up most of the quarter circle, so the area of the quarter circle is certainly between 11 and 14. The area of the whole circle is 4 times as great: between 44 and 56. Check the choices. They are approximately as follows: (A) $8\pi = 25$; (B) $8\pi\sqrt{2} = 36$; (C) $16\pi = 50$; (D) $32\pi = 100$; (E) $64\pi = 200$. The answer is clearly **16π**.
**Use TACTIC 8-5: draw in line segment OQ. Since the area of the square is 8, each side is $\sqrt{8}$, and diagonal OQ is $\sqrt{8}\cdot\sqrt{2} = \sqrt{16} = 4$. But OQ is also a radius, so the area of the circle is $\pi(4)^2 = \mathbf{16\pi}$.

4. **E.** Use TACTIC 8-4. Since the diagram has not been drawn to scale, you are free to change it. AB and AC could each be very short, in which case the sum of their lengths could surely be less than 5. Therefore, none of choices A, B, C, and D could be the answer. The sum **cannot be determined from the information given**.

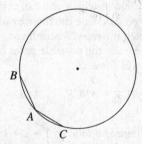

5. **E.** Use TACTIC 8-6: subtract to find the shaded area. The area of square $ABCD$ is 4. The area of $\triangle AED$ is $\frac{2^2\sqrt{3}}{4} = \frac{4\sqrt{3}}{4} = \sqrt{3}$ (see Section 12-J). Then the area of the shaded region is $\mathbf{4 - \sqrt{3}}$.

6. **C.** Use TACTIC 8-6: to get *DE*, subtract *OD* from radius *OE*, which is 4. To get *OD* draw *AO* (TACTIC 8-5). Since $\triangle ADO$ is a 30-60-90 right triangle, *OD* is 2 (one-half of *OA*). Then, *DE* = 4 – 2 = **2**.

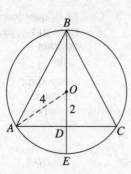

7. **C.** Use TACTIC 8-7: don't do more than you have to. In particular, don't solve for *x*. Here $5x + 13 = 31 \Rightarrow 5x = 18 \Rightarrow 5x + 31 = 18 + 31 = 49 \Rightarrow \sqrt{5x+31} = \sqrt{49} = \mathbf{7}$.

8. **C.** This is a relatively simple ratio, but use TACTIC 8-8 and make sure you get the units right. You need to know that there are 100 cents in a dollar and 16 ounces in a pound.

$$\frac{price}{weight} : \frac{6 \text{ dollars}}{2.25 \text{ pounds}} = \frac{600 \text{ cents}}{36 \text{ ounces}} = \frac{x \text{ cents}}{9 \text{ ounces}}.$$

Now cross-multiply and solve: $36x = 5400 \Rightarrow x = \mathbf{150}$. (If you do this by hand, the arithmetic is easier if you first reduce the fraction: $\frac{600}{36} = \frac{100}{6}$; if you use your calculator, that's not necessary.)

9. **B.** Use TACTIC 8-11. First systematically list the orders in which you can visit the towns, and then calculate the number of ways to follow each itinerary. According to the conditions, here are the possible paths and the number of ways for each:

ABE	ABCE	ACE	ACBE	ADE
1	2	1	2	6

There is a total of 1 + 2 + 1 + 2 + 6 = **12** ways to make the trip.

10. **B.** Use TACTIC 8-14, and add the two equations:

$$10a + 10b = 10 \Rightarrow a + b = 1 \Rightarrow$$

$$\frac{a+b}{2} = \frac{1}{2} = \mathbf{0.5}.$$

(Do not solve for *a* and *b*.)

11. **B.** If you don't see how to do this problem, use TACTIC 8-2: trust the diagram. Estimate the measure of each angle: for example, a = 45, b = 70, c = 30, and d = 120. Then c + d (150) is considerably greater than a + b (115). Choose B as the larger column.

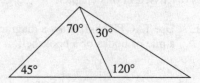

**In fact, *d* by itself is equal to *a* + *b* (an exterior angle of a triangle is equal to the sum of the opposite two interior angles), so c + d > a + b.

12. **B.** From the figure, it appears that *x* and *y* are equal, or nearly so. Use TACTIC 8-4: exaggerate the figure. Draw the diagram with *BC* much greater than *CD*. Now it is clear that *y* is greater than *x*, so column B is greater. **Since *BC* > *CD*, central angle 1 is greater than central angle 2, meaning that x < y.

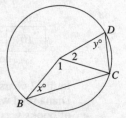

13. **C.** Use TACTIC 8-11. Systematically list all the factors of 30, either individually or in pairs: 1, 30, 2, 15, 3, 10, 5, 6. Of the 8 factors, 4 are even and 4 are odd. The columns are equal (C).

14. **A.** Column A: when 10^3 (1000) is divided by 3, the quotient is 333 and the remainder is 1. Column B: 10^5 is divisible by 5, so the remainder is 0. Column A is greater.

15. **A.** Column A: since c < d, the quotient when *c* is divided by *d* is 0, and the remainder is *c*. Column B: when *d* is divided by *c*, the remainder must be less than *c*. Column A is greater.

16. **(52.5)** Use TACTIC 8-1. Draw a picture of a clock and label it. At 1:15, the minute hand is pointing directly at 3. However, the hour hand is *not* pointing at 1. It was pointing at 1 at 1:00. During the quarter-hour between 1:00 and 1:15, the hour hand moved one-fourth of the way from 1 to 2. Since the measure of the angle between 1 and 2 is 30°, at 1:15 the hour hand has moved 7.5° from 1 toward 2 and still has 22.5° to go. The total degree measure then is 22.5 + 30 = **52.5**.

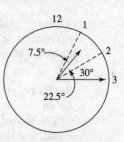

17. **(160)** Use TACTIC 8-11. Systematically list the numbers that contain the digit 1, writing as many as you need to see the pattern. Between 1 and 99 the digit 1 is used 10 times as the units digit (1, 11, 21, ..., 91) and 10 times as the tens digit (10, 11, 12, ..., 19) for a total of 20 times. From 200 to 299, there are 20 more times (the same 20 but preceded by 2). Finally, from 100 to 199 there are 20 more plus 100 numbers where the digit 1 is used in the hundreds place. The total is $20 + 20 + 20 + 100 =$ **160**.

18. $(\dfrac{5}{2}$ or 2.5$)$ Use TACTIC 8-7: don't do more than is necessary. You don't need to solve this system of equations; you don't need to know the values of a and b, only their average. Use TACTIC 8-14. Add the two equations:

$$6a + 6b = 30 \Rightarrow a + b = 5 \Rightarrow$$

$$\frac{a+b}{2} = \frac{5}{2} \text{ or } \textbf{2.5}.$$

19. $(\dfrac{3}{6}$ or $\dfrac{1}{2}$ or .5$)$ Use TACTIC 8-11. Systematically list all of the orders in which the marbles could be drawn. With 4 colors, there would ordinarily have been 24 orders, but since the first marble drawn was red, there are only 6 arrangements for the other 3 colors: BYG, BGY, YGB, YBG, GYB, GBY. In 3 of these 6 the yellow comes before the blue, and in the other 3 the blue comes before the yellow.

Therefore, the probability that the yellow marble will be removed before the blue marble is $\dfrac{3}{6}$ or $\dfrac{1}{2}$ or **.5**.

**By symmetry, it is equally as likely that the yellow marble is drawn before the blue as vice versa (whether or not the first marble drawn is red).

20. $(\dfrac{12}{8}$ or $\dfrac{3}{2}$ or 1.5$)$ The shaded sector is $\dfrac{45}{360} = \dfrac{1}{8}$ of the circle, so its area is $\dfrac{1}{8}$ of 12: $\dfrac{12}{8}$ or $\dfrac{3}{2}$ or **1.5**. (Note that, since $\dfrac{12}{8}$ fits in the grid, it is not necessary to reduce it or to convert it to a decimal. See Chapter 11.)

**If you didn't see that, use TACTIC 8-3 and redraw the figure to scale by making the angle as close as possible to 45°. It is now clear that the sector is $\dfrac{1}{8}$ of the circle (or very close to it).

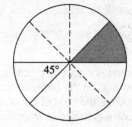

9 Multiple-Choice Questions

- ■ **Testing Tactics**
- ■ **Practice Exercises**
- ■ **Answer Key**
- ■ **Answer Explanations**

Two of the three mathematics sections on the SAT I contain only multiple-choice questions. One of the 30-minute sections has 25 multiple-choice questions, and the 15-minute section has 10. Since in each of these sections the questions proceed from easy to difficult, you should refer to Chapter 2 for advice on how to pace yourself.

On the first page of each of these sections, you will see the following directions:

> In this section *solve each problem*, using any available space on the page for scratchwork. *Then* decide which is the best of the choices given and fill in the corresponding oval on the answer sheet. (Emphasis added.)

The directions are very simple. Basically, they tell you to ignore, at first, the fact that these are multiple-choice questions. Just *solve each problem*, and *then* look at the five choices to see which one is best. As you will learn in this chapter, however, that is not always the best strategy.

In this chapter you will learn all of the important strategies you need to help you answer multiple-choice questions on the SAT I. However, as invaluable as these tactics are, use them only when you need them. *If you know how to solve a problem and are confident that you can do so accurately and reasonably quickly, JUST DO IT!*

Testing Tactics

Tactic 9-1 Test the Choices, Starting with C.

TACTIC 9-1, often called *backsolving*, is useful when you are asked to solve for an unknown and you understand what needs to be done to answer the question, but you want to avoid doing the algebra. The idea is simple: test the various choices to see which one is correct.

NOTE: On the SAT I the answers to virtually all numerical multiple-choice questions are listed in either increasing or decreasing order. Consequently, C is the middle value; and in applying TACTIC 9-1, *you should always start with C*. For example, assume that choices A, B, C, D, and E are given in increasing order. Try C. If it works, you've found the answer. If C doesn't work, you should now know whether you need to test a larger number or a smaller one, and that information permits you to eliminate two more choices. If C is too small, you need a

larger number, so A and B are out; if C is too large, you can eliminate D and E, which are even larger.

Examples 1 and 2 illustrate the proper use of TACTIC 9-1.

Example 1.

> If the average (arithmetic mean) of 2, 7, and x is 12, what is the value of x?
>
> (A) 9　(B) 12　(C) 21　(D) 27　(E) 36

Solution. Use TACTIC 9-1. Test choice C: $x = 21$.

- Is the average of 2, 7, and 21 equal to 12?
- No: $\dfrac{2+7+21}{3} = \dfrac{30}{3} = 10$, which is *too small*.
- Eliminate C; also, since, for the average to be 12, x must be *greater* than 21, eliminate A and B.
- Try choice D: $x = \mathbf{27}$. Is the average of 2, 7, and 27 equal to 12?

• Yes: $\dfrac{2+7+27}{3} = \dfrac{36}{3} = 12$. The answer is **D**.

Every problem that can be solved using TACTIC 9-1 can be solved directly, usually in less time. Therefore, we stress: *if you are confident that you can solve a problem quickly and accurately, just do so.*

Here are two direct methods for solving Example 1, each of which is *faster* than backsolving. (See Section 12-E on averages.) If you know either method, you should use it and save TACTIC 9-1 for problems that you can't easily solve directly.

Direct Solution 1. If the average of three numbers is 12, their sum is 36. Then

$$2 + 7 + x = 36 \Rightarrow 9 + x = 36 \Rightarrow x = \mathbf{27}.$$

Direct Solution 2. Since 2 is *10 less than* 12 and 7 is *5 less than* 12, to compensate, *x* must be *10 + 5 = 15 more than* 12. Then $x = 12 + 15 = \mathbf{27}$.

Example 2.

On Monday, a store owner received a shipment of books. On Tuesday, she sold half of them; on Wednesday, after two more were sold, she had exactly $\dfrac{2}{5}$ of the books left. How many books were in the shipment?

(A) 10   (B) 20   (C) 30   (D) 40   (E) 50

Solution. Use TACTIC 9-1. Test choice C: 30.

• If 30 books were received and half (15) were sold on Tuesday and 2 more on Wednesday, then 17 books were sold in all, and 13 would remain.
• Is 13 exactly $\dfrac{2}{5}$ of 30? No: $\dfrac{2}{5}\overset{6}{\cancel{(30)}}$ is only 12.

Eliminate C.
• Since C (30) is too big, also eliminate D (40) and E (50).
• Try choice B: **20**.
• If 20 books were received and half (10) were sold on Tuesday and 2 more on Wednesday, then 12 were sold and 8 would remain.
• Is 8 exactly $\dfrac{2}{5}$ of 20? Yes: $\dfrac{2}{5}\overset{4}{\cancel{(20)}} = 8$. The answer is **B**.

Using TACTIC 9-1 allows you to avoid the algebra in the following mathematical solution. If *x* represents the number of books in the shipment:

$$x - \frac{1}{2}x - 2 = \frac{2}{5}x \Rightarrow \frac{1}{2}x - 2 = \frac{2}{5}x \Rightarrow \frac{1}{10}x = 2 \Rightarrow x = \mathbf{20}.$$

Some tactics allow you to eliminate a few choices so that you can make an educated guess. On problems where TACTIC 9-1 can be used, it *always* leads you to the right answer. The only reason not to use it on a particular problem is that you can easily solve the problem directly.

Now try applying TACTIC 9-1 to Examples 3 and 4.

Example 3.

If the sum of five consecutive odd integers is 735, what is the largest of these integers?

(A) 155   (B) 151   (C) 145   (D) 143   (E) 141

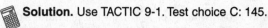 **Solution.** Use TACTIC 9-1. Test choice C: 145.

• If 145 is the largest of the five integers, the integers are 145, 143, 141, 139, and 137. Quickly add them on your calculator. The sum is 705.
• Since 705 is too small, eliminate C, D, and E.
• If you noticed that the amount by which 705 is too small is 30, you should realize that each of the five numbers needs to be increased by 6; therefore, the largest is **151 (B)**.
• If you didn't notice, just try 151, and see that it works.

This solution is easy, and it avoids having to set up and solve the required equation:

$$n + (n + 2) + (n + 4) + (n + 6) + (n + 8) = 735.$$

Example 4.

A competition offers a total of $250,000 in prize money to be shared by the top three contestants. If the money is to be divided among them in the ratio of 1:3:6, what is the value of the largest prize?

(A) $25,000   (B) $75,000   (C) $100,000
(D) $125,000   (E) $150,000

Solution. Use TACTIC 9-1. Test choice C: $100,000.

• If the largest prize is $100,000, the second largest is $50,000 (they are in the ratio of 6:3 = 2:1). The third prize is much less than $50,000, so all three add up to less than $200,000.
• Eliminate A, B, and C; and, since $100,000 is *way* too small, try E, not D.
• Test choice E. The prizes are **$150,000**, $75,000, and $25,000 (one-third of $75,000). Their total *is* $250,000. The answer is **E**.

Again, TACTIC 9-1 lets you avoid the algebra if you can't do it or just don't want to. Here it is: since the three prizes are *x*, 3*x*, and 6*x* [KEY FACT D1],

$$x + 3x + 6x = \$250,000 \Rightarrow 10x = \$250,000 \Rightarrow$$
$$x = \$25,000 \Rightarrow 6x = \mathbf{\$150,000}.$$

Helpful Hint

Don't start with C if some other choice is much easier to work with. If you start with B and it is too small, you may be able to eliminate only two choices (A and B), instead of three, but you will save time if plugging in choice C would be messy.

Example 5.

If $3x = 2(5 - 2x)$, then $x =$

(A) $-\dfrac{10}{7}$ (B) 0   (C) $\dfrac{3}{7}$ (D) 1   (E) $\dfrac{10}{7}$

Solution. Since plugging in 0 is much easier than plugging in $\frac{3}{7}$, start with B: then the left-hand side of the equation is 0, and the right-hand side is 10. The left-hand side is much too small. Eliminate A and B and try something bigger—D, of course; it will be much easier to deal with 1 than with $\frac{3}{7}$ or $\frac{10}{7}$. Now the left-hand side of the equation is 3, and the right-hand side is 6. We're closer, but not there. The answer must be **E**. Notice that we got the right answer without ever plugging in one of those unpleasant fractions. Are you uncomfortable choosing E without checking it? Don't be. If you *know* that the answer is greater than 1, and only one choice is greater than 1, that choice has to be right.

Again, we emphasize that, no matter what the choices are, you backsolve *only* if you can't easily do the algebra. Most students would probably do this problem directly:

$$3x = 2(5 - 2x) \Rightarrow 3x = 10 - 4x \Rightarrow 7x = 10 \Rightarrow x = \frac{10}{7}$$

and save backsolving for a harder problem. You have to determine which method is better for you.

For some multiple-choice questions on the SAT I, you *have to* test the various choices. On these problems you are not really backsolving (there is nothing to solve!); rather you are testing whether a particular choice satisfies a given condition.

Examples 6 and 7 are two such problems. In Example 6, you are asked for the *largest* number satisfying a certain condition. Usually, some of the smaller numbers offered as choices also satisfy the condition, but your job is to find the largest one.

Example 6.

What is the largest integer, n, such that $\frac{112}{2^n}$ is an integer?

(A) 1   (B) 2   (C) 3   (D) 4   (E) 5

Solution. Since you want the *largest* value of n for which $\frac{112}{2^n}$ is an integer, start by testing 5, choice E, the largest of the choices.

• Is $\frac{112}{2^5}$ an integer? No: $\frac{112}{2^5} = \frac{112}{32} = 3.5$.

• Eliminate E and try D: 4. Is $\frac{112}{2^4}$ an integer?

• Yes: $2^4 = 16$, and $\frac{112}{16} = 7$. The answer is **D**.

It doesn't matter whether any of the smaller choices work (you need the *largest*), although in this case they *all* do.

Surprisingly, on a problem that asks for the *smallest* number satisfying a property, you should also start with E, because the choices for these problems are usually given in decreasing order.

It is also better to start with E on questions such as Example 7, in which you are asked "which of the following...?" The right answer is *rarely* one of the first choices.

Sometimes a question asks which of the five choices satisfies a certain condition. Usually, in this situation there is no way to answer the question directly. Rather, you must look at the choices and test each of them until you find one that works. At that point, stop—none of the other choices could be correct. There is no particular order in which to test the choices, except that it makes sense to test the easier choices first. For example, it is usually easier to test whole numbers than fractions and positive numbers than negative ones.

Example 7.

Which of the following is NOT equivalent to $\frac{3}{5}$?

(A) $\frac{24}{40}$ (B) 60%   (C) 0.6   (D) $\frac{3}{7} \times \frac{7}{5}$ (E) $\frac{3}{7} \div \frac{7}{5}$

Solution. Here, we have to test each of the choices until we find one that satisfies the condition that it is *not* equal to $\frac{3}{5}$. If, as you glance at the choices to see if any would be easier to test than the others, you happen to notice that 60% = 0.6, then you can immediately eliminate choices B and C, since it is impossible that both are correct.

• Test choice A. Reduce $\frac{24}{40}$ by dividing the numerator and denominator by 8: $\frac{24}{40} = \frac{3}{5}$.

• Test choice D. $\frac{3}{7} \times \frac{7}{5} = \frac{3}{5}$.

• We now know that E must be the correct answer.

In fact, $\frac{3}{7} \div \frac{7}{5} = \frac{3}{7} \times \frac{5}{7} = \frac{15}{49} \neq \frac{3}{5}$

Tactic 9-2

Replace Variables with Numbers.

Mastery of TACTIC 9-2 is critical for anyone developing good test-taking skills. This tactic can be used whenever the five choices involve the variables in the question. There are three steps:

1. Replace each letter with an easy-to-use number.

2. Solve the problem using those numbers.

3. Evaluate each of the five choices with the numbers you picked to see which choice is equal to the answer you obtained.

Examples 8 and 9 illustrate the proper use of TACTIC 9-2.

Example 8.

If a is equal to b multiplied by c, which of the following is equal to b divided by c?

(A) $\dfrac{a}{bc}$ (B) $\dfrac{ab}{c}$ (C) $\dfrac{a}{c}$ (D) $\dfrac{a}{c^2}$ (E) $\dfrac{a}{bc^2}$

Solution.

- Pick three easy-to-use numbers that satisfy $a = bc$: for example, $a = 6$, $b = 2$, $c = 3$.
- Solve the problem with these numbers: $b \div c = \dfrac{b}{c} = \dfrac{2}{3}$.
- Check each of the five choices to see which one is equal to $\dfrac{2}{3}$:

- (A) $\dfrac{a}{bc} = \dfrac{6}{(2)(3)} = 1$: NO.   (B) $\dfrac{ab}{c} = \dfrac{(6)\cancel{(3)}^1}{\cancel{3}_1} = 6$: NO.

(C) $\dfrac{a}{c} = \dfrac{6}{3} = 2$: NO.   (D) $\dfrac{a}{c^2} = \dfrac{6}{3^2} = \dfrac{6}{9} = \dfrac{2}{3}$: YES!

Still check (E): $\dfrac{a}{bc^2} = \dfrac{6}{2(3^2)} = \dfrac{6}{18} = \dfrac{1}{3}$: NO.
- The answer is **D**.

Example 9.

If the sum of four consecutive odd integers is s, then, in terms of s, what is the greatest of these integers?

(A) $\dfrac{s-12}{4}$ (B) $\dfrac{s-6}{4}$ (C) $\dfrac{s+6}{4}$ (D) $\dfrac{s+12}{4}$

(E) $\dfrac{s+16}{4}$

Solution.

- Pick four easy-to-use consecutive odd integers: say, 1, 3, 5, 7. Then s, their sum, is 16.
- Solve the problem with these numbers: the greatest of these integers is 7.
- When $s = 16$, the five choices are $\dfrac{s-12}{4} = \dfrac{4}{4}$,

$\dfrac{s-6}{4} = \dfrac{10}{4}$, $\dfrac{s+6}{4} = \dfrac{22}{4}$, $\mathbf{\dfrac{s+12}{4} = \dfrac{28}{4}}$, $\dfrac{s+16}{4} = \dfrac{32}{4}$.
- Only $\dfrac{28}{4}$, choice **D**, is equal to 7.

Of course, Examples 8 and 9 can be solved without using TACTIC 9-2 *if your algebra skills are good.* Here are the solutions.

Solution 8. $a = bc \Rightarrow b = \dfrac{a}{c} \Rightarrow b \div c = \dfrac{a}{c} \div c = \dfrac{a}{c^2}$.

Solution 9. Let n, $n + 2$, $n + 4$, and $n + 6$ be four consecutive odd integers, and let s be their sum. Then:

$$s = n + (n + 2) + (n + 4) + (n + 6) = 4n + 12.$$

Therefore:

$$n = \dfrac{s-12}{4} \Rightarrow n + 6 = \dfrac{s-12}{4} + 6 =$$

$$\dfrac{s-12}{4} + \dfrac{24}{4} = \dfrac{s+12}{4}.$$

The important point is that, if you are uncomfortable with the correct algebraic solution, you don't have to omit these questions. You can use TACTIC 9-2 and *always* get the right answer. Of course, even if you can do the algebra, you should use TACTIC 9-2 if you think you can solve the problem faster or will be less likely to make a mistake. This is a good example of what we mean when we say that, with the proper use of these tactics, you can correctly answer many questions that you may not know how to do.

Examples 10 and 11 are somewhat different. You are asked to reason through word problems involving only variables. Most students find problems like these mind-boggling. Here, the use of TACTIC 9-2 is essential; without it, Example 10 is difficult and Example 11 is nearly impossible. TACTIC 9-2 is not easy to master, but with practice you will catch on.

Helpful Hint

Replace the letters with numbers that are easy to use, not necessarily ones that make sense. *It is perfectly OK to ignore reality.* A school can have five students, apples can cost $10 each, trains can go 5 miles per hour or 1000 miles per hour—it doesn't matter.

Example 10.

If a school cafeteria needs c cans of soup each week for each student, and if there are s students in the school, for how many weeks will x cans of soup last?

(A) $\dfrac{cx}{s}$ (B) $\dfrac{xs}{c}$ (C) $\dfrac{s}{cx}$ (D) $\dfrac{x}{cs}$ (E) csx

Solution.

- Replace c, s, and x with three easy-to-use numbers. If a school cafeteria needs 2 cans of soup each week for each student, and if there are 5 students in the school, how many weeks will 20 cans of soup last?
- Since the cafeteria needs $2 \times 5 = 10$ cans of soup per week, 20 cans will last for 2 weeks.
- Which of the choices equals 2 when $c = 2$, $s = 5$, and $x = 20$?
- The five choices become: $\dfrac{cx}{x} = 8$, $\dfrac{xs}{c} = 50$, $\dfrac{x}{cs} = \dfrac{1}{8}$,

$\dfrac{x}{cs} = 2$, $csx = 200$. The answer is **D**.

Example 11.

If p painters can paint h houses in d days, how many houses can five painters, working at the same rate, paint in 2 days?

(A) $\dfrac{dhp}{10}$ (B) $\dfrac{5hp}{2d}$ (C) $\dfrac{2hp}{5d}$ (D) $\dfrac{10h}{dp}$ (E) $\dfrac{10dp}{h}$

Solution.

- Pick three easy-to-use numbers. Suppose that 1 painter can paint 1 house in 1 day.

- Then, in 2 days each painter can paint 2 houses, and 5 painters can paint 10 houses. A quickly drawn chart can keep the numbers straight:

Painters	Houses	Days
1	1	1
1	2	2
5	10	2

- Evaluate the five choices when $p = 1$, $h = 1$, $d = 1$, and find the choice that equals 10:

(A) $\dfrac{dhp}{10} = \dfrac{(1)(1)(1)}{10} = \dfrac{1}{10}$: NO.

(B) $\dfrac{5hp}{2d} = \dfrac{5(1)(1)}{2(1)} = \dfrac{5}{2}$: NO.

(C) $\dfrac{2hp}{5d} = \dfrac{2(1)(1)}{5(1)} = \dfrac{2}{5}$: NO.

(D) $\dfrac{10h}{dp} = \dfrac{10(1)}{(1)(1)} = 10$: YES.

(E) $\dfrac{10dp}{h} = \dfrac{10(1)(1)}{1} = 10$: YES.

- Eliminate A, B, and C. But both D and E are 10. *What now*?
- Change *one* of the numbers, and test only D and E. Suppose that 1 painter could paint 100 houses, instead of just 1, in 1 day. Then 5 painters could paint lots of houses—certainly many more than 10.
- Of D and E, which will be *bigger* if you replace h by 100 instead of 1? In D, the numerator, and hence the whole fraction, which is $\dfrac{10h}{dp}$, will be much bigger. In E, the denominator will be larger and the value of the fraction smaller.
- The answer is **D**.

Example 11 illustrates that replacing a variable by 1 is *not* a good idea in this type of problem. The reason is that multiplying and dividing by 1 give the same result: $3x$ and $\dfrac{3}{x}$ are each equal to 3 when $x = 1$. It is also *not* a good idea to use the same number for different variables: $\dfrac{3a}{b}$ and $\dfrac{3b}{a}$ are each equal to 3 when a and b are equal.

The best choice in Example 11 would be to let $p = 5$ and $d = 2$, and let h be any number at all, say 4. Example 11 would then read, "If 5 painters can paint 4 houses in 2 days, how many houses can 5 painters, working at the same rate, paint in 2 days?" The answer is obviously 4, and only **D** is equal to 4 when $p = 5$ and $d = 2$.

Even though Examples 10 and 11 are much more abstract than Examples 8 and 9, they too can be solved directly and more quickly *if* you can manipulate the variables.

Algebraic Solution 10. If each week the school needs c cans for each of the s students, then it will need cs cans per week. Dividing cs into x gives the number of weeks that x cans will last: $\dfrac{x}{cs}$.

Algebraic Solution 11. Since 1 painter can do $\dfrac{1}{p}$ times the amount of work of p painters, if p painters can paint h houses in d days, then 1 painter can paint $\dfrac{h}{p}$ houses in d days. In 1 day he can paint $\dfrac{1}{d}$ times the number of houses he can paint in d days; so, in 1 day, 1 painter can paint $\dfrac{1}{d} \times \dfrac{h}{p} = \dfrac{h}{dp}$ houses. Of course, in 1 day, 5 painters can paint 5 times as many houses: $\dfrac{5h}{dp}$. Finally, in 2 days these painters can paint twice as many houses: $2\left(\dfrac{5h}{dp}\right) = \dfrac{10h}{dp}$. Even if you could carefully reason this out, why would you want to?

Now, practice TACTIC 9-2 on the following problems.

Example 12.

Nadia will be x years old y years from now. How old was she z years ago?

(A) $x + y + z$ (B) $x + y - z$ (C) $x - y - z$
(D) $y - x - z$ (E) $z - y - x$

Example 13.

If $a = b + \dfrac{1}{2}$, $b = 2c + \dfrac{1}{2}$, and $c = 3d + \dfrac{1}{2}$, which of the following is an expression for d in terms of a?

(A) $\dfrac{a - 2}{6}$ (B) $\dfrac{2a - 3}{6}$ (C) $\dfrac{2a - 3}{12}$

(D) $\dfrac{3a - 2}{18}$ (E) $\dfrac{4a - 3}{24}$

Example 14.

Anne drove for h hours at a constant rate of r miles per hour. How many miles did she go during the final 20 minutes of her drive?

(A) $20r$ (B) $\dfrac{hr}{3}$ (C) $3rh$ (D) $\dfrac{hr}{20}$ (E) $\dfrac{r}{3}$

Example 15.

A factory produces x widgets every hour at a cost of c cents per widget. If the factory operates for h hours and m minutes, how much money will it spend, in dollars, on the production of widgets?

(A) $\dfrac{(h + m)cx}{60}$ (B) $\dfrac{(h + m)cx}{100}$ (C) $\dfrac{(h + 60m)cx}{100}$

(D) $\dfrac{(60h + m)cx}{60}$ (E) $\dfrac{(60h + m)cx}{6000}$

Solution 12. Assume Nadia will be 10 in 2 years. How old was she 3 years ago? If she will be 10 in 2 years, she is 8 now and 3 years ago was 5. Which of the choices equals 5 when $x = 10$, $y = 2$, and $z = 3$? Only $x - y - z$ **(C)**.

Solution 13. Let $d = 1$. Then $c = 3\frac{1}{2}$, $b = 7\frac{1}{2}$, and $a = 8$. Which of the choices equals 1 when $a = 8$? Only $\frac{a-2}{6}$ **(A)**.

Solution 14. If Anne drove at 60 miles per hour for 2 hours, how far did she go in her last 20 minutes? Since 20 minutes is $\frac{1}{3}$ of an hour, she went 20 $\left(\frac{1}{3}$ of $60\right)$ miles. Only $\frac{r}{3}$ **(E)** $= 20$ when $r = 60$ and $h = 2$.

Notice that h is irrelevant. Whether Anne had been driving for 2 hours or 20 hours, the distance she covered in her last 20 minutes would be the same.

 Solution 15. Assume that the factory produces 10 widgets per hour at a cost of 5 cents each. Then, it spends 50 cents per hour on widget production, and in 2 hours and 30 minutes (2.5 hours) it will spend $1.25. Which of the choices is equal to 1.25, or $\frac{5}{4}$, when $x = 10$, $c = 5$, $h = 2$, and $m = 30$? Only $\frac{(60h + m)cx}{6000}$ **(E)**:

$$\frac{[60(2) + 30](10)(5)}{6000} = \frac{(150)(50)}{6000} = \frac{5}{4}.$$

Tactic 9-3 Choose an Appropriate Number.

TACTIC 9-3 is similar to TACTIC 9-2 in that we pick convenient numbers. However, here no variable is given in the problem. TACTIC 9-3 is especially useful in problems involving fractions, ratios, and percents.

Helpful Hint

In problems involving fractions, the best number to use is the least common denominator of all the fractions. In problems involving percents, the easiest number to use is 100. (See Sections 12-B and 12-C.)

Example 16.

At Central High School each student studies exactly one foreign language. Three-fifths of the students take Spanish, and one-fourth of the remaining students take Italian. If all of the others take French, what <u>percent</u> of the students take French?

(A) 10   (B) 15   (C) 20   (D) 25   (E) 30

Solution. The least common denominator of $\frac{3}{5}$ and $\frac{1}{4}$ is 20, so assume that there are 20 students at Central High. (Remember that the numbers you choose don't have to be realistic.) Then the number of students taking Spanish is 12 $\left(\frac{3}{5}$ of $20\right)$. Of the remaining 8 students, 2 $\left(\frac{1}{4}$ of $8\right)$ take Italian. The other 6 take French. Finally, 6 is **30%** of 20. The answer is **E**.

Example 17.

From 1994 to 1995 the number of boys in the school chess club decreased by 20%, and the number of girls in the club increased by 20%. The ratio of girls to boys in the club in 1995 was how many times the ratio of girls to boys in the club in 1994?

(A) $\frac{2}{3}$ (B) $\frac{4}{5}$ (C) 1   (D) $\frac{5}{4}$ (E) $\frac{3}{2}$

Solution. This problem involves percents, so try to use 100. Assume that in 1994 there were 100 boys and 100 girls in the club. Since 20% of 100 is 20, in 1995 there were 120 girls (a 20% increase) and 80 boys (a 20% decrease). See the chart:

Year	Number of Girls	Number of Boys	Ratio of Girls to Boys
1994	100	100	$\frac{100}{100} = 1$
1995	120	80	$\frac{120}{80} = \frac{3}{2}$

The chart shows that the 1994 ratio of 1 was multiplied by $\frac{3}{2}$. The answer is **E**.

Here are two more problems where TACTIC 9-3 is useful.

Example 18.

In a particular triathlon the athletes cover $\frac{1}{24}$ of the total distance by swimming, $\frac{1}{3}$ of it by running, and the rest by bike. What is the ratio of the distance covered by bike to the distance covered by running?

(A) 15:1   (B) 15:8   (C) 8:5   (D) 5:8   (E) 8:15

Example 19.

From 1994 to 1995 the sales of a book decreased by 80%. If the sales in 1996 were the same as in 1994, by what percent did they increase from 1995 to 1996?

(A) 80%   (B) 100%   (C) 120%   (D) 400%   (E) 500%

Solution 18. The least common denominator of the two fractions is 24, so assume that the total distance is 24 miles. Then, the athletes swim for 1 mile and run for 8 $\left(\frac{1}{3}$ of $24\right)$ miles. The remaining 15 miles they cover by bike. Therefore, the required ratio is **15:8 (B)**.

Solution 19. Use TACTIC 9-3, and assume that 100 copies were sold in 1994 (and 1996). Sales dropped by 80 (80% of 100) to 20 in 1995 and then increased by 80, from 20 back to 100, in 1996. The percent increase was

$$\frac{\text{actual increase}}{\text{original amount}} \times 100\% = \frac{80}{20} \times 100\% = \mathbf{400\%\ (D)}.$$

Tactic 9-4
Eliminate Absurd Choices, and Guess.

When you have no idea how to solve a problem, eliminate all the absurd choices and *guess* from among the remaining ones.

In Chapter 2, you read that only very infrequently should you omit a problem that you have time to work on. During the course of an SAT I, you will probably find at least a few multiple-choice questions that you have no idea how to solve. *Do not omit these questions!* Often two or three of the answers are absurd. Eliminate them and *guess*. Occasionally, four of the choices are absurd. When this occurs, your answer is no longer a guess.

What makes a choice absurd? Lots of things. Even if you don't know how to solve a problem, you may realize that:

- the answer must be positive, but some of the choices are negative;
- the answer must be even, but some of the choices are odd;
- the answer must be less than 100, but some choices exceed 100;
- a ratio must be less than 1, but some choices are greater than or equal to 1.

Let's look at several examples. In a few of them the information given is intentionally insufficient to solve the problem, but you will still be able to determine that some of the answers are absurd. In each case the "solution" provided will indicate which choices you should have eliminated. At that point you would simply guess. [See Chapter 2 for a complete discussion of guessing.] Remember: on the SAT I when you have to guess, don't agonize. Just make your choice and then move on.

Example 20.

A region inside a semicircle of radius *r* is shaded. What is its area?

(A) $\frac{1}{4}\pi r^2$ (B) $\frac{1}{3}\pi r^2$ (C) $\frac{1}{2}\pi r^2$ (D) $\frac{2}{3}\pi r^2$ (E) $\frac{3}{4}\pi r^2$

Solution. You may have no idea how to find the area of the shaded region, but you should know that, since the area of a circle is πr^2, the area of a semicircle is $\frac{1}{2}\pi r^2$.

Therefore, the area of the shaded region must be *less than* $\frac{1}{2}\pi r^2$, so eliminate C, D, and E. On an actual problem, if the diagram is drawn to scale, you may be able to make an educated guess between A and B. If not, just choose one or the other.

Example 21.

The average of 5, 10, 15, and *x* is 20. What is *x*?

(A) 0   (B) 20   (C) 25   (D) 45   (E) 50

Solution. If the average of four numbers is 20, and three of them are less than 20, the other one must be greater than 20. Eliminate A and B and guess. If you further realize that, since 5 and 10 are *a lot* less than 20, *x* will probably be *a lot* more than 20, you can eliminate C, as well. Then guess either D or E.

Example 22.

If 25% of 220 equals 5.5% of *w*, what is *w*?

(A) 10   (B) 55   (C) 100   (D) 110   (E) 1000

Solution. Since 5.5% of *w* equals 25% of 220, which is surely greater than 5.5% of 220, *w* must be *greater* than 220. Eliminate A, B, C, and D. The answer *must* be **E**!

Example 22 illustrates an important point. *Even if you know how to solve a problem*, if you immediately see that four of the five choices are absurd, just pick the remaining choice and move on.

Example 23.

A prize of $27,000 is to be divided in some ratio among three people. What is the largest share?

(A) $18,900   (B) $13,500   (C) $8100   (D) $5400
(E) $2700

Solution. If the prize were divided equally, each share would be worth $9000. If it is divided unequally, the largest share is surely *more than* $9000, so eliminate C, D, and E. In an actual question, you would be told what the ratio is, and that information might enable you to eliminate A or B. If not, you would just guess.

Example 24.

A jar contains only red and blue marbles. The ratio of the number of red marbles to the number of blue marbles is 5:3. What percent of the marbles are blue?

(A) 37.5%   (B) 50%   (C) 60%   (D) 62.5%
(E) 80%

Solution. Since there are five red marbles for every three blue ones, there are fewer blue ones than red ones. Therefore, *fewer than half* (50%) of the marbles are blue. Eliminate B, C, D, and E. The answer is **A**.

Example 25.

In the figure at the right, four semicircles are drawn, each centered at the midpoint of one of the sides of square *ABCD*. Each of the four shaded "petals" is the intersection of two of the semicircles. If *AB* = 4, what is the total area of the shaded region?

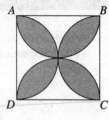

(A) 8π   (B) 32 – 8π   (C) 16 – 8π
(D) 8π – 32   (E) 8π – 16

Solution. The diagram is drawn to scale. Therefore, you may trust it in making your estimate (TACTIC 8-2).

• Since the shaded area *appears* to take up a little more than half of the square, it does.
• The area of the square is 16, so the area of the shaded region must be *about* 9.
    • *Using your calculator*, but only when you need it, check each choice. Since π is slightly more than 3, 8π (which appears in each choice) is somewhat more than 24, approximately 25.

• (A) 8π ≈ 25. More than the whole square: *way* too big.
• (B) 32 – 8π ≈ 7. Too small.
• (C) 16 – 8π is negative. Clearly impossible!
• (D) 8π – 32 is also negative.
• (E) **8π – 16** ≈ 25 – 16 = 9. Finally! The answer is **E**.

Note: Three of the choices are absurd: A is more than the area of the entire square, and C and D are negative and so can be eliminated immediately. No matter what your estimate was, at worst you had to guess between two choices.

Now use TACTIC 9-4 on each of the following problems. Even if you know how to solve them, don't. Practice this technique, and see how many choices you can eliminate *without* actually solving.

Example 26.

In the figure at the right, diagonal *EG* of square *EFGH* is one-half of diagonal *AD* of square *ABCD*. What is the ratio of the area of the shaded region to the area of *ABCD*?

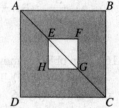

(A) √2:1   (B) 3:4
(C) √2:2   (D) 1:2
(E) 1:2√2

Example 27.

Jim receives a commission of 25¢ for every $20.00 worth of merchandise he sells. What percent is his commission?

(A) $1\frac{1}{4}$%   (B) $2\frac{1}{2}$%   (C) 5%   (D) 25%   (E) 125%

Example 28.

From 1980 to 1990, Michael's weight increased by 25%. If his weight was *W* kilograms in 1990, what was it in 1980?

(A) 1.75*W*   (B) 1.25*W*   (C) 1.20*W*   (D) .80*W*
(E) .75*W*

Example 29.

The average of 10 numbers is –10. If the sum of six of them is 100, what is the average of the other four?

(A) –100   (B) –50   (C) 0   (D) 50   (E) 100

Example 30.

What is 3% of 4%?

(A) 0.07%   (B) 0.12%   (C) 1.2%   (D) 7%   (E) 12%

Solution 26. Obviously, the shaded region is smaller than square *ABCD*, so the ratio must be less than 1. Eliminate A (√2 > 1.4). Also, from the diagram, it is clear that the shaded region is more than half of square *ABCD*, so the ratio is greater than 0.5. Eliminate D and E. Since 3:4 = 0.75 and √2:2 ≈ 0.71, B and C are too close to tell, just by looking, which is right, so guess. (The answer is **B**.)

Solution 27. Clearly, a commission of 25¢ on $20 is quite small. Eliminate D and E, and guess one of the small percents. If you realize that 1% of $20 is 20¢, then you know the answer is a little more than 1%, and you should guess A (maybe B, but definitely not C). (The answer is **A**.)

Solution 28. Since Michael's weight increased, his weight in 1980 was *less than W*. Eliminate A, B, and C and guess. (The answer is **D**.)

Solution 29. Since the average of all 10 numbers is negative, so is their sum. However, the sum of the first six is positive, so the sum (and the average) of the others must be negative. Eliminate C, D, and E. (The answer is **B**.)

Solution 30. Since 3% of a number is just a small part of it, 3% of 4% must be *much less* than 4%. Eliminate D and E, and probably C. (The answer is **B**.)

Practice Exercises

1. If $x^2 + 2x - 6 > x^2 - 2x + 6$, which of the following must be true?

   (A) $x < 3$ (B) $x = 3$ (C) $x > 3$ (D) $x = 4$
   (E) $x \geq 4$

2. Jessica has 4 times as many books as John and 5 times as many as Karen. If Karen has more than 40 books, what is the least number of books that Jessica can have?

   (A) 240 (B) 220 (C) 210 (D) 205 (E) 200

3. Judy is now twice as old as Adam but 6 years ago she was 5 times as old as he was. How old is Judy now?

   (A) 10 (B) 16 (C) 20 (D) 24 (E) 32

4. What is the largest prime factor of 255?

   (A) 5 (B) 15 (C) 17 (D) 51 (E) 255

5. What is the largest integer, n, that satisfies the inequality $n^2 + 8n - 3 < n^2 + 7n + 8$?

   (A) 0 (B) 5 (C) 7 (D) 10 (E) 11

6. If $a < b$ and c is the sum of a and b, which of the following is the positive difference between a and b?

   (A) $2a - c$ (B) $2b - c$ (C) $c - 2b$
   (D) $c - a + b$ (E) $c - a - b$

7. If w widgets cost c cents, how many widgets can you get for d dollars?

   (A) $\dfrac{100dw}{c}$ (B) $\dfrac{dw}{100c}$ (C) $100cdw$

   (D) $\dfrac{dw}{c}$ (E) cdw

8. If 120% of a is equal to 80% of b, which of the following is equal to $a + b$?

   (A) $1.5a$ (B) $2a$ (C) $2.5a$ (D) $3a$ (E) $5a$

9. In the figure at the right, $WXYZ$ is a square whose sides are 12. AB, CD, EF, and GH are each 8, and are the diameters of the four semicircles. What is the area of the shaded region?

   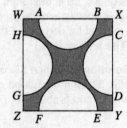

   (A) $144 - 128\pi$ (B) $144 - 64\pi$
   (C) $144 - 32\pi$ (D) $144 - 16\pi$ (E) 16π

10. Which of the following numbers can be expressed as the product of three different integers greater than 1?

    I.   25
    II.   36
    III. 45

    (A) I only (B) II only (C) III only
    (D) II and III only (E) I, II, and III

11. A point is drawn on a rectangular table, 3 feet from one side and 4 feet from an adjacent side. How far, in feet, is the point from the nearest corner of the table?

    (A) $\sqrt{13}$ (B) 5 (C) 7 (D) 25
    (E) It cannot be determined from the information given.

12. What is the average of $4y + 3$ and $2y - 1$?

    (A) $3y + 1$ (B) $3y + 2$ (C) $3y + 4$ (D) $y + 1$
    (E) $y + 2$

13. Judy plans to visit the Boston Museum of Art once each month in 2002 except in July and August, when she plans to go 3 times each month. A single admission costs $3.50, a pass valid for unlimited visits in any 3-month period can be purchased for $18, and an annual pass costs $60.00. What is the least amount, in dollars, that Judy can spend for the number of visits she intends to make?

    (A) 72 (B) 60 (C) 56 (D) 49.5 (E) 48

14. If x and y are integers such that $x^3 = y^2$, which of the following CANNOT be the value of y?

    (A) -1 (B) 1 (C) 8 (D) 16 (E) 27

15. What is a divided by $a\%$ of a?

    (A) $\dfrac{a}{100}$ (B) $\dfrac{100}{a}$ (C) $\dfrac{a^2}{100}$ (D) $\dfrac{100}{a^2}$
    (E) $100a$

16. If an object is moving at a speed of 36 kilometers per hour, how many meters does it travel in 1 second?

    (A) 10 (B) 36 (C) 100 (D) 360 (E) 1000

17. On a certain Russian-American committee, $\dfrac{2}{3}$ of the members are men, and $\dfrac{3}{8}$ of the men are Americans. If $\dfrac{3}{5}$ of the committee members are Russian, what fraction of the members are American women?

    (A) $\dfrac{3}{20}$ (B) $\dfrac{11}{60}$ (C) $\dfrac{1}{4}$ (D) $\dfrac{2}{5}$ (E) $\dfrac{5}{12}$

18. For what value of x is $8^{2x-4} = 16^x$?

   (A) 2   (B) 3   (C) 4   (D) 6   (E) 8

19. If m is a positive integer, which of the following could be true?

   I. m^2 is a prime number
   II. $\sqrt{m}$ is a prime number.
   III. $m^2 = \sqrt{m}$

   (A) I only   (B) II only   (C) III only
   (D) II and III only   (E) I, II, and III

20. If $x\%$ of y is 10, what is y?

   (A) $\dfrac{10}{x}$ (B) $\dfrac{100}{x}$ (C) $\dfrac{1000}{x}$ (D) $\dfrac{x}{100}$

   (E) $\dfrac{x}{10}$

Answer Key

1.	**C**	5.	**D**	9.	**C**	13.	**D**	17.	**A**
2.	**B**	6.	**B**	10.	**B**	14.	**D**	18.	**D**
3.	**B**	7.	**A**	11.	**E**	15.	**B**	19.	**B**
4.	**C**	8.	**C**	12.	**A**	16.	**A**	20.	**C**

Answer Explanations

Note: For many problems, an alternative solution, indicated by two asterisks (**), follows the first solution. When this occurs, one of the solutions is the direct mathematical one and the other is based on one of the tactics discussed in this chapter.

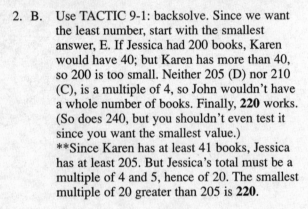

1. **C.** Use TACTIC 9-1: backsolve, starting with C. Must x be greater than 3? Try a number larger than 3; to distinguish it from choices D and E, test 5: $5^2 + 2(5) - 6 = 29$, which is greater than $5^2 - 2(5) + 6 = 21$. Eliminate A, B, and D. Now, to distinguish between C and E, use your calculator to test a number between 3 and 4, say 3.5. It works ($13.25 > 11.25$), so $x > 3$. Eliminate E.
   ** $x^2 + 2x - 6 > x^2 - 2x + 6 \Rightarrow$
   $2x - 6 > -2x + 6 \Rightarrow 4x > 12 \Rightarrow x > 3$.

2. **B.** Use TACTIC 9-1: backsolve. Since we want the least number, start with the smallest answer, E. If Jessica had 200 books, Karen would have 40; but Karen has more than 40, so 200 is too small. Neither 205 (D) nor 210 (C), is a multiple of 4, so John wouldn't have a whole number of books. Finally, **220** works. (So does 240, but you shouldn't even test it since you want the smallest value.)
   Since Karen has at least 41 books, Jessica has at least 205. But Jessica's total must be a multiple of 4 and 5, hence of 20. The smallest multiple of 20 greater than 205 is **220.

3. **B.** Use TACTIC 9-1: backsolve, starting with C. If Judy is now 20, Adam is 10; 6 years ago, they would have been 14 and 4, which is less than 5 times as much. Eliminate C, D, and E, and try a smaller value. If Judy is now **16**, Adam is 8; 6 years ago, they would have been 10 and 2. That's it; 10 is 5 times 2.
   **If Adam is now x, Judy is $2x$; 6 years ago they were $x - 6$ and $2x - 6$, respectively. Solving gives $2x - 6 = 5(x - 6) \Rightarrow x = 8 \Rightarrow 2x = 16$.

4. **C.** Test the choices. Since 255 (E) is divisible by 5, and 51 (D) is divisible by 3, neither is prime. Try C: **17** is prime, and is a factor of 255: $255 \div 17 = 15$.
   **$255 = 5 \times 51 = 5 \times 3 \times 17$.

5. **D.** Using your calculator, test the choices, starting with E (since we want the largest value):
   $$11^2 + 8(11) - 3 = 121 + 88 - 3 = 206,$$
   and
   $$11^2 + 7(11) + 8 = 121 + 77 + 8 = 206.$$
   The two sides are equal. When $n = \mathbf{10}$, however, the left-hand side is smaller:
   $100 + 80 - 3 = 177$ and $100 + 70 + 8 = 178$.
   ** $n^2 + 8n - 3 < n^2 + 7n + 8 \Rightarrow n < 11$.

6. **B.** Use TACTIC 9-2. Pick simple values for a, b, and c. Let $a = 1$, $b = 2$, and $c = 3$. Then $b - a = 1$. Only $2b - c$ is equal to 1.
   ** $c = a + b \Rightarrow a = c - b \Rightarrow$
   $b - a = b - (c - b) = 2b - c$.

7. **A.** Use TACTIC 9-2: replaces variables with numbers. If 2 widgets cost 10 cents, then widgets cost 5 cents each; and for 3 dollars, you can get 60 widgets. Which of the choices equals 60 when $w = 2$, $c = 10$, and $d = 3$?
   Only $\dfrac{100dw}{c}$.
   **Convert d dollars to $100d$ cents, and set the ratios equal: $\dfrac{\text{widgets}}{\text{cents}} = \dfrac{w}{c} = \dfrac{x}{100d} \Rightarrow$
   $x = \dfrac{100dw}{c}$.

8. **C.** Use Tactic 9-3: choose appropriate numbers. Since 120% of 80 = 80% of 120, let $a = 80$ and $b = 120$. Then $a + b = 200$, and $200 \div 80 = \mathbf{2.5}$.

9. **C.** If you don't know how to solve this, you must use TACTIC 9-4: eliminate the absurd choices and guess. Which choices are absurd? Certainly, A and B, both of which are negative. Also, since choice D is about 94, which is much more than half the area of the square, it is much too large. Guess between C (about 43) and E (about 50). If you remember that the way to find shaded areas is to subtract, guess C: **$144 - 32\pi$**.
   The area of the square is $12^2 = 144$. The area of each semicircle is 8π, one-half the area of a circle of radius 4. Together the areas of the semicircles is 32π, and the area of the shaded region is **$144 - 32\pi$.

10. **B.** Treat each of the three Roman numerals as a separate question.

   - 25 has only two positive factors greater than 1 (5 and 25), and so clearly cannot be the product of three different positive factors. (I is false.)
   - 36 can be expressed as the product of three different positive factors: $36 = 2 \times 3 \times 6$. (II is true.)
   - The factors of 45 that are greater than 1 are 3, 5, 9, 15, and 45; no three of them have a product equal to 45. (III is false.)

   Only II is true.

11. **E.** Use TACTIC 8-1: draw a diagram. Clearly, the point is 5 feet from corner *A*. Before picking B as the answer, however, ask yourself whether the point could possibly be closer to another corner of the table. It could, so the answer **cannot be determined from the information given**.

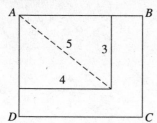

12. **A.** To find the average, add the two quantities and divide by 2:
$$\frac{(4y+3)+(2y-1)}{2} = \frac{6y+2}{2} = 3y+1.$$
   Use TACTIC 9-2. Let $y = 1$. Then $4y + 3 = 7$ and $2y - 1 = 1$. The average of 7 and 1 is $\frac{7+1}{2} = 4$. Of the five choices, only **$3y + 1$ is equal to 4 when $y = 1$.

13. **D.** Judy intends to go to the museum 16 times during the year. Buying a single admission each time would cost $16 \times \$3.50 = \$56$, which is less than the annual pass. If she bought a 3-month pass for June, July, and August, she would pay $18 plus $31.50 for 9 single admissions ($9 \times \$3.50$), for a total expense of **$49.50**, which is the least expensive option.

14. **D.** Use TACTIC 9-1: test the choices. There is no advantage to starting with any particular choice. Here, we started with E. Could $y = 27$? Is there an integer x such that $x^3 = 27^2 = 729$? Use your calculator to test some numbers: $10^3 = 1000$—too large; $9^3 = 729$. Try choice D: 16. Is there an integer x such that $x^3 = 16^2 = 256$? No: $5^3 = 125$, $6^3 = 216$, so 5 and 6 are too small; but $7^3 = 343$, which is too large. The answer is **16**.

15. **B.** $a \div (a\% \text{ of } a) = a \div \left(\frac{a}{100} \cdot a\right) = a \div \left(\frac{a^2}{100}\right) = a \times \frac{100}{a^2} = \frac{100}{a}.$

   **Use TACTICS 9-2 and 9-3: replace *a* by a number, and use 100 since the problem involves percents.

   $$100 \div (100\% \text{ of } 100) = 100 \div 100 = 1.$$

   Test each choice; which one equals 1 when $a = 100$? A and B: $\frac{100}{100} = 1$. Eliminate C, D, and E; and test A and B with another value, 50, for *a*:

   $$50 \div (50\% \text{ of } 50) = 50 \div (25) = 2.$$
   Now, only $\frac{100}{a}$, works: $\frac{100}{50} = 2.$

16. **A.** Set up a ratio:
   $$\frac{\text{distance}}{\text{time}} = \frac{36 \text{ kilometers}}{1 \text{ hour}} =$$
   $$\frac{36,000 \text{ meters}}{60 \text{ minutes}} = \frac{36,000 \text{ meters}}{3600 \text{ seconds}} =$$
   10 meters/second.
   **Use TACTIC 9-1: Test choices, starting with C:

   100 meters/second = 6000 meters/minute = 360,000 meters/hour = 360 kilometers/hour.

   Not only is that too big, but it is too big by a factor of 10. The answer is **10**.

17. **A.** Use TACTIC 9-3: choose appropriate numbers. The LCM of all the denominators is 120, so assume that the committee has 120 members. Then there are $\frac{2}{3} \times 120 = 80$ men and 40 women. Of the 80 men, 30 $\left(\frac{3}{8} \times 80\right)$ are American. Since there are 72 $\left(\frac{3}{5} \times 120\right)$ Russians, there are $120 - 72 = 48$ Americans, of whom 30 are men, so the other 18 are women. Finally, the fraction of American women is $\frac{18}{120} = \frac{3}{20}$. This is illustrated in the Venn diagram below.

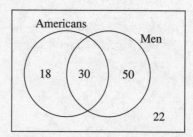

18. D. Use TACTIC 9-1: backsolve, using your calculator. Let $x = 4$: then $8^{2(4)-4} = 8^4 = 4096$, whereas $16^4 = 65,536$. Eliminate A, B, and C, and try a larger value. Let $x = 6$: then $8^{2(6)-4} = 8^8 = 16,777,216$ and $16^6 = 16,777,216$.

    **$8^{2x-4} = 16^x \Rightarrow (2^3)^{2x-4} = (2^4)^x \Rightarrow$ $3(2x - 4) = 4x \Rightarrow 6x - 12 = 4x \Rightarrow$ $2x = 12 \Rightarrow x = 6$.

19. D. Check each statement separately.
    - 1 is not a prime, and for any integer $m > 1$, m^2 is not a prime since it has at least three factors: 1, m, and m^2. (I is false.)
    - If $m = 4$, then $\sqrt{m} = \sqrt{4} = 2$, which is a prime. (II is true.)
    - If $m = 1$, then $m^2 = \sqrt{m}$, since both are equal to 1. (III is true.)
    II and III only are true.

20. C. Use TACTICS 9-2 and 9-3. Since 100% of 10 is 10, let $x = 100$ and $y = 10$. When $x = 100$, choices C and E are each 10. Eliminate A, B, and D, and try some other numbers: 50% of 20 is 10. Of C and E, only $\dfrac{1000}{x} = 20$ when $x = 50$.

10 Quantitative Comparison Questions

- ■ **Testing Tactics**
- ■ **Practice Exercises**
- ■ **Answer Key**
- ■ **Answer Explanations**

In one of the two 30-minute mathematics sections on the SAT I, the first 15 questions are quantitative comparisons, which, like the multiple-choice questions, proceed from easy to difficult. Since, until you started preparing for the PSAT or SAT I, you probably had never seen questions of this type, you are not likely to be familiar with the various strategies for answering them. In this chapter you will learn all of the necessary tactics. After you master them, you will see that quantitative comparisons are the easiest of the three types of mathematics questions, and you will wish that there were more than just 15 of them. Questions 16–25 in this section are grid-in questions, which are discussed in Chapter 11.

On the first page of the SAT I section containing the quantitative comparison questions, you will find the same math facts that appear at the beginning of every mathematics section, as well as directions for answering quantitative comparisons and three examples. It will be similar to this:

Time—30 Minutes
25 Questions

You have 30 minutes to answer the 15 Quantitative Comparison questions and 10 Student-Produced Response questions in this section. You may use any blank space on the page for your work.

Notes:

- You may use a calculator whenever you feel it will be helpful.
- Use the diagrams provided to help you solve the problems. Unless you see the words "Note: Figure not drawn to scale" under a diagram, it has been drawn as accurately as possible. Unless it is stated that a figure is three-dimensional, you may assume it lies in a plane.

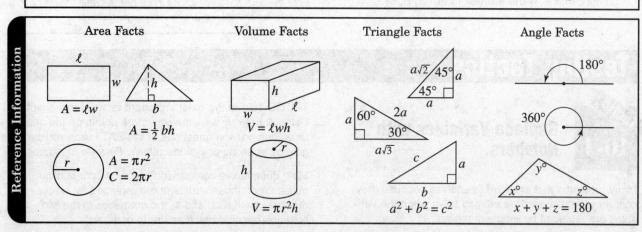

Reference Information

Area Facts

$A = \ell w$

$A = \frac{1}{2} bh$

$A = \pi r^2$
$C = 2\pi r$

Volume Facts

$V = \ell wh$

$V = \pi r^2 h$

Triangle Facts

$a^2 + b^2 = c^2$

Angle Facts

$x + y + z = 180$

Directions for Quantitative Comparison Questions

In each of questions 1–15, two quantities appear in boxes: one in Column A and one in Column B. You must compare them. The correct answer to a question is

A if the quantity in Column A is greater;
B if the quantity in Column B is greater;
C if the two quantities are equal;
D if it is impossible to determine which quantity is greater.

Notes:

- *The correct answer is <u>never</u> E.*
- Sometimes information about one or both of the quantities is centered above the two boxes.
- If the same symbol appears in both columns, it represents the same thing each time.
- All variables represent real numbers.

SAMPLE QUESTIONS		
Column A	Column B	ANSWERS
1. 2^3	3^2	Ⓐ ● Ⓒ Ⓓ Ⓔ
2. a	50	Ⓐ Ⓑ ● Ⓓ Ⓔ
3. $m + n$	mn	Ⓐ Ⓑ Ⓒ ● Ⓔ

(For question 2, a triangle is shown with angle $a°$ at top and angles 60° and 70° at the base.)

(For question 3, the condition $0 < m < n$ is centered above the two boxes.)

Before learning the different strategies for answering this type of question, let's clarify the directions you just read. In quantitative comparison questions there are two quantities, one in Column A and one in Column B, and it is your job to compare them. For these questions there are **only four possible answers**: A, B, C, and D. E is **never** the answer to a quantitative comparison question.

The correct answer to a quantitative comparison question is

A if the quantity in Column A is greater **all the time, no matter what**;
B if the quantity in Column B is greater **all the time, no matter what**;
C if the two quantities are equal **all the time, no matter what**;
D if it is impossible to determine which quantity is greater; that is, **if the answer is not A, B, or C**.

Therefore, *if you can find a single instance* in which the quantity in Column A is greater than the quantity in Column B, you can immediately eliminate two choices: B and C. The answer could be B only if the quantity in Column B were greater **all the time**; but you know of one instance when it isn't. Similarly, the quantities are not equal **all the time**, so the answer can't be C. The correct answer, therefore, *must be* A or D. Even if this is the hardest quantitative comparison on the test, and you have no idea of what to do next, you've narrowed down the correct answer to one of two choices, and you *must* guess. If it turns out that the quantity in Column A *is* greater all the time, then A is the answer; if it isn't, then the answer is D.

Helpful Hint

Right now, memorize the instructions given above for answering quantitative comparison questions. *When you take the SAT I, do not spend even one second reading the directions or looking at the sample problems.*

Testing Tactics

Replace Variables with Numbers.

10-1

Many problems that are hard to analyze because they contain variables become easy to solve when the variables are replaced by simple numbers.

TACTIC 10-1 is the most important tactic in this chapter. Using it properly will earn you more points on the quantitative comparison questions of the SAT I than you can gain by applying any of the others. *Be sure to master it!*

Most quantitative comparison questions contain variables. When those variables are replaced by simple numbers such as 0 and 1, the quantities in the two columns become much easier to compare.

The reason that TACTIC 10-1 is so important is that it *guarantees* that you won't have to leave out any quantitative comparison questions that involve variables and, even more important, that you will get most of those questions right! How is that possible? Try the following example, and then read the explanation very carefully.

Column A	Column B

Example 1.

$$a < b < c < d$$

ab	cd

Solution.

- Replace a, b, c, and d with easy-to-use numbers that satisfy the condition $a < b < c < d$: for example, $a = 1$, $b = 2$, $c = 5$, $d = 10$. [See the guidelines that follow to learn why 1, 2, 3, 4 is *not* the best choice.]
- Evaluate the two columns: $ab = (1)(2) = 2$, and $cd = (5)(10) = 50$.
- Therefore, *in this case*, the quantity in Column B is greater.
- Does that mean that B is the correct answer? Not necessarily. The quantity in Column B is greater this time, but will it be greater **every single time, no matter what**?
- What it does mean is that neither A nor C could possibly be the answer: Column A can't be greater **every single time, no matter what**, because it isn't greater *this* time; and the columns aren't equal **every single time, no matter what**, because they aren't equal *this* time.

The correct answer, therefore, is either B or D; and in the few seconds that it took you to plug in 1, 2, 5, and 10 for a, b, c, and d, you were able to eliminate two of the four choices. If you could do nothing else, you should now guess.

But, of course, *you can and will do something else.* You will try some other numbers. But *which* numbers? Since the first numbers you chose were positive, try some negative numbers this time.

- Let $a = -5$, $b = -3$, $c = -2$, and $d = -1$.
- Evaluate: $ab = (-5)(-3) = 15$ and $cd = (-2)(-1) = 2$.
- Therefore, *in this case*, the quantity in Column A is greater.
- Column B is *not* greater all the time. B is *not* the correct answer.
- The answer is **D**.

NOTE:

1. If for your second substitution you had chosen 3, 7, 8, 10 or 2, 10, 20, 35 or *any* four positive numbers, Column B would have been bigger. No matter how many substitutions you made, Column B would have been bigger each time, and you would have concluded that B was the answer. In fact, if the given condition had been $0 < a < b < c < d$, then B *would have been* the correct answer.

2. Therefore, knowing which numbers to plug in when you are using TACTIC 10-1 is critical. As long as you comply with the conditions written above the columns, you have complete freedom in choosing the numbers. Some choices, however, are much better than others.

Here are some guidelines for deciding which numbers to use when applying TACTIC 10-1.

1. **The very best numbers to use first are 1, 0, and –1.**

2. **Often, fractions between 0 and 1 are useful.**

3. **Occasionally, "large" numbers such as 10 or 100 can be used.**

4. **If there is more than one variable, it is permissible to replace each with the same number.**

5. **If a variable appears more than once in a problem, it must be replaced by the same number each time.**

6. **Do not impose any conditions not specifically stated.** In particular, do not assume that variables must represent integers. For example, 3 is not the only number that satisfies $2 < x < 4$ (2.1, 3.95, and π all work). The expression $a < b < c < d$ does not mean that a, b, c, d are *integers*, let alone *consecutive* integers (which is why we didn't choose 1, 2, 3, and 4 in Example 1), nor does it mean that any or all of these variables are *positive*.

When you replace the variables in a quantitative comparison question with numbers, remember:

If the value in Column A is ever greater:	eliminate B and C— the answer must be A or D.
If the value in Column B is ever greater:	eliminate A and C— the answer must be B or D.
If the two columns are ever equal:	eliminate A and B— the answer must be C or D.

You have learned that, no matter how hard a quantitative comparison question is, as soon as you replace the variables, two choices can *immediately* be eliminated. Then, if you can't decide between the other two, you *must* guess. This guarantees that, in addition to correctly answering all the questions that you know how to solve, you will be able to answer correctly at least half, and probably many more, of the questions that you don't know how to work.

Practice applying TACTIC 10-1 to these examples.

Column A | Column B

Example 2.

$$m > 0 \text{ and } m \neq 1$$

| m^2 | | m^3 |

Example 3.

| $11y$ | | $13y$ |

Example 4.

| $w + 10$ | | $w - 11$ |

Example 5.

| The perimeter of a rectangle whose area is 18 | | The perimeter of a rectangle whose area is 28 |

Example 6.

$$a = \frac{2}{3}t \qquad b = \frac{5}{6}t \qquad c = \frac{3}{5}b$$

| $3a$ | | $4c$ |

Solution 2. Use TACTIC 10-1. Replace m with numbers satisfying $m > 0$ and $m \neq 1$.

	Column A	Column B	Compare	Eliminate
Let $m = 2$.	$2^2 = 4$	$2^3 = 8$	B is greater.	A and C
Let $m = \frac{1}{2}$.	$\left(\frac{1}{2}\right)^2 = \frac{1}{4}$	$\left(\frac{1}{2}\right)^3 = \frac{1}{8}$	A is greater.	B

The answer is **D**.

Solution 3. Use TACTIC 10-1. There are no restrictions on y, so use the best numbers: 1, 0, –1.

	Column A	Column B	Compare	Eliminate
Let $y = 1$.	$11(1) = 11$	$13(1) = 13$	B is greater.	A and C
Let $y = 0$.	$11(0) = 0$	$13(0) = 0$	A and B are equal.	B

The answer is **D**.

Solution 4. Use TACTIC 10-1. There are no restrictions on w, so use the best numbers: 1, 0, –1.

	Column A	Column B	Compare	Eliminate
Let $w = 1$.	$1 + 10 = 11$	$1 - 11 = -10$	A is greater.	B and C
Let $w = 0$.	$0 + 10 = 10$	$0 - 11 = -11$	A is greater.	
Let $w = -1$.	$-1 + 10 = 9$	$-1 - 11 = -12$	A is greater.	

Guess **A**. We let w be a positive number, a negative number, and 0. Each time Column A was greater. That's not proof, but it justifies an educated guess. [The answer is A. Clearly, $10 > -11$; and, if we add w to each side, we get $w + 10 > w - 11$.]

Solution 5. What's this question doing here? How can we use TACTIC 10-1? Where are the variables that we're supposed to replace? Well, in each column there are rectangles, and the variables are their lengths and widths.

Column A	Column B	Compare	Eliminate
Choose a rectangle whose area is 18:	Choose a rectangle whose area is 28:	A and B are equal.	A and B
2, 9	4, 7		
Then the perimeter is $9 + 2 + 9 + 2 = 22$.	Then the perimeter is $7 + 4 + 7 + 4 = 22$.		

Choose a different rectangle of area 18 in Column A, and keep the same rectangle in Column B.

3, 6	4, 7		
Perimeter = $3 + 6 + 3 + 6 = 18$	Perimeter = 22	B is greater.	C

The answer is **D**.

Solution 6. Use TACTIC 10-1. First, try the easiest number: let $t = 0$. Then a, b, and c are each 0, and *in this case*, the columns are equal—they're both 0. Eliminate A and B. Now, try another number for t. The obvious choice is 1, but then a, b, and c will all be fractions. To avoid this complication, let $t = 6$. Then

$$a = \frac{2}{3}(6) = 4, \qquad b = \frac{5}{6}(6) = 5, \quad \text{and} \quad c = \frac{3}{5}(5) = 3.$$

This time, $3a = 3(4) = 12$ and $4b = 4(3) = 12$. *Again, the two columns are equal.*

Choose **C**.

NOTE: You should consider answering this question directly (i.e., without plugging in numbers) *only if you are very comfortable with both fractions and elementary algebra*. Here's the solution:

$$c = \frac{3}{5}b = \frac{3}{5}\left(\frac{5}{6}t\right) = \frac{1}{2}t.$$

Therefore, $2c = t$, and $4c = 2t$. Since $a = \frac{2}{3}t$, $3a = 2t$, so $4c = 3a$. The answer is **C**.

Tactic 10-2

Choose an Appropriate Number.

This is just like TACTIC 10-1. We are replacing a variable with a number, but the variable isn't mentioned in the problem.

Column A	Column B

Example 7.

Every band member is either 15, 16, or 17 years old. One-third of the band members are 16, and twice as many band members are 16 as 15.

The number of 17-year-old band members	The total number of 15- and 16-year-old band members

If the first sentence of Example 7 had been "There are n students in the school band, all of whom are 15, 16, or 17 years old," the problem would have been identical to this one. Using TACTIC 10-1, you could have replaced n with an easy-to-use number, such as 6, and solved: $\frac{1}{3}(6) = 2$ are 16 years old; then 1 is 15, and the remaining 3 are 17. The answer is **C**.

The point of TACTIC 10-2 is that you can plug in numbers even if there are no variables. As discussed in regard to TACTIC 9-3, this is especially useful on problems involving percents, in which case 100 is a good number, and problems involving fractions, in which case the LCD of the fractions is a good choice. However, the use of TACTIC 10-2 is not limited to these situations. Try using TACTIC 10-2 on the three problems that follow.

Column A	Column B

Example 8.

The perimeter of a square and the circumference of a circle are equal.

The area of the circle	The area of the square

Example 9.

Abe, Ben, and Cal divided a cash prize.

Abe took 50% of the money and spent $\frac{3}{5}$ of what he took.

Ben took 40% of the money and spent $\frac{3}{4}$ of what he took.

The amount that Abe spent	The amount that Ben spent

Column A	Column B

Example 10.

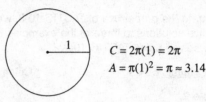

Amy types twice as fast as Kathy.
Kathy charges 50% more per page than Amy.

Amount Amy earns in 9 hours	Amount Kathy earns in 12 hours

Solution 8. First use TACTIC 8-1: draw a diagram.

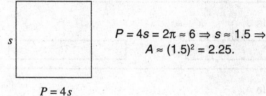

$$C = 2\pi(1) = 2\pi$$
$$A = \pi(1)^2 = \pi \approx 3.14$$

Then use TACTIC 10-2: choose an easy-to-use number. Let the radius of the circle be 1. Then its area is π. If s is the side of the square:

$$P = 4s = 2\pi \approx 6 \Rightarrow s \approx 1.5 \Rightarrow$$
$$A \approx (1.5)^2 = 2.25.$$

$$P = 4s$$
$$A = s^2$$

The answer is **A**.

Solution 9. Use TACTIC 10-2. Assume the prize was \$100. Then Abe took \$50 and spent

$\frac{3}{5}(\$50)^{10}_{1} = \$30$. Ben took \$40 and spent $\frac{3}{4}(\$40)^{10}_{1} = \$30$.

The answer is **C**.

Solution 10. Use TACTIC 10-2. Choose appropriate numbers. Assume Kathy can type 1 page per hour and Amy can type 2. Assume Amy charges \$1.00 per page and Kathy charges \$1.50. Then, in 9 hours, Amy types 18 pages, earning \$18.00. In 12 hours, Kathy types 12 pages, earning $12 \times \$1.50 = \$18.00$. The answer is **C**.

Tactic 10-3

Make the Problem Easier: Do the Same Thing to Each Column.

A quantitative comparison question can be treated as an equation or an inequality. Either:

Column A < Column B, or
Column A = Column B, or
Column A > Column B.

In solving an equation or an inequality, you can always add the same quantity to each side or subtract the same quantity from each side. Similarly, in solving a quantitative comparison problem, you can always add the same quantity to each column or subtract the same quantity from each column. You can also multiply or divide each side of an equation or inequality by the same quantity, *but in the case of <u>inequalities</u> you can do this only if the quantity is positive*. Since you don't know whether the columns are equal or unequal, you cannot multiply or divide by a variable *unless you know that it is positive*. If the quantities in each column are positive, you may square them or take their square roots.

To illustrate the proper use of TACTIC 10-3, we will give alternative solutions to three of the examples that we already solved using TACTIC 10-1.

Column A	Column B

Example 2.

$$m > 0 \text{ and } m \neq 1$$

m^2	m^3

Example 3.

$11y$	$13y$

Example 4.

$w + 10$	$w - 11$

Column A	Column B

Solution 2. Divide each column by m^2 (That's OK—m^2 is positive): $\dfrac{m^2}{m^2} = 1$ $\dfrac{m^3}{m^2} = m$

This is a much easier comparison. Which is greater, m or 1? We don't know. We know $m > 0$ and $m \neq 1$, but m could be greater than or less than 1. The answer is **D**.

Solution 3.
Subtract $11y$
from each column: $11y - 11y = 0$ $13y - 11y = 2y$

Since there are no restrictions, y and $2y$ could be greater than, less than, or equal to 0. The answer is **D**.

Solution 4.
Subtract w
from each column:

$$\begin{array}{r} w + 10 \\ -\ w \\ \hline 10 \end{array} \qquad \begin{array}{r} w - 11 \\ -\ w \\ \hline -11 \end{array}$$

Clearly, 10 is greater than −11. The answer is **A**.

Here are five more examples on which to practice TACTIC 10-3.

Column A	Column B

Example 11.

$\dfrac{1}{3} + \dfrac{1}{4} + \dfrac{1}{9}$	$\dfrac{1}{9} + \dfrac{1}{3} + \dfrac{1}{5}$

Example 12.

$(43 + 59)(17 - 6)$	$(43 + 59)(17 + 6)$

Example 13.

$(43 - 59)(43 - 49)$	$(43 - 59)(43 + 49)$

Example 14.

a is a negative number

a^2	$-a^2$

Example 15.

$\dfrac{\sqrt{20}}{2}$	$\dfrac{5}{\sqrt{5}}$

Column A	Column B

Solution 11.
Subtract
$\dfrac{1}{3}$ and $\dfrac{1}{9}$ from
each column: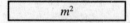

Since $\dfrac{1}{4} > \dfrac{1}{5}$, the answer is **A**.

Solution 12.
Divide each column by $(43 + 59)$:

$$\cancel{(43 + 59)}(17 - 6) \qquad \cancel{(43 + 59)}(17 + 6)$$

Clearly, $(17 + 6) > (17 - 6)$. The answer is **B**.

Solution 13.
CAUTION: $(43 - 59)$ is negative, and you *may not* divide the columns by a negative number.

The easiest alternative: Column A, being the product of two negative numbers, is positive, whereas Column B is negative. The answer is **A**.

| Column A | Column B | | Column A | Column B |

Solution 14.
Add a^2 to each column:

$$a^2 + a^2 = 2a^2 \qquad -a^2 + a^2 = 0$$

Since a is negative, $2a^2$ is positive. The answer is **A**.

Solution 15.
Square each column:

$$\left(\frac{\sqrt{20}}{2}\right)^2 = \frac{20}{4} = 5 \qquad \left(\frac{5}{\sqrt{5}}\right)^2 = \frac{25}{5} = 5$$

The answer is **C**.

Tactic 10-4 — Ask "Could They Be Equal?" and "Must They Be Equal?"

TACTIC 10-4 has many applications, but is most useful when one column contains a variable and the other contains a number. In this situation ask yourself, "Could they be equal?" If the answer is "yes," eliminate A and B, and then ask, "Must they be equal?" If the second answer is "yes," then C is correct; if the second answer is "no," then choose D. When the answer to "Could they be equal?" is "no," we usually know right away what the correct answer is. In both questions: "Could they be equal?" and "Must they be equal," the word *they* refers, of course, to the quantities in Column A and Column B.

Let's look at a few examples.

| Column A | Column B |

Example 16.

The sides of a triangle are 3, 4, and x.

| x | 5 |

Example 17.

$$69 < 4w < 75$$

| w | 18 |

Example 18.

Bank A has 10 tellers and bank B has 20 tellers.
Each bank has more female tellers than male tellers.

| The number of female tellers at bank A | The number of female tellers at bank B |

Example 19.

$$(m + 1)(m + 2)(m + 3) = 720$$

| $m + 2$ | 10 |

| Column A | Column B |

Example 20.

| The perimeter of a rectangle whose area is 21 | 20 |

Solution 16. Could they be equal? Could $x = 5$? Of course. That's the all-important 3-4-5 right triangle. Eliminate A and B. Must they be equal? Must $x = 5$? If you're not sure, try drawing an acute or an obtuse triangle. The answer is "no." Actually, x can be any number satisfying the inequality $1 < x < 7$. (See KEY FACT J12, the triangle inequality, and the figure below.) The answer is **D**.

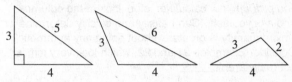

Solution 17. Could they be equal? Could $w = 18$? If $w = 18$, then $4w = 72$, so, they could be equal. Eliminate A and B. Must they be equal? Must $w = 18$? Could w be more or less than 18? BE CAREFUL: $4 \times 17 = 68$, which is too small; and $4 \times 19 = 76$, which is too large. Therefore, the only *integer* that w could be is 18, but w *doesn't have to be an integer*. The *only* restriction is that $69 < 4w < 75$. If $4w$ were 70 or 71.6 or 73, then w would not be 18. The answer is **D**.

Solution 18. Could they be equal? Could the number of female tellers be the same in both banks? No. More than half (i.e., more than 10) of bank B's 20 tellers are female, but bank A has only 10 tellers in all. The answer is **B**.

Solution 19. Could they be equal? Could $m + 2 = 10$? No; if $m + 2 = 10$, then $m + 1 = 9$, $m + 3 = 11$, and $9 \times 10 \times 11 = 990$, which is too large. The answer is *not* C; and since $m + 2$ clearly has to be smaller than 10, the answer is **B**.

Solution 20. Could they be equal? Could a rectangle whose area is 21 have a perimeter of 20? Yes, if its length is 7 and its width is 3: $7 + 3 + 7 + 3 = 20$. Eliminate A and B. Must they be equal? If you're *sure* that there is no other rectangle with an area of 21, then choose C; if you're *not* sure, guess between C and D; if you *know* there are other rectangles of area 21, choose D.

There are other possibilities—lots of them; here are a 7×3 rectangle and a few others:

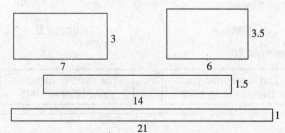

10-5 Don't Calculate: Compare.

Avoid unnecessary calculations. You don't have to determine the exact values of the quantities in Columns A and B; you just have to compare them.

TACTIC 10-5 is the special application of TACTIC 8-7 (Don't do more than you have to) to quantitative comparison questions. The proper use of TACTIC 10-5 allows you to solve many quantitative comparisons without doing tedious calculations, thereby saving you valuable test time that you can use on other questions. *Before you pick up your calculator*, stop, look at the columns, and ask yourself, "Can I easily and quickly determine which quantity is greater without doing any arithmetic?" Consider Examples 21 and 22, which look very similar but really aren't.

Column A	Column B

Example 21.

41×55	47×48

Example 22.

41×55	37×38

Solution 21. Example 21 is very easy. Just use your calculator to multiply: $41 \times 55 = 2255$ and $47 \times 48 = 2256$. The answer is **B**.

Solution 22. Example 22 is even easier. *Don't* multiply. In less time than it takes to pick up your calculator, you can see that $41 > 37$ and $55 > 38$, so clearly $41 \times 55 > 37 \times 38$. The answer is **A**. *You don't get extra credit for taking the time to determine the value of each product!*

Remember: do not start calculating immediately. Always take a second or two to glance at each column. In Example 21 it's not at all clear which product is larger, so you have to multiply. In Example 22, however, no calculations are necessary.

These are problems on which poor test-takers use their calculators and good test-takers think! Practicing TACTIC 10-5 will help you become a good test-taker.

Now, test your understanding of TACTIC 10-5 by solving these problems.

Column A	Column B

Example 23.

The number of years from 1492 to 1929	The number of years from 1429 to 1992

Column A	Column B

Example 24.

$43^2 + 27^2$	$(43 + 27)^2$

Example 25.

$12(34 + 56)$	$12 \times 34 + 12 \times 56$

Example 26.

Howie earned a 75 on each of his first three math tests and an 80 on the fourth and fifth tests.

Howie's average after four tests.	Howie's average after five tests.

Solutions 23–26.

Using Your Calculator to Do the Calculations	Using TACTIC 10-5 to Avoid Doing the Calculations
23. Column A: 1929 − 1492 = 437 Column B: 1992 − 1429 = 563 The answer is **B**.	23. The subtraction is easy enough, but why do it? The dates in Column **B** start earlier and end later. Clearly, they span more years. You don't need to know how many years. The answer is **B**.
24. Column A: $43^2 + 27^2$ = 1849 + 729 = 2578 Column B: $(43 + 27)^2$ = 70^2 = 4900 The answer is **B**.	24. For any positive numbers a and b: $(a + b)^2 > a^2 + b^2$. Do the calculations only if you don't know this fact. The answer is **B**.
25. Column A: 12(34 + 56) = 12(90) = 1080 Column B: $12 \times 34 + 12 \times 56$ = 408 + 672 = 1080 The answer is **C**.	25. Leave your calculator on the desk. This is just the distributive law (KEY FACT A20), which states that, for *any* numbers a, b, c: $a(b + c) = ab + ac$. The answer is **C**.
26. Column A: $\dfrac{75 + 75 + 75 + 80}{4} =$ $\dfrac{305}{4} = 76.25$ Column B: $\dfrac{75 + 75 + 75 + 80 + 80}{5} =$ $\dfrac{385}{5} = 77$ The answer is **B**.	26. Remember that you want to know which average is higher, *not* what the averages are. After four tests Howie's average is clearly less than 80, so an 80 on the fifth test had to *raise* his average (KEY FACT E4). The answer is **B**.

CAUTION: TACTIC 10-5 is important, but *don't spend a lot of time looking for ways to avoid a simple calculation.*

Consider Example 27.

Column A	Column B

Example 27.

$2 + \sqrt{3.5}$	$2\sqrt{3.5}$

 Solution. For this example, most students will find it easier to calculate than to reason the answer out. On your calculator, just get $\sqrt{3.5} \approx 1.87$. Then

$$2 + \sqrt{3.5} \approx 2 + 1.87 = 3.87,$$

whereas $2\sqrt{3.5} \approx 2 \times 1.87 \approx 3.74$. The answer is **A**. (The reasoning is as follows: $2\sqrt{3.5} = \sqrt{3.5} + \sqrt{3.5}$, which is less than $2 + \sqrt{3.5}$ since $\sqrt{3.5} < 2$.)

Tactic 10-6 — Know When to Avoid Choice D.

If the quantities in Columns A and B are both fixed numbers, the answer cannot be D.

Notice that D was not the correct answer to any of the examples discussed under TACTIC 10-5. Those problems had no variables. The quantities in each column were all specific numbers. In each of the next four examples, the quantities in Columns A and B are also fixed numbers. In each case, either the two numbers are equal or one is greater than the other. The answer can *always* be determined, and so D *cannot be the correct answer to any of these problems*. If, while taking the SAT I, you find a problem of this type that you can't solve, just guess: A, B, or C. Now try these four examples.

Column A	Column B

Example 28.

The number of seconds in one day	The number of days in one century

Example 29.

The area of a square whose sides are 4	Twice the area of an equilateral triangle whose sides are 4

Example 30.

Three fair coins are flipped.

The probability of getting one head	The probability of getting two heads

Column A	Column B

Example 31.

The time it takes to drive 40 miles at 35 miles per hour	The time it takes to drive 35 miles at 40 miles per hour

Here's the important point to remember: don't choose D because *you* can't determine which quantity is bigger; choose D only if *nobody* could make this judgment. *You* may or may not know how to compute the number of seconds in a day, the area of an equilateral triangle, or a certain probability, but *these calculations can be made*.

Solutions 28–31.

Direct Calculation	Solution Using Various TACTICS
28. Recall the facts you need and calculate. 60 seconds = 1 minute, 60 minutes = 1 hour, 24 hours = 1 day, 365 days = 1 year, and 100 years = 1 century. Column A: $60 \times 60 \times 24 = 86,400$ Column B: $365 \times 100 = 36,500$ Even if we throw in some extra days for leap years, the answer is clearly **A**.	28. The point of TACTIC 10-6 is that, even if you have no idea how to calculate the number of seconds in a day, you should not omit this question. The answer cannot be D, and it would be an incredible coincidence if these two quantities were actually equal, so eliminate C. *Guess* between A and B.
29. Calculate both areas. (See KEY FACT J15 for the easy way to find the area of an equilateral triangle.) Column A: $A = s^2 = 4^2 = 16$ Column B: $A = \dfrac{s^2\sqrt{3}}{4} = \dfrac{4^2\sqrt{3}}{4} = 4\sqrt{3}$; and *twice* A is $8\sqrt{3} \approx 13.86$. The answer is **A**.	29. Use TACTIC 10-5: don't calculate—compare. Since the height of the triangle is less than 4, its area is less than $\frac{1}{2}(4)(4) = 8$, and twice its area is less than 16, the area of the square. The answer is **A**.

	Direct Calculation	Solution Using Various TACTICS		Direct Calculation	Solution Using Various TACTICS
30.	When a coin is flipped 3 times, there are 8 possible outcomes: HHH, HHT, HTH, HTT, THH, THT, TTH, and TTT. Of these, 3 have one head and 3 have two heads. Each probability is $\frac{3}{8}$. The answer is **C**.	30.	Don't forget TACTIC 10-5. Even if you know how, you don't *have to* calculate the probabilities. When three coins are flipped, getting two heads means getting one tail. Therefore, the probability of two heads equals the probability of one tail, which by symmetry equals the probability of one head. If you don't know how to calculate the probabilities, TACTIC 10-6 allows you to eliminate D and guess.	31.	Since $d = rt$, $t = \frac{d}{r}$ (see Section 12-H). Column A: $\frac{40}{35} \approx 1.142$ hours Column B: $\frac{35}{40} = 0.875$ hour The answer is **A**.	31.	You *do* need to know these formulas, but *not* for this problem. At 35 miles per hour it takes more than 1 hour to drive 40 miles. At 40 miles per hour it takes less than 1 hour to drive 35 miles. Choose **A**.

Practice Questions

	Column A	Column B
	$a < 0$	
1.	$4a$	a^4
	$x > 0$	
2.	$10x$	$\dfrac{10}{x}$
	$ab < 0$	
3.	$(a + b)^2$	$a^2 + b^2$

a, b, and c are the measures of the angles of isosceles triangle ABC.
x, y, and z are the measures of the angles of right triangle XYZ.

	Column A	Column B
4.	The average of a, b, and c	The average of x, y, and z

In the addition problem at the right, each letter stands for a different digit:

$$\begin{array}{r} AB \\ + CD \\ \hline ADC \end{array}$$

5.	A	1
6.	$99 + 299 + 499$	$103 + 305 + 507$

	Column A	Column B
7.	The area of a circle whose radius is 17	The area of a circle whose diameter is 35

Line ℓ goes through $(1,1)$ and $(5,2)$.
Line m is perpendicular to ℓ.

8.	The slope of line ℓ	The slope of line m

x is a positive integer.

9.	The number of multiples of 3 between 100 and $x + 100$	The number of multiples of 7 between 100 and $x + 100$

x, y, and z are three consecutive integers between 300 and 400.

10.	The average (arithmetic mean) of x and z	The average (arithmetic mean) of x, y, and z

$x + y = 5$
$y - x = -5$

11.	y	0

Column A	Column B
Stores A and B sell the same television set. The regular price at store A is 10% less than the regular price at store B.	

	Column A	Column B
12.	The price of the television set when store A has a 10% off sale	The price of the television set when store B has a 20% off sale

	Column A	Column B
13.	$\dfrac{7}{8}$	$\left(\dfrac{7}{8}\right)^5$

$$x > 0$$

	Column A	Column B
14.	$\sqrt{x}$	x

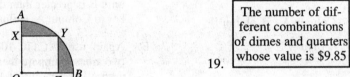

O is the center of the circle of radius 6.
$OXYZ$ is a square.

	Column A	Column B
15.	The area of the shaded region	12

Column A	Column B
The number of square inches in the surface area of a cube is equal to the number of cubic inches in its volume.	

	Column A	Column B
16.	The length of an edge of the cube	6 inches

$$1 < x < 4$$

	Column A	Column B
17.	πx	x^2

$$\frac{5b^2}{7b^2} = \frac{5}{7}$$

	Column A	Column B
18.	b	1

	Column A	Column B
19.	The number of different combinations of dimes and quarters whose value is $9.85	20

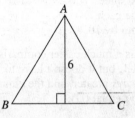

Note: Figure not drawn to scale

	Column A	Column B
20.	The area of $\triangle ABC$	3

Answer Key

1.	**B**	5.	**C**	9.	**D**	13.	**A**	17.	**D**
2.	**D**	6.	**B**	10.	**C**	14.	**D**	18.	**D**
3.	**B**	7.	**B**	11.	**C**	15.	**B**	19.	**C**
4.	**C**	8.	**A**	12.	**A**	16.	**C**	20.	**D**

Answer Explanations

Note: For many problems, an alternative solution, indicated by two asterisks (**), follows the first solution. When this occurs, one of the solutions is the direct mathematical one and the other is based on one of the tactics discussed in this chapter.

1. **B.** Since $a < 0$, $4a$ is negative, whereas a^4 is positive.
   **Use TACTIC 10-1. Replace a with numbers satisfying $a < 0$.

	Column A	Column B	Compare	Eliminate
Let $a = -1$.	$4(-1) = -4$	$(-1)^4 = 1$	B is greater.	A and C
Let $a = -2$.	$4(-2) = -8$	$(-2)^4 = 16$	B is greater.	

   Both times, Column B was greater: choose B.

2. **D.** Use TACTIC 10-1. When $x = 1$, the columns are equal; when $x = 2$, they aren't.
   **Use TACTIC 10-3.

	Column A	Column B
	$10x$	$\dfrac{10}{x}$
Multiply each column by x (this is OK since $x > 0$):	$10x^2$	10
Divide each column by 10:	x^2	1

   This is a much easier comparison. x^2 *could* equal 1, but it doesn't have to. Neither column is *always* greater, and the columns are not *always* equal (D).

3. **B.** Use TACTIC 10-3.

	Column A	Column B
Expand Column A:	$(a + b)^2 =$	
	$a^2 + 2ab + b^2$	$a^2 + b^2$
Subtract $a^2 + b^2$ from each column:	$2ab$	0

   Since it is given that $ab < 0$, then $2ab < 0$.
   **If you can't expand $(a + b)^2$, use TACTIC 10-1. Replace a and b with numbers satisfying $ab < 0$.

	Column A	Column B	Compare	Eliminate
Let $a = 1$ and $b = -1$.	$(1 + -1)^2 =$ 0	$1^2 + (-1)^2 =$ $1 + 1 = 2$	B is greater.	A and C
Let $a = 3$ and $b = -5$.	$(3 + -5)^2 =$ $(-2)^2 = 4$	$3^2 + (-5)^2 =$ $9 + 25 = 34$	B is greater.	

   Both times, Column B was greater: choose B.

4. **C.** The average of three numbers is their sum divided by 3. Since in *any* triangle the sum of the measures of the three angles is 180° (KEY FACT J1), the average in each column is equal to $180 \div 3 = 60$ (C).
   **Use TACTIC 10-1. Pick values for the measures of the angles. For example, in isosceles triangle ABC choose 70,70, 40; in right triangle XYZ, choose 30, 60, 90. Each average is 60. Choose C.

5. **C.** Clearly, A isn't *less* than 1, since 0 can't be the first digit of a number. Could A be *greater* than 1? No, the sum of two 2-digit numbers *must be less than 200* (even 99 + 99 < 200). Therefore, A must be 1, and the columns are equal (C).
   **You could find the complete solution ($A = 1$, $B = 9$, $C = 8$, $D = 0$), but you shouldn't waste your time. (See Section 12-P for the best methods to solve alphanumeric problems.)

6. **B.** This can be solved in less than 30 seconds with a calculator, but in only 5 seconds without one! Use TACTIC 10-5: don't calculate; compare. Each of the three numbers in Column B is greater than the corresponding number in Column A. Column B is greater.

7. **B.** Again, use TACTIC 10-5: don't calculate the two areas; compare them. The circle in Column A has a radius of 17, and so its diameter is 34. Since the circle in Column B has a larger diameter, its area is greater.

8. **A.** Again, use TACTIC 10-5: don't calculate either slope. Quickly, make a rough sketch of line ℓ, going through (1,1) and (5,2), and draw line m perpendicular to it. Line ℓ has a positive slope (it slopes upward), whereas line m has a negative slope. Column A is greater.

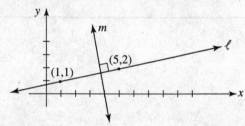

   (*Note:* The slope of ℓ is $\dfrac{1}{4}$, and the slope of m is –4. See Section 12-N for all the facts you need to know about slopes.)
   **If you don't know these facts about slopes, use TACTIC 10-6. The answer cannot be D; and if two lines intersect, their slopes cannot be equal, so eliminate C. Guess A or B.

9. **D.** Every third integer is a multiple of 3, and every seventh integer is a multiple of 7, so in a large interval there will be many more multiples of 3. In a very small interval, however, there may be no multiples or possibly just one

of each. Neither column is *always* greater, and the columns are not *always* equal (D).
**Use TACTIC 10-1. Let $x = 1$. Between 100 and 101 there are *no* multiples of 3 and *no* multiples of 7. Eliminate A and B. Now, choose a large number for x: 100, for example. Between 100 and 200 there are many more multiples of 3 than there are of 7. Eliminate C.

10. **C.** Since x, y, and z are consecutive, $y = x + 1$ and $z = x + 2$.
Column A: x is 1 less than y, and z is 1 more than y. Their average is y.
Column B: the average of three consecutive integers is always the middle one: y. (See Section 12-E.) The columns are equal (C).
**Use TACTIC 10-1: replace x, y, and z with three consecutive integers between 300 and 400—say, 318, 319, and 320, and use your calculator to find the averages.

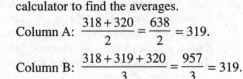

Column A: $\dfrac{318 + 320}{2} = \dfrac{638}{2} = 319$.

Column B: $\dfrac{318 + 319 + 320}{3} = \dfrac{957}{3} = 319$.

11. **C.** Use TACTIC 8-14:
add the equations.
$$x + y = 5$$
$$+ \ y - x = -5$$
$$2y = 0$$
Since $2y = 0$, $y = 0$. The columns are equal (C).
**Use TACTIC 10-4. Could $y = 0$? In each equation, if $y = 0$, then $x = 5$, so y *can* equal 0. Eliminate A and B, and either guess between C and D or try to continue. Must $y = 0$? Yes; when you have two equations in two variables, there is only one solution, so nothing else is possible.

12. **A.** Repeated discounts of a% and b% are *always* less than a single discount of $(a + b)$% (KEY FACT C5). Store A reduced store B's price by 10% and then another 10% when the TV went on sale. That's *less of a discount* than store B's 20% discount, so store A's price is higher. Column A is greater.
**Use TACTIC 10-2: choose an appropriate number. *The best number to use in percent problems is 100*, so assume that the regular price of the television in store B is 100 (the units don't matter). Since 10% of 100 is 10, the regular price in store A is $100 - 10 = 90$.
Column A: 10% of 90 is 9, so the sale price in store A is $90 - 9 = 81$.
Column B: 20% of 100 is 20, so the sale price in store B is $100 - 20 = 80$. (See Section 12-C.)

13. **A.** This is very easy with a calculator (see below), but even easier without one *if* you know KEY FACT A24: If $0 < x < 1$ and $n > 1$,

then $x^n < x$. Since $\dfrac{7}{8}$ is less than 1, then

$\left(\dfrac{7}{8}\right)^5 < \dfrac{7}{8}$. Column A is greater.

**Use your calculator:

$\left(\dfrac{7}{8}\right)^5 = \dfrac{7 \times 7 \times 7 \times 7 \times 7}{8 \times 8 \times 8 \times 8 \times 8} = \dfrac{16,807}{32,768} \approx 0.513$.

Since $\dfrac{7}{8} = 0.875$, Column A is greater. You can find the answer faster with a scientific calculator: just raise $\dfrac{7}{8}$ to the fifth power. But that's still not as fast as just knowing that a positive number less than 1 raised to the fifth power is less than the original number.

14. **D.** Use TACTIC 10-1. When $x = 1$, the columns are equal. When $x = 2$ (or any other positive number), they're not. Neither column is *always* greater, and the columns are not always equal (D).
**Use TACTIC 10-3: do the same thing to each column.

	Column A	Column B
	$\sqrt{x}$	x
Square each column (this is OK since $x > 0$):	x	x^2
Divide each column by x:	1	x

This is a much easier comparison. Although x could equal 1, it doesn't have to.

15. **B.** The area of the shaded region is the area of quarter-circle AOB minus the area of square $OXYZ$. Since $r = OA = 6$, the area of the quarter-circle is $\dfrac{1}{4} \pi r^2 = \dfrac{1}{4} \, 36\pi = 9\pi$. OY, the diagonal of the square, is 6 (since it is a radius of the circle), so OZ, the side of the square, is $\dfrac{6}{\sqrt{2}}$ (KEY FACT J8). Therefore, the area of the square is $\left(\dfrac{6}{\sqrt{2}}\right)^2 = \dfrac{36}{2} = 18$. Finally, the area of the shaded region is $9\pi - 18$, which is approximately 10. Column B is greater.
**The solution above requires several steps. [See Sections 12-J, 12-K, and 12-L to review any of the facts used.] If you can't reason through this solution, you still should answer the question. Use TACTICS 10-5 and 8-2. The shaded region has a definite area, which is either 12, more than 12, or less than 12. Eliminate D. Also, the area of a curved region almost always involves π, so assume that the

area isn't exactly 12. Eliminate C. You can now *guess* between A and B; but if you trust the diagram (as you should), and if you know that the area of the circle is 36π, so that the area of the quarter-circle is 9π or about 28, you can estimate the area of the shaded region. It's less than half of the quarter-circle, so less than 14, and probably less than 12. Guess B.

16. **C.** Use TACTIC 10-4. Could the length of the edge be 6 inches? Test. If each edge measures 6 inches, the area of each face is $6 \times 6 = 36$ square inches. Also, since a cube has six faces, the total surface area is $6 \times 36 = 216$ square inches. The volume of the cube is $6^3 = 216$ cubic inches, so the columns could be equal. Eliminate A and B. If you have a sense that this is the only cube with this property, choose C. In fact, if you had no idea how to do this, you might use TACTIC 10-6, assume that there is only one way, eliminate D, and then guess C.
**The direct solution is simple enough if you know the formulas. The area is $6e^2$, and the volume is e^3: $6e^2 = e^3 \Rightarrow 6 = e$.

17. **D.** There are several ways to do this. Use TACTIC 10-1: plug in a number for x. If $x = 2$, Column A is 2π, which is slightly more than 6, and Column B is $2^2 = 4$. Column A is greater, so eliminate B and C. Must Column A be greater? If the only other number you try is 3, you'll think so, because $3^2 = 9$, but $3\pi > 9$. Remember, however, that x does not have to be an integer: $3.9^2 > 15$, whereas $3.9\pi < 4\pi$, which is a little over 12. Neither column is *always* greater, and the columns are not *always* equal (D).
**Use TACTIC 10-4. Could $\pi x = x^2$? Yes, if $x = \pi$. Must $x = \pi$? No.
**Use TACTIC 10-3. Divide each side by x: now, Column A is π and Column B is x. Which is bigger, π or x? You can't tell.

18. **D.** Since there is a variable in Column A and a number in Column B, use TACTIC 10-4: ask, "Could they be equal?" Could $b = 1$? Of course. Eliminate A and B. Must $b = 1$? In other words, could b be anything else? Sure; if

$b = -1$, $\dfrac{5b^2}{7b^2} = \dfrac{5(-1)^2}{7(-1)^2} = \dfrac{5}{7}$. In fact, b could be *any* number (except 0); and if you see that right away, you don't have to try any numbers. Neither column is *always* greater, and the columns are not *always* equal (D).

19. **C.** Many students would find this question difficult and would tend to omit it. They shouldn't. Whether or not you can figure out how many combinations there are, the answer is some fixed number, and so by TACTIC 10-6 the answer cannot be D. If that's as far as you can get, you should guess A, B, or C. Unless you have some hunch to follow, guess C.
**In fact, the answer is C. Divide 985 by 25 to see the greatest number of quarters there could be: $985 \div 25 = 39.4$. Then there are at most 39 quarters, and 1 combination would be 39 quarters and 1 dime. Since 38 quarters are worth $9.50, and you can't make 35¢ with dimes, you can't have 38 quarters. Very shortly, you should realize that you need an odd number of quarters: 1, 3, 5, ... , 39. This is a list of the first 20 odd numbers. The columns are equal (C).

20. **D.** Use TACTIC 10-4. Could the area of $\triangle ABC = 3$? Since the height is 6, the area would be 3 only if the base were 1: $\dfrac{1}{2}(1)(6) = 3$. Could $BC = 1$? Sure (see the figure). Must the base be 1? Of course not. Neither column is *always* greater, and the columns are not *always* equal (D).

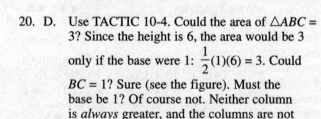

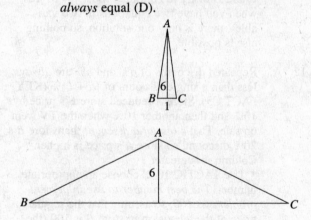

11 Grid-in Questions

- **Practice in Gridding In Numbers**
- **Testing Tactics**
- **Practice Exercises**
- **Answer Key**
- **Answer Explanations**

On the SAT I, the 30-minute section that contains the 15 quantitative comparisons has 10 additional questions for which no choices are given. These are the grid-in problems, which represent the type of question with which you are most familiar—you solve a problem and then write the answer on your answer sheet. The only difference is that, on the SAT I, you must enter the answer on a special grid that can be read by a computer.

The answer sheet for this section will have 10 blank grids, one for each question. Each one will look exactly like the grid on the left, below. After solving a problem, the first step is to write the answer in the four boxes at the top of the grid. You then blacken the appropriate oval under each box. For example, if your answer to a question is 2450, you write 2450 at the top of the grid, one digit in each box, and then in each column blacken the oval that contains the number you wrote at the top of the column. (See the grid on the right, below.) This is not difficult; but there are some special rules concerning grid-in questions, so let's go over them before you practice gridding in some numbers.

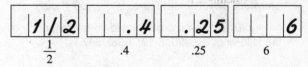

1. The only symbols that appear in the grid are the digits 0 to 9, a decimal point, and a slash (/), used to write fractions. Keep in mind that, since there is

no negative sign, ***the answer to every grid-in question is a positive number or zero***.

2. Be aware that you will receive credit for a correct answer no matter where you grid it. For example, the answer 17 could be gridded in any of three positions:

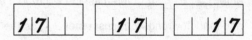

Neverthelesss, we suggest that you consistently ***write all your answers*** the way numbers are usually displayed—***to the right, with blank spaces at the left***.

1/2		.4		.25			6
$\frac{1}{2}$		.4		.25			6

3. ***Never round off your answers***. If a decimal answer will fit in the grid and you round it off, your answer will be marked wrong. For example, if the answer is .148 and you correctly round it off to the nearest hundredth and enter .15, you will receive *no credit*. If a decimal answer will not fit in the grid, enter a decimal point in the first column, followed by the first three digits. For example, if your answer is 0.454545..., enter it as .454. You would receive credit if you rounded it to .455, but don't. You might occasionally make a mistake in rounding, whereas you'll *never* make a mistake if you just copy the first three digits. *Note:* If the correct answer has more than two decimal digits, *you must use all four columns of the grid*. You will receive *no credit* for .4 or .5 or .45. (These answers are not accurate enough.)

4. ***Never write a 0 before the decimal point***. The first column of the grid doesn't even have a 0 in it. If the correct answer is 0.3333..., you must grid it as .333. You can't grid 0.33, and 0.3 is not accurate enough.

5. *Never reduce fractions.*

   - If your answer is a fraction that will fit in the grid, such as $\frac{2}{3}$ or $\frac{4}{18}$ or $\frac{6}{34}$, *just enter it*. Don't waste time reducing it or converting it to a decimal.
   - If your answer is a fraction that won't fit in the grid, do not attempt to reduce it; use your calculator to *convert it to a decimal*. For example, $\frac{24}{65}$ won't fit in a grid—it would require five spaces: 2 4 / 6 5. Don't waste even a few seconds trying to reduce it; just divide on your calculator, and enter .369. Unlike $\frac{24}{65}$, the fraction $\frac{24}{64}$ can be reduced—to $\frac{12}{32}$, which doesn't help, or to $\frac{6}{16}$ or $\frac{3}{8}$, both of which could be entered. *Don't do it!* Reducing a fraction takes time, and you might make a mistake. You won't make a mistake if you just use your calculator: 24 ÷ 64 = .375.

6. *Be aware that you can never enter a mixed number.* If your answer is $2\frac{1}{2}$, you *cannot* leave a space and enter your answer as 2 1/2. Also, if you enter $\boxed{2\ 1\ /\ 2}$, the machine will read it as $\frac{21}{2}$ and mark it wrong. You must enter $2\frac{1}{2}$ as the improper fraction $\frac{5}{2}$ or as the decimal 2.5.

7. Since full credit is given for any equivalent answer, use these guidelines to *enter your answer in the simplest way*. If your answer is $\frac{6}{9}$, you should enter 6/9. (However, credit would be given for any of the following: 2/3, 4/6, 8/12, .666, .667.)

8. Sometimes grid-in questions have more than one correct answer. On these questions, *grid in only one of the acceptable answers*. For example, if a question asked for a positive number less than 100 that was divisible by both 5 and 7, you could enter *either* 35 *or* 70, but not both. Similarly, if a question asked for a number between $\frac{3}{7}$ and $\frac{5}{9}$, you could enter any *one* of more than 100 possibilities: fractions such as $\frac{1}{2}$ and $\frac{4}{9}$ or *any* decimal between .429 and .554—.43 or .499 or .52, for example.

9. *Keep in mind that there is no penalty for a wrong answer to a grid-in question*. Therefore, you might as well guess, even if you have no idea what to do. As you will see shortly, there are some strategies for making intelligent guesses.

10. Be sure to *grid every answer very carefully*. The computer does not read what you have written in the boxes; it reads only the answer in the grid. If the correct answer to a question is 100 and you write 100 in the boxes, but accidentally grid in 200, you get *no* credit.

11. If you know that the answer to a question is 100, can you just grid it in and not bother writing it on top? Yes, you will get full credit, and so some SAT guides recommend that you don't waste time writing the answer. This is terrible advice. Instead, *write each answer in the boxes*. It takes less than 2 seconds per answer to do this, and it definitely cuts down on careless errors in gridding. More important, if you go back to check your work, it is much easier to read what's in the boxes on top than what's in the grid.

12. Be aware that the smallest number that can be gridded is 0; the largest is 9999. No number greater than 100 can have a decimal point. The largest number less than 100 that can be gridded is 99.9; the smallest number greater than 100 that can be gridded is 101.

Practice in Gridding-in Numbers

Now, check your understanding of these guidelines. Assume that the following 10 numbers are your answers to a set of grid-in questions, which will always be questions 16–25 in the section in which they appear. Use the empty numbered grids that follow to enter your answers.

16. 123

17. $\frac{7}{11}$

18. $2\frac{3}{4}$

19. $\frac{8}{30}$

20. 1.1111...

21. 0

22. $\frac{48}{80}$

23. $\frac{83}{100}$

24. $\frac{19}{15}$

25. $3\frac{5}{18}$

16   17 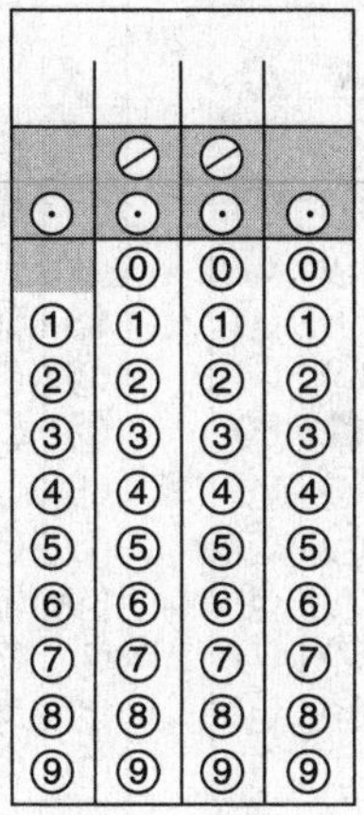   18 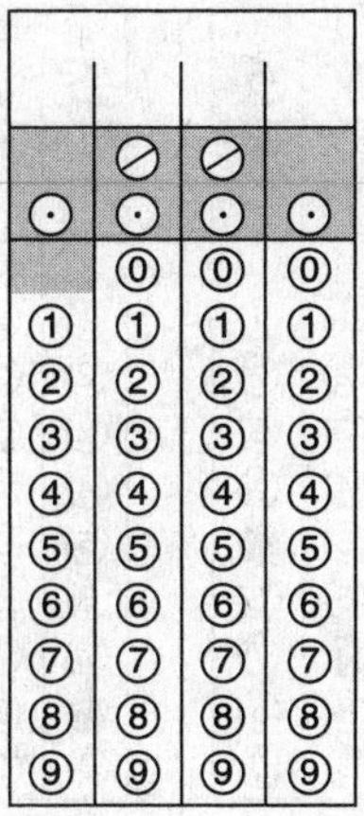   19 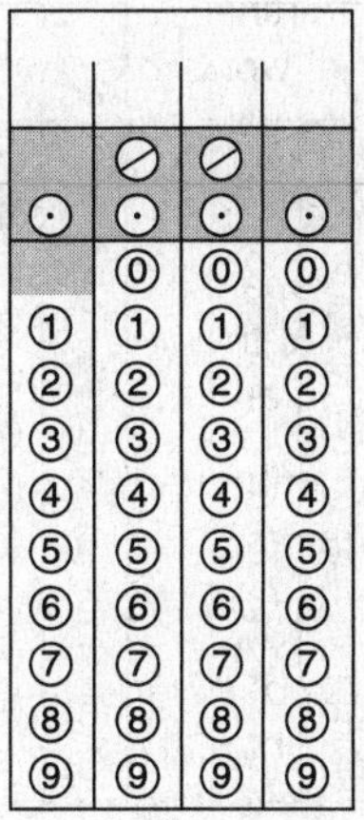   20

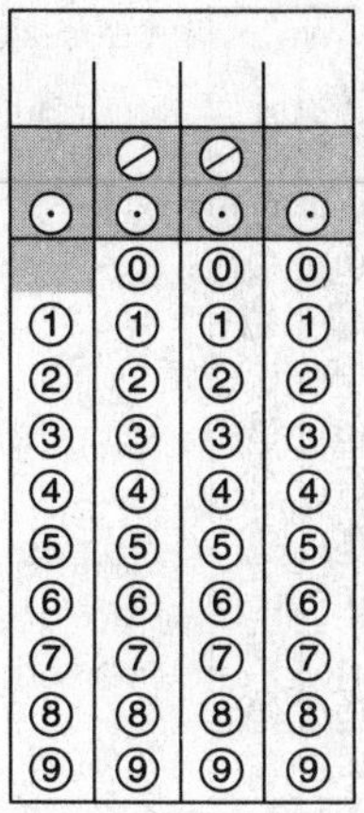

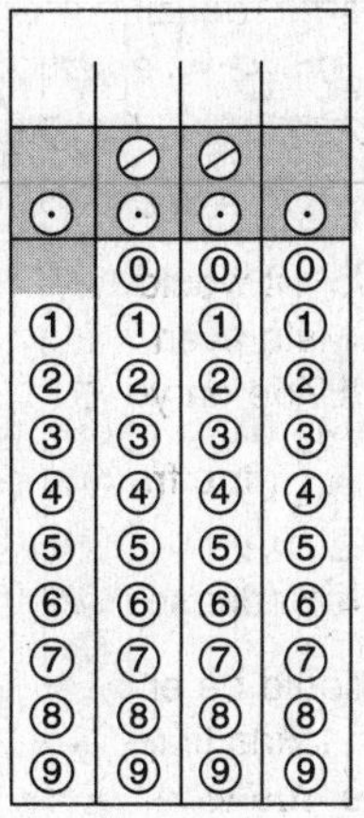

21 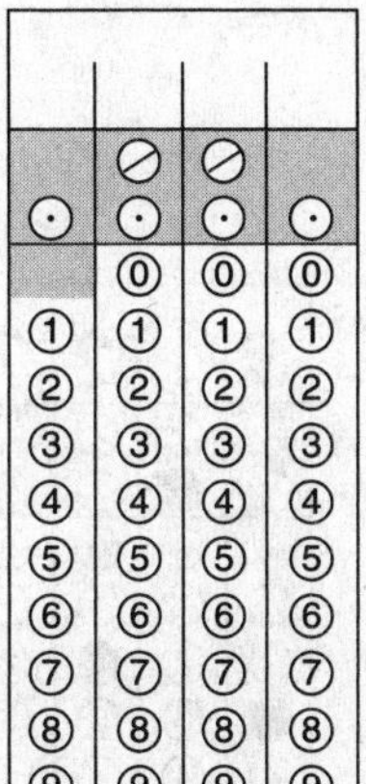   22 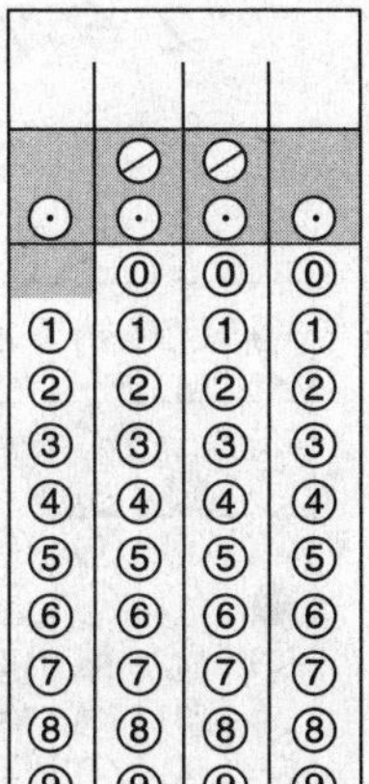   23 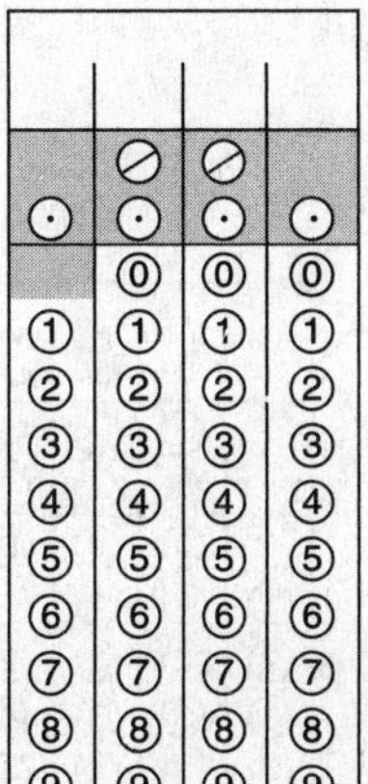   24 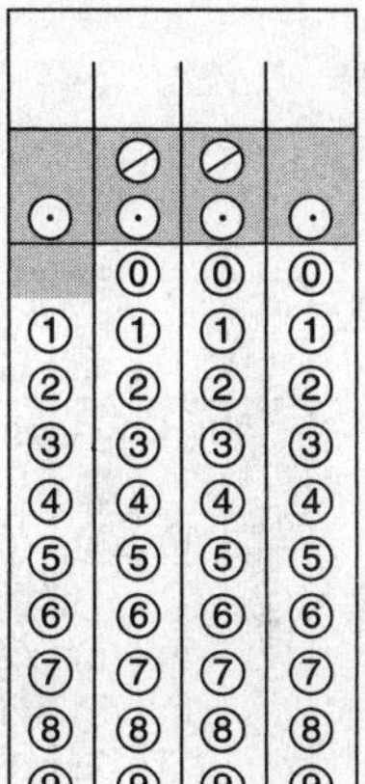   25

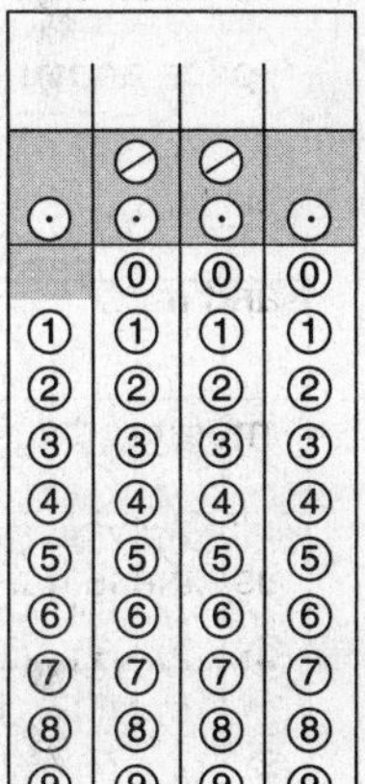

Solutions. Each grid contains the answer we recommend. Other acceptable answers, if any, are written below each grid.

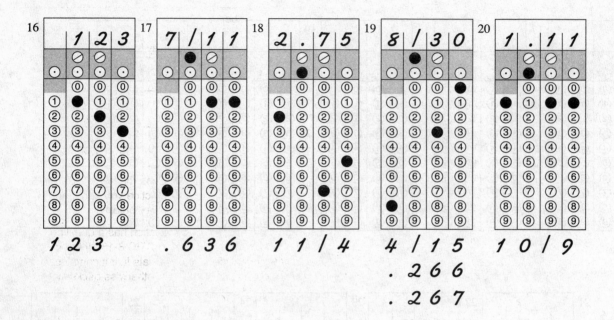

16. 1 2 3

17. . 6 3 6

18. 1 1 / 4
     . 2 6 6
     . 2 6 7

19. 4 / 1 5

20. 1 0 / 9

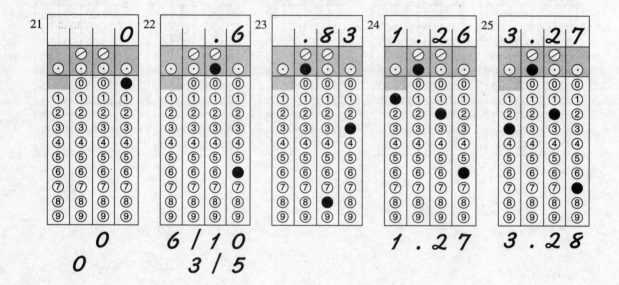

21. 0
     0

22. 6 / 1 0
     3 / 5

23.

24. 1 . 2 7

25. 3 . 2 8

If you missed even one of these, go back and reread the rules for gridding. *You never want to have a correct answer and get no credit because you didn't grid it properly.* Whenever you do practice grid-in problems, actually grid in the answers. Make sure you understand all of these rules *now.* When you actually take the SAT I, don't even look at the gridding instructions.

Many of the tactics that can be used on multiple-choice and quantitative comparison questions don't apply to grid-ins. After all, you can't eliminate choices when there aren't any. However, some strategies can be adapted for these problems.

For example, most of the tactics in Chapter 8 apply also to grid-in problems. You should draw diagrams when appropriate; trust diagrams that have been drawn to scale, and redraw them when they haven't been; make systematic lists when you need to count; and pay attention to units.

Testing Tactics

11-1   Backsolve.

If you think of a grid-in problem as a multiple-choice question in which the choices accidentally got erased, you can still use TACTIC 9-1: test the choices. You just have to make up the choices as you go. Let's illustrate by looking again at Examples 1 and 2 from Chapter 9, except that now the choices are missing.

Example 1.

If the average (arithmetic mean) of 2, 7, and x is 12, what is the value of x?

Example 2.

On Monday, a store owner received a shipment of books. On Tuesday, she sold half of them; on Wednesday, after two more were sold, she had exactly $\frac{2}{5}$ of the books left. How many books were in the shipment?

Instead of starting with choice C, as we did in Chapter 9, we have to pick a starting number. Any number will do, but when the numbers in the problem are 2, 7, and 12, as they are in Example 1, it's more likely that x is 10 or 20 than 100 or 1000. In Example 2, we have no guidance; the shipment might have 10 or 20 books, but it could just as well have 100 or 1000.

Solution 1. You could start with 10; but if you immediately realize that the average of 2, 7, and 10 is less than 10 (so it can't be 12), you'll try a bigger number, say 20. The average of 2, 7, and 20 is

$$\frac{2+7+20}{3} = \frac{29}{3} = 9\frac{2}{3},$$

which is too small. Try $x = 30$:

$$\frac{2+7+30}{3} = \frac{39}{3} = 13,$$

just a bit too big. Since 12 is closer to 13 than it is to $9\frac{2}{3}$, your next choice should be closer to 30 than 20, surely more than 25. Your third try might well be **27**, which works.

Solution 2. Test some values and check whether $\frac{2}{5}$ of the books are left.

Books in Shipment	Number Left on Tuesday	Number Left on Wednesday	
100	50	48	$\frac{48}{100} > \frac{2}{5} = \frac{40}{100}$
50	25	23	$\frac{23}{50} = \frac{46}{100} > \frac{2}{5}$
20	10	8	$\frac{8}{20} = \frac{40}{100} = \frac{2}{5}$: YES!

Depending on where you start, you might have to test four or five numbers, but with practice you can learn to zoom in on the correct answer very quickly.

Often on the SAT I, the grid-in section has a question using a "strange" symbol (see TACTIC 8-13). If the question is strictly numerical, just evaluate it. If it contains variables, solve it directly if possible; otherwise backsolve.

Example 3.

For every positve number $x \neq 20$: $\boxed{x} = 20 + x$ and $\widehat{x} = 20 - x$. If $\frac{\boxed{x}}{\widehat{x}} = 4$, what is the value of x?

Solution. In order for $20 - x$ to be positive, x has to be less than 20.

Try $x = 15$: $\dfrac{20+15}{20-15} = \dfrac{35}{5} = 7$. That's too big.

Try $x = 10$: $\dfrac{20+10}{20-10} = \dfrac{30}{10} = 3$. That's too small.

Try $x = 12$: $\dfrac{20+12}{20-12} = \dfrac{32}{8} = 4$. That's it.

Again, we emphasize that, if you know how to solve a problem directly, and are confident that you can do so accurately, you should not resort to backsolving. *Use this tactic only when you need it.*

Here's how to solve Example 3 algebraically:

$$\frac{20+x}{20-x} = 4 \Rightarrow 20 + x = 80 - 4x \Rightarrow 20 + 5x + 80 \Rightarrow$$
$$5x = 60 \Rightarrow x = 12.$$

11-2   Choose an Appropriate Number.

This is exactly the same as TACTIC 9-3. The most appropriate numbers to choose are 100 for percent problems, the LCD (least common denominator) for fraction problems, and the LCM (least common multiple) of the coefficients for problems involving equations. Each of the problems discussed under TACTIC 9-3 could have been a grid-in, because we didn't even look at the choices until we had the correct answer.

Example 4.

Ball-point pens that used to cost $1.00 for a package of 3 now cost $1.95 for a package of 5. What is the percent increase in the price of these pens? (Do not grid the % sign.)

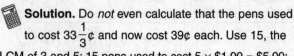 **Solution.** Do *not* even calculate that the pens used to cost $33\frac{1}{3}$¢ and now cost 39¢ each. Use 15, the LCM of 3 and 5: 15 pens used to cost 5 × $1.00 = $5.00; now 15 pens cost 3 × $1.95 = $5.85, an increase of $0.85.

The percent increase is

$$\frac{\text{actual increase}}{\text{original amount}} \times 100\% = \frac{0.85}{5.00} \times 100\% = \textbf{17\%}.$$

(See Section 12-C.)

Example 5.

During an Election Day sale, the price of every television set in a store was reduced by $33\frac{1}{3}$%.

By what percent must these sale prices be raised so that the TVs now sell for their original prices? (Do not grid the % sign.)

Solution. Since this problem involves percents, you should think about using 100. But the fraction $\frac{1}{3}$ is also involved, so 300 is an even better choice. Assume the original price was $300. Since $33\frac{1}{3}$% of 300 = $\frac{1}{3}$ of

300 = 100, the sale price was $200. To restore the price to $300, it must now be raised by $100. The percent increase is

$$\frac{\text{actual increase}}{\text{original amount}} \times 100\% = \frac{100}{200} \times 100\% = \textbf{50\%}.$$

Example 6.

Three-fourths of the members of the chess club are boys; $\frac{2}{5}$ of the boys entered the state tournament; and $\frac{2}{3}$ of the boys who entered won their first-round matches. If 48 of the boys in the club won their first-round matches, how many girls are in the club?

Solution. The LCD of the three fractions in this problem is 60, so for the moment, *assume* that the club has 60 members. Then $\frac{3}{\cancel{4}_1} \times \cancel{60}^{15} = 45$ of them are boys, $\frac{2}{\cancel{5}_1} \times \cancel{45}^{9} = $

18 of the boys entered the tournament, and $\frac{2}{\cancel{3}_1} \times \cancel{18}^{6} = $

12 of the boys who entered won their first-round matches. Since, in fact, 48 of the boys won their first-round matches and 48 = 12 × 4, we need to multiply everything by 4. The club has 240 members of whom 180 are boys and **60** are girls.

Practice Exercises

Directions: Enter your response to these problems on the grids that follow.

1. For what number $b > 0$ is it true that b divided by b% of b equals b?

2. Patty has 150 coins, each of which is a dime or a quarter. If she has $27.90, how many quarters does she have?

3. A fair coin is flipped repeatedly. Each time it lands "heads," Ali gets a point, and whenever it lands "tails," Jason gets a point. The game continues until someone gets 5 points. If the score is now 4 to 3 in Ali's favor, and the probability that Ali will win the game is k times the probability that Jason will win the game, what is the value of k?

4. At a certain university, $\frac{1}{4}$ of the applicants failed to meet minimum standards and were rejected immediately. Of those who met the standards, $\frac{2}{5}$ were accepted. If 1200 applicants were accepted, how many applied?

5. More than half of the members of the Key Club are girls. If $\frac{4}{7}$ of the girls and $\frac{7}{11}$ of the boys in the

Key Club attended the April meeting, what is the smallest number of members the club could have?

6. Jessica copied a column of numbers and added them. The only mistake she made was that she copied one number as 5095 instead of 5.95. If the sum she got was 8545.05, what should the answer have been?

7. Jerry spent $105 for a tool kit and a box of nails. If the tool kit cost $100 more than the nails, how many boxes of nails could be purchased for the price of the tool kit?

8. Ken is now 3 times as old as his younger sister, but in 7 years he will be only twice as old as she will be then. How old is Ken now?

9. The value of an investment increased 50% in 1992 and again in 1993. In each of 1994 and 1995 the value of the investment decreased by 50%. At the end of 1995 the value of the investment was how many times the value at the beginning of 1992?

10. How many integers between 1 and 1000 are the product of two consecutive integers?

1   2   3   4   5

6   7   8   9   10

Answer Key

1. 1 0

2. 8 6

3. 3

4. 4 0 0 0

5. 2 5

6. 3 4 5 6

7. 4 1

8. 2 1

9. 9 / 1 6 or . 5 6 2

10. 3 1

Answer Explanations

1. (10) $b \div (b\% \text{ of } b) = b \div \left(\dfrac{b}{100} \cdot b \right) =$

   $b \div \left(\dfrac{b^2}{100} \right) = b \cdot \left(\dfrac{100}{b^2} \right) = \dfrac{100}{b}.$

   Since this value is to equal b, you have

   $\dfrac{100}{b} = b \Rightarrow b^2 = 100 \Rightarrow b = \mathbf{10}.$

** Use TACTIC 11-1: backsolve. Since this is a percent problem, TACTIC 11-2 suggests starting with $b = 100$:

$100 \div (100\% \text{ of } 100) = 100 \div 100 = 1,$

which does not equal 100. Try $b = 10$:
$10 \div (10\% \text{ of } 10) = 10 \div 1 = \mathbf{10}.$

2. **(86)** If q represents the number of quarters and $150 - q$ the number of dimes, then

$$25q + 10(150 - q) = 2790 \Rightarrow$$
$$25q + 1500 - 10q = 2790 \Rightarrow$$
$$15q = 1290 \Rightarrow q = \mathbf{86}.$$

**To avoid the algebra, use TACTIC 11-1. Pick an easy starting value, say $q = 100$. If this gives a value greater than \$27.90, decrease q; if it gives a value less than \$27.90, increase q.

Number of Quarters	Number of Dimes	Value
100	50	\$25.00 + \$5.00 = \$30.00
80	70	\$20.00 + \$7.00 = \$27.00
85	65	\$21.25 + \$6.50 = \$27.75
86	64	\$21.50 + \$6.40 = \$27.90

3. **(3)** Jason can win only if the next two flips are both tails. The probability of that happening is $\frac{1}{2} \times \frac{1}{2} = \frac{1}{4}$. Therefore, the probability that Ali wins is $1 - \frac{1}{4} = \frac{3}{4}$.

Since $\frac{3}{4} = 3\left(\frac{1}{4}\right)$, $k = \mathbf{3}$.

**Use TACTIC 8-11. Systematically list the possible outcomes of the next two flips and the probability of each outcome.

4. **(4000)** Use TACTIC 11-2: choose an appropriate number. The LCD of $\frac{1}{4}$ and $\frac{2}{5}$ is 20, so *assume* that there were 20 applicants. Then $\frac{1}{4}(20) = 5$ failed to meet the minimum

standards. Of the remaining 15 applicants, $\frac{2}{5}$, or 6, were accepted, so 6 of every 20 applicants were accepted. Set up a proportion:

$$\frac{6}{20} = \frac{1200}{x} \Rightarrow 6x = 24{,}000 \Rightarrow x = \mathbf{4000}.$$

5. **(25)** Since $\frac{4}{7}$ of the girls attended the meeting, the number of girls in the club must be a multiple of 7: 7, 14, 21, ... Similarly, the number of boys in the club must be a multiple of 11: 11, 22, ... Since there are at least 11 boys and there are more girls than boys, there must be at least 14 girls. The smallest possible total is $14 + 11 = \mathbf{25}$.

6. **(3456)** To get the correct sum, subtract the number Jessica added in error and add the number she left out: $8545.05 - 5095 + 5.95 = \mathbf{3456}$.

7. **(41)** The first thing to do is to calculate the prices of the tool kit and the nails. *Be careful*—they are *not* \$100 and \$5. You can get the answer algebraically or by trial and error. If you let x = cost of the nails, then $100 + x$ = cost of the tool kit, and

$$x + (100 + x) = 105 \Rightarrow 2x + 100 = 105 \Rightarrow$$
$$2x = 5 \Rightarrow x = 2.5.$$

Then the nails cost \$2.50, and the tool kit \$102.50. Finally, $102.50 \div 2.50 = \mathbf{41}$.

8. **(21)** Set the problem up algebraically, using a table if that helps you.

Time	Ken's Sister's Age	Ken's Age
Now	x	$3x$
In 7 years	$x + 7$	$3x + 7$

The equation is $3x + 7 = 2(x + 7) \Rightarrow 3x + 7 = 2x + 14 \Rightarrow x = 7$, so Ken is **21** now.
**Use TACTIC 11-2. Pick a value for the sister's age—say, 2. Then Ken is 6. In 7 years, sister and brother will be 9 and 13, respectively. No good; 13 is less than twice 9. Try a bigger number—5. Then Ken is 15, and in 7 years the two will be 12 and 22. That's closer, but still too small. Try 7. Then Ken is 21, and in 7 years his sister and he will be 14 and 28. That's it! (Note that, if you tried a number larger than 7 for the sister's age, in 7 years Ken would be more than twice as old and you would have to try a smaller number.)

9. $\left(.562 \text{ or } \frac{9}{16}\right)$ Use TACTIC 11-2. Pick an easy-to-use starting value—\$100, say. Then the value of the investment at the end of each of the 4 years 1992, 1993, 1994, 1995 was \$150, \$225, \$112.50, \$56.25, so the final value was .5625, or **.562**, times the initial value. Note that some initial values would lead to an answer more easily expressed as a fraction. For example, if you start with \$16, the yearly values would be \$24, \$36, \$18, and \$9, and the

answer would be $\frac{9}{16}$.

10. **(31)** Use TACTIC 8-11. List the integers systematically: $1 \times 2, 2 \times 3, \ldots, 24 \times 25, \ldots$. You don't have to multiply and list the products (2, 6, 12, ... , 600, ...); you just have to know when to stop. The largest product less than 1000 is $31 \times 32 = 992$, so there are **31** numbers.

12 Reviewing Mathematics

This chapter provides a comprehensive review of all of the mathematics that you need to know for the SAT I. Let's start by saying what you *don't* need to know. The SAT I is *not* a test in high school mathematics. There are *no* questions on trigonometry, logarithms, complex numbers, exponential functions, geometric transformations, parabolas, ellipses, statistics, truth tables, or matrices. You will *not* have to graph a straight line, use the quadratic formula, know the equation of a circle, write a geometry proof, do a compass and straightedge construction, prove a trig identity, or solve a complicated word problem. What *do* you need to know?

About 85% of the test questions are divided approximately evenly among topics in arithmetic, elementary algebra, and the fundamentals of geometry. The remaining 15% of the questions represent a few basic miscellaneous topics, such as probability and counting, interpretation of data, and logical reasoning. Most of the arithmetic that you need to know for the SAT I is taught in elementary school, and much of the other material is taught in middle school or junior high school. The only high school math that you need is some elementary algebra and a little basic geometry.

Why, then, if no advanced mathematics is on the SAT I, do so many students find some of the questions difficult? The answer is that the College Board considers the SAT I to be "a test of general reasoning abilities." It attempts to use basic concepts of arithmetic, algebra, and geometry as a method of testing your ability to think logically. The Board is not testing whether you know how to calculate an average, find the area of a circle, use the Pythagorean theorem, or read a bar graph. *It assumes you can.* In fact, because the Board is not even interested in testing your memory, most of the formulas you will need are listed at the beginning of each math section. In other words, the College Board's objective is to use your familiarity with numbers and geometric figures as a way of testing your *logical thinking skills.*

Since, to do well on the SAT I, you must know basic arithmetic, algebra, and geometry, this chapter reviews *everything* you need to know. But that's not enough. You have to be able to use these concepts in ways that may be unfamiliar to you. That's where the advice and tactics from Chapters 8, 9, 10, and 11 come in.

This chapter is divided into 17 sections, numbered 12-A through 12-Q. Each section deals with a different topic, and in it you are given the basic definitions, key facts, and tactics that you need to solve SAT I-type questions on that topic. The especially important facts, which are referenced in the solutions to sample problems and to the Model Tests in PART FOUR, are labeled KEY FACTS and are numbered. Following each KEY FACT is a sample SAT I question that uses that fact. Also included in some sections are test-taking tactics specific to the topics discussed.

Basically, Chapter 12 is broken down as follows:

Topics in Arithmetic	Sections A–E
Topics in Algebra	Sections F–H
Topics in Geometry	Sections I–N
Miscellaneous Topics	Sections O–Q

No topic, however, really belongs to only one category. Average problems are discussed in the arithmetic sections, but on the SAT I you need to be able also to take the average of algebraic expressions and the average of the measures of the angles of a triangle. Most algebra problems involve arithmetic, as well; on many geometry problems you need to use algebra; and several of the problems in the miscellaneous topics sections require a knowledge of arithmetic and/or algebra.

At the end of each section is a set of exercises that consists of a wide variety of multiple-choice, quantitative comparison, and grid-in questions, similar to actual SAT I questions, and utilizing the concepts covered in the section. You should use whichever TACTICS and KEY FACTS from that section that you think are appropriate. If you've mastered the material in the section, you should be able to answer most of the questions. If you get stuck, you can use the various strategies you learned in Chapters 8, 9, 10, and 11; but then you should carefully read the solutions that are provided, so that you understand the correct mathematical way to answer the question. In the solutions a few references are given to TACTICS from Chapters 8, 9, 10, and 11, but the major emphasis here is on doing the mathematics properly.

Finally, one small disclaimer is appropriate. This is not a mathematics textbook—it is a *review* of the essential facts that you need to know to do well on the SAT I. Undoubtedly, you have already learned most, if not all, of them. If, however, you find some topics with which you are unfamiliar or on which you need more information, get a copy of Barron's *Arithmetic the Easy Way*, *Algebra the Easy Way*, and/or *Geometry the Easy Way*. For additional practice on SAT I-type questions, see Barron's *NEW Math Workbook for SAT I*.

Topics in Arithmetic

To do well on the SAT I, you need to feel comfortable with most topics of basic arithmetic. The first five sections of Chapter 12 provide you with a review of the basic arithmetic operations, signed numbers, fractions, decimals, ratios, percents, and averages. Because you will have a calculator with you at the test, you will not have to do long division, multiply three-digit numbers, or perform any other tedious calculations by hand. If you use a calculator with fraction capability, you can even avoid finding least common denominators and reducing fractions.

The solutions to more than one-third of the mathematics questions on the SAT I depend on your knowing the KEY FACTS in these sections. Be sure to review them all.

12-A BASIC ARITHMETIC CONCEPTS

Let's start by reviewing the most important sets of numbers and their properties. On the SAT I the word *number* always means "real number," a number that can be represented by a point on the number line.

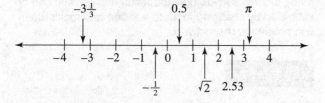

Signed Numbers

The numbers to the right of 0 on the number line are called *positive*, and those to the left of 0 are *negative*. Negative numbers must be written with a *negative sign* (–2); positive numbers can be written with a *plus sign* (+2) but are usually written without a sign (2). All numbers can be called *signed numbers*.

Key Fact A1

For any number *a*, exactly one of the following is true:

- *a* is negative   • *a* = 0   • *a* is positive

The *absolute value* of a number *a*, denoted as $|a|$, is the distance between *a* and 0 on the number line. Since 3 is 3 units to the right of 0 on the number line and –3 is 3 units to the left of 0, both have an absolute value of 3:

- $|3| = 3$ • $|–3| = 3$

Two unequal numbers that have the same absolute value are called *opposites*. For example, 3 is the opposite of –3 and –3 is the opposite of 3.

Key Fact A2

The only number that is equal to its opposite is 0.

| <u>Column A</u> | <u>Column B</u> |

Example 1.

$$a - b = -(a - b)$$

| *a* | *b* |

Solution. Since $-(a - b)$ is the opposite of $a - b$, $a - b = 0$, and so $a = b$ **(C)**.

In arithmetic we are basically concerned with the addition, subtraction, multiplication, and division of numbers. Column 3 of the table below shows the terms used to describe the results of these operations.

Operation	Symbol	Result	Example	
Addition	+	**Sum**	16 is the sum of 12 and 4.	16 = 12 + 4
Subtraction	–	**Difference**	8 is the difference of 12 and 4.	8 = 12 – 4
Multiplication*	×	**Product**	48 is the product of 12 and 4.	48 = 12 × 4
Division	÷	**Quotient**	3 is the quotient of 12 and 4.	3 = 12 ÷ 4

*Multiplication can be indicated also by a dot, parentheses, or the juxtaposition of symbols without any sign: $2^2 \cdot 2^4$, 3(4), 3(x + 2), 3a, 4abc.

Given any two numbers *a* and *b*, we can *always* find their sum, difference, product, and quotient (with a calculator, if necessary), except that we can *never divide by zero*:

- $0 \div 7 = 0$ • $7 \div 0$ is meaningless.

Example 2.

What is the sum of the product and the quotient of 7 and 7?

Solution. Product: $7 \times 7 = 49$. Quotient: $7 \div 7 = 1$. Sum: $49 + 1 = $ **50**.

Key Fact A3

For any number a: $a \times 0 = 0$. Conversely, if the product of two or more numbers is 0, *at least one* of them must be 0:

if $ab = 0$, then $a = 0$ or $b = 0$.

Column A	Column B

Example 3.

The product of the integers from –6 to 3	The product of the integers from –3 to 6

Solution. Before reaching for your calculator, look and think. Each column is the product of 10 numbers, one of which is 0. Then, by KEY FACT A3, each product is 0, and the columns are equal **(C)**.

Key Fact A4

The product and the quotient of two positive numbers or two negative numbers are positive; the product and the quotient of a positive number and a negative number are negative.

×	+	−
+	+	−
−	−	+

÷	+	−
+	+	−
−	−	+

$6 \times 3 = 18$ $6 \times (-3) = -18$ $(-6) \times 3 = -18$ $(-6) \times (-3) = 18$
$6 \div 3 = 2$ $6 \div (-3) = -2$ $(-6) \div 3 = -2$ $(-6) \div (-3) = 2$

To determine whether a product of more than two numbers is positive or negative, count the number of negative factors.

Key Fact A5

• The product of an *even* number of negative factors is positive.
• The product of an *odd* number of negative factors is negative.

Column A	Column B

Example 4.

$(-1)(2)(-3)(4)(-5)$	$(1)(-2)(3)(-4)(5)$

Solution. Column A is negative since the product has three negative factors, whereas Column B is positive since the product has two negative factors. The answer is **B**. This method is faster and easier than multiplying, either mentally or with a calculator.

Key Fact A6

The *reciprocal* of any nonzero number a is $\dfrac{1}{a}$. The product of any number and its reciprocal is 1: $a \left(\dfrac{1}{a} \right) = 1$.

Key Fact A7

• **The sum of two positive numbers is positive.**
• **The sum of two negative numbers is negative.**
• **To find the sum of a positive and a negative number, find the difference of their absolute values and use the sign of the number with the larger absolute value.**

$6 + 2 = 8$ $(-6) + (-2) = -8$

To calculate either $6 + (-2)$ or $(-6) + 2$, take the difference, $6 - 2 = 4$, and use the sign of the number whose absolute value is 6:

$6 + (-2) = 4$ $(-6) + 2 = -4$

Key Fact A8

The sum of any number and its opposite is 0: $a + (-a) = 0$.

Many properties of arithmetic depend on the relationship between subtraction and addition and between division and multiplication. Subtracting a number is the same as adding its opposite, and dividing by a number is the same as multiplying by its reciprocal.

$$a - b = a + (-b) \qquad a \div b = a \left(\frac{1}{b} \right)$$

Many problems involving subtraction and division can be simplified by changing them to addition and multiplication problems, respectively.

Key Fact A9

To subtract signed numbers, change the problem to an addition problem by changing the sign of what is being subtracted, and then use KEY FACT A7.

$2 - 6 = 2 + (-6) = -4$ $2 - (-6) = 2 + (6) = 8$

$(-2) - (-6) = (-2) + (6) = 4$ $(-2) - 6 = (-2) + (-6) = -8$

In each case, the minus sign was changed to a plus sign, and either the 6 was changed to –6 or the –6 was changed to 6.

CALCULATOR HINT

All arithmetic involving signed numbers can be accomplished on *any* calculator, but not all calculators handle negative numbers in the same way. Be sure you know how to enter negative numbers and how to use them on *your* calculator.

Integers

The *integers* are $\{..., -4, -3, -2, -1, 0, 1, 2, 3, 4, ...\}$.

The *positive integers* are $\{1, 2, 3, 4, 5, ...\}$.

The *negative integers* are $\{..., -5, -4, -3, -2, -1\}$.

Note: The integer 0 is neither positive nor negative. Therefore, if an SAT I question asks how many positive numbers have a certain property, and the only numbers with that property are -2, -1, 0, 1, and 2, the answer is 2.

Consecutive integers are two or more integers, written in sequence, each of which is 1 more than the preceding integer. For example:

22, 23   6, 7, 8, 9 $-2, -1, 0, 1$ $n, n+1, n+2, n+3$

Example 5.

If the sum of three consecutive integers is less than 75, what is the greatest possible value of the smallest of the three integers?

Solution. Let the numbers be n, $n+1$, and $n+2$. Then

$$n + (n+1) + (n+2) = 3n + 3 \Rightarrow 3n + 3 < 75 \Rightarrow$$
$$3n < 72 \Rightarrow n < 24.$$

So the most n can be is **23**. (See Section 12-G for help in solving inequalities like this one.)

Of course, you don't *need* to do the algebra (see TACTIC 11-2). Try three consecutive integers near 25, say 24, 25, 26. Their sum is 75, which is *slightly* too big (the sum needs to be *less* than 75), so the numbers must be **23**, 24, 25.

> **CAUTION:** Never assume that *number* means "integer": 3 is not the only number between 2 and 4; there are many others, including 2.5, 3.99, $\frac{10}{3}$, π, and $\sqrt{10}$.

Example 6.

If $2 < x < 4$ and $3 < y < 7$, what is the largest integer value of $x + y$?

Solution. If x and y are integers, the largest value is $3 + 6 = 9$. However, although $x + y$ is to be an integer, neither x nor y must be. If $x = 3.8$ and $y = 6.2$, then $x + y = $ **10**.

The sum, difference, and product of two integers is *always* an integer; the quotient of two integers may be, but is not necessarily, an integer. The quotient $23 \div 10$ can be expressed as $\frac{23}{10}$ or $2\frac{3}{10}$ or 2.3. If the quotient is to be an integer, we can also say that the quotient is 2 and there is a *remainder* of 3.

The way we express the answer depends on the question. For example, if \$23 are to be divided among 10 people, each one will get \$2.30 (2.3 dollars); but if 23 books are to be divided among 10 people, each one will get 2 books and 3 will be left over (the remainder).

 Calculator Shortcut

The standard way to find quotients and remainders is to use long division; but on the SAT I, you *never* do long division: you use your calculator. To find the remainder when 100 is divided by 7, divide on your calculator: $100 \div 7 = 14.285714....$ This tells you that the quotient is 14. To find the remainder, multiply: $14 \times 7 = 98$, and then subtract: $100 - 98 = 2$.

Column A	Column B

Example 7.

The remainder when 999 is divided by 7	The remainder when 777 is divided by 9

 Solution. Don't even consider doing this problem without your calculator.

Column A: $999 \div 7 = 142.71...$; $7 \times 142 = 994$; $999 - 994 = 5$.

Column B: $777 \div 9 = 86.333...$; $9 \times 86 = 774$; $777 - 774 = 3$.

Column **A** is greater.

Example 8.

How many positive integers less than 100 have a remainder of 3 when divided by 7?

Solution. To have a remainder of 3 when divided by 7, an integer must be 3 more than a multiple of 7. For example, when 73 is divided by 7, the quotient is 10 and the remainder is 3: $73 = 10 \times 7 + 3$. Just take the multiples of 7 and add 3:

$\underline{0} \times 7 + 3 = 3$; $\underline{1} \times 7 + 3 = 10$; $\underline{2} \times 7 + 3 = 17$; $...$; $\underline{13} \times 7 + 3 = 94$

There are **14** positive integers less than 100 that have a remainder of 3 when divided by 7.

If a and b are integers, the following four terms are synonymous:

a is a *divisor* of b.	a is a *factor* of b.
b is *divisible* by a.	b is a *multiple* of a.

All these statements mean that, when *b* is divided by *a*, there is no remainder (or, more precisely, the remainder is 0). For example:

3 is a divisor of 12.   3 is a factor of 12.
12 is divisible by 3.   12 is a multiple of 3.

Key Fact A10

Every integer has a finite set of factors (or divisors) and an infinite set of multiples.

The factors of 12:   −12, −6, −4, −3, −2, −1, 1, 2, 3, 4, 6, 12

The multiples of 12:   ... , −48, −36, −24, −12, 0, 12, 24, 36, 48, ...

The only positive divisor of 1 is 1. Every other positive integer has at least two positive divisors: 1 and itself, and possibly many more. For example, 6 is divisible by 1 and 6, as well as by 2 and 3; whereas 7 is divisible only by 1 and 7. Positive integers, such as 7, which have exactly two positive divisors are called *prime numbers* or *primes*. Here are the first few primes:

2, 3, 5, 7, 11, 13, 17, 19, 23.

Memorize this list—it will come in handy. Note that 1 is *not* a prime.

Key Fact A11

Every integer greater than 1 that is not a prime can be written as a product of primes.

To find the prime factorization of any integer, find any two factors: if they're both primes, you are done; if not, factor them. Continue until each factor has been written in terms of primes.

A useful method is to make a *factor tree*.

For example, here are the prime factorizations of 108 and 240:

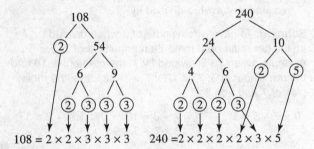

$$108 = 2 \times 2 \times 3 \times 3 \times 3 \qquad 240 = 2 \times 2 \times 2 \times 2 \times 3 \times 5$$

Example 9.

For any positive integer *a*, let $\lceil a \rfloor$ denote the smallest prime factor of *a*. Which of the following is equal to $\lceil 35 \rfloor$?

(A) $\lceil 10 \rfloor$ (B) $\lceil 15 \rfloor$ (C) $\lceil 45 \rfloor$ (D) $\lceil 55 \rfloor$ (E) $\lceil 75 \rfloor$

Solution. Check the first few primes; 35 is not divisible by 2 or 3, but is divisible by 5, so 5 is the *smallest* prime factor of 35, and $\lceil 35 \rfloor = 5$. Now check the five choices: $\lceil 10 \rfloor = 2$, and $\lceil 15 \rfloor$, $\lceil 45 \rfloor$, and $\lceil 75 \rfloor$ are all equal to 3. Only $\lceil 55 \rfloor = 5$. The answer is **D**.

The *least common multiple* (LCM) of two or more integers is the smallest positive integer that is a multiple of each of them. For example, the LCM of 6 and 10 is 30. Infinitely many positive integers are multiples of both 6 and 10, including 60, 90, 180, 600, 6000, and 66,000,000, but 30 is the smallest one.

The *greatest common factor* (GCF) or *greatest common divisor* (GCD) of two or more integers is the largest integer that is a factor of each of them. For example, the only positive integers that are factors of both 6 and 10 are 1 and 2, so the GCF of 6 and 10 is 2. For small numbers, you can often find the GCF and LCM by inspection. For larger numbers, KEY FACTS A12 and A13 are useful.

Key Fact A12

The product of the GCF and LCM of two numbers is equal to the product of the two numbers.

Helpful Hint

It is usually easier to find the GCF than the LCM. For example, you may see immediately that the GCF of 36 and 48 is 12. You can then use KEY FACT A12 to find the LCM: since GCF × LCM = 36 × 48, then

$$\text{LCM} = \frac{\overset{3}{\cancel{36}} \times 48}{\underset{1}{\cancel{12}}} = 3 \times 48 = 144.$$

Key Fact A13

To find the GCF or LCM of two or more integers, first get their prime factorizations.

- The GCF is the product of all the primes that appear in each of the factorizations, using each prime the smallest number of times it appears in any factorization.
- The LCM is the product of all the primes that appear in any of the factorizations, using each prime the largest number of times it appears in any factorization.

For example, let's find the GCF and LCM of 108 and 240. As we saw:

$108 = 2 \times 2 \times 3 \times 3 \times 3$ and $240 = 2 \times 2 \times 2 \times 2 \times 3 \times 5$.

- **GCF**. The primes that appear in both factorizations are 2 and 3. Since 2 appears twice in the factorization of 108 and 4 times in the factorization of 240, we take it twice; 3 appears 3 times in the factorization of 108, but only once in the factorization of 240, so we take it just once. The GCF = $2 \times 2 \times 3$ = **12**.

- **LCM**. We take one of the factorizations and add to it any primes from the other that are not yet listed. We'll start with $2 \times 2 \times 3 \times 3 \times 3$ (108) and look at the primes from 240. There are four 2's; we already wrote two 2's, so we need two more; there is a 3, but we already have that; there is a 5, which we need. The LCM = $(2 \times 2 \times 3 \times 3 \times 3) \times (2 \times 2 \times 5) = 108 \times 20 = \mathbf{2160}$.

Example 10.

What is the smallest number that is divisible by both 34 and 35?

Solution. We are being asked for the LCM of 34 and 35. By KEY FACT A12, the LCM = $\dfrac{34 \times 35}{\text{GCF}}$. The GCF, however, is 1 since no number greater than 1 divides evenly into both 34 and 35. The LCM is $34 \times 35 = \mathbf{1190}$.

The **even numbers** are all the multiples of 2: $\{..., -4, -2, 0, 2, 4, 6, ...\}$.

The **odd numbers** are all the integers not divisible by 2: $\{..., -5, -3, -1, 1, 3, 5, ...\}$.

Note: • The terms *odd* and *even* apply only to integers.
   • Every integer (positive, negative, or 0) is either odd or even.
   • 0 is an even integer; it is a multiple of 2 ($0 = 0 \times 2$).
   • 0 is a multiple of *every* integer ($0 = 0 \times n$).
   • 2 is the only even prime number.

Key Fact A14

The tables below summarize three important facts:

1. **If two integers are both even or both odd, their sum and difference are even.**

2. **If one integer is even and the other odd, their sum and difference are odd.**

3. **The product of two integers is even unless both of them are odd.**

+ and −	even	odd		×	even	odd
even	even	odd		even	even	even
odd	odd	even		odd	even	odd

Exponents and Roots

Repeated addition of the same number is indicated by multiplication:

$$17 + 17 + 17 + 17 + 17 + 17 + 17 = 7 \times 17.$$

Repeated multiplication of the same number is indicated by an exponent:

$$17 \times 17 \times 17 \times 17 \times 17 \times 17 \times 17 = 17^7.$$

In the expression 17^7, 17 is called the **base** and 7 is the **exponent**.

In your math classes you may have seen expressions such as 2^0, 2^{-4}, $2^{\frac{1}{2}}$, or even $2^{\sqrt{2}}$. On the SAT I, although the base, b, can be any number, the only exponents you will see will be positive integers.

Key Fact A15

For any number b: $b^1 = b$, and $b^n = b \times b \times ... \times b$, where b is used as a factor n times.

(i) $2^5 \times 2^3 = (2 \times 2 \times 2 \times 2 \times 2) \times (2 \times 2 \times 2) = 2^8 = 2^{5+3}$

(ii) $\dfrac{2^5}{2^3} = \dfrac{2 \times 2 \times 2 \times 2 \times 2}{2 \times 2 \times 2} = 2 \times 2 = 2^2 = 2^{5-3}$

(iii) $(2^2)^3 = (2 \times 2)^3 = (2 \times 2) \times (2 \times 2) \times (2 \times 2) = 2^6 = 2^{2 \times 3}$

(iv) $2^3 \times 7^3 = (2 \times 2 \times 2) \times (7 \times 7 \times 7) = (2 \times 7)(2 \times 7)(2 \times 7) = (2 \times 7)^3$

These four examples illustrate the four important laws of exponents given in KEY FACT A16.

Key Fact A16

For any numbers b and c and positive integers m and n:

(i) $b^m b^n = b^{m+n}$ (ii) $\dfrac{b^m}{b^n} = b^{m-n}$ (iii) $(b^m)^n = b^{mn}$

(iv) $b^m c^m = (bc)^m$

CAUTION: In (i) and (ii) the bases are the same, and in (iv) the exponents are the same. None of these rules applies to expressions such as $2^5 \times 3^4$, in which both the bases and the exponents are different.

Example 11.

If $2^x = 32$, what is x^2?

Solution. To solve $2^x = 32$, just count (and keep track of) how many 2's you need to multiply to get 32: $2 \times 2 \times 2 \times 2 \times 2 = 32$, so $x = 5$ and $x^2 = \mathbf{25}$.

Example 12.

If $3^a \times 3^b = 3^{100}$, what is the average (arithmetic mean) of a and b?

Solution. Since $3^a \times 3^b = 3^{a+b}$, we see that

$$a + b = 100 \Rightarrow \frac{a+b}{2} = \mathbf{50}.$$

The next KEY FACT is an immediate consequence of KEY FACTS A4 and A5.

Key Fact A17

For any positive integer n:

(i) $0^n = 0$; (ii) if a is positive, a^n is positive;
(iii) if a is negative, a^n is positive if n is even, and negative if n is odd.

Column A	Column B

Example 13.

$(-13)^{10}$	$(-13)^{25}$

Solution. Column A is positive, and Column B is negative, so **A** is greater.

Squares and Square Roots

The exponent that appears most often on the SAT I is 2. It is used to form the square of a number, as in πr^2 (the area of a circle), $a^2 + b^2 = c^2$ (the Pythagorean theorem), or $x^2 - y^2$ (the difference of two squares). Therefore, it is helpful to recognize the *perfect squares*, numbers that are the squares of integers. The squares of the integers from 0 to 15 are as follows:

x	0	1	2	3	4	5	6	7
x^2	0	1	4	9	16	25	36	49

x	8	9	10	11	12	13	14	15
x^2	64	81	100	121	144	169	196	225

There are two numbers that satisfy the equation $x^2 = 9$: $x = 3$ and $x = -3$. The positive number, 3, is called the **square root** of 9 and is denoted by the symbol $\sqrt{9}$.

Clearly, each perfect square has a square root: $\sqrt{0} = 0$, $\sqrt{36} = 6$, $\sqrt{81} = 9$, and $\sqrt{144} = 12$. It is an important fact, however, that *every* positive number has a square root.

Key Fact A18

For any positive number a, there is a positive number b that satisfies the equation $b^2 = a$. That number is called the square root of a: $b = \sqrt{a}$. Therefore, for any positive number a: $\sqrt{a} \times \sqrt{a} = (\sqrt{a})^2 = a$.

The only difference between $\sqrt{9}$ and $\sqrt{10}$ is that the first square root is an integer, while the second one isn't. Since 10 is a little more than 9, we should expect that $\sqrt{10}$ is a little more than $\sqrt{9}$, which is 3. In fact, $(3.1)^2 = 9.61$, which is close to 10; and $(3.16)^2 = 9.9856$, which is very close to 10, so $\sqrt{10} \approx 3.16$. Square roots of integers that aren't perfect squares can be approximated as accurately as we wish, and by pressing the $\sqrt{}$ key on

our calculators we can get much more accuracy than we need for the SAT I. Actually, most answers involving square roots use the square root symbol.

Example 14.

What is the circumference of a circle whose area is 10π?

(A) 5π (B) 10π (C) $\pi\sqrt{10}$ (D) $2\pi\sqrt{10}$
(E) $\pi\sqrt{20}$

Solution. Since the area of a circle is given by the formula $A = \pi r^2$, we have

$$\pi r^2 = 10\pi \Rightarrow r^2 = 10 \Rightarrow r = \sqrt{10}.$$

The circumference is given by the formula $C = 2\pi r$, so $C = 2\pi\sqrt{10}$ **(D)**. (See Section 12-L on circles.)

Key Fact A19

For any positive numbers a and b:

$$\sqrt{ab} = \sqrt{a} \times \sqrt{b} \qquad \text{and} \qquad \sqrt{\frac{a}{b}} = \frac{\sqrt{a}}{\sqrt{b}}.$$

CAUTION: $\sqrt{a+b} \neq \sqrt{a} + \sqrt{b}$. For example:

$$5 = \sqrt{25} = \sqrt{9+16} \neq \sqrt{9} + \sqrt{16} = 3 + 4 = 7.$$

CAUTION: Although it is always true that $(\sqrt{a})^2 = a$, $\sqrt{a^2} = a$ is not true if a is negative: $\sqrt{(-5)^2} = \sqrt{25} = 5$, *not* -5.

Column A	Column B

Example 15.

$\sqrt{x^{20}}$	$(x^5)^2$

Solution. Column A: Since $x^{10}x^{10} = x^{20}$, $\sqrt{x^{20}} = x^{10}$.
Column B: $(x^5)^2 = x^{10}$. The columns are equal **(C)**.

PEMDAS

When a calculation requires performing more than one operation, it is important to carry the operations out in the correct order. For decades students have memorized the sentence "Please Excuse My Dear Aunt Sally," or just the acronym, PEMDAS, to remember the proper order of operations. The letters stand for:

- Parentheses: first do whatever appears in parentheses, following PEMDAS within the parentheses also if necessary.
- Exponents: next evaluate all terms with exponents.
- Multiplication and Division: then do all multiplications and divisions *in order from left to right*—do *not* multiply first and then divide.

- <u>A</u>ddition and <u>S</u>ubtraction: finally, do all additions and subtractions *in order from left to right*—do *not* add first and then subtract.

Here are some worked-out examples.

1. $12 + 3 \times 2 = 12 + 6 = 18$ [Multiply before you add.]
   $(12 + 3) \times 2 = 15 \times 2 = 30$ [First add in the parentheses.]

2. $12 \div 3 \times 2 = 4 \times 2 = 8$ [Just go from left to right.]
   $12 \div (3 \times 2) = 12 \div 6 = 2$ [Multiply first.]

3. $5 \times 2^3 = 5 \times 8 = 40$ [Do exponents first.]
   $(5 \times 2)^3 = 10^3 = 1000$ [Multiply first.]

4. $4 + 4 \div (2 + 6) = 4 + 4 \div 8 = 4 + .5 = 4.5$
   [Do parentheses first, then division.]

5. $100 - 2^2(3 + 4 \times 5) = 100 - 2^2(23) = 100 - 4(23) =$
   $100 - 92 = 8$
   [Do parentheses first (using PEMDAS), then the exponent, then multiplication.]

 Calculator Shortcut

Almost every *scientific* calculator automatically follows PEMDAS; four-function calculators don't. Test each of the above calculations on *your* calculator. Be sure you know whether or not you need to use parentheses or to put anything in memory as you proceed.

There is one situation when you shouldn't start with what's in the parentheses. Consider the following two examples.

(i) What is the value of $7(100 - 1)$?
   Using PEMDAS, you would write $7(100 - 1) = 7(99)$; and then, multiplying on your calculator, you would get **693**. But you can do the arithmetic more quickly in your head if you think of it this way: $7(100 - 1) = 700 - 7 = 693$.

(ii) What is the value of $(77 + 49) \div 7$?
   If you followed the rules of PEMDAS, you would first add: $77 + 49 = 126$, and then divide: $126 \div 7 = $ **18**. This is definitely more difficult and time-consuming than mentally calculating $\dfrac{77}{7} + \dfrac{49}{7} = 11 + 7 = 18$.

Both of these examples illustrate the very important distributive law.

Key Fact A20 (the distributive law)

For any real numbers a, b, and c:

- $a(b + c) = ab + ac$ • $a(b - c) = ab - ac$

and, if $a \neq 0$,

- $\dfrac{b + c}{a} = \dfrac{b}{a} + \dfrac{c}{a}$ • $\dfrac{b - c}{a} = \dfrac{b}{a} - \dfrac{c}{a}$.

Helpful Hint

Many students use the distributive law with multiplication but forget about it with division. Don't make that mistake.

Column A	Column B

Example 16.

$3(x - 7)$	$3x - 7$

Example 17.

$\dfrac{50 + x}{5}$	$10 + x$

Solution 16. Column A = $3x - 21$. The result of subtracting 21 from a number is *always less* than the result of subtracting 7 from that number. Column **B** is greater.

Solution 17.

	Column A	Column B
By the distributive law:	$10 + \dfrac{x}{5}$	$10 + x$
Subtract 10 from each column:	$\dfrac{x}{5}$	x

The columns are equal if $x = 0$, but not if $x = 1$.

The answer is **D**.

Example 18.

If $a = 9 \times 8321$ and $b = 9 \times 7321$, what is the value of $a - b$?

Solution. Of course, you can use your calculator, but you can do the arithmetic faster in your head if you remember the distributive law. In far less time than it takes to write the equation down, you should realize that $a - b = 9(8321) - 9(7321) = 9(1000) = $ **9000**.

NOTE: The proper use of the distributive law is essential in the algebra review in Section 12-F.

Inequalities

The number a is **greater than** the number b, denoted as $a > b$, if a is to the right of b on the number line. Similarly, a is **less than** b, denoted as $a < b$, if a is to the left of b on the number line. Therefore, if a is positive, $a > 0$; and if a is negative, $a < 0$. Clearly, if $a > b$, then $b < a$.

The following KEY FACT gives an important alternative way to describe *greater than* and *less than*.

Key Fact A21

- For any numbers a and b: $a > b$ means that $a - b$ is positive.
- For any numbers a and b: $a < b$ means that $a - b$ is negative.

Key Fact A22

For any numbers a and b, exactly one of the following is true:

$$a > b \quad \text{or} \quad a = b \quad \text{or} \quad a < b.$$

The symbol $\geq$ means **greater than or equal to** and the symbol $\leq$ means **less than or equal to**. The statement "$x \geq 5$" means that x can be 5 or any number greater than 5; the statement "$x \leq 5$" means that x can be 5 or any number less than 5. The statement "$2 < x < 5$" is an abbreviation for the statement "$2 < x$ and $x < 5$." It means that x is a number between 2 and 5 (greater than 2 and less than 5).

Inequalities are very important on the SAT I, especially on the quantitative comparison questions, where you have to determine which of two quantities is greater. KEY FACTS 23 and 24 give some important information about inequalities.

Key Fact A23   The Arithmetic of Inequalities

- **Adding a number to an inequality or subtracting a number from the inequality preserves it.**

  If $a < b$, then $a + c < b + c$ and $a - c < b - c$.
  $3 < 7 \Rightarrow 3 + 100 < 7 + 100 \quad (103 < 107)$
  $3 < 7 \Rightarrow 3 - 100 < 7 - 100 \quad (-97 < -93)$

- **Adding inequalities in the same direction preserves them.**

  If $a < b$ and $c < d$, then $a + c < b + d$.
  $3 < 7$ and $5 < 10 \Rightarrow 3 + 5 < 7 + 10 \quad (8 < 17)$

- **Multiplying or dividing an inequality by a positive number preserves it.**

  If $a < b$, and c is positive, then $ac < bc$ and $\dfrac{a}{c} < \dfrac{b}{c}$.
  $3 < 7 \Rightarrow 3 \times 100 < 7 \times 100 \quad (300 < 700)$
  $3 < 7 \Rightarrow 3 \div 100 < 7 \div 100 \quad \left(\dfrac{3}{100} < \dfrac{7}{100} \right)$

- **Multiplying or dividing an inequality by a negative number reverses it.**

  If $a < b$, and c is negative, then $ac > bc$ and $\dfrac{a}{c} > \dfrac{b}{c}$.
  $3 < 7 \Rightarrow 3 \times (-100) > 7 \times (-100) \quad (-300 > -700)$
  $3 < 7 \Rightarrow 3 \div (-100) > 7 \div (-100) \quad \left(-\dfrac{3}{100} > -\dfrac{7}{100} \right)$

- **Taking negatives reverses an inequality.**

  If $a < b$, then $-a > -b$, and if $a > b$, then $-a < -b$.
  $3 < 7 \Rightarrow -3 > -7$, and $7 > 3 \Rightarrow -7 < -3$.

- **If two numbers are each positive or negative, taking reciprocals reverses an inequality.**

  If a and b are both positive or both negative and $a < b$, then $\dfrac{1}{a} > \dfrac{1}{b}$.

  $3 < 7 \Rightarrow \dfrac{1}{3} > \dfrac{1}{7}$ and $-7 < 3 \Rightarrow \dfrac{1}{-7} > \dfrac{1}{-3}$

Helpful Hint

Be sure you understand KEY FACT A23; it is very useful. Also, review the important properties listed in KEY FACTS A24–A26. These properties come up frequently on the SAT I.

Key Fact A24   Important Inequalities for Numbers Between 0 and 1

- **If $0 < x < 1$, and a is positive, then $xa < a$.**
  For example, $0.85 \times 19 < 19$.
- **If $0 < x < 1$, and m and n are integers with $m > n > 1$, then $x^m < x^n < x$.**

  For example, $\left(\dfrac{1}{2} \right)^5 < \left(\dfrac{1}{2} \right)^2 < \dfrac{1}{2}$.

- **If $0 < x < 1$, then $\sqrt{x} > x$.** For example, $\sqrt{\dfrac{3}{4}} > \dfrac{3}{4}$.

- **If $0 < x < 1$, then $\dfrac{1}{x} > x$. In fact, $\dfrac{1}{x} > 1$.**

  For example, $\dfrac{1}{0.2} > 1 > 0.2$.

Key Fact A25   Properties of Zero

- **0 is the only number that is neither positive nor negative.**
- **0 is smaller than every positive number and greater than every negative number.**
- **0 is an even integer.**
- **0 is a multiple of every integer.**
- **For every number a: $a + 0 = a$ and $a - 0 = a$.**
- **For every number a: $a \times 0 = 0$.**
- **For every integer n: $0^n = 0$.**
- **For every number a (including 0): $a \div 0$ and $\dfrac{a}{0}$ are meaningless symbols. (They are undefined.)**
- **For every number a other than 0: $0 \div a = \dfrac{0}{a} = 0$.**
- **0 is the only number that is equal to its opposite: $0 = -0$.**
- **If the product of two or more numbers is 0, at least one of the numbers is 0.**

Key Fact A26   Properties of 1

- **For any number a: $1 \times a = a$ and $\dfrac{a}{1} = a$.**
- **For any integer n: $1^n = 1$.**
- **1 is a divisor of every integer.**
- **1 is the smallest positive integer.**
- **1 is an odd integer.**
- **1 is the only integer with only one divisor. It is not a prime.**

Exercises on Basic Arithmetic

Multiple-Choice Questions

1. For how many positive integers, a, is it true that $a^2 \le 2a$?

   (A) None   (B) 1   (C) 2   (D) 4   (E) More than 4

2. If $0 < a < b < 1$, which of the following is (are) true?

   I. $a - b$ is negative.

   II. $\dfrac{1}{ab}$ is positive.

   III. $\dfrac{1}{b} - \dfrac{1}{a}$ is positive.

   (A) I only   (B) II only   (C) III only
   (D) I and II only   (E) I, II, and III

3. How many of the numbers in the following list are NOT even numbers?

   $$-64, \ \frac{0}{64}, \ \frac{192}{64}, \ 6.4, \ \sqrt{64}, \ 64^2, \ \frac{64}{1.6}, \ 64\sqrt{2},$$
   $$0.64646464...$$

   (A) 1   (B) 2   (C) 3   (D) 4   (E) 5

4. If a and b are negative, and c is positive, which of the following is (are) true?

   I. $a - b < a - c$

   II. if $a < b$, then $\dfrac{a}{c} < \dfrac{b}{c}$.

   III. $\dfrac{1}{b} < \dfrac{1}{c}$

   (A) I only   (B) II only   (C) III only
   (D) II and III only   (E) I, II, and III

5. At 3:00 A.M. the temperature was 13° below zero. By noon it had risen to 32°. What was the average hourly increase in temperature?

   (A) $\left(\dfrac{19}{9}\right)^{\circ}$ (B) $\left(\dfrac{19}{6}\right)^{\circ}$ (C) 5°   (D) 7.5°

   (E) 45°

6. If $(7^a)(7^b) = \dfrac{7^c}{7^d}$, what is d in terms of a, b, and c?

   (A) $\dfrac{c}{ab}$ (B) $c - a - b$ (C) $a + b - c$ (D) $c - ab$

   (E) $\dfrac{c}{a+b}$

7. A number is "nifty" if it is a multiple of 2 or 3. How many nifty numbers are there between −11 and 11?

   (A) 6   (B) 7   (C) 11   (D) 15   (E) 17

8. If p and q are primes greater than 2, which of the following must be true?

   I. $p + q$ is even.

   II. pq is odd.

   III. $p^2 - q^2$ is even.

   (A) I only   (B) II only   (C) I and II only
   (D) I and III only   (E) I, II, and III

9. If ☺ and ☻ can each be replaced by +, −, or ×, how many different values are there for the expression 2 ☺ 2 ☻ 2?

   (A) 4   (B) 5   (C) 6   (D) 7   (E) 9

Questions 10 and 11 refer to the following definition.

For any positive integer n, $\tau(n)$ represents the number of positive divisors of n.

10. Which of the following is (are) true?

    I. $\tau(5) = \tau(7)$

    II. $\tau(5) \cdot \tau(7) = \tau(35)$

    III. $\tau(5) + \tau(7) = \tau(12)$

    (A) I only   (B) II only   (C) I and II only
    (D) I and III only   (E) I, II, and III

11. What is the value of $\tau(\tau(\tau(12)))$?

    (A) 1   (B) 2   (C) 3   (D) 4   (E) 6

12. Which of the following is equal to $(7^8 \times 7^9)^{10}$?

    (A) 7^{27} (B) 7^{82} (C) 7^{170} (D) 49^{170} (E) 49^{720}

13. If x ✪ y represents the number of integers greater than x and less than y, what is the value of $-\pi$ ✪ $\sqrt{2}$?

    (A) 2   (B) 3   (C) 4   (D) 5   (E) 6

14. If $0 < x < 1$, which of the following lists the numbers in increasing order?

    (A) $\sqrt{x}, x, x^2$ (B) $x^2, x, \sqrt{x}$ (C) $x^2, \sqrt{x}, x$

    (D) $x, x^2, \sqrt{x}$ (E) $x, \sqrt{x}, x^2$

15. If $50^{100} = k(100^{50})$, what is the value of k?

    (A) 2^{50} (B) 25^{50} (C) 50^{50} (D) $\left(\dfrac{1}{2}\right)^{50}$

    (E) $\left(\dfrac{1}{2}\right)^{100}$

Quantitative Comparison Questions

Column A	Column B

16. The product of the odd integers from −7 to 7 | The product of the even integers from −8 to 8

a and *b* are nonzero integers.

17. $a + b$ | ab

18. The remainder when a positive integer is divided by 7 | 7

19. $24 \div 6 \times 4$ | 12

20. $\dfrac{2x - 17}{2}$ | $x - 17$

a and *b* are positive integers with *a* < *b*.

21. The remainder when *a* is divided by *b* | The remainder when *b* is divided by *a*

22. The number of primes that are divisible by 2 | The number of primes that are divisible by 3

n is a positive integer.

23. The number of different prime factors of *n* | The number of different prime factors of n^2

24. The average of 4^3 and 6^3 | 5^3

n is a positive integer.

25. $(-10)^n$ | $(-10)^{n+1}$

n is a positive integer.

26. The remainder when *n* is divided by 11 | The remainder when 100*n* is divided by 11

Column A	Column B

$\dfrac{1}{x}$ is a negative integer.

27. x | -1

28. The number of even positive factors of 30 | The number of odd positive factors of 30

$x^{10} = 100$

29. x^5 | 50

$-1 < a < 0$

30. $\dfrac{1}{a}$ | $\dfrac{1}{a^3}$

Grid-in Questions

31. If 25¢ buys 1.3 French francs, how many francs can be bought for $1.60?

32. At Ben's Butcher Shop 99 pounds of chopped meat is being divided into packages each weighing 2.5 pounds. How many pounds of meat are left when there isn't enough to make another whole package?

33. Maria has two electronic beepers. One of them beeps every 4 seconds; the other beeps every 9 seconds. If they are turned on at exactly the same time, how many times during the next hour will both beepers beep at the same time?

34. If $-7 \le x \le 7$ and $0 \le y \le 12$, what is the greatest possible value of $y - x$?

35. Find an integer that has a remainder of 1 when it is divided by 2, 3, 4, 5, 6, and 7.

36. What is the largest number, x, that can be entered in the grid such that x^2 is an integer?

37. What is the largest number, x, that can be entered in the grid such that $\sqrt{x}$ is an integer?

38. For any integer, a, greater than 1, let $\uparrow a\downarrow$ be the greatest prime factor of a. What is $\uparrow 132 \downarrow$?

39. If the product of four consecutive integers is equal to one of the integers, what is the largest possible value of one of the integers?

40. If x and y are positive integers, and $(13^x)^y = 13^{13}$, what is the average (arithmetic mean) of x and y?

Answer Key

1. **C**	7. **D**	13. **D**	19. **A**	25. **D**
2. **D**	8. **E**	14. **B**	20. **A**	26. **C**
3. **D**	9. **A**	15. **B**	21. **A**	27. **D**
4. **D**	10. **C**	16. **A**	22. **C**	28. **C**
5. **C**	11. **C**	17. **D**	23. **C**	29. **B**
6. **B**	12. **C**	18. **B**	24. **A**	30. **A**

31. **8.32** 32. **1.5** 33. **100** 34. **19** 35. **421** *

36. **9999** 37. **9801** 38. **11** 39. **3** 40. **7**

*Note: Answer to question 35 can be 1 more than any multiple of 420.

Answer Explanations

1. **C.** Since a is positive, we can divide both sides of the given inequality by a: $a^2 \le 2a \Rightarrow a \le 2 \Rightarrow a = 1$ or 2, so that there are two positive integers that satisfy the given inequality.

2. **D.** Since $a < b$, $a - b$ is negative (I is true.) Since a and b are positive, so is their product, ab; and the reciprocal of a positive number is positive. (II is true.) $\dfrac{1}{b} - \dfrac{1}{a} = \dfrac{a-b}{ab}$. We have just seen that the numerator, $a - b$, is negative and the denominator, ab, is positive, so the value of the fraction is negative. (III is false.)

3. **D.** Four numbers in the list are not even numbers: 6.4, $64\sqrt{2}$, and $0.64646464...$, which are not integers, and $\dfrac{192}{64}$, which equals 3.

4. **D.** Since b is negative and c is positive,
$$b < c \Rightarrow -b > -c \Rightarrow a - b > a - c.$$
(I is false.) Since c is positive, dividing by c preserves the inequality. (II is true.) Since b is negative, $\dfrac{1}{b}$ is negative, and so is less than $\dfrac{1}{c}$, which is positive (III is true).

5. **C.** In the 9 hours from 3:00 A.M. to noon, the temperature rose $32 - (-13) = 32 + 13 = 45°$. Therefore, the average hourly increase was $45 \div 9 = 5°$.

6. **B.** $(7^a)(7^b) = 7^{a+b}$, and $\dfrac{7^c}{7^d} = 7^{c-d}$. Therefore:
$$a + b = c - d \Rightarrow a + b + d = c \Rightarrow$$
$$d = c - a - b.$$

7. **D.** There are 15 "nifty" numbers between -11 and 11: 2, 3, 4, 6, 8, 9, 10, their opposites, and 0.

8. **E.** All primes greater than 2 are odd, so p and q are odd, and $p + q$ is even. (I is true.) The product of two odd numbers is odd. (II is true.) Since p and q are odd, so are their squares, and so the difference of the squares is even. (III is true.)

9. **A.** List the nine possible outcomes of replacing ☺ and ☻ by +, –, and ×, and see that there are four different values: –2, 2, 6, 8.

$$2 + 2 + 2 = 6 \quad 2 - 2 - 2 = -2 \quad 2 \times 2 \times 2 = 8$$
$$2 + 2 - 2 = 2 \quad 2 - 2 \times 2 = -2 \quad 2 \times 2 + 2 = 6$$
$$2 + 2 \times 2 = 8 \quad 2 - 2 + 2 = 2 \quad 2 \times 2 - 2 = 2$$

10. **C.** Since 5 and 7 have two positive factors each, $\tau(5) = \tau(7)$. (I is true.) Since 35 has four divisors (1, 5, 7, and 35) and $\tau(5) \cdot \tau(7) = 2 \times 2 = 4$, II is true. The value of $\tau(12)$ is 6, which is *not* equal to $2 + 2$. (III is false.)

11. **C.** $\tau(\tau(\tau(12))) = \tau(\tau(6)) = \tau(4) = 3.$

12. **C.** First, multiply inside the parentheses: $7^8 \times 7^9 = 7^{17}$; then raise to the 10th power: $(7^{17})^{10} = 7^{170}$.

13. **D.** There are five integers (1, 0, –1, –2, –3) that are greater than –3.14 ($-\pi$) and less than 1.41 ($\sqrt{2}$).

14. **B.** For any number, x, between 0 and 1: $x^2 < x$ and $x < \sqrt{x}$.

15. **B.** $50^{100} = k(100^{50}) \Rightarrow (50^{50})(50^{50}) = k(2^{50})(50^{50}) \Rightarrow$
$$k = \frac{50^{50}}{2^{50}} = 25^{50}.$$

16. **A.** Since the product in Column A has four negative factors (–7, –5, –3, –1), it is positive. The product in Column B also has four negative factors, but be careful — it also has the factor 0, and so Column B is 0.

17. **D.** If a and b are each 1, then $a + b = 2$, and $ab = 1$; so Column A is greater. If, however, a and b are each 3, then $a + b = 6$, $ab = 9$, and Column B is greater.

18. **B.** The remainder is *always* less than the divisor.

19. **A.** According to PEMDAS, you divide and multiply from left to right (do *not* do the multiplication first): $24 \div 6 \times 4 = 4 \times 4 = 16$.

20. **A.** By the distributive law,
$$\frac{2x - 17}{2} = \frac{2x}{2} - \frac{17}{2} = x - 8.5,$$
which is greater than $x - 17$ (the larger the number you subtract, the smaller the difference).

21. **A.** Since $a < b$, when a is divided by b, the quotient is 0 and the remainder is a: $a = 0 \times b + a$. When *any* number is divided by a, the remainder must be less than a. Column A is greater.

22. **C.** The only prime divisible by 2 is 2, and the only prime divisible by 3 is 3. The number in each column is 1.

23. **C.** If you make a factor tree for n^2, the first branches are n and n. Then, when you factor each of the n's, you get exactly the same prime factors. (See the example below.)

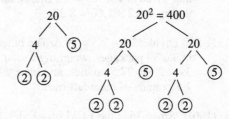

24. **A.** Since $4^3 = 64$ and $6^3 = 216$, their average is
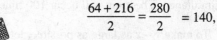
$$\frac{64 + 216}{2} = \frac{280}{2} = 140,$$
which is greater than $5^3 = 125$.

25. **D.** If n is even, then $n + 1$ is odd, and consequently $(-10)^n$ is positive, whereas $(-10)^{n+1}$ is negative. If n is odd, exactly the opposite is true.

26. **C.** The SAT I way to solve this is as follows (see Chapter 10): Pick a value for n; let $n = 13$. Then 11 goes into 13 once with a remainder of 2. How many times does 11 go into 1300? Use your calculator: $1300 \div 11 = 118.18....$ Therefore, 11 goes into 1300 118 times with some remainder: $118 \times 11 = 1298$, and the remainder is 2. Try another value, and then choose C. *Correct mathematical solution.* When n is divided by 11, there is a quotient, q, and a remainder, r: $n = 11q + r$. Therefore, $100n = 1100q + 100r = 1100q + 99r + r = 11(100q + r) + r$.
The remainder is again r. The answer is C.

27. **D.** Since $\frac{1}{-1} = -1$, which is a negative integer, x *could* be –1. Does it have to be? No, if $x = -\frac{1}{2}$, then $\frac{1}{x}$ is –2.

28. **C.** List the factors of 30: 1, 2, 3, 5, 6, 10, 15, 30. Four of them are odd, and four are even.

29. **B.** Since $x^5 x^5 = x^{10} = 100$, $x^5 = 10$, which is less than 50.

30. **A.** The easiest solution is to pick an appropriate value for a: say $-\frac{1}{2}$, and substitute. Then

$$\frac{1}{a} = -2, \text{ whereas } \frac{1}{a^3} = -8.$$

31. **(8.32)** You could set up a proportion (see Section 12-D):

$$\frac{\text{cents}}{\text{francs}} = \frac{25}{1.3} = \frac{160}{x},$$

but the easiest way is to multiply by 4 to find that $1 buys $4 \times 1.3 = 5.2$ francs, and then multiply $5.2 \times 1.60 = 8.32$.

32. **(1.5)** Divide: $99 \div 2.5 = 39.6$. The butchers can make 39 packages, weighing a total of $39 \times 2.5 = 97.5$ pounds, and have $99 - 97.5 = 1.5$ pounds of meat left over.

33. **(100)** Since 36 is the LCM of 4 and 9, the beepers will beep together every 36 seconds. One hour = 60 minutes = 3600 seconds, and so the simultaneous beeping will occur 100 times.

34. **(19)** To make $y - x$ as large as possible, let y be as large as possible (12), and subtract the smallest amount possible ($x = -7$): $12 - (-7) = 19$.

35. **(any multiple of 420 + 1)** The LCM of 2, 3, 4, 5, 6, 7 is 420, so 420 is divisible by each integer, and 421 will leave a remainder of 1 when divided by any of the integers. It is actually quicker, however, to use your calculator to find that the product of all six numbers is 3360, so 3361 works.

36. **(9999)** The largest number that can be entered in the grid is the integer 9999, and the square of any integer is an integer.

37. **(9801)** For $\sqrt{x}$ to be an integer, x must be a perfect square. Since $100^2 = 10,000$, it won't fit, but $99^2 = 9801$, which does fit.

38. **(11)** The easiest way to find the greatest prime factor of 132 is to find its prime factorization: $132 = 2 \times 2 \times 3 \times 11$, so 11 is the greatest prime factor.

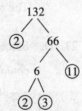

39. **(3)** If all four integers were negative, their product would be positive, and so could not equal one of them. If all four integers were positive, their product would be much greater than any of them (even $1 \times 2 \times 3 \times 4 = 24$). Therefore, the integers must include 0, in which case their product *is* 0. The largest set of four consecutive integers that includes 0 is 0, 1, 2, 3.

40. **(7)** Since $13^{13} = (13^x)^y = 13^{xy}$, then $xy = 13$. The only positive integers whose product is 13 are 1 and 13. Their average is

$$\frac{1 + 13}{2} = 7.$$

12-B FRACTIONS AND DECIMALS

Several questions on the SAT I involve fractions or decimals. In this section we will review all of the important facts on these topics that you need to know for the SAT I. Even if you are using a calculator with fraction capabilities, it is essential that you review all of this material thoroughly. (See Chapter 1 for a discussion of calculators that can perform operations with fractions.)

When a whole is *divided* into n equal parts, each part is called *one-nth* of the whole, written as $\frac{1}{n}$. For example, if a pizza is cut (*divided*) into eight equal slices, each slice is one-eighth $\left(\frac{1}{8}\right)$ of the pizza; a day is *divided* into 24 equal hours, so an hour is one-twenty-fourth $\left(\frac{1}{24}\right)$ of a day; and an inch is one-twelfth $\left(\frac{1}{12}\right)$ of a foot.

- If Sam slept for 5 hours, he slept for five-twenty-fourths $\left(\frac{5}{24}\right)$ of a day.

- If Tom bought eight slices of pizza, he bought eight-eighths $\left(\frac{8}{8}\right)$ of a pie.

- If Joe's shelf is 30 inches long, it measures thirty-twelfths $\left(\frac{30}{12}\right)$ of a foot.

Numbers such as $\frac{5}{24}$, $\frac{8}{8}$, and $\frac{30}{12}$, in which one integer is written over a second integer, are called **fractions**. The center line is called the fraction bar. The number above the bar is called the **numerator**, and the number below the bar is the **denominator**.

> **CAUTION:** The denominator of a fraction can *never* be 0.

- A fraction such as $\frac{5}{24}$, in which the numerator is less than the denominator, is called a **proper fraction**. Its value is less than 1.

- A fraction such as $\frac{30}{12}$, in which the numerator is more than the denominator, is called an **improper fraction**. Its value is greater than 1.

• A fraction such as $\frac{8}{8}$, in which the numerator and denominator are the same, is also an *improper fraction*, but it is equal to 1.

It is useful to think of the fraction bar as a symbol for division. If three pizzas are divided equally among eight people, each person gets $\frac{3}{8}$ of a pizza. If you actually use your calculator to divide 3 by 8, you get $\frac{3}{8} = 0.375$.

Key Fact B1

Every fraction, proper or improper, can be expressed in decimal form (or as a whole number), by dividing the numerator by the denominator. For example:

$$\frac{3}{10} = 0.3 \qquad \frac{3}{4} = 0.75 \qquad \frac{5}{8} = 0.625 \qquad \frac{3}{16} = 0.1875$$

$$\frac{8}{8} = 1 \qquad \frac{11}{8} = 1.375 \qquad \frac{48}{16} = 3 \qquad \frac{100}{8} = 12.5$$

Note: Any number beginning with a decimal point can be written with a 0 to the left of the decimal point. In fact, some calculators will express 3 ÷ 8 as .375, whereas others will print 0.375.

 Calculator Shortcut

On the SAT I, *never* do long division to convert a fraction to a decimal. Use your calculator.

Unlike the examples above, when most fractions are converted to decimals, the division does not terminate after two, three, or four decimal places; rather it goes on forever with some set of digits repeating itself.

$$\frac{2}{3} = 0.666666... \qquad \frac{3}{11} = 0.272727... \qquad \frac{5}{12} = 0.416666...$$

$$\frac{17}{15} = 1.133333...$$

On the SAT I, *you do not need to be concerned with this repetition*. On grid-in problems you just enter as much of the number as will fit in the grid; and on multiple-choice and quantitative comparison questions, all numbers written as decimals terminate.

Although on the SAT I you will have occasion to convert fractions to decimals (by dividing), you will not have to convert decimals to fractions.

Comparing Fractions and Decimals

Key Fact B2

To compare two decimals, follow these rules:

• **Whichever number has the greater number to the left of the decimal point is greater: since 11 > 9, 11.001 > 9.896; and since 1 > 0, 1.234 > 0.8. (Recall that, if a decimal has no number to the left of the decimal point, you may assume that a 0 is there, so 1.234 > .8).**
• **If the numbers to the left of the decimal point are equal (or if there are no numbers to the left of the decimal point), proceed as follows:**

1. **If the numbers do not have the same number of digits to the right of the decimal point, add zeros at the end of the shorter one until the numbers of digits are equal.**

2. **Now, compare the numbers, *ignoring* the decimal point itself.**

For example, to compare 1.83 and 1.823, add a 0 to the end of 1.83, forming 1.830. Now, *thinking of them as whole numbers*, compare the numbers, ignoring the decimal point:

$$1830 > 1823 \Rightarrow 1.830 > 1.823.$$

Column A	Column B

Example 1.

0.2139	0.239

Solution. Do not think that Column A is greater because 2139 > 239. In fact, Column **B** is greater. You can compare the numbers after two digits (21 < 23), or after three digits (213 < 239), or after four digits, if you first add a 0 at the end of 0.239 (2139 < 2390).

 CALCULATOR HINT

KEY FACT B2 enables you to compare decimals just by looking at them. This is definitely the fastest way, but you can also use your calculator. From KEY FACT A21, $a > b$ means that $a - b$ is positive, and $a < b$ means that $a - b$ is negative. To compare, you can just subtract. For example, 1.83 − 1.823 = 0.007, which is positive, so 1.83 > 1.823; 0.2139 − 0.239 = −0.0251, which is negative, so 0.2139 < 0.239.

Key Fact B3

To compare two fractions, use your calculator to convert them to decimals. Then apply KEY FACT B2. This *always* works.

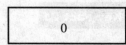 For example, to compare $\frac{1}{3}$ and $\frac{3}{8}$, write

$$\frac{1}{3} = 0.3333... \quad \text{and} \quad \frac{3}{8} = 0.375.$$

Since $0.375 > 0.333$, $\frac{3}{8} > \frac{1}{3}$.

Key Fact B4

When comparing fractions, there are three situations in which it is faster *not* to use your calculator to convert fractions to decimals (although, of course, that will work).

1. **The fractions have the same positive denominator.** Then the fraction with the larger numerator is greater. Just as $9 are more than $7, and 9 books are more than 7 books, 9 tenths is more than 7 tenths: $\frac{9}{10} > \frac{7}{10}$.

2. **The fractions have the same numerator.** Then the fraction with the smaller denominator is greater. If you divide a cake into five equal pieces, each piece is larger than a piece you would get if you had divided the cake into 10 equal pieces: $\frac{1}{5} > \frac{1}{10}$, and similarly $\frac{3}{5} > \frac{3}{10}$.

3. **The fractions are so familiar or easy to work with that you already know the answer.** For example, $\frac{3}{4} > \frac{1}{5}$ and $\frac{11}{20} > \frac{1}{2}$.

Key Fact B5

KEY FACTS B2, B3, and B4 apply to *positive* decimals and fractions. Clearly, any positive number is greater than any negative number. For negative decimals and fractions, use KEY FACT A23, which states that, if $a > b$, then $-a < -b$.

$$\frac{1}{2} > \frac{1}{5} \Rightarrow -\frac{1}{2} < -\frac{1}{5} \quad \text{and} \quad .83 > .829 \Rightarrow -.83 < -.829$$

Example 2.

Which of the following lists the fractions $\frac{2}{3}$, $\frac{5}{8}$, $\frac{7}{11}$, and $\frac{13}{20}$ in order from least to greatest?

(A) $\frac{2}{3}, \frac{5}{8}, \frac{7}{11}, \frac{13}{20}$ (B) $\frac{5}{8}, \frac{7}{11}, \frac{13}{20}, \frac{2}{3}$

(C) $\frac{5}{8}, \frac{13}{20}, \frac{7}{11}, \frac{2}{3}$ (D) $\frac{13}{20}, \frac{7}{11}, \frac{5}{8}, \frac{2}{3}$

(E) $\frac{7}{11}, \frac{13}{20}, \frac{2}{3}, \frac{5}{8}$

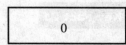 **Solution.** On your calculator convert each fraction to a decimal, writing down the first few decimal places:

$$\frac{2}{3} = 0.666, \quad \frac{5}{8} = 0.625, \quad \frac{7}{11} = 0.636, \quad \text{and} \quad \frac{13}{20} = 0.65.$$

It is now easy to order the decimals:

$$0.625 < 0.636 < 0.650 < 0.666.$$

The answer is **B**.

Column A	Column B

Example 3.

$$0 < x < y$$

$\frac{1}{x} - \frac{1}{y}$	0

Solution. By KEY FACT B4, $x < y \Rightarrow \frac{1}{x} > \frac{1}{y}$, and so, by KEY FACT A21, $\frac{1}{x} - \frac{1}{y}$ is positive. Column **A** is greater.

Equivalent Fractions

If Bill and Al shared a pizza, and Bill ate $\frac{1}{2}$ and Al ate $\frac{4}{8}$, they had exactly the same amount of the pizza. We express this idea by saying that $\frac{1}{2}$ and $\frac{4}{8}$ are *equivalent fractions*: that is, they have the exact same value.

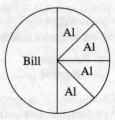

Note: If you multiply both the numerator and the denominator of $\frac{1}{2}$ by 4, you get $\frac{4}{8}$; and if you divide both the numerator and the denominator of $\frac{4}{8}$ by 4, you get $\frac{1}{2}$. This illustrates the next KEY FACT.

Key Fact B6

Two fractions are equivalent if multiplying or dividing both the numerator and the denominator of the first fraction *by the same number* gives the second fraction.

Consider the following two cases.

1. Are $\frac{3}{8}$ and $\frac{45}{120}$ equivalent? There is a number that, when multiplied by 3 gives 45, and there is a number that, when multiplied by 8, gives 120. By KEY FACT B6, if these numbers are the same, the fractions are equivalent. They *are* the same number: $3 \times 15 = 45$ and $8 \times 15 = 120$.

2. Are $\frac{2}{3}$ and $\frac{28}{45}$ equivalent? Since $2 \times 14 = 28$, but $3 \times 14 \neq 45$, they are *not* equivalent. Alternatively, $28 \div 14 = 2$, but $45 \div 14 \neq 3$.

Calculator
Shortcut

To determine whether two fractions are equivalent, convert them to decimals by dividing. For the fractions to be equivalent, the two quotients must be the same.

Example 4

Which of the following is NOT equivalent to $\frac{15}{24}$?

(A) $\frac{45}{72}$ (B) $\frac{60}{96}$ (C) $\frac{180}{288}$ (D) $\frac{5}{8}$ (E) $\frac{3}{5}$

Solution. Just check each choice.

(A) $45 \div 15 = 3$ and $72 \div 24 = 3$, so the fractions are equivalent: $\frac{45}{72} = \frac{15 \times 3}{24 \times 3}$.

(B) $60 \div 15 = 4$ and $96 \div 24 = 4$, so the fractions are equivalent: $\frac{60}{96} = \frac{15 \times 4}{24 \times 4}$.

(C) $180 \div 15 = 12$ and $288 \div 24 = 12$, so the fractions are equivalent: $\frac{180}{288} = \frac{15 \times 12}{24 \times 12}$.

(D) $15 \div 5 = 3$ and $24 \div 8 = 3$, so the fractions are equivalent: $\frac{5}{8} = \frac{15 \div 3}{24 \div 3}$.

(E) $15 \div 3 = 5$ but $24 \div 5 = 4.8$, so the fractions are *not* equivalent.

The answer is **E**.

A fraction is in ***lowest terms*** if no positive integer greater than 1 is a factor of both the numerator and the denominator. For example, $\frac{9}{20}$ is in lowest terms, since no integer greater than 1 is a factor of both 9 and 20; but $\frac{9}{24}$ is not in lowest terms, since 3 is a factor of both 9 and 24.

Key Fact B7

Every fraction can be *reduced* to lowest terms by dividing the numerator and the denominator by their greatest common factor (GCF). If the GCF is 1, the fraction is already in lowest terms.

Calculator
Shortcut

Calculators that have fraction capability either reduce automatically or have a key to reduce. On a regular calculator, see whether some prime can divide evenly into both the numerator and the denominator. On the SAT I, if none of 2, 3, 5, 7, or 11 works, the fraction cannot be reduced.

Helpful Hints

Keep these two facts in mind:

1. On grid-in problems you should never reduce a fraction, such as $\frac{9}{24}$, that fits in a grid; just enter it:

   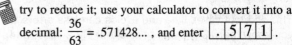 . If a fraction can't fit, such as $\frac{36}{63}$, don't try to reduce it; use your calculator to convert it into a decimal: $\frac{36}{63} = .571428...$, and enter $\boxed{.}\,\boxed{5}\,\boxed{7}\,\boxed{1}$.

   You should reduce a fraction only if you are positive you can do so in *1 or 2 seconds* (faster than you could divide on your calculator), *without making a mistake*. Examples of easy reductions are $\frac{100}{200} = \frac{1}{2}$, $\frac{20}{30} = \frac{2}{3}$, $\frac{2}{120} = \frac{1}{60}$ (see Chapter 11).

2. On multiple-choice questions, on the other hand, the fraction choices are almost always in lowest terms, so you may have to reduce your answer to see which choice is correct. If you can't do this easily, use your calculator to convert your answer to a decimal, and then use your calculator again to check the five choices.

Example 5.

For any positive integer n, $n!$ means the product of all the integers from 1 to n. What is the value of $\frac{6!}{8!}$?

(A) $\frac{1}{56}$ (B) $\frac{1}{48}$ (C) $\frac{1}{8}$ (D) $\frac{1}{4}$ (E) $\frac{3}{4}$

Solution. Assume that you don't see the easy way to do this. On your calculator quickly multiply (or use the ! key if you have one):

$$6! = 1 \cdot 2 \cdot 3 \cdot 4 \cdot 5 \cdot 6 = 720 \quad \text{and}$$
$$8! = 1 \cdot 2 \cdot 3 \cdot 4 \cdot 5 \cdot 6 \cdot 7 \cdot 8 = 40{,}320.$$

You are now faced with reducing $\frac{720}{40{,}320}$. Don't do it.

Use your calculator to divide: $\frac{720}{40{,}320} = 0.0178...$ Now

test the choices, starting with C: $\frac{1}{8} = 0.125$, which is too large. Eliminate C as well as D and E, which are even larger, and try A or B. In fact, $\frac{1}{56} = 0.0178...$**(A)**.

Here's the easy solution:

$$\frac{6!}{8!} = \frac{\overset{1}{\cancel{6 \times 5 \times 4 \times 3 \times 2 \times 1}}}{8 \times 7 \times \underset{1}{\cancel{6 \times 5 \times 4 \times 3 \times 2 \times 1}}} = \frac{1}{8 \times 7} = \frac{1}{56}.$$

This solution takes only a few seconds, but the calculator solution is simple enough and can surely be done in less than a minute.

Arithmetic Operations with Decimals

 Calculator Shortcut

On the SAT I, *all* decimal arithmetic (including whole numbers) that you can't easily do in your head should be done on your calculator.

This shortcut saves time and avoids careless errors. If you know that $12 \times 12 = 144$ and that $1.2 \times 1.2 = 1.44$, fine; but if you're not sure, use your calculator rather than your pencil. You should even use your calculator to multiply 0.2×0.2 if there's any chance that you would get 0.4 instead of 0.04 as the answer.

You should *not* have to use your calculator to multiply or divide any decimal number by a power of 10, because multiplying and dividing by 10 or 100 or 1000 is a calculation you should be able to do easily in your head.

Helpful Hint

Any whole number can be treated as a decimal: $7 = 7$. or 7.0.

Key Fact B8

To multiply any decimal or whole number by a power of 10, move the decimal point as many places to the right as there are 0's in the power of 10, filling in with 0's if necessary.

$$1.35 \times 10 = 13.5 \qquad 1.35 \times 100 = 135$$
$$1.35 \times 1000 = 1350$$

$$23 \times 10 = 230 \qquad 23 \times 100 = 2300$$
$$23 \times 1,000,000 = 23,000,000$$

Key Fact B9

To divide any decimal or whole number by a power of 10, move the decimal point as many places to the left as there are 0's in the power of 10, filling in with 0's if necessary.

$$67.8 \div 10 = 6.78 \qquad 67.8 \div 100 = 0.678$$
$$67.8 \div 1000 = 0.0678$$

$$14 \div 10 = 1.4 \qquad 14 \div 100 = 0.14$$
$$14 \div 1,000,000 = 0.000014$$

| Column A | Column B |

Example 6.

| 3.75×10^4 | $375,000,000 \div 10^4$ |

Solution. In Column A, move the decimal point four places to the right: 37,500.

In Column B, move the decimal point four places to the left: 37,500.

The answer is **C**.

On the SAT I, you *never* have to round off decimal answers. On grid-ins just enter the number, putting in as many digits after the decimal point as fit. For example, enter 3.125 as | 3 | . | 1 | 2 | and .1488 as | . | 1 | 4 | 8 | (see Chapter 11). However, you do have to know how to round off, because *occasionally* there is a question about that procedure.

Key Fact B10

To *round off* a decimal number to any place, follow these rules, which are fully explained with examples in the table below.

- Keep all of the digits to the left of the specified place.
- In that place, keep the digit if the next digit is < 5, and increase that digit by 1 if the next digit is ≥ 5. (*Note:* 9 increased by 1 is 10: put down the 0 and carry the 1.)
- If there are still digits to the left of the decimal point, change them to 0's and eliminate the decimal point and everything that follows it.
- If you are at or beyond the decimal point, stop: don't write any more digits.

For example, here is how to round off 3815.296 to any place.

Round to the Nearest:	Procedure	Answer
thousand	The digit in the thousands place is 3; since the next digit (8) is ≥ 5, increase the 3 to a 4; fill in the 3 places to the left of the decimal point with 0's.	4000
hundred	The digit in the hundreds place is 8; keep everything to the left of it, and keep the 8 since the next digit (1) is < 5; fill in 0's to the left of the decimal point.	3800
ten	The digit in the tens place is 1; keep everything to the left of it, and increase the 1 to a 2 since the next digit (5) is ≥ 5; fill in 0's to the left of the decimal point.	3820

Round to the Nearest:	Procedure	Answer
one	The digit in the ones place is 5; keep everything to the left of it, and keep the 5 since the next digit (2) is < 5; there are no more places to the left of the decimal point, so stop.	3815
tenth	The digit in the tenths place is 2; keep everything to the left of it, and increase the 2 to a 3 since the next digit (9) is ≥ 5; you are beyond the decimal point, so stop.	3815.3
hundredth	The digit in the hundredths place is 9; keep everything to the left of it, and, since the next digit (6) is ≥ 5, increase the 9 to a 10; put down the 0 and carry a 1 into the tenths place: 0.29 becomes 0.30; since you are beyond the decimal point, stop.	3815.30

Example 7.

When 423,890 is rounded off to the nearest thousand, how many digits will be changed?

(A) 0   (B) 1   (C) 2   (D) 3   (E) 4

Solution. When 423,<u>890</u> is rounded off to the nearest thousand, 3 digits are changed: 42<u>4,000</u> **(D)**.

Column A	Column B

Example 8.

419.99 rounded to the nearest ten	419.99 rounded to the nearest tenth

Solution. Column A: To round off 419.99 to the nearest ten, increase the 1 in the tens place to a 2 and change the 9 in the ones place to a 0: 420.

Column B: To round off 419.99 to the nearest tenth, add 1 to the 9 in the tenths column. This results in a 0 in the tenths column and a 1 being carried to the ones column, changing 419 to 420 and yielding 420.0.

Since 420.0 and 420 are equal, the answer is **C**.

Arithmetic Operations with Fractions

Key Fact B11

To multiply two fractions, multiply their numerators and multiply their denominators.

$$\frac{3}{5} \times \frac{4}{7} = \frac{3 \times 4}{5 \times 7} = \frac{12}{35}.$$

Key Fact B12

To multiply a fraction by any other number, write that number as a fraction whose denominator is 1.

$$\frac{3}{5} \times 7 = \frac{3}{5} \times \frac{7}{1} = \frac{21}{5} \qquad \frac{3}{4} \times \pi = \frac{3}{4} \times \frac{\pi}{1} = \frac{3\pi}{4}$$

Before multiplying fractions, reduce. You may reduce by dividing any numerator and any denominator by a common factor.

Example 9.

Express the product $\frac{3}{4} \times \frac{8}{9} \times \frac{15}{16}$ in lowest terms.

Solution. If you just multiply the numerators and denominators (with a calculator, of course), you get $\frac{360}{576}$, which is a nuisance to reduce. Also, dividing on your calculator won't help, since your answer is supposed to be a fraction in lowest terms. It is better to use TACTIC B1 and reduce first:

$$\frac{\overset{1}{\cancel{3}}}{4} \times \frac{\overset{1}{\cancel{8}}}{\underset{3}{\cancel{9}}} \times \frac{\overset{5}{\cancel{15}}}{\underset{2}{\cancel{16}}} = \frac{1 \times 1 \times 5}{4 \times 1 \times 2} = \frac{5}{8}.$$

When a problem requires you to find a fraction *of* a number, multiply.

Example 10.

If $\frac{4}{7}$ of the 350 sophomores at Adams High School are girls, and $\frac{7}{8}$ of the girls play on a team, how many sophomore girls do NOT play on a team?

Solution. There are $\frac{4}{7} \times 350 = 200$ sophomore girls. Of these, $\frac{7}{8} \times 200 = 175$ play on a team. Then, $200 - 175 = $ **25** do not play on a team.

How should you multiply $\frac{4}{7} \times 350$? If you can do this mentally, you should:

$$\frac{4}{\underset{1}{\cancel{7}}} \times \overset{50}{\cancel{350}} = 200.$$

The next step, however, requires you to multiply $\frac{7}{8}$ by 200, and more likely than not you don't *immediately* see that 200 divided by 8 is 25 or that 7 times 25 equals 175:

$$\frac{7}{\cancel{8}_1} \times \overset{25}{\cancel{200}} = 175.$$

For any step that you can't do instantly, you should use your calculator:

$$4 \div 7 \times 350 \times 7 \div 8 = 175.$$

 CALCULATOR HINT

If you are going to use your calculator on a problem, don't bother reducing anything. Given the choice of multiplying $\frac{48}{128} \times 80$ or $\frac{3}{8} \times 80$, you would prefer the second option, but for *your calculator* the first one is just as easy.

The **reciprocal** of any nonzero number, x, is the number $\frac{1}{x}$. The reciprocal of the fraction $\frac{a}{b}$ is the fraction $\frac{b}{a}$.

Key Fact B13

To divide any number by a fraction, multiply that number by the reciprocal of the fraction.

$$20 \div \frac{2}{3} = \frac{\overset{10}{\cancel{20}}}{1} \times \frac{3}{\cancel{2}_1} = 30 \qquad \frac{3}{5} \div \frac{2}{3} = \frac{3}{5} \times \frac{3}{2} = \frac{9}{10}$$

$$\sqrt{2} \div \frac{2}{3} = \frac{\sqrt{2}}{1} \times \frac{3}{2} = \frac{3\sqrt{2}}{2}$$

Helpful Hint

Even if you have a calculator with fraction capability, be sure to review the rules in KEY FACTS B11–B15. Some calculations are easier without a calculator, and no calculator will divide $\sqrt{2}$ by $\frac{2}{3}$ and print out $\frac{3\sqrt{2}}{2}$.

Example 11.

In the meat department of a supermarket, 100 pounds of chopped meat was divided into packages, each of which weighed $\frac{4}{7}$ pound. How many packages were there?

Solution. $100 \div \frac{4}{7} = \frac{\overset{25}{\cancel{100}}}{1} \times \frac{7}{\cancel{4}_1} = 175.$

Key Fact B14

To add or subtract fractions with the same denominator, add or subtract the numerators and keep the denominator.

$$\frac{4}{9} + \frac{1}{9} = \frac{5}{9} \quad \text{and} \quad \frac{4}{9} - \frac{1}{9} = \frac{3}{9} = \frac{1}{3}.$$

To add or subtract fractions with different denominators, first rewrite the fractions as equivalent fractions with the same denominator.

$$\frac{1}{6} + \frac{3}{4} = \frac{2}{12} + \frac{9}{12} = \frac{11}{12}.$$

Note: The *easiest* denominator to find is the product of the denominators ($6 \times 4 = 24$, in this example), but the *best* denominator to use is the *least common denominator*, which is the least common multiple (LCM) of the denominators (12 in this case). Using the least common denominator minimizes the amount of reducing that is necessary to express the answer in lowest terms.

Key Fact B15

If $\frac{a}{b}$ is the fraction of the whole that satisfies some property, then $1 - \frac{a}{b}$ is the fraction of the whole that does *not* satisfy it.

Example 12.

In a jar, $\frac{1}{2}$ of the marbles are red, $\frac{1}{4}$ are white, and $\frac{1}{5}$ are blue. What fraction of the marbles are neither red, white, nor blue?

Solution. The red, white, and blue marbles constitute

$$\frac{1}{2} + \frac{1}{4} + \frac{1}{5} = \frac{10}{20} + \frac{5}{20} + \frac{4}{20} = \frac{19}{20}$$

of the total, so

$$1 - \frac{19}{20} = \frac{20}{20} - \frac{19}{20} = \frac{1}{20}$$

of the marbles are neither red, white, nor blue.

Example 13.

Ali ate $\frac{1}{3}$ of a cake and Jason ate $\frac{1}{4}$ of it. What fraction of the cake was still uneaten?

Example 14.

Ali ate $\frac{1}{3}$ of a cake and Jason ate $\frac{1}{4}$ of what was left. What fraction of the cake was still uneaten?

CAUTION: Be sure to read questions carefully. In Example 13, Jason ate $\frac{1}{4}$ of the cake. In Example 14, however, he ate only $\frac{1}{4}$ of the $\frac{2}{3}$ that was left after Ali had her piece: he ate

$$\frac{1}{\cancel{4}_2} \times \frac{\cancel{2}^1}{3} = \frac{1}{6}$$

of the cake.

Solution 13. $\frac{1}{3} + \frac{1}{4} = \frac{4}{12} + \frac{3}{12} = \frac{7}{12}$ of the cake

was eaten, and $1 - \frac{7}{12} = \frac{5}{12}$ was uneaten.

Solution 14. $\frac{1}{3} + \frac{1}{6} = \frac{2}{6} + \frac{1}{6} = \frac{3}{6} = \frac{1}{2}$ of the

cake was eaten, and the other $\frac{1}{2}$ was uneaten.

Arithmetic Operations with Mixed Numbers

A *mixed number* is a number such as $3\frac{1}{2}$, that consists of an integer followed by a fraction. The mixed number is an abbreviation for the *sum* of the integer and the fraction; so $3\frac{1}{2}$ is an abbreviation for $3 + \frac{1}{2}$.

Every mixed number can be written as an improper fraction, and every improper fraction can be written as a mixed number:

$$3\frac{1}{2} = 3 + \frac{1}{2} = \frac{3}{1} + \frac{1}{2} = \frac{6}{2} + \frac{1}{2} = \frac{7}{2}$$

and $\frac{7}{2} = \frac{6}{2} + \frac{1}{2} = 3 + \frac{1}{2} = 3\frac{1}{2}$.

Key Fact B16

To write a mixed number as an improper fraction, or an improper fraction as a mixed number, follow these rules:

1. To write a mixed number $\left(3\frac{1}{2}\right)$ as an improper fraction, multiply the whole number (3) by the denominator (2), add the numerator (1), and write the sum over the denominator (2): $\frac{3 \times 2 + 1}{2} = \frac{7}{2}$.

2. To write an improper fraction $\left(\frac{7}{2}\right)$ as a mixed number, divide the numerator by the denominator; the quotient (3) is the whole number. Place the remainder (1) over the denominator to form the fractional part $\left(\frac{1}{2}\right)$: $3\frac{1}{2}$.

> **CAUTION:** You can *never* grid in a mixed number. You must change it to an improper fraction or a decimal. (See Chapter 11.)

Key Fact B17

To add mixed numbers, add the integers and also add the fractions.

$$5\frac{1}{4} + 3\frac{2}{3} = (5+3) + \left(\frac{1}{4} + \frac{2}{3}\right) = 8 + \left(\frac{3}{12} + \frac{8}{12}\right) =$$
$$8 + \frac{11}{12} = 8\frac{11}{12}.$$

$$5\frac{3}{4} + 3\frac{2}{3} = (5+3) + \left(\frac{3}{4} + \frac{2}{3}\right) = 8 + \left(\frac{9}{12} + \frac{8}{12}\right) =$$
$$8 + \frac{17}{12} = 8 + 1\frac{5}{12} = 8 + 1 + \frac{5}{12} = 9\frac{5}{12}.$$

Key Fact B18

To subtract mixed numbers, subtract the integers and also subtract the fractions. If, however, the fraction in the second number is greater than the fraction in the first number, you first have to borrow 1 from the integer part.

For example, since $\frac{2}{3} > \frac{1}{4}$, you can't subtract

$5\frac{1}{4} - 3\frac{2}{3}$ until you borrow 1 from the 5:

$$5\frac{1}{4} = 5 + \frac{1}{4} = (4+1) + \frac{1}{4} = 4 + \left(1 + \frac{1}{4}\right) = 4 + \frac{5}{4}.$$

Now, you have

$$5\frac{1}{4} - 3\frac{2}{3} = 4\frac{5}{4} - 3\frac{2}{3} = (4-3) + \left(\frac{5}{4} - \frac{2}{3}\right) =$$
$$1 + \left(\frac{15}{12} - \frac{8}{12}\right) = 1\frac{7}{12}.$$

Key Fact B19

To multiply or divide mixed numbers, change them to improper fractions.

$$1\frac{2}{3} \times 3\frac{1}{4} = \frac{5}{3} \times \frac{13}{4} = \frac{65}{12} = 5\frac{5}{12}.$$

> **CAUTION:** Be aware that $3\left(5\frac{1}{2}\right)$ is *not* $15\frac{1}{2}$; rather:
>
> $$3\left(5\frac{1}{2}\right) = 3\left(5 + \frac{1}{2}\right) = 15 + \frac{3}{2} =$$
> $$15 + 1\frac{1}{2} = 16\frac{1}{2}.$$

 Calculator Shortcut

All arithmetic operations on mixed numbers can be done directly on calculators with fraction capability; there is no need to change the mixed numbers to improper fractions or to borrow.

Complex Fractions

A *complex fraction* is a fraction, such as $\dfrac{1+\dfrac{1}{6}}{2-\dfrac{3}{4}}$, that

has one or more fractions in its numerator or denominator or both.

Key Fact B20

There are two ways to simplify a complex fraction:

1. Multiply *every* term in the numerator and denominator by the least common multiple of all the denominators that appear in the fraction.

2. Simplify the numerator and the denominator, and divide.

To simplify $\dfrac{1+\dfrac{1}{6}}{2-\dfrac{3}{4}}$, multiply each term by 12, the LCM of

6 and 4:

$$\frac{12(1)+\overset{2}{\cancel{12}}\left(\dfrac{1}{\cancel{6}}\right)1}{12(2)-\underset{1}{\overset{3}{\cancel{12}}}\left(\dfrac{3}{\cancel{4}}\right)}=\frac{12+2}{24-9}=\frac{14}{15},$$

or write

$$\frac{1+\dfrac{1}{6}}{2-\dfrac{3}{4}}=\frac{\dfrac{7}{6}}{\dfrac{5}{4}}=\frac{7}{\overset{\cancel{6}}{3}}\times\frac{\overset{2}{\cancel{4}}}{5}=\frac{14}{15}.$$

📟 **Calculator Shortcut**

Remember that, on the SAT I, if you ever get stuck on a fraction problem, you can always convert the fractions to decimals and do all the work on your calculator.

Exercises on Fractions and Decimals

Multiple-Choice Questions

1. A French class has 12 boys and 18 girls. What fraction of the class are boys?

   (A) $\dfrac{2}{5}$ (B) $\dfrac{3}{5}$ (C) $\dfrac{2}{3}$ (D) $\dfrac{3}{4}$ (E) $\dfrac{3}{2}$

2. For how many integers, a, between 30 and 40 is it true that $\dfrac{5}{a}$, $\dfrac{8}{a}$, and $\dfrac{13}{a}$ are all in lowest terms?

   (A) 1   (B) 2   (C) 3   (D) 4   (E) 5

3. What is the value of the product $\dfrac{5}{5}\times\dfrac{5}{10}\times\dfrac{5}{15}\times\dfrac{5}{20}\times\dfrac{5}{25}$?

   (A) $\dfrac{1}{120}$ (B) $\dfrac{1}{60}$ (C) $\dfrac{1}{30}$ (D) $\dfrac{5}{30}$ (E) $\dfrac{1}{2}$

4. Billy won some goldfish at the state fair. During the first week, $\dfrac{1}{5}$ of them died, and during the second week, $\dfrac{3}{8}$ of those still alive at the end of the first week died. What fraction of the original goldfish were still alive after 2 weeks?

   (A) $\dfrac{3}{10}$ (B) $\dfrac{17}{40}$ (C) $\dfrac{1}{2}$ (D) $\dfrac{23}{40}$ (E) $\dfrac{7}{10}$

5. $\dfrac{1}{4}$ is the average (arithmetic mean) of $\dfrac{1}{5}$ and what number?

   (A) $\dfrac{1}{20}$ (B) $\dfrac{3}{10}$ (C) $\dfrac{1}{3}$ (D) $\dfrac{9}{20}$ (E) $\dfrac{9}{40}$

6. If $\dfrac{3}{11}$ of a number is 22, what is $\dfrac{6}{11}$ of that number?

   (A) 6   (B) 11   (C) 12   (D) 33   (E) 44

7. What fractional part of a week is 98 hours?

   (A) $\dfrac{7}{24}$ (B) $\dfrac{24}{98}$ (C) $\dfrac{1}{2}$ (D) $\dfrac{4}{7}$ (E) $\dfrac{7}{12}$

8. $\dfrac{5}{8}$ of 24 is equal to $\dfrac{15}{7}$ of what number?

   (A) 7   (B) 8   (C) 15   (D) $\dfrac{7}{225}$ (E) $\dfrac{225}{7}$

9. Which of the following is less than $\dfrac{5}{9}$?

   (A) $\dfrac{5}{8}$ (B) $\dfrac{21}{36}$ (C) $\dfrac{25}{45}$ (D) $\dfrac{55}{100}$ (E) .565

10. Which of the following is (are) greater than x when $x = \dfrac{9}{11}$?

   I. $\dfrac{1}{x}$

   II. $\dfrac{x+1}{x}$

   III. $\dfrac{x+1}{x-1}$

   (A) I only   (B) I and II only   (C) I and III only
   (D) II and III only   (E) I, II, and III

11. Which of the following statements is true?

   (A) $\dfrac{3}{8} < \dfrac{4}{11} < \dfrac{5}{13}$ (B) $\dfrac{4}{11} < \dfrac{3}{8} < \dfrac{5}{13}$

   (C) $\dfrac{5}{13} < \dfrac{4}{11} < \dfrac{3}{8}$ (D) $\dfrac{4}{11} < \dfrac{5}{13} < \dfrac{3}{8}$

   (E) $\dfrac{3}{8} < \dfrac{5}{13} < \dfrac{4}{11}$

12. If $a = 0.99$, which of the following is (are) less than a?

   I. $\sqrt{a}$
   II. a^2
   III. $\dfrac{1}{a}$

   (A) None   (B) I only   (C) II only   (D) III only
   (E) II and III only

13. Let a, b, c, and d be the result of rounding off 7382.196 to the nearest thousand, hundred, ten, and one, respectively. Which of the following statements is true?

   (A) $d < c < b < a$ (B) $d < c < a < b$
   (C) $a < d < c < b$ (D) $c < d < b < a$
   (E) $a < c < d < b$

14. For what value of x does
   $$\dfrac{(34.56)(7.89)}{x} = (0.3456)(78.9)?$$
   (A) 0.001   (B) 0.01   (C) 0.1   (D) 10   (E) 100

15. For the final step in a calculation, Paul accidentally divided by 1000 instead of multiplying by 1000. What should he do to his answer to correct it?

   (A) Multiply it by 1000.
   (B) Multiply it by 100,000.
   (C) Multiply it by 1,000,000.
   (D) Square it.
   (E) Double it.

Quantitative Comparison Questions

Column A	Column B

16. $\dfrac{5}{13}$ of 47 | $\dfrac{47}{13}$ of 5

$$x = -\dfrac{2}{3} \text{ and } y = \dfrac{3}{5}$$

17. xy | $\dfrac{x}{y}$

18. $\dfrac{1}{\frac{15}{1}{15}}$ | 1

John needed 8 pounds of chicken. At the supermarket, the only packages available weighed $\dfrac{3}{4}$ pound each.

19. The number of packages John needed to buy | 11

20. $\dfrac{100}{2^{100}}$ | $\dfrac{100}{3^{100}}$

$$a \nabla b = \dfrac{a}{b} + \dfrac{b}{a}$$

21. $3 \nabla 4$ | $\dfrac{1}{2} \nabla \dfrac{2}{3}$

22. $\dfrac{2^{100} + 5}{2}$ | $2^{99} + 5$

23. $\left(-\dfrac{1}{2}\right)\left(-\dfrac{3}{4}\right)\left(-\dfrac{5}{6}\right)\left(-\dfrac{7}{8}\right)$ | $\left(-\dfrac{3}{7}\right)\left(-\dfrac{5}{9}\right)\left(-\dfrac{7}{11}\right)$

<u>Column A</u>   <u>Column B</u>

$a = \frac{1}{2}$ and $b = \frac{1}{3}$

24. | $\frac{a}{b}$ | | $\frac{b}{a}$ |

$$\frac{1}{a} + \frac{1}{b} = \frac{1}{c}$$
$$ab = c$$

25. | The average (arithmetic mean) of a and b | | 1 |

---

26. | $\frac{11}{12}$ of $\frac{13}{14}$ | | $\frac{14}{15}$ |

$$c = d + \frac{1}{3}$$

27. | $c - \frac{1}{3}$ | | $d - \frac{1}{3}$ |

---

28. | $\left(\frac{3}{11}\right)^2$ | | $\sqrt{\frac{3}{11}}$ |

$$b < 0$$

29. | $\frac{1}{3}b$ | | $\frac{3}{8}b$ |

$$\frac{3}{x} = \frac{123}{y}$$

30. | y | | $40x$ |

Grid-in Questions

31. One day at Central High School, $\frac{1}{12}$ of the students were absent, and $\frac{1}{5}$ of those present went on a field trip. If the number of students staying in school was 704, how many students are enrolled at Central High?

32. What is a possible value of x if $\frac{3}{5} < \frac{1}{x} < \frac{7}{9}$?

33. What is the value of
$$\frac{\frac{7}{9} \times \frac{7}{9}}{\frac{7}{9} + \frac{7}{9} + \frac{7}{9}}?$$

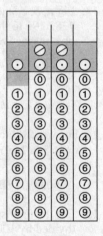

34. If $7a = 3$ and $3b = 7$, what is the value of $\dfrac{a}{b}$?

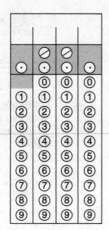

35. If $A = \{1, 2, 3\}$, $B = \{2, 3, 4\}$, and C is the set consisting of all the fractions whose numerators are in A and whose denominators are in B, what is the product of all of the numbers in C?

Answer Key

1. **A**	7. **E**	13. **E**	19. **C**	25. **B**
2. **C**	8. **A**	14. **D**	20. **A**	26. **B**
3. **A**	9. **D**	15. **C**	21. **C**	27. **A**
4. **C**	10. **B**	16. **C**	22. **B**	28. **B**
5. **B**	11. **B**	17. **A**	23. **A**	29. **A**
6. **E**	12. **C**	18. **A**	24. **A**	30. **D**

31.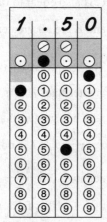

32.

$1.28 < x < 1.67$

33.

34.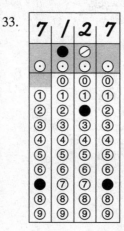

35.

Answer Explanations

1. A. The class has 30 students, of whom 12 are boys. The boys make up $\frac{12}{30} = \frac{2}{5}$ of the class.

2. C. If a is even, then $\frac{8}{a}$ is *not* in lowest terms, since both a and 8 are divisible by 2. The only possibilities are 31, 33, 35, 37, and 39, but $\frac{5}{35} = \frac{1}{7}$ and $\frac{13}{39} = \frac{1}{3}$, so only 31, 33, and 37 (that is, 3 integers) remain.

3. A. Reduce each fraction and multiply:
$$1 \times \frac{1}{2} \times \frac{1}{3} \times \frac{1}{4} \times \frac{1}{5} = \frac{1}{120}.$$
If you multiply on your calculator, you'll get 0.008333, which is less than 0.01, so only choice A is possible.

4. C. *Algebraic solution:* Let x = number of goldfish Billy won. During the first week, $\frac{1}{5}x$ died, so $\frac{4}{5}x$ were still alive. During the second week, $\frac{3}{8}$ of those died and $\frac{5}{8}$ survived:
$$\left(\frac{\cancel{5}^{1}}{\cancel{8}_{2}}\right)\left(\frac{\cancel{4}^{1}}{\cancel{5}_{1}}x\right) = \frac{1}{2}x.$$
The SAT I way (see TACTIC 9-4): Assume that the original number of goldfish was 40, the LCM of the denominators. Then, 8 died the first week $\left(\frac{1}{5} \text{ of } 40\right)$, and 12 of the 32 survivors $\left(\frac{3}{8} \text{ of } 32\right)$ died the second week. In all, 8 + 12 = 20 died; the other 20 $\left(\frac{1}{2} \text{ the original number}\right)$ were still alive.

5. B. The average of $\frac{1}{5}$ and another number, x, is
$$\frac{\frac{1}{5} + x}{2} = \frac{1}{4}.$$
Multiplying both sides by 2 yields
$$\frac{1}{5} + x = \frac{1}{2} \Rightarrow x = \frac{1}{2} - \frac{1}{5} = \frac{5}{10} - \frac{2}{10} = \frac{3}{10}.$$

6. E. Don't bother writing an equation for this one; just think. You know that $\frac{3}{11}$ of the number is 22, and $\frac{6}{11}$ of a number is twice as much as $\frac{3}{11}$ of it: $2 \times 22 = 44$.

7. E. There are 24 hours in a day and 7 days in a week, so there are $24 \times 7 = 168$ hours in a week: $\frac{98}{168} = \frac{7}{12}$.

8. A. If x is the number,
$$\frac{15}{7}x = \frac{5}{\cancel{8}_{1}} \times \cancel{24}^{3} = 15.$$
Then, $\frac{15}{7}x = 15$, which means (dividing by 15) that $\frac{1}{7}x = 1$, so $x = 7$.

9. D. Use your calculator: $\frac{5}{9} = 0.5555555....$ Choice C is also equal to 0.555555...; choices A, B, and E are all greater; only $\frac{55}{100} = 0.55$ is less.

10. B. The reciprocal of a number less than 1 is greater than 1. (I is true). Also, $\frac{x+1}{x} = 1 + \frac{1}{x}$, which is greater than 1. (II is true). When $x = \frac{9}{11}$, $x + 1$ is positive, whereas $x - 1$ is negative. So $\frac{x+1}{x-1}$ is negative, and hence less than 1. (III is false.)

11. B. Use your calculator to convert each fraction to a decimal:
$$\frac{4}{11} = 0.3636..., \quad \frac{3}{8} = 0.375, \quad \frac{5}{13} = 0.3846....$$
This is the correct order.

12. C. Since $a < 1$, then $\sqrt{a} > a$. (I is false.) Since $a < 1$, then $a^2 < a$. (II is true.) The reciprocal of a number less than 1 is greater than 1. (III is false.)

13. E. $a = 7000$, $b = 7400$, $c = 7380$, and $d = 7382$, so $a < c < d < b$.

14. D. There are several easy ways to do this. The fastest is to see that (34.56)(7.89) has four decimal places, whereas (0.3456)(78.9) has five, so the numerator must be divided by 10. The second method is to round off and calculate mentally: since $30 \times 8 = 240$, and

$0.3 \times 80 = 24$, you must divide by 10. Finally, you can do this on your calculator, but you should realize that the first method gives you the correct answer in less time than it takes to punch in 34.56.

15. **C.** Multiplying the incorrect answer by 1000 would undo the final division Paul made—the point at which he should have multiplied by 1000. Then, to correct his error, he would have to multiply again by 1000. In all, he should multiply by $1000 \times 1000 = 1,000,000$.

16. **C.** There's no need for a calculator on this one. Each column equals $\dfrac{5 \times 47}{13}$.

17. **A.** Column A: $-\dfrac{2}{\overset{1}{\cancel{3}}} \times \dfrac{\overset{1}{\cancel{3}}}{5} = -\dfrac{2}{5}$.

    Column B: $-\dfrac{2}{3} \div \dfrac{3}{5} = -\dfrac{2}{3} \times \dfrac{5}{3} = -\dfrac{10}{9}$.

    Finally, $\dfrac{10}{9} > \dfrac{2}{5} \Rightarrow -\dfrac{10}{9} < -\dfrac{2}{5}$.

18. **A.** Column A: $\dfrac{15}{\frac{1}{15}} = 15 \times 15 = 225$—*much larger than 1.*

19. **C.** Column A: $8 \div \dfrac{3}{4} = 8 \times \dfrac{4}{3} = \dfrac{32}{3} = 10\dfrac{2}{3}$.
    Since 10 packages wouldn't be enough
    (10 packages would weigh only $7\dfrac{1}{2}$ pounds),
    John had to buy 11.

20. **A.** When two fractions have the same numerator, the one with the smaller denominator is larger, and $2^{100} < 3^{100}$.

21. **C.** Column B is the sum of two complex fractions:

    $$\dfrac{\frac{1}{2}}{\frac{2}{3}} + \dfrac{\frac{2}{3}}{\frac{1}{2}}.$$

    Simplifying each complex fraction by multiplying numerator and denominator by 6, or treating each one as the quotient of two fractions, we get $\dfrac{3}{4} + \dfrac{4}{3}$, which is exactly the value of Column A.

22. **B.** By the distributive law,

    $$\dfrac{2^{100} + 5}{2} = \dfrac{2^{100}}{2} + \dfrac{5}{2} = 2^{99} + \dfrac{5}{2} < 2^{99} + 5.$$

23. **A.** Since Column A is the product of four negative numbers, it is positive and so is greater than Column B, which, being the product of three negative numbers, is negative.

24. **A.** Column A: $\dfrac{1}{2} \div \dfrac{1}{3} = \dfrac{1}{2} \times \dfrac{3}{1} = \dfrac{3}{2}$. Since Column B is the reciprocal of Column A, Column B $= \dfrac{2}{3}$.

25. **B.** It is given that $\dfrac{1}{c} = \dfrac{1}{a} + \dfrac{1}{b}$, which equals $\dfrac{a+b}{ab}$ which equals $\dfrac{a+b}{c}$ since it is also given that $ab = c$. Therefore:

    $$\dfrac{1}{c} = \dfrac{a+b}{c} \Rightarrow a + b = 1 \Rightarrow \dfrac{a+b}{2} = \dfrac{1}{2}.$$

26. **B.** You don't need to multiply on this one: since $\dfrac{11}{12} < 1$, $\dfrac{11}{12}$ of $\dfrac{13}{14}$ is less than $\dfrac{13}{14}$, which is already less than $\dfrac{14}{15}$.

27. **A.** From the given equation, $c - \dfrac{1}{3} = d$. Then, Column A $= d$, whereas Column B $= d - \dfrac{1}{3}$.

28. **B.** If $0 < x < 1$, then $x^2 < x < \sqrt{x}$. In this question, $x = \dfrac{3}{11}$.

29. **A.** Convert to decimals to verify that $\dfrac{1}{3} < \dfrac{3}{8}$. Multiply both sides by b, remembering to reverse the inequality since b is negative:

    $$\dfrac{1}{3}b > \dfrac{3}{8}b.$$

30. **D.** Since $123 = 41 \times 3$, $y = 41x$, which is greater than $40x$ if x is positive, but less than $40x$ if x is negative.

31. **(960)** If s is the number of students enrolled, $\dfrac{1}{12}s$ is the number who were absent, and $\dfrac{11}{12}s$ is the number who were present. Since $\dfrac{1}{5}$ of those present went on a field trip, $\dfrac{4}{5}$ of them stayed in school. Therefore,

$$704 = \overset{1}{\underset{5}{\cancel{4}}} \times \frac{11}{\underset{3}{\cancel{12}}} s = \frac{11}{15} s \Rightarrow s = 704 \div \frac{11}{15} =$$

$$704 \times \frac{15}{11} = 960.$$

32. $(1.28 < x < 1.67)$ Since $\frac{3}{5} = .6$ and $\frac{7}{9} = .777...,$

$\frac{1}{x}$ can be any number between .6 and .777. If

$\frac{1}{x} = .7 = \frac{7}{10}$, then $x = \frac{10}{7}$ or 1.42; if $\frac{1}{x} =$

$.75 = \frac{3}{4}$, then $x = \frac{4}{3}$ or 1.33; and so on.

33. $\left(\frac{7}{27}\right)$ Don't start by doing the arithmetic. This complex fraction is just

$$\frac{(a)(a)}{a+a+a} = \frac{(a)(a)}{3a} = \frac{a}{3}.$$

Now, replacing a by $\frac{7}{9}$ gives $\frac{7}{9} \div 3 = \frac{7}{27}$.

34. $\left(\frac{9}{49}\right)$ Since $7a = 3$, and $3b = 7 \Rightarrow a = \frac{3}{7}, b = \frac{7}{3}$. So

$$\frac{a}{b} = \frac{3}{7} \div \frac{7}{3} = \frac{3}{7} \times \frac{3}{7} = \frac{9}{49}.$$

35. $\left(\frac{1}{64}\right)$ Nine fractions are formed: $\frac{1}{2}, \frac{1}{3}, \frac{1}{4}, \frac{2}{2}, \frac{2}{3},$

$\frac{2}{4}, \frac{3}{2}, \frac{3}{3}, \frac{3}{4}$. When you multiply, the three 2's and the three 3's in the numerators cancel with the three 2's and three 3's in the denominators. Then, the numerator is 1 and the denominator is $4 \times 4 \times 4 = 64$.

12-C PERCENTS

The word *percent* means "hundredth." We use the symbol "%" to express the word *percent*. For example, "17 percent" means "17 hundredths" and can be written with a % symbol, as a fraction, or as a decimal:

$$17\% = \frac{17}{100} = 0.17.$$

Key Fact C1

To convert a percent to a decimal, or a percent to a fraction, follow these rules:

1. To convert a percent to a decimal, drop the % symbol and move the decimal point two places to

the left, adding 0's if necessary. (Remember that we assume that there is a decimal point to the right of any whole number.)

2. To convert a percent to a fraction, drop the % symbol, write the number over 100, and reduce.

$$25\% = 0.25 = \frac{25}{100} = \frac{1}{4} \qquad 100\% = 1.00 = \frac{100}{100}$$

$$12.5\% = 0.125 = \frac{12.5}{100} = \frac{125}{1000} = \frac{1}{8}$$

$$1\% = 0.01 = \frac{1}{100} \qquad \frac{1}{2}\% = 0.5\% = 0.005 = \frac{5}{100} = \frac{1}{200}$$

$$250\% = 2.50 = \frac{250}{100} = \frac{5}{2}$$

Key Fact C2

To convert a decimal to a percent, or a fraction to a percent, follow these rules:

1. To convert a decimal to a percent, move the decimal point two places to the right, adding 0's if necessary, and add the % symbol.

2. To convert a fraction to a percent, first convert the fraction to a decimal, then do step 1.

$$0.375 = 37.5\% \qquad 0.3 = 30\% \qquad 1.25 = 125\% \qquad 10 = 1000\%$$

$$\frac{3}{4} = 0.75 = 75\% \qquad \frac{1}{3} = 0.33333... = 33.333...\% = 33\frac{1}{3}\%$$

$$\frac{1}{5} = 0.2 = 20\%$$

You should be familiar with the following basic conversions:

$\frac{1}{2} = 50\%$	$\frac{1}{10} = 10\%$	$\frac{6}{10} = \frac{3}{5} = 60\%$
$\frac{1}{3} = 33\frac{1}{3}\%$	$\frac{2}{10} = \frac{1}{5} = 20\%$	$\frac{7}{10} = 70\%$
$\frac{2}{3} = 66\frac{2}{3}\%$	$\frac{3}{10} = 30\%$	$\frac{8}{10} = \frac{4}{5} = 80\%$
$\frac{1}{4} = 25\%$	$\frac{4}{10} = \frac{2}{5} = 40\%$	$\frac{9}{10} = 90\%$
$\frac{3}{4} = 75\%$	$\frac{5}{10} = \frac{1}{2} = 50\%$	$\frac{10}{10} = 1 = 100\%$

Knowing these conversions can help you to solve many problems more quickly. For example, the fastest way to find 25% of 32 is to know that $25\% = \frac{1}{4}$, and that $\frac{1}{4}$ of 32 is 8, *not* to use your calculator.

It is important to keep in mind, however, that *any* problem involving percents can be done on your calculator: to find 25% of 32, write 25% as a decimal and multiply: $32 \times .25 = 8$.

Here is another example of mental math being much faster than calculator math. Since $10\% = \frac{1}{10}$, to take

10% of a number, just divide by 10 by moving the decimal point one place to the left: 10% of 60 is 6. Also, since 5% is half of 10%, then 5% of 60 is 3 (half of 6); and since 30% is 3 times 10%, then 30% of 60 is 18 (3 × 6).

Practice doing this, because improving your ability to do mental math will add valuable points to your score on the SAT I.

Solving Percent Problems

Now, consider these three questions:

(i) What is 45% of 200?
(ii) 90 is 45% of what number?
(iii) 90 is what percent of 200?

Each question can be answered easily by using your calculator, but you must first set the question up properly so that you know what to multiply or divide. In each case, there is one unknown; call it x. Now, just translate each sentence, replacing "is" by "=" and the unknown by x.

(i) $x = 45\%$ of $200 \Rightarrow x = 0.45 \times 200 = 90$.
(ii) $90 = 45\%$ of $x \Rightarrow 90 = 0.45x \Rightarrow x = 90 \div 0.45 = 200$.
(iii) $90 = x\%$ of $200 \Rightarrow 90 = \dfrac{x}{\cancel{100}_1}(\overset{2}{200}) \Rightarrow x = 45$.

Example 1.

Brian gave 20% of his baseball cards to Scott and 15% to Adam. If he still had 520 cards, how many did he have originally?

Solution. Originally, Brian had 100% of the cards (all of them). After he gave away 35% of them, he had 100% − 35% = 65% of them left. So 520 is 65% of what number?

$$520 = .65x \Rightarrow x = 520 \div .65 = \mathbf{800}$$

Example 2.

After Michael gave 110 baseball cards to Sally and 75 to Heidi, he still had 315 left. What percent of his cards did Michael give away?

Solution. Michael gave away a total of 185 cards and had 315 left. Therefore, he started with 185 + 315 = 500 cards. So 185 is what percent of 500?

$$185 = \dfrac{x}{\cancel{100}_1}(\overset{5}{\cancel{500}}) \Rightarrow 5x = 185 \Rightarrow x = 185 \div 5 = \mathbf{37}$$

Michael gave away 37% of his cards.

Since *percent* means "hundredth," the easiest number to use in any percent problem is 100:

$$a\% \text{ of } 100 = \dfrac{a}{100}(100) = a.$$

Key Fact C3

For any positive number a: $a\%$ of 100 is a.

For example, 11.2% of 100 is 11.2; 500% of 100 is 500; and $\frac{1}{2}\%$ of 100 = $\frac{1}{2}$.

Tactic C1

In any problem involving percents, use the number 100.

Example 3.

In 1970 the populations of town A and town B were the same. From 1970 to 1980, however, the population of town A increased by 60% while the population of town B decreased by 60%. In 1980, the population of town B was what percent of the population of town A?

(A) 25%   (B) 36%   (C) 40%   (D) 60%   (E) 120%

Solution. In your math class, you would let x be the population of town A in 1970 and then proceed to set up an algebra problem. *Don't do that on the SAT I.* Assume that the populations of both towns were 100 in 1970. Then, since 60% of 100 is 60, in 1980, the populations were 100 + 60 = 160 (town A) and 100 − 60 = 40 (town B). Then, in 1980, town B's population was $\dfrac{40}{160} = \dfrac{1}{4} = $ **25%** of town A's.

Since $a\%$ of b is $\dfrac{a}{100}(b) = \dfrac{ab}{100}$, and $b\%$ of a is $\dfrac{b}{100}(a) = \dfrac{ba}{100}$ we have the following result.

Key Fact C4

For any positive numbers a and b: $a\%$ of $b = b\%$ of a.

KEY FACT C4 often comes up on the SAT I in quantitative comparison questions: Which is greater, 13% of 87 or 87% of 13? Don't use your calculator—the two quantities are equal.

Percent Increase and Decrease

Key Fact C5

The *percent increase* of a quantity is

$$\dfrac{\text{actual increase}}{\text{original amount}} \times 100\%.$$

The *percent decrease* of a quantity is

$$\dfrac{\text{actual decrease}}{\text{original amount}} \times 100\%.$$

For example:

• If the price of a chair rises from $80 to $100, the actual increase is $20, and the percent increase is

$$\dfrac{\overset{1}{\cancel{20}}}{\underset{4}{\cancel{80}}} \times 100\% = \dfrac{1}{4} \times 100\% = 25\%.$$

• If a $100 chair is on sale for $80, the actual decrease in price is $20, and the percent decrease is

$$\frac{20}{\overset{1}{\cancel{100}}} \times \cancel{100}\% = 20\%.$$

Note that the percent increase in going from 80 to 100 is not the same as the percent decrease in going from 100 to 80.

Key Fact C6

If $a < b$, the percent increase in going from a to b is *always* greater than the percent decrease in going from b to a.

 Calculator Shortcut

To increase a number by $k\%$, multiply it by $(1 + k\%)$; to decrease a number by $k\%$, multiply it by $(1 - k\%)$.

For example:

• The value of a $1600 investment after a 25% increase is $1600(1 + 25\%) = \$1600(1.25) = \$2000$.
• If the investment then loses 25% of its value, it is worth $2000(1 - 25\%) = \$2000(.75) = \$1500$.

Note that, after a 25% increase followed by a 25% decrease, the value is $1500, $100 less than the original amount.

Key Fact C7

An increase of $k\%$ followed by a decrease of $k\%$ is equal to a decrease of $k\%$ followed by an increase of $k\%$, and is *always* less than the original value. The original value is *never* regained.

| Column A | Column B |

Example 4.

Store B always sells furniture at 60% off the list price. Store A sells its furniture at 40% off the list price, but often runs a special sale during which it reduces its prices by 20%.

| The price of a table when it is on sale at store A | The price of the same table at store B |

Solution. Assume that the list price of the table is $100. Store B always sells the table for $40 ($60 off the list price). Store A normally sells the table for $60 ($40 off the list price), but on sale reduces its price by 20%.

Since 20% of 60 is 12, the sale price is $48 ($60 − $12). The price is greater at store **A**.

Note that a decrease of 40% followed by a decrease of 20% is not the same as a single decrease of 60%; it is less. In fact, a decrease of 40% followed by a decrease of 30% wouldn't be as much as a single decrease of 60%.

Key Fact C8

A decrease of $a\%$ followed by a decrease of $b\%$ *always* results in a smaller decrease than a single decrease of $(a + b)\%$. Similarly, an increase of $a\%$ followed by an increase of $b\%$ *always* results in a larger increase than a single increase of $(a + b)\%$. In particular, an increase (or decrease) of $a\%$ followed by another increase (or decrease) of $a\%$ is *never* the same as a single increase (or decrease) of $2a\%$.

| Column A | Column B |

Example 5.

Bill and George were both hired in January at the same salary. Bill got two 35% increases, one in July and another in November. George got one 80% increase in October.

| Bill's salary at the end of the year | George's salary at the end of the year |

 Solution. Since this is a percent problem, assume both starting salaries were $100.

Column A: Bill's salary rose to 100(1.35) = $135, and then to 135(1.35) = $182.25.

Column B: George's salary rose to 100(1.80) = $180.

Column **A** is greater.

Example 6.

In January, the value of a stock increased by 25%; and in February, it decreased by 20%. How did the value of the stock at the end of February compare with its value at the beginning of January?

(A) It was less.
(B) It was the same.
(C) It was 5% greater.
(D) It was more than 5% greater.
(E) It depends on the value of the stock.

Solution. Assume that at the beginning of January the stock was worth $100. Then at the end of January it was worth $125. Since 20% of 125 is 25, during February its value decreased from $125 to $100. The answer is **B**.

Calculator Shortcut

If a number is the result of increasing another number by $k\%$, then, to find the original number, divide by $(1 + k\%)$. Also, if a number is the result of decreasing another number by $k\%$, then to find the original number, divide it by $(1 - k\%)$.

For example, if the population of a town in 1990 was 2760, a number that represents an increase of 15% since 1980, then, to find the population in 1980, divide 2760 by $(1 + 15\%)$: $2760 \div 1.15 = 2400$.

Example 7.

From 1989 to 1990, the number of applicants to a college increased 15% to 5060. How many applicants were there in 1989?

   (A) 759   (B) 4301   (C) 4400   (D) 5819   (E) 5953

Solution. The number of applicants in 1989 was $5060 \div 1.15 = \mathbf{4400\ (C)}$.

Note: Some students find percent problems like Example 7 to be harder than other types. Now, you should be able to solve them correctly. If, however, you get stuck on a problem like this on the SAT I, you still should answer it. In Example 7, since the number of applicants increased from 1989 to 1990, the number in 1989 was clearly less than 5060, so eliminate D and E. Also, 759 (A) is much too small, leaving only B and C as reasonable choices. Therefore, do not omit the question—guess. This situation, in which some of the choices are absurd, is commonplace on the SAT I. (See TACTIC 9-4.)

> **CAUTION:** Percents over 100%, which come up most often on questions involving percent increases, are confusing for many students. Be sure you understand that 100% of a particular number is that number, 200% of a number is 2 times the number, and 1000% of a number is 10 times the number. For example, if the value of an investment rises from $1000 to $5000, the investment is now worth 5 times, or 500%, as much as it was originally; but there has been only a *400%* increase in value:
>
> $$\frac{\text{actual increase}}{\text{original amount}} \times 100\% = \frac{4000}{1000} \times 100\% = 4 \times 100\% = 400\%.$$

Example 8.

The population of a town doubled every 10 years from 1960 to 1990. What was the percent increase in population during this time?

Solution. The population doubled 3 times from, say, 100 to 200 to 400 to 800. Therefore, the population in 1990 was 8 times the population in 1960, but this was an increase of 700 people, or **700%**.

Exercises on Percents

Multiple-Choice Questions

1. Charlie bought a $60 radio on sale at 5% off. How much did he pay, including 5% sales tax?

   (A) $54.15   (B) $57.00   (C) $57.75   (D) $59.85
   (E) $60.00

2. If a is a positive number, 400% of a is what percent of $400a$?

   (A) 0.01   (B) 0.1   (C) 1   (D) 10   (E) 100

3. What percent of 50 is b?

   (A) $\dfrac{b}{50}$ (B) $\dfrac{b}{2}$ (C) $\dfrac{50}{b}$ (D) $\dfrac{2}{b}$ (E) $2b$

4. At Harry's Discount Hardware everything is sold for 20% less than the price marked. If Harry buys tool kits for $80, what price should he mark them if he wants to make a 20% profit on his cost?

   (A) $96   (B) $100   (C) $112   (D) $120
   (E) $125

5. 9 is $\dfrac{1}{3}\%$ of what number?

   (A) 0.03   (B) .27   (C) 3   (D) 300   (E) 2700

6. Mr. Howard was planning on depositing a certain amount of money each month into a college fund for his children. He then decided not to make any contributions during June and July. To make the same annual contribution that he had originally planned, by what percent should he increase his monthly deposits?

   (A) $16\dfrac{2}{3}\%$ (B) 20%   (C) 25%   (D) $33\dfrac{1}{3}\%$

   (E) It cannot be determined from the information given.

7. During his second week on the job, Jason earned $110. This represented a 25% increase over his earnings of the previous week. How much did he earn during his first week of work?

   (A) $82.50   (B) $85.00   (C) $88.00
   (D) $137.50   (E) $146.67

8. What is 10% of 20% of 30%?

   (A) 0.006%   (B) 0.6%   (C) 6%   (D) 60%
   (E) 6000%

9. If 1 micron = 10,000 angstroms, then 100 angstroms is what percent of 10 microns?

(A) 0.0001%   (B) 0.001%   (C) 0.01%   (D) 0.1%
(E) 1%

10. On a test consisting of 80 questions, Marie answered 75% of the first 60 questions correctly. What percent of the other 20 questions did she need to answer correctly for her grade on the entire exam to be 80%.

(A) 85%   (B) 87.5%   (C) 90%   (D) 95%
(E) 100%

Quantitative Comparison Questions

Column A	Column B
11. 500% of 2	200% of 5

n% of 25 is 50.

12. 50% of *n*	25

13. The price of a radio when it is on sale at 30% off	The price of the same radio when it is on sale at $30 off

The price of VCR 1 is 10% more than the price of VCR 2.

14. The price of VCR 1 when it is on sale at 10% off	The price of VCR 2

15. $\frac{1}{2}$% of $\frac{2}{3}$	$\frac{2}{3}$% of $\frac{1}{2}$

a and *b* are positive integers.

16. a% of $\frac{1}{b}$	b% of $\frac{1}{a}$

Bank A pays 5% interest on its savings accounts.
Bank B pays 4% interest on its savings accounts.

17. Percent by which bank B would have to raise its interest rate to match bank A	20%

Column A	Column B

A solution that is 20% sugar is made sweeter by doubling the amount of sugar.

18. The percent of sugar in the new solution	40%

a is an integer greater than 1, and *a* equals *k*% of a^2.

19. k	50

After Judy gave Adam 50% of her money, she had 20% as much as he did.

20. 75% of the amount Adam had originally	150% of the amount Judy had originally

Grid-in Questions

21. A jar contains 2000 marbles. If 61.5% of them are red, 27.2% of them are white, and 10% of them are blue, how many are neither red, white, nor blue?

22. If 25 students took an exam and 4 of them failed, what percent of them passed?

23. There are twice as many girls as boys in an English class. If 30% of the girls and 45% of the boys have already handed in their book reports, what percent of the students have not yet handed in their reports?

24. During a sale a clerk was putting a new price tag on each item. On one radio, he accidentally raised the price by 15% instead of lowering the price by 15%. As a result the price on the tag was $45 too high. What was the original price, in dollars, of the radio?

25. If a person has an income of $100,000, what percent of his income does he pay in federal income tax if the tax rate is as given below?

    15% of the first $30,000 of income,

    28% of the next $30,000 of income, and

    31% of all income in excess of $60,000.

26. The price of a can of soup was increased by 20%. How many cans can be purchased for the amount of money that used to buy 300 cans?

27. An art dealer bought a painting for $1000 and later sold it for $10,000. By what percent did the value of the painting increase?

28. Jar B has 20% more marbles than jar A. What percent of the marbles in jar B have to be moved to jar A, in order that the number of marbles in each jar will be the same?

29. Wendy drew a square. She then erased it and drew a second square whose sides were 3 times the sides of the first square. By what percent was the area of the square increased?

30. In a large jar full of jelly beans, 30% of them are red, and 40% of the red jelly beans are cherry. If 25% of the non-cherry-flavored red jelly beans are raspberry, what percent of all the jelly beans are either cherry or raspberry?

Answer Key

1. **D**	5. **E**	9. **D**	13. **D**	17. **A**
2. **C**	6. **B**	10. **D**	14. **B**	18. **B**
3. **E**	7. **C**	11. **C**	15. **C**	19. **D**
4. **D**	8. **B**	12. **A**	16. **D**	20. **C**

21. **26**

22. **84**

23. **65**

24. **150**

25. **25.3**

26. **250**

27. **900**

28. **8.33** or **25/3**

29. **800**

30. **16.5**

Answer Explanations

1. **D.** Since 5% of 60 is 3, Charlie saved $3, and thus paid $57 for the radio. He then had to pay 5% sales tax on the $57: $.05 \times 57 = 2.85$, so the total cost was $57 + $2.85 = $59.85.

2. **C.** 400% of $a = 4a$, which is 1% of $400a$.

3. **E.** $b = \dfrac{x}{100}(50) \Rightarrow b = \dfrac{x}{2} \Rightarrow x = 2b$.

4. **D.** Since 20% of 80 is 16, Harry wants to get $96 for each tool kit he sells. What price should the tool kits be marked so that, after a 20% discount, the customer will pay $96? If x represents the marked price, then

   $$0.80x = 96 \Rightarrow x = 96 \div .80 = 120.$$

5. **E.** $9 = \dfrac{\frac{1}{3}}{100}x = \dfrac{1}{300}x \Rightarrow x = 9 \times 300 = 2700.$

6. **B.** Assume that Mr. Howard was going to contribute $100 each month, for an annual total of $1200. Having decided not to contribute for 2 months, he would have to contribute the $1200 in 10 monthly deposits of $120 each. This is an increase of $20, and a percent increase of

   $$\dfrac{\text{actual increase}}{\text{original amount}} = \dfrac{20}{100} = 20\%.$$

7. **C.** To find Jason's earnings during his first week, divide his earnings of the second week by 1.25: $110 \div 1.25 = $88.

8. **B.** 10% of 20% of 30% $= .10 \times .20 \times .30 = 0.006 = 0.6\%.$

9. **D.** 1 micron = 10,000 angstroms $\Rightarrow$ 10 microns = 100,000 angstroms; then, dividing both sides by 1000 gives

   $$100 \text{ angstroms} = \dfrac{1}{1000} \text{ (10 microns); and}$$

   $$\dfrac{1}{1000} = 0.001 = 0.1\%.$$

10. **D.** To earn an 80% on the entire exam, Marie needs to correctly answer 64 questions (80% of 80). So far, she has answered 45 questions correctly (75% of 60). Therefore, on the last 20 questions she needs $64 - 45 = 19$ correct answers; and $\dfrac{19}{20} = 95\%$.

11. **C.** Column A: 500% of $2 = 5 \times 2 = 10$.
    Column B: 200% of $5 = 2 \times 5 = 10$.

12. **A.** Since $n\%$ of 25 is 50, then 25% of n is 50, and 50% of n is twice as much: 100. If you don't see that, just solve for n:

    $$\dfrac{n}{100} \times 25 = 50 \Rightarrow \dfrac{n}{4} = 50 \Rightarrow$$
    $$n = 200 \Rightarrow 50\% \text{ of } n = 100.$$

13. **D.** A 30% discount on a $10 radio is much less than $30, whereas a 30% discount on a $1000 radio is much more than $30. (The amounts would be equal only if the regular price of the radio was $100.)

14. **B.** Assume that the price of VCR 2 is $100; then the price of VCR 1 is $110, and on sale at 10% off it costs $11 less: $99.

15. **C.** For *any* numbers a and b: $a\%$ of b is equal to $b\%$ of a.

16. **D.**

Column A	Column B
$a\%$ of $\dfrac{1}{b}$	$b\%$ of $\dfrac{1}{a}$
$\dfrac{a}{100} \times \dfrac{1}{b} = \dfrac{a}{100b}$	$\dfrac{b}{100} \times \dfrac{1}{a} = \dfrac{b}{100a}$

    Multiply by 100: $\quad \dfrac{a}{b} \qquad \dfrac{b}{a}$

    The columns are equal if a and b are equal, and are unequal otherwise.

17. **A.** Bank B would have to increase its rate from 4% to 5%, an actual increase of 1%. This represents a percent increase of

    $$\dfrac{1\%}{4\%} \times 100\% = 25\%.$$

18. **B.** Assume that a vat contains 100 ounces of a solution, of which 20%, or 20 ounces, is sugar (the remaining 80 ounces being water). If the amount of sugar is doubled, there will be 40 ounces of sugar and 80 ounces of water. The sugar will then comprise

    $$\dfrac{40}{120} = \dfrac{1}{3} = 33\dfrac{1}{3}\% \text{ of the solution.}$$

19. **D.** If $a = 2$, then $a^2 = 4$, and $2 = 50\%$ of 4; so the columns could be equal. If $a = 4$, then $a^2 = 16$, and 4 is not 50% of 16; so the columns need not be equal.

20. **C.** Avoid the algebra, and just assume that Judy started with $100. After giving Adam $50, she had $50 left, which was 20%, or one-fifth, of what he had. Then, Adam had $5 \times $50 = 250, which means that originally he had $200. Column A: 75% of $200 = $150. Column B: 150% of $100 = $150. The columns are equal.

21. (26)   Since 61.5 + 27.2 + 10 = 98.7, then 98.7% of the marbles are red, white, or blue, and the other 100% − 98.7% = 1.3% are some other colors. Therefore:

$$1.3\% \text{ of } 2000 = 0.013 \times 2000 = 26.$$

22. (84)   If 4 students failed, then the other 25 − 4 = 21 students passed, and $\frac{21}{25} = 0.84 = 84\%$.

23. (65)   Assume that there are 100 boys and 200 girls in the class. Then, 45 boys (45% of 100) and 60 girls (30% of 200) have handed in their reports. Then, 105 of the 300 students have handed in the reports, and 300 − 105 = 195 have not. What percent of 300 is 195?

$$\frac{195}{300} = 0.65 = 65\%.$$

24. (150)   If p represents the original price, the radio was priced at 1.15p instead of .85p. Since this was a $45 difference:

$$45 = 1.15p - .85p = 0.30p \Rightarrow$$
$$p = 45 \div .30 = 150.$$

25. (25.3)   A person with a $100,000 income would pay 15% of $30,000 plus 28% of $30,000 plus 31% of $40,000:

$$(.15 \times 30{,}000) + (.28 \times 30{,}000) +$$
$$(.31 \times 40{,}000) = 4{,}500 + 8{,}400 + 12{,}400 = 25{,}300$$

and 25,300 is 25.3% of 100,000.

26. (250)   Assume that a can of soup used to cost $1 and that it now costs $1.20 (20% more). Then 300 cans of soup used to cost $300. How many cans costing $1.20 each can be bought for $300?

$$300 \div 1.20 = 250.$$

27. (900)   The increase in the value of the painting was $9,000, and

$$\text{percent increase} = \frac{\text{actual increase}}{\text{original cost}} \times 100\% =$$

$$\frac{9000}{1000} \times 100\% = 900\%.$$

28. $\left(8.33 \text{ or } \frac{25}{3}\right)$ Assume that there are 100 marbles in jar A and 120 in jar B. You may already see that, if 10 marbles are moved, each jar will contain 110. If not, let x be the number of marbles to be moved, and solve the equation:

$$120 - x = 100 + x \Rightarrow 20 = 2x \Rightarrow x = 10.$$

Finally, 10 is what percent of 120?

$$\frac{10}{120} = \frac{1}{12} = 8\frac{1}{3}\%.$$

29. (800)   Assume that the sides of the first square were 1 inch long, so that the area was 1 square inch. Then, the sides of the second square were 3 inches long, and its area was 9 square inches, an increase of 8 square inches or 800%.

30. (16.5)   Since 40% of the red jelly beans are cherry, 60% of the red jelly beans are not cherry. Also, 25% of 60% is 15%, so 15% of the red jelly beans are raspberry and 40% are cherry, for a total of 55%. Therefore, the raspberry and cherry jelly beans constitute 55% of the 30% of the jelly beans that are red. Finally, 55% of 30% is 16.5%.

12-D RATIOS AND PROPORTIONS

A *ratio* is a fraction that compares two quantities that are measured in the *same* units. One quantity is the numerator of the fraction, and the other quantity is the denominator.

For example, if there are 4 boys and 16 girls on the debate team, we say that the ratio of the number of boys to the number of girls on the team is 4 to 16, or $\frac{4}{16}$, often written as 4:16. Since a ratio is just a fraction, it can be reduced or converted to a decimal or a percent. The following are different ways to express the same ratio:

4 to 16   4:16 $\frac{1}{16}$ 2 to 8   2:8 $\frac{2}{8}$

1 to 4   1:4 $\frac{1}{4}$ 0.25   25%

CAUTION: Saying that the ratio of boys to girls on the team is 1:4 does *not* mean that $\frac{1}{4}$ of the team members are boys. It means that, for each boy on the team there are 4 girls, so, of every 5 members of the team, 4 are girls and 1 is a boy. Boys, therefore, make up $\frac{1}{5}$ of the team, and girls $\frac{4}{5}$.

Key Fact D1

If a set of objects is divided into two groups in the ratio of $a{:}b$, then the first group contains $\frac{a}{a+b}$ of the objects and the second group contains $\frac{b}{a+b}$ of the objects.

Example 1.

Last year, the ratio of the number of math tests John passed to the number of math tests he failed was 7:3. What percent of his math tests did John pass?

Solution. John passed $\frac{7}{7+3} = \frac{7}{10} = $ **70%** of his math tests.

Example 2.

If 45% of the students at a college are male, what is the ratio of male students to female students?

Reminder: In problems involving percents, the best number to use is 100.

Solution. Assume that there are 100 students. Then, 45 of them are male, and 55 of them (100 − 45) are female. The ratio of males to females is $\frac{45}{55} = \frac{9}{11}$.

If we know how many boys and girls there are in a club, then, clearly, we know not only the ratio of boys to girls, but also several other ratios. For example, if the club has 7 boys and 3 girls, the ratio of boys to girls is $\frac{7}{3}$, the ratio of girls to boys is $\frac{3}{7}$, the ratio of boys to members is $\frac{7}{10}$, the ratio of members to girls is $\frac{10}{3}$, and so on.

However, if we know a ratio, we *cannot* determine from that fact alone how many objects there are. For example, if a jar contains only red and blue marbles, and if the ratio of red marbles to blue marbles is 3:5, there *may be* 3 red marbles and 5 blue marbles, but *not necessarily*. There may be 300 red marbles and 500 blue ones, since the ratio 300:500 reduces to 3:5. In the same way, all of the following are possibilities for the distribution of the marbles:

Red	6	12	33	51	150	3000	**3x**
Blue	10	20	55	85	250	5000	**5x**

The important thing to observe is that the number of red marbles can be *any* multiple of 3, as long as the number of blue marbles is the *same* multiple of 5.

Key Fact D2

If two numbers are in the ratio of $a:b$, then, for some number x, the first number is ax and the second number is bx. If the ratio is in lowest terms, and if the quantities must be integers, then x is also an integer.

Tactic D1

In any ratio problem, write the letter x after each number and use some given information to solve for x.

Example 3.

If the ratio of boys to girls at a school picnic is 5:3, which of the following could NOT be the number of children at the picnic?

(A) 24   (B) 40   (C) 96   (D) 150   (E) 720

Solution. If $5x$ and $3x$ are the number of boys and the number of girls, respectively, at the picnic, then the number of children present is $5x + 3x = 8x$. Therefore, the number of children must be a multiple of 8. Only **150 (D)** is not divisible by 8.

Note: Assume that the ratio of the number of pounds of cole slaw to the number of pounds of potato salad consumed at the school picnic was 5:3. Then, it is possible that a total of exactly 150 pounds of these foods was eaten: 93.75 pounds of cole slaw and 56.25 pounds of potato salad. In Example 3, however, 150 isn't a possible answer because there has to be a whole number of boys and girls.

Example 4.

The measures of the two acute angles of a right triangle are in the ratio of 5:13. What is the measure of the larger acute angle?

Solution. Let the measure of the smaller angle be $5x$ and the measure of the larger angle be $13x$. Since the sum of the measures of the two acute angles of a right triangle is 90° (KEY FACT J3):

$$5x + 13x = 90 \Rightarrow 18x = 90 \Rightarrow x = 5.$$

Therefore, the measure of the larger angle is $13 \times 5 = $ **65°**.

Ratios can be extended to three or four or more terms. For example, we can say that the ratio of freshmen to sophomores to juniors to seniors in the school band is 6:8:5:8, which means that for every 6 freshmen in the band there are 8 sophomores, 5 juniors, and 8 seniors.

Note: TACTIC D1 applies to extended ratios, as well.

Example 5.

Frannie's Frozen Yogurt sells three flavors: vanilla, chocolate, and coffee. One day, Frannie sold 240 cones, and the ratio of vanilla to chocolate to coffee was 8:17:15. How many chocolate cones were sold that day?

Solution. Let $8x$, $17x$, and $15x$ be the number of vanilla, of chocolate, and of coffee cones sold, respectively. Then:

$$8x + 17x + 15x = 240 \Rightarrow 40x = 240 \Rightarrow x = 6.$$

The number of chocolate cones sold was $17 \times 6 = $ **102**.

Key Fact D3

KEY FACT D1 applies to extended ratios, as well. If a set of objects is divided into three groups in the ratio $a{:}b{:}c$, then the first group contains $\dfrac{a}{a+b+c}$ of the objects, the second $\dfrac{b}{a+b+c}$, and the third $\dfrac{c}{a+b+c}$.

Example 6.

If the ratio of vanilla to chocolate to strawberry cones sold at Frannie's was 8:17:15 on a particular day, what percent of the cones sold were chocolate?

Solution. Chocolate cones made up $\dfrac{17}{8+17+15} = \dfrac{17}{40} = \mathbf{42.5\%}$ of the total.

A jar contains a number of red (R), white (W), and blue (B) marbles. Suppose that R:W = 2:3 and W:B = 3:5. Then, for every 2 red marbles, there are 3 white ones, and for those 3 white ones, there are 5 blue ones. Then, R:B = 2:5, and we can form the extended ratio R:W:B = 2:3:5.

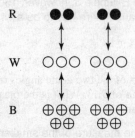

If the ratios were R:W = 2:3 and W:B = 4:5, however, we couldn't combine them as easily. From the diagram below, we see that for every 8 reds there are 15 blues, so R:B = 8:15.

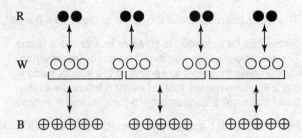

To see this without drawing a picture, we write the ratios as fractions: $\dfrac{R}{W} = \dfrac{2}{3}$ and $\dfrac{W}{B} = \dfrac{4}{5}$. Then, we multiply the fractions:

$$\dfrac{R}{\cancel{W}} \times \dfrac{\cancel{W}}{B} = \dfrac{2}{3} \times \dfrac{4}{5} = \dfrac{8}{15}, \quad \text{so} \quad \dfrac{R}{B} = \dfrac{8}{15}.$$

Not only does this give us R:B = 8:15, but also, if we multiply both W numbers, $3 \times 4 = 12$, we can write the extended ratio: R:W:B = 8:12:15.

Column A	Column B

Example 7.

Jar A and jar B each contain 70 marbles, all of which are red, white, or blue.
In jar A: R:W = 2:3 and W:B = 3:5.
In jar B: R:W = 2:3 and W:B = 4:5.

The number of white marbles in jar A	The number of white marbles in jar B

Solution. From the discussion immediately preceding this example, in jar A the extended ratio R:W:B is 2:3:5, which implies that the white marbles constitute

$$\dfrac{3}{2+3+5} = \dfrac{3}{10} \text{ of the total:}$$

$$\dfrac{3}{\cancel{10}} \times \cancel{70} = 21.$$

In jar B the extended ratio R:W:B is 8:12:15, so the white marbles are $\dfrac{12}{8+12+15} = \dfrac{12}{35}$ of the total:

$$\dfrac{12}{\cancel{35}_1} \times \cancel{70}^2 = 24.$$

The answer is **B**.

A **proportion** is an equation that states that two ratios are equivalent. Since ratios are just fractions, any equation, such as $\dfrac{4}{6} = \dfrac{10}{15}$, in which each side is a single fraction is a proportion. Usually the proportions you encounter on the SAT I involve one or more variables.

Solve proportions by cross-multiplying: if $\dfrac{a}{b} = \dfrac{c}{d}$, then $ad = bc$.

Several problems on the SAT I can be solved by setting up proportions. These problems are usually quite easy and are among the first few in a section.

Example 8.

If $\dfrac{3}{7} = \dfrac{x}{84}$, what is the value of x?

Solution. Cross-multiply:
$3(84) = 7x \Rightarrow 252 = 7x \Rightarrow x = \mathbf{36}$.

Example 9.

If $\dfrac{x+2}{17} = \dfrac{x}{16}$, what is the value of $\dfrac{x+6}{19}$?

Solution. Cross-multiply:

$$16(x + 2) = 17x \Rightarrow 16x + 32 = 17x \Rightarrow x = 32, \text{ so,}$$

$$\frac{x + 6}{19} = \frac{32 + 6}{19} = \frac{38}{19} = 2.$$

Example 10.

A state law requires that on any field trip the ratio of the number of chaperones to the number of students must be at least 1:12. If 100 students are going on a field trip, what is the minimum number of chaperones required?

 Solution. Let x represent the number of chaperones required, and set up a proportion:

$$\frac{\text{number of chaperones}}{\text{number of students}} = \frac{1}{12} = \frac{x}{100}$$

Cross-multiply: $100 = 12x \Rightarrow x = 8.33$. This, of course, is *not* the answer since, clearly, the number of chaperones must be a whole number. Since x is greater than 8, we know that 8 chaperones will not be enough. The answer is **9**.

A *rate* is a fraction that compares two quantities that are measured in *different* units. The word *per* often appears in rate problems: miles per hour, dollars per week, cents per ounce, children per classroom, and so on.

D3

Set rate problems up just like ratio problems. Then, solve the proportions by cross-multiplying.

Example 11.

Sharon read 24 pages of her book in 15 minutes. At this rate, how many pages can she read in 40 minutes?

 Solution. Handle this rate problem exactly like a ratio problem. Set up a proportion and cross-multiply:

$$\frac{\text{pages}}{\text{minutes}} = \frac{24}{15} = \frac{x}{40} \Rightarrow 15x = 40 \times 24 = 960 \Rightarrow x = 64.$$

When the denominator in the given rate is 1 unit (1 minute, 1 mile, 1 dollar), the problem can be solved by a single division or multiplication. Consider Examples 12 and 13.

Example 12.

If Jack types at the rate of 35 words per minute, how long will he take to type 987 words?

Example 13.

If Jack types at the rate of 35 words per minute, how many words can he type in 85 minutes?

To solve, set up the proportions and cross-multiply:

Solution 12. $\dfrac{\text{words typed}}{\text{minutes}} = \dfrac{35}{1} = \dfrac{987}{x} \Rightarrow$

$$35x = 987 \Rightarrow x = \frac{987}{35} = \textbf{14.2 minutes}.$$

Solution 13. $\dfrac{\text{words typed}}{\text{minutes}} = \dfrac{35}{1} = \dfrac{x}{85} \Rightarrow$

$$x = 35 \times 85 = \textbf{2975} \text{ words}.$$

Notice that, in Example 12, all we did was divide 987 by 35, and in Example 13, we multiplied 35 by 85. If you realize that, you don't have to introduce x and set up a proportion. You must know, however, whether to multiply or divide. If you're not absolutely positive which is correct, write the proportion; then you can't go wrong.

> **CAUTION:** In rate problems it is essential that the units in both fractions be the same.

Example 14.

If three apples cost 50¢, how many apples can you buy for $20?

Solution. We have to set up a proportion, but it is *not* $\dfrac{3}{50} = \dfrac{x}{20}$. In the first fraction, the denominator represents *cents*, whereas in the second fraction, the denominator represents *dollars*. The units must be the same. We can change 50 cents to 0.5 dollar, or we can change 20 dollars to 2000 cents:

$$\frac{3}{50} = \frac{x}{2000} \Rightarrow 50x = 6000 \Rightarrow x = \textbf{120} \text{ apples}.$$

On the SAT I, many rate problems involve only variables. These problems are handled in exactly the same way.

Example 15.

If a apples cost c cents, how many apples can be bought for d dollars?

(A) $100acd$ (B) $\dfrac{100d}{ac}$ (C) $\dfrac{ad}{100c}$ (D) $\dfrac{c}{100ad}$

(E) $\dfrac{100ad}{c}$

Solution. First change d dollars to $100d$ cents, set up the proportion and cross-multiply:

$$\frac{\text{apples}}{\text{cents}} = \frac{a}{c} = \frac{x}{100d} \Rightarrow 100ad = cx \Rightarrow x = \frac{\textbf{100}ad}{c} \textbf{ (E)}.$$

Every SAT I has one or two questions like Example 15, and most students find them very difficult. Be sure to do all the exercises at the end of this section, but also see TACTIC 9-2 for another way to handle these problems.

Notice that in rate problems, as one quantity increases or decreases, so does the other. If you are driving at 45 miles per hour, the more hours you drive, the further you go; if you drive fewer miles, less time is required. If chopped meat costs $3.00 per pound, the less you spend, the fewer pounds you get; the more meat you buy, the higher the cost.

In some problems, however, as one quantity increases, the other decreases. These problems *cannot* be solved by setting up a proportion. Consider Examples 16 and 17, which look similar but must be handled differently.

Example 16.

A hospital needs 150 pills to treat 6 patients for a week. How many pills does it need to treat 10 patients for a week?

Example 17.

A hospital has enough pills on hand to treat 10 patients for 14 days. How long will the pills last if there are 35 patients?

Solution 16. Example 16 is a standard rate problem. The more patients there are, the more pills are needed.

The *ratio* or *quotient* remains constant:

$$\frac{150}{6} = \frac{x}{10} \Rightarrow 6x = 1500 = x = \textbf{250}.$$

Solution 17. In Example 17, the situation is different. With more patients, the supply of pills will last for a shorter period of time; if there were fewer patients, the supply would last longer. It is not the ratio that remains constant; it is the *product*.

There are enough pills to last for $10 \times 14 = 140$ patient-days:

$$\frac{140 \text{ patient - days}}{10 \text{ patients}} = 14 \text{ days}$$

$$\frac{140 \text{ patient - days}}{35 \text{ patients}} = \textbf{4 days}$$

$$\frac{140 \text{ patient - days}}{70 \text{ patients}} = 2 \text{ days}$$

$$\frac{140 \text{ patient - days}}{1 \text{ patient}} = 140 \text{ days}$$

Tactic D4

On the SAT, if one quantity increases while another decreases, multiply them; their product is a constant.

Example 18.

If 15 workers can paint a certain number of houses in 24 days, how many days will 40 workers take, working at the same rate, to do the same job?

Solution. Clearly, the more workers there are, the less time will be required, so use TACTIC D4: multiply. The job takes $15 \times 24 = 360$ worker-days:

$$\frac{360 \text{ worker - days}}{40 \text{ workers}} = \textbf{9 days}.$$

Note that it doesn't matter how many houses have to be painted, as long as 15 workers and 40 workers are doing the same job. Even if the question had said, "15 workers can paint 18 houses in 24 days," the number 18 would not have entered into the solution. This number would be important only if the second group of workers was going to paint a different number of houses.

Example 19.

If 15 workers can paint 18 houses in 24 days, how many days will 40 workers take to paint 22 houses?

Solution. This question is similar to Example 18, except that now the jobs that the two groups of workers are doing are different. The solution, however, starts out in exactly the same way.

Just as in Example 18, 40 workers can do in 9 days the *same* job that 15 workers can do in 24 days. Since that job is to paint 18 houses, 40 workers can paint $18 \div 9 = 2$ houses every day. Therefore, they will take **11** days to paint 22 houses.

Exercises on Ratios and Proportions

Multiple-Choice Questions

1. If $\frac{2}{3}$ of the workers in an office are nonsmokers, what is the ratio of smokers to nonsmokers?

   (A) 2:5   (B) 1:2   (C) 3:5   (D) 2:3   (E) 3:2

2. If the ratio of Republicans to Democrats on a committee is 3:5, what percent of the committee members are Democrats?

   (A) 37.5%   (B) 40%   (C) 60%   (D) 62.5%
   (E) It cannot be determined from the information given.

3. If 80% of the applicants to a program were rejected, what is the ratio of the number accepted to the number rejected?

   (A) $\frac{1}{5}$ (B) $\frac{1}{4}$ (C) $\frac{2}{5}$ (D) $\frac{4}{5}$ (E) $\frac{4}{1}$

4. The measures of the three angles in a triangle are in the ratio 1:1:2. Which of the following must be true?

   I. The triangle is isosceles.
   II. The triangle is a right triangle.
   III. The triangle is equilateral.

   (A) None   (B) I only   (C) II only
   (D) I and II only   (E) I and III only

5. A jar contains 50 marbles, each of which is blue or red. If 35 of the marbles are red, which of the following does NOT represent the ratio of the number of red marbles to the number of blue marbles?

   (A) 35:15   (B) $\dfrac{35}{15}$ (C) $\dfrac{7}{3}$ (D) 7:3   (E) $\dfrac{35}{50}$

6. What is the ratio of the circumference of a circle to its radius?

   (A) 1   (B) $\dfrac{\pi}{2}$ (C) $\sqrt{\pi}$ (D) π (E) 2π

7. At Bayview High the ratio of the number of students taking Spanish to the number taking French is 7:2. If 140 students are taking French, how many are taking Spanish?

   (A) 40   (B) 140   (C) 360   (D) 490   (E) 630

8. If $a{:}b = 3{:}5$ and $a{:}c = 5{:}7$, what is the value of $b{:}c$?

   (A) 3:7   (B) 21:35   (C) 21:25   (D) 25:21
   (E) 7:3

9. In the diagram below, $b{:}a = 7{:}2$. What is $b - a$?

   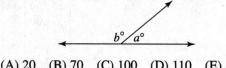

   (A) 20   (B) 70   (C) 100   (D) 110   (E) 160

10. If x is a positive number and $\dfrac{x}{3} = \dfrac{12}{x}$, then $x =$

    (A) 3   (B) 4   (C) 6   (D) 12   (E) 36

11. A snail can move i inches in m minutes. At this rate, how many feet can it move in h hours?

    (A) $\dfrac{5hi}{m}$ (B) $\dfrac{60hi}{m}$ (C) $\dfrac{hi}{12m}$ (D) $\dfrac{5m}{hi}$
    (E) $5him$

12. Barbra can grade t tests in $\dfrac{1}{x}$ hours. At this rate, how many tests can she grade in x hours?

    (A) tx (B) tx^2 (C) $\dfrac{1}{t}$ (D) $\dfrac{x}{t}$ (E) $\dfrac{1}{tx}$

13. If you can buy b bananas for n nickels, how many bananas can you buy for d dimes and q quarters?

    (A) $\dfrac{b}{n}(2d + 5q)$ (B) $\dfrac{b(d+q)}{n}$

    (C) $\dfrac{b}{n}(10d + 25q)$ (D) $\dfrac{10d + 25q}{bn}$

    (E) $\dfrac{d+q}{bn}$

14. A club had 3 boys and 5 girls. During a membership drive the same number of boys and girls joined the club. How many members does the club have now if the ratio of boys to girls is 3:4?

    (A) 12   (B) 14   (C) 16   (D) 21   (E) 28

15. If 500 pounds of mush will feed 20 pigs for a week, for how many days will 200 pounds of mush feed 14 pigs?

    (A) 4   (B) 5   (C) 6   (D) 7   (E) 8

Quantitative Comparison Questions

	Column A	Column B

The ratio of red to blue marbles in a jar was 3:5. The same number of red and blue marbles were added to the jar.

16. | The ratio of red to blue marbles now | 3:5 |

The ratio of the number of boys to girls in the Chess Club is 5:2.
The ratio of the number of boys to girls in the Glee Club is 11:4.

17. | The number of boys in the Chess Club | The number of boys in the Glee Club |

Sharon invited the same number of boys and girls to her party. Everyone who was invited came, and five additional boys showed up. As a result, the ratio of girls to boys at the party was 4:5.

18. | The number of people Sharon invited to her party | 40 |

A large jar is full of marbles. When a single marble is drawn at random from the jar, the probability that it is red is $\dfrac{3}{7}$.

19. | The ratio of the number of red marbles to nonred marbles in the jar | $\dfrac{1}{2}$ |

The radius of circle II is 3 times the radius of circle I.

20. | area of circle II / area of circle I | 3π |

Grid-in Questions

21. If $\frac{a}{9} = \frac{10}{2a}$, what is the value of a^2?

22. Michael drove 135 miles in 2 hours and 30 minutes. At this rate, how many hours will he take to drive 1098 miles?

23. John can read 72 pages per hour. At this rate, how many pages can he read in 72 minutes?

24. If $3a = 2b$ and $3b = 5c$, what is the ratio of a to c?

25. If $\frac{3x-1}{25} = \frac{x+5}{11}$, what is the value of x?

26. The ratio of the number of freshmen to sophomores to juniors to seniors on a college football team is 4:7:6:8. What percent of the team are sophomores?

27. Three associates agreed to split the profit of an investment in the ratio of 2:5:8. If the profit was $3000, what is the difference between the largest share and the smallest?

28. A recipe for stew that feeds 4 people calls for $1\frac{1}{2}$ teaspoons of salt. If 3 teaspoons = 1 tablespoon, how many tablespoons of salt will be needed to make enough stew for 18 people?

29. If $\dfrac{ab}{c} = 7 = \dfrac{rs}{t}$, $r = 3a$, $c = 2t$, and $s = kb$, what is k?

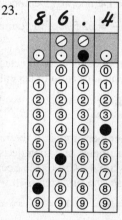

30. If 4 boys can shovel a driveway in 2 hours, how many minutes will 5 boys take to do the job?

Answer Key

1. **B**	5. **E**	9. **C**	13. **A**	17. **D**
2. **D**	6. **E**	10. **C**	14. **B**	18. **C**
3. **B**	7. **D**	11. **A**	15. **A**	19. **A**
4. **D**	8. **D**	12. **B**	16. **A**	20. **B**

21. *45*

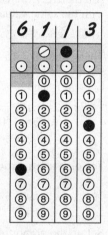

22. *6 1 / 3* or *2 0 . 3*

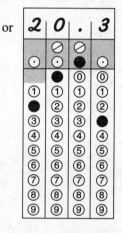

23. *8 6 . 4*

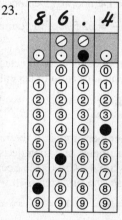

24. *1 0 / 9* or *1 . 1 1*

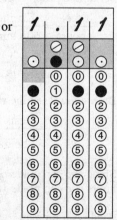

25. *1 7*

26. *2 8*

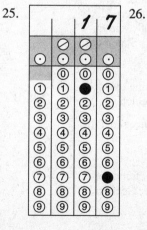

27. *1 2 0 0*

28. 9 / 4 or 2 . 2 5

29. 1 / 6 or . 1 6 6

30. 9 6

Answer Explanations

1. **B.** Of every 3 workers, 2 are nonsmokers, and 1 is a smoker. Then, the ratio of smokers to non-smokers is 1:2.

2. **D.** Of every 8 committee members, 3 are Republicans and 5 are Democrats. Democrats, therefore, make up $\frac{5}{8} = 62.5\%$ of the committee.

3. **B.** If 80% of the applicants were rejected, 20% were accepted, and the ratio of accepted to rejected is $20:80 = 1:4 = \frac{1}{4}$.

4. **D.** It is worth remembering that, if the ratio of the measures of the angles of a triangle is 1:1:2, then the angles are 45-45-90 (see Section 12-J). Otherwise, the first step is to write

   $$x + x + 2x = 180 \Rightarrow 4x = 180 \Rightarrow x = 45.$$

   Since two of the angles have the same measure, the triangle is isosceles. (I is true.) Also, since one of the angles measures 90°, the triangle is a right triangle. (II is true.) Statement III, of course, is false.

5. **E.** There are 35 red marbles and 15 blue ones. The ratio of red to blue is 35:15, which reduces to 7:3. Choice E, $\frac{35}{50}$, reduces to 7:10 and does *not* represent the ratio.

6. **E.** By definition, π is the ratio of the circumference to the diameter of a circle (see Section 12-L), so

   $$\pi = \frac{C}{d} = \frac{C}{2r} \Rightarrow 2\pi = \frac{C}{r}.$$

7. **D.** The number taking Spanish is $7x$, and the number taking French is $2x$, so

   $$2x = 140 \Rightarrow x = 70 \Rightarrow 7x = 490.$$

8. **D.** Since $\frac{a}{b} = \frac{3}{5}, \frac{b}{a} = \frac{5}{3}$, then

   $$\frac{b}{\cancel{a}} \times \frac{\cancel{a}}{c} = \frac{5}{3} \times \frac{5}{7} \Rightarrow \frac{b}{c} = \frac{25}{21}.$$

   Alternatively, we could write equivalent ratios with the same value for a:

   $$a{:}b = 3{:}5 = 15{:}25 \quad \text{and} \quad a{:}c = 5{:}7 = 15{:}21.$$

   Then, when $a = 15$, $b = 25$ and $c = 21$.

9. **C.** Let $b = 7x$ and $a = 2x$. Then

   $$7x + 2x = 180 \Rightarrow 9x = 180 \Rightarrow x = 20 \Rightarrow$$
   $$b = 140 \text{ and } a = 40 \Rightarrow$$
   $$b - a = 140 - 40 = 100.$$

10. **C.** To solve a proportion, cross-multiply:

    $$\frac{x}{3} = \frac{12}{x} \Rightarrow x^2 = 36 \Rightarrow x = 6.$$

11. **A.** Set up the proportion, keeping track of units:

    $$\frac{x \text{ feet}}{h \text{ hours}} = \frac{12x \text{ inches}}{60h \text{ minutes}} = \frac{i \text{ inches}}{m \text{ minutes}} \Rightarrow$$
    $$\frac{x}{5h} = \frac{i}{m} \Rightarrow x = \frac{5hi}{m}.$$

12. **B.** Barbra grades at the rate of

    $$\frac{t \text{ tests}}{\frac{1}{x} \text{ hours}} = \frac{tx \text{ tests}}{1 \text{ hour}}.$$

    Since she can grade tx tests each hour, in x hours she can grade $x(tx) = tx^2$ tests.

13. **A.** Again, set up the proportion, keeping track of units:

    $$\frac{b \text{ bananas}}{n \text{ nickels}} = \frac{b \text{ bananas}}{5n \text{ cents}} = \frac{x \text{ bananas}}{(10d + 25q) \text{ cents}}$$
    $$\Rightarrow \frac{b}{5n} = \frac{x}{10d + 25q} \Rightarrow 5nx = b(10d + 25q)$$

$$\Rightarrow x = \frac{b(\overset{2}{\cancel{10}}d + \overset{5}{\cancel{25}}q)}{\underset{1}{\cancel{5}}n} = \frac{b}{n}(2d + 5q).$$

14. **B.** Suppose that x boys and x girls joined the club. Then, the new ratio of boys to girls would be $(3 + x):(5 + x)$, which we are told is 3:4, and

$$\frac{3+x}{5+x} = \frac{3}{4} \Rightarrow 4(3 + x) = 3(5 + x) \Rightarrow$$

$$12 + 4x = 15 + 3x \Rightarrow x = 3.$$

Therefore, 3 boys and 3 girls joined the existing 3 boys and 5 girls, for a total of 14 members.

15. **A.** Since 500 pounds will last for 20 pig-weeks or 140 pig-days, 200 pounds will last for

$$\frac{200}{500} \times 400 \text{ pig-days} = 56 \text{ pig-days, and}$$

$$\frac{56 \text{ pig-days}}{14 \text{ pigs}} = 4 \text{ days.}$$

16. **A.** Assume that to start there were $3x$ red marbles and $5x$ blue ones and that y marbles of each color were added.

	Column A	Column B
	$\dfrac{3x+y}{5x+y}$	$\dfrac{3}{5}$
Cross-multiply:	$5(3x + y)$	$3(5x + y)$
Distribute:	$15x + 5y$	$15x + 3y$
Subtract $15x$:	$5y$	$3y$

Since y is positive, Column A is greater.

17. **D.** Ratios alone can't answer the question "How many?" There could be 5 boys in the chess club or 500. We can't tell.

18. **C.** Assume that Sharon invited x boys and x girls. When she wound up with x girls and $x + 5$ boys, the girl:boy ratio was 4:5, so

$$\frac{x}{x+5} = \frac{4}{5} \Rightarrow 5x = 4x + 20 \Rightarrow x = 20$$

Sharon invited 40 people
(20 boys and 20 girls).

19. **A.** If the probability of drawing a red marble is $\frac{3}{7}$, 3 out of every 7 marbles are red, and 4 out of every 7 are nonred. Therefore, the ratio red:nonred = 3:4, which is greater than $\frac{1}{2}$.

20. **B.** Assume that the radius of circle I is 1 and the radius of circle II is 3. Then, the areas are π

and 9π, respectively. The area of circle II is 9 times the area of circle I, so Column A = 9, and $3\pi > 9$.

21. **(45)** Cross-multiplying, we get $2a^2 = 90 \Rightarrow a^2 = 45$.

22. $\left(\dfrac{61}{3} \text{ or } 20.3\right)$ Set up a proportion:

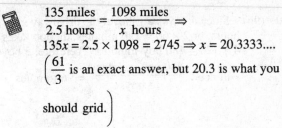

$$\frac{135 \text{ miles}}{2.5 \text{ hours}} = \frac{1098 \text{ miles}}{x \text{ hours}} \Rightarrow$$
$$135x = 2.5 \times 1098 = 2745 \Rightarrow x = 20.3333....$$
$\left(\dfrac{61}{3} \text{ is an exact answer, but 20.3 is what you} \right.$

should grid.$\bigg)$

23. **(86.4)** Set up a proportion:

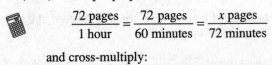

$$\frac{72 \text{ pages}}{1 \text{ hour}} = \frac{72 \text{ pages}}{60 \text{ minutes}} = \frac{x \text{ pages}}{72 \text{ minutes}}$$

and cross-multiply:
$$72 \times 72 = 60x \Rightarrow 5184 = 60x \Rightarrow x = 86.4.$$

24. $\left(\dfrac{10}{9} \text{ or } 1.11\right)$ Multiplying each equation to get the same coefficient of b, gives

$$9a = 6b \text{ and } 6b = 10c \Rightarrow 9a = 10c \Rightarrow \frac{a}{c} = \frac{10}{9}.$$

25. **(17)** Cross-multiplying, we get

$$11(3x - 1) = 25(x + 5) \Rightarrow$$
$$33x - 11 = 25x + 125 \Rightarrow$$
$$8x = 136 \Rightarrow x = 17.$$

26. **(28)** The *fraction* of the team that consists of sophomores is

$$\frac{7}{4+7+6+8} = \frac{7}{25} \quad \text{and} \quad \frac{7}{\underset{1}{\cancel{25}}} \times \overset{4}{\cancel{100}}\% = 28\%$$

27. **(1200)** The shares are $2x$, $5x$, and $8x$, and their sum is 3000:

$$2x + 5x + 8x = 3000 \Rightarrow 15x = 3000 \Rightarrow x = 200,$$
so $8x - 2x = 6x = 1200.$

28. $\left(\dfrac{9}{4} \text{ or } 2.25\right)$ Set up a proportion:

$$\frac{x \text{ tablespoons}}{18 \text{ people}} = \frac{3x \text{ teaspoons}}{18 \text{ people}} = \frac{x \text{ teaspoons}}{6 \text{ people}}.$$

But it is given that 1.5 teaspoons are needed for 4 people, so

$$\frac{x}{6} = \frac{1.5}{4} \Rightarrow 4x = 6(1.5) = 9 \Rightarrow x = \frac{9}{4} = 2.25.$$

29. $\left(\dfrac{1}{6} \text{ or } .166\right)$ In the equation $\dfrac{ab}{c} = \dfrac{rs}{t}$, replace r by $3a$, c by $2t$, and s by kb:

$$\frac{ab}{2t} = \frac{(3a)(kb)}{t} \Rightarrow abt = 6abtk \Rightarrow$$

$$1 = 6k \Rightarrow k = \frac{1}{6} = .166.$$

30. (96)   Since 4 boys can shovel the driveway in 2 hours, or $2 \times 60 = 120$ minutes, the job takes $4 \times 120 = 480$ boy-minutes. Therefore, 5 boys will need $\dfrac{480 \text{ boy - minutes}}{5 \text{ boys}} = 96$ minutes.

12-E AVERAGES

The **average** of a set of n numbers is the sum of those numbers divided by n:

$$\text{average} = \frac{\text{sum of the } n \text{ numbers}}{n} \quad \text{or simply}$$

$$A = \frac{\text{sum}}{n}.$$

If you took three math tests so far this year and your grades were 80, 90, and 76, to calculate your average, you would add the three grades and divide by 3:

$$\frac{80 + 90 + 76}{3} = \frac{246}{3} = 82.$$

The technical name for average is "arithmetic mean," and on the SAT I those words always appear in parentheses—for example, "What is the average (arithmetic mean) of 80, 90, and 76?"

Very often on the SAT I, you are not asked to find an average; rather, you are given the average of a set of numbers and asked to provide some other information. The key to solving all of these problems is to first find the sum of the numbers. Since $A = \dfrac{\text{sum}}{n}$, multiplying both sides by n yields the equation: sum = nA.

Tactic E1

If you know the average, A, of a set of n numbers, multiply A by n to get their sum.

Example 1.

One day a delivery-truck driver picked up 25 packages whose average (arithmetic mean) weight was 14.2 pounds. What was the total weight, in pounds, of all the packages?

 Solution. Use TACTIC E1: $25 \times 14.2 = $ **355**.

NOTE: We do not know how much any individual package weighed or how many packages weighed more or less than 14.2 pounds. All we know is the total weight.

Example 2.

John took five English tests during the first marking period, and his average (arithmetic mean) was 85. If his average after the first three tests was 83, what was the average of his fourth and fifth tests?

(A) 83   (B) 85   (C) 87   (D) 88   (E) 90

 Solution.

• Use TACTIC E1: On his five tests John earned $5 \times 85 = 425$ points.
• Use TACTIC E1 again: On the first three tests he earned $3 \times 83 = 249$ points.
• Subtract: On his last two tests he earned $425 - 249 = 176$ points.
• Calculate his average on his last two tests: $\dfrac{176}{2} = $ **88 (D)**.

NOTE: We cannot determine John's grade on even one of the five tests.

KEY FACT E1

If all the numbers in a set are the same, then that number is the average.

KEY FACT E2

If the numbers in a set are not all the same, then the average must be greater than the smallest number and less than the largest number. Equivalently, at least one of the numbers is less than the average and at least one is greater.

If Mary's test grades are 85, 85, 85, and 85, her average is 85. If Bob's test grades are 76, 83, 88, and 88, his average must be greater than 76 and less than 88. What can we conclude if, after taking five tests, Ellen's average is 90? We know that she earned exactly $5 \times 90 = 450$ points, and that either she got 90 on every test or at least one grade was less than 90 and at least one was over 90. Here are a few of the thousands of possibilities for Ellen's grades:

(a) 90, 90, 90, 90, 90   (b) 80, 90, 90, 90, 100
(c) 83, 84, 87, 97, 99   (d) 77, 88, 93, 95, 97
(e) 50, 100, 100, 100, 100

In (b), 80, the one grade below 90, is *10 points below*, and 100, the one grade above 90, is *10 points above*. In (c), 83 is 7 points below 90, 84 is 6 points below 90, and 87 is 3 points below 90, for a total of 7 + 6 + 3 = *16 points below 90*; 97 is 7 points above 90 and 99 is 9 points above 90, for a total of 7 + 9 = *16 points above 90*.

These differences from the average are called **deviations**, and the situation in these examples is not a coincidence.

KEY FACT E3

The total deviation below the average is equal to the total deviation above the average.

Example 3.

If the average (arithmetic mean) of 25, 31, and x is 37, what is the value of x?

(A) 31   (B) 37   (C) 43   (D) 55   (E) 56

Solution 1. Use KEY FACT E3. Since 25 is 12 less than 37 and 31 is 6 less than 37, the total deviation below the average is $12 + 6 = 18$. Therefore, the total deviation above the average must also be 18. Therefore, $x = 37 + 18 = $ **55 (D)**.

Solution 2. Use TACTIC E1. Since the average of the three numbers is 37, the sum of the three numbers is $3 \times 37 = 111$. Then,

$$25 + 31 + x = 111 \Rightarrow 56 + x = 111 \Rightarrow x = 55.$$

KEY FACT E4

Assume that the average of a set of numbers is A. If a number, x, is added to the set and a new average is calculated, then the new average will be less than, equal to, or greater than A, depending on whether x is less than, equal to, or greater than A, respectively.

Column A	Column B

Example 4.

The average (arithmetic mean) of the integers from 0 to 12	The average (arithmetic mean) of the integers from 1 to 12

Helpful Hint

Remember TACTIC 10-5. We don't have to *calculate* the averages, we just have to *compare* them.

Solution 1. Column B is the average of the integers from 1 to 12, which is surely greater than 1. In Column A we are taking the average of those same 12 numbers and 0. Since the extra number, 0, is less than the Column B average, the Column A average must be *lower* (KEY FACT E4). The answer is **B**.

Solution 2. Clearly, the sum of the 13 integers from 0 to 12 is the same as the sum of the 12 integers from 1 to 12. Since that sum is positive, dividing by 13 in Column A yields a smaller quotient than dividing by 12 in Column B (KEY FACT B4), so B is larger.

Although in solving Example 4 we didn't calculate the averages, we could have:

$$0 + 1 + 2 + 3 + 4 + 5 + 6 + 7 + 8 + 9 + 10 + 11 + 12 = 78$$
$$\text{and} \quad \frac{78}{13} = 6;$$

$$1 + 2 + 3 + 4 + 5 + 6 + 7 + 8 + 9 + 10 + 11 + 12 = 78$$
$$\text{and} \quad \frac{78}{12} = 6.5.$$

Notice that the average of the 13 *consecutive* integers 0, 1,...,12 is the *middle integer*, **6**, and the average of the 12 *consecutive* integers 1, 2,...,12 is the *average of the two middle integers*, **6** and **7**. This is a special case of KEY FACT E5.

KEY FACT E5

Whenever n numbers form an arithmetic sequence (one in which the difference between any two consecutive terms is the same): (i) if n is odd, the average of the numbers is the middle term in the sequence; and (ii) if n is even, the average of the numbers is the average of the two middle terms.

For example, in the arithmetic sequence 6, 9, 12, 15, 18, the average is the middle number, 12; and in the sequence 10, 20, 30, 40, 50, 60, the average is 35, the average of the two middle numbers—30 and 40.

Example 5.

On Thursday, 20 of the 25 students in a chemistry class took a test, and their average was 80. On Friday, the other 5 students took the test, and their average was 90. What was the average for the entire class?

(A) 80   (B) 82   (C) 84   (D) 85   (E) 88

Solution. The class average is calculated by dividing the sum of all 25 test grades by 25.

- The first 20 students earned a total of: $20 \times 80 = 1600$ points
- The other 5 students earned a total of: $5 \times 90 = 450$ points
- Add: altogether the class earned: $1600 + 450 = 2050$ points
- Calculate the class average: $\frac{2050}{25} = $ **82 (B)**.

Notice that the answer to Example 5 is *not* 85, which is the average of 80 and 90. The averages of 80 and 90 were earned by different numbers of students, and so the two averages had to be given different weights in the calculation. For this reason, 82 is called a **weighted average**.

KEY FACT E6

To calculate the weighted average of a set of numbers, multiply each number in the set by the number of times it appears, add all the products, and divide by the total number of numbers in the set.

 The solution to Example 5 should look like this:

$$\frac{20(80)+5(90)}{25} = \frac{1600+450}{25} = \frac{2050}{25} = 82.$$

Helpful Hint

Without doing any calculations, you should immediately realize that, since the grade of 80 is being given more weight than the grade of 90, the average will be closer to 80 than to 90—certainly *less than 85*.

Problems involving *average speed* will be discussed in Section 12-H, but we mention them briefly here because they are closely related to problems on weighted averages.

Example 6.

For the first 3 hours of her trip, Susan drove at 50 miles per hour. Then, because of construction delays, she drove at only 40 miles per hour for the next 2 hours. What was her average speed, in miles per hour, for the entire trip?

 Solution. This is just a weighted average:

$$\frac{3(50)+2(40)}{5} = \frac{150+80}{5} = \frac{230}{5} = 46.$$

Note that in each of the above fractions the numerator is the total distance traveled and the denominator the total time the trip took. This is *always* the way to find an average speed. Consider the following slight variation of Example 6.

Example 6a.

For the first 100 miles of her trip, Susan drove at 50 miles per hour. Then, because of construction delays, she drove at only 40 miles per hour, for the next 120 miles. What was her average speed, in miles per hour, for the entire trip?

Solution. This is not a *weighted* average. Here we immediately know the total distance: 220 miles. To get the total time, find the time for each portion and add: the first 100 miles took 100 ÷ 50 = 2 hours, and the next 120 miles took 120 ÷ 40 = 3 hours. The average speed was $\frac{220}{5}$ = **44 miles per hour.**

Notice that in Example 6, since Susan spent more time traveling at 50 than at 40 miles per hour, her average speed was closer to 50; in Example 6a, however, she spent more time driving at 40 than at 50 miles per hour, so her average speed was closer to 40.

Two other terms associated with averages are **median** and **mode**.

- In a set of *n* numbers arranged in increasing order, the **median** is the middle number (if *n* is odd), or the average of the two middle numbers (if *n* is even).
- The **mode** is the number in the set that occurs most often.

Example 7.

During a 10-day period, Olga received the following number of phone calls each day: 2, 3, 9, 3, 5, 7, 7, 10, 7, 6. What is the average (arithmetic mean) of the median and mode of this set of data?

Solution. The first step is to write the data in increasing order: 2, 3, 3, 5, 6, 7, 7, 7, 9, 10.

- The median is 6.5, the average of the middle two numbers.
- The mode is 7, the number that appears more often than any other.
- The average of the median and the mode is $\frac{6.5+7}{2}$ = **6.75**.

Exercises on Averages

Multiple-Choice Questions

1. Justin's average (arithmetic mean) on four tests is 80. What grade does he need on his fifth test to raise his average to 84?

   (A) 82 (B) 84 (C) 92 (D) 96 (E) 100

2. Judy's average (arithmetic mean) on four tests is 80. Assuming she can earn no more than 100 on any test, what is the least she can earn on her fifth test and still have a chance for an 85 average after seven tests?

   (A) 60 (B) 70 (C) 75 (D) 80 (E) 85

3. Adam's average (arithmetic mean) on four tests is 80. Which of the following CANNOT be the number of tests on which he earned exactly 80 points?

   (A) 0 (B) 1 (C) 2 (D) 3 (E) 4

4. If $x + y = 6$, $y + z = 7$, and $z + x = 9$, what is the average (arithmetic mean) of x, y, and z?

   (A) $\frac{11}{3}$ (B) $\frac{11}{2}$ (C) $\frac{22}{3}$ (D) 11 (E) 22

5. If $a + b = 3(c + d)$, which of the following is the average (arithmetic mean) of a, b, c, and d?

(A) $\dfrac{c+d}{4}$ (B) $\dfrac{3(c+d)}{8}$ (C) $\dfrac{c+d}{2}$ (D) $\dfrac{3(c+d)}{4}$

(E) $c + d$

6. If the average (arithmetic mean) of 5, 6, 7, and w is 8, what is the value of w?

(A) 8 (B) 12 (C) 14 (D) 16 (E) 24

7.

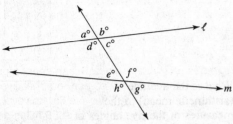

In the diagram above, lines ℓ and m are *not* parallel. If A represents the average (arithmetic mean) of the measures of all eight angles, which of the following is true?

(A) $A = 45°$ (B) $45° < A < 90°$ (C) $A = 90°$
(D) $90° < A < 180°$
(E) It cannot be determined from the information given.

8. What is the average (arithmetic mean) of 2^{10} and 2^{20}?

(A) 2^{15} (B) $2^5 + 2^{10}$ (C) $2^9 + 2^{19}$ (D) 2^{29} (E) 30

9. Let M be the median, and m the mode, of the following set of numbers: 10, 70, 20, 40, 70, 90. What is the average (arithmetic mean) of M and m?

(A) 50 (B) 55 (C) 60 (D) 62.5 (E) 65

10. Which of the following is the average (arithmetic mean) of $x^2 - 10$, $30 - x^2$, and $6x + 10$?

(A) $2x + 10$ (B) $2x + 30$ (C) $3x + 15$
(D) $2x^2 + 6x + 30$ (E) $6x + 10$

Quantitative Comparison Questions

Column A	Column B
The average (arithmetic mean) of the measures of the three angles of an equilateral triangle	The average (arithmetic mean) of the measures of the three angles of a right triangle

11.

Ten students took a test, and the average grade was 80. No one scored exactly 80.

The number of grades over 80	5

12.

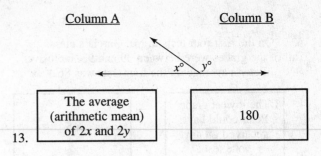

Column A	Column B

The average (arithmetic mean) of $2x$ and $2y$	180

13.

The numbers of boys and girls in a club are the same. The average weight of the boys is 150 pounds. The average weight of the girls is 110 pounds.

The number of boys weighing over 150	The number of girls weighing over 110

14.

The average (arithmetic mean) of 22, 38, x, and y is 15.

$x > 0$

y	0

15.

The average (arithmetic mean) of the *even* numbers between 1 and 11	The average (arithmetic mean) of the *odd* numbers between 2 and 12

16.

The average (arithmetic mean) of 17, 217, 417	The average (arithmetic mean) of 0, 17, 217, 417

17.

$y > 0$

The average (arithmetic mean) of x and y	The average (arithmetic mean) of x, y, and $2y$

18.

Sarah drove from Jacksonville to Tallahassee at an average speed of 60 miles per hour. She returned over the same route at an average speed of 50 miles per hour.

Sarah's average speed for the round trip	55 miles per hour

19.

Column A   Column B

On the first four tests in Mr. Garcia's class,
all of the grades were between 39 and 93, inclusive.
Peter's average on the four tests was 86.

| The lowest grade Peter could have received on any one test | 65 |

20.

23. If $10a + 10b = 35$, what is the average (arithmetic mean) of a and b?

Grid-in Questions

21. What is the average (arithmetic mean) of the positive integers from 1 to 100, inclusive?

24. What is the average (arithmetic mean) of the measures of the five angles in a pentagon?

22. The average (arithmetic mean) weight of the students in the French Club is 150 pounds, and the average weight of the students in the Spanish Club is 130 pounds. If no one is a member of both clubs, if the average weight of all the students is 142 pounds, and if there are 30 members in the French Club, how many members are there in the Spanish Club?

25. Let $[x]$ = the largest integer that is less than or equal to x. For example, $[3.75] = 3$ and $[7] = 7$. What is the average of $[2\pi]$ and $[-\pi]$?

Answer Key

1.	E	5.	E	9.	D	13.	C	17.	A
2.	C	6.	C	10.	A	14.	D	18.	D
3.	D	7.	C	11.	C	15.	B	19.	B
4.	A	8.	C	12.	D	16.	B	20.	C

21. **50.5**   22. **20**   23. **1.75** or **7/4**

24. **108**   25. **1**

Answer Explanations

1. **E.** Use TACTIC E1. For Justin's average on five tests to be 84, he needs a total of $5 \times 84 = 420$ points. So far, he has earned $4 \times 80 = 320$ points. Therefore, he needs 100 points more. *Alternative solution.* Use KEY FACT E3. Assume Justin's first 4 grades were all 80's. His total deviation below 84 is $4 \times 4 = 16$, so his total deviation above 84 must also be 16. He needs $84 + 16 = 100$ points more.

2. **C.** Use TACTIC E1. So far, Judy has earned 320 points. She can survive a low grade on test 5 if she gets the maximum possible on both the sixth and seventh tests. Assume she gets two 100's. Then her total for tests 1, 2, 3, 4, 6, and 7 will be 520. For her seven-test average to be 85, she needs a total of $7 \times 85 = 595$ points. Therefore, she needs at least $595 - 520 = 75$ points.

Alternative solution. Use KEY FACT E3. Assume Judy's first four tests were all 80's. Then her total deviation below 85 would be $4 \times 5 = 20$. Her maximum possible deviation above 85 (assuming 100's on tests 6 and 7) is $15 + 15 = 30$. On test 5 she can deviate at most 10 more points below 85: $85 - 10 = 75$.

3. **D.** Adam could not have earned an 80 on exactly three tests. If he did, his average for those three tests would clearly be 80; and since adding the fourth score didn't change his average, KEY FACT E4 tells us that his fourth score must also be 80. Therefore, it is *not* possible for him to have had exactly three 80's. *Alternative solution.* Could Adam have earned a total of 320 points with:

0 grade of 80?	Easily; for example, 20, 100, 100, 100 or 60, 70, 90, 100.
1 grade of 80?	Lots of ways; 80, 40, 100, 100, for instance.

2 grades of 80?   Yes; 80, 80, 60, 100, for instance.

4 grades of 80?   Sure: 80, 80, 80, 80.

3 grades of 80?   NO! $80 + 80 + 80 + x = 320 \Rightarrow x = 80$, as well.

4. A. Use TACTIC 8-14. Whenever a question involves three equations, add them:

$$
\begin{aligned}
x + y &= 6 \\
y + z &= 7 \\
+\quad z + x &= 9 \\
\hline
2x + 2y + 2z &= 22
\end{aligned}
$$

Divide by 2: $x + y + z = 11$

The average of x, y, and z is $\dfrac{x+y+z}{3} = \dfrac{11}{3}$.

Note: Even if you know how, on the SAT I you should not go through the work of actually solving the equations.

5. E. Calculate the average:

$$
\frac{a+b+c+d}{4} = \frac{3(c+d)+c+d}{4} =
$$
$$
\frac{3c+3d+c+d}{4} = \frac{4c+4d}{4} = c + d
$$

6. C. Use TACTIC E1. The sum of the four numbers is $4 \times 8 = 32$. So

$$
5 + 6 + 7 + w = 32 \Rightarrow
$$
$$
18 + w = 32 \Rightarrow w = 14.
$$

Alternative solution. Use KEY FACT E3. Here, 5 is 3 below 8, 6 is 2 below 8, and 7 is 1 below 8, for a total deviation of $3 + 2 + 1 = 6$ below the average of 8. To compensate, w must be 6 more than 8: $6 + 8 = 14$.

7. C. $a + b + c + d = 360$ and $w + x + y + z = 360$ (see Section 12-I); so the sum of the measures of all eight angles is $360° + 360° = 720°$, and their average, A, is $720° \div 8 = 90°$.

8. C. The average of 2^{10} and 2^{20} is

$$
\frac{2^{10} + 2^{20}}{2} = \frac{2^{10}}{2} + \frac{2^{20}}{2} = 2^9 + 2^{19}.
$$

(See Section 12-A if you had trouble with the exponents.)

Alternative solution. Use your calculator and estimate: 2^{10} is about 1000 and 2^{20} is about 1,000,000. Their average is about 500,000. None of the wrong choices is even close.

9. D. Arrange the numbers in increasing order: 10, 20, 40, 70, 70, 90. The median, M, is the average of the middle two numbers:

$$
\frac{40+70}{2} = 55;
$$

the mode, m, is 70, the number that appears most frequently. The average of M and m, therefore, is the average of 55 and 70, which is 62.5.

10. A. Find the sum of the three expressions, and divide by 3:

$$
(x^2 - 10) + (30 - x^2) + (6x + 10) = 6x + 30
$$

and $\dfrac{6x+30}{3} = 2x + 10$.

Alternative solution. If you get bogged down in the algebra, use TACTIC 9-2. Choose an easy number for x: 1, for example. Then, the three numbers become -9, 29, and 16, whose average is 12. Only A has a value of 12 when $x = 1$. This is also an easy way to check your answer, if you use the first solution.

11. C. In *any* triangle, the sum of the measures of the three angles is $180°$, and the average of their measures is $180° \div 3 = 60°$.

12. D. From KEY FACT E2, we know only that *at least 1 grade was above 80*. In fact, there may have been only 1 (9 grades of 79 and 1 grade of 89, for example), but there could have been 5 or even 9 (for example, 9 grades of 85 and 1 grade of 35).

Alternative solution. The ten students scored exactly 800 points. Ask, "Could the grades be equal?" Could there be exactly 5 grades above 80? Sure: 5 grades of 100 for 500 points and 5 more grades of 60 for the other 300 points. Must they be equal? No, 8 grades of 100 and 2 grades of 0 also total 800.

13. C. The average of $2x$ and $2y$ is $\dfrac{2x+2y}{2} = x + y$, which equals 180 (see Section 12-I).

14. D. It is possible that no boy weighs over 150 (if every single boy weighs exactly 150); on the other hand, it is possible that almost every boy weighs over 150. The same is true for the girls.

15. B. Use TACTIC E1:

$$
22 + 38 + x + y = 4 \times 15 = 60 \Rightarrow
$$
$$
60 + x + y = 60 \Rightarrow x + y = 0.
$$

Since it is given that x is positive, y must be negative and hence is less than 0.

16. B. Don't calculate the averages. Each number in Column A (2, 4, 6, 8, 10) is less than the corresponding number in Column B (3, 5, 7, 9, 11), so the Column A average must be less than the Column B average.

Alternative solution. Either observe that the numbers in each column form an arithmetic sequence, so by KEY FACT E5 the averages are just the middle numbers (6 and 7); or use your calculator and quickly compute each average.

17. A.   Again, don't calculate the averages. The average of the set of numbers in Column A is clearly positive, and by KEY FACT E4, adding 0 to that set in Column B must lower the average.

18. D.   Use KEY FACT E4. If $x < y$, then the average of x and y is less than y, and surely less than $2y$. Therefore, $2y$ has to raise the average. On the other hand, if x is much larger than y, then $2y$ will lower the average.

19. B.   Since Sarah was driving slower, she took more time to return from Tallahassee than to get there, so she spent more time driving at 50 than at 60 miles per hour. Her overall average, therefore, had to be closer to 50 than to 60—it had to be *less* than 55. The alternative is to actually calculate her average speed (54.5454...), but you shouldn't.

20. C.   Since Peter's average was 86, he earned a total of $4 \times 86 = 344$ points. The maximum he could have earned on any one test was 93; and if he did that on three tests, that would account for $3 \times 93 = 279$ points. On the fourth test, he must have scored *at least* $344 - 279 = 65$ points.

21. (50.5)   Clearly, the sequence of integers from 1 to 100 has 100 terms, so by KEY FACT E5 we know that the average of all the numbers is the average of the two middle ones: 50 and 51. The average, therefore, is 50.5.

22. (20)   Let x = number of students in the Spanish Club, and write the weighted average:

$$142 = \frac{30(150) + x(130)}{30 + x} \Rightarrow$$
$$142(30 + x) = 30(150) + 130x \Rightarrow$$
$$4260 + 142x = 4500 + 130x \Rightarrow$$
$$12x = 240 \Rightarrow x = 20.$$

23. (1.75)   Since $10a + 10b = 35$, dividing both sides of the equation by 10 gives $a + b = 3.5$. Therefore, the average of a and b is $3.5 \div 2 = 1.75$.

24. (108)   The average of the measures of the five angles is the sum of their measures divided by 5. The sum is $(5 - 2) \times 180 = 3 \times 180 = 540$ (see Section 12-K), so the average is $540 \div 5 = 108$.

25. (1)   Since π is a little more than 3, 2π is a little more than 6, and $[2\pi] = 6$. Now, be careful: $-\pi$ is a little less than -3, so $[-\pi] = -4$. Therefore, the average of $[2\pi]$ and $[-\pi]$ is the average of 6 and -4, which is 1.

ALGEBRA

For the SAT I you need to know only a small part of the algebra normally taught in a high school elementary algebra course and none of the material taught in an intermediate or advanced algebra course. Sections 12-F, 12-G, and 12-H review only the topics that you need for the SAT I.

12-F POLYNOMIALS

Even though the terms *monomial, binomial, trinomial,* and *polynomial* are not used on the SAT I, you must be able to work with simple polynomials, and the use of these terms will make it easy to discuss the important concepts.

A *monomial* is any number or variable or product of numbers and variables. Each of the following is a monomial:

$$3 \quad -4 \quad x \quad y \quad 3x \quad -4xyz \quad 5x^3 \quad 1.5xy^2 \quad a^3b^4$$

The number that appears in front of the variable or variables in a monomial is called the *coefficient*. The coefficient of $5x^3$ is 5. If there is no number, the coefficient is 1 or -1, because x means $1x$ and $-ab^2$ means $-1ab^2$.

On the SAT I, you are often asked to evaluate a monomial for specific values of the variables.

Example 1.

What is the value of $-3a^2b$ when $a = -4$ and $b = 0.5$?

Solution. Rewrite the expression, replacing the letters a and b by the numbers -4 and 0.5, respectively. Make sure to write each number in parentheses. Then evaluate: $-3(-4)^2(0.5) = -3(16)(0.5) = \mathbf{-24}$.

> **CAUTION:** Be sure you follow PEMDAS: handle exponents before the other operations. In Example 1, you *cannot* multiply -4 by -3, get 12, and then square 12.

A *polynomial* is a monomial or the sum of two or more monomials. Each monomial that makes up the polynomial is called a *term* of the polynomial. Each of the following is a polynomial:

$$2x^2 \quad 2x^2 + 3 \quad 3x^2 - 7 \quad x^2 + 5x - 1$$
$$a^2b + b^2a \quad x^2 - y^2 \quad w^2 - 2w + 1$$

The first polynomial in the above list is a monomial; the second, third, fifth, and sixth polynomials are called *binomials* because each has two terms; the fourth and seventh polynomials are called *trinomials* because each has three terms. Two terms are called *like terms* if they have exactly the same variables and exponents; they can differ only in their coefficients: $5a^2b$ and $-3a^2b$ are like terms, whereas a^2b and b^2a are not.

The polynomial $3x^2 + 4x + 5x + 2x^2 + x - 7$ has six terms, but some of them are like terms and can be combined:

$$3x^2 + 2x^2 = 5x^2 \quad \text{and} \quad 4x + 5x + x = 10x.$$

Therefore, the original polynomial is equivalent to the trinomial $5x^2 + 10x - 7$.

KEY FACT F1

The only terms of a polynomial that can be combined are like terms.

Helpful Hint

To add, subtract, multiply, and divide polynomials, use the usual laws of arithmetic. To avoid careless errors, write each polynomial in parentheses before performing any arithmetic operations.

KEY FACT F2

To add two polynomials, put a plus sign between them, erase the parentheses, and combine like terms.

Example 2.

What is the sum of $5x^2 + 10x - 7$ and $3x^2 - 4x + 2$?

Solution. $(5x^2 + 10x - 7) + (3x^2 - 4x + 2)$
$= 5x^2 + 10x - 7 + 3x^2 - 4x + 2$
$= (5x^2 + 3x^2) + (10x - 4x) + (-7 + 2)$
$= \mathbf{8x^2 + 6x - 5}$.

KEY FACT F3

To subtract two polynomials, change the minus sign between them to a plus sign and change the sign of every term in the second parentheses. Then use KEY FACT F2 to add them: erase the parentheses and combine like terms.

> **CAUTION:** Make sure you get the order right in a subtraction problem.

Example 3.

Subtract $3x^2 - 4x + 2$ from $5x^2 + 10x - 7$.

Solution. Be careful. Start with the second polynomial and subtract the first:

$$(5x^2 + 10x - 7) - (3x^2 - 4x + 2) =$$
$$(5x^2 + 10x - 7) + (-3x^2 + 4x - 2) = \mathbf{2x^2 + 14x - 9}.$$

Example 4.

What is the average (arithmetic mean) of $5x^2 + 10x - 7$, $3x^2 - 4x + 2$, and $4x^2 + 2$?

Solution. As in any average problem, add and divide:

$$(5x^2 + 10x - 7) + (3x^2 - 4x + 2) + (4x^2 + 2) =$$
$$12x^2 + 6x - 3,$$

and by the distributive law (KEY FACT A20):

$$\frac{12x^2 + 6x - 3}{3} = 4x^2 + 2x - 1.$$

KEY FACT F4

To multiply monomials, first multiply their coefficients, and then multiply their variables by adding the exponents (see Section 12-A).

Example 5.

What is the product of $3xy^2z^3$ and $-2x^2y$?

Solution. $(3xy^2z^3)(-2x^2y) = 3(-2)(x)(x^2)(y^2)(y)(z^3) = \mathbf{-6x^3y^3z^3}$.

All other polynomials are multiplied by using the distributive law.

KEY FACT F5

To multiply a monomial by any polynomial, just multiply each term of the polynomial by the monomial.

Example 6.

What is the product of $2a$ and $3a^2 - 6ab + b^2$?

Solution. $2a(3a^2 - 6ab + b^2) = \mathbf{6a^3 - 12a^2b + 2ab^2}$.

On the SAT I, the only other polynomials that you may be asked to multiply are two binomials.

KEY FACT F6

To multiply two binomials, use the so-called FOIL method, which is really nothing more than the distributive law. Multiply each term in the first parentheses by each term in the second parentheses and simplify by combining terms, if possible.

$$(2x - 7)(3x + 2) = (2x)(3x) + (2x)(2) + (-7)(3x) + (-7)(2) =$$

First terms Outer terms Inner terms Last terms

$$6x^2 + 4x - 21x - 14 = 6x^2 - 17x - 14$$

Example 7.

What is the value of $(x - 2)(x + 3) - (x - 4)(x + 5)$?

Solution. First, multiply both pairs of binomials:

$$(x - 2)(x + 3) = x^2 + 3x - 2x - 6 = x^2 + x - 6$$
$$(x - 4)(x + 5) = x^2 + 5x - 4x - 20 = x^2 + x - 20$$

Now, subtract: $(x^2 + x - 6) - (x^2 + x - 20) =$
$x^2 + x - 6 - x^2 - x + 20 = \mathbf{14}$.

KEY FACT F7

The three most important binomial products on the SAT I are these:

- $(x - y)(x + y) = x^2 + xy - yx - y^2 = x^2 - y^2$
- $(x - y)^2 = (x - y)(x - y) = x^2 - xy - yx + y^2 = x^2 - 2xy + y^2$
- $(x + y)^2 = (x + y)(x + y) = x^2 + xy + yx + y^2 = x^2 + 2xy + y^2$

Helpful Hint

If you memorize these products, you won't have to multiply the binomials out each time you need them.

Example 8.

If $a - b = 17.5$ and $a + b = 10$, what is the value of $a^2 - b^2$?

Solution. In Section 12-G, we will review the methods used to solve such a pair of equations; but even if you know how to solve them, *you should not do so here.* You don't need to know the values of a and b to answer this question. The moment you see $a^2 - b^2$, you should think $(a - b)(a + b)$. Then:

$$a^2 - b^2 = (a - b)(a + b) = (17.5)(10) = \textbf{175}.$$

Example 9.

If $x^2 + y^2 = 36$ and $(x + y)^2 = 64$, what is the value of xy?

Solution. Here, $64 = (x + y)^2 = x^2 + 2xy + y^2 = x^2 + y^2 + 2xy = 36 + 2xy$. Therefore:

$$2xy = 64 - 36 = 28 \Rightarrow xy = \textbf{14}.$$

On the SAT I, the only division of polynomials you will have to do is to divide a polynomial by a monomial. You will *not* have to do long division of polynomials.

KEY FACT F8

To divide a polynomial by a monomial, use the distributive law. Then simplify each term by reducing the fraction formed by the coefficients to lowest terms and applying the laws of exponents.

Example 10.

What is the quotient when $32a^2b + 12ab^3c$ is divided by $8ab$?

Solution. By the distributive law,

$$\frac{32a^2b + 12ab^3c}{8ab} = \frac{32a^2b}{8ab} + \frac{12ab^3c}{8ab}.$$

Now reduce each fraction: $\mathbf{4a + \dfrac{3}{2}b^2c}.$

On the SAT I, the most important way to use the three formulas in KEY FACT F7 is to recognize them in reverse. In other words, whenever you see $x^2 - y^2$, you should realize that it can be rewritten as $(x - y)(x + y)$. This process, which is the reverse of multiplication, is called ***factoring***.

Column A	Column B

Example 11.

The value of $x^2 + 4x + 4$ when $x = 95.9$	The value of $x^2 - 4x + 4$ when $x = 99.5$

Solution. Obviously, you don't want to plug in 95.9 and 99.5, even on your calculator (and you know that the SAT I *never* requires you to do tedious arithmetic). Recognize that $x^2 + 4x + 4$ is equal to $(x + 2)^2$ and that $x^2 - 4x + 4$ is equal to $(x - 2)^2$. Then, Column A is $(95.9 + 2)^2 = 97.9^2$, whereas Column B is $(99.5 - 2)^2 = 97.5^2$. Column **A** is greater.

To ***factor*** a polynomial, you must find other polynomials whose product is the original polynomial. For example, since $2x(3x - 5) = 6x^2 - 10x$, then $2x$ and $3x - 5$ are each factors of $6x^2 - 10x$; and since $(a - b)(a + b) = a^2 - b^2$, then $(a - b)$ and $(a + b)$ are each factors of $a^2 - b^2$.

On the SAT I, you will need to do almost no factoring. In fact, other than recognizing the formulas given in KEY FACT F6, the only factoring you are likely to have to do is to remove a common factor from each term of a polynomial. For example, each of the terms of the trinomial $3x^2 + 12x - 27$ is divisible by 3, so you can factor out 3: $3x^2 + 12x - 27 = 3(x^2 + 4x - 9)$. The common factor can contain a variable: $4x^2 + 6xy = 2x(2x + 3y)$.

Example 12.

What is the value of $(1{,}000{,}001)^2 - (999{,}999)^2$?

Solution. Since you're surely not going to square 999,999 by hand, the obvious thing to do is to reach for your calculator. However, some calculators will give an error message if you try to square such a large number, and others will have rounding errors. But even if your calculator could give you the exact answer, you shouldn't use it because you can get the right answer in a few seconds by using your head! This problem is just $a^2 - b^2$, where $a = 1{,}000{,}001$ and $b = 999{,}999$, so change it to $(a - b)(a + b)$:

$$(1{,}000{,}001)^2 - (999{,}999)^2$$
$$= (1{,}000{,}001 - 999{,}999)(1{,}000{,}001 + 999{,}999)$$
$$= (2)(2{,}000{,}000) = \textbf{4{,}000{,}000}.$$

Although the coefficient of any term in a polynomial can be a fraction, such as $\frac{2}{3}x^2 - \frac{1}{2}x$, the variable itself cannot be in the denominator. An expression such as $\frac{3 + x}{x^2}$, which has a variable in the denominator, is called an ***algebraic fraction***. Fortunately, you should have no trouble with algebraic fractions since they are handled just like regular fractions. The rules that you reviewed in Section 12-B for adding, subtracting, multiplying, and dividing fractions apply also to algebraic fractions.

Example 13.

What is the sum of the reciprocals of x^2 and y^2?

Solution. To add $\dfrac{1}{x^2} + \dfrac{1}{y^2}$, you need a common denominator, which is x^2y^2.

Multiply the numerator and denominator of $\dfrac{1}{x^2}$ by y^2 and the numerator and denominator of $\dfrac{1}{y^2}$ by x^2:

$$\frac{1}{x^2} + \frac{1}{y^2} = \frac{y^2}{x^2y^2} + \frac{x^2}{x^2y^2} = \frac{x^2 + y^2}{x^2y^2}.$$

Often, the way to simplify algebraic fractions is to factor the numerator or the denominator or both. Consider Example 14, which is harder than anything you are likely to see on the SAT I but is quite manageable.

Example 14.

What is the value of $\dfrac{4x^3 - x}{(2x+1)(6x-3)}$ when $x = 9999$?

Solution. Don't use FOIL to multiply the denominator. That's going the wrong way. Instead, simplify this fraction by factoring everything you can. First, factor an x out of the numerator, and notice that what's left is the difference of two squares, which can be factored. Then factor out 3 in the second factor in the denominator:

$$\frac{4x^3 - x}{(2x+1)(6x-3)} = \frac{x(4x^2 - 1)}{(2x+1)3(2x-1)} =$$

$$\frac{x\cancel{(2x-1)}\cancel{(2x+1)}}{3\cancel{(2x+1)}\cancel{(2x-1)}} = \frac{x}{3}.$$

Finally, instead of plugging 9999 into the original expression, plug it into $\dfrac{x}{3}$: $9999 \div 3 = \textbf{3333}$.

Exercises on Polynomials

Multiple-Choice Questions

1. If $a^2 - b^2 = 21$ and $a^2 + b^2 = 29$, which of the following could be the value of ab?

   I. -10
   II. $5\sqrt{2}$
   III. 10

   (A) I only   (B) II only   (C) III only
   (D) I and III only   (E) II and III only

2. What is the average (arithmetic mean) of $x^2 + 2x - 3$, $3x^2 - 2x - 3$, and $30 - 4x^2$?

   (A) $\dfrac{8x^2 + 4x + 24}{3}$ (B) $\dfrac{8x^2 + 24}{3}$ (C) $\dfrac{24 - 4x}{3}$
   (D) -12 (E) 8

3. If $a^2 + b^2 = 4$ and $(a - b)^2 = 2$, what is the value of ab?

   (A) 1   (B) $\sqrt{2}$ (C) 2   (D) 3   (E) 4

4. If $\dfrac{1}{a} + \dfrac{1}{b} = \dfrac{1}{c}$ and $ab = c$, what is the average of a and b?

   (A) 0   (B) $\dfrac{1}{2}$ (C) 1   (D) $\dfrac{c}{2}$ (E) $\dfrac{a+b}{2c}$

5. Which of the following is equal to

$$\left(\frac{1}{a} + a\right)^2 - \left(\frac{1}{a} - a\right)^2?$$

   (A) 0   (B) 4   (C) $\dfrac{1}{a^2} - a^2$ (D) $\dfrac{2}{a^2} - 2a^2$

   (E) $\dfrac{1}{a^2} - 4 - a^2$

Quantitative Comparison Questions

Column A	Column B

6. $b < 0$

| $-2b^2$ | $(-2b)^2$ |

7. $a > b$

| $(a - b)(a + b)$ | $(a - b)(a - b)$ |

8. $x = -3$ and $y = 2$

| $-x^2y^3$ | 0 |

9.

| $(x + y)(x - y)$ | $x(y + x) - y(x + y)$ |

10.

| $\dfrac{5x^2 - 20}{x - 2}$ | $4x + 8$ |

Grid-in Questions

11. What is the value of
$\dfrac{a^2 - b^2}{a - b}$ when $a = 17.9$
and $b = 19.7$?

12. If $x^2 - y^2 = 28$ and $x - y = 8$,
what is the average of x and y?

13. What is the value of
$(2x + 3)(x + 6) - (2x - 5)(x + 10)$?

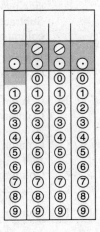

14. What is the value of
$x^2 + 12x + 36$ when $x = 64$?

15. If $\left(\dfrac{1}{a} + a\right)^2 = 100$, what is
the value of $\dfrac{1}{a^2} + a^2$?

Answer Key

1.	D	3.	A	5.	B	7.	D	9.	C
2.	E	4.	B	6.	B	8.	B	10.	D

11. | | 3 | 7 | . | 6 |
12. | 1 | . | 7 | 5 |
13. | | | 6 | 8 |
14. | 4 | 9 | 0 | 0 |
15. | | | 9 | 8 |

Answer Explanations

1. D. Adding the two equations, we get

$$2a^2 = 50 \Rightarrow a^2 = 25 \Rightarrow b^2 = 4.$$

Then, $a = 5$ or -5 and $b = 2$ or -2. The only possibilities for the product ab are 10 and -10. (Only I and III are true.)

2. E. To find the average, take the sum of the three polynomials and then divide by 3. The sum is

$$(x^2 + 2x - 3) + (3x^2 - 2x - 3) + (30 - 4x^2) = 24,$$

and $24 \div 3 = 8$.

3. A. Start by squaring $a - b$:
$(a - b)^2 = a^2 - 2ab + b^2$. Then

$$2 = 4 - 2ab \Rightarrow 2ab = 2 \Rightarrow ab = 1.$$

4. B. $\dfrac{1}{c} = \dfrac{1}{a} + \dfrac{1}{b} = \dfrac{a+b}{ab} = \dfrac{a+b}{c} \Rightarrow$

$$1 = a + b \Rightarrow \dfrac{a+b}{2} = \dfrac{1}{2}.$$

5. B. Expand each square:

$$\left(\frac{1}{a} + a\right)^2 =$$

$$\frac{1}{a^2} + 2\left(\frac{1}{a}\right)(a) + a^2 = \frac{1}{a^2} + 2 + a^2.$$

Similarly, $\left(\dfrac{1}{a} - a\right)^2 = \dfrac{1}{a^2} - 2 + a^2.$

Subtract: $\left(\dfrac{1}{a^2} + 2 + a^2\right) - \left(\dfrac{1}{a^2} - 2 + a^2\right) = 4.$

Alternative solution. Treat this as the difference of two squares problem and factor: $x^2 - y^2 = (x + y)(x - y)$. Then:

$$\left(\frac{1}{a} + a\right)^2 - \left(\frac{1}{a} - a\right)^2 =$$

$$\left[\left(\frac{1}{a} + a\right) + \left(\frac{1}{a} - a\right)\right]\left[\left(\frac{1}{a} + a\right) - \left(\frac{1}{a} - a\right)\right] =$$

$$\left(\frac{2}{a}\right)(2a) = 4.$$

6. B. Since b is negative, b^2 is positive, and so $-2b^2$ is negative. Therefore, Column A is negative, whereas Column B is positive.

	Column A	Column B

7. D. Since $a > b$, then $a - b$ is positive; divide each side by $a - b$: $\quad a + b \qquad a - b$

Subtract a from each column: $\qquad\qquad b \qquad\qquad -b$

If $b = 0$ the columns are equal; if $b = 1$, they aren't.

8. B. Column A: $-(-3)^2 2^3 = -(9)(8) = -72$.
Column B is greater.

9. C. Column B: $x(y + x) - y(x + y) =$
$xy + x^2 - yx - y^2 = x^2 - y^2$.
Column A: $(x + y)(x - y) = x^2 - y^2$.

10. D. Column A: $\dfrac{5x^2 - 20}{x - 2} = \dfrac{5(x^2 - 4)}{x - 2} =$

$$\frac{5(x - 2)(x + 2)}{x - 2} = 5(x + 2).$$

Column B: $4x + 8 = 4(x + 2)$.
If $x = -2$, both columns are 0; for any other value of x, the columns are unequal.

11. (37.6) $\dfrac{a^2 - b^2}{a - b} = \dfrac{(a - b)(a + b)}{a - b} = a + b =$

$$17.9 + 19.7 = 37.6.$$

12. (1.75) Since $x^2 - y^2 = (x - y)(x + y)$, we have:

$$28 = (x - y)(x + y) = 8(x + y) \Rightarrow$$
$$x + y = 28 \div 8 = 3.5.$$

Finally, the average of x and y is $\dfrac{x + y}{2} = \dfrac{3.5}{2}$ = 1.75.

13. (68) First, multiply out both pairs of binomials:

$$(2x + 3)(x + 6) = 2x^2 + 15x + 18$$
and $(2x - 5)(x + 10) = 2x^2 + 15x - 50.$

Now subtract:

$$(2x^2 + 15x + 18) - (2x^2 + 15x - 50) =$$
$$18 - (-50) = 68.$$

Alternative solution. Note that, since this is a grid-in question, the answer must be a (positive) number. All of the x's must cancel out. Therefore, the answer will be the same no matter what x is, so pick a simple value for x. If $x = 0$: $(3)(6) - (-5)(10) = 18 - (-50) = 68$; if $x = 4$: $(11)(10) - (3)(14) = 110 - 42 = 68.$

14. (4900) Of course, you can do this problem on your calculator; but you can do it quicker if you recognize that $x^2 + 12x + 36 = (x + 6)^2$. The value is $(64 + 6)^2 = 70^2 = 4900.$

15. (98) $100 = \left(\dfrac{1}{a} + a\right)^2 = \dfrac{1}{a^2} + 2 + a^2$

$$\Rightarrow \dfrac{1}{a^2} + a^2 = 98.$$

12-G SOLVING EQUATIONS AND INEQUALITIES

The basic principle to which you must adhere in solving any *equation* is that you can manipulate the equation in any way, as long as *you do the same thing to both sides*. For example, you may always add the same number to each side, subtract the same number from each side, multiply or divide each side by the same number (except 0), square each side, take the square root of each side (if the quantities are positive), or take the reciprocal of each side. These comments apply to inequalities, as well, but here you must be very careful because some procedures, such as multiplying or dividing by a negative number and taking reciprocals, reverse inequalities (see KEY FACT A23).

Most of the equations and inequalities that you will have to solve on the SAT I have only one variable and no exponents. The following simple six-step method can be used on all of them.

Example 1.

If $\dfrac{1}{2}x + 3(x - 2) = 2(x + 1) + 1$, what is the value of x?

Solution. Follow the steps outlined in the following table.

Step	What to Do	Example 1
1	Get rid of fractions and decimals by multiplying both sides by the Lowest Common Denominator (LCD).	Multiply each term by 2: $x + 6(x - 2) = 4(x + 1) + 2.$
2	Get rid of all parentheses by using the distributive law.	$x + 6x - 12 = 4x + 4 + 2.$
3	Combine like terms on each side.	$7x - 12 = 4x + 6.$
4	By adding or subtracting, get all the variables on one side.	Subtract $4x$ from each side: $3x - 12 = 6.$
5	By adding or subtracting, get all the plain numbers on the other side.	Add 12 to each side: $3x = 18.$
6	Divide both sides by the coefficient of the variable.*	Divide both sides by 3: $x = \mathbf{6}.$

*If you start with an inequality and in Step 6 you divide by a negative number, remember to reverse the inequality (see KEY FACT A23).

Example 1 is actually much harder than any equation on the SAT I, because it requires all six steps. On the SAT I that never happens. Think of the six steps as a list of questions that must be answered. Ask whether each step is necessary. If it isn't, move on to the next one; if it is, do it.

Let's look at Example 2, which does not require all six steps.

Example 2.

For what real number n is it true that $3(n - 20) = n$?

(A) −10   (B) 0   (C) 10   (D) 20   (E) 30

Solution. Do each of the six steps necessary.

Step	Question	Yes/No	What to Do
1	Are there any fractions or decimals?	No	
2	Are there any parentheses?	Yes	Get rid of them: $3n - 60 = n$
3	Are there any like terms to combine?	No	
4	Are there variables on both sides?	Yes	Subtract n from each side: $2n - 60 = 0$
5	Is there a plain number on the same side as the variable?	Yes	Add 60 to each side: $2n = 60$
6	Does the variable have a coefficient?	Yes	Divide both sides by 2: $n = \mathbf{30}$

Memorize the six steps *in order*, and use this method whenever you have to solve this type of equation or inequality.

Example 3.

Three brothers divided a prize as follows. The oldest received $\frac{2}{5}$ of it, the middle brother received $\frac{1}{3}$ of it, and the youngest received the remaining \$120. What was the value of the prize?

Solution. If x represents the value of the prize, then

$$\frac{2}{5}x + \frac{1}{3}x + 120 = x.$$

Solve this equation using the six-step method.

Step	Question	Yes/No	What to Do
1	Are there any fractions or decimals?	Yes	Get rid of them: multiply by 15*. $$\cancel{15}^{3}\left(\frac{2}{\cancel{5}_1}x\right)+\cancel{15}^{5}\left(\frac{1}{\cancel{3}_1}x\right)+$$ $$15(120) = 15(x)$$ $$6x + 5x + 1800 = 15x$$
2	Are there any parentheses?	No	
3	Are there any like terms to combine?	Yes	Combine them: $11x + 1800 = 15x$.
4	Are there variables on both sides?	Yes	Subtract 11*x* from each side: $1800 = 4x$.
5	Is there a plain number on the same side as the variable?	No	
6	Does the variable have a coefficient?	Yes	Divide both sides by 4: $x = \mathbf{450}$.

*Multiply by 15 since it is the LCM of the two denominators, 3 and 5.

Sometimes on the SAT I, you are given an equation with several variables and asked to solve for one of them in terms of the others.

When you have to solve for one variable in terms of the others, treat all of the others as if they were numbers, and apply the six-step method.

Example 4.

If $a = 3b - c$, what is the value of b in terms of a and c?

Solution. To solve for b, treat a and c as numbers and use the six-step method with b as the variable.

Step	Question	Yes/No	What to Do
1	Are there any fractions or decimals?	No	
2	Are there any parentheses?	No	
3	Are there any like terms to combine?	No	
4	Are there variables on both sides?	No	Remember: the only variable is b.
5	Is there a plain number on the same side as the variable?	Yes	Remember: we're considering c as a number, and it is on the same side as b, the variable. Add c to both sides: $a + c = 3b$.
6	Does the variable have a coefficient?	Yes	Divide both sides by 3: $b = \dfrac{a+c}{3}$.

Sometimes when solving equations, you may see a shortcut. For example, to solve $7(w - 3) = 42$, you can save time if you start by dividing both sides by 7, getting $w - 3 = 6$, rather than using the distributive law to eliminate the parentheses. Similarly, if you have to solve a proportion such as $\frac{x}{7} = \frac{3}{5}$, it is easier to cross-multiply, getting $5x = 21$, than to multiply both sides by 35 to get rid of the fractions (although that's exactly what cross-multiplying accomplishes). Other shortcuts will be illustrated in the problems at the end of the section. If you spot such a shortcut, use it; but if you don't, be assured that the six-step method *always* works.

Helpful Hint

In applying the six-step method, you shouldn't actually write out the table, as we did in Examples 1–4, since it would be too time-consuming. Instead, use the method as a guideline and mentally go through each step, doing whichever ones are required.

Example 5.

If $x - 4 = 11$, what is the value of $x - 8$?

   (A) –15   (B) –7   (C) –1   (D) 7   (E) 15

Solution. Going immediately to Step 5, add 4 to each side of the equation: $x = 15$. But this is *not* the answer. You need the value, not of x, but of $x - 8$: $15 - 8 = \mathbf{7}$ **(D)**.

As in Example 5, on the SAT I you are often asked to solve for something other than the simple variable. In Example 5, we could have been asked for the value of x^2, $x + 4$, $(x - 4)^2$, and so on.

Tactic

G3

As you read each question on the SAT I, in your test booklet circle what you are looking for. Then you will always be sure that you are answering the question that is asked.

Helpful Hint

Very often, solving the equation is *not* the quickest way to answer the question. Consider Example 6.

Example 6.

If $2x - 5 = 98$, what is the value of $2x + 5$?

Solution. First, circle what you are asked for (the value of $2x + 5$), and then look at the question carefully. The best approach is to observe that $2x + 5$ is 10 more than $2x - 5$, so the answer is **108** (10 more than 98). Next best would be to do only one step of the six-step method, and add 5 to both sides: $2x = 103$. Now, add again 5 to both sides: $2x + 5 = 103 + 5 = \mathbf{108}$. The *worst* method would be to divide $2x = 103$ by 2, get $x = 51.5$, and then use that value to calculate $2x + 5$.

Example 7.

If w is an integer, and the average (arithmetic mean) of 3, 4, and w is less than 10, what is the greatest possible value of w?

Solution. Set up the inequality: $\dfrac{3 + 4 + w}{3} < 10$. Step 1 (get rid of fractions by multiplying both sides by 3): $3 + 4 + w < 30$. Step 3 (combine like terms): $7 + w < 30$. Step 5 (subtract 7 from both sides): $w < 23$. Since w is an integer, the most it can be is **22**.

Consider the following variation of Example 7.

Example 7a.

If the average (arithmetic mean) of 3, 4, and w is less than 10, what is the greatest possible value of w that can be entered in the grid?

Solution. Just as in Example 7, we get $w < 23$. The largest number less than 23 that can be entered in a grid is **22.9**.

The six-step method works also when there are variables in denominators.

Example 8.

For what value of x is $\dfrac{4}{x} + \dfrac{3}{5} = \dfrac{10}{x}$?

Solution. Multiply each side by the LCD, $5x$:

$$5x\left(\frac{4}{x}\right) + 5x\left(\frac{3}{5}\right) = 5x\left(\frac{10}{x}\right) \Rightarrow 20 + 3x = 50.$$

Now solve normally:

$$20 + 3x = 50 \Rightarrow 3x = 30 \Rightarrow x = \mathbf{10}.$$

Example 9.

If x is positive, and $y = 5x^2 + 3$, which of the following is an expression for x in terms of y?

   (A) $\sqrt{\dfrac{y}{5} - 3}$ (B) $\sqrt{\dfrac{y - 3}{5}}$ (C) $\dfrac{\sqrt{y - 3}}{5}$

   (D) $\dfrac{\sqrt{y} - 3}{5}$ (E) $\dfrac{\sqrt{y} - \sqrt{3}}{5}$

Solution. The six-step method works when there are no exponents. Let's treat x^2 as a single variable, however, and use the method as far as we can:

$$y = 5x^2 + 3 \Rightarrow y - 3 = 5x^2 \Rightarrow \frac{y - 3}{5} = x^2.$$

Now we take the square root of each side; since x is positive, the only solution is $x = \sqrt{\dfrac{y - 3}{5}}$ **(B)**.

> **CAUTION:** Doing the same thing to each *side* of an equation does *not* mean doing the same thing to each *term* of the equation. Study Examples 10 and 11 carefully.

Example 10.

If $\dfrac{1}{a} = \dfrac{1}{b} + \dfrac{1}{c}$, what is a in terms of b and c?

Note: You *cannot* just take the reciprocal of each term; the answer is *not* $a = b + c$. Here are two solutions.

Solution 1. First add the fractions on the right-hand side:

$$\frac{1}{a} = \frac{1}{b} + \frac{1}{c} = \frac{b + c}{bc}.$$

Now, take the reciprocal of each side: $a = \dfrac{bc}{b + c}$.

Solution 2. Use the six-step method. Multiply each term by abc, the LCD: $abc\left(\dfrac{1}{a}\right) = abc\left(\dfrac{1}{b}\right) + abc\left(\dfrac{1}{c}\right) \Rightarrow bc =$

$ac + ab = a(c + b) \Rightarrow a = \dfrac{bc}{c + b}$.

Example 11.

If $a > 0$ and $a^2 + b^2 = c^2$, what is a in terms of b and c?

Note: You *cannot* take the square root of each term and write $a + b = c$.

Solution. $a^2 + b^2 = c^2 \Rightarrow a^2 = c^2 - b^2$. Now, take the square root of each side: $a = \sqrt{a^2} = \sqrt{c^2 - b^2}$.

Helpful Hint

On a multiple-choice question, if your answer is not among the five choices, check to see whether it is *equivalent* to one of the choices.

Example 12.

If $a = b(c + d)$, what is d in terms of a, b, and c?

(A) $\dfrac{a}{b} - c$ (B) $a - bc$ (C) $\dfrac{a}{bc}$ (D) $\dfrac{a}{bc} - b$

(E) $\dfrac{a - c}{b}$

Solution. We use the six-step method:

$a = b(c + d) \Rightarrow a = bc + bd \Rightarrow a - bc = bd \Rightarrow d = \dfrac{a - bc}{b}$.

Now what? Our answer isn't one of the choices. It is, however, *equivalent* to one of the choices. If we use the distributive law to divide a by b and bc by b, we see that

our answer is just choice **A** in another form:

$$\dfrac{a - bc}{b} = \dfrac{a}{b} - c.$$

There are a few other types of equations that you may need to solve on the SAT I. Fortunately, they are quite easy. You probably will not have to solve a quadratic equation, one in which the variable is raised to the second power. If you do, however, you will not need the quadratic formula, and you will not have to factor a trinomial. Here are two examples.

Example 13.

If x is a positive number and $x^2 + 4 = 125$, what is the value of x?

Solution. When there is an x^2-term, but no x-term, just take the square root:

$$x^2 + 4 = 125 \Rightarrow x^2 = 121 \Rightarrow x = \sqrt{121} = 11.$$

If the equation had been $x^2 + 9 = 125$, the solution would have been $x = \sqrt{116}$, which can be reduced to $\sqrt{4} \times \sqrt{29} = 2\sqrt{29}$.

Calculator Shortcut

If you can easily simplify a square root, that's great; but on the SAT I, you never have to. The answers to grid-in problems don't involve square roots, and if the answer to a multiple-choice question turns out to be $\sqrt{116}$, you can use your calculator to see which of the five choices is equal to 10.77.

Example 14.

What is the largest value of x that satisfies the equation $2x^2 - 3x = 0$?

Solution. When an equation has an x^2-term and an x-term but no constant term, solve by factoring out the x and using the fact that, if the product of two numbers is 0, one of them must be 0 (KEY FACT A3):

$$2x^2 - 3x = 0 \Rightarrow x(2x - 3) = 0$$
$$x = 0 \text{ or } 2x - 3 = 0$$
$$x = 0 \text{ or } 2x = 3$$
$$x = 0 \text{ or } x = 1.5.$$

The largest value is **1.5**.

In another type of equation that occasionally appears on the SAT I, the variable is in the exponent. Equations of this type are particularly easy and are basically solved by inspection.

Example 15.

If $2^{x+3} = 32$, what is the value of 3^{x+2}?

Solution. How many 2's do you have to multiply together to get 32? If you don't know that the answer is 5, just multiply and keep track. Count the 2's on your fingers as you say to yourself, "2 times 2 is 4, times 2 is 8, times 2 is 16, times 2 is 32." Then

$$2^{x+3} = 32 = 2^5 \Rightarrow x + 3 = 5 \Rightarrow x = 2.$$

Therefore, $x + 2 = 4$, and $3^{x+2} = 3^4 = 3 \times 3 \times 3 \times 3 = $ **81**.

Occasionally, both sides of an equation have variables in the exponents. In that case, it is necessary to write both exponentials with the same base.

Example 16.

If $4^{w+3} = 8^{w-1}$, what is the value of w?

Solution. Since it is necessary to have the same base on each side of the equation, write $4 = 2^2$ and $8 = 2^3$. Then

$$4^{w+3} = (2^2)^{w+3} = 2^{2(w+3)} = 2^{2w+6} \text{ and}$$
$$8^{w-1} = (2^3)^{w-1} = 2^{3(w-1)} = 2^{3w-3}.$$

Therefore, $2^{2w+6} = 2^{3w-3} \Rightarrow 2w + 6 = 3w - 3 \Rightarrow w = $ **9**.

Systems of Linear Equations

The equations $x + y = 10$ and $x - y = 2$ each have lots of solutions (infinitely many, in fact). Some of them are given in the tables below.

$x + y = 10$

x	5	6	4	1	1.2	10	20
y	5	4	6	9	8.8	0	-10
$x+y$	10	10	10	10	10	10	10

$x - y = 2$

x	5	6	2	0	2.5	19	40
y	3	4	0	-2	.5	17	38
$x-y$	2	2	2	2	2	2	2

However, only one pair of numbers, $x = 6$ and $y = 4$, satisfy both equations simultaneously: $6 + 4 = 10$ and $6 - 4 = 2$. These numbers, then, are the only solution of the **system of equations** $\begin{cases} x + y = 10 \\ x - y = 2 \end{cases}$.

A system of equations is a set of two or more equations involving two or more variables. To solve such a system, you must find, for all of the variables, values that will make each equation true. In an algebra course you learn several ways to solve systems of equations. On the SAT I, the most useful way is to add or subtract (usually add) the equations. After demonstrating this method, we will show in Example 20 one other way to handle some systems of equations.

Tactic

G4

To solve a system of equations, add or subtract them. If there are more than two equations, add them.

Column A   Column B

Example 17.

$$x + y = 10$$
$$x - y = 2$$

x	y

Solution. Add the two equations:

$$\begin{array}{r} x + y = 10 \\ + \; x - y = 2 \\ \hline 2x \quad\;\; = 12 \\ x = 6 \end{array}$$

Replacing x by 6 in $x + y = 10$ yields $y = 4$, so Column **A** is greater.

On the SAT I, most problems involving systems of equations do *not* require you to solve the systems. These problems usually ask for something other than the value of each variable. Read the questions very carefully, circle what you need, and do not do more than is required.

Example 18.

If $3a + 5b = 10$ and $5a + 3b = 30$, what is the average (arithmetic mean) of a and b?

(A) 2.5   (B) 4   (C) 5   (D) 20
(E) It cannot be determined from the information given.

Solution. Add the two equations:

$$\begin{array}{r} 3a + 5b = 10 \\ + \; 5a + 3b = 30 \\ \hline 8a + 8b = 40 \end{array}$$

Divide both sides by 8: $a + b = 5$

The average of a and b is: $\dfrac{a+b}{2} = \dfrac{5}{2} = $ **2.5 (A)**

Note: It is not only unnecessary to first solve for a and b ($a = 7.5$ and $b = -2.5$) but foolish to do so.

Column A   Column B

Example 19.

$$7a - 3b = 200$$
$$7a + 3b = 100$$

a	b

Solution. Don't actually solve the system. Add the equations: $14a = 300 \Rightarrow 7a = 150$. Replacing $7a$ by 150 in the second equation gives $150 + 3b = 100$; so $3b$, and hence b, must be negative, whereas a is positive: $a > b$, and so Column **A** is greater.

Remember TACTIC 10-5. On quantitative comparison questions, you don't need to know the value of the quantity in each column; you need know only which one is greater.

Occasionally on the SAT I, it is as easy, or easier, to solve a system of equations by substitution.

Tactic

G5

If one of the equations in a system of equations consists of a single variable equal to some expression, substitute that expression for the variable in the other equation.

Column A	Column B

Example 20.

$$x + y = 10$$
$$y = x - 2$$

x	y

Solution. Since the second equation states that a single variable (y) is equal to some expression ($x - 2$), substitute that expression in place of y in the first equation: $x + y = 10$ becomes $x + (x - 2) = 10$. Then,

$$2x - 2 = 10 \Rightarrow 2x = 12 \Rightarrow x = 6.$$

To find the value of y, plug the value of x into one of the two original equations: $y = 6 - 2 = 4$. Column **A** is larger.

Exercises on Equations

Multiple-Choice Questions

1. If $4x + 12 = 36$, what is the value of $x + 3$?

    (A) 3   (B) 6   (C) 9   (D) 12   (E) 18

2. If $4x + 13 = 7 - 2x$, what is the value of x?

    (A) $-\dfrac{10}{3}$ (B) -3 (C) -1 (D) 1   (E) $\dfrac{10}{3}$

3. If $ax - b = c - dx$, what is the value of x in terms of a, b, c, and d?

    (A) $\dfrac{b+c}{a+d}$ (B) $\dfrac{c-b}{a-d}$ (C) $\dfrac{b+c-d}{a}$

    (D) $\dfrac{c-b}{a+d}$ (E) $\dfrac{c}{b} - \dfrac{d}{a}$

4. If $\dfrac{1}{3}x + \dfrac{1}{6}x + \dfrac{1}{9}x = 33$, what is the value of x?

    (A) 3   (B) 18   (C) 27   (D) 54   (E) 72

5. If $\dfrac{a+2b+3c}{3} = \dfrac{a+2b}{2}$, then $c =$

    (A) $\dfrac{a+2b}{6}$ (B) $\dfrac{a+2b}{3}$ (C) $\dfrac{a+2b}{2}$

    (D) $a + 2b$ (E) $\dfrac{1}{2}$

6. If $32^{a+b} = 16^{a+2b}$, then $a =$

    (A) b (B) $2b$ (C) $3b$ (D) $b + 2$ (E) $b - 2$

7. If the average (arithmetic mean) of $3a$ and $4b$ is less than 50, and a is twice b, what is the largest integer value of a?

    (A) 9   (B) 10   (C) 11   (D) 19   (E) 20

8. If $\dfrac{1}{a-b} = 5$, then $a =$

    (A) $b + 5$ (B) $b - 5$ (C) $b + \dfrac{1}{5}$ (D) $b - \dfrac{1}{5}$

    (E) $\dfrac{1-5b}{5}$

9. If $x = 3a + 7$ and $y = 9a^2$, what is y in terms of x?

    (A) $(x - 7)^2$ (B) $3(x - 7)^2$ (C) $\dfrac{(x-7)^2}{3}$

    (D) $\dfrac{(x+7)^2}{3}$ (E) $(x + 7)^2$

10. If $\dfrac{x+3}{2} + 3x = 5(x - 3) + \dfrac{x+23}{5}$, what is the value of x?

    (A) 3   (B) 5   (C) 7   (D) 9   (E) 11

Quantitative Comparison Questions

Column A	Column B

$$a + b = 11$$
$$a - b = 11$$

11.

b	11

$$\dfrac{2^{a-1}}{2^{b+1}} = 8$$

12.

a	b

---

a and b are positive
$$a = b + 0.01$$

13.

a	$10b$

$$4x^2 = 3x$$

14.

x	1

<u>Column A</u>   <u>Column B</u>

Grid-in Questions

$$a + b = 1$$
$$b + c = 2$$
$$c + a = 3$$

21. If $x - 4 = 9$, what is the value of $x^2 - 4$?

15.
| The average (arithmetic mean) of a, b, and c | 1 |

$$3x - 4y = 5$$
$$y = 2x$$

16.
| x | y |

$$\frac{x}{2} - 2 > \frac{x}{3}$$

22. If $\dfrac{a + 5b}{2b} = a - 2b$, what is the value of a when $b = -1$?

17.
| x | 12 |

$$3r - 5s = 17$$
$$2r - 6s = 7$$

18.
| The average (arithmetic mean) of r and s | 10 |

23. If $7x + 10 = 44$, what is the value of $7x - 10$?

$$b > 3a - 2$$
$$a > b$$

19.
| a | 1 |

c and d are positive.
$$\frac{1}{c} = 1 + \frac{1}{d}$$

20.
| c | d |

24. If $a^2 + b^2 = 0$, what is the value of $a^2 - b^2$?

25. If $3x - 4 = 9$, what is the value of $(3x - 4)^2$?

26. If $a = 2b$, $3b = 4c$, and $5c = 6a - 7$, what is the value of c?

27. If $64^{12} = 2^{a-3}$, what is the value of a?

28. If $4y - 3x = 5$, what is the smallest integer value of x for which $y > 100$?

29. If $5^{3x-5} = 25^{x+1}$, what is the value of x?

30. If $x^2 + 3 < 4$ and $2x^2 + 3 > 4$, what is one possible value of x?

Answer Key

1. **C**
2. **C**
3. **A**
4. **D**
5. **A**
6. **A**
7. **D**
8. **C**
9. **A**
10. **C**
11. **B**
12. **A**
13. **D**
14. **B**
15. **C**
16. **A**
17. **A**
18. **B**
19. **B**
20. **B**

21. **1 6 5**

22. **1 / 3** or **. 3 3 3**

23. **2 4**

24. **0**

25. **8 1**

26. **7 / 1 1** or **. 6 3 6**

27. **7 5**

28. **1 3 2**

29. **7**

30. **. 7 5**

$.707 < x < 1$

Answer Explanations

1. C. The easiest method is to recognize that $x + 3$ is $\frac{1}{4}$ of $4x + 12$, and, therefore, equals $\frac{1}{4}$ of 36, which is 9. If you don't see that, solve normally:

$$4x + 12 = 36 \Rightarrow 4x = 24 \Rightarrow x = 6 \Rightarrow x + 3 = 9.$$

2. C. Add $2x$ to each side: $6x + 13 = 7$. Subtract 13 from each side: $6x = -6$. Divide by 6: $x = -1$.

3. A. Treat a, b, c, and d as constants, and use the six-step method to solve for x:

$$ax - b = c - dx \Rightarrow ax - b + dx = c \Rightarrow$$
$$ax + dx = c + b \Rightarrow x(a + d) = b + c \Rightarrow$$
$$x = \frac{b + c}{a + d}.$$

4. D. Multiply both sides by 18, the LCD:

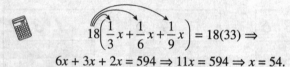

$$18\left(\frac{1}{3}x + \frac{1}{6}x + \frac{1}{9}x\right) = 18(33) \Rightarrow$$
$$6x + 3x + 2x = 594 \Rightarrow 11x = 594 \Rightarrow x = 54.$$

Mentally, it's easier not to multiply 18×33; leave it in that form and divide by 11:

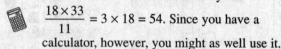

$\frac{18 \times 33}{11} = 3 \times 18 = 54.$ Since you have a calculator, however, you might as well use it.

5. A. If you see right away that the right-hand side is the average of a and $2b$, and that the left-hand side is the average of a, $2b$, and $3c$, you should realize that $3c$ doesn't change the average, which must be equal to the average of a and $2b$:

$$3c = \frac{a + 2b}{2} \Rightarrow c = \frac{a + 2b}{6}.$$

If you don't even think about the averages, just solve normally. Start by cross-multiplying:

$$\frac{a + 2b + 3c}{3} = \frac{a + 2b}{2} \Rightarrow$$
$$2(a + 2b + 3c) = 3(a + 2b) \Rightarrow$$
$$2a + 4b + 6c = 3a + 6b \Rightarrow$$
$$6c = a + 2b \Rightarrow c = \frac{a + 2b}{6}.$$

6. C. $32^{a+b} = (2^5)^{a+b} = 2^{5a+5b}$, and $16^{a+2b} = (2^4)^{a+2b} = 2^{4a+8b}$. Therefore:

$$5a + 5b = 4a + 8b \Rightarrow a + 5b = 8b \Rightarrow a = 3b.$$

7. D. Since $a = 2b$, then $2a = 4b$. Therefore, the average of $3a$ and $4b$ is the average of $3a$ and $2a$, which is $2.5a$. Therefore, $2.5a < 50 \Rightarrow$ $a < 20$, so the largest integer value of a is 19.

8. C. Taking the reciprocal of each side, we get $a - b = \frac{1}{5}$, so $a = b + \frac{1}{5}$.

9. A. If $x = 3a + 7$, then $x - 7 = 3a$ and $a = \frac{x - 7}{3}$. Therefore

$$y = 9a^2 = 9\left(\frac{x - 7}{3}\right)^2 = \overset{1}{\cancel{9}}\frac{(x - 7)^2}{\underset{1}{\cancel{3^2}}} = (x - 7)^2.$$

10. C. Use the six-step method:

1. Multiply by 10, the LCD: $\quad 5(x + 3) + 30x = 50(x - 3) + 2(x + 23)$
2. Clear the parentheses: $\quad 5x + 15 + 30x = 50x - 150 + 2x + 46$
3. Combine like terms: $\quad 35x + 15 = 52x - 104$
4. Get the variable on one side: $\quad 15 = 17x - 104$
5. Add 104 to each side: $\quad 119 = 17x$
6. Divide by 17: $\quad x = 7$

11. B. Adding the two equations, we get $2a = 22$. Therefore, $a = 11$ and $b = 0$.

12. A. Express each side of $\frac{2^{a-1}}{2^{b+1}} = 8$ as a power of 2:

$$8 = 2^3 \quad \text{and} \quad \frac{2^{a-1}}{2^{b+1}} = 2^{(a-1)-(b+1)} = 2^{a-b-2}.$$

Then, $a - b - 2 = 3 \Rightarrow a = b + 5$, and so a is greater.

13. D. If $b = 1$, then $10b = 10$, which is much greater than a, which is 1.01. If $b = 0.0001$, then $10b = 0.001$, which is less than a, which is 0.0101.

14. B. $4x^2 = 3x \Rightarrow 4x^2 - 3x = 0 \Rightarrow x(4x - 3) = 0 \Rightarrow$

$$x = 0 \quad \text{or} \quad 4x - 3 = 0 \Rightarrow$$
$$x = 0 \quad \text{or} \quad 4x = 3 \Rightarrow$$
$$x = 0 \quad \text{or} \quad x = \frac{3}{4}.$$

There are two possible values of x, both of which are less than 1.

15. C. When we add all three equations, we get

$$2a + 2b + 2c = 6 \Rightarrow a + b + c = 3 \Rightarrow$$
$$\frac{a + b + c}{3} = \frac{3}{3} = 1.$$

16. A. Use substitution. Replace y in the first equation with $2x$:

$$3x - 4(2x) = 5 \Rightarrow 3x - 8x = 5 \Rightarrow$$
$$-5x = 5 \Rightarrow x = -1 \Rightarrow y = -2.$$

17. A. Multiply both sides by 6, the LCD:

$$6\left(\frac{x}{2}-2\right) > 6\left(\frac{x}{3}\right) \Rightarrow 3x - 12 > 2x \Rightarrow$$
$$-12 > -x \Rightarrow x > 12.$$

18. B. The first thing to try is adding the equations. That yields $5r - 11s = 24$, which does not appear to be useful. Now try subtracting the equations. That yields $r + s = 10$, so the average of r and s is $\dfrac{r+s}{2} = \dfrac{10}{2} = 5$.

19. B. $a > b$ and $b > 3a - 2 \Rightarrow a > 3a - 2 \Rightarrow$ $-2a > -2$. Now, divide both sides by -2, and be sure to reverse the inequality: $a < 1$.

20. B. Multiply both sides by cd, the LCD of the fractions:

$$cd\left(\frac{1}{c}\right) = cd\left(1 + \frac{1}{d}\right) \Rightarrow$$
$$d = cd + c = c(d + 1) \Rightarrow c = \frac{d}{d+1}.$$

Since d is positive, $d + 1 > 1 \Rightarrow \dfrac{d}{d+1} < d$, so $c < d$.

21. (165) $x - 4 = 9 \Rightarrow x = 13 \Rightarrow x^2 = 169 \Rightarrow$ $x^2 - 4 = 165$.

22. $\left(\dfrac{1}{3} \text{ or } 3.33\right)$ Substitute -1 for b in the given equation and solve:

$$\frac{a-5}{-2} = a + 2 \Rightarrow a - 5 = -2a - 4 \Rightarrow$$
$$3a - 5 = -4 \Rightarrow 3a = 1 \Rightarrow a = \frac{1}{3}.$$

23. (24) Subtracting 20 from each side of $7x + 10 = 44$ gives $7x - 10 = 24$. If you don't see that, subtract 10 from each side, getting $7x = 34$. Then subtract 10 to get $7x - 10 = 24$. The worst alternative is to divide both sides of $7x = 34$ by 7 to get $x = \dfrac{34}{7}$; then you have to multiply by 7 to get back to 34, and then subtract 10.

24. (0) If either a^2 or b^2 were greater than 0, their sum would also be greater. Therefore, each of them is 0, and so is their difference.

25. (81) Be alert. Since you are given the value of $3x - 4$, and want the value of $(3x - 4)^2$, just square both sides: $9^2 = 81$. If you don't see that, you'll waste time solving $3x - 4 = 9$ $\left(x = \dfrac{13}{3}\right)$,

only to use that value to calculate that $3x - 4$ is equal to 9, which you already knew.

26. $\left(\dfrac{7}{11}\right)$ There are several ways to manipulate these equations, substituting for one variable or another. Here is one direct solution. Since $a = 2b$, then $3a = 6b$; and since $3b = 4c$, then $6b = 8c$. Therefore, $3a = 8c$, and $6a = 16c$, so

$$5c = 6a - 7 \Rightarrow 5c = 16c - 7 \Rightarrow$$
$$7 = 11c \Rightarrow c = \frac{7}{11}.$$

27. (75) $2^{a-3} = 64^{12} = (2^6)^{12} = 2^{72} \Rightarrow a - 3 = 72 \Rightarrow$ $a = 75$.

28. (132) First, solve for y in terms of x:

$$4y - 3x = 5 \Rightarrow 4y = 5 + 3x \Rightarrow y = \frac{5+3x}{4}.$$

 Then, since $y > 100$:

$$\frac{5+3x}{4} > 100 \Rightarrow 5 + 3x > 400 \Rightarrow$$
$$3x > 395 \Rightarrow x > 131.666.$$

The smallest integer value of x is 132.

29. (7) $5^{3x-5} = 25^{x+1}$
$= (5^2)^{x+1} = 5^{2(x+1)} \Rightarrow 3x - 5 = 2(x + 1) \Rightarrow$
$3x - 5 = 2x + 2 \Rightarrow x = 7$.

30. $(.707 < x < 1)$ $x^2 + 3 < 4 \Rightarrow x^2 < 1$, and $2x^2 + 3 > 4 \Rightarrow 2x^2 > 1 \Rightarrow x^2 > .5$. Grid in any number between $\sqrt{.5} \approx .707$ and 1.

12-H WORD PROBLEMS

A typical SAT I has several word problems, covering almost every math topic for which you are responsible. In this chapter you have already seen word problems on consecutive integers in Section 12-A, fractions and percents in Sections 12-B and 12-C, ratios and rates in Section 12-D, and averages in Section 12-E. Later in this chapter you will see word problems involving probability and circles, triangles, and other geometric figures. A few of these problems can be solved with just arithmetic, but most of them require basic algebra.

To solve word problems algebraically, you must treat algebra as a foreign language and learn to translate "word for word" from English into algebra, just as you would from English into French or Spanish or any other foreign language. When translating into algebra, we use some letter (often x) to represent the unknown quantity we are trying to determine. It is this translation process that causes difficulty for some students. Once the translation is completed, solving is easy using the techniques we have already reviewed.

Consider the pairs of typical SAT I questions in Examples 1 and 2. The first ones in each pair (1a and 2a) would be considered easy, whereas the second ones (1b and 2b) would be considered harder.

Example 1a.

What is 4% of 4% of 40,000?

Example 1b.

In a lottery, 4% of the tickets printed can be redeemed for prizes, and 4% of those tickets have values in excess of $100. If the state prints 40,000 tickets, how many of them can be redeemed for more than $100?

Example 2a.

If $x + 7 = 2(x - 8)$, what is the value of x?

Example 2b.

In 7 years Erin will be twice as old as she was 8 years ago. How old is Erin now?

Once you translate the words into arithmetic expressions or algebraic equations, Examples 1a and 1b and 2a and 2b are clearly identical. The problem that many students have is doing the translation. It really isn't very difficult, and we'll show you how. First, though, look over the following English to algebra "dictionary."

English Words	Mathematical Meaning	Symbol
Is, was, will be, had, has, will have, is equal to, is the same as	Equals	=
Plus, more than, sum, increased by, added to, exceeds, received, got, older than, farther than, greater than	Addition	+
Minus, fewer, less than, difference, decreased by, subtracted from, younger than, gave, lost	Subtraction	−
Times, of, product, multiplied by	Multiplication	×
Divided by, quotient, per, for	Division	$\div$, $\dfrac{a}{b}$
More than, greater than	Inequality	>
At least	Inequality	≥
Fewer than, less than	Inequality	<
At most	Inequality	≤
What, how many, etc.	Unknown quantity	x (or some other variable)

Let's use our "dictionary" to translate some phrases and sentences.

1. The <u>sum</u> of 5 and some number <u>is</u> 13. $5 + x = 13$
2. John <u>was</u> 2 years <u>younger than</u> Sam. $J = S - 2$
3. Bill has <u>at most</u> $100. $B \le 100$
4. The <u>product</u> of 2 and a number <u>exceeds</u> that number by 5 (is 5 more than). $2N = N + 5$

In translating statements, you first must decide what quantity the variable will represent. Often, this is obvious. Other times there is more than one possibility.

Let's translate and solve the two examples at the beginning of this section, and then we'll look at a few new ones.

Example 1b.

In a lottery, 4% of the tickets printed can be redeemed for prizes, and 4% of those tickets have values in excess of $100. If the state prints 40,000 tickets, how many of them can be redeemed for more than $100?

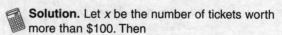 **Solution.** Let x be the number of tickets worth more than $100. Then

$x = 4\%$ of 4% of $40,000 = 0.04 \times 0.04 \times 40,000 = \mathbf{64}$,

which is also the solution to Example 1a.

Example 2b.

In 7 years Erin will be twice as old as she was 8 years ago. How old is Erin now?

Solution. Let x be Erin's age now; 8 years ago she was $x - 8$ and 7 years from now she will be $x + 7$. Then, $x + 7 = 2(x - 8)$, and

$x + 7 = 2(x - 8) \Rightarrow x + 7 = 2x - 16 \Rightarrow 7 = x - 16 \Rightarrow x = \mathbf{23}$,

which is also the solution to Example 2a.

Example 3.

The product of 2 and 8 more than a certain number is 10 times that number. What is the number?

Solution. Let $x =$ unknown number. Then $2(8 + x) = 10x$, and

$2(8 + x) = 10x \Rightarrow 16 + 2x = 10x \Rightarrow 8x = 16 \Rightarrow x = \mathbf{2}$.

Example 4.

If the sum of three consecutive integers is 20 more than the middle integer, what is the smallest of the three?

Solution. Let $n =$ smallest of the three. Then

$$n + (n + 1) + (n + 2) = 20 + (n + 1),$$

and

$n + n + 1 + n + 2 = 20 + n + 1 \Rightarrow 3n + 3 = 21 + n \Rightarrow$
$2n + 3 = 21 \Rightarrow 2n = 18 \Rightarrow n = \mathbf{9}$.

(The integers are 9, 10, and 11.)

Most algebraic word problems on the SAT I are not very difficult. If, after studying this section, you still get stuck on a question, don't despair. Use the tactics that you learned in Chapters 9 and 11. In each of Examples 3 and 4, if you had been given choices, you could have backsolved; and if the questions had been grid-ins, you could have used trial and error (effectively, backsolving by making up your own choices). Here's how.

 Alternative Solution to Example 3. Pick a starting number and test (use your calculator, if necessary).

Try 10: $8 + 10 = 18$ and $2 \times 18 = 36$, but $10 \times 10 = 100$, which is much too big.

Try 5: $8 + 5 = 13$ and $2 \times 13 = 26$, but $10 \times 5 = 50$, which is still too big.

Try 2: $8 + 2 = 10$ and $2 \times 10 = 20$, and $10 \times 2 = 20$. That's it.

Alternative Solution to Example 4. You need three consecutive integers whose sum is 20 more than the middle one. Obviously, 1, 2, 3 and 5, 6, 7 are too small; neither one even adds up to 20.

Try 10, 11, 12: $10 + 11 + 12 = 33$, which is 22 more than 11—a bit too much.

Try 9, 10, 11: $9 + 10 + 11 = 30$, which *is* 20 more than 10.

Of course, if you can do the algebra, that's usually the best way, to handle these problems. On grid-ins you might have to backsolve with several numbers before zooming in on the correct answer; also, if the correct answer was a fraction, such as $\frac{13}{5}$, you might never find it. In the rest of this section, we will stress the proper way of setting up and solving various word problems.

Helpful Hint

In all word problems on the SAT I, remember to circle what you're looking for. Don't answer the wrong question!

Age Problems

Helpful Hint

In problems involving ages, remember that "years ago" means you need to subtract, and "years from now" means you need to add.

Example 5.

In 1980, Judy was 3 times as old as Adam, but in 1984 she was only twice as old as he was. How old was Adam in 1990?

(A) 4   (B) 8   (C) 12   (D) 14   (E) 16

Helpful Hint

It is often very useful to organize the data from a word problem in a table.

Solution. Let x be Adam's age in 1980, and fill in the table below.

Year	Judy	Adam
1980	$3x$	x
1984	$3x + 4$	$x + 4$

Now translate: Judy's age in 1984 was twice Adam's age in 1984:

$$3x + 4 = 2(x + 4)$$
$$3x + 4 = 2x + 8 \Rightarrow x + 4 = 8 \Rightarrow x = 4.$$

Adam was 4 in 1980. However, 4 is *not* the answer to this question. Did you remember to circle what you're looking for? The question *could have* asked for Adam's age in 1980 (choice A) or 1984 (choice B) or Judy's age in any year whatsoever (choice C is 1980, and choice E is 1984); but it didn't. It asked for *Adam's age in 1990*. Since he was 4 in 1980, then 10 years later, in 1990, he was **14 (D)**.

Distance Problems

All distance problems involve one of three variations of the same formula:

$$\text{distance} = \text{rate} \times \text{time} \qquad \text{rate} = \frac{\text{distance}}{\text{time}}$$

$$\text{time} = \frac{\text{distance}}{\text{rate}}$$

These are usually abbreviated as $d = rt$, $r = \frac{d}{t}$, and $t = \frac{d}{r}$.

Example 6.

How much longer, in <u>seconds</u>, is required to drive 1 mile at 40 miles per hour than at 60 miles per hour?

Solution. The time to drive 1 mile at 40 miles per hour is given by

$$t = \frac{1 \text{ mile}}{40 \text{ miles per hour}} = \frac{1}{40} \text{ hour} = \frac{1}{40_2} \times 60^3 \text{ minutes} =$$

$$\frac{3}{2} \text{ minutes} = 1\frac{1}{2} \text{ minutes}.$$

The time to drive 1 mile at 60 miles per hour is given by

$$t = \frac{1 \text{ mile}}{60 \text{ miles per hour}} = \frac{1}{60} \text{ hour} = 1 \text{ minute}.$$

The difference is $\frac{1}{2}$ minute = **30 seconds**.

Note that this solution used the time formula given but required only arithmetic, not algebra. Example 7 requires an algebraic solution.

Example 7.

Mark drove to a meeting at 60 miles per hour. Returning over the same route, he encountered heavy traffic, and was able to drive at only 40 miles per hour. If the return trip took 1 hour longer, how many miles did he drive each way?

(A) 2   (B) 3   (C) 5   (D) 120   (E) 240

Solution. Let x = number of hours Mark took to go, and make a table.

	Rate	Time	Distance
Going	60	x	$60x$
Returning	40	$x + 1$	$40(x + 1)$

Since he drove the same distance going and returning:

$60x = 40(x + 1) \Rightarrow 60x = 40x + 40 \Rightarrow 20x = 40 \Rightarrow x = 2$.

Now be sure to answer the correct question. Choices A, B, and C are the time, in hours, for going, returning, and the round trip; choices D and E are the distances each way and round-trip. You could have been asked for any of the five. If you circled what you're looking for, you won't make a careless mistake. Mark drove **120** miles each way, and so the correct answer is **D**.

The d in the formula $d = rt$ stands for "distance," but it could represent any type of work that is performed at a certain rate, r, for a certain amount of time, t. Example 7 need not be about distance. Instead of driving 120 miles at 60 miles per hour for 2 hours, Mark could have read 120 pages at a rate of 60 pages per hour for 2 hours, or planted 120 flowers at the rate of 60 flowers per hour for 2 hours, or typed 120 words at a rate of 60 words per minute for 2 minutes.

We will end this section with a miscellaneous collection of word problems of the type that you may find on the SAT I. Some of them are similar to problems already discussed in earlier sections.

Example 8.

At 8:00 P.M., the hostess of the party remarked that only $\frac{1}{4}$ of her guests had arrived so far, but that, as soon as 10 more showed up, $\frac{1}{3}$ of the guests would be there. How many people were invited?

Solution. Let x = number of people invited. First, translate the first sentence above into algebra:

$\frac{1}{4}x + 10 = \frac{1}{3}x$. Then, use the six-step method of Section 12-G to solve the equation. Multiply by 12 to get $3x + 120 = 4x$, and then subtract $3x$ from each side: $x = $ **120**.

Example 9.

In a family of three, the father weighed 5 times as much as the child, and the mother weighed $\frac{3}{4}$ as much as the father. If the three of them weighed a total of 390 pounds, how much did the mother weigh?

Helpful Hint

You often have a choice as to what you will let the variable represent. Don't necessarily have it represent what you're looking for; rather, choose what will make the problem easiest to solve.

For example, in this problem it is easier to let x represent the weight of the child, and $5x$ the weight of the father, than to let x represent the weight of the father, and $\frac{1}{5}x$ the weight of the child. The worst choice would be to let x represent the weight of the mother; in that case, since the mother's weight is $\frac{3}{4}$ that of the father's, his weight would be $\frac{4}{3}$ of hers.

Solution. Let x = weight of the child; then $5x$ = weight of the father, and $\frac{3}{4}(5x)$ = weight of the mother. Since their combined weight is 390:

$$x + 5x + \frac{15}{4}x = 390.$$

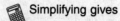 Multiply by 4 to get rid of the fraction:

$$4x + 20x + 15x = 1560.$$

Combine like terms and then divide:

$$39x = 1560 \Rightarrow x = 40.$$

The child weighed 40 pounds, the father weighed $5 \times 40 = 200$ pounds, and the mother weighed $\frac{3}{4}(200) = $ **150 pounds**.

Example 10.

A teacher wrote three consecutive odd integers on the board. She then multiplied the first by 2, the second by 3, and the third by 4. Finally, she added all six numbers and got a sum of 400. What was the smallest number she wrote?

Solution. Let n = first odd integer she wrote. Since the difference between any two consecutive odd integers is 2 (3, 5, 7, 9, etc.), the next consecutive odd integer is $n + 2$ and the third is $n + 4$. The required equation is

$$n + (n + 2) + (n + 4) + 2n + 3(n + 2) + 4(n + 4) = 400.$$

Simplifying gives

$$n + n + 2 + n + 4 + 2n + 3n + 6 + 4n + 16 = 400 \Rightarrow$$
$$12n + 28 = 400 \Rightarrow 12n = 372 \Rightarrow n = \mathbf{31}.$$

Exercises on Word Problems

Multiple-Choice Questions

1. In the afternoon, Judy read 100 pages at the rate of 60 pages per hour; in the evening, when she was tired, she read another 100 pages at the rate of 40 pages per hour. In pages per hour, what was her average rate of reading for the day?

   (A) 45   (B) 48   (C) 50   (D) 52   (E) 55

2. If the sum of five consecutive integers is S, what is the largest of those integers in terms of S?

   (A) $\dfrac{S-10}{5}$ (B) $\dfrac{S+4}{4}$ (C) $\dfrac{S+5}{4}$ (D) $\dfrac{S-5}{2}$

   (E) $\dfrac{S+10}{5}$

3. A jar contains only red, white, and blue marbles. The number of red marbles is $\dfrac{4}{5}$ the number of white ones, and the number of white ones is $\dfrac{3}{4}$ the number of blue ones. If there are 470 marbles in all, how many of them are blue?

   (A) 120   (B) 135   (C) 150   (D) 184   (E) 200

4. As a fund-raiser, the Key Club was selling 2 types of candy: lollipops at 40 cents each and chocolate bars at 75 cents each. On Monday, the members sold 150 candies and raised 74 dollars. How many lollipops did they sell?

   (A) 75   (B) 90   (C) 96   (D) 110   (E) 120

5. On a certain project the only grades awarded were 75 and 100. If 85 students completed the project and the average of their grades was 85, how many earned 100?

   (A) 34   (B) 40   (C) 45   (D) 51   (E) 60

6. Aaron has 3 times as much money as Josh. If Aaron gives Josh $50, Josh will then have 3 times as much money as Aaron. How much money do the two of them have together?

   (A) $75   (B) $100   (C) $125   (D) $150
   (E) $200

7. If $\dfrac{1}{2}x$ years ago Jason was 12, and $\dfrac{1}{2}x$ years from now he will be $2x$ years old, how old will he be $3x$ years from now?

   (A) 18   (B) 24   (C) 30   (D) 54
   (E) It cannot be determined from the information given.

8. Two printing presses working together can complete a job in 2.5 hours. Working alone, press A can do the job in 10 hours. How many hours will press B take to do the job by itself?

   (A) $3\dfrac{1}{3}$ (B) 4   (C) 5   (D) $6\dfrac{1}{4}$ (E) $7\dfrac{1}{2}$

9. Henry drove 100 miles to visit a friend. If he had driven 8 miles per hour faster than he did, he would have arrived in $\dfrac{5}{6}$ of the time he actually took. How many <u>minutes</u> did the trip take?

   (A) 100   (B) 120   (C) 125   (D) 144   (E) 150

10. Since 1950, when Martin graduated from high school, he has gained 2 pounds every year. In 1980 he was 40% heavier than in 1950. What percent of his 1995 weight was his 1980 weight?

    (A) 80   (B) 85   (C) 87.5   (D) 90   (E) 95

Quantitative Comparison Questions

Column A	Column B

Amy is twice as old as she was 10 years ago.
Beth is half as old as she will be in 10 years.

11.

Amy's age now	Beth's age now

Max spent $\dfrac{1}{4}$ of his allowance on Saturday and $\dfrac{1}{3}$ of what was left on Sunday. The rest he put in his savings account.

12.

The amount of his allowance that he spent	The amount of his allowance that he saved

In 8 years, Lindsay will be 3 times as old as she is now.

13.

The number of years until Lindsay will be 6 times as old as she is now	16

<u>Column A</u>   <u>Column B</u>

Liz put exactly 50 cents' worth of postage on an envelope, using only 4-cent stamps and 7-cent stamps.

14.

The number of 4-cent stamps she used	The number of 7-cent stamps she used

---

Car A and car B leave from the same spot at the same time.
Car A travels due north at 40 miles per hour.
Car B travels due east at 30 miles per hour.

15.

Distance from car A to car B 9 hours after they left	450 miles

---

Grid-in Questions

16. What is the greater of two numbers whose product is 900, if the sum of the two numbers exceeds their difference by 30?

17. The number of shells in Fred's collection is 80% of the number in Phil's collection. If Phil has 80 more shells than Fred, how many do they have altogether?

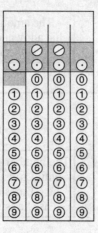

18. Karen played a game several times. She received $5 every time she won and had to pay $2 every time she lost. If the ratio of the number of times she won to the number of times she lost was 3:2, and if she won a total of $66, how many times did she play this game?

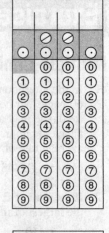

19. Each of the 10 players on the basketball team shot 100 free throws, and the average number of baskets made was 75. When the highest and lowest scores were eliminated, the average number of baskets for the remaining 8 players was 79. What is the fewest number of baskets anyone could have made?

20. In an office there was a small cash box. One day Ann took half of the money plus $1 more. Then Dan took half of the remaining money plus $1 more. Stan then took the remaining $11. How many dollars were originally in the box?

Answer Key

1.	**B**	4.	**D**	7.	**D**	10.	**C**	13.	**A**
2.	**E**	5.	**A**	8.	**A**	11.	**A**	14.	**D**
3.	**E**	6.	**B**	9.	**E**	12.	**C**	15.	**C**

16. **6 0**
17. **7 2 0**
18. **3 0**
19. **1 8**
20. **5 0**

Answer Explanations

1. **B.** Judy's average rate of reading is determined by dividing the total number of pages she read (200) by the total amount of time she spent reading. In the afternoon she read for $\frac{100}{60} = \frac{5}{3}$ hours, and in the evening for $\frac{100}{40} = \frac{5}{2}$ hours, for a total time of

$$\frac{5}{3} + \frac{5}{2} = \frac{10}{6} + \frac{15}{6} = \frac{25}{6} \text{ hours.}$$

Her average rate was

$$200 \div \frac{25}{6} = 200 \times \frac{6}{25} = 48 \text{ pages per hour.}$$

2. **E.** Let the five consecutive integers be n, $n + 1$, $n + 2$, $n + 3$, $n + 4$. Then:

$$S = n + n + 1 + n + 2 + n + 3 + n + 4 = 5n + 10 \Rightarrow 5n = S - 10 \Rightarrow n = \frac{S - 10}{5}.$$

Choice A, $\frac{S - 10}{5}$, is the *smallest* of the integers; the *largest* is

$$n + 4 = \frac{S - 10}{5} + 4 = \frac{S - 10}{5} + \frac{20}{5} = \frac{S + 10}{5}.$$

3. **E.** If b is the number of blue marbles, there are $\frac{3}{4}b$ white ones, and $\frac{4}{5}\left(\frac{3}{4}b\right) = \frac{3}{5}b$ red ones. Then,

$$470 = b + \frac{3}{4}b + \frac{3}{5}b = b\left(1 + \frac{3}{4} + \frac{3}{5}\right) = \frac{47}{20}b,$$

so $b = 470 \div \frac{47}{20} = 470 \times \frac{20}{47} = 200.$

4. **D.** Let x = number of chocolate bars sold; then $150 - x$ = number of lollipops sold. We must use the same units, so we could write 75 cents as 0.75 dollar or 74 dollars as 7400 cents. Let's avoid the decimals: x chocolates sold for $75x$ cents and $(150 - x)$ lollipops sold for $40(150 - x)$ cents. Therefore:

$$7400 = 75x + 40(150 - x) =$$
$$75x + 6000 - 40x = 6000 + 35x \Rightarrow$$
$$1400 = 35x \Rightarrow x = 40$$

and $150 - 40 = 110$.

5. **A.** Let x = number of students earning 100; then $85 - x$ = number of students earning 75. Then:

$$85 = \frac{100x + 75(85 - x)}{85} =$$
$$\frac{100x + 6375 - 75x}{85} = \frac{25x - 6375}{85} \Rightarrow$$
$$7225 = 25x - 6375 \Rightarrow 850 = 25x \Rightarrow x = 34.$$

6. **B.**

	Josh	Aaron
At the beginning	x	$3x$
After the gift	$x + 50$	$3x - 50$

After the gift, Josh will have 3 times as much money as Aaron:

$$x + 50 = 3(3x - 50) \Rightarrow x + 50 = 9x - 150 \Rightarrow$$
$$8x = 200 \Rightarrow x = 25.$$

Therefore, Josh has $25 and Aaron has $75, for a total of $100.

7. D. Since $\frac{1}{2}x$ years ago Jason was 12, he is now

$12 + \frac{1}{2}x$; and $\frac{1}{2}x$ years from now, he will be

$12 + \frac{1}{2}x + \frac{1}{2}x = 12 + x$. At that time he will

be $2x$ years old, so $12 + x = 2x \Rightarrow x = 12$. Thus, he is now $12 + 6 = 18$, and $3x$, or 36, years from now he will be $18 + 36 = 54$.

8. A. Let x = number of hours press B would take working alone.

	Press A Alone	Press B Alone	Together
Part of job that can be completed in 1 hour	$\frac{1}{10}$	$\frac{1}{x}$	$\frac{1}{2.5}$
Part of job that can be completed in 2.5 hours	$\frac{2.5}{10}$	$\frac{2.5}{x}$	1

Write the equation: $\quad \dfrac{2.5}{10} + \dfrac{2.5}{x} = 1$

Multiply each term
by $10x$: $\qquad\qquad 2.5x + 25 = 10x$
Subtract $2.5x$ from
each side: $\qquad\qquad 25 = 7.5x$

Divide each side by 7.5: $\qquad x = 3\frac{1}{3}$ hours

9. E. Let t = time, in hours, and r = rate, in miles per hour, that Henry drove. Then

$$t = \frac{100}{r} \quad \text{and} \quad \frac{5}{6}t = \frac{100}{r+8}.$$

Multiply the second equation by $\frac{6}{5}$:

$$\frac{6}{5}\left(\frac{5}{6}t\right) = \frac{6}{5}\left(\frac{100}{r+8}\right) \Rightarrow t = \frac{600}{5r+40}, \quad \text{so}$$

$$\frac{100}{r} = \frac{600}{5r+40}.$$

Cross-multiply:

$500r + 4000 = 600r \Rightarrow 100r = 4000 \Rightarrow r = 40$.

Henry drove at 40 miles per hour, and the trip took $100 \div 40 = 2.5$ hours $= 150$ minutes. (Had he driven at 48 miles per hour, the trip would have taken 125 minutes.)

10. C. Let x = Martin's weight in 1950. By 1980, he had gained 60 pounds (2 pounds per year for 30 years) and was 40% heavier:

$$60 = 0.40x \Rightarrow x = 60 \div 0.4 = 150.$$

In 1980, he weighed 210 pounds, and 15 years later, in 1995, he weighed 240:

$$\frac{210}{240} = \frac{7}{8} = 87.5\%.$$

11. A. You can do the simple algebra, but you should realize that Amy is as old now as Beth will be in 10 years. If x = Amy's age now:

$$x = 2(x - 10) \Rightarrow x = 2x - 20 \Rightarrow x = 20.$$

Similarly, Beth is now 10 and will be 20 in 10 years.

12. C. Let x = amount Max received for his

allowance. On Saturday, he spent $\frac{1}{4}x$ and still

had $\frac{3}{4}x$; but on Sunday, he spent $\frac{1}{3}$ of that:

$$\frac{1}{3}\left(\frac{3}{4}x\right) = \frac{1}{4}x. \text{ Therefore, he spent } \frac{1}{4} \text{ of his}$$

allowance each day. In 2 days, he spent $\frac{1}{2}$ and

saved $\frac{1}{2}$.

13. A. If x = Lindsay's age now, then $x + 8$ = her age in 8 years, so
$$x + 8 = 3x \Rightarrow 8 = 2x \Rightarrow x = 4.$$
Lindsay will be 6 times as old 20 years from now, when she will be 24.

14. D. If x and y represent the number of 4-cent stamps and 7-cent stamps, respectively that Liz used, then $4x + 7y = 50$. There are infinitely many solutions to this equation, but only two solutions in which x and y are both positive integers: $y = 2$ and $x = 9$ or $y = 6$ and $x = 2$.

15. C. Draw a diagram. In 9 hours, car A drove 360 miles north and car B drove 270 miles east. These are the legs of a right triangle, whose hypotenuse is the distance between them. You can use the Pythagorean theorem if you don't recognize that this is just a 3-4-5 right triangle: the legs are 90×3 and 90×4, and the hypotenuse is $90 \times 5 = 450$.

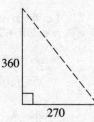

360

270

16. (60) Let x = the greater, and y = the smaller, of the two numbers; then

$$(x + y) = 30 + (x - y) \Rightarrow y = 30 - y \Rightarrow$$
$$2y = 30 \Rightarrow y = 15;$$

and, since $xy = 900$, $x = 900 \div 15 = 60$.

17. (720)   If x = number of shells in Phil's collection, then Fred has $.80x$. Since Phil has 80 more shells than Fred:

$$x = .80x + 80 \Rightarrow .20x = 80 \Rightarrow$$
$$x = 80 \div .20 = 400.$$

Phil has 400 and Fred has 320: a total of 720.

18. (30)   Use TACTIC D1. Karen won $3x$ times and lost $2x$ times, and thus played a total of $5x$ games. Since she got $5 every time she won, she received $\$5(3x) = \$15x$. Also, since she paid $2 for each loss, she paid out $\$2(2x) = \$4x$. Therefore, her net winnings were $\$15x - \$4x = \$11x$, which we are told was $66. Then, $11x = 66 \Rightarrow x = 6$, and so $5x = 30$.

19. (18)   Since the average of all 10 players was 75, the total number of baskets made was $10 \times 75 = 750$. Also, since 8 of the players had an average of 79, they made a total of $8 \times 79 = 632$ points. The other 2 players, therefore, made $750 - 632 = 118$ baskets. The most baskets that the player with the highest number could have made was 100, so the player with the lowest number had to have made at least 18.

20. (50)   You can avoid some messy algebra by working backwards. Put back the $11 Stan took; then put back the extra $1 that Dan took. There is now $12, which means that, when Dan took his half, he took $12. Put that back. Now there is $24 in the box. Put back the extra $1 that Ann took. The box now has $25, so before Ann took her half, there was $50. *Algebraic solution.* Assume that there were originally x dollars in the box. Ann took $\frac{1}{2}x + 1$, leaving $\frac{1}{2}x - 1$. Dan then took $\frac{1}{2}$ of that plus $1 more; he took

$$\frac{1}{2}\left(\frac{1}{2}x - 1\right) + 1 = \frac{1}{4}x - \frac{1}{2} + 1 = \frac{1}{4}x + \frac{1}{2}.$$

Then Stan took $11. Since together they took all x dollars:

$$x = \left(\frac{1}{2}x + 1\right) + \left(\frac{1}{4}x + \frac{1}{2}\right) + 11 = \frac{3}{4}x + 12\frac{1}{2}.$$

Therefore, $12\frac{1}{2} = \frac{1}{4}x \Rightarrow x = 50$.

Geometry

Although about 30% of the math questions on the SAT I involve geometry, you need to know only a relatively small number of facts—far less than you would learn in a geometry course—and, of course, you need provide no proofs. In the next six sections we will review all of the geometry that you need to know to do well on the SAT I. Also, we will present the material exactly as it appears on the SAT I, using the same vocabulary and notation, which may be slightly different from the terminology you have used in your math classes. In particular, the word *congruent* and the symbol "≅" are never used—angles or line segments that have the same measure are considered "equal." There are plenty of sample multiple-choice, quantitative comparison, and grid-in problems for you to solve, and they will show you exactly how these topics are treated on the SAT I.

12-I LINES AND ANGLES

An *angle* is formed by the intersection of two line segments, rays, or lines. The point of intersection is called the *vertex*. On the SAT I, angles are always measured in degrees.

Key Fact I1

Angles are classified according to their degree measures.

- An *acute* angle measures less than 90°.
- A *right* angle measures 90°.
- An *obtuse* angle measures more than 90° but less than 180°.
- A *straight* angle measures 180°.

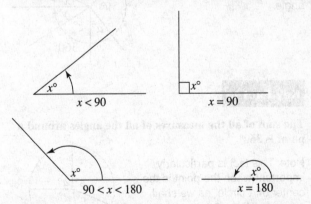

NOTE: A small square like the one in the second figure above *always* means that the angle is a right angle. On the SAT I, if an angle has a square, it must be a 90° angle, *even if the figure has not been drawn to scale.*

Key Fact I2

If two or more angles form a straight angle, the sum of their measures is 180°.

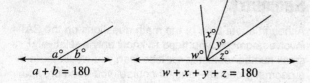

$$a + b = 180$$

$$w + x + y + z = 180$$

Example 1.

In the figure below, R, S, and T are all on line ℓ. What is the average of a, b, c, d, and e?

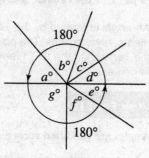

Solution. Since $\angle RST$ is a straight angle, by KEY FACT 12, the sum of a, b, c, d, and e is 180, and so their average is $\dfrac{180}{5} = \textbf{36}$.

In the figure at the right, since $a + b + c + d = 180$ and $e + f + g = 180$, $a + b + c + d + e + f + g = 180 + 180 = 360$.

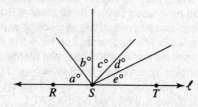

It is also true that $u + v + w + x + y + z = 360$, even though none of the angles forms a straight angle.

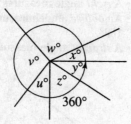

Key Fact 13

The sum of all the measures of all the angles around a point is 360°.

Note: This fact is particularly important when the point is the center of a circle, as we shall see in Section 12-L.

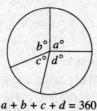

$$a + b + c + d = 360$$

When two lines intersect, four angles are formed. The two angles in each pair of opposite angles are called **vertical angles**.

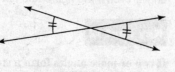

Key Fact 14

Vertical angles have equal measures.

Example 2.

In the figure to the right, what is the value of a?

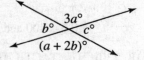

Solution. Because vertical angles are equal:

$$a + 2b = 3a \Rightarrow 2b = 2a \Rightarrow a = b.$$

For the same reason, $b = c$. Therefore, a, b, and c are all equal. Replace each b and c in the figure with a, and add:

$$a + a + 3a + a + 2a = 360 \Rightarrow 8a = 360 \Rightarrow a = \textbf{45}.$$

Consider these vertical angles:

By KEY FACT 14, $a = c$ and $b = d$.

By KEY FACT 12, $a + b = 180$, $b + c = 180$, $c + d = 180$, and $a + d = 180$.

From this it follows that, if any of the four angles are right angles, they all are right angles.

Example 3.

In the figure at the right, what is the value of x?

(A) 6   (B) 8
(C) 10   (D) 20
(E) 40

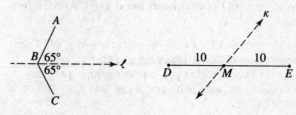

Solution. Since the measures of vertical angles are equal:

$$3x + 10 = 5(x - 2) \Rightarrow 3x + 10 = 5x - 10 \Rightarrow$$
$$3x + 20 = 5x \Rightarrow 20 = 2x \Rightarrow x = 10.$$

The answer is **C**.

In the figures below, line ℓ divides $\angle ABC$ into two equal parts, and line k divides line segment DE into two equal parts. Line ℓ is said to **bisect** the angle, and line k **bisects** the line segment. Point M is called the **midpoint** of segment DE.

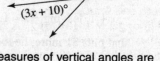

Example 4.

In the figure at the right, lines k, ℓ, and m intersect at O. If line m bisects $\angle AOB$, what is the value of x?

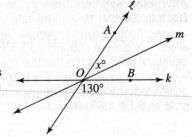

Solution. Here, m$\angle AOB + 130 = 180 \Rightarrow$ m$\angle AOB = 50$; and since $\angle AOB$ is bisected, $x = \mathbf{25}$.

Two lines that intersect to form right angles are called **perpendicular**.

Two lines that never intersect are said to be **parallel**. Consequently, parallel lines form no angles. However, if a third line, called a **transversal**, intersects a pair of parallel lines, eight angles are formed, and the relationships among these angles are very important.

Key Fact 15

If a pair of parallel lines is cut by a transversal that is perpendicular to the parallel lines, all eight angles are right angles.

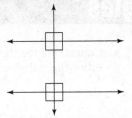

Key Fact 16

If a pair of parallel lines is cut by a transversal that is *not* perpendicular to the parallel lines:

- **Four of the angles are acute, and four are obtuse.**
- **All four acute angles are equal: $a = c = e = g$.**
- **All four obtuse angles are equal: $b = d = f = h$.**
- **The sum of any acute angle and any obtuse angle is 180°: for example, $d + e = 180$, $c + f = 180$, $b + g = 180$, ...**

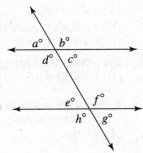

Key Fact 17

If a pair of lines that are not parallel is cut by a transversal, *none* of the statements listed in KEY FACT I6 is true.

You *must* know KEY FACT I6—virtually every SAT I has questions based on it. However, you do *not* need to know the special terms you learned in your geometry class for these pairs of angles; those terms are not used on the SAT I.

Key Fact 18

If a line is perpendicular to each of a pair of lines, then that pair of lines are parallel.

Example 5.

What is the value of x in the figure at the right?

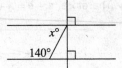

(A) 40
(B) 50
(C) 90
(D) 140

Note: Figure not drawn to scale

(E) It cannot be determined from the information given.

Solution. Despite the fact that the figure has not been drawn to scale, the little squares assure us that the vertical line is perpendicular to both of the horizontal ones, so these lines are parallel. Therefore, the sum of the 140° obtuse angle and the acute angle marked $x°$ is 180°: $x + 140 = 180 \Rightarrow x = \mathbf{40}$.

The answer is **A**.

NOTE: If the two little squares indicating right angles were not in the figure, the answer would be E: "It cannot be determined from the information given." We are not told that the two lines that look parallel are actually parallel; and since the figure is not drawn to scale, we certainly cannot make that assumption. If the lines are not parallel, then $140 + x$ is *not* 180, and x cannot be determined.

Example 6.

In the figure below, AB is parallel to CD. What is the value of x?

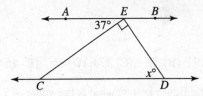

Solution. Let y be the measure of $\angle BED$. Then by KEY FACT I2:

$$37 + 90 + y = 180 \Rightarrow 127 + y = 180 \Rightarrow y = 53.$$

Since AB is parallel to CD, by KEY FACT I6, $x = y \Rightarrow x = \mathbf{53}$.

Example 7.

In the figure below, lines ℓ and k are parallel. What is the value of $a + b$?

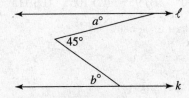

(A) 45 (B) 60 (C) 90 (D) 135
(E) It cannot be determined from the information given.

Solution. If we were asked for the value of either *a* or *b*, the answer would be E—neither one can be determined; but if we are clever, we can find the value of *a* + *b*. We draw a line through the vertex of the angle parallel to ℓ and *k*. Then, looking at the top two lines, we see that *a* = *x*, and looking at the bottom two lines, we have *b* = *y*. Therefore, *a* + *b* = *x* + *y* = **45 (A)**.

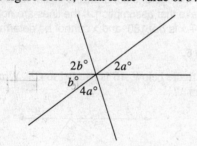

Alternative solution. Draw a different line and use a fact from Section 12-J on triangles. Extend one of the line segments to form a triangle. Since ℓ and *k* are parallel, the measure of the bottom angle in the triangle equals *a*. Now, use the fact that the sum of the measures of the three angles in a triangle is 180° or, even easier, that the given 45° angle is an external angle, and so is equal to the sum of *a* and *b*.

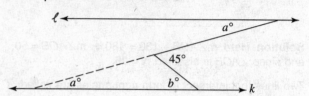

Exercises on Lines and Angles

Multiple-Choice Questions

1. In the figure below, what is the value of *b*?

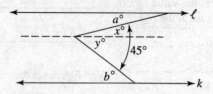

(A) 9   (B) 18   (C) 27   (D) 36   (E) 45

2. In the figure below, what is the value of *x* if
y:*x* = 3:2?

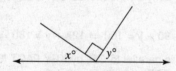

(A) 18   (B) 27   (C) 36   (D) 45   (E) 54

3. What is the measure of the angle formed by the minute and hour hands of a clock at 1:50?

(A) 90°   (B) 95°   (C) 105°   (D) 115°   (E) 120°

4. Concerning the figure below, if *a* = *b*, which of the following statements must be true?

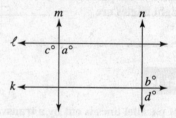

Note: Figure not drawn to scale

I. *c* = *d*.
II. ℓ and *k* are parallel.
III. *m* and ℓ are perpendicular.

(A) None   (B) I only   (C) I and II only
(D) I and III only   (E) I, II, and III

5. In the figure below, *B* and *C* lie on line *n*, *m* bisects ∠*AOC*, and ℓ bisects ∠*AOB*. What is the measure of ∠*DOE*?

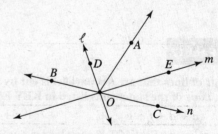

Note: Figure not drawn to scale

(A) 75   (B) 90   (C) 105   (D) 120
(E) It cannot be determined from the information given.

Quantitative Comparison Questions

Column A   Column B

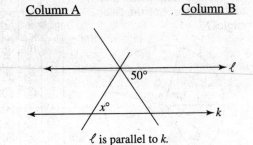

ℓ is parallel to k.

Note: Figure not drawn to scale

6. | x | | 50 |

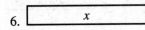

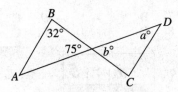

AB is parallel to CD.

7. | a | | b |

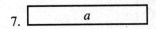

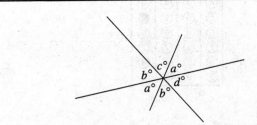

8. | $a + b + c + d$ | | $2a + 2b$ |

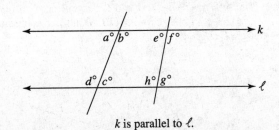

k is parallel to ℓ.

9. | $a + d + f + g$ | | $b + c + e + h$ |

Column A   Column B

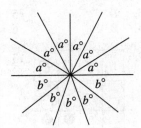

k and ℓ are parallel.

10. | z | | $x + y$ |

Grid-in Questions

11. In the figure below, what is the value of $\dfrac{b + a}{b - a}$?

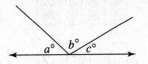

12. In the figure below, $a{:}b = 3{:}5$ and $c{:}b = 2{:}1$. What is the measure of the largest angle?

Note: Figure not drawn to scale

13. A, B, and C are points on a line, with B between A and C. Let M and N be the midpoints of AB and BC, respectively. If $AB{:}BC = 3{:}1$, what is $AB{:}MN$?

14. In the figure below, lines k and ℓ are parallel. What is the value of $y - x$?

15. In the figure below, what is the average (arithmetic mean) of the measures of the five angles?

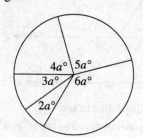

Answer Key

1. **D**	3. **D**	5. **B**	7. **B**	9. **C**
2. **C**	4. **B**	6. **D**	8. **D**	10. **C**

11. *1 1*

12. *1 0 0*

13. *3 / 2*   or   *1 . 5*

14. *4 5*

15. *7 2*

Answer Explanations

1. **D.** Since vertical angles are equal, the two un-marked angles are $2b$ and $4a$. Also, since the sum of all six angles is $360°$:

$$360 = 4a + 2b + 2a + 4a + 2b + b = 10a + 5b.$$

However, since vertical angles are equal, $b = 2a \Rightarrow 5b = 10a$. Hence:

$$360 = 10a + 5b = 10a + 10a = 20a \Rightarrow$$
$$a = 18 \Rightarrow b = 36.$$

2. **C.** Since $x + y + 90 = 180$, then $x + y = 90$. Also, since $y:x = 3:2$, then $y = 3t$ and $x = 2t$. Therefore:

$$3t + 2t = 90 \Rightarrow 5t = 90 \Rightarrow$$
$$t = 18 \Rightarrow x = 2(18) = 36.$$

3. **D.** For problems such as this, always draw a diagram. The measure of each of the 12 central angles from one number to the next on the clock is $30°$. At 1:50 the minute hand is pointing at 10, and the hour hand has gone $\dfrac{50}{60} = \dfrac{5}{6}$ of the way from 1 to 2. Then, from 10 to 1 on the clock is $90°$, and from 1 to the hour hand is $\dfrac{5}{6}(30°) = 25°$, for a total of $90° + 25° = 115°$.

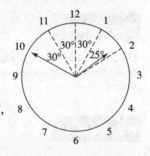

4. **B.** No conclusion can be drawn about the lines; they could form any angles whatsoever. (II and III are both false.) Statement I is true: $c = 180 - a = 180 - b = d$.

5. **B.** $x = \dfrac{1}{2}m\angle AOC$, and $y = \dfrac{1}{2}m\angle AOB$. Therefore,

$$x + y = \dfrac{1}{2}m\angle AOC + \dfrac{1}{2}m\angle AOB =$$

$$\dfrac{1}{2}(m\angle AOC + m\angle AOB) =$$

$$\dfrac{1}{2}(180) = 90.$$

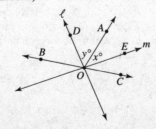

6. **D.** No conclusion can be drawn: x could equal 50 or be more or less.

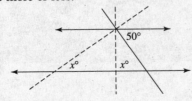

7. **B.** Since $m\angle A + 32 + 75 = 180$, $m\angle A = 73$; and since AB is parallel to CD, $a = 73$, whereas, because vertical angles are equal, $b = 75$.

8. **D.**

	Column A	Column B
	$a + b + c + d$	$2a + 2b$
Subtract a and b from each column:	$c + d$	$a + b$
Since $b = d$, subtract b and d:	c	a

There is no way to determine whether a is less than, greater than, or equal to c.

9. **C.** Since lines k and ℓ are parallel:

$$e + h = a + d = b + c = f + g = 180.$$

Each column is equal to 360.

10. **C.** Extend line segment AB to form a transversal. Then, since $w + z = 180$ and $w + (x + y) = 180$, it follows that $z = x + y$.

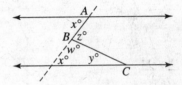

11. **(11)** From the diagram, we see that $6a = 180$, which implies that $a = 30$, and that $5b = 180$, which implies that $b = 36$. Therefore:

$$\dfrac{b + a}{b - a} = \dfrac{36 + 30}{36 - 30} = \dfrac{66}{6} = 11.$$

12. **(100)** Since $a:b = 3:5$, then $a = 3x$ and $b = 5x$; and since $c:b = 2:1$, then $c = 2b = 10x$. Then:

$$3x + 5x + 10x = 180 \Rightarrow 18x = 180 \Rightarrow$$
$$x = 10 \Rightarrow c = 10x = 100.$$

13. $\left(\dfrac{3}{2} \text{ or } 1.5\right)$ If a diagram is not provided on a geometry question, draw one. From the figure below, you can see that $AB:MN = \dfrac{3}{2} = 1.5$.

14. **(45)** Since lines ℓ and k are parallel, the angle marked y in the given diagram and the sum of the angles marked x and 45 are equal: $y = x + 45 \Rightarrow y - x = 45$.

15. **(72)** The markings in the five angles are irrelevant. The sum of the measures of these angles is $360°$, and $360 \div 5 = 72$. If you calculated the measure of each angle, you should have gotten 36, 54, 72, 90, and 108; but you wasted time.

12-J TRIANGLES

More geometry questions on the SAT I pertain to triangles than to any other topic. To answer these questions correctly, you need to know several important facts about the angles and sides of triangles. The KEY FACTS in this section are extremely useful. Read them carefully, a few times if necessary, and *make sure you learn them all.*

Key Fact J1

In any triangle, the sum of the measures of the three angles is 180°: $x + y + z = 180$.

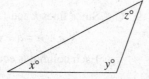

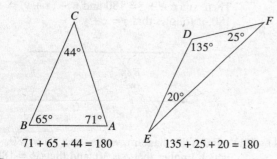

$71 + 65 + 44 = 180$ $135 + 25 + 20 = 180$

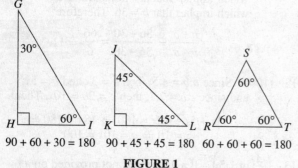

$90 + 60 + 30 = 180$ $90 + 45 + 45 = 180$ $60 + 60 + 60 = 180$

FIGURE 1

Figure 1 illustrates KEY FACT J1 for five different triangles, which will be discussed below.

Example 1.

In the figure below, what is the value of x?

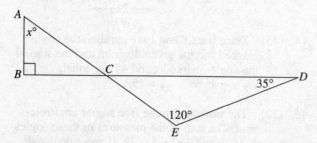

Solution. Use KEY FACT J1 twice: first, for $\triangle CDE$ and then for $\triangle ABC$.

- $m\angle DCE + 120 + 35 = 180 \Rightarrow m\angle DCE + 155 = 180 \Rightarrow m\angle DCE = 25$.
- Since vertical angles are equal, $m\angle ACB = 25$ (see KEY FACT I4).
- $x + 90 + 25 = 180 \Rightarrow x + 115 = 180 \Rightarrow x = \mathbf{65}$.

Example 2.

In the figure at the right, what is the value of a?

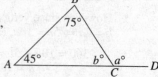

Solution. First find the value of b:

$$180 = 45 + 75 + b = 120 + b \Rightarrow b = 60.$$

Then, $a + b = 180 \Rightarrow a = 180 - b = 180 - 60 = \mathbf{120}$.

In Example 2, $\angle BCD$, which is formed by one side of $\triangle ABC$ and the extension of another side, is called an **exterior angle**. Note that, to find a, we did not have to first find b; we could just have added the other two angles: $a = 75 + 45 = 120$. This is a useful fact to remember.

Key Fact J2

The measure of an exterior angle of a triangle is equal to the sum of the measures of the two opposite interior angles.

Key Fact J3

In any triangle:

- the longest side is opposite the largest angle;
- the shortest side is opposite the smallest angle;
- sides with the same length are opposite angles with the same measure.

CAUTION: In KEY FACT J3 the condition "in any triangle" is crucial. If the angles are not in the same triangle, none of the conclusions holds. For example, in Figure 2 below AB, and DE are *not* equal even though each is opposite a 90° angle; and in Figure 3, QS is not the longest side even though it is opposite the largest angle.

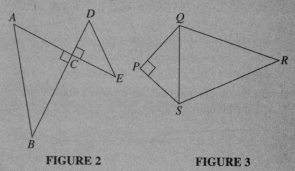

FIGURE 2   **FIGURE 3**

Consider triangles *ABC*, *JKL*, and *RST* in Figure 1.

- In △*ABC*: *BC* is the longest side since it is opposite ∠*A*, the largest angle (71°). Similarly, *AB* is the shortest side since it is opposite ∠*C*, the smallest angle (54°). Therefore, *AB* < *AC* < *BC*.
- In △*JKL*: Angles *J* and *L* have the same measure (45°), so *JK* = *KL*.
- In △*RST*: Since all three angles have the same measure (60°), all three sides have the same length: *RS* = *ST* = *TR*.

Example 3.

Which of the following statements concerning the length of side *YZ* is true?

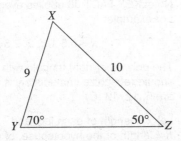

(A) *YZ* < 9
(B) *YZ* = 9
(C) 9 < *YZ* < 10
(D) *YZ* = 10
(E) *YZ* > 10

Solution.

- By KEY FACT J1, m∠*X* + 70 + 50 = 180 ⇒ m∠*X* = 60.
- Then *Y* is the largest angle, *Z* is the smallest, and *X* is in between.
- Therefore, by KEY FACT J3:
  XY < *YZ* < *XZ* ⇒ 9 < *YZ* < 10.
- The answer is **C**.

Classification of Triangles

Name	Lengths of Sides	Measures of Angles	Examples from Figure 1
Scalene	all 3 different	all 3 different	*ABC*, *DEF*, *GHI*
Isosceles	2 the same	2 the same	*JKL*
Equilateral	all 3 the same	all 3 the same	*RST*

Acute triangles are triangles such as *ABC* and *RST*, in which all three angles are acute. An acute triangle can be scalene, isosceles, or equilateral.

Obtuse triangles are triangles such as *DEF*, in which one angle is obtuse and two are acute. An obtuse triangle can be scalene or isosceles.

Right triangles are triangles such as *GHI* and *JKL*, which have one right angle and two acute ones. A right triangle can be scalene or isosceles. The side opposite the 90° angle is called the **hypotenuse**, and by KEY FACT J3 it is the longest side. The other two sides are called the **legs**.

If *x* and *y* are the measures of the acute angles of a right triangle, then by KEY FACT J1: 90 + *x* + *y* = 180, and so *x* + *y* = 90.

Key Fact J4

In any right triangle, the sum of the measures of the two acute angles is 90°.

Column A	Column B

Example 4.

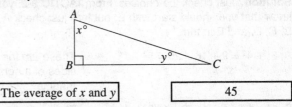

The average of *x* and *y*	45

Solution. Since the diagram indicates that △*ABC* is a right triangle, then, by KEY FACT J4, *x* + *y* = 90. Therefore, the average of *x* and *y* = $\frac{x+y}{2}=\frac{90}{2}$ = 45. The answer is **C**.

The most important facts concerning right triangles are the **Pythagorean theorem** and its converse, which are given in KEY FACT J5 and repeated as the first line of KEY FACT J6.

Key Fact J5

Let *a*, *b*, and *c* be the sides of △*ABC*, with $a \le b \le c$. If △*ABC* is a right triangle, $a^2 + b^2 = c^2$; and if $a^2 + b^2 = c^2$, then △*ABC* is a right triangle.

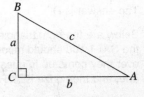

Key Fact J6

Let *a*, *b*, and *c* be the sides of △*ABC*, with $a \le b \le c$.

- $a^2 + b^2 = c^2$ if and only if ∠C is a right angle.
  (△*ABC* is a right triangle.)
- $a^2 + b^2 < c^2$ if and only if ∠C is obtuse.
  (△*ABC* is an obtuse triangle.)
- $a^2 + b^2 > c^2$ if and only if ∠C is acute.
  (△*ABC* is an acute triangle.)

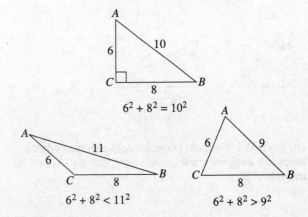

Example 5.

Which of the following are NOT the sides of a right triangle?

(A) 3, 4, 5   (B) 1, 1, $\sqrt{2}$ (C) 1, $\sqrt{3}$, 2

(D) $\sqrt{3}, \sqrt{4}, \sqrt{5}$ (E) 30, 40, 50

Solution. Just check the choices. From TACTIC 9-2, you know that you should start with E, but let's just check A, B, C, D, and E in turn.

A: $3^2 + 4^2 = 9 + 16 = 25 = 5^2$ — These *are* the sides of a right triangle.

B: $1^2 + 1^2 = 1 + 1 = 2 = (\sqrt{2})^2$ — These *are* the sides of a right triangle.

C: $1^2 + (\sqrt{3})^2 = 1 + 3 = 4 = 2^2$ — These *are* the sides of a right triangle.

D: $(\sqrt{3})^2 + (\sqrt{4})^2 = 3 + 4 = 7 \neq (\sqrt{5})^2$ — These *are not* the sides of a right triangle.

E: $30^2 + 40^2 = 900 + 1600 = 2500 = 50^2$ — These *are* the sides of a right triangle.

The answer is **D**.

Below are the right triangles that appear most often on the SAT I. You should recognize them immediately whenever they come up in questions. Carefully study each one, and memorize KEY FACTS J7–J11.

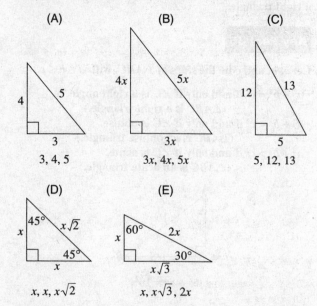

(A) 3, 4, 5

(B) 3x, 4x, 5x

(C) 5, 12, 13

(D) x, x, x√2

(E) x, x√3, 2x

On the SAT I, the most common right triangles whose sides are integers are the 3-4-5 right triangle (A) and its multiples (B).

Key Fact J7

For any positive number x, there is a right triangle whose sides are $3x$, $4x$, $5x$.

For example: $x = 1$ 3, 4, 5 $x = 5$ 15, 20, 25

$x = 2$ 6, 8, 10 $x = 10$ 30, 40, 50

$x = 3$ 9, 12, 15 $x = 50$ 150, 200, 250

$x = 4$ 12, 16, 20 $x = 100$ 300, 400, 500

Note: KEY FACT J6 applies even if x is not an integer. For example:

$$x = 0.5 \quad 1.5, 2, 2.5 \quad x = \pi \quad 3\pi, 4\pi, 5\pi$$

The only other right triangle with integer sides that you should recognize immediately is the one whose sides are 5, 12, 13 (C).

Let x = length of each leg, and h = length of the hypotenuse, of an isosceles right triangle (D). By the Pythagorean theorem (KEY FACT J5), $x^2 + x^2 = h^2$.

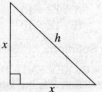

Then, $2x^2 = h^2$, and $h = \sqrt{2x^2} = x\sqrt{2}$.

Key Fact J8

In a 45-45-90 right triangle, the sides are x, x, and $x\sqrt{2}$. Therefore:

- **By multiplying the length of a leg by $\sqrt{2}$, you get the hypotenuse.**
- **By dividing the hypotenuse by $\sqrt{2}$, you get the length of each leg.**

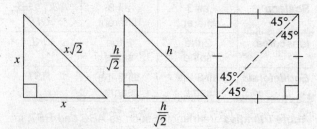

Key Fact J9

The diagonal of a square divides the square into two isosceles right triangles.

The last important right triangle is the one whose angles are 30°, 60°, and 90° (E).

Key Fact J10

An altitude divides an equilateral triangle into two 30-60-90 right triangles.

Let $2x$ be the length of each side of equilateral triangle ABC, in which altitude AD is drawn. Then $\triangle ADB$ is a 30-60-90 right triangle, and its sides are x, $2x$, and h. By the Pythagorean theorem, $x^2 + h^2 = (2x)^2 = 4x^2$, so $h^2 = 3x^2$, and $h = \sqrt{3x^2} = x\sqrt{3}$.

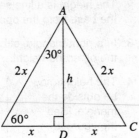

Key Fact J11

In a 30-60-90 right triangle the sides are x, $x\sqrt{3}$, and $2x$.

If you know the length of the shorter leg (x):

- multiply it by $\sqrt{3}$ to get the longer leg;
- multiply it by 2 to get the hypotenuse.

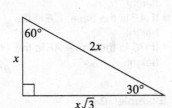

If you know the length of the longer leg (a):

- divide it by $\sqrt{3}$ to get the shorter leg;
- multiply the shorter leg by 2 to get the hypotenuse.

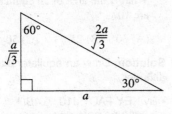

If you know the length of the hypotenuse (h):

- divide it by 2 to get the shorter leg;
- multiply the shorter leg by $\sqrt{3}$ to get the longer leg.

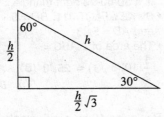

Example 6.

What is the area of a square whose diagonal is 10?

(A) 20 (B) 40 (C) 50 (D) 100 (E) 200

Solution. Draw a diagonal in a square of side s, creating a 45-45-90 right triangle. By KEY FACT J8:

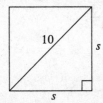

$$s = \frac{10}{\sqrt{2}} \quad \text{and} \quad A = s^2 = \left(\frac{10}{\sqrt{2}}\right)^2 = \frac{100}{2} = 50.$$

The answer is **C**.

[KEY FACT K8 gives the formula for the area of a square based on this example: $A = \frac{d^2}{2}$, where d is the length of a diagonal.]

Example 7.

In the diagram at the right, if $BC = \sqrt{6}$, what is the value of CD?

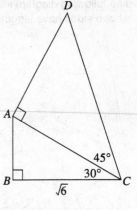

Solution. $\triangle ABC$ and $\triangle DAC$ are 30-60-90 and 45-45-90 right triangles, respectively. Use KEY FACTS J11 and J8.

- Divide the longer leg, BC, by $\sqrt{3}$ to get the shorter leg, AB: $\frac{\sqrt{6}}{\sqrt{3}} = \sqrt{2}$.
- Multiply AB by 2 to get the hypotenuse: $AC = 2\sqrt{2}$.
- Since AC is also a leg of isosceles right triangle DAC, then, to get hypotenuse CD, multiply AC by $\sqrt{2}$: $CD = 2\sqrt{2} \times \sqrt{2} = 2 \times 2 = 4$.

Key Fact J12 (Triangle Inequality)

The sum of the lengths of any two sides of a triangle is greater than the length of the third side.

The best way to remember this is to see that $x + y$, the length of the path from A to C through B, is greater than z, the length of the direct path from A to C.

NOTE: If you subtract x from each side of $x + y > z$, you see that $z - x < y$.

$$x + y > z$$

Key Fact J13

The difference between the lengths of any two sides of a triangle is less than the length of the third side.

Example 8.

If the lengths of two sides of a triangle are 6 and 7, which of the following could be the length of the third side?

I. 1
II. 5
III. 15

(A) None (B) I only (C) II only (D) I and II only
(E) I, II, and III

Solution. Use KEY FACTS J12 and J13.

- The third side must be *less* than $6 + 7 = 13$. (III is false.)
- The third side must be *greater* than $7 - 6 = 1$. (I is false.)
- *Any* number between 1 and 13 could be the length of the third side. (II is true.)

The answer is **C**.

The following diagram illustrates several triangles two of whose sides have lengths of 6 and 7.

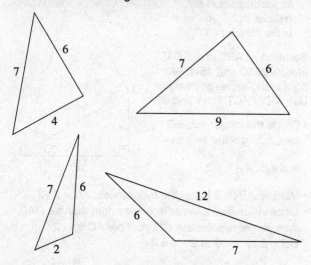

On the SAT I, two other terms that appear regularly in triangle problems are **perimeter** and **area** (see Section 12-K).

Example 9.

In the figure at the right, what is the perimeter of △*ABC*?

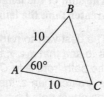

Solution. First, use KEY FACTS J3 and J1 to find the measures of the angles.

- Since *AB = AC*, m∠*B* = m∠*C*. Represent each measure by *x*.
- Then, *x + x +* 60 = 180 ⇒ 2*x* = 120 ⇒ *x* = 60.
- Since the measure of each angle of △*ABC* is 60°, the triangle is equilateral.
- Then, *BC* = 10, and the perimeter is 10 + 10 + 10 = **30**.

Key Fact J14

The area of a triangle is given by $A = \frac{1}{2}bh$, where *b* = base and *h* = height.

Note:

1. *Any* side of the triangle can be taken as the base.

2. The height is a line segment drawn perpendicular to the base from the opposite vertex.

3. In a right triangle, either leg can be the base and the other the height.

4. The height may be outside the triangle. [See the figure at the right.]

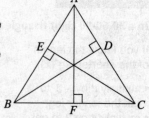

In the figure at the right:

- If *AC* is the base, *BD* is the height.
- If *AB* is the base, *CE* is the height.
- If *BC* is the base, *AF* is the height.

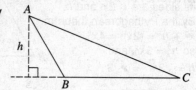

Example 10.

What is the area of an equilateral triangle whose sides are 10?

(A) 30   (B) $25\sqrt{3}$ (C) 50   (D) $50\sqrt{3}$ (E) 100

Solution. Draw an equilateral triangle and one of its altitudes.

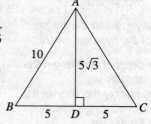

- By KEY FACT J10, △*ABD* is a 30-60-90 right triangle.
- By KEY FACT J11, *BD* = 5 and *AD* = $5\sqrt{3}$.
- The area of △*ABC* = $\frac{1}{2}(10)(5\sqrt{3})$ = **$25\sqrt{3}$ (B)**.

Replacing 10 by *s* in Example 10 yields a very useful result.

Key Fact J15

If *A* represents the area of an equilateral triangle with side *s*, then $A = \frac{s^2\sqrt{3}}{4}$.

Exercises on Triangles

Multiple-Choice Questions

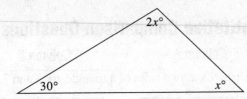

1. In the triangle above, what is the value of x?

    (A) 20   (B) 30   (C) 40   (D) 50   (E) 60

2. What is the area of an equilateral triangle whose altitude is 6?

    (A) 18   (B) $12\sqrt{3}$ (C) $18\sqrt{3}$ (D) 36

    (E) $24\sqrt{3}$

3. Two sides of a right triangle are 12 and 13. Which of the following could be the length of the third side?

    I.   5
    II. 11
    III. $\sqrt{313}$

    (A) I only   (B) II only   (C) I and II only
    (D) I and III only   (E) I, II, and III

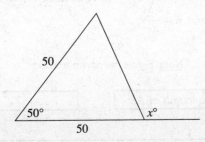

4. What is the value of PS in the triangle above?

    (A) $5\sqrt{2}$ (B) 10   (C) 11   (D) 13   (E) $12\sqrt{2}$

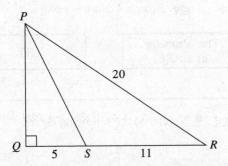

5. What is the value of x in the figure above?

    (A) 80   (B) 100   (C) 115   (D) 120   (E) 130

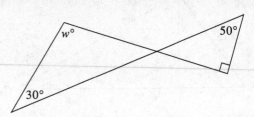

6. In the figure above, what is the value of w?

    (A) 100   (B) 110   (C) 120   (D) 130   (E) 140

Questions 7–8 refer to the following figure.

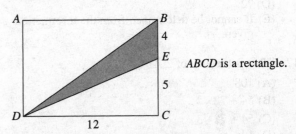

$ABCD$ is a rectangle.

7. What is the area of $\triangle BED$?

    (A) 12   (B) 24   (C) 36   (D) 48   (E) 60

8. What is the perimeter of $\triangle BED$?

    (A) $19 + 5\sqrt{2}$ (B) 28   (C) $17 + \sqrt{185}$
    (D) 32   (E) 36

Questions 9–10 refer to the following figure.

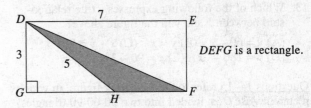

$DEFG$ is a rectangle.

9. What is the area of $\triangle DFH$?

    (A) 3   (B) 4.5   (C) 6   (D) 7.5   (E) 10

10. What is the perimeter of $\triangle DFH$?

    (A) $8 + \sqrt{41}$ (B) $8 + \sqrt{58}$ (C) 16   (D) 17
    (E) 18

Questions 11–12 refer to the following figure.

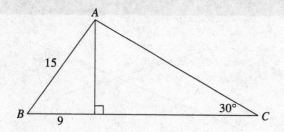

11. What is the perimeter of △ABC?

    (A) 48
    (B) 48 + 12√2
    (C) 48 + 12√3
    (D) 72
    (E) It cannot be determined from the information given.

12. What is the area of △ABC?

    (A) 108
    (B) 54 + 72√2
    (C) 54 + 72√3
    (D) 198
    (E) It cannot be determined from the information given.

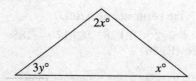

13. Which of the following expresses a true relationship between x and y in the figure above?

    (A) $y = 60 - x$ (B) $y = x$ (C) $x + y = 90$
    (D) $y = 180 - 3x$ (E) $x = 90 - 3y$

Questions 14–15 refer to the following figure, in which rectangle ABCD is divided into two 30-60-90 triangles, a 45-45-90 triangle, and shaded triangle ABF.

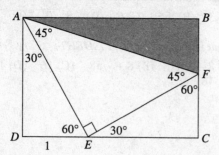

14. What is the perimeter of shaded triangle ABF?

    (A) $\sqrt{2} + 2\sqrt{3}$ (B) $1 + \sqrt{2} + \sqrt{3}$
    (C) $2 + \sqrt{2} + \sqrt{3}$ (D) $2 + 2\sqrt{2} + \sqrt{3}$
    (E) $2\sqrt{2} + 2\sqrt{3}$

15. What is the area of shaded triangle ABF?

    (A) $\dfrac{\sqrt{3}}{2}$ (B) 1   (C) $\dfrac{2\sqrt{3}}{3}$ (D) $\dfrac{\sqrt{3}+1}{2}$

    (E) $\sqrt{2}(\sqrt{3}+1)$

Quantitative Comparison Questions

<u>Column A</u>	<u>Column B</u>

The lengths of two sides of a triangle are 3 and 7.

16.

The length of the third side	11

17.

The ratio of the diagonal to a side of a square	$\sqrt{2}$

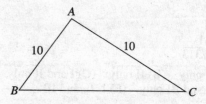

Note: Figure not drawn to scale

18.

The perimeter of △ABC	30

Questions 19–20 refer to the following figure.

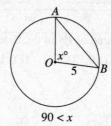

$90 < x$

Note: Figure not drawn to scale

19.

The length of AB	7

20.

The perimeter of △AOB	20

<u>Column A</u>

<u>Column B</u>

21.
| The area of an equilateral triangle whose sides are 10 | The area of an equilateral triangle whose altitude is 10 |

Questions 22–23 refer to the following figure, in which the horizontal and vertical lines divide square *ABCD* into smaller squares.

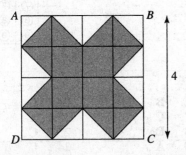

22.
| The perimeter of the shaded region | The perimeter of the square |

23.
| The area of the shaded region | The area of the white region |

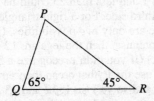

24.
| $a + b$ | c |

Note: Figure not drawn to scale

25.
| *PR* | *QR* |

Grid-in Questions

26. If the difference between the measures of the two smaller angles of a right triangle is 20°, what is the measure, in degrees, of the smallest angle?

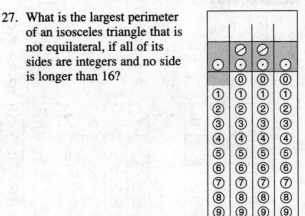

27. What is the largest perimeter of an isosceles triangle that is not equilateral, if all of its sides are integers and no side is longer than 16?

28. Let *P* be the perimeter of an isosceles triangle all of whose sides are integers. If one side is 16 and the triangle is not equilateral, what is the largest value of *P* that will fit in the grid?

29. What is the smallest integer, x, for which x, $x + 5$, and $2x - 15$ can be the lengths of the sides of a triangle?

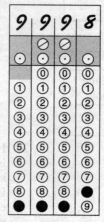

30. If the measures of the angles of a triangle are in the ratio of 1:2:3, and if the perimeter of the triangle is $30 + 10\sqrt{3}$, what is the length of the smallest side?

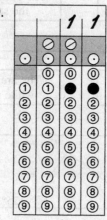

Answer Key

1.	**D**	6.	**B**	11.	**C**	16.	**B**	21.	**B**
2.	**B**	7.	**B**	12.	**C**	17.	**C**	22.	**A**
3.	**D**	8.	**D**	13.	**A**	18.	**D**	23.	**C**
4.	**D**	9.	**B**	14.	**E**	19.	**A**	24.	**C**
5.	**C**	10.	**B**	15.	**B**	20.	**B**	25.	**B**

26. $3\ 5$ 27. $4\ 7$ 28. $9\ 9\ 9\ 8$ 29. $1\ 1$ 30. $1\ 0$

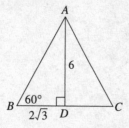

Answer Explanations

1. **D.** $x + 2x + 30 = 180 \Rightarrow 3x + 30 = 180 \Rightarrow 3x = 150 \Rightarrow x = 50$.

2. **B.** Draw altitude AD in equilateral triangle ABC.

A
6
60°
B $2\sqrt{3}$ D C

By KEY FACT J11:

$$BD = \frac{6}{\sqrt{3}} = \frac{6\sqrt{3}}{3} = 2\sqrt{3},$$

and BD is one-half the base. The area is $2\sqrt{3} \times 6 = 12\sqrt{3}$.

3. **D.** If the triangle were not required to be right, by KEY FACTS J11 and J12 *any* number greater than 1 and less than 25 could be the length of the third side. For a right triangle, however, there are only *two* possibilities. (i) If 13 is the hypotenuse, then the legs are 12 and 5. (I is true.) (If you didn't recognize a 5-12-13 triangle, use the Pythagorean theorem: $5^2 + x^2 = 13^2$, and solve.) (ii) If 12 and 13 are the two legs, then use the Pythagorean theorem to find the hypotenuse:

$$12^2 + 13^2 = c^2 \Rightarrow c^2 = 144 + 169 = 313 \Rightarrow c = \sqrt{313}.$$

(III is true.) An 11-12-13 triangle is not a *right* triangle. (II is false.)

4. **D.** Use the Pythagorean theorem twice, unless you recognize the common right triangles in this figure (*which you should*). Since $PR = 20$

and $QR = 16$, $\triangle PQR$ is a $3x$-$4x$-$5x$ right triangle with $x = 4$. Then $PQ = 12$, and $\triangle PQS$ is a right triangle whose legs are 5 and 12. The hypotenuse, PS, therefore, is 13. [If you had difficulty with this question, review the material, but in the meantime remember TACTIC 8-2: trust the diagram. PS is longer than SR, so you can eliminate A, B, and C, and PS is clearly less than QR, so eliminate E.]

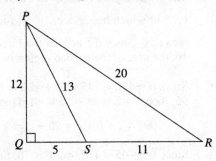

5. **C.** Here,

$$50 + a + b = 180 \Rightarrow a + b = 130,$$

and since the triangle is isosceles, $a = b$. Therefore, a and b are each 65, and $x = 180 - 65 = 115$.

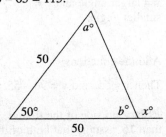

6. **B.** Here, $50 + 90 + a = 180 \Rightarrow a = 40$, and since vertical angles are equal, $b = 40$. Then:

$$40 + 30 + w = 180 \Rightarrow w = 110.$$

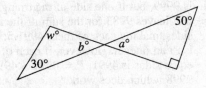

7. **B.** You *could* calculate the area of the rectangle and subtract the area of the two white right triangles, but don't. The shaded area is a triangle whose base is 4 and whose height is 12. The area is $\frac{1}{2}(4)(12) = 24$.

8. **D.** Since both BD and ED are the hypotenuses of right triangles, their lengths can be calculated by the Pythagorean theorem, but again these are triangles you should recognize: the sides of $\triangle DCE$ are 5-12-13, and those of $\triangle BAD$ are 9-12-15 ($3x$-$4x$-$5x$, with $x = 3$). Therefore, the perimeter of $\triangle BED$ is $4 + 13 + 15 = 32$.

9. **B.** Since $\triangle DGH$ is a right triangle, whose hypotenuse is 5 and one of whose legs is 3, the other leg, GH, is 4. Since $GF = DE = 7$, $HF = 3$. Now, $\triangle DFH$ has a base of 3 (HF) and a height of 3 (DG), and its area is

$$\frac{1}{2}(3)(3) = 4.5.$$

10. **B.** For $\triangle DFH$, we already have that $DH = 5$ and $HF = 3$; we need only find DF, which is the hypotenuse of $\triangle DEF$. By the Pythagorean theorem,

$$3^2 + 7^2 = (DF)^2 \Rightarrow (DF)^2 = 9 + 49 = 58 \Rightarrow$$
$$DF = \sqrt{58}.$$

The perimeter is $3 + 5 + \sqrt{58} = 8 + \sqrt{58}$.

11. **C.** $\triangle ADB$ is a right triangle whose hypotenuse is 15 and one of whose legs is 9, so this is a $3x$-$4x$-$5x$ triangle with $x = 3$, and $AD = 12$. Now $\triangle ADC$ is a 30-60-90 triangle, whose shorter leg is 12. Hypotenuse AC is 24, and leg CD is $12\sqrt{3}$, so the perimeter is

$$24 + 15 + 9 + 12\sqrt{3} = 48 + 12\sqrt{3}.$$

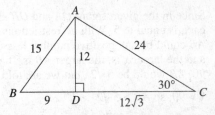

12. **C.** From the solution to Exercise 11, we have the base $(9 + 12\sqrt{3})$ and the height (12) of $\triangle ABC$. Then, the area is

$$\frac{1}{2}(12)(9 + 12\sqrt{3}) = 54 + 72\sqrt{3}.$$

13. **A.** $x + 2x + 3y = 180 \Rightarrow 3x + 3y = 180 \Rightarrow$
$x + y = 60 \Rightarrow y = 60 - x$.

14. **E.**

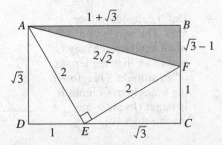

We are given enough information to determine the sides of all the triangles. Both 30-60-90 triangles have sides 1, $\sqrt{3}$, 2; and the 45-45-90 triangle has sides 2, 2, $2\sqrt{2}$. Also, $AB = CD = 1 + \sqrt{3}$, and $BF = AD - CF = \sqrt{3} - 1$.

Then, the perimeter of the shaded triangle is
$1 + \sqrt{3} + \sqrt{3} - 1 + 2\sqrt{2} = 2\sqrt{2} + 2\sqrt{3}$.

15. **B.** The area of $\triangle ABF = \frac{1}{2}(\sqrt{3} + 1)(\sqrt{3} - 1) = \frac{1}{2}(\sqrt{3} - 1) = 1$.

16. **B.** Any side of a triangle must be less than the sum of the other two sides [KEY FACT J12], so the third side is less than $3 + 7 = 10 < 11$.

17. **C.** Draw a diagram. A diagonal of a square is the hypotenuse of each of the two 45-45-90 right triangles formed. The ratio of the hypotenuse to a leg in such a triangle is $\sqrt{2}:1$, so the columns are equal.

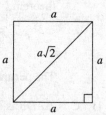

18. **D.** *BC* can be any positive number less than 20 (by KEY FACTS J12 and J13, $BC > 10 - 10 = 0$ and $BC < 10 + 10 = 20$). Therefore, the perimeter can be *any* number greater than 20 and less than 40.

19. **A.** Since in the given figure *OA* and *OB* are radii, each is equal to 5. With no restrictions on *x*, *AB* could be any positive number less than 10; and the larger *x* is, the larger *AB* is. If *x* were 90, *AB* would be $5\sqrt{2}$, but we are told that $x > 90$, so $AB > 5\sqrt{2} > 7$.

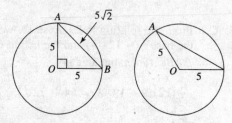

20. **B.** Since *AB* must be less than 10, the perimeter is *less* than 20.

21. **B.** Don't calculate either area. The length of a side of an equilateral triangle is *greater* than the length of an altitude. Therefore, the triangle in Column B is larger (its sides are greater than 10).

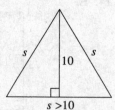

22. **A.** Column A: The perimeter of the shaded region consists of 12 line segments, each of which is the hypotenuse of a white 45-45-90 right triangle whose legs are 1. Then each line segment is $\sqrt{2}$, and the perimeter of the shaded region is $12\sqrt{2} \approx 16.97$.
Column B: The perimeter of the square is 16.

23. **A.** The white region consists of 12 right triangles, each of which has an area of $\frac{1}{2}$, for a total area of 6. Since the area of the large square is 16, the area of the shaded region is $16 - 6 = 10$.

24. **C.** Since $a = 180 - 145 = 35$ and $b = 180 - 125 = 55$, then $a + b = 35 + 55 = 90$. Therefore:
$$180 = a + b + c = 90 + c \Rightarrow c = 90.$$

25. **B.** Since $65 + 45 = 110$, $m\angle P = 70$. Since $\angle P$ is the largest angle, *QR*, the side opposite it, is the largest side.

26. **(35)** Draw a diagram, label it, and then write the equations, letting x = larger angle and y = smaller angle.

$$\begin{array}{rl} x + y = & 90 \\ + x - y = & 20 \\ \hline 2x \quad = & 110 \end{array}$$
Add the equations:

Then $x = 55$, and $y = 90 - 55 = 35$.

27. **(47)** Since no side of the triangle can be longer than 16, assume that both of the equal sides are 16. Then the largest possible value of the third side is 15, making the perimeter $16 + 16 + 15 = 47$.

28. **(9998)** The largest number that can be gridded in is 9999; but if one side of the triangle is 16, that leaves 9983 for the sum of the two equal sides, making each of them 4991.5, which isn't an integer. However, if each of the two equal sides is 4991, $P = 4991 + 4991 + 16 = 9998$, which does work.

29. **(11)** In a triangle the sum of the lengths of any two sides must be greater than the third side. For $x + (x + 5)$ to be greater than $2x - 15$, $2x + 5$ must be greater than $2x - 15$; but that's always true. For $x + (2x - 15)$ to be greater than $x + 5$, $3x - 15$ must be greater than $x + 5$; but $3x - 15 > x + 5$ is true only if $2x > 20$, which means $x > 10$. Grid in 11.

30. **(10)** If the measures of the angles are in the ratio of 1:2:3, then:
$$x + 2x + 3x = 180 \Rightarrow 6x = 180 \Rightarrow x = 30.$$

The triangle is a 30-60-90 right triangle, and the sides are a, $2a$, and $a\sqrt{3}$. The perimeter therefore is $3a + a\sqrt{3} = a(3 + \sqrt{3})$, so

$$a(3 + \sqrt{3}) = 30 + 10\sqrt{3} = 10(3 + \sqrt{3}) \Rightarrow$$
$$a = 10.$$

12-K QUADRILATERALS AND OTHER POLYGONS

A *polygon* is a closed geometric figure made up of line segments. The line segments are called *sides*, and the endpoints of the line segments are called *vertices* (each one is a *vertex*). Line segments inside the polygon drawn from one vertex to another are called *diagonals*.

The simplest polygons, which have three sides, are the triangles, which you studied in Section 12-J. A polygon with four sides is called a *quadrilateral*. There are special names (such as *pentagon* and *hexagon*) for polygons with more than four sides, but you do not need to know any of them for the SAT I.

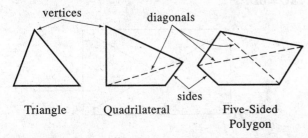

In this section we will present a few facts about polygons in general and then review the key facts you need to know about three special quadrilaterals.

Every quadrilateral has two diagonals. If you draw in either one, you will divide the quadrilateral into two triangles. Since the sum of the measures of the three angles in each of the triangles is 180°, the sum of the measures of the angles in the quadrilateral is 360°.

Key Fact K1

In any quadrilateral, the sum of the measures of the four angles is 360°.

In exactly the same way, any polygon can be divided into triangles by drawing in all of the diagonals emanating from one vertex.

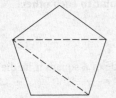 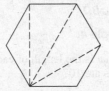

Notice that a five-sided polygon is divided into three triangles, and a six-sided polygon is divided into four triangles. In general, an n-sided polygon is divided into $(n - 2)$ triangles, which leads to KEY FACT K2.

Key Fact K2

The sum of the measures of the n angles in a polygon with n sides is $(n - 2) \times 180°$.

Example 1.

In the figure below, what is the value of x?

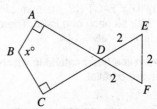

Solution. Since $\triangle DEF$ is equilateral, all of its angles measure 60°; also, since the two angles at vertex D are vertical angles, their measures are equal. Therefore, the measure of $\angle D$ in quadrilateral $ABCD$ is 60°. Finally, since the sum of the measures of all four angles of $ABCD$ is 360°:

$$60 + 90 + 90 + x = 360 \Rightarrow 240 + x = 360 \Rightarrow x = \mathbf{120}.$$

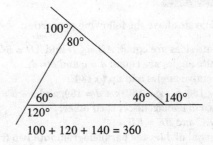

$$100 + 120 + 140 = 360$$

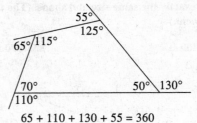

$$65 + 110 + 130 + 55 = 360$$

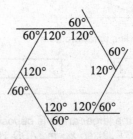

$$60 + 60 + 60 + 60 + 60 + 60 = 360$$

In the polygons in the figure above, one exterior angle has been drawn in at each vertex. Surprisingly, if you add the measures of all of the exterior angles in any of the polygons, the sums are equal.

Key Fact K3

In any polygon, the sum of the exterior angles, taking one at each vertex, is 360°.

Example 2.

A 10-sided polygon is drawn in which each angle has the same measure. What is the measure of each angle?

Solution 1. By KEY FACT K2, the sum of the measures of the 10 angles is $(10 - 2) \times 180 = 8 \times 180 = 1440$. Then, each angle is $1440 \div 10 = \mathbf{144}$.

Solution 2. By KEY FACT K3, the sum of the 10 exterior angles is 360, so each one is 36. Therefore, each interior angle is $180 - 36 = \mathbf{144}$.

A *parallelogram* is a quadrilateral in which both pairs of opposite sides are parallel.

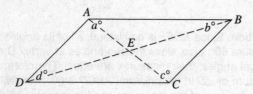

Key Fact K4

Parallelograms have the following properties:

- Opposite sides are equal: $AB = CD$ and $AD = BC$.
- Opposite angles are equal: $a = c$ and $b = d$.
- Consecutive angles add up to 180°:
  $a + b = 180$, $b + c = 180$, $c + d = 180$, and $a + d = 180$.
- The two diagonals bisect each other:
  $AE = EC$ and $BE = ED$.
- A diagonal divides the parallelogram into two triangles that have exactly the same size and shape. (The triangles are congruent.)

Column A	Column B

Example 3.

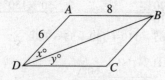

ABCD is a parallelogram.

Solution. In $\triangle ABD$ the larger angle is opposite the larger side [KEY FACT J2]; so $x > m\angle ABD$. However, since AB and CD are parallel lines cut by transversal BD, $y = m\angle ABD$. Therefore, $x > y$ **(A)**.

A *rectangle* is a parallelogram in which all four angles are right angles. Two adjacent sides of a rectangle are usually called the *length* (ℓ) and the *width* (w). Note in the right-hand figure that the length is not necessarily greater than the width.

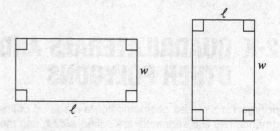

Key Fact K5

Since a rectangle is a parallelogram, all of the properties listed in KEY FACT K4 hold for rectangles. In addition:

- The measure of each angle in a rectangle is 90°.
- The diagonals of a rectangle have the same length:
  $AC = BD$.

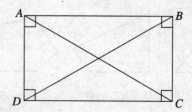

A *square* is a rectangle in which all four sides have the same length.

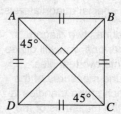

Key Fact K6

Since a square is a rectangle, all of the properties listed in KEY FACTS K4 and K5 hold for squares. In addition:

- All four sides have the same length.
- Each diagonal divides the square into two 45-45-90 right triangles.
- The diagonals are perpendicular to each other:
  $AC \perp BD$.

Example 4.

What is the length of each side of a square if its diagonals are 10?

Solution. Draw a diagram. In square *ABCD*, diagonal *AC* is the hypotenuse of a 45-45-90 right triangle, and side *AB* is a leg of that triangle. By KEY FACT J7,

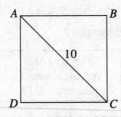

$$AB = \frac{AC}{\sqrt{2}} = \frac{10}{\sqrt{2}} \times \frac{\sqrt{2}}{\sqrt{2}} = \frac{10\sqrt{2}}{2} = 5\sqrt{2}.$$

The *perimeter* (*P*) of any polygon is the sum of the lengths of all of its sides. The only polygons for which we have formulas for the perimeter are the rectangle and the square.

Key Fact K7

In a rectangle, $P = 2(\ell + w)$; in a square, $P = 4s$.

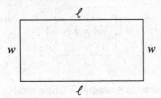

$$P = \ell + w + \ell + w = 2(\ell + w) \qquad P = s + s + s + s = 4s$$

Example 5.

The length of a rectangle is twice its width. If the perimeter of the rectangle is the same as the perimeter of a square of side 6, what is the square of the length of a diagonal of the rectangle?

Solution. Don't do anything until you have drawn diagrams. Perimeter of rectangle = perimeter of square, which is 4(6) = 24. Then

$$2(\ell + w) = 24 \Rightarrow$$
$$\ell + w = 12.$$

But $\ell = 2w$, so

$$2w + w = 3w = 12 \Rightarrow$$
$$w = 4 \text{ (and } \ell = 8).$$

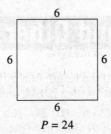

Finally, use the Pythagorean theorem: $d^2 = 4^2 + 8^2 = 16 + 64 = \mathbf{80}.$

In Section 12-J we reviewed the formula for the *area* of a triangle. The only other polygons for which you need to know area formulas are the parallelogram, rectangle, and square.

• Parallelogram: Since the area of each of the two triangles formed by drawing a diagonal in a parallelogram

is $\frac{1}{2}bh$, the area of the parallelogram is twice as great:

$$A = \frac{1}{2}bh + \frac{1}{2}bh = bh.$$

• Rectangle: In a rectangle the same formula holds, except that we usually write $A = \ell w$, using the terms *length* and *width* instead of *base* and *height*.

• Square: In a square the length and width are equal; we label each of them *s* (side), and write $A = s \times s = s^2$. If *d* is the diagonal of a square,

$$d = s\sqrt{2} \Rightarrow d^2 = 2s^2 \Rightarrow s^2 = \frac{1}{2}d^2.$$

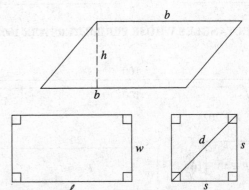

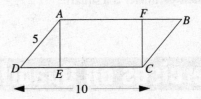

Key Fact K8

Here are the area formulas you need to know:

• For a parallelogram: $A = bh$.
• For a rectangle: $A = lw$.
• For a square: $A = s^2$ or $A = \frac{1}{2}d^2$.

Example 6.

In the figure below, the area of parallelogram *ABCD* is 40. What is the area of rectangle *AFCE*?

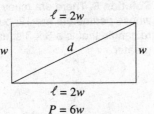

(A) 20   (B) 24   (C) 28   (D) 32   (E) 36

Solution. Since the base, *CD*, is 10 and the area is 40, the height, *AE*, must be 4. Then △*AED* must be a 3-4-5 right triangle with *DE* = 3, which implies that *EC* = 7. The area of the rectangle is $7 \times 4 = \mathbf{28 \ (C)}.$

Two rectangles with the same perimeter can have different areas, and two rectangles with the same area can have different perimeters. These facts are a common source of questions on the SAT I.

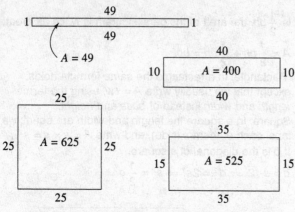

RECTANGLES WHOSE PERIMETERS ARE 100

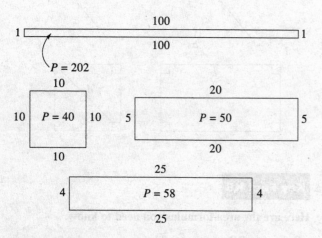

RECTANGLES WHOSE AREAS ARE 100

Key Fact K9

For a given perimeter, the rectangle with the largest area is a square. For a given area, the rectangle with the smallest perimeter is a square.

Column A	Column B

Example 7.

The area of a rectangle whose perimeter is 12	The area of a rectangle whose perimeter is 14

Example 8.

The area of a rectangle whose perimeter is 12	10

Solution 7. Draw any rectangles whose perimeters are 12 and 14, and compute their areas. For the rectangles drawn below, Column A = 8 and Column B = 12.

This time Column B is greater. Is it always? Draw a different rectangle whose perimeter is also 14.

This one has an area of 6. Now Column B isn't greater: choose **D** as the answer.

Solution 8. There are many rectangles of different areas whose perimeters are 12, but the largest area is for a rectangle that is a 3 × 3 square: A = 9. Column **B** is greater.

Exercises on Quadrilaterals and Other Polygons

Multiple-Choice Questions

1. In the figure at the right, the two diagonals divide square *ABCD* into four small triangles. What is the sum of the perimeters of those triangles?

   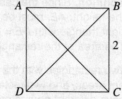

   (A) $2 + 2\sqrt{2}$ (B) $8 + 4\sqrt{2}$
   (C) $8 + 8\sqrt{2}$ (D) 16
   (E) 24

2. If the length of a rectangle is 4 times its width, and if its area is 144, what is its perimeter?

   (A) 6   (B) 24   (C) 30   (D) 60   (E) 96

3. If the angles of a five-sided polygon are in the ratio of 2:3:3:5:5, what is the degree measure of the smallest angle?

   (A) 20   (B) 40   (C) 60   (D) 80   (E) 90

Questions 4–5 refer to a rectangle in which the length of each diagonal is 12, and one of the angles formed by the diagonal and a side measures 30°.

4. What is the area of the rectangle?

    (A) 18   (B) 72   (C) $18\sqrt{3}$ (D) $36\sqrt{3}$
    (E) $36\sqrt{2}$

5. What is the perimeter of the rectangle?

    (A) 18   (B) 24   (C) $12 + 12\sqrt{3}$ (D) $18 + 6\sqrt{3}$
    (E) $24\sqrt{2}$

6. The length of a rectangle is 5 more than the side of a square, and the width of the rectangle is 5 less than the side of the square. If the area of the square is 45, what is the area of the rectangle?

    (A) 20   (B) 25   (C) 45   (D) 50   (E) 70

Questions 7–8 refer to the following figure, in which M, N, O, and P are the midpoints of the sides of rectangle $ABCD$.

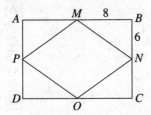

7. What is the perimeter of quadrilateral $MNOP$?

    (A) 24   (B) 32   (C) 40   (D) 48   (E) 60

8. What is the area of quadrilateral $MNOP$?

    (A) 48   (B) 60   (C) 72   (D) 96   (E) 108

Questions 9–10 refer to the following figure, in which M and N are midpoints of two of the sides of square $ABCD$.

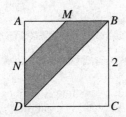

9. What is the perimeter of the shaded region?

    (A) 3   (B) $2 + 3\sqrt{2}$ (C) $3 + 2\sqrt{2}$ (D) 5   (E) 8

10. What is the area of the shaded region?

    (A) 1.5   (B) 1.75   (C) 3   (D) $2\sqrt{2}$ (E) $3\sqrt{2}$

Quantitative Comparison Questions

| Column A | Column B |

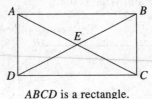

ABCD is a rectangle.

| 11. | The area of $\triangle AED$ | The area of $\triangle EDC$ |

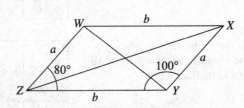

WXYZ is a parallelogram.

| 12. | Diagonal WY | Diagonal XZ |

| 13. | The perimeter of a 30-60-90 right triangle whose longer leg is $2x$ | The perimeter of a five-sided polygon all of whose sides are x |

| 14. | The perimeter of a rectangle whose area is 50 | 28 |

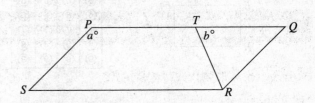

In parallelogram $PQRS$, TR bisects $\angle QRS$.

| 15. | a | $2b$ |

Grid-in Questions

16. In the figure below, *ABCD* is a parallelogram. What is the value of *y* − *z*?

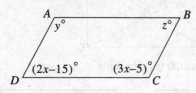

17. In the figure below, what is the sum of the measures of all of the marked angles?

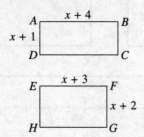

18. If, in the figures below, the area of rectangle *ABCD* is 100, what is the area of rectangle *EFGH*?

A ——*x* + 4—— B
x + 1 [   ]
D ——————— C

E ——*x* + 3—— F
[   ] *x* + 2
H ——————— G

19. How many sides does a polygon have if the measure of each interior angle is 8 times the measure of each exterior angle?

20. In quadrilateral *WXYZ*, the measure of ∠*Z* is 10 more than twice the average of the measures of the other three angles. What is the measure of ∠*Z*?

Answer Key

1. **C**	4. **D**	7. **C**	10. **A**	13. **A**	
2. **D**	5. **C**	8. **D**	11. **C**	14. **A**	
3. **C**	6. **A**	9. **B**	12. **B**	15. **C**	

16. | 5 | 0

17. | 7 | 2 | 0

18. | 1 | 0 | 2

19. | 1 | 8

20. | 1 | 5 | 0

Answer Explanations

1. **C.** Each of the four small triangles is a 45-45-90 right triangle whose hypotenuse is 2. Therefore, each leg is $\frac{2}{\sqrt{2}} = \sqrt{2}$. The perimeter of each small triangle is $2 + 2\sqrt{2}$, and the sum of the perimeters is 4 times as great: $8 + 8\sqrt{2}$.

2. **D.** Draw a diagram and label it.

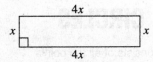

Since the area is 144, then
$$144 = 4x^2 \Rightarrow x^2 = 36 \Rightarrow x = 6.$$
The width is 6, the length is 24, and the perimeter is 60.

3. **C.** The sum of the degree measures of the angles of a five-sided polygon is $(5 - 2) \times 180 = 3 \times 180 = 540$. Then:
$$540 = 2x + 3x + 3x + 5x + 5x = 18x \Rightarrow$$
$$x = 540 \div 18 = 30.$$
The degree measure of the smallest angle is $2x$: $2 \times 30 = 60$.

4. **D.** Draw a diagram and label it. Since $\triangle BCD$ is a 30-60-90 right triangle, BC is 6 (half the hypotenuse) and CD is $6\sqrt{3}$. Then the area of rectangle $ABCD$ is $\ell w = 6(6\sqrt{3}) = 36\sqrt{3}$.

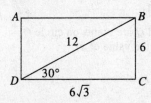

5. **C.** The perimeter of the rectangle is $2(\ell + w) = 2(6 + 6\sqrt{3}) = 12 + 12\sqrt{3}$.

6. **A.** Let x represent the side of the square. Then the dimensions of the rectangle are $(x + 5)$ and $(x - 5)$, and its area is $(x + 5)(x - 5) = x^2 - 25$. Since 45 is the area of the square, $x^2 = 45$, and so $x^2 - 25 = 20$.

7. **C.** Each triangle surrounding quadrilateral *MNOP* is a 6-8-10 right triangle. Then, each side of the quadrilateral is 10, and its perimeter is 40.

8. **D.** The area of each of the triangles is $\frac{1}{2}(6)(8) = 24$, so together the four triangles have an area of 96. The area of the rectangle is $16 \times 12 = 192$. Therefore, the area of quadrilateral *MNOP* is $192 - 96 = 96$.
    Note: Joining the midpoints of the four sides of any quadrilateral creates a parallelogram whose area is one-half the area of the original quadrilateral.

9. **B.** Since M and N are midpoints of sides of length 2, AM, MB, AN, and ND are all equal to 1. Also, $MN = \sqrt{2}$, since it's the hypotenuse of an isosceles right triangle whose legs are 1; and $BD = 2\sqrt{2}$, since it's the hypotenuse of an isosceles right triangle whose legs are 2. Then, the perimeter of the shaded region is $1 + \sqrt{2} + 1 + 2\sqrt{2} = 2 + 3\sqrt{2}$.

10. **A.** The area of $\triangle ABD = \frac{1}{2}(2)(2) = 2$, and the area of $\triangle AMN = \frac{1}{2}(1)(1) = 0.5$. The area of the shaded region is $2 - 0.5 = 1.5$.

11. C. The area of $\triangle AED$ is $\dfrac{1}{2}\,w\!\left(\dfrac{\ell}{2}\right)=\dfrac{\ell w}{4}$. The area

of $\triangle EDC$ is $\dfrac{1}{2}\,\ell\!\left(\dfrac{w}{2}\right)=\dfrac{\ell w}{4}$. *Note:* Each of the

four small triangles has the same area.

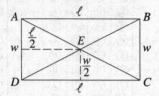

12. B. By KEY FACT J6, since $\angle Z$ is acute and $\angle Y$ is obtuse,

$(WY)^2 < a^2 + b^2$, whereas $(XZ)^2 > a^2 + b^2$.

13. A. Column A: By KEY FACT J11, the shorter leg

of the 30-60-90 right triangle is $\dfrac{2x}{\sqrt{3}}=\dfrac{2\sqrt{3}}{3}\,x$,

and the hypotenuse is twice as large, or

$\dfrac{4\sqrt{3}}{3}\,x$. Then,

$$\text{perimeter} = 2x + \frac{2\sqrt{3}}{3}\,x\ \frac{4\sqrt{3}}{3}\,x =$$

$$\left(2+\frac{2\sqrt{3}}{3}+\frac{4\sqrt{3}}{3}\right)\!x = (2+2\sqrt{3})x.$$

Column B: Clearly, the perimeter of the polygon is $5x$.
Since $2 + 2\sqrt{3} \approx 5.4$, Column A is greater.

14. A. The perimeter of a rectangle of area 50 can be as large as we like, but it is smallest when the rectangle is a square. In that case, each side is $\sqrt{50}$, which is greater than 7, and so the perimeter is greater than 28.

15. C. TR is a transversal cutting parallel sides PQ and RS, so $b = x$ and $2b = 2x$. However, since the opposite angles of a parallelogram are equal, $a = 2x$, so $a = 2b$.

16. (50) The sum of the measures of two consecutive angles of a parallelogram is 180, so

$$180 = (3x - 5) + (2x - 15) = 5x - 20 \Rightarrow$$
$$5x = 200 \Rightarrow x = 40.$$

Since opposite angles of a parallelogram are equal, $y = 3x - 5 = 115$ and $z = 2x - 15 = 65$. Then $y - z = 50$.

17. (720) Each of the 10 marked angles is an exterior angle of the pentagon. If we take one angle at each vertex, the sum of those five angles is

360; the sum of the other five is also 360: $360 + 360 = 720$.

18. (102) The area of rectangle $ABCD =$ $(x + 1)(x + 4) = x^2 + 5x + 4$. The area of rectangle $EFGH = (x + 2)(x + 3) = x^2 + 5x + 6$, which is exactly 2 more than the area of rectangle $ABCD$: $100 + 2 = 102$.

19. (18) The sum of the degree measures of an interior and exterior angle is 180, so $180 = 8x + x = 9x \Rightarrow$ $x = 20$. Since the sum of the degree measures of all the exterior angles of a polygon is 360, there are $360 \div 20 = 18$ angles and, of course, 18 sides.

20. (150) Let W, X, Y, and Z represent the measures of the four angles. Since $W + X + Y + Z = 360$, then $W + X + Y = 360 - Z$. Also:

$$Z = 10 + 2\!\left(\frac{W+X+Y}{3}\right) = 10 + 2\!\left(\frac{360-Z}{3}\right)\!.$$

Then:

$$Z = 10 + \frac{2}{3}(360) - \frac{2}{3}Z = 10 + 240 - \frac{2}{3}Z$$

$$\Rightarrow \frac{5}{3}Z = 250 \Rightarrow Z = 150.$$

12-L CIRCLES

A *circle* consists of all the points that are the same distance from one fixed point, called the *center*. That distance is called the *radius* of the circle. The figure at the right is a circle of radius 1 unit whose center is at the point O. A, B, C, D, and E, which are each 1 unit from O, are all points on circle O. The word *radius* is also used to represent any of the line segments joining the center and a point on the circle. The plural of *radius* is *radii*. In circle O, above, OA, OB, OC, OD, and OE are all radii. If a circle has radius r, each of the radii is r units long.

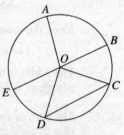

Key Fact L1

Any triangle, such as $\triangle COD$ in the figure above, formed by connecting the endpoints of two radii is isosceles.

Example 1.

If P and Q are points on circle O, what is the value of x?

Solution. Since △*POQ* is isosceles, angles *P* and *Q* have the same measure. Then:

$$70 + x + x = 180 \Rightarrow 2x = 110 \Rightarrow x = 55.$$

A line segment, such as *BE* in circle *O* at the beginning of this section, whose endpoints are on a circle and that passes through the center is called a **diameter**. Since *BE* is made up of two radii, *OB* and *OE*, a diameter is twice as long as a radius.

Key Fact L2

If *d* is the diameter and *r* the radius of a circle, then *d* = 2*r*.

Key Fact L3

A diameter is the longest line segment that can be drawn in a circle.

| Column A | Column B |

Example 2.

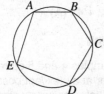

The radius of the circle is $\frac{1}{2}$.

| AB + BC + CD + DE + EA | 5 |

Solution. Since the radius of the circle is $\frac{1}{2}$, the diameter is 1. Therefore, the length of each of the five line segments is less than 1, and the sum of their lengths is less than 5. The answer is **B**.

The total length around a circle, from *A* to *B* to *C* to *D* to *E* and back to *A*, is called the **circumference** of the circle. In every circle the ratio of the circumference to the diameter is exactly the same and is denoted by the symbol π (the Greek letter pi).

Key Fact L4

For every circle:

$$\pi = \frac{\text{circumference}}{\text{diameter}} = \frac{C}{d} \quad \text{or} \quad C = \pi d \quad \text{or} \quad C = 2\pi r.$$

Key Fact L5

The value of π is *approximately* 3.14.

 CALCULATOR HINT

On almost every question on the SAT I that involves circles, you are expected to leave your answer in terms of π, So don't multiply by 3.14 unless you must. If you need an approximation—to test a choice, for example—then use your calculator. If you have a scientific calculator, use the π key. This not only is faster and more accurate than punching in 3.14, but also avoids careless mistakes in entering.

| Column A | Column B |

Example 3.

| The circumference of a circle whose diameter is 12 | The perimeter of a square whose side is 12 |

Solution. Column A: *C* = π*d* = π(12).
Column B: *P* = 4*s* = 4(12).

Since 4 > π, Column **B** is greater. (*Note: P* = 48 and *C* = 12π ≈ 12(3.14) = 37.68, but *you should not have calculated this*.)

An **arc** consists of two points on a circle and all the points between them. If two points, such as *P* and *Q* in circle *O*, are the endpoints of a diameter, they divide the circle into two arcs called **semicircles**. On the SAT I, *arc AB* always refers to the small arc joining *A* and *B*. If we wanted to refer to the large arc going from *A* to *B* through *P* and *Q*, we would say *arc APB* or *arc AQB*.

An angle whose vertex is at the center of a circle is called a **central angle**.

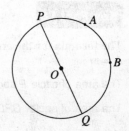

Key Fact L6

The degree measure of a complete circle is 360°.

Key Fact L7

The degree measure of an arc equals the degree measure of the central angle that intercepts it.

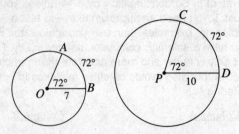

CAUTION: Degree measure is *not* a measure of length. In the circles above, arc *AB* and arc *CD* each measure 72°, even though arc *CD* is much longer.

How long *is* arc *CD*? Since the radius of circle *P* is 10, its circumference is 20π [$2\pi r = 2\pi(10) = 20\pi$]. Since there are 360° in a circle, arc *CD* is $\frac{72}{360}$, or $\frac{1}{5}$, of the circumference: $\frac{1}{5}(20\pi) = 4\pi$.

Key Fact L8

The formula for the area of a circle of radius r is $A = \pi r^2$.

The area of circle *P* above is $\pi(10)^2 = 100\pi$ square units.

The area of sector *CPD* is $\frac{1}{5}$ of the area of the circle:

$\frac{1}{5}(100\pi) = 20\pi.$

Key Fact L9

If an arc measures $x°$, the length of the arc is $\frac{x}{360}(2\pi r)$; and the area of the sector formed by the arc and two radii is $\frac{x}{360}(\pi r^2)$.

Examples 4 and 5 refer to the circle below.

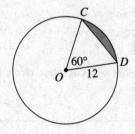

Example 4.

What is the area of the shaded region?

(A) $144\pi - 144\sqrt{3}$ (B) $144\pi - 36\sqrt{3}$ (C) $144\pi - 72$

(D) $24\pi - 36\sqrt{3}$ (E) $24\pi - 72$

Solution. The area of the shaded region is equal to the area of sector *COD* minus the area of $\triangle COD$. The area of the circle is $\pi(12)^2 = 144\pi$. Since $\frac{60}{360} = \frac{1}{6}$, the area of sector *COD* is $\frac{1}{6}(144\pi) = 24\pi$. Since m$\angle O = 60$, m$\angle C$ + m$\angle D = 120$; but $\triangle COD$ is isosceles, so $\angle C = \angle D$. Therefore, each measures 60°, and the triangle is equilateral. Finally, by KEY FACT J14,

$$\text{area of } \triangle COD = \frac{12^2\sqrt{3}}{4} = \frac{144\sqrt{3}}{4} = 36\sqrt{3},$$

so the area of the shaded region is **$24\pi - 36\sqrt{3}$ (D)**.

Example 5.

What is the perimeter of the shaded region?

(A) $12 + 4\pi$ (B) $12 + 12\pi$ (C) $12 + 24\pi$
(D) $12\sqrt{2} + 4\pi$ (E) $12\sqrt{2} + 24\pi$

Solution. Since $\triangle COD$ is equilateral, $CD = 12$. Since

$$\text{circumference of circle} = 2\pi(12) = 24\pi \Rightarrow$$
$$\text{arc } CD = \frac{1}{6}(24\pi) = 4\pi,$$

the perimeter is **$12 + 4\pi$ (A)**.

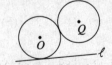 **CALCULATOR HINT**

If you do Examples 4 and 5 correctly, you won't use your calculator at all (except possibly to divide 144 by 4). On multiple-choice questions involving circles, the choices are always in terms of π, so you certainly shouldn't multiply anything by 3.14. However, if you should forget how to find the circumference or area of a circle, you will be happy to have a calculator. Suppose that in Example 5 you see that $CD = 12$, but you don't remember how to find the length of arc *CD*. From the diagram, it is clear that it is slightly longer than *CD*, say 13, so you know that the perimeter is *about* 25. Now, use your calculator. Evaluate each choice to see which one is closest to 25: (A) $12 + 4\pi \approx 12 + 4(3.14) = 24.56$, which is quite close; (B) $12 + 12\pi \approx 49.68$, which is way too large; (C) is even larger; and (E) is larger yet; at 29.5 (D) isn't as absurd as the other wrong choices, but it is still too large. The answer is **A**. You could approximate and test the choices in Example 4 in the same way.

Line ℓ is tangent to circle *O*.
Circles *O* and *Q* are tangent.

The circle is inscribed in the square.   The pentagon is inscribed in the circle.

A line and a circle or two circles are **tangent** if they have only one point of intersection. A circle is **inscribed** in a triangle or square if it is tangent to each side. A polygon is **inscribed** in a circle if each vertex is on the circle.

Example 6.

A is the center of a circle whose radius is 10, and *B* is the center of a circle whose diameter is 10. If these two circles are tangent to one another, what is the area of the circle whose diameter is *AB*?

(A) 30π (B) 56.25π (C) 100π (D) 225π (E) 400π

Solution. Draw a diagram. Since the diameter, *AB*, of the dotted circle is 15, its radius is 7.5 and its area is $\pi(7.5)^2 = \mathbf{56.25\pi}$ **(B)**. (Note that you should use your calculator to square 7.5 but not to multiply by π.)

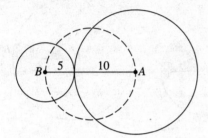

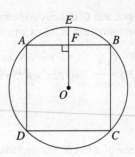

Example 7.

In the figure above, square *ABCD* is inscribed in a circle whose center is *O* and whose radius is 4. If $EO \perp AB$ at *F*, what is the length of *EF*?

(A) 2   (B) $\sqrt{2}$ (C) $2\sqrt{2}$ (D) $4 - \sqrt{2}$ (E) $4 - 2\sqrt{2}$

Solution. Draw diagonal *AC*. Then, $\triangle AFO$ is a 45-45-90 right triangle. Since hypotenuse *AO* is a radius, its length is 4; and by KEY FACT J8:

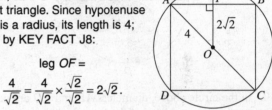

$$\text{leg } OF =$$

$$\frac{4}{\sqrt{2}} = \frac{4}{\sqrt{2}} \times \frac{\sqrt{2}}{\sqrt{2}} = 2\sqrt{2}.$$

$EO = 4$ since it is also a radius. Then

$$EF = EO - OF = \mathbf{4 - 2\sqrt{2}} \text{ (E)}.$$

Exercises on Circles

Multiple-Choice Questions

1. What is the circumference of a circle whose area is 100π?

   (A) 10   (B) 20   (C) 10π (D) 20π (E) 25π

2. What is the area of a circle whose circumference is π?

   (A) $\dfrac{\pi}{4}$ (B) $\dfrac{\pi}{2}$ (C) π (D) 2π (E) 4π

3. What is the area of a circle that is inscribed in a square of area 2?

   (A) $\dfrac{\pi}{4}$ (B) $\dfrac{\pi}{2}$ (C) π (D) $\pi\sqrt{2}$ (E) 2π

4. A square of area 2 is inscribed in a circle. What is the area of the circle?

   (A) $\dfrac{\pi}{4}$ (B) $\dfrac{\pi}{2}$ (C) π (D) $\pi\sqrt{2}$ (E) 2π

Questions 5–6 refer to the following figure.

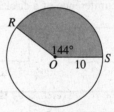

5. What is the length of arc *RS*?

   (A) 8   (B) 20   (C) 8π (D) 20π (E) 40π

6. What is the area of the shaded sector?

   (A) 8   (B) 20   (C) 8π (D) 20π (E) 40π

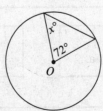

7. In the figure above, what is the value of *x* ?

   (A) 30   (B) 36   (C) 45   (D) 54   (E) 60

8. If A is the area and C the circumference of a circle, which of the following is an expression for A in terms of C?

(A) $\dfrac{C^2}{4\pi}$ (B) $\dfrac{C^2}{4\pi^2}$ (C) $2C\sqrt{\pi}$ (D) $2\,C^2\sqrt{\pi}$

(E) $\dfrac{C^2\sqrt{\pi}}{4}$

9. What is the area of a circle whose radius is the diagonal of a square whose area is 4?

(A) 2π (B) $2\pi\sqrt{2}$ (C) 4π (D) 8π (E) 16π

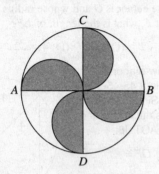

10. In the circle above, diameters AB and CD are perpendicular, and each of the four shaded regions is a semicircle. What is the ratio of the shaded area to the white area?

(A) $\dfrac{3}{4}$ (B) $\dfrac{\pi}{4}$ (C) $\dfrac{1}{1}$ (D) $\dfrac{4}{\pi}$ (E) $\dfrac{4}{3}$

Quantitative Comparison Questions

Column A	Column B

C is the circumference of a circle of radius r

11.

$\dfrac{C}{r}$	6

The circumference of a circle is C inches. The area of the same circle is A square inches.

12.

$\dfrac{C}{A}$	$\dfrac{A}{C}$

13.

The area of a circle of radius 2	The area of a semicircle of radius 3

Column A	Column B

14.

The perimeter of the pentagon	The circumference of the circle

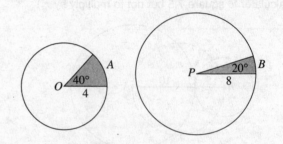

Note: Figures not drawn to scale

15.

The area of sector A	The area of sector B

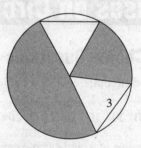

Each of the triangles is equilateral.

16.

The area of the shaded region	6π

Allison and Jessica each took a piece of wire of the same length. Allison bent hers into a circle, and Jessica bent hers into a square.

17.

The area of Allison's circle	The area of Jessica's square

Column A   Column B

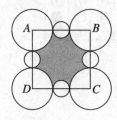

Figure 1   Figure 2

ABCD and *EFGH* are squares, and all the circles are tangent to one another and to the sides of the squares.

18.

| The area of the shaded region in Figure 1 | The area of the shaded region in Figure 2 |

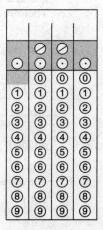

A, B, C, and *D* are the centers of the four large circles, and the sides of square *ABCD* pass through the centers of each small circle.
The large circles have radius 2,
and the small circles have diameter 2.

19.

| Twice the shaded area | The area of the square |

A square and a circle have equal areas.

20.

| The perimeter of the square | The circumference of the circle |

Grid-in Questions

21. The circumference of a circle is $a\pi$ units, and the area of the circle is $b\pi$ square units. If $a = b$, what is the radius of the circle?

22. A 9×12 rectangle is inscribed in a circle. What is the radius of the circle?

23. In the figure below, the ratio of the length of arc *AB* to the circumference of the circle is 2:15. What is the value of *y*?

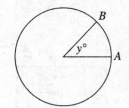

24. If the area of the shaded region is $k\pi$, what is the value of k?

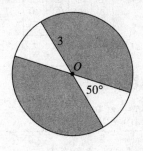

25. The first time after 12:00 that the hour hand and minute hand of a clock form a 90° angle occurs at $A\dfrac{b}{c}$ minutes after 12:00, where A is a positive integer and $\dfrac{b}{c}$ is a fraction written in lowest terms. What is the value of $A + b + c$?

Answer Key

1. **D**	5. **C**	9. **D**	13. **B**	17. **A**
2. **A**	6. **E**	10. **C**	14. **B**	18. **C**
3. **B**	7. **D**	11. **A**	15. **B**	19. **B**
4. **C**	8. **A**	12. **D**	16. **C**	20. **A**

21. $\boxed{2}$ 22. $\boxed{15/2}$ or $\boxed{7.5}$ 23. $\boxed{48}$

24. $\boxed{13/2}$ or $\boxed{6.5}$ 25. $\boxed{31}$

Answer Explanations

1. **D.** $A = \pi r^2 = 100\pi \Rightarrow r^2 = 100 \Rightarrow r = 10$.
$C = 2\pi r = 2\pi(10) = 20\pi$.

2. **A.** $C = 2\pi r = \pi \Rightarrow 2r = 1 \Rightarrow r = \dfrac{1}{2}$.

$A = \pi r^2 = \pi\left(\dfrac{1}{2}\right)^2 = \dfrac{1}{4}\pi = \dfrac{\pi}{4}$.

3. **B.** Draw a diagram. Since the area of square $ABCD$ is 2, $AD = \sqrt{2}$. Then, diameter $EF = \sqrt{2}$ and radius $OE = \dfrac{\sqrt{2}}{2}$,

so area $= \pi\left(\dfrac{\sqrt{2}}{2}\right)^2 = \dfrac{2}{4}\pi = \dfrac{\pi}{2}$.

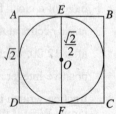

4. **C.** Draw a diagram. Since the area of square $ABCD$ is 2, $AD = \sqrt{2}$. Then diagonal $BD = \sqrt{2} \times \sqrt{2} = 2$. But BD is also a diameter of the circle, so the diameter is 2 and the radius is 1. Therefore, the area is $\pi(1)^2 = \pi$.

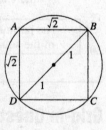

5. **C.** The length of arc $RS = \left(\dfrac{144}{360}\right)2\pi(10) =$

$\left(\dfrac{2}{5}\right)20\pi = 8\pi$. [Note that, instead of reducing $\dfrac{144}{360}$, you could have used your calculator and divided: $144 \div 360 = 0.4$, and $(0.4)(20\pi) = 8\pi$.]

6. **E.** The area of the shaded sector is $\left(\dfrac{144}{360}\right)\pi(10)^2 =$ $\left(\dfrac{2}{5}\right)100\pi = 40\pi$.

7. **D.** The triangle is isosceles, so the third (unmarked) angle is also x:
$$180 = 72 + 2x \Rightarrow 2x = 108 \Rightarrow x = 54.$$

8. **A.** $C = 2\pi r \Rightarrow r = \dfrac{C}{2\pi} \Rightarrow A = \pi\left(\dfrac{C}{2\pi}\right)^2 =$
$$\pi\left(\dfrac{C^2}{4\pi^2}\right) = \dfrac{C^2}{4\pi}.$$

9. **D.** If the area of the square is 4, each side is 2, and the length of a diagonal is $2\sqrt{2}$. The area of a circle whose radius is $2\sqrt{2}$ is $\pi(2\sqrt{2})^2 = 8\pi$.

10. **C.** We could start by letting the radius of the circle be r; but, as in any ratio problem, it is better to use a value. Assume that the radius of the circle is 2. Then the area of the circle is 4π. The radius of each semicircle is 1; and since the area of a circle of radius 1 is π, the area of each semicircle is $\dfrac{1}{2}\pi$, and the total shaded area is $4\left(\dfrac{1}{2}\pi\right) = 2\pi$. The white area is the total area minus the shaded area: $4\pi - 2\pi = 2\pi$. Therefore, the ratio of shade to white is
$$\dfrac{2\pi}{2\pi} = \dfrac{1}{1}.$$

11. **A.** By KEY FACT L4, $\pi = \dfrac{C}{d} = \dfrac{C}{2r} \Rightarrow \dfrac{C}{r} = 2\pi$, which is greater than 6.

12. **D.** Column A: $\dfrac{C}{A} = \dfrac{2\pi r}{\pi r^2} = \dfrac{2}{r}$. Similarly, Column B: $\dfrac{A}{C} = \dfrac{r}{2}$. If $r = 2$, the columns are equal; otherwise, they're not.

13. **B.** Column A: $A = \pi(2)^2 = 4\pi$.
Column B: The area of a circle of radius 3 is $\pi(3)^2 = 9\pi$, and the area of the semicircle is $\dfrac{1}{2}(9\pi) = 4.5\pi$.

14. **B.** There's nothing to calculate here. Each arc of the circle is clearly longer than the corresponding chord, which is a side of the pentagon. Therefore, the circumference of the circle, which is the sum of all the arcs, is greater than the perimeter of the pentagon, which is the sum of all the chords.

15. **B.** The area of sector A is $\dfrac{40}{360}(16\pi) = \dfrac{16\pi}{9}$. The area of sector B is $\dfrac{\overset{1}{\cancel{20}}}{\underset{18}{\cancel{360}}}(64\pi) = \dfrac{64\pi}{18} = \dfrac{32\pi}{9}$, which is twice as large as the area of sector A.

16. **C.** Since the triangles are equilateral, the two white central angles each measure 60°, and their sum is 120°. Then, the white area is $\dfrac{120}{360} = \dfrac{1}{3}$ of the circle, and the shaded area is $\dfrac{2}{3}$ of the circle. Since the area of the circle is $\pi(3)^2 = 9\pi$, the shaded area is $\dfrac{2}{3}(9\pi) = 6\pi$.

17. **A.** If L represents the length of the wire, then L is both the circumference of Allison's circle and the perimeter of Jessica's square.
Column A: $L = 2\pi r \Rightarrow r = \dfrac{L}{2\pi} \Rightarrow$
$$A = \pi\left(\dfrac{L}{2\pi}\right)^2 = \pi\left(\dfrac{L^2}{4\pi^2}\right) = \dfrac{L^2}{4\pi}.$$
Column B: $L = 4s \Rightarrow s = \dfrac{L}{4} \Rightarrow A = \left(\dfrac{L}{4}\right)^2 = \dfrac{L^2}{16}$.
When two fractions have the same numerator, the one with the smaller denominator is greater, and $4\pi < 16$.

18. **C.** In Figure 1, since $BC = 12$, the diameter of each circle is 6, and each radius is 3. Therefore, the area of each circle is 9π, and the total area of the four circles is 36π. Similarly, in Figure 2, the radius of each circle is 2, and so the area of each circle is 4π, and the total area of the nine circles is 36π. In the two figures, the white areas are equal, as are the shaded areas.

19. **B.** Since the side of square $ABCD$ is 6, the area is 36. The white area inside the square consists of four quarter-circles of radius 2 and four semicircles of radius 1. The combined area of the four quarter-circles is 4π, the same as the area of a circle of radius 2; and together the four semicircles have an area of 2π, the same area as two circles of radius 1. Therefore, the total white area inside the square is 6π, which is more than 18 and hence more than half the area of the square. The shaded area, then, is less than half the area of the square, and twice the shaded area is less than the area of the square.

20. **A.** Let A represent the area of the square and the circle.
Column A: $A = s^2 \Rightarrow s = \sqrt{A} \Rightarrow P = 4\sqrt{A}$.
Column B: $A = \pi r^2 \Rightarrow r = \sqrt{\dfrac{A}{\pi}} \Rightarrow$
$$C = 2\pi\left(\dfrac{\sqrt{A}}{\sqrt{\pi}}\right) = 2\sqrt{\pi}\sqrt{A}.$$
Since $\pi < 4$, $\sqrt{\pi} < 2 \Rightarrow 2\sqrt{\pi} < 4$.

21. **(2)** Since $C = a\pi = A$, then $2\pi r = \pi r^2 \Rightarrow 2r = r^2 \Rightarrow r = 2$.

22. (7.5) Draw a diagram. By the Pythagorean theorem (or by recognizing a 3x-4x-5x triangle with $x = 3$), diagonal AC is 15. But AC is also a diameter of the circle, so the diameter is 15 and the radius is 7.5.

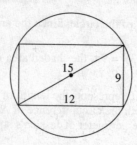

23. (48) Since arc AB is $\dfrac{2}{15}$ of the circumference,

    y is $\dfrac{2}{15} \times 360 = 48$.

24. $\left(\dfrac{13}{2}\text{ or }6.5\right)$ The area of the circle is 9π; and

    since the white region is $\dfrac{100}{360} = \dfrac{5}{18}$ of the

    circle, the shaded region is $\dfrac{13}{18}$ of it:

    $$\dfrac{13}{18} \times 9\pi = \dfrac{13}{2}\pi \text{ or } 6.5\pi.$$

25. (31) In 1 hour, or 60 minutes, the hour hand of a clock moves through an angle of 30°, so it moves through 30 ÷ 60 = 0.5° every minute. In 1 hour, the minute hand moves through 360°, so it moves 6° every minute. Therefore, every minute the minute hand gains 5.5° on the hour hand, so it will

    take $\dfrac{90}{5.5} = \dfrac{180}{11} = 16\dfrac{4}{11}$

    minutes to gain 90°. Finally, $16 + 4 + 11 = 31$.

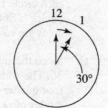

12-M SOLID GEOMETRY

There is very little solid geometry on the SAT I. Basically, all you need to know are the formulas for the volumes and surface areas of rectangular solids (including cubes) and cylinders.

A **rectangular solid** or **box** is a solid formed by six rectangles, called **faces**. The sides of the rectangles are called **edges**. As shown in the diagram that follows, the edges are called the **length**, **width**, and **height**.

A **cube** is a rectangular solid in which the length, width, and height are equal, so that all the edges are the same length.

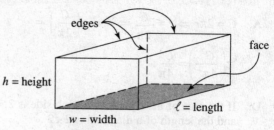

RECTANGULAR SOLID

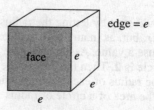

CUBE

The **volume** of a solid, which is the amount of space it occupies, is measured in **cubic units**. One cubic unit is the amount of space occupied by a cube all of whose edges are 1 unit long. In the figure above, if each edge of the cube is 1 inch, the area of each face is 1 square inch, and the volume of the cube is 1 cubic inch.

Key Fact M1

The formula for the volume of a rectangular solid is $V = \ell wh$.

In a cube, all the edges are equal. Therefore, if e is the edge, the formula for the volume is $V = e^3$.

Example 1.

The base of a rectangular tank is 2 feet wide and 4 feet long; the height of the tank is 20 inches. If water is pouring into the tank at the rate of 2 cubic inches per second, how many <u>hours</u> will be required to fill the tank?

Solution. Draw a diagram. Change all units to inches. Then the volume of the tank is $24 \times 48 \times 20 = 23{,}040$ cubic inches. At 2 cubic inches per second:

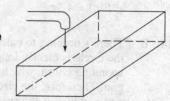

$$\text{required time} = \dfrac{23{,}040}{2} = 11{,}520 \text{ seconds} = \dfrac{11{,}520}{60} =$$

$$192 \text{ minutes} = \dfrac{192}{60} = \textbf{3.2 hours.}$$

The **surface area** of a rectangular solid is the sum of the areas of the six faces. Since the top and bottom faces are equal, the front and back faces are equal, and the left and right faces are equal, we can calculate the area of one face from each pair and then double the sum. In a cube, each of the six faces has the same area.

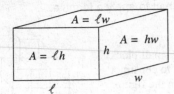

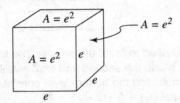

The formula for the surface area of a rectangular solid is $A = 2(\ell w + \ell h + wh)$. The formula for the surface area of a cube is $A = 6e^2$.

Example 2.

The volume of a cube is v cubic yards, and its surface area is a square feet. If $v = a$, what is the length, in inches, of each edge?

Solution. Draw a diagram. If e is the length of the edge in yards, then $3e$ is the length in feet, and $36e$ is the length in inches. Therefore, $v = e^3$ and $a = 6(3e)^2 = 6(9e^2) = 54e^2$.

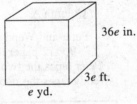

Since $v = a$, $e^3 = 54e^2 \Rightarrow e = 54$; the length of each edge is $36(54) = $ **1944** inches.

A *diagonal* of a box is a line segment joining a vertex on the top of the box to the opposite vertex on the bottom. A box has four diagonals, all the same length. In the box below they are line segments AG, BH, CE, and DF.

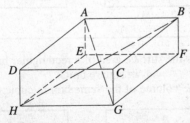

A diagonal of a box is the longest line segment that can be drawn between two points on the box.

If the dimensions of a box are ℓ, w, and h, and if d is the length of a diagonal, then $d^2 = \ell^2 + w^2 + h^2$.

For example, in the box below:

$$d^2 = 3^2 + 4^2 + 12^2 = 9 + 16 + 144 = 169 \Rightarrow d = 13.$$

This formula is really just an extended Pythagorean theorem. *EG* is the diagonal of rectangular base *EFGH*. Since the sides of the base are 3 and 4, *EG* is 5. Now, $\triangle CGE$ is a right triangle whose legs are 12 and 5, so diagonal *CE* is 13. (The only reason we didn't use the Pythagorean theorem is that these triangles are so familiar to us.)

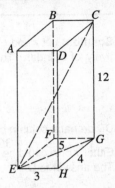

Example 3.

What is the length of a diagonal of a cube whose sides are 1?

Solution. Use the formula:

$$d^2 = 1^2 + 1^2 + 1^2 = 3 \Rightarrow d = \sqrt{3}.$$

Without the formula you would draw a diagram and label it. Since the base is a 1×1 square, its diagonal is $\sqrt{2}$. Then the diagonal of the cube is the hypotenuse of a right triangle whose legs are 1 and $\sqrt{2}$, so

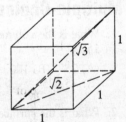

$$d^2 = 1^2 + (\sqrt{2})^2 = 1 + 2 = 3, \quad \text{and} \quad d = \sqrt{3}.$$

A *cylinder* is similar to a rectangular solid except that the base is a circle instead of a rectangle. The volume of a cylinder is the area of its circular base (πr^2) times its height (h). The surface area of a cylinder depends on whether you are envisioning a tube, such as a straw, without a top or bottom, or a can, which has both a top and a bottom.

The formula for the volume, V, of a cylinder whose circular base has radius r and whose height is h is $V = \pi r^2 h$. The surface area, A, of the side of the cylinder is the circumference of the circular base times the height: $A = 2\pi rh$. The area of the top and bottom are each πr^2, so the total area of a can is given by the formula $A = 2\pi rh + 2\pi r^2$.

Column A	Column B

Example 4.

The radius of cylinder II equals the height of cylinder I. The height of cylinder II equals the radius of cylinder I.

The volume of cylinder I	The volume of cylinder II

Solution. Let r and h be the radius and height, respectively, of cylinder I. Then

	Column A	Column B
	$\pi r^2 h$	$\pi h^2 r$
Divide each column by πrh:	r	h

Either r or h could be greater, or the two could be equal. The answer is **D**.

You now know the only formulas you will need. Any other solid geometry questions that may appear on the SAT I will require you to visualize a situation and reason it out, rather than to apply a formula.

Example 5.

How many small blocks are needed to construct the tower in the figure at the right?

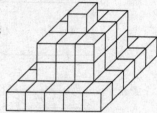

Solution. You need to "see" the answer. The top level consists of 1 block, the second and third levels consist of 9 blocks each, and the bottom layer consists of 25 blocks. The total is $1 + 9 + 9 + 25 = $ **44**.

Exercises on Solid Geometry

Multiple-Choice Questions

1. What is the volume of a cube whose surface area is 150?

    (A) 25   (B) 100   (C) 125   (D) 1000
    (E) 15,625

2. What is the surface area of a cube whose volume is 64?

    (A) 16   (B) 64   (C) 96   (D) 128   (E) 384

3. A solid metal cube of side 3 inches is placed in a rectangular tank whose length, width, and height are 3, 4, and 5 inches, respectively. What is the volume, in cubic units, of water that the tank can now hold?

    (A) 20   (B) 27   (C) 33   (D) 48   (E) 60

4. The height, h, of a cylinder is equal to the edge of a cube. If the cylinder and the cube have the same volume, what is the radius of the cylinder?

    (A) $\dfrac{h}{\sqrt{\pi}}$ (B) $h\sqrt{\pi}$ (C) $\dfrac{\sqrt{\pi}}{h}$ (D) $\dfrac{h^2}{\pi}$ (E) πh^2

5. If the height of a cylinder is 4 times its circumference, what is the volume of the cylinder in terms of its circumference, C?

    (A) $\dfrac{C^3}{\pi}$ (B) $\dfrac{2C^3}{\pi}$ (C) $\dfrac{2C^2}{\pi^2}$ (D) $\dfrac{\pi C^2}{4}$
    (E) $4\pi C^3$

Quantitative Comparison Questions

Column A	Column B

Peter and Wendy each roll a sheet of 9×12 paper to form a cylinder. Peter tapes the two 9-inch edges together. Wendy tapes the two 12-inch edges together.

6.

The volume of Peter's cylinder	The volume of Wendy's cylinder

7.

The volume of a cube whose edges are 5	The volume of a box whose dimensions are 4, 5, and 6

A is the surface area of a rectangular box in square units.
V is the volume of the same box in cubic units.

8.

A	V

Column A	Column B

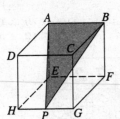

P is a point on edge *GH* of cube *ABCDEFGH*.
Each edge of the cube is 1.

9. The area of △*ABP* | 1

10.

The volume of a sphere whose radius is 1	The volume of a cube whose edge is 1

Grid-in Questions

11. The sum of the lengths of all the edges of a cube is 6 centimeters. What is the volume, in cubic centimeters, of the cube?

12. A 5-foot-long cylindrical pipe has an inner diameter of 6 feet and an outer diameter of 8 feet. If the total surface area (inside and out, including the ends) is $k\pi$, what is the value of k?

13. What is the number of cubic inches in 1 cubic foot?

14. A rectangular tank has a base that is 10 centimeters by 5 centimeters and a height of 20 centimeters. If the tank is half full of water, by how many centimeters will the water level rise if 325 cubic centimeters are poured into the tank?

15. Three identical balls fit snugly into a cylindrical can: the radius of the spheres equals the radius of the can, and the balls just touch the bottom and the top of the can. If the formula for the volume of a sphere is $V = \frac{4}{3}\pi r^3$, what fraction of the volume of the can is taken up by the balls?

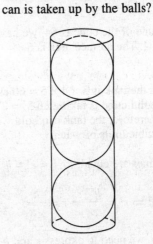

Answer Key

1. **C**	3. **C**	5. **A**	7. **A**	9. **B**
2. **C**	4. **A**	6. **A**	8. **D**	10. **A**

11. `1 / 8` or `.1 2 5`

12. `8 4`

13. `1 7 2 8`

14. `6 . 5`

15. `2 / 3` or `.6 6 6`

Answer Explanations

1. **C.** Since the surface area is 150, each of the six faces of the cube is a square whose area is $150 \div 6 = 25$. Then, each edge is 5, and the volume is $5^3 = 125$.

2. **C.** Since the volume of the cube is 64, we have $e^3 = 64 \Rightarrow e = 4$. The surface area is $6e^2 = 6 \times 16 = 96$.

3. **C.** The volume of the tank is $3 \times 4 \times 5 = 60$ cubic units, but the solid cube is taking up $3^3 = 27$ cubic units. Therefore, the tank can hold $60 - 27 = 33$ cubic units of water.

4. **A.** Since the volumes are equal, $\pi r^2 h = e^3 = h^3$. Therefore,
$$\pi r^2 = h^2 \Rightarrow r^2 = \frac{h^2}{\pi} \Rightarrow r = \frac{h}{\sqrt{\pi}}.$$

5. **A.** Since $V = \pi r^2 h$, we need to express r and h in terms of C. It is given that $h = 4C$; and since

$C = 2\pi r$, then $r = \dfrac{C}{2\pi}$. Therefore,
$$V = \pi \left(\frac{C}{2\pi}\right)^2 (4C) = \pi \left(\frac{C^2}{4\pi^2}\right)(4C) = \frac{C^3}{\pi}.$$

6. **A.** Drawing a diagram makes it easier to visualize the problem. The volume of a cylinder is $\pi r^2 h$. In each case, we know the height but have to determine the radius in order to calculate the volume.

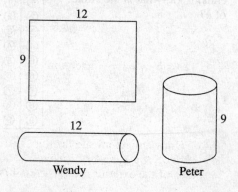

Wendy

Peter

Peter's cylinder has a circumference of 12:

$$2\pi r = 12 \Rightarrow r = \frac{12}{2\pi} = \frac{6}{\pi} \Rightarrow$$

$$V = \pi\left(\frac{6}{\pi}\right)^2(9) = \pi\left(\frac{36}{\pi^2}\right)(9) = \frac{324}{\pi}.$$

Wendy's cylinder has a circumference of 9:

$$2\pi r = 9 \Rightarrow r = \frac{9}{2\pi} \Rightarrow$$

 $$V = \pi\left(\frac{9}{2\pi}\right)^2(12) = \pi\left(\frac{81}{4\pi^2}\right)(12) = \frac{243}{\pi}.$$

7. **A.** Column A: $V = 5^3 = 125$.
   Column B: $V = 4 \times 5 \times 6 = 120$.

8. **D.** There is no relationship between the two columns. If the box is a cube of edge 1, the area is 6 and the volume is 1. If the box is a cube of edge 10, the area is 600 and the volume is 1000.

9. **B.** The base, AB, of $\triangle ABP$ is 1. Since the diagonal is the longest line segment in the cube, the height, h, of the triangle is definitely less than the diagonal, which is $\sqrt{1^2+1^2+1^2} = \sqrt{3}$. Therefore, the area of the triangle is less than

    $\frac{1}{2}(1)\sqrt{3} \approx 0.87$, which is less than 1. (You could also have just calculated the area:

   $h = BG = \sqrt{2}$, so the area is $\frac{1}{2}\sqrt{2} \approx 0.71$.)

10. **A.** You probably don't know how to find the volume of a sphere; fortunately, you don't need to. You should be able to visualize from the given dimensions that the sphere is *much* larger than the cube. (In fact, it is more than 4 times as large.)

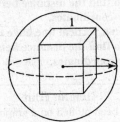

11. $\left(\frac{1}{8} \text{ or } .125\right)$ Since a cube has 12 edges, we have

   $12e = 6 \Rightarrow e = \frac{1}{2}$. Therefore,

   $V = e^3 = \left(\frac{1}{2}\right)^3 = \frac{1}{8}$ or $.125$.

12. **(84)** Draw a diagram and label it. Since the surface of a cylinder is given by $A = 2\pi rh$, the area of the exterior is $2\pi(4)(5) = 40\pi$, and the

area of the interior is $2\pi(3)(5) = 30\pi$. The area of *each* shaded end is the area of the outer circle minus the area of the inner circle: $16\pi - 9\pi = 7\pi$, so

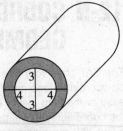

total surface area =
$40\pi + 30\pi + 7\pi + 7\pi = 84\pi \Rightarrow k = 84$.

13. **(1728)** The volume of a cube whose edges are 1 foot can be expressed in either of two ways:

    $(1 \text{ foot})^3 = 1$ cubic foot   or
   $(12 \text{ inches})^3 = 1728$ cubic inches.

14. **(6.5)** Draw a diagram. Since the area of the base is $5 \times 10 = 50$ square centimeters, each 1 centimeter of depth has a volume of 50 cubic centimeters. Therefore, 325 cubic centimeters will raise the water level $325 \div 50 = 6.5$ centimeters.

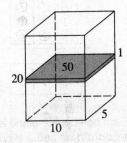

   (Note that we didn't use the fact that the tank was half full, except to be sure that the tank didn't overflow. Since the tank was half full, the water was 10 centimeters deep, and the water level could rise by 6.5 centimeters. Had the tank been three-fourths full, the water would have been 15 centimeters deep, and the extra water would have caused the level to rise 5 centimeters, filling the tank; the rest of the water would have spilled out.)

15. $\left(\frac{2}{3} \text{ or } .666\right)$ To avoid using r, assume that the radii of the spheres and the can are 1. Then the volume of each ball is $\frac{4}{3}\pi(1)^3 = \frac{4}{3}\pi$, and the total volume of the three balls is

   $3\left(\frac{4}{3}\pi\right) = 4\pi$. Since the volume of the can is $\pi(1)^2(6) = 6\pi$, the balls take up $\frac{4\pi}{6\pi} = \frac{2}{3}$ or .666 of the can.

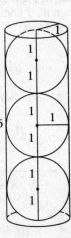

12-N COORDINATE GEOMETRY

The SAT I has very few (typically one or two) questions on coordinate geometry, and they are always considered easy or medium, never hard. Most often they deal with the coordinates of points, occasionally with the slope of a line. You are *never* required to draw a graph.

The coordinate plane is formed by two perpendicular number lines called the **x-axis** and **y-axis**, which intersect at the **origin**. The axes divide the plane into four **quadrants**, labeled, in counterclockwise order, I, II, III, and IV.

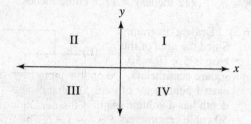

Each point in the plane is assigned two numbers, an **x-coordinate** and a **y-coordinate**, which are written as an ordered pair, **(x, y)**.

• Points to the right of the *y*-axis have positive *x*-coordinates, and those to the left have negative *x*-coordinates.
• Points above the *x*-axis have positive *y*-coordinates, and those below it have negative *y*-coordinates.
• If a point is on the *x*-axis, its *y*-coordinate is 0.
• If a point is on the *y*-axis, its *x*-coordinate is 0.

For example, point *A* in the figure below is labeled (2, 3), since it is 2 units to the right of the *y*-axis and 3 units above the *x*-axis. Similarly, point *B*(–3, –5) is in Quadrant III, 3 units to the left of the *y*-axis and 5 units below the *x*-axis.

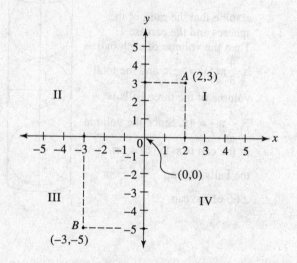

Column A   Column B

Example 1.

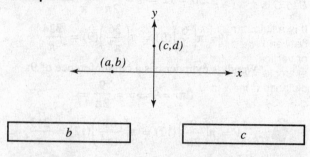

| b | c |

Example 2.

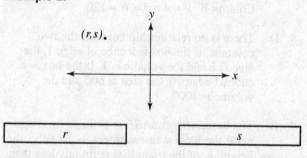

| r | s |

Solution 1. Since (a, b) lies on the *x*-axis, $b = 0$. Since (c, d) lies on the *y*-axis, $c = 0$. The answer is **C**.

Solution 2. Since (r, s) is in Quadrant II, *r* is negative and *s* is positive. The answer is **B**.

Often a question requires you to calculate the distance between two points. This task is easiest when the points lie on the same horizontal or vertical line.

Key Fact N1

• **All the points on a horizontal line have the same *y*-coordinate. To find the distance between them, subtract their *x*-coordinates.**
• **All the points on a vertical line have the same *x*-coordinate. To find the distance between them, subtract their *y*-coordinates.**

Helpful Hint

If the points have been plotted on a graph, you can find the distance between them by counting boxes.

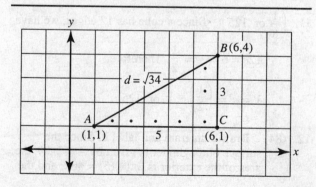

The distance from *A* to *C* is 6 − 1 = 5. The distance from *B* to *C* is 4 − 1 = 3.

It is a little harder, but not much, to find the distance between two points that are not on the same horizontal or vertical line; just use the Pythagorean theorem. For example, in the preceding figure, if *d* represents the distance from *A* to *B*, $d^2 = 5^2 + 3^2 = 25 + 9 = 34 \Rightarrow d = \sqrt{34}$.

CAUTION: You *cannot* count boxes unless the points are on the same horizontal or vertical line. The distance between *A* and *B* is 5, not 4.

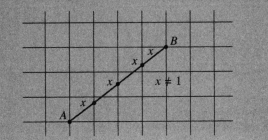

Key Fact N2

The distance, *d*, between two points, $A(x_1, y_1)$ and $B(x_2, y_2)$, can be calculated using the distance formula: $d = \sqrt{(x_2 - x_1)^2 + (y_2 - y_1)^2}$.

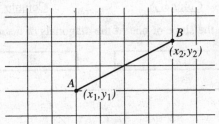

Helpful Hint

The "distance formula" is nothing more than the Pythagorean theorem. If you ever forget the formula, and you need the distance between two points that do not lie on the same horizontal or vertical line, do as follows: create a right triangle by drawing a horizontal line through one of the points and a vertical line through the other, and then use the Pythagorean theorem.

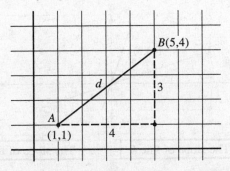

Examples 3–4 refer to the triangle in the following figure.

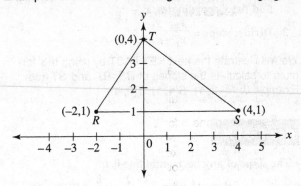

Example 3.

What is the area of △*RST*?

(A) 6   (B) 9   (C) 12   (D) 15   (E) 18

Solution. *R*(−2, 1) and *S*(4, 1) lie on the same horizontal line, so *RS* = 4 − (−2) = 6. Let that be the base of the triangle. Then the height is the distance along the vertical line from *T* to *RS*: 4 − 1 = 3. The area is $\frac{1}{2}(6)(3) = \mathbf{9\ (B)}$.

Example 4.

What is the perimeter of △*RST*?

(A) 13   (B) 14   (C) 16   (D) $11 + \sqrt{13}$ (E) $11 + \sqrt{61}$

Solution. The perimeter is *RS* + *ST* + *RT*. From the solution to Example 3, you know that *RS* = 6. Also, *ST* = 5, since it is the hypotenuse of a 3-4-5 right triangle. To calculate *RT*, use either the distance formula:

$$\sqrt{(-2 - 0)^2 + (1 - 4)^2} = \sqrt{(-2)^2 + (-3)^2} = \sqrt{4 + 9} = \sqrt{13}$$

or the Pythagorean theorem:

$$RT^2 = 2^2 + 3^2 = 4 + 9 = 13 \Rightarrow RT = \sqrt{13}.$$

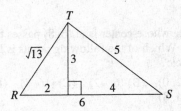

Then the perimeter is $6 + 5 + \sqrt{13} = \mathbf{11 + \sqrt{13}\ (D)}$.

The *slope* of a line is a number that indicates how steep the line is.

Key Fact N3

• **Vertical lines *do not have slopes*.**
• **To find the slope of any other line proceed as follows:**

  1. **Choose any two points, $A(x_1, y_1)$ and $B(x_2, y_2)$ on the line.**

2. Take the differences of the y-coordinates, $y_2 - y_1$, and the x-coordinates, $x_2 - x_1$.

3. Divide: slope $= \dfrac{y_2 - y_1}{x_2 - x_1}$.

We will illustrate the next KEY FACT by using this formula to calculate the slopes of RS, RT, and ST from Example 3: $R(-2, 1)$, $S(4, 1)$, $T(0, 4)$.

Key Fact N4

- The slope of any horizontal line is 0:

$$\text{slope of } RS = \frac{1-1}{4-(-2)} = \frac{0}{6} = 0.$$

- The slope of any line that goes up as you move from left to right is positive:

$$\text{slope of } RT = \frac{4-1}{0-(-2)} = \frac{3}{2}.$$

- The slope of any line that goes down as you move from left to right is negative:

$$\text{slope of } ST = \frac{1-4}{4-0} = -\frac{3}{4}.$$

Column A   Column B

Example 5.

Line ℓ passes through $(1, 2)$ and $(3, 5)$.
Line m is perpendicular to line ℓ.

The slope of ℓ	The slope of m

Solution. First, make a quick sketch. Don't use the formula to calculate the slope of ℓ. Simply notice that ℓ slopes upward, so its slope is positive, and that m slopes downward, so its slope is negative. Column **A** is greater.

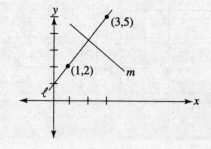

Exercises on Coordinate Geometry

Multiple-Choice Questions

1. If $A(-1, 1)$ and $B(3, -1)$ are the endpoints of one side of square $ABCD$, what is the area of the square?

(A) 12   (B) 16   (C) 20   (D) 25   (E) 36

2. If $P(2, 1)$ and $Q(8, 1)$ are two of the vertices of a rectangle, which of the following could NOT be another of the vertices?

(A) $(2, 8)$ (B) $(8, 2)$ (C) $(2, -8)$ (D) $(-2, 8)$
(E) $(8, 8)$

3. A circle whose center is at $(6, 8)$ passes through the origin. Which of the following points is NOT on the circle?

(A) $(12, 0)$ (B) $(6, -2)$ (C) $(16, 8)$ (D) $(-2, 12)$
(E) $(-4, 8)$

4. What is the slope of the line that passes through (a, b) and $\left(\dfrac{1}{a}, b\right)$?

(A) 0   (B) $\dfrac{1}{b}$ (C) $\dfrac{1-a^2}{a}$ (D) $\dfrac{a^2-1}{a}$
(E) Undefined

5. If $c \neq 0$ and the slope of the line passing through $(-c, c)$ and $(3c, a)$ is 1, which of the following is an expression for a in terms of c?

(A) $-3c$ (B) $-\dfrac{c}{3}$ (C) $2c$ (D) $3c$ (E) $5c$

Quantitative Comparison Questions

Column A   Column B

m is the slope of one of the diagonals of a square.

6.
m^2	1

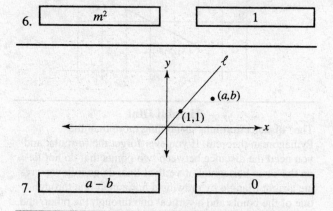

7.
$a - b$	0

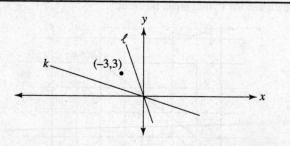

8.
The slope of line k	The slope of line ℓ

Column A   Column B

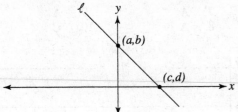

The slope of line ℓ is –0.8.
<u>Note:</u> Figure not drawn to scale

9. | c | | b |

The distance from $(b, 5)$ to $(c, -3)$ is 10.
$b < c$

10. | c – b | | 6 |

Grid-in Questions

11. If the coordinates of $\triangle RST$ are $R(0, 0)$, $S(7, 0)$, and $T(2, 5)$, what is the sum of the slopes of the three sides of the triangle?

12. If the area of circle O below is $k\pi$, what is the value of k?

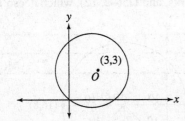

Questions 13–14 concern parallelogram $JKLM$, whose coordinates are $J(-5, 2)$, $K(-2, 6)$, $L(5, 6)$, $M(2, 2)$.

13. What is the area of parallelogram $JKLM$?

14. What is the perimeter of parallelogram $JKLM$?

15. What is the area of quadrilateral $ABCD$?

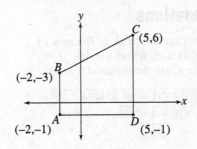

Answer Key

1. **C**	3. **D**	5. **E**	7. **A**	9. **A**
2. **D**	4. **A**	6. **D**	8. **A**	10. **C**

11. `1 . 5`

12. `1 8`

13. `2 8`

14. `2 4`

15. `3 8 . 5` or `7 7 / 2`

Answer Explanations

1. **C.** Draw a diagram and label it. The area of square $ABCD$ is s^2, where $s = AB$.
   To calculate s, use the distance formula:

   $$s = \sqrt{(3 - (-1))^2 + (-1 - 1)^2} = \sqrt{4^2 + (-2)^2} = \sqrt{16 + 4} = \sqrt{20}.$$

   So $s^2 = 20$.

2. **D.** Draw a diagram. Any point whose x-coordinate is 2 or 8 could be another vertex. Of the choices, only $(-2, 8)$ is *not* possible.

   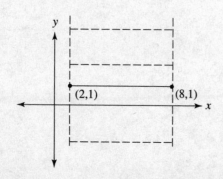

3. **D.** Draw a diagram. The radius of the circle is 10 (since it's the hypotenuse of a 6-8-10 right triangle). Which of the choices are 10 units from $(6, 8)$? First, check the easy ones; E: $(-4, 8)$ and C: $(16, 8)$ are 10 units to the left and right of $(6, 8)$, and B: $(6, -2)$ is 10 units below. What remains is to check A: $(12, 0)$, which works, and D: $(-2, 12)$, which doesn't.

   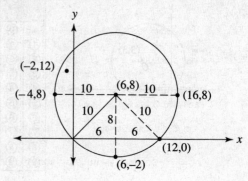

4. **A.** The formula for the slope is $\dfrac{y_2 - y_1}{x_2 - x_1}$; but before using it, look at the question again. Since the y-coordinates are equal, the numerator, and thus the fraction, equals 0.

5. **E.** The slope is equal to

$$\frac{y_2 - y_1}{x_2 - x_1} = \frac{a - c}{3c - (-c)} = \frac{a - c}{4c} = 1 \Rightarrow$$
$$a - c = 4c \Rightarrow a = 5c.$$

6. **D.** If the sides of the square are horizontal and vertical, then m is 1 or -1, and m^2 is 1. But the square could be positioned anyplace, and the slope of a diagonal could be any number.

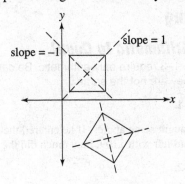

7. **A.** Line ℓ, which goes through $(0, 0)$ and $(1, 1)$ also goes through (a, a); and since (a, b) is below (a, a), $b < a$. Therefore, $a - b$ is positive.

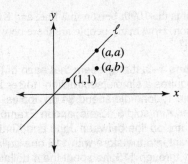

8. **A.** The line going through $(-3, 3)$ and $(0, 0)$ has slope -1. Since ℓ is steeper, its slope is a number such as -2 or -3; since k is less steep, its slope is a number such as -0.5 or -0.3. Therefore, the slope of k is greater. [If you don't realize that, let $(-3, a)$ be on k, and $(-3, b)$ be on ℓ. The slope of $k = \dfrac{a}{-3}$, and the slope of $\ell = \dfrac{b}{-3}$. Since, from the diagram, it is clear that $b > a$, then $\dfrac{b}{-3} < \dfrac{a}{-3}$.]

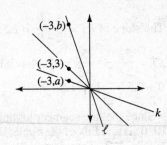

9. **A.** Since (a, b) is on the y-axis, $a = 0$; and since (c, d) is on the x-axis, $d = 0$. Then, by the slope formula,

$$-0.8 = \frac{0 - b}{c - 0} = -\frac{b}{c} \Rightarrow b = 0.8c \Rightarrow b < c.$$

10. **C.** Draw a diagram.

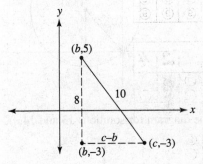

If the hypotenuse of a right triangle is 10 and one of the legs is 8, the other leg is 6 (use the Pythagorean theorem or recognize a $3x$-$4x$-$5x$ right triangle with $x = 2$). Therefore, $c - b = 6$. The columns are equal.

Alternative solution. Since the distance between the two points is 10, by the distance formula

$$10 = \sqrt{(c - b)^2 + (-3 - 5)^2} = \sqrt{(c - b)^2 + (-8)^2}$$
$$= \sqrt{(c - b)^2 + 64}.$$

Squaring both sides gives

$$100 = (c - b)^2 + 64 \Rightarrow$$
$$(c - b)^2 = 36 \Rightarrow c - b = 6.$$

11. **(1.5)** Sketch the triangle, and then calculate the slopes. Since RS is horizontal, its slope is 0.

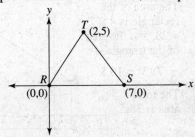

The slope of $RT = \dfrac{5-0}{2-0} = 2.5$. The slope of

$ST = \dfrac{5-0}{2-7} = \dfrac{5}{-5} = -1$. Now add:

$0 + 2.5 + (-1) = 1.5$.

12. (18) Since the line segment joining (3, 3) and (0, 0) is a radius of the circle, the radius equals $3\sqrt{2}$. Therefore,

$$\text{area} = \pi\left(3\sqrt{2}\right)^2 = 18\pi \Rightarrow k = 18.$$

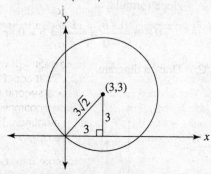

Here is the diagram for solutions 13 and 14.

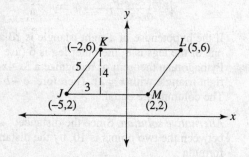

13. (28) The base is 7, and the height is 4. The area is $7 \times 4 = 28$.

14. (24) Sides JM and KL are each 7. Also, sides JK and LM are each the hypotenuse of a 3-4-5 right triangle, and so they are 5. The perimeter is $2(7 + 5) = 24$.

15. (38.5) Draw in line segment BE, dividing quadrilateral $ABCD$ into rectangle $ABED$ and $\triangle BEC$. The area of the rectangle is $4 \times 7 = 28$, and the area of the triangle is $\dfrac{1}{2}(7)(3) = 10.5$. The total area is 38.5.

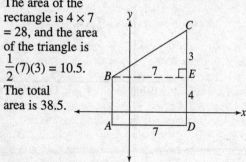

12-O COUNTING AND PROBABILITY

Some questions on the SAT I begin, "How many ...." In these problems you are being asked to count something: how many apples can Maria buy, how many dollars did Jose spend, how many pages did Elizabeth read, how many numbers satisfy a certain property, or how many ways are there to complete a particular task. Sometimes these problems can be handled by simple arithmetic. Other times it helps to use TACTIC 8-11 and systematically make a list. Occasionally it helps to know the counting principle and other strategies that we will review in this section.

Counting

Using Arithmetic to Count

Examples 1–3 require only arithmetic. Be careful, though; they are not the same.

Example 1.

John bought some apples. If he entered the store with $113 and left with $109, how much did the apples cost?

Example 2.

Kim was selling tickets for the school play. One day she sold tickets numbered 109 through 113. How many tickets did she sell that day?

Example 3.

John is the 109th person in a line, and Kim is the 113th person. How many people are there between John and Kim?

Solutions 1–3. It may seem that each of these examples requires a simple subtraction: 113 – 109 = 4. In Example 1, John did spend **$4** on apples. In Example 2, however, Kim sold **5** tickets; and in Example 3, only **3** people are on line between John and Kim! Assume that John went into the store with 113 one-dollar bills, numbered 1 through 113; he spent the 4 dollars numbered 113, 112, 111, and 110, and still had the dollars numbered 1 through 109; Kim sold the 5 tickets numbered 109, 110, 111, 112, and 113; and between John and Kim the 110th, 111th, and 112th persons—3 people— were on line.

In Example 1, you just need to subtract: 113 – 109 = 4. In Example 2, you need to subtract *and then add* 1: 113 – 109 + 1 = 4 + 1 = 5. In Example 3, you need to subtract and then *subtract 1 more*: 113 – 109 – 1 = 3. Although Example 1 is too easy for the SAT I, questions such as Examples 2 and 3 appear frequently, because they're not as obvious and they require that little extra thought. *When do you have to add or subtract 1?*

The issue is whether or not the first and last numbers are included. In Example 1, John spent dollar number

113, but he still had dollar 109 when he left the store. In Example 2, Kim sold both ticket number 109 and ticket 113. In Example 3, neither Kim (the 113th person) nor John (the 109th person) were to be counted.

Key Fact O1

To count how many integers there are between two integers, follow these rules:

- If exactly one of the endpoints is included: subtract.
- If both endpoints are included: subtract and then add 1.
- If neither endpoint is included: subtract and then subtract 1 more.

Example 4.

From 1:09 to 1:13, Elaine read pages 109 through 113 in her English book. What was her rate of reading, in pages per minute?

(A) $\frac{3}{5}$ (B) $\frac{3}{4}$ (C) $\frac{4}{5}$ (D) 1   (E) $\frac{5}{4}$

Solution. Since Elaine read both pages 109 and 113, she read $113 - 109 + 1 = 5$ pages. She started reading during the minute that started at 1:09 (and ended at 1:10). Since she stopped reading at 1:13, she did not read during the minute that began at 1:13 (and ended at 1:14), so she read for $1:13 - 1:09 = 4$ minutes. She read at the rate of $\frac{5}{4}$ pages per minute **(E)**.

Systematically Making a List

When the numbers in a problem are small, it is often better to systematically list all of the possibilities than to risk making an error in arithmetic. In Example 4, rather than even thinking about whether or not to add 1 or subtract 1 after subtracting the numbers of pages, you could have just quickly jotted down the pages Elaine read (109, 110, 111, 112, 113), and then counted them.

Example 5.

Blair has 4 paintings in the basement. She is going to bring up 2 of them and hang 1 in her den and 1 in her bedroom. In how many ways can she choose which paintings go in each room?

(A) 4   (B) 6   (C) 12   (D) 16   (E) 24

Solution. Label the paintings 1, 2, 3, and 4, write B for bedroom and D for den, and make a list.

B-D	B-D	B-D	B-D
1-2	2-2	3-1	4-1
1-3	2-3	3-2	4-2
1-4	2-4	3-4	4-3

There are **12** ways to choose **(C)**.

In Example 5, making a list was feasible, but if Blair had 10 paintings and needed to hang 4 of them, it would be impossible to list all the different ways of hanging them. In such cases we need the *counting principle*.

Using the Counting Principle

Key Fact O2

If two jobs need to be completed and there are *m* ways to do the first job and *n* ways to do the second job, then there are $m \times n$ ways to do one job followed by the other. This principle can be extended to any number of jobs.

In Example 5, the first job was to pick 1 of the 4 paintings and hang it in the bedroom. That could be done in 4 ways. The second job was to pick a second painting to hang in the den. That job could be accomplished by choosing any of the remaining 3 paintings. There are $4 \times 3 = $ **12** ways to hang the 2 paintings.

Now, assume there are 10 paintings to be hung in 4 rooms. The first job is to choose 1 of the 10 paintings for the bedroom. The second job is to choose 1 of the 9 remaining paintings to hang in the den. The third job is to choose 1 of the 8 remaining paintings for, say, the living room. Finally, the fourth job is to pick 1 of the 7 remaining paintings for the dining room. These 4 jobs can be completed in $10 \times 9 \times 8 \times 7 = $ **5040** ways.

Example 6.

How many integers are there between 100 and 1000 all of whose digits are odd?

Solution. We're looking for three-digit numbers, such as 135, 711, 353, and 999, in which all three digits are odd. Note that we are *not* required to use three different digits. Although you certainly wouldn't want to list all of the possibilities, you could count them by listing some of them and seeing whether a pattern develops. In the 100's there are 5 numbers that begin with 11: 111, 113, 115, 117, 119. Similarly, there are 5 numbers that begin with 13: 131, 133, 135, 137, 139; 5 numbers that begin with 15, 5 that begin with 17, and 5 that begin with 19, for a total of $5 \times 5 = 25$ in the 100's. In the same way there are 25 in the 300's, 25 in the 500's, 25 in the 700's, and 25 in the 900's, for a grand total of $5 \times 25 = $ **125**. You can actually do this calculation in less time than it takes to read this paragraph.

The best way to solve Example 6, however, is to use the counting principle. Think of writing a three-digit number as three jobs that need to be done. The first job is to select one of the five odd digits and use it as the digit in the hundreds place. The second job is to select one of the five odd digits to be the digit that goes in the tens place. Finally, the third job is to select one of the five odd digits to be the digit in the units place. Each of these jobs can be done in 5 ways, so the total number of ways is $5 \times 5 \times 5 = 125$.

Using Venn Diagrams

A **Venn diagram** is a figure with two or three overlapping circles, usually enclosed in a rectangle, that is used to solve certain counting problems. To illustrate, assume that a school has 100 seniors. The following Venn diagram, which divides the rectangle into four regions, shows the distribution of those students in the band and the orchestra.

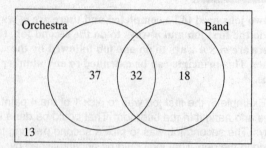

The 32 written in the part of the diagram where the two circles overlap represents the 32 seniors who are in both band and orchestra. The 18 written in the circle on the right represents the 18 seniors who are in the band but not in the orchestra, while the 37 written in the left circle represents the 37 seniors who are in the orchestra but not in the band. Finally, the 13 written in the rectangle outside of the circles represents the 13 seniors who are in neither band nor orchestra. The numbers in all four regions must add up to the total number of seniors: $32 + 18 + 37 + 13 = 100$.

Note that there are 50 seniors in the band—32 who are also in the orchestra and 18 who are not in the orchestra. Similarly, there are $32 + 37 = 69$ seniors in the orchestra. Be careful: the 50 names on the band roster and the 69 names on the orchestra roster add up to 119 names—more than the number of seniors. The reason is that 32 names are on both lists and so have been counted twice. The number of seniors who are in band or orchestra is only $119 - 32 = 87$. Those 87, together with the 13 who are in neither band nor orchestra, make up the total of 100.

On the SAT I, Venn diagrams are used in two ways. Occasionally, you are given a Venn diagram and asked a question about it, as in Example 7. More often, you will come across a problem that you will be able to solve more easily if you draw a Venn diagram, as in Examples 8 and 9.

Example 7.

If the integers from 1 through 15 are each placed in the diagram at the right, which of the following regions is (are) empty?

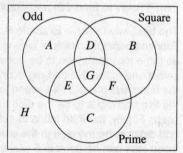

(A) D only (B) F only (C) G only
(D) F and G only (E) D and G only

Solution. The easiest way is just to put each of the numbers from 1 through 15 in the appropriate region. The empty regions are **F and G, (D)**.

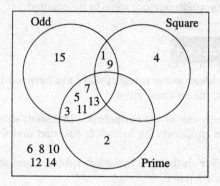

Example 8.

Of the 410 students at Kennedy High School, 240 study Spanish and 180 study French. If 25 students study neither language, how many students study both?

Solution. Draw a Venn diagram. Let x represent the number of students who study both languages, and write x in the part of the diagram where the two circles overlap. Then the number who study only Spanish is $240 - x$, and the number who study only French is $180 - x$. The number who study at least one of the languages is $410 - 25 = 385$, so

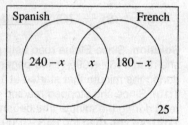

$$385 = (240 - x) + x + (180 - x) = 420 - x \Rightarrow$$
$$x = 420 - 385 = \mathbf{35} \text{ who study both.}$$

Note: No problem *requires* the use of a Venn diagram. On some problems you may even find it easier not to use one. In Example 8, you could have reasoned that, if there were 410 students in the school and 25 didn't study either language, then $410 - 25 = 385$ students studied at least one language. There are 240 names on the Spanish class lists and 180 on the French class lists, a total of $240 + 180 = 420$ names, but those 420 names represent only 385 students. It must be that $420 - 385 = 35$ names are repeated. In other words, 35 students are in both French and Spanish classes.

Helpful Hint

Even though for some problems you may not need a Venn diagram, they are useful. Sometimes they are almost essential.

Example 9.

At Milltown High School, 315 girls play at least one varsity sport; 100 play a fall sport, 150 play a winter sport, and 200 play a spring sport. If 75 girls play exactly two sports, how many play three?

Solution. Draw a Venn diagram, and label each section with what you know. From the diagram at the right, we get the following equation, which fortunately can be simplified:

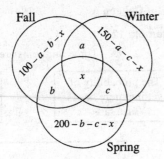

$$315 = (100 - a - b - x) + (150 - a - c - x) +$$
$$(200 - b - c - x) + a + b + c + x$$
$$= 450 - (a + b + c) - 2x$$
$$= 450 - 75 - 2x = 375 - 2x \Rightarrow 2x = 60 \Rightarrow x = 30.$$

The equation would be much more manageable if, instead of using a, b, and c, we just let each of them be 25, or let $a = 0$, $b = 0$, and $c = 75$, as at the right. Then:

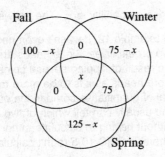

$$315 = 100 - x + 75 - x + 125 - x + 75 + x$$
$$= 375 - 2x \Rightarrow x = 30.$$

Probability

The **probability** that an **event** will occur is a number between 0 and 1, usually written as a fraction, that indicates how likely it is that the event will happen. For example, if you spin the spinner at the right, there are 4 possible outcomes: it is equally likely that the spinner will stop in any of the four regions. There is 1 chance in 4 that it will stop in the region marked 2, so we say that the probability of spinning a 2 is one-fourth and write $P(2) = \frac{1}{4}$. Since 2 is the only even number on the spinner we could also say $P(\text{even}) = \frac{1}{4}$. There are 3 chances in 4 that the spinner will land in a region with an odd number in it, so $P(\text{odd}) = \frac{3}{4}$.

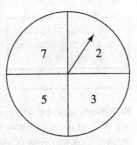

Key Fact O3

If E is any event, the probability that E will occur is given by

$$P(E) = \frac{\text{number of favorable outcomes}}{\text{total number of possible outcomes}},$$

assuming that all of the possible outcomes are equally likely.

In the preceding example, each of the four regions is the same size, so it is equally likely that the spinner will land on the 2, 3, 5, or 7. Therefore:

$$P(\text{odd}) = \frac{\text{number of ways of getting an odd number}}{\text{total number of possible outcomes}} = \frac{3}{4}.$$

Note that the probability of *not* getting an odd number is 1 minus the probability of getting an odd number:

$$1 - \frac{3}{4} = \frac{1}{4}.$$

Let's look at some other probabilities associated with spinning this spinner once:

$$P(\text{number} > 10) =$$
$$\frac{\text{number of ways of getting a number} > 10}{\text{total number of possible outcomes}} = \frac{0}{4} = 0.$$

$$P(\text{prime number}) =$$
$$\frac{\text{number of ways of getting a prime number}}{\text{total number of possible outcomes}} = \frac{4}{4} = 1.$$

$$P(\text{number} < 4) =$$
$$\frac{\text{number of ways of getting a number} < 4}{\text{total number of possible outcomes}} = \frac{2}{4} = \frac{1}{2}.$$

Key Fact O4

Let E be an event, and let $P(E)$ be the probability that it will occur.

- If E is **impossible** (such as getting a number greater than 10), **$P(E) = 0$**.
- If it is **certain** that E will occur (such as getting a prime number), **$P(E) = 1$**.
- In all cases, **$0 \le P(E) \le 1$**.
- The probability that event E will *not* occur is **$1 - P(E)$**.
- If two or more events constitute all the outcomes, the sum of their probabilities is 1.

  [For example, $P(\text{even}) + P(\text{odd}) = \frac{1}{4} + \frac{3}{4} = 1$.]

- The more likely it is that an event will occur, the higher its probability (the closer to 1 it is); the less likely it is that an event will occur, the lower its probability (the closer to 0 it is).

Even though probability is defined as a fraction, we can also write probabilities as decimals or percents. Instead of writing $P(E) = \frac{1}{2}$, we can write $P(E) = .50$ or $P(E) = 50\%$.

Example 10.

An integer between 100 and 999, inclusive, is chosen at random. What is the probability that all the digits of the number are odd?

Solution. By KEY FACT O1, since both endpoints are included, there are $999 - 100 + 1 = 900$ integers between 100 and 999. In Example 6, we saw that there are 125 three-digit numbers all of whose digits are odd. Therefore, the probability is

$$\frac{\text{number of favorable outcomes}}{\text{total number of possible outcomes}} = \frac{125}{900} = \frac{5}{36} \approx .138$$

Key Fact O5

If an experiment is done two (or more) times, the probability that first one event will occur, and then a second event will occur, is the product of the probabilities.

Example 11.

A fair coin is flipped 3 times. What is the probability that the coin will land heads each time?

Solution. When a fair coin is flipped:

$$P(\text{head}) = \frac{1}{2} \text{ and } P(\text{tail}) = \frac{1}{2}.$$

By KEY FACT O5: $P(\text{3 heads}) =$

$P(\text{head 1st time}) \times P(\text{head 2nd time}) \times P(\text{head 3rd time})$

$$= \frac{1}{2} \times \frac{1}{2} \times \frac{1}{2} = \frac{1}{8}.$$

Another way to handle problems such as Example 11 is to make a list of all of the possible outcomes. For example, if a fair coin is tossed three times, the possible outcomes are as follows

head, head, head	head, head, tail
head, tail, head	head, tail, tail
tail, head, head	tail, head, tail
tail, tail, head	tail, tail, tail

On the SAT I, of course, if you choose to list the outcomes, you should abbreviate and just write HHH, HHT, and so on. In any event, there are 8 possible outcomes, and only 1 of them (HHH) is favorable, so the probability is $\frac{1}{8}$.

Column A	Column B

Example 12.

Three fair coins are flipped.

The probability of getting more heads than tails	The probability of getting more tails than heads

Solution. From the list of the 8 possible outcomes previously given, you can see that in 4 of them (HHH, HHT, HTH, THH) there are more heads than tails, and in 4 of them (TTT, TTH, THT, HTT) there are more tails than heads.

Each probability is $\frac{4}{8}$. The answer is **C**.

In Example 12, it wasn't even necessary to calculate the two probabilities. Since heads and tails are equally likely, the result of flipping several coins is just as likely to be more heads as it is to be more tails. This situation is typical of quantitative comparison questions on probability; you usually can tell which of two probabilities is greater without having to calculate either one—another instance where TACTIC 10-5 (don't calculate, compare) is useful.

Column A	Column B

Example 13.

Each of the numbers from 1 to 1000 is written on a slip of paper and placed in a box. Then one slip is removed.

The probability that the number drawn is a multiple of 5	The probability that the number drawn is a multiple of 7

Solution. Since there are more multiples of 5 than there are of 7, it is more likely that a multiple of 5 will be drawn. Column **A** is greater.

Exercises on Counting and Probability

Multiple-Choice Questions

1. A cafeteria has a lunch special, consisting of soup or salad, a sandwich, coffee or tea, and a dessert. If the menu lists 3 soups, 2 salads, 8 sandwiches, and 7 desserts, how many different lunches can you choose? (*Note:* Two lunches are different if they differ in any aspect.)

   (A) 22   (B) 280   (C) 336   (D) 560   (E) 672

2. Dwight Eisenhower was born on October 14, 1890, and died on March 28, 1969. What was his age, in years, at the time of his death?

   (A) 77   (B) 78   (C) 79   (D) 80   (E) 81

3. There are 27 students in Mr. White's homeroom. What is the probability that at least 3 of them have their birthdays in the same month?

   (A) 0   (B) $\frac{3}{27}$ (C) $\frac{3}{12}$ (D) $\frac{1}{2}$ (E) 1

4. A jar has 5 marbles, 1 of each of the colors red, white, blue, green, and yellow. If 4 marbles are removed from the jar, what is the probability that the yellow marble was removed?

(A) $\frac{1}{20}$ (B) $\frac{1}{5}$ (C) $\frac{1}{4}$ (D) $\frac{4}{5}$ (E) $\frac{5}{4}$

5. Let A be the set of primes less than 6, and B be the set of positive odd numbers less than 6. How many different sums of the form $a + b$ are possible if a is in A and b is in B?

(A) 6   (B) 7   (C) 8   (D) 9   (E) 10

6. A printer that can print 1 page in 5 seconds shuts down for 3 minutes to cool off after every hour of operation. How many minutes will the printer take to print 3600 pages?

(A) 300   (B) 312   (C) 315   (D) 18,000
(E) 18,897

7. In the figure at the right, how many paths are there from A to X if the only ways to move are up and to the right?

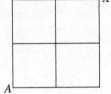

(A) 4   (B) 5   (C) 6
(D) 8   (E) 9

8. A jar contains 20 marbles: 4 red, 6 white, and 10 blue. If you remove 1 marble at a time, randomly, what is the minimum number that you must remove to be certain that you have at least 2 marbles of each color?

(A) 6   (B) 10   (C) 12   (D) 16   (E) 18

9. Jim, Kim, and Tim are playing a mini chess tournament with no ties (two people play each other until one of them wins a game). There are just two matches. First, Jim plays Kim, and then the winner plays Tim. The probability that Jim will beat Kim is $\frac{2}{3}$, that Tim will beat Jim is $\frac{3}{5}$, and that Tim will beat Kim is $\frac{4}{5}$. What is the probability that Kim will win the tournament?

(A) $\frac{1}{15}$ (B) $\frac{1}{5}$ (C) $\frac{1}{3}$ (D) $\frac{2}{5}$ (E) $\frac{8}{15}$

10. At the audition for the school play, n people tried out. If k people went before Judy, who went before Liz, and m people went after Liz, how many people tried out between Judy and Liz?

(A) $n - m - k - 2$ (B) $n - m - k - 1$
(C) $n - m - k$ (D) $n - m - k + 1$
(E) $n - m - k + 2$

Quantitative Comparison Questions

Column A	Column B

11. | The probability of getting no heads when a fair coin is flipped 7 times | The probability of getting 7 heads when a fair coin is flipped 7 times

A jar contains 4 marbles: 2 red and 2 white. 2 marbles are chosen at random.

12. | The probability that the marbles chosen are the same color | The probability that the marbles chosen are different colors

13. | The number of ways to assign a number from 1 to 5 to each of 4 people | The number of ways to assign a number from 1 to 5 to each of 5 people

14. | The probability that 2 people chosen at random were born on the same day of the week | The probability that 2 people chosen at random were born in the same month

15. | The probability that a number chosen at random from the primes between 100 and 199 is odd. | .99

Grid-in Questions

16. Doug works on the second floor of a building. There are 10 doors to the building and 8 staircases from the first to the second floor. Doug decided that each day he would enter by one door and leave by a different one, and go up one staircase and down another. If Doug works 240 days a year, for how many years can he work without ever repeating the same path?

17. There are 100 people on a line. Andy is the 37th person, and Ali is the 67th person. If a person on line is chosen at random, what is the probability that the person is standing between Andy and Ali?

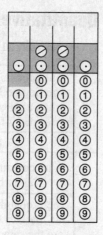

18. How many four-digit numbers have only even digits?

19. How many ways are there to rearrange the letters in the word *elation*, if the first and last letter must each be a vowel?

Questions 20–21 refer to the following diagram. *A* is the set of positive integers less than 20; *B* is the set of positive integers that contain the digit 7; and *C* is the set of primes.

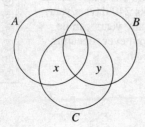

20. How many numbers are members of the region labeled *x*?

21. What is one number less than 50 that is a member of the region labeled *y*?

22. A number is a palindrome if it reads exactly the same from right to left as it does from left to right. For example, 77, 959, and 24742 are all palindromes. If a three-digit number is chosen at random, what is the probability that it is a palindrome?

23. In a group of 100 students, more students are on a team than are members of a club. If 70 are in clubs and 20 are neither on a team nor in a club, what is the minimum number of students who could be both on a team and in a club?

24. In a singles tennis tournament that has 125 entrants, a player is eliminated whenever he or she loses a match. How many matches are played in the entire tournament?

25. A jar contains only red and white marbles. If 1 marble is removed at random, the probability that it is red is $\frac{2}{5}$. After putting another 100 red marbles in the jar, the probability of drawing a red marble is $\frac{3}{5}$. How many marbles were originally in the jar?

Answer Key

1. **D**	4. **D**	7. **C**	10. **A**	13. **C**
2. **B**	5. **B**	8. **E**	11. **C**	14. **A**
3. **E**	6. **B**	9. **A**	12. **B**	15. **A**

16. `2 1` 17. `. 2 9` 18. `5 0 0` 19. `1 4 4 0` 20. `6`

21. `3 7` or `4 7` 22 `1 / 1 0` or `. 1`

23. | 6 1
24. | 1 2 4
25. | 2 0 0

Answer Explanations

1. **D.** You can choose your first course (soup or salad) in 5 ways, your beverage in 2 ways, your sandwich in 8 ways, and your dessert in 7 ways. The counting principle says to multiply: $5 \times 2 \times 8 \times 7 = 560$. (Note that, if you got soup *and* a salad, then, instead of 5 choices for the first course, there would have been $2 \times 3 = 6$ choices for the first two courses.)

2. **B.** President Eisenhower's last birthday was in October 1968. His age at death was $1968 - 1890 = 78$ years.

3. **E.** If there were no month in which at least 3 students had a birthday, then each month would have the birthdays of at most 2 students. But that's not possible; even if there were 2 birthdays in January, 2 in February, ..., and 2 in December, only 24 students would be accounted for. It is guaranteed that, with more than 24 students, at least 1 month will have 3 or more birthdays. The probability is 1.

4. **D.** It is equally likely that any 1 of the 5 marbles will be the one that is not removed. Therefore, the probability that the yellow marble is left is $\frac{1}{5}$, and the probability that it is removed is $\frac{4}{5}$.

5. **B.** $A = \{2, 3, 5\}$ and $B = \{1, 3, 5\}$. Any of the 3 numbers in A could be added to any of the 3 numbers in B, so 9 sums could be formed. However, there could be some duplication. List the sums systematically; first add 1 to each number in A, then 3, and then 5: 3, 4, 6; 5, 6̸, 10; 7, 8, 1̸0̸. There are 7 different sums.

6. **B.** Use the given information to find the rate of pages per hour.

$$\frac{1 \text{ page}}{5 \text{ seconds}} = \frac{12 \text{ pages}}{1 \text{ minute}} = \frac{720 \text{ pages}}{1 \text{ hour}},$$

so 3600 pages will take $3600 \div 720 = 5$ hours, or 300 minutes, of printing time. There will also be 12 minutes (4×3 minutes) when the printer is shut down to cool off, for a total of 312 minutes. Note that there are 5 printing periods and 4 cooling-off periods.

7. **C.** Either label all the vertices and systematically list the possibilities, or systematically trace the diagram. If you start by going from A to B, there are 3 paths: you can get up to the top by BC, EF, or HX, and once there must proceed to the right. Similarly, there are 3 paths if you start by going right from A to D. In all, there are 6 paths from A to X.

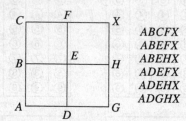

ABCFX
ABEFX
ABEHX
ADEFX
ADEHX
ADGHX

8. **E.** In a problem like this one, the easiest thing to do is to see what could go wrong in your attempt to get 2 marbles of each color. If you were really unlucky, you might remove 10 blue ones in a row, followed by all 6 white ones. At that point you would have 16 marbles, and you still wouldn't have even 1 red. The next 2 marbles, however, must both be red. The answer is 18.

9. **A.** To win the tournament, Kim has to first beat Jim and then beat Tim. The probability that she will beat Jim is $\frac{1}{3}\left(1 - \frac{2}{3}\right)$; then, if she does, her probability of beating Tim is $\frac{1}{5}\left(1 - \frac{4}{5}\right)$. Therefore, her probability of winning the tournament is $\frac{1}{3} \times \frac{1}{5} = \frac{1}{15}$.

10. **A.** It may help to draw a line and label it. Since k people went before Judy, she was number $k + 1$ to try out; and since m people went after Liz, she was number $n - m$ to try out. Then, the number of people to try out between Judy and Liz was

$$(n - m) - (k + 1) - 1 = n - m - k - 2.$$

11. **C.** Don't calculate the probabilities. The probability of no heads is equal to the probability of no tails, but no tails means all heads.

12. **B.** The simplest solution is to notice that, whatever color the first chosen marble is, only 1 more marble of that color, but 2 of the other color, remain in the jar. Therefore, it is twice as likely that the second marble chosen will be a different color than the first one. If you didn't see that, you could have listed the possible outcomes. To distinguish between the 2 reds and the 2 whites, assume that the reds are designated as R_1 and R_2 and the whites as W_1 and W_2. Then the 2 marbles chosen could have been R_1R_2, R_1W_1, R_1W_2, W_1R_1, W_1R_2, or W_1W_2. Of these possibilities, 2 are of the same color and 4 are of different colors.

13. **C.** By the counting principle, Column A is $5 \cdot 4 \cdot 3 \cdot 2$ and Column B is $5 \cdot 4 \cdot 3 \cdot 2 \cdot 1$, which are clearly equal. Alternatively, you can just reason as follows: in Column A, 4 numbers are assigned and 1 is left over; in Column B, 4 numbers are assigned to the first 4 people, and then the 1 number left over is given to the fifth person.

14. **A.** Column A: the probability is $\dfrac{1}{7}$.

Column B: the probability is $\dfrac{1}{12}$.

15. **A.** Every prime between 100 and 199 is odd (the only even prime is 2). Therefore, the probability in Column A is 1, which is greater than .99.

16. **(21)** This is the counting principle at work. Each day Doug has four jobs to do: choose 1 of the 10 doors to enter and 1 of the 9 other doors to exit; choose 1 of the 8 staircases to go up and 1 of the other 7 to come down. This can be done in $10 \times 9 \times 8 \times 7 = 5040$ ways, so on each of 5040 days Doug could choose a different path. To find how many years he can go without repeating, divide: $5040 \div 240 = 21$.

17. **(.29)** There are $67 - 37 - 1 = 29$ people between Andy and Ali. The probability that the person chosen is standing between them is $\dfrac{29}{100} = .29$.

18. **(500)** The easiest way to do this is to use the counting principle. The first digit can be chosen in any of 4 ways (2, 4, 6, 8), whereas the second, third, and fourth digits can be chosen in any of 5 ways (0, 2, 4, 6, 8). Therefore, the total number of four-digit numbers with only even digits is $4 \times 5 \times 5 \times 5 = 500$.

19. **(1440)** Again, use the counting principle. How many ways are there to fill in seven blanks, _ _ _ _ _ _ _, with letters from the word *elation*? Think of this as seven jobs to do. The first job is to choose one of the 4 vowels in the word to be the first letter; the second job is to choose one of the remaining 3 vowels to be the last letter. Thus, there are $4 \times 3 = 12$ ways to choose the first and last letters. Since there are no other restrictions, the five other jobs are to place the remaining 5 letters in the five remaining blanks. There are 5 choices for the first blank, 4 for the next, then 3, then 2, and finally 1. There are $12 \times 5 \times 4 \times 3 \times 2 \times 1 = 1440$ arrangements.

20. **(6)** In the diagram, the region labeled x contains all of the primes less than 20 that do not contain the digit 7. They are 2, 3, 5, 11, 13, 19— 6 numbers in all.

21. **(37 or 47)** Region y consists of primes that contain the digit 7 and are greater than 20.

22. $\left(\dfrac{1}{10} \text{ or } .1\right)$ The simplest solution is to realize that there is 1 palindrome between 100 and 109 (101), 1 between 390 and 399 (393), 1 between 880 and 889 (888), and, in general, 1 out of every 10 numbers.
    Alternative solution. The more direct solution is to count the number of palindromes. Either systematically make a list and notice that there are 10 of them between 100 and 199, and 10 in each of the hundreds from the 100's to the 900's, for a total of 90; or use the counting principle: the first digit can be chosen in any of 9 ways, the second in any of 10 ways, and the third, since it must match the first, in only 1 way ($9 \times 10 \times 1 = 90$). Since there are 900 three-digit numbers, the probability is

$$\frac{90}{900} = \frac{1}{10} \text{ or } .1.$$

23. **(61)** Draw a Venn diagram, letting x be the number of students both on a team and in a club. Since more students are on a team

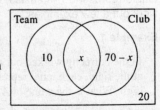

than in a club, $10 + x > 70 \Rightarrow x > 60$. Since x must be an integer, the least it can be is 61.

24. (124)   You could try to break the problem down by saying that, first, 124 of the 125 players would be paired off and play 62 matches. With the 62 losers eliminated, 63 people would be left, the 62 winners and the 1 person who hadn't played yet. You would continue until only 1 person was left. The easy way is to observe that the winner never loses and the other 124 players each lose once. Since each match has exactly one loser, there must be 124 matches.

25. (200)   Let x represent the number of marbles originally in the jar. Since the probability of drawing a red marble is $\dfrac{2}{5}$, the number of red marbles is $\dfrac{2}{5}x$. After 100 red marbles were added, there were $x + 100$ marbles in the jar, of which $\dfrac{2}{5}x + 100$ are red, so

$$\frac{2}{5}x + 100 = \frac{3}{5}(x + 100) = \frac{3}{5}x + 60.$$

Multiplying by 5 gives $2x + 500 = 3x + 300$ $\Rightarrow x = 200$.

12-P LOGICAL REASONING

All of the questions on the SAT I (even the verbal ones) require some logical reasoning. In fact, the official name of the test is the "SAT I Reasoning Test." However, there are often a few questions on the mathematics sections of the SAT I that do not fit into any of the standard mathematics topics. They require "logical reasoning" as opposed to knowledge of a particular fact from arithmetic, algebra, or geometry. Some of the problems don't even involve numbers or geometric figures. In this section and in the exercises that follow it, we will give a variety of examples to illustrate the kinds of "logic" questions that you may encounter.

Alphanumeric Problems

An *alphanumeric problem* is an arithmetic problem in which some or all of the digits have been replaced by letters, and it is your job to determine what numbers the letters represent. The easiest way to explain this is to work out a few examples.

Example 1.

In the correctly worked out addition problem at the right, each letter represents a different digit. What is the value of A?

$$\begin{array}{r} AB \\ + AB \\ \hline BCC \end{array}$$

Solution. Since the two-digit number AB is less than 100, $AB + AB < 200$, implying that BCC is a number

between 100 and 199. No matter what, B must be 1. Now go to the problem, and replace *each B* with a 1.

The addition now looks like this:

$$\begin{array}{r} A1 \\ + A1 \\ \hline 1CC \end{array}$$

Since $1 + 1 = 2$, rewrite the problem again, replacing both C's with 2's.

$$\begin{array}{r} A1 \\ + A1 \\ \hline 122 \end{array}$$

Finally, since $A + A = 12$, then $A = \mathbf{6}$.

Key Fact P1

If the sum of two two-digit numbers is a three-digit number, the first digit of the sum is 1. Similarly, if the sum of two three-digit numbers is a four-digit number, the first digit of the sum is 1.

Example 2.

In the correctly worked out multiplication problem at the right, each letter represents a different digit. What is the value of $A + B + C + D$?

$$\begin{array}{r} ABA \\ \times\ \ \ A \\ \hline CBD5 \end{array}$$

Solution. The first step in the multiplication is to multiply $A \times A$. Since 5 is the only digit whose square ends in 5, A must be 5, so replace *each A* with 5.

The problem now looks like this:

$$\begin{array}{r} 5B5 \\ \times\ \ \ 5 \\ \hline CBD5 \end{array}$$

Since $5 \times 500 = 2500$ and $5 \times 600 = 3000$, the product $CBC5$ is somewhere between. Therefore, $C = 2$ and $B \geq 5$. Rewrite the problem again, replacing C by 2:

$$\begin{array}{r} 5B5 \\ \times\ \ \ 5 \\ \hline 2BD5 \end{array}$$

Since A is 5, B isn't 5, so B is at least 6. Notice that the second digit of $5B5$ and the second digit of $2BD5$ are the same. But $5 \times 5\underline{6}5 = 2\underline{8}25$; so B must be at least 8: $5 \times 5\underline{8}5 = 2\underline{9}25$, which doesn't work, but $5 \times 5\underline{9}5 = 2\underline{9}75$, which does:

$$\begin{array}{r} 595 \\ \times\ \ \ 5 \\ \hline 2975 \end{array}$$

Then $B = 9$ and $D = 7$:

$$A + B + C + D = 5 + 9 + 2 + 7 = \mathbf{23}.$$

Example 2 was harder than any alphanumeric on an SAT I because you had to find the values of all four letters, but the reasoning for each step is exactly what you must be able to do. If the solution wasn't completely clear, go back and reread it.

Sequences

A *sequence* is just a list of numbers separated by commas. It can be finite, such as 1, 3, 5, 7, 9; or it can be infinite, such as 5, 10, 15, 20, 25, ... Each number in the list is called a *term* of the sequence. The terms of a sequence don't have to follow any pattern or rule, but on the SAT I they always do. The most common type of sequence question presents you with a rule for finding the terms of a sequence, and then asks you for a particular term.

P1

Never answer a question involving a sequence without writing out at least the first five terms.

Example 3.

A sequence is formed as follows: the first term is 3, and every other term is 4 more than the term that precedes it. What is the 100th term?

Solution. The sequence begins 3, 7, 11, 15, 19 (7 is 4 more than 3, 11 is 4 more than 7, etc.). Clearly, we could continue writing out the terms, and if the question asked for the 10th term, that would be the easiest thing to do. We are not, however, going to write out 100 terms. What we need now is a little imagination or inspiration. How else could we describe the terms of this sequence? The terms are just 1 less than the corresponding multiples of 4 (4, 8, 12, 16, 20, ...): 7, which is the 2nd term, is 1 less than 2×4; 19, which is the 5th term, is 1 less than 5×4 Now we have the solution. The 100th term is 1 less than 100×4: $400 - 1 = $ **399**.

In Examples 4–6, the sequences S_n are formed as follows:

For any positive integer n: the first term of the sequence S_n is n, and every term after the first is 1 more than twice the preceding term.

Example 4.

What is the value of the smallest term of S_5 that is greater than 100?

Solution. Sequence S_5 proceeds as follows: 5, 11, 23, 47, 95, 191, ..., so the smallest term greater than 100 is **191**.

Example 5.

What is the units digit of the 500th term of S_9?

Solution. Of course, we're not going to write out 500 terms of any sequence, but we *always* write out the first five: 9, 19, 39, 79, 159, ...

There's no question about it: the units digit of *every* term is **9**.

Example 6.

If one of the first 10 terms of S_{1000} is chosen at random, what is the probability that it is odd?

Solution. For any integer m whatsoever, $2m$ is even and $2m + 1$ is odd. The first term of S_{1000} is 1000, but every other term is odd. The probability is $\dfrac{9}{10}$.

In some sequences the terms repeat in a cyclical pattern.

P2

When k numbers form a repeating sequence, to find the nth number, divide n by k and take the remainder r. The rth term and the nth term are the same.

Examples 7–8 refer to the infinite sequence 1, 4, 2, 8, 5, 7, 1, 4, 2, 8, 5, 7, ... , where the six digits 1, 4, 2, 8, 5, and 7 keep repeating in that order.

Example 7.

What is the 500th term of the sequence?

Solution. When 500 is divided by 6, the quotient is 83 ($6 \times 83 = 498$) and the remainder is 2. Therefore, the first 498 terms are just the numbers 1, 4, 2, 8, 5, 7 repeated 83 times. The 498th term is the 83rd 7 in the sequence. Then the pattern repeats again: the 499th term is 1, and the 500th term is **4**.

In this example, notice that the 500th term is the same as the 2nd term. This is because 2 is the remainder when 500 is divided by 6.

Example 8.

What is the sum of the 800th through the 805th terms?

Solution. Don't waste time determining what the 800th term is. Any six consecutive terms of the sequence consist, in some order, of exactly the same six numbers: 1, 4, 2, 8, 5, and 7. Their sum is **27**.

Patterns

Some SAT I questions are based on repeating patterns. These are very similar to repeating sequences, except that the terms don't have to be numbers.

Example 9.

In order to divide the campers at a camp into six teams (the reds, whites, blues, greens, yellows, and browns), the director had all the campers form a line. Then, starting with the first person, each camper on line called out a color, repeating this pattern: red, white, blue, green, yellow, brown, red, white, blue, green, yellow, brown, ... What color was called out by the 500th camper?

(A) red (B) white (C) green (D) yellow
(E) brown

Solution. This is exactly the same as Example 7. When 500 is divided by 6, the quotient is 83 and the remainder is 2. Then, by TACTIC P2, the 500th camper called out the same color as the 2nd camper: **white (B)**.

Example 10.

Last year Elaine's birthday was on Friday. If Susan's birthday was 150 days after Elaine's, how many Sundays were there between Elaine's birthday and Susan's birthday?

Solution. The 7 days of the week repeat in cyclical pattern. Using TACTIC P2, we divide 150 by 7, getting a quotient of 21 and a remainder of 3. Thus, the 150th day after Elaine's birthday was Monday, the same as the 3rd day after her birthday. During the 21 full weeks between Elaine's and Susan's birthdays, there were 21 Sundays, and there was 1 more during the last 3 days, for a total of **22**.

Miscellaneous Logic Problems

Some problems that test your ability to think clearly and logically cannot be categorized. We give one here and a few others in the exercises.

Example 11.

During a visit by the census taker, one child in a family said, "I have twice as many brothers as sisters." Another child in the family said, "I don't. I have the same number of brothers and sisters." How many children are there in the family?

Solution. Since any two boys (or girls) in the family would have the same number of brothers and sisters, the two children who spoke had to be of different sexes. Assume that the second child was a boy. Since he has the same number of brothers and sisters, the family has one more boy than girl. For example, if this child had 2 brothers and 2 sisters, the family would have 3 boys (his 2 brothers and himself) and 2 girls (his 2 sisters), so the possibilities are 2 boys and 1 girl, 3 boys and 2 girls, 4 boys and 3 girls, 5 boys and 4 girls, and so on. In which of these cases would a girl have twice as many brothers as sisters? Only if there were 4 boys and 3 girls, in which case the girl has 4 brothers and 2 sisters. Therefore, there are **7** children in the family.

Exercises on Logical Reasoning

Multiple-Choice Questions

1. In the correctly worked out addition problem at the right, each letter represents a different digit. What is the value of A?

$$
\begin{array}{r}
3A \\
+\,A3 \\
\hline
BBC
\end{array}
$$

   (A) 5   (B) 6   (C) 7   (D) 8   (E) 9

2. In the United States, Thanksgiving is celebrated on the fourth Thursday in November. Which of the following statements are true?

   I. Thanksgiving is the last Thursday in November.
   II. Thanksgiving is never celebrated on November 22.
   III. Thanksgiving cannot be celebrated on the same date 2 years in a row.

   (A) None   (B) I only   (C) II only   (D) III only
   (E) I and III only

3. A gum-ball dispenser is filled with exactly 1000 pieces of gum. The gum balls always come out in the following order: 1 red, 2 blue, 3 green, 4 yellow, and 5 white. After the fifth white, the pattern repeats, starting with 1 red, and so on. What is the color of the last gum ball to come out of the machine?

   (A) red   (B) blue   (C) green   (D) yellow
   (E) white

4. The rectangle below represents a piece of paper that is to be folded at XY so that AB meets CD. It is then to be folded again, so that XY meets CD. Finally, a triangular piece is cut out.

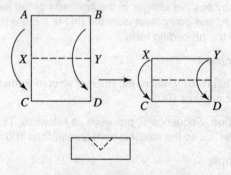

   Like which of the following will the paper look when it is unfolded?

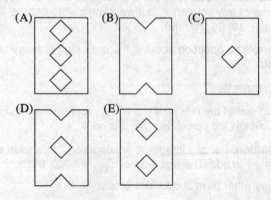

5. In the correctly worked out multiplication problem at the right, each letter represents a different digit. What is the value of $A + B + C$?

$$\begin{array}{r} AB \\ \times\ 3 \\ \hline CBB \end{array}$$

   (A) 12   (B) 15   (C) 18   (D) 21   (E) 27

Quantitative Comparison Questions

Column A	Column B
The digit in the 80th place to the right of the decimal point when $\frac{5}{37}$ is expressed as a decimal	3

6.

$$\begin{array}{r} CBA \\ + DBA \\ \hline E98 \end{array}$$

In the addition problem above, each letter represents a different digit.

7. | A | B |

The first term of sequence A is 10, and every other term is 3 more than the preceding term.
The first term of sequence B is 100, and every other term is 3 less than the preceding term.

8. | The 16th term of sequence A | The 16th term of sequence B |

$$\begin{array}{r} ABCD \\ \times\ 9 \\ \hline EFGH \end{array}$$

In the multiplication problem above, each letter represents a different digit.

9. | The number of letters whose values can be determined | 4 |

Ira, Mark, and Barbara each have quarters and dimes totaling $1.35.
No two of them have the same number of coins.

10. | The total number of dimes they have together | Twice the total number of quarters they have together |

Grid-in Questions

11. In the correctly worked out addition problem below, each letter represents a different digit. What is the number *CBA*?

$$\begin{array}{r} 3A \\ 4A \\ + AA \\ \hline CBA \end{array}$$

12. Three children guessed at the number of jelly beans in a jar. The guesses were 98, 137, and 164. None of the guesses was correct. One guess was off by 12, another by 27, and the third by 39. How many jelly beans were in the jar?

13. The pointer on the dial at the right moves 3 numbers clockwise every minute. If it starts at 1, what number will it be pointing to in exactly 1 hour?

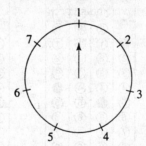

14. A sequence is formed by choosing a number, x, to be the first term. Every term after the first is y more than the preceding term. If the 8th term is 19 and the 12th term is 29, what is xy?

15. The cars on a Ferris wheel are equally spaced around the circumference. They are numbered consecutively, starting with 1. If car 7 is opposite car 25, how many cars are there on the Ferris wheel?

Answer Key

1.	C	3. D	5. B	7. A	9. B
2.	D	4. E	6. C	8. C	10. C

11. 1 3 5

12. 1 2 5

13. 6

14. 3 . 7 5 or 1 5 / 4

15. 3 6

Answer Explanations

1. **C.** By KEY FACT P1,
   $B = 1$, so the sum looks
   like this:

   $$\begin{array}{r} 3A \\ + A3 \\ \hline 11C \end{array}$$

   If $A \le 6$, then the $A + 3$ in each column
   would be a one-digit number, so
   A is at least 7. In fact, 7 works.

   $$\begin{array}{r} 37 \\ + 73 \\ \hline 110 \end{array}$$

2. **D.** If November 1 is a Thursday, then so are
   November 8, 15, 22, and 29. Therefore,
   Thanksgiving could fall on November 22 (II is
   false); and if it does, it is not the last Thursday
   in November (I is false). Assume that on one
   year Thanksgiving falls on Thursday, November X. Then exactly 52 weeks (or $7 \times 52 = 364$
   days) later it will again be Thursday, but it
   won't be November X, because November X
   comes 365 (or 366) days after the preceding
   November X (III is true).

3. **D.** Since the pattern repeats itself after every 15
   gum balls, divide 1000 by 15. The quotient is
   66, and the remainder is 10. Therefore, the
   1000th gum ball is the same color as the 10th,
   which is yellow.

4. **E.** Note that, when the paper was folded, AB was
   at the bottom and so was not cut; eliminate B
   and D. Also, XY, which runs through the center, was at the bottom and was not cut, so there
   is no hole in the middle: eliminate A and C.

5. **B.** Since $AB < 100$, 3 times AB is less
   than $3 \times 100 = 300$, so C is 1 or 2.
   Since 3 times B ends in B, B is
   either 0 or 5. It can't be 0 because
   neither 100 nor 200 is a multiple
   of 3: so $B = 5$.

   $$\begin{array}{r} AB \\ \times\ 3 \\ \hline CBB \end{array}$$

   The simplest thing to do now is test
   whether 155 or 255 is a multiple
   of 3: 155 isn't, but $255 = 3 \times 85$.
   Then $C = 2$ and $A = 8$. Finally,
   $A + B + C = 8 + 5 + 2 = 15$.

   $$\begin{array}{r} A5 \\ \times\ 3 \\ \hline C55 \end{array}$$

6. **C.** First divide 5 by 37 (on your calculator, of
   course): $5 \div 37 = 0.135135135\ldots$. The repeating portion is three digits long, so divide 80 by
   3; the quotient is 26, and since $3 \times 26 = 78$, the
   remainder is 2. Therefore, the digit in the 80th
   place is the same as the one in the 2nd place: 3.

7. **A.** Looking at the units column, we see
   that A must be 4 or 9. If $A = 4$,
   there's nothing to carry, and $B + B$
   must be even, so it can't end in 9.
   Therefore, $A = 9$. Since A and B are
   different, B must be less than 9. (Note that,
   although we didn't have to find B to know that
   A is greater, we could have. Since $A + A = 18$,

   $$\begin{array}{r} CBA \\ + DBA \\ \hline E98 \end{array}$$

   there's 1 to carry, and $B + B + 1$ ends in a 9,
   so B is 4 or 9. Since $A = 9$, $B = 4$.)

8. **C.** To get the 16th term of sequence A, start with
   10 and add 3 fifteen times: $10 + 15 \times 3 = 10 +
   45 = 55$. To get the 16th term of sequence B,
   start with 100 and subtract 3 fifteen times:
   $100 - 15 \times 3 = 100 - 45 = 55$.

9. **B.** The values of three letters can be
   determined. A has to be 1 because
   9 times a number greater than
   2000 will have more than 4 digits.
   E has to be 9 since 9 times a
   number over 1000 is at least 9000.
   B can't be 1 because A is, and B
   has to be less than 2 since 1200
   times 9 is a 5-digit number. So $B = 0$.
   Two possible solutions are shown
   at the right.

   $$\begin{array}{r} 1042 \\ \times\ 9 \\ \hline 9378 \end{array}$$

   $$\begin{array}{r} 1084 \\ \times\ 9 \\ \hline 9756 \end{array}$$

10. **C.** There are only three ways to have \$1.35 in
    quarters and dimes: 1 quarter and 11 dimes, 3
    quarters and 6 dimes, and 5 quarters and 1
    dime. Ira, Mark, and Barbara each had one of
    those combinations. Together, they had a total
    of $1 + 3 + 5 = 9$ quarters and $11 + 6 + 1 = 18$
    dimes. The number of dimes was exactly
    twice the number of quarters.

11. **(135)** A can't be 0, and the only
    other digit A that, multiplied by 3,
    ends in A is 5 ($3 \times 5 = 15$). $A = 5$,
    and $CBA = 35 + 45 + 55 = 135$.

    $$\begin{array}{r} 3A \\ 4A \\ + AA \\ \hline CBA \end{array}$$

12. **(125)** There are lots of ways to reason this out.
    Here is one. The number must be over 100;
    otherwise the guess of 164 would be off by
    more than 64, and none of the guesses were
    that far wrong, Thus, the guess of 98 was too
    low. If it was 12 too low, there would be 110
    jelly beans, but then 164 would be off by 54,
    which isn't right. If 98 was 27 too low, the
    number would be 125, which is 12 less than
    137 and 39 less than 164. That's it.

13. **(6)** To see the pattern develop, write out the loca-
    tions of the pointer for the first few minutes.
    Advancing 3 numbers per minute, it goes from
    $1 \to 4 \to 7 \to 3 \to 6 \to 2 \to 5 \to 1$; and when it is
    back to 1, the whole cycle repeats. To know
    where the pointer will be in 60 minutes, divide
    60 by 7. Since the quotient is 8 and the
    remainder is 4, after 60 minutes the pointer
    will be pointing to the same number it pointed
    to after 4 minutes. Be careful. That number is
    not 3; it's 6. After 1 minute the pointer is at 4,
    after 2 minutes it's at 7, and so on.
    Alternative solution. Since the pointer
    advances 3 numbers per minute, it advances
    $3 \times 60 = 180$ minutes per hour. Dividing 180

by 7 gives a quotient of 25 and a remainder of 5, so the pointer makes 25 complete cycles and then advances 5 more numbers, from 1 to 6.

14. (3.75)   Each term is y more than the preceding term; therefore, the 9th term is $19 + y$, the 10th term is $19 + y + y = 19 + 2y$, the 11th term is $19 + 2y + y = 19 + 3y$, and the 12th term is $19 + 3y + y = 19 + 4y$. But the 12th term is 29, so

$$29 = 19 + 4y \Rightarrow 10 = 4y \Rightarrow y = 2.5.$$

We could now count backward from the 8th term to the 1st term, subtracting 2.5 each time. Instead, note that, to get from the 1st to the 8th term, we had to add 2.5 seven times. Therefore:

$$x + (7 \times 2.5) = 19 \Rightarrow x + 17.5 = 19 \Rightarrow x = 1.5.$$
Finally, $xy = 1.5 \times 2.5 = 3.75$.

15. (36)   Between car 7 and car 25 there are $25 - 7 - 1 = 17$ cars, so there are also 17 cars on the other side of the wheel between car 25 and car 7. In all, there are $17 + 17 + 2 = 36$ cars.

12-Q INTERPRETATION OF DATA

On every SAT I a few questions will require you to interpret and/or manipulate the data that appear in some type of table or graph. The graphs will be no more complicated, and probably simpler, than the ones that you usually see in newspapers and magazines or in your science or social studies textbooks.

You are often asked two questions based on the same set of data. In this case, the first question is usually quite easy, requiring only that you *read* the information in the table or graph. The second question is usually a little more challenging and may ask you to *interpret* the data, or *manipulate* them, or *make a prediction* based on them.

The data can be presented in the columns of a table or displayed graphically. The graphs that appear most often are bar graphs, line graphs, and circle graphs. In this section, we will illustrate each of these and give several examples of the types of questions that may be asked.

Helpful Hint

Before even reading the questions based on a graph or table, take 10 or 15 seconds to look it over. Make sure you understand the information that is being displayed and the units of the quantities involved.

Helpful Hint

After looking over the entire graph, read the first question. Be clear about what is being asked, and circle it in your test booklet. Answer the questions based only on the information provided in the graph.

Although the preceding hint is good advice on *all* SAT I questions, it is particularly important on table and graph problems because there is so much information that can be used, and so many different questions can be asked.

Let's start by looking at a *line graph*. A line graph indicates how one or more quantities change over time. The horizontal axis is usually marked off in units of time; the units on the vertical axis can represent almost any type of numerical data: dollars, weights, exam grades, number of people, and so on.

Here is a typical line graph:

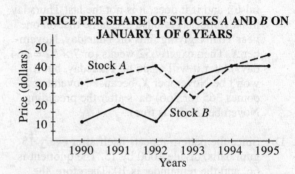

PRICE PER SHARE OF STOCKS A AND B ON JANUARY 1 OF 6 YEARS

Before reading even one of the questions based on the above graph, you should have acquired *at least* the following information: (i) the graph gives the values of two different stocks; (ii) the graph covers the period from January 1, 1990, to January 1, 1995; (iii) during that time, both stocks rose in value.

There are literally dozens of questions that could be asked about the data in this graph. The next seven examples are typical of the types of questions that appear on the SAT I.

Example 1.

What is the difference, in dollars, between the highest and lowest value of a share of stock A?

Solution 1. The lowest value of stock A was \$25 (in 1993); the highest value was \$45 (in 1995). The difference is **\$20**.

Example 2.

On January 1 of what year was the difference in the values of a share of stock A and a share of stock B the greatest?

Solution 2. Just look at the graph. The difference was clearly the greatest in **1992**. (Note that you don't have to calculate what the difference was.)

Example 3.

On January 1 of what year was the ratio of the value of a share of stock A to the value of a share of stock B the greatest?

Solution 3. From 1993 to 1995 the values of the two stocks were fairly close, so those years are not candidates. In 1992, when the difference was greatest, the ratio was 40:15 or 8:3 (or 2.666). In 1990, the difference was less (only $20), but the ratio was 30:10 or 3:1 (or 3). The ratio was greatest in **1990**.

Example 4.

In what year was the percent increase in the value of a share of stock *B* the greatest?

Solution 4. Just look at the graph. Since the slope of the graph is steepest in **1992** (between 1/1/92 and 1/1/93), the rate of growth was greatest then.

Example 5.

During how many years did the value of stock *B* grow at a faster rate than that of stock *A*?

Solution 5. Again, look at the slopes.

In 1990, *B* rose more sharply than *A*. (✓)

In 1991, *B* fell while *A* rose.

In 1992, *B* rose while *A* fell. (✓)

In 1993, *A* rose more sharply than *B*.

In 1994, *A* rose; *B* stayed the same.

B grew at a faster rate during **2** years.

Example 6.

What was the average yearly increase in the value of a share of stock *A* from 1990 to 1995?

Solution 6. Over the 5-year period from January 1, 1990, to January 1, 1995, the value of a share of stock *A* rose from $30 to $45, an increase of $15. The average yearly increase was $15 ÷ 5 years or **$3** per year.

Example 7.

If from 1995 to 2000 the value of each stock increases at the same rate as it did from 1990 to 1995, what will be the ratio of the value of a share of stock *B* to the value of a share of stock *A*?

Solution 7. From 1990 to 1995, the value of stock *A* increased by 50% (from $30 to $45) and the value of stock *B* quadrupled (from $10 to $40). At the same rates, stock *A* will grow from $45 to $67.50 in the years 1995–2000, while stock *B* will grow from $40 to $160. The ratio of the value of a share of stock *B* to the value of a share of stock *A* will be 160 to 67.5, or approximately **2.37**.

In answering these seven questions, we used most (but not all) of the data contained in the graph. On the SAT I, if you had two questions based on that line graph, you can see that there would be many items of information you would not use.

Helpful Hint

On data interpretation questions ignore the extraneous information you are given. Zero in on exactly what you need.

The same information that was given in the preceding line graph, could have been presented in a **table** or in a **bar graph**.

PRICE PER SHARE OF STOCKS *A* AND *B* ON JANUARY 1 OF 6 YEARS

	Prices (dollars)					
Stock	1990	1991	1992	1993	1994	1995
Stock *A*	30	35	40	25	40	45
Stock *B*	10	20	15	35	40	40

PRICE PER SHARE OF STOCKS *A* AND *B* ON JANUARY 1 OF 6 YEARS

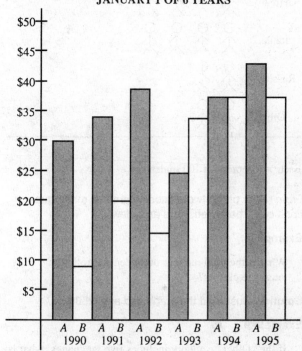

In a bar graph, the taller the bar, the greater is the value of the quantity. Bar graphs can also be drawn horizontally; in this case the longer the bar, the greater is the quantity. You will see examples of each type in the exercises at the end of this section, in the Model Tests, and, of course, on the SAT I.

The following bar graph shows the numbers of students taking courses in the various foreign languages offered at a state college.

NUMBERS OF STUDENTS ENROLLED IN LANGUAGE COURSES AT STATE COLLEGE IN 1995

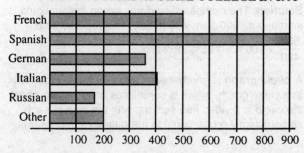

In a slight variation of the horizontal bar graph, the bars are replaced by a string of icons, or symbols. For example, the graph below, in which each picture of a person represents 100 students, conveys the same information as does the preceding bar graph.

NUMBERS OF STUDENTS ENROLLED IN LANGUAGE COURSES AT STATE COLLEGE IN 1995

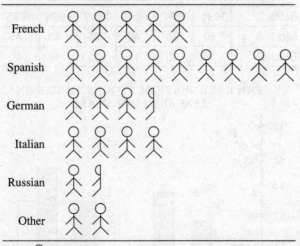

French	
Spanish	
German	
Italian	
Russian	
Other	

Each 人 represents 100 students.

From either of the two preceding graphs, many questions could be asked. Here are a few.

Example 8.

What is the total number of students enrolled in language classes?

Solution. Just read the graph and add: **2500**.

Example 9.

If the "Other" category includes five languages, what is the average (arithmetic mean) number of students studying each language offered at the college?

Solution. There are 2500 students divided among 10 languages (the 5 listed plus the 5 in the "Other" category): $2500 \div 10 = $ **250**.

Example 10.

If the number of students studying Italian next year is the same as the number taking Spanish this year, by what percent will the number of students taking Italian increase?

Solution. The number of students taking Italian would increase by 500 from 400 to 900. This represents a $\frac{500}{400} \times 100\% = $ **125% increase**.

A *circle graph* is another way to present data pictorially. In a circle graph, which is sometimes called a *pie chart*, the circle is divided into sectors, with the size of each sector exactly proportional to the quantity it represents.

For example, the information included in the previous bar graph is presented in the following circle graph.

NUMBERS OF STUDENTS ENROLLED IN LANGUAGE COURSES AT STATE COLLEGE IN 1995

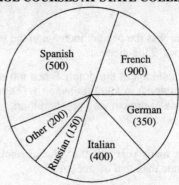

Usually on the SAT I, in each sector of the circle is noted the number of degrees of its central angle or the percent of the total data it contains. For example, in the circle graph above, since 500 of the 2500 language students at State College are studying French, the sector representing French is exactly $\frac{1}{5}$ of the circle. On the SAT I this sector would also be marked either $72°$ $\left(\frac{1}{5} \text{ of } 360°\right)$ or 20% $\left(\frac{1}{5} \text{ of } 100\%\right)$. The SAT I graph would look like one of the graphs below.

DISTRIBUTION OF THE 2500 STUDENTS ENROLLED IN LANGUAGE COURSES

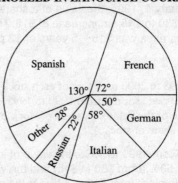

DISTRIBUTION OF THE 2500 STUDENTS ENROLLED IN LANGUAGE COURSES

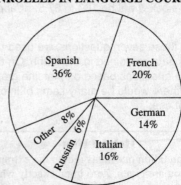

Very often on the SAT I, some data are omitted from a circle graph, and it is your job to determine the missing item. Consider the following circle graph, which shows the distribution of marbles by color in a large jar.

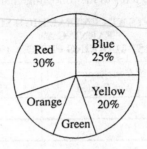

Example 11.

If the jar contains 1200 marbles and there are twice as many orange marbles as there are green, how many green marbles are there?

Solution. Since the red, blue, and yellow marbles constitute 75% of the total (30% + 25% + 20%), the orange and green ones combined account for 25% of the total: 25% of 1200 = 300. Then, since the ratio of orange marbles to green ones is 2:1, there are 200 orange marbles and **100** green ones.

Example 12.

Assume that the jar contains 1200 marbles, and that all of the red ones are removed and replaced by an equal number of marbles, all of which are blue or yellow. If the ratio of blue to yellow marbles remains the same, how many additional yellow marbles are there?

Solution. Since 30% of 1200 is 360, the 360 red marbles were replaced by 360 blue and yellow ones. To maintain the current blue to yellow ratio of 25 to 20, or 5 to 4, $\frac{5}{9}$ of the new marbles would be blue and $\frac{4}{9}$ would be yellow: $\frac{4}{9}$ of 360 = **160**.

Exercises on Interpretation of Data

Multiple-Choice Questions

Questions 1–3 refer to the following graph.

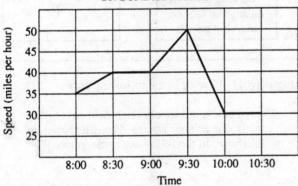

1. For what percent of the time was Marc driving at 40 miles per hour or faster?

    (A) 20   (B) 25   (C) $33\frac{1}{3}$ (D) 40   (E) 50

2. How far, in miles, did Marc drive between 8:30 and 9:00?

    (A) 0   (B) 20   (C) 30   (D) 40
    (E) It cannot be determined from the information given.

3. What was Marc's average speed, in miles per hour, between 8:30 and 9:30?

    (A) 40   (B) $41\frac{2}{3}$ (C) 42.5   (D) 45

    (E) It cannot be determined from the information given.

Questions 4–6 refer to the following graph.

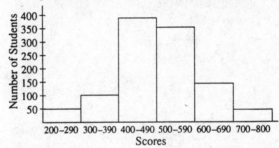

4. How many juniors at Central High School took the SAT I?

    (A) 1000   (B) 1100   (C) 1200   (D) 1250
    (E) 1300

5. What percent of the juniors had Verbal SAT I scores of less than 600?

    (A) $95\frac{5}{11}$ (B) $83\frac{1}{3}$ (C) $81\frac{9}{11}$ (D) 80

    (E) It cannot be determined from the information given.

6. How many juniors had Verbal SAT I scores between 450 and 550?

   (A) 360   (B) 375   (C) 525   (D) 750
   (E) It cannot be determined from the information given.

Questions 7–8 refer to the following graph.

1996 SMITH FAMILY HOUSEHOLD BUDGET

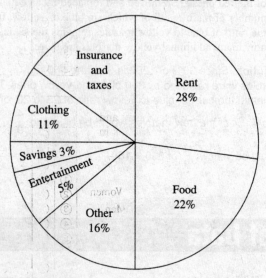

7. If the Smiths' income in 1996 was $40,000, how much more did they spend on insurance and taxes than they did on clothing?

   (A) $1600   (B) $2000   (C) $3200   (D) $4400
   (E) $6000

8. What is the degree measure of the central angle of the sector representing insurance and taxes?

   (A) 45   (B) 54   (C) 60   (D) 72   (E) 90

Quantitative Comparison Questions

Column A	Column B

Questions 9–10 refer to the following chart.

STUDENTS AT CENTRAL HIGH SCHOOL EARNING A's
FIRST MARKING PERIOD, 1995

Number of Courses in Which an A Was Earned	Percent of Students
0	26
1	14
2	24
3	18
4	12
5 or more	x

There are 2500 students at Central High School.

9.

Number of students earning A's in five or more courses	150

During the second marking period, 50% of the students earned at least one more A than they had during the first marking period.

10.

Number of students earning no A's during the second marking period	300

Questions 11–12 refer to the following chart.

Every student at Lincoln High School is taking exactly one science course. The distribution is shown in the following circle graph:

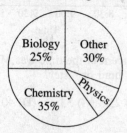

The "other" category, in order of number of students taking each course, consists of astronomy, geology, and ecology.

11.

Number of students taking astronomy	Number of students taking physics

Column A	Column B

200 students transfer to Lincoln High School, and all are placed in biology classes.

12.

Number of students now taking biology	Number of students now taking chemistry

Grid-in Questions

Questions 13–14 refer to the following graph.

DISTRIBUTION OF GRADES ON THE FINAL EXAM IN MATH

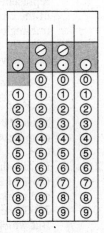

13. If 500 students took the exam, how many earned grades of D?

14. What percent of the students who failed the exam would have had to pass it, in order for the percent of students passing the exam to be at least 88%?

15. The following bar graph shows the number of men and women who earned Ph.D.'s in mathematics at State University in 1996 and 1997.

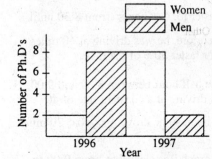

From 1996 to 1997 the number of women earning Ph.D.'s increased by $x\%$, and the number of men earning Ph.D.'s decreased by $y\%$. What is the value of $x - y$?

Answer Key

1.	E		4.	B		7.	A		9.	C
2.	B		5.	C		8.	B		10.	B
3.	C		6.	E						

11.	A
12.	D

13. $2\,5$ 14. $4\,0$ 15. $2\,2\,5$

Answer Explanations

1. **E.** Of the $2\frac{1}{2}$ hours (from 8:00 until 10:30) that Marc was driving, he was going 40 miles per hour or faster for $1\frac{1}{4}$ hours (from 8:30 until 9:45). Therefore, he was driving at 40 miles per hour or faster 50% of the time.

2. **B.** During the half hour between 8:30 and 9:00, Marc was driving at a constant rate of 40 miles per hour, so he drove $\frac{1}{2} \times 40 = 20$ miles.

3. **C.** From the graph it is clear that, from 9:00 to 9:30 Marc's speed increased steadily from 40 to 50 miles per hour and that his average speed was 45 miles per hour. From 8:30 to 9:00 his average speed was clearly 40 miles per hour. So, for the entire hour, he averaged $\frac{40+45}{2} = 42.5$ miles per hour.

4. **B.** Just read the graph carefully, and add the numbers of juniors who had scores in each range:

$$50 + 100 + 400 + 350 + 150 + 50 = 1100.$$

5. **C.** Of the 1100 students, 900 had scores less than 600, and $\frac{900}{1100} = 81\frac{9}{11}\%$.

6. **E.** There is no way of knowing. It is possible, though very unlikely, that all of the scores between 400 and 590 were between 400 and 420 or 570 and 590, and that no one scored between 450 and 550. Undoubtedly, some did, but we can't tell how many.

7. **A.** The total percent for the six categories for which percents are given is

$$28 + 22 + 16 + 5 + 3 + 11 = 85,$$

so the percent of their income that the Smiths spend on insurance and taxes is 15%. Since they spend 11% on clothing, the difference between the two categories is 4%. Finally, 4% of $40,000 is $1600.

8. **B.** Since insurance and taxes take up 15% of the Smiths' income (see solution 7), the sector representing insurance and taxes must be 15% of the circle. The degree measure of the central angle for this sector is 15% of 360 = 54.

9. **C.** First solve for x:

$$26\% + 14\% + 24\% + 18\% + 12\% + x\% = 100\%$$
$$\Rightarrow 94\% + x\% = 100\% \Rightarrow x = 6.$$

Then 6% of 2500 = 150 students earned five or more A's. Columns A and B are equal.

10. **D.** During the first marking period, 650 students (26% of 2500) earned no A's. During the second marking period, 1250 students (50% of 2500) increased the number of A's they earned. But which students? It is possible that all 650 students who had no A's now had at least one A, in which case Column A would be 0. It is also possible, however, that the increase in A's occurred only among those already earning some A's and that none of the 650 students with no A's in the first period earned any A's in the second. In that case, Column A would be 650. The answer is D.

11. **A.** Let x = percent of students taking physics. Then:

$$30\% + 25\% + 35\% + x\% = 100\% \Rightarrow$$
$$90\% + x\% = 100\% \Rightarrow x = 10,$$

so 10% of the students take physics (Column B). Since more students take astronomy than either geology or ecology, astronomy accounts for more than one-third of the 30% in the other category. Therefore, Column A is *more than* 10% of the students.

12. D.   If Lincoln High School originally had 100 students, 25 of them would be taking biology and 35 would be taking chemistry. Clearly, if 200 students transfer into biology classes, there will be many more biology students than chemistry students. However, if there were originally 3000 students in the school, there would be 750 biology students and 1050 chemistry students. Even with the addition of 200 biology students, after the transfer there will still be more students taking chemistry.

13. (25)   Since 20% + 30% + 35% + 10% = 95%, 5% of the students earned grades of D: 5% of 500 = 25.

14. (40)   For the passing rate to have been at least 88%, no more than 60 students (12% of 500) could have failed. Of the 100 students (20% of 500) who actually failed, 40 of them would have had to pass: 40 of 100 is 40%.

15. (225)   Since from 1996 to 1997 the number of women Ph.D's rose from 2 to 8, the actual increase was 6, and the percent increase was $\frac{6}{2} \times 100\% = 300\%$, so $x = 300$. At the same time, the number of men Ph.D's fell from 8 to 2, a decrease of 6; the percent decrease was

$$\frac{6}{8} \times 100\% = \frac{3}{4} \times 100\% = 75\%.$$

Therefore, $y = 75$, and $x - y = 300 - 75 = 225$.

PART FOUR

Test Yourself

13 Seven Model SAT I Tests

- **7 Model Tests**
- **Answer Keys**
- **Self-Evaluations**
- **Answer Explanations**

You are now about to take a major step in preparing yourself to handle an actual SAT I. Before you are 7 Model Tests patterned after current published SATs. Up to now, you've concentrated on specific areas and on general testing techniques. You've mastered tactics and answered practice questions. Now you have a chance to test yourself—thoroughly, repeatedly—before you walk in that test center door.

These 7 Model Tests resemble the actual SAT I, in format, in difficulty, and in content. When you take them, take them as if they *were* the actual SAT I.

Build Your Stamina

Don't start and stop and take time out for a soda or for an important phone call. To do well on the SAT I, you have to focus on the test, the test, and nothing but the test for hours at a time. Many high school students have never had to sit through a three-hour examination before they take their first SAT I. To survive such a long exam takes *stamina*, and, as marathon runners know, the only way to build stamina is to put in the necessary time.

Refine Your Skills

You know how to maximize your score by tackling easy questions first and by eliminating wrong answers whenever you can. Put these skills into practice. If you find yourself spending too much time on any one question, make an educated guess and move on. Remember to check frequently to make sure you are answering the questions in the right spots. This is a great chance for you to get these skills down pat.

Spot Your Weak Points

Do you need a bit more drill in a particular area? After you take each test, consult the self-evaluation section and the answer explanations for that test to pinpoint any areas that need work. *Don't just evaluate your scores.* Build your skills. Read the answer explanations for each question you answered incorrectly, each question you omitted, and each question you answered correctly but found hard. The answer explanation section is tailor-made to help you. You'll find reminders of tactics, definitions of terms, explanations of why the correct answer works. You'll even find an occasional shortcut or two and an explanation of why that incorrect answer didn't work.

Use the answer explanation section to help you spot specific types of questions that you want to review. Suppose, for example, you've omitted answering several reading questions on a test. Going through the answer explanations, you find they all belong to the Inference type. You know right then that you can boost your score by mastering that specific skill.

Take a Deep Breath— and Smile!

It's hard to stay calm when those around you are tense, and you're bound to run into some pretty tense people when you take the SAT I (Not everyone works through this book, unfortunately.) So you may experience a slight case of "exam nerves" on the big day. Don't worry about it.

1. Being keyed up for an examination isn't always bad: you may outdo yourself because you are so worked up.
2. Total panic is unlikely to set in: you know too much.

You know you can handle a three-hour test.

You know you can handle the sorts of questions you'll find on the SAT I.

You know you can omit several questions and *still* score high. Answer correctly only 50–60% of the questions, omitting others, and you'll get a better than average score (and hundreds of solid, well-known colleges are out there right now, looking for serious students with just that kind of score). Answer more than that correctly and you should wind up with a superior score.

Make Your Practice Pay—Approximate the Test

1. Whenever possible, complete an entire Model Test at one sitting.

2. Use a clock or timer.

3. Allow *precisely* 30 minutes for sections 1 through 4 and 15 minutes for sections 5 and 6. (If you have time left over, review your answers or recheck the way you've marked your answer sheet.)

4. After each section, give yourself a one-minute break, and after section 3 take a ten-minute break.

5. Allow no talking in the test room.

6. Work rapidly without wasting time.

Answer Sheet—Test 1

If a section has fewer than 35 questions, leave the extra spaces blank.

Section 1

1 A B C D E	8 A B C D E	15 A B C D E	22 A B C D E	29 A B C D E
2 A B C D E	9 A B C D E	16 A B C D E	23 A B C D E	30 A B C D E
3 A B C D E	10 A B C D E	17 A B C D E	24 A B C D E	31 A B C D E
4 A B C D E	11 A B C D E	18 A B C D E	25 A B C D E	32 A B C D E
5 A B C D E	12 A B C D E	19 A B C D E	26 A B C D E	33 A B C D E
6 A B C D E	13 A B C D E	20 A B C D E	27 A B C D E	34 A B C D E
7 A B C D E	14 A B C D E	21 A B C D E	28 A B C D E	35 A B C D E

Section 2

1 A B C D E	8 A B C D E	15 A B C D E	22 A B C D E	29 A B C D E
2 A B C D E	9 A B C D E	16 A B C D E	23 A B C D E	30 A B C D E
3 A B C D E	10 A B C D E	17 A B C D E	24 A B C D E	31 A B C D E
4 A B C D E	11 A B C D E	18 A B C D E	25 A B C D E	32 A B C D E
5 A B C D E	12 A B C D E	19 A B C D E	26 A B C D E	33 A B C D E
6 A B C D E	13 A B C D E	20 A B C D E	27 A B C D E	34 A B C D E
7 A B C D E	14 A B C D E	21 A B C D E	28 A B C D E	35 A B C D E

Section 3

1 A B C D E	8 A B C D E	15 A B C D E	22 A B C D E	29 A B C D E
2 A B C D E	9 A B C D E	16 A B C D E	23 A B C D E	30 A B C D E
3 A B C D E	10 A B C D E	17 A B C D E	24 A B C D E	31 A B C D E
4 A B C D E	11 A B C D E	18 A B C D E	25 A B C D E	32 A B C D E
5 A B C D E	12 A B C D E	19 A B C D E	26 A B C D E	33 A B C D E
6 A B C D E	13 A B C D E	20 A B C D E	27 A B C D E	34 A B C D E
7 A B C D E	14 A B C D E	21 A B C D E	28 A B C D E	35 A B C D E

Section 4

1 A B C D E	4 A B C D E	7 A B C D E	10 A B C D E	13 A B C D E
2 A B C D E	5 A B C D E	8 A B C D E	11 A B C D E	14 A B C D E
3 A B C D E	6 A B C D E	9 A B C D E	12 A B C D E	15 A B C D E

Section 4 (continued)

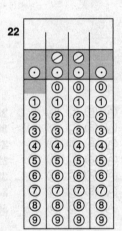

Section 5

1 Ⓐ Ⓑ Ⓒ Ⓓ Ⓔ	8 Ⓐ Ⓑ Ⓒ Ⓓ Ⓔ	15 Ⓐ Ⓑ Ⓒ Ⓓ Ⓔ	22 Ⓐ Ⓑ Ⓒ Ⓓ Ⓔ	29 Ⓐ Ⓑ Ⓒ Ⓓ Ⓔ
2 Ⓐ Ⓑ Ⓒ Ⓓ Ⓔ	9 Ⓐ Ⓑ Ⓒ Ⓓ Ⓔ	16 Ⓐ Ⓑ Ⓒ Ⓓ Ⓔ	23 Ⓐ Ⓑ Ⓒ Ⓓ Ⓔ	30 Ⓐ Ⓑ Ⓒ Ⓓ Ⓔ
3 Ⓐ Ⓑ Ⓒ Ⓓ Ⓔ	10 Ⓐ Ⓑ Ⓒ Ⓓ Ⓔ	17 Ⓐ Ⓑ Ⓒ Ⓓ Ⓔ	24 Ⓐ Ⓑ Ⓒ Ⓓ Ⓔ	31 Ⓐ Ⓑ Ⓒ Ⓓ Ⓔ
4 Ⓐ Ⓑ Ⓒ Ⓓ Ⓔ	11 Ⓐ Ⓑ Ⓒ Ⓓ Ⓔ	18 Ⓐ Ⓑ Ⓒ Ⓓ Ⓔ	25 Ⓐ Ⓑ Ⓒ Ⓓ Ⓔ	32 Ⓐ Ⓑ Ⓒ Ⓓ Ⓔ
5 Ⓐ Ⓑ Ⓒ Ⓓ Ⓔ	12 Ⓐ Ⓑ Ⓒ Ⓓ Ⓔ	19 Ⓐ Ⓑ Ⓒ Ⓓ Ⓔ	26 Ⓐ Ⓑ Ⓒ Ⓓ Ⓔ	33 Ⓐ Ⓑ Ⓒ Ⓓ Ⓔ
6 Ⓐ Ⓑ Ⓒ Ⓓ Ⓔ	13 Ⓐ Ⓑ Ⓒ Ⓓ Ⓔ	20 Ⓐ Ⓑ Ⓒ Ⓓ Ⓔ	27 Ⓐ Ⓑ Ⓒ Ⓓ Ⓔ	34 Ⓐ Ⓑ Ⓒ Ⓓ Ⓔ
7 Ⓐ Ⓑ Ⓒ Ⓓ Ⓔ	14 Ⓐ Ⓑ Ⓒ Ⓓ Ⓔ	21 Ⓐ Ⓑ Ⓒ Ⓓ Ⓔ	28 Ⓐ Ⓑ Ⓒ Ⓓ Ⓔ	35 Ⓐ Ⓑ Ⓒ Ⓓ Ⓔ

Section 6

1 Ⓐ Ⓑ Ⓒ Ⓓ Ⓔ	8 Ⓐ Ⓑ Ⓒ Ⓓ Ⓔ	15 Ⓐ Ⓑ Ⓒ Ⓓ Ⓔ	22 Ⓐ Ⓑ Ⓒ Ⓓ Ⓔ	29 Ⓐ Ⓑ Ⓒ Ⓓ Ⓔ
2 Ⓐ Ⓑ Ⓒ Ⓓ Ⓔ	9 Ⓐ Ⓑ Ⓒ Ⓓ Ⓔ	16 Ⓐ Ⓑ Ⓒ Ⓓ Ⓔ	23 Ⓐ Ⓑ Ⓒ Ⓓ Ⓔ	30 Ⓐ Ⓑ Ⓒ Ⓓ Ⓔ
3 Ⓐ Ⓑ Ⓒ Ⓓ Ⓔ	10 Ⓐ Ⓑ Ⓒ Ⓓ Ⓔ	17 Ⓐ Ⓑ Ⓒ Ⓓ Ⓔ	24 Ⓐ Ⓑ Ⓒ Ⓓ Ⓔ	31 Ⓐ Ⓑ Ⓒ Ⓓ Ⓔ
4 Ⓐ Ⓑ Ⓒ Ⓓ Ⓔ	11 Ⓐ Ⓑ Ⓒ Ⓓ Ⓔ	18 Ⓐ Ⓑ Ⓒ Ⓓ Ⓔ	25 Ⓐ Ⓑ Ⓒ Ⓓ Ⓔ	32 Ⓐ Ⓑ Ⓒ Ⓓ Ⓔ
5 Ⓐ Ⓑ Ⓒ Ⓓ Ⓔ	12 Ⓐ Ⓑ Ⓒ Ⓓ Ⓔ	19 Ⓐ Ⓑ Ⓒ Ⓓ Ⓔ	26 Ⓐ Ⓑ Ⓒ Ⓓ Ⓔ	33 Ⓐ Ⓑ Ⓒ Ⓓ Ⓔ
6 Ⓐ Ⓑ Ⓒ Ⓓ Ⓔ	13 Ⓐ Ⓑ Ⓒ Ⓓ Ⓔ	20 Ⓐ Ⓑ Ⓒ Ⓓ Ⓔ	27 Ⓐ Ⓑ Ⓒ Ⓓ Ⓔ	34 Ⓐ Ⓑ Ⓒ Ⓓ Ⓔ
7 Ⓐ Ⓑ Ⓒ Ⓓ Ⓔ	14 Ⓐ Ⓑ Ⓒ Ⓓ Ⓔ	21 Ⓐ Ⓑ Ⓒ Ⓓ Ⓔ	28 Ⓐ Ⓑ Ⓒ Ⓓ Ⓔ	35 Ⓐ Ⓑ Ⓒ Ⓓ Ⓔ

MODEL SAT I TEST 1   1 1 1 1 1   1

SECTION 1   Time—30 Minutes   Select the best answer to the following questions, then fill in
30 Questions   the appropriate space on your Answer Sheet.

Each of the following sentences contains one or two blanks; these blanks indicate that a word or set of words has been left out. Below the sentence are five words or phrases, lettered A through E. Select the word or set of words that best completes the sentence.

Example:

Fame is ----; today's rising star is all too soon tomorrow's washed-up has-been.

(A) rewarding   (B) gradual
(C) essential   (D) spontaneous
(E) transitory

Ⓐ Ⓑ Ⓒ Ⓓ ●

1. Critics of the welfare system argue that, rather than aiding people's efforts to govern their own lives, it ---- their independence.

(A) supports   (B) saps   (C) hastens
(D) renews   (E) abets

2. The audience failed to warm to the candidate, whose speech contained nothing but empty promises, ----, and clichés.

(A) candor
(B) platitudes
(C) nuances
(D) ingenuity
(E) threats

3. By dint of much practice in the laboratory, the anatomy student became ---- and was able to manipulate her dissecting tools with either hand.

(A) practical
(B) tricky
(C) ambiguous
(D) ambidextrous
(E) ambivalent

4. Like many other pioneers, Dr. Elizabeth Blackwell, founder of the New York Infirmary, the first American hospital staffed entirely by women, faced ridicule from her contemporaries but has received great honor ----.

(A) posthumously
(B) anonymously
(C) privately
(D) prematurely
(E) previously

5. While a great deal of change and modernization has taken place in India since 1947, the basic economic arrangements, values, and family roles have been generally ----.

(A) overturned
(B) stable
(C) modified
(D) complicated
(E) appropriate

6. The hypocrite ---- feelings which he does not possess but which he feels he should display.

(A) conceals
(B) decries
(C) betrays
(D) simulates
(E) condones

7. Deloria has his detractors, but his critics have had amazingly ---- success at shaking his self-confidence or ---- his reputation.

(A) great..repairing
(B) widespread...bolstering
(C) little...denting
(D) small...enhancing
(E) poor...restoring

8. The linguistic ---- of refugee children is ---- their readiness to adopt the language of their new homeland.

(A) conservatism...indicated by
(B) inadequacy...demonstrated by
(C) adaptability...reflected in
(D) philosophy...contradicted by
(E) structure...equivalent to

9. She kept her late parents' furniture, not for any ---- value it had, but for purely ---- reasons.

(A) potential...monetary
(B) ornamental...aesthetic
(C) financial...pecuniary
(D) intrinsic...sentimental
(E) personal...accidental

GO ON TO THE NEXT PAGE

1 1 1 1 1 1 1 1 1 1 1 1

The analogies questions present two words or phrases that are related in some way. Determine which A-through-E answer choice below has a relationship *most* similar to that of the original words or phrases.

Example:

YAWN:BOREDOM:: (A) dream:sleep
(B) anger:madness (C) smile:amusement
(D) face:expression (E) impatience:rebellion

---

10. WORDS:WRITER::
 (A) honor:thief
 (B) mortar:bricklayer
 (C) child:teacher
 (D) batter:baker
 (E) laws:policeman

11. SNOW:DRIFT::
 (A) mountain:boulder
 (B) sand:dune
 (C) pane:glass
 (D) desert:oasis
 (E) mud:rain

12. GRAIN:SILO::
 (A) tree:acorn
 (B) seed:plant
 (C) water:bucket
 (D) druggist:doctor
 (E) furlong:mile

13. SHRUG:INDIFFERENCE::
 (A) grin:deference
 (B) wave:fatigue
 (C) nod:assent
 (D) blink:scorn
 (E) scowl:desire

14. ANGER:CHOLERIC::
 (A) wrath:ironic
 (B) love:bucolic
 (C) island:volcanic
 (D) greed:avaricious
 (E) pride:malicious

15. BLANDISHMENT:ALLURE::
 (A) admonition:warn
 (B) punishment:reward
 (C) scruple:disregard
 (D) invitation:issue
 (E) entertainment:perform

Read each of the passages below, and then answer the questions that follow each passage. The correct response may be stated outright or merely suggested in the passage.

Questions 16–21 are based on the following passage.

The following passage discusses so-called "hot spots," regions of unusual volcanic activity that record the passage of plates over the face of Earth. According to one theory, these hot spots may also contribute to the fracturing of continents and the opening of new oceans.

 Although by far the majority of the world's
active volcanoes are located along the boundaries
of the great shifting plates that make up Earth'
Line surface, more than 100 isolated areas of volcanic
(5) activity occur far from the nearest plate boundary.
Geologists call these volcanic areas hot spots or
mantle plumes. Many of these sources of magma
(the red-hot, molten material within Earth's crust,
out of which igneous rock is formed) lie deep in
(10) the interior of a plate. These so-called intra-plate
volcanoes often form roughly linear volcanic
chains, trails of extinct volcanoes. The Hawaiian
Islands, perhaps the best known example of an
intra-plate volcanic chain, came into being when
(15) the northwest-moving Pacific plate passed over a
relatively stationary hot spot and in doing so initiated this magma-generation and volcano-forma-
tion process. Such a volcanic chain serves as a
landmark signaling the slow but inexorable pas-
(20) sage of the plates.
 No theorist today would deny that the plates
do move. Satellites anchored in space record the
minute movement of fixed sites on Earth, thereby
confirming the motions of the plates. They show
(25) Africa and South America drawing away from
each other, as new lithospheric material wells up
in the sea floor between them in the phenomenon
known as sea-floor spreading. That the two coastlines complement one another is beyond dispute;
(30) a cursory glance at the map reveals the common
geological features that link these separate shores,
reminders of an age eons past when the two continents were joined. In 1963 the Canadian geo-
physicist J. Tuzo Wilson asserted that while Earth

1 1 1 1 1 1 1 1 1 1 1

(35) scientists have constructed the relative motion of
the plates carrying the continents in detail, "the
motion of one plate with respect to another cannot
readily be translated into motion with respect to
the Earth's interior." For this reason, scientists
(40) were unable to determine whether both continents
were moving (diverging in separate directions) or
whether one continent was motionless while the
other was drifting away from it. Wilson hypothe-
sized that hot spots, fixed in Earth's depths, could
(45) provide the necessary information to settle the
question. Using hot spots as a fixed frame of reference, Wilson concluded that the African plate
was motionless and that it had exhibited no movement for 30 million years.
(50)   Wilson's hot-spot hypothesis goes well beyond
this somewhat limited role. He conceives the hot
spots as playing a major part in influencing the
movements of the continental plates. As he wrote
in his seminal essay in *Scientific American,*
(55) "When a continental plate comes to rest over a
hot spot, the material welling up from deeper layers creates a broad dome. As the dome grows it
develops deep fissures; in at least a few cases the
continent may rupture entirely along some of
(60) these fissures, so that the hot spot initiates the formation of a new ocean." The hot spot, flaring up
from Earth's deepest core, may someday cast new
light on the continents' mutability.

16. The term "hot spot" is being used in the passage

(A) rhetorically
(B) colloquially
(C) technically
(D) ambiguously
(E) ironically

17. The author regards the theory that the plates making up the earth's surface move as

(A) tentative
(B) irrefutable
(C) discredited
(D) unanimous
(E) relative

18. According to the passage, which of the following
statements indicates that Africa and South America
once adjoined one another?

I. They share certain common topographic traits.
II. Their shorelines are physical counterparts.
III. The African plate has been stationary for
30 million years.

(A) I only
(B) II only
(C) I and II only
(D) II and III only
(E) I, II, and III

19. The word "constructed" in line 35 most nearly
means

(A) interpreted   (B) built   (C) impeded
(D) restricted   (E) refuted

20. According to Wilson, the hot spot hypothesis eventually may prove useful in interpreting

(A) the boundaries of the plates
(B) the depth of the ocean floor
(C) the relative motion of the plates
(D) current satellite technology
(E) major changes in continental shape

21. In maintaining that fissures in an upwelled dome
can result in the formation of a new ocean (lines
56–61), Wilson has assumed which of the following points?

(A) The fissures are located directly above a hot
    spot.
(B) The dome is broader than the continent upon
    which it rests.
(C) The oceanic depths are immutable.
(D) The fissures cut across the continent, splitting
    it.
(E) No such fissures exist upon the ocean floor.

Questions 22–30 are based on the following passage.

*The following passage is taken from an essay on
Southwestern Native American art.*

        Among the Plains Indians, two separate strains
of decorative art evolved: the figurative, representational art created by the men of the tribe, and
Line the geometric, abstract art crafted by the women.
(5) According to Dunn and Highwater, the artist's
sex governed both the kind of article to be decorated and the style to be followed in its ornamentation. Thus, the decorative works created by
tribesmen consistently depict living creatures
(10) (men, horses, buffalo) or magical beings (ghosts
and other supernatural life-forms). Those created
by women, however, are clearly nonrepresentational: no figures of men or animals appear in this
classically geometric art.
(15)   Art historians theorize that this abstract,
geometric art, traditionally the prerogative of the
women, predates the figurative art of the men.
Descending from those aspects of Woodland
culture that gave rise to weaving, quillwork, and
(20) beadwork, it is a utilitarian art, intended for the
embellishment of ordinary, serviceable objects

GO ON TO THE NEXT PAGE ⟩

1 1 1 1 1 1 1 1 1 1 1

such as parfleche boxes (cases made of rawhide), saddlebags, and hide robes. The abstract designs combine classical geometric figures into formal
(25) patterns: a ring of narrow isosceles triangles arranged on the background of a large central circle creates the well-known "feather and circle" pattern. Created in bold primary colors (red, yellow, blue), sometimes black or green, and
(30) often outlined in dark paint or glue size, these nonrepresentational designs are nonetheless intricately detailed.

  Although the abstract decorations crafted by the women are visually striking, they pale in sig-
(35) nificance when compared to the narrative compositions created by the men. Created to tell a story, these works were generally heroic in nature, and were intended to commemorate a bold and courageous exploit or a spiritual awakening. Unlike
(40) realistic portraits, the artworks emphasized action, not physical likeness. Highwater describes their making as follows: "These representational works were generally drafted by a group of men—often the individuals who had performed the deeds
(45) being recorded—who drew on untailored hide robes and tepee liners made of skins. The paintings usually filled the entire field; often they were conceived at different times as separate pictorial vignettes documenting specific actions. In rela-
(50) tionship to each other, these vignettes suggest a narrative."

  The tribesmen's narrative artwork depicted not only warlike deeds but also mystic dreams and vision quests. Part of the young male's rite
(55) of passage into tribal adulthood involved his discovering his own personal totem or symbolic guardian. By fasting or by consuming hallucinatory substances, the youth opened himself to the revelation of his "mystery object," a symbol that
(60) could protect him from both natural and supernatural dangers.

  What had been in the early 1700s a highly individualistic, personal iconography changed into something very different by the early nine-
(65) teenth century. As Anglos came West in ever greater numbers, they brought with them new materials and new ideas. Just as European glass beads came to replace native porcupine quills in the women's applied designs, cloth eventually
(70) became used as a substitute for animal hides. The emphasis of Plains artwork shifted as well: tribespeople came to create works that celebrated the solidarity of Indians as a group rather than their prowess as individuals.

22. Which of the following titles best summarizes the content of the passage?

 (A) The Ongoing Influence of Plains Indian Art
 (B) Male and Female in Tribal Life
 (C) Indian Art as Narrative and Dream
 (D) Design Specialization In Plains Art
 (E) The History of Indian Representational Art

23. The author cites examples of the work of Plains artists primarily to

 (A) show the differences between male and female decorative styles
 (B) emphasize the functional role of art in Indian life
 (C) describe the techniques employed in the creation of particular works
 (D) illustrate the changes made by Anglo influence on Plains art
 (E) explore the spiritual significance of representational design

24. The word "strains" in line 1 means

 (A) tunes
 (B) pressures
 (C) varieties
 (D) injuries
 (E) pressures

25. In lines 19–20, weaving, quillwork, and beadwork are presented as examples of

 (A) male-dominated decorative arts
 (B) uninspired products of artisans
 (C) geometrically based crafts
 (D) unusual applications of artistic theories
 (E) precursors of representational design

26. With which of the following statements regarding male Plains artists prior to 1800 would the author most likely agree?

 I. They tended to work collaboratively on projects.
 II. They believed art had power to ward off danger.
 III. They derived their designs from classical forms.

 (A) I only
 (B) III only
 (C) I and II only
 (D) II and III only
 (E) I, II, and III

GO ON TO THE NEXT PAGE ⇒

1   1   1   1   1   1   1   1   1   1   1

27. As used in line 43, "drafted" most nearly means

(A) selected
(B) recruited
(C) endorsed
(D) sketched
(E) ventilated

28. According to the passage, dream visions were important to the Plains artist because they

(A) enabled him to foresee influences on his style
(B) suggested the techniques and methods of his art
(C) determined his individual aesthetic philosophy
(D) expressed his sense of tribal solidarity
(E) revealed the true form of his spiritual guardian

29. In its narrative aspect, Plains art resembles LEAST

(A) a cartoon strip made up of several panels
(B) a portrait bust of a chieftain in full headdress
(C) an epic recounting the adventures of a legendary hero
(D) a chapter from the autobiography of a prominent leader
(E) a mural portraying scenes from the life of Martin Luther King

30. According to lines 65–74, the impact of the Anglo presence on Plains art can be seen in the

(A) growth of importance of geometric patterning
(B) dearth of hides available to Plains Indian artists
(C) shift from depicting individuals to depicting the community
(D) emphasis on dream visions as appropriate subject matter for narrative art
(E) growing lack of belief that images could protect one from natural enemies

---

YOU MAY GO BACK AND REVIEW THIS SECTION IN THE REMAINING TIME, BUT DO NOT WORK IN ANY OTHER SECTION UNTIL TOLD TO DO SO.   **S T O P**

SECTION 2

Time—30 Minutes
25 Questions

For each problem in this section determine which of the five choices is correct and blacken in that choice on your answer sheet. You may use any blank space on the page for your work.

Notes:

- You may use a calculator whenever you feel it will be helpful.
- Use the diagrams provided to help you solve the problems. Unless you see the words "<u>Note</u>: Figure not drawn to scale" under a diagram, it has been drawn as accurately as possible. Unless it is stated that a figure is three-dimensional, you may assume it lies in a plane.

Reference Information

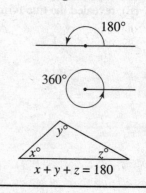

1. If it is now June, what month will it be 100 months from now?

   (A) January (B) April (C) June
   (D) October (E) December

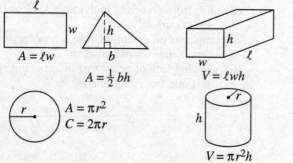

2. In the figure above, what is the value of a?

   (A) 10 (B) 20 (C) 28 (D) 36 (E) 45

3. The Rivertown Little League is divided into d divisions. Each division has t teams, and each team has p players. How many players are there in the entire league?

   (A) $d + t + p$ (B) dtp (C) $\dfrac{pt}{d}$ (D) $\dfrac{dt}{p}$

   (E) $\dfrac{d}{pt}$

4. At the Fancy Furniture Factory, Brian bought two chairs for $299 each and a coffee table for $140. He paid $\dfrac{1}{6}$ of the total cost at the time of purchase and the balance in 12 equal monthly installments. What was the amount of each month's payment?

   (A) $10.25 (B) $37.50 (C) $42.75
   (D) $51.25 (E) $61.50

5. What is the value of n if $2^{n+1} = 32$?

   (A) 4 (B) 5 (C) 6 (D) 7 (E) 8

6. In the figure at the right, what is the value of $a + b + c$?

   (A) 210 (B) 220
   (C) 240 (D) 270
   (E) 280

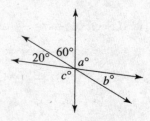

GO ON TO THE NEXT PAGE ⟩

2   2 2 2 2 2 2 2 2 2   2

7. The operation ** is defined as follows: For any positive numbers a and b, $a**b = \sqrt{a + \sqrt{b}}$. Which of the following is an integer?

(A) 11**5   (B) 4**9   (C) 4**16   (D) 7**4
(E) 9**9

Year	1990	1991	1992	1993	1994	1995
Number of tournaments	4	5	10	6	9	12

8. The chart above shows the number of tennis tournaments that Adam entered each year from 1990 through 1995. In what year did he enter 50% more tournaments than the year before?

(A) 1991   (B) 1992   (C) 1993   (D) 1994
(E) 1995

9. If, for any number b, $b\# = b + 1$ and $\#b = b - 1$, which of the following is NOT equal to $(3\#)(\#5)$?

(A) $(1\#)(\#9)$ (B) $7\# + \#9$ (C) $(4\#)(\#4)$

(D) $(7\#)(\#3)$ (E) $\dfrac{15\#}{\#2}$

10. If a is a multiple of 5 and $b = 5a$, which of the following could be the value of $a + b$?

I. 60
II. 100
III. 150

(A) I only   (B) III only   (C) I and III only
(D) II and III only   (E) I, II, and III

11. If Scott can mow $\dfrac{2}{5}$ of a lawn each hour, how many lawns can he mow in h hours?

(A) $\dfrac{2h}{5}$ (B) $\dfrac{5h}{2}$ (C) $h - \dfrac{2}{5}$ (D) $\dfrac{2}{5h}$

(E) $\dfrac{5}{2h}$

12. If $3^a = b$ and $3^c = d$, then $bd =$
(A) 3^{ac} (B) 3^{a+c} (C) 6^{a+c} (D) 9^{ac} (E) 9^{a+c}

13. If r and s are two nonzero numbers and if $78(r + s) = (78 + r)s$, then which of the following MUST be true?

(A) $r = 78$ (B) $s = 78$ (C) $r + s = rs$
(D) $r < 1$ (E) $s < 1$

14. If the average (arithmetic mean) of three consecutive integers is A, which of the following must be true?

I. One of the numbers is equal to A.
II. The average of two of the three numbers is A.
III. A is an integer.

(A) I only   (B) II only   (C) III only
(D) I and II only   (E) I, II, and III

15. A bag contains 25 slips of paper, on each of which a different integer from 1 to 25 is written. Blindfolded, Scott draws one of the slips of paper. He wins if the number on the slip he draws is a multiple of 3 or 5. What is the probability that Scott wins?

(A) $\dfrac{1}{25}$ (B) $\dfrac{8}{25}$ (C) $\dfrac{11}{25}$ (D) $\dfrac{12}{25}$ (E) $\dfrac{13}{25}$

16. If $m^2 = 17$, then what is the value of $(m + 1)(m - 1)$?

(A) $\sqrt{17} - 1$ (B) $\sqrt{17} + 1$ (C) 16   (D) 18
(E) 288

17. What is the value of n if $3^{10} \times 27^2 = 9^2 \times 3^n$?

(A) 6   (B) 10   (C) 12   (D) 15   (E) 30

18. Which of the following points lies in the interior of the circle whose radius is 10 and whose center is at the origin?

(A) $(-9,4)$ (B) $(5,-9)$ (C) $(0,-10)$
(D) $(10,-1)$ (E) $(-6,8)$

GO ON TO THE NEXT PAGE

2   2 2 2 2 2 2 2 2 2   2

19. Assume that p, q, and r are positive integers satisfying the following conditions: (i) $p > q > r$; (ii) p, q, and r are all primes; (iii) $p - q = r$. This information is sufficient to determine the value of which integer or integers?

(A) none of them   (B) p only   (C) q only
(D) r only   (E) p, q, and r

20. If p pencils cost c cents, how many pencils can be bought for d <u>dollars</u>?

(A) cdp (B) $100cdp$ (C) $\dfrac{dp}{100c}$ (D) $\dfrac{100cd}{p}$
(E) $\dfrac{100dp}{c}$

21. If a is increased by 10% and b is decreased by 10%, the resulting numbers will be equal. What is the ratio of a to b?

(A) $\dfrac{9}{11}$ (B) $\dfrac{9}{10}$ (C) $\dfrac{1}{1}$ (D) $\dfrac{10}{9}$ (E) $\dfrac{11}{9}$

22. In the figure at the right, line segments AF and CF partition pentagon $ABCDE$ into a rectangle and two triangles. For which of the following can the value be determined?

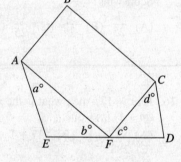

    I. $a + b$
    II. $b + c$
    III. $a + b + c + d$

(A) II only   (B) I and II only
(C) II and III only   (D) I and III only
(E) I, II, and III

23. Which of the following CANNOT be expressed as the sum of two or more consecutive positive integers?

(A) 17   (B) 22   (C) 24   (D) 26   (E) 32

24. The figure at the right consists of four semicircles in a large semicircle. If the small semicircles have radii of 1, 2, 3, and 4, what is the perimeter of the shaded region?

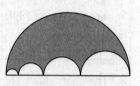

(A) 10π (B) 20π (C) 40π (D) 60π
(E) 100π

25. In the figure at the right, the legs of right triangle ACB are diameters of the two semicircles. If $AB = 4$ what is the sum of the areas of the semicircles?

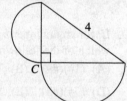

(A) π (B) 2π (C) 4π
(D) 8π (E) 16π

YOU MAY GO BACK AND REVIEW THIS SECTION IN THE REMAINING TIME, BUT DO NOT WORK IN ANY OTHER SECTION UNTIL TOLD TO DO SO.

S T O P

3   3 3 3 3 3 3 3 3 3 3   3

SECTION 3   Time—30 Minutes
35 Questions   Select the best answer to the following questions, then fill in
the appropriate space on your Answer Sheet.

Each of the following sentences contains one or two blanks; these blanks indicate that a word or set of words has been left out. Below the sentence are five words or phrases, lettered A through E. Select the word or set of words that best completes the sentence.

Example:

Fame is ----; today's rising star is all too soon tomorrow's washed-up has-been.

(A) rewarding   (B) gradual
(C) essential   (D) spontaneous
(E) transitory

 Ⓐ Ⓑ Ⓒ Ⓓ ●

1. Like foolish people who continue to live near an active volcano, many of us are ---- about the ---- of atomic warfare and its attendant destruction.
(A) worried...possibility
(B) unconcerned...threat
(C) excited...power
(D) cheered...possession
(E) irritated...news

2. By communicating through pointing and making gestures, Charles was able to overcome any ---- difficulties that arose during his recent trip to Japan.
(A) peripatetic   (B) linguistic   (C) plausible
(D) monetary   (E) territorial

3. It is the task of the International Wildlife Preservation Commission to prevent endangered species from becoming ---- in order that future generations may ---- the great diversity of animal life.
(A) tamed...recollect
(B) evolved...value
(C) extinct...enjoy
(D) specialized...anticipate
(E) widespread...appreciate

4. We find it difficult to translate a foreign text literally because we cannot capture the ---- of the original passage exactly.
(A) novelty
(B) succinctness
(C) connotations
(D) ambivalence
(E) alienation

5. It is remarkable that a man so in the public eye, so highly praised and imitated, can retain his ----.
(A) magniloquence   (B) dogmas   (C) bravado
(D) idiosyncracies   (E) humility

6. For all the ---- involved in the study of seals, we Arctic researchers have occasional moments of pure ---- over some new idea or discovery.
(A) tribulations...despair
(B) hardships...exhilaration
(C) confusions...bewilderment
(D) inconvenience...panic
(E) thrills...delight

7. Despite the growing ---- of Hispanic actors in the American theater, many Hispanic experts feel that the Spanish-speaking population is ---- on the stage.
(A) decrease...inappropriate
(B) emergence...visible
(C) prominence...underrepresented
(D) skill...alienated
(E) number...misdirected

8. As a sportscaster, Cosell was apparently never ----; he made ---- comments about every boxing match he covered.
(A) excited...hysterical
(B) relevant...pertinent
(C) satisfied...disparaging
(D) amazed...awe-struck
(E) impressed...laudatory

9. Even critics who do not ---- Robin Williams' interpretation of the part ---- him as an inventive comic actor who has made a serious attempt to come to terms with one of the most challenging roles of our time.
(A) dissent from...dismiss
(B) cavil at...welcome
(C) agree with...denounce
(D) recoil from...deride
(E) concur with...acknowledge

10. This latest biography of Malcolm X is a nuanced and sensitive picture of a very complex man, ---- analysis of his personality.
(A) an ineffectual   (B) a telling   (C) a ponderous
(D) a simplistic   (E) an overblown

GO ON TO THE NEXT PAGE ▷

3   3   3   3   3   3   3   3   3   3   3   3

The analogies questions present two words or phrases that are related in some way. Determine which A-through-E answer choice below has a relationship *most* similar to that of the original words or phrases.

Example:

YAWN:BOREDOM::   (A) dream:sleep
(B) anger:madness   (C) smile:amusement
(D) face:expression   (E) impatience:rebellion

11. HEART:PUMP::
    (A) lungs:collapse
    (B) appendix:burst
    (C) stomach:digest
    (D) intestine:twist
    (E) teeth:ache

12. MASTER:SERVANT::
    (A) judge:jury
    (B) monarch:subject
    (C) serf:peasant
    (D) capital:labor
    (E) landlord:tenant

13. STANZA:POEM::
    (A) flag:anthem
    (B) story:building
    (C) mural:painting
    (D) program:recital
    (E) rhyme:prose

14. MONGREL:COLLIE::
    (A) goose:gosling
    (B) gem:ruby
    (C) alloy:iron
    (D) pony:bridle
    (E) bleat:sheep

15. MASON:TROWEL::
    (A) potter:clay
    (B) doctor:degree
    (C) carpenter:adze
    (D) preacher:sermon
    (E) sculptor:museum

16. AMASS:WEALTH::
    (A) lavish:bribes
    (B) garner:grain
    (C) disperse:enemy
    (D) refund:deposit
    (E) weigh:value

17. WINCE:PAIN::
    (A) pardon:tolerance
    (B) blush:embarrassment
    (C) cry:anger
    (D) sing:gaiety
    (E) march:patriotism

18. CONNOISSEUR:PAINTING::
    (A) egotist:self
    (B) gourmet:viands
    (C) miser:gold
    (D) jury:criminal
    (E) artist:critic

19. HECKLER:JEER::
    (A) snob:flatter
    (B) grumbler:complain
    (C) mentor:repent
    (D) laughingstock:mock
    (E) miser:weep

20. INIQUITOUS:MALEFACTOR::
    (A) conspicuous:leader
    (B) egregious:philanthropist
    (C) reprehensible:altruist
    (D) renowned:benefactor
    (E) mischievous:prankster

21. SLINK:STEALTH::
    (A) whine:querulousness
    (B) snarl:mockery
    (C) disguise:alias
    (D) praise:friendship
    (E) invest:capital

22. AMUSING:UPROARIOUS::
    (A) puzzling:dumbfounding
    (B) quiet:noisy
    (C) intractable:stubborn
    (D) petty: narrow-minded
    (E) exhausted:weary

23. STANCH:BLEEDING::
    (A) dam:flood
    (B) divert:traffic
    (C) squander:money
    (D) induce:nausea
    (E) color:facts

GO ON TO THE NEXT PAGE

3   3   3   3   3   3   3   3   3   3   3   3

Read the passage below, and then answer the questions that follow the passage. The correct response may be stated outright or merely suggested in the passage.

Questions 24–35 are based on the following passage.

In this excerpt from a novel, Catherine's Aunt Lavinia comes to make her home with Catherine and her father and becomes involved in Catherine's upbringing.

When the child was about ten years old, he
invited his sister, Mrs. Penniman, to come and
stay with him. His sister Lavinia had married a
Line poor clergyman, of a sickly constitution and a
(5)   flowery style of eloquence, and then, at the age of
thirty-three, had been left a widow—without children, without fortune—with nothing but the memory of Mr. Penniman's flowers of speech, a certain vague aroma of which hovered about her own
(10) conversation. Nevertheless, he had offered her a
home under his own roof, which Lavinia accepted
with the alacrity of a woman who had spent the
ten years of her married life in the town of
Poughkeepsie. The Doctor had not proposed to
(15) Mrs. Penniman to come and live with him indefi-
nitely; he had suggested that she should make an
asylum of his house while she looked about for
unfurnished lodgings. It is uncertain whether Mrs.
Penniman ever instituted a search for unfurnished
(20) lodgings, but it is beyond dispute that she never
found them. She settled herself with her brother
and never went away, and, when Catherine was
twenty years old, her Aunt Lavinia was still one
of the most striking features of her immediate
(25) entourage. Mrs. Penniman's own account of the
matter was that she had remained to take charge
of her niece's education. She had given this
account, at least, to everyone but the Doctor, who
never asked for explanations which he could
(30) entertain himself any day with inventing. Mrs.
Penniman, moreover, though she had a good deal
of a certain sort of artificial assurance, shrunk, for
indefinable reasons, from presenting herself to her
brother as a fountain of instruction. She had not a
(35) high sense of humor, but she had enough to prevent her from making this mistake; and her brother, on his side, had enough to excuse her, in her
situation, for laying him under contribution during a considerable part of a lifetime. He therefore
(40) assented tacitly to the proposition which Mrs.
Penniman had tacitly laid down, that it was of
importance that the poor motherless girl should
have a brilliant woman near her. His assent could
only be tacit, for he had never been dazzled by his
(45) sister's intellectual lustre. Save when he fell in
love with Catherine Harrington, he had never
been dazzled, indeed, by any feminine character-

istics whatever; and though he was to a certain
extent what is called a ladies' doctor, his private
(50) opinion of the more complicated sex was not
exalted. He nevertheless, at the end of six months,
accepted his sister's permanent presence as an
accomplished fact, and as Catherine grew older,
perceived that there were in effect good reasons
(55) why she should have a companion of her own
imperfect sex. He was extremely polite to
Lavinia, scrupulously, formally polite; and she
had never seen him in anger but once in her life,
when he lost his temper in a theological discus-
(60) sion with her late husband. With her he never discussed theology, nor, indeed, discussed anything;
he contented himself with making known, very
distinctly in the form of a lucid ultimatum, his
wishes with regard to Catherine.
(65) Once, when the girl was about twelve years
old, he had said to her—
"Try and make a clever woman of her,
Lavinia; I should like her to be a clever woman."
Mrs. Penniman, at this, looked thoughtful a
(70) moment. "My dear Austin," she then inquired,
"do you think it is better to be clever than to be
good?"
From this assertion Mrs. Penniman saw no reason to dissent; she possibly reflected that her own
(75) great use in the world was owing to her aptitude
for many things.
"Of course I wish Catherine to be good," the
Doctor said next day; "but she won't be any the
less virtuous for not being a fool. I am not afraid
(80) of her being wicked; she will never have the salt
of malice in her character. She is 'as good as
good bread,' as the French say; but six years
hence I don't want to have to compare her to
good bread-and-butter."
(85) "Are you afraid she will be insipid? My dear
brother, it is I who supply the butter; so you need
not fear!" said Mrs. Penniman, who had taken in
hand the child's "accomplishments," overlooking
her at the piano, where Catherine displayed a cer-
(90) tain talent, and going with her to the dancing-
class, where it must be confessed that she made
but a modest figure.

GO ON TO THE NEXT PAGE →

3   3 3 3 3 3 3 3 3 3 3   3

24. The word "constitution" in line 4 means

(A) establishment   (B) charter   (C) ambience
(D) physique   (E) wit

25. From the description of how Mrs. Penniman came
to live in her brother's home (lines 1–14), we may
infer all of the following EXCEPT that

(A) she readily became dependent on her brother
(B) she was married at the age of twenty-three
(C) she was physically delicate and in ill health
(D) she had not found living in Poughkeepsie par-
ticularly gratifying
(E) she occasionally echoed an ornate manner of
speech

26. The word "asylum" in line 17 means

(A) institution   (B) sanitarium   (C) refuge
(D) sanction   (E) shambles

27. In the passage the doctor is portrayed most specifically as

(A) benevolent and retiring
(B) casual and easy-going
(C) sadly ineffectual
(D) civil but imperious
(E) habitually irate

28. Lines 31–34 introduce which aspect of the Doctor
and Mrs. Penniman's relationship?

(A) Their mutual admiration
(B) The guilt Mrs. Penniman feels about imposing
on him
(C) The Doctor's burdensome sense of responsibility
(D) His inability to excuse her shortcomings
(E) Her relative lack of confidence in dealing with
him

29. The reason the Doctor gives only tacit assent to Mrs.
Penniman's excuse for living with him is that he

(A) actually regrets ever having allowed her to
move in
(B) does not believe in his sister's purported
brilliance
(C) objects to her taking part in his daughter's
education
(D) is unable to reveal the depth of his respect for
her
(E) does not wish to embarrass his sister with his
praise

30. It can be inferred that the Doctor views children
primarily as

(A) a source of joy and comfort in old age
(B) innocent sufferers for the sins of their fathers
(C) clay to be molded into an acceptable image
(D) the chief objective of the married state
(E) their parents' sole chance for immortality

31. The word "reflected" in line 74 means

(A) mirrored   (B) glittered   (C) considered
(D) indicated   (E) reproduced

32. In lines 83–84, the analogy to "good bread-and-
butter" that the Doctor makes is used to emphasize

(A) the wholesomeness of Catherine's character
(B) his fear that his daughter may prove virtuous
but uninteresting
(C) the discrepancy between Catherine's nature
and her education
(D) his hostility toward his sister's notions of
proper diet
(E) his appreciation of the simple things in life

33. The word "overlooking" in line 88 means

(A) ignoring
(B) slighting
(C) forgiving
(D) watching over
(E) towering above

34. Mrs. Penniman's opinion of her ability to mold
Catherine successfully (lines 85–87) can best be
described as

(A) characteristically modest
(B) moderately ambivalent
(C) atypically judicious
(D) unrealistically optimistic
(E) cynically dispassionate

35. The remarks about Catherine in the last paragraph
reveal her

(A) limited skill as a dancer
(B) virtuosity as a pianist
(C) shyness with her dancing partners
(D) indifference to cleverness
(E) reluctance to practice

YOU MAY GO BACK AND REVIEW THIS SECTION IN THE REMAINING TIME,
BUT DO NOT WORK IN ANY OTHER SECTION UNTIL TOLD TO DO SO.   **STOP**

4   4 4 4 4 4 4 4 4 4 4   4

SECTION 4

Time—30 Minutes
25 Questions

You have 30 minutes to answer the 15 Quantitative Comparison questions and 10 Student-Produced Response questions in this section. You may use any blank space on the page for your work.

Notes:

- You may use a calculator whenever you feel it will be helpful.
- Use the diagrams provided to help you solve the problems. Unless you see the words "Note: Figure not drawn to scale" under a diagram, it has been drawn as accurately as possible. Unless it is stated that a figure is three-dimensional, you may assume it lies in a plane.

Reference Information

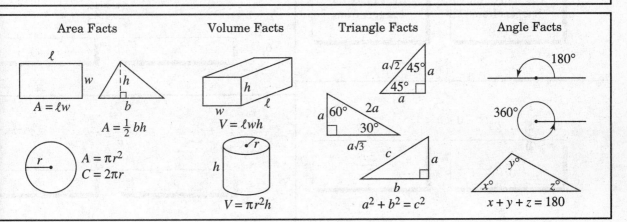

Area Facts

$A = \ell w$

$A = \frac{1}{2} bh$

$A = \pi r^2$
$C = 2\pi r$

Volume Facts

$V = \ell w h$

$V = \pi r^2 h$

Triangle Facts

$a^2 + b^2 = c^2$

Angle Facts

$x + y + z = 180$

Directions for Quantitative Comparison Questions

In each of questions 1–15, two quantities appear in boxes: one in Column A and one in Column B. You must compare them. The correct answer to a question is

A if the quantity in Column A is greater;
B if the quantity in Column B is greater;
C if the two quantities are equal;
D if it is impossible to determine which quantity is greater.

Notes:

- *The correct answer is never E.*
- Sometimes information about one or both of the quantities is centered above the two boxes.
- If the same symbol appears in both columns, it represents the same thing each time.
- All variables represent real numbers.

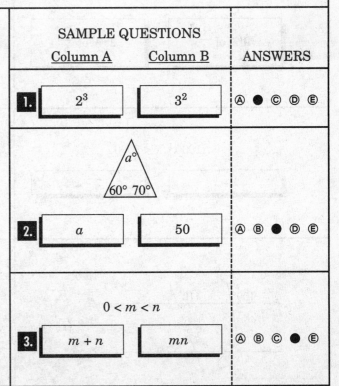

SAMPLE QUESTIONS

Column A	Column B	ANSWERS
1. 2^3	3^2	Ⓐ ● Ⓒ Ⓓ Ⓔ
2. a	50	Ⓐ Ⓑ ● Ⓓ Ⓔ
3. $m + n$	mn	Ⓐ Ⓑ Ⓒ ● Ⓔ

$0 < m < n$

GO ON TO THE NEXT PAGE

4 4 4 4 4 4 4 4 4 4 4 4

SUMMARY DIRECTIONS FOR QUANTITATIVE COMPARISON QUESTIONS

<u>Answer:</u> A if the quantity in Column A is greater;
B if the quantity in Column B is greater;
C if the two quantities are equal;
D if it is impossible to determine which quantity is greater.

	Column A	Column B

1. The sum of the integers from −7 to 3 | The sum of the integers from −3 to 7

2. $0 < a < 1$
$\dfrac{1}{3}\,a$ | $\dfrac{2a}{3}$

3. 40% of $\dfrac{1}{4}$ | 25% of $\dfrac{2}{5}$

4. $1000 < x < 2000$
$1 - x$ | $2 - x$

5.
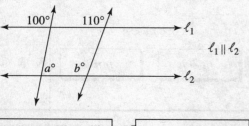
$a + b$ | 190

6. $x > 1$
$xy = 12$
$zx = 25$
y | z

7. $\dfrac{5a}{7b} = \dfrac{5}{7}$
a | b

8. The number of primes between 10 and 20 | The number of primes between 20 and 30

9. The remainder when 3^7 is divided by 10 | The remainder when 7^3 is divided by 10

10. The average (arithmetic mean) of the measures of the three angles of an acute triangle | The average (arithmetic mean) of the measures of the three angles of an obtuse triangle

GO ON TO THE NEXT PAGE

4   4 4 4 4 4 4 4 4 4 4   4

SUMMARY DIRECTIONS FOR QUANTITATIVE COMPARISON QUESTIONS

<u>Answer:</u> A if the quantity in Column A is greater;
B if the quantity in Column B is greater;
C if the two quantities are equal;
D if it is impossible to determine which quantity is greater.

	Column A	Column B
11.	The sum of the areas of two equilateral triangles whose sides are 10	The area of one equilateral triangle whose sides are 20

x and y are positive integers.
$xy = 21$

	Column A	Column B
12.	$x + y$	15

The circumference of a circle is $a\pi$ inches.
The area of the same circle is $b\pi$ square inches.

	Column A	Column B
13.	a	b

	Column A	Column B
14.	The units digit of 14^{14}	The units digit of 16^{16}

From 1980 to 1985 the population of
Mudville decreased 20%.
From 1985 to 1990 the population of
Mudville decreased 20%.
From 1990 to 1995 the population of
Mudville decreased 20%.

	Column A	Column B
15.	The population of Mudville in 1995	One-half the population of Mudville in 1980

GO ON TO THE NEXT PAGE

4　　4　4　4　4　4　4　4　4　4　4　　4

Directions for Student-Produced Response Questions (Grid-ins)

In questions 16–25, first solve the problem, and then enter your answer on the grid provided on the answer sheet. The instructions for entering your answers are as follows:

• First, write your answer in the boxes at the top of the grid.
• Second, grid your answer in the columns below the boxes.
• Use the fraction bar in the first row or the decimal point in the second row to enter fractions and decimal answers.

• Grid only one space in each column.
• Entering the answer in the boxes is recommended as an aid in gridding, but is not required.
• The machine scoring your exam can read only what you grid, so you **must grid in your answers correctly to get credit.**
• If a question has more than one correct answer, grid in only one of them.
• The grid does not have a minus sign, so no answer can be negative.
• A mixed number *must* be converted to an improper fraction or a decimal before it is gridded. Enter $1\frac{1}{4}$ as 5/4 or 1.25; the machine will interpret 1 1/4 as $\frac{11}{4}$ and mark it wrong.
• **All decimals must be entered as accurately as possible.** Here are the three acceptable ways of gridding

$$\frac{3}{11} = 0.272727...$$

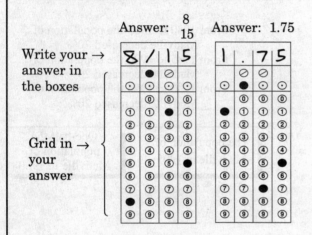

• Note that rounding to .273 is acceptable, because you are using the full grid, but you would receive **no credit** for .3 or .27, because they are less accurate.

16. If a secretary types 60 words per minute, how many minutes will he take to type 330 words?

17. If $2x - 15 = 15 - 2x$, what is the value of x?

GO ON TO THE NEXT PAGE ⟶

4   4 4 4 4 4 4 4 4 4 4   4

18. In the figure at the right, C is the center of the circle. What is the value of c?

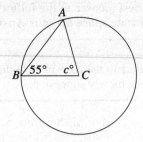

19. Maria is 6 times as old as Tina. In 20 years, Maria will be only twice as old as Tina. How old is Maria now?

20. If r, s, and t are different prime numbers less than 15, what is the greatest possible value of $\frac{r + s}{t}$?

21. If the average (arithmetic mean) of 10, 20, 30, 40, and x is 60, what is the value of x?

22. Line ℓ passes through the origin and point (3,k), where 4 < k < 5. What is one possible value for the slope of line ℓ?

23. At Central High School 50 girls play intramural basketball and 40 girls play intramural volleyball. If 10 girls play both sports, what is the ratio of the number of girls who play only basketball to the number who play only volleyball?

24. If A is the sum of the integers from 1 to 50 and B is the sum of the integers from 51 to 100, what is the value of B − A?

25. In the diagram at the right, O, P, and Q, which are the centers of the three circles, all lie on diameter AB. What is the ratio of the area of the entire shaded region to the area of the white region?

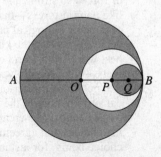

YOU MAY GO BACK AND REVIEW THIS SECTION IN THE REMAINING TIME, BUT DO NOT WORK IN ANY OTHER SECTION UNTIL TOLD TO DO SO.

S T O P

5

The questions that follow the two passages in this section relate to the content of both, and to their relationship. The correct response may be stated outright in the passages or merely suggested.

Questions 1–13 are based on the following passages.

The following passages are excerpted from recent works that discuss the survival of the city in our time. Passage 1 was written by a literary critic and scholar; Passage 2, by an urban planner and sociologist.

Passage 1

When musing on cities over time and in our
time, from the first (whenever it was) to today,
we must always remember that cities are artifacts.
Line Forests, jungles, deserts, plains, oceans—the
(5) organic environment is born and dies and is
reborn endlessly, beautifully, and completely
without moral constraint or ethical control. But
cities—despite the metaphors that we apply to
them from biology or nature ("The city dies when
(10) industry flees"; "The neighborhoods are the vital
cells of the urban organism"), despite the sentimental or anthropomorphic devices we use to
describe cities—are artificial. Nature has never
made a city, and what Nature makes that may
(15) seem like a city—an anthill, for instance—only
seems like one. It is not a city.
Human beings made and make cities, and only
human beings kill cities, or let them die. And
human beings do both—make cities and unmake
(20) them—by the same means: by acts of choice. We
enjoy deluding ourselves in this as in other things.
We enjoy believing that there are forces out there
completely determining our fate, natural forces—
or forces so strong and overwhelming as to be
(25) like natural forces—that send cities through
organic or biological phases of birth, growth, and
decay. We avoid the knowledge that cities are at
best works of art, and at worst ungainly artifacts—but never flowers or even weeds—and that
(30) we, not some mysterious force or cosmic biological system, control the creation and life of a city.
We control the creation and life of a city by
the choices and agreements we make—the basic
choice being, for instance, not to live alone, the
(35) basic agreement being to live together. When
people choose to settle, like the stars, not wander
like the moon, they create cities as sites and symbols of their choice to stop and their agreement
not to separate. Now stasis and proximity, not
(40) movement and distance, define human relationships. Mutual defense, control of a river or har-

bor, shelter from natural forces—all these and
other reasons may lead people to aggregate, but
once congregated, they then live differently and
(45) become different.
A city is not an extended family. That is a tribe
or clan. A city is a collection of disparate families
who agree to a fiction: They agree to live *as if*
they were as close in blood or ties of kinship as in
(50) fact they are in physical proximity. Choosing life
in an artifact, people agree to live in a state of
similitude. A city is a place where ties of proximity, activity, and self-interest assume the role of
family ties. It is a considerable pact, a city. If a
(55) family is an expression of continuity through biology, a city is an expression of continuity through
will and imagination—through mental choices
making artifice, not through physical reproduction.

Passage 2

It is because of this centrality [of the city] that
(60) the financial markets have stayed put. It had been
widely forecast that they would move out en
masse, financial work being among the most
quantitative and computerized of functions. A lot
of the back-office work has been relocated. The
(65) main business, however, is not record keeping
and support services; it is people sizing up other
people, and the center is the place for that.
The problems, of course, are immense. To be
an optimist about the city, one must believe that it
(70) will lurch from crisis to crisis but somehow survive. Utopia is nowhere in sight and probably
never will be. The city is too mixed up for that. Its
strengths and its ills are inextricably bound together. The same concentration that makes the center
(75) efficient is the cause of its crowding and the
destruction of its sun and its light and its scale.
Many of the city's problems, furthermore, are
external in origin—for example, the cruel demo-
graphics of peripheral growth, which are difficult
(80) enough to forecast, let alone do anything about.

GO ON TO THE NEXT PAGE →

5

What has been taking place is a brutal simplification. The city has been losing those functions for which it is no longer competitive. Manufacturing has moved toward the periphery; the back
(85) offices are on the way. The computers are already there. But as the city has been losing functions it has been reasserting its most ancient one: a place where people come together, face-to-face.

More than ever, the center is the place for
(90) news and gossip, for the creation of ideas, for marketing them and swiping them, for hatching deals, for starting parades. This is the stuff of the public life of the city—by no means wholly admirable, often abrasive, noisy, contentious,
(95) without apparent purpose.

But this human congress is the genius of the place, its reason for being, its great marginal edge. This is the engine, the city's true export. Whatever makes this congress easier, more spon-
(100) taneous, more enjoyable is not at all a frill. It is the heart of the center of the city.

1. The author's purpose in Passage 1 is primarily to

   (A) identify the sources of popular discontent with cities
   (B) define the city as growing out of a social contract
   (C) illustrate the difference between cities and villages
   (D) compare cities with blood families
   (E) persuade the reader to change his behavior

2. The author cites the sentence "The neighborhoods are the vital cells of the urban organism" (lines 10–11) as

   (A) an instance of prevarication
   (B) a simple statement of scientific fact
   (C) a momentary digression from his central thesis
   (D) an example of one type of figurative language
   (E) a paradox with ironic implications

3. The author's attitude toward the statements quoted in lines 9–11 is

   (A) respectful
   (B) ambivalent
   (C) pragmatic
   (D) skeptical
   (E) approving

4. According to the author of Passage 1, why is an anthill by definition unlike a city?

   (A) It can be casually destroyed by human beings.
   (B) Its inhabitants outnumber the inhabitants of even the largest city.
   (C) It is the figurative equivalent of a municipality.
   (D) It is a work of instinct rather than of imagination.
   (E) It exists on a far smaller scale than any city does.

5. Mutual defense, control of waterways, and shelter from the forces of nature (lines 41–42) are presented primarily as examples of motives for people to

   (A) move away from their enemies
   (B) build up their supplies of armament
   (C) gather together in settlements
   (D) welcome help from their kinfolk
   (E) redefine their family relationships

6. We can infer from lines 35–37 that roving tribes differ from city dwellers in that these nomads

   (A) have not chosen to settle in one spot
   (B) lack ties of activity and self-interest
   (C) are willing to let the cities die
   (D) have no need for mutual defense
   (E) define their relationships by proximity

7. By saying a city "is a considerable pact" (line 54), the author primarily stresses

   (A) its essential significance
   (B) its speculative nature
   (C) the inevitable agreement
   (D) the moral constraints
   (E) its surprising growth

8. To the author of Passage 1, to live in a city is

   (A) an unexpected outcome
   (B) an opportunity for profit
   (C) an act of volition
   (D) a pragmatic solution
   (E) an inevitable fate

9. Underlying the forecast mentioned in lines 61–62 is the assumption that

   (A) the financial markets are similar to the city in their need for quantitative data
   (B) computerized tasks such as record keeping can easily be performed at remote sites
   (C) computerized functions are not the main activity of these firms
   (D) the urban environment is inappropriate for the proper performance of financial calculations
   (E) either the markets would all move or none of them would relocate

10. The word "scale" in line 76 means

   (A) series of musical tones
   (B) measuring instrument
   (C) relative dimensions
   (D) thin outer layer
   (E) means of ascent

GO ON TO THE NEXT PAGE

5

11. The "congress" referred to in line 96 is

(A) a city council
(B) the supreme legislative body
(C) a gathering of individuals
(D) an enjoyable luxury
(E) an intellectual giant

12. The author of Passage 2 differs from the author of Passage 1 in that he

(A) argues in favor of choosing to live alone
(B) disapproves of relocating support services to the outskirts of the city

(C) has no patience with the harshness inherent in public life
(D) believes that in the long run the city as we know it will not survive
(E) is more outspoken about the city's difficulties

13. Compared to Passage 1, Passage 2 is

(A) more lyrical and less pragmatic
(B) more impersonal and less colloquial
(C) more sentimental and less definitive
(D) more practical and less detached
(E) more objective and less philosophical

YOU MAY GO BACK AND REVIEW THIS SECTION IN THE REMAINING TIME, BUT DO NOT WORK IN ANY OTHER SECTION UNTIL TOLD TO DO SO.

S T O P

6   6 6 6 6 6 6 6 6 6   6

SECTION 6

Time—15 Minutes
10 Questions

For each problem in this section determine which of the five choices is correct and blacken in that choice on your answer sheet. You may use any blank space on the page for your work.

Notes:

• You may use a calculator whenever you feel it will be helpful.

• Use the diagrams provided to help you solve the problems. Unless you see the words "Note: Figure not drawn to scale" under a diagram, it has been drawn as accurately as possible. Unless it is stated that a figure is three-dimensional, you may assume it lies in a plane.

Reference Information

Area Facts | Volume Facts | Triangle Facts | Angle Facts

$A = \ell w$

$A = \frac{1}{2} bh$

$A = \pi r^2$
$C = 2\pi r$

$V = \ell wh$

$V = \pi r^2 h$

$a^2 + b^2 = c^2$

$x + y + z = 180$

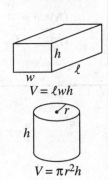

1. In the figure above, what is the value of a?

   (A) 30   (B) 36   (C) 45   (D) 72
   (E) It cannot be determined from the information given.

---

2. $A = \{2, 3, 4\}$, and $B = \{3, 4, 6\}$. If a is in A and b is in B, how many different values are there for the product ab?

   (A) 4   (B) 6   (C) 7   (D) 8   (E) 9

Questions 3–4 are based on information in the following table.

TEAM PARTICIPATION BY CLASS AT CENTRAL H. S. IN 1995

Class	Number of Students	Percent of Students
Freshman	180	15
Sophomore	120	x
Junior	y	40
Senior	z	w
Total	t	100

---

3. What is the value of t, the total number of students on teams?

   (A) 450   (B) 750   (C) 1200   (D) 1800
   (E) It cannot be determined from the information given.

---

4. What is the value of z, the number of seniors on teams?

   (A) 360   (B) 420   (C) 630   (D) 800
   (E) It cannot be determined from the information given.

---

5. Which of the following CANNOT be expressed as the sum of three consecutive integers?

   (A) 18   (B) 24   (C) 28   (D) 33   (E) 36

GO ON TO THE NEXT PAGE

6   6 6 6 6 6 6 6 6 6   6

6. Given that $x \neq y$ and that $(x - y)^2 = x^2 - y^2$, which of the following MUST be true?

    I. $x = 0$

    II. $y = 0$

    III. $x = -y$

(A) I only (B) II only (C) III only
(D) I and II only (E) I, II, and III

7. An international convention has a total of d delegates from c countries. If each country is represented by the same number of delegates, how many delegates does each country have?

(A) $c + d$ (B) cd (C) $\dfrac{c}{d}$ (D) $\dfrac{d}{c}$ (E) $\dfrac{c + d}{c}$

8. Bob and Jack share an apartment. If each month Bob pays a dollars and Jack pays b dollars, what percent of the total cost does Bob pay?

(A) $\dfrac{a}{b}\%$ (B) $\dfrac{b}{a}\%$ (C) $\dfrac{a}{a + b}\%$

(D) $\dfrac{100a}{b}\%$ (E) $\dfrac{100a}{a + b}\%$

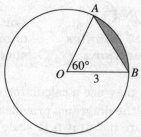

9. In the figure above, the radius of circle O is 3, and $m\angle AOB = 60$. What is the perimeter of the shaded region?

(A) $3 + \dfrac{\pi}{2}$ (B) $\sqrt{3} + \pi$ (C) $3 + \pi$

(D) $2\sqrt{3} + \pi$ (E) It cannot be determined from the information given.

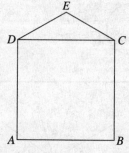

10. In the figure above, the area of square $ABCD$ is 100, and the area of isosceles triangle DEC is 10. Find the distance from A to E.

(A) 11 (B) 12 (C) $\sqrt{146}$ (D) 13 (E) $\sqrt{244}$

YOU MAY GO BACK AND REVIEW THIS SECTION IN THE REMAINING TIME, BUT DO NOT WORK IN ANY OTHER SECTION UNTIL TOLD TO DO SO.

STOP

Answer Key

Note: The letters in brackets following the Mathematical Reasoning answers refer to the sections of Chapter 12 in which you can find the information you need to answer the questions. For example, **1. C [E]** means that the answer to question 1 is C, and that the solution requires information found in Section 12-E: Averages.

Section 1   Verbal Reasoning

1.	B	7.	C	13.	C	19.	A	25.	C
2.	B	8.	C	14.	D	20.	E	26.	C
3.	D	9.	D	15.	A	21.	D	27.	D
4.	A	10.	D	16.	C	22.	D	28.	E
5.	B	11.	B	17.	B	23.	A	29.	B
6.	D	12.	C	18.	C	24.	C	30.	C

Section 2   Mathematical Reasoning

1.	D [P]	6.	B [I]	11.	A [D]	16.	C [F]	21.	A [C]
2.	C [J]	7.	D [A]	12.	B [A]	17.	C [A]	22.	A [K]
3.	B [A]	8.	D [Q, C]	13.	B [A]	18.	A [L, N]	23.	E [A]
4.	D [A]	9.	C [A]	14.	E [E]	19.	D [A]	24.	B [L]
5.	A [A, G]	10.	C [A]	15.	D [O]	20.	E [D]	25.	B [J, L]

Section 3   Verbal Reasoning

1.	B	8.	C	15.	C	22.	A	29.	B
2.	B	9.	E	16.	B	23.	A	30.	C
3.	C	10.	B	17.	B	24.	D	31.	C
4.	C	11.	C	18.	B	25.	C	32.	B
5.	E	12.	B	19.	B	26.	C	33.	D
6.	B	13.	B	20.	E	27.	D	34.	D
7.	C	14.	C	21.	A	28.	E	35.	A

Section 4   Mathematical Reasoning

Quantitative Comparison Questions

1.	B [A]	4.	B [A]	7.	C [B]	10.	C [E, J]	13.	D [L]
2.	B [B]	5.	C [I]	8.	A [A]	11.	B [J]	14.	C [A, P]
3.	C [B, C]	6.	B [G, B]	9.	A [A]	12.	D [A]	15.	A [C]

Grid-in Questions

16. [D] 5.5   *or* 11/2

17. [G] 7.5   *or* 15/2

18. [J] 70

19. [H] 30

20. [F] 12

21. [E] 2 0 0

22. [N] 1 . 5

$$\frac{4}{3} < x < \frac{5}{3}$$
or
$$1.33 < x < 1.67$$

23. [O] 4 / 3

or 1.33

24. [A] 2 5 0 0

25. [L] 1 3 / 3

or 4.33

Section 5 Verbal Reasoning

1. **B**	4. **D**	7. **A**	10. **C**
2. **D**	5. **C**	8. **C**	11. **C**
3. **D**	6. **A**	9. **B**	12. **E**

13. **E**

Section 6 Mathematical Reasoning

1. **B [I]**	3. **C [Q, C]**	5. **C [A]**	7. **D [B]**	9. **C [J, L]**
2. **C [A, O]**	4. **B [Q, A]**	6. **B [F, G]**	8. **E [B, C]**	10. **D [J, K]**

Calculate Your Raw Score

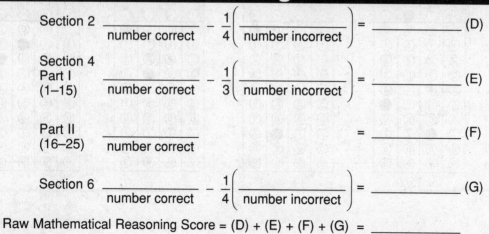

Verbal Reasoning

Section 1 _____ − $\frac{1}{4}$ (_____) = _____ (A)
number correct   number incorrect

Section 3 _____ − $\frac{1}{4}$ (_____) = _____ (B)
number correct   number incorrect

Section 5 _____ − $\frac{1}{4}$ (_____) = _____ (C)
number correct   number incorrect

Raw Verbal Reasoning Score = (A) + (B) + (C) = _____

Mathematical Reasoning

Section 2 _____ − $\frac{1}{4}$ (_____) = _____ (D)
number correct   number incorrect

Section 4
Part I _____ − $\frac{1}{3}$ (_____) = _____ (E)
(1–15)   number correct   number incorrect

Part II _____ = _____ (F)
(16–25) number correct

Section 6 _____ − $\frac{1}{4}$ (_____) = _____ (G)
number correct   number incorrect

Raw Mathematical Reasoning Score = (D) + (E) + (F) + (G) = _____

Evaluate Your Performance

	Verbal Reasoning	Mathematical Reasoning
Superior	67–78	51–60
Very Good	60–66	45–50
Good	52–59	40–44
Satisfactory	44–51	35–39
Average	36–43	30–34
Needs Further Study	29–35	25–29
Needs Intensive Study	21–28	20–24
Inadequate	0–20	0–19

Identify Your Weaknesses

Verbal Reasoning

Question Type	Question Numbers			Chapter to Study
	Section 1	Section 3	Section 5	
Sentence Completion	1, 2, 3, 4, 5, 6, 7, 8, 9	1, 2, 3, 4, 5, 6, 7, 8, 9, 10		Chapter 4
Analogy	10, 11, 12, 13, 14, 15	11, 12, 13, 14, 15, 16, 17, 18, 19, 20, 21, 22, 23		Chapter 5
Reading Comprehension	16, 17, 18, 19, 20, 21, 22, 23, 24, 25, 26, 27, 28, 29, 30	24, 25, 26, 27, 28, 29, 30, 31, 32, 33, 34, 35	1, 2, 3, 4, 5, 6, 7, 8, 9, 10, 11, 12, 13	Chapter 6

Identify Your Weaknesses

Mathematical Reasoning

Skill Area	Question Numbers			Pages to Study
	Section 2	**Section 4**	**Section 6**	
Basics of Arithmetic	3, 4, 5, 7, 9, 10, 12, 13, 17, 19, 23	1, 4, 8, 9, 12, 14, 24	2, 4, 5	331–338
Fractions and Decimals		2, 3, 6, 7	7, 8	344–352
Percents	8, 21	3, 15	3, 8	358–361
Ratios	11, 20	10, 16		366–370
Averages	14	21		376–378
Polynomials	16	20	6	383–386
Equations and Inequalities	5	6, 17	6	389–402
Word Problems		19		399–402
Lines and Angles	6	5	1	407–410
Triangles	2, 25	10, 11, 18	9, 10	414–418
Quadrilaterals	22		10	425–428
Circles	18, 24, 25	13, 25	9	432–435
Solid Geometry				440–442
Coordinate Geometry	18	22		446–448
Counting and Probability	15	23	2	452–456
Logical Reasoning	1	14		462–464
Data Interpretation	8		3, 4	468–471

Answer Explanations

Section 1   Verbal Reasoning

1. **B.** To *sap* or weaken the recipient's self-suffi-ciency would be contrary to the recipient's true welfare.

    The phrase "argument *against*" is your clue to look for a "negative" verb. Therefore, you can eliminate any answer choices with positive verbs.

    Choices A, C, and D all have positive associa-tions. If the welfare system supported, has-tened, or renewed independence in people, that would be an argument for the system, not against it. Choice E makes no sense in the sentence. That leaves you with Choice B.
    (Examples)

2. **B.** The word *platitudes* (trite, commonplace remarks) complements *empty promises* and *clichés* (overworked phrases). The three linked phrases support the same thought.

    Remember to watch for signal words that link one part of the sentence to another. The pres-ence of *and* linking items in a series indicates that the missing word may be a synonym or near-synonym for the linked words.
    (Support Signal)

3. **D.** Someone able to manipulate things with both hands is *ambidextrous*, capable of using both hands with equal ease.

    The presence of *and* indicates that the missing word supports or explains the other linked words.
    (Definition Pattern)

4. **A.** *Posthumously* means after one's death. Some-one who faced ridicule during her lifetime ("from her contemporaries") could only gain honor *after* death. Word Parts Clue: *Post* means *after*.

    Watch for signals that link one part of the sen-tence to another. *But* signals a contrast. This indicates that the missing word must be an antonym or near-antonym for *from her con-temporaries*.
    (Contrast Signal)

5. **B.** Despite the changes produced by modernization, certain aspects of Indian life have remained *stable* (firmly established; resistant to change).

    Again, watch for signals that link one part of the sentence to another. *While* in the opening clause signals a contrast. This indicates that the missing word must be an antonym or near-antonym for *change*.
    (Contrast Signal)

6. **D.** A *hypocrite* (someone who pretends to be vir-tuous) would fake feelings he thinks he should show. *Simulates* means pretends or feigns.

    Choice A is incorrect. It would not be logical for a hypocrite to *conceal* or hide something he thinks he should display.

    Choice B is incorrect. It would not be logical for a hypocrite to *decry* or criticize a feeling he thinks he should show.

    Choice C is incorrect. If a hypocrite does not possess certain feelings, he cannot *betray* them or reveal them unintentionally.

    Choice E is incorrect. It would not be logical for a hypocrite to merely *condone* or excuse a feeling he thinks he should show.
    (Definition)

7. **C.** The fact that Deloria has detractors or critics leads one to expect his confidence might be shaken. However, the opposite has occurred. The critics have had *little* success at shaking his self-confidence or *denting* or damaging his reputation.

    Note the use of *but* signalling the contrast.
    (Contrast Signal)

8. **C.** A readiness to adopt or adjust to new things is *adaptability*.

    Remember, before you look at the answer choices, to read the sentence and think of a word that makes sense. Likely Words: "versa-tility," "ability."   (Definition Patterns)

9. **D.** *Intrinsic* value is inherent value, value that essentially belongs to an object, not merely *sentimental* value. She did not keep the furni-ture because it was worth money or was beau-tiful (inherent, "real" value). She kept it for emotional reasons (sentimental value).

    The words *not for...but for* signal a contrast, telling you that the missing words must be antonyms or near-antonyms. You can immedi-ately eliminate Choices B and C as synonym or near-synonym pairs.   (Contrast Signal)

10. **D.** A *writer* creates a book out of *words*. A *baker* creates a cake out of *batter*.
    (Worker and Material)

11. **B.** A ridge of *snow* is a *drift*. A ridge of *sand* is a *dune*.   (Definition)

12. **C.** *Grain* is kept in a *silo*; *water* is kept in a *bucket*.   (Function)

13. **C.** A *shrug* indicates *indifference* or lack of con-cern; a *nod* indicates *assent* or agreement.
    (Action and Its Significance)

14. **D.** A person characterized by *anger* is defined as *choleric*; a person characterized by *greed* is defined as *avaricious*.

    Beware Eye-Catchers: Choice A is incorrect. Don't be fooled because *anger* is a synonym for *wrath*.   (Synonym Variant)

15. A. A *blandishment* (something tending to flatter or entice) by definition *allures* (entices); an *admonition* (warning; caution) by definition *warns*. (Degree of Intensity)

16. C. The author uses the term "hot spot" to indicate a geological phenomenon; she uses the term *technically*, as it is used in the scientific discipline.
Choice B is incorrect. In its informal or colloquial sense, a hot spot is a nightclub.

17. B. The author states that no theorist today would deny the movement of the plates. Thus, she clearly regards the theory that the plates move as *irrefutable*, unable to be contradicted or disproved.

18. C. Choice C is correct. You can arrive at it by the process of elimination.
Statement I is correct. There are "common geographical features that link these separate shores" (lines 30–31). These indicate the continents were once joined. Therefore, you can eliminate Choices B and D.
Statement II is correct. The "coastlines complement one another" (lines 28–29); they are *physical counterparts*. This indicates the continents were once joined. Therefore, you can eliminate Choice A.
Statement III is not correct. Though it is true that the African plate has been motionless for ages, this fact is not stated as proof that Africa and South America once were joined. Therefore, you can eliminate Choice E.
Only Choice C is left. It is the correct answer.

19. A. In constructing the relative motion of the plate in detail, geologists have worked out or *interpreted* the movements involved.

20. E. Choice E is correct. The concluding sentence of the passage states that hot spots "may someday cast new light on the continents' mutability," helping to explain their tendency to change in shape, even break apart and form a new ocean.
Choice A is incorrect. Line 43 indicates that hot spots are seldom located near the boundaries of plates. Thus, they would be unlikely to provide useful information about plate boundaries.
Choice B is incorrect. It is unsupported by the passage.
Choice C is incorrect. Hot spots have proved useful in studying the *respective* motion of the plates, not their relative motion (lines 35–39).
Choice D is incorrect. According to the passage, satellite technology has proved useful in recording the movement of fixed sites on

Earth. The hot spot hypothesis, however, is not mentioned as interpreting current satellite technology.

21. D. Wilson states that "the continent may rupture *entirely* along some of these fissures, *so that* the hot spot initiates the formation of a new ocean" (lines 60–61). Note the use of "so that" to indicate cause and effect. *If* the fissures split the continent, then water from the surrounding oceans may pour into the rift, in process starting off the formation of a new ocean.

22. D. The opening sentence introduces the subject of "specialization by the artist's sex and role in the group" and its impact on the style. These artists specialize or limit themselves to certain designs. The subsequent paragraphs discuss the men's and women's traditional designs. The title that best summarizes this content is *Design Specialization in Plains Arts.*
Choice A is incorrect. The passage does not discuss the continuing or ongoing effect of Plains art.
Choice B is too broad to be correct. The passage deals specifically with male and female *artistic roles* in the tribe, not with male and female roles in general.
Choice C is too narrow to be correct. While the passage discusses male Indian art in terms of narrative and dream, it also discusses several other topics.
Choice E is too narrow to be correct. The passage deals with Indian abstract or geometrical art as well as Indian representational art.
Remember, when asked to choose a title, watch out for choices that are too specific or too broad.

23. A. Throughout the passage the author is supporting his thesis that male and female Indian artists specialized in different sorts of designs. Thus, when he describes specific examples of their work, he is doing so to point out these differences in decorative styles.
Choice B is incorrect. The passage mentions that women's art, for example, appears on functional objects (lines 20–23); however, it stresses these objects' designs, not their usefulness.
Choice C is incorrect. The passage mentions artistic materials and patterns in some detail; it barely touches on technique (*how* the artists worked).
Choices D and E are incorrect. By the time the author mentions Anglo influence (lines 65–67) and the spiritual significance of emblems (lines 57–61), he no longer is discussing specific works of art.

24. C. The two separate strains of decorative art discussed are two separate *varieties* or kinds of

decorative art. Remember, when answering a vocabulary-in-context question, test each answer choice by substituting it in the sentence for the word in quotes.

25. **C.** The crafts of weaving, quillwork, and bead-work are presented as descending from the same aspect of Woodland culture that the women's geometric art does. Thus, they are presented as examples of *geometrically based crafts*.

26. **C.** You can arrive at the correct answer through the process of elimination.
The author would agree with statement I. He states in line 43 that Indian men worked in groups (*corporately*) on projects. Therefore, you can eliminate Choices B and D.
The author also would agree with Statement II. He states in lines 57–61 that the dream images or emblems could "protect him from...dangers" and thus could *ward off danger*. Therefore, you can eliminate Choice A.
The author would *not* agree with Statement III. In lines 15–17 he assigns the use of classical or abstract forms not to the men, but to the women. Therefore, you can eliminate Choice E.
Only Choice C remains. It is the correct answer.

27. **D.** In drafting a representational piece of art, the men were *sketching* it, drawing a preliminary version of it on the hide.
Again, in vocabulary-in-context questions, substitute the answer choices in the original sentence.

28. **E.** Lines 52–61 talk of the discovery of personal omens or emblems through dream quests and tell of their protective nature. These emblems can thus be described as *spiritual guardians*.
Choices A and C are incorrect. They are not mentioned in the passage.
Choice B is incorrect. The dream vision suggests the artist's subject matter (his omen or emblem), not his methods or technique.
Choice D is also incorrect. Group solidarity is mentioned in the passage, but *not* in connection with the dreams.

29. **B.** Choice B, the portrait bust, lacks a narrative aspect: it tells no heroic story. Therefore, it does *not* resemble Plains art in its narrative aspect. Choice B is correct.
Choice A, the cartoon strip, has a narrative aspect: it tell a story in panels or "pictorial vignettes."
Choice C, the epic, has a narrative aspect: it tells a heroic story.

Choice D, the autobiography, tells a personal story.
Choice E, the mural showing scenes from the life of George Washington, an American hero, clearly resembles Plains art.

30. **C.** The concluding sentences of the passage stress the growing emphasis on depicting the group or *community* in Plains art.
Choice A is incorrect. Nothing is said to indicate that geometric patterning increased in importance in the 1800s.
Choice B is incorrect. Though during this period cloth came into use as a substitute for animal hides, this does not necessarily mean that the Plains Indians had fewer hides available to them. Instead, they may simply have had greater access to cloth through the Anglo settlers and traders.
Choices D and E are incorrect. Nothing in passage suggests either possibility.

Section 2 Mathematical Reasoning

In each mathematics section, for many problems, an alternative solution, indicated by two asterisks (**), follows the first solution. When this occurs, one of the solutions is the direct mathematical one and the other is based on one of the tactics discussed in Chapters 8–12.

1. **D.** Since $100 = 12 \times 8 + 4$, 100 months is 4 months more than 8 years. Therefore, 8 years from now it will again be June, and 4 months later it will be **October**.

   Look for a pattern. Since there are 12 months in a year, after every 12 months it will again be June; that is, it will be June after 12, 24, 36, 48,... months. Therefore, 96 (8×12) months from now it will again be June. Count 4 more months to **October.

2. **C.** The sum of the measures of the three angles of a triangle is 180°, so write the equation and use the six-step method of Section 12-G to solve it:
$$40 + 2a + 3a = 180 \Rightarrow 40 + 5a = 180 \Rightarrow$$
$$5a = 140 \Rightarrow a = 28.$$

   **To answer this question, you must know that the sum of the measures of the three angles of a triangle is 180°. If you know this, but want to avoid the algebra, use TACTIC 9-1: backsolve. If you start with C, as you should, you get the right answer immediately.

   Use TACTIC 8-2. If you trust the diagram, there are lots of ways to go. If a were 45, $2a$ would be 90, which is clearly wrong. Likewise, if a were 10, $2a$ would be 20, which is also way off. In fact, S appears to be *about* a 90° angle, so $3a \approx 90$, which means $a \approx 30$. Choose **28.

3. **B.** Since d divisions each have t teams, multiply to get dt teams; and since each team has p players, multiply the number of teams (dt) by p to get the total number of players: **dtp.** On any more difficult problem of this type, you should definitely use TACTIC 9-2 (see below and the solution to question 20).

    Use TACTIC 9-2. Pick three numbers for t, d, and p; the numbers should be easy to use, not necessarily realistic. Assume that there are 2 divisions, each consisting of 4 teams, so there are 2 × 4 = 8 teams. Then assume that each team has 10 players, for a total of 8 × 10 = 80 players. Now check the choices. Which one is equal to 80 when $d = 2$, $t = 4$, and $p = 10$? Only **dtp.

4. **D.** Brian's total cost was $299 + $299 + $140 = $738. At the time of purchase, he paid $123 $\left(\frac{1}{6}\text{ of }\$738\right)$ and paid the balance of $615 ($738 − $123) in 12 monthly installments: $615 ÷ 12 = **$51.25.**

5. **A.** You should recognize the first few powers of 2: 2, 4, 8, 16, 32, 64. Since $32 = 2^5$, then $n + 1 = 5$, and $n = 4$.

    Use TACTIC 9-1. Backsolve, starting with 6, choice C: $6 + 1 = 7$, and $2^7 = 128$—too large. Eliminate C, D, and E, leaving A and B. Since 128 was much too large, try **4, the correct answer.

6. **B.** The unmarked angle opposite the 60° angle also measures 60° (KEY FACT I4), and the sum of the measures of all six angles in the diagram is 360° (KEY FACT I3). Then
    $$360 = a + b + c + 20 + 60 + 60 = a + b + c + 140.$$
    Subtracting 140 from each side, we get $a + b + c = $ **220.**

7. **D.** There's nothing to do except check each choice.
    7**4 $= \sqrt{7 + \sqrt{4}} = \sqrt{7 + 2} = \sqrt{9} = 3$, which is an integer. The answer is D. Once you find the answer, don't waste time trying the other choices—they won't work.

8. **D.** As in question 7, check the answers. In **1994** Adam entered 3 more tournaments than in 1993, an increase of $\frac{3}{6} = \frac{1}{2} = 50\%$.

    (From 1990 to 1991 the increase was 25%, from 1991 to 1992 it was 100%, from 1995 to 1996 it was 33⅓%, and from 1992 to 1993 there was a decrease.)

9. **C.** The first step is to calculate (3#)(#5) = (3 + 1) (5 − 1) = 4 × 4 = 16. Now check each answer until you find one that is *not* 16. The other four choices are all equal to 16. C: **(4#)(#4)** = (4 + 1)(4 − 1) = 5 × 3 = 15 ≠ 16.

10. **C.** Since a is a multiple of 5, $a = 5n$ for some integer n. Also, $b = 5a$, so $a + b = a + 5a = 6a = 6(5n) = 30n$. Then $a + b$ must be a multiple of 30. Now check I, II, and III. I: Could $a + b = 60$? Yes, $60 = 30 \times 2$ ($a = 10$ and $b = 50$). Eliminate A, B, and D. II: Could $a + b = 100$? No, 100 is not a multiple of 30. Eliminate E. The answer must be C: **I and III**. Note that we didn't have to check III, but, yes, $a + b$ could be 150 (with $n = 5$, $a = 25$, and $b = 125$).

    **Use TACTIC 9-2: a must be a multiple of 5, so just try $a = 5, 10, 15, \ldots$.

a	5	10	15	20	25
$b = 5a$	25	50	75	100	125
$a + b$	30	**60**	90	120	**150**

    After two or three tries you can guess that $a + b$ must be a multiple of 30.

11. **A.** Just multiply: $\frac{2}{5}(h) = \frac{2h}{5}$.

    **Use TACTIC 9-2. Pick an easy-to-use number for h: 2, for example. Scott can mow $\frac{2}{5}$ of a lawn in the first hour and another $\frac{2}{5}$ of a lawn in the second hour, for a total of $\frac{4}{5}$ of a lawn. Check the choices. Only $\frac{2h}{5}$ is $\frac{4}{5}$ when $h = 2$. (Note that, if you replaced h by 1, both A and D would work.)

12. **B.** $bd = (3^a)(3^c) = \mathbf{3^{a+c}}$. (KEY FACT A16).

    **Use TACTIC 9-2. Pick easy-to-use numbers for a and c; $a = 1$ and $c = 2$, for example. Then $b = 3^1 = 3$ and $d = 3^2 = 9$, so $bd = 27$. Check the choices. Only $\mathbf{3^{a+c}}$ works.

13. **B.** Use the distributive law:
    $$78(r + s) = 78r + 78s \text{ and}$$
    $$(78 + r)s = 78s + rs.$$
    Then, $78r + 78s = 78s + rs$, which implies that $78r = rs$. Since it is given that $r \ne 0$, we can divide both sides by r to get $s = \mathbf{78}$.

14. **E.** The average of three consecutive integers is always the middle one, which is an integer and is equal to the average of the smallest and largest of the three integers. Therefore, **I, II, and III** are all true.

    **Use TACTIC 9-2. Pick three consecutive integers: 2, 3, 4. Their average is $\frac{2+3+4}{3} = \frac{9}{3} = 3$, which *is* an integer (III) and which is one of the numbers (I). Also, the average of 2 and 4 is 3, so II is true. (Note that the problem asks which statements *must* be true. Here we showed only that *in this case* all three statements are true.) You could try three consecutive negative integers, as well.

15. **D.** Between 1 and 25, the 8 multiples of 3 and 5 multiples of 5 would all make Scott a winner. That looks like 13 (8 + 5) winning numbers, but the number 15 has been counted twice, so we must subtract 1. There are only 12 winning numbers, and the probability is $\frac{12}{25}$.

    **The simplest thing to do here is to quickly list which of the 25 numbers will make Scott a winner. Just consider each number and ask, "Is it a multiple of 3 or 5?" The answers are 1 – no, 2 – no, 3 – yes, 4 – no, 5 – yes, and so on. The winning numbers are 3, 5, 6, 9, 10, 12, 15, 18, 20, 21, 24, 25. There are 12 of them. The probability is $\frac{12}{25}$.

16. **C.** $(m + 1)(m - 1) = m^2 - 1 = 17 - 1 = \mathbf{16}$.

    Use your calculator. Since $m^2 = 17$, $m = \sqrt{17} \approx 4.123....$ Multiply $5.123 \times 3.123 = 15.999$. Choose **16. If you don't round off, your calculator will probably give you 16, exactly.

17. **C.** $3^{10} \times 27^2 = 3^{10} \times (3^3)^2 = 3^{10} \times 3^6 = 3^{16}$. Also, $9^2 \times 3^n = (3^2)^2 \times 3^n = 3^4 \times 3^n = 3^{4+n}$ so, $3^{16} = 3^{4+n}$ and $16 = 4 + n$. Then $n = \mathbf{12}$.

    **Use your calculator. $9^2 \times 3^n = 81 \times 3^n$ and $3^{10} \times 27^2 = 43046721$, so $3^n = 43046721 \div 81 = 531441$. Now just keep taking powers of 3 until you get to $3^{12} = 531441$. (If you have a scientific calculator, use the power button; if not, just keep multiplying $3 \times 3 \times 3....$)

18. **A.** Find the distance from each point to (0,0), the center of the circle. We're looking for a point that is *less than* 10 units from the center.

    The distance from (a,b) to (0,0) equals $\sqrt{(a-0)^2 + (b-0)^2} = \sqrt{a^2 + b^2}$. Check each point. A: **(–9,4)** $\sqrt{(-9)^2 + 4^2} = \sqrt{81 + 16} = \sqrt{97} < 10$ (KEY FACT N2).

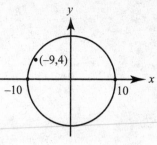

**Clearly, (0,–10) is 10 units from the origin, and so is *on* the circle. Also, since (10,0) is on the circle, (10,–1) is *outside*. The others are too close to call without knowing the formula or using the Pythagorean theorem, so if you're not sure, guess.

19. **D.** Since 2 is the smallest prime and since p and q are each bigger than r, neither p nor q can be 2. Therefore, both p and q are odd (2 is the only even prime), which means that $p - q$ is even (KEY FACT A14). But $p - q = r$, so r *must be* 2. However, there are many possibilities for p and q: $5 - 3 = 2$, $13 - 11 = 2$, $31 - 29 = 2$, etc. Therefore, the answer is *r* only.

20. **E.** Since p pencils cost c cents, each pencil costs $\frac{c}{p}$ cents. By dividing the number of cents we have by $\frac{c}{p}$, we can find out how many pencils we can buy. Since d dollars equals $100d$ cents, we divide $100d$ by $\frac{c}{p}$, which is equivalent to multiplying $100d$ by $\frac{p}{c}$:

$$100d(\frac{p}{c}) = \frac{100dp}{c}.$$

**Use TACTIC 9-2. Assume that 2 pencils cost 10 cents; then pencils cost 5 cents each or 20 for a dollar. For 3 dollars, we can buy 60 pencils. Which of the choices equals 60 when $p = 2$, $c = 10$, and $d = 3$? Only $\frac{100dp}{c}$.

21. **A.** $a + 10\%(a) = a + 0.1a = 1.1a$. Also, $b - 10\%(b) = b - 0.1b = 0.9b$. Then, $1.1a = 0.9b$, and $\frac{a}{b} = \frac{.9}{1.1} = \frac{9}{11}$.

    **If after increasing a and decreasing b the results are equal, a must be smaller than b, so *the ratio of a to b must be less than 1*. Eliminate choices C, D, and E. Now, either test choices A and B or just guess. To test B, pick two numbers in the ratio of 9 to 10—90 and 100, for example. Then 90 increased by 10% is 99, and 100 decreased by 10% is 90. The results are not equal, so eliminate B. The answer is $\frac{9}{11}$. (110 decreased by 10% *is* 99.)

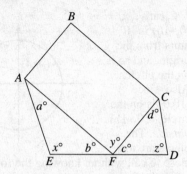

22. A. Since DE is a line segment, $b + y + c = 180$ (KEY FACT I2); and since F is a corner of a rectangle, $y = 90$. Therefore, $b + 90 + c = 180$, and $b + c = 90$. (II is true.) If we knew the value of x, we could determine the value of $a + b$, but we don't. Nor do we know the value of any of the other angles, including z. Therefore, **II only** is true.

23. E. Any odd number can be expressed as the sum of two consecutive integers: $8 + 9 = 17$. Eliminate A. Next try the sum of three consecutive integers: $7 + 8 + 9 = 24$. Eliminate C. Now try the sum of four consecutive integers: $4 + 5 + 6 + 7 = 22$ and $5 + 6 + 7 + 8 = 26$. Eliminate B and D. The answer must be **32**.

24. B. In the given figure, the diameters of the four small semicircles are 2, 4, 6, and 8, so the diameter of the large semicircle is $2 + 4 + 6 + 8 = 20$, and its radius is 10. The perimeter of the shaded region is the sum of the circumferences of all five semicircles. Since the circumference of a semicircle is π times its radius, the perimeter is $\pi + 2\pi + 3\pi + 4\pi + 10\pi = \mathbf{20\pi}$.

25. B. Let x and y be the radii of the two semicircles. Then the legs of right triangle ACB are $2x$ and $2y$, and by the Pythagorean theorem $(2x)^2 + (2y)^2 = 4^2$.

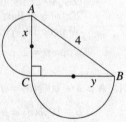

Then $4x^2 + 4y^2 = 16$, and $x^2 + y^2 = 4$. Since the area of a semicircle of radius r is $\frac{1}{2}\pi r^2$, the sum of the areas of the semicircles is

$$\frac{1}{2}\pi x^2 + \frac{1}{2}\pi y^2 = \frac{1}{2}\pi(x^2 + y^2) = \frac{1}{2}\pi(4) = \mathbf{2\pi}.$$

Use TACTIC 9-2. Pick numbers a and b for the legs of the triangle. For example, if a is 2, then by the Pythagorean theorem $2^2 + b^2 = 4^2$.

Then $b^2 = 12$ and $b = \sqrt{12} = 2\sqrt{3}$, so the radii of the semicircles are 1 and $\sqrt{3}$. Now, just calculate the area of each semicircle and add:

$$\frac{1}{2}\pi + \frac{3}{2}\pi = \mathbf{2\pi}.$$

Section 3 Verbal Reasoning

1. B. Many writers have compared people who seem *unconcerned* about the *threat* of atomic warfare to people who live in areas of danger and lack the sense to move away.
Remember, in double-blank sentences, go through the answer choices, testing the *first* words in each choice and eliminating those that don't fit.
Choice A does not fit. *Foolish* people would be *unworried* rather than worried about living near an active volcano.
Choice C also seems unlikely. Even extremely foolish people would not be *cheered* about atomic warfare. (Examples)

2. B. Gestures are useful when words are unavailable or when a person has *linguistic* difficulties, as in dealing with a foreign language.
Remember, before you look at the choices, read the sentence and think of a word that makes sense.
Likely Words: translation, language, vocabulary. (Examples)

3. C. Preservationists would not want a species to die out or become *extinct*, but instead want it to survive for the enjoyment of generations to come. (Definition)

4. C. *Connotations* (the implications or overtones a word carries in addition to its primary meaning) are most difficult to translate.
Remember, before you look at the choices, read the sentence and think of a word that makes sense.
Likely Words: subtleties, nuances, meaning. (Cause and Effect Signal)

5. E. It is difficult for a celebrity to keep his *humility*, or sense of his own *unimportance*, while the world is telling him how important he is.
Remember, before you look at the choices, read the sentence and think of a word that makes sense.
Likely Words: modesty, humbleness, humility. (Implicit Contrast Signal)

6. B. In spite of the difficulties or *hardships* involved in their research, the researchers have some moments of *exhilaration* or cheer.

Remember to watch for signal words that link one part of the sentence to another. The use of "for all the" in the opening clause sets up a contrast. The missing words must be antonyms or near-antonyms. You can immediately eliminate Choices A, C, and E as synonym or near synonym pairs.

(Contrast Signal)

7. C. Although some Hispanic actors are *prominent* (widely and popularly known), the group as a whole is felt to be *underrepresented* (not represented adequately).

Remember to watch for signal words that link one part of the sentence to another. The use of "despite" sets up a contrast. The missing words must be antonyms or near-antonyms. Only Choice C is such a pair.

(Contrast Signal)

8. C. Someone *never satisfied* would be likely to make *disparaging* (belittling or carping) comments.

Remember to watch for signal words that link one part of the sentence to another. The use of "never" in the opening clause sets up a contrast. The missing words must be antonyms or near-antonyms. You can immediately eliminate Choices A, B, and D as synonym or near-synonym pairs.

(Contrast Signal)

9. E. Even those who do not agree or *concur* with the way Williams plays his part *acknowledge* or grant that he is a serious, inventive actor.

Note that the second missing word must be a positive term. This allows you to eliminate Choices A, C, and D: you would not be likely to *dismiss* (ignore), *denounce* (condemn), or *deride* (treat scornfully) someone you regarded as both a serious and an imaginative actor.

(Argument Pattern)

10. B. The biography is described positively as "nuanced" (subtle) and "sensitive." To complete the thought, we need another positive term. A *telling* analysis is effective; it reveals much that would otherwise go unnoticed.

Note that you are looking for a word with positive associations. Therefore, you can eliminate any word with negative ones. Choices A, C, D, and E all have negative associations. Only Choice B can be correct.

(Support Pattern)

11. C. The function of the *heart* is to *pump*; the function of the *stomach* is to *digest*.   (Function)

12. B. By definition, a *servant* is bound to do the bidding of his or her *master*; a *subject* is bound to do the bidding of his or her *monarch*.

Beware Eye-Catchers: Choice E is incorrect. Although a *landlord* and a *tenant* have a "working relationship," the tenant is not bound to do the bidding of the landlord.

(Function)

13. B. A *stanza* is a subdivision of a *poem*; a *story* is a subdivision of a *building*.   (Part to Whole)

14. C. A *mongrel* is a mixed breed while a *collie* is a pure breed. An *alloy* is a mixture of metals. *Iron* is a single metal.

Choice A is incorrect. A gosling is a young goose.

Choice B is incorrect. A ruby is a kind of gem.

Choice C is incorrect. A bridle is a piece of restraining harness for a horse or pony.

Choice E is incorrect. A bleat is the cry of a sheep.   (Part to Whole)

15. C. A *trowel* is a tool used by a *mason*; an *adze* is a tool used by a *carpenter*.

Remember, if more than one answer appears to fit the relationship in your sentence, look for a narrower approach. "A mason uses a trowel" is too broad a test sentence; it could fit both Choices A and C. While a *potter* uses *clay* in his work, it is his material, not his tool.

(Worker and Tool)

16. B. One seeks to *amass* (gather) *wealth* to preserve it; one seeks to *garner* (collect) *grain* to store it.   (Purpose)

17. B. Those who *wince* indicate *pain*; those who *blush* indicate *embarrassment*.

(Action and Its Significance)

18. B. A *connoisseur* is an expert in the field of art or *paintings*. A *gourmet* is an expert in the field of food or *viands*.

Remember, if more than one answer appears to fit the relationship in your sentence, look for a narrower approach. "A connoisseur enjoys paintings" is too broad a framework; it could fit Choices B and C. A miser enjoys gold, but he is not necessarily a discerning judge of its artistic or aesthetic qualities.

(Function)

19. B. A *heckler* is someone who *jeers* or mocks; a *grumbler* is someone who *complains*.

Beware Eye-Catchers: Choice D is incorrect. A *heckler* does the jeering; a laughingstock, however, is the one who gets mocked.

(Definition)

20. E. A *malefactor* (evildoer) is by definition *iniquitous* (wicked); a *prankster* (person who plays tricks on others) is by definition *mischievous*.

(Defining Characteristics)

21. **A.** To *slink* is to show *stealth*, to move sneakily; to *whine* is to show *querulousness*, to speak petulantly.   (Defining Characteristic)

22. **A.** Something *uproarious* is extremely *amusing*; something *dumbfounding* is extremely *puzzling*.

Note that Choices C, D, and E are all pairs of synonyms. Eliminate them: the correct answer must belong to a different analogy type.   (Degree of Intensity)

23. **A.** One must *stanch bleeding* to stop the flow of blood; one must *dam* a *flood* to prevent an overflow of water.   (Function)

24. **D.** In describing Mr. Penniman's constitution as sickly, James is referring to the clergyman's delicate physical condition or *physique*.

25. **C.** The author portrays Mrs. Penniman's late husband as sickly. Nothing in the passage, however, allows us to infer that *she* is sickly. Therefore, Choice C is correct.

You can arrive at the correct answer by using the process of elimination.

The passage cites Mrs. Penniman's "alacrity" or willingness to accept her brother's offer. Thus, she readily becomes dependent on him. Choice A is supported by the passage. Therefore, it is incorrect.

The passage states that Mrs. Penniman was widowed at the age of thirty-three and that she had been married for ten years. This suggests that she was married at twenty-three. Choice B is supported by the passage. Therefore, it is incorrect.

The passage describes Mrs. Penniman's willingness to move as "the alacrity of a woman who had spent the ten years of her married life in Poughkeepsie." This suggests she did not think much of Poughkeepsie. Choice D is supported by the passage. Therefore, it is incorrect. The memory of Mr. Penniman's "flowers of speech" hovered about Mrs. Penniman's conversation (lines 7–10). This suggests she at times echoed her late husband's ornate conversational style. Choice E is supported by the passage. Therefore, it is incorrect.

Only Choice C is left. It is the correct answer.

26. **C.** As the widow of a poor clergyman, Mrs. Penniman has been left essentially penniless. She cannot afford to stay in whatever housing she shared with her late husband. Thus, her brother offers to let her take temporary *refuge* in his home.

Choices A and B are incorrect. Though an asylum can be an institution, such as a sanitarium or orphanage, the word is used here in its more general sense of *place of refuge*.

27. **D.** Choice D is correct. The Doctor is *civil*: "polite . . . , scrupulously, formally polite" (line 57); he is also domineering or *imperious*, never discussing anything, but issuing ultimatums instead (lines 62–63).

Choice A is incorrect. While the Doctor provides his widowed sister with a home, he does not do so in a particularly kindly or benevolent manner.

Choice B is incorrect. The Doctor is formal, not casual.

Choice C is incorrect. The Doctor is neither powerless nor ineffectual. He is the center of authority in his home.

Choice E is incorrect. The Doctor is not habitually angry or irate; his sister has seen him in a temper only once in her life (lines 57–58).

28. **E.** Mrs. Penniman tells all her friends that she has kept on living with her brother in order to supervise his daughter's education. She never says this to him. Why not? She "shrunk . . . from presenting herself to her brother as a fountain of instruction." Her self-assurance is largely artificial; she *lacks the confidence* or presumption to try to pass herself off as a brilliant woman to him.

29. **B.** If the Doctor were to back up Mrs. Penniman's story and say he needed his sister to take charge of Catherine's education, he would be lying. Lines 44–45 state he "had never been dazzled by his sister's intellect." The Doctor *does not believe in his sister's brilliance*. Unwilling to lie overtly, he keeps silent, giving only tacit (unspoken) assent to her excuse.

30. **C.** The Doctor asks his sister to try and make a clever woman of his daughter (lines 67–68). This implies that he views children as *clay to be molded*.

Choices A, B, D, and E are all unsupported by the passage.

31. **C.** In reflecting about herself, Mrs. Penniman is contemplating or *considering* her status.

Note that in line 69 Mrs. Penniman looks *thoughtful*. *Reflection* is a synonym for *thought*.

32. **B.** Choice B is correct. The Doctor knows that Catherine is good. Goodness alone, however, does not satisfy him: he finds goodness ("good bread-and-butter") bland and dull. He wants his daughter, like his dinner, to have spice. But Catherine will never have the salt of malice or mischievousness in her to make her lively and interesting. ("Salt" here means an element that gives liveliness, piquancy, or zest.) Thus, he fears that, lacking cleverness, she will turn out *virtuous but uninteresting*.

33. **D.** In overlooking Catherine at the piano, Mrs. Penniman is *watching over* or keeping an eye on Catherine's performance. This is another example of Mrs. Penniman's supervision of her niece's education in womanly accomplishments.

34. **D.** Mrs. Penniman tells her brother he needn't fear about Catherine's growing up to be insipid or uninteresting; after all, Catherine is being raised by her "clever" aunt. The reader knows, however, that Mrs. Penniman is not particularly clever. She is unlikely to mold Catherine into the sort of young woman the Doctor would admire. Thus, in her assurances to her brother, Mrs. Penniman is *unrealistically optimistic*.

35. **A.** In stating that Catherine "made but a modest figure" on the dance floor, the passage indicates her moderate or *limited skill as a dancer*. "But" here means only. Her skill was *only* modest or limited.
    Choice B is incorrect. *Virtuosity* means expertise, extreme skill or talent. Catherine had only "a certain talent" at the piano, not the talent of an expert.
    Choice C is incorrect. *Modest* here means moderate or limited. It does not indicate shyness on her part.
    Choice D is incorrect. Nothing in the passage suggests Catherine is indifferent to cleverness.
    Choice E is incorrect. It is unsupported by the passage.

Section 4   Mathematical Reasoning
Quantitative Comparison Questions

1. **B.** In each column, the sum includes the numbers from -3 to 3. All the other numbers in Column A are negative, and all those in Column B are positive, so B is greater. (Note that we didn't calculate either sum. We just used TACTIC 10-5 and compared the columns. Of course, we *could have* quickly calculated each sum.)

2. **B.** Since $\frac{1}{3} < \frac{2}{3}$ and a is positive, $\frac{1}{3}a < \frac{2}{3}a$.
   Column B is greater. (KEY FACT A23). Note that it is irrelevant that $a < 1$.
   **Use TACTIC 10-1. Replace a with $\frac{1}{2}$, and see that Column B is greater. Eliminate A and C. Try another number between 0 and 1; Column B is again greater. Guess B.

3. **C.** Just calculate. Column A: $\frac{1}{4} \times 40\% = 10\%$.

Column B: $\frac{2}{5} \times 25\% = 10\%$.

Columns A and B are equal (C).
**If you realize that $\frac{1}{4} = 25\%$ and that $\frac{2}{5} = 40\%$, then each column is just $25\% \times 40\%$, and so they are equal (C).

4. **B.** Use TACTIC 10-3. Add x to each column. Column A = 1 and Column B = 2. Column B is greater. It is irrelevant that $1000 < x < 2000$.
   **Use TACTIC 10-1. Plug in one or two numbers. Column B is always greater. Remember: $-1499 < -1498$ (KEY FACT A23).

5. **C.** By KEY FACTS I2 and I3, $c = 80$ and $d = 110$. Since ℓ_1 and ℓ_2 are parallel, then, by KEY FACT I6, $a = c = 80$ and $b = d = 110$. Therefore $a + b = 80 + 110 = 190$. The columns are equal (C).

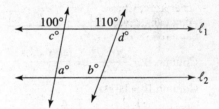

6. **B.** Column A: $y = \frac{12}{x}$. Column B: $z = \frac{25}{x}$. If two fractions have the same *positive* denominator, the one with the larger numerator—here, B—is greater (KEY FACT B4).
   **Use TACTIC 10-1. Let $x = 2$. Then $y = 6$ and $z = 12.5$. In this case, Column B is greater, so eliminate A and C. Try another value; Column B is again greater. Guess B.

7. **C.** Since $\frac{5a}{7b} = \frac{5}{7}$ then $\frac{a}{b} = 1$. Therefore, $a = b$; the columns are equal (C).
   **Cross-multiply: $35a = 35b \Rightarrow a = b$ (C).

8. **A.** There are four primes between 10 and 20: 11, 13, 17, and 19, but only two primes between 20 and 30: 23 and 29. Column A is greater. (Note: It's worth memorizing the list of primes up to at least 25. If you haven't done so, remember that, other than 2 and 5, *every* prime ends in either 1, 3, 7, or 9, so those are the only numbers you need to check.)

9. **A.** Column A: $3^7 = 2187$, which, when divided by 10, has a quotient of 218 and a remainder of 7 ($2187 = 10 \times 218 + 7$). Column B: $7^3 = 343$, which, when divided by 10, has a quotient of 34 and a remainder of 3 ($343 = 10 \times 34 + 3$). Column A is greater.

10. **C.**   The average of the measures of the three angles of *any* triangle is $180° \div 3 = 60°$. The columns are equal (C).

   **Use TACTIC 10-1. Pick an acute triangle: say the measures of the angles are 50°, 60°, and 70°. Their average is 60°. Choose an obtuse triangle: say the measures of the angles are 100°, 40°, and 40°. Again, the average is 60°. The columns are equal (C).

11. **B.**   If you draw a diagram, it is immediately clear that the area of the large triangle is *more than* twice the area of the small one. In fact, it is 4 times as great. Column B is larger.

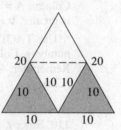

   **Use the formula for the area of an equilateral triangle of side *s*:

   $$A = \frac{s^2 \sqrt{3}}{4} \text{ (KEY FACT J15).}$$

   Column A $= 2 \times \dfrac{10^2 \sqrt{3}}{4} = \dfrac{200 \sqrt{3}}{4}$.

   Column B $= \dfrac{20^2 \sqrt{3}}{4} = \dfrac{400 \sqrt{3}}{4}$.

   Column B is larger.

   **If you don't know the formula used above, use $A = \dfrac{1}{2} bh$. To get *h*, remember that, in an equilateral triangle of side *s*, the altitude (height) creates a 30-60-90 right triangle (KEY FACT J10), and the height is $\dfrac{s}{2} \sqrt{3}$.

12. **D.**   If $x = 3$ and $y = 7$ (or vice versa), then $x + y = 10$, and Column B is greater. Eliminate A and C. If $x = 1$ and $y = 21$ (or vice versa), then $x + y = 22$. This time, Column A is greater. Eliminate B. Neither column is *always* greater, and the two columns are not *always* equal.

13. **D.**   Let *r*, *C*, and *A* represent the radius, circumference, and area of the circle:

   $$C = 2\pi r = a\pi \text{ and } a = \frac{2\pi r}{{}_1\pi} = 2r.$$

   Similarly,

   $$A = \pi r^2 = b\pi \Rightarrow b = \frac{\pi r^2}{{}_1\pi} = r^2.$$

   The value of Column A is $2r$, and the value of Column B is r^2. Which is greater? Dividing each by *r* yields 2 in Column A and *r* in Column B. Since there are no restrictions, *r* could be greater than, less than, or equal to 2. Neither column is *always* greater, and the two columns are not *always* equal (D).

   **Use TACTIC 10-1. Let $r = 1$. Then $C = 2\pi$ and $A = \pi$; so $a = 2$ and $b = 1$. Column B is

greater: eliminate A and C. Try $r = 2$. Now, $C = 4\pi$ and $A = 4\pi$; $a = b$ and the columns are equal. Eliminate B. The answer is D.

14. **C.**   You can't use your calculator to look at the units digits of these numbers because they're too large (14^{14} has 15 digits!). But you can use it to see that, in Column A, $14^2 = 196$, $14^3 = 2744$, $14^4 = 38416$, and that the units digits of the powers of 14 alternate 4, 6, 4, 6, 4,.... The number 14 to an even power has a units digit of 6. In Column B, *every* power of 16 ends in 6: 16, 256, 4096, 65536,.... Therefore Columns A and B are each equal to 6, and the answer is C. (<u>Note:</u> You don't need your calculator at all. You don't need to know even the first few powers of 14 or 16; you need know only what they end in. It is easy to reason that the product of any two numbers ending in 4 is a number ending in 6, and that the product of a number ending in 6 and a number ending in 4 is a number ending in 4, and so on.)

15. **A.**   Note that, when a number is decreased by 20%, what remains is 80% of the original: 80% of 80% of 80% $= .8 \times .8 \times .8 = .512 = 51.2\%$, which is greater than 50%. Column A is larger.

   **Use TACTIC 10-2. *Assume* that in 1980 the population of Mudville was 100. Then, in 1985 it was 80, in 1990 it was 64, and in 1995 it was 51.2, which is greater than 50, one-half of the 1980 population.

Grid-in Questions

16. $\left(5.5 \text{ or } \dfrac{11}{2}\right)$ Divide. By calculator: $330 \div 60 = \mathbf{5.5}$.

   By hand: $\dfrac{330}{60} = \dfrac{33}{6} = \dfrac{11}{2}$.

    **Set up a proportion using the ratio $\dfrac{\text{words}}{\text{minutes}}$:

   $\dfrac{60}{1} = \dfrac{330}{x}$. Cross-multiply: $60x = 330$. Divide by 60: $x = \mathbf{5.5}$.

17. $\left(7.5 \text{ or } \dfrac{15}{2}\right)$ Notice that the left-hand side $(2x - 15)$ of the equation is the negative of the right-hand side $(15 - 2x)$, meaning that each side is equal to 0 ($a = -a \Rightarrow a = 0$). Therefore $2x - 15 = 0 \Rightarrow 2x = 15 \Rightarrow x = \mathbf{7.5}$ or $\dfrac{\mathbf{15}}{\mathbf{2}}$.

   **Just solve the equation:
   $2x - 15 = 15 - 2x \Rightarrow 4x - 15 = 15 \Rightarrow$
   $4x = 30 \Rightarrow x = \mathbf{7.5}$.

**Use TACTIC 11-1. Quickly test some values of x:

x	1	5	7	8	7.5
$2x - 15$	-13	-5	-1	1	0
$15 - 2x$	13	5	1	-1	0

18. (70) Since all of the radii of a circle have the same length, $CA = CB$. Therefore, m$\angle A$ = m$\angle B$ = 55°. Therefore $c = 180 - (55 + 55) = 180 - 110 = \textbf{70}$.

19. (30) Let x = Tina's age, and write the algebraic equation. If it helps, quickly make a table:

	Now	In 20 Years
Tina's age	x	$x + 20$
Maria's age	$6x$	$6x + 20$

$6x + 20 = 2(x + 20) \Rightarrow$
$6x + 20 = 2x + 40 \Rightarrow$
$4x = 20 \Rightarrow x = 5$
(Tina's age)

Be careful. The question asks for *Maria's* age: $6x = \textbf{30}$.

Use TACTIC 11-1. Test some values. If Tina is 1, Maria is 6; in 20 years, their ages will be 21 and 26. Maria will be less than twice as old as Tina. If Tina is 10, Maria is 60, and in 20 years their ages will be 30 and 80. Maria will be more than twice as old as Tina. Try 5. Then their ages are 5 and **30, and in 20 years they will be 25 and 50. That's it!

20. (12) To make a fraction as large as possible, make the numerator as large, and the denominator as small, as you can. Let r and s be 11 and 13, the largest primes less than 15, and let $t = 2$, the smallest prime. Then
$$\frac{r + s}{t} = \frac{11 + 13}{2} = \textbf{12}.$$

21. (200) By TACTIC E1, if the average of five numbers is 60, their sum is $5 \times 60 = 300$. The first four in the question add up to 100 $(10 + 20 + 30 + 40)$, so the fifth number, x, is **200** $(300 - 100)$.

Use TACTIC 11-1. Test some numbers. Since the average, 60, is greater than each of the four given numbers, the fifth number must be substantially greater than 60. Try 100 to start. The average of 10, 20, 30, 40, and 100 is 40. That's too small. Try a larger number—150 or **200 or 300. Zoom in.

22. (1.5 or any number between $\frac{4}{3}$ or 1.33 and $\frac{5}{3}$ or 1.67) Pick a value for k: 4.5 say, and use the

slope formula. The slope of the line through $(0,0)$ and $(3,4.5)$ is $\frac{4.5 - 0}{3 - 0} = \frac{4.5}{3} = 1.5$, so grid in **1.5**.

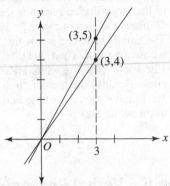

Draw a quick sketch. The line through the origin and $(3,4)$ has slope $\frac{4}{3}$. Likewise, the slope of the line through the origin and $(3,5)$ is $\frac{5}{3}$. Therefore, the slope could be any number **greater than $\frac{4}{3}$ (1.33) and less than $\frac{5}{3}$ (1.67), expressed as a fraction or decimal: $\frac{3}{2}$ or 1.5 or 1.6 and so on.

23. $\left(\frac{4}{3} \text{ or } 1.33\right)$ Mentally, or by using a Venn

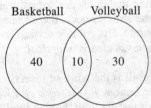

diagram, determine the number of girls who play only one sport. 40 play only basketball and 30 play only volleyball. The ratio is 40:30. Grid in $\frac{4}{3}$ or **1.33**.

24. (2500) The equation is as follows:
$B - A = (51+52+53+...+99+100) - (1+2+3+...+49+50)$
$= (51-1)+(52-2)+(53-3)+...+(99-49)+(100-50)$
$= 50 + 50 + 50 + ... + 50 + 50 = 50 \times 50 = \textbf{2500}$.

** If you know the formula, $\frac{n(n + 1)}{2}$, for adding up the first n positive integers, you can use it:
$A = \frac{50(51)}{2} = 25(51) = 1275$. B is the sum of the integers from 1 to 100 minus the sum of the integers from 1 to 50:
$B = \frac{100(101)}{2} - 1275 = 50(101) - 1275 = 5050 - 1275 = 3875$.
Finally, $B - A = 3875 - 1275 = \textbf{2500}$.

25. $\left(\frac{13}{3} \text{ or } 4.33\right)$ Pick a simple number for the radius of circle Q—say, 1. Then the radius of circle P is 2, and the radius of circle O is 4. The area of the large shaded region is the area of circle O minus the area of circle P: $16\pi - 4\pi = 12\pi$. The small shaded region is just circle Q, whose area is π. Then, the total shaded area is $12\pi + \pi = 13\pi$. The white area is the area of circle P minus the area of circle Q: $4\pi - \pi = 3\pi$. Finally, the ratio of the entire shaded area to the white area is

$$\frac{13\pi}{3\pi} = \frac{13}{3} \text{ or } \mathbf{4.33}.$$

Section 5   Verbal Reasoning

1. B.   Throughout Passage 1 the author reiterates that human beings make cities, that the creation of a city is an act of choice, that a city is the result of an agreement or pact. In all these ways, he *defines the city as growing out of a social contract* by which human beings choose to bind themselves.

2. D.   The sentences quoted within the parentheses are illustrations of the sort of metaphors we use in describing cities. Thus, they are examples *of one type of figurative language*.

3. D.   Insisting that cities are not natural but artificial, the author rejects these metaphors as inaccurate. His attitude toward the statements he quotes is clearly *skeptical*.

4. D.   An anthill is the work of insects rather than of human beings. *It is a work of instinct rather than of imagination*, human intelligence, and choice; therefore, by the author's definition, it is not like a city.

5. C.   The author cites these factors as "reasons (that) may lead people to aggregate" or *gather together in settlements*.

6. A.   The nomads have chosen to wander like the moon. The logical corollary of that is that they *have not chosen to settle in one spot*.

7. A.   The author clearly is impressed by the magnitude of the choice people make when they agree to live as if mere geographical links, "ties of proximity," can be as strong as blood relationships. In proclaiming a city "a considerable pact," he stresses the *essential significance* or weightiness of this agreement.

8. C.   To the author, "a city is an expression of continuity through will and imagination." Thus, to live in a city is *an act of volition* (will).

9. B.   One would predict such a mass exodus of financial firms only if one assumed that the firms could do their work just as well at distant locations as they could in the city. Thus, the basic assumption underlying the forecast is that *computerized tasks such as record keeping* (the major task of most financial institutions) *can easily be performed at remote sites*.

10. C.   The city's concentration of people necessitates the enormous size of its buildings. These outsized buildings destroy the scale or *relative dimensions* of the city as it was originally envisioned by its planners.

11. C.   The human congress is described in the next-to-last paragraph. It is the *gathering of individuals*, bringing about the vital exchange of ideas and opinions, that the city makes possible.

12. E.   While the author of Passage 1 talks in terms of abstractions that keep people dwelling together in cities (the city as pact, the city as an expression of will and imagination), the author of Passage 2 openly mentions the concrete ills that threaten the city: overcrowding, overbuilding of outsize skyscrapers that block the sun, loss of businesses to the suburbs (with the attendant loss of tax revenues). Given his perspective as an urban planner and sociologist, he is inevitably moved to talk about the city's difficulties.

13. E.   The author of Passage 1 muses about the nature of the city, defining it and dwelling on its significance. He is *philosophical*. Without romanticizing the city, the author of Passage 2 discusses both its strengths and weaknesses. Though he emphasizes the importance of the city, he tries to be impartial or *objective*. Compared to Passage 1, Passage 2 is *more objective and less philosophical*.

Section 6   Mathematical Reasoning

1. B.   By KEY FACT I2, $a + a + a + a + a = 180$ $\Rightarrow 5a = 180 \Rightarrow a = 36$.

2. C.   Use TACTIC 8-11: list systematically. Take 2, the first number in A, multiply it by each number in B, and jot down each product: 6, 8, 12. Now, take 3, the next number in A, multiply it by each number in B, and write down each *new* product: 9,   , 18. Note that, when we got to $3 \times 4 = 12$, we didn't list 12, because we already had the product 12 from 2×6. The complete list is: 6, 8, 12; 9, 18; 16, 24. There are **7** different values of ab.

3. C.   15% of t, the total number of students, is 180. Then

$$.15t = 180 \Rightarrow t = \frac{180}{.15} = \mathbf{1200}.$$

Use TACTIC 9-1. Try choice C, 1200. Look at the table. Is 15% of **1200 equal to 180? Yes!

4. **B.** There are 480 juniors on teams (40% of 1200). Then z, the number of seniors on teams, is $1200 - (180 + 120 + 480) = 1200 - 780 = \mathbf{420}$.

**The sophomores account for 10% $\left(\frac{\overset{1}{\cancel{120}}}{\underset{10}{\cancel{1200}}}\right)$ of the students on teams, so the percentage, w, of seniors is

$$100 - (15 + 10 + 40) = 100 - 65 = 35.$$

Finally, 35% of 1200 is **420**.

5. **C.** The sum of three consecutive integers can be expressed as

$$n + (n + 1) + (n + 2) = 3n + 3 = 3(n + 1),$$

and so must be a multiple of 3. Only **28** is *not* a multiple of 3.
**Quickly add up sets of three consecutive integers: $4 + 5 + 6 = 15$, $5 + 6 + 7 = 18$, $6 + 7 + 8 = 21$, and so on, and see the pattern (they're all multiples of 3); or cross off the choices as you come to them.

6. **B.** We are given that: $x^2 - y^2 = (x - y)^2$
   - Expand: $x^2 - y^2 = x^2 - 2xy + y^2$
   - Subtract x^2 from each side: $-y^2 = -2xy + y^2$
   - Add y^2 to each side:
   $$0 = 2y^2 - 2xy \Rightarrow 0 = 2y(y - x)$$

   Either $y = 0$ or $y - x = 0$; but it is given that $x \ne y$, so $y - x \ne 0$. Therefore, it *must* be that $y = 0$. (II is true.) If we replace y by 0 in the original equation, we get $x^2 = x^2$, which is true for *any* value of x. Therefore, it is not true that x must equal 0. (I is false.) Also, it is not true that $x = -y$. (III is false.) Then **II only** is true.
   **Look at the choices. *If $x = 0$, then $-y^2 = (-y)^2 = y^2$ which means that $y = 0$, which is impossible since $x \ne y$. (I is false.) Eliminate A, D, and E. If $y = 0$, then $(x)^2 = x^2$, which is always true *no matter what x is*, so *y could be* 0. Don't eliminate B yet.
   $$x = -y \Rightarrow x^2 = y^2 \Rightarrow x^2 - y^2 = 0$$
   but $(x - y)^2 = (x + x)^2 = (2x)^2 = 4x^2$, which clearly does not have to be 0. Eliminate C. The answer must be B.

7. **D.** Divide the number of delegates, d, by the number of countries, c: $\dfrac{d}{c}$.

   **Use TACTIC 9-2. Pick some simple numbers. If there are a total of 10 delegates from 2 countries, then, clearly, each country has 5 delegates.
   Only $\dfrac{d}{c} = 5$ when $d = 10$ and $c = 2$.

8. **E.** The total rent is $a + b$, so Bob's fractional share is $\dfrac{a}{a + b}$. To convert to a percent, simply multiply by 100%: $\dfrac{100a}{a + b}\%$.

   **Use TACTIC 9-2. Pick two easy-to-use numbers. If Bob pays \$1 and Jack pays \$2, then Bob pays $\dfrac{1}{3}$, or $33\dfrac{1}{3}\%$, of the rent. Only $\dfrac{100a}{a + b}\% = 33\dfrac{1}{3}\%$ when $a = 1$ and $b = 2$.

9. **C.** Since each radius is 3, $OA = OB$, and by KEY FACT J3 $m\angle A = m\angle B$. Then, $60 + x + x = 180 \Rightarrow x = 60$. Therefore $\triangle AOB$ is equilateral, and $AB = 3$. The length of arc AB is $\dfrac{60}{360} = \dfrac{1}{6}$ of the circumference.

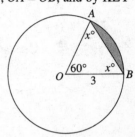

$C = 2\pi(3) = 6\pi$, so the length of arc $AB = \pi$. The perimeter of the region, then, is $3 + \pi$.

**Use TACTIC 8-2: trust the diagram. AB looks about the same as OB, so assume it is 3, and arc AB is clearly slightly bigger. Hence, the perimeter is a little more than 6. Choices A and B are both less than 5 (use your calculator), which is definitely too small. Between C and D *guess*. C, $3 + \pi$, is the better guess, because *AB might be* exactly 3.

10. **D.** Draw in segment $EXY \perp AB$. Then $XY = 10$ since it is the same length as a side of the

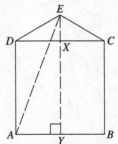

square. EX is the height of $\triangle ECD$, whose base is 10 and whose area is 10, so

$$EX = 2\left[\frac{1}{2}bh = \frac{1}{2}(10)(2) = 10\right], \text{ and } EY = 12.$$

Since $\triangle ECD$ is isosceles, $DX = 5$, so $AY = 5$. Finally, recognize $\triangle AYE$ as a 5-12-13 right triangle, or use the Pythagorean theorem to find the hypotenuse, AE, of the triangle:
$$(AE)^2 = 5^2 + 12^2 = 25 + 144 = 169,$$
so $AE = \mathbf{13}$.

Answer Sheet—Test 2

If a section has fewer than 35 questions, leave the extra spaces blank.

Section 1

1 Ⓐ Ⓑ Ⓒ Ⓓ Ⓔ	8 Ⓐ Ⓑ Ⓒ Ⓓ Ⓔ	15 Ⓐ Ⓑ Ⓒ Ⓓ Ⓔ	22 Ⓐ Ⓑ Ⓒ Ⓓ Ⓔ	29 Ⓐ Ⓑ Ⓒ Ⓓ Ⓔ
2 Ⓐ Ⓑ Ⓒ Ⓓ Ⓔ	9 Ⓐ Ⓑ Ⓒ Ⓓ Ⓔ	16 Ⓐ Ⓑ Ⓒ Ⓓ Ⓔ	23 Ⓐ Ⓑ Ⓒ Ⓓ Ⓔ	30 Ⓐ Ⓑ Ⓒ Ⓓ Ⓔ
3 Ⓐ Ⓑ Ⓒ Ⓓ Ⓔ	10 Ⓐ Ⓑ Ⓒ Ⓓ Ⓔ	17 Ⓐ Ⓑ Ⓒ Ⓓ Ⓔ	24 Ⓐ Ⓑ Ⓒ Ⓓ Ⓔ	31 Ⓐ Ⓑ Ⓒ Ⓓ Ⓔ
4 Ⓐ Ⓑ Ⓒ Ⓓ Ⓔ	11 Ⓐ Ⓑ Ⓒ Ⓓ Ⓔ	18 Ⓐ Ⓑ Ⓒ Ⓓ Ⓔ	25 Ⓐ Ⓑ Ⓒ Ⓓ Ⓔ	32 Ⓐ Ⓑ Ⓒ Ⓓ Ⓔ
5 Ⓐ Ⓑ Ⓒ Ⓓ Ⓔ	12 Ⓐ Ⓑ Ⓒ Ⓓ Ⓔ	19 Ⓐ Ⓑ Ⓒ Ⓓ Ⓔ	26 Ⓐ Ⓑ Ⓒ Ⓓ Ⓔ	33 Ⓐ Ⓑ Ⓒ Ⓓ Ⓔ
6 Ⓐ Ⓑ Ⓒ Ⓓ Ⓔ	13 Ⓐ Ⓑ Ⓒ Ⓓ Ⓔ	20 Ⓐ Ⓑ Ⓒ Ⓓ Ⓔ	27 Ⓐ Ⓑ Ⓒ Ⓓ Ⓔ	34 Ⓐ Ⓑ Ⓒ Ⓓ Ⓔ
7 Ⓐ Ⓑ Ⓒ Ⓓ Ⓔ	14 Ⓐ Ⓑ Ⓒ Ⓓ Ⓔ	21 Ⓐ Ⓑ Ⓒ Ⓓ Ⓔ	28 Ⓐ Ⓑ Ⓒ Ⓓ Ⓔ	35 Ⓐ Ⓑ Ⓒ Ⓓ Ⓔ

Section 2

1 Ⓐ Ⓑ Ⓒ Ⓓ Ⓔ	8 Ⓐ Ⓑ Ⓒ Ⓓ Ⓔ	15 Ⓐ Ⓑ Ⓒ Ⓓ Ⓔ	22 Ⓐ Ⓑ Ⓒ Ⓓ Ⓔ	29 Ⓐ Ⓑ Ⓒ Ⓓ Ⓔ
2 Ⓐ Ⓑ Ⓒ Ⓓ Ⓔ	9 Ⓐ Ⓑ Ⓒ Ⓓ Ⓔ	16 Ⓐ Ⓑ Ⓒ Ⓓ Ⓔ	23 Ⓐ Ⓑ Ⓒ Ⓓ Ⓔ	30 Ⓐ Ⓑ Ⓒ Ⓓ Ⓔ
3 Ⓐ Ⓑ Ⓒ Ⓓ Ⓔ	10 Ⓐ Ⓑ Ⓒ Ⓓ Ⓔ	17 Ⓐ Ⓑ Ⓒ Ⓓ Ⓔ	24 Ⓐ Ⓑ Ⓒ Ⓓ Ⓔ	31 Ⓐ Ⓑ Ⓒ Ⓓ Ⓔ
4 Ⓐ Ⓑ Ⓒ Ⓓ Ⓔ	11 Ⓐ Ⓑ Ⓒ Ⓓ Ⓔ	18 Ⓐ Ⓑ Ⓒ Ⓓ Ⓔ	25 Ⓐ Ⓑ Ⓒ Ⓓ Ⓔ	32 Ⓐ Ⓑ Ⓒ Ⓓ Ⓔ
5 Ⓐ Ⓑ Ⓒ Ⓓ Ⓔ	12 Ⓐ Ⓑ Ⓒ Ⓓ Ⓔ	19 Ⓐ Ⓑ Ⓒ Ⓓ Ⓔ	26 Ⓐ Ⓑ Ⓒ Ⓓ Ⓔ	33 Ⓐ Ⓑ Ⓒ Ⓓ Ⓔ
6 Ⓐ Ⓑ Ⓒ Ⓓ Ⓔ	13 Ⓐ Ⓑ Ⓒ Ⓓ Ⓔ	20 Ⓐ Ⓑ Ⓒ Ⓓ Ⓔ	27 Ⓐ Ⓑ Ⓒ Ⓓ Ⓔ	34 Ⓐ Ⓑ Ⓒ Ⓓ Ⓔ
7 Ⓐ Ⓑ Ⓒ Ⓓ Ⓔ	14 Ⓐ Ⓑ Ⓒ Ⓓ Ⓔ	21 Ⓐ Ⓑ Ⓒ Ⓓ Ⓔ	28 Ⓐ Ⓑ Ⓒ Ⓓ Ⓔ	35 Ⓐ Ⓑ Ⓒ Ⓓ Ⓔ

Section 3

1 Ⓐ Ⓑ Ⓒ Ⓓ Ⓔ	8 Ⓐ Ⓑ Ⓒ Ⓓ Ⓔ	15 Ⓐ Ⓑ Ⓒ Ⓓ Ⓔ	22 Ⓐ Ⓑ Ⓒ Ⓓ Ⓔ	29 Ⓐ Ⓑ Ⓒ Ⓓ Ⓔ
2 Ⓐ Ⓑ Ⓒ Ⓓ Ⓔ	9 Ⓐ Ⓑ Ⓒ Ⓓ Ⓔ	16 Ⓐ Ⓑ Ⓒ Ⓓ Ⓔ	23 Ⓐ Ⓑ Ⓒ Ⓓ Ⓔ	30 Ⓐ Ⓑ Ⓒ Ⓓ Ⓔ
3 Ⓐ Ⓑ Ⓒ Ⓓ Ⓔ	10 Ⓐ Ⓑ Ⓒ Ⓓ Ⓔ	17 Ⓐ Ⓑ Ⓒ Ⓓ Ⓔ	24 Ⓐ Ⓑ Ⓒ Ⓓ Ⓔ	31 Ⓐ Ⓑ Ⓒ Ⓓ Ⓔ
4 Ⓐ Ⓑ Ⓒ Ⓓ Ⓔ	11 Ⓐ Ⓑ Ⓒ Ⓓ Ⓔ	18 Ⓐ Ⓑ Ⓒ Ⓓ Ⓔ	25 Ⓐ Ⓑ Ⓒ Ⓓ Ⓔ	32 Ⓐ Ⓑ Ⓒ Ⓓ Ⓔ
5 Ⓐ Ⓑ Ⓒ Ⓓ Ⓔ	12 Ⓐ Ⓑ Ⓒ Ⓓ Ⓔ	19 Ⓐ Ⓑ Ⓒ Ⓓ Ⓔ	26 Ⓐ Ⓑ Ⓒ Ⓓ Ⓔ	33 Ⓐ Ⓑ Ⓒ Ⓓ Ⓔ
6 Ⓐ Ⓑ Ⓒ Ⓓ Ⓔ	13 Ⓐ Ⓑ Ⓒ Ⓓ Ⓔ	20 Ⓐ Ⓑ Ⓒ Ⓓ Ⓔ	27 Ⓐ Ⓑ Ⓒ Ⓓ Ⓔ	34 Ⓐ Ⓑ Ⓒ Ⓓ Ⓔ
7 Ⓐ Ⓑ Ⓒ Ⓓ Ⓔ	14 Ⓐ Ⓑ Ⓒ Ⓓ Ⓔ	21 Ⓐ Ⓑ Ⓒ Ⓓ Ⓔ	28 Ⓐ Ⓑ Ⓒ Ⓓ Ⓔ	35 Ⓐ Ⓑ Ⓒ Ⓓ Ⓔ

Section 4

1 Ⓐ Ⓑ Ⓒ Ⓓ Ⓔ	4 Ⓐ Ⓑ Ⓒ Ⓓ Ⓔ	7 Ⓐ Ⓑ Ⓒ Ⓓ Ⓔ	10 Ⓐ Ⓑ Ⓒ Ⓓ Ⓔ	13 Ⓐ Ⓑ Ⓒ Ⓓ Ⓔ
2 Ⓐ Ⓑ Ⓒ Ⓓ Ⓔ	5 Ⓐ Ⓑ Ⓒ Ⓓ Ⓔ	8 Ⓐ Ⓑ Ⓒ Ⓓ Ⓔ	11 Ⓐ Ⓑ Ⓒ Ⓓ Ⓔ	14 Ⓐ Ⓑ Ⓒ Ⓓ Ⓔ
3 Ⓐ Ⓑ Ⓒ Ⓓ Ⓔ	6 Ⓐ Ⓑ Ⓒ Ⓓ Ⓔ	9 Ⓐ Ⓑ Ⓒ Ⓓ Ⓔ	12 Ⓐ Ⓑ Ⓒ Ⓓ Ⓔ	15 Ⓐ Ⓑ Ⓒ Ⓓ Ⓔ

Section 4 (continued)

Grid-in answer boxes 16–25.

Section 5

1 Ⓐ Ⓑ Ⓒ Ⓓ Ⓔ	8 Ⓐ Ⓑ Ⓒ Ⓓ Ⓔ	15 Ⓐ Ⓑ Ⓒ Ⓓ Ⓔ	22 Ⓐ Ⓑ Ⓒ Ⓓ Ⓔ	29 Ⓐ Ⓑ Ⓒ Ⓓ Ⓔ
2 Ⓐ Ⓑ Ⓒ Ⓓ Ⓔ	9 Ⓐ Ⓑ Ⓒ Ⓓ Ⓔ	16 Ⓐ Ⓑ Ⓒ Ⓓ Ⓔ	23 Ⓐ Ⓑ Ⓒ Ⓓ Ⓔ	30 Ⓐ Ⓑ Ⓒ Ⓓ Ⓔ
3 Ⓐ Ⓑ Ⓒ Ⓓ Ⓔ	10 Ⓐ Ⓑ Ⓒ Ⓓ Ⓔ	17 Ⓐ Ⓑ Ⓒ Ⓓ Ⓔ	24 Ⓐ Ⓑ Ⓒ Ⓓ Ⓔ	31 Ⓐ Ⓑ Ⓒ Ⓓ Ⓔ
4 Ⓐ Ⓑ Ⓒ Ⓓ Ⓔ	11 Ⓐ Ⓑ Ⓒ Ⓓ Ⓔ	18 Ⓐ Ⓑ Ⓒ Ⓓ Ⓔ	25 Ⓐ Ⓑ Ⓒ Ⓓ Ⓔ	32 Ⓐ Ⓑ Ⓒ Ⓓ Ⓔ
5 Ⓐ Ⓑ Ⓒ Ⓓ Ⓔ	12 Ⓐ Ⓑ Ⓒ Ⓓ Ⓔ	19 Ⓐ Ⓑ Ⓒ Ⓓ Ⓔ	26 Ⓐ Ⓑ Ⓒ Ⓓ Ⓔ	33 Ⓐ Ⓑ Ⓒ Ⓓ Ⓔ
6 Ⓐ Ⓑ Ⓒ Ⓓ Ⓔ	13 Ⓐ Ⓑ Ⓒ Ⓓ Ⓔ	20 Ⓐ Ⓑ Ⓒ Ⓓ Ⓔ	27 Ⓐ Ⓑ Ⓒ Ⓓ Ⓔ	34 Ⓐ Ⓑ Ⓒ Ⓓ Ⓔ
7 Ⓐ Ⓑ Ⓒ Ⓓ Ⓔ	14 Ⓐ Ⓑ Ⓒ Ⓓ Ⓔ	21 Ⓐ Ⓑ Ⓒ Ⓓ Ⓔ	28 Ⓐ Ⓑ Ⓒ Ⓓ Ⓔ	35 Ⓐ Ⓑ Ⓒ Ⓓ Ⓔ

Section 6

1 Ⓐ Ⓑ Ⓒ Ⓓ Ⓔ	8 Ⓐ Ⓑ Ⓒ Ⓓ Ⓔ	15 Ⓐ Ⓑ Ⓒ Ⓓ Ⓔ	22 Ⓐ Ⓑ Ⓒ Ⓓ Ⓔ	29 Ⓐ Ⓑ Ⓒ Ⓓ Ⓔ
2 Ⓐ Ⓑ Ⓒ Ⓓ Ⓔ	9 Ⓐ Ⓑ Ⓒ Ⓓ Ⓔ	16 Ⓐ Ⓑ Ⓒ Ⓓ Ⓔ	23 Ⓐ Ⓑ Ⓒ Ⓓ Ⓔ	30 Ⓐ Ⓑ Ⓒ Ⓓ Ⓔ
3 Ⓐ Ⓑ Ⓒ Ⓓ Ⓔ	10 Ⓐ Ⓑ Ⓒ Ⓓ Ⓔ	17 Ⓐ Ⓑ Ⓒ Ⓓ Ⓔ	24 Ⓐ Ⓑ Ⓒ Ⓓ Ⓔ	31 Ⓐ Ⓑ Ⓒ Ⓓ Ⓔ
4 Ⓐ Ⓑ Ⓒ Ⓓ Ⓔ	11 Ⓐ Ⓑ Ⓒ Ⓓ Ⓔ	18 Ⓐ Ⓑ Ⓒ Ⓓ Ⓔ	25 Ⓐ Ⓑ Ⓒ Ⓓ Ⓔ	32 Ⓐ Ⓑ Ⓒ Ⓓ Ⓔ
5 Ⓐ Ⓑ Ⓒ Ⓓ Ⓔ	12 Ⓐ Ⓑ Ⓒ Ⓓ Ⓔ	19 Ⓐ Ⓑ Ⓒ Ⓓ Ⓔ	26 Ⓐ Ⓑ Ⓒ Ⓓ Ⓔ	33 Ⓐ Ⓑ Ⓒ Ⓓ Ⓔ
6 Ⓐ Ⓑ Ⓒ Ⓓ Ⓔ	13 Ⓐ Ⓑ Ⓒ Ⓓ Ⓔ	20 Ⓐ Ⓑ Ⓒ Ⓓ Ⓔ	27 Ⓐ Ⓑ Ⓒ Ⓓ Ⓔ	34 Ⓐ Ⓑ Ⓒ Ⓓ Ⓔ
7 Ⓐ Ⓑ Ⓒ Ⓓ Ⓔ	14 Ⓐ Ⓑ Ⓒ Ⓓ Ⓔ	21 Ⓐ Ⓑ Ⓒ Ⓓ Ⓔ	28 Ⓐ Ⓑ Ⓒ Ⓓ Ⓔ	35 Ⓐ Ⓑ Ⓒ Ⓓ Ⓔ

MODEL SAT I TEST 2   1 1 1 1 1   1

Each of the following sentences contains one or two blanks; these blanks indicate that a word or set of words has been left out. Below the sentence are five words or phrases, lettered A through E. Select the word or set of words that best completes the sentence.

Example:

Fame is ----; today's rising star is all too soon tomorrow's washed-up has-been.

(A) rewarding   (B) gradual
(C) essential   (D) spontaneous
   (E) transitory

1. Although he is ---- about the problems that still confront blacks in ballet, Mitchell nevertheless is optimistic about the future, especially that of his own dance company.

(A) hopeful   (B) uninformed   (C) abstract
   (D) realistic   (E) unconcerned

2. Despite all its ---- , a term of enlistment in the Peace Corps can be both stirring and satisfying to a college graduate still undecided on a career.

(A) rewards   (B) renown   (C) adventures
   (D) romance   (E) frustrations

3. Although he had the numerous films to his credit and a reputation for technical ---- , the moviemaker lacked originality; all his films were sadly ---- of the work of others.

(A) skill...independent
(B) ability...unconscious
(C) expertise...derivative
(D) competence...contradictory
(E) blunders...enamored

4. John Gielgud crowns a distinguished career of playing Shakespearean roles by giving a performance that is ---- .

(A) mediocre
(B) outmoded
(C) superficial
(D) unsurpassable
(E) insipid

5. Those interested in learning more about how genetics applies to trees will have to ---- the excellent technical journals where most of the pertinent material is ---- .

(A) subscribe to...ignored
(B) suffer through...located
(C) rely on...unrepresented
(D) resort to...found
(E) see through...published

6. Rent control restrictions on small apartment owners may unfortunately ---- rather than alleviate housing problems.

(A) resolve   (B) diminish   (C) castigate
   (D) minimize   (E) exacerbate

7. In the light of Dickens's description of the lively, even ---- dance parties of his time, Sharp's approach to country dancing may seem overly formal, suggesting more ---- than is necessary.

(A) sophisticated...expertise
(B) rowdy...decorum
(C) prudish...propriety
(D) lewd...ribaldry
(E) enjoyable...vitality

8. It is said that the custom of shaking hands originated when primitive men held out empty hands to indicate that they had no ---- weapons and were thus ---- disposed.

(A) lethal...clearly
(B) concealed...amicably
(C) hidden...harmfully
(D) murderous...ill
(E) secret...finally

9. The biochemistry instructor urged that we take particular care of the ---- chemicals to prevent their evaporation.

(A) insoluble   (B) superficial   (C) extraneous
   (D) volatile   (E) insipid

GO ON TO THE NEXT PAGE ⟩

1   1   1   1   1   1   1   1   1   1   1   1

The analogies questions present two words or phrases that are related in some way. Determine which A-through-E answer choice below has a relationship *most* similar to that of the original words or phrases.

Example:

YAWN:BOREDOM::   (A) dream:sleep
(B) anger:madness   (C) smile:amusement
(D) face:expression   (E) impatience:rebellion

 Ⓐ Ⓑ ● Ⓓ Ⓔ

---

10. PEA:POD::
    (A) orange:section
    (B) bean:crock
    (C) pumpkin:stem
    (D) nut:shell
    (E) potato:stew

11. THERMOMETER:HEAT::
    (A) filament:light
    (B) chronometer:color
    (C) odometer:waves
    (D) Geiger counter:radiation
    (E) barometer:electricity

12. AIRPLANE:HANGAR::
    (A) ship:channel
    (B) jet:runway
    (C) helicopter:pad
    (D) motorcycle:sidecar
    (E) automobile:garage

13. FROWN:DISPLEASURE::
    (A) blush:pallor
    (B) smile:commiseration
    (C) sneer:contempt
    (D) snore:relief
    (E) smirk:regret

14. CANDLE:TALLOW::
    (A) banana:peel
    (B) temple:altar
    (C) statue:bronze
    (D) fireplace:hearth
    (E) furniture:polish

15. REBUTTAL:DISPROVE::
    (A) narration:summarize
    (B) qualification:limit
    (C) refutation: conclude
    (D) contention:clarify
    (E) annotation:define

Read each of the passages below, and then answer the questions that follow each passage. The correct response may be stated outright or merely suggested in the passage.

Questions 16–21 are based on the following passage.

The following passage is taken from a major historical text on life in the Middle Ages.

To the world when it was half a thousand years younger, the outlines of all things seemed more clearly marked than to us. The contrast
Line between suffering and joy, between adversity and
(5) happiness, appeared more striking. All experience had yet to the minds of men the directness and absoluteness of the pleasure and pain of child-life. Every event, every action, was still embodied in expressive and solemn forms, which raised them
(10) to the dignity of a ritual. For it was not merely the great facts of birth, marriage, and death which, by their sacredness, were raised to the rank of mysteries; incidents of less importance, like a journey, a task, a visit, were equally attended by a thou-
(15) sand formalities: benedictions, ceremonies, formulae.
    Calamities and indigence were more afflicting than at present; it was more difficult to guard against them, and to find solace. Illness and
(20) health presented a more striking contrast; the cold and darkness of winter were more real evils. Honors and riches were relished with greater avidity and contrasted more vividly with surrounding misery. We, at the present day, can
(25) hardly understand the keenness with which a fur coat, a good fire on the hearth, a soft bed, a glass of wine, were formerly enjoyed.
    Then, again, all things in life were of a proud or cruel publicity. Lepers sounded their rattles
(30) and went about in processions, beggars exhibited their deformity and their misery in churches. Every order and estate, every rank and profession, was distinguished by its costume. The great lords never moved about without a glorious display of
(35) arms and liveries, exciting fear and envy. Executions and other public acts of justice, hawking,

GO ON TO THE NEXT PAGE →

1   1   1   1   1   1   1   1   1   1   1   1

marriages and funerals, were all announced by
cries and processions, songs and music. The lover
wore the colors of his lady; companions the
(40) emblem of their confraternity; parties and servants
the badges or blazon of their lords. Between town
and country, too, the contrast was very marked. A
medieval town did not lose itself in extensive suburbs of factories and villas; girded by its walls, it
(45) stood forth as a compact whole, bristling with
innumerable turrets. However tall and threatening
the houses of noblemen or merchants might be, in
the aspect of the town the lofty mass of the
churches always remained dominant.
(50)   The contrast between silence and sound, darkness and light, like that between summer and winter, was more strongly marked than it is in our
lives. The modern town hardly knows silence or
darkness in their purity, nor the effect of a soli-
(55) tary light or a single distant cry.
    All things presenting themselves to the mind in
violent contrasts and impressive forms, lent a tone
of excitement and of passion to everyday life and
tended to produce the perpetual oscillation
(60) between despair and distracted joy, between cruelty and pious tenderness which characterizes life
in the Middle Ages.

16. The author's main purpose in this passage is best
defined as an attempt to show how

(A) extremes of feeling and experience marked the
Middle Ages
(B) the styles of the very poor and the very rich
complemented each other
(C) twentieth century standards of behavior cannot
be applied to the Middle Ages
(D) the Middle Ages developed out of the Dark
Ages
(E) the medieval spirit languished five hundred
years ago

17. According to lines 10–16, surrounding an activity
with formalities makes it

(A) less important
(B) more stately
(C) less expensive
(D) more indirect
(E) less solemn

18. The author's use of the term "formulae" (line 16)
could best be interpreted to mean which of the following?

(A) set forms of words for rituals
(B) mathematical rules or principles
(C) chemical symbols
(D) nourishment for infants
(E) prescriptions for drugs

19. The word "order" in line 32 means

(A) command
(B) harmony
(C) sequence
(D) physical condition
(E) social class

20. According to the passage, well above the typical
medieval town there towered

(A) houses of worship
(B) manufacturing establishments
(C) the mansions of the aristocracy
(D) great mercantile houses
(E) walled suburbs

21. To the author, the Middle Ages seem to be all the
following EXCEPT

(A) routine and boring
(B) festive and joyful
(C) dignified and ceremonious
(D) passionate and turbulent
(E) harsh and bleak

Questions 22–30 are based on the following passage.

The following passage is excerpted from Hunger of
Memory, *the autobiography of the Mexican-American
writer Richard Rodriguez, who speaks of lessons he
learned as the child of working-class immigrant parents.*

I remember to start with that day in
Sacramento—a California now nearly thirty years
past—when I first entered a classroom, able to
Line   understand some fifty stray English words.
(5)   The third of four children, I had been preceded
to a neighborhood Roman Catholic school by an
older brother and sister. Each afternoon they
returned, as they left in the morning, always
together, speaking in Spanish as they climbed the
(10) five steps of the porch. And their mysterious
books, wrapped in shopping-bag paper, remained
on the table next to the door, closed firmly behind
them.
    An accident of geography sent me to a school
(15) where all my classmates were white, many the
children of doctors and lawyers and business
executives. All my classmates certainly must have
been uneasy on that first day of school—as most
children are uneasy—to find themselves apart
(20) from their families in the first institution of their
lives. But I was astonished.

GO ON TO THE NEXT PAGE

1 1 1 1 1 1 1 1 1 1 1

The nun said, in a friendly but oddly impersonal voice, "Boys and girls, this is Richard Rodriguez." (I heard her sound out: *Rich-heard Road-*
(25) *ree-guess*.) It was the first time I had heard anyone name me in English. "Richard," the nun
repeated more slowly, writing my name down in
her black leather book. Quickly I turned to see
my mother's face dissolve in a watery blur behind
(30) the pebbled glass door.

Many years later there is something called
bilingual education—a scheme proposed in the
late 1960s by Hispanic-American social activists,
later endorsed by a congressional vote. It is a pro-
(35) gram that seeks to permit non-English-speaking
children, many from lower class homes, to use
their family language as the language of school.
(Such is the goal its supporters announce.) I hear
them and am forced to say no: It is not possible
(40) for a child—any child—ever to use his family's
language in school. Not to understand this is to
misunderstand the public uses of schooling and to
trivialize the nature of intimate life—a family's
"language."

(45) Memory teaches me what I know of these matters; the boy reminds the adult. I was a bilingual
child, a certain kind—socially disadvantaged—
the son of working-class parents, both Mexican
immigrants.

(50) In the early years of my boyhood, my parents
coped very well in America. My father had steady
work. My mother managed at home. They were
nobody's victims. Optimism and ambition led
them to a house (our home) many blocks from the
(55) Mexican south side of town. We lived among
gringos and only a block from the biggest,
whitest houses. It never occurred to my parents
that they couldn't live wherever they chose. Nor
was the Sacramento of the fifties bent on teaching
(60) them a contrary lesson. My mother and father
were more annoyed than intimidated by those two
or three neighbors who tried initially to make us
unwelcome. ("Keep your brats away from my
sidewalk!") But despite all they achieved, perhaps
(65) because they had so much to achieve, any deep
feeling of ease, the confidence of "belonging"
in public was withheld from them both. They
regarded the people at work, the faces in crowds,
as very distant from us. They were the others, *los*
(70) *gringos*. That term was interchangeable in their
speech with another, even more telling, *los ameri-*
canos.

22. The family members in the passage are discussed
primarily in terms of

(A) the different personalities of each
(B) the common heritage they shared
(C) the ambitions they possessed

(D) their interaction with the English-speaking
world
(E) their struggle against racial discrimination

23. The author's description of his older brother and
sister's return from school (lines 7–10) suggests
that they

(A) enjoyed exploring the mysteries of American
culture
(B) were afraid to speak English at home
(C) wished to imitate their English-speaking class-
mates
(D) readily ignored the need to practice using
English
(E) regretted their inability to make friends

24. What initially confused the author on his first day
of school?

(A) His mother's departure took him by surprise.
(B) Hearing his name in English disoriented him.
(C) His older brother and sister had told him lies
about the school.
(D) He had never before seen a nun.
(E) He had never previously encountered white
children.

25. The word "scheme" in line 32 means

(A) conspiracy
(B) diagram
(C) plan
(D) outline
(E) goal

26. The author rejects bilingual education on the
grounds that

(A) allowing students to use their family's language in school presents only trivial difficulties to teachers
(B) its champions fail to see that public education
must meet public needs, not necessarily personal ones
(C) most students prefer using standard English
both at home and in the classroom
(D) the proposal was made only by social activists
and does not reflect the wishes of the
Hispanic-American community
(E) it is an unnecessary program that puts a heavy
financial burden upon the taxpayer

GO ON TO THE NEXT PAGE ▷

1   1 1 1 1 1 1 1 1 1   1

27. In lines 45–49, the author most likely outlines his specific background in order to

   (A) emphasize how far he has come in achieving his current academic success
   (B) explain the sort of obstacles faced by the children of immigrants
   (C) indicate what qualifies him to speak authoritatively on the issue
   (D) dispel any misunderstandings about how much he remembers of his childhood
   (E) evoke the reader's sympathy for socially disadvantaged children

28. The author's attitude toward his parents (lines 50–72) can best be described as

   (A) admiring   (B) contemptuous   (C) indifferent
   (D) envious   (E) diffident

29. Which of the following statements regarding Mexican-Americans in Sacramento would be most true to the author's experiences?

   (A) They were unable to find employment.
   (B) They felt estranged from the community as a whole.
   (C) They found a ready welcome in white neighborhoods.
   (D) They took an active part in public affairs.
   (E) They were unaware of academic institutions.

30. The word "telling" as used in line 71 means

   (A) outspoken
   (B) interchangeable
   (C) unutterable
   (D) embarrassing
   (E) revealing

YOU MAY GO BACK AND REVIEW THIS SECTION IN THE REMAINING TIME, BUT DO NOT WORK IN ANY OTHER SECTION UNTIL TOLD TO DO SO.   **S T O P**

Reference Information

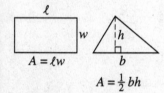

Area Facts — $A = \ell w$, $A = \frac{1}{2}bh$, $A = \pi r^2$, $C = 2\pi r$

Volume Facts — $V = \ell w h$, $V = \pi r^2 h$

Triangle Facts — $a^2 + b^2 = c^2$

Angle Facts — $x + y + z = 180$

---

1. If $5c + 3 = 3c + 5$, what is the value of c?

   (A) –1   (B) 0   (C) 1   (D) 3   (E) 5

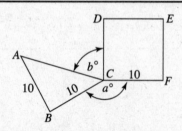

2. In the figure above, C is the only point that right triangle ABC and square $CDEF$ have in common. What is the value of $a + b$?

   (A) 135   (B) 180   (C) 210   (D) 225   (E) 270

3. A lacrosse team raised some money. They used 74% of the money to buy uniforms, 18% for equipment, and the remaining $216 for a team party. How much money did they raise?

   (A) $2400   (B) $2450   (C) $2500   (D) $2600
   (E) $2700

4. If $\frac{3}{4}$ of a number is 7 more than $\frac{1}{6}$ of the number, what is $\frac{5}{3}$ of the number?

   (A) 12   (B) 15   (C) 18   (D) 20   (E) 24

5. For all positive numbers a and b, let $a\,\square\,b = \sqrt{ab}$. If $n > 1$, what does $n\,\square\,\frac{1}{n}$ equal?

   (A) $\sqrt{n}$ (B) $\sqrt{n^2}$ (C) $\dfrac{1}{\sqrt{n}}$ (D) $\dfrac{1}{\sqrt{n^2}}$ (E) 1

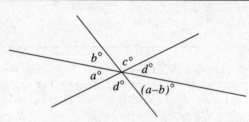

Note: Figure not drawn to scale

6. In the figure above, what is the value of b?

   (A) 30   (B) 36   (C) 45   (D) 60   (E) 72

GO ON TO THE NEXT PAGE

2   2 2 2 2 2 2 2 2 2   2

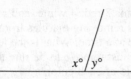

Note: Figure not drawn to scale

7. In the figure above, if x is 150 more than y, what is the value of y?

   (A) 10   (B) 15   (C) 20   (D) 25   (E) 30

8. Heidi wrote the number 1 on 1 slip of paper, the number 2 on 2 slips of paper, the number 3 on 3 slips of paper, the number 4 on 4 slips of paper, the number 5 on 5 slips of paper, and the number 6 on 6 slips of paper. All the slips of paper were placed in a bag, and Sally drew 1 slip at random. What is the probability that the number on the slip Sally drew was odd?

   (A) $\frac{1}{9}$ (B) $\frac{1}{7}$ (C) $\frac{3}{7}$ (D) $\frac{1}{2}$ (E) $\frac{4}{7}$

9. Sandrine is now 5 times as old as Nicholas, but 7 years from now she will be 3 times as old as he will be then. How old is Sandrine now?

   (A) 15   (B) 20   (C) 21   (D) 25   (E) 35

10. For how many positive numbers a is it true that $a \times a \times a = a + a + a$?

   (A) 0   (B) 1   (C) 2   (D) 3   (E) more than 3

11. Last year Jose sold a painting for $2000. If he made a 25% profit on the sale, how much had he paid for the painting?

   (A) $1200   (B) $1500   (C) $1600
   (D) $2400   (E) $2500

12. For any positive integer $n > 1$, $n!$ represents the product of the first n positive integers. For example, $3! = 1 \times 2 \times 3 = 6$. Which of the following are equal to $\frac{10!}{8!}$?

   I. $5! - 4! - 3!$
   II. $\frac{5!}{4!}$
   III. $15(3!)$

   (A) I only   (B) II only   (C) III only
   (D) I and III only   (E) I, II, and III

13. Let the lengths of the sides of a triangle be represented by $x + 3$, $2x - 3$, and $3x - 5$. If the perimeter of the triangle is 25, what is the length of the shortest side?

   (A) 5   (B) 7   (C) 8   (D) 10   (E) It cannot be determined from the information given.

14. A rectangle is twice as long as it is wide. If the width is a, what is the length of a diagonal?

   (A) $a\sqrt{2}$ (B) $a\sqrt{3}$ (C) $a\sqrt{5}$ (D) $3a$ (E) $5a$

15. If $abc = 1$, which of the following could be the number of integers among a, b, and c?

   I. 1
   II. 2
   III. 3

   (A) none   (B) I only   (C) I and II only
   (D) I and III only   (E) I, II, and III

16. At Essex High School 100 students are taking chemistry and 80 students are taking biology. If 20 students are taking both chemistry and biology, what is the ratio of the number of students taking only chemistry to the number taking only biology?

   (A) $\frac{3}{4}$ (B) $\frac{1}{1}$ (C) $\frac{5}{4}$ (D) $\frac{4}{3}$ (E) It cannot be determined from the information given.

17. In the figure above, a small square is drawn inside a large square. If the shaded area and the white area are equal, what is the ratio of the side of the large square to the side of the small square?

   (A) $\frac{\sqrt{2}}{1}$ (B) $\frac{2}{1}$ (C) $\frac{2\sqrt{2}}{1}$ (D) $\frac{2}{\sqrt{2}-1}$

   (E) It cannot be determined from the information given.

GO ON TO THE NEXT PAGE

2 2 2 2 2 2

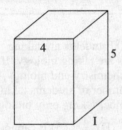

18. In rectangle *ABCD* above, diagonal *AC* makes a 30° angle with side *AD*. If *AC* = 10, what is the area of the rectangle?

(A) $25\sqrt{2}$ (B) $25\sqrt{3}$ (C) 48 (D) 50 (E) 100

19. The value of 10 pounds of gold is *d* dollars, and a pound of gold has the same value as *p* pounds of silver. What is the value, in dollars, of one pound of silver?

(A) $\dfrac{d}{10p}$ (B) $\dfrac{10p}{d}$ (C) $\dfrac{dp}{10}$

(D) $\dfrac{p}{10d}$ (E) $\dfrac{10d}{p}$

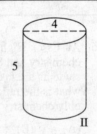

I   II

20. Of the figures above, container I is a rectangular solid whose base is a square 4 inches on a side, and container II is a cylinder whose base is a circle of diameter 4 inches. The height of each container is 5 inches. How much more water, in cubic inches, will container I hold than container II?

(A) $4(4-\pi)$ (B) $20(4-\pi)$ (C) $80(\pi-1)$
(D) $80(1-\pi)$ (E) It cannot be determined from the information given.

21. A bag contains 3 red, 4 white, and 5 blue marbles. Jason begins removing marbles from the bag at random, one at a time. What is the least number of marbles he must remove to be sure that he has at least 1 marble of each color?

(A) 3   (B) 6   (C) 8   (D) 10   (E) 12

22. The distance between Ali's house and college is exactly 135 miles. If she drove $\dfrac{2}{3}$ of the distance in 135 minutes, what was her average speed, in miles per hour?

(A) 40   (B) 45   (C) 60   (D) 67.5   (E) It cannot be determined from the information given.

23. If $x + 2y = a$ and $x - 2y = b$, which of the following is an expression for *xy*?

(A) ab (B) $\dfrac{a+b}{2}$ (C) $\dfrac{a-b}{2}$ (D) $\dfrac{a^2-b^2}{4}$

(E) $\dfrac{a^2-b^2}{8}$

24. What is the maximum number of points of intersection between a square and a circle?

(A) less than 4   (B) 4   (C) 6   (D) 8
(E) more than 8

25. The average (arithmetic mean) weight of five students is 150.4 pounds. If no student weighs less than 130 pounds and if no two students' weights are within 5 pounds of each other, what is the most, in pounds, that any one of the students can weigh?

(A) 172   (B) 192   (C) 202   (D) 232
(E) It cannot be determined from the information given.

YOU MAY GO BACK AND REVIEW THIS SECTION IN THE REMAINING TIME, BUT DO NOT WORK IN ANY OTHER SECTION UNTIL TOLD TO DO SO.   **S T O P**

3   3 3 3 3 3 3 3 3 3 3   3

SECTION 3   **Time—30 Minutes**
35 Questions   Select the best answer to the following questions, then fill in
the appropriate space on your Answer Sheet.

Each of the following sentences contains one or two
blanks; these blanks indicate that a word or set of words
has been left out. Below the sentence are five words or
phrases, lettered A through E. Select the word or set of
words that best completes the sentence.

Example:

Fame is ----; today's rising star is all too soon
tomorrow's washed-up has-been.

(A) rewarding   (B) gradual
 (C) essential   (D) spontaneous
  (E) transitory

1. Because our supply of fossil fuel has been sadly
---- , we must find ---- sources of energy.

(A) stored...hoarded
(B) compensated...significant
(C) exhausted...inefficient
(D) increased...available
(E) depleted...alternate

2. He is much too ---- in his writings: he writes a page
when a sentence should suffice.

(A) devious   (B) lucid   (C) verbose
 (D) efficient   (E) pleasant

3. In apologizing to the uncredited photographer, the
editor said that he ---- that this ---- use of copy-
righted photographs had taken place.

(A) deplored....legitimate
(B) conceded...inevitable
(C) regretted...unauthorized
(D) admitted...warranted
(E) acknowledged...appropriate

4. The herb Chinese parsley is an example of what we
mean by an acquired taste: Westerners who originally ---- it eventually come to ---- its flavor in
Oriental foods.

(A) relish...enjoy
(B) dislike...welcome
(C) savor...abhor
(D) ignore...detest
(E) discern...recognize

5. The abundance and diversity of insects is the
cumulative effect of an extraordinarily low ----
rate: bugs endure.

(A) metabolic
(B) density
(C) extinction
(D) percentage
(E) standard

6. Because he was ---- in the performance of his
duties, his employers could not ---- his work.

(A) derelict...quarrel over
(B) dilatory...grumble at
(C) undisciplined...object to
(D) assiduous...complain about
(E) mandatory...count on

7. British ---- contemporary art has been an obstacle
even for modern artists now revered as great, such
as Francis Bacon and Lucian Freud, who were ----
for years before winning acceptance.

(A) veneration of...eulogized
(B) indifference to...dismissed
(C) disdain for...lauded
(D) ignorance of...studied
(E) intolerance of...vindicated

8. Pre-Spanish art in Mexico is not a ---- art; they are
mistaken who see in its bold simplifications or
wayward conceptions an inability to ---- technical
difficulties.

(A) formal...ignore
(B) graphic...understand
(C) primitive...nurture
(D) crude...overcome
(E) revolutionary...instigate

GO ON TO THE NEXT PAGE

3   3 3 3 3 3 3 3 3 3 3   3

9. Are we to turn into spineless ---- , afraid to take a ---- stand, unable to answer a question without pussyfooting?

(A) disciples...positive
(B) hedonists...compromising
(C) criminals...defiant
(D) critics...constructive
(E) equivocators...forthright

10. The heretofore peaceful natives, seeking ---- the treachery of their supposed allies, became, ---- enough according to their perspective, embittered and vindictive.

(A) acquiescence in...understandably
(B) magnanimity towards...logically
(C) evidence of...impartially
(D) retribution for ...justifiably
(E) exoneration of...ironically

The analogies questions present two words or phrases that are related in some way. Determine which A-through-E answer choice below has a relationship *most* similar to that of the original words or phrases.

Example:

YAWN:BOREDOM::   (A) dream:sleep
(B) anger:madness   (C) smile:amusement
(D) face:expression   (E) impatience:rebellion

---

11. ROOSTER:HEN::

(A) duck:drake
(B) dog:cat
(C) gander:gosling
(D) swan:drake
(E) gander:goose

12. CHAIRMAN:GAVEL::

(A) conductor:baton
(B) violinist:bow
(C) orator:dais
(D) teacher:blackboard
(E) pianist:keys

13. VIOLA:INSTRUMENT::

(A) color:sound
(B) spectrum:shade
(C) trumpet:drum
(D) chisel:tool
(E) fiddle:bass

14. TRUNK:BOUGH::

(A) hook:eye
(B) leaf:branch
(C) detour:highway
(D) torso:arm
(E) keg:flask

15. COBBLER:SHOES::

(A) mechanic:automobile
(B) carpenter:saw
(C) painter:easel
(D) spy:plans
(E) interrogator:questions

16. BREEZE:TORNADO::

(A) ice:floe
(B) trickle:gusher
(C) conflagration:flame
(D) river:stream
(E) eruption:volcano

17. FELICITY:SORROW::

(A) celerity:speed
(B) agility:clumsiness
(C) concept:scheme
(D) congratulations:benediction
(E) ignorance:bliss

18. DISBAND:ORGANIZATION::

(A) merge:corporation
(B) demobilize:army
(C) discharge:employer
(D) expand:capacity
(E) respect:order

19. ASSURANCE:FEAR::

(A) opiate:pain
(B) insurance:premium
(C) cigarette:cough
(D) confidence:man
(E) narcotic:drug

20. MARSUPIAL:OPOSSUM::

(A) rodent:squirrel
(B) fish:whale
(C) kangaroo:hare
(D) unicorn:lion
(E) carnivore:herbivore

GO ON TO THE NEXT PAGE

3   3 3 3 3 3 3 3 3 3 3   3

21. PRIDE:LION::

(A) lair:bear
(B) bevy:quail
(C) horn:unicorn
(D) ensign:banner
(E) flame:phoenix

22. PROPITIATION:APPEASE::

(A) harassment:vex
(B) inauguration:terminate
(C) retribution:vindicate
(D) incitement:mollify
(E) renovation:raze

23. OSTRACISM:CENSURE::

(A) love:marriage
(B) success:promotion
(C) applause:approval
(D) editing:composition
(E) loyalty:tribute

Read the passage below, and then answer the questions that follow the passage. The correct response may be stated outright or merely suggested in the passage.

Questions 24–35 are based on the following passage.

The following excerpt is taken from "Life on the Rocks: the Galapagos" by the writer Annie Dillard. Like Charles Darwin, originator of the theory of evolution, Dillard visited the Galapagos Islands in the Pacific. In this passage she muses on the islands, on Darwin, and on the evolutionary process.

Charles Darwin came to the Galapagos in 1835, on the *Beagle*; he was twenty-six. He threw the marine iguanas as far as he could into the
Line water; he rode the tortoises and sampled their
(5) meat. He noticed that the tortoises' carapaces varied wildly from island to island; so also did the forms of various mockingbirds. He made collections. Nine years later he wrote in a letter, "I am almost convinced (quite contrary to the opinion I
(10) started with) that species are not (it is like confessing a murder) immutable." In 1859 he published *On the Origin of Species*, and in 1871 *The Descent of Man*. It is fashionable now to disparage Darwin's originality; not even the surliest of
(15) his detractors, however, faults his painstaking methods or denies his impact.

It all began in the Galapagos, with these finches. The finches in the Galapagos are called Darwin's finches; they are everywhere in the
(20) islands, sparrowlike, and almost identical but for their differing beaks. At first Darwin scarcely noticed their importance. But by 1839, when he revised his journal of the *Beagle* voyage, he added a key sentence about the finches' beaks:
(25) "Seeing this gradation and diversity of structure in one small, intimately related group of birds, one might really fancy that from an original paucity of birds in this archipelago, one species

had been taken and modified for different ends."
(30) And so it was.

The finches come when called. I don't know why it works, but it does. Scientists in the Galapagos have passed down the call: you say psssssh psssssh psssssh psssssh until you run out
(35) of breath; then you say it again until the island runs out of birds. You stand on a flat of sand by a shallow lagoon rimmed in mangrove thickets and call the birds right out of the sky. It works anywhere, from island to island.
(40) Once, on the island of James, I was standing propped against a leafless *palo santo* tree on a semiarid inland slope, when the naturalist called the birds.

From other leafless *palo santo* trees flew the
(45) yellow warblers, speckling the air with bright bounced sun. Gray mockingbirds came running. And from the green prickly pear cactus, from the thorny acacias, sere grasses, bracken and manzanilla, from the loose black lava, the bare dust,
(50) the fern-hung mouths of caverns or the tops of sunlit logs—came the finches. They fell in from every direction like colored bits in a turning kaleidoscope. They circled and homed to a vortex, like a whirlwind of chips, like draining water. The tree
(55) on which I leaned was the vortex. A dry series of puffs hit my cheeks. Then a rough pulse from the tree's thin trunk met my palm and rang up my arm—and another, and another. The tree trunk agitated against my hand like a captured cricket: I

GO ON TO THE NEXT PAGE ➡

(60) looked up. The lighting birds were rocking the tree. It was an appearing act: before there were barren branches; now there were birds like leaves.

Darwin's finches are not brightly colored; they are black, gray, brown, or faintly olive. Their *(65)* names are even duller: the large ground finch, the medium ground finch, the small ground finch; the large insectivorous tree finch; the vegetarian tree finch; the cactus ground finch, and so forth. But the beaks are interesting, and the beaks' origins *(70)* even more so.

Some finches wield chunky parrot beaks modified for cracking seeds. Some have slender warbler beaks, short for nabbing insects, long for probing plants. One sports the long chisel beak of *(75)* a woodpecker; it bores wood for insect grubs and often uses a twig or cactus spine as a pickle fork when the grub won't dislodge. They have all evolved, fanwise, from one bird.

The finches evolved in isolation. So did every- *(80)* thing else on earth. With the finches, you can see how it happened. The Galapagos islands are near enough to the mainland that some strays could hazard there; they are far enough away that those strays could evolve in isolation from parent *(85)* species. And the separate islands are near enough to each other for further dispersal, further isolation, and the eventual reassembling of distinct species. (In other words, finches blew to the Galapagos, blew to various islands, evolved into *(90)* differing species, and blew back together again.) The tree finches and the ground finches, the woodpecker finch and the warbler finch, veered into being on isolated rocks. The witless green sea shaped those beaks as surely as it shaped the *(95)* beaches. Now on the finches in the *palo santo* tree you see adaptive radiation's results, a fluorescent spray of horn. It is as though an archipelago were an arpeggio, a rapid series of distinct but related notes. If the Galapagos had been one uni- *(100)* fied island, there would be one dull note, one super-dull finch.

24. Dillard's initial portrayal of Darwin (lines 1–5) primarily conveys a sense of his

(A) methodical research
(B) instant commitment
(C) youthful playfulness
(D) lack of original thought
(E) steadiness of purpose

25. From lines 8–11 one can conclude that Darwin originally viewed species as

(A) unchanging   (B) original   (C) ambiguous
(D) evolutionary   (E) indistinguishable

26. In the phrase "It all began in the Galapagos" (line 17), "It" refers to the origins of

(A) sentient life
(B) distinct species of creatures
(C) Darwin's theory of evolution
(D) controlled experimentation
(E) Darwin's interest in nature

27. The word "ends" in line 29 means

(A) borders   (B) extremities   (C) limits
(D) purposes   (E) deaths

28. The use of the phrase "run out" two times (lines 32–36) emphasizes the

(A) waste of energy involved
(B) difference between the actions of humans and birds
(C) impatience of the naturalists calling the birds
(D) nervousness of the author in strange situations
(E) overwhelming response of the birds

29. The word "lighting" in line 60 means

(A) illuminating
(B) landing
(C) shining
(D) weightless
(E) flapping

30. The pulse that Dillard feels (lines 56–58) is most likely

(A) the agitated beating of her heart
(B) the rhythm of the birds' touching down
(C) the leaping of crickets against the tree
(D) a painful throbbing in her arm
(E) the wind of the birds' passing

31. Dillard's physical description of the finches (lines 71–77) chiefly serves to

(A) contrast their overall drabness with their variety in one specific aspect
(B) illustrate the predominance of tree finches over ground finches
(C) emphasize the use of memorable names to distinguish different species
(D) convey a sense of the possibilities for further evolution in the finch family
(E) distinguish them from the warblers and mockingbirds found in the islands

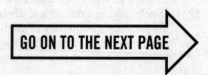
GO ON TO THE NEXT PAGE

32. Lines 77–78 suggest that the finches' beaks evolved in ways that

(A) mimicked a fanlike shape
(B) protected the birds from attack
(C) captured Darwin's interest
(D) enhanced the birds' attractiveness
(E) enabled them to reach nourishment

33. The word "hazard" in line 83 means

(A) venture
(B) speculate
(C) be imperiled
(D) run aground
(E) develop

34. The "fluorescent spray of horn" referred to by the author in lines 96–97 is most likely

(A) a series of musical notes
(B) a flock of birds
(C) the birds' shiny beaks
(D) branches of the *palo santo* tree
(E) a primitive musical instrument

35. In the final paragraph, the author does all of the following EXCEPT

(A) restate an assertion
(B) make a comparison
(C) define a term
(D) refute an argument
(E) describe a sequence of events

YOU MAY GO BACK AND REVIEW THIS SECTION IN THE REMAINING TIME, BUT DO NOT WORK IN ANY OTHER SECTION UNTIL TOLD TO DO SO.   **S T O P**

4   4   4   4   4   4   4   4   4   4   4   4

SECTION 4

Time—30 Minutes
25 Questions

You have 30 minutes to answer the 15 Quantitative Comparison questions and 10 Student-Produced Response questions in this section. You may use any blank space on the page for your work.

Notes:

- You may use a calculator whenever you feel it will be helpful.
- Use the diagrams provided to help you solve the problems. Unless you see the words "Note: Figure not drawn to scale" under a diagram, it has been drawn as accurately as possible. Unless it is stated that a figure is three-dimensional, you may assume it lies in a plane.

Reference Information

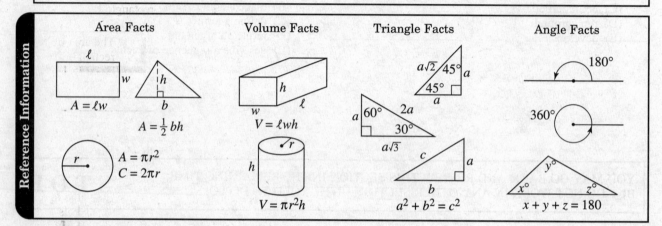

Area Facts

$A = \ell w$

$A = \frac{1}{2} bh$

$A = \pi r^2$
$C = 2\pi r$

Volume Facts

$V = \ell wh$

$V = \pi r^2 h$

Triangle Facts

$a^2 + b^2 = c^2$

Angle Facts

$x + y + z = 180$

Directions for Quantitative Comparison Questions

In each of questions 1–15, two quantities appear in boxes: one in Column A and one in Column B. You must compare them. The correct answer to a question is

A if the quantity in Column A is greater;
B if the quantity in Column B is greater;
C if the two quantities are equal;
D if it is impossible to determine which quantity is greater.

<u>Notes:</u>

- *The correct answer is never E.*
- Sometimes information about one or both of the quantities is centered above the two boxes.
- If the same symbol appears in both columns, it represents the same thing each time.
- All variables represent real numbers.

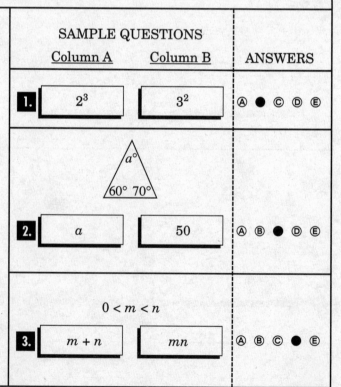

SAMPLE QUESTIONS

	Column A	Column B	ANSWERS
1.	2^3	3^2	Ⓐ ● Ⓒ Ⓓ Ⓔ
2.	a	50	Ⓐ Ⓑ ● Ⓓ Ⓔ
3.	$m + n$	mn	Ⓐ Ⓑ Ⓒ ● Ⓔ

2. (triangle with $a°$, $60°$, $70°$)

3. $0 < m < n$

GO ON TO THE NEXT PAGE

4 4 4 4 4 4 4 4 4 4 4

SUMMARY DIRECTIONS FOR QUANTITATIVE COMPARISON QUESTIONS

<u>Answer</u>: A if the quantity in Column A is greater;
B if the quantity in Column B is greater;
C if the two quantities are equal;
D if it is impossible to determine which quantity is greater.

Column A	Column B

1. The product of the integers from −7 to 3 | The product of the integers from −3 to 7

2. The least multiple of 6 that is greater than 80 | The largest multiple of 7 that is less than 90

x and *y* are positive.
$x + y = 1$

3. xy | 1

$a > 0, b > 0$
$a \neq b$

4. $\dfrac{a}{b}$ | $\left(\dfrac{a}{b}\right)^3$

5. c | d

6. The largest prime factor of 51 | The largest prime factor of 78

Column A	Column B

The length of rectangle II is 10% more than the length of rectangle I.
The width of rectangle II is 10% less than the width of rectangle I.

7. The area of rectangle I | The area of rectangle II

1 dollar is worth 4.9 francs.
5 shekels are worth 8.4 francs.

8. The value of 1 dollar | The value of 3 shekels

$0 < a < b < 1$

9. $\sqrt{a+b}$ | $\sqrt{a} + \sqrt{b}$

$x < y$

10. The average (arithmetic mean) of *x* and *y* | The average (arithmetic mean) of *x*, *y*, and *y*

GO ON TO THE NEXT PAGE ⟩

4   4   4   4   4   4   4   4   4   4   4   4

SUMMARY DIRECTIONS FOR QUANTITATIVE COMPARISON QUESTIONS

Answer: A if the quantity in Column A is greater;
B if the quantity in Column B is greater;
C if the two quantities are equal;
D if it is impossible to determine which quantity is greater.

Column A	Column B

$$1 < a < b < 2$$

11. ab | $a + b$

The measures of the angles in $\triangle$I are in the ratio of 1:2:3.
The measures of the angles in $\triangle$II are in the ratio of 2:7:9.

12. The measure of the largest angle of $\triangle$I | The measure of the largest angle of $\triangle$II

500 children were asked, "What is your favorite green vegetable?" The table below shows how many children chose each vegetable. The vegetables are listed in order from most popular to least. There were no ties.

Vegetable	Number of Children
Broccoli	189
String beans	a
Peas	b
Spinach	95
Asparagus	c

13. c | 30

Column A	Column B

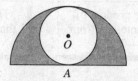

The circle with center O is inscribed in the semicircle with center A.

14. The area of the shaded region | The area of the white region

Column A	Column B

The average (arithmetic mean) of n numbers is 17.
The average of those n numbers and 25 is 21.

15. n | 2

GO ON TO THE NEXT PAGE

4 4 4 4 4 4 4 4 4 4 4

Directions for Student-Produced Response Questions (Grid-ins)

In questions 16–25, first solve the problem, and then enter your answer on the grid provided on the answer sheet. The instructions for entering your answers are as follows:

- First, write your answer in the boxes at the top of the grid.
- Second, grid your answer in the columns below the boxes.
- Use the fraction bar in the first row or the decimal point in the second row to enter fractions and decimal answers.

- Grid only one space in each column.
- Entering the answer in the boxes is recommended as an aid in gridding, but is not required.
- The machine scoring your exam can read only what you grid, so you **must grid in your answers correctly to get credit.**
- If a question has more than one correct answer, grid in only one of them.
- The grid does not have a minus sign, so no answer can be negative.
- A mixed number *must* be converted to an improper fraction or a decimal before it is gridded. Enter $1\frac{1}{4}$ as 5/4 or 1.25; the machine will interpret 1 1/4 as $\frac{11}{4}$ and mark it wrong.

- **All decimals must be entered as accurately as possible.** Here are the three acceptable ways of gridding

$$\frac{3}{11} = 0.272727...$$

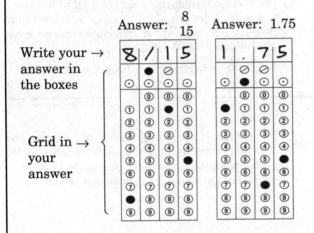

Answer: $\frac{8}{15}$ Answer: 1.75

Write your → answer in the boxes

Grid in → your answer

Answer: 100

Either position is acceptable

3/11   .272   .273

- Note that rounding to .273 is acceptable, because you are using the full grid, but you would receive **no credit** for .3 or .27, because they are less accurate.

16. If $7a = (91)(13)$, what is the value of $\sqrt{a}$?

17. If a, b, and c are positive numbers with $a = \frac{b}{c^2}$, what is the value of c when $a = 44$ and $b = 275$?

GO ON TO THE NEXT PAGE ⟶

4   4 4 4 4 4 4 4 4 4 4   4

18. What is the area of a right triangle whose hypotenuse is 25 and one of whose legs is 15?

19. In 1980, Elaine was 8 times as old as Adam, and Judy was 3 times as old as Adam. Elaine is 20 years older than Judy. How old was Adam in 1988?

20. If $x + y = 10$ and $x - y = 11$, what is the value of $x^2 - y^2$?

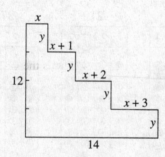

21. In the figure above, all of the line segments meet to form right angles. What is the perimeter of the figure?

22. If $a = 2b$, $3b = 4c$, and $5c = 6d$, what is the ratio of a to d?

23. If the average (arithmetic mean) of a, b, c, d, and e is 95, and the average of a, b, and e is 100, what is the average of c and d?

24. The average (arithmetic mean) of a set of 9 numbers is 99. After one of the numbers is deleted from the set, the average of the remaining numbers is 89. What number was deleted?

25. Two circular tables have diameters of 35 inches and 25 inches, respectively. The area of the larger table is what percent <u>more</u> than the area of the smaller table? (Grid in your answer without a percent sign.)

YOU MAY GO BACK AND REVIEW THIS SECTION IN THE REMAINING TIME, BUT DO NOT WORK IN ANY OTHER SECTION UNTIL TOLD TO DO SO.   **S T O P**

5

The questions that follow the two passages in this section relate to the content of both, and to their relationship.
The correct response may be stated outright in the passages or merely suggested.

Questions 1–13 are based on the following passages.

*The following passages are adapted from essays on
detective fiction, often known as mysteries. In the first,
the poet W. H. Auden discusses the detective story's
magic formula. In the second, historian Robin Winks
assesses what we do when we read mysteries.*

Passage 1

    The most curious fact about the detective story
is that it makes its greatest appeal precisely to
those classes of people who are most immune to
Line other forms of daydream literature. The typical
(5) detective story addict is a doctor or clergyman or
scientist or artist, i.e., a fairly successful professional man with intellectual interests and well-
read in his own field, who could never stomach
the *Saturday Evening Post* or *True Confessions* or
(10) movie magazines or comics.
    It is sometimes said that detective stories are
read by respectable law-abiding citizens in order
to gratify in fantasy the violent or murderous
wishes they dare not, or are ashamed to, translate
(15) into action. This may be true for readers of
thrillers (which I rarely enjoy), but it is quite false
for the reader of detective stories. On the contrary, the magical satisfaction the latter provide
(which makes them escape literature, not works
(20) of art) is the illusion of being dissociated from the
murderer.
    The magic formula is an innocence which is
discovered to contain guilt; then a suspicion of
being the guilty one; and finally a real innocence
(25) from which the guilty other has been expelled, a
cure effected, not by me or my neighbors, but by
the miraculous intervention of a genius from outside who removes guilt by giving knowledge of
guilt. (The detective story subscribes, in fact, to
(30) the Socratic daydream: "Sin is ignorance.")
    If one thinks of a work of art which deals with
murder, *Crime and Punishment* for example, its
effect on the reader is to compel an identification
with the murderer which he would prefer not to
(35) recognize. The identification of fantasy is always
an attempt to avoid one's own suffering: the identification of art is a compelled sharing in the suffering of another. Kafka's *The Trial* is another
instructive example of the difference between a
(40) work of art and the detective story. In the latter it

is certain that a crime has been committed and,
temporarily, uncertain to whom guilt should be
attached; as soon as this is known, the innocence
of everyone else is certain. (Should it turn out that
(45) after all no crime has been committed, then all
would be innocent.) In *The Trial*, on the other
hand, it is the guilt that is certain and the crime
that is uncertain; the aim of the hero's investigation is not to prove his innocence (which would
(50) be impossible for he knows he is guilty), but to
discover what, if anything, he has done to make
himself guilty. K, the hero, is, in fact, a portrait of
the kind of person who reads detective stories for
escape.
(55)   The fantasy, then, which the detective story
addict indulges is the fantasy of being restored to
the Garden of Eden, to a state of innocence,
where he may know love as love and not as the
law. The driving force behind this daydream is
(60) the feeling of guilt, the cause of which is
unknown to the dreamer. The fantasy of escape is
the same, whether one explains the guilt in
Christian, Freudian, or any other terms. One's
way of trying to face the reality, on the other
(65) hand, will, of course, depend very much on one's
creed.

Passage 2

    Detective fiction creates for us an anonymity;
within it, we may constitute the last law on earth,
making decisions (to be "proved" right or wrong)
(70) as we go, responsible for them, tricked, disappointed, triumphant, joyful, honest as to our mistakes, setting the record straight. As we make
leaps of faith between evidence and decision in
our daily lives—to board this bus, to choose that
(75) doctor, to add these pounds—so we make leaps of
faith between evidence and conclusion, through
the public historiography and the private autobiography that we read. We learn how to define
evidence, to use up our intellectual shoe leather in
(80) pursuit of an operable truth, to take joy from the

GO ON TO THE NEXT PAGE ➡

5

receding horizon and pleasure in the discovery that the answer has not yet been found, that there is more work to be done. We learn that what peo-ple believe to be true is as important as the objec-
(85) tive truth defined by the researcher/detective. In Marlowe and Archer we meet people who have no *use* for their conclusions, no desire for vengeance, who know that society will supply the uses while they may engage in the happy ambigu-
(90) ity of simply finding the facts, which, inert, take on life when embedded in a context of cause and effect.

Ultimately one reads detective fiction because it involves judgments—judgments made, passed
(95) upon, tested. In raising questions about purpose, it raises questions about cause and effect. In the end, like history, such fiction appears to, and occasionally does, decode the environment; appears to and occasionally does tell one what to
(100) *do*; appears to and occasionally does set the record straight. Setting the record straight ought to matter. Detective fiction, in its high serious-ness, is a bit like a religion, in pursuit of truths best left examined at a distance. As with all fine
(105) literature, history, philosophy, as with the written word wherever employed creatively, it can lead us to laughter in our frustration, to joy in our experience, and to tolerance for our complexities. It begins as Hawthorne so often does, and as the
(110) best of historians do, with a personal word, diffi-dent, apparently modest, in search of the subject by asking, What is the question? It ends, as histo-rians who have completed their journey often do, with an authoritative tone, the complex explained,
(115) the mystery revealed.

1. The word "curious" in line 1 means

   (A) inquisitive
   (B) unusual
   (C) sensitive
   (D) prying
   (E) salutary

2. The opening paragraph of Passage 1 suggests that the author would consider *True Confessions* and movie magazines as

   (A) sources of factual data about society
   (B) worthwhile contemporary periodicals
   (C) standard forms of escapist literature
   (D) the typical literary fare of professionals
   (E) less addictive than detective fiction

3. The author of Passage 1 asserts that readers of detec-tive fiction can most accurately be described as

   (A) believers in the creed of art for art's sake
   (B) people bent on satisfying an unconscious thirst for blood

   (C) dreamers unable to face the monotony of everyday reality
   (D) persons seeking momentary release from a vague sense of guilt
   (E) idealists drawn to the comforts of organized religion

4. The word "translate" in line 14 means

   (A) decipher
   (B) move
   (C) explain
   (D) convey
   (E) convert

5. Which best describes what the author is doing in citing the example of Kafka's *The Trial* (lines 46–54)?

   (A) Dramatizing the plot of a typical detective story
   (B) Analyzing its distinctive qualities as a work of art
   (C) Refuting a common opinion about readers of detective fiction
   (D) Demonstrating the genius of the outside inves-tigator
   (E) Discrediting a theory about Kafka's narrative

6. In Passage 1, the author's attitude toward detective fiction can best be described as one of

   (A) fastidious distaste
   (B) open skepticism
   (C) profound veneration
   (D) aloof indifference
   (E) genuine appreciation

7. In context, "use up our intellectual shoe leather" (line 79) suggests that readers of mysteries

   (A) suffer in the course of arriving at the truth
   (B) are attempting to escape from overly strenuous intellectual pursuits
   (C) work hard mentally, much as detectives do physically
   (D) have only a limited supply of time to devote to detective fiction
   (E) grow hardened to crime in the course of their reading

GO ON TO THE NEXT PAGE

5

8. In lines 78–83, the author of Passage 2 finds the prospect of additional work

    (A) burdensome (B) unexpected (C) unfounded
    (D) delightful (E) deceptive

9. Passage 2 suggests that Marlowe and Archer are most likely

    (A) murder victims
    (B) fictional detectives
    (C) prominent novelists
    (D) literary scholars
    (E) rival theorists

10. As used in line 106, the word "employed" most nearly means

    (A) hired (B) used (C) commissioned
    (D) remunerated (E) labored

11. According to lines 109–112, the detective story starts by

    (A) setting the record straight
    (B) simplifying the difficulties of the case
    (C) humanizing the investigating detective
    (D) introducing the characters under suspicion
    (E) defining the problem to be solved

12. Both passages are primarily concerned with the question of

    (A) whether detective stories gratify a taste for violence
    (B) why people enjoy reading detective fiction
    (C) how detectives arrive at their conclusions
    (D) why some people resist the appeal of escapist literature
    (E) whether detective stories can be considered works of art

13. The author of Passage 1 would most likely react to the characterization of detective fiction presented in lines 93–115 by pointing out that

    (A) reading detective fiction is an escape, not a highly serious pursuit
    (B) other analyses have shown the deficiencies of this characterization
    (C) this characterization reflects the author's lack of taste
    (D) this characterization is neither original nor objective
    (E) the realities of the publishing trade justify this characterization

---

YOU MAY GO BACK AND REVIEW THIS SECTION IN THE REMAINING TIME, BUT DO NOT WORK IN ANY OTHER SECTION UNTIL TOLD TO DO SO.   **S T O P**

6   6 6 6 6 6 6 6 6 6   6

Reference Information

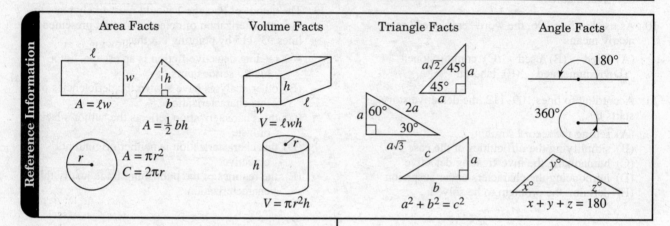

Area Facts
$A = \ell w$
$A = \frac{1}{2}bh$
$A = \pi r^2$
$C = 2\pi r$

Volume Facts
$V = \ell wh$
$V = \pi r^2 h$

Triangle Facts
$a^2 + b^2 = c^2$

Angle Facts
$x + y + z = 180$

1. If $2x - 1 = 9$, what is $10x - 5$?

   (A) 35   (B) 45   (C) 55   (D) 75   (E) 95

2. If in the figure above, $\ell_1 \parallel \ell_2$, which of the following statements about $a + b$ is true?

   (A) $a + b < 180$ (B) $a + b = 180$
   (C) $180 < a + b \le 270$ (D) $270 < a + b \le 360$
   (E) It cannot be determined from the information given.

Note: Figure not drawn to scale

3. Which of the following expressions has the greatest value?

   (A) $4 \times 4 \div 4 + 4$ (B) $4 \div 4 \times 4 + 4$
   (C) $4 \times 4 - 4 \times 4$ (D) $4 \div 4 + 4 \times 4$
   (E) $4 + 4 \times 4 - 4$

4. Hoover High School has 840 students, and the ratio of the number of students taking Spanish to the number not taking Spanish is 4:3. How many of the students take Spanish?

   (A) 280   (B) 360   (C) 480   (D) 560   (E) 630

GO ON TO THE NEXT PAGE

6 6 6 6 6 6 6 6 6 6 6

5. Of the 200 seniors at Monroe High School, exactly 40 are in the band, 60 are in the orchestra, and 10 are in both. How many students are in neither the band nor the orchestra?

(A) 80   (B) 90   (C) 100   (D) 110   (E) 120

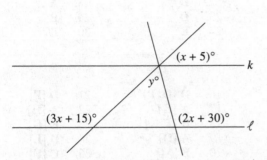

6. In the figure above, if $k \parallel \ell$, what is the value of y?

(A) 40   (B) 45   (C) 50   (D) 60   (E) 65

7. If, for any numbers a and b, $a \circledcirc b$ represents the average of a and b, which of the following MUST be true?

I. $a \circledcirc (a \circledcirc a) = a$

II. $a \circledcirc b = b \circledcirc a$

III. $a \circledcirc (b \circledcirc c) = (a \circledcirc b) \circledcirc c$

(A) I only   (B) II only   (C) I and II only
(D) II and III only   (E) I, II, and III

Model	Number Sold (1000's)
A	⊕⊕⊕⊕⊕⊕⊕⊕
B	⊕⊕⊕⊕⊕⊕⊕⊕⊕⊕

8. If the selling price of model B is 60% more than the selling price of model A, what percent of the total sales do the sales of model A represent?

(A) 25%   (B) 36%   (C) 40%   (D) 50%
(E) 60%

9. If $x = \frac{2}{3}(x + y)$, which of the following is an expression for x in terms of y ?

(A) $\frac{2}{3}y$ (B) y (C) $\frac{3}{2}y$ (D) $2y$

(E) $3y$

10. Let P and Q be points 2 inches apart, and let A be the area, in square inches, of a circle that passes through P and Q. Which of the following is the set of all possible values of A?

(A) $0 < A$ (B) $0 < A \leq \pi$ (C) $A = \pi$
(D) $A > \pi$ (E) $A \geq \pi$

YOU MAY GO BACK AND REVIEW THIS SECTION IN THE REMAINING TIME, BUT DO NOT WORK IN ANY OTHER SECTION UNTIL TOLD TO DO SO.   **S T O P**

Answer Key

Note: The letters in brackets following the Mathematical Reasoning answers refer to the sections of Chapter 12 in which you can find the information you need to answer the questions. For example, **1. C [E]** means that the answer to question 1 is C, and that the solution requires information found in Section 12-E: Averages.

Section 1 Verbal Reasoning

1.	D	7.	B	13.	C	19.	E	25.	C
2.	E	8.	B	14.	C	20.	A	26.	B
3.	C	9.	D	15.	B	21.	A	27.	C
4.	D	10.	D	16.	A	22.	D	28.	A
5.	D	11.	D	17.	B	23.	D	29.	B
6.	E	12.	E	18.	A	24.	B	30.	E

Section 2 Mathematical Reasoning

1.	C [G]	6.	B [I]	11.	C [C]	16.	D [D, P]	21.	D [P]
2.	D [I]	7.	B [I]	12.	D [A]	17.	A [K]	22.	A [H]
3.	E [C]	8.	C [O]	13.	B [K, G]	18.	B [J, K]	23.	E [G]
4.	D [G]	9.	E [H]	14.	C [K]	19.	A [D]	24.	D [L]
5.	E [A]	10.	B [A]	15.	E [A]	20.	B [M]	25.	C [E]

Section 3 Verbal Reasoning

1.	E	8.	D	15.	A	22.	A	29.	B
2.	C	9.	E	16.	B	23.	C	30.	B
3.	C	10.	D	17.	B	24.	C	31.	A
4.	B	11.	E	18.	B	25.	A	32.	E
5.	C	12.	A	19.	A	26.	C	33.	A
6.	D	13.	D	20.	A	27.	D	34.	C
7.	B	14.	D	21.	B	28.	E	35.	D

Section 4 Mathematical Reasoning

Quantitative Comparison Questions

1.	C [A]	4.	D [A]	7.	A [C, K]	10.	B [E]	13.	B [Q, P]
2.	C [A]	5.	A [J]	8.	B [D]	11.	B [A]	14.	C [L]
3.	B [A]	6.	A [A]	9.	B [A]	12.	C [D, J]	15.	B [E]

Grid-in Questions

16. [A] 13

17. [A] 2.5 *or 5/2*

18. [J] 150

19. [H] 12

20. [F, G] 110

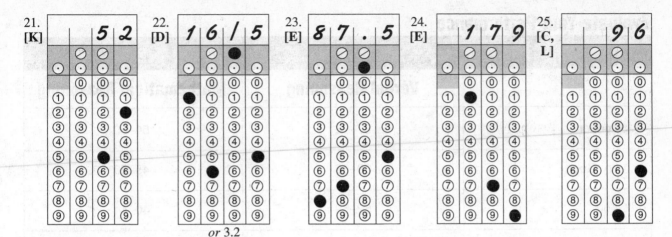

21. [K] **5 2**
22. [D] **1 6 / 5**   *or 3.2*
23. [E] **8 7 . 5**
24. [E] **1 7 9**
25. [C, L] **9 6**

Section 5   Verbal Reasoning

1. **B**	4. **E**	7. **C**	10. **B**	13. **A**
2. **C**	5. **B**	8. **D**	11. **E**	
3. **D**	6. **E**	9. **B**	12. **B**	

Section 6   Mathematical Reasoning

1. **B [G]**	3. **D [A]**	5. **D [O]**	7. **C [E]**	9. **D [G]**
2. **E [I]**	4. **C [D]**	6. **E [I, G]**	8. **B [Q, E]**	10. **E [L]**

Calculate Your Raw Score

Verbal Reasoning

Section 1 $\dfrac{}{\text{number correct}} - \dfrac{1}{4}\left(\dfrac{}{\text{number incorrect}}\right) = \underline{}$ (A)

Section 3 $\dfrac{}{\text{number correct}} - \dfrac{1}{4}\left(\dfrac{}{\text{number incorrect}}\right) = \underline{}$ (B)

Section 5 $\dfrac{}{\text{number correct}} - \dfrac{1}{4}\left(\dfrac{}{\text{number incorrect}}\right) = \underline{}$ (C)

Raw Verbal Reasoning Score = (A) + (B) + (C) = $\underline{}$

Mathematical Reasoning

Section 2 $\dfrac{}{\text{number correct}} - \dfrac{1}{4}\left(\dfrac{}{\text{number incorrect}}\right) = \underline{}$ (D)

Section 4
Part I
(1–15) $\dfrac{}{\text{number correct}} - \dfrac{1}{3}\left(\dfrac{}{\text{number incorrect}}\right) = \underline{}$ (E)

Part II
(16–25) $\dfrac{}{\text{number correct}} = \underline{}$ (F)

Section 6 $\dfrac{}{\text{number correct}} - \dfrac{1}{4}\left(\dfrac{}{\text{number incorrect}}\right) = \underline{}$ (G)

Raw Mathematical Reasoning Score = (D) + (E) + (F) + (G) = $\underline{}$

Evaluate Your Performance

	Verbal Reasoning	Mathematical Reasoning
Superior	67–78	51–60
Very Good	60–66	45–50
Good	52–59	40–44
Satisfactory	44–51	35–39
Average	36–43	30–34
Needs Further Study	29–35	25–29
Needs Intensive Study	21–28	20–24
Inadequate	0–20	0–19

Identify Your Weaknesses

Verbal Reasoning

Question Type	Question Numbers			Chapter to Study
	Section 1	Section 3	Section 5	
Sentence Completion	1, 2, 3, 4, 5, 6, 7, 8, 9	1, 2, 3, 4, 5, 6, 7, 8, 9, 10		Chapter 4
Analogy	10, 11, 12, 13, 14, 15	11, 12, 13, 14, 15, 16, 17, 18, 19, 20, 21, 22, 23		Chapter 5
Reading Comprehension	16, 17, 18, 19, 20, 21, 22, 23, 24, 25, 26, 27, 28, 29, 30	24, 25, 26, 27, 28, 29, 30	1, 2, 3, 4, 5, 6, 7, 8, 9, 10, 11, 12, 13	Chapter 6

Identify Your Weaknesses

Mathematical Reasoning

Skill Area	Question Numbers			Pages to Study
	Section 2	Section 4	Section 6	
Basics of Arithmetic	5, 10, 12, 15	1, 2, 3, 6, 9, 11, 16, 17	3	331–338
Fractions and Decimals	12, 15	4		344–352
Percents	3, 11	7, 25	9	358–361
Ratios	16, 19	8, 12, 22	4	366–370
Averages	25	10, 15, 23, 24	7, 8	376–378
Polynomials	10	20		383–386
Equations and Inequalities	1, 4, 13, 23	20	1, 6	389–394
Word Problems	9, 22	19		399–402
Lines and Angles	2, 6, 7		2, 6	407–410
Triangles	18	5, 12, 18		414–418
Quadrilaterals	13, 14, 17, 18	7, 21		425–428
Circles	24	14, 25	10	432–435
Solid Geometry	20			440–442
Coordinate Geometry				446–448
Counting and Probability	8	13	5	452–456
Logical Reasoning	16, 21	13		462–464
Data Interpretation			8	468–471

Answer Explanations
Section 1   Verbal Reasoning

1. **D.** Mitchell is optimistic about the future of African-Americans in ballet. However, he is not blindly optimistic. Instead, he is *realistic* about the problems blacks face.
Remember to watch for signal words that link one part of the sentence with another. The use of "Although" in the opening clause sets up a contrast. The missing word must be an antonym for "optimistic."   (Contrast Signal)

2. **E.** *Frustrations* or limitations are by definition not satisfying.
Again, remember to watch for signal words that link one part of the sentence with another. The use of "Despite" in the opening clause sets up a contrast. The missing word must be an antonym for "stirring and satisfying." Note, too, that you are looking for a word with negative associations. Therefore, you can eliminate any word with positive ones. Choices A, B, C, and D all have positive ones. Only Choice E can be correct.   (Contrast Signal)

3. **C.** *Derivative* means unoriginal. Unoriginal work derives from or comes from the work of others. The moviemaker is unoriginal despite his reputation for skill or *expertise*.
The word "sadly" is your clue to look for a negative word to fill in the second blank. Therefore, you can eliminate any word with positive associations.   (Definition)

4. **D.** One crowns a career with a triumph, in this case an *unsurpassable* performance.
Remember, before you look at the choices, read the sentence and think of a word that makes sense. Words like magnificent, superlative, and matchless come to mind. Note that you are looking for a word with positive associations. Therefore, you can eliminate any word with negative ones. Choices A, B, C, and E all have negative associations. Only Choice D can be correct.   (Examples)

5. **D.** Students of genetics will have to turn or *resort to* respected journals where relevant information is *found*.
Choice A is incorrect. Excellent journals would be unlikely to ignore relevant materials.
Choice B is incorrect. An interested student of genetics would enjoy reading an excellent journal in the field. Such a student would not be likely to suffer through it.
Choice C is incorrect. Pertinent material logically would be represented in an excellent technical journal.

Choice E is incorrect. We would be unlikely to complain about excellent technical journals.   (Argument Pattern)

6. **E.** Rather than alleviating or easing problems, rent control may worsen or *exacerbate* them. The signal words "rather than" indicate that the missing word must be an antonym or near-antonym for "alleviate."
You can immediately eliminate *resolve*, *diminish* and *minimize*, which make no sense in the context.   (Contrast Signal)

7. **B.** This sentence sets up a contrast between Dickens's image of country dancing and Sharp's. Dickens views country dances as "lively, even *(something)*." In this context, *even* acts as an intensifier: it points up just how *very* lively these country dances could get. The first missing word must be a synonym for *very lively*.
Look at the first word of each answer choice. *Sophisticated*, *prudish*, and *lewd* are highly unlikely choices as synonyms for *very lively*. You can immediately eliminate Choices A, C, and D. *Enjoyable* also seems an unlikely choice: liveliness, carried to an extreme, does not by definition become more enjoyable. You probably can eliminate Choice E. Only Choice B is left. Could lively dances grow so lively that they might become disorderly, *rowdy* affairs? They could.
Consider the second word in Choice B. Sharp's image of dancing is excessively formal. It is not rowdy. It suggests more *decorum* and propriety than the behavior Dickens described. The correct answer is Choice B.   (Contrast Pattern)

8. **B.** By showing that they had no hidden or *concealed* weapons, they were showing themselves to be friendly or *amicably* disposed. Because the first word of any one of these answer choices could work, you have to try out each entire pair before eliminating any of the choices.   (Cause and Effect Signal)

9. **D.** By definition, *volatile* substances tend to evaporate (convert from a liquid state into a vapor).
Beware Eye-Catchers. Choice A is incorrect. *Insoluble* substances cannot be dissolved in liquid. Such substances are unlikely to evaporate.   (Definition)

10. **D.** Just as the *pea* grows within the *pod*, the *nut* grows within the *shell*.   (Part to Whole)

11. **D.** A *thermometer* measures temperature or *heat*; a *Geiger counter* measures *radiation*.

Choice A is incorrect. A filament (the conductor inside a light bulb) gives off light; it doesn't measure light.

Choice B is incorrect. A chronometer measures time, not color.

Choice C is incorrect. An odometer measures distance, not waves.

Choice E is incorrect. A barometer measures atmospheric pressure, not electricity.

(Function)

12. E. A *hangar* is a place for servicing and storing *airplanes*; a *garage* is a place for servicing and storing *automobiles*.

If your original sentence was "An airplane is found in a hangar," Choices A, B, C, and E would all have made good analogies. If more than one answer appears to fit your original sentence, you need to state the relationship more precisely. (Definition)

13. C. A *frown* indicates *displeasure*; a *sneer* indicates *contempt* or scorn.

(Action and Its Significance)

14. C. A *candle* may be made of *tallow*; a *statue*, of *bronze*. (Composition)

15. B. A *rebuttal* (refutation or contradiction) by definition attempts to *disprove*. A *qualification* (restriction or modification) by definition attempts to *limit*.

Note that a secondary meaning of *qualification* is being used here. (Definition)

16. A. The opening paragraph, with its talk of clearly marked outlines and contrasts "between suffering and joy," and the concluding sentence, with its mentions of "violent contrasts" and "the perpetual oscillation between despair and joy" emphasize the author's main idea: the Middle Ages were marked by extremes.

Choice B is incorrect. Though the author depicts aspects of the lives of the very rich and the very poor, he does not stress the notion that their styles complemented one another.

Choice C is incorrect. The author's concern is for the Middle Ages, not for the twentieth century.

Choices D and E are incorrect. They are unsupported by the text.

Remember, when asked to find the main idea, be sure to check the opening and the summary sentences of each paragraph.

17. B. The cloaking of minor activities (journeys, visits, etc.) with forms (line 9) "raised them to the dignity of a ritual"; in other words, the forms (fixed or formal ways of doing things) made the acts *more dignified*.

Choices A, C, D, and E are incorrect. They are not supported by the passage.

Remember, when asked about specific details in the passage, spot key words in the question and scan the passage to find them (or their synonyms).

Key Word: formalities.

18. A. The linking of "formulae" with "ceremonies" (formal series of acts) and "benedictions" (words of blessing) suggests that these formulae are most likely *set forms of words for rituals*.

Note how the use of the colon suggests that all three words that follow are examples of "formalities."

19. E. Treat this vocabulary-in-context question as if it were a sentence completion exercise. "Every ____ and estate, every rank and profession, was distinguished by its costume." Which of the answer choices best fills in the blank? *Estate* (major political or social class), *rank* (separate class in a social system), and *profession* (body of people engaged in an occupation) are all examples of groups or classes of people. Thus, in this context, an order is a *social class*.

Note how the use of "and" and of the commas to group together these terms suggests that all four of these nouns are similar in meaning.

20. A. The last sentence of the third paragraph states that the lofty churches, the houses of worship, towered above the town. The churches always "remained dominant."

When asked about specific details, spot the key words in the question and scan the passage to find them (or their variants).

Key Words: above, towered.

21. A. In cataloging the extremes of medieval life, the author in no way suggests that the Middle Ages were *boring*.

Choice B is incorrect. The author portrays the Middle Ages as festive and joyful; he says they were filled with vivid pleasures and proud celebrations.

Choice C is incorrect. The author portrays the Middle Ages as filled with ceremony and ritual.

Choice D is incorrect. The author portrays the Middle Ages as passionate and turbulent; he mentions the "tone of excitement and of passion" in everyday life.

Choice E is incorrect. The author suggests the Middle Ages were harsh and bleak; he portrays them as cold and miserable.

22. D. Richard's introduction to school, his parents' reaction to their unfriendly neighbors, his brother and sister's silence about their classroom experiences—all these instances illus-

trate the family members' interaction with the *English-speaking world.*

23. **D.** The older children return home speaking Spanish, abandoning the English taught in the classroom. What is more, "their mysterious books . . . remained on the table next to the door, closed firmly behind them." Clearly, they *readily ignored the need to practice using English* at home.

24. **B.** The author's statement that it "was the first time I had heard anyone name me in English" supports Choice B. In addition to finding himself apart from his family, the usual experience of new pupils, he finds himself stripped of his name, his identity. Being addressed in such a strange and impersonal manner rattles him.
Choice A is incorrect. All the students were uneasy to find themselves separated from their families.
Choices C and D are incorrect. Nothing in the passage supports them.
Choice E is incorrect. The narrator lived in a *gringo* neighborhood; he must have seen white children.

25. **C.** Bilingual education is a scheme or *plan* that seeks to permit non-English-speaking children to use their native languages in school.
Choice E is incorrect. As used in the sentence, bilingual education is a plan or program. Establishing such a plan is the goal of bilingual education's supporters.

26. **B.** Bilingual education's supporters wish to have non-English-speaking children taught in the language they customarily use at home. Rodriguez feels they have missed an important point. To him, the job of public education is to teach children to function effectively in the society in which they live. To do so, they must learn to use public language, the language we use *outside* the home. He believes that the champions of bilingual education *fail to see that public education must meet public needs, not necessarily personal ones.*

27. **C.** Rodriguez has just given his opinion on a controversial topic. He now must convince his readers that he knows what he is talking about. To do so, he cites specific aspects of his background that prove he knows something about bilingual education. In other words, he *indicates what qualifies him to speak authoritatively on the issue.*

28. **A.** The author's assertions in the last paragraph that his parents coped very well and that they were nobody's victims, indicate that his basic attitude toward them is *admiring.*

29. **B.** Statement B is true to the author's experience: they *felt estranged* from the *gringos'* world.
Choice A is incorrect. Richard's father found steady work.
Choice C is incorrect. Although Sacramento as a whole was not determined to keep Mexicans out of white neighborhoods, some neighbors tried to frighten away Richard's family.
Choice D is incorrect. Lacking confidence in public, Richard's parents remained detached from community affairs.
Choice E is incorrect. Richard's parents sent their children to Roman Catholic schools; they were involved with academic institutions.

30. **E.** For Richard's parents to call white people *los americanos*, "the Americans," implies that on some level they did not consider themselves Americans. This is a *telling* or *revealing* comment that points up the degree of alienation Richard's parents felt.

Section 2   Mathematical Reasoning

In each mathematics section, for many problems, an alternative solution, indicated by two asterisks (**), follows the first solution. When this occurs, one of the solutions is the direct mathematical one and the other is based on one of the tactics discussed in Chapters 8–12.

1. **C.** Use the six-step method of TACTIC G1 on the given equation, $5c + 3 = 3c + 5$:
$$5c + 3 = 3c + 5 \Rightarrow 2c + 3 = 5 \Rightarrow$$
$$2c = 2 \Rightarrow c = \mathbf{1}.$$

   **Use TACTIC 9-1. Backsolve, starting with C.

2. **D.** Since $\triangle ABC$ is an isosceles right triangle, $x = 45$; also, $y = 90$, since it is a corner of square *CDEF*. Therefore, $a + b = 360 - (45 + 90) = 360 - 135 = \mathbf{225}$.

   **Use TACTIC 8-2: trust the diagram. Clearly, 135 and 180 are too small, and 270 is too large. Guess between 210 and 225.

3. **E.** Since $74\% + 18\% = 92\%$, the $216 spent on the party represents the other 8% of the money raised. Then
$$0.08m = 216 \Rightarrow m = 216 \div 0.08 = \mathbf{2700}.$$

4. **D.** Let the number be x, and write the equation: $\frac{3}{4}x = 7 + \frac{1}{6}x$.

Multiply both sides by 12: $9x = 84 + 2x$

Subtract $2x$ from each side and divide by 7: $7x = 84$
$$x = 12$$

Be careful: 12 is *not* the answer. You were asked for $\frac{5}{3}$ of the number: $\frac{5}{\cancel{3}}(\cancel{12}^{4}) = \mathbf{20}$.

5. **E.** Here, $n \square \frac{1}{n} = \sqrt{n\left(\frac{1}{n}\right)} = \sqrt{1} = \mathbf{1}$.

**Use TACTIC 9-3. Pick an easy-to-use number, say 2. (Note that 1 would *not* be a good choice because then each of the five choices would be 1.)

Then, $2 \square \frac{1}{2} = \sqrt{2\left(\frac{1}{2}\right)} = \sqrt{1} = 1$. Only **1**

equals 1 when $n = 2$.

6. **B.** Since vertical angles have the same measure (KEY FACT I4), $c = d$, $d = a$, and $b = a - b \Rightarrow a = 2b$. Therefore, $c = d = a = 2b$. Also, the sum of the measures of all six angles is 360° (KEY FACT I3), so $a + b + c + d + a - b + d = 2a + c + 2d = 360$. Replacing c, d, and a by $2b$ yields $10b = 360 \Rightarrow b = \mathbf{36}$.

7. **B.** Since the two angles, x and y, form a straight angle, $x + y = 180$ (KEY FACT I2). Also, it is given that $x = y + 150$. Therefore, $(y + 150) + y = 180 \Rightarrow 2y + 150 = 180 \Rightarrow 2y = 30 \Rightarrow y = \mathbf{15}$.

**Use TACTIC 9-1: backsolve. Start with 20, choice C. If $y = 20$, then $x = 170$, but $20 + 170 = 190$, which is too large. Eliminate C, D, and E, and try A or B. B works.

8. **C.** There is a total of $1 + 2 + 3 + 4 + 5 + 6 = 21$ slips of paper. Since odd numbers are written on $1 + 3 + 5 = 9$ of them, the probability of drawing an odd number is $\frac{9}{21} = \frac{3}{7}$.

9. **E.** Set up a table.

Time	Nicholas	Sandrine
Now	x	$5x$
In 7 years	$x + 7$	$5x + 7$

Then
$5x + 7 = 3(x + 7) \Rightarrow 5x + 7 = 3x + 21 \Rightarrow$
$2x = 14 \Rightarrow x = 7$.
Sandrine, therefore, is **35**.

**Use TACTIC 9-1, but since Sandrine is 5 times as old as Nicholas, avoid C, the only answer that is not a multiple of 5. Try B, 20. Then Nicholas is 4. In 7 years, he'll be 11 and Sandrine will be 27, which is less than 3 times as old. Try a larger number: 25 or 35.

10. **B.** The given equation can be written as $a^3 = 3a$. Since a is positive, we can divide each side by a: $a^2 = 3$. There is only **1** positive number that satisfies this equation: $\sqrt{3}$. (Note that 0 and $-\sqrt{3}$ also satisfy the original equation, but neither of these is positive.)

11. **C.** Jose made a 25% profit, so if he bought it for x, he sold it for
$$x + 0.25x = 1.25x = 2000 \Rightarrow$$
$$x = 2000 \div 1.25 = \mathbf{1600}.$$

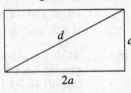

12. **D.** The fraction $\frac{10!}{8!}$ reduces to $10 \times 9 = 90$.

Now, evaluate the three choices.

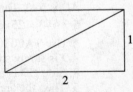

I: $5! - 4! - 3! = 120 - 24 - 6 = 90$ (true).

II: $\frac{5!}{4!} = 5$ (false).

III: $15(3!) = 15(6) = 90$ (true).

I and III only are true.

13. **B.** Write the equation and use the six-step method (TACTIC G1) to solve it:

Set up the equation:
$(x + 3) + (2x - 3) + (3x - 5) = 25$

Collect like terms: $6x - 5 = 25$

Add 5 to each side: $6x = 30$

Divide each side by 6: $x = 5$

Plugging in 5 for x, we get the lengths of the sides: 8, **7**, and 10.

14. **C.** Use TACTIC 8-1: draw a diagram and label it. Use the Pythagorean theorem to find d, the length of the diagonal:
$a^2 + (2a)^2 = d^2 \Rightarrow$
$a^2 + 4a^2 = d^2 \Rightarrow$
$5a^2 = d^2 \Rightarrow d = a\sqrt{5}$.

**Use TACTIC 9-2. Let $a = 1$. Then use TACTIC 8-1, and draw the rectangle (to scale); that is, let the width be 1 and the length be 2. Now use TACTIC 8-2: trust your eyes. Clearly, the diagonal is longer than 2 and shorter than 3 (the width plus the length is 3). The answer *must* be $a\sqrt{5}$, the *only* choice between 2 and 3, when $a = 1$.

15. E. Could exactly one of a, b, and c be an integer? Sure; $(4)\left(\frac{1}{2}\right)\left(\frac{1}{2}\right) = 1$. Could exactly two of a,

b, and c be integers? Yes; $(1)(2)\left(\frac{1}{2}\right) = 1$.

Could all three be integers? Yes again: $(1)(1)(1) = 1$. *Be careful:* the question does *not* require a, b, and c to be different numbers. Statements **I, II, and III** are all true.

16. D. Draw a Venn diagram. Of the 100 students taking chemistry, 20 take biology, and 80 don't; they take *only* chemistry. Similarly, of the 80 students taking biology, 20 also take chemistry, and 60 take *only* biology. The desired ratio is

$80{:}60 = 4{:}3 = \dfrac{4}{3}$.

17. A. Let S be a side of the large square, and s a side of the small square. The area of the white region is just s^2, whereas the area of the shaded region is $S^2 - s^2$. Therefore,

$S^2 - s^2 = s^2 \Rightarrow S^2 = 2s^2 \Rightarrow \dfrac{S^2}{s^2} = 2 \Rightarrow \dfrac{S}{s} = \sqrt{2}.$

The ratio of the side of the large square to the side of the small

square is $\dfrac{\sqrt{2}}{1}$.

****Redraw the diagram with the small square in the corner of the large one. If the ratio were 2:1, the white area would be much smaller than the shaded area, so the small square must be larger and the ratio is less than 2:1. Only $\dfrac{\sqrt{2}}{1}$ is less than 2:1.

18. B. AC is the hypotenuse of a 30-60-90 right triangle. By KEY FACT J11, CD, the leg opposite the 30° angle, is 5 (half the hypotenuse), and AD is $5\sqrt{3}$. Then the area of the rectangle is $5 \times 5\sqrt{3} = \mathbf{25\sqrt{3}}$.

****Use TACTIC 8-2: trust the diagram. Side AD is surely shorter than the hypotenuse, say 8. Side CD is about half the hypotenuse, say 5. Then the area is *about* 40. Eliminate C, D, and E. Use your calculator to evaluate A (≈ 35.4) and B (≈ 43.3) and then guess.

19. A. Set up a proportion: $\dfrac{\text{dollars}}{\text{pounds}}$

$\dfrac{d \text{ dollars}}{10 \text{ pounds of gold}} = \dfrac{d \text{ dollars}}{10p \text{ pounds of silver}} = \dfrac{x \text{ dollars}}{1 \text{ pound of silver}}$

So, $\dfrac{d}{10p} = \dfrac{x}{1} \Rightarrow x = \dfrac{d}{10p}$

20. B. The formulas for the volumes of a rectangular solid and a cylinder are $V = \ell wh$ and $V = \pi r^2 h$, respectively. (Remember that these formulas are given to you on the first page of every SAT I math section.) The volume of container I is $(4)(4)(5) = 80$ cubic inches. Since the diameter of container II is 4, its radius is 2, and so its volume is $\pi(2^2)(5) = 20\pi$. The difference in volumes is $80 - 20\pi = \mathbf{20(4 - \pi)}$.

****If you don't know, or can't use, the formulas, you must guess. If you knew the formulas, you *could* answer the question, so eliminate E. Also, D is out since $1 - \pi$ is negative. If that's all you know, guess among A, B, and C. If you know that the volume of the rectangular solid is 80, but you don't know the volume of the cylinder, eliminate C, which is over 160, and guess between A and B. *Don't leave this question out.*

21. D. If Jason were really unlucky, what could go wrong in his attempt to get 1 marble of each color? Well, his first nine picks *might* yield 5 blue marbles and 4 white ones. But then the tenth marble would be red, and he would have at least 1 of each color. The answer is **10**.

22. A. 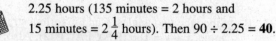 To find the average speed, in miles per hour, divide the distance, in miles, by the time, in hours. Ali drove 90 miles $\left(\frac{2}{3} \text{ of } 135\right)$ in 2.25 hours (135 minutes $= 2$ hours and 15 minutes $= 2\frac{1}{4}$ hours). Then $90 \div 2.25 = \mathbf{40}$.

****It should be clear that there is enough information to find Ali's average speed, so eliminate E. Remember that 60 miles per hour is 1 mile per minute. Since Ali drove for 135 minutes and covered less than 135 miles, she was going slower than 60 mph. Eliminate C and D and guess.

23. E. The easiest way to solve this is to use TACTIC 9-2. Let $x = 2$ and $y = 1$. Then $xy = 2$, $a = 4$, and $b = 0$. Now, plug in 4 for a and 0 for b, and see which of the five choices is equal to 2. Only E works: $\dfrac{a^2 - b^2}{8} = \dfrac{4^2 - 0^2}{8} = \dfrac{16}{8} = 2.$

****Here is the correct algebraic solution.

Add the two equations:
$$\begin{array}{r} x + 2y = a \\ + \quad x - 2y = b \\ \hline 2x = a + b \end{array}$$

Divide by 2: $\qquad x = \dfrac{a + b}{2}$

Multiply the second equation by -1, and add it to the first:
$$\begin{array}{r} x + 2y = a \\ + \; -x + 2y = -b \\ \hline 4y = a - b \end{array}$$

Divide by 4: $y = \dfrac{a-b}{4}$

Then $xy = \dfrac{a+b}{2} \cdot \dfrac{a-b}{4} = \dfrac{a^2-b^2}{8}$.

This is the type of algebra you want to avoid.

24. **D.** A circle can cross each side of a square at most twice. The answer is $2 \times 4 = \mathbf{8}$.

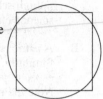

25. **C.** Since the average of the five students' weights is 150.4 pounds, their total weight is $5 \times 150.4 = 752$ pounds (TACTIC E1). No student weighs less than 130 and none is within 5 pounds of another, so the least that the four lightest students can weigh is 130, 135, 140, and 145 pounds, for a total of 550 pounds. The heaviest student, therefore, cannot exceed $752 - 550 = \mathbf{202}$ pounds.

Section 3   Verbal Reasoning

1. **E.** The *depletion* or exhaustion of our energy sources would lead us to seek *alternate* sources.
   Remember, in double-blank sentences, go through the answer choices, testing the *first* words in each choice and eliminating those that don't fit.
   Note that you are looking for a word with negative associations. Therefore, you can eliminate any word with positive ones. Choices A, B, and D all have positive associations. Only Choices C or E can be correct. Turning to the second words of these two choices, you can eliminate Choice C: it would make no sense to seek *inefficient* energy sources.
   (Cause and Effect Signal)

2. **C.** *Verbose* means overly wordy. The second clause of the sentence provides an example that brings the abstract term *verbose* to life.
   (Examples)

3. **C.** The publisher is apologizing for having used the photographs without the photographer's permission. He *regrets* printing them without *authorization*.
   To answer this question correctly, you *must* check the second word of each answer choice.
   (Definition Pattern)

4. **B.** To acquire a taste for something, you must originally not have that taste or even *dislike* it; you acquire the taste by growing to like or *welcome* it.
   Note how the second clause of the sentence serves to clarify what is meant by the term "acquired taste."   (Example)

5. **C.** Bugs are abundant or plentiful because they endure. They endure because they have an extremely low *extinction* or death rate.
   (Cause and Effect Pattern)

6. **D.** *Assiduous* work, work performed industriously or diligently, should not lead employers to *complain*.
   Note that the use of *because* in the opening clause signals that a cause and effect relationship is at work here.
   (Cause and Effect Signal)

7. **B.** The key word here is *obstacle*. What sort of attitude toward modern art would present an *obstacle* or hindrance to artists? Clearly, a negative one. You therefore can eliminate any answer choice that is positive. *Veneration* (awed respect) is highly positive. Eliminate Choice A.
   Indifference (lack of caring), *disdain* (scorn), *ignorance*, and *intolerance* are all negative terms. You must check the second word of Choices B, C, D, and E. Bacon and Freud are now accepted, respected artists. In years past, they were viewed differently. They were *dismissed* or rejected as insignificant. The correct answer is Choice B.
   Note that a secondary meaning of *dismissed* is involved here.   (Contrast Pattern)

8. **D.** To the author of this sentence, pre-Spanish art in Mexico is praiseworthy. It is not *crude* art but strong art. He likes its bold simplifications and asserts they are not the result of the artists' inability to *overcome* or conquer the technical difficulties involved.
   Note how the second clause of the sentence serves to clarify what the author means by his assertion that pre-Spanish art is not crude.
   Be careful with sentences containing negative words and prefixes. The words "not," "mistaken," and "inability" all affect the sentence's meaning.

9. **E.** To pussyfoot is to refrain from committing oneself, to be wary of stating one's views candidly. People unable or afraid to take *forthright* stands are, by definition, *equivocators*.
   (Definition Pattern)

10. D. Given treachery on the part of their allies, it is likely that the natives would seek vengeance or *retribution*. It is also likely that they would feel *justified* in doing so.

Test the first word in each answer choice. Betrayed natives who have become bitter would be unlikely to seek *acquiescence* (agreement) or *magnanimity* (generosity of spirit; nobility of mind) or *exoneration* (vindication). You can immediately rule out Choices A, B, and E.   (Cause and Effect Pattern)

11. E. The *rooster* is the male of the species; the *hen*, the female. Likewise, the *gander* is the male of its species; the *goose*, the female.
(Gender)

12. A. A *chairman* uses a *gavel* to conduct meetings. A *conductor* uses a *baton* to conduct musical performances.

Remember, if more than one answer appears to fit the relationship in your test sentence, look for a narrower approach. "A chairman uses a gavel" is too broad a framework; it could fit Choices B, C, D, and E, as well as Choice A.   (Worker and Tool)

13. D. A *viola* is a kind of *instrument*; a *chisel* is a kind of *tool*.   (Member and Class)

14. D. Just as a *bough* branches off from a tree's *trunk*, an *arm* branches off from a person's *torso*.   (Part to Whole)

15. A. A *cobbler* repairs *shoes*, and a *mechanic* repairs *automobiles*.

Remember, if more than one answer appears to fit the relationship in your sentence, look for a narrower approach. "A cobbler works with shoes" is too broad a framework; it could fit Choices B, C, D, and E. You need to find a more specific relationship between the original pair.   (Function)

16. B. Just as a *breeze* is a less intense wind than a *tornado* (violent windstorm), a *trickle* is a less intense outpouring of liquid than a *gusher*.
(Degree of Intensity)

17. B. *Felicity* (happiness; bliss) and *sorrow* are antonyms; *agility* (nimbleness) and *clumsiness* are antonyms.   (Antonyms)

18. B. To *disband* an *organization* is to dismiss it from service or break it up. To *demobilize* an *army* is to dismiss it from service or break it up. Remember Analogy Tactic 4: Watch out for errors stemming from reversals. Choice C is incorrect. The employer is the person who discharges or dismisses someone from service. He is not the one who is discharged.
(Purpose)

19. A. *Assurance* will allay (calm or quiet) *fear*; an *opiate* will allay *pain*.   (Function)

20. A. One example of a *marsupial* (mammal that carries its young in a pouch) is an *opossum*; one example of a *rodent* is a *squirrel*. Answering some analogy questions requires specialized technical vocabulary typically used in high school science, literature, and social science classes.   (Class and Member)

21. B. A *pride* is a company or group of *lions*. Similarly, a *bevy* is a flock or group of birds, especially *quails*.

Note the use of a secondary meaning of the familiar-looking noun *pride*.

Use the process of elimination to find the correct answer. If you know that a pride is a group of lions, you can eliminate Choices A, C, D, and E. (A lair is a bear's den, not a group of bears; a minnow is a kind of fish, not a group of fish). By process of elimination, a *bevy* must be a group of quails.
(Group and Member)

22. A. *Propitiation* (conciliation; soothing) is intended to *appease* (calm or mollify); likewise, *harassment* (persecution) is intended to *vex* or annoy.

Watch out for eye-catchers. *Vindicate* means exonerate or clear. It is not a synonym for being *vindictive* or vengeful.
(Synonym Variant)

23. C. *Ostracism* (banishment from society) signifies *censure* (expression of disapproval). *Applause* signifies *approval*.
(Action and Its Significance)

24. C. Consider the activities Dillard describes Darwin participating in. He threw marine iguanas into the ocean, just for the sport of it; he went for rides on the backs of giant tortoises, as children today do on visits to the zoo. Thus, Dillard's initial picture of Darwin gives us a sense of his *youthful playfulness*.

25. A. In 1844, Darwin has come to the conclusion that species are *not* immutable (unable to change). He now believes that species do change. This conclusion is the *opposite* of what he originally thought. In other words, he originally viewed species as *unchanging*.

In answering questions about passages containing parenthetical comments, you may find it useful to read the passage *without* the remarks in parentheses. ("I am almost convinced . . . that species are not . . . immutable.") Once you have the basic idea, go back to the parenthetical comments to see how they modify what is being stated.

Note, by the way, the importance of negative words and prefixes here. Darwin says he almost believes that species are *not* immutable. In other words, he almost believes that species *are* mutable, able to evolve or change.

26. **C.** The observations that led Darwin to formulate the theory of evolution—the records Darwin made of the minute differences among the different types of finch—took place in the Galapagos. Thus, Dillard asserts that *Darwin's theory of evolution* and all it has meant to modern society began right there.

27. **D.** A single species of finch had been taken and modified to meet different *purposes*, to serve different ends. Again, treat this vocabulary-in-context question as if it were a sentence completion exercise. Go back to the original sentence and substitute each of the different answer choices for the word in quotes.

28. **E.** To say pssssssh pssssssh pssssssh pssssssh until you run out of breath is an everyday sort of thing: if you kept on breathing out that way, you'd naturally exhaust your supply of oxygen. However, to say it until an island runs out of birds—that's something else again. The idea that an island could run out of birds, that bird after bird after bird could come swooping down from the sky until there were no more birds left anywhere around—this image emphasizes the *overwhelming response of the birds.*

29. **B.** *Lighting* here means *landing* or coming to rest on a branch.

30. **B.** As each bird lands or touches down on a branch, the impact rocks the slender tree. It is the rhythm made by these repeated impacts that Dillard feels as "a rough pulse from the tree's thin trunk" against her hand.

31. **A.** Dillard spends one paragraph describing the finches as *drab*, dull creatures. In the next paragraph she shows how they can be differentiated by their distinctive beaks. Thus, her description of the finches chiefly serves to *contrast their overall drabness with their variety in one specific aspect.*

32. **E.** Short beaks are described as good for nabbing or catching insects. Long beaks are described as good for probing or poking deep into plants. Chisel beaks are described as good for digging grubs out of trees. What do these beaks have in common? They all *enable the finches to reach a specific source of nourishment*; they have evolved to meet a particular need.

33. **A.** Since the Galapagos are relatively close to the mainland, some mainland birds might have *ventured* or taken the risk of flying there.

34. **C.** Strip down the sentence, rephrasing it in its shortest form: "You see . . . on the finches . . . a fluorescent spray of horn." *Horn* here means a hard projection, in this case a bright, shiny one. It is the author's poetic way of referring to *the birds' shiny beaks.*

35. **D.** Use the process of elimination to find the correct answer to this question.
In the parenthetical comment beginning "In other words" (lines 88–90), the author restates an assertion. Therefore, you can eliminate Choice A.
The author compares an archipelago to an arpeggio. Therefore, you can eliminate Choice B.
The author defines an arpeggio as "a rapid series of distinct but related notes." Therefore, you can eliminate Choice C.
In the parenthetical comment beginning "In other words" (lines 88–90), the author describes a sequence of events. Therefore, you can eliminate Choice E.
Only Choice D is left. It is the correct answer. The author never *refutes or disproves an argument.*

Section 4   Mathematical Reasoning

Quantitative Comparison Questions

1. **C.** Each column is the product of 11 integers, one of which is 0. Since 0 times any number is 0, each column is 0. The columns are equal (C).

2. **C.** Column A: the multiples of 6 are 0, 6, 12, ..., 72, 78, 84... . The smallest one greater than 80 is 84. Column B: the multiples of 7 are 0, 7, 14, ... , 77, 84, 91... . The largest one less than 90 is 84. The columns are equal (C).

3. **B.** Since x and y are positive, $x + y = 1 \Rightarrow$ $x < 1$ and $y < 1 \Rightarrow xy < 1$ (KEY FACT A24: the product of positive numbers less than 1 is less than 1). Column B is greater.

4. **D.** Use TACTIC 10-1. Replace the variables with numbers. If $a = 1$ and $b = 2$, then Column A is $\frac{1}{2}$ and Column B is $\left(\frac{1}{2}\right)^3 = \frac{1}{8}$. This time A is larger; eliminate B and C. If $a = 2$ and $b = 1$, Column A is 2 and Column B is $2^3 = 8$.
This time B is larger; eliminate A. Neither column is *always* greater, and the two columns are not *always* equal (D).

5. A. In any triangle, if one side is longer than a second side, the angle opposite the longer side is greater than the angle opposite the shorter side (KEY FACT J3), so $c > d$. Column A is greater. (It is irrelevant that the third angle is 135°)

6. A. Column A: $51 = 1 \times 51 = 3 \times 17$. The largest *prime* factor is 17.
Column B:

$78 = 1 \times 78 = 2 \times 39 = 3 \times 26 = 6 \times 13$. The largest *prime* factor is 13. Column A is greater.

7. A. Let ℓ = length and w = width of rectangle I. Then 1.1ℓ = length and $0.9w$ = width of rectangle II. Column A is ℓw, but Column B is $(1.1\ell)(.9w) = 0.99\ell w$. Column A is greater.

    **Use TACTIC 10-2. Choose easy-to-use numbers. Since percents are involved, use 100. Assume that rectangle I is a 100×100 square; then its area is 10,000. Then rectangle II is 110×90, and its area is 9900. In this case, Column A is larger, so eliminate B and C. With a calculator you can try other values. Column A is always greater.

8. B. Column B: 3 shekels = $\frac{3}{5}$ (5 shekels) =

    $\frac{3}{5}$ (8.4 francs) = 5.04 francs. Column A:

    1 dollar = 4.9 francs. Column B is greater.

    **Since 8.4 francs = 5 shekels, 1 franc = $\frac{5}{8.4}$

    shekels, and so 1 dollar = 4.9 francs =

    $4.9\left(\frac{5}{8.4}\right)$ shekels ≈ 2.9 shekels, which is less

    than 3 shekels.

9. B.

Column A	Column B
$\sqrt{a+b}$	$\sqrt{a} + \sqrt{b}$

    Since the quantities in each column are positive, square them (TACTIC 10-3): $a + b$ $a + 2\sqrt{ab} + b$

    Subtract $a + b$ from each column: 0 $2\sqrt{ab}$

    Since a and b are positive, $2\sqrt{ab}$ is positive and Column B is greater.

    **Use TACTIC 10-1: Plug in easy-to-use

    numbers that satisfy the conditions, and use your calculator.
    Let $a = 0.1$ and $b = 0.9$. Column A is $\sqrt{0.1 + 0.9} = \sqrt{1} = 1$.
    Column B is $\sqrt{0.1} + \sqrt{0.9} \approx 0.32 + 0.95 = 1.27$. Column B is greater; eliminate A and C. Try other values; each time Column B is larger. Guess B.

10. B. The average of x and y is less than y, so having another y raises the average (KEY FACT E4). Column B is greater.

    **Use TACTIC 10-1. Plug in numbers. Column A: the average of 2 and 4 is 3. Column B: the average of 2, 4, and 4 is surely more than 3, because the extra 4 raises the average (it's 3.333). The answer is B.

11. B. Column A: since $b < 2$, $ab < 2a$.
Column B: since $b > a$, $b + a > a + a = 2a$. Column B is greater.

    **Use TACTIC 10-1. Plug in numbers that
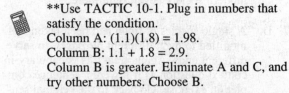
    satisfy the condition.
    Column A: $(1.1)(1.8) = 1.98$.
    Column B: $1.1 + 1.8 = 2.9$.
    Column B is greater. Eliminate A and C, and try other numbers. Choose B.

12. C. In each triangle the largest angle is the sum of the two smaller ones ($3 = 1 + 2$ and $9 = 2 + 7$), so each is a 90° angle. The columns are equal (C).

    **Use TACTIC D2. In ratio problems, write x after each number and solve.
    Column A: $x + 2x + 3x = 180 \Rightarrow 6x = 180 \Rightarrow x = 30 \Rightarrow 3x = 90$.
    Column B: $2x + 7x + 9x = 180 \Rightarrow 18x = 180 \Rightarrow x = 10 \Rightarrow 9x = 90$.

13. B. The *least* that a and b can be are 97 and 96. Therefore, the top four choices were selected by at least $189 + 97 + 96 + 95 = 477$ of the 500 children. Then, c is *at most* 23 (less if a and b are larger), and surely less than 30. Column B is greater.

14. C. If r is the radius of the white circle, $2r$ is the radius of the shaded semicircle. The area of the white circle is πr^2. The area of the semicircle is $\frac{1}{2}\pi(2r)^2 = \frac{1}{2}\pi(4r^2) = 2\pi r^2$, so the area of the shaded region is $2\pi r^2 - \pi r^2 = \pi r^2$. The columns are equal (C).

    **The solution is even easier if you use TACTIC 10-1. Let the radius of the circle be 1 instead of r, and proceed as above. The area of each region is π.

15. B. If the average of n numbers is 17, their sum is $17n$. To find the average of those n numbers and 25, divide $17n + 25$ by $n + 1$:

    $$\frac{17n + 25}{n + 1} = 21 \Rightarrow 17n + 25 = 21n + 21 \Rightarrow$$

    $$4n = 4 \Rightarrow n = 1$$

    Column B is greater.

Grid-in Questions

16. (13) Use your calculator:

$$a = \frac{(91)(13)}{7} = 169 \Rightarrow \sqrt{a} = \sqrt{169} = \mathbf{13}.$$

17. $\left(2.5 \text{ or } \frac{5}{2}\right)$ Replace a by 44 and b by 275:
$$44 = \frac{275}{c^2} \Rightarrow 44c^2 = 275 \Rightarrow$$

$$c^2 = \frac{275}{44} = 6.25.$$

Then, $c = \sqrt{6.25} = \mathbf{2.5}.$

18. (150) Draw and label the right triangle. By the Pythagorean theorem:
$15^2 + b^2 = 25^2 \Rightarrow$
$225 + b^2 = 625 \Rightarrow$
$b^2 = 400 \Rightarrow b = 20.$
The area of the triangle
is $\frac{1}{2}(15)(20) = \mathbf{150}.$

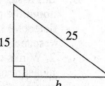

[You can save some work if you recognize this as a 3-4-5 triangle in which each side has been multiplied by 5 (15-20-25).]

19. (12) Let x = Adam's age in 1980. Then, in 1980, Judy's age was $3x$ and Elaine's age was $8x$. Since Elaine is 20 years older than Judy, $8x = 3x + 20 \Rightarrow 5x = 20 \Rightarrow x = 4.$ Therefore, in 1988, Adam was $4 + 8 = \mathbf{12}.$

**Use TACTIC 11-1. Test numbers and zoom in.

Adam	Judy	Elaine	Difference between Elaine and Judy
10	30	80	50, much too big
5	15	40	25, slightly too big
4	12	32	20, that's it

20. (110) Here, $x^2 - y^2 = (x + y)(x - y) = 10 \times 11 = \mathbf{110}.$

**Add the two equations: $2x = 21$, so $x = 10.5$. Since $10.5 + y = 10$, then $y = -.5$. Using your calculator, you get:
$x^2 - y^2 = (10.5)^2 - (.5)^2 = 110.25 - .25 = \mathbf{110}.$

21. (52) Ignore the x's and the y's. In any "staircase" the perimeter is just twice the sum of the height and the length, so the perimeter is
$$2(12 + 14) = 2(26) = \mathbf{52}.$$

22. $\left(\frac{16}{5} \text{ or } 3.2\right)$ Since $a = 2b$, $b = \frac{4}{3}c$, and $c = \frac{6}{5}d$:

$$a = 2\left(\frac{4}{3}c\right) = \frac{8}{3}\left(\frac{6}{5}d\right) = \frac{16}{5}d \Rightarrow$$

$$\frac{a}{d} = \frac{16}{5} \text{ or } \mathbf{3.2}.$$

**Use TACTIC 11-2. If we let $d = 1$, $c = \frac{6}{5}$.

That's OK, but it's easier if we avoid fractions. We'll let $d = 5$. Then, $c = 6$, $b = \frac{4}{3}(6) = 8$, and $a = 2(8) = 16$, so $\frac{a}{d} = \mathbf{\frac{16}{5}}.$

23. (87.5) If the average of 5 numbers (a, b, c, d, e) is 95, the sum of these numbers is $5 \times 95 = 475$ (TACTIC E1). Similarly, the sum of the 3 numbers (a, b, e) whose average is 100 is 300, leaving 175 $(475 - 300)$ as the sum of the 2 remaining numbers, c and d. The average of these 2 numbers is their sum divided by 2: average of c and d = $175 \div 2 = \mathbf{87.5}.$

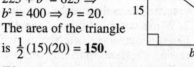

24. (179) If the average of a set of 9 numbers is 99, their sum is $9 \times 99 = 891$. If deleting one number reduces the average of the remaining 8 numbers to 89, the sum of those 8 numbers must be $8 \times 89 = 712$. So the deleted number was $891 - 712 = 179$.

25. (96) Since the diameters of the tables are in the ratio of 35:25, or 7:5, the ratio of their areas is $7^2:5^2 = 49:25$. Convert the ratio to a percent: $49:25 = \frac{49}{25} = \frac{196}{100} = 196\%$. The area of the larger table is 196% of the area of the small one, or is **96%** *more* than the area of the small one.

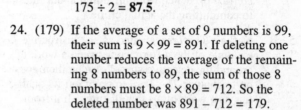

With your calculator, actually calculate the areas. The radius of the larger table is 17.5, so its area is $\pi(17.5)^2 = 306.25\pi$. Similarly, the radius of the smaller table is 12.5, and its area is $\pi(12.5)^2 = 156.25\pi$. The difference in the areas is $306.25\pi - 156.25\pi = 150\pi$, and 150π is **96% of 156.25π
$\left(\frac{150\pi}{156.25\pi} = \frac{150}{156.25} = 0.96\right).$

Section 5   Verbal Reasoning

1. B. Auden finds it curious or *unusual* that detective fiction *most* appeals to people who are *least* likely to find other forms of escapist literature appealing.

2. C. In lines 1–4, Auden states that typical readers of detective fiction do not find other forms of daydream or escapist literature appealing. In that context he then states that the typical mystery fan could not stomach or tolerate *True Confessions* and movie magazines. This suggests that Auden considers these magazines *standard examples of escapist literature.*

3. D. In the closing paragraph of Passage 1, Auden states that readers of detective fiction indulge in a fantasy of escape or release that is prompted by a "feeling of guilt, the cause of which is

unknown to the dreamer." Thus, they are *seeking release from a vague sense of guilt*.
Choice A is incorrect. Nothing in the passage supports it.
Choice B is incorrect. Auden denies that readers of detective fiction are bent on satisfying "violent or murderous wishes."
Choice C is incorrect. Although Auden depicts readers of detective fiction as dreamers, he depicts them as dreamers impelled by a sense of guilt, not by a sense of boredom.
Choice E is incorrect. Nothing in the passage supports it.

4. **E.** To translate murderous wishes into action is to *convert* or switch from dreaming about murder to committing the actual crime.

5. **B.** Kafka's *The Trial* is cited as an "instructive example of the difference between a work of art and the detective story." Auden then goes on to analyze *The Trial* to point out its qualities as a work of art that distinguish it from mere detective fiction.
Choice A is incorrect. *The Trial* is a work of art, not a detective story.
Choice C is incorrect. Auden is not discussing readers of detective fiction in lines 46–54.
Choice D is incorrect. The outside investigator, the genius who removes guilt by giving knowledge of guilt, is a figure out of the detective story; he has no place in the work of art. Although K investigates his situation, he is trapped inside it; he is no genius from outside.
Choice E is incorrect. There is nothing in the passage to support it.

6. **E.** Auden explicitly disassociates himself from the readers of thrillers (which he rarely enjoys). However, he associates himself with the readers of detective fiction ("me and my neighbors"), those who are caught up in the mystery, but, unlike the outside investigator, unable to solve it. This suggests he is a fan of detective fiction, one who views it with *genuine appreciation*.
Choices A, B, C, and D are incorrect. Nothing in the passage suggests them.

7. **C.** In the phrase "use up our intellectual shoe leather," the author of Passage 2 evokes a familiar image of the detective wearing out his or her shoe leather while pounding the pavements in search of clues. Readers of mysteries do not physically pound the pavements searching for clues. However, they do *work hard mentally, much as detectives do physically*.

8. **D.** The author writes of taking "pleasure in the discovery . . . that there is more work to be done." This suggests that he finds the prospect of additional work pleasing or *delightful*.

9. **B.** Throughout Passage 2 the author is discussing detective fiction. Immediately before mentioning Marlowe and Archer and their search for the facts, the author refers to the objective truth defined or discovered by the researcher/detective. This juxtaposition suggests that Marlowe and Archer are *fictional detectives*.

10. **B.** To employ a word is to *use* it.

11. **E.** The statement that the detective story begins "in search of the subject . . .(and) asking, What is the question?" suggests that the story must start by *defining the problem that is to be solved* in the course of the investigation.

12. **B.** In Passage 1, Auden goes on at some length about the psychological satisfaction readers of detective fiction derive from their literary "escape" from their sense of guilt. In Passage 2, Winks describes (also at some length) the pleasure readers of detective fiction get from raising questions, pursuing truths, making judgments. In both passages, the authors are primarily concerned with the question of *why people enjoy reading detective fiction*.

13. **A.** In characterizing detective fiction as "a bit like a religion" and linking it "with all fine literature, history, philosophy," Winks clearly goes further than Auden would. Auden stresses that detective stories are "escape literature, not works of art" (lines 19–20). Thus, Auden would most likely react to Winks's somewhat exalted view of detective fiction by reiterating that *reading detective fiction is an escape, not a highly serious pursuit*.

Section 6   Mathematical Reasoning

1. **B.** Multiplying both sides of $2x - 1 = 9$ by 5 yields $10x - 5 = \textbf{45}$.

   **Just solve:
   $2x - 1 = 9 \Rightarrow 2x = 10 \Rightarrow x = 5 \Rightarrow$
   $10x = 50 \Rightarrow 10x - 5 = \textbf{45}$.

2. **E.** Since the measures of corresponding angles are equal, $a = b$ (KEY FACT I6). Since the figure is not drawn to scale, the angles could just as well be acute as obtuse, as shown in the figure at the right. The sum $a + b$ **cannot be determined from the information given.**

3. D. Since there are no parentheses, you must be careful to follow the proper order of operations (PEMDAS). Do multiplications and divisions left to right *before* any additions and subtractions.

A: $4 \times 4 \div 4 + 4 = 16 \div 4 + 4 = 4 + 4 = 8$
B: $4 \div 4 \times 4 + 4 = 1 \times 4 + 4 = 4 + 4 = 8$
C: $4 \times 4 - 4 \times 4 = 16 - 16 = 0$
D: $4 \div 4 + 4 \times 4 = 1 + 16 = 17$, the greatest value
E: $4 + 4 \times 4 - 4 = 4 + 16 - 4 = 20 - 4 = 16$

4. C. Let $4x$ and $3x$ be the numbers of students taking and not taking Spanish, respectively. Then $4x + 3x = 840 \Rightarrow 7x = 840 \Rightarrow x = 120$. The number taking Spanish is $4(120) = \mathbf{480}$.

**Use TACTIC 9-1. Try choice C. If 480 students take Spanish, $840 - 480 = 360$ do not. Is $\frac{480}{360} = \frac{4}{3}$ a true proportion?

Yes. Cross-multiply: $480 \times 3 = 360 \times 4$.

5. D. Draw a Venn diagram. Since 10 seniors are in *both* band and orchestra, 30 are in band only and 50 are in orchestra only. Therefore, $10 + 30 + 50 = 90$ seniors are in at least one group, and the remaining **110** are in neither.

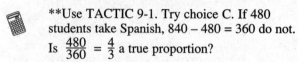

6. E. Since $k \| \ell$, two interior angles on the same side of the transversal are supplementary (KEY FACT I6), so $z + (3x + 15) = 180$. But $z = x + 5$ (KEY FACT I4: vertical angles are equal).

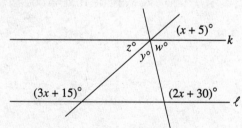

Then, $(3x + 15) + (x + 5) = 180 \Rightarrow 4x + 20 = 180 \Rightarrow 4x = 160 \Rightarrow x = 40$, so $z = x + 5 = 45$. Also, $w + (2x + 30) = 180$; but $2x + 30 = 80 + 30 = 110$, so $w = 70$. Finally, $w + y + z = 180 \Rightarrow 70 + y + 45 = 180 \Rightarrow 115 + y = 180 \Rightarrow y = \mathbf{65}$.

7. C. Check each of the three statements. Since the average of a and a is a, I is true. Clearly, the average of a and b is the same as the average of b and a, so II is also true. Note that $a \circledcirc (b \circledcirc c)$ is *not* the average of the three numbers a, b, and c. To calculate this aver-

age, you first take the average of b and c and then take the average of that result and a. Then,
$$a \circledcirc (b \circledcirc c) =$$
$$\frac{a + \left(\frac{b + c}{2}\right)}{2} = \frac{2a + b + c}{4},$$
whereas
$$(a \circledcirc b) \circledcirc c = \frac{\left(\frac{a + b}{2}\right) + c}{2} = \frac{a + b + 2c}{4},$$

and these are equal only if $a = c$. Therefore, III is false and **I and II only** are true.

**Use TACTIC 9-2: plug in some easy numbers. You probably don't need to do this for I and II, but for III it may be a lot easier than the analysis above:
$2 \circledcirc (4 \circledcirc 6) =$
$2 \circledcirc 5 = 3.5$, whereas
$(2 \circledcirc 4) \circledcirc 6 =$
$3 \circledcirc 6 = 4.5$. III is false.

8. B. As always, with a percent problem use a simple number such as 10 or 100. Assume that model A sells for \$10; then, since 60% of 10 is 6, model B sells for \$16. The chart tells you that 9000 model A's and 10,000 model B's were sold, for a total of
$\$10(9000) + \$16(10,000) =$
$\$90,000 + \$160,000 = \$250,000$.
The sales of model A (\$90,000) represent **36%** of the total sales (\$250,000).

9. D. The best approach is to use the six-step method from Section 12-G.
To get rid of the fractions, multiply both sides of the equation by 3: $3x = 2(x + y)$
Use the distributive law to get rid of the parentheses: $3x = 2x + 2y$
Subtract $2x$ from each side: $x = 2y$

10. E. If PQ is a diameter of the circle, then the radius is 1 and A, the area, is π. This is the smallest possible value of A, but A can actually be any number larger than π if the radius is made arbitrarily large, as shown by the figures below.

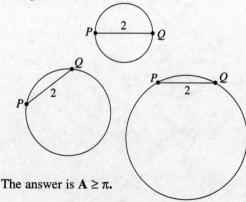

The answer is $\mathbf{A \geq \pi}$.

Answer Sheet—Test 3

If a section has fewer than 35 questions, leave the extra spaces blank.

Section 1

1 Ⓐ Ⓑ Ⓒ Ⓓ Ⓔ   8 Ⓐ Ⓑ Ⓒ Ⓓ Ⓔ   15 Ⓐ Ⓑ Ⓒ Ⓓ Ⓔ   22 Ⓐ Ⓑ Ⓒ Ⓓ Ⓔ   29 Ⓐ Ⓑ Ⓒ Ⓓ Ⓔ
2 Ⓐ Ⓑ Ⓒ Ⓓ Ⓔ   9 Ⓐ Ⓑ Ⓒ Ⓓ Ⓔ   16 Ⓐ Ⓑ Ⓒ Ⓓ Ⓔ   23 Ⓐ Ⓑ Ⓒ Ⓓ Ⓔ   30 Ⓐ Ⓑ Ⓒ Ⓓ Ⓔ
3 Ⓐ Ⓑ Ⓒ Ⓓ Ⓔ   10 Ⓐ Ⓑ Ⓒ Ⓓ Ⓔ   17 Ⓐ Ⓑ Ⓒ Ⓓ Ⓔ   24 Ⓐ Ⓑ Ⓒ Ⓓ Ⓔ   31 Ⓐ Ⓑ Ⓒ Ⓓ Ⓔ
4 Ⓐ Ⓑ Ⓒ Ⓓ Ⓔ   11 Ⓐ Ⓑ Ⓒ Ⓓ Ⓔ   18 Ⓐ Ⓑ Ⓒ Ⓓ Ⓔ   25 Ⓐ Ⓑ Ⓒ Ⓓ Ⓔ   32 Ⓐ Ⓑ Ⓒ Ⓓ Ⓔ
5 Ⓐ Ⓑ Ⓒ Ⓓ Ⓔ   12 Ⓐ Ⓑ Ⓒ Ⓓ Ⓔ   19 Ⓐ Ⓑ Ⓒ Ⓓ Ⓔ   26 Ⓐ Ⓑ Ⓒ Ⓓ Ⓔ   33 Ⓐ Ⓑ Ⓒ Ⓓ Ⓔ
6 Ⓐ Ⓑ Ⓒ Ⓓ Ⓔ   13 Ⓐ Ⓑ Ⓒ Ⓓ Ⓔ   20 Ⓐ Ⓑ Ⓒ Ⓓ Ⓔ   27 Ⓐ Ⓑ Ⓒ Ⓓ Ⓔ   34 Ⓐ Ⓑ Ⓒ Ⓓ Ⓔ
7 Ⓐ Ⓑ Ⓒ Ⓓ Ⓔ   14 Ⓐ Ⓑ Ⓒ Ⓓ Ⓔ   21 Ⓐ Ⓑ Ⓒ Ⓓ Ⓔ   28 Ⓐ Ⓑ Ⓒ Ⓓ Ⓔ   35 Ⓐ Ⓑ Ⓒ Ⓓ Ⓔ

Section 2

1 Ⓐ Ⓑ Ⓒ Ⓓ Ⓔ   8 Ⓐ Ⓑ Ⓒ Ⓓ Ⓔ   15 Ⓐ Ⓑ Ⓒ Ⓓ Ⓔ   22 Ⓐ Ⓑ Ⓒ Ⓓ Ⓔ   29 Ⓐ Ⓑ Ⓒ Ⓓ Ⓔ
2 Ⓐ Ⓑ Ⓒ Ⓓ Ⓔ   9 Ⓐ Ⓑ Ⓒ Ⓓ Ⓔ   16 Ⓐ Ⓑ Ⓒ Ⓓ Ⓔ   23 Ⓐ Ⓑ Ⓒ Ⓓ Ⓔ   30 Ⓐ Ⓑ Ⓒ Ⓓ Ⓔ
3 Ⓐ Ⓑ Ⓒ Ⓓ Ⓔ   10 Ⓐ Ⓑ Ⓒ Ⓓ Ⓔ   17 Ⓐ Ⓑ Ⓒ Ⓓ Ⓔ   24 Ⓐ Ⓑ Ⓒ Ⓓ Ⓔ   31 Ⓐ Ⓑ Ⓒ Ⓓ Ⓔ
4 Ⓐ Ⓑ Ⓒ Ⓓ Ⓔ   11 Ⓐ Ⓑ Ⓒ Ⓓ Ⓔ   18 Ⓐ Ⓑ Ⓒ Ⓓ Ⓔ   25 Ⓐ Ⓑ Ⓒ Ⓓ Ⓔ   32 Ⓐ Ⓑ Ⓒ Ⓓ Ⓔ
5 Ⓐ Ⓑ Ⓒ Ⓓ Ⓔ   12 Ⓐ Ⓑ Ⓒ Ⓓ Ⓔ   19 Ⓐ Ⓑ Ⓒ Ⓓ Ⓔ   26 Ⓐ Ⓑ Ⓒ Ⓓ Ⓔ   33 Ⓐ Ⓑ Ⓒ Ⓓ Ⓔ
6 Ⓐ Ⓑ Ⓒ Ⓓ Ⓔ   13 Ⓐ Ⓑ Ⓒ Ⓓ Ⓔ   20 Ⓐ Ⓑ Ⓒ Ⓓ Ⓔ   27 Ⓐ Ⓑ Ⓒ Ⓓ Ⓔ   34 Ⓐ Ⓑ Ⓒ Ⓓ Ⓔ
7 Ⓐ Ⓑ Ⓒ Ⓓ Ⓔ   14 Ⓐ Ⓑ Ⓒ Ⓓ Ⓔ   21 Ⓐ Ⓑ Ⓒ Ⓓ Ⓔ   28 Ⓐ Ⓑ Ⓒ Ⓓ Ⓔ   35 Ⓐ Ⓑ Ⓒ Ⓓ Ⓔ

Section 3

1 Ⓐ Ⓑ Ⓒ Ⓓ Ⓔ   8 Ⓐ Ⓑ Ⓒ Ⓓ Ⓔ   15 Ⓐ Ⓑ Ⓒ Ⓓ Ⓔ   22 Ⓐ Ⓑ Ⓒ Ⓓ Ⓔ   29 Ⓐ Ⓑ Ⓒ Ⓓ Ⓔ
2 Ⓐ Ⓑ Ⓒ Ⓓ Ⓔ   9 Ⓐ Ⓑ Ⓒ Ⓓ Ⓔ   16 Ⓐ Ⓑ Ⓒ Ⓓ Ⓔ   23 Ⓐ Ⓑ Ⓒ Ⓓ Ⓔ   30 Ⓐ Ⓑ Ⓒ Ⓓ Ⓔ
3 Ⓐ Ⓑ Ⓒ Ⓓ Ⓔ   10 Ⓐ Ⓑ Ⓒ Ⓓ Ⓔ   17 Ⓐ Ⓑ Ⓒ Ⓓ Ⓔ   24 Ⓐ Ⓑ Ⓒ Ⓓ Ⓔ   31 Ⓐ Ⓑ Ⓒ Ⓓ Ⓔ
4 Ⓐ Ⓑ Ⓒ Ⓓ Ⓔ   11 Ⓐ Ⓑ Ⓒ Ⓓ Ⓔ   18 Ⓐ Ⓑ Ⓒ Ⓓ Ⓔ   25 Ⓐ Ⓑ Ⓒ Ⓓ Ⓔ   32 Ⓐ Ⓑ Ⓒ Ⓓ Ⓔ
5 Ⓐ Ⓑ Ⓒ Ⓓ Ⓔ   12 Ⓐ Ⓑ Ⓒ Ⓓ Ⓔ   19 Ⓐ Ⓑ Ⓒ Ⓓ Ⓔ   26 Ⓐ Ⓑ Ⓒ Ⓓ Ⓔ   33 Ⓐ Ⓑ Ⓒ Ⓓ Ⓔ
6 Ⓐ Ⓑ Ⓒ Ⓓ Ⓔ   13 Ⓐ Ⓑ Ⓒ Ⓓ Ⓔ   20 Ⓐ Ⓑ Ⓒ Ⓓ Ⓔ   27 Ⓐ Ⓑ Ⓒ Ⓓ Ⓔ   34 Ⓐ Ⓑ Ⓒ Ⓓ Ⓔ
7 Ⓐ Ⓑ Ⓒ Ⓓ Ⓔ   14 Ⓐ Ⓑ Ⓒ Ⓓ Ⓔ   21 Ⓐ Ⓑ Ⓒ Ⓓ Ⓔ   28 Ⓐ Ⓑ Ⓒ Ⓓ Ⓔ   35 Ⓐ Ⓑ Ⓒ Ⓓ Ⓔ

Section 4

1 Ⓐ Ⓑ Ⓒ Ⓓ Ⓔ   4 Ⓐ Ⓑ Ⓒ Ⓓ Ⓔ   7 Ⓐ Ⓑ Ⓒ Ⓓ Ⓔ   10 Ⓐ Ⓑ Ⓒ Ⓓ Ⓔ   13 Ⓐ Ⓑ Ⓒ Ⓓ Ⓔ
2 Ⓐ Ⓑ Ⓒ Ⓓ Ⓔ   5 Ⓐ Ⓑ Ⓒ Ⓓ Ⓔ   8 Ⓐ Ⓑ Ⓒ Ⓓ Ⓔ   11 Ⓐ Ⓑ Ⓒ Ⓓ Ⓔ   14 Ⓐ Ⓑ Ⓒ Ⓓ Ⓔ
3 Ⓐ Ⓑ Ⓒ Ⓓ Ⓔ   6 Ⓐ Ⓑ Ⓒ Ⓓ Ⓔ   9 Ⓐ Ⓑ Ⓒ Ⓓ Ⓔ   12 Ⓐ Ⓑ Ⓒ Ⓓ Ⓔ   15 Ⓐ Ⓑ Ⓒ Ⓓ Ⓔ

Section 4 (continued)

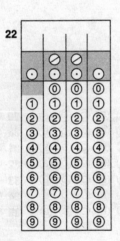

Grid-in answer boxes numbered 16 through 25.

Section 5

1 Ⓐ Ⓑ Ⓒ Ⓓ Ⓔ	8 Ⓐ Ⓑ Ⓒ Ⓓ Ⓔ	15 Ⓐ Ⓑ Ⓒ Ⓓ Ⓔ	22 Ⓐ Ⓑ Ⓒ Ⓓ Ⓔ	29 Ⓐ Ⓑ Ⓒ Ⓓ Ⓔ
2 Ⓐ Ⓑ Ⓒ Ⓓ Ⓔ	9 Ⓐ Ⓑ Ⓒ Ⓓ Ⓔ	16 Ⓐ Ⓑ Ⓒ Ⓓ Ⓔ	23 Ⓐ Ⓑ Ⓒ Ⓓ Ⓔ	30 Ⓐ Ⓑ Ⓒ Ⓓ Ⓔ
3 Ⓐ Ⓑ Ⓒ Ⓓ Ⓔ	10 Ⓐ Ⓑ Ⓒ Ⓓ Ⓔ	17 Ⓐ Ⓑ Ⓒ Ⓓ Ⓔ	24 Ⓐ Ⓑ Ⓒ Ⓓ Ⓔ	31 Ⓐ Ⓑ Ⓒ Ⓓ Ⓔ
4 Ⓐ Ⓑ Ⓒ Ⓓ Ⓔ	11 Ⓐ Ⓑ Ⓒ Ⓓ Ⓔ	18 Ⓐ Ⓑ Ⓒ Ⓓ Ⓔ	25 Ⓐ Ⓑ Ⓒ Ⓓ Ⓔ	32 Ⓐ Ⓑ Ⓒ Ⓓ Ⓔ
5 Ⓐ Ⓑ Ⓒ Ⓓ Ⓔ	12 Ⓐ Ⓑ Ⓒ Ⓓ Ⓔ	19 Ⓐ Ⓑ Ⓒ Ⓓ Ⓔ	26 Ⓐ Ⓑ Ⓒ Ⓓ Ⓔ	33 Ⓐ Ⓑ Ⓒ Ⓓ Ⓔ
6 Ⓐ Ⓑ Ⓒ Ⓓ Ⓔ	13 Ⓐ Ⓑ Ⓒ Ⓓ Ⓔ	20 Ⓐ Ⓑ Ⓒ Ⓓ Ⓔ	27 Ⓐ Ⓑ Ⓒ Ⓓ Ⓔ	34 Ⓐ Ⓑ Ⓒ Ⓓ Ⓔ
7 Ⓐ Ⓑ Ⓒ Ⓓ Ⓔ	14 Ⓐ Ⓑ Ⓒ Ⓓ Ⓔ	21 Ⓐ Ⓑ Ⓒ Ⓓ Ⓔ	28 Ⓐ Ⓑ Ⓒ Ⓓ Ⓔ	35 Ⓐ Ⓑ Ⓒ Ⓓ Ⓔ

Section 6

1 Ⓐ Ⓑ Ⓒ Ⓓ Ⓔ	8 Ⓐ Ⓑ Ⓒ Ⓓ Ⓔ	15 Ⓐ Ⓑ Ⓒ Ⓓ Ⓔ	22 Ⓐ Ⓑ Ⓒ Ⓓ Ⓔ	29 Ⓐ Ⓑ Ⓒ Ⓓ Ⓔ
2 Ⓐ Ⓑ Ⓒ Ⓓ Ⓔ	9 Ⓐ Ⓑ Ⓒ Ⓓ Ⓔ	16 Ⓐ Ⓑ Ⓒ Ⓓ Ⓔ	23 Ⓐ Ⓑ Ⓒ Ⓓ Ⓔ	30 Ⓐ Ⓑ Ⓒ Ⓓ Ⓔ
3 Ⓐ Ⓑ Ⓒ Ⓓ Ⓔ	10 Ⓐ Ⓑ Ⓒ Ⓓ Ⓔ	17 Ⓐ Ⓑ Ⓒ Ⓓ Ⓔ	24 Ⓐ Ⓑ Ⓒ Ⓓ Ⓔ	31 Ⓐ Ⓑ Ⓒ Ⓓ Ⓔ
4 Ⓐ Ⓑ Ⓒ Ⓓ Ⓔ	11 Ⓐ Ⓑ Ⓒ Ⓓ Ⓔ	18 Ⓐ Ⓑ Ⓒ Ⓓ Ⓔ	25 Ⓐ Ⓑ Ⓒ Ⓓ Ⓔ	32 Ⓐ Ⓑ Ⓒ Ⓓ Ⓔ
5 Ⓐ Ⓑ Ⓒ Ⓓ Ⓔ	12 Ⓐ Ⓑ Ⓒ Ⓓ Ⓔ	19 Ⓐ Ⓑ Ⓒ Ⓓ Ⓔ	26 Ⓐ Ⓑ Ⓒ Ⓓ Ⓔ	33 Ⓐ Ⓑ Ⓒ Ⓓ Ⓔ
6 Ⓐ Ⓑ Ⓒ Ⓓ Ⓔ	13 Ⓐ Ⓑ Ⓒ Ⓓ Ⓔ	20 Ⓐ Ⓑ Ⓒ Ⓓ Ⓔ	27 Ⓐ Ⓑ Ⓒ Ⓓ Ⓔ	34 Ⓐ Ⓑ Ⓒ Ⓓ Ⓔ
7 Ⓐ Ⓑ Ⓒ Ⓓ Ⓔ	14 Ⓐ Ⓑ Ⓒ Ⓓ Ⓔ	21 Ⓐ Ⓑ Ⓒ Ⓓ Ⓔ	28 Ⓐ Ⓑ Ⓒ Ⓓ Ⓔ	35 Ⓐ Ⓑ Ⓒ Ⓓ Ⓔ

MODEL SAT I TEST 3   1 1 1 1 1 1   1

SECTION 1   Time—30 Minutes   Select the best answer to the following questions, then fill in the
30 Questions   appropriate space on your Answer Sheet.

Each of the following sentences contains one or two
blanks; these blanks indicate that a word or set of words
has been left out. Below the sentence are five words or
phrases, lettered A through E. Select the word or set of
words that best completes the sentence.

Example:

Fame is ----; today's rising star is all too soon
tomorrow's washed-up has-been.

(A) rewarding   (B) gradual
(C) essential   (D) spontaneous
(E) transitory

Ⓐ Ⓑ Ⓒ Ⓓ ●

1. Archaeologists are involved in ---- Mayan temples
in Central America, uncovering the old ruins in
order to learn more about the civilization they represent.

(A) demolishing   (B) incapacitating
(C) excavating   (D) worshiping
(E) adapting

2. Afraid that the ---- nature of the plays being presented would corrupt the morals of their audiences,
the Puritans closed the theaters in 1642.

(A) mediocre
(B) fantastic
(C) profound
(D) lewd
(E) witty

3. The governor's imposition of martial law on the
once-peaceful community was the last straw, so far
as the lawmakers were concerned: the legislature
refused to function until martial law was ----.

(A) reaffirmed   (B) reiterated   (C) inaugurated
(D) rescinded   (E) prolonged

4. The sergeant suspected that the private was ---- in
order to avoid going on the ---- march scheduled
for that morning.

(A) malingering...arduous
(B) proselytizing...interminable
(C) invalidating...threatened
(D) exemplary...leisurely
(E) disgruntled...strenuous

5. The incidence of smoking among women, formerly
----, has grown to such a degree that lung cancer,
once a minor problem, has become the chief ---- of
cancer-related deaths among women.

(A) negligible...cause
(B) minor...antidote
(C) preeminent...cure
(D) relevant...modifier
(E) pervasive...opponent

6. The columnist was almost ---- when he mentioned
his friends, but he was unpleasant and even ----
when he discussed people who irritated him.

(A) recalcitrant...laconic
(B) reverential...acrimonious
(C) sensitive...remorseful
(D) insipid...militant
(E) benevolent...stoical

7. An experienced politician who knew better than to
launch a campaign in troubled political waters, she
intended to wait for a more ---- occasion before she
announced her plans.

(A) propitious
(B) provocative
(C) unseemly
(D) questionable
(E) theoretical

8. Wemmick, the soul of kindness in private, is oblig-
ed in ---- to be uncompassionate and even ---- on
behalf of his employer, the harsh lawyer Jaggers.

(A) conclusion...careless
(B) principle...contradictory
(C) theory...esoteric
(D) court...judicious
(E) public...ruthless

9. In one instance illustrating Metternich's consuming
----, he employed several naval captains to purchase books abroad for him, eventually adding an
entire Oriental library to his ---- collection.

(A) foresight...indifferent
(B) altruism...eclectic
(C) bibliomania...burgeoning
(D) avarice...inadvertent
(E) egocentricity...magnanimous

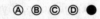

GO ON TO THE NEXT PAGE ➤

1   1   1   1   1   1   1   1   1   1   1

The analogies questions present two words or phrases that are related in some way. Determine which A-through-E answer choice below has a relationship *most* similar to that of the original words or phrases.

Example:

YAWN:BOREDOM::   (A) dream:sleep
(B) anger:madness   (C) smile:amusement
(D) face:expression   (E) impatience:rebellion

Ⓐ Ⓑ ● Ⓓ Ⓔ

10. BARBER:SHEARS::
(A) baker:batter
(B) dentist:drill
(C) patient:prescription
(D) architect:blueprint
(E) butcher:sausages

11. PUCK:HOCKEY::
(A) net:tennis
(B) goal:soccer
(C) ball:golf
(D) rod:fishing
(E) helmet:football

12. HILLOCK:MOUNTAIN::
(A) hassock:stool
(B) pond:lake
(C) spice:herb
(D) gravel:sand
(E) tree:lumber

13. MENTOR:COUNSEL::
(A) poet:criticism
(B) plea:mercy
(C) bodyguard:protection
(D) sermon:conscience
(E) judge:lawyer

14. CHAUVINISM:COUNTRY::
(A) frugality:money
(B) patriotism:authority
(C) gluttony:food
(D) jingoism:loyalty
(E) criticism:book

15. SEDULOUS:DILIGENCE::
(A) ambitious:vanity
(B) haughty:obsequiousness
(C) lush:barrenness
(D) ingenuous:naivete
(E) devious:diversity

Read each of the passages below, and then answer the questions that follow each passage. The correct response may be stated outright or merely suggested in the passage.

Questions 16–21 are based on the following passage.

The following passage on the formation of oil is excerpted from a novel about oil exploration written by Alistair MacLean.

Five main weather elements act upon rock. Frost and ice fracture rock. It can be gradually eroded by airborne dust. The action of the seas,
Line whether through the constant movement of tides
(5) or the pounding of heavy storm waves, remorse-lessly wears away the coastlines. Rivers are immensely powerful destructive agencies—one has but to look at the Grand Canyon to appreciate their enormous power. And such rocks as escape
(10) all these influences are worn away over the eons by the effect of rain.

Whatever the cause of erosion, the net result is the same. The rock is reduced to its tiniest possible constituents—rock particles or, simply, dust.
(15) Rain and melting snow carry this dust down to the tiniest rivulets and the mightiest rivers, which, in turn, transport it to lakes, inland seas and the coastal regions of the oceans. Dust, however fine and powdery, is still heavier than water, and
(20) whenever the water becomes sufficiently still, it will gradually sink to the bottom, not only in lakes and seas but also in the sluggish lower reaches of rivers and where flood conditions exist, in the form of silt.
(25) And so, over unimaginably long reaches of time, whole mountain ranges are carried down to the seas, and in the process, through the effects of gravity, new rock is born as layer after layer of dust accumulates on the bottom, building up to a
(30) depth of ten, a hundred, perhaps even a thousand feet, the lowermost layers being gradually com-pacted by the immense and steadily increasing pressures from above, until the particles fuse together and reform as a new rock.

GO ON TO THE NEXT PAGE ➡

1 1 1 1 1 1 1 1 1 1 1

(35)   It is in the intermediate and final processes of the new rock formation that oil comes into being. Those lakes and seas of hundreds of millions of years ago were almost choked by water plants and the most primitive forms of aquatic life. On
(40) dying, they sank to the bottom of the lakes and seas along with the settling dust particles and were gradually buried deep under the endless layers of more dust and more aquatic and plant life that slowly accumulated above them. The pass-
(45) ing of millions of years and the steadily increasing pressures from above gradually changed the decayed vegetation and dead aquatic life into oil.

    Described this simply and quickly, the process sounds reasonable enough. But this is where the
(50) gray and disputatious area arises. The conditions necessary for the formation of oil are known; the cause of the metamorphosis is not. It seems probable that some form of chemical catalyst is involved, but this catalyst has not been isolated.
(55) The first purely synthetic oil, as distinct from secondary synthetic oils such as those derived from coal, has yet to be produced. We just have to accept that oil is oil, that it is there, bound up in rock strata in fairly well-defined areas throughout
(60) the world but always on the sites of ancient seas and lakes, some of which are now continental land, some buried deep under the encroachment of new oceans.

16. According to the author, which of the following statements is (are) true?

   I. The action of the seas is the most important factor in erosion of the earth's surface.
   II. Scientists have not been able to produce a purely synthetic oil in the laboratory.
   III. Gravity plays an important role in the formation of new rock.

(A) I only
(B) II only
(C) III only
(D) I and III only
(E) II and III only

17. The Grand Canyon is mentioned in the first paragraph to illustrate

(A) the urgent need for dams
(B) the devastating impact of rivers
(C) the effect of rain
(D) a site where oil may be found
(E) the magnificence of nature

18. According to the author, our understanding of the process by which oil is created is

(A) biased   (B) systematic   (C) erroneous
(D) deficient   (E) adequate

19. We can infer that prospectors should search for oil deposits

(A) wherever former seas existed
(B) in mountain streambeds
(C) where coal deposits are found
(D) in the Grand Canyon
(E) in new rock formations

20. The author does all of the following EXCEPT

(A) describe a process
(B) state a possibility
(C) cite an example
(D) propose a solution
(E) mention a limitation

21. The word "reaches" in line 23 means

(A) grasps
(B) unbroken stretches
(C) range of knowledge
(D) promontories
(E) juxtapositions

Questions 22–30 are based on the following passage.

The following passage is excerpted from a book on the meaning and importance of fairy tales by the noted child psychologist, Bruno Bettelheim.

    Plato—who may have understood better what forms the mind of man than do some of our contemporaries who want their children exposed only
Line to "real" people and everyday events—knew what
(5) intellectual experiences make for true humanity. He suggested that the future citizens of his ideal republic begin their literary education with the telling of myths, rather than with mere facts or so-called rational teachings. Even Aristotle, mas-
(10) ter of pure reason, said: "The friend of wisdom is also a friend of myth."

    Modern thinkers who have studied myths and fairy tales from a philosophical or psychological viewpoint arrive at the same conclusion, regard-
(15) less of their original persuasion. Mircea Eliade, for one, describes these stories as "models for human behavior [that,] by that very fact, give meaning and value to life." Drawing on anthropological parallels, he and others suggest that myths
(20) and fairy tales were derived from, or give symbolic expression to, initiation rites or other *rites of passage*—such as metaphoric death of an old, inadequate self in order to be reborn on a higher

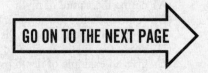

GO ON TO THE NEXT PAGE

1   1   1   1   1   1   1   1   1   1   1

plane of existence. He feels that this is why these
(25) tales meet a strongly felt need and are carriers of
such deep meaning.

Other investigators with a depth-psychological
orientation emphasize the similarities between the
fantastic events in myths and fairy tales and those
(30) in adult dreams and daydreams—the fulfillment
of wishes, the winning out over all competitors,
the destruction of enemies—and conclude that
one attraction of this literature is its expression of
that which is normally prevented from coming to
(35) awareness.

There are, of course, very significant differences between fairy tales and dreams. For example, in dreams more often than not the wish fulfillment is disguised, while in fairy tales much of
(40) it is openly expressed. To a considerable degree,
dreams are the result of inner pressures that have
found no relief, of problems that beset a person to
which he knows no solution and to which the
dream finds none. The fairy tale does the oppo-
(45) site: it projects the relief of all pressures and not
only offers ways to solve problems but promises
that a "happy" solution will be found.

We cannot control what goes on in our dreams.
Although our inner censorship influences what we
(50) may dream, such control occurs on an unconscious level. The fairy tale, on the other hand, is
very much the result of common conscious and
unconscious content having been shaped by the
conscious mind, not of one particular person, but
(55) the consensus of many in regard to what they
view as universal human problems, and what they
accept as desirable solutions. If all these elements
were not present in a fairy tale, it would not be
retold by generation after generation. Only if a
(60) fairy tale met the conscious and unconscious
requirements of many people was it repeatedly
retold, and listened to with great interest. No
dream of a person could arouse such persistent
interest unless it was worked into a myth, as was
(65) the story of the pharaoh's dream as interpreted by
Joseph in the Bible.

There is general agreement that myths and fairy
tales speak to us in the language of symbols representing unconscious content. Their appeal is simul-
(70) taneously to our conscious mind, and to our need
for ego-ideals as well. This makes it very effective; and in the tales' content, inner psychological
phenomena are given body in symbolic form.

22. In the opening paragraph, the author quotes Plato
and Aristotle primarily in order to

(A) define the nature of myth
(B) contrast their opposing points of view
(C) support the point that myths are valuable
(D) prove that myths originated in ancient times
(E) give an example of depth psychology

23. The author's comment about people who wish their
children exposed only to actual historic persons and
commonplace events (lines 3–4) suggests he primarily views such people as

(A) considerate of their children's welfare
(B) misguided in their beliefs
(C) determined to achieve their ends
(D) more rational than the ancients
(E) optimistic about human nature

24. By "Plato . . . knew what intellectual experiences
make for true humanity" (lines 4–5), the author
means that

(A) Plato comprehended the effects of the intellectual life on real human beings
(B) Plato realized how little a purely intellectual
education could do for people's actual well-
being
(C) Plato grasped which sorts of experiences
helped promote the development of truly
humane individuals
(D) actual human beings are transformed by reading the scholarly works of Plato
(E) human nature is a product of mental training
according to the best philosophical principles

25. The word "persuasion" in line 15 means

(A) enticement
(B) convincing force
(C) political party
(D) opinion
(E) gullibility

26. Lines 12–18 suggest that Mircea Eliade is most
likely

(A) a writer of children's literature
(B) a student of physical anthropology
(C) a twentieth century philosopher
(D) an advocate of practical education
(E) a contemporary of Plato

27. In line 69, the word "appeal" most nearly means

(A) plea
(B) wistfulness
(C) prayer
(D) request
(E) attraction

GO ON TO THE NEXT PAGE

1   1 1 1 1 1 1 1 1 1   1

28. It can be inferred from the passage that the author's interest in fairy tales centers chiefly on their

(A) literary qualities
(B) historical background
(C) factual accuracy
(D) psychological relevance
(E) ethical weakness

29. Which of the following best describes the author's attitude toward fairy tales?

(A) Reluctant fascination
(B) Wary skepticism
(C) Scornful disapprobation
(D) Indulgent tolerance
(E) Open approval

30. According to the passage, fairy tales differ from dreams in which of the following characteristics?

I. Their shared nature of their creation
II. Their convention of a happy ending
III. Their enduring general appeal

(A) I only
(B) II only
(C) I and II only
(D) II and III only
(E) I, II, and III

YOU MAY GO BACK AND REVIEW THIS SECTION IN THE REMAINING TIME, BUT DO NOT WORK IN ANY OTHER SECTION UNTIL TOLD TO DO SO.　　**S T O P**

2   2 2 2 2 2 2 2 2 2   2

SECTION 2

Time—30 Minutes
25 Questions

For each problem in this section determine which of the five choices is correct and blacken in that choice on your answer sheet. You may use any blank space on the page for your work.

Notes:

- You may use a calculator whenever you feel it will be helpful.
- Use the diagrams provided to help you solve the problems. Unless you see the words "Note: Figure not drawn to scale" under a diagram, it has been drawn as accurately as possible. Unless it is stated that a figure is three-dimensional, you may assume it lies in a plane.

Reference Information

Area Facts	Volume Facts	Triangle Facts	Angle Facts

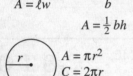
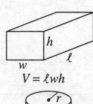
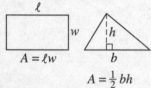
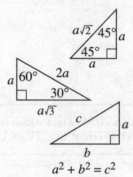
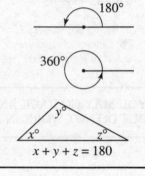

Area Facts: $A = \ell w$, $A = \frac{1}{2}bh$, $A = \pi r^2$, $C = 2\pi r$

Volume Facts: $V = \ell wh$, $V = \pi r^2 h$

Triangle Facts: $a^2 + b^2 = c^2$

Angle Facts: $x + y + z = 180$

---

1. If $3x = 12$, $5x =$
   (A) 2.4   (B) 14   (C) 15   (D) 20   (E) 60

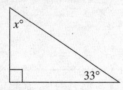

2. In the figure above, $x =$
   (A) 33   (B) 57   (C) 67   (D) 123   (E) 147

3. If $8 - (8 - m) = 8$, then $m =$
   (A) −16   (B) −8   (C) 0   (D) 8   (E) 16

4. In a class, 20 children were sharing equally the cost of a present for their teacher. When 4 of the children decided not to contribute, each of the other children had to pay $1.50 more. How much, in dollars, did the present cost?
   (A) 50   (B) 80   (C) 100   (D) 120   (E) 150

5. If $\frac{5}{9}$ of the members of the school chorus are boys, what is the ratio of girls to boys in the chorus?
   (A) $\frac{4}{9}$ (B) $\frac{4}{5}$ (C) $\frac{5}{4}$ (D) $\frac{9}{4}$
   (E) It cannot be determined from the information given.

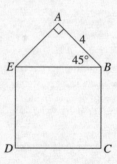

6. In the figure above, what is the perimeter of pentagon $ABCDE$, formed by right triangle EAB and square $BCDE$?
   (A) 20   (B) $8 + 12\sqrt{2}$ (C) $8 + 16\sqrt{2}$
   (D) $8 + 12\sqrt{3}$ (E) 32

7. If Wally's Widget Works is open exactly 20 days each month and produces 80 widgets each day it is open, how many years will it take to produce 96,000 widgets?
   (A) less than 5   (B) 5
   (C) more than 5 but less than 10   (D) 10
   (E) more than 10

GO ON TO THE NEXT PAGE

2   2 2 2 2 2 2 2 2 2   2

8. If $x^4 = 10$, what is x^6?

(A) $10\sqrt{10}$ (B) 100 (C) $100\sqrt{10}$

(D) 1000 (E) $1000\sqrt{10}$

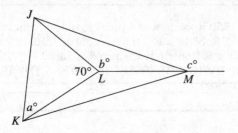

9. In the figure above, $JL = KL = LM$ and m$\angle JLK =$ 70°. This information is sufficient to determine the value of which of the following?

(A) a only   (B) b only   (C) a and b only
(D) b and c only   (E) a, b, and c

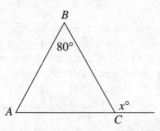

Note: Figure not drawn to scale

10. If, in the figure above, BC is the longest side of $\triangle ABC$ and x is an integer, what is the smallest possible value of x?

(A) 100   (B) 130   (C) 141   (D) 160
(E) 161

11. If $\dfrac{a+3}{5}$ is an integer, what is the remainder when a is divided by 5?

(A) 1   (B) 2   (C) 3   (D) 4
(E) It cannot be determined from the information given.

12. Brigitte's average (arithmetic mean) on her six math tests this marking period is 75. Fortunately for Brigitte, her teacher drops each student's lowest grade, and this raises Brigitte's average to 85. What was her lowest grade?

(A) 20   (B) 25   (C) 30   (D) 40   (E) 50

13. If m is an integer, which of the following could be true?

   I. $\dfrac{17}{m}$ is an even integer.

   II. $\dfrac{m}{17}$ is an even integer.

   III. $17m$ is a prime.
(A) I only   (B) II only   (C) III only
(D) I and II only   (E) II and III only

14. Max purchased some shares of stock at $10 per share. Six months later the stock was worth $20 per share. What was the percent increase in the value of Max's investment?
(A) 20%   (B) 50%   (C) 100%   (D) 200%
(E) The answer depends on the number of shares purchased.

15. Benjamin can type a full report in h hours. At this rate, how many reports can he type in m minutes?

(A) $\dfrac{mh}{60}$ (B) $\dfrac{60m}{h}$ (C) $\dfrac{m}{60h}$ (D) $\dfrac{60h}{m}$

(E) $\dfrac{h}{60m}$

16. The estate of a wealthy man was distributed as follows: 10% to his wife, 5% divided equally among his three children, 5% divided equally among his five grandchildren, and the balance to a charitable trust. If the trust received $1,000,000, how much did each grandchild inherit?
(A) $10,000   (B) $12,500   (C) $20,000
(D) $62,500   (E) $100,000

17. If A, B, C, and D lie on the same straight line, and if $AC = 2CD = 3BD$, what is the value of the ratio $\dfrac{BC}{CD}$?

(A) $\dfrac{1}{6}$ (B) $\dfrac{1}{3}$ (C) $\dfrac{1}{2}$ (D) $\dfrac{5}{3}$

(E) It cannot be determined from the information given.

18. A car going 40 miles per hour set out on an 80-mile trip at 9:00 A.M. Exactly 10 minutes later, a second car left from the same place and followed the same route. How fast, in miles per hour, was the second car going if it caught up with the first car at 10:30 A.M.?
(A) 45   (B) 50   (C) 53   (D) 55   (E) 60

GO ON TO THE NEXT PAGE ▷

19. In the figure above, what is the ratio of y to x?

(A) $\dfrac{1}{5}$ (B) $\dfrac{1}{4}$ (C) $\dfrac{1}{3}$ (D) $\dfrac{1}{2}$

(E) It cannot be determined from the information given.

Questions 20–21 refer to the following definition.
For any positive integer n, $\boxed{n}$ represents the sum of the integers from 1 to n. For example,
$\boxed{5} = 1 + 2 + 3 + 4 + 5 = 15$.

20. Which of the following is equal to $\boxed{10} - \boxed{9}$?

(A) $\boxed{1}$ (B) $\boxed{2}$ (C) $\boxed{3}$ (D) $\boxed{4}$ (E) $\boxed{5}$

---

21. If $\boxed{1000} = 50{,}500$ and $\boxed{10} = 55$, what is the value of $\boxed{1010}$?

(A) 50,555   (B) 55,555   (C) 60,500

(D) 60,555   (E) 65,555

---

22. At Harry's Hardware, a hammer costs d dollars and c cents. What is the cost, in dollars, of h hammers?

(A) $\dfrac{hd + c}{100}$ (B) $\dfrac{h(c + d)}{100}$ (C) $h(100c + d)$

(D) $\dfrac{100hd + hc}{100}$ (E) $100cdh$

23. A school's honor society has 100 members: 40 boys and 60 girls, of whom 30 are juniors and 70 are seniors. What is the smallest possible number of senior boys in the society?

(A) 0   (B) 5   (C) 10   (D) 15   (E) 20

---

24. In 1950 Roberto was 4 times as old as Juan. In 1955 Roberto was 3 times as old as Juan. In what year was Roberto twice as old as Juan?

(A) 1960   (B) 1965   (C) 1970   (D) 1975

(E) 1980

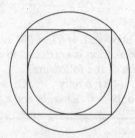

25. In the figure above, the small circle is inscribed in the square, which is inscribed in the large circle. What is the ratio of the area of the large circle to the area of the small circle?

(A) $\sqrt{2}:1$ (B) $\sqrt{3}:1$ (C) $2:1$ (D) $2\sqrt{2}:1$

(E) It cannot be determined from the information given.

YOU MAY GO BACK AND REVIEW THIS SECTION IN THE REMAINING TIME, BUT DO NOT WORK IN ANY OTHER SECTION UNTIL TOLD TO DO SO.

S T O P

3   3 3 3 3 3 3 3 3 3 3   3

Select the best answer to the following questions, then fill in the
appropriate space on your Answer Sheet.

Each of the following sentences contains one or two
blanks; these blanks indicate that a word or set of words
has been left out. Below the sentence are five words or
phrases, lettered A through E. Select the word or set of
words that best completes the sentence.

Example:

Fame is ----; today's rising star is all too soon
tomorrow's washed-up has-been.

(A) rewarding   (B) gradual
(C) essential   (D) spontaneous
(E) transitory

1. The civil rights movement did not emerge from
obscurity into national prominence overnight; on
the contrary, it captured the public's imagination
only ----.
(A) fruitlessly
(B) unimpeachably
(C) momentarily
(D) expeditiously
(E) gradually

2. Most of the settlements that grew up near the logging camps were ---- affairs, thrown together in a
hurry because people needed to live on the job.
(A) protracted   (B) unobtrusive   (C) nomadic
(D) ramshackle   (E) banal

3. Quick-breeding and immune to most pesticides,
cockroaches are so ---- that even a professional
exterminator may fail to ---- them.
(A) vulnerable...eradicate
(B) widespread...discern
(C) fragile...destroy
(D) hardy...eliminate
(E) numerous...detect

4. The seventeenth-century writer Mary Astell was a
rare phenomenon, a single woman who maintained
and even ---- a respectable reputation while earning
a living by her pen.
(A) eclipsed   (B) impaired   (C) decimated
(D) avoided   (E) enhanced

5. An optimistic supporter of the women's movement,
Kubota contends that recent ---- by Japanese
women in the business world are meaningful and
indicative of ---- opportunity to come.
(A) advances...diminished
(B) strides...greater
(C) innovations...marginal
(D) retreats...theoretical
(E) failures...hidden

6. The patient bore the pain ----, neither wincing nor
whimpering when the incision was made.
(A) histrionically   (B) stoically
(C) sardonically   (D) poorly
(E) marginally

7. The actor's stories of backstage feuds and rivalry
might be thought ---- were there not so many cor-
roborating anecdotes from other theatrical personalities.
(A) pantomime   (B) ambiguity
(C) approbation   (D) hyperbole
(E) vainglory

8. The ---- ambassador was but ---- linguist; yet he
insisted on speaking to foreign dignitaries in their
own tongues without resorting to a translator's aid.
(A) eminent...an indifferent
(B) visiting...a notable
(C) revered...a talented
(D) distinguished...a celebrated
(E) ranking...a sensitive

9. Nowadays life models—men and women who pose
in the nude for artists—seem curiously ----, relics
of a bygone age when art students labored amid
skeletons and anatomical charts, learning to draw
the human body as painstakingly as medical students learn to ---- it.
(A) anachronistic...sketch
(B) archaic...dissect
(C) contemporary...diagnose
(D) stereotyped...examine
(E) daring...cure

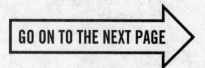

GO ON TO THE NEXT PAGE

10. Although Roman original contributions to government, jurisprudence, and engineering are commonly acknowledged, the artistic legacy of the Roman world continues to be judged widely as ---- the magnificent Greek traditions that preceded it.

(A) an improvement on
(B) an echo of
(C) a resolution of
(D) a precursor of
(E) a consummation of

The analogies questions present two words or phrases that are related in some way. Determine which A-through-E answer choice below has a relationship *most* similar to that of the original words or phrases.

Example:

YAWN:BOREDOM::   (A) dream:sleep
(B) anger:madness   (C) smile:amusement
(D) face:expression   (E) impatience:rebellion

Ⓐ Ⓑ ● Ⓓ Ⓔ

---

11. AUTOMOBILE:GASOLINE::

(A) train:caboose
(B) cow:milk
(C) airplane:propeller
(D) man:food
(E) disease:germs

12. COMPOSER:SYMPHONY::

(A) tragedian:playwright
(B) actor:comedy
(C) conductor:orchestra
(D) director:movie
(E) poet:sonnet

13. WEARISOME:REFRESHING::

(A) wrathful:irrational
(B) tedious:dull
(C) original:scintillating
(D) lengthy:brief
(E) truthful:courageous

14. FOLLOW:STALK::

(A) regret:rejoice
(B) look:spy
(C) execute:condemn
(D) lurk:hide
(E) beckon:gesture

15. DAMPEN:DRENCH ::

(A) glide:drift
(B) gambol:play
(C) simmer:boil
(D) stagnate:flow
(E) ignite:quench

16. ALLAY:PAIN::

(A) mollify:fright
(B) cancel:order
(C) arbitrate:dispute
(D) mitigate:punishment
(E) testify:court

17. EXERTION:FATIGUE::

(A) school:graduation
(B) exercise:atrophy
(C) sedation:tranquillity
(D) effort:results
(E) morality:lechery

18. ENMITY:FOE::

(A) civility:pacifist
(B) avarice:miser
(C) vanity:celebrity
(D) piety:atheist
(E) humility:friend

19. CARDIOLOGY:HEART::

(A) pathology:maps
(B) apology:sorrow
(C) tautology:education
(D) pharmacology:drugs
(E) orthography:religion

20. BACTERIUM:COLONY::

(A) microbe:disease
(B) fish:shoal
(C) stockade:settlement
(D) virus:immunization
(E) sovereign:kingdom

21. SHUN:PARIAH::

(A) hunt:predator
(B) transmute:alchemist
(C) beg:mendicant
(D) flatter:sycophant
(E) ridicule:butt

GO ON TO THE NEXT PAGE ➡

22. TURNCOAT:TREACHEROUS::
    (A) seamstress:generous
    (B) firebrand:mysterious
    (C) mountebank:serious
    (D) spoilsport:notorious
    (E) killjoy:lugubrious

23. MELLIFLUOUS:CACOPHONY::
    (A) vinegary:acidity
    (B) fragrant:noisomeness
    (C) sweet:euphony
    (D) somber:discord
    (E) ironic:sarcasm

Read the passage below, and then answer the questions that follow the passage. The correct response may be stated outright or merely suggested in the passage.

Questions 24–35 are based on the following passage.

Rock musicians often affect the role of social revolutionaries. The following passage is taken from an unpublished thesis on the potential of rock and roll music to contribute to political and social change.

It should be clear from the previous arguments that rock and roll cannot escape its role as a part of popular culture. One important part of that role
Line is its commercial nature. Rock and roll is "big
(5) corporation business in America and around the globe. As David De Voss has noted: 'Over fifty U.S. rock artists annually earn from $2 million to $6 million. At last count, thirty-five artists and fifteen additional groups make from three to
(10) seven times more than America's highest paid business executive.'"
Perhaps the most damning argument against rock and roll as a political catalyst is suggested by John Berger in an essay on advertising. Berger
(15) argues that "publicity turns consumption into a substitute for democracy. The choice of what one eats (or wears or drives) takes the place of significant political choice." To the extent that rock and roll is big business, and that it is marketed like
(20) other consumer goods, rock and roll also serves this role. Our freedom to choose the music we are sold may be distracting us from more important concerns. It is this tendency of rock and roll, fought against but also fulfilled by punk, that Julie
(25) Burchill and Tony Parsons describe in *The Boy Looked at Johnny: The Obituary of Rock and Roll.*
Never mind, kid, there'll soon be another washing-machine/spot-cream/rock-band on the market to solve all your problems and
(30) keep you quiet/off the street/distracted from the real enemy/content till the next pay-day. Anyhow, God Save Rock and Roll. . . it made you a consumer, a potential Moron. . . IT'S ONLY ROCK AND ROLL AND IT'S
(35) PLASTIC, PLASTIC, YES IT IS!!!!!!
This is a frustrating conclusion to reach, and it is especially frustrating for rock and roll artists who are dissatisfied with the political systems in which they live. If rock and roll's ability to pro-
(40) mote political change is hampered by its popularity, the factor that gives it the potential to reach significant numbers of people, to what extent can rock and roll artists act politically? Apart from charitable endeavors, with which rock and roll
(45) artists have been quite successful at raising money for various causes, the potential for significant political activity promoting change appears quite limited.
The history of rock and roll is filled with rock
(50) artists who abandoned, at least on vinyl, their political commitment. Bob Dylan, who, by introducing the explicit politics of folk music to rock and roll, can be credited with introducing the political rock and roll of the sixties, quickly aban-
(55) doned politics for more personal issue. John Lennon, who was perhaps more successful than any other rock and roll artist at getting political material to the popular audience, still had a hard time walking the line between being overtly polit-
(60) ical but unpopular and being apolitical and extremely popular. In 1969 "Give Peace a Chance" reached number fourteen on the Billboard singles charts. 1971 saw "Power to the People" at number eleven. But the apolitical
(65) "Instant Karma" reached number three on the charts one year earlier. "Imagine," which mixed personal and political concerns, also reached number three one year later. Lennon's most political album, *Some Time in New York City*, pro-
(70) duced no hits. His biggest hits, "Whatever Gets You Through the Night" and "Starting Over," which both reached number one on the charts, are apolitical. Jon Wiener, in his biography of Lennon, argues that on "Whatever Gets You
(75) Through the Night," "it seemed like John was turning himself into Paul, the person without political values, who put out Number One songs and who managed to sleep soundly. Maybe that's

GO ON TO THE NEXT PAGE

why John (Lennon) told Elton John that 'What-
(80) ever Gets You Through the Night' was 'one of
my least favorites.'" When, after leaving music
for five years, Lennon returned in 1980 with the
best-selling *Double Fantasy* album, the subject of
his writing was "caring, sharing, and being a
(85) whole person."

    The politically motivated rock and roll artist's
other option is to maintain his political commitment without fooling himself as to the ultimate
impact his work will have. If his music is not
(90) doomed to obscurity by the challenge it presents
to its listeners the artist is lucky. But even such
luck can do nothing to protect his work from the
misinterpretation it will be subjected to once it is
popular. Tom Greene of the Mekons expresses
(95) the frustration such artists feel when he says,
"You just throw your hands up in horror and try
and . . . I don't know. I mean, what can you do?
How can you possibly avoid being a part of the
power relations that exist?" The artist's challenge
(100) is to *try* to communicate with his audience. But
he can only take responsibility for his own intentions. Ultimately, it is the popular audience that
must take responsibility for what it does with the
artist's work. The rock and roll artist cannot cause
(105) political change. But, if he is very lucky, the popular audience might let him contribute to the
change it makes.

24. De Voss's comparison of the salaries of rock stars
and corporate executives (lines 8–11) is cited primarily in order to

(A) express the author's familiarity with current
pay scales
(B) argue in favor of higher pay for musical artists
(C) refute the assertion that rock and roll stars are
underpaid
(D) support the view that rock and roll is a major
industry
(E) indicate the lack of limits on the wages of popular stars

25. The word "consumption" in line 15 means

(A) supposition
(B) beginning a task
(C) using up goods
(D) advertising a product
(E) culmination

26. In the quotation cited in lines 27–35, Burchill and
Parsons most likely run the words "washing-
machine/spot-cream/rock-band" together to indicate that

(A) to the consumer they are all commodities
(B) they are products with universal appeal

(C) advertisers need to market them differently
(D) rock music eliminates conventional distinctions
(E) they are equally necessary parts of modern
society

27. The word "plastic" in the Burchill and Parsons
quotation (line 35) is being used

(A) lyrically
(B) spontaneously
(C) metaphorically
(D) affirmatively
(E) skeptically

28. Their comments in lines 32–33 suggest that
Burchill and Parsons primarily regard consumers as

(A) invariably dimwitted
(B) markedly ambivalent
(C) compulsively spendthrift
(D) unfamiliar with commerce
(E) vulnerable to manipulation

29. The author's comments about Bob Dylan (lines
51–55) chiefly suggest that

(A) Dylan readily abandoned political rock and roll
for folk music
(B) folk music gave voice to political concerns
long before rock and roll music did
(C) rock and roll swiftly replaced folk music in the
public's affections
(D) Dylan lacked the necessary skills to convey his
political message musically
(E) Dylan betrayed his fans' faith in him by turning away from political commentary

30. Wiener's statement quoted in lines 75–78 suggests
that

(A) John had no desire to imitate more successful
performers
(B) John was unable to write Number One songs
without help from Paul
(C) because Paul lacked political values, he wrote
fewer Number One songs than John did
(D) as an apolitical performer, Paul suffered less
strain than John did
(E) John disliked "Whatever Gets You Through
the Night" because it had been composed by
Paul

GO ON TO THE NEXT PAGE

3 3 3 3 3 3 3 3 3 3 3 **3**

31. In lines 70–85, "Starting Over" and the *Double Fantasy* album are presented as examples of

   (A) bold applications of John's radical philosophy
   (B) overtly political recordings without general appeal
   (C) profitable successes lacking political content
   (D) uninspired and unpopular rock and roll records
   (E) unusual recordings that effected widespread change

32. The word "maintain" in line 87 means

   (A) repair   (B) contend   (C) subsidize
    (D) brace   (E) keep

33. As quoted in lines 96–99, Tom Greene of the Mekons feels particularly frustrated because

   (A) his work has lost its initial popularity
   (B) he cannot escape involvement in the power structure
   (C) his original commitment to political change has diminished
   (D) he lacks the vocabulary to make coherent political statements
   (E) he is horrified by the price he must pay for political success

34. The author attributes the success of the politically motivated rock and roll artist to

   (A) political influence
   (B) challenging material
   (C) good fortune
   (D) personal contacts
   (E) textual misinterpretation

35. In the last paragraph, the author concludes that the rock and roll artist's contribution to political change is

   (A) immediate
   (B) decisive
   (C) indirect
   (D) irresponsible
   (E) blatant

YOU MAY GO BACK AND REVIEW THIS SECTION IN THE REMAINING TIME, BUT DO NOT WORK IN ANY OTHER SECTION UNTIL TOLD TO DO SO.   **S T O P**

4   4 4 4 4 4 4 4 4 4 4   4

SECTION 4

Time—30 Minutes
25 Questions

You have 30 minutes to answer the 15 Quantitative Comparison questions and 10 Student-Produced Response questions in this section. You may use any blank space on the page for your work.

Notes:

- You may use a calculator whenever you feel it will be helpful.
- Use the diagrams provided to help you solve the problems. Unless you see the words "Note: Figure not drawn to scale" under a diagram, it has been drawn as accurately as possible. Unless it is stated that a figure is three-dimensional, you may assume it lies in a plane.

Reference Information

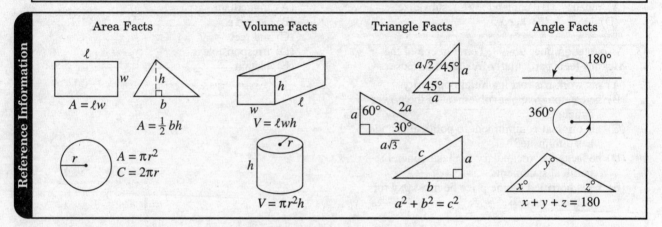

Area Facts

$A = \ell w$

$A = \frac{1}{2}bh$

$A = \pi r^2$
$C = 2\pi r$

Volume Facts

$V = \ell w h$

$V = \pi r^2 h$

Triangle Facts

$a^2 + b^2 = c^2$

Angle Facts

$x + y + z = 180$

Directions for Quantitative Comparison Questions

In each of questions 1–15, two quantities appear in boxes: one in Column A and one in Column B. You must compare them. The correct answer to a question is

   A if the quantity in Column A is greater;
   B if the quantity in Column B is greater;
   C if the two quantities are equal;
   D if it is impossible to determine which quantity is greater.

Notes:

- *The correct answer is never E.*
- Sometimes information about one or both of the quantities is centered above the two boxes.
- If the same symbol appears in both columns, it represents the same thing each time.
- All variables represent real numbers.

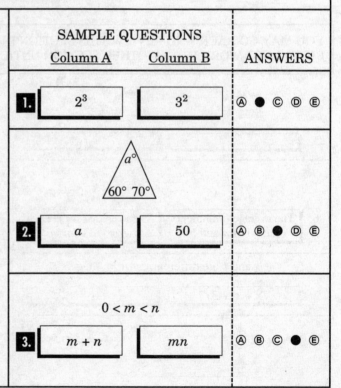

SAMPLE QUESTIONS

Column A	Column B	ANSWERS
1. 2^3	3^2	Ⓐ ● Ⓒ Ⓓ Ⓔ
2. a	50	Ⓐ Ⓑ ● Ⓓ Ⓔ
3. $m + n$	mn	Ⓐ Ⓑ Ⓒ ● Ⓔ

$0 < m < n$

GO ON TO THE NEXT PAGE

4   4 4 4 4 4 4 4 4 4 4   4

SUMMARY DIRECTIONS FOR QUANTITATIVE COMPARISON QUESTIONS

<u>Answer</u>: A if the quantity in Column A is greater;
B if the quantity in Column B is greater;
C if the two quantities are equal;
D if it is impossible to determine which quantity is greater.

Column A	Column B

1. The sum of the positive divisors of 19 | The product of the positive divisors of 19

m and *n* are positive integers.
$$mn = 25$$

2. m | n

a and *b* are primes.
$$a + b = 12$$

3. b | 8

$$a < b < c$$
$$abc = 0$$

4. a | 0

$x°$ $x°$
$y°$
$y°$
$y°$
$60°$ $y°$

Note: Figure not drawn to scale

5. y | 20

$$\frac{a+b}{c+d} = 1$$

6. The average (arithmetic mean) of a and b | The average (arithmetic mean) of c and d

x and *y* are different nonzero integers.

7. $(x + y + 3)^2$ | $(x + y - 3)^2$

$b°$
$a°$ $c°$

8. $a + b - c$ | 0

Column A	Column B

$$a < 0$$

9. $(2a)^3$ | $2a^3$

x people require 10 days to complete a job. Working at the same rate, $x - 5$ people require A days.

10. A | 20

$$x^5 = \frac{13}{17}$$

11. x | $\left(\frac{13}{17}\right)^5$

12. The total surface area of a cube whose sides are each s | The total surface area of a rectangular solid whose length, width, and height are $s - 1$, s, and $s + 1$, respectively

$$xy \neq 0$$

13. $(x + y)^2 - (x^2 - y^2)$ | $2xy$

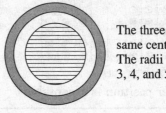

The three circles have the same center.
The radii of the circles are 3, 4, and 5.

14. The area of the shaded region | The area of the striped region

A wooden cube whose edges are 3 inches is painted red. The cube is then cut into 27 cubes whose edges are 1 inch.

15. The total surface area of all of the unpainted faces | 100 square inches

GO ON TO THE NEXT PAGE

4   4   4   4   4   4   4   4   4   4   4   4

Directions for Student-Produced Response Questions (Grid-ins)

In questions 16–25, first solve the problem, and then enter your answer on the grid provided on the answer sheet. The instructions for entering your answers are as follows:
- First, write your answer in the boxes at the top of the grid.
- Second, grid your answer in the columns below the boxes.
- Use the fraction bar in the first row or the decimal point in the second row to enter fractions and decimal answers.

- Grid only one space in each column.
- Entering the answer in the boxes is recommended as an aid in gridding, but is not required.
- The machine scoring your exam can read only what you grid, so you **must grid in your answers correctly to get credit.**
- If a question has more than one correct answer, grid in only one of them.
- The grid does not have a minus sign, so no answer can be negative.
- A mixed number *must* be converted to an improper fraction or a decimal before it is gridded. Enter $1\frac{1}{4}$ as 5/4 or 1.25; the machine will interpret 1 1/4 as $\frac{11}{4}$ and mark it wrong.
- **All decimals must be entered as accurately as possible.** Here are the three acceptable ways of gridding

$$\frac{3}{11} = 0.272727\ldots$$

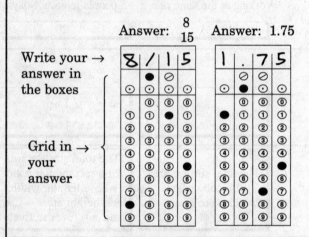

Answer: $\frac{8}{15}$ Answer: 1.75

Write your → answer in the boxes

Grid in → your answer

Answer: 100

Either position is acceptable

- Note that rounding to .273 is acceptable, because you are using the full grid, but you would receive **no credit** for .3 or .27, because they are less accurate.

---

16. If $a = 3$ and $b = -3$, what is the value of $3a - 2b$?

17. If $a:b:c = 6:7:11$, what is the value of $c - a$?

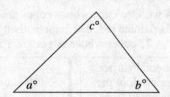

18. What is the perimeter of a right triangle if the length of its two smallest sides are 15 and 36?

19. There are 250 people on a line outside a theater. If Jack is the 25th person from the front, and Jill is the 125th person from the front, how many people are between Jack and Jill?

GO ON TO THE NEXT PAGE

4   4   4   4   4   4   4   4   4   4   4   **4**

20. Each integer from 1 to 50 whose units digit is a 7 is written on a separate slip of paper. If the slips are placed in a box and one is picked at random, what is the probability that the number picked is prime?

21. Five people shared a prize of $100. Each one received a whole number of dollars, and no two people received the same amount. If the largest share was $30 and the smallest share was $15, what is the most money that the person with the third largest share could have received?

22. Jessica created a sequence of five numbers. She chose a number for the first term and got each successive term by using the following rule: alternately add 6 to the preceding term and double the preceding term. The second term of Jessica's sequence was 6 more than the first, the third term was double the second, the fourth term was 6 more than the third, and the fifth term was double the fourth. If the fifth number was 1996, what number did Jessica choose for the first term?

23. The sum of three different positive integers is 12. Let g be the greatest possible product of the three integers, and let ℓ be the least possible product of the integers. What is the value of $g - \ell$?

24. In a right triangle, $\frac{1}{4}$ of the length of the longer leg is equal to $\frac{3}{5}$ of the length of the shorter leg. What is the ratio of the length of the hypotenuse to the length of the shorter leg?

25. How many times between midnight and noon of the same day will the minute hand and the hour hand of a clock form a right angle?

YOU MAY GO BACK AND REVIEW THIS SECTION IN THE REMAINING TIME, BUT DO NOT WORK IN ANY OTHER SECTION UNTIL TOLD TO DO SO.   **S T O P**

5

The questions that follow the two passages in this section relate to the content of both, and to their relationship. The correct response may be stated outright in the passages or merely suggested.

Questions 1–13 are based on the following passages.

The following passages are taken from memoirs by two young American writers, each of whom records his reaction to the prospect of visiting his ancestral homeland.

Passage 1

Thomas Wolfe said that going home again is like stepping into a river. You cannot step into the same river twice; you cannot go home again.
Line After a very long time away, you will not find the
(5) same home you left behind. It will be different, and so will you. It is quite possible that home will not be home at all, meaningless except for its sentimental place in your heart. At best it will point the long way back to where you started, its value
(10) lying in how it helped to shape you and in the part of home you have carried away.

Alex Haley went to Africa in the mid-sixties. Somehow he had managed to trace his roots back to a little village called Juffure, upriver from
(15) Banjul in the forests of The Gambia. It was the same village from which his ancestors had been stolen and forced into slavery. In some way Haley must have felt he was returning home: a flood of emotions, an awakening of the memories hidden
(20) in his genes.

Those were the two extremes between which I was trapped. I could not go home again, yet here I was. Africa was so long ago the land of my ancestors that it held for me only a symbolic sig-
(25) nificance. Yet there was enough to remind me that what I carry as a human being has come in part from Africa. I did not feel African, but was beginning to feel not wholly American anymore either. I felt like an orphan, a waif without a
(30) home.

I was not trying to find the village that had once been home to my people, nor would I stand and talk to people who could claim to be my relatives, as Haley had done. The thought of running
(35) into someone who looked like a relative terrified me, for that would have been too concrete, too much proof. My Africanism was abstract and I wanted it to remain so. I did not need to hear the names of my ancient ancestors or know what they
(40) looked like. I had seen the ways they loved their children in the love of my father. I would see

their faces and their smiles one day in the eyes of my children.

Haley found what he was seeking. I hardly
(45) knew what I was looking for, except perhaps to know where home once was, to know how much of me is really me, how much of being black has been carried out of Africa.

Passage 2

I am a *Sansei*, a third-generation Japanese-
(50) American. In 1984, through luck and through some skills as a poet, I traveled to Japan. My reasons for going were not very clear.

At the time, I'd been working as an arts administrator in the Writers-in-the-Schools pro-
(55) gram, sending other writers to grade schools and high schools throughout Minnesota. It wasn't taxing, but it didn't provide the long stretches needed to plunge into my own work. I had applied for a U.S./Japan Creative Artist Exchange Fellowship
(60) mainly because I wanted time to write.

Japan? That was where my grandparents came from; it didn't have much to do with my present life.

For me Japan was cheap baseballs, Godzilla,
(65) weird sci-fi movies like *Star Man,* where you could see the strings that pulled him above his enemies, flying in front of a backdrop so poorly made even I, at eight, was conscious of the fakery. Then there were the endless hordes storming G.I.'s in
(70) war movies. Before the television set, wearing my ever-present Cubs cap, I crouched near the sofa, saw the enemy surrounding me. I shouted to my men, hurled a grenade. I fired my gun. And the Japanese soldiers fell before me, one by one.
(75) So, when I did win the fellowship, I felt I was going not as an ardent pilgrim, longing to return to the land of his grandparents, but more like a contestant on a quiz show who finds himself winning a trip to Bali or the Bahamas. Of course, I
(80) was pleased about the stipend, the plane fare for me and my wife, and the payments for Japanese lessons, both before the trip and during my stay. I was also excited that I had beat out several

GO ON TO THE NEXT PAGE ➡

hundred candidates in literature and other fields
(85) for one of the six spots. But part of me wished the
prize was Paris, not Tokyo. I would have preferred French bread and Brie over *sashimi* and
rice, Baudelaire and Proust over Basho and
Kawabata, structuralism and Barthes over Zen
(90) and D. T. Suzuki.
      This contradiction remained. Much of my life I
had insisted on my Americanness, had shunned
most connections with Japan and felt proud I
knew no Japanese; yet I *was* going to Japan as a
(95) poet, and my Japanese ancestry was there in my
poems—my grandfather, the relocation camps,
the *hibakusha* (victims of the atomic bomb), a
picnic of *Nisei* (second-generation Japanese-
Americans), my uncle who fought in the 442nd.
(100) True, the poems were written in blank verse,
rather than *haiku*, *tanka*, or *haibun*. But perhaps
it's a bit disingenuous to say that I had no longing
to go to Japan; it was obvious my imagination
had been traveling there for years, unconsciously
(105) swimming the Pacific, against the tide of my family's emigration, my parents' desire, after the
internment camps, to forget the past.

1. Wolfe's comment referred to in lines 1–6 represents

(A) a digression from the author's thesis
(B) an understatement of the situation
(C) a refutation of the author's central argument
(D) a figurative expression of the author's point
(E) an example of the scientific method

2. Judging from lines 8–11, the most positive outcome of your attempting to go home again would
be for you to

(A) find the one place you genuinely belong
(B) recognize the impossibility of the task
(C) grasp how your origins have formed you
(D) reenter the world of your ancestors
(E) decide to stay away for shorter periods of time

3. Throughout Passage 1, the author primarily seeks
to convey

(A) his resemblance to his ancestors
(B) his ambivalence about his journey
(C) the difficulties of traveling in a foreign country
(D) his need to deny his American origins
(E) the depth of his desire to track down his roots

4. The statement "I could not go home again, yet here
I was" (lines 22–23) represents

(A) a paradox
(B) a prevarication
(C) an interruption
(D) an analogy
(E) a fallacy

5. The word "held" in line 24 means

(A) grasped
(B) believed
(C) absorbed
(D) accommodated
(E) possessed

6. By "my own work" (line 58), the author of Passage
2 refers to

(A) seeking his ancestral roots
(B) teaching in high school
(C) writing a travel narrative
(D) creating poetry
(E) directing art programs

7. The word "taxing" in lines 56–57 means

(A) imposing
(B) obliging
(C) demanding
(D) accusatory
(E) costly

8. The author's purpose in describing the war movie
incident (lines 70–74) most likely is to

(A) indicate the depth of his hatred for the
Japanese
(B) show the extent of his self-identification as an
American
(C) demonstrate the superiority of American films
to their Japanese counterparts
(D) explore the range of his interest in contempo-
rary art forms
(E) explain why he had a particular urge to travel
to Japan

9. By "a trip to Bali or the Bahamas" (line 79) the
author wishes to convey

(A) his love for these particular vacation sites
(B) the impression that he has traveled to these
places before
(C) his preference for any destination other than
Japan
(D) his sense of Japan as just another exotic desti-
nation
(E) the unlikelihood of his ever winning a second
trip

GO ON TO THE NEXT PAGE

5

10. The author's attitude toward winning the fellow-ship can best be described as one of

(A) graceful acquiescence
(B) wholehearted enthusiasm
(C) unfeigned gratitude
(D) frank dismay
(E) marked ambivalence

11. The author concludes Passage 2 with

(A) a rhetorical question
(B) a eulogy
(C) an epitaph
(D) an extended metaphor
(E) a literary allusion

12. Both passages are primarily concerned with the subject of

(A) ethnic identity
(B) individual autonomy
(C) ancestor worship
(D) racial purity
(E) genealogical research

13. Which of the following statements from Passage 1 does not have a parallel idea conveyed in Passage 2?

(A) Africa "held for me only a symbolic signifi-cance" (lines 24–25)
(B) "I did not feel African" (line 27)
(C) "I felt like an orphan, a waif without a home" (lines 29–30)
(D) "I hardly knew what I was looking for" (lines 44–45)
(E) "an awakening of the memories hidden in his genes" (lines 19–20)

YOU MAY GO BACK AND REVIEW THIS SECTION IN THE REMAINING TIME, BUT DO NOT WORK IN ANY OTHER SECTION UNTIL TOLD TO DO SO.   **S T O P**

6   6 6 6 6 6 6 6 6 6   6

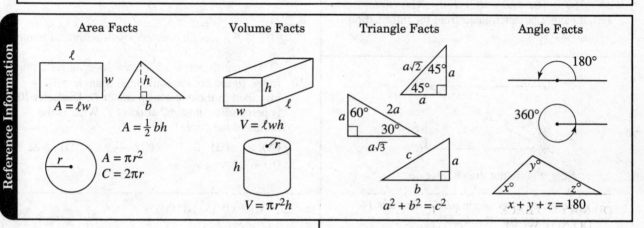

SECTION 6

Time—15 Minutes
  10 Questions

Notes:

For each problem in this section determine which of the five choices is correct and blacken in that choice on your answer sheet. You may use any blank space on the page for your work.

- You may use a calculator whenever you feel it will be helpful.
- Use the diagrams provided to help you solve the problems. Unless you see the words "Note: Figure not drawn to scale" under a diagram, it has been drawn as accurately as possible. Unless it is stated that a figure is three-dimensional, you may assume it lies in a plane.

Reference Information

Area Facts

$A = \ell w$

$A = \frac{1}{2} bh$

$A = \pi r^2$
$C = 2\pi r$

Volume Facts

$V = \ell wh$

$V = \pi r^2 h$

Triangle Facts

$a^2 + b^2 = c^2$

Angle Facts

$x + y + z = 180$

---

1. If $3x = 36$, then $\dfrac{x}{3} =$
   (A) 3   (B) 4   (C) 6   (D) 9   (E) 12

2. If $a\left(\dfrac{7}{11}\right) = \left(\dfrac{7}{11}\right)b$, then $\dfrac{a}{b} =$

   (A) $\dfrac{49}{121}$ (B) $\dfrac{7}{11}$ (C) 1

   (D) $\dfrac{11}{7}$ (E) $\dfrac{121}{49}$

3. The weights, in kilograms, of five students are 48, 56, 61, 52, and 57. If 1 kilogram = 2.2 pounds, how many of the students weigh over 120 pounds?
   (A) 1   (B) 2   (C) 3   (D) 4   (E) 5

4. From 1980 to 1990, the value of a share of stock of XYZ Corporation doubled every year. If in 1990 a share of the stock was worth $80, in what year was it worth $10?
   (A) 1984   (B) 1985   (C) 1986   (D) 1987
   (E) 1988

5. The average (arithmetic mean) of two numbers is a. If one of the numbers is 10, what is the other?
   (A) $2a + 10$ (B) $2a - 10$ (C) $2(a - 10)$

   (D) $\dfrac{10 + a}{2}$ (E) $\dfrac{10 - a}{2}$

6. The chart below shows the value of an investment on January 1 of each year from 1990 to 1995. During which year was the percent increase in the value of the investment the greatest?

Year	Value
1990	$150
1991	$250
1992	$450
1993	$750
1994	$1200
1995	$1800

   (A) 1990   (B) 1991   (C) 1992   (D) 1993
   (E) 1994

GO ON TO THE NEXT PAGE

6   6   6   6   6   6   6   6   6   6   6

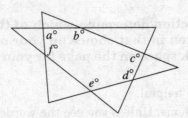

7. In the figure above, what is the value of
$a + b + c + d + e + f$?
(A) 360   (B) 540   (C) 720   (D) 900
(E) It cannot be determined from the information given.

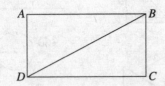

Note: Figure not drawn to scale

8. If the perimeter of rectangle $ABCD$ above is 14, what is the perimeter of $\triangle BCD$?

(A) 7   (B) 12   (C) $7 + \sqrt{29}$ (D) $7 + \sqrt{37}$
(E) It cannot be determined from the information given.

9. Jordan has taken five math tests so far this semester. If he gets a 70 on his next test, that grade will lower his test average (arithmetic mean) by 4 points. What is his average now?
(A) 74   (B) 85   (C) 90   (D) 94   (E) 95

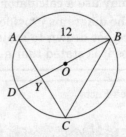

10. In the figure above, equilateral triangle ABC is inscribed in the circle with center O. Diameter BD is perpendicular to AC at point Y. What is the radius of the circle?

(A) 6   (B) $2\sqrt{3}$ (C) $4\sqrt{3}$ (D) $6\sqrt{2}$
(E) $6\sqrt{3}$

YOU MAY GO BACK AND REVIEW THIS SECTION IN THE REMAINING TIME, BUT DO NOT WORK IN ANY OTHER SECTION UNTIL TOLD TO DO SO.   **S T O P**

Answer Key

Note: The letters in brackets following the Mathematical Reasoning answers refer to the sections of Chapter 12 in which you can find the information you need to answer the questions. For example, **1. C [E]**, means that the answer to question 1 is C, and that the solution requires information found in Section 12–E: Averages.

Section 1   Verbal Reasoning

1.	C	7.	A	13.	C	19.	A	25.	D
2.	D	8.	E	14.	C	20.	D	26.	C
3.	D	9.	C	15.	D	21.	B	27.	E
4.	A	10.	B	16.	E	22.	C	28.	D
5.	A	11.	C	17.	B	23.	B	29.	E
6.	B	12.	B	18.	D	24.	C	30.	E

Section 2   Mathematical Reasoning

1.	D [G]	6.	B [J, K]	11.	B [A, G]	16.	B [C]	21.	D [A, P]
2.	B [J]	7.	B [A]	12.	B [E]	17.	E [D, I]	22.	D [D]
3.	D [G]	8.	A [A]	13.	E [A]	18.	A [D, H]	23.	C [O]
4.	D [G]	9.	A [J]	14.	C [C]	19.	B [I, J]	24.	C [H]
5.	B [D]	10.	E [J]	15.	C [D]	20.	D [A, P]	25.	C [J, L]

Section 3   Verbal Reasoning

1.	E	8.	A	15.	C	22.	E	29.	B
2.	D	9.	B	16.	D	23.	B	30.	D
3.	D	10.	B	17.	C	24.	D	31.	C
4.	E	11.	D	18.	B	25.	C	32.	E
5.	B	12.	E	19.	D	26.	A	33.	B
6.	B	13.	D	20.	B	27.	C	34.	C
7.	D	14.	B	21.	E	28.	E	35.	C

Section 4   Mathematical Reasoning

Quantitative Comparison Questions

1.	A [A]	4.	D [A]	7.	D [F]	10.	D [D]	13.	A [F]
2.	D [A]	5.	D [J]	8.	C [J]	11.	A [A]	14.	C [L]
3.	B [A]	6.	C [E]	9.	B [A]	12.	A [M]	15.	A [M]

Grid-in Questions

16.
[A]   1 5

17.
[D, J]   3 7 . 5

18.
[J]   9 0

19.
[O]   9 9

20.
[A, O]   4 / 5

or 0.8

21. [A, P] `1 9`
22. [F, P] `4 9 0`
23. [A] `4 2`
24. [D, J] `1 3 / 5` *or* 2.6
25. [P, I] `2 2`

Section 5   Verbal Reasoning

1. **D**	4. **A**	7. **C**	10. **E**	13. **C**
2. **C**	5. **E**	8. **B**	11. **D**	
3. **B**	6. **D**	9. **D**	12. **A**	

Section 6   Mathematical Reasoning

1. **B [G]**	3. **C [D]**	5. **B [E, G]**	7. **C [K]**	9. **D [E, G]**
2. **C [G]**	4. **D [B]**	6. **B [Q, C]**	8. **E [J, K]**	10. **C [L, J]**

Calculate Your Raw Score

Verbal Reasoning

Section 1 $\dfrac{}{\text{number correct}} - \dfrac{1}{4}\left(\dfrac{}{\text{number incorrect}}\right) = \underline{}$ (A)

Section 3 $\dfrac{}{\text{number correct}} - \dfrac{1}{4}\left(\dfrac{}{\text{number incorrect}}\right) = \underline{}$ (B)

Section 5 $\dfrac{}{\text{number correct}} - \dfrac{1}{4}\left(\dfrac{}{\text{number incorrect}}\right) = \underline{}$ (C)

Raw Verbal Reasoning Score = (A) + (B) + (C) = $\underline{}$

Mathematical Reasoning

Section 2 $\dfrac{}{\text{number correct}} - \dfrac{1}{4}\left(\dfrac{}{\text{number incorrect}}\right) = \underline{}$ (D)

Section 4
Part I
(1–15) $\dfrac{}{\text{number correct}} - \dfrac{1}{3}\left(\dfrac{}{\text{number incorrect}}\right) = \underline{}$ (E)

Part II
(16–25) $\dfrac{}{\text{number correct}} = \underline{}$ (F)

Section 6 $\dfrac{}{\text{number correct}} - \dfrac{1}{4}\left(\dfrac{}{\text{number incorrect}}\right) = \underline{}$ (G)

Raw Mathematical Reasoning Score = (D) + (E) + (F) + (G) = $\underline{}$

Evaluate Your Performance

	Verbal Reasoning	**Mathematical Reasoning**
Superior	67–78	51–60
Very Good	60–66	45–50
Good	52–59	40–44
Satisfactory	44–51	35–39
Average	36–43	30–34
Needs Further Study	29–35	25–29
Needs Intensive Study	21–28	20–24
Inadequate	0–20	0–19

Identify Your Weaknesses

Verbal Reasoning

Question Type	Question Numbers			Chapter to Study
	Section 1	**Section 3**	**Section 5**	
Sentence Completion	1, 2, 3, 4, 5, 6, 7, 8, 9	1, 2, 3, 4, 5, 6, 7, 8, 9, 10		Chapter 4
Analogy	10, 11, 12, 13, 14, 15	11, 12, 13, 14, 15, 16, 17, 18, 19, 20, 21, 22, 23		Chapter 5
Reading Comprehension	16, 17, 18, 19, 20, 21, 22, 23, 24, 25, 26, 27, 28, 29, 30	24, 25, 26, 27, 28, 29, 30	1, 2, 3, 4, 5, 6, 7, 8, 9, 10, 11, 12, 13	Chapter 6

Identify Your Weaknesses

Mathematical Reasoning

Skill Area	Question Numbers			Pages to Study
	Section 2	**Section 4**	**Section 6**	
Basics of Arithmetic	7, 8, 11, 13, 20, 21	1, 2, 3, 4, 9, 11, 16, 20, 21, 23		331–338
Fractions and Decimals	13		4	344–352
Percents	14, 25		6	358–361
Ratios	5, 15, 17, 18, 22	10, 17, 24	3	366–370
Averages	12	6	5, 9	376–378
Polynomials		7, 13, 22		383–386
Equations and Inequalities	1, 3, 4, 11		1, 2, 5, 9	389–394
Word Problems	18, 24			399–402
Lines and Angles	17, 19	25		407–410
Triangles	2, 6, 9, 10, 16, 19	5, 8, 17, 18, 24	8, 10	414–418
Quadrilaterals	6		7, 8	425–428
Circles	16	14	10	432–435
Solid Geometry		12, 15		440–442
Coordinate Geometry				446–448
Counting and Probability	23	19, 20		452–456
Logical Reasoning	20, 21	21, 22, 25		462–464
Data Interpretation			6	468–471

Answer Explanations

Section 1   Verbal Reasoning

1. **C.** To uncover buried ruins is to *excavate* them. Notice the use of the comma to set off the phrase that defines the missing word.
(Definition)

2. **D.** Puritans (members of a religious group following a pure standard of morality) would be offended by *lewd* (lecherous, obscene) material and would fear it might corrupt theatergoers.
(Argument Pattern)

3. **D.** *Rescind* means to cancel or withdraw. The lawmakers were so angered by the governor's enactment of martial law that they refused to work until it was canceled.
The phrase "the last straw" refers to the straw that broke the camel's back. *Because* the governor had exceeded his bounds, the lawmakers essentially went on strike.
(Cause and Effect Pattern)

4. **A.** *Malingering* means pretending illness to avoid duty. Faced with an *arduous* or hard campaign, a private might well try to get out of doing the work.
(Argument Pattern)

5. **A.** What was once a minor problem is now a major cause of death; what was formerly *negligible* (insignificant; minor and thus of no consequence) has become the chief *cause* of cancer-related deaths. Note how the two phrases set off by commas ("formerly..."; "once...") balance one another and are similar in meaning. Remember, in double-blank sentences, go through the answer choices, testing the *first* words in each choice and eliminating those that don't fit.
(Argument Pattern)

6. **B.** The columnist was almost *reverential* (worshipful) in what he wrote about those he liked, but he savagely attacked those he disliked. "Even" here serves as an intensifier.
Acrimonious (stinging or bitter in nature) is a stronger word than *unpleasant*. It emphasizes how *very* unpleasant the columnist could become.
(Contrast Signal)

7. **A.** *Propitious* means favorable. It would be sensible to wait for a favorable moment to reveal plans.
Remember, before you look at the choices, read the sentence and think of a word that makes sense.
Likely Words: appropriate, fitting, favorable.
(Examples)

8. **E.** Wemmick's private kindness is contrasted with his *public* harshness or *ruthlessness*. Note here the use of "even" as an intensifier: to be *ruthless* or relentless is more blameworthy then merely to be *uncompassionate* or hardhearted.
(Contrast Pattern)

9. **C.** Metternich hires ships' captains to buy books to add to his growing, *burgeoning* collection. This is an example of his great passion for books or *bibliomania*.
Word Parts Clue: *Biblio-* means book; *mania* means passion or excessive enthusiasm.
(Example)

10. **B.** The *barber* uses his *shears* (scissors) to trim hair; the *dentist* uses his *drill* to bore holes in teeth.
(Worker and Tool)

11. **C.** A *puck* (a black rubber disk) is struck by a stick in playing *hockey*. A *ball* is struck by a club in playing *golf*.
Remember, if more than one answer appears to fit the relationship in your sentence, look for a narrower approach. "A puck is used in playing hockey" is too broad a test sentence.
(Function)

12. **B.** A *hillock* is defined as a little hill, a natural elevation of land smaller than a *mountain*. A *pond* is a body of water smaller than a *lake*.
(Relative Size)

13. **C.** A *mentor* (wise and trusted counselor) provides one with *counsel* (advice). A *bodyguard* provides one with *protection*.
(Definition)

14. **C.** *Chauvinism* is excessive patriotism or extreme love of *country*. *Gluttony* is extreme desire for *food*.
(Definition)

15. **D.** Someone *sedulous* (industrious) exhibits *diligence*; likewise someone *ingenuous* (innocent; unsophisticated) exhibits *naivete* (lack of sophistication).
(Synonym Variant)

16. **E.** You can arrive at the correct answer by the process of elimination.
Statement I is false. While sea action plays a part in erosion, the author does not say it is the most important factor in erosion.
Therefore, you can eliminate Choices A and D.
Statement II is true. The first purely synthetic oil "has yet to be produced." Therefore, you can eliminate Choice C.
Statement III is true. New rock is born or created "through the effects of gravity."
Therefore, you can eliminate Choice B.
Only Choice E is left. It is the correct answer.

17. B.   The author mentions the Grand Canyon in the context of speaking of rivers as "immensely powerful destructive agencies." The dramatic canyon illustrates the *devastating impact* a river can have.

18. D.   In the last paragraph the author states that "the cause of the metamorphosis" of decayed vegetation and dead aquatic life into oil is not known. We lack full understanding of the process by which oil is created; therefore, our understanding is *deficient*.
Choice C is incorrect. Our knowledge is not *erroneous* or false; it is simply incomplete.

19. A.   The last sentence states that oil is always found "on the sites of ancient seas and lakes."

20. D.   The author describes several processes (erosion, rock formation, oil formation). He states the possibility that a chemical catalyst is involved in oil formation. He cites the Grand Canyon as an example of what a river can do to the land. He mentions the limitation of our ability to produce oil synthetically. However, he never proposes a solution to any problem.

21. B.   The term *reaches* here refers to the vast, *unbroken stretches* of time it takes for the mountains to erode and, out of their dust, for new rock to be formed at the bottom of the sea.

22. C.   The author presents these favorable comments about the value of myths in order to support his general thesis that myths and fairy tales perform valuable psychological and educational functions.

23. B.   The author looks on contemporary parents who want their children exposed only to "real" people and everyday events as mistaken. Stating that Plato may have known more about what shapes people's minds than these modern parents do, he suggests that his contemporaries may be *misguided in their beliefs*.

24. C.   As used in this sentence, "make for" means help to promote or maintain. The author is asserting that Plato understood which sorts of experiences worked to *promote the development of* true humanity.

25. D.   No matter what they originally believe—regardless of their original persuasion or *opinion*—contemporary theorists who study myths and fairy tales come to the same conclusion.
Remember, when answering a vocabulary-in-context question, test each answer choice by substituting it in the sentence for the word in quotes.

26. C.   The opening sentences of the second paragraph suggest that Eliade is a modern thinker who has studied myths from a philosophical or psychological view.
Note the use of the phrase "for one" in the sentence describing Eliade. "For one" indicates that Eliade is one of a group. In this case he is one example of the group of *twentieth century philosophers* who have explored the nature of myths.

27. E.   The author has been discussing what there is about a fairy tale that attracts and holds its audience's interest. He concludes that their *attraction* or appeal is at one and the same time to our conscious mind and to our unconscious mind as well.
Again, when answering a vocabulary-in-context question, test each answer choice by substituting it in the sentence for the word in quotes.

28. D.   Like Eliade and other modern thinkers, the author is concerned with the tales' meeting strongly felt needs and providing desirable solutions to human problems—in other words, their *psychological relevance*.

29. E.   The author's citation of the favorable comments of Plato, Aristotle, and Eliade (and his lack of citation of any unfavorable comments) indicates his attitude is one of *approval*.

30. E.   Use the process of elimination to answer this question.
Characteristic I illustrates a way in which fairy tales differ from dreams. Fairy tales are shaped by the conscious minds of many people (*shared creation*). Dreams, however, are created by an individual's unconscious mind. Therefore, you can eliminate Choices B and D.
Characteristic II illustrates a second way in which fairy tales differ from dreams. Fairy tales promise a happy solution to problems (*happy ending*). Dreams, on the other hand, do not necessarily offer any solutions to problems. Therefore, you can eliminate Choice A.
Characteristic III illustrates a third way in which fairy tales differ from dreams. Unlike dreams, which usually interest only the dreamer, fairy tales arouse persistent interest in many people (*general appeal*). Therefore, you can eliminate Choice C.
Only Choice E is left. It is the correct answer.

Section 2   Mathematical Reasoning

In each mathematics section, for many problems, an alternative solution, indicated by two asterisks (**), follows the first solution. When this occurs, one of the solutions is the direct mathematical one and the other is based on one of the tactics discussed in Chapters 8–12.

1. **D.** $3x = 12 \Rightarrow x = 4 \Rightarrow 5x = \mathbf{20}$.

2. **B.**   The sum of the measures of the three angles in any triangle is 180° (KEY FACT J1), so $90 + 33 + x = 180 \Rightarrow 123 + x = 180 \Rightarrow x = \mathbf{57}$.

3. **D.**   Clearing the parentheses in the original equation gives $8 - 8 + m = 8$, so $m = \mathbf{8}$.
**Use TACTIC 9-1: backsolve. Replace m by 0, choice C: $8 - (8 - 0) = 8 - 8 = 0$. This is too small; eliminate A, B, C. Let $m = \mathbf{8}$, choice D. It works!

4. **D.**   Let x be the amount, in dollars, that each of the 20 children were going to contribute; then $20x$ represents the cost of the present. When 4 children dropped out, the remaining 16 each had to pay $(x + 1.50)$ dollars, so
$$16(x + 1.5) = 20x \Rightarrow 16x + 24 = 20x \Rightarrow$$
$$24 = 4x \Rightarrow x = 6,$$
and so the cost of the present was $20 \times 6 = \mathbf{120}$ dollars.
Use TACTIC 9-1: backsolve. Try choice C, 100. If the present cost $100, then each of the 20 children would have had to pay $5. When 4 dropped out, the remaining 16 would have had to pay $100 ÷ 16 = $6.25 apiece, an increase of $1.25. Since the actual increase was $1.50, the gift was more expensive. Eliminate A, B, and C. Try D, **120; it works.

5. **B.**   Use TACTIC 9-3: pick an easy-to-use number. Since $\dfrac{5}{9}$ of the members are boys, assume there are 9 members, 5 of whom are boys. Then the other 4 are girls, and the ratio of girls to boys is 4 to 5, or $\dfrac{\mathbf{4}}{\mathbf{5}}$.

6. **B.**   Triangle EAB is a 45-45-90 triangle; then by KEY FACT J8, $AE = 4$ and BE $= 4\sqrt{2}$. Since $BCDE$ is a square, each of its sides is also equal to $4\sqrt{2}$, so the perimeter is
$$4 + 4 + 4\sqrt{2} + 4\sqrt{2} + 4\sqrt{2} = \mathbf{8 + 12\sqrt{2}}.$$
**Use TACTIC 8-2: trust the diagram. BC is clearly longer than AB, which is 4, but not nearly twice as long. A good guess would be between 5 and 6. Then the perimeter is between

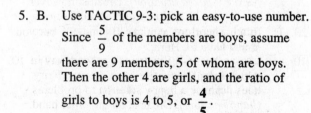

23 $(4 + 4 + 5 + 5 + 5)$ and 26 $(4 + 4 + 6 + 6 + 6)$. Now, use your calculator; to the nearest whole number, the five choices are: 20, 25, 31, 29, 32. Obviously, the right one is **B**.

7. **B.**   Wally produces 80 widgets per day × 20 days per month × 12 months per year = 19,200 widgets per year; $96,000 ÷ 19,200 = \mathbf{5}$.

8. **A.**   If $x^4 = 10$, then (taking the square root of each side) $x^2 = \sqrt{10}$, and $x^6 = x^4 \cdot x^2 = \mathbf{10\sqrt{10}}$.
**If $x^4 = 10$, then $x^8 = x^4 \cdot x^4 = 10 \times 10 = 100$, so x^6 is surely less. Only $10\sqrt{10}$ is less than 100.
**Use your calculator. The fourth root of 10, $(10^{.25})$, is approximately 1.78, which when raised to the sixth power, (1.78^6), is approximately 32. Only $\mathbf{10\sqrt{10}}$ is anywhere near 32.

9. **A.**   Since $JL = KL$, the angles opposite them have the same measure (KEY FACT J3). Then, $d = a$, and we *can* find the value of a $(a + a + 70 = 180)$, but that's it. Since b and e are not necessarily equal (see the diagram), we *cannot* determine b or c. The answer is a **only**.

10. **E.**   Since $BC > AC$, $y > 80$ (KEY FACT J3), but $y + z = 100$. Therefore, $z < 20$, meaning that x must be greater than 160. Since x is an integer, it must be at least **161**.
**Use TACTIC 9-1: backsolve. Start with 100, the smallest choice. If $x = 100$, then $z = 80$, which would leave only 20° for y. This is *way too small*, since y is supposed to be the largest angle. Try something much bigger for x.

11. **B.**   Pick an integer, 2 say. Then
$$\frac{a+3}{5} = 2 \Rightarrow a + 3 = 10 \Rightarrow a = 7,$$
and 5 goes into 7 once with a remainder of **2**.

12. **B.**   On six tests combined, Brigitte earned a total of $6 \times 75 = 450$ points (TACTIC E1). The total of her five best grades is $5 \times 85 = 425$ points, so her lowest grade was $450 - 425 = \mathbf{25}$.
**Assume that Brigitte's five best grades were each 85. Then each one has a deviation of 10 points above the average of 75, and the total deviation above 75 is $5 \times 10 = 50$ points. Therefore, her one bad grade must have been 50 points below 75.

13. E.   Check each statement. The only factors of 17 are ±1 and ±17. If m is any of these, $\frac{17}{m}$ is an odd integer. (I is false.) Eliminate A and D. Could $\frac{m}{17}$ be an even integer? Sure, it could be *any* even integer; for example, if $m = 34$, $\frac{m}{17} = 2$, and if $m = 170$, $\frac{m}{17} = 10$. (II is true.) Eliminate C. Could $17m$ be a prime? Yes, if $m = 1$. (III is true.) The true statements are **II and III only**.

14. C.   The percent increase in Max's investment is $\frac{\text{actual increase}}{\text{original value}} \times 100\%$. Each share was originally worth $10, and the actual increase in value of each share was $10. Max's percent increase in value $= \frac{10}{10} \times 100\% = \mathbf{100\%}$.

15. C.   The number, n, of reports Benjamin can type is equal to the rate, in reports *per minute*, at which he types times the number of minutes he types. Then

$$n = \frac{1 \text{ report}}{h \text{ hours}} \times m \text{ minutes}$$

$$= \frac{1 \text{ report}}{60h \text{ minutes}} \times m \text{ minutes} = \frac{m}{60h} \text{ reports}.$$

**Use TACTIC 9-3: pick some easy to use numbers. Suppose Benjamin can type 1 report every 2 hours, and he types for 60 minutes; he will complete half of a report. Which of the five choices equals $\frac{1}{2}$ when $h = 2$ and $m = 60$? Only $\frac{m}{60h}$.

16. B.   The trust received 80% of the estate (10% went to the man's wife, 5% to his children, and 5% to his grandchildren). If E represents the value of the estate, then
$$0.80E = 1,000,000 \Rightarrow$$
$E = 1,000,000 \div 0.80 = 1,250,000.$
Each grandchild received 1% (one-fifth of 5%) of the estate, or **$12,500**.

17. E.   Use TACTIC 8-1: draw a diagram. Since this is a ratio problem, immediately plug in a number (TACTIC 9-2). To avoid fractions, use 6, the LCM of the numbers in the question. Let $AC = 6$; then

A———6———C

A——6——•——3——D
　　　　C

A——3——•——3——C
　　　D

A————6————•——3——•—2—B
　　　　　C　　D

A——3——•—2—•—1—C
　　D　B

$CD = 3$, with D on either side of C. $BD = 2$, but B could be on either side of D, and so we have no way of knowing length BC. The value of the ratio $\frac{BC}{CD}$ **cannot be determined from the information given**.

18. A.   At 10:30 A.M. the first car had been going 40 miles per hour for 1.5 hours, and so had gone $40 \times 1.5 = 60$ miles. The second car covered the same 60 miles in 1 hour and 20 minutes, or $1\frac{1}{3} = \frac{4}{3}$ hours. Therefore, its rate was

$$60 \div \frac{4}{3} = 60 \times \frac{3}{4} = \mathbf{45} \text{ miles per hour.}$$

19. B.   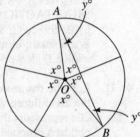 Since $5x = 360$ (KEY FACT I3), $x = 72$ and $m\angle AOB = 2x = 144$. Since $OA = OB$ (they are both radii), $\triangle AOB$ is isosceles:

$$2y + 144 = 180 \Rightarrow 2y = 36 \Rightarrow y = 18.$$

Then $\frac{y}{x} = \frac{18}{72} = \mathbf{\frac{1}{4}}$.

**It should be clear that the values of x and y can be determined, so eliminate E, and use TACTIC 8-2: trust the diagram; x appears to be about 70 and y about 20. Then, $\frac{y}{x} \approx$

$$\frac{20}{70} = \frac{1}{3.5},$$ and you should *guess* between $\frac{1}{3}$ and $\frac{1}{4}$.

20. D.   It's not hard to calculate $\boxed{10}$ and $\boxed{9}$, but you don't have to. Here, $\boxed{10} - \boxed{9} = (1 + 2 + \cdots + 9 + 10) - (1 + 2 + \cdots + 9) = 10$. Now, calculate the choices: Only $\boxed{4} = 1 + 2 + 3 + 4 = 10$.

21. D. $\boxed{1010} = (1 + 2 + ... + 1000) + (1001 + 1002 + \cdots + 1010)$. The sum in the first parentheses is just $\boxed{1000} = 50,500$. The sum in the second parentheses is $(1000 + 1) + (1000 + 2) + \cdots + (1000 + 10)$, which can be written as $(1000 + 1000 + ... + 1000) + (1 + 2 + ... + 10) = 10,000 + 55$. The total is
$$50,500 + 10,000 + 55 = \mathbf{60,555}.$$

22. D.   Since c cents $= \frac{c}{100}$ dollars, the cost, in dollars, of 1 hammer is $d + \frac{c}{100}$, and the cost

of h hammers is

$$h\left(d + \frac{c}{100}\right) = h\left(\frac{100d + c}{100}\right) = \frac{100hd + hc}{100}.$$

**Use TACTIC 9-3. Plug in easy-to-use numbers. If 1 hammer costs 1 dollar and 50 cents, then 2 hammers cost 3 dollars. Which of the choices equals 3 when $d = 1$, $c = 50$, and $h = 2$? Only $\dfrac{100hd + hc}{100}$. Remember: don't waste time getting the exact value of each choice; as soon as you can see that it doesn't equal 3, eliminate it. For example, choices C and E are gigantic.

23. **C.** Draw a Venn diagram and label each region. Let x be the number of senior boys. Then $40 - x$ is the number of boys who are not seniors (i.e., are juniors), and $70 - x$ is the number of seniors who are not boys (i.e., are girls). Then

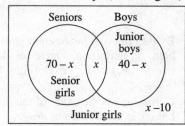

number of junior girls =
$100 - [(40 - x) + x + (70 - x)] =$
$100 - [110 - x] = x - 10$.
Since the number of junior girls must be at least 0, $x - 10 \geq 0 \Rightarrow x \geq \mathbf{10}$.
Use TACTIC 9-1. Backsolve, but since we want the smallest number, start with A. If there are no senior boys, then all 40 boys are juniors and all 70 seniors are girls; but that's 110 people. Eliminate A. If there are 5 senior boys, there will be 35 junior boys and 65 senior girls, a total of 105. Finally, check **10, which works.

24. **C.** Make tables to determine Roberto's and Juan's ages.

Table 1		
	1950	1955
Roberto	$4x$	$4x + 5$
Juan	x	$x + 5$

Table 2		
	1950	$1950 + t$
Roberto	40	$40 + t$
Juan	10	$10 + t$

Let x represent Juan's age in 1950, and fill in Table 1 as shown. In 1955, Roberto was 3 times as old as Juan, so
$4x + 5 = 3(x + 5) = 3x + 15 \Rightarrow x = 10$.
Now, make a second table in which t represents the number of years since 1950 (see Table 2). Then, if Roberto is to be twice as old,
$40 + t = 2(10 + t) = 20 + 2t \Rightarrow t = 20$.
This occurs in $1950 + 20 = \mathbf{1970}$.
**This result can also be established by trial and error. Use TACTIC 9-3. Guess an age for

Juan, and test it. In 1950, if Juan was 5, Roberto was 20; 5 years later they were 10 and 25 (but Roberto was *less* than 3 times as old). Try 10. Now, if in 1950 Juan and Roberto were 10 and 40, respectively, in 1960 they were 20 and 50, in 1965 they were 25 and 55, and in **1970** they were 30 and 60—that's it!

25. **C.** Let r and R be the radii of the two circles. From the figure, you can see that $\triangle OAB$ is a 45-45-90 right triangle, and so $R = r\sqrt{2}$ (KEY FACT J8). Therefore,

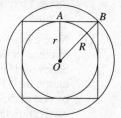

$$\frac{\text{area of large circle}}{\text{area of small circle}} = \frac{\pi R^2}{\pi r^2} = \frac{\pi\left(r\sqrt{2}\right)^2}{\pi r^2} = \frac{2\pi r^2}{\pi r^2} = 2.$$

The ratio is **2:1**.
**Do exactly the same thing except use TACTIC 9-2. Let $r = 1$; then $R = \sqrt{2}$, and the ratio is $\dfrac{\pi\left(\sqrt{2}\right)^2}{\pi(1)^2} = \dfrac{2\pi}{\pi} = \mathbf{2{:}1}$.

Section 3   Verbal Reasoning

1. **E.** The first clause states that the movement did not become famous instantly or "overnight." Instead, it gained fame step by step, or *gradually*.
Remember to watch for signal words that link one part of the sentence to another. The use of "on the contrary" here sets up a contrast. The missing word must be an antonym for *overnight*.   (Contrast Signal)

2. **D.** Buildings constructed in such a hurry would tend to be *ramshackle*, loosely held together affairs.   (Definition)

3. **D.** Immune to most pesticides, cockroaches are thus tough or *hardy* and hard to *eliminate*. Remember, in double-blank sentences, go through the answer choices, testing the *first* word in each choice and eliminating those that don't fit. You can immediately eliminate Choices A and C.   (Cause and Effect Pattern)

4. **E.** The intensifier "even" indicates that Astell did more than merely maintain a good reputation; she improved or *enhanced* it.
                    (Intensifier Signal)

5. **B.** Kubota is hopeful about the success of the women's movement. Thus, she maintains that the recent forward steps or *strides* made by

Japanese women in business mean even *greater* chances for women in future days.
(Support Signal)

6. B. *Stoically* describes how a person bears pain with great courage.
The presence of *and* linking the two clauses indicates that the missing word continues the thought expressed in the phrase "did not wince or whimper."   (Support Signal)

7. D. Note the use of "might." Without the support of other stories, the actor's stories might not be believed. If people need such supporting testimony, their first response to the stories must be one of disbelief. They must think them exaggerations or *hyperbole.* "Were there not" is a short way of saying "If there were not."
(Argument)

8. A. This is a case in which you can't eliminate any of the answer choices by checking the first words of each answer pair: all are terms that could describe an ambassador. In this case, the *eminent* ambassador was only an *indifferent* (mediocre) linguist; nevertheless, he insisted on trying to speak foreign languages without help.
Remember to watch for signal words that link one part of the sentence to another. The use of "yet" in the second clause sets up a contrast. Note that "but" here means "only." That's your clue to be on the lookout for a belittling or negative word.   (Contrast Signal)

9. B. To the author, nude models seem *archaic,* suited to an earlier day when art students spent as much time learning to draw the human body as medical students today spend learning to *dissect* or cut it up.
Remember, in double-blank sentences, go through the answer choices, testing the *first* words in each choice and eliminating those that don't fit. By definition, a relic or remnant of a bygone age is outdated or old-fashioned. You can immediately eliminate Choices C and E.
(Definition)

10. B. The view of Rome's contributions to government, law, and engineering is wholly positive: these additions to human knowledge are generally acknowledged or recognized. *In contrast,* Rome's original contributions to art are *not* recognized: they are seen as just an *echo* or imitation of the art of ancient Greece. Note that "although" sets up a contrast.
(Contrast Signal)

11. D. *Gasoline* provides the energy for an *automobile; food,* the energy for a *man.* (Function)

12. E. A *symphony* is written by a *composer*; a *sonnet* is written by a *poet.*
(Worker and Creation)

13. D. *Wearisome* (fatiguing; tiresome) and *refreshing* are opposites; *lengthy* and *brief* are opposites.   (Antonyms)

14. B. To *stalk* someone is to *follow* or draw near him stealthily or secretly. Similarly, to *spy* on someone is to *look* at or observe him stealthily.   (Manner)

15. C. To *dampen* something is less intense than to *drench* it; to *simmer* something is less intense than to *boil* it.   (Degree of Intensity)

16. D. To *allay pain* is to lessen it; to *mitigate* a punishment to reduce its severity.   (Function)

17. C. *Exertion* (vigorous effort) causes *fatigue; sedation* (administration of a tranquilizing drug) causes *tranquility* or calm.
(Cause and Effect)

18. B. By definition, a *foe* or enemy feels *enmity* or hate. By definition, a *miser* or skinflint feels *avarice* or greed.   (Defining Characteristic)

19. D. *Cardiology* is the study of the *heart*; *pharmacology* is the science of *drugs.*
Word Parts Clue: *Card-* (as in cardiac) means heart; *-logy* means science or study.
(Definition)

20. B. A *bacterium* is a member of a *colony* (group of bacteria growing together). A *fish* is a member of a *shoal* or school.
(Member and Group)

21. E. By definition, one *shuns* (avoids) a *pariah* (outcast). Likewise, one *ridicules* a *butt* (laughingstock).
Remember to watch out for errors stemming from reversals. *Pariah* is the object of the verb *shun*; he is the person being shunned. In contrast, *predator* is the subject of the verb *hunt*; he is the person who hunts, *not* the person being hunted. The grammatical relationship is reversed.   (Defining Characteristic)

22. E. A *turncoat* (renegade; someone who switches to the opposite party) is by definition *treacherous*; a *killjoy* (someone who spoils the pleasure of others) is by definition *lugubrious* or gloomy.   (Definition)

23. B. *Cacophonous* (harshly dissonant) is the opposite of *mellifluous* (sweet-sounding). By definition, *cacophony* is not *mellifluous.* Similarly, *noisome* (offensive of smell) is the opposite of *fragrant.* By definition, *noisomeness* is not *fragrant.* The relationship is a variant on an antonym.   (Antonym Variant)

24. D. The sentence immediately preceding the De Voss quotation asserts that rock and roll is "big corporation business." The De Voss quote is used to support this view that rock and roll is a major industry, for, by showing that many rock stars earn far more than major corporate executives do, it indicates the impact that the music business has on America's economy.

25. C. *Consumption* here refers to using up *consumer* goods, such as foodstuffs, clothes, and cars.

26. A. The washing machine, spot cream, and rock band are all "on the market" (lines 28–29): they are all being marketed as *commodities*, and they all serve equally well to distract the consumer from more essential concerns.

27. C. *Plastic* here is being used *metaphorically* or figuratively. It creates an image of rock and roll as somehow synthetic, dehumanized, even mercenary, as in *plastic smiles* or *plastic motel rooms* or *plastic money*.

28. E. To Burchill and Parsons, the consumer is "a potential Moron" who can be kept quiet and content by being handed consumer goods as a distraction. Thus, the consumer is someone who is *vulnerable to manipulation* by the enemy.

29. B. Dylan is given credit for "introducing the explicit politics of folk music to rock and roll." Clearly, this implies that, at the time Dylan introduced politics to rock, folk music was already an openly political medium through which artists expressed their convictions. It was only after Dylan's introduction of political ideas into his lyrics that other rock and roll artists began to deal with political materials. In other words, *folk music gave voice to political concerns long before rock and roll music did.*

30. D. Wiener makes three points about Paul: he lacked political values (was *apolitical*), wrote highly successful nonpolitical songs ("Number One hits"), and managed to sleep soundly. Clearly, this suggests that John, who attempted to express his political values through his songs and as a result had difficulty putting out Number One hits, didn't always sleep soundly. This in turn implies that, as an apolitical performer who had a relatively easy time turning out hits, *Paul suffered less strain than John did.*

31. C. The author describes Lennon's apolitical "Starting Over" as one of his "biggest hits" (line 70). Similarly, she describes the highly personal *Double Fantasy* album as "best-selling" (line 83). Thus, she clearly offers them as examples of *profitable successes lacking political content.*

32. E. The artist's task is to *keep* or preserve his political commitment without deluding himself about how much influence his songs will have.
    Treat vocabulary-in-context questions as if they are sentence completion exercises. Always substitute each of the answer choices in place of the quoted word in the original sentence.

33. B. Greene asks how one can "possibly avoid being a part of the power relations that exist?" He feels trapped. The more popular his music is, the more his work is subject to misinterpretation, and the more he is involved in the power relations of the music industry. As a politically committed artist, he is frustrated because *he cannot escape involvement* in the very power relations he condemns.

34. C. Throughout the last paragraph, the author reiterates that, given the difficulty of his material, the politically motivated artist is lucky to gain any degree of popular success. She clearly attributes any such success to pure luck or *good fortune.*

35. C. The author states that the "rock and roll artist cannot cause political change" (lines 104–105). In other words, he has no direct, immediate effect on the political situation. However, he may be able to make an *indirect* contribution to political change by influencing his audience and thus contributing to the change it makes.

Section 4   Mathematical Reasoning

Quantitative Comparison Questions

1. A. The only positive divisors of 19 are 1 and 19. Column A: $1 + 19 = 20$. Column B: $1 \times 19 = 19$. Column A is greater.

2. D. Use TACTIC 10-4. Could m and n be equal? Sure, if each is 5. Eliminate A and B. Must they be equal? No, not if $m = 1$ and $n = 25$. Eliminate C, as well. Neither column is *always* greater, and the two columns are not *always* equal (D).

3. B. The only primes whose sum is 12 are 5 and 7, both of which are less than 8. [Note: $1 + 11 = 12$, but 1 is not a prime (KEY FACT A26).] Column B is greater.

4. D. Use TACTIC 10-4. Could $a = 0$? Yes; $0 < 1 < 2$ and $0 \cdot 1 \cdot 2 = 0$. Eliminate A and B. Must $a = 0$? No; since $abc = 0$, either a or b or c must be 0, but not necessarily a: $-1 < 0 < 5$ and $-1 \cdot 0 \cdot 5 = 0$. Eliminate C. Neither column is *always* greater, and the two columns are not *always* equal (D).

5. D. Use TACTIC 10-4. Could $y = 20$? Yes, if the large triangle were equilateral, x would be 30 and y would be 20. Must $y = 20$? No, if $x = 45$, $y = 10$. (Note: Since the figure is not drawn to scale, the triangle could be *any* triangle with a 60° angle.) Neither column is *always* larger, and the columns are not *always* equal (D).

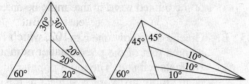

6. C. Since $\dfrac{a+b}{c+d} = 1$, then $a + b = c + d \Rightarrow$
    $\dfrac{a+b}{2} = \dfrac{c+d}{2}$. The columns are equal.
    **Use TACTIC 10-1. Pick any simple numbers: for example, $a = 1$, $b = 3$, $c = 2$, and $d = 2$. Both averages are 2.

7. D. Use TACTIC 10-1. Since neither x nor y can be 0, and x and y must be different, let $x = 1$ and $y = -1$. Then $x + y = 0$, and each column equals 9. Eliminate A and B. But, of course, these two quantities are not always equal (try 1 and 2), so eliminate C. Neither column is *always* greater, and the columns are not *always* equal (D).
    **You can expand each column partially or completely, but this is clearly a time when it is better to avoid the algebra.

8. C. Since the measure of an exterior angle of a triangle is equal to the sum of the measures of the two opposite interior angles (KEY FACT J2], $c = a + b \Rightarrow$ $a + b - c = 0$. The columns are equal (C).
    **Use TACTIC 10-1: plug in easy-to-use numbers. If $a = 60$ and $b = 70$, then $d = 50 \Rightarrow$ $c = 130$, and $60 + 70 - 130 = 0$.

9. B. Column A $= (2a)^3 = 2^3 a^3 = 8a^3$ (KEY FACT A16), which is *less* than $2a^3$, since a^3 is negative (KEY FACT A23). Column B is greater.
    **Use TACTIC 10-1. Let $a = -1$. Then Column A is $(-2)^3 = -8$ and Column B is -2. Column B is greater, so eliminate A and C. When other negative values are substituted for a, Column B is still greater. Guess B.

10. D. Use TACTIC 10-4. Could $A = 20$, that is, could $x - 5$ people take twice as long as x people? Yes, if there are half as many people working: if $x = 10$ and $x - 5 = 5$. Must $A = 20$? No, not if there are any other numbers of people. Neither column is *always* greater, and the columns are not *always* equal (D).
    **Use TACTIC 10-1. Since the number of people working on a job must be positive, $x - 5 \geq 1$, and so $x \geq 6$. So, you can't use 1, 0, -1, or fractions. Try 6, the smallest number you can use, and then a large number. If 6 people need 10 days to complete the job, then $6 - 5 = 1$ person will require 60 days. Column A is greater; eliminate B and C. If 100 people need 10 days, then 95 people would need a little more than 10 days, but clearly far less than 20 days. Eliminate A. The answer is D.

11. A. Column B $= \left(\dfrac{13}{17}\right)^5 = (x^5)^5 = x^{25}$. Since
    $0 < x < 1$, $x^{25} < x$. Column A is greater.
    **Use a scientific calculator: $\left(\dfrac{13}{17}\right)^5 \approx 0.26$,
    whereas $x \approx 0.95$ (raise $\dfrac{13}{17}$ to the $\dfrac{1}{5}$ or 0.2
    power). Even with a regular calculator, you
    can get $\left(\dfrac{13}{17}\right)^5 \approx 0.26$ and reason that x must
    be much larger, since $(.26)^5 \approx 0.001$, which is
    much less than $\dfrac{13}{17}$.

12. A. The surface area of the cube in Column A is $6s^2$. The rectangular solid in Column B, shown in the figure at the right, has 2 faces whose areas are each $s^2 - 1$, 2 faces with areas $s^2 - s$, and 2 faces with areas $s^2 + s$, for a total area of $6s^2 - 2$. Column A is greater.
    **Use TACTIC 10-1. Let $s = 2$. Then Column A $= 6(2)^2 = 24$, whereas Column B is $2(2 + 3 + 6) = 2(11) = 22$. Eliminate B and C. Try any other value for s; as shown above, Column B will be 2 less than Column A.

13. A. Avoid the algebra. Use TACTIC 10-1. If x and y are each 1, then Column A is 4 and Column B is 2. Eliminate B and C. If $x = 1$ and $y = -1$, Column A is 0, whereas Column B is -2. Again, Column A is greater. Choose A.
    **Simplify the expression in Column A: $(x + y)^2 - (x^2 - y^2) = x^2 + 2xy + y^2 - x^2 + y^2 = 2xy + 2y^2$, which is greater than $2xy$, since $2y^2$ is positive. Column A is greater.

14. **C.** The area of the shaded region is the area of the large circle, 25π, minus the area of the middle circle, 16π: $25\pi - 16\pi = 9\pi$. The striped region is just a circle of radius 3. Its area is 9π. The columns are equal (C).

15. **A.** The surface area of the uncut red cube is $6(3)^2 = 54$. The surface area of each small cube is $6(1)^2 = 6$. Then the total surface area of the 27 small cubes is $27 \times 6 = 162$. Of the 162 small faces, 54 are painted red and $162 - 54 = 108$ are unpainted. Column A is greater.

Grid-in Questions

16. **(15)** Evaluate $3a - 2b$: $3(3) - 2(-3) = 3(3) + 2(3) = 9 + 6 = $ **15**.

17. **(37.5)** Use TACTIC D1. In a ratio problem write the letter x after each number. Then, $a = 6x$, $b = 7x$, and $c = 11x$; and since the sum of the measures of the angles of a triangle is $180°$: $6x + 7x + 11x = 180 \Rightarrow 24x = 180 \Rightarrow x = 7.5$. Then $c - a = 11x - 6x = 5x = 5(7.5) = $ **37.5**. [Note that we did *not* have to find the value of any of the angles (TACTIC 8-7)].

18. **(90)** Draw a right triangle and label the two legs 15 and 36. To calculate the perimeter, you need only find the length of the hypotenuse and then add the lengths of the three sides. Before using the Pythagorean theorem, ask yourself whether this is a multiple of one of the basic right triangles you know: 3-4-5 or 5-12-13. It is: $15 = 3 \times 5$ and $36 = 3 \times 12$, so the hypotenuse is $3 \times 13 = 39$. The perimeter is $3(5 + 12 + 13) = 3 \times 30 = $ **90**.
    **If you don't recognize the triangle, use Pythagoras and your calculator:
    $15^2 + 36^2 = c^2 \Rightarrow c^2 = 225 + 1296 = 1521$
    $\Rightarrow c = 39$.
    The perimeter is $15 + 36 + 39 = $ **90**.

19. **(99)** From the 124 people in front of Jill, remove Jack plus the 24 people in front of Jack: $124 - 25 = $ **99**.
    **It may be easier for you to see this if you draw a diagram (TACTIC 8-1):

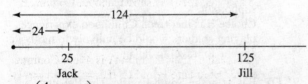

20. **$\left(\dfrac{4}{5} \text{ or } 0.8\right)$** There are five integers less than 50 whose units digit is 7: 7, 17, 27, 37, and 47. Of these, four (all but 27) are prime. Then, the probability of drawing a prime is $\dfrac{4}{5}$.

21. **(19)** Draw a diagram. For the third-place share to be as large as possible, the fourth-place share must be as small as possible. However, it must be more than $15, so let it be $16. Then the amount, in dollars, left for second and third places is $100 - (30 + 16 + 15) = 100 - 61 = 39$. The second-place share could be $20, and the third-place share $19.
    Use TACTIC 11-2. Try a number. Third place must be less than 30 and more than 15; try 20. Then second place must be at least 21 and fourth place at least 16. But $30 + 21 + 20 + 16 + 15 = 102$, which is a *little* too big. Try a little smaller number, such as **19, which works.

22. **(490)** Let x be the number Jessica chose. Then the other terms are as follows:

Term	2	3	4	5
Expression	$x + 6$	$2(x + 6) = 2x + 12$	$2x + 12 + 6 = 2x + 18$	$2(2x + 18) = 4x + 36$

Finally, $4x + 36 = 1996 \Rightarrow 4x = 1960 \Rightarrow x = $ **490**.
**Use TACTIC 11-2. Try some numbers. Using your calculator, start with any number that seems reasonable and quickly add 6, double, add 6, double.

$100 \to 106 \to 212 \to 218 \to 436$	Way too small. Try 500.
$500 \to 506 \to 1012 \to 1018 \to 2036$	A bit too large. Try 490.
$490 \to 496 \to 992 \to 1998 \to 1996$	That's it!

You might not zero in on the correct answer that quickly, but it shouldn't take long.

23. **(42)** Use TACTIC 8-11. Systematically list all the ways of expressing 12 as the sum of three different positive integers, and calculate each product.

Integers	Product	Integers	Product
9, 2, 1	18	6, 5, 1	30
8, 3, 1	24	6, 4, 2	48
7, 4, 1	28	5, 4, 3	60
7, 3, 2	42		

Then $g = 60$, $\ell = 18$, and $g - \ell = $ **42**.

24. **$\left(\dfrac{13}{5} \text{ or } 2.6\right)$** Use TACTIC 8-1. Draw a right triangle, and label the shorter leg a, the longer leg b, and the hypotenuse c.

Then $\dfrac{1}{4}b = \dfrac{3}{5}a \Rightarrow b = \dfrac{12}{5}a$. *Stop.*
This is a question about right triangles, so if the 12 and the 5 in that fraction make you think of a 5-12-13 triangle,

check it out: $\frac{1}{4}(12) = 3$ and $\frac{3}{5}(5) = 3$. It

works. The ratio is $\frac{13}{5}$.

**If you didn't see that, use the Pythagorean theorem:

$$c^2 = a^2 + \left(\frac{12}{5}a\right)^2 =$$

$$a^2 + \frac{144}{25}a^2 = \frac{25}{25}a^2 + \frac{144}{25}a^2 = \frac{169}{25}a^2 \Rightarrow$$

$$c = \sqrt{\frac{169}{25}a^2} = \frac{13}{5}a \Rightarrow \frac{c}{a} = \frac{13}{5}.$$

25. (22) *Be careful.* It may seem as though a right angle is formed 24 times — twice each hour (e.g., at *about* 12:15 and 12:45, actually at 12:16 $\frac{4}{11}$ and 12:49 $\frac{1}{11}$); but this is the last problem in the set and cannot be quite that easy. In fact, a right angle is formed twice each hour; but between 2:00 and 3:00 this occurs at *about* 2:27 and at 3:00 *exactly,* and between 3:00 and 4:00 it occurs at *exactly* 3:00 and *about* 3:33. Therefore, 3:00 gets counted twice and so does 9:00. The answer, then, is **22.**

Section 5   Verbal Reasoning

1. D.   Wolfe is making a point through a simile, a type of *figurative expression.* Going home again, he says, is *like* stepping into a river, through which new water constantly flows. Each time you step into the river, it will be different; each time you try to return home, it too will be different.

2. C.   The author of Passage 1 states that *at best* the journey home will point you to your origins, "to where you started," and will let you know how your origins have "helped to shape you." In other words, the most positive outcome of your attempting to go home would be for you to *grasp how your origins have formed you.*

3. B.   The author feels trapped between Wolfe's certainty that one cannot go home again and Haley's certainty that one *can* do so, that one can find the way back to one's ancestral homeland and return to one's roots. He is torn between extremes, uncertain about just what he is looking for—his conflicting desires clearly show that he is *ambivalent about his journey.*
Choice A is incorrect. The author has no desire to know what his ancestors looked like. He is not seeking to convey his resemblance to them.

Choices C and D are incorrect. Nothing in the passage supports them.
Choice E is incorrect. Though on one level the author deeply desires to trace his roots (as Haley did), on another he feels attempting to do so is a meaningless exercise. Thus, he chiefly conveys his ambivalence about his journey.

4. A.   A *paradox* is a seemingly contradictory statement that may perhaps be true in fact. Here the author was, in Africa, his ancestral homeland, but it did not feel like home to him. He clearly found his situation paradoxical.

5. E.   Africa held or *possessed* symbolic significance for the author of this passage.
Remember, when answering a vocabulary-in-context question, try substituting each answer choice in the original sentence for the word in quotes.

6. D.   Though the author earns his living as an arts administrator, he thinks of himself as a poet, a creative artist. When he says he needed time for his own work, he is referring to his work *creating poetry.*

7. C.   The author essentially looks down on his administrative work. Though it is time-consuming, leaving him with little time to compose poetry, it is not a taxing or *demanding* job.

8. B.   The author describes a scene in which he, a Japanese-American child watching old World War II movies, playacted being an American G.I. shooting down Japanese soldiers. Rather than siding with the Japanese soldiers whom he physically resembled, he took the part of their opponents. This episode serves to show how much he *identified himself as an American.*
Choice A is incorrect. The author had no particular hatred for Japan or the Japanese. He merely felt they did not have much to do with his life.
Choice C is incorrect. Though he has mentioned the fakery of Japanese films, he does not describe the American-made war movies in order to show that they are better than Japanese films.
Choice D is incorrect. Nothing in the passage supports it.
Choice E is incorrect. Childhood experiences playing soldiers would be unlikely to motivate anyone to travel to Japan.

9. D.   Bali is in the South Pacific. The Bahamas are in the Caribbean. The primary thing these islands have in common is that they are classic *exotic destinations* for vacationers.

10. E.   Like the author of Passage 1, the author of Passage 2 feels *marked ambivalence* about his

prospective journey. He is happy to have won the fellowship, but unhappy at the prospect of having to spend a year in a country he finds relatively unappealing.

11. **D.** In the final lines of Passage 2, the author creates a picture of his imagination as a swimmer, "unconsciously swimming the Pacific" toward Japan, going against tide of his family's earlier movement from Japan to America. This picture is *an extended metaphor* or image.

12. **A.** In both passages, the authors are concerned about their racial or *ethnic identity*. The author of Passage 1 is seeking to discover "how much of being black" comes from his African origins. The author of Passage 2 has to a degree denied his ethnic identity ("Much of my life I had insisted on my Americanness, had shunned most connections with Japan and felt proud I knew no Japanese") and yet has celebrated his Japanese heritage in his verse.
Choice B is incorrect. The authors are not seeking to establish their independence as individuals. They are seeking to discover the nature of their ties to their ancestral homelands.
Choice C is incorrect. While the authors may wish to learn more about their ancestors, they do not worship them.
Choice D is incorrect. There is nothing in either passage to support it.
Choice E is incorrect. While Passage 1 mentions Haley's attempts to trace his roots, its author has no such attempts in mind. Passage 2's author never mentions genealogical research at all.

13. **C.** Use the process of elimination to arrive at the correct answer to this question.
The author of Passage 2 insists that Japan "didn't have much to do with" his present life. This parallels the statement in Passage 1 that Africa held "only a symbolic significance" to the author. Therefore, Choice A is incorrect.
The author of Passage 2 asserts that he "had insisted on" his Americanness and "felt proud" of knowing no Japanese. Like the author of Passage 1, who "did not feel African," the Japanese-American author of Passage 2 did not feel Japanese. Therefore, Choice B is incorrect.
The author of Passage 2 states that his "reasons for going (to Japan) were not very clear." He hardly knew why he was going there. This parallels the comment in Passage 1 that its author "hardly knew what" he was looking for in Africa. Therefore, Choice D is incorrect.
The image of "memories hidden in (one's) genes" awakening has its counterpart in Mura's image of how his poetic imagination had been returning to his ancestral past, "unconsciously swimming the Pacific." Therefore, Choice E is incorrect.

Only Choice C is left. It is the correct answer. Passage 1's author is so torn between Africa and America that he comes to feel like a "waif without a home." There is nothing corresponding to this idea in Passage 2. Throughout Passage 2, its author insists on his Americanness, identifies with the G.I's in World War II movies. He clearly feels America is his home.

Section 6   Mathematical Reasoning

1. **B.** $3x = 36 \Rightarrow x = 12 \Rightarrow \dfrac{x}{3} = \mathbf{4}.$

2. **C.** If $\dfrac{7}{11} a = \dfrac{7}{11} b$, then $a = b$, and $\dfrac{a}{b} = \mathbf{1}.$

3. **C.** Set up a proportion:
$$\frac{2.2 \text{ pounds}}{1 \text{ kilogram}} = \frac{120 \text{ pounds}}{x \text{ kilograms}}. \text{ Then}$$
$$2.2x = 120 \Rightarrow x = \frac{120}{2.2} = 54.54\ldots$$

 Therefore, the **3** students weighing more than 120 pounds are the 3 who weigh more than 54.54 kilograms.
**Quickly multiply by 2.2: $56 \times 2.2 = 123.2$, so 56, 57, and 61 kilograms are all more than 120 pounds. The other two weights are less.

4. **D.** Since the value of a share doubled every year, each year it was worth *half* as much as the following year. In 1990 a share was worth $80, so in 1989 it was worth half as much, or $40; in 1988 it was worth $20; and in **1987** it was worth $10.
Use TACTIC 9-1: backsolve, starting with C, 1986. If a share was worth $10 in 1986, then it was worth $20 in 1987, $40 in 1988, $80 in 1989. That's a year too soon. Start a year later—1987**.

5. **B.** If a is the average of 10 and some other number, x, then
$$a = \frac{10 + x}{2} \Rightarrow 2a = 10 + x \Rightarrow x = \mathbf{2a - 10}.$$
**Use TACTIC 9-2. Pick a number for a, say 5. Since 5 is the average of 10 and 0, check the five choices to see which one equals 0 when $a = 5$. Only B: $2(5) - 10 = 0$.

6. **B.** The percent increase in a quantity is
 $\dfrac{\text{actual increase}}{\text{original}} \times 100\%$ (KEY FACT C5).

For *each* year calculate the actual increase

and divide. For example, in 1990 the increase was \$100 (from \$150 to \$250), so the percent increase was $\dfrac{100}{150} \times 100\% = 66.66\%$. In **1991** the increase was \$200 and the percent increase was $\dfrac{200}{250} \times 100\% = 80\%$. Check the other choices; this is the greatest.

7. **C.**   The interior of the star is a hexagon, a six-sided polygon. By KEY FACT K2, the sum of the six angles in a hexagon is $(6 - 2)180 = 4(180) = $ **720**.
    **Use TACTIC 8-2: trust the diagram. Since each of the six angles clearly measures more than 100° but less than 150°, the total is more than 600 but less than 900. Only **720 is in that range.

8. **E.**   The perimeter, P, of $\triangle BCD = $ $BC + CD + BD$. Since $BC + CD = 7$ (it is one-half the perimeter of rectangle $ABCD$), $P = 7 + BD$. But BD cannot be determined, since it depends on the length of sides BC and CD. Both rectangles in the figure at the right have perimeters that are 14, but the values of BD are different. The perimeter of $\triangle BCD$ **cannot be determined from the information given.**

9. **D.**   If a represents Jordan's average after five tests, then he has earned a total of $5a$ points (TACTIC E1). A grade of 70 on the sixth test will lower his average 4 points to $a - 4$. Therefore
    $$a - 4 = \frac{5a + 70}{6} \Rightarrow 6(a - 4) = 5a + 70 \Rightarrow$$
    $$6a - 24 = 5a + 70 \Rightarrow 6a = 5a + 94 \Rightarrow a = \mathbf{94}.$$

****Assume that Jordan's average is a because he earned a on each of his first five tests. Since, after getting a 70 on his sixth test, his average will be $a - 4$, the deviation on each of the first five tests is 4, for a total deviation above the average of 20 points. Then the total deviation below the average must also be 20 (KEY FACT E3). Therefore, 70 is 20 less than the new average of $a - 4$: $70 = (a - 4) - 20 \Rightarrow a = 94$.
****Use TACTIC 9-1: backsolve, starting with choice C, 90. If Jordan's five-test average is 90, he has 450 points and a 70 on the sixth test will give him a total of 520 points, and an average of $520 \div 6 = 86.666$. The 70 lowered his average 3.3333 points, which is not enough. Eliminate A, B, and C. Try D, 94. It works.

10. **C.**   Altitude BY bisects AC, so $AY = 6$. Draw radius OA, creating 30-60-90 right triangle AYO. By KEY FACT J11:
    $$OY = \frac{AY}{\sqrt{3}} = \frac{6}{\sqrt{3}} = \frac{6}{\sqrt{3}} \times \frac{\sqrt{3}}{\sqrt{3}} = \frac{6\sqrt{3}}{3} = 2\sqrt{3},$$
    and the hypotenuse, OA, which is also the radius of the circle, is 2 times OY, or $\mathbf{4\sqrt{3}}$.
    ****Use TACTIC 8-2: trust the diagram. After drawing OA, compare OA and AB. Clearly, OA is more than half of AB, so $OA > 6$. Eliminate A and B ($2\sqrt{3} \approx 3.4$). However, OA looks to be less than two-thirds of AB; so $OA < 8$. Eliminate D ($6\sqrt{2} \approx 8.4$). Guess C.

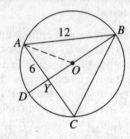

Answer Sheet—Test 4

If a section has fewer than 35 questions, leave the extra spaces blank.

Section 1

1 Ⓐ Ⓑ Ⓒ Ⓓ Ⓔ   8 Ⓐ Ⓑ Ⓒ Ⓓ Ⓔ   15 Ⓐ Ⓑ Ⓒ Ⓓ Ⓔ   22 Ⓐ Ⓑ Ⓒ Ⓓ Ⓔ   29 Ⓐ Ⓑ Ⓒ Ⓓ Ⓔ
2 Ⓐ Ⓑ Ⓒ Ⓓ Ⓔ   9 Ⓐ Ⓑ Ⓒ Ⓓ Ⓔ   16 Ⓐ Ⓑ Ⓒ Ⓓ Ⓔ   23 Ⓐ Ⓑ Ⓒ Ⓓ Ⓔ   30 Ⓐ Ⓑ Ⓒ Ⓓ Ⓔ
3 Ⓐ Ⓑ Ⓒ Ⓓ Ⓔ   10 Ⓐ Ⓑ Ⓒ Ⓓ Ⓔ   17 Ⓐ Ⓑ Ⓒ Ⓓ Ⓔ   24 Ⓐ Ⓑ Ⓒ Ⓓ Ⓔ   31 Ⓐ Ⓑ Ⓒ Ⓓ Ⓔ
4 Ⓐ Ⓑ Ⓒ Ⓓ Ⓔ   11 Ⓐ Ⓑ Ⓒ Ⓓ Ⓔ   18 Ⓐ Ⓑ Ⓒ Ⓓ Ⓔ   25 Ⓐ Ⓑ Ⓒ Ⓓ Ⓔ   32 Ⓐ Ⓑ Ⓒ Ⓓ Ⓔ
5 Ⓐ Ⓑ Ⓒ Ⓓ Ⓔ   12 Ⓐ Ⓑ Ⓒ Ⓓ Ⓔ   19 Ⓐ Ⓑ Ⓒ Ⓓ Ⓔ   26 Ⓐ Ⓑ Ⓒ Ⓓ Ⓔ   33 Ⓐ Ⓑ Ⓒ Ⓓ Ⓔ
6 Ⓐ Ⓑ Ⓒ Ⓓ Ⓔ   13 Ⓐ Ⓑ Ⓒ Ⓓ Ⓔ   20 Ⓐ Ⓑ Ⓒ Ⓓ Ⓔ   27 Ⓐ Ⓑ Ⓒ Ⓓ Ⓔ   34 Ⓐ Ⓑ Ⓒ Ⓓ Ⓔ
7 Ⓐ Ⓑ Ⓒ Ⓓ Ⓔ   14 Ⓐ Ⓑ Ⓒ Ⓓ Ⓔ   21 Ⓐ Ⓑ Ⓒ Ⓓ Ⓔ   28 Ⓐ Ⓑ Ⓒ Ⓓ Ⓔ   35 Ⓐ Ⓑ Ⓒ Ⓓ Ⓔ

Section 2

1 Ⓐ Ⓑ Ⓒ Ⓓ Ⓔ   8 Ⓐ Ⓑ Ⓒ Ⓓ Ⓔ   15 Ⓐ Ⓑ Ⓒ Ⓓ Ⓔ   22 Ⓐ Ⓑ Ⓒ Ⓓ Ⓔ   29 Ⓐ Ⓑ Ⓒ Ⓓ Ⓔ
2 Ⓐ Ⓑ Ⓒ Ⓓ Ⓔ   9 Ⓐ Ⓑ Ⓒ Ⓓ Ⓔ   16 Ⓐ Ⓑ Ⓒ Ⓓ Ⓔ   23 Ⓐ Ⓑ Ⓒ Ⓓ Ⓔ   30 Ⓐ Ⓑ Ⓒ Ⓓ Ⓔ
3 Ⓐ Ⓑ Ⓒ Ⓓ Ⓔ   10 Ⓐ Ⓑ Ⓒ Ⓓ Ⓔ   17 Ⓐ Ⓑ Ⓒ Ⓓ Ⓔ   24 Ⓐ Ⓑ Ⓒ Ⓓ Ⓔ   31 Ⓐ Ⓑ Ⓒ Ⓓ Ⓔ
4 Ⓐ Ⓑ Ⓒ Ⓓ Ⓔ   11 Ⓐ Ⓑ Ⓒ Ⓓ Ⓔ   18 Ⓐ Ⓑ Ⓒ Ⓓ Ⓔ   25 Ⓐ Ⓑ Ⓒ Ⓓ Ⓔ   32 Ⓐ Ⓑ Ⓒ Ⓓ Ⓔ
5 Ⓐ Ⓑ Ⓒ Ⓓ Ⓔ   12 Ⓐ Ⓑ Ⓒ Ⓓ Ⓔ   19 Ⓐ Ⓑ Ⓒ Ⓓ Ⓔ   26 Ⓐ Ⓑ Ⓒ Ⓓ Ⓔ   33 Ⓐ Ⓑ Ⓒ Ⓓ Ⓔ
6 Ⓐ Ⓑ Ⓒ Ⓓ Ⓔ   13 Ⓐ Ⓑ Ⓒ Ⓓ Ⓔ   20 Ⓐ Ⓑ Ⓒ Ⓓ Ⓔ   27 Ⓐ Ⓑ Ⓒ Ⓓ Ⓔ   34 Ⓐ Ⓑ Ⓒ Ⓓ Ⓔ
7 Ⓐ Ⓑ Ⓒ Ⓓ Ⓔ   14 Ⓐ Ⓑ Ⓒ Ⓓ Ⓔ   21 Ⓐ Ⓑ Ⓒ Ⓓ Ⓔ   28 Ⓐ Ⓑ Ⓒ Ⓓ Ⓔ   35 Ⓐ Ⓑ Ⓒ Ⓓ Ⓔ

Section 3

1 Ⓐ Ⓑ Ⓒ Ⓓ Ⓔ   8 Ⓐ Ⓑ Ⓒ Ⓓ Ⓔ   15 Ⓐ Ⓑ Ⓒ Ⓓ Ⓔ   22 Ⓐ Ⓑ Ⓒ Ⓓ Ⓔ   29 Ⓐ Ⓑ Ⓒ Ⓓ Ⓔ
2 Ⓐ Ⓑ Ⓒ Ⓓ Ⓔ   9 Ⓐ Ⓑ Ⓒ Ⓓ Ⓔ   16 Ⓐ Ⓑ Ⓒ Ⓓ Ⓔ   23 Ⓐ Ⓑ Ⓒ Ⓓ Ⓔ   30 Ⓐ Ⓑ Ⓒ Ⓓ Ⓔ
3 Ⓐ Ⓑ Ⓒ Ⓓ Ⓔ   10 Ⓐ Ⓑ Ⓒ Ⓓ Ⓔ   17 Ⓐ Ⓑ Ⓒ Ⓓ Ⓔ   24 Ⓐ Ⓑ Ⓒ Ⓓ Ⓔ   31 Ⓐ Ⓑ Ⓒ Ⓓ Ⓔ
4 Ⓐ Ⓑ Ⓒ Ⓓ Ⓔ   11 Ⓐ Ⓑ Ⓒ Ⓓ Ⓔ   18 Ⓐ Ⓑ Ⓒ Ⓓ Ⓔ   25 Ⓐ Ⓑ Ⓒ Ⓓ Ⓔ   32 Ⓐ Ⓑ Ⓒ Ⓓ Ⓔ
5 Ⓐ Ⓑ Ⓒ Ⓓ Ⓔ   12 Ⓐ Ⓑ Ⓒ Ⓓ Ⓔ   19 Ⓐ Ⓑ Ⓒ Ⓓ Ⓔ   26 Ⓐ Ⓑ Ⓒ Ⓓ Ⓔ   33 Ⓐ Ⓑ Ⓒ Ⓓ Ⓔ
6 Ⓐ Ⓑ Ⓒ Ⓓ Ⓔ   13 Ⓐ Ⓑ Ⓒ Ⓓ Ⓔ   20 Ⓐ Ⓑ Ⓒ Ⓓ Ⓔ   27 Ⓐ Ⓑ Ⓒ Ⓓ Ⓔ   34 Ⓐ Ⓑ Ⓒ Ⓓ Ⓔ
7 Ⓐ Ⓑ Ⓒ Ⓓ Ⓔ   14 Ⓐ Ⓑ Ⓒ Ⓓ Ⓔ   21 Ⓐ Ⓑ Ⓒ Ⓓ Ⓔ   28 Ⓐ Ⓑ Ⓒ Ⓓ Ⓔ   35 Ⓐ Ⓑ Ⓒ Ⓓ Ⓔ

Section 4

1 Ⓐ Ⓑ Ⓒ Ⓓ Ⓔ   4 Ⓐ Ⓑ Ⓒ Ⓓ Ⓔ   7 Ⓐ Ⓑ Ⓒ Ⓓ Ⓔ   10 Ⓐ Ⓑ Ⓒ Ⓓ Ⓔ   13 Ⓐ Ⓑ Ⓒ Ⓓ Ⓔ
2 Ⓐ Ⓑ Ⓒ Ⓓ Ⓔ   5 Ⓐ Ⓑ Ⓒ Ⓓ Ⓔ   8 Ⓐ Ⓑ Ⓒ Ⓓ Ⓔ   11 Ⓐ Ⓑ Ⓒ Ⓓ Ⓔ   14 Ⓐ Ⓑ Ⓒ Ⓓ Ⓔ
3 Ⓐ Ⓑ Ⓒ Ⓓ Ⓔ   6 Ⓐ Ⓑ Ⓒ Ⓓ Ⓔ   9 Ⓐ Ⓑ Ⓒ Ⓓ Ⓔ   12 Ⓐ Ⓑ Ⓒ Ⓓ Ⓔ   15 Ⓐ Ⓑ Ⓒ Ⓓ Ⓔ

Section 4 (continued)

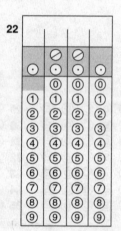

16 17 18 19 20

21 22 23 24 25

Section 5

1 Ⓐ Ⓑ Ⓒ Ⓓ Ⓔ	8 Ⓐ Ⓑ Ⓒ Ⓓ Ⓔ	15 Ⓐ Ⓑ Ⓒ Ⓓ Ⓔ	22 Ⓐ Ⓑ Ⓒ Ⓓ Ⓔ	29 Ⓐ Ⓑ Ⓒ Ⓓ Ⓔ
2 Ⓐ Ⓑ Ⓒ Ⓓ Ⓔ	9 Ⓐ Ⓑ Ⓒ Ⓓ Ⓔ	16 Ⓐ Ⓑ Ⓒ Ⓓ Ⓔ	23 Ⓐ Ⓑ Ⓒ Ⓓ Ⓔ	30 Ⓐ Ⓑ Ⓒ Ⓓ Ⓔ
3 Ⓐ Ⓑ Ⓒ Ⓓ Ⓔ	10 Ⓐ Ⓑ Ⓒ Ⓓ Ⓔ	17 Ⓐ Ⓑ Ⓒ Ⓓ Ⓔ	24 Ⓐ Ⓑ Ⓒ Ⓓ Ⓔ	31 Ⓐ Ⓑ Ⓒ Ⓓ Ⓔ
4 Ⓐ Ⓑ Ⓒ Ⓓ Ⓔ	11 Ⓐ Ⓑ Ⓒ Ⓓ Ⓔ	18 Ⓐ Ⓑ Ⓒ Ⓓ Ⓔ	25 Ⓐ Ⓑ Ⓒ Ⓓ Ⓔ	32 Ⓐ Ⓑ Ⓒ Ⓓ Ⓔ
5 Ⓐ Ⓑ Ⓒ Ⓓ Ⓔ	12 Ⓐ Ⓑ Ⓒ Ⓓ Ⓔ	19 Ⓐ Ⓑ Ⓒ Ⓓ Ⓔ	26 Ⓐ Ⓑ Ⓒ Ⓓ Ⓔ	33 Ⓐ Ⓑ Ⓒ Ⓓ Ⓔ
6 Ⓐ Ⓑ Ⓒ Ⓓ Ⓔ	13 Ⓐ Ⓑ Ⓒ Ⓓ Ⓔ	20 Ⓐ Ⓑ Ⓒ Ⓓ Ⓔ	27 Ⓐ Ⓑ Ⓒ Ⓓ Ⓔ	34 Ⓐ Ⓑ Ⓒ Ⓓ Ⓔ
7 Ⓐ Ⓑ Ⓒ Ⓓ Ⓔ	14 Ⓐ Ⓑ Ⓒ Ⓓ Ⓔ	21 Ⓐ Ⓑ Ⓒ Ⓓ Ⓔ	28 Ⓐ Ⓑ Ⓒ Ⓓ Ⓔ	35 Ⓐ Ⓑ Ⓒ Ⓓ Ⓔ

Section 6

1 Ⓐ Ⓑ Ⓒ Ⓓ Ⓔ	8 Ⓐ Ⓑ Ⓒ Ⓓ Ⓔ	15 Ⓐ Ⓑ Ⓒ Ⓓ Ⓔ	22 Ⓐ Ⓑ Ⓒ Ⓓ Ⓔ	29 Ⓐ Ⓑ Ⓒ Ⓓ Ⓔ
2 Ⓐ Ⓑ Ⓒ Ⓓ Ⓔ	9 Ⓐ Ⓑ Ⓒ Ⓓ Ⓔ	16 Ⓐ Ⓑ Ⓒ Ⓓ Ⓔ	23 Ⓐ Ⓑ Ⓒ Ⓓ Ⓔ	30 Ⓐ Ⓑ Ⓒ Ⓓ Ⓔ
3 Ⓐ Ⓑ Ⓒ Ⓓ Ⓔ	10 Ⓐ Ⓑ Ⓒ Ⓓ Ⓔ	17 Ⓐ Ⓑ Ⓒ Ⓓ Ⓔ	24 Ⓐ Ⓑ Ⓒ Ⓓ Ⓔ	31 Ⓐ Ⓑ Ⓒ Ⓓ Ⓔ
4 Ⓐ Ⓑ Ⓒ Ⓓ Ⓔ	11 Ⓐ Ⓑ Ⓒ Ⓓ Ⓔ	18 Ⓐ Ⓑ Ⓒ Ⓓ Ⓔ	25 Ⓐ Ⓑ Ⓒ Ⓓ Ⓔ	32 Ⓐ Ⓑ Ⓒ Ⓓ Ⓔ
5 Ⓐ Ⓑ Ⓒ Ⓓ Ⓔ	12 Ⓐ Ⓑ Ⓒ Ⓓ Ⓔ	19 Ⓐ Ⓑ Ⓒ Ⓓ Ⓔ	26 Ⓐ Ⓑ Ⓒ Ⓓ Ⓔ	33 Ⓐ Ⓑ Ⓒ Ⓓ Ⓔ
6 Ⓐ Ⓑ Ⓒ Ⓓ Ⓔ	13 Ⓐ Ⓑ Ⓒ Ⓓ Ⓔ	20 Ⓐ Ⓑ Ⓒ Ⓓ Ⓔ	27 Ⓐ Ⓑ Ⓒ Ⓓ Ⓔ	34 Ⓐ Ⓑ Ⓒ Ⓓ Ⓔ
7 Ⓐ Ⓑ Ⓒ Ⓓ Ⓔ	14 Ⓐ Ⓑ Ⓒ Ⓓ Ⓔ	21 Ⓐ Ⓑ Ⓒ Ⓓ Ⓔ	28 Ⓐ Ⓑ Ⓒ Ⓓ Ⓔ	35 Ⓐ Ⓑ Ⓒ Ⓓ Ⓔ

MODEL SAT I TEST 4 1 1 1 1 1 1 1

SECTION 1 **Time—30 Minutes**
30 Questions **Select the best answer to the following questions, then fill in the appropriate space on your Answer Sheet.**

Each of the following sentences contains one or two blanks; these blanks indicate that a word or set of words has been left out. Below the sentence are five words or phrases, lettered A through E. Select the word or set of words that best completes the sentence.

Example:

Fame is ----; today's rising star is all too soon tomorrow's washed-up has-been.

(A) rewarding   (B) gradual
  (C) essential   (D) spontaneous
   (E) transitory

Ⓐ Ⓑ Ⓒ Ⓓ ●

1. Although in his seventies at the time of the interview, Picasso proved alert and insightful, his faculties ---- despite the inevitable toll of the years.

   (A) atrophied   (B) diminished   (C) intact
    (D) useless   (E) impaired

2. While the 1940s are most noted for the development of black modern dance, they are also ---- because they were the last gasp for tap dancing.

   (A) irrelevant
   (B) unfounded
   (C) significant
   (D) speculative
   (E) contemporary

3. People who take megadoses of vitamins and minerals should take care: though beneficial in small quantities, in large amounts these substances may have ---- effects.

   (A) admirable
   (B) redundant
   (C) intangible
   (D) toxic
   (E) minor

4. The number of black hawks has ---- because the encroachments of humans on their territory have caused them to ---- their customary breeding places.

   (A) multiplied..endure
   (B) extrapolated..alter
   (C) increased..locate
   (D) diminished..accept
   (E) dwindled..shun

5. Although Britain's film makers often produce fine films, they are studiously ---- and rarely aim at a mass market.

   (A) commercial
   (B) viable
   (C) derivative
   (D) elitist
   (E) collaborative

6. MacDougall's former editors remember him as a ---- man whose ---- and exhaustive reporting was worth the trouble.

   (A) domineering..wearisome
   (B) congenial..pretentious
   (C) popular..supercilious
   (D) fastidious..garbled
   (E) cantankerous..meticulous

7. The opossum is ---- the venom of snakes in the rattlesnake subfamily and thus views the reptiles not as ---- enemies but as a food source.

   (A) vulnerable to..natural
   (B) conscious of..mortal
   (C) impervious to..lethal
   (D) sensitive to..deadly
   (E) defenseless against..potential

8. Breaking with established musical conventions, Stravinsky was ---- composer whose heterodox works infuriated the traditionalists of his day.

   (A) a derivative
   (B) an iconoclastic
   (C) an uncontroversial
   (D) a venerated
   (E) a trite

9. A code of ethics governing the behavior of physicians during epidemics did not exist until 1846 when it was ---- by the American Medical Association.

   (A) rescinded
   (B) promulgated
   (C) presupposed
   (D) depreciated
   (E) implied

GO ON TO THE NEXT PAGE

1   1   1   1   1   1   1   1   1   1   1   1

The analogies questions present two words or phrases that are related in some way. Determine which A-through-E answer choice below has a relationship *most* similar to that of the original words or phrases.

Example:

YAWN:BOREDOM::   (A) dream:sleep
(B) anger:madness   (C) smile:amusement
(D) face:expression   (E) impatience:rebellion

Ⓐ Ⓑ ● Ⓓ Ⓔ

---

10. DOG:MAMMAL::

(A) wolf:pack
(B) tree:forest
(C) insect:antenna
(D) snake:reptile
(E) kennel:house

11. TELLER:BANK::

(A) guest:motel
(B) architect:blueprint
(C) actor:rehearsal
(D) patient:hospital
(E) teacher:school

12. VISIONARY:PRACTICAL::

(A) dilettante:amateurish
(B) braggart:modest
(C) rebel:revolutionary
(D) connoisseur:cultivated
(E) retainer:loyal

13. INSUBORDINATION:SOLDIER::

(A) enrollment:student
(B) indignation:heckler
(C) autonomy:government
(D) disobedience:child
(E) diligence:worker

14. TUMBLER:BEVERAGE::

(A) quiver:arrows
(B) juggler:orange
(C) quibbler:revenge
(D) glutton:food
(E) gambler:lottery

15. EPHEMERAL:MAYFLY::

(A) ravenous:cobra
(B) graceful:gazelle
(C) succulent:mosquito
(D) amorphous:butterfly
(E) hasty:spider

Read each of the passages below, and then answer the questions that follow each passage. The correct response may be stated outright or merely suggested in the passage.

Questions 16–21 are based on the following passage.

Are Americans today overworked? The following passage is excerpted from a book published in 1991 on the unexpected decline of leisure in American life.

Faith in progress is deep within our culture. We have been taught to believe that our lives are better than the lives of those who came before us.
Line The ideology of modern economics suggests that
(5) material progress has yielded enhanced satisfaction and well-being. But much of our confidence about our own well being comes from the assumption that our lives are easier than those of earlier generations. I have already disputed the
(10) notion that we work less than medieval European peasants, however poor they may have been. The field research of anthropologists gives another view of the conventional wisdom.

The lives of so-called primitive peoples are
(15) commonly thought to be harsh—their existence dominated by the "incessant quest for food." In fact, primitives do little work. By contemporary standards, we'd have to judge them very lazy. If the Kapauku of Papua work one day, they do no
(20) labor on the next. !Kung Bushmen put in only two and a half days per week and six hours per day. In the Sandwich Islands of Hawaii, men work only four hours per day. And Australian aborigines have similar schedules. The key to
(25) understanding why these "stone age peoples" fail to act like us—increasing their work effort to get more things—is that they have limited desires. In the race between wanting and having, they have kept their wanting low—and, in this way, ensure
(30) their own kind of satisfaction. They are materially poor by contemporary standards, but in at least one dimension—time—we have to count them richer.

GO ON TO THE NEXT PAGE ▶

1   1   1   1   1   1   1   1   1   1   1

I do not raise these issues to imply that we
(35) would be better off as Polynesian natives or
medieval peasants. Nor am I arguing that
"progress" has made us worse off. I am, instead,
making a much simpler point. We have paid a
price for prosperity. Capitalism has brought a dra-
(40) matically increased standard of living, but at the
cost of a much more demanding worklife. We are
eating more, but we are burning up those calories
at work. We have color televisions and compact
disc players, but we need them to unwind after a
(45) stressful day at the office. We take vacations, but
we work so hard throughout the year that they
become indispensable to our sanity. The conventional wisdom that economic progress has given
us more things *as well as* more leisure is difficult
(50) to sustain.

16. According to the author, we base our belief that
American people today are well off on the assumption that

(A) America has always been the land of opportunity
(B) Americans particularly deserve to be prosper-
ous
(C) people elsewhere have an inferior standard of
living
(D) people elsewhere envy the American way of
life
(E) our faith in progress will protect us as a nation

17. The author regards "the conventional wisdom"
(line 13) with

(A) resentment
(B) skepticism
(C) complacency
(D) apprehension
(E) bewilderment

18. In lines 18–22, the Kapauku tribesmen and the
!Kung Bushmen are presented as examples of

(A) malingerers who turn down opportunities to
work
(B) noble savages with little sense of time
(C) people who implicitly believe in progress
(D) people unmotivated by a desire for consumer
goods
(E) people obsessed by their constant search for
food

19. The word "raise" in line 34 means

(A) elevate
(B) increase
(C) nurture
(D) bring up
(E) set upright

20. The primary purpose of the passage is to

(A) dispute an assumption
(B) highlight a problem
(C) ridicule a theory
(D) answer a criticism
(E) counter propaganda

21. The last four sentences of the passage (lines 41–50)
provide

(A) a recapitulation of a previously made argument
(B) an example of the argument that has been pro-
posed earlier
(C) a series of assertions and qualifications with a
conclusion
(D) a reconciliation of two opposing viewpoints
(E) a reversal of the author's original position

Questions 22–30 are based on the following passage.

*The following passage, written in the twentieth century,
is taken from a discussion of John Webster's 17th-cen-
tury drama "The Duchess of Malfi."*

The curtain rises; the Cardinal and Daniel de
Bosola enter from the right. In appearance, the
Cardinal is something between an El Greco cardi-
Line nal and a Van Dyke noble lord. He has the tall,
(5) spare form—the elongated hands and features—of
the former; the trim pointed beard, the imperial
repose, the commanding authority of the latter.
But the El Greco features are not really those of
asceticism or inner mystic spirituality. They are
(10) the index to a cold, refined but ruthless cruelty in
a highly civilized controlled form. Neither is the
imperial repose an aloof mood of proud detachment. It is a refined expression of satanic pride of
place and talent.
(15) To a degree, the Cardinal's coldness is artifi-
cially cultivated. He has defined himself against
his younger brother Duke Ferdinand and is the
opposite to the overwrought emotionality of the
latter. But the Cardinal's aloof mood is not one of
(20) bland detachment. It is the deliberate detachment
of a methodical man who collects his thoughts
and emotions into the most compact and formidable shape—that when he strikes, he may strike
with the more efficient and devastating force. His
(25) easy movements are those of the slowly circling
eagle just before the swift descent with the

GO ON TO THE NEXT PAGE

1   1 1 1 1 1   1   1   1   1   1

exposed talons. Above all else, he is a man who
never for a moment doubts his destined authority
as a governor. He derisively and sharply rebukes
(30) his brother the Duke as easily and readily as he
mocks his mistress Julia. If he has betrayed his
hireling Bosola, he uses his brother as the tool to
win back his "familiar." His court dress is a long
brilliant scarlet cardinal's gown with white cuffs
(35) and a white collar turned back over the red, both
collar and cuffs being elaborately scalloped and
embroidered. He wears a small cape, reaching
only to the elbows. His cassock is buttoned to the
ground, giving a heightened effect to his already
(40) tall presence. Richelieu would have adored his
neatly trimmed beard. A richly jeweled and orna-
mented cross lies on his breast, suspended from
his neck by a gold chain.

Bosola, for his part, is the Renaissance "famil-
(45) iar" dressed conventionally in somber black with
a white collar. He wears a chain about his neck, a
suspended ornament, and a sword. Although a
"bravo," he must not be thought of as a leather-
jacketed, heavy-booted tough, squat and swarthy.
(50) Still less is he a sneering, leering, melodramatic
villain of the Victorian gaslight tradition. Like his
black-and-white clothes, he is a colorful contradiction, a scholar-assassin, a humanist-hangman;
introverted and introspective, yet ruthless in
(55) action; moody and reluctant, yet violent. He is a
man of scholarly taste and subtle intellectual discrimination doing the work of a hired ruffian. In
general effect, his impersonator must achieve sup-
pleness and subtlety of nature, a highly complex,
(60) compressed, yet well restrained intensity of temperament. Like Duke Ferdinand, he is inwardly
tormented, but not by undiluted passion. His dominant emotion is an intellectualized one: that of
disgust at a world filled with knavery and folly,
(65) but in which he must play a part and that a lowly,
despicable one. He is the kind of rarity that
Browning loved to depict in his Renaissance
monologues.

22. The primary purpose of the passage appears to
be to

(A) provide historical background on the
Renaissance church
(B) describe ecclesiastical costuming and
pageantry
(C) analyze the appearances and moral natures of
two dramatic figures
(D) explain why modern audiences enjoy *The
Duchess of Malfi*
(E) compare two interpretations of a challenging
role

23. The word "spare" in line 5 means

(A) excessive
(B) superfluous
(C) pardonable
(D) lean
(E) inadequate

24. In lines 24–27, the author most likely compares the
movements of the Cardinal to those of a circling
eagle in order to emphasize his

(A) flightiness
(B) love of freedom
(C) eminence
(D) spirituality
(E) mercilessness

25. The Cardinal's "satanic pride of place" (lines
13–14) refers to his glorying in his

(A) faith
(B) rank
(C) residence
(D) immobility
(E) wickedness

26. As used in the third paragraph, the word "bravo"
most nearly means

(A) a courageous man
(B) a national hero
(C) a clergyman
(D) a humanist
(E) a mercenary killer

27. In describing Bosola (lines 44–68), the author
chiefly uses which of the following literary techniques?

(A) Rhetorical questions
(B) Unqualified assertions
(C) Comparison and contrast
(D) Dramatic irony
(E) Literary allusion

28. The word "discrimination" in lines 56–57 means

(A) prejudice
(B) villainy
(C) discretion
(D) favoritism
(E) discernment

GO ON TO THE NEXT PAGE

1   1   1   1   1   1   1   1   1   1   1

29. According to lines 61–66, why does Bosola suffer torments?

(A) His master the Cardinal berates him for performing his duties inadequately.
(B) He feels intense compassion for the pains endured by the Cardinal's victims.
(C) He is frustrated by his inability to attain a higher rank in the church.
(D) He feels superior to the villainy around him, yet must act the villain himself.
(E) He lacks the intellectual powers for scholarly success, but cannot endure common fools.

30. The author of the passage assumes that the reader is

(A) familiar with the paintings of El Greco and Van Dyke
(B) disgusted with a world filled with cruelty and folly
(C) ignorant of the history of the Roman Catholic Church
(D) uninterested in psychological distinctions
(E) unacquainted with the writing of Browning

YOU MAY GO BACK AND REVIEW THIS SECTION IN THE REMAINING TIME, BUT DO NOT WORK IN ANY OTHER SECTION UNTIL TOLD TO DO SO.   **S T O P**

2   2 2 2 2 2 2 2 2 2   2

SECTION 2

Time—30 Minutes
25 Questions

For each problem in this section determine which of the five choices is correct and blacken in that choice on your answer sheet. You may use any blank space on the page for your work.

Notes:

- You may use a calculator whenever you feel it will be helpful.
- Use the diagrams provided to help you solve the problems. Unless you see the words "Note: Figure not drawn to scale" under a diagram, it has been drawn as accurately as possible. Unless it is stated that a figure is three-dimensional, you may assume it lies in a plane.

Reference Information

| Area Facts | Volume Facts | Triangle Facts | Angle Facts |

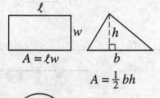
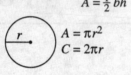

$A = \ell w$

$A = \frac{1}{2} bh$

$A = \pi r^2$
$C = 2\pi r$

$V = \ell w h$

$V = \pi r^2 h$

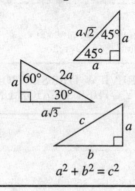

$a^2 + b^2 = c^2$

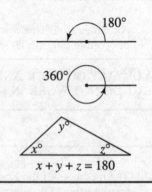

$x + y + z = 180$

---

1. If $2x + 4x + 6x = -12$, then $x =$

   (A) -1 (B) $-\frac{1}{2}$ (C) 0 (D) $\frac{1}{2}$ (E) 1

2. If $(w + 12) - 12 = 12$, then $w =$

   (A) -12 (B) 0 (C) 12 (D) 24 (E) 36

Questions 3–4 refer to the information in the following table, which shows the number of students in each of the five fifth-grade classes at Taft Elementary School and, for each class, the number of students in the school band.

Class	Number of Students	Number in Band
A	20	5
B	30	7
C	23	5
D	27	6
E	25	6

3. What is the average (arithmetic mean) number of students per class?

   (A) 23 (B) 24 (C) 24.5 (D) 25 (E) 26

4. Which class has the highest percent of students in the band?

   (A) A (B) B (C) C (D) D (E) E

5. What is the product of 1.1 and 1.9 rounded to the nearest tenth?

   (A) 1.5 (B) 1.7 (C) 2.0 (D) 2.1 (E) 3.0

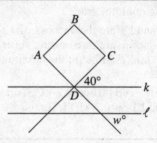

6. In the figure above, lines k and ℓ are parallel, and line k passes through D, one of the corners of square $ABCD$. What is the value of w?

   (A) 30 (B) 40 (C) 45 (D) 50 (E) 60

GO ON TO THE NEXT PAGE ▶

2   2   2   2   2   2   2   2   2   2   2

7. If 24 of the 40 students in a club are girls, what is the ratio of boys to girls in the club?

(A) 2:5   (B) 3:5   (C) 2:3   (D) 3:2   (E) 5:2

8. Steve took a bike trip in which he covered half the total distance on Monday. After going 100 kilometers on Tuesday, he determined that he still had 10% of the trip to complete. What was the total length, in kilometers, of the trip?

(A) 200   (B) 250   (C) 400   (D) 500   (E) 600

9. A number, x, is chosen at random from the set of positive integers less than 10. What is the probability that $\dfrac{9}{x} > x$?

(A) $\dfrac{1}{5}$ (B) $\dfrac{2}{9}$ (C) $\dfrac{1}{3}$ (D) $\dfrac{2}{3}$ (E) $\dfrac{7}{9}$

10. The members of the French Club conducted a fundraising drive. The average (arithmetic mean) amount of money raised per member was $85. Then Jean joined the club and raised $50. This lowered the average to $80. How many members were there before Jean joined?

(A) 4   (B) 5   (C) 6   (D) 7   (E) 8

11. R, S, and T are points with $RT = 2RS$. Which of the following could be true?

   I. R, S, and T are the vertices of a right triangle.
   II. R, S, and T are three of the vertices of a square.
   III. R, S, and T all lie on the circumference of a circle.

(A) I only   (B) III only   (C) I and II only
(D) I and III only   (E) I, II, and III

12. At Music Outlet the regular price for a CD is d dollars. How many CDs can be purchased for m dollars when the CDs are on sale at 50% off the regular price?

(A) $\dfrac{m}{50d}$ (B) $\dfrac{md}{50}$ (C) $\dfrac{md}{2}$ (D) $\dfrac{m}{2d}$

(E) $\dfrac{2m}{d}$

13. There are 12 men on a basketball team, and in a game 5 of them play at any one time. If the game is 1 hour long, and if each man plays exactly the same amount of time, how many minutes does each man play?

(A) 10   (B) 12   (C) 24   (D) 25   (E) 30

14. The volume of pitcher I is A ounces, and the volume of pitcher II is B ounces, with $B > A$. If pitcher II is full of water and pitcher I is empty, and if just enough water is poured from pitcher II to fill pitcher I, what fraction of pitcher II is now full?

(A) $\dfrac{1}{2}$ (B) $\dfrac{1}{B}$ (C) $\dfrac{A}{B}$ (D) $\dfrac{A-B}{B}$

(E) $\dfrac{B-A}{B}$

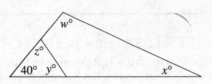

15. In the figure above, $w + x + y + z =$

(A) 140   (B) 280   (C) 300   (D) 320   (E) 360

$$\begin{array}{r} AB \\ + CD \\ \hline AAA \end{array}$$

16. In the addition problem above, A, B, C, and D are different non-zero digits. What is the value of C?

(A) 1   (B) 3   (C) 5   (D) 7   (E) 9

$$x + y = 10 \qquad y + z = 15 \qquad x + z = 17$$

17. What is the average (arithmetic mean) of x, y, and z?

(A) 7   (B) 14   (C) 15   (D) 21
(E) It cannot be determined from the information given.

GO ON TO THE NEXT PAGE

18. A number of people boarded a bus at the terminal. At the first stop, half of the passengers got off and 1 got on. At the second stop, $\frac{1}{3}$ of the passengers on the bus got off and 1 got on. If the bus then had 15 passengers, how many were there when the bus left the terminal?

(A) 40   (B) 48   (C) 58   (D) 60   (E) 62

19. The route from Peter's house to Wendy's house is exactly 10 miles. At the same time, Peter and Wendy each left home and walked toward the other's house. If Peter walked at a rate of 4 miles per hour, and they met 4 miles from Wendy's house, how fast, in miles per hour, did Wendy walk?

(A) 2   (B) $2\frac{2}{3}$ (C) $3\frac{1}{2}$ (D) 4   (E) 6

20. $A = \{2, 3\}$ $B = \{4, 5\}$ $C = \{6, 7\}$

In how many ways is it possible to pick 1 number from each set, so that the 3 numbers could be the lengths of the three sides of a triangle?

(A) 0   (B) 2   (C) 4   (D) 6   (E) 8

21. If a, b, and c are positive numbers such that $3a = 4b = 5c$, and if $a + b = kc$, what is the value of k?

(A) $\frac{12}{35}$ (B) $\frac{5}{7}$ (C) $\frac{10}{7}$ (D) $\frac{7}{5}$ (E) $\frac{35}{12}$

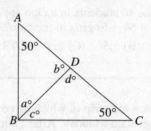

Note: Figure not drawn to scale.

22. Which of the following statements concerning the triangle in the figure above must be true?

   I. $c = 80 - a$
   II. $c = b - 50$
   III. $a + b = c + d$

(A) I only   (B) II only   (C) I and II only
(D) I and III only   (E) I, II, and III

23. If c carpenters can build a garage in d days, how many days will it take e carpenters, working at the same rate, to build 2 garages?

(A) $\frac{2cd}{e}$ (B) $\frac{2d}{ce}$ (C) $\frac{2e}{ce}$ (D) $\frac{cd}{2e}$

(E) $\frac{ce}{2d}$

24. If $a^2 \neq b^2$, then $\dfrac{a^2 - b^2}{b^2 - a^2} + \dfrac{a - b}{b - a} =$

(A) –2   (B) 0   (C) 2   (D) $\dfrac{a+b}{a-b}$ (E) $\dfrac{a-b}{b-a}$

25. Let A = total area of five circles of radius r, and let B = total area of three circles of radius s. If $A = B$, then $\dfrac{r}{s} =$

(A) $\dfrac{3}{5}$ (B) $\dfrac{\sqrt{3}}{\sqrt{5}}$ (C) $\dfrac{3\pi}{5}$ (D) $\dfrac{\sqrt{3\pi}}{\sqrt{5}}$

(E) $\dfrac{\sqrt{3}}{\sqrt{5}}\pi$

YOU MAY GO BACK AND REVIEW THIS SECTION IN THE REMAINING TIME, BUT DO NOT WORK IN ANY OTHER SECTION UNTIL TOLD TO DO SO.   **STOP**

3 3 3 3 3 3 3 3 3 3 3 **3**

SECTION 3   Time—30 Minutes
35 Questions   Select the best answer to the following questions, then fill in
the appropriate space on your Answer Sheet.

Each of the following sentences contains one or two blanks; these blanks indicate that a word or set of words has been left out. Below the sentence are five words or phrases, lettered A through E. Select the word or set of words that best completes the sentence.

Example:

Fame is ----; today's rising star is all too soon tomorrow's washed-up has-been.

(A) rewarding   (B) gradual
(C) essential   (D) spontaneous
(E) transitory

1. The critics were distressed that an essayist of such glowing ---- could descend to writing such dull, uninteresting prose.

(A) obscurity   (B) ill-repute   (C) shallowness
(D) promise   (E) amiability

2. Famous in her time and then forgotten, the 17th-century Dutch painter Judith Leyster was ---- obscurity when, in 1993, the Worcester Art Museum organized the first retrospective exhibition of her work.

(A) resigned to
(B) rewarded with
(C) rescued from
(D) indifferent to
(E) worthy of

3. The testimony of eyewitnesses is notoriously ----; emotion and excitement all too often cause our minds to distort what we see.

(A) judicious
(B) interdependent
(C) credible
(D) unreliable
(E) gratifying

4. Although Henry was not in general a sentimental man, occasionally he would feel a touch of ---- for the old days and would contemplate making a brief excursion to Boston to revisit his childhood friends.

(A) exasperation   (B) chagrin   (C) nostalgia
(D) lethargy   (E) anxiety

5. We had not realized how much people ---- the library's old borrowing policy until we received complaints once it had been ----.

(A) enjoyed...continued
(B) disliked...administered
(C) respected...imitated
(D) ignored...lauded
(E) appreciated...superseded

6. During the Dark Ages, hermits and other religious ---- fled the world to devote themselves to silent contemplation.

(A) renegades   (B) skeptics   (C) altruists
(D) recluses   (E) convictions

7. No real life hero of ancient or modern days can surpass James Bond with his nonchalant ---- of death and the ---- with which he bears torture.

(A) contempt...distress
(B) disregard...fortitude
(C) veneration...guile
(D) concept...terror
(E) ignorance...fickleness

8. Even though the basic organization of the brain does not change after birth, details of its structure and function remain ---- for some time, particularly in the cerebral cortex.

(A) plastic   (B) immutable   (C) essential
(D) unavoidable   (E) static

9. Lavish in visual beauty, the film *Lawrence of Arabia* also boasts ---- of style: it knows how much can be shown in a shot, how much can be said in a few words.

(A) extravagance   (B) economy   (C) autonomy
(D) frivolity   (E) arrogance

10. Unlike the highly ---- Romantic poets of the previous century, Arnold and his fellow Victorian poets were ---- and interested in moralizing.

(A) rhapsodic...lyrical
(B) frenetic...distraught
(C) emotional...didactic
(D) sensitive...strange
(E) dramatic...warped

GO ON TO THE NEXT PAGE

3 3 3 3 3 3 3 3 3 3 3 3

The analogies questions present two words or phrases that are related in some way. Determine which A-through-E answer choice below has a relationship *most* similar to that of the original words or phrases.

Example:

YAWN:BOREDOM::   (A) dream:sleep
(B) anger:madness   (C) smile:amusement
 (D) face:expression   (E) impatience:rebellion

Ⓐ Ⓑ ● Ⓓ Ⓔ

11. JOURNALIST:TYPEWRITER::

(A) surgeon:bones
(B) carpenter:lumber
(C) poet:beauty
(D) floorwalker:flower
(E) electrician:pliers

12. MUTTON:SHEEP::

(A) bleat:lamb
(B) sow:pig
(C) hide:buffalo
(D) beef:steer
(E) calf:cow

13. ENTRY:DIARY::

(A) sonnet:ballad
(B) paragraph:prose
(C) missive:epistle
(D) episode:serial
(E) book:leaf

14. MURAL:WALL::

(A) statue:courtyard
(B) painting:portrait
(C) quarry:stone
(D) etching:paper
(E) watercolor:tempera

15. LIBRETTO:AUTHOR::

(A) aria:tenor
(B) score:composer
(C) drama:reviewer
(D) chisel:sculptor
(E) portfolio:architect

16. TETHER:HORSE::

(A) safari:tiger
(B) specimen:animal
(C) brand:calf
(D) muzzle:dog
(E) fetters:prisoner

17. BLIND:SIGHT::

(A) diabetic:sugar
(B) indigent:tact
(C) amnesiac:memory
(D) benevolent:charity
(E) misanthropic:hate

18. PECKISH:STARVING::

(A) proper:seemly
(B) rural:urban
(C) plain:hideous
(D) drunken:sober
(E) sterile:contaminated

19. POET:ODE::

(A) philosopher:nature
(B) dramatist:scenery
(C) sculptor:marble
(D) seamstress:gown
(E) astronomer:planet

20. TIME:SCYTHE::

(A) liberty:sickle
(B) justice:scales
(C) honesty:badge
(D) ignorance:chains
(E) freedom:mountaintop

21. VIRTUOSO:EXPERIENCED::

(A) rogue:knavish
(B) democrat:dictatorial
(C) saint:naive
(D) leader:deferential
(E) evildoer:repentant

22. CAUSTIC:CORRODE::

(A) aesthetic:judge
(B) chaotic:erupt
(C) hypnotic:mesmerize
(D) defunct:revive
(E) durable:harden

23. CARAPACE:TURTLE::

(A) speed:hare
(B) chameleon:lizard
(C) amphibian:frog
(D) shell:snail
(E) kennel:dog

GO ON TO THE NEXT PAGE ▶

Read the passage below, and then answer the questions that follow the passage. The correct response may be stated outright or merely suggested in the passage.

Questions 24–35 are based on the following passage.

In this adaptation of an excerpt from a short story set in Civil War times, a man is about to be hanged. The first two paragraphs set the scene; the remainder of the passage presents a flashback to an earlier, critical encounter.

A man stood upon a railroad bridge in Northern Alabama, looking down into the swift waters twenty feet below. The man's hands were
Line behind his back, the wrists bound with a cord. A
(5) rope loosely encircled his neck. It was attached to a stout cross-timber above his head, and the slack fell to the level of his knees. Some loose boards laid upon the sleepers supporting the metals of the railway supplied a footing for him and his execu-
(10) tioners—two private soldiers of the Federal army, directed by a sergeant, who in civil life may have been a deputy sheriff. At a short remove upon the same temporary platform was an officer in the uniform of his rank, armed. He was a captain. A
(15) sentinel at each end of the bridge stood with his rifle in the position known as 'support'—a formal and unnatural position, enforcing an erect carriage of the body. It did not appear to be the duty of these two men to know what was occurring at the
(20) center of the bridge; they merely blockaded the two ends of the foot plank which traversed it.

The man who was engaged in being hanged was apparently about thirty-five years of age. He was a civilian, if one might judge from his dress,
(25) which was that of a planter. His features were good—a straight nose, firm mouth, broad fore-head, from which his long, dark hair was combed straight back, falling behind his ears to the collar of his well-fitting frock coat. He wore a mous-
(30) tache and pointed beard, but no whiskers; his eyes were large and dark grey and had a kindly expres-sion that one would hardly have expected in one whose neck was in the hemp. Evidently this was no vulgar assassin. The liberal military code
(35) makes provision for hanging many kinds of peo-ple, and gentlemen are not excluded.

Peyton Farquhar was a well-to-do planter, of an old and highly respected Alabama family. Being a slave-owner, and, like other slave-own-
(40) ers, a politician, he was naturally an original secessionist and ardently devoted to the Southern cause. Circumstances had prevented him from taking service with the gallant army that had fought the disastrous campaigns ending with the
(45) fall of Corinth, and he chafed under the inglorious restraint, longing for the release of his energies, the larger life of the soldier, the opportunity for distinction. That opportunity, he felt, would come, as it comes to all in war time. Meanwhile, he did
(50) what he could. No service was too humble for him to perform in aid of the South, no adventure too perilous for him to undertake if consistent with the character of a civilian who was at heart a soldier, and who in good faith and without too
(55) much qualification assented to at least a part of the frankly villainous dictum that all is fair in love and war.

One evening while Farquhar and his wife were sitting near the entrance to his grounds, a grey-
(60) clad soldier rode up to the gate and asked for a drink of water. Mrs. Farquhar was only too happy to serve him with her own white hands. While she was gone to fetch the water, her husband approached the dusty horseman and inquired
(65) eagerly for news from the front.

"The Yanks are repairing the railroads," said the man, "and are getting ready for another advance. They have reached the Owl Creek bridge, put it in order, and built a stockade on the
(70) other bank. The commandant has issued an order, which is posted everywhere, declaring that any civilian caught interfering with the railroad, its bridges, tunnels, or trains, will be summarily hanged. I saw the order."

(75) "How far is it to the Owl Creek bridge?" Farquhar asked.

"About thirty miles."

"Is there no force on this side of the creek?"

"Only a picket post half a mile out, on the rail-
(80) road, and a single sentinel at this end of the bridge."

"Suppose a man—a civilian and a student of hanging—should elude the picket post and per-haps get the better of the sentinel," said Farquhar,
(85) smiling, "what could he accomplish?"

The soldier reflected. "I was there a month ago," he replied. "I observed that the flood of last winter had lodged a great quantity of driftwood against the wooden pier at the end of the bridge.
(90) It is now dry and would burn like tow."

GO ON TO THE NEXT PAGE ⇒

The lady had now brought the water, which the soldier drank. He thanked her ceremoniously, bowed to her husband, and rode away. An hour later, after nightfall, he repassed the plantation,
(95) going northward in the direction from which he had come. He was a Yankee scout.

24. The word "civil" in line 11 means

(A) polite
(B) individual
(C) legal
(D) collective
(E) nonmilitary

25. In cinematic terms, the first two paragraphs most nearly resemble

(A) a wide-angle shot followed by a close-up
(B) a sequence of cameo appearances
(C) a trailer advertising a feature film
(D) two episodes of an ongoing serial
(E) an animated cartoon

26. In lines 30–33, by commenting on the planter's amiable physical appearance, the author suggests that

(A) he was innocent of any criminal intent
(B) he seemed an unlikely candidate for execution
(C) the sentinels had no need to fear an attempted escape
(D) the planter tried to assume a harmless demeanor
(E) the eyes are the windows of the soul

27. The author's tone in discussing "the liberal military code" (line 34) can best be described as

(A) approving
(B) ironic
(C) irked
(D) regretful
(E) reverent

28. Peyton Farquhar would most likely consider which of the following a good example of how a citizen should behave in wartime?

(A) He should use even underhanded methods to support his cause.
(B) He should enlist in the army without delay.
(C) He should turn to politics as a means of enforcing his will.
(D) He should avoid involving himself in disastrous campaigns.
(E) He should concentrate on his duties as a planter.

29. The word "consistent" in line 52 means

(A) unfailing
(B) agreeable
(C) dependable
(D) constant
(E) compatible

30. In line 55, the word "qualification" most nearly means

(A) competence
(B) eligibility
(C) restriction
(D) reason
(E) liability

31. It can be inferred from lines 61–62 that Mrs. Farquhar is

(A) sympathetic to the Confederate cause
(B) uninterested in news of the war
(C) too proud to perform menial tasks
(D) reluctant to ask her slaves to fetch water
(E) inhospitable by nature

32. Farquhar's inquiry about what a man could accomplish (lines 82–85) illustrates which aspect of his character?

(A) Morbid longing for death
(B) Weighty sense of personal responsibility
(C) Apprehension about his family's future
(D) Keenly inquisitive intellect
(E) Romantic vision of himself as a hero

33. From Farquhar's exchange with the soldier (lines 75–90), we can infer that Farquhar most likely is going to

(A) sneak across the bridge to join the Confederate forces
(B) attempt to burn down the bridge to halt the Yankee advance
(C) remove the driftwood blocking the Confederates' access to the bridge
(D) attack the stockade that overlooks the Owl Creek bridge
(E) undermine the pillars that support the railroad bridge

GO ON TO THE NEXT PAGE

3   3 3 3 3 3 3 3 3 3 3 **3**

34. As used in the next-to-last paragraph, "tow" is

(A) an act of hauling something
(B) a tugboat
(C) a railroad bridge
(D) a highly combustible substance
(E) a picket post

35. We may infer from lines 93–96 that

(A) the soldier has deserted from the Southern army
(B) the soldier has lost his sense of direction
(C) the scout has been tempting Farquhar into an unwise action
(D) Farquhar knew the soldier was a Yankee scout
(E) the soldier returned to the plantation unwillingly

YOU MAY GO BACK AND REVIEW THIS SECTION IN THE REMAINING TIME, BUT DO NOT WORK IN ANY OTHER SECTION UNTIL TOLD TO DO SO.   **S T O P**

4   ·4   4   4   4   4   4   4   4   4   4   4   4

SECTION 4

Time—30 Minutes
25 Questions

You have 30 minutes to answer the 15 Quantitative Comparison questions and 10 Student-Produced Response questions in this section. You may use any blank space on the page for your work.

Notes:

- You may use a calculator whenever you feel it will be helpful.
- Use the diagrams provided to help you solve the problems. Unless you see the words "Note: Figure not drawn to scale" under a diagram, it has been drawn as accurately as possible. Unless it is stated that a figure is three-dimensional, you may assume it lies in a plane.

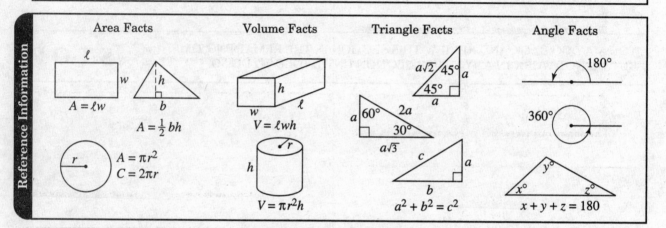

Reference Information

Area Facts

$A = \ell w$

$A = \frac{1}{2} bh$

$A = \pi r^2$
$C = 2\pi r$

Volume Facts

$V = \ell w h$

$V = \pi r^2 h$

Triangle Facts

$a^2 + b^2 = c^2$

Angle Facts

$x + y + z = 180$

Directions for Quantitative Comparison Questions

In each of questions 1–15, two quantities appear in boxes: one in Column A and one in Column B. You must compare them. The correct answer to a question is

A if the quantity in Column A is greater;
B if the quantity in Column B is greater;
C if the two quantities are equal;
D if it is impossible to determine which quantity is greater.

Notes:

- *The correct answer is never E.*
- Sometimes information about one or both of the quantities is centered above the two boxes.
- If the same symbol appears in both columns, it represents the same thing each time.
- All variables represent real numbers.

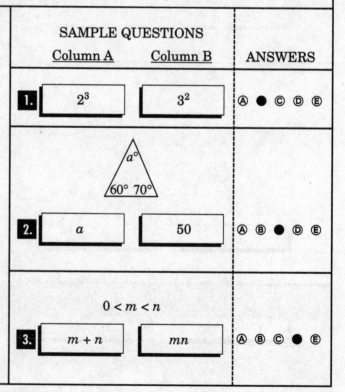

SAMPLE QUESTIONS

Column A	Column B	ANSWERS
1. 2^3	3^2	Ⓐ ● Ⓒ Ⓓ Ⓔ
2. a	50	Ⓐ Ⓑ ● Ⓓ Ⓔ
3. $m + n$	mn	Ⓐ Ⓑ Ⓒ ● Ⓔ

$0 < m < n$

GO ON TO THE NEXT PAGE

4   4 4 4 4 4 4 4 4 4 4   4

SUMMARY DIRECTIONS FOR QUANTITATIVE COMPARISON QUESTIONS

Answer: A if the quantity in Column A is greater;
B if the quantity in Column B is greater;
C if the two quantities are equal;
D if it is impossible to determine which quantity is greater.

Column A   Column B

Column A   Column B

1. $(-7)^4$ -7^4

$a > b > 0$

6. a^3b ab^3

2.   65% of a $\frac{2}{3}$ of a

$-1 < a < 0$

7. $\dfrac{1}{a^6}$ $\dfrac{1}{a^5}$

$A = \{1, 2, 3\}$
$B = \{3, 4, 5\}$

3.   A number picked at random from A A number picked at random from B

$xy = 10$
$x < y$

8. x 3

4. $a + b$ $c + d$

3 beeps = 2 clicks
4 beeps = 5 tweets

9.   1 click   2 tweets

5.   17.6% of 83   83.6% of 17

GO ON TO THE NEXT PAGE →

4   4 4 4 4 4 4 4 4 4 4   4

Column A	Column B

$ab = 0$

10. $(a + b)^2$ $(a - b)^2$

$a > 0$

11.   The average (arithmetic mean) of 1, 2, and $-a$ The average (arithmetic mean) of -1, -2, and a

---

Note: Figure not drawn to scale

12. $r + t$ s

$0 < a < 1$

13.   The area of a square whose side is a The area of a circle whose diameter is a

---

Column A	Column B

A wooden cube whose edges are 4 inches is painted red. The cube is then cut into 64 small cubes whose edges are 1 inch.

14.   The number of small cubes that have exactly three red faces   The number of small cubes that have no red faces

---

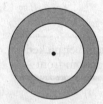

The radius of the large circle is R.
The radius of the small circle is r.
The areas of the shaded region and the white region are equal.

15. $\dfrac{R}{r}$ 1.5

GO ON TO THE NEXT PAGE

4   4 4 4 4 4 4 4 4 4 4   4

Directions for Student-Produced Response Questions (Grid-ins)

In questions 16–25, first solve the problem, and then enter your answer on the grid provided on the answer sheet. The instructions for entering your answers are as follows:

- First, write your answer in the boxes at the top of the grid.
- Second, grid your answer in the columns below the boxes.
- Use the fraction bar in the first row or the decimal point in the second row to enter fractions and decimal answers.

- Grid only one space in each column.
- Entering the answer in the boxes is recommended as an aid in gridding, but is not required.
- The machine scoring your exam can read only what you grid, so you **must grid in your answers correctly to get credit.**
- If a question has more than one correct answer, grid in only one of them.
- The grid does not have a minus sign, so no answer can be negative.
- A mixed number *must* be converted to an improper fraction or a decimal before it is gridded. Enter $1\frac{1}{4}$ as 5/4 or 1.25; the machine will interpret 1 1/4 as $\frac{11}{4}$ and mark it wrong.
- **All decimals must be entered as accurately as possible.** Here are the three acceptable ways of gridding

$$\frac{3}{11} = 0.272727...$$

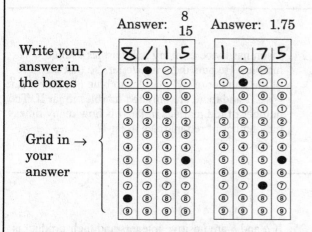

Answer: $\frac{8}{15}$ Answer: 1.75

Write your → answer in the boxes

Grid in → your answer

Answer: 100

Either position is acceptable

3/11   .272   .273

- Note that rounding to .273 is acceptable, because you are using the full grid, but you would receive **no credit** for .3 or .27, because they are less accurate.

16. If $a \otimes b = (a^2 + b^2) - (a^2 - b^2)$, what is the value of $6 \otimes 7$?

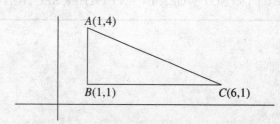

17. In the figure above, what is the area of $\triangle ABC$?

GO ON TO THE NEXT PAGE

4　　4　4　4　4　4　4　4　4　4　4　　4

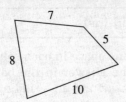

18. A square, not shown, has the same perimeter as the quadrilateral above. What is the length of a side of the square?

19. A factory can produce 1 gizmo every 333 seconds. How many <u>hours</u> will it take to produce 40 gizmos?

20. If the average (arithmetic mean) of a, b, and 10 is 100, what is the average of a and b?

21. If the rent on an apartment goes up 10% every year, next year's rent will be how many times last year's rent?

22. Boris was 26 years old in 1970, when his daughter, Olga, was born. In what year was Boris exactly 3 times as old as Olga?

23. When 25 students took a quiz, the grades they earned ranged from 2 to 10. If exactly 22 of them passed, by earning a grade of 7 or higher, what is the highest possible average (arithmetic mean) the class could have earned on the quiz?

24. Jason has twice as many red marbles as blue marbles. He puts them in two jars so that the ratio of the number of red marbles to blue marbles in jar I is 2:7 and there are only red marbles in jar II. The number of red marbles in jar II is how many times the number of red marbles in jar I?

25. If a and b are positive integers and their product is 3 times their sum, what is the value of $\frac{1}{a}+\frac{1}{b}$?

YOU MAY GO BACK AND REVIEW THIS SECTION IN THE REMAINING TIME, BUT DO NOT WORK IN ANY OTHER SECTION UNTIL TOLD TO DO SO.　　**S T O P**

5

| SECTION 5 | Time—15 Minutes
13 Questions | Select the best answer to the following questions, then fill in
the appropriate space on your Answer Sheet. |

The questions that follow the two passages in this section relate to the content of both, and to their relationship. The correct response may be stated outright in the passages or merely suggested.

Questions 1–13 are based on the following passages.

The following passages deal with the exotic world of subatomic physics. Passage 1, written by a popularizer of contemporary physics, was published in 1985. Passage 2 was written nearly 15 years later.

Passage 1

The classical idea of matter was something with solidity and mass, like wet stone dust pressed in a fist. If matter was composed of
Line atoms, then the atoms too must have solidity and
(5) mass. At the beginning of the twentieth century the atom was imagined as a tiny billiard ball or a granite pebble writ small. Then, in the physics of Niels Bohr, the miniature billiard ball became something akin to a musical instrument, a finely
(10) tuned Stradivarius 10 billion times smaller than the real thing. With the advent of quantum mechanics, the musical instrument gave way to pure music. On the atomic scale, the solidity and mass of matter dissolved into something light and
(15) airy. Suddenly physicists were describing atoms in the vocabulary of the composer—"resonance," "frequency," "harmony," "scale." Atomic electrons sang in choirs like seraphim, cherubim, thrones, and dominions. Classical distinctions
(20) between matter and light became muddled. In the new physics, light bounced about like particles, and matter undulated in waves like light.

In recent decades, physicists have uncovered elegant subatomic structures in the music of mat-
(25) ter. They use a strange new language to describe the subatomic world: *quark, squark, gluon, gauge, technicolor, flavor, strangeness, charm.* There are *up* quarks and *down* quarks, *top* quarks and *bottom* quarks. There are particles with *truth*
(30) and *antitruth*, and there are particles with *naked beauty*. The simplest of the constituents of ordinary matter—the proton, for instance—has taken on the character of a Bach fugue, a four-part counterpoint of matter, energy, space, and time.
(35) At matter's heart there are arpeggios, chromatics, syncopation. On the lowest rung of the chain of being, Creation dances.

Already, the astronomers and the particle physicists are engaged in a vigorous dialogue.
(40) The astronomers are prepared to recognize that the large-scale structure of the universe may have been determined by subtle interactions of particles in the first moments of the Big Bang. And the particle physicists are hoping to find confirmation
(45) of their theories of subatomic structure in the astronomers' observations of deep space and time. The snake has bitten its tail and won't let go.

Passage 2

Consider a dew drop, poised at the tip of a grass blade. Only one millimeter in diameter, this
(50) tiny dew drop is composed of a billion trillion molecules of water, each consisting of two hydrogen atoms and one oxygen atom (H_2O). At the onset of the twentieth century, this was the accepted view of the nature of matter. Atoms
(55) were seen as matter's basic building blocks, elementary or fundamental particles that could not be divided into anything smaller.

This relatively simple picture, however, changed drastically as physicists came to explore
(60) the secrets of the subatomic world. The once-indivisible atom, split, was revealed to consist of a nucleus made up of protons and neutrons around which electrons orbited. Protons and neutrons, in turn, were composed of even smaller subatomic
(65) particles whimsically dubbed quarks. At first, theorists claimed that all matter was made of three fundamental particles: electrons and paired up and down quarks. Later, however, experiments with powerful accelerators and colliding particle beams
(70) suggested the existence of other pairs of quarks, three generations in all, whose mass increased with each generation. Lightest of all were the first generation quarks, up and down, which combined to create the basic protons and neutrons; some-
(75) what heavier were the second generation quarks, strange and charm, the building blocks of the more esoteric particles produced in the physicists' labs. Then in 1977 a team headed by Fermilab physicist Leon Lederman uncovered the possibili-
(80) ty of a third generation of quarks. Using new accelerators with higher energies, they produced a short-lived heavy particle, the upsilon, whose

GO ON TO THE NEXT PAGE

5

properties suggested it could not be made of the
four quarks then known. They concluded it must
(85) be made of a fifth quark, which they named bottom, whereupon scientists throughout the world
set off in hot pursuit of bottom's hypothetical
partner, top.

The hunt for the top quark consumed the
(90) world's particle physicists for nearly twenty
years. It was their Grail, and they were as determined as any knight of King Arthur's court to
succeed in their holy quest. To Harvard theorist
Sheldon Glashow in 1994, it was "not just anoth-
(95) er quark. It's the last blessed one, and the sooner
we find it, the better everyone will feel." Indeed,
they had to find it, for the Standard Model of particle physics, the theoretical synthesis that
reduced the once-maddening hordes of particles
(100) (the so-called "particle zoo") to just a few primary components, hinged upon its existence.
Physicists likened the missing quark to the keystone of an arch: the Standard Model, like an
arch, was supported by all its constituents, but it
(105) was the keystone, the last piece to go in, that
ensured the structure's stability.

In 1995 the physicists found the keystone to
their arch, and with it, new questions to answer.
Surprisingly the top quark was far heavier than
(110) theorists had predicted, nearly twice as heavy in
fact. Fermilab physicist Alvin Tollestrup originally had estimated top to weight at least as much as
a silver atom. At the hunt's end, top was determined to have a mass similar to that of an atom of
(115) gold. (With an atomic weight of 197, a gold atom
is made up of hundreds of up and down quarks.)
The question thus remains, why is top so massive? Why does any fundamental particle have
mass? With its astonishing heft, the top quark
(120) should help clarify the hidden mechanisms that
make some particles massive while others have
no mass at all.

1. Which of the following would be the most appropriate title for the Passage 1?

(A) Linguistic Implications of Particle Physics
(B) The Influence of Music on Particle Interactions
(C) Matter's Transformation: The Music of
Subatomic Physics
(D) Trends in Physics Research: Eliminating the
Quark
(E) The Impossible Dream: Obstacles to Proving
the Existence of Matter

2. The author of Passage 1 refers to quarks, squarks,
and charms (paragraph 2) primarily in order to

(A) demonstrate the similarity between these particles and earlier images of the atom
(B) make a distinction between appropriate and
inappropriate terms
(C) object to suggestions of similar frivolous names
(D) provide examples of idiosyncratic nomenclature in contemporary physics
(E) cite preliminary experimental evidence supporting the existence of subatomic matter

3. The author's tone in the second paragraph of
Passage 1 can best be described as one of

(A) scientific detachment
(B) moderate indignation
(C) marked derision
(D) admiring wonder
(E) qualified skepticism

4. "Matter's heart" mentioned in line 35 is

(A) outer space
(B) the subatomic world
(C) the language of particle physics
(D) harmonic theory
(E) flesh and blood

5. In line 47, the image of the snake biting its tail is
used to emphasize

(A) the dangers of circular reasoning
(B) the vigor inherent in modern scientific dialogue
(C) the eventual triumph of the classical idea of
matter
(D) the unity underlying the astronomers' and particle physicists' theories
(E) the ability of contemporary scientific doctrine
to swallow earlier theories

6. The word "properties" in line 83 most nearly
means

(A) lands   (B) titles   (C) investments
(D) civilities   (E) characteristics

7. Glashow's comment in lines 94–96 reflects his

(A) apprehension
(B) impatience
(C) imagination
(D) jubilation
(E) spirituality

GO ON TO THE NEXT PAGE

8. The references to the "keystone" of the arch (lines 102–103) serve to

(A) diminish the top quark's status to that of a commodity

(B) provide an accurate physical description of the elusive particle

(C) highlight the contrast between appearance and reality

(D) give an approximation of the top quark's actual mass

(E) illustrate the importance of the top quark to subatomic theory

9. The word "hinged" (line 101) most nearly means

(A) folded   (B) vanished   (C) remarked
(D) depended   (E) weighed

10. The author of Passage 2 does all of the following EXCEPT

(A) cite an authority

(B) use a simile

(C) define a term

(D) pose a question

(E) deny a possibility

11. The author of Passage 2 mentions the gold atom (lines 114–115) primarily to

(A) clarify the monetary value of the top quark

(B) explain what is meant by atomic weight

(C) illustrate how hefty a top quark is compared to other particles

(D) suggest the sorts of elements studied in high-energy accelerators

(E) demonstrate the malleability of gold as an element

12. As Passage 2 suggests, since the time Passage 1 was written, the Standard Model has

(A) determined even more whimsical names for the subatomic particles under discussion

(B) taken into account the confusion of the particle physicists

(C) found theoretical validation through recent experiments

(D) refuted significant aspects of the Big Bang theory of the formation of the universe

(E) collapsed for lack of proof of the existence of top quarks

13. The author of Passage 2 would most likely react to the characterization of the constituents of matter in lines 31–37 by pointing out that

(A) this characterization has been refuted by prominent physicists

(B) the characterization is too fanciful to be worthwhile

(C) the most recent data on subatomic particles support this characterization

(D) this characterization supersedes the so-called Standard Model

(E) the current theoretical synthesis is founded on this characterization

YOU MAY GO BACK AND REVIEW THIS SECTION IN THE REMAINING TIME, BUT DO NOT WORK IN ANY OTHER SECTION UNTIL TOLD TO DO SO.   **S T O P**

6   6   6   6   6   6   6   6   6   6   6

SECTION 6
Time—15 Minutes
10 Questions

For each problem in this section determine which of the five choices is correct and blacken in that choice on your answer sheet. You may use any blank space on the page for your work.

Notes:
- You may use a calculator whenever you feel it will be helpful.
- Use the diagrams provided to help you solve the problems. Unless you see the words "Note: Figure not drawn to scale" under a diagram, it has been drawn as accurately as possible. Unless it is stated that a figure is three-dimensional, you may assume it lies in a plane.

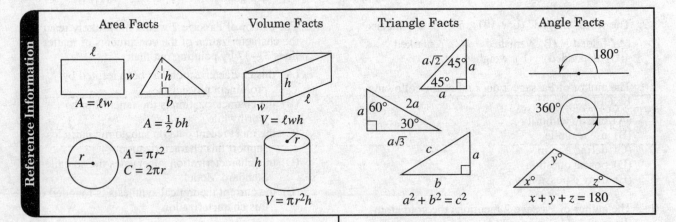

Reference Information

Area Facts
$A = \ell w$
$A = \frac{1}{2}bh$
$A = \pi r^2$
$C = 2\pi r$

Volume Facts
$V = \ell wh$
$V = \pi r^2 h$

Triangle Facts
$a^2 + b^2 = c^2$

Angle Facts
$x + y + z = 180$

1. If $\dfrac{1}{a} + \dfrac{1}{a} + \dfrac{1}{a} = 12$, then $a =$

(A) $\dfrac{1}{12}$ (B) $\dfrac{1}{4}$ (C) $\dfrac{1}{3}$ (D) 3   (E) 4

2. What is the value of $2x^2 - 3x - 7$ when $x = -5$?
(A) 28   (B) 42   (C) 58   (D) 78   (E) 108

Questions 3–4 refer to the information in the following bar graph, which shows the number of books read in January 1995 by the five members of a book club.

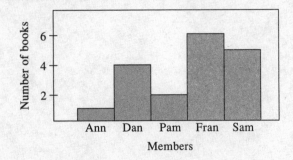

3. What was the total number of books read in January 1995 by the members of the club?
(A) 14   (B) 15   (C) 16   (D) 17   (E) 18

4. What percent of the members read more books than the average (arithmetic mean) number of books read?
(A) 20%   (B) 40%   (C) 50%   (D) 60%   (E) 80%

5. What is the diameter of a circle whose area is A?

(A) $2\sqrt{\dfrac{A}{\pi}}$ (B) $\sqrt{\dfrac{A}{\pi}}$ (C) $\dfrac{A}{2\pi}$ (D) $\dfrac{A}{\pi}$

(E) $\dfrac{2\sqrt{A}}{\pi}$

6. Laurie inherited 40% of her father's estate. After paying a tax equal to 30% of her inheritance, what percent of her father's estate did she own?
(A) 10%   (B) 12%   (C) 25%   (D) 28%   (E) 30%

GO ON TO THE NEXT PAGE

6   6   6   6   6   6   6   6   6   6   6

7. What is the value of a if a is positive and
   $a \times a \times a = a + a + a$?

   (A) $\frac{1}{3}$ (B) $\sqrt{3}$ (C) 3   (D) $3\sqrt{3}$ (E) 9

8. What is the volume, in cubic inches, of a cube
   whose surface area is 60 square inches?

   (A) $10\sqrt{10}$ (B) $15\sqrt{15}$ (C) $60\sqrt{60}$
   (D) 1000   (E) 3375

9. If the circumference of circle I is equal to the
   diameter of circle II, what is the ratio of the area
   of circle II to the area of circle I?

   (A) $\frac{1}{\pi^2}$ (B) $\sqrt{\pi}$ (C) π (D) π^2 (E) $4\pi^2$

10. If A is 25 kilometers east of B, which is 12 kilome-
    ters south of C, which is 9 kilometers west of D,
    how far, in kilometers, is A from D?

    (A) 20   (B) $5\sqrt{34}$ (C) $5\sqrt{41}$ (D) $10\sqrt{13}$
    (E) 71

YOU MAY GO BACK AND REVIEW THIS SECTION IN THE REMAINING TIME,
BUT DO NOT WORK IN ANY OTHER SECTION UNTIL TOLD TO DO SO.   **S T O P**

Answer Key

Note: The letters in brackets following the Mathematical Reasoning answers refer to the sections of Chapter 12 in which you can find the information you need to answer the questions. For example, **1. C [E]**, means that the answer to question 1 is C, and that the solution requires information found in Section 12-E: Averages.

Section 1   Verbal Reasoning

1. C	7. C	13. D	19. D	25. B
2. C	8. B	14. A	20. A	26. E
3. D	9. B	15. B	21. C	27. C
4. E	10. D	16. C	22. C	28. E
5. D	11. E	17. B	23. D	29. D
6. E	12. B	18. D	24. E	30. A

Section 2   Mathematical Reasoning

1. A [G]	6. D [I]	11. D [J, K, L]	16. E [P]	21. E [G]
2. C [G]	7. C [D]	12. E [C, D]	17. A [E]	22. E [J]
3. D [Q, E]	8. B [C]	13. D [A]	18. A [G]	23. A [D]
4. A [Q, C]	9. B [A, O]	14. E [B, M]	19. B [H]	24. A [F]
5. D [B]	10. C [E, G]	15. B [J]	20. C [J]	25. B [L]

Section 3   Verbal Reasoning

1. D	8. A	15. B	22. C	29. E
2. C	9. B	16. E	23. D	30. C
3. D	10. C	17. C	24. E	31. A
4. C	11. E	18. C	25. A	32. E
5. E	12. D	19. D	26. B	33. B
6. D	13. D	20. B	27. B	34. D
7. B	14. D	21. A	28. A	35. C

Section 4   Mathematical Reasoning

Quantitative Comparison Questions

1. A [A]	4. A [N]	7. A [A]	10. C [A, F]	13. A [K, L]
2. D [C, B]	5. A [C]	8. D [G]	11. D [F]	14. C [M]
3. D [O]	6. A [A]	9. B [D, G]	12. C [J]	15. B [L]

Grid-in Questions

16. [F]   98
17. [J,N]   7.5
18. [K]   7.5
19. [K,D]   3.7
20. [E]   145

21.
[C] 1 . 2 1

22.
[H] 1 9 8 3

23.
[E] 9 . 3 6

24.
[D,H] 6

25.
[B] 1 / 3

or .333

Section 5   Verbal Reasoning

1. C	4. B	7. B	10. E	13. B
2. D	5. D	8. E	11. C	
3. D	6. E	9. D	12. C	

Section 6   Mathematical Reasoning

1. B [B, G]	3. E [Q]	5. A [L]	7. B [A]	9. D [L, D]
2. C [A, F]	4. D [Q, C, E]	6. D [C]	8. A [M]	10. A [J, K]

Calculate Your Raw Score

Verbal Reasoning

Section 1 $\dfrac{}{\text{number correct}} - \dfrac{1}{4}\left(\dfrac{}{\text{number incorrect}}\right) = $ _____ (A)

Section 3 $\dfrac{}{\text{number correct}} - \dfrac{1}{4}\left(\dfrac{}{\text{number incorrect}}\right) = $ _____ (B)

Section 5 $\dfrac{}{\text{number correct}} - \dfrac{1}{4}\left(\dfrac{}{\text{number incorrect}}\right) = $ _____ (C)

Raw Verbal Reasoning Score = (A) + (B) + (C) = _____

Mathematical Reasoning

Section 2 $\dfrac{}{\text{number correct}} - \dfrac{1}{4}\left(\dfrac{}{\text{number incorrect}}\right) = $ _____ (D)

Section 4
Part I
(1–15) $\dfrac{}{\text{number correct}} - \dfrac{1}{3}\left(\dfrac{}{\text{number incorrect}}\right) = $ _____ (E)

Part II
(16–25) $\dfrac{}{\text{number correct}}$ $ = $ _____ (F)

Section 6 $\dfrac{}{\text{number correct}} - \dfrac{1}{4}\left(\dfrac{}{\text{number incorrect}}\right) = $ _____ (G)

Raw Mathematical Reasoning Score = (D) + (E) + (F) + (G) = _____

Evaluate Your Performance

	Verbal Reasoning	Mathematical Reasoning
Superior	67–78	51–60
Very Good	60–66	45–50
Good	52–59	40–44
Satisfactory	44–51	35–39
Average	36–43	30–34
Needs Further Study	29–35	25–29
Needs Intensive Study	21–28	20–24
Inadequate	0–20	0–19

Identify Your Weaknesses

Verbal Reasoning

Question Type	Question Numbers			Chapter to Study
	Section 1	Section 3	Section 5	
Sentence Completion	1, 2, 3, 4, 5, 6, 7, 8, 9	1, 2, 3, 4, 5, 6, 7, 8, 9, 10		Chapter 4
Analogy	10, 11, 12, 13, 14, 15	11, 12, 13, 14, 15, 16, 17, 18, 19, 20, 21, 22, 23		Chapter 5
Reading Comprehension	16, 17, 18, 19, 20, 21, 22, 23, 24, 25, 26, 27, 28, 29, 30	24, 25, 26, 27, 28, 29, 30	1, 2, 3, 4, 5, 6, 7, 8, 9, 10, 11, 12, 13	Chapter 6

Identify Your Weaknesses

Mathematical Reasoning

Skill Area	Question Numbers			Pages to Study
	Section 2	Section 4	Section 6	
Basics of Arithmetic	1, 2, 9, 13	1, 6, 7, 10	2, 7	331–338
Fractions and Decimals	5, 14	2, 25	1	344–352
Percents	4, 8, 12	2, 5, 21	4, 6	358–361
Ratios	7, 12, 23	9, 19, 24	9	366–370
Averages	3, 10, 17	20, 23	4	376–378
Polynomials	24	10, 11, 16	2	383–386
Equations and Inequalities	10, 18, 21	8, 9	1	389–394
Word Problems	19	22, 24		399–402
Lines and Angles	6			407–410
Triangles	11, 15, 20, 22	12, 17	10	414–418
Quadrilaterals	11	13, 18, 19	10	425–428
Circles	11, 25	13, 15	5, 9	432–435
Solid Geometry	14	14	8	440–442
Coordinate Geometry		4		446–448
Counting and Probability	9	3		452–456
Logical Reasoning	16			462–464
Data Interpretation	3, 4		3, 4	468–471

Answer Explanations

Section 1   Verbal Reasoning

1. **C.** If one is alert and insightful, one's faculties (mental powers) are *intact* (sound or whole).
Note how the phrase set off by the comma restates and clarifies the idea that Picasso has continued to be perceptive and alert.
(Contrast Signal)

2. **C.** *While* suggests a contrast between the fates of the two dance forms during the 1940s. The decade was *most* noted for the growth of Black modern dance. However, it was also noteworthy or *significant* for the decline of tap dancing.
(Contrast Signal)

3. **D.** Something beneficial or helpful in small amounts may be *toxic* (poisonous) in large amounts.
Remember to watch for signal words that link one part of the sentence to another. The use of "though" in the second clause sets up a contrast. The missing word must be an antonym or near-antonym for beneficial.
(Argument Pattern)

4. **E.** The encroachments or trespassing of human beings on the hawk's territory would frighten the birds, leading them to *shun* or avoid their usual locations for breeding. Frightened away from their nests, disturbed in their breeding routines, the hawks would have fewer offspring. Thus, their numbers would diminish or *dwindle*.
You can immediately eliminate Choices A, B, and C. Choices A and C you can rule out on the basis of general knowledge: when humans come close, wild birds abandon their nests (and their eggs): they have fewer offspring. Choice B you can rule out on the basis of usage. People may *extrapolate* or make projections on the basis of known data about the number of hawks. The "number of black hawks," however, doesn't extrapolate anything.
(Argument Pattern)

5. **D.** To aim at a mass market is to try to appeal to the lowest common denominator. British films rarely do this. Instead of trying to appeal to the masses, they try to appeal to the elite. They are thus *elitist*.
(Contrast Signal)

6. **E.** The key phrase here is "worth the trouble." What sort of person creates trouble for his employers? Not a *congenial* (agreeable) or *popular* one. You can immediately eliminate Choices B and C. A *cantankerous* (bad-tempered) employee creates problems. However,

if he turns in *meticulous* (very careful and exact) work, his employers may think he's worth the trouble he makes.
Note that, after eliminating the answer choices whose first word does not work in the sentence, you must check the second words of the remaining answer choices. A *domineering* (bossy) or *fastidious* (fussy) employee might create problems around the newspaper office. However, he would not get on his employers' good side by turning in *wearisome* (boring) or *garbled* (confused) stories.
(Argument)

7. **C.** Because the opossum is *impervious* to (unharmed by) the poison, it can treat the rattlesnake as a potential source of food and not as a *lethal* or deadly enemy.
Note the cause and effect signal "thus." The nature of the opossum's response to the venom explains *why* it can look on a dangerous snake as an easy prey.
(Cause and Effect Signal)

8. **B.** By definition, someone who breaks with established convention is *iconoclastic* or nonconformist. Go through the answer choices, eliminating anything you can.
Choices A and E are incorrect. Someone who departs from tradition is unlikely to be *derivative* (lacking originality) or *trite* (commonplace; timeworn).
Choices C and D are incorrect. Someone who infuriates (enrages) the traditionalists is controversial, not *uncontroversial*, and is unlikely to be *venerated* (deeply respected) by them.
This is one of the last sentence completion questions, so its answer is an extremely difficult word.
(Definition Pattern)

9. **B.** If the code did not exist until 1846, it could not have been *rescinded* (canceled), *presupposed* (required as an already existing condition), or *depreciated* (disparaged) at that time. It makes most sense that the code was *promulgated* or made known to the public by the A.M.A. at that time.
(Definition)

10. **D.** A *dog* is a *mammal*; a *snake*, a *reptile*.
(Member and Class)

11. **E.** A *teller's* working place is a *bank*; a *teacher's*, a *school*.
(Worker and Workplace)

12. **B.** A *visionary* (dreamer) is not *practical*; a *braggart* (boaster) is not *modest*.
(Antonym Variant)

13. **D.** What is *disobedience* in a child is *insubordination* in a soldier.
(Defining Characteristic)

14. A. A *tumbler* is a container for *beverages*; a *quiver* is a container for *arrows*.
Consider secondary meanings of the capitalized words as well as their primary meanings. Here a *tumbler* is a stemless drinking glass, not an acrobat.   (Definition)

15. B. A *mayfly* is known to be *ephemeral* (short-lived); a *gazelle* is known to be *graceful*.
                    (Defining Characteristic)

16. C. According to the author, "We have been taught to believe that our lives are better than the lives of those who came before us" and the lives of those today who live in similarly "primitive" circumstances. We base our belief that we Americans are well off today the assumption that people in earlier generations and people living in "primitive" circumstances have an *inferior standard of living*.

17. B. The conventional wisdom is that the lives of primitive peoples are filled with toil. The author, however, states that primitives do little work. Thus, she regards the conventional wisdom with *skepticism* or doubt.

18. D. According to the author, these "stone age peoples" have limited desires. They are not motivated by any particular *desire for consumer goods* or other material comforts.

19. D. To raise an issue is to bring it up for discussion.

20. A. Throughout the passage the author *disputes the assumption* made by the conventional wisdom that our economic progress has been an unmitigated blessing. She argues instead that we "have paid a price for prosperity."

21. C. The author makes an assertion: "We are eating more." She then qualifies or limits her assertion: "but we are burning up those calories at work." She repeats this pattern of assertion followed by qualification. She then draws her conclusion: it is hard to support the conventional wisdom that economic progress has been an unmixed blessing for us.

22. C. The author provides the reader both with physical details of dress and bearing and with comments about the motives and emotions of the Cardinal and Bosola.
Choice A is incorrect. The passage scarcely mentions the church. Choice B is incorrect. The description of ecclesiastical costumes is only one item in the description of the Cardinal. Choice D is incorrect. While audiences today might well enjoy seeing the characters acted as described here, the author does not cite specific reasons why the play might appeal to modern audiences. Choice E is incorrect. The author's purpose is to describe two separate roles, not to compare two interpretations of a single role.

23. D. "Spare" is being used to describe the Cardinal's physical appearance. He is tall and *lean*.

24. E. The eagle is poised to strike "with exposed talons." It, like the Cardinal, gathers itself together to strike with greater force. The imagery suggests the Cardinal's *mercilessness*. Choice A is incorrect. The Cardinal is not *flighty* (light-headed and irresponsible); he is cold and calculating. Choice B is incorrect. He loves power, not freedom. Choice C is incorrect. An eagle poised to strike with bare claws suggests violence, not *eminence* (fame and high position). Choice D is incorrect. Nothing in the passage suggests he is spiritual.
Beware of eye-catchers. "Eminence" is a title of honor applied to cardinals in the Roman Catholic church. Choice C may attract you for this reason.

25. B. The Cardinal glories in his place in the hierarchy of the Church: his *rank* or status as an ecclesiastical lord.

26. E. Although Bosola is not a "leather-jacketed" hoodlum, he is a hired "assassin," a "hangman" (despite his scholarly taste and humanist disposition).

27. C. Answer this question by using the process of elimination.
Choice A is incorrect. In describing Bosola the author makes no use of *rhetorical questions* (questions asked solely to produce an effect).
Choice B is incorrect. Though the author makes many assertions about Bosola, he limits or *qualifies* many of them. For example, the author asserts that Bosola "is inwardly tormented." He then immediately qualifies his assertion, adding "but not by undiluted passion." Thus, the author does not chiefly use *unqualified assertions* in describing Bosola.
Choice D is incorrect. *Dramatic irony* is irony built in to a speech or a situation, which the audience understands, but which the characters onstage have yet to grasp. The author does not use this literary technique in describing Bosola.
Choice E is incorrect. The author makes one brief literary allusion (to Browning's verse monologues). He does not chiefly use *literary allusions* in describing Bosola.
Only Choice C is left. It is the correct answer. Throughout the passage's final paragraph, the author describes Bosola through *comparisons* ("Like his black-and-white clothes," "Like

Duke Ferdinand") and *contrasts* ("not . . . a leather-jacketed, heavy-booted tough," "Still less . . . a sneering, leering melodramatic villain").

28. **E.**   The author is contrasting the two sides of Bosola, the scholar and the assassin. As a scholar, he is a man of perceptive intellect, noted for discrimination or *discernment*.

29. **D.**   Lines 61–66 state that Bosola "is inwardly tormented ... (by) disgust at a world filled with knavery and folly, ... in which he must play a part and that a lowly, despicable one." The villainy and foolishness around him disgust him. He feels intellectually superior to the evil around him, *yet must act the villain himself.*

30. **A.**   The casual references to the elongated hands and features of El Greco's work and to the trim beards and commanding stances in the work of Van Dyke imply that the author assumes the reader has seen examples of both painters' art.

Section 2   Mathematical Reasoning

In each mathematics section, for many problems, an alternative solution, indicated by two asterisks(**), follows the first solution. When this occurs, one of the solutions is the direct mathematical one and the other is based on one of the tactics discussed in Chapters 8–12.

1. **A.**   If $2x + 4x + 6x = -12$, then $12x = -12$ and $x = -1$.
   **Note that x *must* be negative, so only A and B are possible. Test these choices.

2. **C.**   The left-hand side of $(w + 12) - 12 = 12$ is just w, so $w = 12$.
   **Of course, you can use TACTIC 9-1: back-solve, starting (and ending) with C.

3. **D.**   The average is just the sum of the number of students in the five classes (125) divided by 5: $125 \div 5 = 25$.

4. **A.**   In class **A**, one-fourth, or 25% (5 of 20), of the students are in the band. In each of the other classes, the number in the band is *less than* one-fourth of the class.

5. **D.**   Use your calculator: $1.1 \times 1.9 = 2.09$, which, to the nearest tenth, is **2.1**.

6. **D.**   Since *ABCD* is a square, $y = 90$. Then $x + 90 + 40 = 180 \Rightarrow x = 50$.

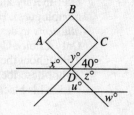

Then $x = z = u = w = 50$ [When parallel lines are cut by a transversal, the four acute angles have the same measure (KEY FACT I6)].
**Use TACTIC 8-2: trust the diagram; w appears to be slightly more than a 45° angle.

7. **C.**   If 24 of the students are girls, then $40 - 24 = 16$ are boys. The ratio of boys to girls is 16:24 which reduces to **2:3**.
   **Even if you can't do the above, there are clearly fewer boys than girls, and so the ratio must be less than 1:1. Eliminate D and E and guess.

8. **B.**   Since 50% of the trip was completed on Monday and 10% of the trip is left, the 100 kilometers traveled on Tuesday represents the other 40% of the total distance, d, so
   $$0.40d = 100 \Rightarrow d = 100 \div 0.40 = 250.$$
   Estimate. Since half of the trip was completed Monday, the 100 kilometers traveled on Tuesday plus the 10% still to go constitutes the other half. The 100 kilometers by itself is slightly less than half, and 200 kilometers would be slightly less than the whole distance. Of the choices, only **250 is possible.

9. **B.**   There are nine positive integers less than 10: 1, 2, ... , 9. For which of them is $\frac{9}{x} > x$? Only 1 and 2: $\frac{9}{1} > 1$ and $\frac{9}{2} > 2$. When $x = 3$, $\frac{9}{x} = x$, and for all the others $\frac{9}{x} < x$. The probability is $\frac{2}{9}$.

10. **C.**   Let n represent the number of members of the club before Jean joined. These members raised a total of $85n$ dollars (KEY FACT E1). After Jean was in the club, the total raised was $85n + 50$, the average was 80, and the number of members was $n + 1$: $\dfrac{85n + 50}{n + 1} = 80$

   Cross-multiply: $85n + 50 = 80(n + 1)$
   Distribute: $85n + 50 = 80n + 80$
   Subtract $80n$ and 50 from each side $5n = 30$
   Divide by 5: $n = 6$
   **Assume that each of the original members raised $85. The only one who raised less than the average of $80 was Jean, who raised $50, so the total deviation below the average was 30. Therefore the total deviation above the mean was also 30 (KEY FACT E3). Since the deviation of each original member is 5, there must be $30 \div 5 = 6$ of them.
   **Use TACTIC 9-1: backsolve. Try 6, choice C. If there were 6 members, the total raised

would be $6 \times 85 = 510$. Now add Jean's 50 and the total goes to 560 for 7 members; and $560 \div 7 = 80$. It works!

11. D. Draw pictures. R, S, T *could be* the vertices of a right triangle (I is true.) R, S, T *could not be* the vertices of a square: $RT = \sqrt{2}\,RS$.

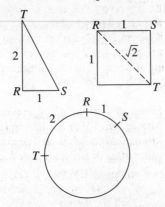

(II is false.) R, S, T *could* all lie on a circle. In fact, the only way they couldn't would be if they all were on the same line. (III is true.) Statements **I and III only** are true.

12. E. At the regular price, a CD costs d dollars, so at 50% off it costs $\dfrac{d}{2}$ dollars. To find out how many you can buy, divide the amount of money, m, by the price per CD, $\dfrac{d}{2}$:

$$m \div \frac{d}{2} = m \times \frac{2}{d} = \frac{2m}{d}.$$

**Use TACTIC 9-2: plug in easy-to-use numbers. If a CD regularly costs \$10, then on sale at 50% off, they cost \$5 each. How many can be purchased on sale for \$20? The answer is 4. Which of the choices equals 4 when $d = 10$ and $m = 20$?

Only $\dfrac{2m}{d}$.

13. D. Since the game takes 1 hour, or 60 minutes, and there are always 5 men playing, there is a total of $5 \times 60 = 300$ man-minutes of playing time. If that amount of time is evenly divided among the 12 players, each one plays $300 \div 12 = \mathbf{25}$ minutes.
**Estimate. If 5 men played the first 10 minutes, and 5 other men played the next 10 minutes, who's left to play the rest of the game? Try the choices: 10 and 12 are much too small, so eliminate A and B. If 5 men played for 30 minutes, and 5 other men played the next 30 minutes, the game would be over and 2 men wouldn't have played at all. Since 30 is too large, eliminate E. The answer must be 24 or 25. Guess.

14. E. When A ounces of water are removed from pitcher II, that pitcher will contain $B - A$ ounces. Since its capacity is B, pitcher II will be $\dfrac{B - A}{B}$ full.

**Use TACTIC 9-3: plug in easy-to-use numbers. Suppose pitcher II holds 10 ounces and pitcher I holds 3. Then, if 3 ounces are poured from pitcher II into pitcher I, pitcher II will have 7 ounces and be $\dfrac{7}{10}$ full. Which of the choices equals $\dfrac{7}{10}$ when $B = 10$ and $A = 3$?

Only $\dfrac{B - A}{B}$.

15. B. In $\triangle ABC$, $w + x + 40 = 180 \Rightarrow w + x = 140$. Similarly, in $\triangle ADE$, $y + z + 40 = 180 \Rightarrow y + z = 140$. Then $w + x + y + z = 140 + 140 = \mathbf{280}$.

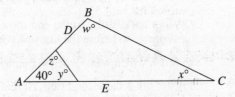

Use TACTIC 8-2: trust the diagram; w, x, y, and z appear to be *about* 100, 45, 60, and 80, respectively, for a total of 285. Your estimate may well be slightly more or less, but should surely be between 240 and 310. With anything less than 300, guess **280; if your estimate is over 300, you might pick 320.

16. E. The sum of 2 two-digit numbers must be less than 200, so $A = 1$ and the sum is 111. Since B and D are positive, $B + D$ cannot be 1, and so must be 11, which means that a 1 is carried into the tens column. In the tens column we must add 1 (for A), the 1 we carried, and C, and the sum is 11. Then $1 + 1 + C = 11$, and $C = \mathbf{9}$.

$$\begin{array}{r} 1B \\ + \underline{CD} \\ 111 \end{array}$$

B, D can be any digits whose sum is 11.

$C = 9$

17. A. Use TACTIC 8-14: when you have more than two equations, add them.

$$\begin{array}{r} x + y = 10 \\ y + z = 15 \\ + \underline{x + z = 17} \\ 2x + 2y + 2z = 42 \end{array}$$

Divide by 2: $\quad x + y + z = 21$

To get the average, divide the sum by 3: $\dfrac{x+y+z}{3} = \dfrac{21}{3} = 7$

(Note: You *could* solve for x, y, z, but you shouldn't.)

18. **A.** Let $x =$ the number of passengers originally on the bus, and keep track of the comings and goings. At the first stop half the people got off, leaving $\dfrac{1}{2}x$ on the bus, and 1 more got on: $\dfrac{1}{2}x + 1$. At the second stop $\dfrac{1}{3}$ of the passengers got off, leaving two-thirds on the bus, and 1 person got on: $\dfrac{2}{3}\left(\dfrac{1}{2}x+1\right) + 1$.

This simplifies to $\dfrac{1}{3}x + \dfrac{2}{3} + 1$, which equals 15, so

$$\dfrac{1}{3}x + \dfrac{2}{3} = 14 \Rightarrow x + 2 = 42 \Rightarrow x = \mathbf{40}.$$

Work backwards. At the end there were 15 passengers, so before the last one got on, there were 14, which was $\dfrac{2}{3}$ of the number before any got off at the second stop. At that point there were 21 passengers, meaning that, before 1 person got on at the first stop, there were 20, which is half of **40, the original number.
**Use TACTIC 9-1: backsolve. Start with C, 58: 29 got off and 1 got on; then there were 30; 10 got off and 1 got on; then there were 21, but we should have only 15. Since 58 is too big, eliminate C, D, and E. Try A or B; A works.

19. **B.** Since Peter walked 6 miles at a rate of 4 miles per hour, it took him $1\dfrac{1}{2}$ or $\dfrac{3}{2}$ hours. Since Wendy walked 4 miles in the same time, she was walking at a rate of

$$4 \div \dfrac{3}{2} = 4 \times \dfrac{2}{3} = \dfrac{8}{3} = \mathbf{2\dfrac{2}{3}} \text{ miles per hour.}$$

20. **C.** According to the triangle inequality (KEY FACT J10), the sum of the lengths of two sides of a triangle must be greater than the length of the third side. There is only one way to pick a number, a, from A and a number, b, from B so that their sum is greater than 7: $a = 3$ and $b = 5$. There are three ways to choose a and b so that their sum is greater than 6: $a = 2$ and $b = 5$; $a = 3$ and $b = 4$; and $a = 3$ and $b = 5$. So in all there are **4** ways to pick the lengths of the three sides.

21. **E.** If $3a = 4b = 5c$, then $a = \dfrac{5}{3}c$ and $b = \dfrac{5}{4}c$, so

$$a + b = \left(\dfrac{5}{3} + \dfrac{5}{4}\right)c = \dfrac{35}{12}c.$$

Then $k = \dfrac{35}{12}$.

**Use TACTIC 9-2: plug in easy-to-use numbers. The factors 3, 4, 5 suggest the number 60. Let $a = 20$, $b = 15$, $c = 12$. Then $a + b = 35$, so $35 = 12k \Rightarrow k = \dfrac{35}{12}$.

22. **E.** In $\triangle ABC$, $\angle B$ measures $80°$, so $a + c = 80$ and $c = 80 - a$. (I is true.) Since the measure of an exterior angle of a triangle equals the sum of the measures of the two opposite interior angles (KEY FACT J2), $b = c + 50 \Rightarrow c = b - 50$. (II is true.) Since $a + b = 130$ and $c + d = 130$, then $a + b = c + d$. (III is true.) Statements **I, II, and III** are true.

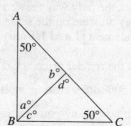

23. **A.** If c carpenters can build a garage in d days, then 1 carpenter will take c times as long, or cd days, and 2 cd days to build 2 garages. Finally, if the work is divided up among e carpenters, they will take $\dfrac{2cd}{e}$ days.

**Use TACTIC 9-2: plug in easy-to-use numbers. If 2 carpenters can build a garage in 10 days, they will take 20 days to build 2 garages. It will take 4 carpenters half as long: 10 days. Which choice is equal to 10 when $c = 2$, $d = 10$, and $e = 4$? Only $\dfrac{2cd}{e}$. Remember: test each choice with your calculator, and eliminate a choice as soon as you can see that it is not equal to 10.

24. **A.** This question is easier than it seems at first. In each fraction, the numerator is the negative of the denominator, so each fraction equals -1 and the sum of the fractions is **-2**.
**Of course, you can use TACTIC 9-2: plug in numbers. If $a = 1$ and $b = 2$, then each fraction is equal to -1.

25. B.   Here $A = 5\pi r^2$ and $B = 3\pi s^2$, so

Divide both sides by π:

$$5\pi r^2 = 3\pi s^2$$
$$5r^2 = 3s^2$$

Divide both sides by $5s^2$:

$$\frac{r^2}{s^2} = \frac{3}{5}$$

Take the square root of each side: $\dfrac{r}{s} = \dfrac{\sqrt{3}}{\sqrt{5}}$.

Section 3   Verbal Reasoning

1. D.   The critics would regret any lapse on the part of a *promising* writer.
The adjective *glowing* is your clue that you are looking for a word with positive associations. Therefore, you can eliminate any word with negative ones. Choices A, B, and C have negative associations. Only Choices D or E can be correct.   (Cause and Effect Pattern)

2. C.   To be the subject of a major exhibition would surely *rescue* a forgotten artist from obscurity (the state of being unknown).
(Cause and Effect Pattern)

3. D.   If we see things in a distorted or altered fashion, our testimony is *unreliable*.
Note how the second clause serves to clarify or define the meaning of the missing word. Remember, before you look at the choices, read the sentence and think of a word that makes sense.
Likely Words: undependable, misleading.
(Definition)

4. C.   A longing for old friends and familiar scenes is *nostalgia* or homesickness.
Remember, before you look at the choices, read the sentence and think of a word that makes sense.
Likely Words: homesickness, nostalgia, yearning.   (Definition)

5. E.   Borrowers would complain that an old, *appreciated* borrowing policy had been set aside or *superseded*.
Remember, in double-blank sentences, go through the answer choices, testing the *first* words in each choice and eliminating those that don't fit. The fact that the new policy has received complaints indicates that the old policy was viewed positively. You can immediately eliminate Choice B, *disliked*, and Choice D, *ignored*. Both are negative terms.
(Contrast Pattern)

6. D.   People who shut themselves away from society are, by definition, hermits or *recluses*.
(Definition)

7. B.   Heroic virtues include *disregard* or ignoring of death and *fortitude* or courage in the face of torture. Through it all, Bond remains nonchalant or cool.   (Examples)

8. A.   *Even though* signals a contrast. The brain's fundamental organization does not change. However, the details of the brain's organization do change: they remain *plastic*, pliable, capable of being molded or shaped.
(Contrast Signal)

9. B.   The key phrase here is "in a few words." Although the movie is lavish in its beauty, it is not lavish in its use of words or film. Instead, it demonstrates *economy* of style.   (Definition)

10. C.   The Romantic poets can be described as *emotional*; Arnold and the later "moralizing" Victorian era poets can be described as *didactic* (interested in teaching).
Remember to watch for signal words that link one part of the sentence to another. The use of "unlike" in the opening clause sets up a contrast. The missing words must be antonyms or near-antonyms. You can immediately eliminate Choices A and B as synonyms or near-synonym pairs.   (Contrast Signal)

11. E.   A *typewriter* is a tool used by a *journalist*; a pair of *pliers* is a tool used by an *electrician*.
(Worker and Tool)

12. D.   The meat of a *sheep* is called *mutton*; the meat of a *steer* is called *beef*.   (Definition)

13. D.   An *entry* is one day's record that is part of a *diary*; an *episode* is one separate performance that is part of a *serial*.   (Part to Whole)

14. D.   A *mural* (wall painting) is painted on a *wall*; an *etching* is imprinted on *paper*.
(Defining Characteristic)

15. B.   A *libretto* (the words of an opera or musical play) is written by an *author*; the *score* (musical arrangement), by a *composer*.
(Worker and Creation)

16. E.   To restrict the movements of a *horse*, a *tether* is used. To restrict those of a *prisoner*, *shackles* are used.   (Function)

17. C.   A *blind* person suffers from a loss of *sight*. Similarly, an *amnesiac* suffers from a loss of *memory*.   (Antonym Variant)

18. C.   *Peckish* (slightly hungry) is less extreme a condition than *starving*. *Plain* (homely, unattractive) is less extreme a condition than *hideous* (extremely ugly).
(Degree of Intensity)

19. D. A *poet* writes or creates an *ode* (lyric poem); a *seamstress* sews or creates a *gown*.
                                                (Worker and Creation)

20. B. The symbol of *time* is a bearded man carrying a *scythe*; the symbol of *justice* is a blindfolded woman carrying a *scale*.
                          (Symbol and the Abstraction It Represents)

21. A. A *virtuoso* (expert performer) is by definition *experienced*; a *rogue* (scoundrel) is by definition *knavish*.   (Synonym Variant)

22. C. Something *caustic* (biting; corrosive) by definition *corrodes* (eats away); something *hypnotic* (tending to induce a sleep-like trance) by definition *mesmerizes* (hypnotizes).
                                                (Definition)

23. D. A *carapace* (hard case) protects a *turtle*; a *shell* protects a *snail*.   (Function)

24. E. Substitute the answer choices in the original sentence. The sergeant is a person who might have been a deputy sheriff before he joined the army—that is, in his civil or *nonmilitary* life.

25. A. Paragraph 1 presents a general picture of the man on the bridge, the executioners and the officer standing nearby, the sentinels at the far ends of the bridge. Cinematically, it is like *a wide-angle shot* of the whole panorama. Paragraph 2 takes a closer look at the man, examining his clothes, his face, his expression. It is as if the camera has moved in for *a close-up* shot.

26. B. The author's comment that the man "had a kindly expression that one would hardly have expected in one whose neck was in the hemp" suggests that he is *an unlikely candidate for execution* and that some unusual circumstances must have brought him to this fate.

27. B. In calling the military code "liberal" because it doesn't exclude members of the upper classes from being executed, the author is being highly *ironic*. Generally, people would like regulations to be interpreted liberally to permit them to do the things they want. Here, the liberal military code is permitting the man to be hanged. Clearly, the gentleman facing execution would have preferred the code to be less liberal in this case.

28. A. Farquhar agrees readily with the saying that all is fair in love and war. This implies he is willing to use underhanded or unfair methods to support the Southern cause.

29. E. Farquhar has no objection to performing humble errands or undertaking dangerous tasks as long as these tasks are appropriate to someone who sees himself as a sort of "undercover soldier," a secret agent of the Confederacy. Anything he does must be consistent or *compatible* with his image of himself in this role.

30. C. At heart a soldier, Farquhar fundamentally agrees that all's fair in war. He doesn't particularly qualify or restrict his commitment to this viewpoint: he's ready to go out and do something underhanded for his cause without much *restriction* as to what he's willing to do.

31. A. Mrs. Farquhar's readiness to fetch water for the gray-clad Confederate soldier suggests some degree of sympathy on her part for the Confederate cause.
        Choices B and D are incorrect. There is nothing in the passage to suggest either of them. Choices C and E are incorrect. Mrs. Farquhar's action, in hospitably fetching water "with her own white hands," contradicts them.

32. E. Earlier in the passage, Farquhar is described as frustrated by "the inglorious restraint" preventing his serving the Southern cause. He sees the life of the soldier as larger than that of the civilian, a life filled with opportunities for distinction, for renown. Thus, when he speaks about someone managing to sneak past the guards and accomplishing something for the cause, he is *envisioning himself as a hero*.

33. B. Farquhar wishes to prevent the Yankee advance. To do so, he must somehow damage the railroad, its bridges, its tunnels, or its trains. The soldier tells him that some highly flammable driftwood is piled up at the base of the wooden railroad bridge. Clearly, it would make sense for Farquhar to try to set fire to the driftwood in order to destroy the bridge.

34. D. The phrase "burn like tow" and the reference to dry driftwood suggest that tow will catch fire readily. Remember, when asked to give the meaning of an unfamiliar word, to look for nearby context clues.

35. C. The scout is a Yankee soldier disguised as a member of the enemy. By coming to the Farquhars' plantation in Confederate disguise, he is able to learn they are sympathetic to the enemy. By telling Farquhar of the work on the bridge, stressing both the lack of guards and the abundance of fuel, he is tempting Farquhar into an attack on the bridge (and into an ambush). The scout's job is to locate potential enemies and draw them out from cover.

Section 4   Mathematical Reasoning

Quantitative Comparison Questions

1. **A.** Column A is positive, and Column B is negative. Remember PEMDAS: $(-7)^4 =$ $(-7)(-7)(-7)(-7)$, whereas $-7^4 = -(7)(7)(7)(7)$. Column A is greater.

2. **D.** Since $\frac{2}{3} = 66\frac{2}{3}\%$, which is clearly more than 65%, it *appears* that Column B is greater. *Be careful!* That would be true if a were positive, but no restrictions are placed on a. If $a = 0$, the columns are equal; if a is negative, Column A is greater. Neither column is *always* greater, and the columns are not *always* equal (D).
   **Use TACTIC 10-1. Just let $a = 0$, and then let $a = 1$.

3. **D.** If the number picked from B is 4 or 5, it will be greater than any number picked from A. If, however, the numbers picked from A and B are both 3, the columns are equal. Neither column is *always* greater, and the columns are not *always* equal. (D).

4. **A.** Since (a,b) is on the positive portion of the x-axis, a is positive and $b = 0$, so $a + b$ is positive. Also, since (c,d) is on the negative portion of the y-axis, c is negative and $d = 0$, so $c + d$ is negative. Column A is greater.

5. **A.** It looks as though the columns *may* be equal (without the .6 in each percent they would be), but don't chance it. Use your calculator and multiply. Column A: $.176 \times 83 = 14.608$. Column B: $.836 \times 17 = 14.212$. Column A is greater.

6. **A.** Use TACTIC 10-3.

Column A	Column B
a^3b	ab^3

   Since a and b are positive, divide each column by ab:

   $$\frac{a^3b}{ab} = a^2 \qquad \frac{ab^3}{ab} = b^2$$

   Take the square root of each side: a b

   Since it is given that $a > b$, Column A is greater.
   **Use TACTIC 10-1: plug in numbers. If $a = 2$ and $b = 1$, Column A is 8 and Column B is 2, so eliminate B and C. Try some other numbers. A is always greater.

7. **A.** Since a is negative, a^5 is negative, whereas a^6 is positive (KEY FACT A5). Column A is greater.

8. **D.** *Be careful!* It is *not* given that x and y are integers; $x = 1$, $y = 10$ and $x = 2$, $y = 5$ are not the only values of x and y satisfying the conditions. In these cases, x is less than 3, so Column B is greater. But $x = 3$, $y = \frac{10}{3}$ also satisfies the conditions, and in this case the columns are equal. Neither column is *always* greater, and the columns are not *always* equal (D). (Note that x could be even greater than 3; it could be anything less than $\sqrt{10} \approx 3.16$.)
   **Use TACTIC 10-4. Could $x = 3$? Yes. Must $x = 3$? No. (See above.)

9. **B.** Use b, c, and t for "beeps," "clicks," and "tweets," respectively. Then the given equations are: $3b = 2c$ and $4b = 5t$ Multiply the first equation by 4 and the second by 3: $12b = 8c$ and $12b = 15t$ Then $8c = 15t \Rightarrow c = \frac{15}{8}t < 2t$, so 1 click is less than 2 tweets. Column B is greater.

10. **C.** Since $ab = 0$, either a or b is 0 (KEY FACT A3). If $a = 0$, each column is b^2, whereas if $b = 0$, each column is a^2. Either way, the columns are equal (C).
    **Column A $= a^2 + 2ab + b^2$, and Column B $= a^2 - 2ab + b^2$. After subtracting $a^2 + b^2$ from each column, compare $2ab$ and $-2ab$: both are 0.

11. **D.** Use TACTIC 10-1: replace the variable with a number. Let $a = 1$. Then Column A is the average of 1, 2, and –1: $\frac{1+2+(-1)}{3} = \frac{2}{3}$, and Column B is the average of –1, –2, and 1: $\frac{(-1)+(-2)+1}{3} = -\frac{2}{3}$. In this case Column A is greater, so eliminate B and C. Let $a = 10$. Now Column A is $\frac{1+2+(-10)}{3} = -\frac{7}{3}$, whereas Column B is $\frac{(-1)+(-2)+10}{3} = \frac{7}{3}$. This time B is greater. Neither column is *always* greater, and the columns are not *always* equal (D).

12. **C.** Since $6^2 + 8^2 = 10^2$ ($36 + 64 = 100$), the triangle, despite its appearance, is a right triangle and $s = 90$ (KEY FACT J6). Also, in a right triangle the sum of the measures of the two acute angles is 90° (KEY FACT J4), so $r + t = 90$. The columns are equal (C).

13. **A.** Column A: the area of a square of side a is a^2 (KEY FACT K8). Column B: since the diameter of the circle is a, the radius is $\frac{1}{2}a$. Then, by KEY FACT L8, the area of the circle is $\pi\left(\frac{1}{2}a\right)^2 = \frac{\pi}{4}a^2$, which is less than a^2, since $\frac{\pi}{4} < 1$. Column A is greater.

14. **C.** Draw a diagram, and on each small cube write the number of red faces it has. The cubes with three red faces are the eight corners. The cubes with no red faces are the "inside" ones that can't be seen. If you cut off the top and bottom rows, the front and back rows, and the left and right rows, you are left with a small 2-inch cube none of whose faces is red. That 2-inch cube is made up of eight 1-inch cubes. The columns are equal (C).

15. **B.** The area of the large circle is πR^2, and the area of the small circle is πr^2, so the area of the shaded region is $\pi R^2 - \pi r^2 = \pi(R^2 - r^2)$. Since the shaded region and the white region have the same area,

$$\pi(R^2 - r^2) = \pi r^2 \Rightarrow R^2 - r^2 = r^2 \Rightarrow$$
$$R^2 = 2r^2 \Rightarrow \frac{R^2}{r^2} = 2 \Rightarrow \frac{R}{r} = \sqrt{2},$$

which is *less* than 1.5. Column B is greater.

Grid-in Questions

16. **(98)** The easiest way is to simplify first: $(a^2 + b^2) - (a^2 - b^2) = 2b^2$. Then $6 \otimes 7 = 2(7^2) = 2(49) = \mathbf{98}$.
**If you don't think to simplify (or you can't), just do the arithmetic:
$$(6^2 + 7^2) - (6^2 - 7^2) = (36 + 49) - (36 - 49) =$$
$$85 - (-13) = 85 + 13 = \mathbf{98}.$$

17. **(7.5)** Here, $\triangle ABC$ is a right triangle and its area is given by $\frac{1}{2}(AB)(BC)$. Since AB is vertical, find its length by subtracting the y-coordinates: $AB = 4 - 1 = 3$. Similarly, since BC is horizontal, find its length by subtracting the x-coordinates: $BC = 6 - 1 = 5$. Then
$$\text{area of } \triangle ABC = \frac{1}{2}(3)(5) = \frac{15}{2} = \mathbf{7.5}.$$

18. **(7.5)** The perimeter of the quadrilateral in the figure is 30 $(5 + 7 + 8 + 10)$. Then $4s = 30$, where s is a side of the square, and $s = \mathbf{7.5}$.

19. **(3.7)** To produce 40 gizmos takes $40 \times 333 = 13{,}320$ seconds. Since there are 60 seconds in a minute and 60 minutes in an hour, there are $60 \times 60 = 3600$ seconds in an hour; $13{,}320 \div 3600 = \mathbf{3.7}$ hours.
**$13{,}320$ seconds $\div 60 = 222$ minutes, and 222 minutes $\div 60 = \mathbf{3.7}$ hours.

20. **(145)** Since the average of a, b, and 10 is 100, their sum is 300 (TACTIC E1). Then
$$a + b + 10 = 300 \Rightarrow a + b = 290 \Rightarrow$$
$$\frac{a+b}{2} = \frac{290}{2} = \mathbf{145}.$$

Since 10 is 90 less than 100, then a and b together must be 90 more than 100 (KEY FACT E3). Assume each is 45 more than 100; that is, a and b are both 145. Then their average is **145.

21. **(1.21)** Use TACTIC 11-2. Since this is a percent problem, assume the rent *last year* was \$100. Since 10% of 100 is 10, this year the rent went up \$10 to \$110. Now, 10% of 110 is 11, so next year the rent will go up \$11 to \$121. Finally, 121 is $\mathbf{1.21} \times 100$.

22. **(1983)**

Year	Boris's Age	Olga's Age
1970	26	0
1970 + x	26 + x	x

The equation is $26 + x = 3x \Rightarrow 26 = 2x \Rightarrow x = 13$. Boris was 3 times as old as Olga 13 years after 1970, in **1983** (when they were 39 and 13, respectively).

23. **(9.36)** The class average will be highest when all the grades are as high as possible. Assume that all 22 students who passed earned 10's. Of the 3 who failed, 1 received a grade of 2; but assume that the other 2 students had 6's, the highest failing grade. Then the total is $22 \times 10 + 2 + 2 \times 6 = 220 + 2 + 12 = 234$, so the highest possible class average is $234 \div 25 = \mathbf{9.36}$.

24. **(6)** Let $2x$ and $7x$ represent the number of red and blue marbles, respectively, in jar I. Then in total there are $7x$ blue marbles and $14x$ red ones. Since there are $2x$ red marbles in jar I, there are $12x$ red marbles in jar II. So there are **6** times as many red marbles in jar II as there are in jar I.
**Do the same analysis, except let $x = 1$. Then jar I contains 2 red and 7 blue marbles, whereas jar II contains 12 red ones.

25. $(\frac{1}{3})$ Adding the fractions, we get $\frac{1}{a} + \frac{1}{b} = \frac{a+b}{ab}$.

But it is given that ab is 3 times $(a + b)$.

Therefore, $\frac{a+b}{ab} = \frac{1}{3}$.

Section 5   Verbal Reasoning

1. **C.** The opening paragraph discusses changes in the idea of matter, emphasizing the use of musical terminology to describe the concepts of physics. The second paragraph then goes on to develop the theme of the music of matter. Choice B is incorrect. Music does not directly influence the interactions of particles; physicists merely use musical terms to describe these interactions.

2. **D.** The author mentions these terms as examples of what he means by the strange new language or *idiosyncratic nomenclature* of modern particle physics.

3. **D.** In his references to the elegance of the newly discovered subatomic structures and to the dance of Creation, the author conveys his *admiration* and *wonder*.

4. **B.** "Matter's heart," where the physicist can observe the dance of Creation, is *the subatomic world*, the world of quarks and charms.

5. **D.** The image of the snake swallowing its tail suggests that the astronomers' and physicists' theories are, at bottom, one and the same. In other words, there is an *underlying unity* connecting them.

6. **E.** The properties of the upsilon particle that implied it could not be made of up, down, strange, or charm quarks were its *characteristics* or attributes.

7. **B.** Glashow is eager for the end of the hunt. His words ("last blessed one," "the sooner...the better") reflect his *impatience*.

8. **E.** The keystone of the arch (the wedge-shaped block that is inserted last into the arch and locks the other pieces in place) completes the arch. By comparing the top quark to the keystone, the author of Passage 2 *illustrates the importance of the top quark to subatomic theory.*

9. **D.** The physicists had to find the top quark because their theory *depended* on the top's existence.

10. **E.** The author of Passage 2 cites authorities (Glashow, Tollestrup) and uses similes ("like an arch"). She defines the Standard Model as the theoretical synthesis that reduced the zoo of subatomic particles to a manageable number. She poses a question about what makes certain particles more massive than others. However, she *never denies a possibility*.

11. **C.** Physicists are familiar with the weight of a gold atom. In stating that the top was determined to weigh about as much as a gold atom, the author is illustrating just *how hefty* or massive a top quark is.

12. **C.** The 1995 experiments succeeded: The physicists found the keystone to their arch. From this we can infer that the Standard Model was not disproved but instead received its *validation*.

13. **B.** In lines 35–36, the author of Passage 1 develops a fanciful metaphor for the nature of matter. To him, subatomic matter is like a Bach fugue, filled with arpeggios. While the author of Passage 2 resorts to some figurative language ("Grail," "keystone") in attempting to describe the top quark, she is more factual than figurative: she never uses any metaphor as extended as the metaphor "the music of matter." Thus, her most likely reaction to lines 36–37 would be to point out that this metaphor *is too fanciful to be worthwhile.*

Section 6   Mathematical Reasoning

1. **B.** Solve the given equation: $\frac{1}{a} + \frac{1}{a} + \frac{1}{a} = 12$

Add the fractions: $\frac{3}{a} = 12$

Multiply both sides by a: $3 = 12a$

Divide both sides by 12: $a = \frac{3}{12} = \frac{1}{4}$.

**You can use TACTIC 9-1: backsolve; try choice C. If $a = \frac{1}{3}$, then $\frac{1}{a} = 3$, so the left-hand side equals 9. That's too small. Now, *be careful*: a fraction gets bigger when its denominator gets *smaller* (KEY FACT B4). Eliminate C, D, and E, and try a smaller value for a: $\frac{1}{4}$ works.

2. **C.** If $x = -5$, then

$$2x^2 - 3x - 7 = 2(-5)^2 - 3(-5) - 7 =$$
$$2(25) + 15 - 7 = \mathbf{58}.$$

3. **E.** Carefully read the values from the chart. Ann, Dan, Pam, Fran, and Sam read 1, 4, 2, 6, and 5 books, respectively. The sum is **18**.

4. **D.** The average number of books read by the five members is the sum, 18 (calculated in the solution to question 3), divided by 5: 3.6. Three of the five members, or **60%**, read more than 3.6 books.

5. **A.** The formula for the area of a circle is: $A = \pi r^2$

    Divide both sides by π: $r^2 = \dfrac{A}{\pi}$

    Take the square root of each side: $r = \sqrt{\dfrac{A}{\pi}}$

    The diameter is twice the radius: $d = 2r = 2\sqrt{\dfrac{A}{\pi}}$

    **Let the radius of the circle be 1. Then the area is π, and the diameter is 2. Which of the five choices is equal to 2 when $A = \pi$? Only $2\sqrt{\dfrac{A}{\pi}}$.

6. **D.** If Laurie had to pay 30% of the value of her inheritance in taxes, she still owned 70% of her inheritance: 70% of 40% is **28%** $(0.70 \times 0.40 = 0.28)$.
    Assume the estate was worth $100. Laurie received 40%, or $40. Her tax was 30% of $40, or $12. She still had $28, or **28%, of the $100 estate.

7. **B.** Write the given equation as: $a^3 = 3a$
    Since a is positive, divide both sides by a: $a^2 = 3$
    Take the square root of each side: $a = \sqrt{3}$

    **Use TACTIC 9-1: test the choices, starting with C.

8. **A.** If e is the edge of the cube, the surface area, A, is $6e^2$ and the volume, V, is e^3 (KEY FACTS M1 and M2). Then

    $$A = 6e^2 = 60 \Rightarrow e^2 = 10 \Rightarrow e = \sqrt{10} \Rightarrow$$
    $$V = \left(\sqrt{10}\right)^3 = \left(\sqrt{10}\right)\left(\sqrt{10}\right)\left(\sqrt{10}\right) = \mathbf{10\sqrt{10}}.$$

9. **D.** Let r = radius of circle I, and let R = radius of circle II. Then $2R$ is the diameter of circle II, and $2\pi r$ is the circumference of circle I.

    It is given that: $2\pi r = 2R$
    Divide both sides by 2: $R = \pi r$

    Then $\dfrac{\text{area of circle II}}{\text{area of circle I}} = \dfrac{\pi R^2}{\pi r^2} = \dfrac{\pi(\pi r)^2}{\pi r^2}$

    $$= \dfrac{\pi^3 r^2}{\pi r^2} = \pi^2$$

    **Use TACTIC 9-2. Pick some easy-to-use number, such as 1, for the radius of circle I. Then the circumference of circle I is 2π, which is the diameter of circle II, and the radius of circle II is π (one-half its diameter). The area of a circle is given by $A = \pi r^2$, so the area of circle I is $\pi(1) = \pi$, and the area of circle II is $\pi(\pi^2) = \pi^3$. Finally, the ratio of their areas is $\dfrac{\pi^3}{\pi} = \pi^2$.

10. **A.** Use TACTIC 8-1: draw a diagram. In the figure below, form rectangle $BCDE$ by drawing $DE \perp AB$. Then, $BE = 9$, $AE = 16$, and $DE = 12$. Finally, $DA = \mathbf{20}$, because right triangle AED is a 3-4-5 triangle in which each side is multiplied by 4. If you don't realize that, use the Pythagorean theorem to get DA:

    $$(DA)^2 = (AE)^2 + (DE)^2 = 256 + 144 = 400$$
    $$\Rightarrow DA = \mathbf{20}.$$

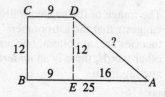

Answer Sheet—Test 5

If a section has fewer than 35 questions, leave the extra spaces blank.

Remove answer sheet by cutting on dotted line

Section 1

1 Ⓐ Ⓑ Ⓒ Ⓓ Ⓔ	8 Ⓐ Ⓑ Ⓒ Ⓓ Ⓔ	15 Ⓐ Ⓑ Ⓒ Ⓓ Ⓔ	22 Ⓐ Ⓑ Ⓒ Ⓓ Ⓔ	29 Ⓐ Ⓑ Ⓒ Ⓓ Ⓔ
2 Ⓐ Ⓑ Ⓒ Ⓓ Ⓔ	9 Ⓐ Ⓑ Ⓒ Ⓓ Ⓔ	16 Ⓐ Ⓑ Ⓒ Ⓓ Ⓔ	23 Ⓐ Ⓑ Ⓒ Ⓓ Ⓔ	30 Ⓐ Ⓑ Ⓒ Ⓓ Ⓔ
3 Ⓐ Ⓑ Ⓒ Ⓓ Ⓔ	10 Ⓐ Ⓑ Ⓒ Ⓓ Ⓔ	17 Ⓐ Ⓑ Ⓒ Ⓓ Ⓔ	24 Ⓐ Ⓑ Ⓒ Ⓓ Ⓔ	31 Ⓐ Ⓑ Ⓒ Ⓓ Ⓔ
4 Ⓐ Ⓑ Ⓒ Ⓓ Ⓔ	11 Ⓐ Ⓑ Ⓒ Ⓓ Ⓔ	18 Ⓐ Ⓑ Ⓒ Ⓓ Ⓔ	25 Ⓐ Ⓑ Ⓒ Ⓓ Ⓔ	32 Ⓐ Ⓑ Ⓒ Ⓓ Ⓔ
5 Ⓐ Ⓑ Ⓒ Ⓓ Ⓔ	12 Ⓐ Ⓑ Ⓒ Ⓓ Ⓔ	19 Ⓐ Ⓑ Ⓒ Ⓓ Ⓔ	26 Ⓐ Ⓑ Ⓒ Ⓓ Ⓔ	33 Ⓐ Ⓑ Ⓒ Ⓓ Ⓔ
6 Ⓐ Ⓑ Ⓒ Ⓓ Ⓔ	13 Ⓐ Ⓑ Ⓒ Ⓓ Ⓔ	20 Ⓐ Ⓑ Ⓒ Ⓓ Ⓔ	27 Ⓐ Ⓑ Ⓒ Ⓓ Ⓔ	34 Ⓐ Ⓑ Ⓒ Ⓓ Ⓔ
7 Ⓐ Ⓑ Ⓒ Ⓓ Ⓔ	14 Ⓐ Ⓑ Ⓒ Ⓓ Ⓔ	21 Ⓐ Ⓑ Ⓒ Ⓓ Ⓔ	28 Ⓐ Ⓑ Ⓒ Ⓓ Ⓔ	35 Ⓐ Ⓑ Ⓒ Ⓓ Ⓔ

Section 2

1 Ⓐ Ⓑ Ⓒ Ⓓ Ⓔ	8 Ⓐ Ⓑ Ⓒ Ⓓ Ⓔ	15 Ⓐ Ⓑ Ⓒ Ⓓ Ⓔ	22 Ⓐ Ⓑ Ⓒ Ⓓ Ⓔ	29 Ⓐ Ⓑ Ⓒ Ⓓ Ⓔ
2 Ⓐ Ⓑ Ⓒ Ⓓ Ⓔ	9 Ⓐ Ⓑ Ⓒ Ⓓ Ⓔ	16 Ⓐ Ⓑ Ⓒ Ⓓ Ⓔ	23 Ⓐ Ⓑ Ⓒ Ⓓ Ⓔ	30 Ⓐ Ⓑ Ⓒ Ⓓ Ⓔ
3 Ⓐ Ⓑ Ⓒ Ⓓ Ⓔ	10 Ⓐ Ⓑ Ⓒ Ⓓ Ⓔ	17 Ⓐ Ⓑ Ⓒ Ⓓ Ⓔ	24 Ⓐ Ⓑ Ⓒ Ⓓ Ⓔ	31 Ⓐ Ⓑ Ⓒ Ⓓ Ⓔ
4 Ⓐ Ⓑ Ⓒ Ⓓ Ⓔ	11 Ⓐ Ⓑ Ⓒ Ⓓ Ⓔ	18 Ⓐ Ⓑ Ⓒ Ⓓ Ⓔ	25 Ⓐ Ⓑ Ⓒ Ⓓ Ⓔ	32 Ⓐ Ⓑ Ⓒ Ⓓ Ⓔ
5 Ⓐ Ⓑ Ⓒ Ⓓ Ⓔ	12 Ⓐ Ⓑ Ⓒ Ⓓ Ⓔ	19 Ⓐ Ⓑ Ⓒ Ⓓ Ⓔ	26 Ⓐ Ⓑ Ⓒ Ⓓ Ⓔ	33 Ⓐ Ⓑ Ⓒ Ⓓ Ⓔ
6 Ⓐ Ⓑ Ⓒ Ⓓ Ⓔ	13 Ⓐ Ⓑ Ⓒ Ⓓ Ⓔ	20 Ⓐ Ⓑ Ⓒ Ⓓ Ⓔ	27 Ⓐ Ⓑ Ⓒ Ⓓ Ⓔ	34 Ⓐ Ⓑ Ⓒ Ⓓ Ⓔ
7 Ⓐ Ⓑ Ⓒ Ⓓ Ⓔ	14 Ⓐ Ⓑ Ⓒ Ⓓ Ⓔ	21 Ⓐ Ⓑ Ⓒ Ⓓ Ⓔ	28 Ⓐ Ⓑ Ⓒ Ⓓ Ⓔ	35 Ⓐ Ⓑ Ⓒ Ⓓ Ⓔ

Section 3

1 Ⓐ Ⓑ Ⓒ Ⓓ Ⓔ	8 Ⓐ Ⓑ Ⓒ Ⓓ Ⓔ	15 Ⓐ Ⓑ Ⓒ Ⓓ Ⓔ	22 Ⓐ Ⓑ Ⓒ Ⓓ Ⓔ	29 Ⓐ Ⓑ Ⓒ Ⓓ Ⓔ
2 Ⓐ Ⓑ Ⓒ Ⓓ Ⓔ	9 Ⓐ Ⓑ Ⓒ Ⓓ Ⓔ	16 Ⓐ Ⓑ Ⓒ Ⓓ Ⓔ	23 Ⓐ Ⓑ Ⓒ Ⓓ Ⓔ	30 Ⓐ Ⓑ Ⓒ Ⓓ Ⓔ
3 Ⓐ Ⓑ Ⓒ Ⓓ Ⓔ	10 Ⓐ Ⓑ Ⓒ Ⓓ Ⓔ	17 Ⓐ Ⓑ Ⓒ Ⓓ Ⓔ	24 Ⓐ Ⓑ Ⓒ Ⓓ Ⓔ	31 Ⓐ Ⓑ Ⓒ Ⓓ Ⓔ
4 Ⓐ Ⓑ Ⓒ Ⓓ Ⓔ	11 Ⓐ Ⓑ Ⓒ Ⓓ Ⓔ	18 Ⓐ Ⓑ Ⓒ Ⓓ Ⓔ	25 Ⓐ Ⓑ Ⓒ Ⓓ Ⓔ	32 Ⓐ Ⓑ Ⓒ Ⓓ Ⓔ
5 Ⓐ Ⓑ Ⓒ Ⓓ Ⓔ	12 Ⓐ Ⓑ Ⓒ Ⓓ Ⓔ	19 Ⓐ Ⓑ Ⓒ Ⓓ Ⓔ	26 Ⓐ Ⓑ Ⓒ Ⓓ Ⓔ	33 Ⓐ Ⓑ Ⓒ Ⓓ Ⓔ
6 Ⓐ Ⓑ Ⓒ Ⓓ Ⓔ	13 Ⓐ Ⓑ Ⓒ Ⓓ Ⓔ	20 Ⓐ Ⓑ Ⓒ Ⓓ Ⓔ	27 Ⓐ Ⓑ Ⓒ Ⓓ Ⓔ	34 Ⓐ Ⓑ Ⓒ Ⓓ Ⓔ
7 Ⓐ Ⓑ Ⓒ Ⓓ Ⓔ	14 Ⓐ Ⓑ Ⓒ Ⓓ Ⓔ	21 Ⓐ Ⓑ Ⓒ Ⓓ Ⓔ	28 Ⓐ Ⓑ Ⓒ Ⓓ Ⓔ	35 Ⓐ Ⓑ Ⓒ Ⓓ Ⓔ

Section 4

1 Ⓐ Ⓑ Ⓒ Ⓓ Ⓔ	4 Ⓐ Ⓑ Ⓒ Ⓓ Ⓔ	7 Ⓐ Ⓑ Ⓒ Ⓓ Ⓔ	10 Ⓐ Ⓑ Ⓒ Ⓓ Ⓔ	13 Ⓐ Ⓑ Ⓒ Ⓓ Ⓔ
2 Ⓐ Ⓑ Ⓒ Ⓓ Ⓔ	5 Ⓐ Ⓑ Ⓒ Ⓓ Ⓔ	8 Ⓐ Ⓑ Ⓒ Ⓓ Ⓔ	11 Ⓐ Ⓑ Ⓒ Ⓓ Ⓔ	14 Ⓐ Ⓑ Ⓒ Ⓓ Ⓔ
3 Ⓐ Ⓑ Ⓒ Ⓓ Ⓔ	6 Ⓐ Ⓑ Ⓒ Ⓓ Ⓔ	9 Ⓐ Ⓑ Ⓒ Ⓓ Ⓔ	12 Ⓐ Ⓑ Ⓒ Ⓓ Ⓔ	15 Ⓐ Ⓑ Ⓒ Ⓓ Ⓔ

Section 4 (continued)

16–20: grid-in answer boxes (numbered 16, 17, 18, 19, 20), each with blank fraction/decimal bubbles and digit columns 0–9.

21–25: grid-in answer boxes (numbered 21, 22, 23, 24, 25), each with blank fraction/decimal bubbles and digit columns 0–9.

Section 5

1 Ⓐ Ⓑ Ⓒ Ⓓ Ⓔ	8 Ⓐ Ⓑ Ⓒ Ⓓ Ⓔ	15 Ⓐ Ⓑ Ⓒ Ⓓ Ⓔ	22 Ⓐ Ⓑ Ⓒ Ⓓ Ⓔ	29 Ⓐ Ⓑ Ⓒ Ⓓ Ⓔ
2 Ⓐ Ⓑ Ⓒ Ⓓ Ⓔ	9 Ⓐ Ⓑ Ⓒ Ⓓ Ⓔ	16 Ⓐ Ⓑ Ⓒ Ⓓ Ⓔ	23 Ⓐ Ⓑ Ⓒ Ⓓ Ⓔ	30 Ⓐ Ⓑ Ⓒ Ⓓ Ⓔ
3 Ⓐ Ⓑ Ⓒ Ⓓ Ⓔ	10 Ⓐ Ⓑ Ⓒ Ⓓ Ⓔ	17 Ⓐ Ⓑ Ⓒ Ⓓ Ⓔ	24 Ⓐ Ⓑ Ⓒ Ⓓ Ⓔ	31 Ⓐ Ⓑ Ⓒ Ⓓ Ⓔ
4 Ⓐ Ⓑ Ⓒ Ⓓ Ⓔ	11 Ⓐ Ⓑ Ⓒ Ⓓ Ⓔ	18 Ⓐ Ⓑ Ⓒ Ⓓ Ⓔ	25 Ⓐ Ⓑ Ⓒ Ⓓ Ⓔ	32 Ⓐ Ⓑ Ⓒ Ⓓ Ⓔ
5 Ⓐ Ⓑ Ⓒ Ⓓ Ⓔ	12 Ⓐ Ⓑ Ⓒ Ⓓ Ⓔ	19 Ⓐ Ⓑ Ⓒ Ⓓ Ⓔ	26 Ⓐ Ⓑ Ⓒ Ⓓ Ⓔ	33 Ⓐ Ⓑ Ⓒ Ⓓ Ⓔ
6 Ⓐ Ⓑ Ⓒ Ⓓ Ⓔ	13 Ⓐ Ⓑ Ⓒ Ⓓ Ⓔ	20 Ⓐ Ⓑ Ⓒ Ⓓ Ⓔ	27 Ⓐ Ⓑ Ⓒ Ⓓ Ⓔ	34 Ⓐ Ⓑ Ⓒ Ⓓ Ⓔ
7 Ⓐ Ⓑ Ⓒ Ⓓ Ⓔ	14 Ⓐ Ⓑ Ⓒ Ⓓ Ⓔ	21 Ⓐ Ⓑ Ⓒ Ⓓ Ⓔ	28 Ⓐ Ⓑ Ⓒ Ⓓ Ⓔ	35 Ⓐ Ⓑ Ⓒ Ⓓ Ⓔ

Section 6

1 Ⓐ Ⓑ Ⓒ Ⓓ Ⓔ	8 Ⓐ Ⓑ Ⓒ Ⓓ Ⓔ	15 Ⓐ Ⓑ Ⓒ Ⓓ Ⓔ	22 Ⓐ Ⓑ Ⓒ Ⓓ Ⓔ	29 Ⓐ Ⓑ Ⓒ Ⓓ Ⓔ
2 Ⓐ Ⓑ Ⓒ Ⓓ Ⓔ	9 Ⓐ Ⓑ Ⓒ Ⓓ Ⓔ	16 Ⓐ Ⓑ Ⓒ Ⓓ Ⓔ	23 Ⓐ Ⓑ Ⓒ Ⓓ Ⓔ	30 Ⓐ Ⓑ Ⓒ Ⓓ Ⓔ
3 Ⓐ Ⓑ Ⓒ Ⓓ Ⓔ	10 Ⓐ Ⓑ Ⓒ Ⓓ Ⓔ	17 Ⓐ Ⓑ Ⓒ Ⓓ Ⓔ	24 Ⓐ Ⓑ Ⓒ Ⓓ Ⓔ	31 Ⓐ Ⓑ Ⓒ Ⓓ Ⓔ
4 Ⓐ Ⓑ Ⓒ Ⓓ Ⓔ	11 Ⓐ Ⓑ Ⓒ Ⓓ Ⓔ	18 Ⓐ Ⓑ Ⓒ Ⓓ Ⓔ	25 Ⓐ Ⓑ Ⓒ Ⓓ Ⓔ	32 Ⓐ Ⓑ Ⓒ Ⓓ Ⓔ
5 Ⓐ Ⓑ Ⓒ Ⓓ Ⓔ	12 Ⓐ Ⓑ Ⓒ Ⓓ Ⓔ	19 Ⓐ Ⓑ Ⓒ Ⓓ Ⓔ	26 Ⓐ Ⓑ Ⓒ Ⓓ Ⓔ	33 Ⓐ Ⓑ Ⓒ Ⓓ Ⓔ
6 Ⓐ Ⓑ Ⓒ Ⓓ Ⓔ	13 Ⓐ Ⓑ Ⓒ Ⓓ Ⓔ	20 Ⓐ Ⓑ Ⓒ Ⓓ Ⓔ	27 Ⓐ Ⓑ Ⓒ Ⓓ Ⓔ	34 Ⓐ Ⓑ Ⓒ Ⓓ Ⓔ
7 Ⓐ Ⓑ Ⓒ Ⓓ Ⓔ	14 Ⓐ Ⓑ Ⓒ Ⓓ Ⓔ	21 Ⓐ Ⓑ Ⓒ Ⓓ Ⓔ	28 Ⓐ Ⓑ Ⓒ Ⓓ Ⓔ	35 Ⓐ Ⓑ Ⓒ Ⓓ Ⓔ

MODEL SAT I TEST 5

1 1 1 1 1 1

SECTION **1**   Time—30 Minutes   Select the best answer to the following questions, then fill in
                 30 Questions   the appropriate space on your Answer Sheet.

Each of the following sentences contains one or two blanks; these blanks indicate that a word or set of words has been left out. Below the sentence are five words or phrases, lettered A through E. Select the word or set of words that best completes the sentence.

Example:

Fame is ----; today's rising star is all too soon tomorrow's washed-up has-been.

(A) rewarding   (B) gradual
 (C) essential   (D) spontaneous
  (E) transitory

Ⓐ Ⓑ Ⓒ Ⓓ ●

---

1. He felt that the uninspiring routine of office work was too ---- for someone of his talent and creativity.

   (A) diverse   (B) insatiable   (C) exacting
    (D) enthralling   (E) prosaic

2. The museum arranged the fossils in ---- order, placing the older fossils dating from the Late Ice Age on the first floor and the more recent fossils on the second floor.

   (A) alphabetical
   (B) chronological
   (C) random
   (D) arbitrary
   (E) retrospective

3. With the evolution of wings, insects were able to ---- to the far ecological corners, across deserts and bodies of water, to reach new food sources and inhabit a wider variety of promising environmental niches.

   (A) relate   (B) disperse   (C) transgress
    (D) revert   (E) ascend

4. Having recently missed out on the Matisse retrospective, which has taken Paris and New York by storm, and on the tour of great paintings from Philadelphia's Barnes collection, London is becoming ---- in the competition to show ---- international art exhibitions.

   (A) a trend-setter...major
   (B) an also-ran...blockbuster
   (C) a world-beater...itinerant
   (D) a mecca...distinguished
   (E) a connoisseur...esoteric

5. What most ---- the magazine's critics is the manner in which its editorial opinions are expressed—too often as if only an idiot could see things any other way.

   (A) belies
   (B) impedes
   (C) riles
   (D) placates
   (E) identifies

6. Despite her compassionate nature, the new nominee to the Supreme Court was single-minded and ---- in her strict ---- the letter of the law.

   (A) merciful...interpretation of
   (B) uncompromising...adherence to
   (C) dilatory...affirmation of
   (D) vindictive...deviation from
   (E) lenient...dismissal of

7. Although he generally observed the adage "Look before you leap," in this instance he was ---- acting in an unconsidered fashion.

   (A) chary of
   (B) impervious to
   (C) precipitate in
   (D) hesitant about
   (E) conventional in

8. Surrounded by a retinue of sycophants who invariably ---- her singing, Callas wearied of the constant adulation and longed for honest criticism.

   (A) orchestrated
   (B) thwarted
   (C) assailed
   (D) extolled
   (E) reciprocated

9. There is nothing ---- or provisional about Moore's early critical pronouncements; she deals ---- with what were then radical new developments in poetry.

   (A) tentative...confidently
   (B) positive...expertly
   (C) dogmatic...arbitrarily
   (D) shallow...superficially
   (E) imprecise...inconclusively

GO ON TO THE NEXT PAGE ➡

1 1 1 1 1 1 1 1 1 1 1

The analogies questions present two words or phrases that are related in some way. Determine which A-through-E answer choice below has a relationship *most* similar to that of the original words or phrases.

Example:

YAWN:BOREDOM:: (A) dream:sleep
(B) anger:madness (C) smile:amusement
(D) face:expression (E) impatience:rebellion

10. STAGE:ACTOR::

(A) quarry:sculptor
(B) library:lecturer
(C) baton:conductor
(D) safe:banker
(E) rink:skater

11. BEAM:DELIGHT::

(A) frown:indifference
(B) glower:anger
(C) yawn:assurance
(D) grin:compassion
(E) snarl:grief

12. CREST:WAVE::

(A) basin:water
(B) crown:tree
(C) sand:dune
(D) mountain:range
(E) dregs:wine

13. MAXIM:PROVERBIAL::

(A) generalization:specific
(B) question:interrogative
(C) dialogue:poetic
(D) hypothesis:ingenious
(E) symbol:obscure

14. ASCETIC:INTEMPERANCE::

(A) hypocrite:brevity
(B) fanatic:zeal
(C) bigot:idolatry
(D) altruist:fidelity
(E) miser:extravagance

15. DIATRIBE:INVECTIVE::

(A) elegy:mirth
(B) encomium:praise
(C) statute:limitation
(D) circumlocution:clarity
(E) parody:performance

Read each of the passages below, and then answer the questions that follow each passage. The correct response may be stated outright or merely suggested in the passage.

Questions 16–21 are based on the following passage.

The following passage is taken from Jane Austen's novel Persuasion. *In this excerpt we meet Sir Walter Elliot, father of the heroine.*

Vanity was the beginning and end of Sir
Walter Elliot's character: vanity of person and of
situation. He had been remarkably handsome in
Line his youth, and at fifty-four was still a very fine
(5) man. Few women could think more of their personal appearance than he did, nor could the valet
of any new-made lord be more delighted with the
place he held in society. He considered the blessing of beauty as inferior only to the blessing of a
(10) baronetcy; and the Sir Walter Elliot, who united
these gifts, was the constant object of his warmest
respect and devotion.

His good looks and his rank had one fair claim
on his attachment, since to them he must have
(15) owed a wife of very superior character to anything deserved by his own. Lady Elliot had been
an excellent woman, sensible and amiable, whose

judgment and conduct, if they might be pardoned
the youthful infatuation which made her Lady
(20) Elliot, had never required indulgence afterwards.
She had humored, or softened, or concealed his
failings, and promoted his real respectability for
seventeen years; and though not the very happiest
being in the world herself, had found enough in
(25) her duties, her friends, and her children, to attach
her to life, and make it no matter of indifference
to her when she was called on to quit them. Three
girls, the two eldest sixteen and fourteen, was an
awful legacy for a mother to bequeath, an awful
(30) charge rather, to confide to the authority and
guidance of a conceited, silly father. She had,
however, one very intimate friend, a sensible,
deserving woman, who had been brought, by
strong attachment to herself, to settle close by her,
(35) in the village of Kellynch; and on her kindness
and advice Lady Elliot mainly relied for the best

GO ON TO THE NEXT PAGE

1   1   1   1   1   1   1   1   1   1   1

help and maintenance of the good principles and
instruction which she had been anxiously giving
her daughters.

(40)   This friend and Sir Walter did not marry,
whatever might have been anticipated on that
head by their acquaintance. Thirteen years had
passed away since Lady Elliot's death, and they
were still near neighbors and intimate friends, and
one remained a widower, the other a widow.

(45)   That Lady Russell, of steady age and character, and extremely well provided for, should have
no thought of a second marriage, needs no apology to the public, which is rather apt to be unrea-
sonably discontented when a woman *does* marry

(50) again, than when she does *not;* but Sir Walter's
continuing in singleness requires explanation. Be
it known, then, that Sir Walter, like a good father
(having met with one or two disappointments in
very unreasonable applications), prided himself

(55) on remaining single for his dear daughters' sake.

16. According to the passage, Sir Walter Elliot's vanity
centered on his

   I. physical attractiveness
  II. possession of a title
 III. superiority of character

(A) I only
(B) II only
(C) I and II
(D) I and III
(E) I, II, and III

17. The narrator speaks well of Lady Elliot for all of
the following EXCEPT

(A) her concealment of Sir Walter's shortcomings
(B) her choice of an intimate friend
(C) her guidance of her three daughters
(D) her judgment in falling in love with Sir Walter
(E) her performance of her wifely duties

18. It can be inferred that over the years Lady Elliot
was less than happy because of

(A) her lack of personal beauty
(B) her separation from her most intimate friend
(C) the disparity between her character and that of
    her husband
(D) the inferiority of her place in society
(E) her inability to teach good principles to her
    wayward daughters

19. Lady Elliot's emotions regarding her approaching
death were complicated by her

(A) pious submissiveness to her fate
(B) anxieties over her daughters' prospects
(C) resentment of her husband's potential remarriage
(D) lack of feeling for her conceited husband
(E) reluctance to face the realities of her situation

20. The phrase "make it no matter of indifference to
her when she was called upon to quit them" (lines
26–27) is an example of

(A) ironic understatement
(B) effusive sentiment
(C) metaphorical expression
(D) personification
(E) parable

21. The applications made by Sir Walter (line 54) were
most likely

(A) professional
(B) insincere
(C) marital
(D) mournful
(E) fatherly

Questions 22–30 are based on the following passage.

The following passage is excerpted from a text on
Native American history. Here, the author describes
how certain major Indian nations related to the
European powers during the 1700s.

   By the end of the seventeenth century the
coastal tribes along most of the Atlantic seaboard
had been destroyed, dispersed, or subjected
Line directly to European control. Yet the interior
(5) tribes—particularly those who had grouped themselves into confederations—remained powers
(and were usually styled nations) who dealt with
Europeans on a rough plane of equality.
Throughout the eighteenth century, the Creeks,
(10) Choctaws, Chickasaws, Cherokees, and Iroquois,
as well as the tribes of the Old Northwest, alternately made war and peace with the various
European powers, entered into treaties of alliance
and friendship, and sometimes made cessions of
(15) territory as a result of defeat in war. As the imperial power of France and Great Britain expanded
into the interior, those powerful Indian nations
were forced to seek new orientations in their policy. For each Indian nation the reorientation was
(20) different, yet each was powerfully affected by the
growth of European settlements, population, and
military power. The history of the reorientation of
Iroquois policy toward the Europeans may serve
as an example of the process that all the interior
(25) nations experienced in the eighteenth century.
   The stability that had marked the Iroquois
Confederacy's generally pro-British position was
shattered with the overthrow of James II in 1688,

GO ON TO THE NEXT PAGE

1 1 1 1 1 1 1 1 1 1 1 1

the colonial uprisings that followed in Massachu-
(30) setts, New York, and Maryland, and the commencement of King William's War against Louis
XIV of France. The increasing French threat to
English hegemony in the interior of North
America was signalized by French-led or French-
(35) inspired attacks on the Iroquois and on outlying
colonial settlements in New York and New
England. The high point of the Iroquois response
was the spectacular raid of August 5, 1689, in
which the Iroquois virtually wiped out the French
(40) village of Lachine, just outside Montreal. A coun-
terraid by the French on the English village of
Schenectady in March, 1690, instilled an appropriate measure of fear among the English and
their Iroquois allies.
(45)   The Iroquois position at the end of the war,
which was formalized by treaties made during the
summer of 1701 with the British and the French,
and which was maintained throughout most of the
eighteenth century, was one of "aggressive neu-
(50) trality" between the two competing European
powers. Under the new system the Iroquois initiated a peace policy toward the "far Indians,"
tightened their control over the nearby tribes, and
induced both English and French to support their
(55) neutrality toward the European powers by appropriate gifts and concessions.
        By holding the balance of power in the sparse-
ly settled borderlands between English and
French settlements, and by their willingness to
(60) use their power against one or the other nation if
not appropriately treated, the Iroquois played the
game of European power politics with effectiveness. The system broke down, however, after the
French became convinced that the Iroquois were
(65) compromising the system in favor of the English
and launched a full-scale attempt to establish
French physical and juridical presence in the Ohio
Valley, the heart of the borderlands long claimed
by the Iroquois. As a consequence of the ensuing
(70) Great War for Empire, in which Iroquois neutrality was dissolved and European influence moved
closer, the play-off system lost its efficacy and a
system of direct bargaining supplanted it.

22. The author's primary purpose in this passage is to
    (A) denounce the imperialistic policies of the
        French
    (B) disprove the charges of barbarism made
        against the Indian nations
    (C) expose the French government's exploitation
        of the Iroquois balance of power
    (D) describe and assess the effect of European mil-
        itary power on the policy of an Indian nation
    (E) show the inability of the Iroquois to engage in
        European-style diplomacy

23. Which of the following best captures the meaning
    of the word "styled" in line 7?
    (A) Arranged
    (B) Designated
    (C) Brought into conformity with
    (D) Dismissed as
    (E) Made fashionable

24. In writing that certain of the interior tribes "dealt
    with Europeans on a rough plane of equality" (lines
    7–8), the author
    (A) agrees that the Europeans treated the Indians
        with unnecessary roughness
    (B) concedes that the Indians were demonstrably
        superior to the Europeans
    (C) acknowledges that European-Indian relations
        were not those of absolute equals
    (D) emphasizes that the Europeans wished to treat
        the Indians equitably
    (E) suggests that the coastal tribes lacked essential
        diplomatic skills

25. The author most likely has chosen to discuss the
    experience of the Iroquois because he regards it as
    (A) singular
    (B) colorful
    (C) representative
    (D) ephemeral
    (E) obscure

26. It can be inferred from the passage that the author's
    attitude toward the Iroquois leadership can best be
    described as one of
    (A) suspicion of their motives
    (B) respect for their competence
    (C) indifference to their fate
    (D) dislike of their savagery
    (E) pride in their heritage

27. With which of the following statements would the
    author be LEAST likely to agree?
    (A) The Iroquois were able to respond effectively
        to French acts of aggression.
    (B) James II's removal from the throne caused dis-
        sension to break out among the colonies.
    (C) The French begrudged the British their alleged
        high standing among the Iroquois.
    (D) Iroquois negotiations involved playing one
        side against the other.
    (E) The Iroquois ceased to hold the balance of
        power early in the eighteenth century.

GO ON TO THE NEXT PAGE ▶

1   1   1   1   1   1   1   1   1   1   1

28. The author attributes such success as the Iroquois policy of aggressive neutrality had to

(A) their readiness to fight either side
(B) ties of loyalty to the British
(C) French physical presence in the borderlands
(D) the confusion of the European forces
(E) European reliance on formal treaties

29. The word "compromising" in line 65 means

(A) humiliating   (B) jeopardizing   (C) revealing
(D) yielding   (E) conceding

30. The final three paragraphs of the passage provide

(A) an instance of a state of relationships described earlier
(B) a modification of a thesis presented earlier
(C) a refutation of an argument that has been made earlier
(D) a summary of the situation referred to earlier
(E) an allusion to the state of events depicted earlier

YOU MAY GO BACK AND REVIEW THIS SECTION IN THE REMAINING TIME, BUT DO NOT WORK IN ANY OTHER SECTION UNTIL TOLD TO DO SO.

S T O P

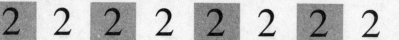

SECTION 2

Time—30 Minutes
25 Questions

For each problem in this section determine which of the five choices is correct and blacken in that choice on your answer sheet. You may use any blank space on the page for your work.

Notes:

- You may use a calculator whenever you feel it will be helpful.
- Use the diagrams provided to help you solve the problems. Unless you see the words "Note: Figure not drawn to scale" under a diagram, it has been drawn as accurately as possible. Unless it is stated that a figure is three-dimensional, you may assume it lies in a plane.

Reference Information

Area Facts   Volume Facts   Triangle Facts   Angle Facts

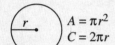
$A = \ell w$

$A = \frac{1}{2} bh$

$A = \pi r^2$
$C = 2\pi r$

$V = \ell w h$

$V = \pi r^2 h$

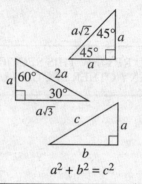

$a^2 + b^2 = c^2$

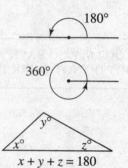

$x + y + z = 180$

---

1. Which of the following numbers has the same digit in the hundreds and hundredths places?

    (A) 2200.0022   (B) 2224.2442   (C) 2242.4242
    (D) 2246.2462   (E) 2246.6422

2. Beth has twice as many baseball cards as Bruce. If Beth has b cards, how many cards does Bruce have?

    (A) $2b$ (B) b^2 (C) $\frac{b}{2}$ (D) $\frac{2}{b}$ (E) $b + 2$

3. Alexis programmed her VCR to record for exactly 225 minutes. If it began recording at 9:05 A.M., at what time did it stop recording?

    (A) 11:30 A.M.   (B) 12:00 P.M.   (C) 12:30 P.M.
    (D) 12:50 P.M.   (E) 1:00 P.M.

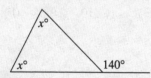

4. In the figure above, what is the value of x?

    (A) 40   (B) 60   (C) 70   (D) 80   (E) 140

5. Mr. Brock wrote a number on the blackboard. When he added 3 to the number, he got the same result as when he multiplied the number by 3. What was the number he wrote?

    (A) –3   (B) 0   (C) 1.5   (D) $\sqrt{3}$ (E) 3

6. What positive number n satisfies the equation $(16)(16)(16)n = \dfrac{(64)\,(64)}{n}$?

    (A) $\frac{1}{4}$ (B) 1   (C) 4   (D) 8   (E) 16

7. If the difference of two numbers is greater than the sum of the numbers, which of the following must be true?

    (A) Neither number is negative.
    (B) At least one of the numbers is negative.
    (C) Exactly one of the numbers is negative.
    (D) Both numbers are negative.
    (E) None of these statements must be true.

GO ON TO THE NEXT PAGE

8. $(3a^2b^3)^3 =$
   (A) $9a^5b^6$ (B) $9a^6b^9$ (C) $27a^5b^6$ (D) $27a^6b^9$
   (E) $27a^8b^{27}$

9. Anne-Marie was x years old y years ago. How old will she be in z years?
   (A) $x + y + z$ (B) $x - y + z$ (C) $z - x - y$
   (D) $y - x + z$ (E) $x - y - z$

10. 10 is what percent of A?
    (A) $10A\%$ (B) $\dfrac{1}{10A}\%$ (C) $\dfrac{10}{A}\%$ (D) $\dfrac{100}{A}\%$
    (E) $\dfrac{1000}{A}\%$

11. A rectangle has a perimeter equal to the circumference of a circle of radius 3. If the width of the rectangle is 3, what is its length?
    (A) $3\pi - 3$ (B) $4.5\pi - 3$ (C) $6\pi - 3$ (D) $9\pi - 3$
    (E) It cannot be determined from the information given.

12. If Anthony had 3 times as many marbles as he actually has, he would have $\dfrac{1}{3}$ as many marbles as Billy has. What is the ratio of the number of marbles Anthony has to the number of marbles Billy has?
    (A) $\dfrac{1}{9}$ (B) $\dfrac{1}{3}$ (C) $\dfrac{1}{1}$ (D) $\dfrac{3}{1}$ (E) $\dfrac{9}{1}$

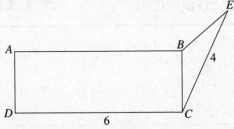

13. In the figure above, $BC = BE$. If R represents the perimeter of rectangle $ABCD$, and T represents the perimeter of $\triangle CBE$, what is the value of $R - T$?
    (A) 2 (B) 8 (C) 20 (D) $12 - 4\sqrt{2}$
    (E) It cannot be determined from the information given.

14. Two cylindrical tanks have the same height, but the radius of one tank equals the diameter of the other. If the volume of the larger is $k\%$ more than the volume of the smaller, $k =$
    (A) 50 (B) 100 (C) 200 (D) 300 (E) 400

Questions 15–16 refer to the following definition.

W	X
Y	Z

is a *number square* if $W + Z = X + Y$ and $2W = 3X$.

15. If

3	X
Y	7

is a *number square*, what is the value of Y?
    (A) 0 (B) 2 (C) 4 (D) 6 (E) 8

16. If

W	X
Y	W

is a *number square*, $Y =$
    (A) $\dfrac{3}{4}W$ (B) W (C) $\dfrac{4}{3}W$ (D) $3W$ (E) $4W$

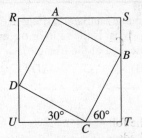

17. In the figure above, if the perimeter of square $ABCD$ is 8, what is the perimeter of square $RSTU$?
    (A) $4 + 4\sqrt{3}$ (B) $8\sqrt{3}$ (C) 12 (D) 16
    (E) It cannot be determined from the information given.

18. If $x + y = a$, $y + z = b$, and $x + z = c$, what is the average (arithmetic mean) of x, y, and z?
    (A) $\dfrac{a + b + c}{2}$ (B) $\dfrac{a + b + c}{3}$ (C) $\dfrac{a + b + c}{4}$
    (D) $\dfrac{a + b + c}{6}$ (E) It cannot be determined from the information given.

19. What is the remainder when 5^{20} is divided by 100?
    (A) 0 (B) 5 (C) 10 (D) 25 (E) 50

GO ON TO THE NEXT PAGE

2   2 2 2 2 2 2 2 2 2   2

20. A circular grass field has a circumference of $120\sqrt{\pi}$ meters. If Eric can mow 400 square meters of grass per hour, how many hours will he take to mow the entire field?

(A) 4   (B) 5   (C) 6   (D) 8   (E) 9

21. If $X = \dfrac{ab^2}{c}$, what is the result on X of doubling a, tripling b, and quadrupling c?

(A) X is multiplied by 1.5.   (B) X is multiplied by 3.
(C) X is multiplied by 4.5.   (D) X is multiplied by 6.
(E) X is multiplied by 9.

22. A sequence of numbers begins 1, 1, 1, 2, 2, 3 and then repeats this pattern of six numbers forever. What is the sum of the 135th, 136th, and 137th numbers in the sequence?

(A) 3   (B) 4   (C) 5   (D) 6   (E) 7

23. A square and an equilateral triangle each have sides of length 5. What is the ratio of the area of the square to the area of the triangle?

(A) $\dfrac{4}{3}$ (B) $\dfrac{16}{9}$ (C) $\dfrac{\sqrt{3}}{4}$ (D) $\dfrac{4\sqrt{3}}{3}$ (E) $\dfrac{16\sqrt{3}}{9}$

24. If r and s are positive numbers satisfying the inequality $\dfrac{r}{s} < \dfrac{r+1}{s+1}$, which of the following must be true?

(A) $r < s$ (B) $s < r$ (C) $r > 1$ (D) $s > 1$
(E) r and s can be any numbers as long as $r \neq s$.

25. The measures of the three angles of a triangle are in the ratio of 5:5:10, and the length of the longest side is 10. From this information, which of the following can be determined?

  I. The area of the triangle

  II. The perimeter of the triangle

  III. The lengths of each of the three altitudes

(A) I only   (B) II only   (C) III only
(D) I and II only   (E) I, II, and III

YOU MAY GO BACK AND REVIEW THIS SECTION IN THE REMAINING TIME, BUT DO NOT WORK IN ANY OTHER SECTION UNTIL TOLD TO DO SO.   **S T O P**

3   3 3 3 3 3 3 3 3 3 3 3   3

SECTION 3   Time—30 Minutes
35 Questions   Select the best answer to the following questions, then fill in
the appropriate space on your Answer Sheet.

Each of the following sentences contains one or two blanks; these blanks indicate that a word or set of words has been left out. Below the sentence are five words or phrases, lettered A through E. Select the word or set of words that best completes the sentence.

Example:

Fame is ----; today's rising star is all too soon tomorrow's washed-up has-been.

(A) rewarding   (B) gradual
(C) essential   (D) spontaneous
(E) transitory

1. She pointed out that his resume was ---- because it merely recorded his previous positions and failed to highlight the specific skills he had mastered in each job.

(A) disinterested
(B) inadequate
(C) conclusive
(D) obligatory
(E) detailed

2. Because it was already known that retroviruses could cause cancer in animals, it seemed only ---- to search for similar cancer-causing viruses in human beings.

(A) culpable   (B) charitable   (C) hypothetical
(D) logical   (E) negligent

3. Her ---- is always a source of irritation: she never uses a single word when she can substitute a long clause or phrase in its place.

(A) frivolity   (B) verbosity   (C) ambivalence
(D) cogency   (E) rhetoric

4. It is ---- to try to destroy pests completely with chemical poisons, for as each new chemical pesticide is introduced, the insects gradually become ---- to it.

(A) useless...drawn
(B) pointless...vulnerable
(C) futile...resistant
(D) wicked...indifferent
(E) worthwhile...immune

5. Ms. Ono ---- gives interviews because she believes the news media have ---- her and treated her badly.

(A) frequently...publicized
(B) rarely...misrepresented
(C) seldom...eulogized
(D) reluctantly...acclaimed
(E) gradually...evaded

6. Totem craftsmanship reached its ---- in the 19th century, when the introduction of metal tools enabled carvers to execute more sophisticated designs.

(A) roots
(B) conclusion
(C) antithesis
(D) reward
(E) apex

7. As delicate and ---- as insect bodies are, it is remarkable that over the ages enough of them have ----, preserved in amber, for scientists to trace insect evolution.

(A) beautiful...disappeared
(B) fragile...survived
(C) impervious...multiplied
(D) refined...awakened
(E) indestructible...evolved

8. Unfortunately, the current Broadway season offers some ---- fare that sounds markedly like imitations of previous hits.

(A) epic
(B) radical
(C) formulaic
(D) incongruous
(E) challenging

9. For those who admire realism, Louis Malle's recent film succeeds because it consciously ---- the stuff of legend and tells ---- story as it might actually unfold with fallible people in earthly time.

(A) rejects..a derivative
(B) anticipates..an antiquated
(C) shuns..an unembellished
(D) emulates..an ethereal
(E) exaggerates..a mythic

GO ON TO THE NEXT PAGE

10. Crabeater seal, the common name of *Lobodon carcinophagus*, is a ----, since the animal's staple diet is not crabs, but krill.

    (A) pseudonym
    (B) misnomer
    (C) delusion
    (D) digression
    (E) compromise

The analogies questions present two words or phrases that are related in some way. Determine which A-through-E answer choice below has a relationship *most* similar to that of the original words or phrases.

Example:

YAWN:BOREDOM::   (A) dream:sleep
(B) anger:madness   (C) smile:amusement
   (D) face:expression   (E) impatience:rebellion

---

11. CHIEF:TRIBE::

    (A) mascot:troop
    (B) voter:senate
    (C) partner:marriage
    (D) captain:team
    (E) musician:band

12. ATLAS:MAPS::

    (A) album:photographs
    (B) road:signs
    (C) automobile:wheels
    (D) star:planets
    (E) circus:acrobats

13. NOVELIST:PLOT::

    (A) dramatist:acts
    (B) architect:blueprint
    (C) sculptor:chisel
    (D) magician:legerdemain
    (E) composer:notes

14. SPINE:CACTUS::

    (A) backbone:man
    (B) quill:porcupine
    (C) root:oak
    (D) pit:olive
    (E) binding:book

15. JACKKNIFE:DIVER::

    (A) sword:fencer
    (B) fairway:golfer
    (C) strike:umpire
    (D) cartwheel:gymnast
    (E) easel:painter

16. ISLAND:ARCHIPELAGO::

    (A) team:player
    (B) sphere:hemisphere
    (C) star:galaxy
    (D) multitude:horde
    (E) continent:peninsula

17. INVENTORY:MERCHANDISE::

    (A) repertory:theater
    (B) roster:members
    (C) gadget:profits
    (D) bankruptcy:debts
    (E) dormitory:college

18. INTEREST:FASCINATION::

    (A) dislike:abhorrence
    (B) delusion:gullibility
    (C) exertion:fatigue
    (D) science:witchcraft
    (E) bonfire:torch

19. RENEGADE:FAITH::

    (A) glutton:appetite
    (B) zealot:suspicion
    (C) visionary:dream
    (D) maverick:herd
    (E) hermit:cave

20. OLFACTORY:NOSE::

    (A) peripheral:eyes
    (B) gustatory:tongue
    (C) ambulatory:patient
    (D) tactile:ears
    (E) perfunctory:skin

21. INDIGENT:WEALTH::

    (A) irate:sobriety
    (B) taciturn:silence
    (C) painstaking:meticulousness
    (D) frivolous:seriousness
    (E) scholarly:wit

GO ON TO THE NEXT PAGE

3 **3** **3** **3** **3** **3** **3** **3** **3** **3** **3** **3**

22. LABYRINTHINE:MAZE::

   (A) circuitous:logic
   (B) perfidious:treachery
   (C) insolvent:funds
   (D) orderly:chaos
   (E) fastidious:taste

23. SCOTCH:RUMOR::

   (A) divert:traffic
   (B) broach:topic
   (C) suppress:riot
   (D) singe:fire
   (E) spread:gossip

Read the passage below, and then answer the questions that follow the passage. The correct response may be stated outright or merely suggested in the passage.

Questions 24–35 are based on the following passage.

The writer John Updike muses on the significance of Mickey Mouse.

Cartoon characters have soul as Carl Jung defined it in his *Archetypes and the Collective Unconscious*: "soul is a life-giving demon who
Line plays his elfin game above and below human
(5) existence." Without the "leaping and twinkling of the soul," Jung says, "man would rot away in his greatest passion, idleness." The Mickey Mouse of the thirties shorts was a whirlwind of activity, with a host of unsuspected skills and a reluctant
(10) heroism that rose to every occasion. Like Chaplin and Douglas Fairbanks and Fred Astaire, he acted out our fantasies of endless nimbleness, of perfect weightlessness. Yet withal, there was nothing aggressive or self-promoting about him, as there
(15) was about Popeye. Disney, interviewed in the thirties, said, "Sometimes I've tried to figure out why Mickey appealed to the whole world. Everybody's tried to figure it out. So far as I know, nobody has. He's a pretty nice fellow who
(20) never does anybody any harm, who gets into scrapes through no fault of his own, but always manages to come up grinning." This was perhaps Disney's image of himself: for twenty years he did Mickey's voice in the films, and would often
(25) say, "There's a lot of the Mouse in me." Mickey was a character created with his own pen, and nurtured on Disney's memories of his mouse-ridden Kansas City studio and of the Missouri farm where his struggling father tried for a time to
(30) make a living. Walt's humble, scrambling beginnings remained embodied in the mouse, whom the Nazis, in a fury against the Mickey-inspired Allied legions (the Allied code word on D-Day was "Mickey Mouse"), called "the most miser-
(35) able ideal ever revealed...mice are dirty."
   But was Disney, like Mickey, just "a pretty nice fellow"? He was until crossed in his driving perfectionism, his Napoleonic capacity to marshal men and take risks in the service of an artistic and
(40) entrepreneurial vision. He was one of those great Americans, like Edison and Henry Ford, who

invented themselves in terms of a new technology. The technology—in Disney's case, film animation—would have been there anyway, but
(45) only a few driven men seized the full possibilities and made empires. In the dozen years between *Steamboat Willie* and *Fantasia*, the Disney studios took the art of animation to heights of ambition and accomplishment it would never have
(50) reached otherwise, and Disney's personal zeal was the animating force. He created an empire of the mind, and its emperor was Mickey Mouse.
   The thirties were Mickey's conquering decade. His image circled the globe. In Africa, tribesmen
(55) painfully had tiny mosaic Mickey Mouses inset into their front teeth, and a South African tribe refused to buy soap unless the cakes were embossed with Mickey's image. Nor were the high and mighty immune to Mickey's elemental
(60) appeal—King George V and Franklin Roosevelt insisted that all film showings they attended include a dose of Mickey Mouse. But other popular phantoms, like Felix the Cat, have faded, where Mickey has settled into the national collec-
(65) tive consciousness. The television program revived him for my children's generation, and the theme parks make him live for my grandchildren's. Yet survival cannot be imposed through weight of publicity. Mickey's persistence springs
(70) from something unhyped, something timeless in the image that has allowed it to pass in status from a fad to an icon.
   To take a bite out of our imaginations, an icon must be simple. The ears, the wiggly tail, the red
(75) shorts, give us a Mickey. Donald Duck and Goofy, Bugs Bunny and Woody Woodpecker are inextricably bound up with the draftsmanship of the artists who make them move and squawk, but Mickey floats free. It was Claes Oldenburg's pop
(80) art that first alerted me to the fact that Mickey

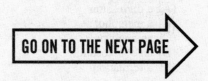
GO ON TO THE NEXT PAGE

Mouse had passed out of the realm of commercially generated image into that of artifact. A new
Disney gadget, advertised on television, is a cam-
(85) era-like box that spouts bubbles when a key is
turned; the key consists of three circles, two
mounted on a larger one, and the image is unmistakably Mickey. Like yin and yang, like the
Christian cross and the star of Israel, Mickey can
(90) be seen everywhere—a sign, a rune, a hieroglyph-
ic trace of a secret power, an electricity we want
to plug into. Like totem poles, like African masks,
Mickey stands at that intersection of abstraction
and representation where magic connects.

24. The author's attitude toward Popeye in lines 13–15
is primarily

(A) nostalgic
(B) deprecatory
(C) apathetic
(D) vindictive
(E) reverent

25. By describing Mickey's skills as "unsuspected" and
his heroism as "reluctant" (line 9), the author primarily conveys Mickey's

(A) unassuming nature
(B) unrealistic success
(C) contradictory image
(D) ignominious failings
(E) idealistic character

26. The word "scrapes" in line 21 means

(A) abrasions
(B) harsh sounds
(C) small economies
(D) discarded fragments
(E) predicaments

27. By saying "There's a lot of the Mouse in me" (line
25), Disney revealed

(A) his inability to distinguish himself as an indi-
vidual
(B) the extent of his identification with his creation
(C) the desire to capitalize on his character's popu-
larity
(D) his fear of being surpassed by a creature he
produced
(E) his somewhat negative image of himself

28. The reference to the Nazis' comments on Mickey
(lines 32–35) can best be described as

(A) a digression
(B) a metaphor
(C) an analysis
(D) an equivocation
(E) a refutation

29. The word "crossed" in line 37 means

(A) traversed
(B) confused
(C) intersected
(D) encountered
(E) opposed

30. The author views Disney as all of the following
EXCEPT

(A) a self-made man
(B) a demanding artist
(C) an enterprising businessman
(D) the inventor of film animation
(E) an empire-builder

31. The references to the African tribesmen (lines
54–58) and to Franklin Roosevelt (line 60) primarily serve to

(A) demonstrate the improbability of Mickey's
reaching such disparate audiences
(B) dispel a misconception about the nature of
Mickey's popularity
(C) support the assertion that people of all back-
grounds were drawn to Mickey Mouse
(D) show how much research the author has done
into the early history of Disney cartoons
(E) answer the charges made by critics of Disney's
appeal

32. The distinction made between a "fad" and an
"icon" (lines 68–72) can best be summarized as
which of the following?

(A) The first is a popular fashion, the second
attracts only a small group.
(B) The first involves a greater degree of audience
involvement than the second.
(C) The first is less likely to need publicity than
the second.
(D) The first is less enduring in appeal than is the
second.
(E) The first conveys greater prestige than the
second.

33. The phrase "take a bite out of our imaginations"
(line 73) most nearly means

(A) injure our creativity
(B) reduce our innovative capacity
(C) cut into our inspiration
(D) capture our fancies
(E) limit our visions

GO ON TO THE NEXT PAGE

34. The author's description of the new Disney gadget (lines 83–88) does which of the following?

    (A) It suggests that popular new product lines are still being manufactured by Disney.
    (B) It demonstrates that even a rudimentary outline can convey the image of Mickey.
    (C) It illustrates the importance of television advertising in marketing new products.
    (D) It disproves the notion that Disney's death has undermined his mercantile empire.
    (E) It refutes the author's assertion that Mickey's survival springs from something unhyped.

35. Which of the following most resembles the new Disney gadget (lines 82–87) in presenting Mickey as an artifact?

    (A) A comic book presenting the adventures of Mickey Mouse
    (B) A rubber mask realistically portraying Mickey's features
    (C) A Mickey Mouse watch on which Mickey's hands point at the time
    (D) A Mickey Mouse waffle iron that makes waffles in the shape of three linked circles
    (E) A framed cell or single strip from an original Mickey Mouse animated film

YOU MAY GO BACK AND REVIEW THIS SECTION IN THE REMAINING TIME, BUT DO NOT WORK IN ANY OTHER SECTION UNTIL TOLD TO DO SO.

S T O P

4 4 4 4 4 4 4 4 4 4 4 **4**

SECTION 4

Time—30 Minutes
25 Questions

You have 30 minutes to answer the 15 Quantitative Comparison questions and 10 Student-Produced Response questions in this section. You may use any blank space on the page for your work.

Notes:

- You may use a calculator whenever you feel it will be helpful.

- Use the diagrams provided to help you solve the problems. Unless you see the words "<u>Note</u>: Figure not drawn to scale" under a diagram, it has been drawn as accurately as possible. Unless it is stated that a figure is three-dimensional, you may assume it lies in a plane.

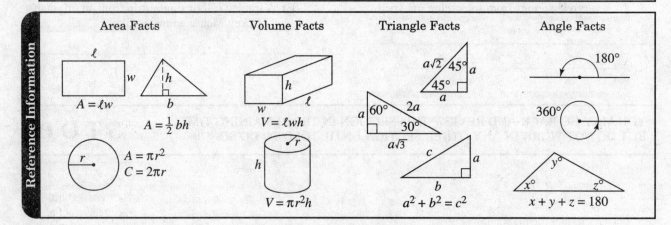

Reference Information

Area Facts Volume Facts Triangle Facts Angle Facts

$A = \ell w$

$A = \frac{1}{2} bh$

$A = \pi r^2$
$C = 2\pi r$

$V = \ell wh$

$V = \pi r^2 h$

$a^2 + b^2 = c^2$

$x + y + z = 180$

Directions for Quantitative Comparison Questions

In each of questions 1–15, two quantities appear in boxes: one in Column A and one in Column B. You must compare them. The correct answer to a question is

  A if the quantity in Column A is greater;
  B if the quantity in Column B is greater;
  C if the two quantities are equal;
  D if it is impossible to determine which quantity is greater.

Notes:

- *The correct answer is never E.*
- Sometimes information about one or both of the quantities is centered above the two boxes.
- If the same symbol appears in both columns, it represents the same thing each time.
- All variables represent real numbers.

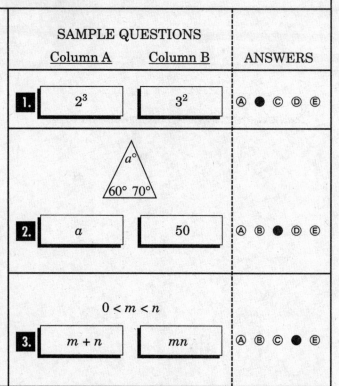

SAMPLE QUESTIONS

Column A   Column B   ANSWERS

1. 2^3 3^2 Ⓐ ● Ⓒ Ⓓ Ⓔ

2. a 50   Ⓐ Ⓑ ● Ⓓ Ⓔ

$0 < m < n$

3. $m + n$ mn Ⓐ Ⓑ Ⓒ ● Ⓔ

GO ON TO THE NEXT PAGE

4   4   4   4   4   4   4   4   4   4   4   **4**

SUMMARY DIRECTIONS FOR QUANTITATIVE COMPARISON QUESTIONS

<u>Answer</u>: A if the quantity in Column A is greater;
               B if the quantity in Column B is greater;
               C if the two quantities are equal;
               D if it is impossible to determine which quantity is greater.

<u>Column A</u>   <u>Column B</u>

1.   4.798 rounded to the nearest hundredth   4.849 rounded to the nearest tenth

2. 2^{1000} 1000^2

Note: Figure not drawn to scale

3. c 5

$$a \neq 0$$
$$ab = a^2$$

4. a b

<u>Column A</u>   <u>Column B</u>

$$A = 7x - 3$$

5.   The value of A when $x = -10$ The value of $-A$ when $x = 10$

n is an odd positive integer.

6.   The number of prime factors of n The number of prime factors of $2n$

7.   The average (arithmetic mean) of all the positive multiples of 5 less than 26   The average (arithmetic mean) of all the positive multiples of 7 less than 26

Stores A and B normally sell a particular radio for the same price.

8.   The price of the radio when it's on sale at store A for $20 off   The price of the radio when it's on sale at store B for 20% off

GO ON TO THE NEXT PAGE ▷

4   4 4 4 4 4 4 4 4 4 4   4

SUMMARY DIRECTIONS FOR QUANTITATIVE COMPARISON QUESTIONS

<u>Answer</u>: A if the quantity in Column A is greater;
  B if the quantity in Column B is greater;
  C if the two quantities are equal;
  D if it is impossible to determine which quantity is greater.

Column A   Column B   Column A   Column B

Note: Figure not drawn to scale

9. x y

$ab = 0$

10. $(a + b)^2$ $(a - b)^2$

$x = -7$

11. x^{200} $(7x^{99})^2$

On a test $\frac{4}{7}$ of the boys and $\frac{7}{11}$ of the girls earned over 90.

12.   The number of   The number of
      students receiving   students receiving
      grades over 90   grades of 90 or less

$x^2 - x - 5 = 0$

13. $x^2 - 5$ x

Jack and Jill each bought the same TV set using a 10% off coupon. Jack's cashier took 10% off the price and then added 8.5% sales tax. Jill's cashier first added the tax and then took 10% off the total price.

14.   The amount Jack paid   The amount Jill paid

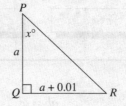

Note: Figure not drawn to scale

15. x 60

GO ON TO THE NEXT PAGE ⇨

Directions for Student-Produced Response Questions (Grid-ins)

In questions 16–25, first solve the problem, and then enter your answer on the grid provided on the answer sheet. The instructions for entering your answers are as follows:
- First, write your answer in the boxes at the top of the grid.
- Second, grid your answer in the columns below the boxes.
- Use the fraction bar in the first row or the decimal point in the second row to enter fractions and decimal answers.

Answer: $\frac{8}{15}$ Answer: 1.75

Write your → answer in the boxes

Grid in → your answer

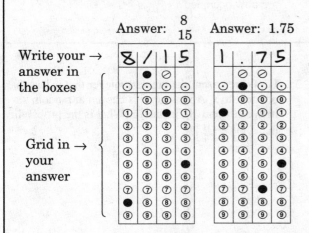

Answer: 100

Either position is acceptable

- Grid only one space in each column.
- Entering the answer in the boxes is recommended as an aid in gridding, but is not required.
- The machine scoring your exam can read only what you grid, so you **must grid in your answers correctly to get credit.**
- If a question has more than one correct answer, grid in only one of them.
- The grid does not have a minus sign, so no answer can be negative.
- A mixed number *must* be converted to an improper fraction or a decimal before it is gridded. Enter $1\frac{1}{4}$ as 5/4 or 1.25; the machine will interpret 1 1/4 as $\frac{11}{4}$ and mark it wrong.
- **All decimals must be entered as accurately as possible.** Here are the three acceptable ways of gridding

$$\frac{3}{11} = 0.272727...$$

3/11   .272   .273

- Note that rounding to .273 is acceptable, because you are using the full grid, but you would receive **no credit** for .3 or .27, because they are less accurate.

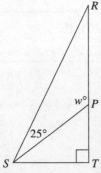

16. In the figure above, if *PS* bisects ∠*RST*, what is the value of *w*?

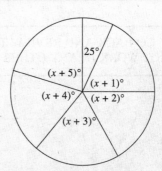

17. What is the value of *x* in the figure above?

GO ON TO THE NEXT PAGE

4   4 4 4 4 4 4 4 4 4   **4**

18. Two white cards measuring 3" × 5" are placed on a 9" × 12" piece of red construction paper so that they do not overlap. What is the area, in square inches, of the uncovered part of the red paper?

19. If 80% of the adult population of a village are registered to vote, and 60% of those registered actually voted in a particular election, what percent of the adults in the village did NOT vote in that election?

20. If Henry drove 198 kilometers between 10:00 A.M. and 1:40 P.M., what was his average speed, in kilometers per hour?

21. The first term of a sequence is 1. Starting with the second term, each term is 1 less than 3 times the preceding term. What is the smallest number greater than 100 in the sequence?

22. Each stockholder of XYZ Corporation belongs to either Group A or Group B. Exactly 10% of the stockholders are in Group A, and collectively they own 80% of the stock. Let a represent the average number of shares of stock owned by the members of Group A, and b represent the average number of shares of stock owned by the members of Group B. If $a = kb$, what is the value of k?

23. In a jar containing only red and blue marbles, 40% of the marbles are red. If the average weight of a red marble is 40 grams and the average weight of a blue marble is 60 grams, what is the average weight, in grams, of all the marbles in the jar?

24. A school group charters three identical buses and occupies $\frac{4}{5}$ of the seats. After $\frac{1}{4}$ of the passengers leave, the remaining passengers use only two of the buses. What fraction of the seats on the two buses are now occupied?

25. Let [x] represent the greatest integer that is less than or equal to x. An integer a is chosen at random between 1 and 10, inclusive. What is the probability that $\left[\frac{a}{5}\right] = \left[\frac{a}{4}\right]$?

YOU MAY GO BACK AND REVIEW THIS SECTION IN THE REMAINING TIME, BUT DO NOT WORK IN ANY OTHER SECTION UNTIL TOLD TO DO SO.   **S T O P**

5

The questions that follow the two passages in this section relate to the content of both, and to their relationship.
The correct response may be stated outright in the passages or merely suggested.

Questions 1–13 are based on the following passages.

*The following passages are excerpted from popular
articles on dolphins, the first dating from the 1960s, the
second written in 1990.*

Passage 1

Most of the intelligent land animals have prehensile, grasping organs for exploring their environment—hands in human beings and their
Line   anthropoid relatives, the sensitive inquiring trunk
(5)   in the elephant. One of the surprising things about
the dolphin is that his superior brain is unaccom-
panied by any type of manipulative organ. He
has, however, a remarkable range-finding ability
involving some sort of echo-sounding. Perhaps
(10)   this acute sense—far more accurate than any that
human ingenuity has been able to devise artifi-
cially—brings him greater knowledge of his
watery surroundings than might at first seem possible. Human beings think of intelligence as
(15)   geared to things. The hand and the tool are to us
the unconscious symbols of our intellectual attainment. It is difficult for us to visualize another
kind of lonely, almost disembodied intelligence
floating in the wavering green fairyland of the
(20)   sea—an intelligence possibly near or comparable
to our own but without hands to build, to transmit
knowledge by writing, or to alter by one hairs-
breadth the planet's surface. Yet at the same time
there are indications that this is a warm, friendly,
(25)   and eager intelligence quite capable of coming to
the assistance of injured companions and striving
to rescue them from drowning. Dolphins left the
land when mammalian brains were still small and
primitive. Without the stimulus provided by agile
(30)   exploring fingers, these great sea mammals have
yet taken a divergent road toward intelligence of a
high order. Hidden in their sleek bodies is an
impressively elaborated instrument, the reason for
whose appearance is a complete enigma. It is as
(35)   though both the human being and the dolphin
were each part of some great eye which yearned
to look both outward on eternity and inward to
the sea's heart—that fertile entity like the mind in
its swarming and grotesque life.

Passage 2

(40)   Nothing about dolphins has been more widely
or passionately discussed over the centuries than
their supposed intelligence and communicative
abilities. In fact, a persistent dogma holds that
dolphins are among the most intelligent of ani-
(45)   mals and that they communicate with one another
in complex ways. Implicit in this argument is the
belief that dolphin cultures are at least as ancient
and rich as our own. To support the claim of high
intelligence amongst dolphins, proponents note
(50)   that they have large brains, live in societies
marked as much by co-operative as by competitive interactions and rapidly learn the artificial
tasks given to them in captivity. Indeed, dolphins
are clearly capable of learning through observa-
(55)   tion and have good memories. People who spend
time with captive dolphins are invariably
impressed by their sense of humor, playfulness,
quick comprehension of body language, command of situations, mental agility, and emotional
(60)   resilience. Individual dolphins have distinctive
personalities and trainers often speak of being
trained by their subjects, rather than the other way
round.

The extremely varied repertoires of sounds
(65)   made by dolphins are often invoked as *prima
facie* evidence of advanced communication abilities. In addition, some "scientific" experiments
done by John Lilly and his associates during the
1950s and 1960s were claimed to show that dol-
(70)   phins communicate not only with one another but
also with humans, mimicking human speech and
reaching out across the boundaries that divide us.

These conclusions about dolphin intelligence
and communication have not withstood critical
(75)   scrutiny. While they have fueled romantic speculation, their net impact has been to mislead.
Rather than allowing dolphins to be discovered
and appreciated for what they are, Lilly's vision
has forced us to measure these animals' value
(80)   according to how close they come to equalling or
exceeding our own intelligence, virtue, and spiritual development.

GO ON TO THE NEXT PAGE

5

The issues of dolphin intelligence and communication have been inseparable in most people's
(85) minds, and the presumed existence of one has been taken as proof of the other, a classic case of begging the question. Not surprisingly then, most experiments to evaluate dolphin intelligence have measured the animals' capacity for cognitive pro-
(90) cessing as exhibited in their understanding of the rudiments of language.

From the early work of researchers like Dwight Batteau and Jarvis Bastian through the more recent work of Louis Herman and associ-
(95) ates, dolphins have been asked to accept simple information, in the form of acoustic or visual symbols representing verbs and nouns, and then to act on the information following a set of commands from the experimenter.

(100) The widely publicized results have been somewhat disappointing. Although they have demonstrated that dolphins do have the primary skills necessary to support understanding and use of a language, they have not distinguished the dol-
(105) phins from other animals in this respect. For example, some seals, animals we do not normally cite as members of the intellectual or communicative elite, have been found to have the same basic capabilities.

(110) What, then, do the results of experiments to date mean? Either we have not devised adequate tests to permit us to detect, measure, and rank intelligence as a measure of a given species' ability to communicate, or we must acknowledge that
(115) the characteristics that we regard as rudimentary evidence of intelligence are held more commonly by many "lower" animals than we previously thought.

1. According to Passage 1, which of the following statements about dolphins is true?

   (A) They have always been water-dwelling creatures.
   (B) They at one time possessed prehensile organs.
   (C) They lived on land in prehistoric times.
   (D) Their brains are no longer mammalian in nature.
   (E) They developed brains to compensate for the lack of a prehensile organ.

2. The author of Passage 1 suggests that human failure to understand the intelligence of the dolphin is due to

   (A) the inadequacy of human range-finding equipment
   (B) a lack of knowledge about the sea
   (C) the want of a common language
   (D) the primitive origins of the human brain
   (E) the human inclination to judge other life by our own

3. In Passage 1, the author's primary purpose is apparently to

   (A) examine the dolphin's potential for surpassing humankind
   (B) question the need for prehensile organs in human development
   (C) refute the theory that dolphins are unable to alter their physical environment
   (D) reassess the nature and extent of dolphin intelligence
   (E) indicate the superiority of human intelligence over that of the dolphin

4. The word "acute" in line 10 means

   (A) excruciating
   (B) severe
   (C) keen
   (D) sudden and intense
   (E) brief in duration

5. The "impressively elaborated instrument" referred to in line 33 is best interpreted to mean which of the following?

   (A) A concealed manipulative organ
   (B) An artificial range-finding device
   (C) A complex, intelligent brain
   (D) The dolphin's hidden eye
   (E) An apparatus for producing musical sounds

6. According to the author's simile in lines 38–39, the human mind and the heart of the sea are alike in that both

   (A) teem with exotic forms of life
   (B) argue in support of intelligence
   (C) are necessary to the evolution of dolphins
   (D) are directed outward
   (E) share a penchant for the grotesque

7. Which of the following best characterizes the tone of Passage 1?

   (A) Restrained skepticism
   (B) Pedantic assertion
   (C) Wondering admiration
   (D) Amused condescension
   (E) Ironic speculation

GO ON TO THE NEXT PAGE

5

8. The author of Passage 2 puts quotation marks around the word *scientific* in line 67 to indicate he

(A) is faithfully reproducing Lilly's own words
(B) intends to define the word later in the passage
(C) believes the reader is unfamiliar with the word as used by Lilly
(D) advocates adhering to the scientific method in all experiments
(E) has some doubts as to how scientific those experiments were

9. The author of Passage 2 maintains that the writings of Lilly and his associates have

(A) overstated the extent of dolphin intelligence
(B) been inadequately scrutinized by critics
(C) measured the worth of the dolphin family
(D) underrated dolphins as intelligent beings
(E) established criteria for evaluating dolphin intelligence

10. By calling the argument summarized in lines 83–86 a classic case of begging the question, the author of Passage 2 indicates he views it with

(A) trepidation
(B) optimism
(C) detachment
(D) skepticism
(E) credulity

11. Which of the following would most undercut the studies on which the author bases his conclusion in lines 110–118?

(A) Evidence proving dolphin linguistic abilities to be far superior to those of other mammals
(B) An article recording attempts by seals and walruses to communicate with human beings
(C) The reorganization of current intelligence tests by species and level of difficulty
(D) A reassessment of the definition of the term "lower animals"
(E) The establishment of a project to develop new tests to detect intelligence in animals

12. The author of Passage 2 would find Passage 1

(A) typical of the attitudes of Lilly and his associates
(B) remarkable for the perspective it offers
(C) indicative of the richness of dolphin culture
(D) supportive of his fundamental point of view
(E) intriguing for its far-reaching conclusions

13. Compared to Passage 2, Passage 1 is

(A) more figurative
(B) less obscure
(C) more objective
(D) more current
(E) less speculative

YOU MAY GO BACK AND REVIEW THIS SECTION IN THE REMAINING TIME, BUT DO NOT WORK IN ANY OTHER SECTION UNTIL TOLD TO DO SO.   **STOP**

6   6 6 6 6 6 6 6 6 6 6   6

SECTION 6

Time—15 Minutes
10 Questions

For each problem in this section determine which of the five choices is correct and blacken in that choice on your answer sheet. You may use any blank space on the page for your work.

Notes:

- You may use a calculator whenever you feel it will be helpful.
- Use the diagrams provided to help you solve the problems. Unless you see the words "Note: Figure not drawn to scale" under a diagram, it has been drawn as accurately as possible. Unless it is stated that a figure is three-dimensional, you may assume it lies in a plane.

Reference Information

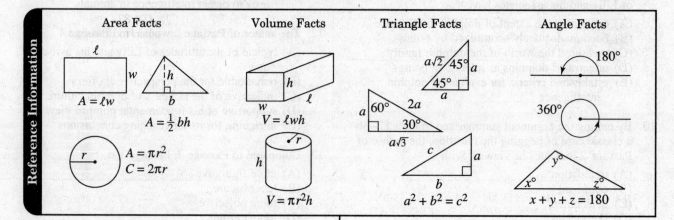

Area Facts

$A = \ell w$

$A = \frac{1}{2} bh$

$A = \pi r^2$
$C = 2\pi r$

Volume Facts

$V = \ell w h$

$V = \pi r^2 h$

Triangle Facts

$a^2 + b^2 = c^2$

Angle Facts

$x + y + z = 180$

---

1. If an alarm beeps at a constant rate of 16 beeps per minute, how many minutes will it take to beep 88 times?

   (A) 5   (B) 5.5   (C) 6.5   (D) 23.5   (E) 1408

2. Each of the following is equal to $\frac{1}{2}$ % EXCEPT

   (A) $\dfrac{\frac{1}{2}}{100}$ (B) $\dfrac{1}{200}$ (C) 0.005   (D) $\dfrac{5}{1000}$

   (E) $\dfrac{1\%}{2\%}$.

3. $\{[(a \times a) + a] \div a\} - a =$
   (A) 0   (B) 1   (C) a (D) $a^2 - a$ (E) $a^2 - a + 1$

4. How many primes less than 1000 are divisible by 7?

   (A) none   (B) 1   (C) more than 1 but less than 142
   (D) 142   (E) more than 142

5. If the average (arithmetic mean) of the measures of two angles of a quadrilateral is 60°, what is the average of the measures of the other two angles?

   (A) 60°   (B) 90°   (C) 120°   (D) 180°   (E) 240°

6. If m is an integer and m, $m + 1$, and $m + 2$ are the lengths of the sides of a triangle, which of the following could be the value of m?

   I. 1
   II. 10
   III. 100

   (A) I only   (B) II only   (C) III only
   (D) II and III only   (E) I, II, and III

GO ON TO THE NEXT PAGE

6   6   6   6   6   6   6   6   6   6   6   6

7. What is the measure, in degrees, of the smaller angle formed by the hour hand and the minute hand of a clock at 11:20?

(A) 120   (B) 130   (C) 135   (D) 140   (E) 150

9. 10% more than 10% less than x is what percent of $10x$?

(A) 9%   (B) 9.9%   (C) 10%   (D) 99%
(E) 100%

8. The following table lists the salaries in 1980 of five people and the percent changes in their salaries from 1980 to 1990.

Name	1980 Salary	Percent Change
Ada	$32,000	+35
Bob	$40,000	+11
Cal	$35,000	+25
Dan	$50,000	−12
Eve	$42,000	+6

Who had the highest salary in 1990?

(A) Ada   (B) Bob   (C) Cal   (D) Dan   (E) Eve

10. So far this year, Adam has played 30 games of chess and has won only 6 of them. What is the minimum number of additional games he must play, given that he is sure to lose at least one-third of them, so that for the year he will have won more games than he lost?

(A) 25   (B) 34   (C) 57   (D) 87
(E) It is not possible for Adam to do this.

YOU MAY GO BACK AND REVIEW THIS SECTION IN THE REMAINING TIME, BUT DO NOT WORK IN ANY OTHER SECTION UNTIL TOLD TO DO SO.   S T O P

Answer Key

Note: The letters in brackets following the Mathematical Reasoning answers refer to the sections of Chapter 12 in which you can find the information you need to answer the questions. For example, **1. C [E]** means that the answer to question 1 is C, and that the solution requires information found in Section 12-E: Averages.

Section 1   Verbal Reasoning

1. E	7. C	13. B	19. B	25. C
2. B	8. D	14. E	20. A	26. B
3. B	9. A	15. B	21. C	27. E
4. B	10. E	16. C	22. D	28. A
5. C	11. B	17. D	23. B	29. B
6. B	12. B	18. C	24. C	30. A

Section 2   Mathematical Reasoning

1. C [A]	6. B [G]	11. A [K, L]	16. C [G]	21. C [A]
2. C [G]	7. B [A]	12. A [D, H]	17. A [J, K]	22. C [P]
3. D [A]	8. D [A]	13. B [K, G]	18. D [E, G]	23. D [J, K]
4. C [J]	9. A [H]	14. D [M, C]	19. D [A]	24. A [A, D]
5. C [G]	10. E [C]	15. E [G]	20. E [H, L]	25. E [J]

Section 3   Verbal Reasoning

1. B	8. C	15. D	22. B	29. E
2. D	9. C	16. C	23. C	30. D
3. B	10. B	17. B	24. B	31. C
4. C	11. D	18. A	25. A	32. D
5. B	12. A	19. D	26. E	33. D
6. E	13. B	20. B	27. B	34. B
7. B	14. B	21. D	28. A	35. D

Section 4   Mathematical Reasoning

Quantitative Comparison Questions

1. C [B]	4. C [A]	7. A [E]	10. C [F]	13. C [F]
2. A [A]	5. B [A]	8. D [C]	11. C [A]	14. C [C]
3. D [J]	6. B [A]	9. D [J]	12. A [B]	15. D [J]

Grid-in Questions

16. [J]	17. [I, G]	18. [K]	19. [C]	20. [D, H]
1 1 5	6 4	7 8	5 2	5 4

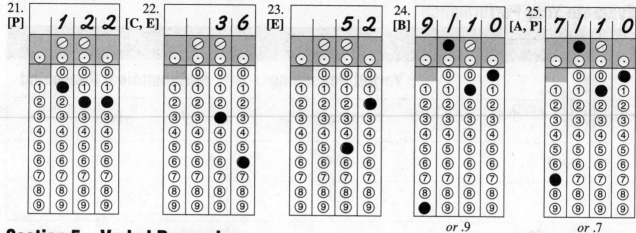

21. [P] 1 2 2
22. [C, E] 3 6
23. [E] 5 2
24. [B] 9 / 1 0   *or .9*
25. [A, P] 7 / 1 0   *or .7*

Section 5   Verbal Reasoning

1. C
2. E
3. D
4. C
5. C
6. A
7. C
8. E
9. A
10. D
11. A
12. A
13. A

Section 6   Mathematical Reasoning

1. B [D]
2. E [B, C]
3. B [A]
4. B [A]
5. C [K]
6. D [J]
7. D [I, P]
8. E [C, Q]
9. B [C]
10. C [G, H]

Calculate Your Raw Score

Verbal Reasoning

Section 1 $\dfrac{}{\text{number correct}} - \dfrac{1}{4}\left(\dfrac{}{\text{number incorrect}} \right) = \underline{}$ (A)

Section 3 $\dfrac{}{\text{number correct}} - \dfrac{1}{4}\left(\dfrac{}{\text{number incorrect}} \right) = \underline{}$ (B)

Section 5 $\dfrac{}{\text{number correct}} - \dfrac{1}{4}\left(\dfrac{}{\text{number incorrect}} \right) = \underline{}$ (C)

Raw Verbal Reasoning Score = (A) + (B) + (C) = \underline{}

Mathematical Reasoning

Section 2 $\dfrac{}{\text{number correct}} - \dfrac{1}{4}\left(\dfrac{}{\text{number incorrect}} \right) = \underline{}$ (D)

Section 4
Part I
(1–15) $\dfrac{}{\text{number correct}} - \dfrac{1}{3}\left(\dfrac{}{\text{number incorrect}} \right) = \underline{}$ (E)

Part II
(16–25) $\dfrac{}{\text{number correct}} = \underline{}$ (F)

Section 6 $\dfrac{}{\text{number correct}} - \dfrac{1}{4}\left(\dfrac{}{\text{number incorrect}} \right) = \underline{}$ (G)

Raw Mathematical Reasoning Score = (D) + (E) + (F) + (G) = \underline{}

Evaluate Your Performance

	Verbal Reasoning	Mathematical Reasoning
Superior	67–78	51–60
Very Good	60–66	45–50
Good	52–59	40–44
Satisfactory	44–51	35–39
Average	36–43	30–34
Needs Further Study	29–35	25–29
Needs Intensive Study	21–28	20–24
Inadequate	0–20	0–19

Identify Your Weaknesses

Verbal Reasoning

Question Type	Question Numbers			Chapter to Study
	Section 1	Section 3	Section 5	
Sentence Completion	1, 2, 3, 4, 5, 6, 7, 8, 9	1, 2, 3, 4, 5, 6, 7, 8, 9, 10		Chapter 4
Analogy	10, 11, 12, 13, 14, 15	11, 12, 13, 14, 15, 16, 17, 18, 19, 20, 21, 22, 23		Chapter 5
Reading Comprehension	16, 17, 18, 19, 20, 21, 22, 23, 24, 25, 26, 27, 28, 29, 30	24, 25, 26, 27, 28, 29, 30	1, 2, 3, 4, 5, 6, 7, 8, 9, 10, 11, 12, 13	Chapter 6

Identify Your Weaknesses

Mathematical Reasoning

Skill Area	Question Numbers			Pages to Study
	Section 2	Section 4	Section 6	
Basics of Arithmetic	1, 3, 7, 8, 19, 21, 24	1, 2, 4, 5, 6, 11, 25	3, 4	331–338
Fractions and Decimals		12, 24	2	344–352
Percents	10, 14	8, 14, 19, 22	2, 8, 9	358–361
Ratios	12, 24	20	1, 8	366–370
Averages	18	7, 22, 23		376–378
Polynomials		10, 13		383–386
Equations and Inequalities	2, 5, 6, 13, 15, 16, 18	17	10	389–394
Word Problems	9, 12, 20	20	10	399–402
Lines and Angles		17	7	407–410
Triangles	4, 17, 23, 25	3, 9, 15, 16	6	414–418
Quadrilaterals	11, 13, 17, 23	18	5	425–428
Circles	11, 20			432–435
Solid Geometry	14			440–442
Coordinate Geometry				446–448
Counting and Probability				452–456
Logical Reasoning	22	21, 25	7	462–464
Data Interpretation				468–471

Answer Explanations

Section 1   Verbal Reasoning

1. **E.** The subject considers himself talented and creative and thinks office work is uninspiring, dull, in a word *prosaic*.
Note that the missing word must be a synonym or near-synonym for "uninspiring." Connected by the linking *was*, both words describe or define the office routine.
(Definition)

2. **B.** A *chronological* order is one arranged in order of time. The missing word is an adjective describing the order in which the museum arranged the fossils. The second part of the sentence defines that order: from older to more recent in time.
Word Parts Clue: *Chron-* means time.
(Definition)

3. **B.** Thanks to the development of wings, insects were able to *disperse* or scatter over the earth's surface. Thus, they were able to reach new habitats and untapped sources of nourishment.
(Cause and Effect Pattern)

4. **B.** For London to miss out on (fail to attract) two major international art exhibitions marks it as a failure or *also-ran* in the highly competitive world of international art museums.
(Cause and Effect Pattern)

5. **C.** The critics are *riled* or irritated by the condescending, superior tone of the magazine's editorials.
Note how the section of the sentence following the hyphen illustrates what aspect of the magazine annoys its critics.   (Example)

6. **B.** *Although* the Supreme Court nominee had a compassionate nature, nevertheless she was strict and unbending (*uncompromising*) in sticking or *adhering* to the law.
Note that "although" signals a contrast. Look at the first word of each answer choice to see if it is an antonym for "compassionate by nature." You can immediately eliminate Choices A, C, and E.
Choice D is incorrect. Someone *truly* compassionate by nature would not be *vindictive* or vengeful.   (Contrast Signal)

7. **C.** To observe the adage "Look before you leap" is to be cautious. In this instance, however, the subject did *not* look before he leaped. Instead, he was *precipitate* (hasty, rash) in acting in a thoughtless, unconsidered manner.
Again, "although" signals a contrast. Look at each answer choice to see if it is an antonym for being cautious.   (Contrast Signal)

8. **D.** Callas longed for honest criticism. She had grown tired of *adulation* (praise) because she had been surrounded by a group of people who constantly *extolled* (praised) her singing. (A retinue of sycophants is a group of flatterers in attendance on an important personage.) Remember, before you look at the choices, read the sentence and think of a word that makes sense.
Likely Words: praised, admired.   (Examples)

9. **A.** Moore's criticism was *not* unsure (*tentative*) or provisional. It was sure or confident: she wrote *confidently*.
Remember to watch for signal words that link one part of the sentence to another. The presence of *or* linking items in a series indicates that the missing word may be a synonym or near-synonym for "provisional," the other linked word.
This sentence contrasts two ideas *without* using a signal word. The contrast is implicit in the juxtaposition of the two clauses.
(Contrast Pattern)

10. **E.** An *actor* performs on a *stage*. A *skater* performs at a *rink*.   (Worker and Workplace)

11. **B.** To *beam* (smile radiantly) is to show *delight*. To *glower* (scowl sullenly) is to show *anger*.
(Action and Significance)

12. **B.** The *crest* is the top of a *wave*. The *crown* is the top of the *tree*.   (Part to Whole)

13. **B.** A *maxim* is defined as an expression that is *proverbial* in nature. A *question* is defined as an expression that is *interrogative* in nature.
(Definition)

14. **E.** An *ascetic* (person who leads a life of self-denial) shuns *intemperance* (lack of moderation; indulgence in passions). A *miser* (person who lives wretchedly in order to save money) shuns *extravagance* (wasteful spending).
(Person and Thing Avoided)

15. **B.** A *diatribe* is a bitter and abusive speech. It consists of *invective* (abuse). An *encomium* is a laudatory speech. It consists of *praise*.
(Definition)

16. **C.** Choice C is correct. You can arrive at it by the process of elimination.
Statement I is true. Sir Walter's vanity was "vanity of person." He was vain about his personal appearance, his *physical attractiveness*. Therefore, you can eliminate Choice B.

Statement II is true. Sir Walter's vanity was also vanity "of situation." He was vain about his position in society, his titled rank. Therefore, you can eliminate Choices A and D. Statement III is untrue. Sir Walter's wife, not Sir Walter, was superior in character. Therefore, you can eliminate Choice E. Only Choice C is left. It is the correct answer.

17. **D.** The narrator does *not* commend Lady Elliot for falling in love with Sir Walter, calling it a "youthful infatuation," the only misjudgment in an otherwise blameless life. Therefore, Choice D is correct.

The narrator speaks well of Lady Elliot for concealing Sir Walter's shortcomings: she has "promoted his real respectability." Choice A is supported by the passage. Therefore, it is incorrect.

The narrator commends Lady Elliot for her choice of a friend: she has chosen "a sensible, deserving woman," one who even moves into the neighborhood to be near her. Choice B is supported by the passage. Therefore, it is incorrect.

The narrator speaks well of the way Lady Elliot guides her daughters: she has given them "good principles and instruction." Choice C is supported by the passage. Therefore, it is incorrect.

Choice E is incorrect. The narrator clearly commends Lady Elliot in her performance of her duties as a wife.

18. **C.** The narrator's statement that Lady Elliot was "not the very happiest being in the world herself" is preceded by a list of all Lady Elliot had to do to cover up for her "conceited, silly" husband. Thus we can infer that the cause of her unhappiness was the difference or *disparity* between her character and that of her husband.

Choice A is incorrect. Nothing in the passage suggests Lady Elliot lacks beauty. Indeed, we suspect that Sir Walter, so conscious of his own beauty, would not have chosen an unattractive wife.

Choice B is incorrect. Lady Elliot's best friend had moved to be near her; they were not separated.

Choice D is incorrect. Lady Elliot's social position was, at least in Sir Walter's eyes, superior, not inferior.

Choice E is incorrect. Nothing in the passage suggests that Lady Elliot's daughters were wayward.

19. **B.** Choice B is correct. The narrator tells little directly of Lady Elliot's feelings about dying. However, such phrases as "Three girls...was an awful legacy to bequeath" and "anxiously giving her daughters (instruction)" show us something of her mind. Her concern centers not on herself but on those she must leave behind: her daughters. Her emotions as she faces death are complicated by *anxieties over her daughters' prospects*.

Choice A is incorrect. Nothing in the passage suggests resignation or pious submissiveness on her part.

Choices C and D are incorrect. Both are unsupported by the passage.

Choice E is also incorrect. Lady Elliot clearly has faced the reality of her approaching death: she realizes that she is abandoning her daughters to the care of her conceited, silly husband.

20. **A.** Lady Elliot in "quitting her family" is not simply taking a trip: she is dying. We expect a person facing death to react strongly, emotionally. Instead, the narrator states that Lady Elliot was merely attached enough to life to make dying no matter of indifference to her. That is clearly an *understatement*. It is an example of *irony*, the literary technique that points up the contradictions in life, in this case the contradiction between the understated expression and the deeply felt reality.

21. **C.** Sir Walter's applications have been *marital* ones. In his conceit, he has applied for the hand in marriage of some women who were far too good for him (his applications were *unreasonable*). Sensibly enough, these women have turned him down (he has been *disappointed* in his proposals of matrimony). However, his conceit is undiminished: he prides himself on remaining single for his dear daughters' sake.

22. **D.** The opening sentence describes the shattering of the Iroquois leadership's pro-British policy. The remainder of the passage describes how Iroquois policy changed to reflect changes in European military goals.

Choice A is incorrect. The passage is expository, not accusatory.

Choice B is incorrect. Nothing in the passage suggests that such charges were made against the Iroquois.

Choice C is incorrect. It is unsupported by the passage.

Choice E is incorrect. The passage demonstrates the Iroquois were able to play European power politics.

Remember, when asked to find the main idea, be sure to check the opening and summary sentences of each paragraph.

23. **B.** The Europeans *designated* or called these confederations of Indian tribes nations, giving them the same title they used for European states.

24. C. In this sentence, "rough" means approximate, as in "a rough guess." The tribes dealt with Europeans as approximate equals, *not as exact or absolute equals*.

25. C. The author presents the Iroquois Confederacy's experience "as an example of the process that *all* the interior nations experienced." Thus, he regards what happened to the Iroquois as *representative* or typical of the experiences of the other interior tribes.

26. B. In lines 61–63, the author states that the Iroquois "played the game of European power politics with effectiveness." Thus, he shows *respect for their competence*.
None of the other choices is supported by the passage.
Remember, when asked to determine the author's attitude or tone, look for words that convey value judgments.

27. E. Lines 45–63 indicate that in the early 1700s and through most of the eighteenth century the Iroquois *did* hold the balance of power. Therefore, Choice E is the correct answer.
Choice A is incorrect. The raid on Lachine was an effective response to French aggression, as was the Iroquois-enforced policy of aggressive neutrality.
Choice B is incorrect. James II's overthrow was followed by colonial uprisings.
Choice C is incorrect. In response to the Iroquois leaders' supposed favoring of the British (lines 63–69), the French went to war.
Choice D is incorrect. This sums up the policy of aggressive neutrality.

28. A. Lines 57–60 indicate that the Iroquois played the game of power politics with effectiveness "by their willingness to use their power against one or the other nation." In other words, they were ready to fight either side.
Choice B is incorrect. Ties of loyalty may actually have hampered the Iroquois; the French fear that the Iroquois were compromising the system in favor of the British led to the eventual breakdown of the policy of neutrality.
Choice C is incorrect. French presence in the borderlands would have been a challenge to Iroquois power.
Choices D and E are incorrect. They are unsupported by the passage.

29. B. The French believed that the Iroquois were *jeopardizing* or undermining the system of Iroquois neutrality by making decisions that favored the English.

30. A. The opening paragraph describes the changing state of relationships between the European

powers and the tribes of the interior during the eighteenth century. As more and more French and English settlers moved into the interior, the Indian nations had to find new ways of dealing with the encroaching French and English populations. The paragraph concludes by stating that the "history of the reorientation of Iroquois policy toward the Europeans may serve as an example of the process that all the interior nations experienced in the eighteenth century." Thus, the next three paragraphs, which sum up the Iroquois' experience, provide *an instance or example of the changing state of relationships described earlier*.

Section 2   Mathematical Reasoning

In each mathematics section, for many problems, an alternative solution, indicated by two asterisks (**), follows the first solution. When this occurs, one of the solutions is the direct mathematical one and the other is based on one of the tactics discussed in Chapters 8–12.

1. C. Just look at each number carefully. The hundreds place is the third from the left of the decimal point, and the hundredths place is the second to the right of the decimal point: **2242.4242**.

2. C. If Beth has twice as many cards as Bruce, Bruce has half as many as Beth: $\frac{b}{2}$.
**This is so easy that you shouldn't have to plug in a number, but you could: If Beth has 10 cards, Bruce has 5, and only $\frac{b}{2}$ equals 5 when b is 10.

3. D. To convert 225 minutes to hours, divide by 60: the quotient is 3 and the remainder is 45. Therefore, 225 minutes from 9:05 is 3 hours and 45 minutes from 9:05 A.M. which is **12:50 P.M.**
**If you divide 225 by 60 on your calculator, you get 3.75; then you have to convert 0.75, or $\frac{3}{4}$, of an hour to 45 minutes.

4. C. By KEY FACT J2, the measure of an exterior angle of a triangle is equal to the sum of the measures of the two opposite interior angles, so $140 = x + x = 2x \Rightarrow x = $ **70**. If you don't know this fact, let the third angle in the triangle be y. Then $140 + y = 180 \Rightarrow y = 40$; and $40 + x + x = 180 \Rightarrow x = $ **70**.

5. C. Let x be Mr. Brock's number.
Then $x + 3 = 3x \Rightarrow 3 = 2x \Rightarrow x = $ **1.5**.
**Use TACTIC 9-1: backsolve. Start with C: $1.5 + 3 = 4.5$ and $1.5 \times 3 = 4.5$. It works.

6. **B.** The easiest solution is to quickly reduce, either by dividing by 16 (if you recognize that $64 = 4 \times 16$) or by repeatedly dividing each side by 8: $^1\cancel{(16)}\cancel{(16)}\cancel{(16)}\,n = \dfrac{^4\cancel{(64)}\cancel{(64)}^4}{n}$.

Then $n = \dfrac{1}{n} \Rightarrow n = \mathbf{1}$.

**Of course, you can rewrite the equation as
$$n^2 = \dfrac{(64)(64)}{(16)(16)(16)}$$
and use your calculator: $n^2 = \mathbf{1}$.

7. **B.** Let x and y be the two numbers: $x - y > x + y \Rightarrow -y > y \Rightarrow 0 > 2y \Rightarrow y$ is negative. Therefore, **at least one of the numbers is negative**. [Note that there are no restrictions on x: $x - (-1) = x + 1$, which is greater than $x + (-1) = x - 1$, no matter what x is.]

8. **D.** By the laws of exponents (KEY FACT A16), $(3a^2b^3)^3 = 3^3(a^2)^3(b^3)^3 = \mathbf{27a^6b^9}$.

**Use TACTIC 9-2: substitute numbers. If a and b are 1, $(3a^2b^3)^3 = 3^3 = 27$. Eliminate A and B. If $a = 1$ and $b = 2$, $(3a^2b^3)^3 = (3 \cdot 1 \cdot 8)^3 = 24^3$. Use your calculator to evaluate $24^3 = 13{,}824$; then test choices C (which doesn't work) and D: $\mathbf{27a^6b^9}$.

9. **A.** If y years ago Anne-Marie was x years old, she is now $x + y$, and in z years she will be $\mathbf{x + y + z}$.

**Use TACTIC 9-2: substitute numbers. If 2 years ago Anne-Marie was 10, how old will she be in 3 years? She is now 12 and in 3 years will be 15. Only $x + y + z$ (A) equals 15 when $x = 10$, $y = 2$, and $z = 3$.

10. **E.** Solve the equation, $10 = \dfrac{x}{100}A$:

$$1000 = xA \Rightarrow x = \dfrac{\mathbf{1000}}{A}\%.$$

**Use TACTIC 9-2: substitute an easy-to-use number. 10 is 100% of 10. Which choices are equal to 100% when $A = 10$? Both A and E. Eliminate B, C, and D, and try another number: 10 is 50% of 20. Of A and E, only $\dfrac{\mathbf{1000}}{A}$ equals 50 when $A = 20$.

11. **A.** Refer to the figures at the right. The circumference of a circle of radius 3 is 6π (KEY FACT L4). By KEY FACT K7, the perimeter of a rectangle is $2(\ell + w)$, so

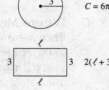

$$6\pi = 2(\ell + 3) \Rightarrow$$
$$\ell + 3 = 3\pi \Rightarrow \ell = \mathbf{3\pi - 3}.$$

12. **A.** Let x be the number of marbles that Anthony has. Then $3x$ is $\dfrac{1}{3}$ the number of marbles Billy has, so Billy has $9x$ marbles. The ratio is $x:9x$ or **1:9**.

Use TACTIC 9-3: pick an easy-to-use number. Assume that Anthony has 1 marble. If he had 3 times as many, he would have 3; and if 3 is $\dfrac{1}{3}$ the number that Billy has, Billy has 9. The ratio is **1:9.

13. **B.** It is given that $BE = BC$; also $BC = AD$, since they are opposite sides of a rectangle. Label each of them w, as shown in the figure.

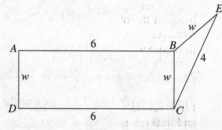

Then $R = 12 + 2w$ and $T = 4 + 2w$, so $R - T = \mathbf{8}$.

14. **D.** The volume of the small tank is $\pi r^2 h$, and the volume of the large tank is $\pi(2r)^2 h$, which equals $4\pi r^2 h$, so the large tank is 4 times the size of the small one. *Be careful!* This is an *increase* of 300% not 400%. (4 is 3 more than 1, so is 300% more than 1.) Therefore, $k = \mathbf{300}$.

15. **E.** Since $W = 3$ and $2W = 3X$, then $3X = 6 \Rightarrow X = 2$. Therefore
$$3 + 7 = 2 + Y \Rightarrow Y = 10 - 2 = \mathbf{8}.$$

16. **C.** By definition, $W + W = X + Y \Rightarrow 2W = X + Y$; but the definition also states that $2W = 3X$, so $X = \dfrac{2}{3}W$. Therefore
$$2W = \dfrac{2}{3}W + Y \Rightarrow Y = \dfrac{4}{3}W.$$

17. **A.** If the hypotenuse of a 30-60-90 right triangle is 2, the legs are 1 and $\sqrt{3}$. Therefore, each side of square $RSTU$ is $1 + \sqrt{3}$, and the perimeter is 4 times that value: $\mathbf{4 + 4\sqrt{3}}$.

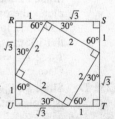

18. **D.** Use TACTIC 8-14. When you have three equations, add them:

$$\begin{array}{r} x + y = a \\ y + z = b \\ +\ \underline{\ x + z = c\ } \\ 2x + 2y + 2z = a + b + c \end{array}$$

Divide by 2: $\qquad x + y + z = \dfrac{a+b+c}{2}$

Divide by 3: $\qquad \dfrac{x+y+z}{3} = \dfrac{a+b+c}{6}$

**Use TACTIC 9-2: substitute for the variables. Let $x = 1$, $y = 2$, and $z = 3$. Then the average of x, y, and z is 2. When $a = 1 + 2 = 3$, $b = 2 + 3 = 5$, and $c = 1 + 3 = 4$, which of the choices equals 2? Only $\dfrac{a+b+c}{6}$.

19. **D.** When an integer is divided by 100, the remainder is just the last two digits of that integer (100 goes into <u>273</u> 2 times with a remainder of <u>73</u>). Except for 5 itself, every power of 5 ends in the digits <u>**25**</u>: 25, 125, 625, 3125, ...

20. **E.** Since $C = 2\pi r$ (KEY FACT L4),
$2\pi r = 120\sqrt{\pi} \Rightarrow r = \dfrac{120\sqrt{\pi}}{2\pi} = \dfrac{60\sqrt{\pi}}{\pi}$.

Then, by KEY FACT L8, area of the field =
$\pi\left(\dfrac{60\sqrt{\pi}}{\pi}\right)^2 = \pi\dfrac{3600\pi}{\pi^2} = 3600$ square meters.

Finally, since Eric can mow 400 square meters of grass per hour, he will take $3600 \div 400 = \mathbf{9}$ hours to mow the entire field.

21. **C.** Replacing a by $2a$, b by $3b$, and c by $4c$ gives
$\dfrac{(2a)(3b)^2}{4c} = \dfrac{2a(9b^2)}{4c} = \dfrac{9}{2}\left(\dfrac{ab^2}{c}\right) = \dfrac{9}{2}X = 4.5X$.
In words, **X is multiplied by 4.5.**

**Use TACTIC 9-2. Let $a = 1$, $b = 2$,

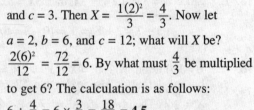 and $c = 3$. Then $X = \dfrac{1(2)^2}{3} = \dfrac{4}{3}$. Now let

$a = 2$, $b = 6$, and $c = 12$; what will X be?
$\dfrac{2(6)^2}{12} = \dfrac{72}{12} = 6$. By what must $\dfrac{4}{3}$ be multiplied to get 6? The calculation is as follows:

$6 \div \dfrac{4}{3} = 6 \times \dfrac{3}{4} = \dfrac{18}{4} = \mathbf{4.5}$.

22. **C.** Since the pattern has six digits, divide 135 by 6. The quotient is 22, and the remainder is 3. Since $22 \times 6 = 132$, the 132nd number completes the pattern for the 22nd time. Then the 133rd, 134th, and <u>135</u>th numbers are 1's, and the <u>136</u>th and <u>137</u>th are 2's; and their sum is $\underline{1} + \underline{2} + \underline{2} = \mathbf{5}$.

23. **D.** Since you need a ratio, the length of the side is irrelevant. The area of a square is s^2, and the area of an equilateral triangle is $\dfrac{s^2\sqrt{3}}{4}$ (KEY FACT J15). Then the ratio is

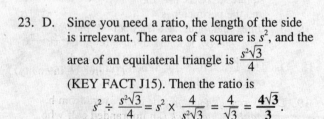 $s^2 \div \dfrac{s^2\sqrt{3}}{4} = s^2 \times \dfrac{4}{s^2\sqrt{3}} = \dfrac{4}{\sqrt{3}} = \dfrac{4\sqrt{3}}{3}$.

Of course, you could have used 5 instead of s; and if you forgot the formula for the area of an equilateral triangle, you could have used $A = \dfrac{1}{2}bh$.

24 **A.** Cross-multiply: $r(s + 1) < s(r + 1) \Rightarrow$
$rs + r < rs + s \Rightarrow \mathbf{r < s.}$
(Note that, since s is positive, the order of the inequality is preserved. Also, if r and s are integers, then $s > 1$, but they need not be integers.)

**Use Tactic 9-2: Try some numbers.
If $r = 1$ and $s = 1$, the inequality is false.
If $r = 1$ and $s = 2$, only A, D, and E are satisfied, so eliminate B and C. If trying one or two more numbers doesn't eliminate any other choices, guess.

25. **E.** If you think to reduce the ratio 5:5:10 to 1:1:2, fine; if not, just write
$\qquad 180 = 5x + 5x + 10x = 20x \Rightarrow x = 9 \Rightarrow$
$\qquad$ the angles measure 45, 45, and 90.
If you know the length of any side of a 45-45-90 right triangle, you can find the other sides and hence the area (I), the perimeter (II) and the lengths of the altitudes, two of which are the legs (III). Statements **I, II, and III** are true. (*Note:* You should not waste any time actually finding the area, the perimeter, or the altitudes.)

Section 3   Verbal Reasoning

1. **B.** The words "merely" and "failed to highlight" indicate that the woman is dissatisfied with the job-seeker's resume. It lacks some qualities she thinks it needs. It is *inadequate*, not up to standards, deficient.
Note that you are looking for a word with negative associations. Therefore, you can eliminate any word with positive ones. Choices C and E both have positive associations. Only Choices A, B, or D can be correct.
$\qquad$ (Examples)

2. **D.** Most medical research is aimed at helping human beings. Therefore, having discovered something about the cause of a disease affecting animals, it would be perfectly reasonable or *logical* for researchers to wish to apply their findings to the treatment of humans. Remember, before you look at the choices, read the sentence and think of a word that makes sense.
Watch for signal words that link one part of the sentence to another. The use of "Because" in the opening clause is a cause signal. Ask yourself what would be a logical next step after finding out that a kind of virus caused cancer in animals.   (Cause and Effect Signal)

3. B. The subject's *verbosity*, her tendency to use too many words, is what's irritating. The second clause defines the first.   (Definition)

4. C. It would be pointless or *futile* to try to poison pests chemically if the creatures eventually became *resistant* to or able to withstand the effect of each new poison you introduced. Choice C is correct.
Remember, watch for signal words that link one part of the sentence to another. The conjunction "for" connecting the two halves of the sentence signals you to expect a *cause and effect* relationship between them.
    (Cause and Effect Signal)

5. B. The key phrase here is "treated her badly." *Because* the news media have treated her badly and *misrepresented* her, distorting or misstating her comments, Ms. Ono does not like to give interviews. Therefore, she gives them *rarely*.
Remember to watch for signal words that link one part of the sentence to another. The use of "because" introducing the second clause sets up a pattern of cause and effect. Note also the use of the support signal *and*, here letting you know that the second missing word must be a synonym or near-synonym for "treated her badly."
    (Cause and Effect Signal/Support Signal)

6. E. The introduction of metal tools significantly improved totem craftsmanship: *because* the carvers had better tools, they could do better, "more sophisticated" or advanced work. Thus, thanks to the introduction of metal tools, totem craftsmanship reached its high point or *apex*.   (Cause and Effect Pattern)

7. B. *Because* insect bodies are *fragile* or breakable, it is surprising that enough of them have *survived* (lasted in an unbroken condition) for scientists to draw conclusions about the way insects species changed over time.
The key word here is "remarkable." It signals a built-in contrast between what one might expect to have happened and what actually did happen.   (Implicit Contrast Signal)

8. C. There are two key words here, "unfortunately" and "imitations." "Unfortunately" indicates that the missing word has negative connotations: the plays currently showing on Broadway are pretty poor. "Imitations" defines in just what way these plays are poor. They are copies of hit plays, imitations trying to follow a once-sucessful *formula* or pattern that no longer works. In other words, they are *formulaic* fare.   (Definition)

9. C. Admirers of realism would not esteem "the stuff of legend"; they prefer fallible, ordinary people to mythic figures who seem larger-than-life. They thus prefer a film that *shuns* or rejects make-believe in order to tell a plain, *unembellished* tale.
Note the cause-and-effect signal *because*. The sentence explains why Malle's realistic film succeeds.   (Cause and Effect Signal)

10. B. Because these seals eat far more krill than crabs, it *misnames* them to call them crabeater seals. The term is thus a *misnomer*, a name that's wrongly applied to someone or something. Beware eye-catchers. Choice A is incorrect. A *pseudonym* isn't a mistaken name; it's a false name that an author adopts.
Remember, this is the tenth sentence completion question of a set of ten. If you have to guess, try the *least* familiar word among the answers.   (Cause and Effect Signal)

11. D. The *chief* is the leader of the *tribe*. The *captain* is the leader of the *team*.   (Function)

12. A. An *atlas* is a book of *maps*. An *album* is a book of *photographs*.   (Part to Whole)

13. B. Just as a *novelist* creates a *plot* as a guide for a novel in progress, an *architect* creates a *blueprint* as a guide for a building in progress. Remember, if more than one word appears to fit the relationship in your sentence, look for a narrower approach. "A novelist uses a plot" is too broad a framework; it could fit Choices A, C, D, and E.   (Worker and Creation)

14. B. A *spine* is a sharp-pointed outgrowth on a *cactus*; a *quill* is a sharp-pointed bristle on a *porcupine*.   (Part to Whole)

15. D. A *diver* performs a *jackknife* (a special kind of dive). A *gymnast* performs a *cartwheel* (a special kind of acrobatic feat).   (Function)

16. C. An *archipelago* is a cluster of *islands*. A *galaxy* is a cluster of *stars*.   (Part to Whole)

17. B. An *inventory* lists *merchandise* or assets. A *roster* lists *members* (the roster of the New York Mets lists team members, for example).   (Defining Characteristic)

18. A. *Interest* is a less intense feeling than *fascination*. *Dislike* is a less intense feeling than *abhorrence* (loathing, detestation).   (Degree of Intensity)

19. D. A *renegade* denies or turns away from his faith. A *maverick* (an unbranded calf who doesn't follow its mother; a member of a

group who refuses to conform) turns away from the *herd.* (Person and Thing Avoided)

20. **B.** *Olfactory* refers to the sense of smell; the organ involved in this is the *nose. Gustatory* refers to the sense of taste; the organ involved in this is the *tongue.* (Defining Characteristic)

21. **D.** Someone *indigent* (poor, needy) lacks riches or *wealth.* Someone *frivolous* (light-minded, superficial) lacks *seriousness.*
(Antonym Variant)

22. **B.** A *maze* (an intricate pattern of interconnecting and branching passages) is by definition *labyrinthine* or mazelike. *Treachery* (treason or betrayal of trust) is by definition *perfidious* (deceitful; treacherous). (Definition)

23. **C.** To *scotch* or block a *rumor* is to crush it. To *suppress* or quell a *riot* is to crush it.
(Purpose)

24. **B.** The author contrasts Popeye with Mickey, referring to Popeye as "aggressive" and "self-promoting." These relatively negative terms indicate that the author's attitude toward Popeye is *deprecatory* or disparaging.

25. **A.** Unlike Popeye, Mickey does not promote or boast about himself: he lets his skills remain unsuspected. Similarly, when danger strikes, Mickey does not push himself forward: he is a reluctant hero. These traits reveal Mickey's modest, *unassuming nature.*

26. **E.** The scrapes Mickey gets into are *predicaments* or difficult situations.

27. **B.** Immediately before quoting Disney's assertion that there was a lot of the Mouse in him, the author states that the image of Mickey as a pretty nice, harmless, good-natured sort of guy "was perhaps Disney's image of himself." Disney pictured himself as Mickey, scrambling and struggling and yet always managing to come up grinning. Thus, by saying "There's a lot of the Mouse in me," Disney revealed *the extent of his identification with his creation.*

28. **A.** The author has been developing Disney's positive image of Mickey as a pretty nice fellow, showing how Disney's background led to his identifying himself with the humble, scrambling mouse. He then suddenly goes off on a side topic, explaining why the Nazis during World War II had a negative image of Mickey. Clearly, he is *digressing,* straying from the subject at hand.

29. **E.** Disney is described as being nice "until crossed." If someone *opposed* him and stood in the way of his reaching his artistic and business goals, he quit being nice.

30. **D.** Disney was *not* the inventor of film animation. As the passage indicates, the technology "would have been there anyway."

31. **C.** Both President Roosevelt, who insisted on being shown Mickey Mouse cartoons, and the African tribesmen, who insisted on having Mickey's image set into their teeth, are examples of people around the globe who enjoyed Mickey Mouse. The author uses these examples to *support his assertions* that Mickey's image was known around the world—it was popular all over Africa as well as in the States—and that powerful people as well as primitive tribesmen, *people of all backgrounds, were drawn to Mickey Mouse.*

32. **D.** "(S)omething timeless in the image" transforms its status from that of a fad or passing fancy to that of an icon (a sign that stands for the object it represents because of some resemblance between the two; often a sacred image venerated by people). *The fad is clearly less enduring in appeal than the icon.*

33. **D.** The author wishes to show how strong a hold Mickey has on America's collective awareness. To do so, he revitalizes a familiar cliché. Mickey does not simply grab our imaginations; he takes a bite out of them. In other words, he forcefully *captures our fancies.*

34. **B.** The key shaped out of three connected circles does not present a realistic, detailed likeness of Mickey Mouse. It fails to show his nose, his eyes, his mouth—the usual identifying features. Nevertheless, this simple, bare outline is *unmistakably* Mickey: anyone who looks at it knows it is an image of Mickey Mouse. This clearly shows that *even a rudimentary outline can convey the image of Mickey.*

35. **D.** The new Disney gadget is described as representing Mickey's image in the simplest, most rudimentary fashion: "three circles, two mounted on a larger one, (whose) image is unmistakably Mickey." Only the waffle iron, turning out its three-ringed, featureless (but unmistakable) Mickey Mouse waffles, presents Mickey as an artifact, a manufactured object, rather than as the commercially generated, representational image of the familiar cartoon figure in red shorts.

Section 4   Mathematical Reasoning

Quantitative Comparison Questions

1. C.   Column A: 4.798 is between 4.79 and 4.80; it is closer to 4.80. Column B: 4.849 is between 4.8 and 4.9; it is closer to 4.8. The columns are equal (C). (See Section 12-B for rules on rounding.)

2. A.   It's not even close. Column B is 1,000,000, but Column A is so large that you get an error message on a scientific calculator—2^{1000} is actually more than 300 digits long! Even on a four-function calculator you can quickly get $2^{10} = 1024 \Rightarrow 2^{20} = 1024 \times 1024 > 1,000,000$. Column A is greater.

3. D.   Use TACTIC 10-4. Could the columns be equal? Could $c = 5$? Sure, if this is a 3-4-5 right triangle. Must $c = 5$? No; if the triangle is not a right triangle, c could be less than or more than 5. Neither column is *always* greater, and the columns are not *always* equal (D). (*Note*: Since the figure is not drawn to scale, do *not* assume that the triangle has a right angle, and do *not* attempt to measure.)

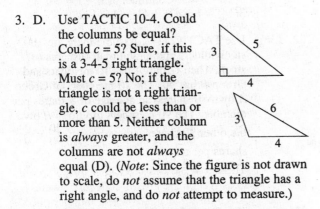

4. C.   Since $a \neq 0$, divide each side of $ab = a^2$ by a, which yields $a = b$. The columns are equal (C).

5. B.   Column A: $7(-10) - 3 = -70 - 3 = -73$. Column B: since $-A = -7x + 3$, then $-7(10) + 3 = -70 + 3 = -67$. Column B is greater.

6. B.   Every factor of n is a factor of $2n$, but 2 is a prime factor of $2n$ that is not a factor of n (since n is odd). Therefore, $2n$ has more prime factors than n. Column B is greater.

    **Use TACTIC 10-1. Replace n by an odd number. Let $n = 5$; 5 has 1 prime factor (5), whereas 10 has 2 prime factors (2 and 5). Eliminate A and C. Try $n = 15$; 15 has 2 prime factors (3 and 5), whereas 30 has 3 prime factors (2, 3, and 5). Choose B.

7. A.   Column A: there are 5 positive multiples of 5 less than 26: 5, 10, 15, 20, 25; their average is 15, the middle one (KEY FACT E5). Column B: there are 3 positive multiples of 7 less than 26: 7, 14, 21; their average is 14. Column A is greater.

8. D.   Use TACTIC 10-4. Could the columns be equal? Could a $20 discount be the same as a 20% discount? Yes, if the radio cost $100. Must they be equal? No, not if the radio cost anything other than $100. Neither column is *always* greater, and the columns are not *always* equal (D).

    **Use TACTIC 10-2. If the regular price of the radio was $20, on sale store A would be giving it away, while store B would be charging $16. On the other hand, if the radio cost $1000, on sale store A would be selling it for $980 and store B for $800.

9. D.   Use TACTIC 10-4. Could x and y be equal. Yes; if a and b are each 90, then x and y are each 40. Must they be equal? No; see the figure at the right, in which $x < y$. Neither column is *always* greater, and the columns are not *always* equal (D). (Don't trust the diagram. The only thing that's guaranteed is that $x + y = 80$.)

10. C.   Column A: $(a + b)^2 = a^2 + 2ab + b^2 = a^2 + b^2$ (since $ab = 0$). Column B: $(a - b)^2 = a^2 - 2ab + b^2 = a^2 + b^2$ (since $ab = 0$). The columns are equal (C). **Use TACTIC 10-1. Let $a = 0$ and $b = 1$. Then $(a + b)^2 = (0 + 1)^2 = 1$ and $(a - b)^2 = (0 - 1)^2 = 1$. Eliminate A and B, and try other values where either a or b is 0 ($ab = 0$). The answer is C.

11. C.   Your calculator won't help; these numbers are too large. Column A: $(-7)^{200} = 7^{200}$. Column B: $\{7(-7)^{99}\}^2 = 7^2(-7)^{198} = 7^2(7)^{198}$. The columns are equal (C).

12. A.   It makes no difference how many students took the test or how many were boys and how many were girls. More than half the boys *and* more than half the girls scored over 90, so more grades were over 90 than were 90 or below. Column A is greater.

    **Use TACTIC 10-2. Assume 7 boys and 11 girls took the exam. Then 11 students (4 boys and 7 girls) got over 90, and the other 7 got 90 or less.

13. C.   This one is easier than it looks. Don't try to factor, and don't solve. Just add x to both sides of the given equation to get $x^2 - 5 = x$. The columns are equal (C).

14. C. Let P = price of the TV set. Then Jack paid $1.085(0.90P)$ whereas Jill paid $0.90(1.085P)$. The columns are equal (C).

**As always, if you have any hesitancy about the algebraic expressions, the best strategy is to use TACTIC 10-2 and choose a convenient number: assume the TV cost $100. Then Jack paid $90 plus $7.65 tax (8.5% of $90) for a total of $97.65. Jill's cashier rang up $100 plus $8.50 tax and then deducted $10.85 (10% of $108.50) for a final cost of $97.65.

15. D. Since $PQ < QR$, $x > 45$ and m$\angle R$ is less than 45; but that is the *only* thing we know about x. It *appears* as if PQ and QR are almost equal, in which case the acute angles opposite them would be almost equal: x would be slightly more than 45 and m$\angle P$ slightly less. Surely, x would be less than 30. However, that's not true if a is very small.

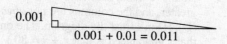

0.001
$0.001 + 0.01 = 0.011$

If $a = 0.001$, then $a + .01 = 0.011$, in which case QR is more than 10 times greater than PQ, and x is large, certainly greater than 60.

Grid-in Questions

16. (115) We can find any or all of the angles in the figure. The easiest way to find w is to note that the measure of $\angle PST = 25°$ and so $w = 25 + 90 = 115$.

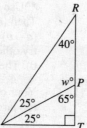

17. (64) Since the sum of the six angles is 360° (KEY FACT I3), $5x + 40 = 360 \Rightarrow 5x = 320 \Rightarrow x = 64$.

18. (78) The area of the red paper is $9 \times 12 = 108$ square inches. The area of each 3×5 card is 15 square inches, so $108 - 15 - 15 = 78$.

19. (52) If there are x adults in the village, then $.8x$ of them are registered and $.6(.8x) = .48x$ voted. Therefore, $x - .48x = .52x$, or **52%**, of the adults did not vote.

The above solution is straightforward, but there is no reason to use x. Use TACTIC 11-2, and assume there are 100 adults. Then 80 of them are registered and 60% of 80 = 48 of them voted; 52 did not vote, which is $\frac{52}{100}$ or **52%.

20. (54) To find Henry's average speed, in kilometers per hour, divide the distance he went, in kilometers, (198), by the time it took, in hours. Henry drove for 3 hours and 40 minutes, which is $3\frac{2}{3}$ hours

(40 minutes = $\frac{40}{60}$ hour = $\frac{2}{3}$ hour). Henry's average speed is

$198 \div 3\frac{2}{3} = 198 \div \frac{11}{3} = 198 \times \frac{3}{11} = 54$.

21. (122) Write out the first few terms, being careful to follow the directions. The first term is 1. The second term is 1 less than 3 times the first term: $3(1) - 1 = 2$. The third term is 1 less than 3 times the second term: $3(2) - 1 = 5$. Continue: $3(5) - 1 = 14$; $3(14) - 1 = 41$; $3(41) - 1 = 122$.

22. (36) Use TACTIC 11-2. Assume there are 100 stockholders and a total of 100 shares of stock. Then Group A has 10 members and Group B has 90. The 10 members of Group A own 80 shares, an average of 8 shares per member. The 90 members of Group B own the other 20 shares, an average of $\frac{20}{90} = \frac{2}{9}$ shares per member.

Then, $8 = \frac{2}{9}k \Rightarrow k = 8 \times \frac{9}{2} = 36$.

23. (52) This is a weighted average (KEY FACT E6):

$\frac{40\%(40) + 60\%(60)}{100\%} = \frac{16 + 36}{1} = 52$.

**If you prefer, assume there are 100 marbles, 40 of which are red and 60 of which are blue:

$\frac{40(40) + 60(60)}{100} = \frac{1600 + 3600}{100} = 52$.

24. ($\frac{9}{10}$ or .9) If there are x seats on each bus, then the group is using $\frac{4}{5}(3x) = \frac{12}{5}x$ seats. After $\frac{1}{4}$ of passengers get off, $\frac{3}{4}$ of them, or $\frac{3}{4}(\frac{12}{5}x) = \frac{9}{5}x$, remain. The fraction of the $2x$ seats now being used on the two buses is $\frac{\frac{9}{5}x}{2x} = \frac{\frac{9}{5}}{2} = \frac{9}{10}$.

**Again, you can use TACTIC 11-2 to avoid working with x. Assume there are 20 seats on each bus. At the beginning, the group is using 48 of the 60 seats on the three buses $[\frac{4}{\underset{1}{5}}(\overset{12}{60}) = 48]$. When 12

people left $[\frac{1}{\underset{1}{4}}(\overset{12}{48}) = 12]$, the 36 remaining

people used $\frac{36}{40} = \mathbf{\frac{9}{10}}$ of the 40 seats on two

buses.

25. $\left(\mathbf{\frac{7}{10}} \text{ or } \mathbf{.7}\right)$ The easiest thing to do is just check

each possible value from $a = 1$ to $a = 10$. If

a is 1, 2, or 3, $\dfrac{a}{4}$ and $\dfrac{a}{5}$ are each less than

1, and so $\left[\dfrac{a}{4}\right] = \left[\dfrac{a}{5}\right] = 0$. $\left[\dfrac{4}{4}\right] = 1$,

whereas $\left[\dfrac{4}{5}\right] = 0$, so $\left[\dfrac{a}{4}\right]$ and $\left[\dfrac{a}{5}\right]$ are

not equal when $a = 4$. When $a = 5$, 6, or 7

$\dfrac{a}{4}$ and $\dfrac{a}{5}$ are each between 1 and 2, and

so $\left[\dfrac{a}{4}\right] = \left[\dfrac{a}{5}\right] = 1$. $\left[\dfrac{8}{4}\right]$ and $\left[\dfrac{9}{4}\right]$ are

each 2, whereas $\left[\dfrac{8}{5}\right]$ and $\left[\dfrac{9}{5}\right]$ are each 1.

Finally, $\left[\dfrac{10}{4}\right] = \left[\dfrac{10}{5}\right] = 2$. For 7 of the

10 integers from 1 to 10, $\left[\dfrac{a}{4}\right] = \left[\dfrac{a}{5}\right]$.

Section 5 Verbal Reasoning

1. C. Passage 1 states: "Dolphins left the land when mammalian brains were still small and primitive." This indicates that dolphins were once land animals, mammals like ourselves, whose evolutionary development took them back into the sea.

2. E. The passage indicates that human beings think of intelligence in terms of our own ability to manipulate our environment—our ability to build and do all sorts of things with our hands. Since dolphins have no hands, we have trouble appreciating their high level of intelligence.

3. D. Passage 1 attempts to *reassess the nature and extent of dolphin intelligence*, first giving reasons why human beings may have trouble appreciating how intelligent dolphins really are and then, in the concluding sentence,

reflecting how dolphin intelligence (that looks "inward to the sea's heart") may complement human intelligence (that looks "outward on eternity").

4. C. The dolphin's acute echo-sounding sense is a sharp, *keen* sense that enables the dolphin to sound or measure the ocean depths by using echoes.

5. C. The entire passage has concentrated on the dolphin's brain, so it is safe to assume that this is what is meant by the "impressively elaborated instrument." The items listed in the other answer choices have not been mentioned at all. Note that Choice B, an artificial range-finding device, is incorrect because the dolphin's range-finding ability is entirely natural, not artificial.

6. A. The sea's heart is like the human mind in that it swarms or *teems* (abounds) with grotesque or *exotic forms of life*.

7. C. The author's tone is distinctly *admiring*. The passage speaks of the dolphins' "remarkable range-finding ability," mentions their care for each other, and repeatedly praises dolphin intelligence.

8. E. The quotation marks here indicate that the word in quotes is being used in a special sense (often an ironic one). In this case, as the next paragraph makes abundantly clear, the author is critical of both the results and the influence of Lilly's experiments. He *has some doubts as to how scientific those experiments were*.

9. A. According to the author, by claiming that "dolphins communicate not only with one another but also with humans, mimicking human speech and reaching out across the boundaries that divide us," Lilly and his associates have *overstated* their case, misrepresenting *the extent of dolphin intelligence*. Choice B is incorrect. In stating that Lilly's conclusions have not withstood (stood up against) critical scrutiny, the author indicates that they *have* been critically scrutinized to an appropriate degree.

10. D. "Begging the question" refers to assuming the truth of the very point whose truth or falsehood you're trying to establish. The author of Passage 2 considers the reasoning in this argument flawed; he views it with doubt or *skepticism*.

11. A. If dolphins were proven far superior in linguistic capability to seals and other lower animals, that clearly would contradict the results of the studies the author cites and would thus *undercut* or weaken their impact.

12. A. In its glorification of dolphin intelligence as something that equals or possibly exceeds human intelligence, Passage 1 seems *typical of the attitudes of Lilly and his associates.*

13. A. Passage 1 is filled with images. The sea is a "wavering green fairyland." The dolphin's brain is an "impressively elaborated instrument." Mammals take "a divergent road." The passage concludes with an elaborate simile. It is clearly more *figurative* than Passage 2.
Choice B is incorrect. With its enigmatic references to some "impressively elaborated instrument" and to a "great eye" staring at eternity, Passage 1 is far more *obscure* than Passage 2.
Choice C is incorrect. Passage 1 is heavily slanted in favor of the superiority of dolphin intelligence. It is not *more objective* or impartial than Passage 2, which attempts to give a short survey of research on dolphin intelligence, summing up current experiments and providing historical background.
Choice D is incorrect. The italicized introduction indicates that Passage 2 was written almost thirty years after Passage 1. By definition, it presents a more *current*, up-to-date view of the topic. *Always pay attention to information contained in the introductions to the reading passages.*
Choice E is incorrect. Passage 1's conclusion is sheer conjecture or *speculation.*

Section 6 Mathematical Reasoning

1. B. 88 beeps ÷ 16 beeps per minute = **5.5** minutes. If you prefer, set up a ratio and cross-multiply:
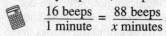
$$\frac{16 \text{ beeps}}{1 \text{ minute}} = \frac{88 \text{ beeps}}{x \text{ minutes}}.$$

2. E. $\frac{1}{2}\%$ *means* $\frac{1}{2}$ (or 0.5) divided by 100, which
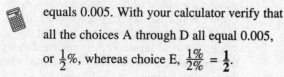
equals 0.005. With your calculator verify that all the choices A through D all equal 0.005, or $\frac{1}{2}\%$, whereas choice E, $\frac{1\%}{2\%} = \frac{1}{2}$.

3. B. $\{[(a \times a) + a] \div a\} - a =$
$\{[a^2 + a] \div a\} - a =$
$\frac{a^2 + a}{a} - a = a + 1 - a = \mathbf{1}.$

**Use TACTIC 9-2. Let $a = 2$; then
$\{[(2 \times 2) + 2] \div 2\} - 2 =$
$\{[4 + 2] \div 2\} - 2 = \{6 \div 2\} - 2 = 3 - 2 = \mathbf{1}.$

4. B. There is *only* **1** prime divisible by 7, namely, 7.

5. C. The sum of the measures of the four angles of any quadrilateral is 360° (KEY FACT K1). If the average of the measures of two of them is 60°, then they total 120° (TACTIC E1), leaving 240° for the other two angles, so their average is **120°**.
**Draw a quadrilateral, two of whose angles measure 60°, and estimate the measures of the other angles. None of the wrong choices is even close.

6. D. Just check each choice. Is there a triangle whose sides are 1, 2, 3? No, the sum of any two sides of a triangle must be *greater* than the third side (KEY FACT J12). (I is false.) Are there triangles whose sides are 10, 11, 12 and 100, 101, 102? Yes. (II and III are true.) Statements **II and III only** are true.

7. D. Draw a diagram. The minute hand, of course, is pointing right at 4. The hour hand, however, is *not* pointing at 11. It was pointing at 11 at 11:00, 20 minutes, or $\frac{1}{3}$ hour, ago. The hour hand is now one-third of the way between 11 and 12, so there are 20 degrees between the hour hand and 12 and another 120 degrees to 4, a total of **140** degrees.
**If you can't figure the answer out exactly, guess. From the diagram, you should see that the angle is considerably more than 120. Eliminate at least A and B, and probably see that E is too big.

8. E. Calculate each 1990 salary by multiplying each 1980 salary by (1 + the percent change). **Eve** had the highest 1990 salary, $42,000(1.06) = $44,520.

9. B. Use TACTIC 9-2: substitute a simple number for x. Since this is a percent problem, choose 10 or 100. Let $x = 10$: 10% less than 10 is 9, and 10% more than 9 is 9.9. Now, what percent of 100 ($10x$) is 9.9? The answer is **9.9%**.

10. C. Assume Adam loses the minimum number, one-third, of the remaining games. Say he loses x games and wins $2x$ games. Then, in total, he will have $6 + 2x$ wins and $24 + x$ losses. Finally, $6 + 2x > 24 + x \Rightarrow 2x > 18 + x \Rightarrow x > 18 \Rightarrow x$ is at least 19. He has at least 19 additional losses and 38 additional wins, for a total of **57** more games.
Avoid the algebra and zoom in by trial and error. If Adam plays 30 more games, losing 10 and winning 20, he'll have 34 losses and 26 wins—not enough. If he plays 60 more games, losing 20 and winning 40, he'll have 46 wins and 44 losses. Close enough, pick **57.

Answer Sheet—Test 6

If a section has fewer than 35 questions, leave the extra spaces blank.

Section 1

1 Ⓐ Ⓑ Ⓒ Ⓓ Ⓔ	8 Ⓐ Ⓑ Ⓒ Ⓓ Ⓔ	15 Ⓐ Ⓑ Ⓒ Ⓓ Ⓔ	22 Ⓐ Ⓑ Ⓒ Ⓓ Ⓔ	29 Ⓐ Ⓑ Ⓒ Ⓓ Ⓔ
2 Ⓐ Ⓑ Ⓒ Ⓓ Ⓔ	9 Ⓐ Ⓑ Ⓒ Ⓓ Ⓔ	16 Ⓐ Ⓑ Ⓒ Ⓓ Ⓔ	23 Ⓐ Ⓑ Ⓒ Ⓓ Ⓔ	30 Ⓐ Ⓑ Ⓒ Ⓓ Ⓔ
3 Ⓐ Ⓑ Ⓒ Ⓓ Ⓔ	10 Ⓐ Ⓑ Ⓒ Ⓓ Ⓔ	17 Ⓐ Ⓑ Ⓒ Ⓓ Ⓔ	24 Ⓐ Ⓑ Ⓒ Ⓓ Ⓔ	31 Ⓐ Ⓑ Ⓒ Ⓓ Ⓔ
4 Ⓐ Ⓑ Ⓒ Ⓓ Ⓔ	11 Ⓐ Ⓑ Ⓒ Ⓓ Ⓔ	18 Ⓐ Ⓑ Ⓒ Ⓓ Ⓔ	25 Ⓐ Ⓑ Ⓒ Ⓓ Ⓔ	32 Ⓐ Ⓑ Ⓒ Ⓓ Ⓔ
5 Ⓐ Ⓑ Ⓒ Ⓓ Ⓔ	12 Ⓐ Ⓑ Ⓒ Ⓓ Ⓔ	19 Ⓐ Ⓑ Ⓒ Ⓓ Ⓔ	26 Ⓐ Ⓑ Ⓒ Ⓓ Ⓔ	33 Ⓐ Ⓑ Ⓒ Ⓓ Ⓔ
6 Ⓐ Ⓑ Ⓒ Ⓓ Ⓔ	13 Ⓐ Ⓑ Ⓒ Ⓓ Ⓔ	20 Ⓐ Ⓑ Ⓒ Ⓓ Ⓔ	27 Ⓐ Ⓑ Ⓒ Ⓓ Ⓔ	34 Ⓐ Ⓑ Ⓒ Ⓓ Ⓔ
7 Ⓐ Ⓑ Ⓒ Ⓓ Ⓔ	14 Ⓐ Ⓑ Ⓒ Ⓓ Ⓔ	21 Ⓐ Ⓑ Ⓒ Ⓓ Ⓔ	28 Ⓐ Ⓑ Ⓒ Ⓓ Ⓔ	35 Ⓐ Ⓑ Ⓒ Ⓓ Ⓔ

Section 2

1 Ⓐ Ⓑ Ⓒ Ⓓ Ⓔ	8 Ⓐ Ⓑ Ⓒ Ⓓ Ⓔ	15 Ⓐ Ⓑ Ⓒ Ⓓ Ⓔ	22 Ⓐ Ⓑ Ⓒ Ⓓ Ⓔ	29 Ⓐ Ⓑ Ⓒ Ⓓ Ⓔ
2 Ⓐ Ⓑ Ⓒ Ⓓ Ⓔ	9 Ⓐ Ⓑ Ⓒ Ⓓ Ⓔ	16 Ⓐ Ⓑ Ⓒ Ⓓ Ⓔ	23 Ⓐ Ⓑ Ⓒ Ⓓ Ⓔ	30 Ⓐ Ⓑ Ⓒ Ⓓ Ⓔ
3 Ⓐ Ⓑ Ⓒ Ⓓ Ⓔ	10 Ⓐ Ⓑ Ⓒ Ⓓ Ⓔ	17 Ⓐ Ⓑ Ⓒ Ⓓ Ⓔ	24 Ⓐ Ⓑ Ⓒ Ⓓ Ⓔ	31 Ⓐ Ⓑ Ⓒ Ⓓ Ⓔ
4 Ⓐ Ⓑ Ⓒ Ⓓ Ⓔ	11 Ⓐ Ⓑ Ⓒ Ⓓ Ⓔ	18 Ⓐ Ⓑ Ⓒ Ⓓ Ⓔ	25 Ⓐ Ⓑ Ⓒ Ⓓ Ⓔ	32 Ⓐ Ⓑ Ⓒ Ⓓ Ⓔ
5 Ⓐ Ⓑ Ⓒ Ⓓ Ⓔ	12 Ⓐ Ⓑ Ⓒ Ⓓ Ⓔ	19 Ⓐ Ⓑ Ⓒ Ⓓ Ⓔ	26 Ⓐ Ⓑ Ⓒ Ⓓ Ⓔ	33 Ⓐ Ⓑ Ⓒ Ⓓ Ⓔ
6 Ⓐ Ⓑ Ⓒ Ⓓ Ⓔ	13 Ⓐ Ⓑ Ⓒ Ⓓ Ⓔ	20 Ⓐ Ⓑ Ⓒ Ⓓ Ⓔ	27 Ⓐ Ⓑ Ⓒ Ⓓ Ⓔ	34 Ⓐ Ⓑ Ⓒ Ⓓ Ⓔ
7 Ⓐ Ⓑ Ⓒ Ⓓ Ⓔ	14 Ⓐ Ⓑ Ⓒ Ⓓ Ⓔ	21 Ⓐ Ⓑ Ⓒ Ⓓ Ⓔ	28 Ⓐ Ⓑ Ⓒ Ⓓ Ⓔ	35 Ⓐ Ⓑ Ⓒ Ⓓ Ⓔ

Section 3

1 Ⓐ Ⓑ Ⓒ Ⓓ Ⓔ	8 Ⓐ Ⓑ Ⓒ Ⓓ Ⓔ	15 Ⓐ Ⓑ Ⓒ Ⓓ Ⓔ	22 Ⓐ Ⓑ Ⓒ Ⓓ Ⓔ	29 Ⓐ Ⓑ Ⓒ Ⓓ Ⓔ
2 Ⓐ Ⓑ Ⓒ Ⓓ Ⓔ	9 Ⓐ Ⓑ Ⓒ Ⓓ Ⓔ	16 Ⓐ Ⓑ Ⓒ Ⓓ Ⓔ	23 Ⓐ Ⓑ Ⓒ Ⓓ Ⓔ	30 Ⓐ Ⓑ Ⓒ Ⓓ Ⓔ
3 Ⓐ Ⓑ Ⓒ Ⓓ Ⓔ	10 Ⓐ Ⓑ Ⓒ Ⓓ Ⓔ	17 Ⓐ Ⓑ Ⓒ Ⓓ Ⓔ	24 Ⓐ Ⓑ Ⓒ Ⓓ Ⓔ	31 Ⓐ Ⓑ Ⓒ Ⓓ Ⓔ
4 Ⓐ Ⓑ Ⓒ Ⓓ Ⓔ	11 Ⓐ Ⓑ Ⓒ Ⓓ Ⓔ	18 Ⓐ Ⓑ Ⓒ Ⓓ Ⓔ	25 Ⓐ Ⓑ Ⓒ Ⓓ Ⓔ	32 Ⓐ Ⓑ Ⓒ Ⓓ Ⓔ
5 Ⓐ Ⓑ Ⓒ Ⓓ Ⓔ	12 Ⓐ Ⓑ Ⓒ Ⓓ Ⓔ	19 Ⓐ Ⓑ Ⓒ Ⓓ Ⓔ	26 Ⓐ Ⓑ Ⓒ Ⓓ Ⓔ	33 Ⓐ Ⓑ Ⓒ Ⓓ Ⓔ
6 Ⓐ Ⓑ Ⓒ Ⓓ Ⓔ	13 Ⓐ Ⓑ Ⓒ Ⓓ Ⓔ	20 Ⓐ Ⓑ Ⓒ Ⓓ Ⓔ	27 Ⓐ Ⓑ Ⓒ Ⓓ Ⓔ	34 Ⓐ Ⓑ Ⓒ Ⓓ Ⓔ
7 Ⓐ Ⓑ Ⓒ Ⓓ Ⓔ	14 Ⓐ Ⓑ Ⓒ Ⓓ Ⓔ	21 Ⓐ Ⓑ Ⓒ Ⓓ Ⓔ	28 Ⓐ Ⓑ Ⓒ Ⓓ Ⓔ	35 Ⓐ Ⓑ Ⓒ Ⓓ Ⓔ

Section 4

1 Ⓐ Ⓑ Ⓒ Ⓓ Ⓔ	4 Ⓐ Ⓑ Ⓒ Ⓓ Ⓔ	7 Ⓐ Ⓑ Ⓒ Ⓓ Ⓔ	10 Ⓐ Ⓑ Ⓒ Ⓓ Ⓔ	13 Ⓐ Ⓑ Ⓒ Ⓓ Ⓔ
2 Ⓐ Ⓑ Ⓒ Ⓓ Ⓔ	5 Ⓐ Ⓑ Ⓒ Ⓓ Ⓔ	8 Ⓐ Ⓑ Ⓒ Ⓓ Ⓔ	11 Ⓐ Ⓑ Ⓒ Ⓓ Ⓔ	14 Ⓐ Ⓑ Ⓒ Ⓓ Ⓔ
3 Ⓐ Ⓑ Ⓒ Ⓓ Ⓔ	6 Ⓐ Ⓑ Ⓒ Ⓓ Ⓔ	9 Ⓐ Ⓑ Ⓒ Ⓓ Ⓔ	12 Ⓐ Ⓑ Ⓒ Ⓓ Ⓔ	15 Ⓐ Ⓑ Ⓒ Ⓓ Ⓔ

Section 4 (continued)

16   17   18   19   20

21   22   23   24   25

Section 5

1 Ⓐ Ⓑ Ⓒ Ⓓ Ⓔ	8 Ⓐ Ⓑ Ⓒ Ⓓ Ⓔ	15 Ⓐ Ⓑ Ⓒ Ⓓ Ⓔ	22 Ⓐ Ⓑ Ⓒ Ⓓ Ⓔ	29 Ⓐ Ⓑ Ⓒ Ⓓ Ⓔ
2 Ⓐ Ⓑ Ⓒ Ⓓ Ⓔ	9 Ⓐ Ⓑ Ⓒ Ⓓ Ⓔ	16 Ⓐ Ⓑ Ⓒ Ⓓ Ⓔ	23 Ⓐ Ⓑ Ⓒ Ⓓ Ⓔ	30 Ⓐ Ⓑ Ⓒ Ⓓ Ⓔ
3 Ⓐ Ⓑ Ⓒ Ⓓ Ⓔ	10 Ⓐ Ⓑ Ⓒ Ⓓ Ⓔ	17 Ⓐ Ⓑ Ⓒ Ⓓ Ⓔ	24 Ⓐ Ⓑ Ⓒ Ⓓ Ⓔ	31 Ⓐ Ⓑ Ⓒ Ⓓ Ⓔ
4 Ⓐ Ⓑ Ⓒ Ⓓ Ⓔ	11 Ⓐ Ⓑ Ⓒ Ⓓ Ⓔ	18 Ⓐ Ⓑ Ⓒ Ⓓ Ⓔ	25 Ⓐ Ⓑ Ⓒ Ⓓ Ⓔ	32 Ⓐ Ⓑ Ⓒ Ⓓ Ⓔ
5 Ⓐ Ⓑ Ⓒ Ⓓ Ⓔ	12 Ⓐ Ⓑ Ⓒ Ⓓ Ⓔ	19 Ⓐ Ⓑ Ⓒ Ⓓ Ⓔ	26 Ⓐ Ⓑ Ⓒ Ⓓ Ⓔ	33 Ⓐ Ⓑ Ⓒ Ⓓ Ⓔ
6 Ⓐ Ⓑ Ⓒ Ⓓ Ⓔ	13 Ⓐ Ⓑ Ⓒ Ⓓ Ⓔ	20 Ⓐ Ⓑ Ⓒ Ⓓ Ⓔ	27 Ⓐ Ⓑ Ⓒ Ⓓ Ⓔ	34 Ⓐ Ⓑ Ⓒ Ⓓ Ⓔ
7 Ⓐ Ⓑ Ⓒ Ⓓ Ⓔ	14 Ⓐ Ⓑ Ⓒ Ⓓ Ⓔ	21 Ⓐ Ⓑ Ⓒ Ⓓ Ⓔ	28 Ⓐ Ⓑ Ⓒ Ⓓ Ⓔ	35 Ⓐ Ⓑ Ⓒ Ⓓ Ⓔ

Section 6

1 Ⓐ Ⓑ Ⓒ Ⓓ Ⓔ	8 Ⓐ Ⓑ Ⓒ Ⓓ Ⓔ	15 Ⓐ Ⓑ Ⓒ Ⓓ Ⓔ	22 Ⓐ Ⓑ Ⓒ Ⓓ Ⓔ	29 Ⓐ Ⓑ Ⓒ Ⓓ Ⓔ
2 Ⓐ Ⓑ Ⓒ Ⓓ Ⓔ	9 Ⓐ Ⓑ Ⓒ Ⓓ Ⓔ	16 Ⓐ Ⓑ Ⓒ Ⓓ Ⓔ	23 Ⓐ Ⓑ Ⓒ Ⓓ Ⓔ	30 Ⓐ Ⓑ Ⓒ Ⓓ Ⓔ
3 Ⓐ Ⓑ Ⓒ Ⓓ Ⓔ	10 Ⓐ Ⓑ Ⓒ Ⓓ Ⓔ	17 Ⓐ Ⓑ Ⓒ Ⓓ Ⓔ	24 Ⓐ Ⓑ Ⓒ Ⓓ Ⓔ	31 Ⓐ Ⓑ Ⓒ Ⓓ Ⓔ
4 Ⓐ Ⓑ Ⓒ Ⓓ Ⓔ	11 Ⓐ Ⓑ Ⓒ Ⓓ Ⓔ	18 Ⓐ Ⓑ Ⓒ Ⓓ Ⓔ	25 Ⓐ Ⓑ Ⓒ Ⓓ Ⓔ	32 Ⓐ Ⓑ Ⓒ Ⓓ Ⓔ
5 Ⓐ Ⓑ Ⓒ Ⓓ Ⓔ	12 Ⓐ Ⓑ Ⓒ Ⓓ Ⓔ	19 Ⓐ Ⓑ Ⓒ Ⓓ Ⓔ	26 Ⓐ Ⓑ Ⓒ Ⓓ Ⓔ	33 Ⓐ Ⓑ Ⓒ Ⓓ Ⓔ
6 Ⓐ Ⓑ Ⓒ Ⓓ Ⓔ	13 Ⓐ Ⓑ Ⓒ Ⓓ Ⓔ	20 Ⓐ Ⓑ Ⓒ Ⓓ Ⓔ	27 Ⓐ Ⓑ Ⓒ Ⓓ Ⓔ	34 Ⓐ Ⓑ Ⓒ Ⓓ Ⓔ
7 Ⓐ Ⓑ Ⓒ Ⓓ Ⓔ	14 Ⓐ Ⓑ Ⓒ Ⓓ Ⓔ	21 Ⓐ Ⓑ Ⓒ Ⓓ Ⓔ	28 Ⓐ Ⓑ Ⓒ Ⓓ Ⓔ	35 Ⓐ Ⓑ Ⓒ Ⓓ Ⓔ

MODEL SAT I TEST 6   1 1 1 1 1   1

SECTION 1   **Time—30 Minutes**   Select the best answer to the following questions, then fill in the
             30 Questions   appropriate space on your Answer Sheet.

Each of the following sentences contains one or two
blanks; these blanks indicate that a word or set of words
has been left out. Below the sentence are five words or
phrases, lettered A through E. Select the word or set of
words that best completes the sentence.

Example:

Fame is ----; today's rising star is all too soon
tomorrow's washed-up has-been.

(A) rewarding   (B) gradual
 (C) essential   (D) spontaneous
   (E) transitory

---

1. His critical reviews were enjoyed by many of his
audience, but the subjects of his analysis dreaded
his comments; he was vitriolic, devastating, irritating and never ----.

  (A) analytic   (B) personal   (C) constructive
   (D) uncharitable   (E) controversial

2. Despite the team members' resentment of the new
coach's training rules, they ---- them as long as he
did not ---- them too strictly.

  (A) embraced...follow
  (B) condemned...formulate
  (C) questioned...interpret
  (D) challenged...implement
  (E) tolerated...apply

3. Given the ---- state of the published evidence, we
do not argue here that exposure to low-level
microwave energy is either hazardous or safe.

  (A) inconclusive
  (B) satisfactory
  (C) definitive
  (D) immaculate
  (E) exemplary

4. Tacitus' descriptions of Germanic tribal customs
were ---- by the ---- state of communications in his
day, but they match the accounts of other contemporary writers.

  (A) defined...inconsequential
  (B) limited...primitive
  (C) enriched...antiquated
  (D) contradicted...thriving
  (E) muddled...suspended

5. No matter how ---- the revelations of the coming
years may be, they will be hard put to match those
of the past decade, which have ---- transformed our
view of the emergence of Mayan civilization.

  (A) minor...dramatically
  (B) profound...negligibly
  (C) striking...radically
  (D) bizarre...nominally
  (E) questionable...possibly

6. Because of its inclination to ----, most Indian art is
---- Japanese art, where symbols have been minimized and meaning has been conveyed by the merest suggestion.

  (A) exaggerate...related to
  (B) imitate...superior to
  (C) understate...reminiscent of
  (D) overdraw...similar to
  (E) sentimentalize...supportive of

7. Irony can, after a fashion, become a mode of
escape: to laugh at the terrors of life is in some
sense to ---- them.

  (A) overstate   (B) revitalize   (C) corroborate
   (D) evade   (E) license

8. The contract negotiations were often surprisingly
----, deteriorating at times into a welter of accusations and counter-accusations.

  (A) perspicacious
  (B) phlegmatic
  (C) sedate
  (D) acrimonious
  (E) propitious

9. Black religion was in part a protest movement—a
protest against a system and a society that was ----
designed to ---- the dignity of a segment of God's
creation.

  (A) unintentionally...reflect
  (B) explicitly...foster
  (C) inevitably...assess
  (D) deliberately...demean
  (E) provocatively...enhance

GO ON TO THE NEXT PAGE →

1 1 1 1 1 1 1 1 1 1 1

The analogies questions present two words or phrases that are related in some way. Determine which A-through-E answer choice below has a relationship *most* similar to that of the original words or phrases.

Example:

YAWN:BOREDOM:: (A) dream:sleep
(B) anger:madness (C) smile:amusement
(D) face:expression (E) impatience:rebellion

 Ⓐ Ⓑ ● Ⓓ Ⓔ

10. SCRAPBOOK:CLIPPINGS::
   (A) newspaper:headlines
   (B) record:label
   (C) album:stamps
   (D) almanac:dates
   (E) bulletin:tacks

11. AVALANCHE:SNOW::
   (A) igloo:ice
   (B) deluge:water
   (C) sleet:hail
   (D) dew:rain
   (E) current:air

12. SHIP:FOUNDER::
   (A) government:reform
   (B) union:strike
   (C) business:organize
   (D) building:collapse
   (E) crew:muster

13. SQUIRM:DISCOMFORT::
   (A) chortle:distress
   (B) fume:anger
   (C) snarl:confusion
   (D) waddle:embarrassment
   (E) shrug:determination

14. RUTHLESS:SYMPATHY::
   (A) pathetic:pity
   (B) belligerent:detachment
   (C) lethargic:fatigue
   (D) heedless:intelligence
   (E) outspoken:reticence

15. CLIQUE:EXCLUSIVE::
   (A) congregation:benevolent
   (B) mob:disorderly
   (C) sorority:representative
   (D) troupe:renowned
   (E) flock:wayward

Read each of the passages below, and then answer the questions that follow each passage. The correct response may be stated outright or merely suggested in the passage.

Questions 16–21 are based on the following passage.

The following passage is taken from Civilisation, *a book based on the scripts for the television series of the same name. In this excerpt, author Kenneth Clark introduces the audience to the Europe of the 13th–15th centuries: the Gothic world.*

     I am in the Gothic world, the world of chivalry, courtesy, and romance; a world in which serious things were done with a sense of play—where
Line even war and theology could become a sort of
(5) game; and when architecture reached a point of extravagance unequalled in history. After all the great unifying convictions that inspired the medieval world, High Gothic art can look fantastic and luxurious—what Marxists call conspicu-
(10) ous waste. And yet these centuries produced some of the greatest spirits in the history of man, amongst them St. Francis of Assisi and Dante. Behind all the fantasy of the Gothic imagination there remained, on two different planes, a sharp
(15) sense of reality. Medieval man could see things

very clearly, but he believed that these appearances should be considered as nothing more than symbols or tokens of an ideal order, which was the only true reality.
(20)   The fantasy strikes us first, and last; and one can see it in the room in the Cluny Museum in Paris hung with a series of tapestries known as *The Lady with the Unicorn*, one of the most seductive examples of the Gothic spirit. It is poet-
(25) ical, fanciful and profane. Its ostensible subject is the four senses. But its real subject is the power of love, which can enlist and subdue all the forces of nature, including those two emblems of lust and ferocity, the unicorn and the lion. They kneel
(30) before this embodiment of chastity, and hold up the corners of her cloak. These wild animals have become, in the heraldic sense, her supporters. And all round this allegorical scene is what the

GO ON TO THE NEXT PAGE ⟶

1 1 1 1 1 1 1 1 1 1 1

medieval philosophers used to call *natura natu-*
(35) *rans*—nature naturing—trees, flowers, leaves
galore, birds, monkeys, and those rather obvious
symbols of nature naturing, rabbits. There is even
nature domesticated, a little dog, sitting on a
cushion. It is an image of worldly happiness at its
(40) most refined, what the French call the *douceur de
vivre*, which is often confused with civilization.
　　We have come a long way from the powerful
conviction that induced medieval knights and
ladies to draw carts of stone up the hill for the
(45) building of Chartres Cathedral. And yet the
notion of ideal love, and the irresistible power of
gentleness and beauty, which is emblematically
conveyed by the homage of these two fierce
beasts, can be traced back for three centuries, to
(50) days long before these tapestries were conceived.

16. The author distinguishes the Medieval imagination
    from the Gothic on the basis of the latter's
    (A) heraldic sense
    (B) respect for tradition
    (C) elaborateness of fancy
    (D) philosophical unity
    (E) firm belief

17. The word "point" in line 5 means
    (A) tip　(B) component　(C) message
    　(D) motive　(E) degree

18. The author cites St. Francis and Dante (line 12) pri-
    marily in order to
    (A) identify the inspiration for the design of the
        Unicorn tapestries
    (B) illustrate the source of the great convictions
        that animated the Medieval world
    (C) demonstrate his acquaintance with the writings
        of great thinkers of the period
    (D) refute the notion that the Gothic period pro-
        duced nothing but extravagance
    (E) support his contention that theology could
        become a sort of game

19. The author thinks of the Unicorn tapestries as
    exemplifying the essence of the Gothic imagination
    because
    (A) their allegorical nature derives from medieval
        sources
    (B) their use as wall hangings expresses the realis-
        tic practicality of the Gothic mind
    (C) they demonstrate the wastefulness and extrava-
        gance of the period
    (D) they combine worldly and spiritual elements in
        a celebration of love
    (E) they confuse the notion of civilization with
        worldly happiness

20. By "this embodiment of chastity" (line 30) the
    author is referring to
    (A) the unicorn
    (B) the Gothic spirit
    (C) St. Francis
    (D) the lady
    (E) the Cluny Museum

21. According to the final paragraph, in the Middle
    Ages some members of the nobility demonstrated
    the depth of their faith by
    (A) designing tapestries symbolic of courtly love
    (B) paying homage to aristocratic ladies
    (C) choosing to refine their notions of worldly
        happiness
    (D) hauling stones used to construct Chartres
        Cathedral
    (E) following the Franciscan ideal of living in har-
        mony with nature

Questions 22–30 are based on the following passage.

*African elephants now are an endangered species. The
following passage, taken from an article written in
1989, discusses the potential ecological disaster that
might occur if the elephant were to become extinct.*

　　The African elephant—mythic symbol of a
continent, keystone of its ecology and the largest
land animal remaining on earth—has become the
Line object of one of the biggest, broadest international
(5) efforts yet mounted to turn a threatened species
off the road to extinction. But it is not only the
elephant's survival that is at stake, conservationists say. Unlike the endangered tiger, unlike even
the great whales, the African elephant is in great
(10) measure the architect of its environment. As a
voracious eater of vegetation, it largely shapes the
forest-and-savanna surroundings in which it lives,
thereby setting the terms of existence for millions
of other storied animals—from zebras to gazelles
(15) to giraffes and wildebeests—that share its habitat.
And as the elephant disappears, scientists and
conservationists say, many other species will also
disappear from vast stretches of forest and savanna, drastically altering and impoverishing whole
(20) ecosystems.
　　It is the elephant's metabolism and appetite
that make it a disturber of the environment and
therefore an important creator of habitat. In a constant search for the 300 pounds of vegetation it
(25) must have every day, it kills small trees and

GO ON TO THE NEXT PAGE ➡

1   1   1   1   1   1   1   1   1   1   1

underbrush and pulls branches off big trees as
high as its trunk will reach. This creates innumerable open spaces in both deep tropical forests and
in the woodlands that cover part of the African
(30) savannas. The resulting patchwork, a mosaic of
vegetation in various stages of regeneration, in
turn creates a greater variety of forage that
attracts a greater variety of other vegetation-eaters
than would otherwise be the case.

(35)   In studies over the last twenty years in southern Kenya near Mount Kilimanjaro, Dr. David
Western has found that when elephants are
allowed to roam the savannas naturally and normally, they spread out at "intermediate densities."
(40) Their foraging creates a mixture of savanna
woodlands (what the Africans call bush) and
grassland. The result is a highly diverse array of
other plant-eating species: those like the zebra,
wildebeest and gazelle, that graze; those like the
(45) giraffe, bushbuck and lesser kudu, that browse on
tender shoots, buds, twigs and leaves; and plant-
eating primates like the baboon and vervet mon-
key. These herbivores attract carnivores like the
lion and cheetah.

(50)   When the elephant population thins out, Dr.
Western said, the woodlands become denser and
the grazers are squeezed out. When pressure from
poachers forces elephants to crowd more densely
onto reservations, the woodlands there are knocked
(55) out and the browsers and primates disappear.

    Something similar appears to happen in dense
tropical rain forests. In their natural state, because
the overhead forest canopy shuts out sunlight and
prevents growth on the forest floor, rain forests
(60) provide slim pickings for large, hoofed plant-
eaters. By pulling down trees and eating new
growth, elephants enlarge natural openings in the
canopy, allowing plants to regenerate on the forest floor and bringing down vegetation from the
(65) canopy so that smaller species can get at it.

    In such situations, the rain forest becomes hos-
pitable to large plant-eating mammals such as
bongos, bush pigs, duikers, forest hogs, swamp
antelopes, forest buffaloes, okapis, sometimes
(70) gorillas and always a host of smaller animals that
thrive on secondary growth. When elephants disappear and the forest reverts, the larger animals
give way to smaller, nimbler animals like monkeys, squirrels and rodents.

22. The passage is primarily concerned with

(A) explaining why elephants are facing the threat
     of extinction
(B) explaining difficulties in providing sufficient
     forage for plant-eaters
(C) explaining how the elephant's impact on its
     surroundings affects other species

(D) distinguishing between savannas and rain
     forests as habitats for elephants
(E) contrasting elephants with members of other
     endangered species

23. The word "mounted" in line 5 means

(A) ascended
(B) increased
(C) launched
(D) attached
(E) exhibited

24. In the opening paragraph, the author mentions
tigers and whales in order to emphasize which
point about the elephant?

(A) Like them, it faces the threat of extinction.
(B) It is herbivorous rather than carnivorous.
(C) It moves more ponderously than either the
     tiger or the whale.
(D) Unlike them, it physically alters its environ-
     ment.
(E) It is the largest extant land mammal.

25. A necessary component of the elephant's ability to
transform the landscape is its

(A) massive intelligence
(B) threatened extinction
(C) ravenous hunger
(D) lack of grace
(E) ability to regenerate

26. The author's style can best be described as

(A) hyperbolic
(B) naturalistic
(C) reportorial
(D) esoteric
(E) sentimental

27. It can be inferred from the passage that

(A) the lion and the cheetah commonly prey upon
     elephants
(B) the elephant is dependent upon the existence of
     smaller plant-eating mammals for its survival
(C) elephants have an indirect effect on the hunt-
     ing patterns of certain carnivores
(D) the floor of the tropical rain forest is too over-
     grown to accommodate larger plant-eating
     species
(E) the natural tendency of elephants is to crowd
     together in packs

GO ON TO THE NEXT PAGE →

1   1   1   1   1   1   1   1   1   1   1   1

28. The passage contains information that would answer which of the following questions?

I. How does the elephant's foraging affect its surroundings?
II. How do the feeding patterns of gazelles and giraffes differ?
III. What occurs in the rain forest when the elephant population dwindles?

(A) I only
(B) II only
(C) I and II only
(D) II and III only
(E) I, II, and III

29. The word "host" in line 70 means

(A) food source for parasites
(B) very large number
(C) provider of hospitality
(D) military force
(E) angelic company

30. Which of the following statements best expresses the author's attitude toward the damage to vegetation caused by foraging elephants?

(A) It is an unfortunate by-product of the feeding process.
(B) It is a necessary but undesirable aspect of elephant population growth.
(C) It fortuitously results in creating environments suited to diverse species.
(D) It has the unexpected advantage that it allows scientists access to the rain forest.
(E) It reinforces the impression that elephants are a disruptive force.

YOU MAY GO BACK AND REVIEW THIS SECTION IN THE REMAINING TIME, BUT DO NOT WORK IN ANY OTHER SECTION UNTIL TOLD TO DO SO.   **S T O P**

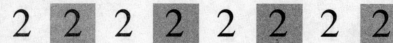

SECTION 2

**Time—30 Minutes
25 Questions**

For each problem in this section determine which of the five choices is correct and blacken in that choice on your answer sheet. You may use any blank space on the page for your work.

Notes:

* You may use a calculator whenever you feel it will be helpful.
* Use the diagrams provided to help you solve the problems. Unless you see the words "<u>Note</u>: Figure not drawn to scale" under a diagram, it has been drawn as accurately as possible. Unless it is stated that a figure is three-dimensional, you may assume it lies in a plane.

Reference Information

Area Facts	Volume Facts	Triangle Facts	Angle Facts

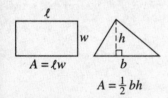

$A = \ell w$

$A = \frac{1}{2}bh$

$A = \pi r^2$
$C = 2\pi r$

$V = \ell wh$

$V = \pi r^2 h$

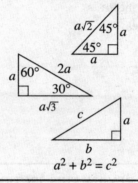

$a^2 + b^2 = c^2$

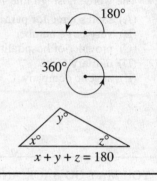

$x + y + z = 180$

---

1. If $a - 5 = 0$, what is the value of $a + 5$?

   (A) –10   (B) –5   (C) 0   (D) 5   (E) 10

2. What is 50% of 50% of 50?

   (A) 0.125   (B) 0.5   (C) 1.25   (D) 5.0   (E) 12.5

3. How many minutes did John take, driving at 20 miles per hour, to go the same distance that Mary took 30 minutes to drive at 60 miles per hour?

   (A) 10   (B) 30   (C) 60   (D) 90   (E) 180

4. Which of the following is an expression for "the product of 5 and the average (arithmetic mean) of x and y"?

   (A) $\dfrac{5x+y}{2}$ (B) $\dfrac{5x+5y}{2}$ (C) $\dfrac{5+x+y}{3}$

   (D) $5 + \dfrac{x+y}{2}$ (E) $\dfrac{5+5x+5y}{3}$

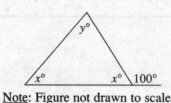

Note: Figure not drawn to scale

5. In the figure above, what is the value of y?

   (A) 20   (B) 40   (C) 50   (D) 80
   (E) It cannot be determined from the information given.

6. Assume that light travels at 300,000 kilometers per second, and that a light-minute is the distance that light travels in 1 minute. If the sun is 150,000,000 kilometers from Earth, how many light-minutes is it from the sun to Earth?

   (A) 0.002   (B) 0.12   (C) $8\frac{1}{3}$ (D) 20

   (E) 500

GO ON TO THE NEXT PAGE

7. If it is now 1:15, what time will it be when the hour hand has moved through an angle of 10°?

   (A) 1:25   (B) 1:35   (C) 2:15   (D) 3:15
   (E) 11:15

8. If d is the length of a diagonal of a square, what does d^2 represent?

   (A) the area of the square
   (B) twice the area of the square
   (C) $\dfrac{1}{2}$ the area of the square
   (D) 4 times the area of the square
   (E) $\dfrac{1}{4}$ the area of the square

9. If $a < b < c < d$ and the average (arithmetic mean) of a, b, c, and d is 10, which of the following must be true?

   I. $a + d = b + c$
   II. $a < 10$ and $d > 10$
   III. $b < 10$ and $c > 10$

   (A) I only   (B) II only   (C) I and II only
   (D) I and III only   (E) I, II, and III

10. A woman takes a horse out of a stable and rides it 3 miles north, 8 miles east, and then 3 miles north again to her house. How far is it, in miles, from the stable to her house?

    (A) 10   (B) 12   (C) 14   (D) 16
    (E) It cannot be determined from the information given.

11. What is the length of each of the five equal sides of a regular pentagon if the perimeter of the pentagon is equal to the perimeter of a square whose area is 25?

    (A) 4   (B) 5   (C) 10   (D) 20   (E) 25

12. Two sides of a right triangle are 5 and 6. Which of the following could be the length of the third side?

    I. $\sqrt{11}$ II. $\sqrt{31}$ III. $\sqrt{61}$

    (A) I only   (B) III only   (C) I and II only
    (D) I and III only   (E) I, II, and III

Questions 13–14 refer to the following definition.

For any numbers a, b, and c,

$$\triangle_{b\ \ c}^{\ \ a} = abc - (a + b + c).$$

13. $\triangle_{5\ \ 2}^{\ \ 3} = ?$

    (A) 0   (B) 5   (C) 10   (D) 20   (E) 30

14. For which of the following equations is it true that there is exactly one positive integer that satisfies it?

    I. $\triangle_{0\ \ a}^{\ \ a} = 0$
    II. $\triangle_{a\ \ a}^{\ \ a} = 0$
    III. $\triangle_{2a\ 3a}^{\ \ a} = 0$

    (A) none   (B) I only   (C) III only
    (D) I and III only   (E) I, II, and III

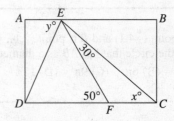

Note: Figure not drawn to scale

15. In the figure above, rectangle $ABCD$ has been partitioned into four triangles. If $DF = EF$, what is the value of $x + y$?

    (A) 60   (B) 75   (C) 85   (D) 90   (E) 105

16. Megan wrote down all of the three-digit numbers that can be written using each of the numerals 1, 2, and 3 exactly once. What is the average (arithmetic mean) of the numbers that Megan wrote?

    (A) 213   (B) 222   (C) 231   (D) 233   (E) 333

GO ON TO THE NEXT PAGE

2   2 2 2 2 2 2 2 2 2   2

17. Aaron was 24 when his daughter Sarah was born. If Aaron is now 3 times as old as Sarah, how many years ago was Aaron 4 times as old as Sarah?

(A) 4   (B) 6   (C) 8   (D) 12   (E) 18

---

18. A relation # is defined on the set of real numbers as follows: $a \# b$ is true if and only if $a - 3 > b + 3$. Which of the following must be true?

   I. $3 \# (-3)$ II. $10 \# 5$ III. $7c \# c$

(A) none   (B) I only   (C) II only   (D) III only
(E) I and III only

---

19. The population density of a region is the number of people living in the region per square mile. Jackson County is a rectangle whose length is ℓ miles and whose width is w miles. How many people live in Jackson County if its population density is d?

(A) $d\ell w$ (B) $\dfrac{\ell w}{d}$ (C) $\dfrac{d}{\ell w}$ (D) $\dfrac{2(\ell + w)}{d}$

(E) $\dfrac{\ell + w}{2d}$

---

20. If A is point $(-4,1)$ and B is point $(2,1)$, what is the area of the circle that has AB as a diameter?

(A) 3π (B) 6π (C) 9π (D) 12π (E) 36π

---

21. Mrs. James gave a test to her two geometry classes. The 24 students in her first-period class had a class average (arithmetic mean) of 78. The average of the 26 students in her second-period class was 83. What was the average for all students taking the exam?

(A) 79.4   (B) 80.5   (C) 80.6   (D) 81.2
(E) 81.4

---

22. If x is an even number, then each of the following must be true EXCEPT

(A) $2x + 7$ is odd
(B) $3x^2 + 5$ is odd
(C) $x^3 - x^2 + x - 1$ is odd
(D) $3x + 4$ is even
(E) $(3x - 5)(5x - 3)$ is even

---

23. If $x = 2y - 5$ and $z = 16y^3$, what is z in terms of x?

(A) $\left(\dfrac{x+5}{2}\right)^3$ (B) $\dfrac{(x+5)^3}{2}$ (C) $2(x+5)^3$

(D) $4(x+5)^3$ (E) $8(x+5)^3$

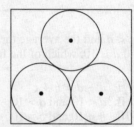

24. In the figure above, each circle is tangent to the other two circles and to the sides of the rectangle. If the diameter of each circle is 10, what is the area of the rectangle?

(A) 300   (B) 400   (C) $100 + 200\sqrt{3}$

(D) $200 + 100\sqrt{3}$

(E) It cannot be determined from the information given.

---

25. If the sum of all the positive even integers less than 1000 is A, what is the sum of all the positive odd integers less than 1000?

(A) $A - 998$ (B) $A - 499$ (C) $A + 1$

(D) $A + 500$ (E) $\dfrac{A}{2} + 999$

YOU MAY GO BACK AND REVIEW THIS SECTION IN THE REMAINING TIME, BUT DO NOT WORK IN ANY OTHER SECTION UNTIL TOLD TO DO SO.   **S T O P**

3   3 3 3 3 3 3 3 3 3 3   3

SECTION 3   Time—30 Minutes
35 Questions   Select the best answer to the following questions, then fill in the
appropriate space on your Answer Sheet.

Each of the following sentences contains one or two blanks; these blanks indicate that a word or set of words has been left out. Below the sentence are five words or phrases, lettered A through E. Select the word or set of words that best completes the sentence.

Example:

Fame is ----; today's rising star is all too soon tomorrow's washed-up has-been.

(A) rewarding   (B) gradual
(C) essential   (D) spontaneous
(E) transitory

1. Either the Polynesian banquets at Waikiki are ----, or the one I visited was a poor example.

    (A) delicious   (B) impeccable   (C) overrated
    (D) untasted   (E) unpopular

2. Given the ---- nature of wood, the oldest totem poles of the Northwest Coast Indians eventually fell to decay; only a few still stand today.

    (A) resilient   (B) combustible   (C) malleable
    (D) perishable   (E) solid

3. Lee, who refrained from excesses in his personal life, differed markedly from Grant, who ---- notorious drinking bouts with his cronies.

    (A) deprecated
    (B) minimized
    (C) indulged in
    (D) shunned
    (E) compensated for

4. The college librarian initiated a new schedule of fines for overdue books with the ----, if not the outright encouragement, of the faculty library committee.

    (A) skepticism   (B) acquiescence   (C) scorn
    (D) applause   (E) disapprobation

5. At first ---- were simply that: straightforward first-hand testimonials about the ---- of a product.

    (A) trademarks...contents
    (B) creeds...excellence
    (C) prejudices...flaws
    (D) reprimands...benefits
    (E) endorsements...virtues

6. By nature Toshiro was ----, given to striking up casual conversations with strangers he encountered at bus stops or check-out stands.

    (A) diffident
    (B) observant
    (C) reticent
    (D) gregarious
    (E) laconic

7. In the absence of native predators to stop their spread, imported deer ---- to such an inordinate degree that they overgrazed the countryside and ---- the native vegetation.

    (A) thrived...threatened
    (B) propagated...cultivated
    (C) suffered...abandoned
    (D) flourished...scrutinized
    (E) dwindled...eliminated

8. He was habitually so docile and ---- that his friends could not understand his sudden ---- his employers.

    (A) accommodating...outburst against
    (B) incorrigible...suspicion of
    (C) truculent...virulence toward
    (D) erratic...envy of
    (E) hasty...cordiality toward

9. That Mr. Willis's newest film is No. 1 at the box office this week is a testament to the star's ---- power and not to the reviews, which were ---- at best.

    (A) waning...indifferent
    (B) ongoing...glowing
    (C) drawing...modest
    (D) increasing...matchless
    (E) unique...superb

10. The campus police who monitored the demonstrations had little respect for the student protesters, generally speaking of them in ---- terms.

    (A) hyperbolic
    (B) euphemistic
    (C) pejorative
    (D) derivative
    (E) uncertain

GO ON TO THE NEXT PAGE

The analogies questions present two words or phrases that are related in some way. Determine which A-through-E answer choice below has a relationship *most* similar to that of the original words or phrases.

Example:

YAWN:BOREDOM::   (A) dream:sleep
(B) anger:madness   (C) smile:amusement
(D) face:expression   (E) impatience:rebellion

Ⓐ Ⓑ ● Ⓓ Ⓔ

11. BRAKE:AUTOMOBILE::
(A) pad:helicopter
(B) ship:fleet
(C) reins:horse
(D) helmet:motorcycle
(E) boot:saddle

12. AREA:SQUARE::
(A) diagonal:rectangle
(B) volume:cube
(C) angle:triangle
(D) radius:circle
(E) base:cylinder

13. COLLEAGUES:PROFESSION::
(A) kinsfolk:family
(B) spectators:game
(C) exiles:country
(D) rivals:team
(E) passengers:subway

14. TERMITE:WOOD::
(A) moth:wool
(B) silkworm:silk
(C) oyster:shell
(D) anthracite:coal
(E) terrace:stone

15. TALLY:VOTES::
(A) census:population
(B) taxation:revenue
(C) government:laws
(D) team:athletes
(E) election:candidates

16. CEASE-FIRE:HOSTILITIES::
(A) alimony:divorce
(B) battery:missiles
(C) lull:storm
(D) bonfire:kindling
(E) apology:insult

17. INTEREST:USURY::
(A) concern:disregard
(B) thrift:prodigality
(C) debit:credit
(D) frugality:parsimony
(E) pleasure:utility

18. BOOK:SPINE::
(A) film:clip
(B) ladder:rung
(C) skeleton:backbone
(D) newspaper:column
(E) light:switch

19. CACOPHONY:EAR::
(A) calligraphy:eye
(B) piquancy:taste
(C) stench:nose
(D) tracheotomy:throat
(E) retina:eye

20. EULOGY:PRAISE::
(A) elegy:death
(B) slander:disparagement
(C) paean:anger
(D) reproof:confirmation
(E) satire:vanity

21. OUTFOX:CUNNING::
(A) outline:thought
(B) outstrip:speed
(C) outreach:charity
(D) outrank:bravery
(E) outrage:wrath

22. BRONZE:PATINA::
(A) wood:veneer
(B) plaque:honor
(C) mold:yeast
(D) iron:rust
(E) lead:tin

23. EMBROIL:STRIFE::
(A) chafe:restriction
(B) embarrass:pride
(C) emulate:model
(D) annul:marriage
(E) imperil:danger

GO ON TO THE NEXT PAGE

3   3   3   3   3   3   3   3   3   3   3

Read the passage below, and then answer the questions that follow the passage. The correct response may be stated outright or merely suggested in the passage.

In this excerpt from his autobiographical Narrative of the Life of an American Slave, *the abolitionist Frederick Douglass tells how he, as a young child, learned the value of learning to read and write.*

Mr. and Mrs. Auld were both at home, and met me at the door with their little son Thomas, to take care of whom I had been given. And here I
Line saw what I had never seen before; it was a white
(5) face beaming with the most kindly emotions; it was the face of my new mistress, Sophia Auld. I wish I could describe the rapture that flashed through my soul as I beheld it. It was a new and strange sight to me, brightening up my pathway
(10) with happiness. Little Thomas was told, there was his Freddy,—and I was told to take care of little Thomas; and thus I entered upon the duties of my new home with the most cheering prospect ahead.
(15) My new mistress proved to be all she appeared when I first met her at the door,—a woman of the kindest heart and feelings. She had never had a slave under her control previously to myself, and prior to her marriage she had been dependent
(20) upon her own industry for a living. She was by trade a weaver; and by constant application to her business, she had been in a good degree preserved from the blighting and dehumanizing effects of slavery. I was utterly astonished at her goodness.
(25) I scarcely knew how to behave towards her. My early instruction was all out of place. The crouching servility, usually so acceptable a quality in a slave, did not answer when manifested toward her. Her favor was not gained by it; she seemed to
(30) be disturbed by it. She did not deem it impudent or unmannerly for a slave to look her in the face. The meanest slave was put fully at ease in her presence, and none left without feeling better for having seen her. But alas! this kind heart had but
(35) a short time to remain such. The fatal poison of irresponsible power was already in her hands, and soon commenced its infernal work.
Very soon after I went to live with Mr. and Mrs. Auld, she very kindly commenced to teach
(40) me the A, B, C. After I had learned this, she assisted me in learning to spell words of three or four letters. Just at this point of my progress, Mr. Auld found out what was going on, and at once forbade Mrs. Auld to instruct me further, telling
(45) her that it was unlawful, as well as unsafe, to teach a slave to read. Further, he said, "If you give a slave an inch, he will take an ell. A slave should know nothing but to obey his master—to

do as he is told to do. Learning would *spoil* the
(50) best slave in the world. Now," said he, "if you teach that boy (speaking of myself) how to read, there would be no keeping him. It would forever unfit him to be a slave. He would at once become unmanageable, and of no value to his master. As
(55) to him, it could do him no good, but a great deal of harm. It would make him discontented and unhappy." These words sank deep into my heart, stirred up sentiments within that lay slumbering, and called into existence an entirely new train of
(60) thought. I now understood what had been to me a most perplexing difficulty—to wit, the white man's power to enslave the black man. From that moment I understood the pathway from slavery to freedom. Though conscious of the difficulty of
(65) learning without a teacher, I set out with high hope, and a fixed purpose, at whatever cost of trouble, to learn how to read. The very decided manner with which my master spoke, and strove to impress his wife with the evil consequences of
(70) giving me instruction, served to convince me that he was deeply sensible of the truths he was uttering. It gave me the best assurance that I might rely with the utmost confidence on the results which, he said, would flow from teaching me to
(75) read. What he most dreaded, that I most desired. What he most loved, that I most hated. That which to him was a great evil, to be carefully shunned, was to me a great good, to be diligently sought; and the argument which he so warmly
(80) urged, against my learning to read, only served to inspire me with a desire and determination to learn. In learning to read, I owe almost as much to the bitter opposition of my master, as to the kindly aid of my mistress. I acknowledge the
(85) benefit of both.

24. According to the opening paragraph, the author's initial reaction toward joining the Aulds' household was primarily one of

(A) absolute astonishment
(B) marked pleasure
(C) carefree nonchalance
(D) quiet resignation
(E) subdued nostalgia

GO ON TO THE NEXT PAGE

25. To some degree, the author attributes Mrs. Auld's freedom from the common attitudes of slave owners to her

    (A) abolitionist upbringing
    (B) personal wealth
    (C) indifference to her husband
    (D) experiences as a mother
    (E) concentration on her trade

26. Which of the following best explains why the author felt his "early instruction was all out of place" (lines 25–26)?

    (A) It failed to include instruction in reading and writing.
    (B) It did not prepare him to take adequate care of the Aulds' son Thomas.
    (C) It did not train him to assist Mrs. Auld with her weaving.
    (D) It had been displaced by the new instructions he received from the Aulds.
    (E) It insisted on an obsequiousness that distressed his new mistress.

27. The word "answer" in line 28 most nearly means

    (A) acknowledge
    (B) retort
    (C) reply
    (D) serve
    (E) atone

28. By "this kind heart had but a short time to remain such" (lines 34–35) the author primarily intends to convey that Mrs. Auld

    (A) had only a brief time in which to do her work
    (B) was fated to die in the near future
    (C) was unable to keep her temper for extended periods of time
    (D) had too much strength of will to give in to the softer emotions
    (E) was destined to undergo a change of character shortly

29. It can be inferred from the passage that all of the following were characteristic of Mrs. Auld at the time the author first met her EXCEPT

    (A) diligence in labor
    (B) dislike of fawning
    (C) gentleness of spirit
    (D) disdain for convention
    (E) benevolent nature

30. For which of the following reasons does Mr. Auld forbid his wife to educate her slave?

    I. Providing slaves with an education violates the law.
    II. He believes slaves lack the capacity for education.
    III. He fears education would leave the slave less submissive.

    (A) I only
    (B) III only
    (C) I and II only
    (D) I and III only
    (E) I, II, and III

31. We can assume on the basis of Mr. Auld's comment in lines 46–47 that

    (A) he is willing to give his slaves the inch they request
    (B) he uses the term *ell* to signify a letter of the alphabet
    (C) Mrs. Auld is unfamiliar with standard forms of measurement
    (D) an ell is a much larger unit of length than an inch
    (E) slaves are far less demanding than he realizes

32. The author's main purpose in this passage is to

    (A) describe a disagreement between a woman and her husband
    (B) analyze the reasons for prohibiting the education of slaves
    (C) describe a slave's discovery of literacy as a means to freedom
    (D) dramatize a slave's change in attitude toward his mistress
    (E) portray the downfall of a kindhearted woman

33. The word "sensible" in line 71 means

    (A) logical
    (B) prudent
    (C) intelligent
    (D) conscious
    (E) sensory

GO ON TO THE NEXT PAGE ⟶

3 3 3 3 3 3 3 3 3 3 3 **3**

34. The tone of the author in acknowledging his debt to his master (lines 82–85) can best be described as

(A) sentimental and nostalgic
(B) cutting and ironic
(C) petulant and self-righteous
(D) resigned but wistful
(E) angry and impatient

35. Which of the following definitions of "education" is closest to the author's view of education as presented in the passage?

(A) Education makes people easy to govern, but impossible to enslave.
(B) Education is the best provision for old age.
(C) Education has for its object the formation of character.
(D) Education has produced a vast population able to read but unable to distinguish what is worth reading.
(E) Education begins and ends with the knowledge of human nature.

YOU MAY GO BACK AND REVIEW THIS SECTION IN THE REMAINING TIME, BUT DO NOT WORK IN ANY OTHER SECTION UNTIL TOLD TO DO SO.   **S T O P**

4   4   4   4   4   4   4   4   4   4   4   4

SECTION 4

Time—30 Minutes
25 Questions

You have 30 minutes to answer the 15 Quantitative Comparison questions and 10 Student-Produced Response questions in this section. You may use any blank space on the page for your work.

Notes:

- You may use a calculator whenever you feel it will be helpful.
- Use the diagrams provided to help you solve the problems. Unless you see the words "<u>Note</u>: Figure not drawn to scale" under a diagram, it has been drawn as accurately as possible. Unless it is stated that a figure is three-dimensional, you may assume it lies in a plane.

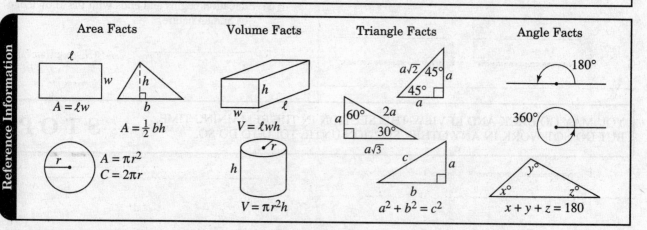

Reference Information

Area Facts

$A = \ell w$

$A = \frac{1}{2} bh$

$A = \pi r^2$
$C = 2\pi r$

Volume Facts

$V = \ell w h$

$V = \pi r^2 h$

Triangle Facts

$a^2 + b^2 = c^2$

Angle Facts

$x + y + z = 180$

Directions for Quantitative Comparison Questions

In each of questions 1–15, two quantities appear in boxes: one in Column A and one in Column B. You must compare them. The correct answer to a question is

A if the quantity in Column A is greater;
B if the quantity in Column B is greater;
C if the two quantities are equal;
D if it is impossible to determine which quantity is greater.

Notes:

- *The correct answer is <u>never</u> E.*
- Sometimes information about one or both of the quantities is centered above the two boxes.
- If the same symbol appears in both columns, it represents the same thing each time.
- All variables represent real numbers.

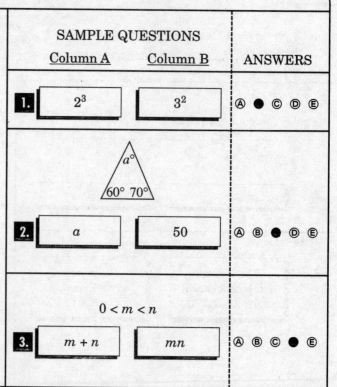

SAMPLE QUESTIONS

Column A	Column B	ANSWERS
1. 2^3	3^2	Ⓐ ● Ⓒ Ⓓ Ⓔ
2. a	50	Ⓐ Ⓑ ● Ⓓ Ⓔ
3. $m + n$	mn	Ⓐ Ⓑ Ⓒ ● Ⓔ

$0 < m < n$

GO ON TO THE NEXT PAGE

4   4 4 4 4 4 4 4 4 4 4   4

SUMMARY DIRECTIONS FOR QUANTITATIVE COMPARISON QUESTIONS

<u>Answer</u>: A if the quantity in Column A is greater;
B if the quantity in Column B is greater;
C if the two quantities are equal;
D if it is impossible to determine which quantity is greater.

<u>Column A</u>	<u>Column B</u>

$n = -1$

1. $(n + n^2)^2$ 0

$a < 0$

2. 60% of $3a$ 30% of $6a$

$$\dfrac{x}{3} = \dfrac{x}{\frac{1}{3}}$$

3. x 0

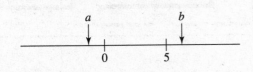

4. $a - b$ -5

---

5. The average (arithmetic mean) of $4x$, $7x$, and 100 The average (arithmetic mean) of x, $10x$, and 100

<u>Column A</u>	<u>Column B</u>

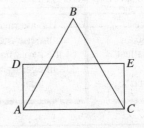

$\triangle ABC$ is equilateral. Perimeter of $\triangle ABC =$ perimeter of rectangle $ADEC$.

6. AB $2EC$

$0 < ab < 1$

7. $\dfrac{a}{b}$ 1

At XYZ Corporation the ratio of the number of male employees to the number of female employees is 3:2.
20% of the males and 30% of the female employees attended the company picnic.

8. The number of male employees at the picnic   The number of female employees at the picnic

---

9. The area of a square whose sides are 10   The area of a square whose diagonals are 15

GO ON TO THE NEXT PAGE ➔

4   4 4 4 4 4 4 4 4 4 4   4

Column A	Column B

10.

The average (arithmetic mean) of the two smallest even integers greater than a	The average (arithmetic mean) of the two smallest odd integers greater than a

---

The areas of a square and a circle are equal.

11.

The perimeter of the square	The circumference of the circle

$$a + b = 24$$
$$a - b = 25$$

12.

b	0

$$\frac{a-b}{c-a} = 1$$

13.

The average (arithmetic mean) of b and c	a

Column A	Column B

E is a point on line CD, and $ABCD$ is a rectangle.

14.

The area of $\triangle ABC$	The area of $\triangle ABE$

The figure below consists of four circles with the same center.
The radii of the four circles are 1, 2, 3, and 4.

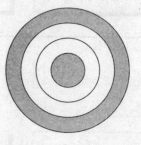

15.

The area of the shaded region	The area of the white region

GO ON TO THE NEXT PAGE

4   4 4 4 4 4 4 4 4 4 4   4

Directions for Student-Produced Response Questions (Grid-ins)

In questions 16–25, first solve the problem, and then enter your answer on the grid provided on the answer sheet. The instructions for entering your answers are as follows:

- First, write your answer in the boxes at the top of the grid.
- Second, grid your answer in the columns below the boxes.
- Use the fraction bar in the first row or the decimal point in the second row to enter fractions and decimal answers.

- Grid only one space in each column.
- Entering the answer in the boxes is recommended as an aid in gridding, but is not required.
- The machine scoring your exam can read only what you grid, so you **must grid in your answers correctly to get credit.**
- If a question has more than one correct answer, grid in only one of them.
- The grid does not have a minus sign, so no answer can be negative.
- A mixed number *must* be converted to an improper fraction or a decimal before it is gridded. Enter $1\frac{1}{4}$ as 5/4 or 1.25; the machine will interpret 1 1/4 as $\frac{11}{4}$ and mark it wrong.

- **All decimals must be entered as accurately as possible.** Here are the three acceptable ways of gridding

$$\frac{3}{11} = 0.272727...$$

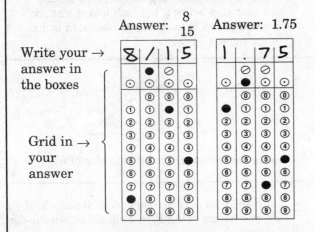

Answer: $\frac{8}{15}$ Answer: 1.75

Write your → answer in the boxes

Grid in → your answer

Answer: 100

Either position is acceptable

3/11   .272   .273

- Note that rounding to .273 is acceptable, because you are using the full grid, but you would receive **no credit** for .3 or .27, because they are less accurate.

16. What is the value of $\dfrac{1}{5} + \dfrac{2}{10} + \dfrac{3}{15} + \dfrac{4}{20} + \dfrac{5}{25}$?

17. If $ab = 20$ and $a = -5$, what is the value of $a^2 - b^2$?

GO ON TO THE NEXT PAGE ⇒

4   4   4   4   4   4   4   4   4   4   4   **4**

18. If $\frac{2}{3}$ of x equals $\frac{3}{4}$ of x, what is $\frac{4}{5}$ of x?

19. A clock chimes every hour to indicate the time, and also chimes once every 15 minutes on the quarter-hour and half-hour. For example, it chimes 3 times at 3:00, once at 3:15, once at 3:30, once at 3:45, and 4 times at 4:00. What is the smallest number of times the clock could chime in an interval of $2\frac{1}{2}$ hours?

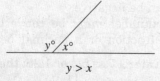

$$y > x$$

<u>Note</u>: Figure not drawn to scale

20. For the figure above, what is the largest value of x that will fit in the grid?

21. The average (arithmetic mean) amount of savings of 10 students is $60. If 3 of the students have no savings at all, and each of the others has at least $25, including John, who has exactly $130, what is the largest amount, in dollars, that any one student could have?

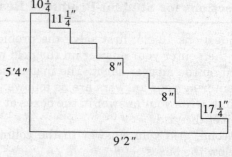

22. In the stair unit in the figure above, all the angles are right angles. The left side is 5 feet 4 inches, and the bottom is 9 feet 2 inches. Each vertical riser is 8 inches. The top step is 10.25 inches, and each step below it is 1 inch longer than the preceding step. What is the perimeter, in inches, of the figure?

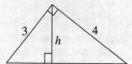

23. In the figure above, what is the value of h?

24. Let a and b be positive numbers such that $a\%$ of $a\%$ of b equals c. If $a^2\%$ of b equals kc, what is the value of k?

25. For how many positive three-digit numbers is the average of the three digits equal to 2?

YOU MAY GO BACK AND REVIEW THIS SECTION IN THE REMAINING TIME, BUT DO NOT WORK IN ANY OTHER SECTION UNTIL TOLD TO DO SO.   **S T O P**

5

The questions that follow the two passages in this section relate to the content of both, and to their relationship. The correct response may be stated outright in the passages or merely suggested.

Questions 1–13 are based on the following passages.

The following passages deal with the importance of money to Americans. The first is taken from a commencement address made by the American philosopher George Santayana in 1904. The second is taken from an essay written by the British poet W. H. Auden in 1963.

Passage 1

American life, everyone has heard, has extraordinary intensity; it goes at a great rate. This is not due, I should say, to any particular urgency in
Line the object pursued. Other nations have more
(5) pressing motives to bestir themselves than America has: and it is observable that not all the new nations, in either hemisphere, are energetic. This energy can hardly spring either from unusually intolerable conditions which people wish to
(10) overcome, nor from unusually important objects which they wish to attain. It springs, I should venture to say, from the harmony which subsists between the task and the spirit, between the mind's vitality and the forms which, in America,
(15) political and industrial tradition has taken on. It is sometimes said that the ruling passion in America is the love of money. This seems to me a complete mistake. The ruling passion is the love of *business*, which is something quite different. The
(20) lover of money would be jealous of it; he would spend it carefully; he would study to get out of it the most he could. But the lover of business, when he is successful, does not much change his way of living; he does not think out what further
(25) advantages he can get out of his success. His joy is in that business itself and in its further operation, in making it greater and better organized and a mightier engine in the general life. The adventitious personal profit in it is the last thing he
(30) thinks of, the last thing he is skillful in bringing about; and the same zeal and intensity is applied in managing a college, or a public office, or a naval establishment, as is lavished on private business, for it is not a motive of personal gain
(35) that stimulates to such exertions. It is the absorbing, satisfying character of the activities themselves; it is the art, the happiness, the greatness of them. So that in beginning life in such a society,

which has developed a native and vital tradition
(40) out of its practice, you have good reason to feel that your spirit will be freed, that you will begin to realize a part of what you are living for.

Passage 2

Political and technological developments are rapidly obliterating all cultural differences and it
(45) is possible that, in a not remote future, it will be impossible to distinguish human beings living on one area of the earth's surface from those living on any other, but our different pasts have not yet been completely erased and cultural differences
(50) are still perceptible. The most striking difference between an American and a European is the difference in their attitudes towards money. Every European knows, as a matter of historical fact, that, in Europe, wealth could only be acquired at
(55) the expense of other human beings, either by conquering them or by exploiting their labor in factories. Further, even after the Industrial Revolution began, the number of persons who could rise from poverty to wealth was small; the vast major-
(60) ity took it for granted that they would not be much richer nor poorer than their fathers. In consequence, no European associates wealth with personal merit or poverty with personal failure.

To a European, money means power, the free-
(65) dom to do as he likes, which also means that, consciously or unconsciously, he says: "I want to have as much money as possible myself and others to have as little money as possible."

In the United States, wealth was also acquired
(70) by stealing, but the real exploited victim was not a human being but poor Mother Earth and her creatures who were ruthlessly plundered. It is true that the Indians were expropriated or exterminated, but this was not, as it had always been in
(75) Europe, a matter of the conqueror seizing the wealth of the conquered, for the Indian had never realized the potential riches of his country. It is also true that, in the Southern states, men lived on the labor of slaves, but slave labor did not make
(80) them fortunes; what made slavery in the South all

GO ON TO THE NEXT PAGE

5

the more inexcusable was that, in addition to being morally wicked, it didn't even pay off handsomely.

Thanks to the natural resources of the country,
(85) every American, until quite recently, could reasonably look forward to making more money than his father, so that, if he made less, the fault must be his; he was either lazy or inefficient. What an American values, therefore, is not the possession
(90) of money as such, but his power to make it as a proof of his manhood; once he has proved himself by making it, it has served its function and can be lost or given away. In no society in history have rich men given away so large a part of their for-
(95) tunes. A poor American feels guilty at being poor, but less guilt than an American *rentier** who has inherited wealth but is doing nothing to increase it; what can the latter do but take to drink and psychoanalysis?

*A *rentier* lives on a fixed income from rents and investments.

1. The word "spring" in line 8 means

   (A) leap
   (B) arise
   (C) extend
   (D) break
   (E) blossom

2. The lover of business (lines 22–38) can be described as all of the following EXCEPT

   (A) enthusiastic
   (B) engrossed
   (C) enterprising
   (D) industrious
   (E) mercenary

3. The author of Passage 1 maintains that Americans find the prospect of improving business organizations

   (A) pleasurable
   (B) problematic
   (C) implausible
   (D) wearing
   (E) unanticipated

4. In line 28, "engine" most nearly means

   (A) artifice
   (B) locomotive
   (C) mechanical contrivance
   (D) financial windfall
   (E) driving force

5. The author of Passage 1 contends that those who grow up in American society will be influenced by its native traditions to

   (A) fight the intolerable conditions afflicting their country
   (B) achieve spiritual harmony through meditation
   (C) find self-fulfillment through their business activities
   (D) acknowledge the importance of financial accountability
   (E) conserve the country's natural resources

6. In lines 43–48 the author of Passage 2 asserts that technological advances

   (A) are likely to promote greater divisions between the rich and the poor
   (B) may eventually lead to worldwide cultural uniformity
   (C) can enable us to tolerate any cultural differences between us
   (D) may make the distinctions between people increasingly easy to discern
   (E) destroy the cultural differences they are intended to foster

7. The word "striking" in line 50 means

   (A) attractive
   (B) marked
   (C) shocking
   (D) protesting
   (E) commanding

8. In taking it for granted that they would not be much richer nor poorer than their fathers (lines 59–61), Europeans do which of the following?

   (A) They express a preference.
   (B) They refute an argument.
   (C) They qualify an assertion.
   (D) They correct a misapprehension.
   (E) They make an assumption.

9. According to lines 84–88, to Americans the failure to surpass one's father in income indicates

   (A) a dislike of inherited wealth
   (B) a lack of proper application on one's part
   (C) a fear of the burdens inherent in success
   (D) the height of fiscal irresponsibility
   (E) the effects of a guilty conscience

GO ON TO THE NEXT PAGE

5

10. The author's description of the likely fate of the American *rentier* living on inherited wealth is

(A) astonished
(B) indulgent
(C) sorrowful
(D) sympathetic
(E) ironic

11. In Passage 2 the author does all of the following EXCEPT

(A) make a categorical statement
(B) correct a misapprehension
(C) draw a contrast
(D) pose a question
(E) cite an authority

12. The authors of both passages most likely would agree that Americans engage in business

(A) on wholly altruistic grounds
(B) as a test of their earning capacity
(C) only out of economic necessity
(D) regardless of the example set by their parents
(E) for psychological rather than financial reasons

13. Compared to the attitude toward Americans expressed in Passage 1, the attitude toward them expressed in Passage 2 is

(A) more admiring
(B) less disapproving
(C) more cynical
(D) less patronizing
(E) more chauvinistic

YOU MAY GO BACK AND REVIEW THIS SECTION IN THE REMAINING TIME, BUT DO NOT WORK IN ANY OTHER SECTION UNTIL TOLD TO DO SO.   S T O P

6   6   6   6   6   6   6   6   6   6   6

SECTION 6

Time—15 Minutes
10 Questions

For each problem in this section determine which of the five choices is correct and blacken in that choice on your answer sheet. You may use any blank space on the page for your work.

Notes:

• You may use a calculator whenever you feel it will be helpful.

• Use the diagrams provided to help you solve the problems. Unless you see the words "Note: Figure not drawn to scale" under a diagram, it has been drawn as accurately as possible. Unless it is stated that a figure is three-dimensional, you may assume it lies in a plane.

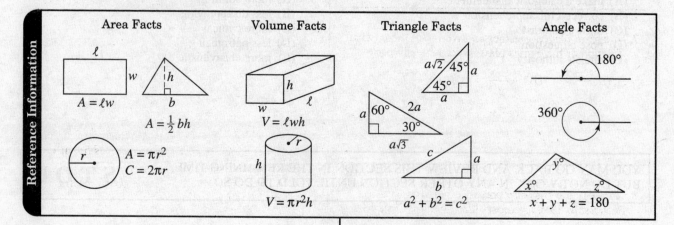

Reference Information

Area Facts
$A = \ell w$
$A = \frac{1}{2} bh$
$A = \pi r^2$
$C = 2\pi r$

Volume Facts
$V = \ell wh$
$V = \pi r^2 h$

Triangle Facts
$a^2 + b^2 = c^2$

Angle Facts
$x + y + z = 180$

---

1. If $a = -2$, what is the value of $a^4 - a^3 + a^2 - a$?

    (A) –30   (B) –10   (C) 0   (D) 10   (E) 30

2. If a mixture of nuts consists of 3 pounds of peanuts, 1 pound of walnuts, and 5 pounds of cashews, by weight, what fraction of the mixture is peanuts?

    (A) $\frac{1}{9}$ (B) $\frac{1}{5}$ (C) $\frac{1}{3}$ (D) $\frac{3}{8}$ (E) $\frac{1}{2}$

3. When a digital clock reads 3:47, the sum of the digits is 14. How many minutes after 3:47 will the sum of the digits be 20 for the first time?

    (A) 42   (B) 132   (C) 192   (D) 251   (E) 301

4. Gilda drove 650 miles at an average speed of 50 miles per hour. How many miles per hour faster would she have had to drive in order for the trip to have taken 1 hour less?

    (A) $6\frac{2}{3}$ (B) $4\frac{2}{3}$ (C) $4\frac{1}{3}$ (D) $4\frac{1}{6}$

    (E) $3\frac{1}{3}$

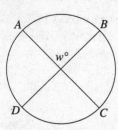

AC and *BD* are diameters.

Note: Figure not drawn to scale

5. In the figure above, if $w = 40$, what is the ratio of the total length of arcs *AB* and *CD* to the circumference?

    (A) $\frac{1}{9}$ (B) $\frac{2}{9}$ (C) $\frac{1}{4}$ (D) $\frac{2}{5}$ (E) $\frac{1}{2}$

GO ON TO THE NEXT PAGE

6   6   6   6   6   6   6   6   6   6   6

6. Phil's Phone Shop sells three models of cellular phones, priced at $100, $125, and $225. In January, Phil sold exactly the same number of each model. What percent of the total income from the sales of cellular phones was attributable to sales of the cheapest model?

(A) $22\frac{2}{9}\%$ (B) $28\frac{4}{7}\%$ (C) $33\frac{1}{3}\%$ (D) $44\frac{4}{9}\%$

(E) It cannot be determined from the information given.

7. If a team played g games and won w of them, what fraction of the games played did the team lose?

(A) $\dfrac{w-g}{w}$ (B) $\dfrac{w-g}{g}$ (C) $\dfrac{g-w}{g}$

(D) $\dfrac{g}{g-w}$ (E) $\dfrac{g-w}{w}$

8. In 1980, the cost of p pounds of potatoes was d dollars. In 1990, the cost of $2p$ pounds of potatoes was $\frac{1}{2}d$ dollars. By what percent did the price of potatoes decrease from 1980 to 1990?

(A) 25%   (B) 50%   (C) 75%   (D) 100%
(E) 400%

9. If a square and an equilateral triangle have equal perimeters, what is the ratio of the area of the triangle to the area of the square?

(A) $\dfrac{4\sqrt{3}}{9}$ (B) $\dfrac{3}{4}$ (C) $\dfrac{1}{1}$ (D) $\dfrac{4}{3}$

(E) It cannot be determined from the information given.

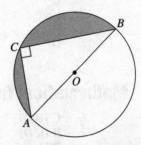

10. In the figure above, AB is a diameter of circle O. If $AC = 6$ and the radius of the circle is 5, what is the perimeter of the shaded region?

(A) $14 + 5\pi$ (B) $17 + 5\pi$ (C) $14 + 10\pi$
(D) $17 + 10\pi$ (E) $24 + 5\pi$

YOU MAY GO BACK AND REVIEW THIS SECTION IN THE REMAINING TIME, BUT DO NOT WORK IN ANY OTHER SECTION UNTIL TOLD TO DO SO.   **S T O P**

Answer Key

Note: The letters in brackets following the Mathematical Reasoning answers refer to the sections of Chapter 12 in which you can find the information you need to answer the questions. For example, **1. C [E]**, means that the answer to question 1 is C, and that the solution requires information found in Section 12-E: Averages.

Section 1 Verbal Reasoning

1.	C	7.	D	13.	B	19.	D	25.	C
2.	E	8.	D	14.	E	20.	D	26.	C
3.	A	9.	D	15.	B	21.	D	27.	C
4.	B	10.	C	16.	C	22.	C	28.	E
5.	C	11.	B	17.	E	23.	C	29.	B
6.	C	12.	D	18.	D	24.	D	30.	C

Section 2 Mathematical Reasoning

1.	E [G]	6.	C [D, H]	11.	A [K]	16.	B [E]	21.	C [E]
2.	E [C]	7.	B [I, D]	12.	D [J]	17.	A [H]	22.	E [A, G]
3.	D [D]	8.	B [J, K]	13.	D [A]	18.	A [A, G]	23.	C [G]
4.	B [A, E]	9.	B [E]	14.	C [G]	19.	A [D]	24.	D [K, L]
5.	A [J]	10.	A [J]	15.	C [I, J]	20.	C [L, N]	25.	D [A, P]

Section 3 Verbal Reasoning

1.	C	8.	A	15.	A	22.	D	29.	D
2.	D	9.	C	16.	C	23.	E	30.	D
3.	C	10.	C	17.	D	24.	B	31.	D
4.	B	11.	C	18.	C	25.	E	32.	C
5.	E	12.	B	19.	C	26.	E	33.	D
6.	D	13.	A	20.	B	27.	D	34.	B
7.	A	14.	A	21.	B	28.	E	35.	A

Section 4 Mathematical Reasoning

Quantitative Comparison Questions

1.	C [A]	4.	B [A]	7.	D [A, B]	10.	D [E]	13.	C [E, G]
2.	C [C]	5.	C [E]	8.	C [C, D]	11.	A [K, L]	14.	C [J, K]
3.	C [G, A]	6.	C [J, K]	9.	B [K]	12.	B [G, A]	15.	C [L]

Grid-in Questions

16. [B] **1**

17. [A] **9**

18. [A, B] **0**

19. [P] **11**

20. [I] **89.9**

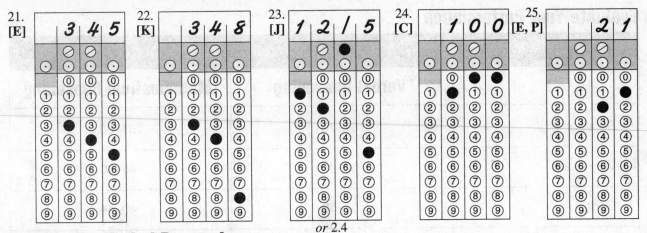

or 2.4

Section 5   Verbal Reasoning

1. **B**	4. **E**	7. **B**	10. **E**	13. **C**
2. **E**	5. **C**	8. **E**	11. **E**	
3. **A**	6. **B**	9. **B**	12. **E**	

Section 6   Mathematical Reasoning

1. **E [A]**	3. **C [P]**	5. **B [L]**	7. **C [B]**	9. **A [J, K]**
2. **C [B]**	4. **D [H]**	6. **A [C]**	8. **C [C, D]**	10. **A [J, L]**

Calculate Your Raw Score

Verbal Reasoning

Section 1 $\dfrac{}{\text{number correct}} - \dfrac{1}{4}\left(\dfrac{}{\text{number incorrect}}\right) = \underline{}$ (A)

Section 3 $\dfrac{}{\text{number correct}} - \dfrac{1}{4}\left(\dfrac{}{\text{number incorrect}}\right) = \underline{}$ (B)

Section 5 $\dfrac{}{\text{number correct}} - \dfrac{1}{4}\left(\dfrac{}{\text{number incorrect}}\right) = \underline{}$ (C)

Raw Verbal Reasoning Score = (A) + (B) + (C) = \underline{}

Mathematical Reasoning

Section 2 $\dfrac{}{\text{number correct}} - \dfrac{1}{4}\left(\dfrac{}{\text{number incorrect}}\right) = \underline{}$ (D)

Section 4
Part I
(1–15) $\dfrac{}{\text{number correct}} - \dfrac{1}{3}\left(\dfrac{}{\text{number incorrect}}\right) = \underline{}$ (E)

Part II
(16–25) $\dfrac{}{\text{number correct}} = \underline{}$ (F)

Section 6 $\dfrac{}{\text{number correct}} - \dfrac{1}{4}\left(\dfrac{}{\text{number incorrect}}\right) = \underline{}$ (G)

Raw Mathematical Reasoning Score = (D) + (E) + (F) + (G) = \underline{}

Evaluate Your Performance

	Verbal Reasoning	Mathematical Reasoning
Superior	67–78	51–60
Very Good	60–66	45–50
Good	52–59	40–44
Satisfactory	44–51	35–39
Average	36–43	30–34
Needs Further Study	29–35	25–29
Needs Intensive Study	21–28	20–24
Inadequate	0–20	0–19

Identify Your Weaknesses

Verbal Reasoning

Question Type	Question Numbers			Chapter to Study
	Section 1	Section 3	Section 5	
Sentence Completion	1, 2, 3, 4, 5, 6, 7, 8, 9	1, 2, 3, 4, 5, 6, 7, 8, 9, 10		Chapter 4
Analogy	10, 11, 12, 13, 14, 15	11, 12, 13, 14, 15, 16, 17, 18, 19, 20, 21, 22, 23		Chapter 5
Reading Comprehension	16, 17, 18, 19, 20, 21, 22, 23, 24, 25, 26, 27, 28, 29, 30	24, 25, 26, 27, 28, 29, 30	1, 2, 3, 4, 5, 6, 7, 8, 9, 10, 11, 12, 13	Chapter 6

Identify Your Weaknesses

Mathematical Reasoning

Skill Area	Question Numbers			Pages to Study
	Section 2	Section 4	Section 6	
Basics of Arithmetic	4, 13, 18, 22, 25	1, 3, 4, 7, 12, 17, 18	1	331–338
Fractions and Decimals		7, 16, 18	2, 7	344–352
Percents	2	2, 8, 24	6, 8	358–361
Ratios	3, 6, 7, 19	8	8	366–370
Averages	4, 9, 16, 21	5, 10, 13, 21, 25		376–378
Polynomials				383–386
Equations and Inequalities	1, 14, 18, 22, 23	3, 12, 13		389–394
Word Problems	6, 17		4	399–402
Lines and Angles	7, 15	20		407–410
Triangles	5, 8, 10, 12, 15	6, 14, 23	9, 10	414–418
Quadrilaterals	8, 11, 24	6, 9, 11, 14, 22	9	425–428
Circles	20, 24	11, 15	5, 10	432–435
Solid Geometry				440–442
Coordinate Geometry	20			446–448
Counting and Probability				452–456
Logical Reasoning	25	19, 25	3	462–464
Data Interpretation				468–471

Answer Explanations

Section 1   Verbal Reasoning

1. C.   The reviewer was vitriolic (as biting as acid), devastating (destructive), and irritating (annoying). He was not *constructive* or helpful. *Never* signals a contrast. The missing word must be an antonym or near-antonym for the three adjectives in the series.
   Note that you are looking for a word with positive associations. Therefore, you can eliminate any word with negative ones. Choices D and E have negative associations. Only Choices A, B, or C can be correct. Choice C is preferable.   (Contrast Signal)

2. E.   The team members *tolerated* or put up with the coach's rules as long as the coach was not too strict in *applying* them.
   Despite signals a contrast. You expect people who resent rules to fight them or disobey them. Instead, the team members put up with them. Remember, in double-blank sentences, go through the answer choices, testing the *first* words in each choice and eliminating those that don't fit. You can immediately eliminate Choices B, C, and D.   (Contrast Signal)

3. A.   If we still cannot make up our minds whether low-level microwave radiation is dangerous or safe, our evidence must be too weak for us to be able to decide; it must be *inconclusive*. Remember, before you look at the choices, read the sentence and think of a word that makes sense.
   Likely Words: incomplete, uncorroborated, unverified.   (Argument Pattern)

4. B.   Tacitus' descriptions were *limited* or hindered by the crude (*primitive*) state of communications.
   But signals a contrast. The fact that Tacitus' descriptions match those of other writers of his time implies that they are reasonable descriptions for that period. They are adequate *in spite of* the limitations they suffered from.   (Contrast Signal)

5. C.   If future archaeological discoveries will be "hard put to match" the revelations of the past ten years, the past decade's discoveries must have been truly remarkable ones, ones that *radically* or fundamentally changed the field. Even *striking* or dramatic discoveries could not compare with such revelations.
               (Argument Pattern)

6. C.   Indian art recalls (*is reminiscent of*) Japanese art because, like Japanese art, it minimizes; it *understates*.

The clause following "Japanese art" gives *examples* of what Japanese art is like: it suggests; it does not state directly or overstate. Look at the first word of each answer pair. If the first word means states directly or overstates, then the second word must mean "is unlike," because it is unlike Japanese art to overstate. If the first word means suggests or understates, then the second word must mean "is like," because it is like Japanese art to understate.   (Examples)

7. D.   If irony has become a way of escape, then its job is to help people escape or *evade* life's terrors.
   Note that the second clause defines what is meant by irony as a *mode of escape*. It clarifies the phrase's meaning.   (Definition)

8. D.   The negotiations have degenerated or deteriorated; they have become *acrimonious* or bitter. The phrase following the blank gives an example of what the sessions are like. They are degenerating into a welter or turmoil of accusations.
   Note that you are looking for a word with negative associations. Therefore, you can eliminate any word with positive ones. Choices A, C, and E all have positive associations. Only Choice B or Choice D can be correct. Choice C, *phlegmatic* (slow and stolid; undemonstrative), is an inappropriate word to describe a wild turmoil of accusations. By process of elimination, the correct answer must be *acrimonious*, Choice D.   (Examples)

9. D.   One would protest a system *deliberately* or intentionally designed to *demean* (degrade or debase) human dignity.
   Choices A, B, and E are incorrect. One would be unlikely to protest a system that reflected, fostered (nourished), or enhanced (improved) human dignity.
   Choice C is also incorrect. *Assess* (evaluate) is inappropriate in the context.   (Definition)

10. C.   A *scrapbook* is a blank book for keeping a collection of *clippings*. An *album* is a blank book for keeping a collection of *stamps*.
               (Part to Whole)

11. B.   An *avalanche* is a sudden great or overwhelming rush of *snow*. A *deluge* is a sudden great or overwhelming rush of *water*.
               (Defining Characteristic)

12. D.   A *ship* that *founders* gives way and sinks. A *building* that *collapses* gives way and falls down.   (Function)

13. **B.**   To *squirm* or wriggle is to show *discomfort* (mental or physical uneasiness). To *fume* or seethe is to show *anger*.
(Action and Its Significance)

14. **E.**   Someone *ruthless* (merciless, pitiless) lacks *sympathy*. Someone *outspoken* (candid, frank, unreserved in speech) lacks *reticence* (reserve, restraint in speaking).   (Antonym Variant)

15. **B.**   A *clique* (narrow, exclusive group of persons) is by definition *exclusive* (inclined to shut others out). A *mob* (rowdy, unruly group) is by definition *disorderly*. (Defining Characteristic)

16. **C.**   In the opening paragraph the writer speaks of the Gothic world in terms of play and extravagance, of the fantastic and the luxurious. In other words, he speaks of it in terms of its *elaborateness of fancy* or fantasy.
Choices A and B are incorrect. They are unsupported by the passage.
Choices D and E are incorrect. They are attributes of the Medieval imagination, not of the Gothic.

17. **E.**   For architecture to reach a point of extravagance unequalled in history is for it to achieve an unparalleled *degree* of lavishness and excess.

18. **D.**   The author has just described the extraordinary degree of wastefulness and excess in the Gothic period. He then notes something somewhat paradoxical. Despite the worldly extravagance of the period, it produced the saintly Francis of Assisi and the religious poet Dante. By citing these two great spirits, the author corrects a potential misapprehension. He thus *refutes the notion that the Gothic period produced nothing but extravagance*.

19. **D.**   The tapestries combine worldly elements (mythological beasts that symbolize lust and ferocity, wild creatures that symbolize fertility) with spiritual ones (the lady who embodies chastity) to express "the power of love."
Choice A is incorrect. It is unsupported by the passage.
Choice B is incorrect. Though the Gothic imagination has a "sharp sense of reality" (lines 14–15), it is more inclined to be playful than to be practical.
Choice C is incorrect. Nothing in the passage suggests that wall hangings are wasteful.
Choice E is incorrect. It is unsupported by the passage.

20. **D.**   The tapestries are known as *The Lady with the Unicorn*. In the central tapestry, the lion and the unicorn kneel before *the lady*, who gently, irresistibly, subdues the forces of nature.

21. **D.**   To draw carts of stones up the hill for the building of Chartres Cathedral is to *haul the stones used to construct the cathedral*. In doing such hard manual labor, the noble knights and ladies showed the depth of their conviction or belief.

22. **C.**   The author's emphasis is on the elephant as an important "creator of habitat" for other creatures.

23. **C.**   To mount an effort to rescue an endangered species is to *launch* or initiate a campaign.

24. **D.**   The elephant is the architect of its environment in that it *physically alters its environment*, transforming the landscape around it.

25. **C.**   The author states that it is the elephant's metabolism and appetite—in other words, its voracity or *ravenous hunger*—that leads to its creating open spaces in the woodland and transforming the landscape.

26. **C.**   In this excerpt from a newspaper article, the author objectively reports the effect of the decline in the elephant population on other species that inhabit the savanna. His style can best be described as *reportorial*.

27. **C.**   Since the foraging of elephants creates a varied landscape that attracts a diverse group of plant-eating animals and since the presence of these plant-eaters in turn attracts carnivores, it follows that elephants *have an indirect effect on the hunting patterns of carnivores*.

28. **E.**   You can arrive at the correct answer choice through the process of elimination.
Question I is answerable on the basis of the passage. The elephant's foraging opens up its surroundings by knocking down trees and stripping off branches. Therefore, you can eliminate Choices B and D.
Question II is answerable on the basis of the passage. Gazelles are grazers; giraffes are browsers. Therefore, you can eliminate Choice A.
Question III is answerable on the basis of the passage. The concluding sentence states that when elephants disappear the forest reverts. Therefore, you can eliminate Choice C.
Only Choice E is left. It is the correct answer.

29. **B.**   The author is listing the many species that depend on the elephant as a creator of habitat. Thus, the host of smaller animals is the *very large number* of these creatures that thrive in the elephant's wake.

30. **C.** The author is in favor of the effect of elephants on the environment; he feels an accidental or *fortuitous result* of their foraging is that it allows a greater variety of creatures to exist in mixed-growth environments.

Section 2 Mathematical Reasoning

In each mathematics section, for many problems, an alternative solution, indicated by two asterisks (**), follows the first solution. When this occurs, one of the solutions is the direct mathematical one and the other is based on one of the tactics discussed in Chapters 8–12.

1. **E.** $a - 5 = 0 \Rightarrow a = 5 \Rightarrow a + 5 = \mathbf{10}$.

2. **E.** Use your calculator *only* if you don't realize that $50\% = \dfrac{1}{2}$. Otherwise, just say $\dfrac{1}{2}$ of 50 is 25, and $\dfrac{1}{2}$ of 25 is **12.5**.

3. **D.** Going at $\dfrac{1}{3}$ of Mary's speed, John took 3 times as long: $3 \times 30 = \mathbf{90}$.

4. **B.** The average of x and y is $\dfrac{x+y}{2}$, and the product of that fraction and 5 is
$$5\left(\frac{x+y}{2}\right) = \frac{5x + 5y}{2}.$$

   **It's easier and quicker to do this directly, so substitute for x and y only if you get stuck or confused. If $x = 2$ and $y = 4$, their average is 3; and the product of 5 and 3 is 15. Only $\dfrac{5x + 5y}{2}$ is equal to 15 when $x = 2$ and $y = 4$.

5. **A.** Since $x + 100 = 180$, $x = 80$; also,
$$180 = y + x + x = y + 80 + 80 = y + 160$$
$$\Rightarrow y = \mathbf{20}.$$

6. **C.** In 1 minute light will travel
$$(300{,}000 \text{ km/sec})(60 \text{ sec}) =$$
$$18{,}000{,}000 \text{ kilometers.}$$
Therefore, light will travel 150,000,000 kilometers in $\dfrac{150{,}\cancel{000}{,}\cancel{000}}{18{,}\cancel{000}{,}\cancel{000}} = 8\dfrac{1}{3}$ minutes.

7. **B.** Every hour the hour hand moves through 30° $\left(\dfrac{1}{12} \text{ of } 360°\right)$. It will move through 10° in $\dfrac{1}{3}$ hour, or 20 minutes; and 20 minutes after 1:15 the time is **1:35**.

8. **B.** Draw a square, and let the sides be 1. Then, by KEY FACTS J8 and J10, the diagonal, d, is $\sqrt{2}$, and $d^2 = 2$. Since the area of the square is 1, d^2 is **twice the area of the square.**

   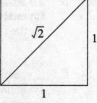

   **By KEY FACT K8, the area of a square = $\dfrac{d^2}{2}$.

9. **B.** Since the average of a, b, c, and d is 10, their sum is 40. The only other condition is that they be in increasing order. The numbers could be 1, 2, 3, and 34, in which case both I and III are false. This guarantees that the answer is **II only**, but let's just verify that II is true: in any set of numbers that are not all equal, the smallest number in the set is less than the average of the numbers, and the greatest number is more than their average.

10. **A.** Use TACTIC 8-1: Draw a diagram, and label all the line segments. Now add two segments to create a right triangle. Since the legs are 6 and 8, the hypotenuse is **10**.

    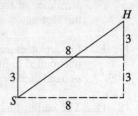

    **Use TACTIC 9-4: eliminate the absurd choices and guess. The woman rode 14 miles. Clearly, the direct path is shorter; eliminate C, D, and E. Since it's probably *much* shorter, eliminate B, as well.

11. **A.** Since the area of the square is 25, its sides are 5, and its perimeter is 20. Since the perimeter of the pentagon is also 20, each of its sides is **4**.

    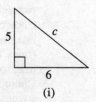

12. **D.** Either (i) 5 and 6 are the lengths of the two legs, or (ii) 5 is the length of a leg, and 6 is the hypotenuse. In either case use the Pythagorean theorem:

    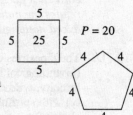

    (i) $5^2 + 6^2 = c^2 \Rightarrow$
    $c^2 = 61 \Rightarrow c = \sqrt{61}$;
    or
    (ii) $a^2 + 5^2 = 6^2 \Rightarrow$
    $a^2 = 36 - 25 = 11 \Rightarrow a = \sqrt{11}.$

    Statements **I and II only** are true.

13. **D.** By definition, 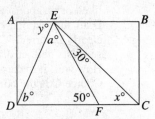 $= (5)(3)(2) - (5 + 3 + 2)$
    $= 30 - 10 = \textbf{20}$.

14. **C.** Check each choice to see which equation has *exactly one positive integer solution*.

    I. For *every* number a: $(0)(a)(-a) = 0$ and
        $0 + a + (-a) = 0$, so for *every* positive integer a,

        $= 0 - 0 = 0$. (I is false.)

    II. $= 0 \Rightarrow a^3 - 3a = 0 \Rightarrow a^3 = 3a$. We're
        looking for *positive* solutions, so assume
        $a \neq 0$, and divide by a: $a^2 = 3 \Rightarrow a = \pm \sqrt{3}$.
        But $\sqrt{3}$ is not an integer. (II is false.)

    III. $= 0 \Rightarrow 6a^3 - 6a = 0 \Rightarrow 6a^3 = 6a \Rightarrow$
        $a^2 = 1$. This equation has *one* positive integer
        solution, $a = 1$. (III is true.)

    Statement **III only** is true.

15. **C.** There are many ways to get the values of x and y; here's the easiest. Since $\angle EFD$ is an exterior angle of $\triangle FEC$, $50 = 30 + x \Rightarrow x = 20$ (KEY FACT J2). Since $DF = EF$, then $a = b$ and

    $$a + b + 50 = 180 \Rightarrow a + b = 130,$$

    so a and b are 65 each. But since the opposite sides of a rectangle are parallel, $b = y$, so $y = 65$ and $x + y = 20 + 65 = \textbf{85}$.

16. **B.** It's possible to reason the answer out without writing down and adding up all the numbers, but it won't save any time. Systematically list them: 123, 132, 213, 231, 312, 321. Use your calculator: the sum is 1332, and the average is $1332 \div 6 = \textbf{222}$.

17. **A.** Organize the data in a table. Assume Aaron was 4 times as old as Sarah after x years and 3 times as old after y years.

Time	Aaron's Age	Sarah's Age
When Sarah was born	24	0
x years later	$24 + x$	x
y years later	$24 + y$	y

$24 + x = 4x \Rightarrow 3x = 24 \Rightarrow x = 8$;
$24 + y = 3y \Rightarrow 2y = 24 \Rightarrow y = 12$.
Aaron was 4 times as old as Sarah **4** years ago. (They are now 36 and 12; 4 years ago they were 32 and 8.)

**To avoid the algebra, you can just use trial and error. In less time than it takes to explain it, you can make a little table:

Years from now	3	6	8	10	12
Aaron's age	27	30	32	34	36
Sarah's age	3	6	8	10	12

After 3 years, Aaron's 9 times as old; after 6 years he's 5 times as old; and so on.

18. **A.** Check each of the three statements:
    (I) $3 \# (-3)$ is true if $3 - 3 > -3 + 3$. Is it?
         Is $0 > 0$? No, I is false.
    (II) $10 \# 5$ is true if $10 - 3 > 5 + 3$. Is it?
          Is $7 > 8$? No, II is false.
    (III) $7c \# c$ is true if $7c - 3 > c + 3$. Is it?
          Only if $6c > c$, which is true only if c is
          positive, but not if c is 0 or negative. III
          is false.

    None of the statements is true.

19. **A.** Write the equation from the definition given:
    $$\text{density} = \frac{\text{population}}{\text{area}}.$$ Then, if the population is p,
    $$d = \frac{p}{\ell w} \Rightarrow p = \textbf{d\ell w}.$$

    **Use TACTIC 9-2: replace the letters with easy-to-use numbers. Let $\ell = 2$ and $w = 3$. Then the area is 6; and if the population is 60, the density is 10 people per square mile. Only $d\ell w$ equals 60 when $\ell = 2$, $w = 3$, and $d = 10$.

20. **C.** Use TACTIC 8-1: Draw a diagram. Since the distance between $(-4,1)$ and $(2,1)$ is 6, the diameter of the circle is 6 and the radius is 3. Then the area is $\pi(3)^2 = \textbf{9}\boldsymbol{\pi}$.

    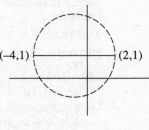

21. **C.** This question calls for a weighted average. The students in the first-period class earned a total of $24 \times 78 = 1872$ points, and the students in the second-period class earned $26 \times 83 = 2158$ points. In total, the 50 students earned $1872 + 2158 = 4030$ points, so their average was
    $$\frac{4030}{50} = \textbf{80.6}.$$

    The average of 78 and 83 is 80.5. However, since the group of students averaging 83 is *slightly* larger than the group with the 78 average, the average must be *slightly* greater than 80.5. Eliminate A and B and guess. There's no guarantee, but certainly, **80.6 is *slightly* greater than 80.5.

22. **E.** If x is even, then every multiple of x is even and x^n is even for any positive integer n. So, x, $2x$, $3x$, $5x$, x^2, $3x^2$, and x^3 are all even. Finally, the sum of any two even numbers is even, and the sum of an even number and an odd number is odd. Therefore, choices A–D are all true. Choice E is the product of two odd numbers and so is odd.

    **Use TACTIC 9-2 and replace x with a simple even number, such as 2. Then evaluate each of the choices to see which one is not true. When $x = 2$, $(3x - 5)(5x - 3) = (1)(7) = 7$, which is odd. Choice E is not true.

23. **C.** 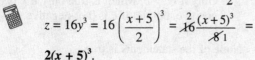 $x = 2y - 5 \Rightarrow 2y = x + 5 \Rightarrow y = \dfrac{x+5}{2}$, so

    $$z = 16y^3 = 16\left(\frac{x+5}{2}\right)^3 = \cancel{16}^{2}\frac{(x+5)^3}{\cancel{8}^{1}} =$$

    $2(x + 5)^3$.

    Use TACTIC 9-2: replace the letters with numbers. Let $y = 2$; then $x = -1$ and $z = 16(2)^3 = 16(8) = 128$. Which of the five choices equals 128 when $x = -1$? Only **$2(x + 5)^3$.

24. **D.** The length of the rectangle is clearly 20, the length of two diameters. The width of the rectangle is $10 + h$, where h is the

    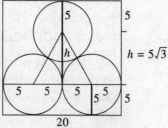

    height of the equilateral triangle formed by joining the centers of the three circles. Since the sides of that triangle are 10, the height is $5\sqrt{3}$ (KEY FACT J11). Then the width is $10 + 5\sqrt{3}$ and the area is $20(10 + 5\sqrt{3}) =$

    $200 + 100 + \sqrt{3}$.

    **Use TACTIC 8-2: trust the diagram. Clearly, the length is 20, and the width is much more than 10, but less than 20. You should even see that the width must be more than 15, so the area is between 300 and 400.

25. **D.** Let B be the sum of all the positive odd integers less than 1000.

    $$A = 2 + 4 + 6 + 8 + \cdots + 996 + 998$$
    $$\downarrow \; \downarrow \; \downarrow \; \downarrow \qquad\quad \downarrow \qquad \downarrow$$
    $$B = (1 + 3 + 5 + 7 + \cdots + 995 + 997) + 999$$

    A is the sum of 499 even integers, each of which is 1 more than the corresponding odd integer in B. Then $(1 + 3 + 5 + \cdots + 997) = A - 499$, and $B = (A - 499) + 999 = A + 500$.

Section 3   Verbal Reasoning

1. **C.** The sentence implies that Polynesian banquets are usually reputed to be good. The speaker was disappointed by the banquet. Two possibilities exist: either this banquet was a poor one, or the banquets in general are *overrated* (too highly valued).
   Note how the "either...or" structure sets up a contrast between the two clauses.
   (Contrast Signal)

2. **D.** If something falls into decay or disintegrates, by definition it must be *perishable* or subject to decay.　　　　(Cause and Effect)

3. **C.** Since Lee avoided or refrained from excesses, Grant, his opposite, must have *indulged in* or satisfied his taste for excesses.
   The key words in this sentence are "differed markedly." They set up the contrast between the two men.
   Note that you are looking for a word that suggests Grant enjoyed drinking. Therefore, you can eliminate any word that suggests he disliked or disapproved of it. Choices A, B, and D all suggest dislike or disapproval. They are clearly incorrect. Choice E, *compensated for*, suggests neither disapproval nor dislike. However, it makes no sense in the context. Choice C is the correct answer.
   (Contrast Pattern)

4. **B.** The librarian has the committee's *acquiescence* or agreement; they assent but do not go so far as to encourage or spur on the librarian. Their support is of a lesser degree.
   Note how the "with the...if not the" structure signals that the missing word and the noun *encouragement* must differ in meaning to some degree.
   Remember, before you look at the choices, read the sentence and think of a word that makes sense.
   Likely Words: agreement, permission, consent, approval

5. **E.** An *endorsement* is a testimonial or statement recommending a product for its *virtues* or good qualities.
   Beware Eye-Catchers. Choice A is incorrect. Though products have trademarks, trademarks are not statements of a product's contents; they are names or logos manufacturers use to identify their products.　　　(Definition)

6. **D.** Someone given to starting casual conversations with total strangers is by definition *gregarious* or sociable.　　　(Definition)

7. **A.** With no enemies to stop their spread, the deer must have done well or *thrived*. They

did so well that they "overgrazed" or ate too much grass. This *threatened* (was bad for) the vegetation.

Note how the "to such a degree…that" structure signals cause and effect.

Remember, in double-blank sentences, go through the answer choices, testing the *first* words in each choice and eliminating those that don't fit. You can immediately eliminate Choices C and E. (Cause & Effect Signal)

8. A. His friends could not understand his outburst because he was usually dutiful (*docile*) and helpful (*accommodating*).

Remember, watch for signal words that link one part of the sentence to another. The presence of *and* linking items in a series indicates that the missing word may be a synonym or near-synonym for the other linked words. In this case, *docile* and *accommodating* are near-synonyms. (Support Signal)

9. C. To be No. 1 at the box office, a film must attract or draw a large audience. That attests to its star's *drawing* power, particularly if the film didn't receive especially good reviews.

To say that the film's reviews were *modest* at best is *not* high praise. It indicates that even the best of the reviews were lukewarm or middling. (Contrast Pattern)

10. C. Looking down on the demonstrators (viewing them "with little respect"), the police would most likely talk about them in negative or *pejorative* terms. (Definition)

11. C. Applying the *brake* slows or stops an *automobile*. Pulling on the *reins* slows or stops a *horse*. (Function)

12. B. *Area* measures the size of a *square*. *Volume* measures the size of a *cube*. (Defining Characteristic)

13. A. *Colleagues* (professional associates) share a common *profession*. *Kinsfolk* (relatives) share a common *family*. (Defining Characteristic)

14. A. A *termite* feeds on (and eats away) *wood*. In its larval stage, a *moth* feeds on (and eats away) *wool*.

Beware Eye-Catchers: Choice B is incorrect. A silkworm makes silk; it does not feed on it. (Function)

15. A. A *tally* is a recorded account of *votes*. A *census* is a recorded account of *population*.

Beware Eye-Catchers: Choice E is incorrect. An election is a choice among candidates; it is not a recorded account of candidates. (Definition)

16. C. A *cease-fire* is a temporary pause in *hostilities* (acts of warfare). A *lull* is a temporary pause in a *storm*. (Defining Characteristic)

17. D. *Usury* (exorbitant interest) is an excessive or extreme form of *interest*. *Parsimony* (miserliness; excessive thrift) is an excessive or extreme form of *frugality* (economy; thrift).

Use the process of elimination to improve your guessing odds. The word pairs in Choices A, B, and C are all antonyms. Since they all belong to the same analogy type, none of the three can be the correct answer. Eliminate all three. (Degree of Intensity)

18. C. The *spine* (back or bound edge) forms the axis of a *book*. The *backbone* (spinal column) forms the axis of a *skeleton*.

Beware Eye-Catchers: Choice D is incorrect. A newspaper is made up of many columns; a book has only one spine. (Function)

19. C. *Cacophony* (harsh discordant sound) is distasteful to the *ear*. A *stench* (foul smell) is distasteful to the *nose*.

Remember, if more than one answer appears to fit the relationship in your sentence, look for a narrower approach. "Cacophony is perceived by the ear" is too general a framework. It would fit both Choice A and Choice C. (Defining Characteristic)

20. B. A *eulogy* is an expression of *praise*. A *slander* (statement damaging someone's reputation) is an expression of *disparagement* (depreciation, scorn).

Beware Eye-Catchers: Choice A is incorrect. An elegy is an expression of sorrow over a death. It is not an expression of death. (Definition)

21. B. To *outfox* someone is to surpass that person in *cunning*; to *outstrip* someone is to surpass that person in *speed*. (Defining Characteristic)

22. D. Ancient *bronze* works are coated with a greenish rust called *patina*. Exposed *iron* also becomes coated with *rust*. (Defining Characteristic)

23. E. To *embroil* someone is to involve her in conflict or *strife*. To *imperil* someone is to involve her in peril or *danger*. (Defining Characteristic)

24. B. The author describes his rapture or great joy when he first saw his new owner's smiling face. Clearly, his immediate response to the prospect of living with the Aulds was chiefly one of *marked* (distinct) *pleasure*.

25. E. Lines 21–22 state that "by constant application to her business, (Mrs. Auld) had been in a good degree preserved from the blighting and dehumanizing effects of slavery." Mrs. Auld has applied herself to her business or trade of weaving. She has *concentrated on this trade*. Because she has not owned slaves but has kept herself busy with her own work, she has been relatively unaffected by slavery and has not adopted the inhumane attitudes typical of slave owners.

26. E. The sentences immediately following Douglass's comment about his early instruction clarify what he had been taught. He had been taught to behave in a slavish, *obsequious* fashion. However, "her favor was not gained by (crouching servility); she seemed to be disturbed by it" (lines 29–30). In other words, the *obsequiousness in which he had been drilled distressed his new mistress*.

27. D. Fawning and cringing did not *serve* the purpose of pleasing Mrs. Auld; such slavish behavior did not do at all in this particular situation.

28. E. According to Douglass, at the time he met her Mrs. Auld was a kind, loving woman who had not yet had the experience of owning slaves. Thus, she had been kept free of "the blighting and dehumanizing effects of slavery" (lines 23–24). However, she now owned a slave—Douglass himself—and would inevitably be affected by her power over him. Her kind heart would cease to be kind: she *was destined to undergo a change of character* as she became corrupted by her participation in the institution of slavery.

29. D. The passage does not suggest that a *disdain* or scorn for convention is typical of Mrs. Auld. Therefore, Choice D is correct.
     Mrs. Auld was noted for "constant application to her business" (lines 21–22). This implies that *diligence in labor* was one of her characteristics. Therefore, Choice A is incorrect.
     Mrs. Auld seemed "disturbed" by "crouching servility" (lines 26–27). This implies that a *dislike of fawning* was one of her characteristics. Therefore, Choice B is incorrect.
     Mrs. Auld was kindhearted (lines 16–17) and able to put people at ease (lines 32–33). This implies that *gentleness of spirit* was one of her characteristics. Therefore, Choice C is incorrect.
     Mrs. Auld voluntarily began to teach the narrator. She wished him well. This implies that a *benevolent nature* was one of her characteristics. Therefore, Choice E is incorrect.

30. D. Choice D is correct. You can arrive at it by the process of elimination.

Statement I is true. In line 45 Mr. Auld tells his wife that instructing slaves is unlawful: it *violates the law*. Therefore, you can eliminate Choice B.
Statement II is untrue. Since Mr. Auld is so concerned that education would spoil his slaves, he must believe that slaves *can* be taught. Therefore, you can eliminate Choices C and E.
Statement III is true. Mr. Auld states that a slave who was able to read would become "unmanageable" (line 54). Therefore, you can eliminate Choice A.
Only Choice D is left. It is the correct answer.

31. D. Mr. Auld is arguing that Mrs. Auld should not give Douglass reading lessons. To convince her, he cites a variant of the proverb "If you give him an inch, he'll take a mile." (In other words, he'll take a lot *more* than you originally planned to give him.) A mile is a much larger unit of length than an inch. We can assume that *an ell is a much larger unit of length than an inch*, also.

32. C. The author's purpose in this passage is to show how he discovered that learning to read was vital for him if he wanted to be free. The bulk of the passage deals with learning to read—the author's introduction to it, his master's arguments against it, his own increased determination to succeed in it.
     Choice A is incorrect. It is the cause of their disagreement that is central, not the existence of their disagreement.
     Choice B is incorrect. The author lists, but does not analyze, the master's reasons for forbidding his wife to teach her slave.
     Choice D is incorrect. It is unsupported by the passage.
     Choice E might seem a possible answer, but it is too narrow in scope. Only the last two sentences of the first paragraph stress Mrs. Auld's moral downfall.

33. D. Douglass states that his master "was deeply sensible of the truths he was uttering." In other words, his master was highly *conscious* that he was saying the truth; he felt sure that only evil consequences would come from teaching a slave to read.

34. B. The author's tone is strongly ironic. He knows full well that, in opposing his education, his master did not intend to *benefit* him. Thus, by acknowledging his "debt" to his master, the author is underlining his master's defeat.
     Choice A is incorrect. The author is not filled with loving sentiment and warmth when he thinks of his harsh master.

Choice C is incorrect. The author neither whines nor congratulates himself on his own moral superiority.
Choice D is incorrect. The author is not resigned or submissive; he certainly is not wistful or longing for the days gone by.
Choice E is incorrect. Although the author still feels anger at the institution of slavery, when he thinks of his master's defeat he feels triumphant as well.

35. **A.** The author wholly believes his master's statement that learning would make him unmanageable. In other words, education would make him *impossible to enslave.*
Choice B is incorrect. The author is concerned with education for freedom, not for old age.
Choices C, D, and E are incorrect. They are unsupported by the passage.

Section 4   Mathematical Reasoning
Quantitative Comparison Questions

1. **C.** Column A: $[(-1) + (-1)^2]^2 = [(-1) + 1]^2 = [0]^2 = 0$. The columns are equal (C).

2. **C.** Column A: 60% of $3a = .60 \times 3a = 1.8a$.
Column B: 30% of $6a = .30 \times 6a = 1.8a$.
The columns are equal (C).
**Although it is irrelevant that a is negative, if you use TACTIC 10-1, just pick an easy-to-use negative number. This is a percent problem, so choose -100 and in your head or with a calculator take 60% of -300 and 30% of -600.

3. **C.** Cross-multiply: $\frac{1}{3}x = 3x$. If a and b are unequal, the *only way* that ax can equal bx is if $x = 0$. The columns are equal (C).
**Use TACTIC 10-4. Could $x = 0$? Yes: $0 \div 3$ and $0 \div \frac{1}{3}$ are both equal to 0. Eliminate A and B. Must $x = 0$. Yes: a linear equation can have only one solution.

4. **B.** Clearly, the distance between a and b is greater than 5; and since $a < b$, then $b - a > 5$. Therefore, $a - b < -5$. Column B is greater.
**Use TACTIC 10-1: pick values for a and b. If $a = -1$ and $b = 6$, then $a - b = -7$, which is less than -5.

5. **C.** Column A: $\frac{4x + 7x + 100}{3} = \frac{11x + 100}{3}$.
Column B: $\frac{x + 10x + 100}{3} = \frac{11x + 100}{3}$.
The columns are equal (C).
**Pick any number for x, and calculate the average in each column.

6. **C.** Of course, side AC of the rectangle is equal to side AC of the triangle, and $DE = AC = BC$. Therefore, the sum of the two widths, $AD + EC$, equals AB, the third side of the triangle. Then $AB = AD + EC = 2EC$. The columns are equal (C).
**Pick a value for AC, say 10. Then the perimeters of both the triangle and the rectangle are 30. Since AC and DE are 10, their sum is 20, and the other 10 comes from the two widths, which must be 5 each.

7. **D.** Could $\frac{a}{b} = 1$? Sure, if $a = b = 0.5$. Must they be equal? No, not if $a = 1$ and $b = 0.5$. Neither column is *always* greater, and the columns are not *always* equal (D).

8. **C.** Let the numbers of male and female employees be $3x$ and $2x$, respectively. Then Column A = $20\%(3x) = 0.6x$ and Column B = $30\%(2x) = 0.6x$. The columns are equal (C).
**Do the same thing, except use a number. Assume there are 300 men and 200 women, and calculate.

9. **B.** If the side of a square is 10, its diagonal is $10\sqrt{2} \approx 14$ (KEY FACTS J8 and J9). The square in Column B is greater.
**The area of the square in Column A is $10^2 = 100$. The area of the square in Column B is $\frac{1}{2}15^2 = \frac{1}{2}(225) = 112.5$.

10. **D.** Let $a = 1$. Then Column A = 3 (the average of 2 and 4), whereas Column B = 4 (the average of 3 and 5). Eliminate A and C. Let $a = 2$. Now, Column A = 5 (the average of 4 and 6), and Column B is still 4. Eliminate B. Neither column is *always* greater, and the columns are not *always* equal (D).

11. **A.** Let the radius of the circle be 1. Then the area of the circle is π. Since the area of the square is also π, each side of the square is $\sqrt{\pi}$. Then the perimeter of the square is $4\sqrt{\pi}$, and the circumference of the circle is 2π. Which is greater $4\sqrt{\pi}$ or 2π? Use your calculator; the answer is $4\sqrt{\pi}$. Column A is greater.

12. **B.** You don't *have to* solve for a and b. If $a - b > a + b$, then b is negative, and Column B is greater.
**You *could* solve. Adding the two equations yields
$$2a = 49 \Rightarrow a = 24.5 \Rightarrow b = -0.5.$$

13. C. $\dfrac{a-b}{c-a} = 1 \Rightarrow a - b = c - a \Rightarrow 2a =$

$b + c \Rightarrow a = \dfrac{b+c}{2}$. The columns are equal.

**Since you have an equation with three variables, pick values for two of them and find the third. Let $a = 2$ and $b = 1$.

Then $\dfrac{2-1}{c-2} = 1 \Rightarrow c = 3$. The average of b and c is 2, which equals a.

14. C.   Draw diagrams. The triangles in the two columns have the same base, AB, and the same height, BC, the distance between the two parallel sides.

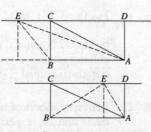

The areas of $\triangle ABC$ and $\triangle ABE$ are equal. The columns are equal (C).

15. **(C)** Since the entire region is a circle of radius 4, its area is $\pi(4)^2 = 16\pi$. The white region is a circle of radius 3 minus the small, shaded circle of radius 1, so its area is $9\pi - \pi = 8\pi$. Therefore, the area of the white region is one-half of the total area, and the area of the shaded region is the other half. The columns are equal (C).

Grid-in Questions

16. (1) $\dfrac{1}{5} + \dfrac{2}{10} + \dfrac{3}{15} + \dfrac{4}{20} + \dfrac{5}{25} =$

$\dfrac{1}{5} + \dfrac{1}{5} + \dfrac{1}{5} + \dfrac{1}{5} + \dfrac{1}{5} = \dfrac{5}{5} = \mathbf{1}$.

17. (9) $ab = 20$ and $a = -5 \Rightarrow -5b = 20 \Rightarrow b = -4$, so
$a^2 - b^2 = 25 - 16 = \mathbf{9}$.

18. (0)   If $a \neq b$ and $ax = bx$, then x must be 0. Therefore
$\dfrac{2}{3}x = \dfrac{3}{4}x \Rightarrow x = 0 \Rightarrow \dfrac{4}{5}x = \mathbf{0}$.

19. (11)   Between 12:10 A.M. and 2:40 P.M., for example, the clock chimes once every 15 minutes, beginning at 12:15 and continuing to 2:30, except twice at 2:00: a total of **11** times.

20. (89.9)   Since $y > x$, then y must be greater than 90 and x less than 90. The largest number less than 90 that can fit in the grid is **89.9**.

21. (345)   Since the average amount of savings for the 10 students is $60, the total amount they have all saved is $600 (TACTIC E1). John has $130, and 3 students have no savings at all. If 5 other students have $125 total ($25 each, the least possible), then the tenth student will have $600 − $130 − $125 = **$345**.

22. (348)   You don't need to add up the lengths of the steps. Together, all the horizontal steps are equal to the bottom, and all the vertical risers are equal to the left side. The sum of the left side, 5 feet 4 inches, or 64 inches, and the bottom, 9 feet 2 inches, or 110 inches, is half the perimeter. The perimeter is $2(64 + 110) = 2(174) = \mathbf{348}$.
**Of course, if you don't see this, you can add everything. For the sum of the lengths of the steps, you could use the formula for adding up an arithmetic sequence, but don't: just reach for your calculator.

23. $\left(\dfrac{12}{5} \text{ or } 2.4\right)$ Since the area of a right triangle is $\dfrac{1}{2}$ the product of its legs, the area is $\dfrac{1}{2}(3)(4) = 6$.

But the area can also be calculated as $\dfrac{1}{2}bh$. Since this is a 3-4-5 triangle, the base is 5, so
$6 = \dfrac{1}{2}(5)h \Rightarrow 5h = 12 \Rightarrow h = \dfrac{12}{5}$ or **2.4**.

**There are *several* other ways to get this answer if you know more than the basic geometry required for the SAT I. For example, the little triangle on the left in the figure is similar to the large one, and the ratio of the hypotenuse of the small triangle to the hypotenuse of the large triangle is 3:5. Then, $3:5 = h: 4 \Rightarrow h = \mathbf{2.4}$.

24. (100) $c = a\%$ of $a\%$ of $b = \dfrac{a}{100} \times \dfrac{a}{100} \times b =$

$\dfrac{a^2 b}{10,000}$, and $kc = a^2\%$ of $b = \dfrac{a^2}{100}b$. Then

$\dfrac{a^2 b}{100} = kc = k\dfrac{a^2 b}{10,000} \Rightarrow \dfrac{1}{100} = \dfrac{k}{10,000} \Rightarrow$
$100k = 10,000 \Rightarrow k = \mathbf{100}$.
**Use TACTIC 11-2: replace the variables with numbers. If $a = 10$ and $b = 100$, 10% of (10% of 100) = 10% of 10 = 1, so $c = 1$; but $(10)^2\%$ of 100 = 100% of 100 = 100. Then $kc = 100 \Rightarrow k = \mathbf{100}$.

25. (21)   Since the average of the three digits is 2, the sum of the digits is 6. The simplest thing is to list them. If there are only a few, list them all; if it seems that there will be too many to list, look for a pattern. The list starts this way: 105, 114, 123, 132, 141, 150, so there are 6 positive three-digit numbers in the 100's. Continue: 204, 213, 222, 231, 240; there are 5 in the 200's. You can conclude, correctly, that there are 4 in the 300's, 3 in the 400's, 2 in the 500's, and 1 in the 600's. The total is $6 + 5 + 4 + 3 + 2 + 1 = \mathbf{21}$. If you don't spot the pattern, just continue the list: 303, 312, ... , 501, 510, 600.

Section 5   Verbal Reasoning

1. **B.** The energy of American life springs or *arises* from various factors.
   Remember, when answering a vocabulary-in-context question, test each answer choice, substituting it in the sentence for the word in quotes.

2. **E.** Use the process of elimination to answer this question.
   Choice A is incorrect. The lover of business is *enthusiastic*; he applies zeal or enthusiasm to the task at hand.
   Choice B is incorrect. The lover of business is *engrossed* in his work because of its "absorbing, satisfying character" (lines 35–36).
   Choice C is incorrect. The lover of business is *enterprising*, industriously devoting himself to making the business "greater and better organized" (line 27).
   Choice D is incorrect. The lover of business is *industrious*; he applies himself to the task at hand with "zeal and intensity" (line 31).
   Only Choice E is left. It is the correct answer. The lover of business is *not* ruled by the love of money or material advantages. He is clearly not *mercenary*.

3. **A.** Lines 25–28 plainly state that American lovers of business find joy or pleasure in making businesses greater and better organized. Thus, Americans clearly must find the prospect of improving business organizations *pleasurable*.

4. **E.** The word *engine* here is used metaphorically to indicate a *driving force* in society. The lover of business wants his organization to be a powerful force in the world.

5. **C.** The concluding sentence of Passage 1 states that "in beginning life in a society (that) has developed a native and vital tradition" of business, young people will come to "realize a part of what (they) are living for." In other words, they will be influenced to *find self-fulfillment* or self-realization *through their business activities*.

6. **B.** The author states that technological advances have wiped out cultural differences so thoroughly that the time may come when "it will be impossible to distinguish human beings living on one area of the earth's surface from those living on any other." In other words, he asserts that these advances *may eventually lead to worldwide cultural sameness or uniformity*.

7. **B.** A striking difference is *marked* or noticeable; it immediately strikes the eye.

8. **E.** To take something for granted is to accept it without question or objection, in other words, to *assume* it.

9. **B.** If a man made less money than his father did, Americans assumed the fault was his. His failure to surpass his father in income was proof that he had not worked hard enough ("was lazy") or had not worked effectively ("was...inefficient"). In other words, he had not *applied himself properly* to the task.

10. **E.** Rather than enjoy his inherited wealth, the *rentier* is "doomed" to a life of drunkenness or psychoanalysis. Clearly, the author feels no sympathy for the sufferings of this poor little rich man. Instead, he views the *rentier* with objectively sardonic *irony*.

11. **E.** Use the process of elimination to answer this question.
    Choice A is incorrect. The assertion "In no society in history have rich men given away so large a part of their fortunes" is a *categorical statement*.
    Choice B is incorrect. The author *corrects a misapprehension* about how profitable slave labor was to Southern slave owners.
    Choice C is incorrect. Throughout the passage the author *contrasts* the European and American attitudes toward money.
    Choice D is incorrect. In the passage's final sentence, the author *poses a question*.
    Only Choice E is left. It is the correct answer. Throughout the passage, the author never refers to or *cites an authority*.

12. **E.** The author of Passage 1 asserts that American men engage in business for the sheer love of business activities. The author of Passage 2 asserts they do so out of a sense of Oedipal rivalry with their fathers. However, both authors would agree that Americans engage in business *for psychological rather than financial reasons*.

13. **C.** The author of Passage 1 is making a commencement address to students about to graduate from an American college. Appropriately enough, he addresses them positively, expressing an optimistic view of American traditions and society. The British author of Passage 2, however, has a far *more cynical* view of Americans, who are (in his opinion) far less rational than their European counterparts.

Section 6   Mathematical Reasoning

1. **E.**   *Be careful* with the minus signs and the negatives:
$$(-2)^4 - (-2)^3 + (-2)^2 - (-2) =$$
$$16 - (-8) + 4 - (-2) = 16 + 8 + 4 + 2 = \mathbf{30}.$$

2. **C.**   The weight of the mixture is $9\,(3 + 1 + 5)$ pounds, of which 3 pounds are peanuts.
Hence, the desired fraction is $\dfrac{3}{9} = \dfrac{1}{3}$.

3. **C.**   The largest possible sum of the digits for the minutes is 14, when it is 59 minutes after the hour. Therefore, the first time that the sum of all the digits can be 20 occurs when the hour is 6: at 6:59 we have $6 + 5 + 9 = 20$. Since 6:59 is 3 hours and 12 minutes after 3:47, and since 3 hours is 180 minutes, this sum of 20 will occur after $180 + 12 = \mathbf{192}$ minutes.

4. **D.**   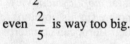 Driving at 50 miles per hour, Gilda took $650 \div 50 = 13$ hours for the trip. In order for the trip to have taken only 12 hours, she would have had to drive at a rate of
$$650 \div 12 = 54\tfrac{1}{6} \text{ miles per hour, or}$$
$4\dfrac{1}{6}$ miles per hour faster.

5. **B.**   Since $w = 40$, arc AB is $\dfrac{40}{360} = \dfrac{1}{9}$ of the circumference. Arc CD is the same length, so the total length of the two arcs is $\dfrac{\mathbf{2}}{\mathbf{9}}$ of the circumference.
**The two arcs add up to 80°, which is less than 90°, a quarter of the circle. Therefore, the answer is less than $\dfrac{1}{4}$: eliminate C, D, and E.
Also, since $\dfrac{1}{9} = 0.111...$, which is much too small, eliminate A.
**Use TACTIC 8-3: redraw the diagram.

Clearly, the two arcs take up more than $\dfrac{1}{9}$, but much less than $\dfrac{1}{2}$, of the circumference; even $\dfrac{2}{5}$ is way too big. Eliminate A, D, and E,

and guess between $\dfrac{2}{9} = 0.222$ and

$\dfrac{1}{4} = 0.25$, which are too close to distinguish just by looking.

6. **A.**   Assume Phil sold only one phone of each model. Then his total sales were \$450 (\$100 + \$125 + \$225), so $\dfrac{100}{450} = \dfrac{2}{9}$ of the total sales were attributable to the cheapest phone.

Changing to percents gives:
$$\frac{2}{9} = \frac{2}{9}(100)\% = \mathbf{22\tfrac{2}{9}\%}.$$

7. **C.**   If a team won w of the g games it played, it lost the rest: $g - w$. The fraction is $\dfrac{g-w}{g}$.
**Use TACTIC 9-2: plug in easy-to-use numbers. If the team won 2 of its 3 games, it lost $\dfrac{1}{3}$ of them. Only $\dfrac{g-w}{g}$ equals $\dfrac{1}{3}$ when $g = 3$ and $w = 2$.

8. **C.**   Since, in 1990, $2p$ pounds of potatoes cost $\dfrac{1}{2}d$ dollars, p pounds cost half as much: $\dfrac{1}{2}\left(\dfrac{1}{2}d\right)$
$= \dfrac{1}{4}d$. This is $\dfrac{1}{4}$, or 25%, as much as the cost in 1980, which represents a decrease of **75%**.
**In this type of problem it is often easier to use TACTIC 9-2. Assume that 1 pound of potatoes cost \$100 in 1980. Then in 1990, 2 pounds cost \$50, so 1 pound cost \$25. This is a decrease of \$75 in the cost of 1 pound of potatoes, and
$$\text{percent decrease} = \frac{\text{decrease}}{\text{original cost}}(100\%)$$
$$= \frac{75}{100}(100\%)$$
$$= \mathbf{75\%}.$$

9. **A.**   Use TACTIC 9-3. Choose an appropriate number for the common perimeter. Any number will work; but since a triangle has 3 sides and a square has 4 sides, 12 is a good choice. Then, each side of the square = 3, and the area is $3^2 = 9$. Each side of the equilateral triangle $= 4$, and the area is $\dfrac{4^2\sqrt{3}}{4} = 4\sqrt{3}$. (KEY FACT J15). The ratio is $\dfrac{4\sqrt{3}}{9}$.

10. **A.**   Since the radius of circle O is 5, diameter $AB = 10$. Also, since $\triangle ACB$ is a right triangle whose hypotenuse, AB, is 10 and one of whose legs is 6, the other leg, BC, is 8. (If you don't recognize this as a 6-8-10 triangle, use the Pythagorean theorem.) The circumference of a circle whose diameter is 10 is 10π, so the length of the semicircle is 5π. The perimeter is the sum of the lengths of the semicircle and the two legs of the triangle: $6 + 8 + 5\pi = \mathbf{14 + 5\pi}$.

Answer Sheet—Test 7

If a section has fewer than 35 questions, leave the extra spaces blank.

Section 1

1 Ⓐ Ⓑ Ⓒ Ⓓ Ⓔ	8 Ⓐ Ⓑ Ⓒ Ⓓ Ⓔ	15 Ⓐ Ⓑ Ⓒ Ⓓ Ⓔ	22 Ⓐ Ⓑ Ⓒ Ⓓ Ⓔ	29 Ⓐ Ⓑ Ⓒ Ⓓ Ⓔ
2 Ⓐ Ⓑ Ⓒ Ⓓ Ⓔ	9 Ⓐ Ⓑ Ⓒ Ⓓ Ⓔ	16 Ⓐ Ⓑ Ⓒ Ⓓ Ⓔ	23 Ⓐ Ⓑ Ⓒ Ⓓ Ⓔ	30 Ⓐ Ⓑ Ⓒ Ⓓ Ⓔ
3 Ⓐ Ⓑ Ⓒ Ⓓ Ⓔ	10 Ⓐ Ⓑ Ⓒ Ⓓ Ⓔ	17 Ⓐ Ⓑ Ⓒ Ⓓ Ⓔ	24 Ⓐ Ⓑ Ⓒ Ⓓ Ⓔ	31 Ⓐ Ⓑ Ⓒ Ⓓ Ⓔ
4 Ⓐ Ⓑ Ⓒ Ⓓ Ⓔ	11 Ⓐ Ⓑ Ⓒ Ⓓ Ⓔ	18 Ⓐ Ⓑ Ⓒ Ⓓ Ⓔ	25 Ⓐ Ⓑ Ⓒ Ⓓ Ⓔ	32 Ⓐ Ⓑ Ⓒ Ⓓ Ⓔ
5 Ⓐ Ⓑ Ⓒ Ⓓ Ⓔ	12 Ⓐ Ⓑ Ⓒ Ⓓ Ⓔ	19 Ⓐ Ⓑ Ⓒ Ⓓ Ⓔ	26 Ⓐ Ⓑ Ⓒ Ⓓ Ⓔ	33 Ⓐ Ⓑ Ⓒ Ⓓ Ⓔ
6 Ⓐ Ⓑ Ⓒ Ⓓ Ⓔ	13 Ⓐ Ⓑ Ⓒ Ⓓ Ⓔ	20 Ⓐ Ⓑ Ⓒ Ⓓ Ⓔ	27 Ⓐ Ⓑ Ⓒ Ⓓ Ⓔ	34 Ⓐ Ⓑ Ⓒ Ⓓ Ⓔ
7 Ⓐ Ⓑ Ⓒ Ⓓ Ⓔ	14 Ⓐ Ⓑ Ⓒ Ⓓ Ⓔ	21 Ⓐ Ⓑ Ⓒ Ⓓ Ⓔ	28 Ⓐ Ⓑ Ⓒ Ⓓ Ⓔ	35 Ⓐ Ⓑ Ⓒ Ⓓ Ⓔ

Section 2

1 Ⓐ Ⓑ Ⓒ Ⓓ Ⓔ	8 Ⓐ Ⓑ Ⓒ Ⓓ Ⓔ	15 Ⓐ Ⓑ Ⓒ Ⓓ Ⓔ	22 Ⓐ Ⓑ Ⓒ Ⓓ Ⓔ	29 Ⓐ Ⓑ Ⓒ Ⓓ Ⓔ
2 Ⓐ Ⓑ Ⓒ Ⓓ Ⓔ	9 Ⓐ Ⓑ Ⓒ Ⓓ Ⓔ	16 Ⓐ Ⓑ Ⓒ Ⓓ Ⓔ	23 Ⓐ Ⓑ Ⓒ Ⓓ Ⓔ	30 Ⓐ Ⓑ Ⓒ Ⓓ Ⓔ
3 Ⓐ Ⓑ Ⓒ Ⓓ Ⓔ	10 Ⓐ Ⓑ Ⓒ Ⓓ Ⓔ	17 Ⓐ Ⓑ Ⓒ Ⓓ Ⓔ	24 Ⓐ Ⓑ Ⓒ Ⓓ Ⓔ	31 Ⓐ Ⓑ Ⓒ Ⓓ Ⓔ
4 Ⓐ Ⓑ Ⓒ Ⓓ Ⓔ	11 Ⓐ Ⓑ Ⓒ Ⓓ Ⓔ	18 Ⓐ Ⓑ Ⓒ Ⓓ Ⓔ	25 Ⓐ Ⓑ Ⓒ Ⓓ Ⓔ	32 Ⓐ Ⓑ Ⓒ Ⓓ Ⓔ
5 Ⓐ Ⓑ Ⓒ Ⓓ Ⓔ	12 Ⓐ Ⓑ Ⓒ Ⓓ Ⓔ	19 Ⓐ Ⓑ Ⓒ Ⓓ Ⓔ	26 Ⓐ Ⓑ Ⓒ Ⓓ Ⓔ	33 Ⓐ Ⓑ Ⓒ Ⓓ Ⓔ
6 Ⓐ Ⓑ Ⓒ Ⓓ Ⓔ	13 Ⓐ Ⓑ Ⓒ Ⓓ Ⓔ	20 Ⓐ Ⓑ Ⓒ Ⓓ Ⓔ	27 Ⓐ Ⓑ Ⓒ Ⓓ Ⓔ	34 Ⓐ Ⓑ Ⓒ Ⓓ Ⓔ
7 Ⓐ Ⓑ Ⓒ Ⓓ Ⓔ	14 Ⓐ Ⓑ Ⓒ Ⓓ Ⓔ	21 Ⓐ Ⓑ Ⓒ Ⓓ Ⓔ	28 Ⓐ Ⓑ Ⓒ Ⓓ Ⓔ	35 Ⓐ Ⓑ Ⓒ Ⓓ Ⓔ

Section 3

1 Ⓐ Ⓑ Ⓒ Ⓓ Ⓔ	8 Ⓐ Ⓑ Ⓒ Ⓓ Ⓔ	15 Ⓐ Ⓑ Ⓒ Ⓓ Ⓔ	22 Ⓐ Ⓑ Ⓒ Ⓓ Ⓔ	29 Ⓐ Ⓑ Ⓒ Ⓓ Ⓔ
2 Ⓐ Ⓑ Ⓒ Ⓓ Ⓔ	9 Ⓐ Ⓑ Ⓒ Ⓓ Ⓔ	16 Ⓐ Ⓑ Ⓒ Ⓓ Ⓔ	23 Ⓐ Ⓑ Ⓒ Ⓓ Ⓔ	30 Ⓐ Ⓑ Ⓒ Ⓓ Ⓔ
3 Ⓐ Ⓑ Ⓒ Ⓓ Ⓔ	10 Ⓐ Ⓑ Ⓒ Ⓓ Ⓔ	17 Ⓐ Ⓑ Ⓒ Ⓓ Ⓔ	24 Ⓐ Ⓑ Ⓒ Ⓓ Ⓔ	31 Ⓐ Ⓑ Ⓒ Ⓓ Ⓔ
4 Ⓐ Ⓑ Ⓒ Ⓓ Ⓔ	11 Ⓐ Ⓑ Ⓒ Ⓓ Ⓔ	18 Ⓐ Ⓑ Ⓒ Ⓓ Ⓔ	25 Ⓐ Ⓑ Ⓒ Ⓓ Ⓔ	32 Ⓐ Ⓑ Ⓒ Ⓓ Ⓔ
5 Ⓐ Ⓑ Ⓒ Ⓓ Ⓔ	12 Ⓐ Ⓑ Ⓒ Ⓓ Ⓔ	19 Ⓐ Ⓑ Ⓒ Ⓓ Ⓔ	26 Ⓐ Ⓑ Ⓒ Ⓓ Ⓔ	33 Ⓐ Ⓑ Ⓒ Ⓓ Ⓔ
6 Ⓐ Ⓑ Ⓒ Ⓓ Ⓔ	13 Ⓐ Ⓑ Ⓒ Ⓓ Ⓔ	20 Ⓐ Ⓑ Ⓒ Ⓓ Ⓔ	27 Ⓐ Ⓑ Ⓒ Ⓓ Ⓔ	34 Ⓐ Ⓑ Ⓒ Ⓓ Ⓔ
7 Ⓐ Ⓑ Ⓒ Ⓓ Ⓔ	14 Ⓐ Ⓑ Ⓒ Ⓓ Ⓔ	21 Ⓐ Ⓑ Ⓒ Ⓓ Ⓔ	28 Ⓐ Ⓑ Ⓒ Ⓓ Ⓔ	35 Ⓐ Ⓑ Ⓒ Ⓓ Ⓔ

Section 4

1 Ⓐ Ⓑ Ⓒ Ⓓ Ⓔ	4 Ⓐ Ⓑ Ⓒ Ⓓ Ⓔ	7 Ⓐ Ⓑ Ⓒ Ⓓ Ⓔ	10 Ⓐ Ⓑ Ⓒ Ⓓ Ⓔ	13 Ⓐ Ⓑ Ⓒ Ⓓ Ⓔ
2 Ⓐ Ⓑ Ⓒ Ⓓ Ⓔ	5 Ⓐ Ⓑ Ⓒ Ⓓ Ⓔ	8 Ⓐ Ⓑ Ⓒ Ⓓ Ⓔ	11 Ⓐ Ⓑ Ⓒ Ⓓ Ⓔ	14 Ⓐ Ⓑ Ⓒ Ⓓ Ⓔ
3 Ⓐ Ⓑ Ⓒ Ⓓ Ⓔ	6 Ⓐ Ⓑ Ⓒ Ⓓ Ⓔ	9 Ⓐ Ⓑ Ⓒ Ⓓ Ⓔ	12 Ⓐ Ⓑ Ⓒ Ⓓ Ⓔ	15 Ⓐ Ⓑ Ⓒ Ⓓ Ⓔ

Section 4 (continued)

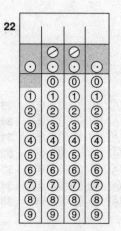

Grid-in answer boxes numbered 16, 17, 18, 19, 20, 21, 22, 23, 24, 25.

Section 5

1 Ⓐ Ⓑ Ⓒ Ⓓ Ⓔ	8 Ⓐ Ⓑ Ⓒ Ⓓ Ⓔ	15 Ⓐ Ⓑ Ⓒ Ⓓ Ⓔ	22 Ⓐ Ⓑ Ⓒ Ⓓ Ⓔ	29 Ⓐ Ⓑ Ⓒ Ⓓ Ⓔ
2 Ⓐ Ⓑ Ⓒ Ⓓ Ⓔ	9 Ⓐ Ⓑ Ⓒ Ⓓ Ⓔ	16 Ⓐ Ⓑ Ⓒ Ⓓ Ⓔ	23 Ⓐ Ⓑ Ⓒ Ⓓ Ⓔ	30 Ⓐ Ⓑ Ⓒ Ⓓ Ⓔ
3 Ⓐ Ⓑ Ⓒ Ⓓ Ⓔ	10 Ⓐ Ⓑ Ⓒ Ⓓ Ⓔ	17 Ⓐ Ⓑ Ⓒ Ⓓ Ⓔ	24 Ⓐ Ⓑ Ⓒ Ⓓ Ⓔ	31 Ⓐ Ⓑ Ⓒ Ⓓ Ⓔ
4 Ⓐ Ⓑ Ⓒ Ⓓ Ⓔ	11 Ⓐ Ⓑ Ⓒ Ⓓ Ⓔ	18 Ⓐ Ⓑ Ⓒ Ⓓ Ⓔ	25 Ⓐ Ⓑ Ⓒ Ⓓ Ⓔ	32 Ⓐ Ⓑ Ⓒ Ⓓ Ⓔ
5 Ⓐ Ⓑ Ⓒ Ⓓ Ⓔ	12 Ⓐ Ⓑ Ⓒ Ⓓ Ⓔ	19 Ⓐ Ⓑ Ⓒ Ⓓ Ⓔ	26 Ⓐ Ⓑ Ⓒ Ⓓ Ⓔ	33 Ⓐ Ⓑ Ⓒ Ⓓ Ⓔ
6 Ⓐ Ⓑ Ⓒ Ⓓ Ⓔ	13 Ⓐ Ⓑ Ⓒ Ⓓ Ⓔ	20 Ⓐ Ⓑ Ⓒ Ⓓ Ⓔ	27 Ⓐ Ⓑ Ⓒ Ⓓ Ⓔ	34 Ⓐ Ⓑ Ⓒ Ⓓ Ⓔ
7 Ⓐ Ⓑ Ⓒ Ⓓ Ⓔ	14 Ⓐ Ⓑ Ⓒ Ⓓ Ⓔ	21 Ⓐ Ⓑ Ⓒ Ⓓ Ⓔ	28 Ⓐ Ⓑ Ⓒ Ⓓ Ⓔ	35 Ⓐ Ⓑ Ⓒ Ⓓ Ⓔ

Section 6

1 Ⓐ Ⓑ Ⓒ Ⓓ Ⓔ	8 Ⓐ Ⓑ Ⓒ Ⓓ Ⓔ	15 Ⓐ Ⓑ Ⓒ Ⓓ Ⓔ	22 Ⓐ Ⓑ Ⓒ Ⓓ Ⓔ	29 Ⓐ Ⓑ Ⓒ Ⓓ Ⓔ
2 Ⓐ Ⓑ Ⓒ Ⓓ Ⓔ	9 Ⓐ Ⓑ Ⓒ Ⓓ Ⓔ	16 Ⓐ Ⓑ Ⓒ Ⓓ Ⓔ	23 Ⓐ Ⓑ Ⓒ Ⓓ Ⓔ	30 Ⓐ Ⓑ Ⓒ Ⓓ Ⓔ
3 Ⓐ Ⓑ Ⓒ Ⓓ Ⓔ	10 Ⓐ Ⓑ Ⓒ Ⓓ Ⓔ	17 Ⓐ Ⓑ Ⓒ Ⓓ Ⓔ	24 Ⓐ Ⓑ Ⓒ Ⓓ Ⓔ	31 Ⓐ Ⓑ Ⓒ Ⓓ Ⓔ
4 Ⓐ Ⓑ Ⓒ Ⓓ Ⓔ	11 Ⓐ Ⓑ Ⓒ Ⓓ Ⓔ	18 Ⓐ Ⓑ Ⓒ Ⓓ Ⓔ	25 Ⓐ Ⓑ Ⓒ Ⓓ Ⓔ	32 Ⓐ Ⓑ Ⓒ Ⓓ Ⓔ
5 Ⓐ Ⓑ Ⓒ Ⓓ Ⓔ	12 Ⓐ Ⓑ Ⓒ Ⓓ Ⓔ	19 Ⓐ Ⓑ Ⓒ Ⓓ Ⓔ	26 Ⓐ Ⓑ Ⓒ Ⓓ Ⓔ	33 Ⓐ Ⓑ Ⓒ Ⓓ Ⓔ
6 Ⓐ Ⓑ Ⓒ Ⓓ Ⓔ	13 Ⓐ Ⓑ Ⓒ Ⓓ Ⓔ	20 Ⓐ Ⓑ Ⓒ Ⓓ Ⓔ	27 Ⓐ Ⓑ Ⓒ Ⓓ Ⓔ	34 Ⓐ Ⓑ Ⓒ Ⓓ Ⓔ
7 Ⓐ Ⓑ Ⓒ Ⓓ Ⓔ	14 Ⓐ Ⓑ Ⓒ Ⓓ Ⓔ	21 Ⓐ Ⓑ Ⓒ Ⓓ Ⓔ	28 Ⓐ Ⓑ Ⓒ Ⓓ Ⓔ	35 Ⓐ Ⓑ Ⓒ Ⓓ Ⓔ

MODEL SAT I TEST 7

1 1 1 1 1 1

SECTION 1   Time—30 Minutes   Select the best answer to the following questions, then fill in
                30 Questions   the appropriate space on your Answer Sheet.

Each of the following sentences contains one or two blanks; these blanks indicate that a word or set of words has been left out. Below the sentence are five words or phrases, lettered A through E. Select the word or set of words that best completes the sentence.

Example:

Fame is ----; today's rising star is all too soon tomorrow's washed-up has-been.

(A) rewarding   (B) gradual
(C) essential   (D) spontaneous
  (E) transitory

Ⓐ Ⓑ Ⓒ Ⓓ ●

---

1. In view of the interrelationships among a number of the African American leaders treated in this anthology, there is inevitably a certain amount of ---- among some of the essays presented here.

(A) overlapping
(B) inaccuracy
(C) pomposity
(D) exaggeration
(E) objectivity

2. As surprising as the new findings are, Dr. Wilson said he would not characterize them as ----.

(A) sound   (B) revolutionary   (C) equitable
  (D) evident   (E) abstruse

3. The best Eskimo carvings of all ages seem to possess a powerful ability to ---- the great barriers of language and time and communicate ---- with us.

(A) leap over...temporarily
(B) reach across...directly
(C) rise above...verbally
(D) pass through...infrequently
(E) leave behind...anonymously

4. The developing brain can be likened to a highway system that ---- use: less traveled roads may be abandoned, popular roads broadened, and new ones added where they are needed.

(A) suffers from
(B) evolves with
(C) detours around
(D) atrophies with
(E) buckles under

5. British collectors are notorious for their ---- of interest in ---- art, much preferring to collect antiques and "important" pictures by long-dead artists.

(A) wealth...modern
(B) growth...abstract
(C) lack...posthumous
(D) resurgence...innovative
(E) dearth...contemporary

6. Although Barbara Tuchman never earned a graduate degree, she nonetheless ---- a scholarly career as a historian noted for her vivid style and ---- erudition.

(A) interrupted...deficient
(B) relinquished...immense
(C) abandoned...capricious
(D) pursued...prodigious
(E) followed...scanty

7. The systems analyst hesitated to talk to strangers about her highly specialized work, fearing it was too ---- for people uninitiated in the computer field to understand.

(A) intriguing   (B) derivative   (C) frivolous
  (D) esoteric   (E) rudimentary

8. In Victorian times, countless Egyptian mummies were ground up to produce dried mummy powder, hailed by quacks as a near-magical ---- able to cure a wide variety of ailments.

(A) toxin
(B) indisposition
(C) symptom
(D) panacea
(E) placebo

9. Like a martinet, Norman ---- his subordinates to ---- rigidly to the rules.

(A) disciplined…adapt
(B) constrained…adhere
(C) coaxed…refer
(D) accustomed…object
(E) coerced…demur

GO ON TO THE NEXT PAGE →

1 1 1 1 1 1 1 1 1 1 1

The analogies questions present two words or phrases that are related in some way. Determine which A-through-E answer choice below has a relationship *most* similar to that of the original words or phrases.

Example:

YAWN:BOREDOM::   (A) dream:sleep
(B) anger:madness   (C) smile:amusement
(D) face:expression   (E) impatience:rebellion

 Ⓐ Ⓑ ● Ⓓ Ⓔ

10. MUFFLER:NECK::
   (A) lace:collar
   (B) elbow:arm
   (C) sash:waist
   (D) cuticle:finger
   (E) skirt:hem

11. BARGE:VESSEL::
   (A) cargo:hold
   (B) brake:automobile
   (C) shovel:implement
   (D) squadron:plane
   (E) link:chain

12. ARMORY:WEAPONS::
   (A) penitentiary:guards
   (B) warehouse:merchandise
   (C) courthouse:laws
   (D) bank:mortgages
   (E) hospital:wards

13. COMPETITOR:VIE::
   (A) sluggard:haste
   (B) hypocrite:condemn
   (C) renegade:accuse
   (D) mutineer:revolt
   (E) snob:edify

14. DARING:FOOLHARDY::
   (A) strong:sturdy
   (B) loyal:optimistic
   (C) respectful:obsequious
   (D) astute:perceptive
   (E) wistful:benevolent

15. RUBBLE:BUILDING::
   (A) bauble:jewelry
   (B) blight:plant
   (C) shards:pottery
   (D) blister:skin
   (E) compost:heap

Read each of the passages below, and then answer the questions that follow each passage. The correct response may be stated outright or merely suggested in the passage.

Questions 16–21 are based on the following passage.

The following passage is excerpted from an article on the immune system that appeared in a popular magazine in 1987.

    An oft-used, but valuable, analogy compares the immune system with an army. The defending troops are the white blood cells called lympho-
Line cytes, born in the bone marrow, billeted in the
(5) lymph nodes and spleen, and on exercise in the blood and lymph systems. A body can muster some 200,000,000 cells, making the immune system comparable in mass to the liver or brain.
    The lymphocytes are called to action when the
(10) enemy makes itself known. They attack anything foreign. Their job is to recognize the enemy for what it is, and then destroy it. One of the key features of the immune system is its specificity. Inoculation with smallpox provokes an attack on
(15) any smallpox virus, but on nothing else. This specificity of response depends on the lympho-

cyte's ability to identify the enemy correctly by the molecules on its surface, called antigens.
    An antigen is an enemy uniform. It can be a
(20) protein on the surface of a cold virus, or it can be a protein on the surface of a pollen grain, in which case the immune response takes the form of an allergy. An antigen can also be a protein on the surface of a transplanted organ, in which case
(25) the immune response "rejects" the transplant. Organs can therefore be transplanted only between closely related people—in whom the antigens are the same—or into people treated with a drug that suppresses the immune system, such
(30) as cyclosporin.

GO ON TO THE NEXT PAGE

1   1   1   1   1   1   1   1   1   1   1

In the 1940s, an Australian immunologist, Sir Frank Macfarlane Burnet, proposed a theory that helped explain how lymphocytes recognize and are activated by specific foreign antigens.
(35) The clonal selection theory, as it was called, suggested that the innate immune system was not a homogeneous mass of more or less identical lymphocytes, but rather was made up of millions of different families called clones. The members
(40) of each clone carry on their surfaces a receptor that is capable of identifying and binding to just one foreign antigen (or a part of it called the determinant).

Thus, when a foreign body carrying that anti-
(45) gen appears, the antigen binds to the receptor of only those lymphocyte clones which are capable of recognizing it. Once the antigen binds to the receptor it stimulates the lymphocyte to divide, which generates more identical copies of itself.
(50) These clone members then attack the foreign entity which carries the antigen.

This implies that the immune system works on a "ready-made" basis. A person's immune system inherits the knowledge of all foreign antigens to
(55) which it might be exposed. The sum of this inheritance increases as new threats are met.

16. The author's primary purpose in the passage is to do which of the following?

   (A) Demonstrate the inadequacy of an analogy.
   (B) Advocate a method to strengthen the immune system.
   (C) Compare the immune system to the brain.
   (D) Clarify the workings of the body's defense system.
   (E) Correct an outmoded view of a bodily process.

17. The word "mass" in line 8 means

   (A) bulk
   (B) function
   (C) company
   (D) lump
   (E) stack

18. The author provides information to answer which of the following questions?

   (A) What is the process by which antigens are produced?
   (B) What is the mechanism by which cyclosporin suppresses the immune system?
   (C) What is the process that prevents closely related persons from developing dissimilar antigens?
   (D) How does inoculation with smallpox wear off over a period of years?
   (E) Where do the body's lymphocytes originate?

19. It can be inferred from lines 23–30 that treatment with cyclosporin might result in which of the following?

   I.   An increased susceptibility to invasion by disease
   II. The rejection of a transplanted organ
   III. An increased effectiveness of antigens

   (A) I only
   (B) II only
   (C) I and II only
   (D) I and III only
   (E) I, II, and III

20. In describing the immune system, the author does all of the following EXCEPT

   (A) define a term
   (B) illustrate through a comparison
   (C) quote an authoritative source
   (D) give an approximation
   (E) develop an extended metaphor

21. As stated in the final three paragraphs, the clonal selection theory explains

   (A) why the body's immune system may reject transplanted organs
   (B) where and when specific foreign antigens enter the body
   (C) why dividing lymphocytes produce exactly identical copies
   (D) how the immune system tailors its response to specific antigens
   (E) why the immune system is composed of more or less identical lymphocytes

Questions 22–30 are based on the following passage.

The following passage is excerpted from a short story with a simple, thought-provoking title: "Ruin."

My father was a cattle rancher in Jamaica. One day after the war he had become sick after eating a bad piece of frozen meat, and that was it.
Line Suddenly all our cane went down and men began
(5) putting up fences. By himself my father took the Oracabessa launch to Cuba, went up into the mountains he said, and came back a week later with a Cuban he had known during the war in North Africa. Pappy was his name, and he had
(10) two teeth in his mouth and looked thin and stupid, but knew cattle.

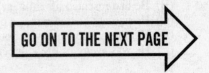

1   1   1   1   1   1   1   1   1   1   1

It was a risk for my father to take the Oracabessa launch across the straits in September. It
was only ninety miles, but September in Jamaica
(15) is the time for bad storms; they come up quickly.
He was very daring, my mother told me, after the
war, and I remember it a bit myself. All the men
were a little like that. My mother said that after El
Alamain my father thought he could do anything.
(20) He was impetuous, like a young boy, the war having taught him both how temporary life is, and
how valuable.

He had been a cane grower all his life, that
was what he knew, but he was willing to learn
(25) cattle. He put every penny, every quattie of what
we had, into a small herd, and a prize black bull
that came from Corpus Christi in October and
was lowered from the freighter to the dock, hung
from a bright yellow sling. When the yellow sash
(30) was dropped away and we could see the bull's
blackness and the rotations of green that were its
eyes, my father was a proud man. The bull looked
up and snorted, its eyes fixed on the mountain,
and Pappy said with a hideous gentle smile that it
(35) smelled the herd, and that the sea voyage had
done it no good.

Our house had red tiles on the roof. They
glowed vermilion in the sun. We heard drums on
Friday and Saturday nights; drifting up from the
(40) town, the sound was marvelous and frightening.
When my father was troubled he walked down
the mountain on the winding road, and stayed for
a long time on the wall overlooking the sea. It was
terribly hot and still in the morning. Everyone
(45) wore white. I was often aware of carrion rotting
unseen in some soft place.

I was quite surprised when, a week after we
took the bull off the ship, Pappy ran onto the ter-
race and turning his straw hat rapidly in his hands
(50) announced that the bull had gone wild and was
killing the other animals. My father got up slowly
and put down the *Gleaner*. He was in white pants
and a white shirt, and he was stained beautifully
with colors, for he had been painting fish and
(55) fruit. I followed him to his room where I watched
him load a .30-06, pushing in the dull brass car-
tridges one by one. He seemed to be angry and
perhaps a little frightened. I was frightened for
him.

22. The narrator states all of the following about his
father EXCEPT:

(A) He was audacious and impulsive.
(B) He had resented his military service.
(C) He had not started out as a cattle rancher.
(D) His journey to Cuba was potentially dangerous.
(E) He was aware of life's impermanence.

23. The narrator most likely uses the phrase "and that
was it" (line 3) to pinpoint the moment that

(A) his father first ate frozen meat
(B) he understood his father's weakness
(C) his father left home for good
(D) Pappy first entered his life
(E) his father decided to try raising cattle

24. It can be inferred from the passage that the father
most likely sought out Pappy

(A) because he missed his days in North Africa
(B) out of pity for Pappy's poverty
(C) to find a cure for his food-poisoning
(D) because he needed Pappy's guidance
(E) because he knew how to navigate a launch

25. As used in the passage, a "quattie" (line 25) is most
likely

(A) a breed of cattle
(B) a stalk of sugar cane
(C) a Jamaican coin
(D) one fourth of the estate
(E) an agricultural tool

26. Pappy's comment in lines 34–36 can best be taken
to mean that

(A) the sea journey had failed to cure the bull's
illness
(B) the herd of cattle had developed an unfortunate
odor
(C) the bull was upset to be parted from the cattle
on the boat
(D) he had expected the sea voyage to improve the
bull's disposition
(E) he realized that being transported had angered
the bull

27. Pappy most likely turned his straw hat rapidly in
his hands

(A) to fan himself in the terrible heat
(B) because he wished to demonstrate his dexterity
(C) to chase away the maddened bull
(D) because he was agitated by the news he
brought
(E) to dissipate the smell of wet paint

GO ON TO THE NEXT PAGE ⇒

1   1 1 1 1 1 1 1 1 1   1

28. In lines 45–46, the reference to carrion rotting is used to

(A) emphasize the poor sanitation of the islands
(B) indicate the lack of refrigeration during the period
(C) criticize the father's farm management
(D) foreshadow the destruction of the cattle
(E) point out one of the causes of food-poisoning

29. In the light of the events narrated in lines 47–59, the father's pride on acquiring the new bull seems

(A) warranted   (B) idiosyncratic
(C) rhetorical   (D) understated   (E) ironic

30. In the passage as a whole, the narrator is most concerned with

(A) excusing his father's cowardice
(B) reliving a childhood adventure
(C) praising his father's ability to take risks
(D) understanding his family's financial undoing
(E) overcoming his sense of nostalgia

YOU MAY GO BACK AND REVIEW THIS SECTION IN THE REMAINING TIME, BUT DO NOT WORK IN ANY OTHER SECTION UNTIL TOLD TO DO SO.

S T O P

SECTION 2

Time—30 Minutes
25 Questions

For each problem in this section determine which of the five choices is correct and blacken in that choice on your answer sheet. You may use any blank space on the page for your work.

Notes:

- You may use a calculator whenever you feel it will be helpful.
- Use the diagrams provided to help you solve the problems. Unless you see the words "<u>Note</u>: Figure not drawn to scale" under a diagram, it has been drawn as accurately as possible. Unless it is stated that a figure is three-dimensional, you may assume it lies in a plane.

Reference Information

Area Facts	Volume Facts	Triangle Facts	Angle Facts

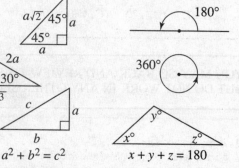

$A = \ell w$ $A = \frac{1}{2} bh$ $A = \pi r^2$ $C = 2\pi r$ $V = \ell wh$ $V = \pi r^2 h$ $a^2 + b^2 = c^2$ $x + y + z = 180$

---

1. What is the value of n if $(8 - 3)(8 - n) = 40$?

    (A) –3   (B) 0   (C) 3   (D) 5   (E) 8

2. Debbie saves $8 every day. If 11 days ago she had $324, how many dollars will she have 11 days from now?

    (A) 148   (B) 236   (C) 412   (D) 500   (E) 566

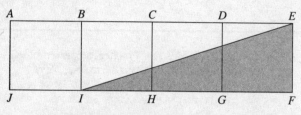

3. In the figure above, rectangle *AEFJ* is divided into four equal squares. What is the ratio of the area of the shaded region to the area of the white region?

    (A) 3:8   (B) 3:5   (C) 5:8   (D) 3:4   (E) 7:8

4. One positive number is $\frac{1}{3}$ of another number. If the product of the numbers is 12, what is their sum?

    (A) 4   (B) 6   (C) 8   (D) 10   (E) 12

5. In the figure above, what is the average of a, b, c, and d?

    (A) 60   (B) 70   (C) 80   (D) 90
    (E) It cannot be determined from the information given.

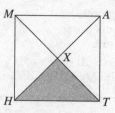

6. In square *MATH* above, if $MX = 3$, what is the area of the shaded triangle?

    (A) $\frac{9}{4}$ (B) $\frac{9\sqrt{3}}{4}$ (C) 4.5   (D) 9   (E) 18

GO ON TO THE NEXT PAGE

2 2 2 2 2 2 2 2 2 2 **2**

7. A rectangle has the same area as a circle of radius 4. If the width of the rectangle is 2, what is its length?

(A) $\dfrac{8}{\pi}$ (B) $\dfrac{16}{\pi}$ (C) 2π (D) 4π (E) 8π

8. Sharon saw 5 movies this month. Each was at least $1\dfrac{1}{2}$ hours long, and the total running time of all 5 was 8 hours and 40 minutes. If the average length of the first 3 movies was 100 minutes, what is the greatest possible length, in minutes, of any of the movies?

(A) 110 (B) 120 (C) 130 (D) 140 (E) 150

9. What is the area of the circle whose center is at the origin and that passes through point $(3,-3)$?

(A) $3\sqrt{2}\,\pi$ (B) 3π (C) 9π (D) 18π (E) 36π

10. Amy had to file c cards. After she had filed d of them, what percent of the cards were still unfiled?

(A) $100(c-d)\%$ (B) $\dfrac{c-d}{100}\%$ (C) $\dfrac{c-d}{100c}\%$

(D) $\dfrac{100(c-d)}{d}\%$ (E) $\dfrac{100(c-d)}{c}\%$

11. For any number x, $\bigcirc\!\!\!x = x^2$ and $\boxed{x} = \sqrt{x}$.
If $\bigcirc\!\!\!a = \boxed{b}$, what is $\bigcirc\!\!\!b$?
(A) a (B) a^2 (C) a^4 (D) a^8 (E) a^{16}

12. If p, q, and r are prime numbers, which of the following could be true?

   I. $p + q$ is prime.
   II. $p + q + r$ is prime.
   III. qr is prime.

(A) I only (B) II only (C) I and II only
(D) II and III only (E) I, II, and III

13. Isabelle typed $\dfrac{3}{5}$ of her report in 3.2 hours. At the same rate, how many more <u>minutes</u> will she need to finish typing the report?

(A) $2\dfrac{2}{15}$ (B) $76\dfrac{4}{5}$ (C) 128 (D) 192
(E) 320

Questions 14–15 refer to the following definition.

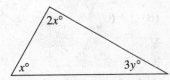

$\boxed{a}\;\boxed{b}\;\boxed{c}\;\boxed{d}\;\boxed{e}$ is a *number strip* if b is the average (arithmetic mean) of a and c, c is the average of b and d, and d is the average of c and e.

14. If $\boxed{3}\;\boxed{7}\;\boxed{c}\;\boxed{d}\;\boxed{e}$ is a number strip, what is the value of e?

(A) 5.5 (B) 11 (C) 13 (D) 17 (E) 19

15. If $\boxed{a}\;\boxed{b}\;\boxed{c}\;\boxed{d}\;\boxed{e}$ is a number strip, which of the following is an expression for e in terms of a and b?

(A) $\dfrac{a+b+c+d}{4}$ (B) $\dfrac{b+c+d}{3}$ (C) $4b - 3a$

(D) $6b - 4a$ (E) $7b - 10a$

16. If x, y, and z are integers with $x < y < z$, and $y = 50$, what is the greatest possible value of $x + y - z$?

(A) -2 (B) 2 (C) 48 (D) 52
(E) It cannot be determined from the information given.

17. For the figure above, which of the following is an expression for x in terms of y?

(A) y (B) $60 - y$ (C) $y - 60$ (D) $180 - 3y$
(E) $90 - y$

18. A cube whose edges are 3 inches is painted blue. The cube is then cut into smaller cubes, all of which have edges that are 1 inch long. How many of the small cubes have no paint on them?

(A) 0 (B) 1 (C) 3 (D) 4 (E) 9

GO ON TO THE NEXT PAGE

2 2 2 2 2 2 2 2 2 2

19. In 1995, Greg rented several movies. From January through April he rented an average (arithmetic mean) of m movies per month, and from May through December he rented an average of n movies per month. What was the average number of movies he rented each month in 1995?

(A) $m + n$ (B) $2m + 4n$ (C) $\dfrac{m+n}{2}$

(D) $\dfrac{m+n}{12}$ (E) $\dfrac{m+2n}{3}$

20. The measures of the angles of a triangle are in the ratio of 1:2:3. What is the ratio of the length of the smallest side to the length of the longest side?

(A) $1:\sqrt{2}$ (B) $1:\sqrt{3}$ (C) 1:2   (D) 1:3
(E) It cannot be determined from the information given.

21. If a, b, and c are positive integers and $\dfrac{1}{a}+\dfrac{1}{b}+\dfrac{1}{c} = 1$, what is the largest possible value of $a + b + c$?

(A) 3   (B) 8   (C) 9   (D) 10   (E) 11

22. In the figure above, the shaded region is bounded by two semicircles and two sides of a square. If the perimeter of the shaded region is $4 + 2\pi$, what is the area of the shaded region?

(A) $4 - 2\pi$ (B) $4 - \pi$ (C) $4 + 2\pi$
(D) $16 - 4\pi$ (E) $4\pi - 16$

23. If x is a positive integer, which of the following CANNOT be an integer?

(A) $\sqrt{x-1}$ (B) $\sqrt{x^2-1}$ (C) $\dfrac{x+4}{x-2}$

(D) $\dfrac{x+4}{x+2}$ (E) $\dfrac{5}{x+1}$

24. Joanna walked $m + \dfrac{2}{3}$ miles at a rate of $r + \dfrac{1}{2}$ miles per hour. For how many <u>minutes</u> did she walk?

(A) $\dfrac{40(3m+2)}{2r+1}$ (B) $\dfrac{6m+4}{6r+3}$ (C) $60\left(\dfrac{m}{r}+\dfrac{4}{3}\right)$

(D) $\dfrac{3m+2}{2r+1}$ (E) $60\left(\dfrac{3m+2}{2r+1}\right)$

25. Mr. Smith can process 10 claims per hour, and his assistant can process 5 claims per hour. If they each processed the same number of claims, what was the average amount of time, in <u>minutes</u>, taken for a claim to be processed?

(A) 6   (B) $6\dfrac{2}{3}$ (C) 7.5   (D) 8   (E) 9

YOU MAY GO BACK AND REVIEW THIS SECTION IN THE REMAINING TIME, BUT DO NOT WORK IN ANY OTHER SECTION UNTIL TOLD TO DO SO.   **S T O P**

3   3 3 3 3 3 3 3 3 3 3   3

SECTION 3   **Time—30 Minutes**   **Select the best answer to the following questions, then fill in**
35 Questions   **the appropriate space on your Answer Sheet.**

Each of the following sentences contains one or two
blanks; these blanks indicate that a word or set of words
has been left out. Below the sentence are five words or
phrases, lettered A through E. Select the word or set of
words that best completes the sentence.

Example:

Fame is ----; today's rising star is all too soon
tomorrow's washed-up has-been.

(A) rewarding   (B) gradual
(C) essential   (D) spontaneous
(E) transitory

1. Advances in health care have lengthened life spans,
   lowered infant mortality rates, and, thus, ---- the
   overpopulation problem.

   (A) eliminated
   (B) aggravated
   (C) minimized
   (D) distorted
   (E) discouraged

2. The plot of the motion picture *Hoosiers* is ----;
   we have all seen this story, the tale of an underdog
   team going on to win a championship, in one form
   or another countless times.

   (A) inept   (B) absorbing   (C) intricate
   (D) controversial   (E) trite

3. Although Josephine Tey is arguably as good a mystery writer as Agatha Christie, she is clearly far less
   ---- than Christie, having written only six books in
   comparison to Christie's sixty.

   (A) coherent
   (B) prolific
   (C) equivocal
   (D) pretentious
   (E) gripping

4. Being cynical, he was reluctant to ---- the ---- of
   any kind act until he had ruled out all possible
   secret, uncharitable motives.

   (A) question...benevolence
   (B) acknowledge...wisdom
   (C) credit...unselfishness
   (D) endure...loss
   (E) witness...outcome

5. Most Antarctic animals ---- depend on the tiny
   shrimplike krill, either feeding on them directly,
   like the humpback whale, or consuming species
   that feed on them.

   (A) seldom
   (B) ultimately
   (C) preferably
   (D) immediately
   (E) marginally

6. Through her work at the Center for the Family in
   Transition, Wallerstein has come to see divorce not
   as a single circumscribed event but as a process
   that begins during the failing marriage and extends
   over many years, a ---- of changing family relationships.

   (A) continuum
   (B) termination
   (C) parody
   (D) denial
   (E) curtailment

7. Physicists dream of a unified theory of matter that
   could replace the present ---- of mutually inconsistent theories that litter the field.

   (A) bonanza   (B) concord   (C) dearth
   (D) integration   (E) clutter

8. Because he had assumed that the child's first,
   fierce rush of grief would quickly ----, Murdstone
   was astonished to find him still ----.

   (A) subside...disconsolate
   (B) fade...irresolute
   (C) elapse...disingenuous
   (D) escalate...forlorn
   (E) dwindle...dormant

9. Dr. Smith cautioned that the data so far are not sufficiently ---- to warrant dogmatic assertions by
   either side in the debate.

   (A) hypothetical
   (B) tentative
   (C) controversial
   (D) unequivocal
   (E) imponderable

GO ON TO THE NEXT PAGE

3 3 3 3 3 3 3 3 3 3 3   3

10. Americans have always been rightfully ---- unnecessary government coercion, feeling that the government should use its powers sparingly.

    (A) disarmed by
    (B) chary about
    (C) dependent on
    (D) amenable to
    (E) enthusiastic about

The analogies questions present two words or phrases that are related in some way. Determine which A-through-E answer choice below has a relationship *most* similar to that of the original words or phrases.

Example:

YAWN:BOREDOM::   (A) dream:sleep
(B) anger:madness   (C) smile:amusement
(D) face:expression   (E) impatience:rebellion

---

11. CLASP:BRACELET::

    (A) hook:coat
    (B) buckle:belt
    (C) diamond:ring
    (D) wrist:watch
    (E) cuff:trousers

12. REAM:PAPER::

    (A) skin:tissue
    (B) envelope:letter
    (C) cord:wood
    (D) swatch:cloth
    (E) chisel:stone

13. TROUGH:PIGS::

    (A) carton:eggs
    (B) den:bears
    (C) manger:cattle
    (D) flock:sheep
    (E) corral:horses

14. WHIFF:SCENT::

    (A) musk:fragrance
    (B) whistle:tune
    (C) tide:wave
    (D) blaze:light
    (E) puff:smoke

15. EXTRACT:TOOTH::

    (A) trim:hair
    (B) expend:energy
    (C) protract:argument
    (D) uproot:stump
    (E) insert:plug

16. RUSTLE:CATTLE::

    (A) bleat:sheep
    (B) swim:fish
    (C) pan:gold
    (D) speculate:stock
    (E) hijack:cargo

17. RUFFLE:COMPOSURE::

    (A) flounce:turmoil
    (B) flourish:prosperity
    (C) provoke:discussion
    (D) adjust:balance
    (E) upset:equilibrium

18. GRISLY:RECOIL::

    (A) sudden:rebound
    (B) tainted:purify
    (C) flagging:invigorate
    (D) heartrending:weep
    (E) craven:quail

19. PURIST:CORRECTNESS::

    (A) miser:generosity
    (B) saint:elevation
    (C) nomad:refuge
    (D) judge:accuracy
    (E) martinet:discipline

20. PULVERIZE:DUST::

    (A) analyze:argument
    (B) vaporize:mist
    (C) petrify:fear
    (D) permeate:odor
    (E) solidify:fluid

21. NECROMANCER:WITCHCRAFT::

    (A) martyr:excellence
    (B) glutton:abstinence
    (C) swindler:duplicity
    (D) ingenue:fascination
    (E) politician:graft

GO ON TO THE NEXT PAGE

22. LUMINARY:ILLUSTRIOUS::

    (A) zealot:intense
    (B) miser:prodigal
    (C) atheist:radical
    (D) dignitary:conceited
    (E) celebrity:wealthy

23. DOGGEREL:POET::

    (A) symphony:composer
    (B) easel:painter
    (C) caption:cartoonist
    (D) soliloquy:playwright
    (E) potboiler:novelist

Read the passage below, and then answer the questions that follow the passage. The correct response may be stated outright or merely suggested in the passage.

Questions 24–35 are based on the following passage.

The following passage is excerpted from the 40th anniversary edition of a standard work on African Americans, first published in 1948.

There can be no doubt that the emergence of Negro writers in the post-war period stemmed, in part, from the fact that they were inclined to
Line exploit the opportunity to write about themselves.
(5) It was more than that, however. The movement that has been variously called the Harlem Renaissance, the Black Renaissance, and the New Negro Movement was essentially a part of the growing interest of American literary circles in
(10) the immediate and pressing social and economic problems facing the country. This increasing interest coincided with two developments in Negro life that fostered the growth of the New Negro Movement. The migration that began dur-
(15) ing the war had thrown the destiny of blacks into their own hands more than ever before. They developed a responsibility and a self-confidence that they had not previously known. During the war they learned from their president the promise
(20) of freedom, and on the battlefield black men served their country. They began to see the discrepancies between the promise of freedom and the reality of their experiences. They became defiant, bitter, and impatient.
(25) In the riots and clashes that followed the war, blacks fought back with surprising audacity. By this time, moreover, they had achieved a level of articulation that enabled them to transform their feelings into a variety of literary forms. Despite
(30) their intense feelings of hate and hurt, they possessed enough restraint and objectivity to use their materials artistically. They were sufficiently in touch with the main currents of American literary thought to adapt the accepted forms of expres-
(35) sion to their own material, thus gaining a wider audience. These two factors, the keener realization of injustice and the improvement of the

capacity for expression, produced a crop of black writers who constituted the Harlem Renaissance.
(40) Those who contributed to the literature of the Harlem Renaissance were deeply aware of their belonging to a group that not only was a minority but also was set apart in numerous ways. If black writers accepted this separateness, they did so not
(45) because they wanted to be what others wanted them to be (that is, a distinct and even exotic group in the eyes of patronizing whites), but because their experiences had given them some appreciation of their own unique cultural heritage.
(50) The plantation, the slave quarters, the proscriptions even in freedom, the lynchings and the riots, the segregation and discrimination had created a body of common experiences that, in turn, helped to promote the idea of a distinct and authentic
(55) cultural community. In the years following the First World War, this community's spokesmen protested their social and economic wrongs. They stood for full equality, but they celebrated the strength of their own integrity as a people. While
(60) they had a vision of social and economic freedom, they cherished the very unhappy experiences that had drawn them closer together. They also had a vision, as Nathan Huggins has suggested, "of themselves as actors and creators of a peo-
(65) ple's birth (or rebirth)...."
The writers of the Harlem Renaissance, bitter and cynical as some of them were, were more intent on confronting American racists than on embracing the doctrines of the Socialists and
(70) Communists. The editor of the *Messenger* ventured the opinion that the new Negro was the "product of the same world-wide forces that have brought into being the great liberal and radical movements that are now seizing the reins of

GO ON TO THE NEXT PAGE

(75) political, social, and economic power in all the civilized countries of the world." Such forces may have produced the new Negro, but the more articulate of the group did not seek to subvert American constitutional government. Indeed, the
(80) writers of the Harlem Renaissance were not so much revolting against the system as they were protesting the unjust operation of the system. In this approach they proved as characteristically American as any writers of the period. Like their
(85) white contemporaries, black writers were merely becoming more aware of America's pressing social problems, and, like the others, were willing to use their art not only to contribute to the great body of American literature but also to improve
(90) the civilization of which they were a part.

    All the black writers of this period cannot be described as crusaders, however, for not all of them assumed this role. Some were not immediately concerned with the injustices heaped on
(95) Negroes. Some contrived their poems, novels, and songs merely for the sake of art, while others took up their pens to escape the sordid aspects of their existence. If an element of race exists in the work of these writers, it is because their material flows
(100) out of their individual and group experiences reflecting the emergence of a distinct cultural community. This is not to say that such writings were ineffective as protest literature, but rather that not all the authors were conscious crusaders
(105) for a better world. As a matter of fact, it was this detachment, this objectivity, that made it possible for many of the writers of the Harlem Renaissance to achieve a nobility of expression and a poignancy of feeling in their writings that placed
(110) them among the great masters of recent American literature.

24. The word "stemmed" in line 2 means

(A) checked
(B) arose
(C) stripped
(D) branched
(E) restrained

25. The Harlem Renaissance, the Black Renaissance, and the New Negro Movement are

(A) groups that competed for the same supporters
(B) literary terms that are no longer in common use
(C) alternate names for the same social and cultural phenomenon
(D) programs to acquaint African Americans with the dominant culture
(E) organizations that exploited Negro writers

26. The author views the behavior of blacks in the riots and clashes following World War I (lines 25–26) as

(A) counterproductive
(B) commonplace
(C) hostile
(D) daring
(E) violent

27. A primary factor in the increasing acceptance of black writers was their

(A) degree of emotional intensity
(B) support from the president and other prominent figures
(C) adoption of the prevalent literary modes
(D) migration from the countryside to the cities
(E) restrained use of literary allusions

28. In analyzing the black writers' acceptance of their separateness (lines 43–65), the author

(A) condemns their willingness to be cut off from the mainstream
(B) finds a positive aspect of a largely negative experience
(C) suggests additional reasons for their desire for full integration
(D) welcomes the exoticism implicit in black culture
(E) questions the logic underlying their decision

29. The word "embracing" in line 69 means

(A) hugging
(B) accommodating
(C) adopting
(D) containing
(E) transforming

30. Which of the following is implied by the statement that the writers of the Harlem Renaissance "were not so much revolting against the system as they were protesting the unjust operation of the system" (lines 80–82)?

(A) Black writers played only a minor part in protesting the injustices of the period.
(B) Left to itself, the system was sure to operate justly.
(C) Black writers in general were not opposed to the system as such.
(D) In order for the system to operate justly, blacks must seize the reins of power in America.
(E) Black writers were too caught up in aesthetic philosophy to identify the true nature of the conflict.

GO ON TO THE NEXT PAGE

3   3 3 3 3 3 3 3 3 3 3   3

31. The word "assumed" in line 93 means

    (A) believed in   (B) took on   (C) simulated
    (D) usurped   (E) suspected

32. In reference to the achievements of the Harlem Renaissance, the passage conveys primarily a sense of

    (A) protest   (B) betrayal   (C) nostalgia
    (D) urgency   (E) admiration

33. The author is primarily concerned with

    (A) arguing that the literature of the Harlem Renaissance arose from the willingness of black writers to portray their own lives
    (B) depicting the part played by socially conscious black writers in a worldwide ideological and literary crusade
    (C) providing examples of the injustices protested by the writers of the Harlem Renaissance
    (D) describing the social and political background that led to the blossoming of the Harlem Renaissance
    (E) analyzing stages in the development of the New Negro Movement into the Harlem Renaissance

34. In the course of the passage, the author does all of the following EXCEPT

    (A) quote an authority
    (B) qualify assertions
    (C) cite examples
    (D) dismiss a possibility
    (E) pose a question

35. The passage supplies information for answering which of the following questions?

    (A) What factors led black writers in the postwar period to abandon the accepted literary forms of the day?
    (B) Who were the leading exponents of protest literature during the Harlem Renaissance?
    (C) Why were the writers of the Harlem Renaissance in rebellion against foreign ideological systems?
    (D) How did black writers in the postwar period define the literary tradition to which they belonged?
    (E) In what larger literary and social context did the black writers of the postwar period compose their works of protest?

YOU MAY GO BACK AND REVIEW THIS SECTION IN THE REMAINING TIME, BUT DO NOT WORK IN ANY OTHER SECTION UNTIL TOLD TO DO SO.   **S T O P**

4   4   4   4   4   4   4   4   4   4   4   4

SECTION 4

**Time—30 Minutes
25 Questions**

You have 30 minutes to answer the 15 Quantitative Comparison questions and 10 Student-Produced Response questions in this section. You may use any blank space on the page for your work.

Notes:

- You may use a calculator whenever you feel it will be helpful.
- Use the diagrams provided to help you solve the problems. Unless you see the words "Note: Figure not drawn to scale" under a diagram, it has been drawn as accurately as possible. Unless it is stated that a figure is three-dimensional, you may assume it lies in a plane.

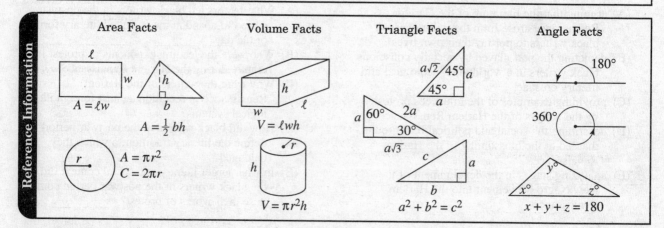

Reference Information

Area Facts

$A = \ell w$

$A = \frac{1}{2}bh$

$A = \pi r^2$
$C = 2\pi r$

Volume Facts

$V = \ell wh$

$V = \pi r^2 h$

Triangle Facts

$a^2 + b^2 = c^2$

Angle Facts

$x + y + z = 180$

Directions for Quantitative Comparison Questions

In each of questions 1–15, two quantities appear in boxes: one in Column A and one in Column B. You must compare them. The correct answer to a question is

- A if the quantity in Column A is greater;
- B if the quantity in Column B is greater;
- C if the two quantities are equal;
- D if it is impossible to determine which quantity is greater.

Notes:

- *The correct answer is never E.*
- Sometimes information about one or both of the quantities is centered above the two boxes.
- If the same symbol appears in both columns, it represents the same thing each time.
- All variables represent real numbers.

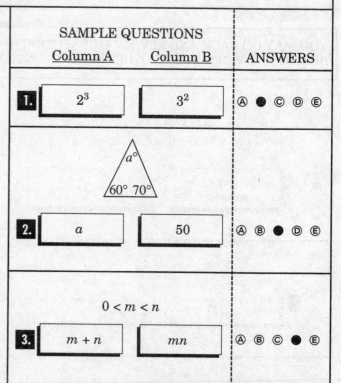

SAMPLE QUESTIONS

Column A	Column B	ANSWERS
1. 2^3	3^2	Ⓐ ● Ⓒ Ⓓ Ⓔ
2. a	50	Ⓐ Ⓑ ● Ⓓ Ⓔ
3. $m + n$	mn	Ⓐ Ⓑ Ⓒ ● Ⓔ

(question 2 figure: triangle with angles $a°$, $60°$, $70°$)

(question 3: $0 < m < n$)

GO ON TO THE NEXT PAGE

4   4 4 4 4 4 4 4 4 4 4   4

SUMMARY DIRECTIONS FOR QUANTITATIVE COMPARISON QUESTIONS

<u>Answer</u>: A if the quantity in Column A is greater;
B if the quantity in Column B is greater;
C if the two quantities are equal;
D if it is impossible to determine which quantity is greater.

Column A	Column B

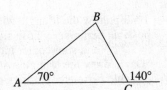

Note: Figure not drawn to scale

1.

AC	BC

2.

$5(r + t)$	$5r + t$

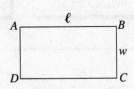

$ABCD$ is a rectangle.
$7 < \ell < 9$ and $5 < w < 7$

3.

The area of the rectangle	50

$ab = 48$

4.

$a + b$	50

5.

$(-1)^{100}$	$(-1)^{125}$

Column A	Column B

When the four-digit number $ABCD$ is divided by 10, the remainder is 7.

6.

D	7

The length of rectangle II is twice the length of rectangle I.
The width of rectangle II is half the width of rectangle I.

7.

The perimeter of rectangle I	The perimeter of rectangle II

$x > 0$ and $y > 0$
$x^{20} = 4$ and $y^{10} = 2$

8.

x	y

Let $x \circledast y$ be the average (arithmetic mean) of x and y.
$a < b < c$

9.

$(a \circledast b) \circledast c$	$a \circledast (b \circledast c)$

GO ON TO THE NEXT PAGE

4   4 4 4 4 4 4 4 4 4 4   4

SUMMARY DIRECTIONS FOR QUANTITATIVE COMPARISON QUESTIONS

Answer: A if the quantity in Column A is greater;
B if the quantity in Column B is greater;
C if the two quantities are equal;
D if it is impossible to determine which quantity is greater.

Column A	Column B

Questions 10–11 refer to the following definition.

$\lfloor A \rfloor$ is the number formed by
reversing the digits of A.
For example, $\lfloor 347 \rfloor = 743$ and $\lfloor 200 \rfloor = 002 = 2$.

10.

The number of integers between 100 and 200 for which $\lfloor A \rfloor = A$	10

11.

The number of two-digit integers for which $\lfloor A \rfloor < A$	The number of two-digit integers for which $\lfloor A \rfloor > A$

A small ice cream cone costs $1.00.
A large ice cream cone costs $1.50.
On a particular day, 60% of the cones
sold were small.

12.

The average (arithmetic mean) price of all cones sold that day	$1.20

Column A	Column B

Phillip drew the triangle with the smallest
possible perimeter whose sides were 5, 13,
and some other integer.
David drew the triangle with the greatest
possible perimeter whose sides were 5, 13,
and some other integer.

13.

The perimeter of David's triangle minus the perimeter of Phillip's triangle	8

14.

The remainder when 10^{100} is divided by 5^{75}	The remainder when 10^{100} is divided by 75^5

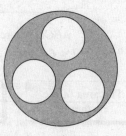

Each small circle has radius r, and the large
circle has radius R.
The areas of the shaded region and the white
region are equal.

15.

$\dfrac{R}{r}$	2

GO ON TO THE NEXT PAGE ⟹

4 4 4 4 4 4 4 4 4 4 4 4 4

Directions for Student-Produced Response Questions (Grid-ins)

In questions 16–25, first solve the problem, and then enter your answer on the grid provided on the answer sheet. The instructions for entering your answers are as follows:
- First, write your answer in the boxes at the top of the grid.
- Second, grid your answer in the columns below the boxes.
- Use the fraction bar in the first row or the decimal point in the second row to enter fractions and decimal answers.

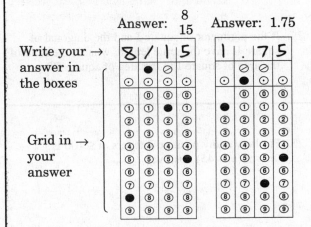

Answer: $\frac{8}{15}$ Answer: 1.75

Write your → answer in the boxes

Grid in → your answer

Answer: 100

Either position is acceptable

- Grid only one space in each column.
- Entering the answer in the boxes is recommended as an aid in gridding, but is not required.
- The machine scoring your exam can read only what you grid, so you **must grid in your answers correctly to get credit.**
- If a question has more than one correct answer, grid in only one of them.
- The grid does not have a minus sign, so no answer can be negative.
- A mixed number *must* be converted to an improper fraction or a decimal before it is gridded. Enter $1\frac{1}{4}$ as 5/4 or 1.25; the machine will interpret 1 1/4 as $\frac{11}{4}$ and mark it wrong.
- **All decimals must be entered as accurately as possible.** Here are the three acceptable ways of gridding

$$\frac{3}{11} = 0.272727...$$

3/11   .272   .273

- Note that rounding to .273 is acceptable, because you are using the full grid, but you would receive **no credit** for .3 or .27, because they are less accurate.

---

16. What is the area, in square inches, of a rectangle whose perimeter is 80 inches and whose length is 3 times its width?

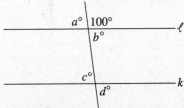

Lines ℓ and k are parallel.

17. In the figure above, what is the value of $a + b + c + d$?

GO ON TO THE NEXT PAGE ⟶

4   4 4 4 4 4 4 4 4 4 4   4

18. If A is the median of $\{1, 2, 3, \ldots, 10\}$ and B is the median of $\{1, 2, 3, \ldots, 11\}$, what is the average (arithmetic mean) of A and B?

19. Jean spent $125 for a camera and some film. The camera cost $100 more than the film. What percent of the cost of the two items did Jean spend for the camera?

20. Al, Bob, Carol, and Diane shared a $1000 prize. Bob got twice as much as Al, Carol got 3 times as much as Al, and Diane got $100. How much, in dollars, did Al get?

21. If a and b are positive numbers for which $\dfrac{10}{7}a = \dfrac{7}{10}b$, what is the ratio of a to b?

22. If x, y, and z are different positive integers less than 10, what is the greatest possible value of $\dfrac{x^2 - y}{z}$?

23. There are 25 students in a class, 36% of whom are girls. If the average (arithmetic mean) weight of the girls is 120 pounds and the average weight of the boys is 150 pounds, what is 10 times the average weight of the children in the class?

24. If the perimeter of square I and the diagonal of square II have the same length, what is the ratio of the area of square I to the area of square II?

25. For how many positive integers $m \le 100$ is $(m - 5)(m - 45)$ positive?

| YOU MAY GO BACK AND REVIEW THIS SECTION IN THE REMAINING TIME, BUT DO NOT WORK IN ANY OTHER SECTION UNTIL TOLD TO DO SO. | **S T O P** |

5

Questions 1–13 are based on the following passages.

The following passages are excerpted from essays about flying.

Passage 1

Flying alone in an open plane is the purest
experience of flight possible. That pure experience is felt at its most intense in acrobatic flying,
Line when you are upside down, or pointed at the sky
(5) or at the earth, and moving in ways that you can
only in the unsubstantial medium of the air.
Acrobatic flying is a useless skill in its particulars—nobody *needs* to do a loop or a roll, not
even a fighter pilot—but this skill extends your
(10) control of the plane and yourself and makes
extreme actions in the sky comfortable. When
you reach the top of a loop, upside down and
engine at full throttle, and tilt your head back to
pick up the horizon line behind you, you are as
(15) far outside instinctive human behavior as you can
go—hanging in space, the sky below you and the
earth above, inscribing a circle on emptiness. And
then the nose drops across the horizon; your
speed increases and the plane scoops through into
(20) normal flight, and you are back in the normal
world, with the earth put back in its place. The
going out and coming back are what makes a loop
so satisfying.

After a while, that is. At first it was terrifying,
(25) like being invited to a suicide that you didn't
want to commit. "This is a loop," my instructor
said casually. He lowered the plane's nose to gain
airspeed, and then pulled sharply up. The earth,
and my stomach, fell away from me; and we were
(30) upside down, and I could feel gravity clawing at
me, pulling me out into the mile of empty space
between me and the ground. I grabbed at the sides
of the cockpit and hung on until gravity was on
my side again.
(35) "You seemed a little nervous that time," the
instructor said when the plane was right side up
again. "You've got to have confidence in that seat
belt, or you'll never do a decent loop. So this
time, when we get on top, I want you to put both
(40) arms out of the cockpit." And I did it. It was like
stepping off a bridge, but I did it, and the belt
held, and the plane came round. And after that I
could fly a loop. It was, as I said, satisfying.

Passage 2

The black plane dropped spinning, and flat-
(45) tened out spinning the other way; it began to
carve the air into forms that built wildly and
musically on each other and never ended.
Reluctantly, I started paying attention. Rahm
drew high above the world an inexhaustibly glori-
(50) ous line; it piled over our heads in loops and
arabesques. The plane moved every way a line
can move, and it controlled three dimensions, so
the line carved massive and subtle slits in the air
like sculptures. The plane looped the loop, seem-
(55) ing to arch its back like a gymnast; it stalled,
dropped, and spun out of it climbing; it spiraled
and knifed west on one side's wings and back
east on another; it turned cartwheels, which must
be physically impossible; it played with its own
(60) line like a cat with yarn. How did the pilot know
where in the air he was? If he got lost, the ground
would swat him.

His was pure energy and naked spirit. I have
thought about it for years. Rahm's line unrolled in
(65) time. Like music, it split the bulging rim of the
future along its seam. It pried out the present. We
watchers waited for the split-second curve of
beauty in the present to reveal itself. The human
pilot, Dave Rahm, worked in the cockpit right at
(70) the plane's nose; his very body tore into the
future for us and reeled it down upon us like a
curling peel.

Like any fine artist, he controlled the tension
of the audience's longing. You desired, unwitting-
(75) ly, a certain kind of roll or climb, or a return to a
certain portion of the air, and he fulfilled your
hope slantingly, like a poet, or evaded it until you
thought you would burst, and then fulfilled it surprisingly, so you gasped and cried out.
(80) The oddest, most exhilarating and exhausting
thing was this: he never quit. The music had no
periods, no rests or endings; the poetry's beautiful
sentence never ended; the line had no finish; the
sculptured forms piled overhead, one into another
(85) without surcease. Who could breathe, in a world
where rhythm itself had no periods?

GO ON TO THE NEXT PAGE

5

I went home and thought about Rahm's performance that night, and the next day, and the next.

I had thought I knew my way around beauty a
(90) little bit. I knew I had devoted a good part of my life to it, memorizing poetry and focusing my attention on complexity of rhythm in particular, on force, movement, repetition, and surprise, in both poetry and prose. Now I had stood among
(95) dandelions between two asphalt runways in Bellingham, Washington, and begun learning about beauty. Even the Boston Museum of Fine Arts was never more inspiring than this small northwestern airport on this time-killing Sunday
(100) afternoon in June. Nothing on earth is more gladdening than knowing we must roll up our sleeves and move back the boundaries of the humanly possible once more.

1. According to the author of Passage 1, training in acrobatic flying

(A) has only theoretical value
(B) expands a pilot's range of capabilities
(C) is an essential part of general pilot training
(D) comes naturally to most pilots
(E) should only be required of fighter pilots

2. The word "medium" in line 6 means

(A) midpoint
(B) appropriate occupation
(C) method of communication
(D) environment
(E) compromise

3. To "pick up the horizon line" (line 14) is to

(A) lift it higher
(B) spot it visually
(C) measure its distance
(D) choose it eagerly
(E) increase its visibility

4. Passage 1 suggests that the author's grabbing at the sides of the cockpit (lines 32–34) was

(A) instinctive
(B) terrifying
(C) essential
(D) habit-forming
(E) life-threatening

5. By putting both arms out of the cockpit (lines 37–42), the author

(A) chooses the path of least resistance
(B) enables himself to steer the plane more freely
(C) relies totally on his seat belt to keep him safe
(D) allows himself to give full expression to his nervousness
(E) is better able to breathe deeply and relax

6. The author's use of the word "satisfying" (line 43) represents

(A) a simile
(B) an understatement
(C) a fallacy
(D) a euphemism
(E) a hypothesis

7. The author of Passage 2 mentions her initial reluctance to watch the stunt flying (line 48) in order to

(A) demonstrate her hostility to commercial entertainment
(B) reveal her fear of such dangerous enterprises
(C) minimize her participation in aerial acrobatics
(D) indicate how captivating the demonstration was
(E) emphasize the acuteness of her perceptions

8. By fulfilling "your hope slantingly" (lines 76–77), the author means that

(A) the pilot flew the plane at an oblique angle
(B) Rahm distorted the desires of his audience
(C) the pilot had a bias against executing certain kinds of rolls
(D) Rahm refused to satisfy the audience's expectations directly
(E) the pilot's sense of aesthetic judgment was askew

9. The references in Passage 2 to "asphalt runways" (line 95) and "the Boston Museum of Fine Arts" (line 97) serve to

(A) illuminate the differences between the East and the Pacific Northwest
(B) evoke traditional aesthetics in order to discredit unorthodox notions of beauty
(C) give a sense of how far the author has had to travel
(D) show how unlikely a setting this was for such a profound aesthetic experience
(E) convey a faithful picture of the two places

10. At the end of Passage 2, the author is left feeling

(A) empty in the aftermath of the stunning performance she has seen
(B) jubilant at the prospect of moving from Boston to Washington
(C) exhilarated by her awareness of new potentials for humanity
(D) glad that she has not wasted any more time memorizing poetry
(E) surprised by her response to an art form she had not previously believed possible

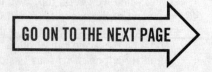
GO ON TO THE NEXT PAGE

5

11. The author of Passage 2 does all of the following EXCEPT

(A) pose a question
(B) develop a simile
(C) refute an argument
(D) state a conclusion
(E) draw a contrast

12. Compared to Passage 2, Passage 1 is

(A) less informative
(B) more tentative
(C) more argumentative
(D) more speculative
(E) less lyrical

13. How would the author of Passage 2 most likely react to the assessment of acrobatic flying in lines 7–11?

(A) She would consider it too utilitarian an assessment of an aesthetic experience.
(B) She would reject it as an inaccurate description of the pilot's technique.
(C) She would admire it as a poetic evocation of the pilot's art.
(D) She would criticize it as a digression from the author's main point.
(E) She would regard it as too effusive to be appropriate to its subject.

YOU MAY GO BACK AND REVIEW THIS SECTION IN THE REMAINING TIME, BUT DO NOT WORK IN ANY OTHER SECTION UNTIL TOLD TO DO SO.   **S T O P**

6   **6**   **6**   **6**   **6**   **6**   **6**   **6**   **6**   **6**   **6**

SECTION 6

Time—15 Minutes
10 Questions

For each problem in this section determine which of the five choices is correct and blacken in that choice on your answer sheet. You may use any blank space on the page for your work.

Notes:

- You may use a calculator whenever you feel it will be helpful.
- Use the diagrams provided to help you solve the problems. Unless you see the words "Note: Figure not drawn to scale" under a diagram, it has been drawn as accurately as possible. Unless it is stated that a figure is three-dimensional, you may assume it lies in a plane.

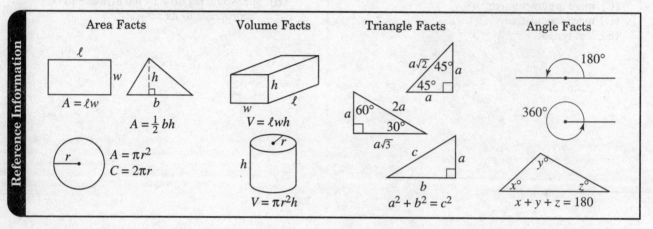

Reference Information

1. If the ratio of the number of boys to girls in a club is 3:5, what percent of the club members are girls?

    (A) 37.5%   (B) 40%   (C) 50%   (D) 60%
    (E) 62.5%

2. Neil paid $357, including 5% sales tax, for a suit. What was the cost of the suit, not counting the tax?

    (A) $339.15   (B) $340.00   (C) $342.00
    (D) $352.00   (E) $374.85

3. If $3x + 5 = 91$, what is the value of $\sqrt{3x - 5}$?

    (A) 7   (B) 8   (C) 9   (D) 10   (E) 11

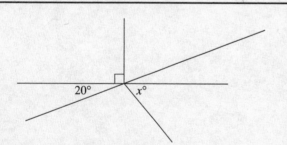

4. In the figure above, what is the value of x?

    (A) 20   (B) 70   (C) 60   (D) 110
    (E) It cannot be determined from the information given.

5. If n is an even integer, what is the sum of the smallest even integer greater than $5n + 6$ and the largest even integer less than $4n + 9$?

    (A) $9n + 13$ (B) $9n + 14$ (C) $9n + 15$
    (D) $9n + 16$ (E) $9n + 17$

6. In a class of 40 students, 13 have their own TV's and 18 have their own computers. If 16 have neither a TV nor a computer, how many students have both?

    (A) 0   (B) 3   (C) 6   (D) 7   (E) 11

7. A set of numbers is called "special" if the product of any two different numbers in the set is also in the set. For example, {0, 1, 2} is a special set. Which of the following numbers could be inserted in {0, 1, 2} so that the resulting set of four numbers would also be special?

    (A) –2   (B) –1   (C) $\dfrac{1}{2}$ (D) 4

    (E) none of them

GO ON TO THE NEXT PAGE

6   6 6 6 6 6 6 6 6 6 6   6

8. If Karen was born on Friday, September 13, which of the following could be the day of the week on which her third birthday falls?

       I. Monday
      II. Tuesday
    III. Friday

(A) I only (B) II only (C) III only
(D) I and II only (E) I and III only

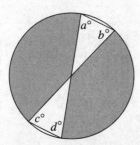

9. In the figure above, the diameter of the circle is 20 and the area of the shaded region is 80π. What is the value of $a + b + c + d$?

(A) 144   (B) 216   (C) 240   (D) 270   (E) 288

10. Each of s students was informed that he or she had won a scholarship and that a fund of d dollars would be divided equally among them. The committee then decided to choose a additional winners and to divide the fund equally among all winners. How much more money, in dollars, would each original winner have received if the additional winners were not named?

(A) $\dfrac{ad}{s(s+a)}$ (B) $\dfrac{d}{s+a}$ (C) $\dfrac{d}{s-a}$

(D) $\dfrac{d}{s(s+a)}$ (E) $\dfrac{ad}{s(s-a)}$

YOU MAY GO BACK AND REVIEW THIS SECTION IN THE REMAINING TIME, BUT DO NOT WORK IN ANY OTHER SECTION UNTIL TOLD TO DO SO.   **S T O P**

Answer Key

<u>Note</u>: The letters in brackets following the Mathematical Reasoning answers refer to the sections of Chapter 12 in which you can find the information you need to answer the questions. For example, **1. C [E]**, means that the answer to question 1 is C, and that the solution requires information found in Section 12-E: Averages.

Section 1   Verbal Reasoning

1. A	7. D	13. D	19. A	25. C
2. B	8. D	14. C	20. C	26. E
3. B	9. B	15. C	21. D	27. D
4. B	10. C	16. D	22. B	28. D
5. E	11. C	17. A	23. E	29. E
6. D	12. B	18. E	24. D	30. D

Section 2   Mathematical Reasoning

1. B [A]	6. C [J, K]	11. D [A]	16. C [A]	21. E [B]
2. D [A]	7. E [K, L]	12. C [A]	17. B [J, G]	22. B [K, L]
3. B [D, J, K]	8. C [E]	13. C [D]	18. B [M, P]	23. D [A]
4. C [G]	9. D [L, N]	14. E [E]	19. E [E]	24. A [H]
5. B [E, I]	10. E [B, C]	15. C [E, G]	20. C [D, J]	25. E [H, E]

Section 3   Verbal Reasoning

1. B	8. A	15. D	22. A	29. C
2. E	9. D	16. E	23. E	30. C
3. B	10. B	17. E	24. B	31. B
4. C	11. B	18. D	25. C	32. E
5. B	12. C	19. E	26. D	33. D
6. A	13. C	20. B	27. C	34. E
7. E	14. E	21. C	28. B	35. E

Section 4   Mathematical Reasoning

Quantitative Comparison Questions

1. C [J]	4. D [A]	7. D [K]	10. C [O]	13. C [J]
2. D [A]	5. A [A]	8. C [A]	11. A [O]	14. B [A, B]
3. D [K]	6. C [A]	9. A [E, B]	12. C [C]	15. A [L]

Grid-in Questions

16. [K] 300

17. [I] 320

18. [E] 5.75

19. [C,H] 90

20. [H] 150

or 23/4

21. [D] `. 4 9`

22. [A] `7 9`

23. [E] `1 3 9 2`

24. [K] `1 / 8`

or .125

25. [A,O] `5 9`

Section 5   Verbal Reasoning

1.	B	4.	A	7.	D	10.	C	13.	A
2.	D	5.	C	8.	D	11.	C		
3.	B	6.	B	9.	D	12.	E		

Section 6   Mathematical Reasoning

1.	E [C, D]	3.	C [G]	5.	D [A, F]	7.	C [A]	9.	E [L, J]
2.	B [C]	4.	E [I]	6.	D [O]	8.	D [P]	10.	A [B, F]

Calculate Your Raw Score

Verbal Reasoning

Section 1 $\dfrac{}{\text{number correct}} - \dfrac{1}{4}\left(\dfrac{}{\text{number incorrect}}\right) = \underline{}$ (A)

Section 3 $\dfrac{}{\text{number correct}} - \dfrac{1}{4}\left(\dfrac{}{\text{number incorrect}}\right) = \underline{}$ (B)

Section 5 $\dfrac{}{\text{number correct}} - \dfrac{1}{4}\left(\dfrac{}{\text{number incorrect}}\right) = \underline{}$ (C)

Raw Verbal Reasoning Score = (A) + (B) + (C) = _____

Mathematical Reasoning

Section 2 $\dfrac{}{\text{number correct}} - \dfrac{1}{4}\left(\dfrac{}{\text{number incorrect}}\right) = \underline{}$ (D)

Section 4
Part I
(1–15) $\dfrac{}{\text{number correct}} - \dfrac{1}{3}\left(\dfrac{}{\text{number incorrect}}\right) = \underline{}$ (E)

Part II
(16–25) $\dfrac{}{\text{number correct}} = \underline{}$ (F)

Section 6 $\dfrac{}{\text{number correct}} - \dfrac{1}{4}\left(\dfrac{}{\text{number incorrect}}\right) = \underline{}$ (G)

Raw Mathematical Reasoning Score = (D) + (E) + (F) + (G) = _____

Evaluate Your Performance

	Verbal Reasoning	Mathematical Reasoning
Superior	67–78	51–60
Very Good	60–66	45–50
Good	52–59	40–44
Satisfactory	44–51	35–39
Average	36–43	30–34
Needs Further Study	29–35	25–29
Needs Intensive Study	21–28	20–24
Inadequate	0–20	0–19

Identify Your Weaknesses

Verbal Reasoning

Question Type	Question Numbers			Chapter to Study
	Section 1	Section 3	Section 5	
Sentence Completion	1, 2, 3, 4, 5, 6, 7, 8, 9	1, 2, 3, 4, 5, 6, 7, 8, 9, 10		Chapter 4
Analogy	10, 11, 12, 13, 14, 15	11, 12, 13, 14, 15, 16, 17, 18, 19, 20, 21, 22, 23		Chapter 5
Reading Comprehension	16, 17, 18, 19, 20, 21, 22, 23, 24, 25, 26, 27, 28, 29, 30	24, 25, 26, 27, 28, 29, 30	1, 2, 3, 4, 5, 6, 7, 8, 9, 10, 11, 12, 13	Chapter 6

Identify Your Weaknesses

Mathematical Reasoning

Skill Area	Question Numbers			Pages to Study
	Section 2	**Section 4**	**Section 6**	
Basics of Arithmetic	1, 2, 11, 12, 16, 23	2, 4, 5, 6, 8, 14, 22, 25	5, 7	331–338
Fractions and Decimals	10, 21	9, 14	10	344–352
Percents	10	12, 19	1, 2	358–361
Ratios	3, 13, 20	21	1	366–370
Averages	5, 8, 14, 15, 19, 25	9, 18, 23		376–378
Polynomials			5, 10	383–386
Equations and Inequalities	4, 15, 17		3	389–394
Word Problems	24, 25	19, 20		399–402
Lines and Angles	5	17	4	407–410
Triangles	3, 6, 17, 20	1, 13	9	414–418
Quadrilaterals	3, 6, 7, 22	3, 7, 16, 24		425–428
Circles	7, 9, 22	15	9	432–435
Solid Geometry	18			440–442
Coordinate Geometry	9			446–448
Counting and Probability		10, 11, 25	6	452–456
Logical Reasoning	18		7	462–464
Data Interpretation				468–471

Answer Explanations

Section 1 Verbal Reasoning

1. **A.** Because the African American leaders were involved with one another, an essay dealing with one of them inevitably will also mention others of them. In other words, there's inevitably some *overlapping* among these essays. (Argument)

2. **B.** Though the new findings are surprising, they do not completely overturn established principles: they are not *revolutionary*.
Watch out for little words like *not*. They have a big effect on a sentence's meaning. (Contrast Pattern)

3. **B.** Great art has the ability to touch an audience. Here, it *reaches across* barriers to communicate *directly* with us.
Note that the sentence views these Eskimo carvings positively. They are the best carvings of all ages, and are able to communicate with us in a strong, positive way—*directly*. (Support Signal)

4. **B.** The key word "developing" anticipates the description of the way a highway system changes and grows. The road network is described as similar to the brain, which also *evolves with* use, developing and changing. (Comparison)

5. **E.** The collectors prefer to buy the works of long-dead artists. Therefore, they do not care to collect *contemporary* art. In fact, they are notorious (infamous) for their *dearth* or lack of interest in current art. (Contrast Pattern)

6. **D.** Tuchman is unusual because she *pursued* a scholarly career and became noted for *prodigious* (great; amazing) learning even though she never completed the standard graduate studies in her field. (Contrast Signal)

7. **D.** The systems analyst was reluctant to talk to ordinary people about her work because she thought it was too *esoteric* (obscure and specialized) for them to understand. (Argument)

8. **D.** A medicine that is said to "cure a wide variety of ailments" is by definition a *panacea*. (Definition)

9. **B.** A martinet is by definition a strict disciplinarian. Such a person would *constrain* (require or compel his or her underlings to *adhere* to (comply with; follow) all rules and regulations. (Definition)

10. **C.** One wears a *muffler* around one's *neck*; one wears a *sash* around one's *waist*. (Defining Characteristic)

11. **C.** A *barge* is a kind of *vessel* or ship; a *shovel* is a kind of *implement* or tool. (Class and Member)

12. **B.** An *armory* is a place of storage for *weapons*. A *warehouse* is a place of storage for *merchandise*. (Function)

13. **D.** A *competitor* is someone who *vies* or competes. A *mutineer* is someone who *revolts* or rebels. (Definition)

14. **C.** To be *foolhardy* or rashly bold is to carry being *daring* to a negative extreme. To be *obsequious* or slavishly attentive is to carry being *respectful* to a negative extreme. (Degree of Intensity)

15. **C.** By definition, *rubble* (waste fragments of brick) is what is left when a *building* is destroyed. *Shards* (fragments of earthenware) are what are left when *pottery* is destroyed. (Defining Characteristic)

16. **D.** The author is developing the military analogy in order to explain the immune system, the body's system of defense.
Choice A is incorrect. The author is not critical of the analogy; he draws on it in order to explain a complex system. Choice B is incorrect. The passage is expository, not persuasive: it explains, it doesn't argue. Choice C is incorrect. The author compares the mass of the immune system to that of the brain. However, that is only a passing reference. Choice E is incorrect. In developing the military analogy, the author is clarifying our picture of the immune system; he is not correcting a view that is out-of-date.

17. **A.** If you put together all the cells making up the immune system, you would have something about as big as the liver or brain. In other words, you'd have something that you could compare in mass or *bulk* to familiar bodily organs.

18. **E.** Lines 3–4 state that the lymphocytes are "born in the bone marrow." This answers the question as to where the body's lymphocytes *originate*.

19. **A.** Cyclosporin is a drug that suppresses the body's immune system. The immune system protects the body from foreign invaders, such as viruses. Suppression or inhibition of the immune system might well make the body

more susceptible to disease. It would not, however, make the body more likely to reject a transplanted organ, nor would it be likely to increase the effectiveness of antigens. Indeed, treatment by cyclosporin makes the body less likely to reject a transplanted organ. Presumably it also makes the immune system less responsive to the presence of antigens.

20. C. Though the author mentions the Australian immunologist Sir Frank Macfarlane Burnet, he never directly quotes Burnet's words or those of any other medical authority.
Choice A is incorrect. The author identifies *lymphocytes* as white blood cells. He states that *antigens* are protein molecules on a substance's surface that trigger the immune response. Choice B is incorrect. The passage is based on the comparison made between the immune system and an army. Choice D is incorrect. The author estimates the number of white blood cells available for mustering at approximately 200,000,000. Choice E is incorrect. By the use of military terminology ("troops," "billeted," "muster," "uniform") the author develops the central metaphor comparing the immune system to an army.

21. D. Lines 31–34 state that the clonal selection theory "helped explain how lymphocytes recognize and are activated by *specific foreign antigens*." In the immune system, lymphocyte families known as clones spot the enemy (the foreign antigens) and multiply to meet the threat. The immune system works on a "ready-made" basis, tailoring its response in accordance with its inherited knowledge of all foreign antigens to which it might be exposed.

22. B. The narrator never indicates that his father felt bitter about his army service. Choice A is incorrect. The narrator describes his father as "daring" and "impetuous." Choice C is incorrect. The narrator indicates that his father had been a sugarcane grower before he took up cattle ranching. Choice D is incorrect. Paragraph 2 stresses the riskiness of the trip during the stormy season. Choice E is incorrect. The narrator states his father had learned from the war that life was temporary.

23. E. Look at the context of the phrase. The very next words are "Suddenly all our cane went down and men began putting up fences." Why? They are putting up fences in order to be ready to enclose the cattle the father is about to buy. The father has sensed there is a market for good, fresh, untainted meat, and has immediately decided to try his hand at raising cattle.

24. D. Pappy "knew cattle." The father knew cane-growing, but wanted to learn cattle. This suggests that the father sought out Pappy *because he needed Pappy's guidance* in his new endeavor.

25. C. A quattie, like a penny, is a kind of *Jamaican coin*.

26. E. The bull has just been ferried on a freighter and unloaded by being hung from a sling. Pappy sees it snorting and rolling its eyes, and says the sea voyage had done it no good. He *realizes that being transported has angered the bull*.

27. D. Pappy had just had a frightening experience: he had seen the maddened bull attack the other cattle. Clearly, he would be *agitated by the news he brought*.

28. D. Throughout this short story, the author prepares the reader for the family's economic ruin. Here, he mentions rotting meat, both reminding the reader of the spoiled meat that inspired the father to try cattle-ranching and *foreshadowing* or hinting at *the eventual destruction of the herd*.

29. E. Given that the prize bull, the father's pride and joy, goes wild and destroys the herd, the father's pride in acquiring him seems highly *ironic*. Clearly, when he purchased the bull, the father had not expected this tragic outcome.

30. D. In this excerpt, the narrator is taking a retrospective look at events that took place in his childhood. (Note the mother's comments, in lines 16–19: they make it clear that the narrator is looking back.) His father abandoned cane-growing for cattle-ranching, a new, risky venture. He put all the family's money into buying a small herd and a prize bull. That bull went mad, attacking the herd. The passage concludes with the father's loading a rifle. What does this set of events suggest? First, it suggests the father would try to kill the prize bull. Other cattle were already dead or so badly injured that they, too, would have to be killed. The father had spent all he had on cattle; he had no money left to buy a new herd. He had cut down his sugar cane. He had taken a risk and lost. As the story's title suggests, he was destined for ruin. And years later his son would look back, trying to *come to terms with his family's financial undoing*.

Section 2   Mathematical Reasoning

In each mathematics section, for many problems, an alternative solution, indicated by two asterisks (**), follows the first solution. When this occurs, one of the solutions is the direct mathematical one and the other is based on one of the tactics discussed in Chapters 8–12.

1. **B.** $40 = (8 - 3)(8 - n) = 5(8 - n) = 40 - 5n \Rightarrow$
   $5n = 0 \Rightarrow n = \mathbf{0}.$

2. **D.**   In 11 days Debbie saves $88. If 11 days ago she had $324, she now has $324 + $88 = $412, and 11 days from now will have $412 + $88 = **$500**.

3. **B.**   Let each side of the small squares = 1. The white area consists of a square, *ABIJ*, whose area is 1 and $\triangle EBI$. Triangles *EFI* and *EBI* are each right triangles whose legs are 1 and 3. Therefore, the area of each triangle is $\frac{1}{2}(1)(3) = 1.5$. The shaded area is 1.5, and the white area is 2.5 (1.5 + 1). The ratio is 1.5:2.5, which equals **3:5**.

4. **C.**   Let the numbers be x and $\frac{1}{3}x$. Then

   $$12 = x\left(\frac{1}{3}x\right) = \frac{1}{3}x^2 \Rightarrow x^2 = 36 \Rightarrow$$
   $$x = 6 \quad \text{or} \quad x = -6.$$

   Since the numbers are positive, $x = 6$, $\frac{1}{3}x = 2$, and their sum is **8**.
   **You can avoid the algebra by just testing pairs of small numbers, in which one number is 3 times the other: 1 and 3? No. 2 and 6? Yes.

5. **B.**   Since vertical angles are equal, the measure of the unmarked angle is 40°. Then

   $$a + b + c + d + 40 + 40 = 360 \Rightarrow$$
   $$a + b + c + d = 280 \Rightarrow$$
   $$\frac{a+b+c+d}{4} = \frac{280}{4} = \mathbf{70}.$$

6. **C.**   Triangle *MAX* is a 45-45-90 right triangle, so

   $$MX = 3 \Rightarrow AX = 3 \Rightarrow$$
   $$\text{area of } \triangle MAX = \frac{1}{2}(3)(3) = \mathbf{4.5},$$

   which is also the area of the shaded triangle.
   **$MX = 3 \Rightarrow MT = 6 \Rightarrow$ area of square = $\frac{1}{2}(6)^2 = 18$. Then the area of the shaded triangle is $18 \div 4 = \mathbf{4.5}$.

7. **E.**   The area of a circle of radius 4 is 16π, so the area of the rectangle is also 16π. Since the

area of a rectangle is ℓw and it is given that the width is 2, we have $16\pi = \ell w = 2\ell \Rightarrow \ell = \mathbf{8\pi}$.

8. **C.**   The total length of all 5 movies was 8 hours and 40 minutes, or 480 + 40 = 520 minutes. The total length of the first 3 movies was $3 \times 100 = 300$ minutes, leaving 520 – 300 = 220 minutes for the other 2. If 1 movie was 90 minutes, the shortest length possible, the other would have been 220 – 90 = **130** minutes long. Is it possible that any of the first 3 was longer than that? No. Even if 2 of them were as short as possible, 90 minutes each, they would take 180 minutes, leaving only 300 – 180 = 120 minutes for the third.

9. **D.**   Draw a diagram. By the Pythagorean theorem, $r^2 = 3^2 + 3^2 = 9 + 9 = 18$. Since the formula for the area of a circle is $A = \pi r^2$, we get $A = 18\pi$.

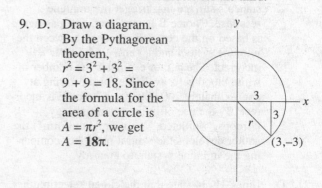

10. **E.**   If d of the cards were filed, $c - d$ were still unfiled, so the fraction of the cards that were unfiled was $\frac{c-d}{c}$. To get the percent, multiply the fractional part by 100%: $\frac{100(c-d)}{c}$%.
    **Use TACTIC 9-2. If Amy had 10 cards to file, then, after she filed 2 of them, 80% (8 of the 10) were still unfiled. Only $\frac{100(c-d)}{c}$ equals 80% when $c = 10$ and $d = 2$.

11. **D.**   Since $\boxed{b} = \textcircled{a} = a^2$, and $\boxed{b} = \sqrt{b}$, then
    $$\sqrt{b} = a^2 \Rightarrow b = a^4 \Rightarrow \textcircled{b} = (a^4)^2 = a^8.$$
    **Use TACTIC 9-2: replace a with a simple number. If $a = 1$, then all five choices = 1, so let $a = 2$. Then $\boxed{b} = \textcircled{2} = 2^2 = 4$, so
    $$\sqrt{b} = 4 \Rightarrow b = 16 \Rightarrow \textcircled{b} = 16^2 = (2^4)^2 = \mathbf{2^8}.$$

12. **C.**   Since $2 + 3 = 5$, so I could be true. Also, $3 + 5 + 11 = 19$, so II could be true. Since qr is divisible by 1, q, r, and qr, it cannot be prime, so III is false. Statements **I and II only** are true.

13. **C.**   First convert 3.2 hours to minutes by multiplying by 60: $3.2 \times 60 = 192$. Since $\frac{3}{5}$ of the report took 192 minutes, divide by 3 to find

how long $\frac{1}{5}$ of the report took: $192 \div 3 = 64$.

Then $\frac{2}{5}$ of the report will take twice as long:
$2 \times 64 = \mathbf{128}$ minutes.

**By dividing 192 by $\frac{3}{5}$, you can find that the whole report would take 320 minutes; then take $\frac{2}{5}$ of that.

**Note that, since more than half has been typed, the answer is less than 192. Eliminate D and E. Also eliminate A, which is ridiculously small. At worst, guess between B and C, but note that even $76\frac{4}{5}$ seems too small.

14. E.   Since 7 has to be the average of 3 and c, then $3 + c = 14 \Rightarrow c = 11$. Now 11 is the average of 7 and d, so $7 + d = 22 \Rightarrow d = 15$. Finally, since 15 is the average of 11 and e, then $11 + e = 30 \Rightarrow e = \mathbf{19}$.

15. C.   Since b is the average of a and c, then $a + c = 2b \Rightarrow c = 2b - a$. Also, since c is the average of b and d, then $b + d = 2c = 4b - 2a \Rightarrow d = 3b - 2a$. Finally, since d is the average of c and e,

$$c + e = 2d \Rightarrow (2b - a) + e = 6b - 4a \Rightarrow$$
$$e = \mathbf{4b - 3a}.$$

**Note that choices A and B aren't given in terms of just a and b; eliminate them. Next, use the number strip determined in exercise 14: $\boxed{3 \mid 7 \mid 11 \mid 15 \mid 19}$. Which choices are equal to 19 when $a = 3$ and $b = 7$? Unfortunately, both C ($4 \times 7 - 3 \times 3 = 28 - 9$) and E ($7 \times 7 - 10 \times 3 = 49 - 30$) equal 19, but at least you can also eliminate D. If you have no other ideas, guess between C and E.

16. C.   To make $x + y - z$ as large as possible, let x and y be as large as they can and then subtract the smallest number possible. Since it is given that $y = 50$, and that $x < y < z$, the greatest possible value of $x + y - z = 49 + 50 - 51 = \mathbf{48}$.

17. B.   Since the sum of the three measures is 180°:
$$180 = x + 2x + 3y = 3x + 3y = 3(x + y) \Rightarrow$$
$$x + y = 60 \Rightarrow x = \mathbf{60 - y}.$$

**Use TACTIC 9-2. Pick an easy-to-use value for x, say 10. Then
$10 + 20 + 3y = 180 \Rightarrow 3y = 150 \Rightarrow y = 50$.
Which of the choices equals 10 when y is 50? Only $\mathbf{60 - y}$.

18. B.   This question just requires good visualization. Think of the cube as being cut into three slices,

as in the figure below. All 9 little cubes in the top row and in the bottom row are painted, and all but the center cube in the middle row is painted. Only **1** small cube is unpainted.

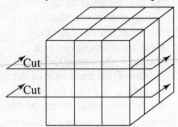

19. E.   In the 4 months from January to April, Greg rented $4m$ movies; and in the 8 months from May to December, he rented $8n$ movies. In total, he rented $4m + 8n$ movies in 12 months, for a monthly average of $\frac{4m + 8n}{12} = \frac{m + 2n}{3}$.

**Of course, this is the type of problem where you can use TACTIC 9-2 and plug in numbers. Pick any small numbers for m and n, and solve.

20. C.   It's worth remembering that, when the three angles of a triangle are in the ratio of 1:2:3, the triangle is a 30-60-90 right triangle. (If you don't know that, solve the equation $x + 2x + 3x = 180$.) In a 30-60-90 right triangle the sides are a, $a\sqrt{3}$, and $2a$, so the desired ratio is $a:2a = \mathbf{1:2}$.

21. E.   There aren't too many possibilities. One of them is $\frac{1}{3} + \frac{1}{3} + \frac{1}{3} = 1$; if the fractions were all smaller than $\frac{1}{3}$, the sum would be too small. What if one of the fractions is $\frac{1}{2}$?

Then the other two have to add up to $\frac{1}{2}$: $\frac{1}{4} + \frac{1}{4}$ works, so $a + b + c$ could be $2 + 4 + 4 = 10$.

Could one of the fractions be less than $\frac{1}{4}$?

Yes; $\frac{1}{2} + \frac{1}{3} = \frac{5}{6}$, so the third fraction could be $\frac{1}{6}$: $\frac{1}{2} + \frac{1}{3} + \frac{1}{6} = 1$, and $2 + 3 + 6 = \mathbf{11}$.
You could try to find something bigger; but since 11 is the largest of the five choices, don't waste valuable time.

**You should see that $\frac{1}{3} + \frac{1}{3} + \frac{1}{3} = 1$, so the answer is at least 9. Eliminate A and B. Also, the answer 9 is probably too easy for question 21, so eliminate C. If you can't figure out the answer, just guess.

22. **B.** The perimeter of the shaded region is given as $4 + 2\pi$. You can easily prove that the lengths of the curved parts of the region are 2π and that the straight edges have a total length of 4, but you should just assume these

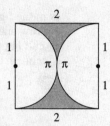

values. Then each side of the square is 2, and its area is 4. From that subtract π, the area of a circle (two semicircles) of radius 1: $\mathbf{4 - \pi}$.

**Eliminate choices A and E, which are negative. If you guess correctly that each side of the square is 2, then you know that the area of the square is 4 and the shaded area is much less. Eliminate choices C and D.

23. **D.** Check each choice. (A) If $x = 5$, $\sqrt{x-1} = 2$. (B) This one is tougher; the only possibility is $x = 1$, in which case $\sqrt{x^2 - 1} = 0$. If you don't see that immediately, keep B under consideration, and test the rest. (C) If $x = 3$, $\dfrac{x+4}{x-2} = 7$ (4, 5, and 8 also work). (D) For positive x, $\dfrac{x+4}{x+2}$ is always greater than 1 but less than 2 (if $x = 0$, the fraction equals 2); $\dfrac{x+4}{x+2}$ cannot be an integer—that's it. If you didn't reason that out, check E: $\dfrac{5}{x+1}$ is an integer if $x = 4$. You should have eliminated at least A, C, and E.

24. **A.** Dividing the distance, in miles, that Joanna walked by her rate, in miles per hour, gives the amount of time in <u>hours</u>, that she walked:

$\left(\dfrac{m + \dfrac{2}{3}}{r + \dfrac{1}{2}} \right)$. Simplify the complex fraction by

multiplying every term in the numerator and denominator by 6: $\dfrac{6m+4}{6r+3} = \dfrac{2(3m+2)}{3(2r+1)}$.

Finally, multiply by 60 to get the amount of time in <u>minutes</u>:

$$\overset{20}{\cancel{60}}\left(\dfrac{2(3m+2)}{\underset{1}{\cancel{3}}(2r+1)} \right) = \dfrac{40(3m+2)}{2r+1}.$$

**Complex fractions are never fun, but they are a bit easier if you have simple numbers

 instead of letters. Assume Joanna walked $2\dfrac{2}{3}$

miles at a rate of $1\dfrac{1}{2}$ miles per hour, and work the problem out.

25. **E.** From the wording of the question it is clear that it doesn't matter how many claims were processed, as long as Mr. Smith and his assistant each processed the same number. Pick an easy number; assume each person processed 10 claims. Mr. Smith did his 10 in 1 hour, and his assistant did his 10 in 2 hours. Then 3 hours, or 180 minutes, were used to process 20 claims: an average of $180 \div 20 = \mathbf{9}$ minutes per claim.

Section 3   Verbal Reasoning

1. **B.** To *aggravate* a problem is to make it worse. When people live longer and fewer babies die, overpopulation is made worse.
(Cause and Effect)

2. **E.** A plot that people have seen over and over again is by definition *trite* (stale; overdone). Note that the second clause gives you the information you need to fill in the word missing in the first clause.   (Definition)

3. **B.** If Tey has written fewer books than Christie, then by definition Tey is the less *prolific* (productive) writer. The sentence contrasts the two writers in terms of both quality and quantity.
(Contrast Signal)

4. **C.** By definition, someone cynical finds it difficult to *credit* or believe in the *unselfishness* of people's actions.   (Definition)

5. **B.** If most of these animals either eat krill directly or eat it indirectly (by eating other animals that live on krill), then *ultimately*, in the final analysis, they depend on krill.   (Definition)

6. **A.** Wallerstein views divorce as a *continuum* or continuous series of changing relationship. Note how the "not as...but as" structure sets up the contrast.   (Contrast Signal)

7. **E.** The field is littered by a *clutter* or chaotic jumble of contradictory theories. Choice A is incorrect. While *bonanza* means abundance, it is an abundance of good things, a desired abundance. Here the abundance of theories is undesired; it is a confusion, not a blessing.   (Definition)

8. **A.** If you expected someone's grief to die down or *subside* quickly, you would be surprised to find that he continued to grieve and was hopelessly unhappy (*disconsolate*).
(Cause and Effect Signal)

9. D. Only *unequivocal* (clear and unmistakable) data could justify either side's making dogmatic, authoritative assertions. Note how important the word "not" is in this sentence.
(Argument)

10. B. If Americans believe the government should use its powers sparingly, then they must be *chary* or cautious about the government's using unnecessary force.
(Argument/Definition)

11. B. A *clasp* is the fastening on a *bracelet*. A *buckle* is the fastening on a *belt*. (Function)

12. C. A *ream* is a unit of quantity for *paper*; a *cord* is a unit of quantity for *wood*.
(Defining Characteristic)

13. C. A *trough* is a feeding bin for *pigs*; a *manger* is a feeding bin for *cattle*. (Function)

14. E. A *whiff* is a slight gust or puff of odor or *scent*. A *puff* is a small, brief blast of vapor or *smoke*. Beware of eye-catchers. Choice A is incorrect. *Musk* refers to a type of fragrance; *whiff* refers to an amount of *scent*.
(Defining Characteristic)

15. D. To *extract* a *tooth* is to pull it out or remove it. To *uproot* a tree *stump* is to pull it out or remove it. (Purpose)

16. E. To *rustle cattle* is to steal them. To *hijack cargo* is to steal it. Note that you are dealing with a secondary meaning of the verb *rustle* here. (Defining Characteristic)

17. E. To *ruffle* someone's *composure* is to disturb or trouble his self-possession. To *upset* someone's *equilibrium* is to disturb or trouble his balance. (Function)

18. D. Something *grisly* or gruesome causes one to *recoil* or flinch. Something *heartrending* or severely distressing causes one to *weep*.
(Cause and Effect)

19. E. A *purist* (stickler for correctness) by definition is someone who insists on *correctness*. A *martinet* (strict disciplinarian) by definition is someone who insists on *discipline*.
Beware of eye-catchers. Choice D is incorrect. While accuracy is related to correctness, judges are not defined as people who insist on accuracy. (Defining Characteristic)

20. B. To *pulverize* something is to convert it to powder or *dust*. To *vaporize* something is to convert it to vapor or *mist*. (Definition)

21. C. A *necromancer* or sorcerer practices *witchcraft*. A *swindler* or trickster practices *duplicity* (deceit). (Defining Characteristic)

22. A. A *luminary* (notable person) is by definition *illustrious* (renowned). A *zealot* (fanatic; extremist) is by definition *intense*.
(Defining Characteristic)

23. E. *Doggerel* is trivial or inferior verse produced by a *poet*. A *potboiler* is a trivial or inferior literary work produced by a *novelist*.
(Worker and Article Created)

24. B. The writers' emergence stemmed or *arose* from their willingness to take the opportunity to write about black lives. Always substitute the answer choices in the original sentence.

25. C. In lines 5–11, the author refers to the "movement that has been variously called the Harlem Renaissance, the Black Renaissance, and the New Negro Movement." He is discussing the historic black literary movement that both affirmed African American culture and worked to bridge the chasm between the races through literature and art. The Harlem Renaissance, the Black Renaissance, and the New Negro Movement are *alternate names* for this *social and cultural phenomenon*.

26. D. The author describes blacks fighting back in the riots "with surprising audacity." He is impressed that blacks *dared* to strike back against the injustices they had endured for so long.

27. C. The author states that black writers "were sufficiently in touch with the main currents of American literary thought to adapt the accepted forms of expression to their own material, thus gaining a wider audience." They used the *prevalent literary modes* (short stories, sonnets, novels, plays)—the accepted forms of expression—to bring their material to a wider audience. In doing so, they became increasingly accepted as writers.

28. B. The author casts a positive light on the writers' acceptance of their separateness, emphasizing that the sufferings of blacks "had drawn them closer together" and had given them a vision of their mission as a people.

29. C. Again, substitute the answer choices in the original context. By embracing a doctrine, you *adopt* or espouse that doctrine: you come to believe in it, and defend its teachings.

30. C.   The writers were more involved with fighting problems in the system than with attacking the system itself. This suggests that fundamentally they *were not opposed to* the democratic system of government.
Choice A is incorrect. The fact that the writers did not revolt against the system does not imply that they played only a minor part in fighting abuses of the system. Choices B, D and E are incorrect. None is suggested by the statement.

31. B.   To assume the role of crusader is to act the part. Not all black writers in the period assumed or *took on* this particular role.

32. E.   The author's use of such terms as "nobility of expression" and "great masters of recent American literature" make it clear his attitude is one of *admiration*.

33. D.   The concluding sentence of paragraph 2 states two major factors that produced the crop of black writers who made up the Harlem Renaissance. The following two paragraphs continue the discussion of these social and political factors.
Choice A is incorrect. The opening sentence indicates that the willingness of black writers to portray their own lives was a factor in the Harlem Renaissance. Yet the next sentence makes it clear that this willingness was only *part* of what was going on. Choice B is incorrect. The author is concerned with these writers as part of an American literary movement, not a worldwide crusade. Choice C is incorrect. The author cites examples of specific injustices in passing. Choice E is incorrect. It is unsupported by the passage.

34. E.   Use the process of elimination to find the correct answer to this question.
Choice A is incorrect. In lines 62–65, the author *quotes an authority*, citing the historian Nathan Huggins.
Choice B is incorrect. Throughout the passage, the author makes assertions (black writers "stood for full equality" with whites) and then proceeds to qualify or modify them ("but they celebrated...their own integrity as a people").
Choice C is incorrect. The author cites examples of the trials suffered by blacks: "the slave quarters, the proscriptions even in freedom, the lynchings and the riots."
Choice D is incorrect. In lines 43–49 the author dismisses or rejects the possibility that black writers accepted their separateness because they wanted to be a distinct and possibly even exotic group.
Only Choice E is left. It is the correct answer. Throughout the passage the author never *poses or asks a question*.

35. E.   The passage discusses the growing interest of American literary circles in the social and economic problems of the country, the effects of the First World War, and the impact of the liberal and radical political movements of the period on whites and blacks alike.
Choice A is unanswerable on the basis of the passage. If anything, the passage indicates that black writers did not abandon the accepted literary forms of the day. Choice B is unanswerable on the basis of the passage, which mentions no specific names. Choice C is unanswerable on the basis of the passage. While the passage indicates black writers may have been influenced by foreign ideological systems, it nowhere suggests that the writers were *in rebellion against* these systems. Choice D is unanswerable on the basis of the passage. No such information is supplied.

Section 4   Mathematical Reasoning
Quantitative Comparison Questions

1. C.   Since by KEY FACT J2 the measure of an exterior angle of a triangle is equal to the sum of the measures of the two opposite interior angles,

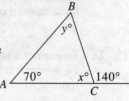

$140 = 70 + y$, and so $y = 70$. Therefore, angles A and B are equal, and by KEY FACT J3 so are the sides opposite them: $AC = BC$. The columns are equal (C).
**If you don't know the theorem about the exterior angle, first find x: $x + 140 = 180 \Rightarrow x = 40$. Then, since the sum of the measures of the three angles of a triangle is 180, $y = 70$.

2. D.   Column A: by the distributive law, $5(r + t) = 5r + 5t$. Subtracting $5r$ from each column, compare $5t$ and t. They are equal if $t = 0$ and are unequal otherwise. Neither column is *always* greater, and the columns are not *always* equal (D).

3. D.   If $\ell = 8$ and $w = 6$, the area of the rectangle is 48, in which case Column B is greater. But if $\ell = 8.5$ and $w = 6$, the area is 51, in which case Column A is greater. Remember: neither ℓ nor w has to be an integer. Neither column is *always* greater, and the columns are not *always* equal (D).

4. D.   If a and b had to be integers, the greatest $a + b$ could is 49 (when the numbers are 1 and 48). Just as in question 3, however, the variables do not have to be integers. If $a = 0.1$,

and $b = 480$, then $ab = 48$, and $a + b = 480.1$. Neither column is *always* greater, and the columns are not *always* equal (D).

5. **A.** Since 100 is even, $(-1)^{100} = 1$, whereas, since 125 is odd, $(-1)^{125} = -1$. Column A is greater.

6. **C.** When *any* number is divided by 10, the remainder is the units digit. (For example, $3457 = 10 \times 345 + 7$: the quotient is 345, and the remainder is 7.) The columns are equal (C).

7. **D.** If ℓ represents the length and w the width of rectangle I, then 2ℓ and $0.5w$ are the length and the width of rectangle II. Then Column A is $2\ell + 2w$, and Column B is $4\ell + w$. Subtracting 2ℓ and w from each column gives w in Column A and 2ℓ in Column B. You are not given any relationship between w and ℓ, so you can't determine the perimeters. Remember that length is not necessarily greater than width. Neither column is *always* greater, and the columns are not *always* equal (D).
    **You can use TACTIC 10-1 and solve this problem by picking values for ℓ and w as long as you remember that w can be much greater than ℓ.

8. **C.** Since $y^{10} = 2$, then $(y^{10})^2 = 2^2$, so $y^{20} = 4$. Therefore, $x^{20} = y^{20}$, implying that $x = y$, since x and y are both positive. The columns are equal (C).

9. **A.** Column A: $(a \circledast b) \circledast c = \left(\dfrac{a+b}{2}\right) \circledast c =$

    $\dfrac{\dfrac{a+b}{2}+c}{2}$. Simplify the complex fraction by

    multiplying every term in the numerator and denominator by 2: $\dfrac{a+b+2c}{4}$.

    Similarly, Column B: $a \circledast (b \circledast c) =$

    $a \circledast \left(\dfrac{b+c}{2}\right) = \dfrac{a+\dfrac{b+c}{2}}{2} = \dfrac{2a+b+c}{4}$.

	$\dfrac{a+b+2c}{4}$	$\dfrac{2a+b+c}{4}$
Multiply each column by 4:	$a + b + 2c$	$2a + b + c$
Subtract $a + b + c$ from each column:	c	a

    Since it is given that $c > a$, Column A is greater.
    **Wouldn't you rather do this with numbers? Just pick any three numbers, and calculate the averages. Column A will be greater. Doing it once, you eliminate B and C. Do it twice, using numbers like 1, 0, and −1, and you can choose A with confidence.

10. **C.** If $\lfloor A \rfloor = A$, then A reads the same forward and backward. The only numbers between 100 and 200 with this property are 101, 111, 121, ... , 191. There are 10 such numbers in all. The columns are equal (C).

11. **A.** Of the 90 two-digit numbers, 9 numbers (11, 22, ... , 99) satisfy $\lfloor A \rfloor = A$. Of the other 81, 45 satisfy $\lfloor A \rfloor < A$ and 36 satisfy $\lfloor A \rfloor > A$. The easiest way to see this is to list the numbers systematically. In the 10's there is 1 number $(01 < 10)$; in the 20's there are 2 numbers $(02 < 20$ and $12 < 21)$; in the 30's there are 3 numbers; ... ; in the 90's there are 9 numbers: $1 + 2 + \cdots + 9 = 45$. Column A is greater.

12. **C.** Don't solve this algebraically. Since this is a percent problem, just plug in 100 for the number of cones sold. Then 60 small cones were sold for \$60, and 40 large cones were sold for $40 \times \$1.50 = \$60$. Therefore, 100 cones were sold for a total of \$120, and the average price was \$1.20. The columns are equal (C).

13. **C.** Let $x =$ length of the third side of a triangle whose other two sides are 5 and 13. By the triangle inequality,

    $$(13 - 5) < x < (13 + 5) \Rightarrow 8 < x < 18.$$

    Since Phillip's and David's triangles have integer sides, Phillip's third side is 9 and David's is 17. Since the other two sides are equal, the difference between their perimeters is the same as the difference between their third sides: $17 - 9 = 8$. The columns are equal (C).

14. **B.** Column A: 10^{100} is evenly divisible by 5^{75}. (Just imagine a fraction whose numerator is the product of 100 10's and whose denominator is the product of 75 5's. Each 5 divides into one of the 10's.) Then Column A is 0. Column B: 10^{100} is not evenly divisible by 75^5, since 75^5 is divisible by 3, but 10^{100} is not. Since there will be a remainder, Column B is greater than 0 and therefore greater than Column A.

15. **A.** Since the area of each small circle is πr^2, the area of the white region is $3\pi r^2$. Also, since the area of the large circle is πR^2, the area of the shaded region is $\pi R^2 - 3\pi r^2 = \pi(R^2 - 3r^2)$. Since the areas of the white region and shaded region are equal:

    $$3\pi r^2 = \pi(R^2 - 3r^2) \Rightarrow 3r^2 = R^2 - 3r^2 \Rightarrow$$
    $$R^2 = 6r^2 \Rightarrow \frac{R^2}{r^2} = 6 \Rightarrow \frac{R}{r} = \sqrt{6},$$

    which is greater than 2. Column A is greater.

Grid-in Questions

16. (300)   Draw a diagram, and label it. If the width of the rectangle is w, the length is $3w$ and the perimeter is

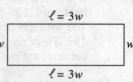

$w + 3w + w + 3w = 8w = 80$, so $w = 10$. Finally, the area is $\ell w = 30 \times 10 = $ **300**.
****Use TACTIC 11-2. Don't try to guess the area; guess the width and length. Pick a value for the width: 5, say. Then the length will be 15 and the perimeter will be $5 + 15 + 5 + 15 = 40$—too small. In fact, just half of what you need. Try 10.

17. (320)   Since $a + 100 = 180$, $a = 80$. But since ℓ and k are parallel, the four acute angles are all equal: $80 = a = b = c = d$, so their sum is $4 \times 80 = $ **320**.

18. $\left(5.75 \text{ or } \dfrac{23}{4}\right)$ The median of the 11 numbers 1, 2,

3, ... , 11 is the middle one: 6. The median of the 10 numbers 1, 2, 3, ... , 10 is the average of the two middle ones: $\dfrac{5+6}{2} = 5.5$. Finally, the average of 6 and 5.5 is **5.75** or $\dfrac{23}{4}$.

19. (90)   If x = the cost of the film, then $100 + x$ = price of the camera, and

$$125 = x + (100 + x) = 2x + 100 \Rightarrow$$
$$2x = 25 \Rightarrow x = 12.5,$$

which is 10% of the total cost of 125. The camera cost **90%** of the total.

20. (150)   Since Diane got $100, the other three shared the remaining $900. If x represents Al's share, then Bob got $2x$ and Carol got $3x$. Then

$$900 = x + 2x + 3x = 6x \Rightarrow x = 150.$$

21. (.49)   Cross-multiply: $100a = 49b$, so

$a = \dfrac{49}{100}b \Rightarrow \dfrac{a}{b} = \dfrac{49}{100}$. Since $\dfrac{49}{100}$ can't

fit in the grid, write it as a decimal: **.49**.

22. (79)   To make a large fraction, you need as large a numerator as possible and as small a denominator as possible. The greatest value that $x^2 - y$ can have is 80, by letting $x = 9$ and $y = 1$. Then, since x, y, and z are different, the least that z can be is 2, and the value of the fraction will be $\dfrac{80}{2}$ or 40. However, if you interchange

x and y, you get 79 for the numerator ($9^2 - 2$) and 1 for the denominator: $\dfrac{79}{1}$ or **79**.

23. (1392)   Since 36% of 25 is 9, there are 9 girls and $25 - 9 = 16$ boys in the class. The total weight of the 9 girls is $9 \times 120 = 1080$ pounds, and the total weight of the 16 boys is $16 \times 150 = 2400$ pounds. Therefore, the average weight of all 25 students is

$$\frac{1080 + 2400}{25} = \frac{3480}{25} = 139.2,$$

and 10 times the average is **1392**.

24. $\left(\dfrac{1}{8} \text{ or } .125\right)$ Draw and label a diagram. Let s

represent a side of square I. Then the perimeter of square I and the diagonal of square II are each $4s$, and the area of square I is s^2. The easiest way to get the area of square II is to

use the formula $A = \dfrac{1}{2}d^2$ (KEY FACT K8):

$$A = \frac{1}{2}(4s)^2 = \frac{1}{2}16s^2 = 8s^2.$$

Then, the ratio of the two areas is $\dfrac{s^2}{8s^2} = \dfrac{1}{8}$ or **.125**.

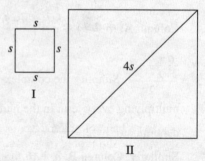

****Proceed exactly as above, except that, to find the area of square II, find the length of a side and square it. Since the diagonal is $4s$, by KEY FACT J8 (or by the Pythagorean

theorem), each side is $\dfrac{4s}{\sqrt{2}}$. Then the area is

$$\left(\frac{4s}{\sqrt{2}}\right)^2 = \frac{16s^2}{2} = 8s^2.$$

****Use TACTIC 11-2: plug in an easy-to-use number. For example, let a side of square I be 1; then the perimeter of square I is 4. The diagonal of square II is also 4, so the area of square I is 1 and the area of square II is 8.

25. (59)   For $(m - 5)(m - 45)$ to be positive, either both factors are positive or both factors are negative. For $(m - 5)$ to be negative, m must be less than 5, so $m = 1, 2, 3,$ or 4 (4 values).

For $(m - 45)$ to be positive, m must be greater than 45, so $m = 46, 47, \ldots, 100$ (55 values). The answer is **59**. [Note that from 46 to 100 there are $100 - 46 + 1 = 55$ integers, just as there are $4 - 1 + 1 = 4$ integers from 1 to 4 (KEY FACT O1).]

Section 5   Verbal Reasoning

1. **B.** In extending the pilot's control of the plane and making extreme actions (loops, sudden swerves, dives, and so forth) comfortable, acrobatic flying *extends a pilot's range of capabilities*.

2. **D.** The medium of the air is the *environment* in which flying creatures function.

3. **B.** In the course of doing a loop, you lose sight of the horizon and must tilt your head backward to catch sight of the horizon line again. Thus, to pick up the horizon line is to *spot it visually*.

4. **A.** Earlier in the passage, the author describes the experience of doing a loop as being "as far outside instinctive human behavior as you can go." In grabbing at the sides of the cockpit during the loop, the author has responded to his fear of falling in an *instinctive*, involuntary manner.
Choice B is incorrect. The experience of doing a loop was terrifying; grabbing the sides of the cockpit was not. Choice C is incorrect. It was not essential for the author to grab the sides of the cockpit; his seat belt was strong enough to keep him from falling out of the plane. Choice D is incorrect. The author did not wind up making a habit of grabbing the sides of the cockpit; he did it only that once. Choice E is incorrect. The experience of doing a loop may have seemed life-threatening; grabbing the sides of the cockpit was not.

5. **C.** The instructor tells the author to put his arms out of the cockpit so that he can learn to have confidence in his seat belt's ability to hold him in the plane. He does so, *relying totally on his seat belt to keep him safe*.

6. **B.** By stressing the terror that went into learning how to fly a loop, the author makes you feel that *satisfying* is an extremely mild word to describe the exhilaration of overcoming such an extreme fear and mastering such an unnatural skill. It is clearly an *understatement*.

7. **D.** The author was not a fan of stunt-flying; she was reluctant to pay attention to the aerial display. Therefore, this particular aerial display

must have been unusually *captivating* to capture her attention.

8. **D.** The author describes the audience's longing for a particular effect in the stunt-flying demonstration ("a certain kind of roll or climb, or a return to a certain portion of the air"). The members of the audience supposedly know what they want. Rahm, however, will not give them what they want. He *refuses to satisfy their expectations directly* but gives them something unexpected—and even more satisfying—instead.

9. **D.** By contrasting the small, weed-filled northwestern airport (a place to kill time on a Sunday afternoon) with the imposing, art-filled Boston Museum of Fine Arts (a place to seek aesthetic inspiration), the author points up just *how unlikely a setting the airport was for such a profound aesthetic experience*.

10. **C.** By "moving back the boundaries of the humanly possible" the author is talking about becoming aware *of new potentials for humanity*. This new knowledge leaves her gladdened and *exhilarated*.

11. **C.** Use the process of elimination to answer this question. The author poses two questions in the course of the passage. ("How did the pilot know…?" "Who could breathe…?") Therefore, you can eliminate Choice A. She develops several similes ("like a gymnast," "like a cat," "like a curling peel"). You can eliminate Choice B. She states what she has learned from the experience, concluding that "(n)othing on earth is more gladdening than knowing we must roll up our sleeves and move back the boundaries of the humanly possible once more." You can eliminate Choice D. She contrasts the Boston Museum of Fine Arts with the Bellingham airport. You can eliminate Choice E. However, she never disproves or *refutes an argument*. Only Choice C is left. It is the correct answer.

12. **E.** Passage 1 is both descriptive and informative. In recounting the story of the flying lesson, it is anecdotal. However, in comparison with Passage 2, it is not particularly poetic or *lyrical*.

13. **A.** The author of Passage 1 talks about how useful acrobatic flying is in improving the skills of pilots. The author of Passage 2, however, looks on acrobatic flying as *an aesthetic experience*: she responds to Rahm's aerial demonstration as a new form of beauty, a performance that engages her aesthetically. Therefore, she would most likely consider the assessment of aerial flying in Passage 1 *too*

utilitarian (concerned with practical usefulness) to be appropriate for an aesthetic
experience.

Section 6   Mathematical Reasoning

1. **E.** Since the ratio of the number of boys to girls
   is 3:5, the number of boys is $3x$, the number of
   girls is $5x$, and the total number of members is
   $3x + 5x = 8x$. The girls make up $\frac{5x}{8x} = \frac{5}{8} =$
   62.5% of the members.

2. **B.** Since $357 was the cost of the suit including
   5% tax, *divide* 357 by 1.05: $357 \div 1.05 = \mathbf{340}$.
   (If c is the cost of the suit, $357 = c + 0.05c =$
   $1.05c$.)

3. **C.** $3x + 5 = 91 \Rightarrow 3x = 86 \Rightarrow 3x - 5 = 81 \Rightarrow$
   $\sqrt{3x-5} = \sqrt{81} = \mathbf{9}$. (Note that, since the
   given equation and what you want both
   involve $3x$, you should *not* solve for x.)

4. **E.** Since vertical angles are equal, $a = 20$, and so
   $x + y = 160$. We can see that $b = 70$; but there
   are no other vertical angles, and **it is impossible to determine x or y from the information given.**

   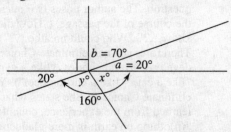

5. **D.** Since any multiple of an even integer is even,
   $4n$ and $5n$ are both even. Then $5n + 6$ is even
   (it's the sum of two even numbers); add 2 to
   get the next even integer: $5n + 8$. But $4n + 9$ is
   odd (it's the sum of an even and an odd number); subtract 1 to get the next lower even
   number: $4n + 8$. Finally, take the sum:
   $5n + 8 + 4n + 8 = \mathbf{9n + 16}$.
   **This is a perfect situation for TACTIC 9-2.
   Let $n = 2$. Then $5n + 6 = 16$, and the next
   even number is 18; $4n + 9 = 17$, and the even
   number just less than 17 is 16: $18 + 16 = 34$.
   Only $9n + 16 = 34$ when $n = 2$.

6. **D.** Since 16 of the 40 students have neither a TV
   nor a computer, 24 students have at least one,
   possibly both. Since 18 of those 24 have computers, 6 of them have TV's but no computer.
   But since 13 have TV's, it must be that **7** students have both TV's and computers.
   **A Venn diagram may make this problem
   easier.

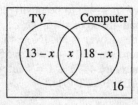

From the diagram:
$$13 - x + x + 18 - x = 24 \Rightarrow$$
$$31 - x = 24 \Rightarrow x = \mathbf{7}.$$

7. **C.** Just check each choice. A: $\{-2, 0, 1, 2\}$ isn't
   special because it doesn't contain $-2 \times 2 = -4$.
   B: $\{-1, 0, 1, 2\}$ isn't special because it doesn't
   contain $-1 \times 2 = -2$. D: $\{4, 0, 1, 2\}$ isn't
   special because 4×2 isn't in the set.

   C: $\{\frac{1}{2}, 0, 1, 2\}$ *is* special—each of the products

   $\frac{1}{2} \times 0$, $\frac{1}{2} \times 1$, and $\frac{1}{2} \times 2$ is in the set.

8. **E.** Since $52 \times 7 = 364$, a normal 365-day year
   consists of 52 weeks plus 1 day. Therefore, 1
   year, or 365 days, after Friday, September 13,
   it will be Saturday, September 13; the following year September 13 will be on Sunday; and
   the year after that September 13 will be on a
   Monday. So, if there are no leap years,
   Karen's third birthday will fall on a Monday.
   (I is true). If one of the three years is a 366-
   day leap year, that year the day will advance
   by 2 (since 366 days is 2 days more than 52
   weeks). If this occurs, Karen's third birthday
   will fall on a Tuesday. (II is true). These are
   the only two possibilities; it is impossible for
   her third birthday to be on a Friday.

9. **E.** Since the diameter of the circle is 20, the
   radius is 10 and the area is 100π. Also, since
   the area of the shaded region is 80π, it is
   $\frac{80}{100} = \frac{4}{5}$ of the circle, and the white area is $\frac{1}{5}$
   of the circle. Then the sum of the measures of
   the two white central angles is $\frac{1}{5}$ of 360°, or
   72°. The sum of the measures of all six angles
   in the triangles is 360°, so
   $$a + b + c + d = 360 - 72 = \mathbf{288}.$$

10. **A.** Each of the original winners expected the fund
    of d dollars to be divided among s students, in
    which case each of them would have received
    $\frac{d}{s}$ dollars. Instead, the fund was divided among
    $s + a$ students, and each received $\frac{d}{s+a}$ dollars.
    This represents a loss to each of the original
    winners of

$$\frac{d}{s} - \frac{d}{s+a} = \frac{d(s+a)-ds}{s(s+a)} = \frac{ds+ad-ds}{s(s+a)} =$$

$$\frac{ad}{s(s+a)}.$$

**Unless you are comfortable with the algebra, plug in numbers. If 2 students were going to share $100, each would have received $50.

If there were 3 more winners, each of the 5 would receive $20, a $30 loss to the original 2 winners. Which of the choices is equal to 30 when $s = 2$, $a = 3$, and $d = 100$? Only $\dfrac{ad}{s(s+a)}$.

Remember that you don't have to get the exact value of each choice; you just have to determine whether it is equal to 30.

PART FIVE

Organize Your Admissions Game Plan

14 Getting Into College

- **Choosing a College**
- **From Application to Acceptance**
- **Meeting the Cost**

Choosing a College

The current rise in the number of high school graduates has created a return to the college entrance pressures of thirty years ago, when colleges had to turn away some well-qualified applicants because of the great number of college-bound high school seniors and the limited space for the entering freshman class. Under pressure to be accepted by the best college possible, students today routinely apply to well over a dozen schools, in some cases applying to institutions they know only by name. What these students fail to realize is that choosing a good college is not the same thing as choosing the best-ranked or most prestigious college. Choosing a good college means choosing the best college for you.

The Best College for You

What is the best college for you? It's not necessarily Harvard or Yale. The conventional wisdom that, over a lifetime, a Harvard degree is a better investment than a degree from State U. has been challenged: a recent article in *Fortune* showed no financial difference between alumni who had spent four years at Harvard and their counterparts who had spent four years at public universities. Instead of choosing a college for *its* name, choose one where you stand a chance to make *your* name. Choose a college where you can be comfortable and where you can succeed.

Gathering Information
College Directories
There are a number of guides available. *Profiles of American Colleges* (Barron's Educational Series, Inc., Hauppauge, N.Y. 11788) is a comprehensive directory. It features complete, succinct descriptions of more than 1600 four-year colleges including such items as admission standards, costs, student life, and courses of study. Colleges are indexed alphabetically and by admissions competitive rating. Three charts present at-a-glance data about the colleges: Index of College Majors, Colleges at a Glance, and In-state Cost Ranges Directory. Other valuable information regarding applying to college, financial aid, selecting a major, and information for international students is also included.

The College Catalog
Consult college catalogs in your school or public library and write for those in which you seem to have a genuine interest. Observe the number of courses offered. Look for the strength of the faculty in the subject areas that are of most interest to you. Remember that a fantastic physics department is of no use to you if you never plan to enter a science laboratory. A magnificent music department will not help you if you are tone deaf. Examine descriptions of the library, science laboratories, and other facilities in areas of interest to you. Consider the types of internship programs and study abroad programs the school has to offer. Look at the graduation and job placement rates. Information in a catalog may save you a time-consuming, expensive visit to a campus that is not a college for you.

The Internet
Explore the wide range of college and university web sites on the Internet. Take virtual tours of campuses, consult on-line catalogs, even fill out your admissions applications on-line. Consult the College Board's own site, *www.collegeboard.org*, as well as services such as *www.embark.com*, which link you to many academic institutions and allow you to apply simultaneously to multiple schools.

Exploring the Campus
Planning Your Visit to a College Campus
If the college you are visiting is near your home, you should walk on the college grounds and talk to currently enrolled students. You should become familiar with the buildings, visit the library, and ask permission to enter laboratories, classrooms, and dormitories. You should inquire whether you may receive a guided tour.

In most cases, however, the college of interest to you may be far from home. This involves expense and special preparation. From a practical point of view, these visits should be confined to those colleges in which you have a sincere interest—probably your top two or three choices. Before you select which campuses to visit, obtain a video or interactive computer program from the schools you think you are interested in and do some "virtual" visiting. This will help you to be selective in deciding which campuses to actually visit. Be alert to advertisements on your school bulletin boards and in local papers of group tours to several campuses during a school holiday period. These relatively inexpensive trips are generally organized by bus companies or travel agents.

There are at least two schemes for making visits to colleges:

1. The visit planned through the admissions office, complete with a formal interview and a guided campus tour.

2. The visit informally arranged with a student you know who already attends the school. In this case, a casual weekend visit should be planned during which time you can ask questions and examine all the interesting places and facilities on campus.

Ideally, if time and money permit, you should plan both types of visits to the two or three schools you are most seriously considering.

If you are taking the trip on your own, you should make certain arrangements ahead of time. If you are planning a formal visit, you should write to the admissions office telling them of your contemplated trip. Perhaps you should give them an alternate date to suit the convenience of the busy office. In many cases a member of the staff will chat with you, perhaps take notes of impressions made by you, and you may leave with a feeling of encouragement to file an application.

To save time and money, try to include colleges in the same geographic area on the same trip. It is foolish to attempt to visit more than two colleges in one day; in fact, it is advisable to devote at least a full day to exploring each of those universities you are seriously considering. If an overnight stay is involved, be sure to make reservations considerably in advance. Some colleges are in a position to recommend accommodations in their areas. If the opportunity exists, ask to spend the night in a typical dormitory with the students themselves.

If possible, your parents should accompany you. Most colleges are interested in seeing parents, though they may want some time alone with the prospective student. The wise parent and prospective student will withhold judgment of a college until they get back home and can make an objective judgment about the entire trip.

Relax throughout the visit. Don't make it a hasty, pressure-filled shopping trip. Regard it as an inspection, an educational experience, where you are learning first hand about institutions you have heard about. You'll find that the trip will tell you more about the college you really want and about what colleges expect of you.

Just before you make the trip, re-read the catalog. Make notes on specific things you would like to see, such as a particular arts center or a language laboratory. Make notes on specific questions you have. When you speak to a college official, do not hesitate to discuss finances, scholarships, and work opportunities as well as your high school record. After all, if you decide to apply to this college, its officials are going to learn of your financial situation eventually. Tactfully, you may ask for some estimate of your chances for admission. Most probably you will not get any firm commitment, but a word of encouragement may be sufficient at this time.

What You Should Look for on the Campus Tour

Devote a good deal of time to an examination of the college library. Get an idea of the size of its collections, its study facilities, and other special features such as listening rooms. Make time in your visit to attend several classes, possibly choosing those that are of special interest to you. Be sure to visit a typical dormitory room, dining hall, student lounge, the college's athletic and recreational facilities, and, if you so desire, fraternity or sorority houses. If a student guide accompanies you on your tour, feel free to ask about any aspect of college life. The guide will welcome some clue about your interests—sports, dramatics, debate, and so forth—and may include a visit to the headquarters for such activities if time permits. But it's up to you to see what interests you—the responsibility is not the college tour guide's.

Whether you are touring the campus alone or with your parents, make it your business to talk to students. Tell them who you are. Very often they will tell you that they were in your position a few years ago. Observe their patterns of speech, their dress, and ask yourself if you belong there. Feel free to ask them about gripes; more than likely, they'll express their likes and dislikes without being asked.

Obtain a copy of the college newspaper. What problems seem to face the students? Does the newspaper seem to reflect the atmosphere of the campus? What is the general tone, morale, and quality of the paper?

After the visit, make some notes on your reactions to the college; they'll be useful later on when you're trying to evaluate various institutions, and they may suggest some additional points for discussion with your guidance counselors and parents.

How the College Board Can Help You Select a College

The SAT Program of the College Board can help you select a college that will satisfy your educational goals through its Student Search Service, which is free. The Student Search Service helps colleges find students with characteristics they are seeking. To take advantage of this service, you simply indicate on your registration form for SAT I that you want to participate.

From Application to Acceptance

Applying for Admission

The first step in the application procedure is to obtain applications from the colleges you're planning to apply to. You do this by writing (a postcard is quite acceptable) or calling the admissions office of each school and asking them to mail you an application.

When you receive the application forms, you will be asked to deliver certain parts to your high school authorities so that they may fill out the data in connection with the evaluation of your school record. Your parents may be asked to fill out one section with information regarding your personal health. Another part of the application will delve into your family background, your past history, and your interests and hobbies, as well as your plans for the future.

Filling Out the Application

Neatness counts. Read the entire application before you start to write, and then put it away in a safe place. Writing for a second application may not count in your favor. When you are ready to answer the questions, jot down the facts you must collect. Collect all your data on scrap paper and have some reliable person such as a teacher or guidance counselor review the answers and make suggestions for the necessary mechanical corrections. Some colleges require that all parts of the application be completed in the handwriting of the applicant. In such cases, write out the corrected answers very carefully. If permitted, type or print the answers on the application form.

If a photograph is requested, choose one that is simple and does you justice. Do not use a snapshot with extraneous background. It is not wise to use a photograph that shows you in unusual dress or attire.

Many applications require you to write an essay. This is an interesting, decisive, and revealing part of the application. A superb, original, thoughtful, literate, and mature life story can tip the scales in your favor, if all the phases of the application are satisfactory. A poor essay, on the other hand, might provide sufficient reason for rejection. This does not mean that you should hire a "ghost writer." Members of an admissions board are quick to detect "masterpieces" written by well-meaning parents or friends of the family. The next chapter, "Writing Your Application Essay," will show you how to write your own masterpiece.

Evaluation of Your School Record

This is by far the most significant part of the application. Officers of admissions committees were not at all surprised at a recent study that showed that about half of the first year dropouts left school for academic reasons, which included poor grades in college and poor high school preparation.

Some colleges communicate with your high school as soon as your application is filed. Others ask you to deliver a special form to your principal, headmaster, or guidance counselor. The college will want to know if you have met or will meet the entrance requirements. They will therefore request a transcript of your high school record.

In examining this record, the committee looks for grades and the subjects completed. They look for subjects that gave the applicant difficulty and take into account such extenuating circumstances as temporary illness, or lack of interest in certain (but not all) subjects. They attempt to determine whether the student elected challenging courses, and are on the lookout for students who took easy courses in order to raise their averages.

Your standing in the class is quite significant. This is a direct way of comparing you with the other students in your graduating class. If you have high grades, but a low rank in your class, it is sometimes a sign that the marking system in your school suffers from inflation. If you attend a specialized school for selected or gifted pupils, then class standing needs special consideration, for you are being compared with special students. Finally, if you attend a very small school, your achievement involves small numbers and therefore carries less significance.

Extracurricular Activities

Activities outside the classroom, both in school and in the community, are important. They afford the opportunity to develop personal talents, to pursue special interests, and to stimulate qualities of initiative and leadership. However, admissions officers are not impressed with a long list of rather insignificant activities, most of which merely involved occasional passive attendance at meetings. These make an attractive listing in a high school yearbook but do not impress the scrutinizing eye of a college admissions officer, who is more concerned with any elected and appointed offices you might have held, and those activities you might have engaged in that suggest definite signs of leadership in your character, and who is also very interested in your ability to play an unusual musical instrument, paint a canvas, or write a line of poetry.

Certainly no good college will entirely put aside its other standards for admission for a good extracurricular record. However, all other things being equal, in choosing one of two applicants, the admissions office will generally choose the student who participated in out-of-class activities.

Letters of Reference

Many colleges will ask you to submit the names and addresses of people who will furnish information regarding your character. Of course, common courtesy requires that you first ask the individual for permission to use his or her name. In choosing these individuals, it is well to bear in mind that they will be requested to give answers to such questions as:

1. Are you related to the applicant?

2. How long have you known the applicant?

3. In what capacity have you been in contact with the applicant?

4. Give any evidences of good moral character, leadership, maturity, and consideration for others that you have had the opportunity to observe in the applicant.

Some colleges send you forms to be given to people who can furnish information about your character. It is courteous to supply each of these people with a stamped envelope addressed to the office of admissions. The people you might ask for recommendations include:

1. teacher of a subject in which you excel

2. instructor, teacher, or coach of a creative activity in which you excel (e.g., art, music, drama)

3. advisor of a club or service activity in which you participated

4. coach of a team on which you served

5. scout leader

6. sponsor of a youth group

7. religious leader

8. professional or business person active in your community

9. camp counselor or director

10. employer of your part-time or summer position

11. public official

Keep in mind that college personnel are not likely to be swayed by letters containing empty platitudes and sweeping praise. They read scores of these letters every day. Certainly they want to know your accomplishments and strong points, those things that make you different from the other applicants; but at the same time they are anxious to learn about a flesh and blood person, not the subject of some glorious ode. The typically general, impersonal recommendation of some well-known personality will have less impact on admissions officers than a warm, sensitive letter from a less well-known individual who intimately knows you and is therefore in a better position to appraise your particular qualities.

Avoid suggesting as references individuals who will not answer the college questionnaire promptly. Similarly, do not use individuals who might not show good judgment, neatness, or taste in corresponding with the admissions office of the college.

The Personal Interview

There is no uniformity among the schools as to the time for holding the interview. It may occur after all other factors determining admission have been inspected and tentatively approved, or it may occur before the secondary school records and test scores have been received. In addition, while some schools require an interview, others consider the interview only a way to give you more information about the school.

If an interview is required, you should write early in the school year for an appointment. If the interview is optional but you can arrange for one, you should also make an appointment. (Where distance makes a visit impractical, a local alumnus may be assigned to talk with you.) Plan your trip to the college so that you arrive punctually. Your appearance and dress should be in good taste. Remember you are not going to a formal dance, nor to a sporting event. Make certain that your shoes are shined, your hair is combed, and your fingernails are clean. Dress conservatively. Be careful about odors of perfumes, tobacco, or foods. This is the day when you should start breaking the habit of chewing gum.

As far as the interview itself is concerned, the best advice is to be yourself. Since this is not an interview for a role as actor or actress, you should relax and answer all questions with frankness and honesty. If you do not possess a particular characteristic for which they are looking, you may not be happy at this school. The interviewer may give you some valuable counsel and send you off to the school where you really belong.

If you haven't ever experienced such an interview you will be wondering about the topics of conversation and the general tone of this event. It will be informal, and it is safe to say that it will be conducted on a most pleasant level. You will perhaps discuss people and things you like or dislike. Again, be honest. Perhaps the official interviewing you likes jazz music himself. Even if he doesn't, he won't hold it against you if you do. Don't hide your distastes or weaknesses. Some of our poor high school mathematics students have gone on to become college professors in other fields.

You may be asked about your career plans. If you are not certain about your future, state that as a fact. It is not a sign of weakness. Most students enter college with only vague ideas about what they want to do after graduation. If you have applied to other colleges, don't hesitate to mention them if that question comes up.

Towards the close of the interview you may be given an opportunity to ask questions about the college. Don't feel that you have to ask a question and then hastily compose a question, which may show your unfamiliarity with data furnished in the catalog. It may be wiser to say that you have no questions to ask about the school.

Your College Board Scores

Colleges use standardized scores to enable them to compare students from different schools. A high school record alone cannot be a yardstick of academic promise. Grading standards differ among high schools. Class standing in a small high school is not as significant as it is in a large city school. The standing in a specialized school is of little significance except for those at the very top. Entrance examinations afford equal opportunity to each college-bound student.

Do not, however, feel that you are a failure because you fell short of an 800 on your SAT I. Bear in mind that the average SAT I scores on a national basis are somewhere between 400 and 500 reported on a scale of 200 to 800. Even highly competitive schools admit students with a wide range of scores.

A college that reported a median score of 610 in the verbal part of the SAT for its freshman class indicated that 25% of freshmen scored between 550 and 559, 14% received 500 to 549, and 6% had scores between 400 and 450. For the mathematics part of the SAT the same school reported a median score of 700, but 20% of the admitted students received scores between 500 and 599.

Another school, reporting an average of 669 in the verbal part of the SAT for the 500 accepted applicants, indicated that 33 of them scored between 550 and 599, and 10 scored below 550. It is interesting to note that this school failed to accept 15 applicants with SAT verbal scores of 700 to 749 and one applicant with a score above 750.

Thus we see that College Board scores are important, but additional criteria matter as well. It is well to repeat that SAT I scores are used to supplement such factors as high school grades, class rank, and personal qualities. Another factor that admissions officers are reporting is that they are giving special consideration to applicants with low SAT I scores from deprived areas or to applicants for whom English is not the native language. Of course, these college-bound students must present evidence of academic promise.

To Sum It Up

You will gain admission to college on the basis of your school record, your personality, your extracurricular activities, the impressions you made on others, and your performance on college entrance examinations. Your acceptance is an indication that the college has faith in your ability to succeed in that school.

Meeting the Cost

Types of Financial Aid

The main types of financial aid are grants and scholarships, loans, and student employment. Grants are awarded on the basis of need and do not have to be repaid. These may come from federal or state government agencies, college funds, or special programs. Scholarships are similar to grants, and usually are awarded on the basis of academic achievement and/or financial need. College employment offices often furnish on or off-campus jobs to help supplement other forms of aid. Finally, low-interest loans that do not have to be repaid until after graduation can help pay for college. Loans are also available for parents.

Chief Sources of Financial Aid

There are four main sources of financial aid: the federal government, state governments, private sources, and the colleges themselves.

Federal Government

The federal government has five main student aid programs: the Pell Grant Program, the Supplemental Educational Opportunity Grant (SEOG), the College Work-Study Program (CWS), Carl Perkins Loans (formerly, National Direct Student Loans), and Parent Loans for Undergraduate Students (PLUS).

The Pell Grant Program, the largest of the federal student aid grant programs, and SEOG are the two main federal grant programs. They are both based on need, and they do not have to be repaid. College Work-Study is a student employment program that provides on- and off-campus jobs for students who demonstrate need. Carl Perkins Loans and Stafford Loans are both low-interest loan programs. Monies borrowed through these loan programs do not have to be repaid until after graduation unless you take out an unsubsidized Stafford Loan or a PLUS Loan. Then the interest must be paid monthly.

In addition to the federal student aid programs already mentioned, the Veterans Administration provides two types of funds—G.I. Bill benefits and War Orphan benefits—to veterans of all wars and to the children of deceased or entirely disabled veterans whose disability or death was service-related. Contact a local office of the Veterans Administration for details on eligibility.

State Government

Most states have some type of scholarship or grant program for residents. These are usually based on achievement in high school and scores on college entrance examinations, but need is often also a determining factor. Often the scholarship or grant applies only if the student attends a college in that state. Some states also have loan programs.

Private Sources

Many individual scholarships are available from labor unions, benevolent societies, patriotic organizations, and business. Look in your high school guidance office and in your local library for information on private scholarships such as these as well as local scholarships available in your community. Awards made available by local fraternal societies, women's clubs, civic and business organizations, ethnic and religious groups, alumni, and PTAs are numerous but usually modest in dollars and cents value. Your parents' employer or labor union may turn out to be another source of aid.

The largest independently funded scholarship program in the United States is administered by the National Merit Scholarship Corporation and is funded by company foundations and colleges and universities. Scholarship recipients are selected on the basis of their score on the Preliminary SAT/National Merit Scholarship Qualifying Test (PSAT/NMSQT), other academic factors, and their character. For further information, write to the National Merit Scholarship Corporation, One American Plaza, Evanston, Illinois 60201, and ask for the PSAT/NMSQT Student Bulletin.

Colleges

Nearly every college offers a number of scholarships and grants that range from partial payment of tuition to complete payment of all expenses. These grants are awarded in recognition of academic achievement and/or financial need. Special scholarships may be given to attract outstanding athletes or students with special talents in such areas as music, drama, or journalism.

In addition to their own scholarship and grant funds, colleges often act as agents of distribution for federal and state programs.

Since each college has different scholarships, grants, loans, and student-employment opportunities to offer, and since there is an often enormous difference in the amount of money available for student aid from one college to another, it is important that you get your information about student aid directly from the financial aid office of each college you are thinking of applying to as soon as possible. Many colleges and universities award scholarships and grants on a first-come, first-served basis.

How to Apply for Financial Aid

Most need-based financial aid programs, whether they are government programs, private programs, or individual college programs, require applicants to file the Free Application for Federal Student Aid (FAFSA). More than one form may be required. Some schools will require you to complete the PROFILE form. All financial aid forms ask the applicant to itemize all family information and financial data pertinent to the candidate's application for aid.

It is important to find out which form or forms the colleges you are applying to require. Some schools will want their own aid application filed in addition to the FAFSA and PROFILE. And some government and private programs request additional forms as well; they use one of the three as an initial qualifying form but then require a separate application for their program.

All forms are available from your high school guidance counselor or local college financial aid offices.

We've left the most important facts about applying for financial aid for last: (1) you must apply for financial aid; you are not automatically considered for aid when you apply to a college; (2) apply as early as possible so that you have the best possible chance at a share of the available funds before they are used up on applicants who applied for aid earlier; (3) you must reapply for financial aid each year; (4) reapply if your family's financial circumstances change; and (5) you can appeal your financial aid award. There is no getting away from the fact that you'll have to do some research, and that you and your parents will have to spend some time filling out some rather detailed forms. But there is no way to get around this paperwork when you're applying for any kind of financial aid. So be patient and be thorough; hopefully, your efforts will pay off.

15 Writing Your Application Essay

- **What the Colleges Look For**
- **The Questions That Colleges Ask**
- **Pitfalls to Avoid**
- **Composing Your Essay**
- **Presenting Your Essay**
- **In Addition to Your Essay**

On the day you seal and mail your college application, your job—at least for the present—is done. But the work of the admissions committee at the college of your choice has just begun. At selective colleges—those that receive three or more applications for each place in the freshman class—college officials screen applications with agonizing care.

Each section of your application, from SAT scores to extra-curricular activities, contributes another piece to your portrait. But a thoughtful, well-written essay endows your portrait with life. It is like a window into your mind and personality. Unlike an A in chemistry or a B+ in English, it reveals your uniqueness, your attitudes on life, your creativity, your aims, and your drive. And perhaps most important, it demonstrates your writing ability. The gift of saying what you want to say in clear, correct, and interesting language sometimes offsets shortcomings in almost any other part of your application.

What the Colleges Look For

Colleges seek a generous mix of bright, confident, and positive students who will contribute actively to campus life for the next four years. Basically, your essay tells the colleges whether you're the sort of person they are looking for. It puts the finishing touches on your application. A three-sport high school athlete, for example, could use the essay to prove that his mind is as fit as his body. A serious scholar could prove that he has a sense of humor. Whatever your attributes, admissions people want you to think of your essay as an opportunity to present yourself honestly, openly, and intelligently.

Your transcript and list of activities have already told them what you have done. From your essay they hope to learn why.

Although you probably won't be admitted to a college solely on the strength of your essay, a well-written and sincere piece of writing can tip the balance in your favor. Conversely, a poor and sloppy essay can shut the door in your face. Nevertheless, some college officials claim, fewer than half of all application essays show evidence of real, honest effort. Still, at every college that requires an essay, your work will be read thoughtfully and seriously. At most colleges a team of two or more people will read every essay. At one prestigious school, up to five admissions people sometimes read an essay before the applicant is accepted. It's that important, according to that school's officials.

Colleges Want to Know What Makes You Tick

Because colleges want to get to know you, the cardinal rule of writing an application essay is to be yourself. Don't make the fatal mistake of trying to guess what a college wants. Admissions people don't want anything in particular except for you to portray yourself accurately and honestly. They don't ask trick questions on an application.

Pick a subject you care about—something significant and familiar to you. Nothing will flop faster than an impersonal essay full of sweeping generalizations about issues in the news or philosophical questions that have puzzled scholars for ages. If you're interested in current events, that's fine, but admissions people can read about apartheid and nuclear disarmament in *Newsweek*. If you're going to write about a current issue, make sure you have done more than read the newspaper: go to a rally, march in a parade, circulate a petition, give a speech in your history class. In short, show personal commitment and involvement in whatever you write about.

Try to make your essay the one that only you could write. After all, it should set you apart in some way from every other applicant. That doesn't mean it must be worthy of a Pulitzer Prize, only that it ought to be uniquely personal. It ought to sound like you.

The Questions That Colleges Ask

Colleges have invented numerous ways to test your essay-writing skills. Sometimes you're assigned just one 250 to 300 word essay, sometimes more. Some applications give you choices, others don't. While some give you no directions on what to write—as though to test your ingenuity—others state specific guidelines, in part to see whether you can follow directions.

Although application questions differ in detail from one college to the next, they all ask you to write about the same general subject: YOU! Your task is always the same—to project personal qualities not apparent in other places on your application.

The mass of application questions fall into five broad categories, each with opportunities for you to project yourself onto the paper, but each with perils to watch out for:

1. Why go to college, and why here?
2. Who are you?
3. Would you tell us a story about yourself?
4. What is important to you?
5. What would you like to tell us about yourself?

Responses to these questions frequently overlap. If, for instance, you were to write an essay that describes an important personal value—say, your love of the outdoors—you might frame it in the form of a story about a rafting trip down the Colorado River. At the same time you would be defining who you are—in this case, perhaps an adventurous out-doorsman or a recently-converted city-slicker.

Why Go to College? Why Here?

From questions about your plans for the future, colleges hope to discern your route for the next four years. What will the college experience mean to you? Will you study or will you party? Have you thought about why you're going to college at all? Expecting a look at your educational map, colleges often make inquiries such as these:

Why do you want to go to college?

Why do you want to go to this college in particular?

What are your career objectives and how will college help you achieve them?

How will this college help you fulfill your goals and aspirations?

What will your presence add to this college?

No one answer to such questions is preferable to another. If you aim to be a physicist for IBM, that's fine. But no college seeks to fill its classrooms with only one type of student. In the main, colleges try to keep their enrollments balanced. It's not a weakness, therefore, to admit that you don't know how you want to spend the rest of your life. College is for exploring. In fact, liberal-arts students frequently come to campuses with receptive and open minds. More than likely, they'll rummage through many of the offerings on which a college has built its reputation.

As you explain your intentions to a college, consider these essay-writing hints:

DO
■ Answer the question.

■ Scrutinize the college's offerings before writing a word. If you expect to major in, say, ecology, be sure the college has an environmental studies program.

■ Think hard about what you hope to get out of college, avoiding clichés such as "I want an education," and "I want to get a good, well-paying job," and "I want to be a success in my chosen field."

■ Try to figure out why this college appeals to you. Did the college reps make it sound exciting? Did you visit the campus and feel good vibrations? Is there a particular program that has attracted your interest?

■ Focus on educational or personal reasons for going to college, not on social, economic, or family reasons.

DON'T
■ Don't flatter the college. Yale, Stanford, and all the other top colleges already know that they're good.

■ Don't stress that you love the college's location, size, or appearance. By applying there, you have implied that those characteristics are acceptable to you.

■ Don't tell a college that it's your "safe" school.

■ Don't write that you're going to college because you don't know what else to do.

Finally, don't take any of these precautions as the last word in application essay-writing. Use them at your discretion. But don't ignore them unless you have a sound reason for doing so. Jim D, for example, came right out and told

Bowdoin he wanted to go there precisely because of its location. "Like Thoreau," Jim wrote, "I feel most alive near wild streams and forests."

Answers That Worked

Marian T's after school work in a fabric shop inspired her love of fashion and developed her flair for design. "In college," Marian wrote, "I plan to major in fine arts."

David B studied four languages in high school. Because of his bent toward languages and foreign cultures, he wants a career in international affairs as a businessman or diplomat, but he said, "A stint in the Peace Corps will come first."

Lisa C loves to read. "I can't imagine a career more suited to me than librarian in a school or a public library," she wrote.

Wendy W has wide and wandering interests. Last year it was dance, this year it is Greenpeace. Wendy thinks of college as a place for "accumulating more interests, for meeting people, for working hard, and ultimately, for finding a niche in life to fill."

Andy S has always taken the hardest courses. He doesn't know why, except that doing well in tough courses has made him feel good. "I hope to continue feeling good in college," he quipped.

Deena R admires one of her high school English teachers. Since he's told her wonderful stories of Williams College, she'd like to go there, too. "I plan to major in English," she wrote, "and find out if Mr. Stern's stories are true."

Karen S's "most joyful and gratifying high school experience" has been working with mentally retarded children. In college she'll major in special education.

Mark D lost his father and a brother last year. Yet he has retained his essential optimism. He wrote that "there is still a promise in life for me. There are so many things which I have not yet experienced, but inevitably must." That's why he wants to go to college.

Don E has met many people through playing guitar at festivals and nightspots. He thrives on people whose style of living differs from his. Don asked, "What better place than a giant university is there for finding a variety of people?"

Becky B is thinking of a career in acting. She expects a college education to help her become a more complete person. "My wish," she wrote, "is not only to be a good actor but also a good person, and my belief is that they might be the same thing."

Who Are You?

Colleges have heard what others think of you—teachers, counselors, interviewers. With self-assessment questions, they hope to learn what you think of yourself. Do you know who you are? Are you aware of how others react to you?

Would you like to change in some way? Self-knowledge is often thought to be a prerequisite for understanding the world, and an essay that demonstrates that you know yourself well will give your application a big boost. To check the depth of your insight, colleges ask questions like these:

What is important to you?

How would you describe yourself as a human being?

How might a freshman roommate describe you?

Write your own recommendation to college.

If you could strengthen one aspect of yourself, what would it be? Why?

What quality do you like best in yourself? What quality do you like least?

Imagine yourself as a book or other object. How would people react to you?

What makes you different from other people?

In your response, readers hope to find clues to your personality. Unless you present yourself as a bizarre monster, they won't necessarily care whether you are soft-spoken or loud, a realist or a dreamer, a liberal or a rock-hard conservative. But they'll give you short shrift if they think you are a fake. Above all, then, in writing "who-are-you" essays, be truthful with yourself—as truthful as you've ever been before.

Telling the truth doesn't mean you must bare your soul and disclose your deepest secrets. Colleges don't need to know about your sex life, psychiatric treatment, or drug and drinking problems. On the other hand, you needn't portray yourself as a saint. Students have written successful essays about their cynicism, frustration, greed, and their favorite vices. In the end, let good taste govern your choice of material. It you have doubts, switch topics. Jenny G wrote an essay about a family drug problem, thought the better of it afterwards, and wrote another, highlighting her good judgment.

DO

■ Answer the question.

■ Be as honest as you can. Search for qualities you really have, not those you just wish for.

■ Emphasize specific, observable qualities that show your distinctive personality. Imagine that your reader will someday have to pick you out in a crowd.

■ Illustrate your qualities with specific examples. Use telling anecdotes to support your opinions of yourself.

■ Ask people who know you well whether they agree with your self-analysis.

DON'T

■ Don't be evasive. Stand up for what you think about yourself.

■ Don't be too cute or coy. Sincerity is preferable.

■ Don't choose a characteristic merely to impress the college.

■ Don't write everything you know about yourself. Focus on one or two of your outstanding qualities.

■ Don't write an essay fit for *True Confessions.*

Remember that you can violate every rule and still write a compelling essay. Just be aware of the perils.

Answers That Worked

Suzannah R thinks of herself as a dynamo in danger of burning out by age 20. But she can't control her energy level. She's impatient and often intolerant of others' laid-back attitudes. But, she added, "As I have grown older, I feel I am learning to accept other people's shortcomings."

Betsy S wrote four paragraph-long sketches of important moments in her life. Each one—a sail with her father, her mother's remarriage, a breakfast at summer school, and a skiing trip in Vermont—has shaped her personality in some way.

Nancy S explained that "anxiety over taking tests has resulted in scores that reflect neither my academic achievement nor my enthusiasm for learning." Nancy has tried "every trick in the book" to overcome test anxiety, but none seems to work. She appealed to the college to be understanding.

David V said, "The most important fact to know about me is that I am a black person in a white society." David considers himself an outsider and expects to continue feeling alienated as long as racial prejudice exists.

Ellen E contrasted her goofing off early in high school ("personal problems and just plain stupidity") with her productive junior and senior years. In effect, she was reborn during the summer between 10th and 11th grade.

Allison R has fought shyness all her life. She recounted three moments in her life when shyness defeated her. In contrast, she told of three recent incidents that have helped to raise her self-esteem.

Steve M sees himself as a latter-day Clarence Darrow, always standing in defense of the little guy, often taking the minority point of view in class, just to generate a little controversy. If others consider him obnoxious, he claimed, "it's a small price to pay for a life full of heated debates and discussions."

John K sees himself as a character in a movie. When he's alone he pretends he's Brad Pitt, playing the role of a yuppie bachelor. He even hums background film music when he's driving or jogging.

Brendan B is a gourmet cook. He loves to eat. "You are what you eat," he believes, so he defined himself by the food he enjoys most. From meat and potatoes, for example, he has gained a strong will. From French sauces, he has derived a subtle sense of humor.

Nicole W is a perfectionist. From schoolwork to keeping her room in order, she cannot allow herself to do anything shabbily or incompletely. She is worried about "getting a slob for a college roommate."

Dena P, a gymnast since age eight, works like a demon to be number one. Ever striving for perfection, she wrote, "I know now that when it comes to making commitments, I can be ready to make them."

Doug W is an adopted Korean orphan. He sees himself as a child of two cultures. While a double identity causes confusion in others, he feels "more fortunate and richer" than his American classmates.

Jennifer B defines herself as a human computer. Instead of brains she has memory boards and micro-circuitry inside her head. Everything about computers comes so easily and naturally to her that she said, "I must have been conceived in a Nintendo factory."

Would You Tell Us a Story About Yourself?

Telling stories is a most natural thing to do. When you come home from school you tell what happened that day. You tell friends what Donna said to Fred and how Kathy felt afterwards.

The story you write for a college application isn't expected to be like a superbly crafted tale by Poe or O. Henry, but just an autobiographical account of an experience. It should tell about something that happened and what it meant to you. A good story both entertains and informs the reader. A story written for a college does even more. It suggests your values, clarifies your attitudes, and better yet, breathes life into your personality.

While storytelling possibilities are limitless, application questions usually direct you to identify and discuss a noteworthy time in your life:

Write about a significant experience or event in your life and what it meant to you.

Write an original essay about a humorous personal experience.

What is it that you have done that best reflects your personality?

Describe a challenging situation and how you responded.

Comment on an experience that helped you discern or define a value you hold.

What is the most difficult thing you've ever done?

Write about a group endeavor in which you participated and describe your contribution.

In response to any of these topics, you can write a story about last night or pick an event from the time you wore diapers. The experience can have been instantaneous or long-lived, a once-in-a-lifetime occasion or a daily occurrence. It can have taken place in a schoolroom, a ballroom, a mountaintop—anywhere, in fact, including inside your head.

An event need not have been earth-shaking to inspire a story. Almost everything you do from the moment you wake up holds possibilities. If you haven't noticed how life is crammed with moments of drama, cast off those blurry lenses and start to look for the hidden realities behind the daily face of things: In a disagreement with your brother, in an encounter with a former girlfriend, or in a teacher's criticism you might find the ingredients for an insightful, dramatic essay. Simply by making a list of ten things that happened yesterday and another ten things that occurred last week, you might trigger more than one essay idea.

If you want to write about the time you made headlines, that's great. But most people lead ordinary lives. Taking a common experience and interpreting it as only you can is a perfectly acceptable way to handle the task of writing an application essay.

DO

■ Answer the question.

■ Choose an experience you remember well. Details will make or break your story.

■ Pick an experience you can dramatize. Let the reader hear people speaking and see people acting.

■ Focus on a specific incident or event.

■ Make yourself the central character in the story.

DON'T

■ Don't think that a commonplace event can't be turned into an uncommonly good story.

■ Don't choose a complicated event unless you can explain it briefly. Fill in background, but focus on what happened.

■ Don't lie. But if you must fabricate material for effect, be sure it has the ring of truth.

■ Don't ramble. Rambling stories are boring.

■ Don't explain your point with a lecture on what the reader is supposed to notice. Let the story make its own point.

Answers That Worked

Ted B collects things: match-box cars, license plates, matchbook covers, and rocks. From his hobby he has learned about design, geography, advertising, and geology. Interior decorating, too, for after five years of collecting, he literally wallpapered the foyer of his house with matchbook covers.

Pete S was riding in a car with his brother. At a stoplight a pretty girl in a neighboring car smiled at him. Pete looked away. Afterwards, he berated himself and resolved to become more outgoing and more responsive to others.

Colin V is Catholic. Last year on May 6 his Jewish godson was born. As a result, Colin's eyes have been opened to the world of Jewish customs. "I look at everything differently, now," Colin wrote.

Jenny B's hard-of-hearing grandfather lives with the family. Whenever Jenny tries to help the old man, he rebuffs her. A blow-up occurred after Jenny knocked too loudly on his door to summon him to the phone. The incident has caused her to reflect at length on the needs of the aged.

Mary G, from a middle-class family, works in a slum area soup kitchen with her church group. She'll never be a social reformer, but the work, she claims, has made her "more sensitive to the needs of the poor and homeless."

Roy O's summer at a lake with his father building a cabin gave him time to think about how lucky he was to have been born in the USA into a fairly well-to-do family. "I'll never take the blessings of life for granted again," he wrote.

Liz H and her twin sister Mary have rarely been apart. Lately, Liz has found it necessary to seek her own identity and has taken up running as a way to get away. Her hours of solitude on the road have helped to strengthen the bonds with her sister.

Sandy M says, "Sunday is always spent gathering the scattered fragments of my life." It's the day she uses to catch up on schoolwork, gain some perspective on her social life, make peace with her parents, and look in the mirror for a long time trying to figure out who she is.

Lauren S has always been plagued by insecurity. An off-hand remark by an art teacher ("Hey, you're good!") has helped her to build confidence and work that much harder in her courses. She's beginning to see signs of how good she really is.

Lisa R's parents were divorced. The complex legal negotiations that accompanied the split, while painful to her, so fascinated Lisa that she plans to become a lawyer.

Robert S thinks that he has been ostracized at his school because of his ragged appearance. Instead of wearing a jacket and tie to an honor society interview, he showed up in his jeans. The incident heightened his awareness that people are judged by superficialities, not by their character.

What Is Important to You?

Would you rather hear a Bach cantata or a Pearl Jam CD? Would you prefer to go bowling or spend an afternoon in an art museum? Do you like fast foods or nouvelle cuisine? To a great extent, your preferences define you. Hoping for a glimpse of your taste and your biases, many colleges ask you to write a "choice" essay. But rather than give you a menu of choices, they tell you to come up with one of your own: your favorite quotation, an influential person in your life, a significant book you've read.

What is your favorite quotation? Explain your choice.

What have you read that has had special significance for you? Explain.

Identify a person who has had a significant influence on you and describe that influence.

Tell us about a personal, local, national, or international issue of particular concern to you.

What is your favorite noun? What does it mean to you?

If you could invent anything, what would you create? Discuss.

If you could affect the outcome of human history by changing a particular event, what event would you choose? How would you change it, and why?

If you could spend an evening with any prominent person—living, deceased, or fictional—whom would you choose, and why?

What you choose when responding to such questions is important. But the rationale for your choice is even more important and should make up the heart of your essay.

The key to writing a forceful response is that your choice has some direct, personal bearing on your life. A quotation from Shakespeare may sound impressive, but if you pick it only for effect, you'd be better off with a rap lyric or a maxim of your grandmother's. Before you select an important world issue like terrorism or over-population, be sure you've been personally touched by it. Instead of decrying the evils of apartheid, tell what you've done to support divestment. If you write on a book, don't limit yourself to school reading. What you've read on your own tells far more about you than any class assignment.

If you are wavering between two equally good choices, tip your scales toward less popular subjects. Conversations with Columbus, Lincoln, and Martin Luther King, Jr. have already been written. So have numerous essays about cures for cancer and AIDS. Many students have already written about altering human history by eliminating war, pre-

venting the birth of Hitler, and scrubbing the flight of TWA 800. They have also expressed concerns about child labor, capital punishment, poor people, and women's rights. Countless others have been influenced by a grandparent, a sibling with a handicap, a teacher, or a virtuous public figure.

Nevertheless, the last word on all these subjects hasn't yet been written. Although admissions staffers may frown on still more essays about peace or pollution, they'll welcome any essay that's genuine, insightful and interesting.

DO

■ Answer the question.

■ Choose a subject that you care about.

■ Let your head and heart be your source of material.

■ Think of at least three very good personal reasons for your choice.

■ Try out more than one answer. Submit the one that you like best.

DON'T

■ Don't choose a topic merely to look good.

■ Don't be self-conscious about your choice. Just tell the truth.

■ Don't choose a subject that requires research. Let your experience guide you.

Answers That Worked

Lisa D, born in South Africa, came to the United States at age 11. Her anti-apartheid essay recalls her black nurse, who was forbidden to enter the park where Lisa and her friends played hopscotch and tag.

Amy B thinks that Seinfeld would make an ideal dinner companion. She admires Seinfeld's humor, his understanding, and his impatience with hypocrisy.

Jenny B has been fascinated with space flight ever since second grade, when the elementary school librarian introduced her to a sci-fi book, *Matthew Looney, the Boy from the Moon*. In college Jenny expects to major in physics or astronomy.

Luke J chose the word "family" as his favorite noun. To explain, he wrote a moving portrait of a close-knit family. Five times in the last ten years the family has moved. Luke's father works overseas for months at a time. Yet, Luke derives stability from his family, despite its fragmented life.

Robert B refuted the old adage, "You can't compare apples and oranges," by writing a tongue-in-cheek comparison of the two fruits. As a result, he wonders about the validity of other pieces of wisdom. He plans to research next "You can't tell a book by its cover" and "Absence makes the heart grow fonder."

Carl G, who has a deaf kid brother, wrote about *Dancing Without Music: Deafness in America,* a book that persuaded him and his parents to introduce young Danny to other deaf people as a way to help the boy find an identity as a hearing-impaired person.

Karen S would like to interview Margaret Mead. Being a young woman, Karen looks ahead to the problems of balancing a family and a career. Since reading Mead's autobiography, *Blackberry Winter,* Karen thinks that Mead would have some sound advice to give her.

Gary K wrote about Steven, his mentally retarded brother. All his life, Gary has been Steven's fun committee, psychiatrist-at-home, and teacher. Gary wept recently after he found Steven eating pineapple from a can. It had taken Gary six weeks to teach Steven how to use a can-opener.

Jordana S said that her favorite cartoon character, Linus from "Peanuts," has qualities that she envies: stability, self-confidence, and grace under pressure. As for his security blanket, "Linus carries it to show that he's secure enough not to worry what others think about his carrying it."

Joanna L named Miss B, her elementary school gym teacher, as a significant person in her life. Miss B so intimidated Joanna that "even today the smell of a gymnasium and the sight of orange mats stimulate feelings of terror and dread."

What Would You Like to Tell Us About Yourself?

Perhaps the toughest writing assignment is the one without a suggested topic. "Tell us anything you'd like, anything to help us know you better," says the application.

> We would welcome any comments you care to make about yourself.

> The essay is an important part of your application. It will help admissions officers gain a more complete picture of you. Use the essay to tell about yourself.

> If there is anything else you would like to tell us about you, please explain on an additional sheet.

> Please use this page to give us any information you think would be helpful to us as we consider your application.

> The purpose of this application is to help us learn about you. Is there additional information we should know which will help us to make an informed decision?

> To better understand you, what else should we know?

Without restrictions, you may literally send in anything. Starting from scratch, you can cook up a totally new piece of writing. Or you may submit a poem, a story, or a paper you've written for school or for yourself. Applicants who have written for publications often send samples of their writing. But if you include a previously written piece, don't just pull it from your files and throw it in the envelope. Carefully explain on a new cover page what it is and why you chose it.

DO

- Pick something important—something that matters to you.

- Consider explaining anything unusual that has influenced your school or home life.

- Use a style of writing that sounds like you.

- Write the sort of piece (e.g., essay, poem, internal monologue) you've written successfully in the past.

DON'T

- Don't turn down the college's invitation to write more about yourself.

- Don't put on airs or try to impress the college. Be yourself.

- Don't repeat what you've written elsewhere on your application.

- Don't try to use a form or style of writing for the first time unless you have a record of successful writing experiments.

- Don't write the essay—or any other part of your application—the night before it's due.

Another word of caution: Try to avoid submitting a reheated essay, one you've written for another application. A college which asks an open-ended question won't appreciate an essay entitled "My Most Significant Academic Experience" or "I'd like to spend an evening with...." Naturally, you can use bits and pieces from your other college essays, but rework your material, disguise it, change its focus—do all you can to keep the college from suspecting that you're sending in a secondhand sample of your work. In a pinch you may, of course, need to send the same essay to two or more colleges. Or your essay may be so good you feel compelled to use it again. In either case, courteously tell the second or third college what you have done and why. Your decency will be appreciated.

Answers That Worked

Bonnie W asserted that writing the college essay helped her sort out her feelings about herself. She has finally accepted the fact that she is a non-conformist "I used to run with the 'in' crowd," she wrote, "but now I don't give a damn. I can breathe."

Lillian S, a student of karate, wrote about how it feels to break a board with her bare hand. Writing about karate, she said, has heightened her concentration as she trains to earn a black belt.

Kevin B wrote a funny piece on being a New Yorker. On a recent trip to Massachusetts with the school band, his overnight host expected him to come equipped with a switchblade and chains. The folks in the Bay State seemed disappointed by his "normal" behavior and appearance.

Jenny J wrote a collection of fables, each concluding with a moral or maxim to illustrate a strongly held conviction. One story ended, "Be satisfied with who you are." Another, "Don't turn your back on anyone in pursuit of power."

Pitfalls to Avoid

Trying to Impress

Colleges ask for an essay largely because they want to get to know you. If you give them only what you think they want, you're being dishonest, posing as someone you are not. An imposter, for example, may try to pass himself or herself off as a seriously committed poet. But if the rest of the application makes no reference to writing poetry, working on publications, or taking poetry courses, admissions officials may question the validity of the applicant's claim. Therefore, it often makes sense to choose a subject that explains or amplifies something that appears elsewhere on the application.

On the other hand, don't hesitate to write on a personal subject that adds a new piece to your portrait. Just make it honest. Don't invent fiction that poses as fact. If you're not fascinated by politics, don't write on a political topic. If you don't thrive on art and music and books, don't try to pass yourself off as a humanist. Almost any topic will do, in fact, as long as it portrays the true you.

Trying to Include Everything

Don't expect to write an autobiography in 300 to 500 words. Yes, you can cover the highlights, but you won't reveal what lies below the surface—the facts that distinguish you from hundreds of other applicants. Besides, many of the highlights of your life already appear in other parts of the application—in your list of activities, travels, and interests. Therefore, don't use the "what-I-did-in-high-school-and-what-I-learned-from-it" approach. It's common and uninspired.

It's far better to focus on one topic, to show the depth of your feeling and thought in one very small area. Focusing on a single area may be tough when you've done a lot with your life. But by targeting one activity you can show how hard you've thrown yourself into it. You can also include specific details about yourself, details which make you more distinctive.

Boasting

Since most of us have been taught not to brag and boast, we usually don't puff ourselves up too much. We don't want to appear conceited. Yet, if you don't tell the college that you are a gourmet cook, a whiz at fixing stereos, or an ace rock-climber, who will? The problem, though, is that self-impressed people rarely impress others. So, if you're good at something, tell the college, of course, but don't shout. A champion with a touch of reserve or a sense of humor is always more endearing than a braggart.

One high school senior named Eliot, evidently dazzled by his own musical achievement, didn't realize how immodest he sounded when he declared, "My extraordinary talent and accomplishments in the field of music are sufficiently noteworthy to warrant my inclusion in the highly-exclusive all-county orchestra." Although Eliot may deserve respect for his musicianship, he could probably use a lesson in modesty.

Actually, modesty is rather easy to learn. Just say that you consider yourself lucky to have great talent. Or tell how you've struggled to attain success, then add that you're still trying to do better. For instance, Susan, another exceptional musician, wrote, "As a violinist, I have discovered wonderful feelings of accomplishment, surpassed only by the knowledge that this is only the beginning of a lifetime's experience."

The "Jock" Essay

Admissions personnel are rarely impressed by the so-called "jock" essay, the one which predictably tells the reader what you learned from being first-string left tackle or playing goalie on the field hockey team. Every reasonably successful athlete has learned self-discipline, courage, and sportsmanship on the field. If a sport has truly been a crucial part of your life, your essay will have to show how. But you'll have to do more than write the typical story of how you won the race or how losing it helped to build your character.

Raymond, an all-star high school baseball player, wrote an essay about his career on the diamond. But instead of summarizing his pitching and hitting records, he wrote a tongue-in-cheek analysis of his statistics. He said, for instance, that his 1.87 e.r.a. was close to 50% of his batting average (.400). "Does that make me only half as good a pitcher as I am a slugger?" he asked rhetorically. He went on to say that he registered ten strikeouts in one game. That same week he struck out with three different girls. "Am I a better pitcher or a better boyfriend?" he wondered.

In a more serious essay, Linda, a varsity tennis player, described the thoughts going through her head during a match. While she should have been concentrating on beating her opponent, she thought about doing her calculus homework, about the school carnival she helped to organize, about taking her driver's test, about an oil painting she was working on, and about attending a weekend retreat with her church youth group. Although Linda lost the tennis match, she wrote a winning essay that revealed not only her interests and concerns, but also told of her anxiety about trying to do too much and ending up doing nothing well.

The Travelogue

Travel is probably the most popular subject chosen for a college essay. Applicants seem extraordinarily fond of turning their travels into "significant experience" stories. But while travel has virtues galore, writing about it can be perilous. Colleges take a dim view of essays that are little more than personal narratives of "My Trip to Hawaii" or "What I Learned While Biking in Belgium." Even worse are those glorified itineraries, essays that list in order the national parks or countries you visited on that teen tour last summer.

But an admissions committee will welcome a well-written travel piece that reveals your personal and unique response to the experience. For instance, Barry, a tourist in Europe last year, wrote of awakening in the middle of the night in Switzerland and peering across the moonlit mountains to the Jungfrau. It was one of those memorable moments, he wrote, when "life's pieces come together"; he'd never been happier. He could not understand exactly why, but he preserved the experience in a sonnet (submitted with his essay) which he had completed as the sun came up the next morning.

Jodi, another European traveler, wrote of the irony she observed in a family trip. Her mother and father were on the verge of separation, but during the family's tour through Italy, France, and Spain, her parents seemed to make peace. How odd, Jodi thought, to leave home in order to preserve the home.

Barry and Jodi's travel pieces worked because they focused on a particular moment or idea. If all you can say, however, is that travel has broadened your life, made you more well-rounded or more tolerant of others, you'd be better off keeping the memories of your unforgettable trip in a scrapbook.

Straining to Be Funny

Although essays that contain gimmicks like puns, coined words, slang, and fractured English may attract attention among thousands of conventionally written essays, your cleverness could tarnish your otherwise sterling application. Like an ill-timed wisecrack, it could miss the funny bone of a weary admissions dean. That doesn't mean that humor is out of place in an application essay. On the contrary. Readers will relish something playful, satirical or whimsical. But don't overdo it. Tread lightly and cautiously with jokes and sarcasm. Humor is very difficult to write well. What you and your friends may think is uproarious in the school lunchroom could fall on its face in the admissions office.

Give your wit a workout in the application, but test your humor on an impartial adult before you send it to a college. If you're not usually a funny person, don't try to become one on your application. David Lettermans are not made overnight.

Being Too Creative

Some colleges, hoping to draw out the uniqueness in your personality, make unusual requests on their applications. Penn asks you to send page 217 of your autobiography, Stanford wants to know what you'd stow in a time capsule, and Dartmouth tells you to write your own question and answer it. Bates asks you to write your own recommendation, while Goucher instructs you to invent something and discuss it.

Such questions aren't meant to catch you. They don't have correct answers. It doesn't matter at Goucher whether you invent a cure for AIDS or a digital belt buckle. Colleges just want to get to know you better and see if you can think and write. When Swarthmore asks you to travel through time, choose a stopping place, and explain your choice, they're not interested in your mastery of history—your transcript contains that information. They'd rather hear why you picked the Jazz Age or the day Mt. Vesuvius exploded.

An off-beat question doesn't obligate you to write an off-beat answer. Just make your answer sound like you. If you are naturally creative, write a creative piece. But unusual creativity is not essential. You can bring out your best in a sober, sensitive, and sincere essay as well. You'll never be penalized for a clearly written, thoughtful essay that accurately reflects your beliefs and feelings.

Being Too Ordinary

While an odd-ball essay question may inspire quirky answers, an ordinary question shouldn't tempt you to write an ordinary response. A typical question—this one from Bates—might ask, "What personal or academic experiences were particularly rewarding for you (a project, teacher, piece of writing or research, a particular course of study)?" Although the question suggests that you write about school, you are free to pick any experience whatever. You may be better off, in fact, if you choose a unique personal experience. Finding you own topic demonstrates your initiative. You can also bet that most other people will play it safe and write about school. Don't run with the crowd. Take the less-travelled route, and choose a topic that is distinctively yours.

As you think about your essay, keep asking two key questions: What's unique about me? and What do I want my reader to think of me? You might begin, for example, by simply making a list of adjectives that describe what you like about yourself. Then make another list of what you dislike. Don't worry if the second list is longer than the first—most people are pretty hard on themselves. Study these lists for patterns, contradictions, and unusual combinations. How, for instance, might a person who "doesn't rest until a job is done" also consider himself "lazy"? Then rank the qualities in the order of importance. Which quality would you be most reluctant to give up? Which would you relinquish first? Which are you proudest of? Which would you most like to change? While you're answering such questions, you are beginning to define yourself and figure out what makes you unique. Think also of anecdotes or stories that illustrate each quality, as though you'd been asked for proof that you are "mysterious," "flirtatious" or "living in the past." Perhaps your best story could ultimately be developed into an essay that shows the true you.

You might also distinguish yourself from others by answering questions such as these:

What are you good at?

What are you trying to get better at?

What has been your greatest success? Your greatest failure?

What three words would you like engraved on your tombstone?

What is your strongest conviction?

What would you do with a million dollars?

If the world were to end one year from today, how would you spend your remaining time?

Generating thoughtful responses to often whimsical questions might trigger any number of possibilities for your essay.

Composing Your Essay

You probably won't get out of high school without writing some sort of essay on *Macbeth*—or if not *Macbeth,* then on the Great Depression or dissecting a frog. By this time in your life, in fact, you've probably written enough essays to fill a large book. When writing those essays, perhaps you sat down, spilled your thoughts onto the page and handed in your paper. Or maybe you wrote a rough draft and went back later to reorganize and rephrase your ideas. Possibly, you thought out ahead of time what you wanted to say and prepared a list of ideas or an outline. Maybe you used a combination of methods, varying them from time to time according to the purpose and importance of the essay.

Everyone who writes uses a process of some kind. Some processes seem to work better than others. The variations are endless, and no one process is always better than another. The best one—the one you should use—is the process which helps you do your best writing.

Warming Up

The quality of your essay may depend in part on your warm-ups. Since writing forces you to do strenuous mental work, a warming-up period can help to prepare you. Once you know the question on your application, you're likely to start thinking about your response. Make lists. Toss ideas back and forth in your head. Tell someone what you're thinking. Keep a notebook in your pocket because a great thought may hit you at any time. Keep pen and pad by your bed to record a 4 A.M. inspiration. Do some freewriting. Think hard about what you want your readers to think of you. In short, do something to activate your writing muscles.

Some people call this part of the process "pre-writing." You might call it getting yourself "psyched." Whatever the name, it's the time you spend testing possible topics and tuning up to write. It may even include finding a quiet, uncluttered place to work, gathering together a pen, paper, a typewriter or word-processor and a dictionary. And it involves laying aside many hours of time for solitary, unhurried work.

Warm-up time should also include a search for the point, or focus, of your essay. Identifying a topic isn't enough. Now you must focus on what you'll say about it. The sharper your focus, the better. You can't expect to write everything in a 300- to 500-word essay.

Maybe the surest way to narrow your topic is to begin writing. If your essay seems dull and disappointing after a couple of paragraphs, you're probably being too vague, too impersonal, or both. But keep at it as long as you can, for you may discover the point of your essay at any time. Be prepared, however, to face the fact that you could write yourself into a dead end. Not every topic will work. If you're blocked on all sides, you have no choice but to grit your teeth, turn to another topic, and start over.

Writing the Essay

By the time some writers begin to compose their essays, they more or less know that they'll reach their destination using the famous five-paragraph essay formula. Other writers will start more tentatively, knowing their general direction, but not finding the specific route until they get there.

Neither method excels the other, for much depends on the subject matter and intent of the writer. The first method follows a simple, clear-cut formula, which may not win a prize for originality but can help to turn a muddle of ideas into a model of clarity. It has a beginning, a middle, and an end. You can call on it any time you need to set ideas in order. Each step has its place and purpose.

The Five-Paragraph Essay Formula

Title

Introduction

Body: Point 1
Point 2
Point 3

Conclusion

In reality, however, writers rarely follow "The Formula." In fact, you may never see a formula essay in print. Yet a majority of college essays, even those which take circuitous paths between the beginning and end, adhere to some sort of three-step organization. In the *introduction* writers tell readers what they plan to tell them. In the *body* they tell them. And in the *conclusion* they tell them what they told them. Since all writers differ, however, you find endless variations within each step.

The Introduction: Grabbing the Reader's Interest

The best essays usually begin with something catchy, something to lure the readers into the piece. Basically, it's a hook—a phrase, sentence, or idea that will nab the readers' interest so completely that they'll keep on reading almost in spite of themselves. Once you've hooked your readers, you can lead them anywhere.

1. Start with an incident, real or invented, that leads the readers gracefully to the point of your essay.

2. State a provocative idea in an ordinary way or an ordinary idea in a provocative way. Either will spark the readers' interest.

3. Use a quotation—not necessarily a famous one. Shakespeare's or your grandmother's will do, as long as the quote relates to the topic of your essay.

4. Knock down a commonly held assumption or define a word in a new and surprising way.

5. Ask an interesting question or two which you will answer in your essay.

In any collection of good essays you'd no doubt find other worthy techniques for writing a compelling opening. Even a direct statement that introduces your topic may be appropriate. Whatever your opening, though, it must fit your writing style and personality. Work hard at getting it right, but at the same time, not too hard. A forced opening may obscure the point of your essay, or worse, dim the reader's enthusiasm for finding out what you have to say. Furthermore, an opening that comprises, say, more than a quarter of your essay is probably too long.

The Body: Putting the Pieces Together

Order is important. What should come first? second? third? In most writing the best order is the clearest order, the arrangement your readers can follow with the least effort.

There is no single way to get from the beginning of a piece of writing to the end. The route you take will vary according to what you want to do to your readers. Whether you want to shock, sadden, inspire, move, or entertain them, each purpose will have its own best order. In story-telling, the events are often placed in the sequence they occur. But to explain a childhood memory or define who you are, to stand up for women's rights or describe a poignant moment—each may take some other kind of arrangement. No one plan is superior to another, provided you have a valid reason for using it.

The plan that fails is the aimless one, the one in which ideas are arranged solely on the basis of the order in which they popped into your head. To guard against aimlessness, rank your ideas in order of importance either before you start or while you're writing drafts. Although your first idea may turn out to be your best, you probably should save it for later in your essay. Giving it away at the start is self-defeating. To hold your readers' interest, it's better to work toward your best point, not away from it. If you have, say, three main points to make, save the strongest for last. Launch your essay with your second-best, and tuck your least favorite between the other two.

In a typical college essay, a body consisting of three sections will be just about right. Why three? Mainly because three is a number that works. When you can make three statements about a subject, you probably know what you're talking about. One is too simple, two is still pretty shallow, three is thoughtful. Psychologically, three creates a sense of wholeness, like the beginning, middle, and end of a story. Each point doesn't necessarily receive equal treatment. You might manage one point with a single paragraph, while the others get more. But each point has to be distinctive. Your third point mustn't be a rerun of the first or second.

It shouldn't be difficult to break the main point of most essays into at least three secondary points, regardless of their topic or form. A narrative essay, for example, naturally breaks into a beginning, middle, and end. A process is likely to have at least three steps, some of which may be broken into sub-steps. In an essay of comparison and contrast, you ought to be able to find at least three similarities and differences to write about. A similar division into thirds applies to essays of cause and effect, definition, description, and certainly to essays of argumentation.

The Conclusion: Giving a Farewell Gift

When you reach the end of your essay, you can lift your pen off the page and be done with it. Or you can present your readers with a little something to remember you by: a gift—an idea to think about, a line to chuckle over, a memorable phrase or quotation. Whatever you give, the farewell gift must fit the content, style, and mood of your essay. A tacked-on ending will puzzle, not delight, your readers.

Some writers think that endings are more important than beginnings. After all, by the time readers arrive at your conclusion, the memory of your introduction may have already begun to fade. A stylish ending, though, will stick with readers and influence their feelings not only about your essay, but also about its writer. Therefore, choose a farewell gift thoughtfully. Be particular. Send your reader off feeling good, laughing, weeping, angry, thoughtful or thankful, but above all, glad that they stayed with your essay to the end.

1. Have some fun with your ending. Readers may remember your sense of humor long after forgetting other details about you.

2. End with an apt quotation, drawn either from the essay itself or from elsewhere.

3. Create a sense of completeness by recalling something you said earlier in your essay.

4. Fill in what took place between the end of a story and the present time.

5. Tell the readers how an unresolved issue was settled.

6. Ask a rhetorical question that springs naturally from your essay.

7. Speculate on what might occur in the future.

Some essays don't need an extended conclusion. When they're over, they're over. But at the end of an essay the readers should feel that they've arrived somewhere. In a sense, your whole essay has prepared them to arrive at a certain destination. Your introduction should have told them approximately where you're taking them. En route you developed ideas that moved them toward the conclusion. And at the end they shouldn't be at all surprised to find that they are there. You don't want a reader to say, "Oh, now I see what you've been driving at."

When choosing an ending let your instinct guide you. A tacked-on ending is, well—tacky. Always ask whether your ending maintains the spirit and style of the whole essay. An ending to avoid, though, is the summary. Trust your readers to know what you wrote in your two- or three-page essay. To say everything again is not only boring, it could be annoying. Your essay isn't a textbook. A chapter review isn't necessary. On the other hand, a quick general reiteration of the essay's theme and a memorable tag line could drive home your essay's main point. It's worth trying.

Presenting Your Essay

Appearance

Would you like to hear a sad but true story? It's about Robert, a high school senior, a good student likely to be accepted wherever he applied. He wrote his essay with care but sent it in looking as though he'd stored it in his jeans for a week. Robert was rejected. The admissions people concluded that Robert couldn't be seriously interested in their college if he submitted such a sloppy-looking piece of work.

Obviously, there's a lesson in Robert's tale: Don't send in an essay that looks anything less than gorgeous. Present your essay with pride. That is, make it neat, crisp, easy-to-read, accurately typed, in all respects as close to perfect as it can be. Its appearance speaks for you as clearly as its contents.

Unless the college asks for an essay written in your own hand, type it, preferably on a computer or word processor, where corrections can be made easily. Be sure your printer is letter-quality or close to it. Dot-matrix prepared copy is often hard to read unless the ribbon is brand new. If you do not own a computer, one may be available at your school or public library; or try a friend. If all else fails, use an electric typewriter with a fresh ribbon. A handwritten essay must be as legible as you can make it. If your penmanship is flawed, then print. Keep a bottle of white-out handy. In short, do all you can to make your essay easy on the eyes.

Use high-quality white paper, 8 1/2 by 11 inches. Separate continuous computer paper into sheets and remove the perforated edges. Double-space for ease of reading. Center the text on the page, and leave at least a one-inch margin all around. Number your pages. If you're asked to write more than one essay, designate which is which with the question number or topic on the application.

Many colleges give you a word limit. They mean business, so stick to the number of words they ask for. It's permissible to go over or under by, say, ten percent, but more may count against you. Some applications provide a few inches of space for your answer. Rather than fill up every square millimeter with type or with miniscule writing, cut words from your piece. What you may lose in content, you'll make up in legibility. In a pinch, you can reduce the size of your type on the computer or with a photocopying machine and glue the reduced version neatly onto the application.

It goes without saying that cross-outs and last-minute insertions using arrows, asterisks, paragraph markers or carets are not acceptable. Don't change anything on your final copy unless you are prepared to retype the whole page. This is where a computer comes in very handy! Aim to make your essay letter-perfect. In all respects, neatness counts.

Proofreading

To proofread well, you need fresh eyes. Therefore, your best proofreading method is to let someone else do it. Xerox five copies of your essay and have five reliable readers scour your piece for flaws in grammar, punctuation, and spelling.

But if you're on your own, put your essay aside for a few days, if possible. Then read it slowly, once for the sense of it and once for mechanics. Read it a line at a time, keeping a hawklike watch on every letter, word, and mark of punctuation. You might even cut a narrow horizontal window out of a spare sheet of paper. Move the window over your essay a line at a time. Concentrate on that line only, reading it once forward and once back. On the backward reading you'll lose the sense of the meaning, allowing you to keep your mind on the spelling.

In Addition to Your Essay

Some colleges want more than an essay from you. They ask for paragraph-long responses to any number of questions—why you chose that particular college, which extracurricular activity you like the most, your favorite book, career plans, honors, and so on. Whatever your answers, write them with the same care as your essay. Start with drafts. Revise and edit. Use your most interesting writing style. Since you're usually limited to less than half a dozen lines, get to the point promptly and express yourself concisely. Be attentive to the sound and appearance of your responses.

Some questions invite you to reply with a list of some kind—travels, prizes, alumni connections. If you can, however, respond with a thoughtful, well-developed paragraph. Not only will your answer be more interesting to read, you'll have the opportunity to highlight the items that matter. Moreover, the reader will note that you took

the trouble to write a coherent, lucid paragraph and that you have more than just a college essay in your writing repertoire.

When an application asks, "Is there additional information we should know?" try to reply with an emphatic "Yes!" Since your essay won't have told them everything, grab this chance to explain more of yourself or to show your interests and accomplishments. Applicants frequently send their creative work—a short story, a collection of poetry, articles written for the school paper, slides of artwork, photos—almost anything that fits into an envelope or small package. Don't overdo it, though. One carefully chosen term paper will suffice to reveal your love of history. One chapter of your novel is more than admissions people will have time to read, anyway. Quality, not quantity, counts.

Whatever you send, prepare it with the same high standards you used on your essay. Written material should be typed, photos and artwork should be attractively displayed and clearly explained or captioned. Before you mail a tape of your music or a video of your gymnastic performance, wind it to the starting spot. Make certain that it works and that it contains only what you want the college to hear or see. Also, submit only a few minutes, worth of material—not your whole concert or routine.

Your Friend, the Mail Carrier

What a glorious feeling it will be to turn your application and essay over to the U.S. Postal Service. Before you do, however, make photocopies. Once in the mail, you'll never see them again. Then sit back and rejoice. Pat yourself on the back for a job well done. Relax and wait for the momentous day when the postman brings you the *fat* envelope—the one containing information about housing, courses, freshman orientation and, of course, the letter which begins, "It gives me great pleasure to tell you that you have been accepted in the class of...."

If you would like more information and step-by-step guidance in writing your college application essay, see *Writing a Successful College Application Essay*. It was written by George Ehrenhaft, who wrote this chapter, and is also published by Barron's Educational Series, Inc.

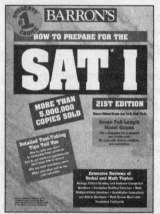

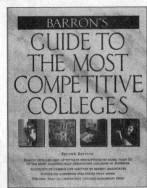